INTRODUCTION TO LITERATURE

NEW EDITION

EDWARD J. GORDON

BETTY YVONNE WELCH • WILLIAM ELLER

GINN AND COMPANY

Acknowledgments

Grateful acknowledgement is due to the following publishers, authors, and other holders of copyright material for permission to use selections from their publications.

APPLETON-CENTURY-CROFTS: "Roland Sees the King," Roland Becomes a Knight," from *Famous Legends Adapted for Children* by Emeline G. Crommelin; "Bill," from *Yellow Gentians and Blue,* by Zona Gale. Copyright, 1927, by D. Appleton and Company; renewed, 1955. By permission of Appleton-Century.

MRS. GEORGE BAMBRIDGE: "Tommy," from *Barrack Room Ballads,* by Rudyard Kipling.

A. S. BARNES & COMPANY, INC.: "Bonny Barbara Allan," "The Crafty Farmer," and "Lord Randal," from *The Ballad Book,* edited by MacEdward Leach. Used by permission.

THE BODLEY HEAD LTD.: "Our Lady's Juggler," from *Mother of Pearl,* by Anatole France.

BOY'S LIFE MAGAZINE: "Patrol at Valley Forge," by Russell Gordon Carter. By permission of the author and *Boy's Life,* published by the Boy Scouts of America.

BRANDT & BRANDT: "Thomas Jefferson," from *A Book of Americans,* by Rosemary and Stephen Vincent Benét, Holt, Rinehart and Winston, Inc. Copyright, 1933 by Rosemary and Stephen Vincent Benét. Copyright renewed 1961 by Rosemary Carr Benét.

CURTIS BROWN, LTD.: "Death at Suppertime," by Phyllis McGinley. Reprinted by permission of the author. Copyright 1948 by The New Yorker Magazine, Inc.

MRS. RUSSELL GORDON CARTER: "Patrol at Valley Forge," by Russell Gordon Carter.

THE CLARENDON PRESS: "Robin Hood and Alan a Dale," from *The Oxford Book of Ballads,* edited by Sir Arthur Quiller-Couch.

FRANK MARSHALL DAVIS: "Rain," by Frank Marshall Davis.

DODD, MEAD & COMPANY: "Our Lady's Juggler," reprinted by permission of Dodd, Mead & Company from *Mother of Pearl,* by Anatole France; "The Cremation of Sam McGee," reprinted by permission of Dodd, Mead & Company from *Collected Poems of Robert Service.*

DOUBLEDAY & COMPANY, INC.: "The Gift of the Magi," from *The Four Million,* by O. Henry; "Tommy," by Rudyard Kipling, from the book *Collected Verse by Rudyard Kipling.* Reprinted by permission of Mrs. George Bambridge and Doubleday & Company, Inc.

CONSTANCE GARLAND DOYLE AND ISABEL GARLAND LORD: "A Day's Pleasure," from *Main-Travelled Roads,* by Hamlin Garland.

E. P. DUTTON & CO., INC.: "Young Washington, The Embassy to the French Forts, 1753," from the book *I Sing the Pioneer,* by Arthur Guiterman. Copyright 1926, by E. P. Dutton & Co., Inc. Renewal, 1954, by Mrs. Vida Lindo Guiterman. Reprinted by permission of the publishers.

FARRAR, STRAUS & GIROUX, INC.: "Where Are the Children?" Reprinted, *in slightly adapted form,* by permission of Farrar, Straus & Giroux, Inc. from *My Mother's House and Sido* by Colette, translated by Una Vicenzo Troubridge and Enid McLeod. Copyright 1953 by Farrar, Straus & Young, Inc.

AMBROSE FLACK: "The Strangers That Came to Town," by Ambrose Flack. © Copyright 1952 by Crowell Collier Publishing Co.; appeared originally in *Woman's Home Companion.* Reprinted by permission of the author.

HARPER & ROW, PUBLISHERS: "Leaves," from *Copper Sun,* by Countee Cullen. Copyright 1927 by Harper & Brothers; renewed 1955 by Ida M. Cullen. By permission of Harper & Row, Publishers; "Jumping Mouse," abridged from pp. 66–85 in *Seven Arrows* by Hyemeyohsts Storm. Copyright © 1972 by Hyemeyohsts Storm. Reprinted by permission of Harper & Row, Publishers, Inc.; excerpt from pp. 138–144 in *The Adventures of Huckleberry Finn* by Mark Twain, Harper & Row.

Preface

Introduction to Literature is designed to further students' enjoyment and understanding of literature in two ways: first, to increase their awareness of the world by presenting them with new ideas to consider; and second, to give them some of the basic means of analyzing ideas in literature.

Four ideas, or themes, for students to consider are presented visually on pages viii–xv. These themes — Human Love, Human Strength, the Darker Side of Human Nature, and Death — recur throughout the selections of this book. Pages xvi–xix present students with one of the facets of the reader-writer relationship. The selections within the anthology are arranged in eight units with varying organizations to show students some ways of approaching literature. For instance, the first units are organized by elements of literature (i.e., Plot, Character); the fourth unit is organized by theme (i.e., Building America); other units are organized by types of literature (i.e., Poetry, Drama).

Each unit begins by explaining its purpose and some of the ideas or techniques which are presented in more detail throughout the unit. Each of the selections is then introduced by a headnote which discusses a key literary technique used in the selection. The questions that follow the selections reinforce the material in the headnotes and help students respond fully to the ideas in the selection. Further activities, including writing assignments, are often suggested. (A complete listing of these writing assignments is included on pages xx–xxii.) Attention is also given to increasing vocabulary and to vocabulary-building techniques, such as the use of context, connotation, prefixes, and suffixes.

Several supplementary aids are included at the end of the book. Biographical sketches of the authors of the selections are useful for giving students additional background and suggestions for further reading. Definitions of literary terms used in the book, as well as additional terms some teachers may wish to introduce, follow the biographical sketches. Each definition also refers the reader to pages on which the term is further discussed. Unfamiliar words which students will encounter often in reading, as well as vocabulary-exercise words, are defined in a glossary. Difficult words which are rarely used, proper names, and allusions are footnoted in the text.

By reading the selections, studying the material in the unit introductions and headnotes, and discussing the questions which follow the selections, the students should greatly increase both their understanding and enjoyment of the world of literature.

Human Love

Can love happen between any two people?

It happens between friends . . .

Elysium is as far as to
The very nearest Room
If in that Room a Friend await
Felicity or Doom—
—*from* "Elysium is as far as to"
  EMILY DICKINSON

children and parents . . . and lovers.

But I, being poor, have only my dreams;
I have spread my dreams under your feet;
Tread softly because you tread on my dreams.
—*from* "He Wishes for the Cloths of Heaven"
W. B. YEATS

Can it happen between strangers?

"You gonna take me to jail?" asked the boy, bending over the sink.

"Not with that face, I would not take you nowhere," said the woman. "Here I am trying to get home to cook me a bite to eat, and you snatch my pocketbook! Maybe you ain't been to your supper either, late as it be. Have you?"

—*from* "Thank You, M'am"
LANGSTON HUGHES

the old and the young?

The patience and humility of the face she loved so well was a better lesson to Jo than the wisest lecture, the sharpest reproof.

—from *Little Women*
LOUISA MAY ALCOTT

people of different races?

Can we make love happen or do we have to let it happen?

Selections Illustrating the Theme of *Human Love*

Human Strength

"Would you like to have some Medicine Power?"
Frog asked.

"Medicine Power? Me?" asked little Mouse. "Yes,
yes! If it is Possible."

"Then Crouch as Low as you Can, and then
Jump as High as you are Able! You will have your
Medicine!" Frog said.

—from "The Story of Jumping Mouse"
HYEMEYOHSTS STORM

Is strength a matter of physical stamina and courage, a matter of attitude, or both?

"What shall I say, brave Adm'r'l, say,
 If we sight naught but seas at dawn?"
"Why you shall say at break of day:
 'Sail on! sail on! sail on! and on!"

—from "Columbus"
JOAQUIN MILLER

What makes a person psychologically strong?

Now I say to you, my friends, even though we have the difficulties of today and tomorrow, I still have a dream . . . I have a dream that one day this nation will rise up and live out the true meaning of its creed: "We hold these truths to be self-evident, that all men are created equal."

—MARTIN LUTHER KING

Pandora hastened to replace the lid; but, alas! the whole contents of the jar had escaped, one thing only excepted, which lay at the bottom, and that was *hope*.

—*from* "Prometheus and Pandora"
THOMAS BULFINCH

Selections Illustrating the Theme of *Human Strength*

The Darker Side of Human Nature

The darkness of a child's mean streak . . .

. . . I had found Geraldine and one of her devotees kicking my cap around. I stood rooted to the bottom stair, watching, my heart sick. "This yours?" Geraldine asked, picking it up and tossing it at me disdainfully. "Crazy kind of a cap." I wept when I got home that night, for the beauty that had gone out of my cap-and-mittens set, and for being in the wrong.
—*from* "You Never Know"
NANCY HALE

the darkness of a group of people making up stories about a neighbor . . .

The women started in on Mrs. Duvitch because she "never showed her face." . . . this gave rise to the rumor that she was the victim of an obscure skin disease and that every morning she shook the scales out of the bed sheet.
—*from* "The Strangers That Came to Town"
AMBROSE FLACK

the darkness of anger and hate . . .

"I hated that woman," Charles recalls. "All of a sudden, and for the very first time in my life, I hated somebody, really hated somebody. . . . These are the people, I thought to myself, who made me believe all my life that they were superior to me, an African."
—*from* "My Journey Is Still Long"
CHARLES L. SANDERS

the darkness of insanity . . .

True!—nervous—very, very dreadfully nervous I had been and am; but why *will* you say that I am mad?
—*from* "The Telltale Heart"
EDGAR ALLAN POE

Why do most people avoid thinking about the darker side of human nature?

His head is bowed. He thinks on men and kings.
Yea, when the sick world cries, how can he sleep?
Too many peasants fight, they know not why,
Too many homesteads in black terror weep.
—*from* "Abraham Lincoln Walks at Midnight"
VACHEL LINDSAY

Can we begin to understand human nature without looking at the darker side?

Selections Illustrating the Theme of *The Darker Side of Human Nature*

Death

"Death" and "the dead" are emotionally charged words. People often avoid using them if some other word or expression is handy. They say "pass away," "expire," "the deceased," "the departed." Like the darker side of human nature, death often embarrasses and frightens those who believe in the importance of human life and the importance of the individual human being.

Some people's beliefs free them from the fear of death.

"Tom," she said faintly, far away, "in the Southern Seas there's a day in each man's life when he knows it's time to shake hands with all his friends and say good-by and sail away, and he does, and it's natural—it's just his time."

—from "Good-by, Grandma"
Ray Bradbury

But I trust in that last great roundup
When the Rider shall cut the big herd,
That the cowboy will be represented
In the earmark and brand of the Lord.
    —"The Cowboy's Dream"
    Anonymous

An aura of mystery sometimes surrounds the idea of death.

Full fathom five thy father lies:
  Of his bones are coral made;
Those are pearls that were his eyes . . .
      —*from* "Ariel's Song"
      WILLIAM SHAKESPEARE

What is the idea in this passage from "Ariel's Song"? What is your idea of death?

Selections Illustrating the Theme of *Death*

The Writer and Literature

Full fathom five thy father lies;
  Of his bones are coral made;
Those are pearls that were his eyes;
  Nothing of him that doth fade
But suffer a sea change
Into something rich and strange.
Sea nymphs hourly ring his knell:
  . . . Ding-dong.
Hark! now I hear them—Ding-dong bell.
—"Ariel's Song," *from* The Tempest
WILLIAM SHAKESPEARE

Much of literature is like the father drowned in *The Tempest*. Is he dead? Yes and no—emphatically "no!" But how can something be both dead and not dead? Why start your study of literature with riddles? Let's answer a riddle with a riddle. The poet above has his mischievous sprite end the puzzling song with, "Nothing of him that doth fade / But suffer a sea change / Into something rich and strange." What has happened? In Ariel's song a man dies, leaving the world as we know it. But, in death, the man's skeleton changes into a thing of beauty in another world. The song seems to say that in time familiar things may become transformed into things "rich and strange" which remind us of what we once knew. The sea bell which the spirit hears reminds him of this fascinating relationship.

The worlds of literature are much like the puzzle posed by the song. Things can "die" and still live; the past can also be the present. Many of the stories you will read this year will remind you of other stories. Regardless of the "sea change" caused by time and individual writers, there may be echoes of other stories. That framework which we call "plot" will seem to appear time and time again, always familiar, but never exactly the same. Why is it that stories we've heard before crop up again and again? Another question might get us closer to the answer. When is the past the present? When we say "the past," we may be thinking about what generally goes under the title of "History," records of battles, victories, kings, ceremonies, invasions. And behind these records lie stories of people who really lived. The records of these lives are of value to us because they record the human experiences that continually occur. Literature, the re-creation of the past, is a type of history. It records the *why* of past lives, as well as the *when* and the *what*. Yet, unlike history, it is also a record of things which were *not* done, of things which were dreamed about. Literature records what is imagined as well as what happens. It is a record of dreams and imagination, as well as of fact. Here is where the past becomes the present.

If we listen to the voices of the past, we find ourselves asking the same questions, wondering about the same things as our parents and ancestors did: What is love? What is death? What is friendship? What is strength? Are men naturally good? These questions ring out again and again to remind us of those who asked them before. And where do we find answers to these questions? In addition to personal observations, we find answers in the stories men have saved. Around us and before us we see familiar patterns of acting and reacting to life. When these patterns occur in literature we call them *plots*.

The reading you did in elementary school and much of the movie and television viewing you have done have equipped you very well to deal with plot. In fact, you are already so used to dealing with the concept that you talk of it in a kind of shorthand. For instance, if someone asks you what a specific movie was like, you might respond, "Oh, it was another of those Westerns, the good-guy—bad-guy type," or "It was a girl-next-door romance," or "It was the generation gap story again." In each case, your questioner probably would give a knowing nod and not press you for further details. You gave a recognizable plot framework, and he found it easy to sketch in details of action, and even character. Even pre-schoolers, very young children, possess this ability to predict what will happen. Part of this ability is due to sheer repetition: they hear their favorite stories again and again. But part of it is also due to the fact that when they are given certain circumstances they expect certain consequences. Thus, they can finish incomplete stories with a remarkable degree of accuracy.

At this point, you might be asking, "If I knew, or sensed, what plot was when I was very young, why are we discussing it now?" A partial answer lies in Ariel's song: familiar things can undergo changes. Plots may be passed down from generation to generation with different details of name and place. This is one kind of change. But we, too, may change in time. And as we change, we may see the same plot differently.

The child's favorite story may be more than just an entertaining story to the older person, for the older person can look at the fairy tale world and see similarities between it and his own. For instance, the good-guy—bad-guy Western may appeal to a six-year-old because he identifies with the good guy and feels a personal victory when he wins. The older reader knows, from observation and personal experience, that in life the "good" does not always win out over the "bad." Perhaps he would like it to, and so fashions his plots around what he would like to be true. The usual plots that you see in many Westerns and spy shows reflect man's tendency to shape his stories around what he feels to be important. Let's look, for a moment, at some of the oldest stories that we have inherited, the fables.

For generations fables have appealed to people of all ages. Children have been entertained by their fanciful, "fabulous" characters. They are amused that animals talk "like real people." They are very much interested in what happens, but don't usually worry over why it happens. Why do you think Aesop, a man who is supposed to have lived over 2,000 years ago, wrote the following fable? And why do you think it has been passed on to you?

The Fox and the Crow

A fox once saw a crow fly off with a piece of cheese in its beak and settle on a branch of a tree. "That's for me, as I am a fox," said Master Reynard, and he walked up to the foot of the tree. "Good day, Mistress Crow," he cried. "How well you are looking today: how glossy your feathers; how bright your eye. I feel sure your voice must surpass that of other birds, just as your figure does; let me hear but one song from you that I may greet you as the queen of birds." The crow lifted up her head and began to caw her best, but the moment she opened her mouth the piece of cheese fell to the ground, only to be snapped up by Master Fox. "That will do," said he. "That was all I wanted. In exchange for your cheese I will give you a piece of advice for the future—"

Have you ever been outfoxed? If so, whose fault was it? What important bit of advice is Aesop passing on to you? What bit of experience has he preserved in the rich form of the fable? And under how many other different forms have you seen this story? How many times have you seen the story played out with real people? Perhaps Aesop and many other story tellers used animals rather than people because it softened their criticism or observation. Plots, then, arise as much out of human nature as out of a desire to report a chain of events. It is human nature to ask questions as well as to give answers. The world of stories has a rich treasury of questions.

Man has always wanted to know how the earth was created, why there are seasons, why there are storms, why there is misery, what the limits are of his power and knowledge. To answer these great questions about himself and the universe he has fashioned superhumans, or gods. The animals in fables act out moral truths; the gods of the Greek and Roman myths (and, indeed, those of every land) act out what men have thought to be natural and universal truths, truths about human nature, about man's desire to know and control both that and the world around him. In the space age, these stories might have a special significance.

Did you know that centuries ago, probably before man could even write, man was launching a type of moon-shot? Legend has it that there once lived on Crete a craftsman so ingenious that he invented a maze, a labyrinth, from which no man could escape without clues. This craftsman, Daedalus, was treasured by King Minos, but was also a source of irritation. The restless mind which had created the maze from which there was no escape was not content to stay in one place. The King, not wanting to lose Daedalus, forbade him passage from the island. So Daedalus and his son Icarus invented wings. But, let the story speak for itself. Daedalus speaks to his son, Icarus:

> ". . . Follow me, and remember the wings on your shoulders are not natural wings, like those of Cupid. We are men and must use tools to do what the gods can do for themselves. Even with our tools we must always fall short of them. If you fly too near the sea, the feathers will become wet and heavy, and you will drown; if you fly up into the air as the gods do, the wax will melt in the sun long before you reach Olympus. Then your wings will fall off and you will perish. . . ." Up, up Icarus went, soaring into the bright sun. In vain Daedalus called to him. He was only a black speck by now. At last he was coming down. He was coming very fast, much too fast. In another second Daedalus caught sight of the boy, whirling headlong. The framework was still on his shoulders, but the feathers had all fallen off, as the hot sun had melted the wax. One moment he saw him; then with a mighty splash Icarus hit the water and was gone. Daedalus circled round over the sea, not daring to go too low lest his own wings become soaked. . . .
>
> Daedalus flew on. He reached the land at last, . . . but he would neither use his wings nor teach others how to make them. He had learned man's limitations. . . .

Does the Space Age have any use for this story? Underneath its "rich and strange" details does it recognize a familiar truth?

As you wander through the world of stories, look for the familiar in the strange, and the riches in what is around you and within you. When you read "Once upon a time . . . ," remember that the "time" may really be now.

Composition Assignments

To the Teacher

Additional writing assignments may be found in the *Teachers' Handbook and Key* as "Additional Assignments" or "Suggested Unit Reviews." The composition assignments below are taken directly from the students' texts, most often from the "Further Activities" sections.

To the Student

Many of the stories you will read this year are concerned with people—how they act, think, and feel. Others are concerned primarily with ideas—the ideas that affect all people. In the composition assignments below you will have an opportunity to become a writer—to tell stories, to say how you feel and think, to react to what the writers in the book have said. In this way, you are not simply asked to read and believe what you read. You have the opportunity to become a writer.

Assignment	Location	Page
1. Develop the statement "A reader of 'Bill' finishes with a feeling of pity," by explaining the statement, by telling for whom you felt pity, and by pointing out incidents in the story that caused that feeling.	FA[1]	5
2. Choose a topic about which you have special knowledge or interest, then describe this special interest including the most important details to interest your reader.	FA2	24
3. Explain what you think Mallory in "Top Man" meant by his statement about Mt. Everest, "I want to climb it because it is there." Tell why you think his answer is a good or poor one.	FA3	25
4. Write a report of the murder in "The Telltale Heart" as it might have been written by one of the policemen.	FA1	38
5. Describe your first impression of someone about whom you later changed your mind, telling what made you change your mind.	FA1	69
6. Discuss how the story "The Strangers That Came to Town" would be different if a character other than Andy had told it.	FA2	69
7. Rewrite "The Pocketbook Game" as a dialogue, including details about what Marge did and said at various times.	FA	71
8. Describe a ceremony, tradition, or object which is important to your family, telling the background of that item and why it is important.	FA	83

---

[1]The abbreviation *FA* refers to the "Further Activities" sections of the text.

²The abbreviation *UL* refers to the "Understanding Literature" sections of the text.

Contents

Building America   177

Myths, Fables, and Legends   245

MYTHS

FABLES

LEGENDS

The One-Act Play   357

Poetry   410

Famous Characters in Literature 500

Plot

THE BEGINNINGS of literature grew from the universal desire to tell and to hear a good story. The good storyteller, whose main object is to entertain you, tries to take you out of your world into another. He or she convinces you that something is happening (plot) to someone (character) somewhere (setting). Over the thousands of years that people have spent as tellers of tales, they have invented ways of putting a story together so that it will convince you of its reality. That last word—reality—is a complicated one. It does not mean that the story is really happening; it means that while you read, you believe that it is. And this makes all the difference.

Some people are so dull that they could not convince anyone that the sun will rise tomorrow morning. But good writers have convinced many children, during a story, that a cow could jump over the moon, that the Pied Piper of Hamelin could lead all the children away from their parents, or that Alice could have fallen down a rabbit hole. Given the chance, a good storyteller will take you into many new places and adventures.

The storyteller usually creates a story by organizing a series of related incidents into a plot. The good writer does not just tell you what happens; to do so would be mere reporting. The writer has to select from what happened those moments that are the most important to the story. And the incidents which make up the plot are related to one another. Because the character in the story is in a particular situation, he or she does something and may be led then to do something else. You can think of a plot as a chain of incidents, each link joined to the next. When you read a short story, therefore, the first question you should ask is: What happens? And then: How is each event related to the one before it?

It is believed that when the author of this story, Zona Gale, was working for the newspaper *New York World*, she was asked by the editor to check up on this advertisement which had appeared in the paper:

> A man with a few months to live would
> like nice people to adopt his little girl,
> six, blue eyes, curls. References required.

The following short story is based on what Zona Gale found out.

Bill

Zona Gale

IMPROVING YOUR READING: A writer has to interest you early in the story. One way is to make good use of *suspense*, usually by setting a question in the reader's mind. The question is not openly stated, but is suggested by the action of the story. In this story Miss Gale begins: "Bill was thirty when his wife died, and little Minna was four. Bill's carpenter shop was in the yard of his house, so he thought that he could keep up his home for Minna and himself." The question, then, that causes the suspense is: Will Bill be able to take care of his daughter until she is old enough to take care of herself? You read on then to find the answer.

BILL WAS THIRTY when his wife died, and little Minna was four. Bill's carpenter shop was in the yard of his house, so he thought that he could keep up his home for Minna and himself. All day while he worked at his bench, she played in the yard, and when he was obliged to be absent for a few hours, the woman next door looked after her. Bill could cook a little, coffee and bacon and fried potatoes and flapjacks, and he found bananas and sardines and crackers useful. When the woman next door said this was not the diet for four-year-olds, he asked her to teach him to cook oatmeal and vegetables, and though he always burned the dishes in which he cooked these things, he cooked them every day. He swept, all but the corners, and he dusted, dabbing at every object; and he complained that after he had cleaned the windows he could not see out as well as he could before. He washed and patched Minna's little garments and mended her doll. He found a kitten for her so that she wouldn't be lonely. At night he heard her say her prayer, kneeling in the middle of the floor with her hands folded, and speaking like lightning. If he forgot the prayer, he either woke her up, or else he made her say it the first thing next morning. He himself used to try to

2

pray: "Lord, make me do right by her if you see me doing wrong." On Sundays he took her to church and sat listening with his head on one side, trying to understand, and giving Minna peppermints when she rustled. He stopped work for a day and took her to the Sunday-school picnic. "Her mother would of," he explained. When Minna was old enough to go to kindergarten, Bill used to take her morning or afternoon, and he would call for her. Once he dressed himself in his best clothes and went to visit the school. "I think her mother would of," he told the teacher, diffidently.[1] But he could make little of the colored paper and the designs and the games, and he did not go again. "There's some things I can't be any help to her with," he thought.

Minna was six when Bill fell ill. On a May afternoon he went to a doctor. When he came home he sat in his shop for a long time and did nothing. The sun was beaming through the window in bright squares. He was not going to get well. It might be that he had six months. . . . He could hear Minna singing to her doll.

When she came to kiss him that night, he made an excuse, for he must never kiss her now. He held her at arm's length, looked in her eyes, said: "Minna's a big girl now. She doesn't want Papa to kiss her." But her lip curled and she turned away sorrowful, so the next day Bill went to another doctor to make sure. The other doctor made him sure.

1 diffidently: shyly.

He tried to think what to do. He had a sister in Nebraska, but she was a tired woman. His wife had a brother in the city, but he was a man of many words. And little Minna . . . there were things known to her which he himself did not know— matters of fairies and the words of songs. He wished that he could hear of somebody who would understand her. And he had only six months. . . .

Then the woman next door told him bluntly that he ought not to have the child there, and him coughing as he was; and he knew that his decision was already upon him.

One whole night he thought. Then he advertised in a city paper:

A man with a few months more to live would like nice people to adopt his little girl, six, blue eyes, curls. References required.

They came in a limousine, as he had hoped that they would come. Their clothes were as he had hoped. They had with them a little girl who cried: "Is this my little sister?" On which the woman in the smart frock said sharply:

"Now then, you do as Mama tells you and keep out of this or we'll leave you here and take this darling little girl away with us."

So Bill looked at this woman and said steadily that he had now other plans for his little girl. He watched the great blue car roll away. "For the land sake!" said the woman next door when she heard. "You done her out of a fortune. You hadn't the right—a man in your health." And when other cars came, and he let them go, this woman told her husband that Bill ought to be reported to the authorities.

The man and woman who walked into Bill's shop one morning were still mourning their own little girl. The woman was not sad—only sorrowful, and the man, who was tender of her, was a carpenter. In a blooming of his hope and his dread, Bill said to them: "You're the ones." When they asked: "How long before we can have her?" Bill said: "One day more."

That day he spent in the shop. It was summer and Minna was playing in the yard. He could hear the words of her songs. He cooked their supper and while she ate, he watched. When he had tucked her in her bed, he stood in the dark hearing her breathing. "I'm a little girl tonight—kiss me," she had said, but he shook his head. "A big girl, a big girl," he told her.

When they came for her the next morning, he had her ready and her little garments were ready, washed and mended, and he had mended her doll. "Minna's never been for a visit!" he told her buoyantly. And when she ran toward him, "A big girl, a big girl," he reminded her.

He stood and watched the man and woman walking down the street with Minna between them. They had brought her a little blue parasol in case the parting should be hard. This parasol Minna held bobbing above her head, and she was so absorbed in looking up at the blue silk that she did not remember to turn and wave her hand.

Understanding Literature

1. What do you learn, in the first paragraph, of the situation in which Bill and Minna find themselves at the opening of the story?
2. What change in the situation is described in the second paragraph? How does the change increase the suspense?
3. What drives Bill to put the advertisement in the paper?
4. How does he treat the woman in the limousine? Why does he treat her this way?
5. Why does he approve of the man and woman who came? How does the author contrast the attitude of the first woman toward her daughter with the attitude of the couple toward Minna?
6. The author never says how Bill feels toward Minna; instead, she has him act out his attitude. The reader has to draw his own conclusion. How does Bill feel toward his daughter? How does he feel in the last paragraph? How does Minna feel at the end?

Further Activity

When an author writes a story, a poem, or a play, he expects the reader to have an emotional reaction to it. In this story he wants the reader to feel a sense of pity.

Write a paragraph that begins with the following sentence: "A reader of 'Bill' finishes with a feeling of pity." In the second sentence tell for whom you had a sense of pity. In the next few sentences point out two incidents in the story that aroused this feeling in you.

Have you ever wanted to conquer a mountain? This challenge is difficult for many people to understand, but one purpose of literature is to help you better understand other people, their desires, ideals, and ways of living. As you read the adventure "Top Man," try to predict the ending. It is an unusual one.

Top Man

James Ramsey Ullman

IMPROVING YOUR READING: In every story there must first be a *conflict* which needs to be resolved. Otherwise, there would be no story. In "Top Man" there are two problems: one is the conflict of man against man, and the other is the conflict of man against nature. Notice how the story develops around these two conflicts.

FOCUSING ON WORDS: Unless you are familiar with climbing, you will need to learn the following words in order to enjoy and understand this story fully: *gorge, summit, avalanche, precipices, glacier, reconnaissance, crevasse, outcroppings, traverse, rarefied, pinnacle, chimney.* If you need to use the glossary, be sure to find the definition which fits the word as it would be used in a story about mountain climbing.

THE GORGE BENT. The walls fell steeply away, and we came out on the edge of a bleak boulder-strewn valley.

And there it was.

Osborn saw it first. He had been leading the column, threading his way slowly among the huge rockmasses of the gorge's mouth. Then he came to the first flat bare place and stopped. He neither pointed nor cried out, but every man behind him knew instantly what it was. The long file sprang taut, like a jerked rope. As swiftly as we could, but in complete silence, we came out one by one into the open space where Osborn stood and raised our eyes with his.

In the records of the Indian Topographical Survey it says: "Kalpurtha: altitude 27,930 ft. The highest peak in the Garhwal Himalayas. Also known as K₃. A Tertiary formation of sedimentary limestone . . .''

There were men among us who had spent months of their lives—in some cases years—reading, thinking, planning about what now lay before us; but at that moment statistics and geology, knowledge, thought and plans, were as remote and forgotten as the far-away western cities from which we had come. We were men bereft of everything but eyes, everything but the single electric perception: *there it was!*

Before us the valley stretched into miles of rocky desolation. To right and left it was bounded by low ridges, which, as the eye followed them, slowly mounted and drew closer together, until the valley was no longer a valley at all, but a narrowing, rising corridor between the cliffs. What happened then I can describe only as a stupendous crash of music. At the end of the corridor and above it—so far above it that it shut out half the sky—hung the blinding white mass of K_3.

It was like the many pictures I had seen, and at the same time utterly unlike them. The shape was there, and the familiar distinguishing features: the sweeping skirt of glaciers; the monstrous vertical precipices of the face and the jagged ice line of the east ridge; finally the symmetrical summit pyramid that transfixed the sky. But whereas in the pictures the mountain had always seemed unreal —a dream-image of cloud, snow and crystal—it was now no longer an image at all. It was a mass: solid, palpable,[1] appalling. We were still too far away to see the windy whipping of its snowplumes or to hear the cannonading of its avalanches, but in that sudden silent moment every man of us was for the first time aware of it not as a picture in his mind, but as a thing, an antagonist. For all its twenty-eight thousand feet of lofty grandeur it seemed, somehow, less to tower than to crouch—a white-hooded giant, secret and remote, but living. Living and on guard.

I turned my eyes from the dazzling glare and looked at my companions. Osborn still stood a little in front of the others. He was absolutely motionless, his young face tense and shining, his eyes devouring the mountain as a lover's might devour the form of his beloved. One could feel in the very set of his body the overwhelming desire that swelled in him to act, to come to grips, to conquer. A little behind him were ranged the other white men of the expedition: Randolph, our leader, Wittmer and Johns, Dr. Schlapp and Bixler. All were still, their eyes cast upward. Off to one side a little stood Nace, the Englishman, the only one among us who was not staring at K_3 for the first time. He had been the last to come up out of the gorge and stood now with arms folded on his chest, squinting at the great peak he had known so long and fought so tirelessly and fiercely. His lean British face, under its mask of stubble and windburn, was expressionless. His lips were a thin line, and his eyes seemed almost shut. Behind the sahibs[2] ranged the porters, bent forward over their staffs, their brown seamed faces straining upward from beneath their loads.

For a long while no one spoke or moved. The only sounds were the soft hiss of our breathing and the pounding of our hearts.

Through the long afternoon we wound slowly between the great boulders of the valley and at sundown pitched camp in the bed of a dried-up stream. The porters ate their rations in silence, wrapped themselves in their blankets and fell asleep under the stars. The rest of

1 **palpable:** easily seen.

2 **sahibs:** masters.

us, as was our custom, sat close about the fire that blazed in the circle of tents, discussing the events of the day and the plans for the next. It was a flawlessly clear Himalayan night, and K₃ tiered up into the blackness like a gigantic beacon lighted from within. There was no wind, but a great tide of cold air crept down the valley from the ice fields above, penetrating our clothing, pressing gently against the canvas of the tents.

"Another night or two and we'll be needing the sleeping bags," commented Randolph.

Osborn nodded. "We could use them tonight would be my guess."

Randolph turned to Nace. "What do you say, Martin?"

The Englishman puffed at his pipe a moment. "Rather think it might be better to wait," he said at last.

"Wait? Why?" Osborn jerked his head up.

"Well, it gets pretty nippy high up, you know. I've seen it thirty below at twenty-five thousand on the east ridge. The longer we wait for the bags, the better acclimated³ we'll get."

Osborn snorted. "A lot of good being acclimated will do, if we have frozen feet."

"Easy, Paul, easy," cautioned Randolph. "It seems to me Martin's right."

Osborn bit his lip, but said nothing. The other men entered the conversation, and soon it had veered to other matters: the weather, the porters and pack animals, routes, camps and strategy, the inevitable inexhaustible topics of the climber's world.

There were all kinds of men among the eight of us, men with a great diversity of background and interest. Sayre Randolph whom the Alpine Club had named leader of our expedition, had for years been a well-known explorer and lecturer. Now in his middle fifties, he was no longer equal to the grueling physical demands of high climbing, but served as planner and organizer of the enterprise. Wittmer was a Seattle lawyer, who had recently made a name for himself by a series of difficult ascents in the Coast Range of British Columbia. Johns was an Alaskan, a fantastically strong able sourdough,⁴ who had been a ranger in the U.S. Forestry Service and had accompanied many famous Alaskan expeditions. Schlapp was a practicing physician from Milwaukee, Bixler a government meteorologist with a talent for photography. I, at the time, was an assistant professor of geology at an eastern university.

Finally, and pre-eminently,⁵ there were Osborn and Nace. I say "pre-eminently," because even at this time, when we had been together as a party for little more than a month, I believe all of us realized that these were the two key men of our venture. None, to my knowledge, ever expressed it in words, but the conviction was none the less there that if any of us were eventually to stand on the summit of K₃, it would be one of

---

3 acclimated (ăk/lə māt/ĭd): used to the climate.

4 sourdough: Alaskan prospector or explorer.
5 pre-eminently (prĭ ĕm/ə nənt lĭ): above all others.

them, or both. They were utterly dissimilar men. Osborn was twenty-three and a year out of college, a compact buoyant mass of energy and high spirits. He seemed to be wholly unaffected by either the physical or mental hazards of mountaineering and had already, by virtue of many spectacular ascents in the Alps and Rockies, won a reputation as the most skilled and audacious of younger American climbers. Nace was in his forties—lean, taciturn, introspective.[6] An official in the Indian Civil Service, he had explored and climbed in the Himalayas for twenty years. He had been a member of all four of the unsuccessful British expeditions to K_3, and in his last attempt had attained to within five hundred feet of the summit, the highest point which any man had reached on the unconquered giant. This had been the famous tragic attempt in which his fellow climber and lifelong friend, Captain Furness, had slipped and fallen ten thousand feet to his death. Nace never mentioned his name, but on the steel head of his ice ax were engraved the words: *TO MARTIN FROM JOHN.* If fate were to grant that the ax of any one of us should be planted upon the summit of K_3, I hoped it would be this one.

Such were the men who huddled about the fire in the deep still cold of a Himalayan night. There were many differences among us, in temperament as well as in background. In one or two cases, notably that of Osborn and Nace, there had already been a certain amount of friction, and as the venture continued and the struggles and hardships of the actual ascent began, it would, I knew, increase. But differences were unimportant. What mattered—all that mattered—was that our purpose was one: to conquer the monster of rock and ice that now loomed above us in the night; to stand for a moment where no man, no living thing, had ever stood before. To that end we had come from half a world away, across oceans and continents to the fastnesses[7] of inner Asia. To that end we were prepared to endure cold, exhaustion and danger, even to the last extremity of human endurance. . . . Why? . . . There is no answer, and at the same time every man among us knew the answer; every man who has ever looked upon a great mountain and felt the fever in his blood to climb and conquer knows the answer. George Leigh Mallory, greatest of mountaineers, expressed it once and for all when he was asked why he wanted to climb unconquered Everest.

"I want to climb it," said Mallory, "because it is there."

Day after day we crept on and upward. Sometimes the mountain was brilliant above us, as it had been when we first saw it; sometimes it was partially or wholly obscured by tiers of clouds. The naked desolation of the valley was unrelieved by any motion, color or sound, and, as we progressed, the great rock walls

6 taciturn, introspective (tăs′ə tûrn′, ĭn′trə spĕkt′ĭv): silent, thoughtful.

7 fastnesses: strongholds; fortresses.

that enclosed it grew so high and steep that its floor received the sun for less than two hours each day. The rest of the time it lay in ashen half-light, its gloom intensified by the dazzling brilliance of the ice slopes above. As long as we remained there we had the sensation of imprisonment; it was like being trapped at the bottom of a deep well or in a sealed court between tall skyscrapers. Soon we were thinking of the ascent of the shining mountain not only as an end in itself, but as an escape.

In our nightly discussions around the fire our conversation narrowed more and more to the immediate problems confronting us, and during them I began to realize that the tension between Osborn and Nace went deeper than I had at first surmised.[8] There was rarely any outright argument between them—they were both far too able mountain men to disagree on fundamentals—but I saw that at almost every turn they were rubbing each other the wrong way. It was a matter of personalities, chiefly. Osborn was talkative, enthusiastic, optimistic, always chafing to be up and at it, always wanting to take the short straight line to the given point. Nace, on the other hand, was matter-of-fact, cautious, slow. He was the apostle of trial and error and watchful waiting. Because of his far greater experience and intimate knowledge of K_3 Randolph almost invariably followed his advice, rather than Osborn's, when a

difference of opinion arose. The younger man usually capitulated[9] with good grace, but I could tell that he was irked.

During the days in the valley I had few occasions to talk privately with either of them, and only once did either mention the other in any but the most casual manner. Even then, the remarks they made seemed unimportant and I remember them only in view of what happened later.

My conversation with Osborn occurred first. It was while we were on the march, and Osborn, who was directly behind me, came up suddenly to my side. "You're a geologist, Frank," he began without preamble.[10] "What do you think of Nace's theory about the ridge?"

"What theory?" I asked.

"He believes we should traverse under it from the glacier up. Says the ridge itself is too exposed."

"It looks pretty mean through the telescope."

"But it's been done before. He's done it himself. All right, it's tough —I'll admit that. But a decent climber could make it in half the time the traverse will take."

"Nace knows the traverse is longer," I said. "But he seems certain it will be much easier for us."

"Easier for *him* is what he means." Osborn paused, looking moodily at the ground. "He was a great climber in his day. It's a shame a man can't be honest enough with himself to know when he's through." He fell

8 surmised: guessed; imagined.

9 capitulated (kə pĭch′ə lāt′): yielded; agreed.
10 preamble: introduction.

silent and a moment later dropped back into his place in line.

It was that same night, I think, that I awoke to find Nace sitting up in his blanket and staring at the mountain.

"How clear it is," I whispered.

The Englishman pointed. "See the ridge?"

I nodded, my eyes fixed on the great twisting spine of ice that climbed into the sky. I could see now, more clearly than in the blinding sunlight, its huge indentations and jagged wind-swept pitches.[11] "It looks impossible," I said.

"No, it can be climbed. Trouble is, when you've made it you're too done in for the summit."

"Osborn seems to think its shortness would make up for its difficulty."

Nace was silent a long moment before answering. Then for the first and only time I heard him speak the name of his dead companion. "That's what Furness thought," he said quietly. Then he lay down and wrapped himself in his blanket.

For the next two weeks the uppermost point of the valley was our home and workshop. We established our base camp as close to the mountain as we could, less than half a mile from the tongue of its lowest glacier, and plunged into the arduous tasks of preparation for the ascent. Our food and equipment were unpacked, inspected and sorted, and finally repacked in lighter loads for transportation to more advanced camps. Hours were spent poring over maps and charts and studying the intricate heights above us through telescope and binoculars. Under Nace's supervision, a thorough reconnaissance of the glacier was made and the route across it laid out; then began the backbreaking labor of moving up supplies and establishing the chain of camps.

Camps I and II were set up on the glacier itself, in the most sheltered sites we could find. Camp III we built at its upper end, as near as possible to the point where the great rock spine of K_3 thrust itself free of ice and began its precipitous[12] ascent. According to our plans, this would be the advance base of operations during the climb. The camps to be established higher up, on the mountain proper, would be too small and too exposed to serve as anything more than one or two nights' shelter. The total distance between the base camp and Camp III was only fifteen miles, but the utmost daily progress of our porters was five miles, and it was essential that we should never be more than twelve hours' march from food and shelter. Hour after hour, day after day, the long file of men wound up and down among the hummocks and crevasses of the glacier, and finally the time arrived when we were ready to advance.

Leaving Dr. Schlapp in charge of eight porters at the base camp, we proceeded easily and on schedule, reaching Camp I the first night, Camp II the second and the advance

11 **pitches:** slopes.

12 **precipitous** (prĭ sĭp'ə təs): steep.

base the third. No men were left at Camps I and II, inasmuch as they were designed simply as caches[13] for food and equipment; and furthermore we knew we would need all the man power available for the establishment of the higher camps on the mountain proper.

For more than three weeks now the weather had held perfectly, but on our first night at the advance base, as if by malignant[14] prearrangement of nature, we had our first taste of the fury of a high Himalayan storm. It began with great streamers of lightning that flashed about the mountain like a halo; then heavily through the weird glare snow began to fall. The wind rose. At first it was only sound—a remote, desolate

moaning in the night high above us —but soon it descended, sucked down into the deep valley as if into an enormous funnel. Hour after hour it howled about the tents with hurricane frenzy, and the wild flapping of the canvas dinned in our ears like machine-gun fire.

There was no sleep for us that night or the next. For thirty-six hours the storm raged without lull, while we huddled in the icy gloom of the tents, exerting our last ounce of strength to keep from being either buried alive or blown into eternity. At last, on the third morning, it was over, and we came out into a world transformed by a twelve-foot cloak of snow. No single landmark remained as it had been before, and our supplies and equipment were in the wildest confusion. Fortunately

13 **caches** (kăsh'əz): hiding places.
14 **malignant:** evil.

there had not been a single serious injury, but it was another three days before we had regained our strength and put the camp in order.

Then we waited. The storm did not return, and the sky beyond the ridges gleamed flawlessly clear; but night and day we could hear the thunder of avalanches on the mountain above us. To have ventured so much as one step into that savage vertical wilderness before the new-fallen snow froze tight would have been suicidal. We chafed[15] or waited patiently, according to our individual temperaments, while the days dragged by.

It was late one afternoon that Osborn returned from a short reconnaissance up the ridge. His eyes were shining and his voice jubilant. "It's tight," he cried. "Tight as a drum. We can go!" All of us stopped whatever we were doing. His excitement leapt like an electric spark from one to another. "I went about a thousand feet, and it's sound all the way. What do you say, Sayre? Tomorrow?"

Randolph hesitated, then looked at Nace.

"Better give it another day or two," said the Englishman.

Osborn glared at him. "Why?" he challenged.

"It's generally safer to wait until—"

"Wait! Wait!" Osborn exploded. "Don't you ever think of anything but waiting? Man, the snow's firm, I tell you!"

"It's firm down here," Nace replied

quietly, "because the sun hits it only two hours a day. Up above it gets the sun for twelve hours. It may not have frozen yet."

"The avalanches have stopped."

"That doesn't necessarily mean it will hold a man's weight."

"It seems to me that Martin's point—" Randolph began.

Osborn wheeled on him. "Sure," he snapped. "I know. Martin's right. The cautious bloody English are always right. Let him have his way, and we'll be sitting here chewing our nails until the mountain falls down on us." His eyes flashed to Nace. "Maybe with a little less of that bloody cautiousness you English wouldn't have made such a mess of Everest. Maybe your pals Mallory and Furness wouldn't be dead."

"Osborn!" commanded Randolph sharply.

The youngster stared at Nace for another moment, breathing heavily. Then abruptly he turned away.

The next two days were clear and windless, but we still waited, following Nace's advice. There were no further brushes between him and Osborn, but an unpleasant air of restlessness and tension hung over the camp. I found myself chafing almost as impatiently as Osborn himself for the moment when we would break out of that maddening inactivity and begin the assault.

At last the day came. With the first paling of the sky a roped file of men, bent almost double beneath heavy loads, began slowly to climb the ice slope, just beneath the jagged line of the east ridge. In accordance

---

15 chafed (chāft): became irritated; fretted.

with prearranged plan, we proceeded in relays, this first group consisting of Nace, Johns, myself and eight porters. It was our job to ascend approximately two thousand feet in a day's climbing and establish Camp IV at the most level and sheltered site we could find. We would spend the night there and return to the advance base next day, while the second relay, consisting of Osborn, Wittmer and eight more porters, went up with their loads. This process was to continue until all necessary supplies were at Camp IV, and then the whole thing would be repeated between Camps IV and V and V and VI. From VI, at an altitude of about 26,000 feet, the ablest and fittest men —presumably Nace and Osborn— would make the direct assault on the summit. Randolph and Bixler were to remain at the advance base throughout the operations, acting as directors and co-ordinators. We were under the strictest orders that any man—sahib or porter—who suffered illness or injury should be brought down immediately.

How shall I describe those next two weeks beneath the great ice ridge of K₃? In a sense there was no occurrence of importance, and at the same time everything happened that could possibly happen, short of actual disaster. We established Camp IV, came down again, went up again, came down again. Then we crept laboriously higher. With our axes we hacked uncountable thousands of steps in the gleaming walls of ice. Among the rocky outcroppings of the cliffs we clung to holds and strained

at ropes until we thought our arms would spring from their sockets. Winds swooped down on us, battered us and passed, and the air grew steadily colder and more difficult to breathe. One morning two of the porters awoke with their feet frozen black; they had to be sent down. A short while later Johns developed an uncontrollable nosebleed and was forced to descend to a lower camp. Wittmer was suffering from racking headaches and I from a continually dry throat. But providentially,[16] the one enemy we feared the most in that icy gale-lashed hell did not again attack us. No snow fell. And day by day, foot by foot, we ascended.

It is during ordeals like this that the surface trappings of a man are shed and his secret mettle[17] laid bare. There were no shirkers or quitters among us—I had known that from the beginning—but now, with each passing day, it became more manifest[18] which were the strongest and ablest among us. Beyond all argument, these were Osborn and Nace.

Osborn was magnificent. All the boyish impatience and moodiness which he had exhibited earlier were gone, and, now that he was at last at work in his natural element, he emerged as the peerless mountaineer he was. His energy was inexhaustible, his speed, both on rock and ice, almost twice that of any other man in the party. He was always discovering new routes and short cuts.

16 **providentially:** luckily; miraculously.
17 **mettle:** spirit; disposition.
18 **more manifest:** plainer; more obvious.

PLOT

Often he ascended by the ridge itself, instead of using the traverse beneath it, as had been officially prescribed; but his craftsmanship was so sure and his performance so brilliant that no one ever thought of taking him to task. Indeed, there was such vigor, buoyancy and youth in everything he did that it gave heart to all the rest of us.

In contrast, Nace was slow, methodical, unspectacular. Since he and I worked in the same relay, I was with him almost constantly, and to this day I carry in my mind the clear image of the man: his tall body bent almost double against shimmering slopes of ice; his lean brown face bent in utter concentration on the problem in hand, then raised searchingly to the next; the bright prong of his ax rising, falling, rising, falling with tireless rhythm, until the steps in the glassy incline were so wide and deep that the most clumsy of the porters could not have slipped from them had he tried. Osborn attacked the mountain head on. Nace studied it, sparred with it, wore it down. His spirit did not flap from his sleeve like a pennon;[19] it was deep inside him—patient, indomitable.[20]

The day soon came when I learned from him what it is to be a great mountaineer. We were making the ascent from Camp IV to V, and an almost perpendicular ice wall had made it necessary for us to come out for a few yards on the exposed crest of the ridge. There were six of us in the party, roped together, with Nace leading, myself second and four porters bringing up the rear. The ridge at this particular point was free of snow, but razor-thin, and the rocks were covered with a smooth glaze of ice. On either side the mountain dropped away in sheer precipices of five thousand feet.

Suddenly the last porter slipped. I heard the ominous scraping of boot nails behind me and, turning, saw a gesticulating[21] figure plunge sideways into the abyss. There was a scream as the next porter was jerked off too. I remember trying frantically to dig into the ridge with my ax, realizing at the same time it would no more hold against the weight of the falling men than a pin stuck in a wall. Then I heard Nace shout, "Jump!" As he said it, the rope went tight about my waist, and I went hurtling after him into space on the opposite side of the ridge. After me came the nearest porter. . . .

What happened then must have happened in five yards and a fifth of a second. I heard myself cry out, and the glacier, a mile below, rushed up at me, spinning. Then both were blotted out in a violent spasm,[22] as the rope jerked taut. I hung for a moment, an inert mass, feeling that my body had been cut in two, then I swung in slowly to the side of the mountain. Above me the rope lay tight and motionless across the crest of the ridge, our weight exactly counterbalancing that of the men who had fallen on the far slope.

19 **pennon:** flag; banner.
20 **indomitable:** unconquerable.

21 **gesticulating:** gesturing; suddenly motioning.
22 **spasm:** sudden movement; convulsion.

Nace's voice came up from below. "You chaps on the other side!" he shouted. "Start climbing slowly. We're climbing too."

In five minutes we had all regained the ridge. The porters and I crouched panting on the jagged rocks, our eyes closed, the sweat beading our faces in frozen drops. Nace carefully examined the rope that again hung loosely between us.

"All right men," he said presently. "Let's get on to camp for a cup of tea."

Above Camp V the whole aspect of the ascent changed. The angle of the ridge eased off, and the ice, which lower down had covered the mountain like a sheath, lay only in scattered patches between the rocks. Fresh enemies, however, instantly appeared to take the place of the old. We were now laboring at an altitude of more than 25,000 feet— well above the summits of the highest surrounding peaks—and day and night, without protection or respite,[23] we were buffeted[24] by the fury of the wind. Worse than this was that the atmosphere had become so rarified it could scarcely support life. Breathing itself was a major physical effort, and our progress upward consisted of two or three painful steps followed by a long period of rest in which our hearts pounded wildly and our burning lungs gasped for air. Each of us carried a small cylinder of oxygen in his pack, but we used it only in emergencies and

found that, while its immediate effect was salutary,[25] it left us later even worse off than before. My throat dried and contracted until it felt as if it were lined with brass. The faces of all of us, under our beards and windburn, grew haggard and strained.

But the great struggle was now mental as much as physical. The lack of air induced a lethargy[26] of mind and spirit; confidence and the powers of thought and decision waned, and dark foreboding crept out from the secret recesses of the subconscious. The wind seemed to carry strange sounds, and we kept imagining we saw things which we knew were not there. The mountain, to all of us, was no longer a mere giant of rock and ice; it had become a living thing, an enemy, watching us, waiting for us, hostile, relentless and aware. Inch by inch we crept upward through that empty forgotten world above the world, and only one last thing remained to us of human consciousness and human will: to go on. To go on.

On the fifteenth day after we had first left the advance base we pitched Camp VI at an altitude of almost 26,000 feet. It was located near the uppermost extremity of the east ridge, directly beneath the so-called shoulder of the mountain. On the far side of the shoulder the vast north face of K_3 fell sheer to the glaciers, two miles below. And above it and to the left rose the symmetrical bulk of the summit pyramid. The top-

---

23 respite (rĕs'pĭt): relief; time of rest.
24 buffeted: struck repeatedly.

25 salutary (săl'yə tĕr'ĭ): helpful; beneficial.
26 lethargy (lĕth'ər jĭ): inaction.

most rocks of its highest pinnacle were clearly visible from the shoulder, and the intervening two thousand feet seemed to offer no insuperable obstacles.

Camp VI, which was in reality no camp at all, but a single tent, was large enough to accommodate only three men. Osborn established it with the aid of Wittmer and one porter; then, the following morning, Wittmer and the porter descended to Camp V, and Nace and I went up. It was our plan that Osborn and Nace should launch the final assault —the next day, if the weather held— with myself in support, following their progress through binoculars and going to their aid or summoning help from below if anything went wrong. As the three of us lay in the tent that night, the summit seemed already within arm's reach, victory securely in our grasp.

Then the blow fell. With malignant timing, which no power on earth could have made us believe was a simple accident of nature, the mountain hurled at us its last line of defense. It snowed.

For a day and a night the great flakes drove down upon us, swirling and swooping in the wind, blotting out the summit, the shoulder, everything beyond the tiny white-walled radius of our tent. Hour after hour we lay in our sleeping bags, stirring only to eat or to secure the straining rope and canvas. Our feet froze under their thick layers of wool and rawhide. Our heads and bodies throbbed with a dull nameless aching, and time crept over our numbed

minds like a glacier. At last, during the morning of the following day, it cleared. The sun came out in a thin blue sky, and the summit pyramid again appeared above us, now whitely robed in fresh snow. But still we waited. Until the snow either froze or was blown away by the wind it would have been the rashest courting of destruction for us to have ascended a foot beyond the camp. Another day passed. And another.

By the third nightfall our nerves were at the breaking point. For hours on end we had scarcely moved or spoken, and the only sounds in all the world were the endless moaning of the wind outside and the harsh sucking noise of our breathing. I knew that, one way or another, the end had come. Our meager food supply was running out; even with careful rationing there was enough left for only two more days.

Presently Nace stirred in his sleeping bag and sat up. "We'll have to go down tomorrow," he said quietly.

For a moment there was silence in the tent. Then Osborn struggled to a sitting position and faced him.

"No," he said.

"There's still too much loose snow above. We can't make it."

"But it's clear. As long as we can see—"

Nace shook his head. "Too dangerous. We'll go down tomorrow and lay in a fresh supply. Then we'll try again."

"Once we go down we're licked. You know it."

Nace shrugged. "Better to be

licked than—" The strain of speech was suddenly too much for him and he fell into a paroxysm[27] of coughing. When it had passed there was a long silence.

Suddenly Osborn spoke again. "Look, Nace," he said, "I'm going up tomorrow."

The Englishman shook his head. "I'm going—understand?"

For the first time since I had known him I saw Nace's eyes flash in anger. "I'm the senior member of this group," he said. "I forbid you to go!"

Osborn jerked himself to his knees, almost upsetting the tiny tent. "You forbid me? This may be your fifth time on the mountain, and all that, but you don't *own* it! I know what you're up to. You haven't got it in you to make the top yourself, so you don't want anyone else to make it. That's it, isn't it? Isn't it?" He sat down again suddenly, gasping for breath.

Nace looked at him with level eyes. "This mountain has beaten me four times," he said softly. "It killed my best friend. It means more to me to climb it than anything else in the world. Maybe I'll make it and maybe I won't. But if I do, it will be as a rational intelligent human being—not as a fool throwing my life away."

He collapsed into another fit of coughing and fell back in his sleeping bag. Osborn, too, was still. They lay there inert,[28] panting, too exhausted for speech.

27 **paroxysm** (păr′ək sĭz′əm)**:** fit; attack.
28 **inert:** motionless; inactive.

It was hours later that I awoke from dull uneasy sleep. In the faint light I saw Nace fumbling with the flap of the tent.

"What is it?" I asked.

"Osborn. He's gone."

The words cut like a blade through my lethargy. I struggled to my feet and followed Nace from the tent.

Outside, the dawn was seeping up the eastern sky. It was very cold, but the wind had fallen and the mountain seemed to hang suspended in a vast stillness. Above us the summit pyramid climbed bleakly into space, like the last outpost of a spent and lifeless planet. Raising my binoculars, I swept them over the gray waste. At first I saw nothing but rock and ice; then, suddenly, something moved.

"I've got him," I whispered.

As I spoke, the figure of Osborn sprang into clear focus against a patch of ice. He took three or four slow upward steps, stopped, went on again. I handed the glasses to Nace.

The Englishman squinted through them, returned them to me and reentered the tent. When I followed he had already laced his boots and was pulling on his outer gloves.

"He's not far," he said. "Can't have been gone more than half an hour." He seized his ice ax and started out again.

"Wait," I said. "I'm going with you."

Nace shook his head. "Better stay here."

"I'm going with you," I said.

He said nothing further, but waited while I made ready. In a few moments we left the tent, roped up and started off.

Almost immediately we were on the shoulder and confronted with the paralyzing two-mile drop of the north face; but we negotiated[29] the short exposed stretch without mishap and in ten minutes were working up the base of the summit pyramid. The going here was easier, in a purely climbing sense: the angle of ascent was not steep, and there was firm rock for hand- and foot-holds between the patches of snow and ice. Our progress, however, was creepingly slow. There seemed to be literally no air at all, and after almost every step we were forced to rest, panting and gasping as we leaned forward against our axes. My heart swelled and throbbed with every movement until I thought it would explode.

The minutes crawled into hours, and still we climbed. Presently the sun came up. Its level rays streamed across the clouds, far below, and glinted from the summits of distant peaks. But, although the pinnacle of K_3 soared a full three thousand feet above anything in the surrounding world, we had scarcely any sense of height. The wilderness of mountain valley and glacier that spread beneath us to the horizon was flattened and remote, an unreal insubstantial landscape seen in a dream. We had no connection with it, or it with us. All living, all awareness, purpose and will, were concentrated in the next step, and the next; to put one foot before the other; to breathe; to ascend. We struggled on in silence.

I don't know how long it was since we had left the camp—it might have been two hours, it might have been six—when we suddenly sighted Osborn. We had not been able to find him again since our first glimpse through the binoculars; but now, unexpectedly and abruptly, as we came up over a bulge of rock, there he was. He was at a point, only a few yards above us, where the mountain steepened into an almost vertical wall. The smooth surface directly in front of him was obviously unclimbable, but two alternate routes were presented. To the left, a chimney cut obliquely[30] across the wall, forbiddingly steep, but seeming to offer adequate holds. To the right was a gentle slope of snow that curved upward and out of sight behind the rocks. As we watched, Osborn ascended to the edge of the snow, stopped and probed it with his ax. Then, apparently satisfied that it would bear his weight he stepped out on the slope.

I felt Nace's body tense. "Paul!" he cried out.

His voice was too weak and hoarse to carry. Osborn continued his ascent.

Nace cupped his hands and called his name again, and this time Osborn turned. "Wait!" cried the Englishman.

Osborn stood still, watching us, as we struggled up the few yards to the

---

29 **negotiated:** passed (as an obstacle).

30 **obliquely** (ə blēk′lī): in a sloping or slanting line.

PLOT

edge of the snow slope. Nace's breath came in shuddering gasps, but he climbed faster than I had ever seen him climb before.

"Come back!" he called. "Come off the snow!"

"It's all right. The crust is firm," Osborn called back.

"But it's melting. There's—" Nace paused, fighting for air. "There's nothing underneath!"

In a sudden sickening flash I saw what he meant. Looked at from directly below, at the point where Osborn had come to it, the slope on which he stood appeared as a harmless covering of snow over the rocks. From where we were now, however, a little to one side, it could be seen that it was in reality no covering at all, but merely a cornice or unsupported platform clinging to the side of the mountain. Below it was not rock, but ten thousand feet of blue air.

"Come back!" I cried. "Come back!"

Osborn hesitated, then took a downward step. But he never took the next. For in that same instant the snow directly in front of him disappeared. It did not seem to fall or to break away. It was just soundlessly and magically no longer there. In the spot where Osborn had been about to set his foot there was now revealed the abysmal drop of the north face of K_3.

I shut my eyes, but only for a second, and when I reopened them Osborn was still, miraculously, there. Nace was shouting, "Don't move! Don't move an inch!"

"The rope—" I heard myself saying.

The Englishman shook his head. "We'd have to throw it, and the impact would be too much. Brace yourself and play it out." As he spoke, his eyes were traveling over the rocks that bordered the snow bridge. Then he moved forward.

I wedged myself into a cleft in the wall and let out the rope which extended between us. A few yards away Osborn stood in the snow, transfixed, one foot a little in front of the other. But my eyes now were on Nace. Cautiously, but with astounding rapidity, he edged along the rocks beside the cornice. There was a moment when his only support was an inch-wide ledge beneath his feet, another where there was nothing under his feet at all, and he supported himself wholly by his elbows and hands. But he advanced steadily, and at last reached a shelf wide enough for him to turn around on. At this point he was perhaps six feet away from Osborn.

"It's wide enough here to hold both of us," he said in a quiet voice. "I'm going to reach out my ax. Don't move until you're sure you have a grip on it. When I pull, jump."

He searched the wall behind him and found a hold for his left hand. Then he slowly extended his ice ax, head foremost, until it was within two feet of Osborn's shoulder. "Grip it!" he cried suddenly. Osborn's hands shot out and seized the ax. "Jump!"

There was a flash of steel in the sunlight and a hunched figure hurtled inward from the snow to the ledge. Simultaneously another figure hurtled out. The haft of the ax jerked suddenly from Nace's hand, and he lurched forward and downward. A violent spasm convulsed my body as the rope went taut. Then it was gone. Nace did not seem to hit the snow; he simply disappeared through it, soundlessly. In the same instant the snow itself was gone. The frayed, yellow end of broken rope spun lazily in space. . . .

Somehow my eyes went to Osborn. He was crouched on the ledge, where Nace had been a moment before, staring dully at the ax he held in his hands. Beyond his head, not two hundred feet above, the white untrodden pinnacle of K_3 stabbed the sky.

Perhaps ten minutes passed, perhaps a half hour. I closed my eyes and leaned forward motionless against the rock, my face against my arm. I neither thought nor felt; my body and mind alike were enveloped in a suffocating numbness. Through it at last came the sound of Osborn moving. Looking up, I saw he was standing beside me.

"I'm going to try for the top," he said tonelessly.

I merely stared at him.

"Will you come?"

"No," I said.

Osborn hesitated; then turned and began slowly climbing the steep chimney above us. Halfway up he paused, struggling for breath. Then he resumed his laborious upward progress and presently disappeared beyond the crest.

I stayed where I was, and the hours passed. The sun reached its zenith above the peak and sloped away behind it. And at last I heard above me the sound of Osborn returning. As I looked up, his figure appeared at the top of the chimney and began the descent. His clothing was in tatters, and I could tell from his movements that only the thin flame of his will stood between him and collapse. In another few minutes he was standing beside me.

"Did you get there?" I asked dully.

He shook his head. "I couldn't make it," he answered. "I didn't have what it takes."

We roped together silently and began the descent to the camp.

There is nothing more to be told of the fifth assault on K₃—at least not from the experiences of the men who made it. Osborn and I reached Camp V in safety, and three days later the entire expedition gathered at the advance base. It was decided, in view of the tragedy that had occurred, to make no further attempt on the summit, and by the end of the week we had begun the evacuation of the mountain.

It remained for another year and other men to reveal the epilogue.[31]

The summer following our attempt a combined English-Swiss expedition stormed the peak successfully. After weeks of hardship and struggle they attained the topmost pinnacle of the giant, only to find that what should have been their great moment of triumph was, instead, a moment of the bitterest disappointment. For when they came out at last upon the summit they saw that they were *not* the first. An ax stood there. Its haft was embedded in rock and ice and on its steel head were the engraved words: *TO MARTIN FROM JOHN*.

They were sporting men. On their return to civilization they told their story, and the name of the conqueror of K₃ was made known to the world.

31 epilogue (ĕp′ə lôg′): conclusion to the story.

Understanding Literature

1. What are the two kinds of conflict in this story?
2. A person's character is usually revealed through what he says and what he does. What do the statements and actions of Osborn and Nace reveal about their characters? In what ways are the two men alike? In what ways are they different?
3. What details in the story indicate that its author knows what mountain climbing is like?
4. Summarize the story of the ice ax on which was engraved: *To Martin from John*. Who was John? What had happened to him?
5. Randolph, the leader of the expedition, usually followed the advice of Nace. Why?

6. Which character in "Top Man" tells the story? Why did the author use this character instead of Nace or Osborn to tell the story?

7. Although this story is probably not true, it is related very convincingly. How does the use of "I" to tell the story help to make it seem true? How does the author keep the "I," the narrator of the story, on the scene?

8. What incidents suggest the struggle going on inside of the men? What details suggest the physical strain they undergo? What are the signs of growing danger in the story?

9. After the descent the narrator says, "It remained for another year and other men to reveal the epilogue." What was the epilogue? Why had Osborn not told the others that he had reached the top? Why had he placed Nace's ice ax there?

Further Activities

1. After the men on the expedition first see the towering Kalpurtha, each feels that the mountain is an *antagonist* (par. 7). *Antagonist* is a key word, one you must know before you will fully understand the story and the men. Notice the way *antagonist* is explained and defined in the remainder of the paragraph. Define *antagonist* in your own words. Then look up the word in the glossary. Why is the mountain described as an antagonist?

2. When you are writing, it is best to choose a topic about which you have definite understanding or experience. James Ullman's writing skill, for example, is due partly to his extensive travels (Brazil, Hawaii, Russia, Africa, the Alps, and the Andes) and to his experience in mountain climbing. *The White Tower*, a best-selling novel, also illustrates Ullman's knowledge of mountains and mountain climbing.

   Select a topic about which you have some special knowledge, such as photography, cooking, chemistry, building models, or any one of a number of possibilities. Your special knowledge might be the outgrowth of some type of lesson—music, dance, horseback riding. Or perhaps you are particularly interested and skilled in a certain sport.

   After you have decided on a topic, write two or three paragraphs in which you describe this special interest, including those details which are most important. Plan your beginning sentence most carefully so that it will immediately arouse the reader's interest. Remember that this beginning sentence will probably be your *topic sentence*, although a topic sentence can occur any place within the paragraph.

Before copying your rough draft, rework and proofread it carefully. Will it make sense to a reader who does not have your background about the subject? Have you said exactly what you want to say? Are all the words spelled correctly? Are your punctuation, grammar, and capitalization correct?

3. Why do people climb mountains? dive to the bottom of the sea? go into outer space? In the story Ullman quotes the famous mountaineer, George Leigh Mallory, who, when asked why he wanted to climb Mount Everest, answered, "I want to climb it because it is there."

   Write a paragraph in which you explain what you think Mallory meant by his statement, and indicate why you feel that his answer is a good one or a poor one.

Mark Twain, whose real name was Samuel Clemens, is known to everyone as the author of *Tom Sawyer* and *Huckleberry Finn*. He was a newspaperman in California when, in 1865, he wrote "The Celebrated Jumping Frog of Calaveras County." When the story was printed in the East, it made Twain a national celebrity. Suddenly it seemed that everyone was reading and talking about the famous frog which could jump so well "that he'd nail a fly every time as fur as he could see him."

The Celebrated Jumping Frog of Calaveras County

Mark Twain

IMPROVING YOUR READING: The first question you ask of a story is: What happens? In answering the question, you are talking about *plot*, the connected incidents leading to a *climax*, the point of highest interest. In the following story you see a man tricked. If Mark Twain had described the trick alone, he would have been writing an anecdote instead of a short story. Instead, he describes a series of connected incidents; he shows you what led up to the trick, how it came about. The trick itself is the climax.

IN COMPLIANCE with the request of a friend of mine, who wrote me from the East, I called on good-natured, garrulous[1] old Simon Wheeler, and inquired after my friend's friend, Leonidas W. Smiley, as requested to do, and I hereunto append[2] the result. I have a lurking suspicion that *Leonidas W. Smiley* is a myth; that my friend never knew such a personage; and that he only conjectured[3] that if I asked old Wheeler about him, it would remind him of his infamous *Jim* Smiley, and he would go to work and bore me to death with some exasperating reminiscence[4] of him as

long and as tedious as it should be useless to me. If that was the design, it succeeded.

I found Simon Wheeler dozing comfortably by the barroom stove of the dilapidated tavern in the decaying mining camp of Angel's, and I noticed that he was fat and bald-headed, and had an expression of winning gentleness and simplicity upon his tranquil countenance.[5] He roused up, and gave me good day. I told him a friend of mine had commissioned me to make some inquiries about a cherished companion of his boyhood named *Leonidas W. Smiley* —Rev. *Leonidas W. Smiley*, a young

1 **garrulous** (găr′ə ləs): talkative.
2 **append:** attach.
3 **conjectured:** guessed.
4 **reminiscence** (rĕm′ə nĭs′əns): remembered experience.

5 **countenance:** face.

minister of the Gospel, who he had heard was at one time a resident of Angel's Camp. I added that if Mr. Wheeler could tell me anything about this Rev. Leonidas W. Smiley, I would feel under many obligations to him.

Simon Wheeler backed me into a corner and blockaded me there with his chair, and then sat down and reeled off the monotonous narrative which follows this paragraph. He never smiled, he never frowned, he never changed his voice from the gentle-flowing key to which he tuned his initial sentence, he never betrayed the slightest suspicion of enthusiasm; but all through the interminable[6] narrative there ran a vein of impressive earnestness and sincerity, which showed me plainly that, so far from his imagining that there was anything ridiculous or funny about his story, he regarded it as a really important matter, and admired its two heroes as men of transcendent genius in *finesse*.[7] I let him go on in his own way, and never interrupted him once.

"Rev. Leonidas W. H'm, Reverend Le—well, there was a feller here once by the name of *Jim* Smiley, in the winter of '49—or maybe it was the spring of '50—I don't recollect exactly, somehow, though what makes me think it was one or the other is because I remember the big flume[8] warn't finished when he first come to the camp; but anyway, he was the curiosest man about always betting on anything that turned up you ever see, if he could get anybody to bet on the other side; and if he couldn't he'd change sides. Any way that suited the other man would suit *him*—any way just so's he got a bet, *he* was satisfied. But still he was lucky, uncommon lucky; he most always come out winner. He was always ready and laying for a chance; there couldn't be no solit'ry thing mentioned but that feller'd offer to bet on it, and take ary side you please, as I was just telling you. If there was a horse race, you'd find him flush or you'd find him busted at the end of it; if there was a dog fight, he'd bet on it; if there was a cat fight, he'd bet on it; if there was a chicken fight, he'd bet on it; why, if there was two birds setting on a fence, he would bet you which one would fly first; or if there was a camp meeting, he would be there reg'lar to bet on Parson Walker, which he judged to be the best exhorter[9] about here, and so he was, too, and a good man. If he even see a straddlebug start to go anywheres, he would bet you how long it would take him to get to—to wherever he was going to, and if you took him up, he would foller that straddlebug to Mexico but what he would find out where he was bound for and how long he was on the road. Lots of the boys here has seen that Smiley, and can tell you about him. Why, it never made no difference to *him*—he'd bet on *any* thing—the dangdest feller. Parson Walker's

---

6 interminable (ĭn tûr′mə nə bəl): endless.
7 transcendent . . . *finesse*: exceptional talent in strategy.
8 flume: channel for carrying water.

9 exhorter: one who advises or urges.

wife laid very sick once, for a good while, and it seemed as if they warn't going to save her; but one morning he come in, and Smiley up and asked him how she was, and he said she was considable better—thank the Lord for his inf'nite mercy—and coming on so smart that with the blessing of Prov'dence she'd get well yet; and Smiley, before he thought, says: 'Well, I'll resk two-and-a-half she don't anyway.'

"Thish-yer Smiley had a mare—the boys called her the fifteen-minute nag, but that was only in fun, you know, because, of course, she was faster than that—and he used to win money on that horse, for all she was so slow and always had the asthma, or the distemper, or the consumption, or something of that kind. They used to give her two or three hun-dred yards start, and then pass her under way; but always at the fag end of the race she'd get excited and desperate like, and come cavorting and straddling up, and scattering her legs around limber, sometimes in the air, and sometimes out to one side among the fences, and kicking up m-o-r-e dust and raising m-o-r-e racket with her coughing and sneez-ing and blowing her nose—and *al-ways* fetch up at the stand just about a neck ahead, as near as you could cipher it down.

"And he had a little small bull pup, that to look at him you'd think he warn't worth a cent but to set around and look ornery and lay for a chance to steal something. But as soon as money was up on him he was a dif-ferent dog; his underjaw'd begin to stick out like the fo'castle of a steamboat, and his teeth would uncover and shine like the furnaces. And a dog might tackle him and bullyrag him, and bite him, and throw him over his shoulder two or three times, and Andrew Jackson—which was the name of the pup—Andrew Jackson would never let on but what *he* was satisfied, and hadn't expected nothing else—and the bets being doubled and doubled on the other side all the time, till the money was all up; and then all of a sudden he would grab that other dog jest by the j'int of his hind leg and freeze to it—not chaw, you understand, but only just grip and hang on till they throwed up the sponge, if it was a year. Smiley always come out winner on that pup, till he harnessed a dog once that didn't have no hind legs, because they'd been sawed off in a circular saw, and when the thing had gone along far enough, and the money was all up, and he come to make a snatch for his pet holt, he see in a minute how he'd been imposed on,[10] and how the other dog had him in the door, so to speak, and he 'peared surprised, and then he looked sorter discouraged-like and didn't try no more to win the fight, and so he got shucked out bad. He give Smiley a look, as much as to say his heart was broke, and it was *his* fault, for putting up a dog that hadn't no hind legs for him to take holt of, which was his main dependence in a fight, and then he limped off a piece and laid down and died. It was a good pup, was that Andrew Jackson, and would have made a name for hisself if he'd lived, for the stuff was in him and he had genius—I know it, because he hadn't no opportunities to speak of, and it don't stand to reason that a dog could make such a fight as he could under them circumstances if he hadn't no talent. It always makes me feel sorry when I think of that last fight of his'n, and the way it turned out.

"Well, thish-yer Smiley had rat-tarriers, and chicken cocks, and tom-cats and all them kind of things, till you couldn't rest, and you couldn't fetch nothing for him to bet on but he'd match you. He ketched a frog one day, and took him home, and said he cal'lated[11] to educate him; and so he never done nothing for three months but set in his back yard and learn that frog to jump. And you bet you he *did* learn him, too. He'd give him a little punch behind, and the next minute you'd see that frog whirling in the air like a dough-nut—see him turn one summerset, or maybe a couple, if he got a good start, and come down flat-footed and all right, like a cat. He got him up so in the matter of ketching flies, and kep' him in practice so constant, that he'd nail a fly every time as fur as he could see him. Smiley said all a frog wanted was education, and he could do 'most anything—and I believe him. Why, I've seen him set Dan'l Webster down here on this floor—Dan'l Webster was the name of the frog—and sing out, 'Flies, Dan'l, flies!' and quicker'n you could wink he'd spring straight up and snake a fly off'n the

10 **imposed on:** here, tricked; cheated.   11 **cal'lated:** calculated.

counter there, and flop down on the floor ag'in as solid as a gob of mud, and fall to scratching the side of his head with his hind foot as indifferent as if he hadn't no idea he'd been doin' any more'n any frog might do. You never see a frog so modest and straightfor'ard as he was, for all he was so gifted. And when it come to fair and square jumping on a dead level, he could get over more ground at one straddle than any animal of his breed you ever see. Jumping on a dead level was his strong suit, you understand; and when it come to that, Smiley would ante up money on him as long as he had a red. Smiley was monstrous proud of his frog, and well he might be, for fellers that had traveled and been everywheres all said he laid over any frog that ever *they* see.

"Well, Smiley kep' the beast in a little lattice box, and he used to fetch him down town sometimes and lay for a bet. One day a feller—a stranger in the camp, he was—come acrost him with his box, and says:

" 'What might it be that you've got in the box?'

"And Smiley says, sorter indifferent-like: 'It might be a parrot, or it might be a canary, maybe, but it ain't —it's only just a frog.'

"And the feller took it, and looked at it careful, and turned it round this way and that, and says: 'H'm—so 'tis. Well, what's *he* good for?'

" 'Well,' Smiley says, easy and careless, 'he's good enough for *one* thing, I should judge—he can outjump any frog in Calaveras county.'

"The feller took the box again, and took another long, particular look, and give it back to Smiley, and says, very deliberate, 'Well,' he says, 'I don't see no p'ints about that frog that's any better'n any other frog.'

" 'Maybe you don't,' Smiley says. 'Maybe you understand frogs and maybe you don't understand 'em; maybe you've had experience, and maybe you ain't only a amature,[12] as it were. Anyways, I've got *my* opinion, and I'll resk forty dollars that he can outjump any frog in Calaveras county.'

"And the feller studied a minute, and then says, kinder sad like, 'Well, I'm only a stranger here, and I 'ain't got no frog; but if I had a frog, I'd bet you.'

"And then Smiley says, 'That's all right—that's all right—if you'll hold my box a minute, I'll go and get you a frog.' And so the feller took the box, and put up his forty dollars along with Smiley's, and set down to wait.

"So he set there a good while thinking and thinking to hisself, and then he got the frog out and prized his mouth open and took a teaspoon and filled him full of quail shot— filled him pretty near up to his chin— and set him on the floor. Smiley he went to the swamp and slopped around in the mud for a long time, and finally he ketched a frog, and fetched him in, and give him to this feller, and says:

" 'Now, if you're ready, set him alongside of Dan'l, with his forepaws just even with Dan'l's, and I'll give

12 **amature:** amateur.

the word.' Then he says, 'One—two —three—*git!*' and him and the feller touched up the frogs from behind, and the new frog hopped off lively, but Dan'l give a heave, and hysted up his shoulders—so—like a Frenchman, but it warn't no use—he couldn't budge; he was planted as solid as a church, and he couldn't no more stir than if he was anchored out. Smiley was a good deal surprised, and he was disguted too, but he didn't have no idea what the matter was, of course.

"The feller took the money and started away; and when he was going out at the door, he sorter jerked his thumb over his shoulder—so—at Dan'l, and says again, very deliberate, 'Well,' he says, 'I don't see no p'ints about that frog that's any better'n any other frog.'

"Smiley he stood scratching his head and looking down at Dan'l a long time, and at last he says, 'I do wonder what in the nation that frog throw'd off for—I wonder if there ain't something the matter with him —he 'pears to look mighty baggy, somehow.' And he ketched Dan'l by the nap of the neck, and hefted him, and says, 'Why, blame my cats if he don't weigh five pound!' and turned him upside down and he belched out a double handful of shot. And then he see how it was, and he was the maddest man—he set the frog down and took out after that feller, but he never ketched him. And—"

Here Simon Wheeler heard his name called from the front yard, and got up to see what was wanted. And turning to me as he moved away, he said: "Just set where you are, stranger, and rest easy—I ain't going to be gone a second."

But, by your leave, I did not think that a continuation of the history of the enterprising vagabond *Jim* Smiley would be likely to afford me much information concerning the Rev. *Leonidas* W. Smiley, and so I started away.

At the door I met the sociable Wheeler returning, and he buttonholed me and recommenced:

"Well, thish-yer Smiley had a yaller one-eyed cow that didn't have no tail, only just a short stump like a bannanner, and—"

However, lacking both time and inclination, I did not wait to hear about the afflicted cow, but took my leave.

Understanding Literature

1. In this story there is a double plot: the story of the "I" who is telling the whole tale, and the story told by Simon Wheeler. What do you learn in the opening paragraphs about the "I"? about Simon Wheeler?
2. In the fourth paragraph Wheeler begins telling the story of Jim Smiley. How does Smiley spend his time? Tell in your own words the anecdotes about Smiley described in the fourth paragraph.

3. Tell the stories of Smiley and his mare and of Smiley and his bull pup. How is the story of the bull pup like the story of the frog?

4. Repeated phrases are always important in a story. Twice "the feller" in the story says, "I don't see no p'ints about that frog that's any better'n any other frog." How does Smiley react the first time it is said? How does he react the second time?

5. Look back at the first three paragraphs and at the ending (after Smiley's story). What is the "I" in the story like? What is his reaction to the story? What is your reaction to the story?

6. Find examples of Mark Twain's use of exaggeration or over-statement.

Edgar Allan Poe, one of America's greatest writers, was a master of the short horror story. Here he is concerned not so much with a murder as with a man's reaction to it. What is going on inside the mind of the narrator, the teller of the tale?

The Telltale Heart

Edgar Allan Poe

IMPROVING YOUR READING: A writer establishes the *mood* of his story by the way he describes how different things look, feel, and sound. A dark, empty house at night is quite different from a pond in bright sunlight; each scene creates a different mood. Thus an author can change the mood by the way he uses light or dark and sound or silence, and by shifting from one scene to another. How does Poe build the mood, or atmosphere, in this story?

TRUE!—NERVOUS—very, very dreadfully nervous I had been and am; but why *will* you say that I am mad? The disease had sharpened my senses —not destroyed—not dulled them. Above all was the sense of hearing acute. I heard all things in the heaven and in the earth. I heard many things in hell. How, then, am I mad? Hearken! and observe how healthily—how calmly I can tell you the whole story.

It is impossible to say how first the idea entered my brain; but once conceived, it haunted me day and night. Object there was none. Passion there was none. I loved the old man. He had never wronged me. He had never given me insult. For his gold I had no desire. I think it was his eye! yes, it was this! One of his eyes resembled that of a vulture—a pale blue eye, with a film over it. Whenever it fell upon me, my blood ran cold; and so by degrees—very gradually—I made up my mind to take the life of the old man, and thus rid myself of the eye forever.

Now this is the point. You fancy me mad. Madmen know nothing. But you should have seen *me*. You should have seen how wisely I proceeded—with what caution—with what foresight—with what dissimulation[1] I went to work! I was never kinder to the old man than during the whole week before I killed him. And every night, about midnight, I turned the latch of his door and opened it—oh, so gently! And then, when I had made an opening sufficient for my head, I put in a dark lantern, all closed, closed, so that no light shone out, and then I thrust in my head. Oh, you would have laughed to see how cunningly I

1 **dissimulation** (dĭ sĭm′yə lā′shən): pretense; deception.

thrust it in! I moved it slowly—very, very slowly, so that I might not disturb the old man's sleep. It took me an hour to place my whole head within the opening so far that I could see him as he lay upon his bed. Ha!—would a madman have been so wise as this? And then, when my head was well in the room, I undid the lantern cautiously—oh, so cautiously—cautiously (for the hinges creaked)—I undid it just so much that a single thin ray fell upon the vulture eye. And this I did for seven long nights—every night just at midnight—but I found the eye always closed; and so it was impossible to do the work; for it was not the old man who vexed me, but his Evil Eye. And every morning, when the day broke, I went boldly into the chamber, and spoke courageously to him, calling him by name in a hearty tone, and inquiring how he had passed the night. So you see he would have been a very profound old man, indeed, to suspect that every night, just at twelve, I looked in upon him while he slept.

Upon the eighth night I was more than usually cautious in opening the door. A watch's minute hand moves more quickly than did mine. Never before that night had I *felt* the extent of my own powers—of my sagacity.[2] I could scarcely contain my feelings of triumph. To think that there I was, opening the door, little by little, and he not even to dream of my secret deeds or thoughts. I fairly chuckled at the idea; and perhaps he

heard me; for he moved on the bed suddenly, as if startled. Now you may think that I drew back—but no. His room was as black as pitch with the thick darkness (for the shutters were close fastened, through fear of robbers), and so I knew that he could not see the opening of the door, and I kept pushing it on steadily, steadily.

I had my head in, and was about to open the lantern, when my thumb slipped upon the tin fastening, and the old man sprang up in the bed, crying out—"Who's there?"

I kept quite still and said nothing. For a whole hour I did not move a muscle, and in the meantime I did not hear him lie down. He was still sitting up in the bed listening—just as I have done, night after night, hearkening to the death watches in the wall.

Presently I heard a slight groan, and I knew it was the groan of mortal terror. It was not a groan of pain or of grief—oh, no!—it was the low stifled sound that arises from the bottom of the soul when overcharged with awe. I knew the sound well. Many a night, just at midnight, when all the world slept, it has welled up from my own bosom, deepening, with its dreadful echo, the terrors that distracted me. I say I knew it well. I knew what the old man felt, and pitied him, although I chuckled at heart. I knew that he had been lying awake ever since the first slight noise, when he had turned in the bed. His fears had been ever since growing upon him. He had been trying to fancy them causeless, but could not. He had been saying to

2 **sagacity** (sə găs′ə tĭ): shrewdness; cunning.

PLOT

himself—"It is nothing but the wind in the chimney—it is only a mouse crossing the floor," or "it is merely a cricket which has made a single chirp." Yes, he has been trying to comfort himself with these suppositions; but he had found all in vain. *All in vain;* because Death, in approaching him, had stalked with his black shadow before him, and enveloped the victim. And it was the mournful influence of the unperceived[3] shadow that caused him to feel—although he neither saw nor heard—to *feel* the presence of my head within the room.

When I had waited a long time, very patiently, without hearing him lie down, I resolved to open a little—a very, very little crevice in the lantern. So I opened it—you cannot imagine how stealthily, stealthily—until, at length, a single dim ray, like the thread of the spider, shot from out of the crevice and full upon the vulture eye.

It was open—wide, wide open—and I grew furious as I gazed upon it. I saw it with perfect distinctness—all a dull blue, with a hideous veil over it that chilled the very marrow in my bones; but I could see nothing else of the old man's face or person: for I had directed the ray as if by instinct, precisely upon the damned spot.

And now have I not told you that what you mistake for madness is but over-acuteness of the senses?—now, I say, there came to my ears a low, dull, quick sound, such as a watch makes when enveloped in cotton. I knew *that* sound well too. It was the beating of the old man's heart. It increased my fury, as the beating of a drum stimulates the soldier into courage.

But even yet I refrained and kept still. I scarcely breathed. I held the lantern motionless. I tried how steadily I could maintain the ray upon the eye. Meantime the hellish tattoo[4] of the heart increased. It grew quicker and quicker, and louder and louder every instant. The old man's terror *must* have been extreme! It grew louder, I say, louder every moment!—do you mark me well? I have told you that I am nervous: so I am. And now at the dead hour of the night, amid the dreadful silence of that old house, so strange a noise as this excited me to uncontrollable terror. Yet, for some minutes longer I refrained and stood still. But the beating grew louder, louder! I thought the heart must burst. And now a new anxiety seized me—the sound would be heard by a neighbor! The old man's hour had come! With a loud yell, I threw open the lantern and leaped into the room. He shrieked once—once only. In an instant I dragged him to the floor, and pulled the heavy bed over him. I then smiled gaily, to find the deed so far done. But, for many minutes, the heart beat on with a muffled sound. This, however, did not vex me; it would not be heard through the wall. At length it ceased. The old man

---

3 **unperceived:** unseen. 4 **tattoo:** here, beating; drumming.

was dead. I removed the bed and examined the corpse. Yes, he was stone, stone dead. I placed my hand upon the heart and held it there many minutes. There was no pulsation. He was stone dead. His eye would trouble me no more.

If still you think me mad, you will think so no longer when I describe the wise precautions I took for the concealment of the body. The night waned, and I worked hastily, but in silence. First of all I dismembered the corpse. I cut off the head and the arms and the legs.

I then took up three planks from the flooring of the chamber, and deposited all between the scantlings. I then replaced the boards so cleverly, so cunningly, that no human eye—not even *his*—could have detected anything wrong. There was nothing to wash out—no stain of any kind—no blood spot whatever. I had been too wary for that. A tub had caught all —ha! ha!

When I had made an end of these labors, it was four o'clock—still dark as midnight. As the bell sounded the hour, there came a knocking at the street door. I went down to open it with a light heart—for what had I *now* to fear? There entered three men, who introduced themselves, with perfect suavity,[5] as officers of the police. A shriek had been heard by a neighbor during the night; suspicion of foul play had been aroused; information had been lodged at the police office, and they (the officers) had been deputed[6] to search the premises.

I smiled—for *what* had I to fear? I bade the gentlemen welcome. The shriek, I said, was my own in a dream. The old man, I mentioned, was absent in the country. I took my visitors all over the house. I bade them search—search *well*. I led them, at length, to *his* chamber. I showed them his treasures, secure, undisturbed. In the enthusiasm of my confidence, I brought chairs into the room, and desired them *here* to rest from their fatigues, while I myself, in the wild audacity of my perfect triumph, placed my own seat upon the very spot beneath which reposed the corpse of the victim.

The officers were satisfied. My *manner* had convinced them. I was singularly at ease. They sat, and while I answered cheerily, they chatted familiar things. But, ere long, I felt myself getting pale and wished them gone. My head ached, and I fancied a ringing in my ears: but still they sat and still they chatted. The ringing became more distinct:— it continued and became more distinct: I talked more freely to get rid of the feeling: but it continued and gained definitiveness—until, at length, I found that the noise was *not* within my ears.

No doubt I now grew *very* pale;— but I talked more fluently,[7] and with a heightened voice. Yet the sound increased—and what could I do? It was *a low, dull, quick sound—such a*

5 **suavity** (swăv′ə tǐ): here, smooth politeness.
6 **deputed:** assigned.
7 **more fluently:** more easily; faster.

sound as a watch makes when enveloped in cotton. I gasped for breath—and yet the officers heard it not. I talked more quickly—more vehemently; but the noise steadily increased. I arose and argued about trifles, in a high key and with violent gesticulations,[8] but the noise steadily increased. Why *would* they not be gone? I paced the floor to and fro with heavy strides, as if excited to fury by the observation of the men—but the noise steadily increased. Oh God! what *could* I do? I foamed—I raved—I swore! I swung the chair upon which I had been sitting, and grated it upon the boards, but the noise arose over all and continually increased. It grew louder—louder—louder! And still the men chatted pleasantly, and smiled. Was it possible they heard not? Almighty God! —no, no! They heard!—they suspected!—they *knew!*—they were making a mockery of my horror!—this I thought, and this I think. But anything was better than this agony! Anything was more tolerable than this derision! I could bear those hypocritical smiles no longer! I felt that I must scream or die!—and now —again!—hark! louder! louder! louder! *louder!*—

"Villains!" I shrieked, "dissemble[9] no more! I admit the deed!—tear up the planks!—here, here!—it is the beating of his hideous heart!"

---

8 **gesticulations** (jĕs tĭk′yə lā′shənz): gestures.

9 **dissemble** (dĭ sĕm′bəl): pretend.

Understanding Literature

1. What is the setting of the story? Point out specific phrases that show where the story takes place.
2. Why does the narrator take the police to the old man's chamber?
3. The narrator of the story states several times that the reader may think that he is a madman, but that he is not. Is he a madman? What evidence can you find for your answer?
4. In what manner does the murderer reveal the hiding place of the body to the police?
5. Where do you suppose the narrator, the "I," is when he tells the story?
6. What use is made of sound or lack of sound in the events of the story? If you read aloud a section of the story, following the rhythm of the lines, you will find that the author tries to imitate the beating of a heart. Note especially the paragraph beginning "No doubt I now grew *very* pale. . . ." In what way does the sound of this paragraph differ from the sound of the earlier ones?
7. Point out places where Poe uses light and dark to create a particular mood.

Further Activities

1. Write a one-paragraph report on the murder as it might have been written by one of the policemen.
2. At some time in your life you have probably felt fear or fright. When you got over this fear, you might have found that it was quite ridiculous; you may have even laughed about it. Prepare a short talk in which you describe a time when you were frightened. Perhaps you will want to use some of the words Poe used to establish a mood of fear.

   Think through your talk so that you can be brief and to the point. Probably more time should be spent on planning your beginning sentence than on any other. Your first sentence should immediately arouse the interest of your listeners. The closing sentence is next in importance.

   If you are called upon to tell about your experience, work to appear poised, look at your audience so that everyone feels included, and be enthusiastic and expressive about what you have to tell.

Focusing on Words

A suffix is a letter or group of letters added to the end of a word or to the root of a word. The suffix *phobia* signifies fear or dislike of something. For example, *claustrophobia* is fear of being enclosed in a small area. *Acrophobia* is a fear of high places. If you see, therefore, the suffix *-phobia* added to the stem word, you will know it means a fear of something. Often *phobia* is used alone in a sentence as in "He has a phobia about lightning." Find and define five other words ending in *-phobia*.

Langston Hughes, one of the best-known Black American authors, wrote poetry, non-fiction, and fiction. This short story concerns a boy who wanted something very badly, and a woman he met while trying to get it. Could such a boy or such a woman really have lived?

Thank You, M'am

Langston Hughes

IMPROVING YOUR READING: The first paragraph of this story is a lot like the first paragraph of a newspaper story. It tells you a great deal very quickly—*what* is happening, *whom* it is happening to, *where* it is happening, *how* it is happening. The author could have taken several pages of dialogue and description to tell all that he tells in the first paragraph. Does the matter-of-fact writing in this paragraph help you to get involved in the story more quickly?

SHE WAS a large woman with a large purse that had everything in it but hammer and nails. It had a long strap and she carried it slung across her shoulder. It was about eleven o'clock at night, and she was walking alone, when a boy ran up behind her and tried to snatch her purse. The strap broke with the single tug the boy gave it from behind. But the boy's weight, and the weight of the purse combined caused him to lose his balance so, instead of taking off full blast as he had hoped, the boy fell on his back on the sidewalk, and his legs flew up. The large woman simply turned around and kicked him right square in his blue jeaned sitter. Then she reached down, picked the boy up by his shirt front, and shook him until his teeth rattled.

After that the woman said, "Pick up my pocketbook, boy, and give it here."

She still held him. But she bent down enough to permit him to stoop and pick up her purse. Then she said, "Now ain't you ashamed of yourself?"

Firmly gripped by his shirt front, the boy said, "Yes'm."

The woman said, "What did you want to do it for?"

The boy said, "I didn't aim to."

She said, "You a lie!"

By that time two or three people passed, stopped, turned to look, and some stood watching.

"If I turn you loose, will you run?" asked the woman.

"Yes'm," said the boy.

"Then I won't turn you loose," said the woman. She did not release him.

"I'm very sorry, lady, I'm sorry," whispered the boy.

"Um-hum! And your face is dirty. I got a great mind to wash your face for you. Ain't you got nobody home to tell you to wash your face?"

"No'm," said the boy.

"Then it will get washed this evening," said the large woman, starting up the street, dragging the frightened boy behind her.

He looked as if he were fourteen or fifteen, frail and willow-wild[1], in tennis shoes and blue jeans.

The woman said, "You ought to be my son. I would teach you right from wrong. Least I can do right now is to wash your face. Are you hungry?"

"No'm," said the being-dragged boy. "I just want you to turn me loose."

"Was I bothering you when I turned that corner?" asked the woman.

"No'm."

"But you put yourself in contact with *me*," said the woman. "If you think that that contact is not going to last awhile, you got another thought coming. When I get through with you, sir, you are going to remember Mrs. Luella Bates Washington Jones."

Sweat popped out on the boy's face and he began to struggle. Mrs. Jones stopped, jerked him around in front of her, put a half-nelson[2] about his

1 **willow-wild:** as wild as a willow tree.

2 **half-nelson:** a wrestling term; a hold in which one arm is put under the same arm of the other person, and the hand is put on the back of his neck.

neck, and continued to drag him up the street. When she got to her door, she dragged the boy inside, down a hall, and into a large kitchenette-furnished room at the rear of the house. She switched on the light and left the door open. The boy could hear other roomers laughing and talking in the large house. Some of their doors were open, too, so he knew he and the woman were not alone. The woman still had him by the neck in the middle of her room.

She said, "What is your name?"

"Roger," answered the boy.

"Then, Roger, you go to that sink and wash your face," said the woman, whereupon she turned him loose—at last. Roger looked at the door—looked at the woman—looked at the door— *and went to the sink.*

"Let the water run until it gets warm," she said. "Here's a clean towel."

"You gonna take me to jail?" asked the boy, bending over the sink.

"Not with that face, I would not take you nowhere," said the woman. "Here I am trying to get home to cook me a bite to eat and you snatch my pocketbook! Maybe you ain't been to your supper either, late as it be. Have you?"

"There's nobody home at my house," said the boy.

"Then we'll eat," said the woman. "I believe you're hungry—or been hungry—to try to snatch my pocketbook."

"I wanted a pair of blue suede shoes," said the boy.

"Well, you didn't have to snatch my pocketbook to get some suede shoes," said Mrs. Luella Bates Washington Jones. "You could of asked me."

"M'am?"

The water dripping from his face, the boy looked at her. There was a long pause. A very long pause. After he had dried his face and not knowing what else to do dried it again, the boy turned around, wondering what next. The door was open. He could make a dash for it down the hall. He could run, run, run, run, run!

The woman was sitting on the day-bed. After awhile she said, "I were young once and I wanted things I could not get."

There was another long pause. The boy's mouth opened. Then he frowned, but not knowing he frowned.

The woman said, "Um-hum! You thought I was going to say *but*, didn't you? You thought I was going to say, *but I didn't snatch people's pocketbooks.* Well, I wasn't going to say that." Pause. Silence. "I have done things, too, which I would not tell you, son—neither tell God, if he didn't already know. So you set down while I fix us something to eat. You might run that comb through your hair so you will look presentable."

In another corner of the room behind a screen was a gas plate and an icebox. Mrs. Jones got up and went behind the screen. The woman did not watch the boy to see if he was going to run now, nor did she watch her purse which she left behind her on the day-bed. But the boy took care to sit on the far side of the room where he thought she could easily see him out of the corner of her eye, if she wanted to. He did not trust the woman *not* to trust him. And he did not want to be mistrusted now.

"Do you need somebody to go to the store," asked the boy, "maybe to get some milk or something?"

"Don't believe I do," said the woman, "unless you just want sweet milk yourself. I was going to make cocoa out of this canned milk I got here."

"That will be fine," said the boy.

She heated some lima beans and ham she had in the icebox, made the cocoa, and set the table. The woman did not ask the boy anything about where he lived, or his folks, or anything else that would embarrass him. Instead, as they ate, she told him about her job in a hotel beauty-shop that stayed open late, what the work was like, and how all kinds of women came in and out, blondes, red-heads, and Spanish. Then she cut him a half of her ten-cent cake.

"Eat some more, son," she said.

When they were finished eating she got up and said, "Now, here, take this ten dollars and buy yourself some blue suede shoes. And next time, do not make the mistake of latching onto *my* pocketbook *nor nobody else's*—because shoes come by devilish like that will burn your feet. I got to get my rest now. But I wish you would behave yourself, son, from here on in."

She led him down the hall to the front door and opened it. "Goodnight! Behave yourself, boy!" she said, looking out into the street.

The boy wanted to say something else other than, "Thank you, m'am," to Mrs. Luella Bates Washington Jones, but he couldn't do so as he turned at the barren stoop and looked back at the large woman in the door. He barely managed to say, "Thank you," before she shut the door. And he never saw her again.

Understanding Literature

1. Why did the boy want to steal the woman's purse?
2. Why did the woman take the boy home with her?
3. Was the boy different at the end of the story from what he was at the beginning?
4. Why do you think the boy never saw the woman again?

Poor Sam McGee loves gold, but he cannot stand cold weather. How can he survive in the Yukon?

Poems that tell a story are called *narrative poems*. They use the same devices, such as setting, exposition, and mood, that you find in short stories.

The Cremation of Sam McGee

Robert W. Service

There are strange things done in the midnight sun
*   By the men who moil[1] for gold;*
The Arctic trails have their secret tales
*   That would make your blood run cold;*
The Northern Lights have seen queer sights,
*   But the queerest they ever did see*
Was that night on the marge[2] of Lake Lebarge
*   I cremated Sam McGee.*

Now Sam McGee was from Tennessee, where the cotton blooms and blows.
Why he left his home in the South to roam 'round the Pole, God only knows.
He was always cold, but the land of gold seemed to hold him like a spell;
Though he'd often say in his homely way that "he'd sooner live in hell."

On a Christmas Day we were mushing our way over the Dawson trail
Talk of your cold! through the parka's fold it stabbed like a driven nail.
If our eyes we'd close, then the lashes froze till sometimes we couldn't see;
It wasn't much fun, but the only one to whimper was Sam McGee.

And that very night, as we lay packed tight in our robes beneath the snow,
And the dogs were fed, and the stars o'erhead were dancing heel and toe,
He turned to me, and "Cap," says he, "I'll cash in this trip, I guess;
And if I do, I'm asking that you won't refuse my last request."

Well, he seemed so low that I couldn't say no; then he says with a sort of moan:
"It's the cursèd cold, and it's got right hold till I'm chilled clean through to the bone.
Yet 'taint being dead—it's my awful dread of the icy grave that pains;
So I want you to swear that, foul or fair, you'll cremate my last remains."

---

1 moil: work; toil.   2 marge: here, shore.

A pal's last need is a thing to heed, so I swore I would not fail;
And we started on at the streak of dawn; but God! he looked ghastly pale.
He crouched on the sleigh, and he raved all day of his home in Tennessee;
And before nightfall a corpse was all that was left of Sam McGee.

There wasn't a breath in that land of death, and I hurried, horror-driven,
With a corpse half hid that I couldn't get rid, because of a promise given;
It was lashed to the sleigh, and it seemed to say: "You may tax your brawn
   and brains,
But you promised true, and it's up to you to cremate those last remains."

Now a promise made is a debt unpaid, and the trail has its own stern code.
In the days to come, though my lips were dumb, in my heart how I cursed
   that load.
In the long, long night, by the lone firelight, while the huskies, round in a
   ring,
Howled out their woes to the homeless snows—O God! how I loathed the
   thing.

And every day that quiet clay seemed to heavy and heavier grow;
And on I went, though the dogs were spent and the grub was getting low;
The trail was bad, and I felt half mad, but I swore I would not give in;
And I'd often sing to the hateful thing, and it hearkened with a grin.

Till I came to the marge of Lake Lebarge, and a derelict[3] there lay;
It was jammed in the ice, but I saw in a trice it was called the "Alice May."
And I looked at it, and I thought a bit, and I looked at my frozen chum;
Then "Here," said I, with a sudden cry, "is my cre-ma-tor-eum."

Some planks I tore from the cabin floor, and I lit the boiler fire;
Some coal I found that was lying around, and I heaped the fuel higher;
The flames just soared, and the furnace roared—such a blaze you seldom see;
And I burrowed a hole in the glowing coal, and I stuffed in Sam McGee.

Then I made a hike, for I didn't like to hear him sizzle so;
And the heavens scowled, and the huskies howled; and the wind began to
   blow.
It was icy cold, but the hot sweat rolled down my cheeks, and I don't
   know why;
And the greasy smoke in an inky cloak went streaking down the sky.

3 derelict: abandoned vessel.

I do not know how long in the snow I wrestled with grisly fear;
But the stars came out and they danced about ere again I ventured near;
I was sick with dread, but I bravely said: "I'll just take a peep inside.
I guess he's cooked, and it's time I looked;" . . . then the door I opened wide.

And there sat Sam, looking cool and calm, in the heart of the furnace roar;
And he wore a smile you could see a mile, and he said: "Please close that
   door.
It's fine in here, but I greatly fear you'll let in the cold and storm—
Since I left Plumtree, down in Tennessee, it's the first time I've been warm."

> *There are strange things done in the midnight sun*
>   *By the men who moil for gold;*
> *The Arctic trails have their secret tales*
>   *That would make your blood run cold;*
> *The Northern Lights have seen queer sights,*
>   *But the queerest they ever did see*
> *Was that night on the marge of Lake Lebarge*
>   *I cremated Sam McGee.*

Understanding Literature

1. What is the setting of the poem?
2. What is Sam's predicament, his unfortunate situation, as described in stanzas 4 and 5? Why does he want to be cremated?
3. How does the narrator try to cremate Sam? How does it affect Sam? Where is the climax of the poem?
4. What is the mood of the poem? How does the author create this mood?

Some stories sound almost too incredible to be real. The story of Kofi Akakpo, a teen-ager from Ghana, is one such tale. His incredible journey all started with the search for an American pen pal. The selection below is excerpted from an article entitled "The Odyssey of Charles Wayo" and includes part of the journal Kofi (Charles) kept on his trek.

"My Journey Is Still Long"

Charles L. Sanders

IMPROVING YOUR READING: Some of the elements of fiction are found in both biography and autobiography (the account of a person's life, written by that person). The best biographies include *conflict*, or a problem to be solved, and *suspense*. *Setting* may also play an important part in true stories. All are found in the true story of Kofi Akakpo (Charles Wayo). Ask yourself: Could this story have taken place somewhere else or at another time?

ONE WALKS THROUGH the villages of mud-and-wattle huts that ring Accra, Ghana, and sees women frying great baskets of fish and plantain which they spoon over *kenkey* and sell to anyone who will buy. They cook the seafood, fruit, and millet goo right on the street and keep the pots warm by banking their fires with dry leaves and wads of newspapers and magazines.

An old copy of a magazine was about to be tossed into such a fire one day in 1962 when 12-year-old Kofi Akakpo, a Hausa tribesman in the village of Nima, pulled it from a pile of waste paper, sat under a jacaranda tree, and became fasci-nated by the pictures of the people who looked like Hausas but had fine houses and clothes and cars and lived across the sea in the U.S.A.

Kofi kept the magazine for weeks, showed it to everyone in his village, and searched each page for the name of someone who might become his "pen pal" and tell him all about America and its people who looked like him. In the "Letters to the Editor," he saw a name he liked: Charles W. Simmons, Capt., U.S. Air Force. There was an APO number, and Kofi began writing down all the things he wanted to say. He wrote that he was a poor boy who had learned to read and write at a school where he worked as a clean-up boy. He said he swept the classrooms before dawn and then stood outside a window or door each day to listen to others recite their lessons. He studied the blackboards, he said, and rewrote everything on them before washing them for the next day's classes. In case Capt. Simmons would not believe his story, he gave as a reference the name of the man who ran the school.

The boy wrote that he wanted an education in America so that he could return to Africa and become a leader of his people. If Capt. Simmons helped him, he would "be your slave for a period of ten years." Then Kofi Akakpo signed the letter with a new name: Charles W. Wayo. The "Charles W." was, of course, the first name and initial of Capt. Simmons. The "Wayo" was Hausa for "man with smart brain." Then the boy walked to the post office in Accra and sent the letter on its way.

Capt. Simmons was impressed. He began writing to the boy, and he and friends sent him money, books, and clothes, and paid for a year of school. Charles (everyone was calling him that by now) won highest honors in his class and soon became First Boy in the entire school.

But Charles still dreamed of an education in American schools. By late 1963, when he was 14, he had decided what he would do. "I am leaving Ghana," he wrote to Capt. Simmons. "I am coming to you so that I will have a chance to complete my studies and then come back home to be the kind of leader that Africa needs."

Recalls Capt. Simmons, who was stationed in Ankara, Turkey, at the time: "I wrote back and praised his ambition, but I didn't think much more about his coming to me. After all, he was just a little kid, he was an entire continent away from me, and I wasn't able to send for him."

But Charles had made up his mind. He had saved 24 Ghanaian *cedis* (about $25) from the money that Capt. Simmons had sent him. He had gone to the U.S. Information Service Library in Accra and checked a map of the world. On the map, Turkey was, after all, only a few inches from Accra.

Getting up very early one morning, he put on a shirt and his khaki shorts. He took another shirt and made a bundle containing a towel, a pencil, and a writing pad. He told his mother that he was going into the bush to trap birds. His mother, who is, he says, a very beautiful woman who smiles all the time and is called Dede Aku, told him to come to her and hold her hand. "I think she knew I was planning something big because she looked real scared," Charles says. But, speaking Hausa, she told him to "come back home before the sun goes to bed."

Charles went into the bush, sat under a tree, said his prayers, cried a little, then began talking to God as if he were speaking to someone he knew real well: "Now look," he said. "This is going to be a real dangerous trip, and I have nobody to go with me but You and Death. It's up to You to protect me, because I'm going to find Captain Simmons. Good-bye."

He walked into Accra, stopped at a gas station, and bought a small calendar and a map. Then he went to a market and bought two or three loaves of bread and a pound of onions. He put everything into his bundle and headed in a direction he thought was north. He thinks he walked about 45 miles the first day. That night he sat under a tree and ate a little of the bread and an onion. Then he opened his blue writing pad and wrote the first of the entries that would become a remarkable diary of his long journey, his fears and loneliness, his struggle to survive the bush and the desert, and his frequent talks to a God who he believed would protect him from everything:

1st Jan. 1964

This night I am going to sleep in the bush here. I have left home all alone without the knowledge of my parents to go to look for my friend Capt. Charles Wesley Simmons of the US Air Force. I am about 45 miles from home (I mean Nima). My friend, the above, lives in Turkey. I am going to walk until I get to him. I must have to go to school. I am poor, I have no money, I can't get anywhere but walk. Legs were made before engines. With me are two friends— God and Death. Anyway, I am scared a little bit. God help me. Good night. Till tomorrow.

2nd Jan. 1964

Tonight, the sky is bright. I can see clearly. I have walked a lot and my legs are angry. I don't want to quarrel with them. So both of us must rest. I am about 100 miles from home now. I am almost beginning to know what lies ahead. I have bread and fried fish in my bundle. The fish is smelling, so I will eat all quick. The day's walk has been interesting. I saw many creatures. God is great. Never have I seen such beautiful animals playing all over in their kingdom. They did not bother me, except one antelope which kept running in the direction I am heading. I wondered why. Well, I am sleepy, so I will climb up an orange tree and pass the night peacefully. Good night.

3rd Jan. 1964

Today I passed many villages and picked some food on the village markets. Nobody bothered me. The night is cold. Oh, I remember home. I am very homesick. Tonight, I can imagine my parents sitting by the warm coal-pot fire, while I am very cold here. Anyway who asked me to leave the house? Nobody. I must bear the cold as a man. I have only khaki shorts on and my jumper. The mosquitoes are having a great feast on my legs. May God help me from fever. I am tired, so good night.

4th Jan. 1964

I was nearly killed yesterday. This is how: I was asleep for about two hours when I felt something heavy on my stomach. Opened my eyes. A big black snake crawling over me, heading opposite direction. Nearly screamed. Somebody held my throat and pressed my body very strong and still till my would-be assailant towed itself away. I regained consciousness. I don't think I can sleep tonight, just sit here and continue tomorrow. I don't think I am far away from Togo now. Good night.

Month after month Charles followed the north-south route from Agadés into Algeria, past the old French Foreign Legion outpost of Tamanrasset (formerly Ft. Laperrine), across the Tropic of Cancer, into the desert way-stations of In Salah, El Goléa, Ghardaia—the 1,000-mile route which leads straight up to Algiers on the Mediterranean. He spent long periods pacing himself, moving when he could from outpost to outpost, walking most of the way, but accepting rides on camels and on the one or two trucks that passed. It took him weeks to cross, for example, the Ahaggar—the mountain range which is one of the most cruel of all Sahara areas. It is here that the sun is so intense that the normally gray-brown rock has turned black, and hard-blown sand has polished the sides of mountains until they appear as huge mirrors that reflect the sun into one's eyes with an unbearable glare. At first, Charles tried covering his eyes with his hands and looking out through the spaces between his fingers, while using his shirt to cover his head. But the rocks cut his feet and the sand was too hot to bear. He tore the shirt into shreds, wrapped his feet, and told himself, he says, that "God will not let my brains boil." He began walking at night, hiding from the sun during the day in the shade of rocks and dunes. Somewhere between Agadés and In Salah, Charles made these entries in his diary:

5th July 1965

I am losing my strength very fast, so I must write something about myself before I die, so that you will know who I was. My name is Charles Wayo. My mother is called Dede Aku, my father is of the poorest family of Kwashie. They live in house No. E6/12 in the village of Nima, near Accra, Ghana. I left my home to find my friend, Capt. Charles W. Simmons, US Air Force, TUSLOG DOT30 APO254, New York. I had no money to take a plane, so I walked. Bury me where you find me and no ceremonies. Don't let my parents see my body for they will die. They love me and I love them, too. Tell them I have gone to the Houses of the Sun, and tell the world that I am sorry that I have not lived to my word. But I have no power over death. Tell my brother that I loved him and still love him. Tell him to clothe himself with manhood and get some education and one day he will be great. I am growing weaker now. Bye. There comes something now I cannot see well.

12th July 1965

This story is too miraculous to tell you here. But I will say it in short. Some French army men riding on the Sahara picked me up while dying. So, after all, God has taken mercy on my youth and granted me another pardon. Now the Frenchmen have left me with two month's supply of food after treating me for three days. They can't keep anyone longer than that. They brought me somewhere and said I should sit here and a truck will come soon and pick me up. I have sardines, some strange long bread which could be used to spank someone. I have a water can, etc. May the Lord guard, guide, and protect those men. And I was picked up again by some Arabs yesterday, and I am riding on top of a truck now. It is about 24 feet long and well packed with goods. I am enjoying it. The two men are sitting in front and I am right at the back. I am moving much faster now. . . .

Within two months, Charles had made his way to El Goléa in north-central Algeria. Then, riding on a cart with an old Arab, he reached Ghardaia by October. From there he walked on to the villages of Laghouat and Djelfa. In each place he made friends with Arabs, and they gave him water and such food as they had. At Djelfa, the Sahara had ended and Charles began seeing signs pointing to Algiers and the sea. He reached Algiers at the end of October. In his diary he wrote:

1st Nov. 1965

I am well glad to see such a fantastic city as Algiers. It is beautiful, and being here means that Wayo has conquered the Sahara. I am now halfway to Turkey, and only God knows that this is really me. I will not write anymore in my diary, for I am cold and still have a long way to go. Maybe I will write again when I reach my goal. Now I am going to Morocco, for someone has told me it is better to get to Turkey from there. Good-bye.

Following railroad tracks, Charles slipped across the border into Morocco and made his way to Fez and Meknes, then to Rabat, and finally to Tangier. He went to the Tangier docks, slipped aboard a ferry, and hid among barrels. Hours later he found himself across the Strait of Gibraltar at the port of Algeciras, Spain. He had reached Europe at last, but the route he had taken had landed him thousands of miles west of the Turkish city where Capt. Simmons lived.

In Spain, Charles underwent a remarkable change. This was the first "white" country he had ever seen, and, as he walked through Algeciras, he saw poor white people for the first time. No white man he had seen in Africa had been poor. But on the streets of Algeciras he saw white beggars—white people who were hungry, whose clothes were as ragged as his. As he left the city, following the signs that pointed toward Madrid, he saw white peasants along the road. In Cadiz, a beggar woman reached out and pleaded with him for a coin.

"I hated that woman," Charles recalls. "All of a sudden, and for the very first time in my life, I hated somebody, really hated somebody. I hated that woman and all the white people I was seeing in their own country for the first time. These are the people, I thought to myself, who made me believe all my life that they were superior to me, an African. These are the people whose books made me think that their cities were so rich that even the streets shone like mirrors and nobody was ever hungry and nobody ever wanted a place to sleep. I looked at those people who had not only conquered Africa, but had set themselves up as masters of the whole world, and I hated them for making me and my brother and my parents and so many other people of Africa believe that we would never have what white men had, and that we weren't supposed to ever hope for the same things. Just look there, I thought, one of them is begging me, and I'm one of those Africans that they've always said are useless, without brains, fit only to be slaves."

In Seville, Charles passed a cathedral and felt only contempt for the nuns and priests who he knew must be inside saying their prayers. He despised even those Spaniards who waved to him and called him "Amigo," and he pushed away the hands that tried to brush dirt from his hair. In Madrid, he stole fruit from the markets not only because he was hungry, but because, he says, he wanted to see how it felt to take something from white people for the first time.

The hate was with him, he says, until he made his way across the border at Hendaye and began walking through southern France. "I walked into the first little French village knowing that I looked real bad," he remembers. "I had on an old overcoat that a man had given me in Morocco when winter began setting in, and that old coat was filthy and smelling, and my hair must have been about four inches long. People stared at me and spoke in French, which I couldn't understand. But when I pointed to my stomach, they understood that I was hungry and gave me food. When I got into a village and cupped my hands to my mouth, the French knew that I was thirsty and gave me water. In one village I just said the word 'Paris' and some people took me by the hands, led me to a road, gave me food, and smiled as I waved good-bye. I walked all the way to Paris and none of the people in the villages treated me bad. They treated me just like the African village people had done, and I knew for the first time that white people and black people could be just the same. I knew they could be poor, and get sick and everything, one just like the other. I stopped hating white people, and, if anything, I became more determined than ever to reach my goal and show them that Africans can build trains and buildings and big ships, too, and even be superior to them in some ways."

In Paris, Charles met an American couple who listened to his story, then helped him telephone Capt. Simmons to say that he was safe and on his way. Capt. Simmons sent him $50, but Charles lost the money before he could get to a train. "I felt so stupid about losing it," he says, "that I didn't want to phone him a second time. I just started walking all over again."

Charles was an old hand at slipping across borders ("Sometimes the border guards would ask for a passport, but I'd shake my head, then they'd look me up and down, shake their heads, and wave me on through"), so he had no trouble getting into Germany. He stayed in Aachen for a while, then went on to Cologne. It was here that he learned to hitchhike. "I met some boys on the road," he says, "and they showed me how to put my finger up in the air and make cars stop." He hitchhiked to Bonn, then walked to Wiesbaden, then followed the *autobahn* to Mannheim, Frankfurt, and Munich. Then he walked over the Austrian border which, he says, "was the easiest of all to cross." He thumbed his way across Austria, crossed into Yugoslavia, and began walking toward Belgrade. At Zagreb, he met an old couple who gave him food. "They watched me eat," he recalls, "and put their hands to their hearts to tell me they were my friends. Then I pointed toward the sky and spread my hands over them, which meant 'God bless you.' They understood and both of them cried."

A Swiss tourist gave Charles a ride into Belgrade, then he walked on to Dimitrovgrad. To get across the Bulgarian border he used sign language to make some farmers understand. They hid him under hay in their cart, crossed a border checkpoint, and kept him out of sight until they reached Sofia. Charles was very near to Ankara now. Only the Turkish border remained. "When I got there," he says, "I started figuring out how I'd slip past this last gate between me and Capt. Simmons. Then I saw an old man with a very long beard. I think he was Greek, but he could speak a little English and understand what I wanted to do. He thought for a while, then told me to grab his hand and talk real fast when we came close to the crossing point. I did just like he said and we walked right past the guards. I spent two days with that old man because he told me he had some friends who would be coming along to take a truck load of dates to Istanbul. Sure enough, they came and I rode all the way to Istanbul."

In Istanbul, Charles met four white American sailors from the S.S. *Saratoga*. He told them his story. Though one sailor asked him, "If you're a real African, where's the elephant bone you're supposed to wear in your nose?" he took him to the train station, bought a ticket to Ankara, and sent him on his way.

Charles thinks about the trip now and says, "When that train got to Ankara, I just didn't believe I was really me. I thought about the bush and the Sahara and all the things I had been through on that long journey, and then there I was in the very city where Capt. Simmons lived. I prayed to God and thanked him for guarding and guiding me, then I started trying to find my friend.

"The first thing I did was ask somebody where the American Embassy was located. Then I went there to see if they had Capt. Simmons's address. They said no, but there was a Marine guard there and he showed me where the Air Force officers lived."

It was the end of May, 1966—nearly 2½ years since the day that Charles had left his village home, and his heart was pounding, he says, as he stopped airman after airman and asked, "Do you know Capt. Charles W. Simmons? Do you know where he lives?" Finally someone showed Charles the Simmons apartment, and he says his hands were trembling with excitement as he walked upstairs and knocked on the door. He knocked twice, three times, again and again. But nobody was at home. "I sat right down on the steps and cried," he says, "but then a Negro airman came into the building and saw me there. I told him what had happened, and he said, 'Aw, fellow, come on in my house and relax. Simmons and his family will be back later on.'"

Hours later a car drove into the parking lot and a man, a woman, and some children got out and went into the apartment that had the Simmons name on the door. Charles went there and knocked again. When the door opened, he was so scared that he couldn't say a word. But then a very kind-faced man shouted, "You're Charles Wayo, aren't you?" Charles managed to say "Yes, sir, it's me." The man grabbed him and said "Well, I'll just be...." Charles's friend had been found.

Understanding Literature

1. Why did Kofi Akakpo (Charles Wayo) choose Captain Charles Simmons to be his pen pal?
2. Why did Kofi Akakpo change his name? Why was the new name so appropriate?
3. What dangers faced Wayo on his journey? How did he overcome them?
4. What change in Wayo's outlook took place in Spain? What caused this change? Was it permanent?
5. The title of this excerpt comes from a section of the Wayo story not printed in this book. What might have made Charles Wayo say "my journey is still long," even though he reached his destination, the Simmons home?

CHARLES L. SANDERS

Characterization

You READ literature partly to learn more about how people act and why they act that way. Reading, then, is important because it helps you to understand other people and to understand yourself.

In literature you judge a character in much the same way that you judge people in real life. Ordinarily you decide on a person's character by observing what he says, what he does, and, sometimes, by what others say about him. When John asks you about Joe, he says, "What's he like?" You base your answer on how you have seen Joe act and from what you have heard him say. In literature the author presents a person in action, and expects you to draw the conclusions which will answer the question, "What's he like?" Your answer will be determined by how thoughtfully you read.

In the following selections the characterization is very carefully done. The emphasis is on *motivation*, on why people act as they do.

One of the important things you need to understand in dealing with other people is that you seldom really know them. You get quick impressions of new people and then cling to those impressions. You do not know, at first, *why* they do what they do. As you get to know people better, you should be willing to change your mind. In the following story is an expression of an important idea: To know all is to forgive all. What does this statement mean? How does it relate to the story?

The Strangers That Came to Town

Ambrose Flack

IMPROVING YOUR READING: As a story begins and people move onto the scene, you should ask, "What are they like?" When you answer this question, you have judged the characters of the people; you speak of them as honest, cruel, or generous, for example. You are able to make this judgment because of the *characterization*. The author does not usually tell you what people are like; he lets them act out their characters. When Andy, who tells the following story, drops a cake of soap in the tub of fish, he shows a streak of cruelty. When his father carries out a series of acts, you see that he is fair. As you read, observe what people do and say, and then draw conclusions about what kinds of people they are.

THE FIRST OF April came dark and stormy, with silver whips of lightning cracking open the lowering clouds that seemed to skim the treetops. My brother Tom and I, recovering from chest colds, tired of reading and listening to the radio, turned to the big living-room window of our house on Syringa Street.

"Here they come, Mother," cried Tom when a big truck drove up in the teeming rain and stopped in front of the empty cottage across the street.

Mother hurried in from the kitchen and we three looked out. That truck, we knew, contained the Duvitch family and all their earthly possessions.

Mr. Duvitch and the biggest boy carefully helped Mrs. Duvitch from the seat and walked her into the house, supporting her all the way. Another big boy, carrying a well-bundled baby, followed. A stream of young Duvitches, accompanied by a big brown houndlike dog, poured out of the back of the truck and stood in a huddle in the rain.

The barnyard sounds we heard escaped from two crates of hens the Duvitches had fetched along and from a burlap bag in which a small flock of ducks had been stowed. While the livestock made noises according to its kind, the Duvitches were quiet—almost solemn. They showed no elation at finding themselves in a new neighborhood and a very pretty neighborhood at that.

All afternoon Mother, Tom and myself had been watching out for them, with rather mixed emotions. For the Duvitches were immigrants and the first of their nationality to settle in our small smug town. Coming to our obscure part of the state a year before, they had moved into a rotting old farmhouse two miles north of town, long abandoned. After the slashing hurricane of mid-March, the moss-rotten dwelling looked like the house in the fairy tale that remained standing only because it did not know which way to fall and the Duvitches were forced to give it up.

"I wonder if Mrs. Duvitch is ill," murmured Mother, looking through the rain at the dreary street scene.

"She must be," said Tom. "I wonder if it'll be all right for Andy and me to help 'em move in their stuff."

This request, as Mother well knew, was not inspired by genuine feeling for the Duvitches but by curiosity and she shook her head. It was a strict family rule that any illness which kept us out of school would automatically keep us indoors.

But the Duvitches got along very well without help from us. As it turned out, they were old hands at moving. For years before coming to America they had been on the move, to escape starvation, separation, possible assassination. Every child capable of two-legged locomotion pitched in and helped carry the things from the truck. In no time at all, it seemed, the truck was empty

and the Duvitches were shut up tight in their new home.

That was the signal for Mother to step into the kitchen. She returned swathed[1] in her hooded raincoat, carrying a basket containing a vacuum jug of chicken soup, a baked tuna-fish dish, steaming hot; a loaf of fresh bread and a chocolate cake. These she took to the house across the street and gave basket and all to the boy who answered her knock. It wasn't her plan to stop for a visit that day but to wait a week or so and call when the Duvitches were all settled.

The next day when the three of us —Mother, Tom and myself—were having lunch, we heard a faint tap at the back door. I answered it and there stood a pale dark-eyed boy, looking very solemn, holding our basket. It contained the empty vacuum jug, casserole dish and cake plate, all of which shone, and a tiny very shapely potted rose tree, in exquisite pink-tipped bud, the handsomest plant—and the only plant of its kind—ever seen in that neighborhood.

"I send them a few scraps of food," murmured Mother, a few seconds later, deeply touched, "and get this queenly gift!"

That was our last traffic with the Duvitch family for over two years. When Mother stopped to visit them a week after their coming, the little girl who opened the door a few inches said, "Mamma sick; she stay in bed today." Mrs. Duvitch never crossed the street to our house and Mother, a

1 swathed: wrapped.

CHARACTERIZATION

rather formal woman, made no further attempts to see the family. But Father disagreed when she remarked that she thought the Duvitches probably wished to be left alone.

Syringa Street seemed to be a friendly street. It was a crooked maple-shady country lane that wound through the town without losing its charm. The sidewalk here and there was almost lost in weeds and the ditches, in places, were brightened by clumps of orange day lilies. Widely spaced cottages, some of them smothered in vines, only seemed to make the neighborhood more rural. There were brilliant flower gardens, vegetable plots, fruit trees—and a few henhouses. The children, who enjoyed all the benefits of country life while actually living in town, were quite numerous. Behind the façades of the street's dwellings there was probably no more greed, envy, superstition or intolerance than lurked behind the doors of any average dwelling in any average American town. The cardinal[2] virtues, no doubt, were all represented. Yes, Syringa Street seemed to be a friendly street.

But the Duvitches were marked people. They were the one struggling family in a prosperous community—and poverty, amid prosperity, is often embarrassing and irritating to the prosperous. They were considered unattractive physically. They were so meek! The Duvitches never fought back.

The women started in on Mrs. Du-

vitch because she "never showed her face." It is true, she was rarely if ever seen in the daytime, emerging from her dwelling only after dark in warm weather, to sit on the veranda, where she found privacy behind the ragged trumpet creeper.[3] But this gave rise to the rumor that she was the victim of an obscure skin disease and that every morning she shook scales out of the bed sheet. (When my father heard that one, he went out to the pantry and mixed himself a tall drink.)

Mr. Duvitch, too, was classified as an untouchable. His job, a rather malodorous[4] one, was with the local rendering plant[5] as a laborer. It followed that the Syringa Street young, meeting him on the street, sometimes stopped their noses as they passed him by—a form of torment all the more acute when Mr. Duvitch had to share it with the children that happened to be with him.

Black hard luck seemed to be their lot.

A few weeks after they moved to Syringa Street they suffered a tragedy they were all summer in recovering from—Mr. Duvitch lost two weeks' pay while gathering mushrooms in Tamarack Swamp. Inside of a year and a half, three Duvitch boys had lost, among them, by various mishaps, two fingers, one eye and an ear lobe. They were forever being cut up, bruised, mutilated by things falling, breaking, cracking and exploding.

A mild case of typhoid, mass cases

3 trumpet creeper: a climbing plant with trumpet-shaped flowers.
4 malodorous: ill-smelling.
5 rendering plant: a plant which makes industrial fats and oils from livestock carcasses.

2 cardinal: chief; most important.

of whooping cough and measles—all plagued the family within a year of their arrival. Their only bright spot here was Dr. Switzer, one of the town's kindliest souls. He declined to accept fees, but was several times seen leaving the Duvitch cottage, carrying off a handsome house plant and looking very pleased. The Duvitches' dog, Kasimar, acted just like the family to which he belonged—like one of the world's poorest canine relations. He seemed to be afraid of his own shadow and no one had ever heard him bark or growl.

Because they cast their eyes on the sidewalk as one passed them by and spoke only when spoken to, the young Duvitches, like their parents, were considered antisocial. They were regarded as born scavengers too, for they spent hours foraging[6] in the town dump, where they often picked up their footgear, some of their pants and shirts and furnishings for the house as well. They went on country excursions to gather watercress, dandelion greens, mushrooms and wild berries; and the few apples and tomatoes they occasionally concealed under their blouses didn't make the farmers on whom they poached much poorer. Tom and I raided tomato patches and robbed apple trees just for the fun of it.

That first September four Duvitches—Irving, Benny, Abe and Esther—registered at the local grammar school. Mrs. Lovejoy, the principal, said they were bright, conscientious, pathetically eager but almost pathologically[7] shy. Before she could put a stop to it, some of their classmates scoffed at the leaf-lard-and-black-bread sandwiches they ate for lunch, huddled in one corner of the recreation room, dressed in their boiled-out ragpickers' clothes. After school they headed straight for home, never lingering on the playground.

Even the tradesmen to whom the Duvitches gave good money were either curt[8] with them or downright rude. Mrs. Frithjof Kinsella, the proprietor of the general store and a big jolly Viking who could be heard two blocks away, extended credit to almost everybody in town and had a way of insulting her customers so heartily that they all loved her for it. The Duvitches, however, Mrs. Kinsella very carefully *did not insult* (a form of insult in itself) and neither did she extend them credit.

But Mother, remembering the potted rose tree, always had a friendly word and a smile for the young Duvitches when she saw them and a bone for Kasimar when he found courage to venture across the road. Father was the only man on Syringa Street who tipped his hat to sixteen-year-old pock-marked Maria Duvitch, otherwise quite pretty, when he met her coming home from her piece-work job in Miller's Box Factory. It may have been that their European travail[9] made it easy for them to endure such a trifle as humiliation in America.

"I think," said Father one fine Sat-

6 **foraging:** searching for provisions.

7 **pathologically:** abnormally.
8 **curt:** short in language.
9 **travail:** torment.

CHARACTERIZATION

urday morning in July two years after the Duvitches had come to Syringa Street, "that it would be very pleasant for Andy, Tom and myself to pitch our tent out at Durston's Pond and spend the night. We could fish and swim. That is," he added, "if Mother can spare us."

"I can spare you very well," Mother said cheerfully.

She had a notion it did menfolk good to get away from their women occasionally and in this instance the sacrifice came easily, because camp life was little to her liking. She packed a hamper of food, Tom and I fetched the tent from the attic and Father looked over his fishing tackle. An hour after lunch we were driving through rolling farm country out to Durston's Pond, four miles north of town.

We often had the serene little lake all to ourselves but on our arrival that afternoon we found half a dozen male Duvitches in possession. They had been fishing for several hours, casting from the shore, dropping their lines over the wooden bridge that spanned Cat Creek where it flowed into the pond and trolling for bass from a flat-bottomed rowboat.

Tom and I, Philistines[10] like our friends, ignored the Duvitch boys but Father went up to Mr. Duvitch, who was fishing from the shore, and put out his hand.

"Good afternoon, Mr. Duvitch! It's nice to see you and the boys here. What a beautiful day! Are Mrs. Duvitch and the girls all well?"

10 **Philistines:** here, insensitive people.

Mr. Duvitch was a little fellow, a lean starveling of a man with watery blue eyes and a kicked-about look. Gratitude for being agreeably noticed showed in his mosquito-bitten face as he took Father's hand and his tremulous smile showed broken teeth.

"I know the mosquitoes are biting," Father went on pleasantly, "but are the fish?"

Proudly, oh, so proudly, Mr. Duvitch exhibited the catch that would probably feed his family for the better part of a week: a fine mess of bass, perch and sunfish, all of them alive, as far as I could see, and swimming around in the oaken washtub in which they had been dropped. Father gave Mr. Duvitch hearty congratulations and said we couldn't hope to do as well but that we'd try.

We three pitched the tent on a little knoll over the pond, and then Father, with a happy sigh, lay down on the blanket for a nap in the sun. Tom and I played a game of chew-the-peg on the grassy bank above the water and, later on, made several trips to the tent, for the camera, the field glasses, the sun lotion. On a trip for a cold drink from the vacuum jug and to fetch towels and soap, we stopped to look again at the Duvitches' catch of fish.

Mr. Duvitch and the boys had moved away and were fishing in a a small arm of the pond below us. None of them seemed visible. Tom and I, our glances meeting over the big cake of soap in my hand, were similarly and wickedly inspired—the thing was irresistible. We held a brief whispering conversation; and then, egged on[11] by him and quite willing on my own, I played a shameful trick on the Duvitches, the memory of which will come back to the end of my days to plague me. Without considering further, I dropped the cake of soap into the tub of fish.

"Let's go," whispered Tom after we had watched the soap sink to the bottom.

We swam out to the raft, diving and frolicking in the deep water. After a while the Duvitches, calling it a day, assembled at a spot on the shore below our tent, happy in the knowledge of a good catch to take home.

In a little while Tom and I could hear their muffled exclamations of disbelief and dismay. Father woke up and joined our neighbors in a conclave,[12] looking down at the tub of fish near his feet. After a few moments he produced the whistle he carried on all our country excursions and blew it piercingly three times, the proclamation of emergency. This meant that Tom and I must come at once.

Looking as guilty as we felt, we swam in and joined the group gathering around the tub. In the midst of our stricken neighbors stood Father, holding the half-melted cake of soap in his palm silently but accusingly, for the fish had perished miserably in the soapy water and were unfit to eat. Not only had Tom and I snatched precious food from their mouths but we had brazenly[13] advertised the contempt[14] in which we held them.

Father's eyes were narrow slits of blue fire in his white face. I had never seen him so angry. One look at Tom and me told him everything. Words would have been superfluous[15] and my brother and I bowed our heads in acknowledgment of our guilt.

"You will begin," Father said in a voice I didn't recognize, "by saying you're sorry."

Our stunned neighbor wiped his blinking eyes as he listened to our mumbled words, which Father made us repeat when they were inaudible. But there was no hostility, no animosity[16] toward us in the man and it was obvious also that he considered himself too humble to receive an apology, finding it, like most of life's troubles, a mockery to be endured without protest. His sons showed no resentment, either, only a kind of resignation in their minds, which carried almost atavistic memories[17] of century-old oppression by country barons and landed gentry.

One-eyed Manny Duvitch, as it turned out, had told Father he had seen me drop something in the tub of fish (before he learned that it had been a cake of soap). Now he looked guiltier than Tom and I. Because he had been the witness and accuser, it was as if he considered himself to be the trouble-maker, deserving the punishment. The two real culprits were the young lords of the ruling manor,

14 **contempt:** scorn.
15 **superfluous:** unnecessary.
16 **animosity:** ill-will; resentment.
17 **atavistic memories:** memories inherited from ancestors.

11 **egged on:** encouraged.
12 **conclave:** private meeting.
13 **brazenly:** boldly; impudently.

CHARACTERIZATION

with unlimited license, exempt from chastisement.[18] To Manny, the fortunate, the well-to-do, were also the privileged.

"Do you realize," said Father coldly, looking from Tom to me, "that in certain primitive communities the sort of stunt you've pulled would be punishable by death?"

Tom and I did not reply.

"Turn over the tub," said Father abruptly, addressing us as if we were strangers.

We turned it over. The gray soapy water ran away in bubbly rivulets, disappearing in the coarse mat of turf, and the poisoned fish lay exposed on the grass—quiet, strangled, open-mouthed—and somehow looking as if they were mutely[19] protesting their horrid unnatural fate.

"Count the fish," Father ordered us, his voice like steel.

Tom and I got down on our knees.

"How many are there?" demanded Father.

"Sixty-one," I said.

"How many bass?"

"Twelve."

Father handed Mr. Duvitch two dollars, the price of a day's rental of the rowboat. Then, looking both the avenging angel and executioner, he ordered Tom and me, with our tackle and bait, off the land we had disgraced—into exile, out on Durston's Pond.

"And you are not to come back," he gave out in the same steely tones, "until you've caught sixty-one fish to repay Mr. Duvitch. See to it that among them you bring in at least a dozen bass."

Father stepped up to the tent on the knoll to fetch our shirts and dungarees. These he rolled into a tight ball and shot like a bolt into the rowboat. He then turned his back to us and, thus disowned, Tom and I lost no time in rowing out on the pond. Father's decisions, even with Mother present, were never reversed and swift execution, from which there was no appeal, followed his sentences.

Out in the middle of the big pond we dropped anchor, threaded our steel rods and, baiting our hooks, began to fish. I knew that if it took us all summer to catch them, we dared not set foot ashore without sixty-one fish. Almost at once Tom pulled in a good-sized bass and ten minutes later two yellow perch were added to our string. The crestfallen Duvitches went home. Father threw himself on the blanket, furiously smoking a cigar. That was about four in the afternoon.

Oh, the mosquitoes! They were bad enough at the time, and while the light held, but after we had been fishing for three hours and had caught eight fish, they swarmed out of the dark Hades of swampland surrounding the pond like Lucifer's[20] angels, in legions.

After an hour of it we wanted to leap overboard. They got in our ears, our noses, our eyes, even in our mouths, and nestling in our hair, they bit through to our scalps. I remembered tales of Indian prisoners in Alaska, stripped by their captors and turned loose on the tundra,[21] where they died of the mosquitoes in two hours. Several times we slipped over the side of the boat, immersing ourselves in the water to escape the bloodthirsty clouds. The night dragged on while the whining swarms grew thicker.

"Andy, what time is it?"

"Ten o'clock, Tom."

"Is that all?" Tom groaned and pulled in another bass and killed six or eight mosquitoes in one slap. Two hours passed and midnight was ghostly on Durston's Pond.

The moon, bright as day, sailed high in the purple sky, dimming the starfire, casting a great white shaft of quivering radiance on the water, but it was all hideous. The big yellow disk sank in a gauzy cloudbank, then disappeared for good and the stars shone out with renewed splendor.

"Andy, what *time* is it?"

"Two o'clock, Tom."

The treetops whispered as if in conspiracy against us. Owls hooted —mockingly we thought—and bats circled over our heads, making us feel thoroughly damned. Our only solace[22] was the campfire Father kept burning near the tent, which flared like a beacon light in the dark. We went on fishing as our tormentors bit and sang. Each hour was an eternity of frenzy and I fairly panted for the light of dawn to come, but even now

20 **Lucifer's:** the Devil's.

21 **tundra:** treeless plain.
22 **solace:** comfort.

I cannot decide which was worse, that night with the mosquitoes on Durston's Pond or the following day in the blistering heat.

"Andy—"

"It's four o'clock, Tom, and we've got sixteen fish."

Dawn came but even I, a highly impressionable youngster of seventeen, did not enjoy that calm effulgent[23] majesty of daybreak. A long stretch on Durston's Pond, under the July sun, still faced us.

The rising sun was red, casting glimmering circles of rose-colored light on the windless surface of the pond. The mosquitoes thinned, the fish continued to bite. But as we fished the sun mounted steadily and by eleven it had fulfilled its awful prophecy and became a ball of fire in the cloudless skies. Tom and I began to bake in the heat waves that shimmered over the pond and we were steamed in the scalding vapory mist.

"I wish it was night again, Andy," groaned Tom after sweating out two hours of it. "This is worse than the mosquitoes."

"At least we won't get any infections from our bites, Tom," I said feebly. "The sun's cauterizing[24] them."

"We might get sunstrokes, though. We're liable to, without our hats. But I don't care if I do. I'd rather be unconscious."

Tom was only fifteen and I think he hated me that day. I, the older, should have been his protector against participation in crime, not his accomplice. I wanted to row him in, then come back to finish the business alone, but there on the green Eden-like shore stood Father—the archangel bearing the fiery sword, stationed by the Lord at the gates of Paradise to bar the way.

Tom and I weighed our hooks down to the deep cold water. We caught two more bass and half a dozen sunfish.

By one o'clock groups of people gathered on the shore, for word of the drama that was being enacted on Durston's Pond had spread through the town. Some of the visitors praised Father for his stern discipline; others berated[25] him. He went right on reading his magazine and smoking his cigar, as indifferent to their praise as he was to their criticism.

Local fishermen who knew the lake and something about the angling ability of the average youngster made gloomy estimates as to the possible length of our exile on the water. A few had us fishing until the snow flew. They made bets too. Would Tom and I have the guts to stick it out? Most of the bets were against us.

But we sat there in the rowboat, without food, through the hottest day of the summer.

No breeze stirred. No cloud obscured the sun. Even the bird life of the swamp, usually a medley of song, was silent and dead. Tom was drooping visibly in the glare and I tried hard not to look at his scorched face.

---

23 **effulgent:** radiant; brightly shining.
24 **cauterizing:** burning; searing.

25 **berated:** criticized.

Between three and four we dropped lines in a school of yellow perch and pulled up no less than twenty. The bass continued to bite in the deep black holes off the swamp, which bristled with tree trunks. Benumbed, half-blinded, moving like automatons,[26] Tom and I geared ourselves for the home stretch.

When the sun, dropping low, had lost its fury and the hard blue enamel of the sky began to pale, I pulled up the thirteenth bass, which was our sixty-first fish.

Turned lobster-red, fairly devoured, famished and drooping from lack of sleep, we put together our rods and with our remaining strength rowed to where Father was waiting.

He received us coolly, making no comment on our condition. At once he asked to see the fish and we held them up by the strings.

"Count them," he said.

Obviously we would receive permission to land only when we had produced the required number, which was the price of our freedom.

"Sixty-one," said Tom.

"Including thirteen bass," I added.

"Very good," said Father in businesslike tones. "We will now restore to Mr. Duvitch his rightful property."

Tom and I took care not to play the part of triumphant heroes, even of redeemed sinners—that would not have suited our parent. Certainly, in appearance, we were more damned than redeemed. But when we tottered out of the rowboat something in me was quietly rejoicing. I guessed

that Father was secretly proud of our fortitude and I realized, too, that all through the night he had suffered with us.

We walked through the crowd of visitors on the lake shore, climbed into the car and silently drove to the Duvitch cottage. Mrs. Duvitch and the children were not visible but we found Mr. Duvitch sitting on the porch.

When he saw Tom and me and we silently handed him the strings of fish, he gulped and swallowed hard. For a moment he could not speak. Then, in a voice that was raw with emotion, he protested that he had not wished us to suffer so. Suppose we had fallen overboard in the dark?

"Will you shake hands with the boys?" asked Father.

Instead, Mr. Duvitch broke down. My brother and I did not know where to look and during those moments we suffered more acutely than we had suffered in the clouds of mosquitoes and under the broiling sun. After our neighbor had composed himself, he seized our hands and bowed his head over them. There was something Biblical, like a picture in the Old Testament, in the man's gesture. Anyway, it was my greatest lesson in humility.

When Mother, who had heard about our exile on the pond from a neighbor, saw us she burst into tears. She tried to embrace us but we drew back painfully. While she was rubbing salves and ointments on our seared backs and necks, somebody knocked at the kitchen door and Father opened it to find Mrs. Duvitch

26 automatons (ô tŏm′ə tŏnz′): automatic machines; robots.

standing there, her face and skin as undefiled as the Virgin's—the first time she had crossed the street to our house.

In her pale swaying hand Mrs. Duvitch held a porcelain teacup, ornamented with pink rosebuds and golden leaves—a relic from the old country and, as it turned out, her most cherished possession.

Her voice, thin and wispy from fright and shock, was difficult to follow. But we gathered that she had brought the teacup over as a peace offering and as a plea for our forgiveness to her family for the living purgatory,[27] no matter whose fault, through which my brother and I had passed. When Mother declined the teacup and assured Mrs. Duvitch that she would not have it otherwise with Tom and me, our neighbor, unable to find her tongue, made a little eloquent sign with her hands that was for thanks and that looked like a silent blessing. She quietly turned and went away; and again I felt that I had witnessed a scene from the Old Testament.

Mother continued her ministrations[28] to Tom and me and put us to bed. Despite our skin, which stuck to sheet and pillowcase, we slept like creatures drugged.

"It is high time," Tom and I heard Father say calmly, sanely, to Mother around noon next day when we woke up, "for this senseless feeling against the Duvitches to stop and I'm willing to do still more to stop it. Tonight we are having supper with them.

I've just seen Mr. Duvitch and he remarked that since Andy and Tom caught the fish, he'd feel better if we all shared in them. I suggested a fish-fry picnic supper and with a few hints from me, and some encouragement, he invited us over. It may be an ordeal but we ought to be able to bear it."

We walked across the street at six o'clock, not knowing what to expect. All the Duvitches, dressed in their Sunday best, bright and flushed and shining as we had never seen them, received us at the door as if we had been royalty. They looked at Tom and me and delicately looked away— I shuddered when I thought of what my brother and I would have had to endure had this been any other family.

Instead of a wretched abode we found a scantily furnished home that shone with cleanliness and smelled of spicy garden pinks. In its almost barren simplicity there was something comely.[29] A few of the stands, chairs and tables had the intimate quality of what is fashioned by the human hand. These, together with odds and ends the family had brought from the old country and others resurrected from the town dump and mended, painted, waxed and polished, made for a kind of native household harmony. The house plants (no window was without several) delighted Mother. Mrs. Duvitch was raising little orange and lemon trees from seed and experimenting with a pine-

27 **purgatory:** prolonged punishment.
28 **ministrations:** actions of aid and comfort.

29 **comely:** pleasant; attractive.

apple plant growing in a butter tub.

At once we were conscious of a remarkable difference in the demeanor[30] of the family. The children, thrilled by their first party, by the family's first recognition in this country, kept showing their pleasure in wide delighted smiles. I couldn't believe they were the same timid downcast youngsters one met on the street and saw in school; they seemed to have been touched by a wand. The Duvitches' home was their castle: sustained and animated[31] by the security of its four walls, shut away from a world of contempt and hostility, they were complete human beings. In their own house their true personalities emerged.

As the host Mr. Duvitch was a man we were seeing for the first time. Overjoyed to have neighbors in his house, he was so full of himself that I was conscious of an invisible stature in him which made him seem quite as tall as Father. He beamed and feasted his eyes on us. Saying very little, he managed to make us feel a great deal and he constantly sought his wife's eyes with glances of delight over the wonder of what was happening.

David, the oldest boy, helped his father serve a bottle of homemade blackberry wine.

We ate fried fish and good food of the American picnic variety at a long plank table set out in the back yard under an apple tree. The young Duvitches passed things politely, never helping themselves first: and their thanks upon receiving a dish were almost ceremonial. They waited patiently for their plates and ate every scrap of food.

Father kept the conversation going. His every word was listened to, every childish eye riveted on him while he spoke.

Tom and I, fascinated by the family's metamorphosis,[32] almost forgot about our blisters and our stings. As Father told stories and jokes, we discovered that the Duvitches had a gift for gaiety, for laughter, all but extinguished but still capable of resurrection. They were merry people who had suffered too much. How strange to see the boys and girls throw back their heads and laugh when Father said something that was funny, but not terribly funny.

After supper we were ushered to the open summer kitchen, the coolest room in the house, for entertainment. David played folk songs on his accordion. Mr. Duvitch turned out to be an amateur ventriloquist; he made the dog Kasimar talk Polish, the cat Jan talk Russian and a doll named Sophia talk English. Mrs. Duvitch read aloud to us, translating as she went along, a letter her mother had received from the great actress Modjeska, whom her family had known long ago.

I could tell that the Duvitches were a great revelation to Father and that he had enjoyed the evening tremendously.

"To think," he murmured as if talking to himself, while we were cross-

30 **demeanor:** behavior.
31 **sustained and animated:** supported and strengthened.

32 **metamorphosis:** transformation.

CHARACTERIZATION

ing the street, "that they should turn out to be gentle people of cultivation and accomplishment. Looked down on and ignored by their inferiors!"

I like to believe that the oil paintings of George Washington, Abraham Lincoln and Thomas Jefferson, which hung in our living room, helped to establish the Duvitches in our community. Even the fountain tinkling in the lily pool in our garden might have helped. In that town, oil paintings and flowing fountains were the symbols of wealth and aristocracy. Only a few mansions on Sycamore Hill were adorned with such.

Because our home was graced with these symbols, we had always been classified with the town's great, which gave us such prestige in the neighborhood that people often followed our lead. Obviously the Duvitches were important in Father's eyes, shown by the rigorous sentence he had imposed on Tom and me for our misuse of them. Added to that, we had recognized the family by taking a meal with them in their own house. People, often persuaded to accept what we accepted, to believe what we believed, began to think the Duvitches must really count, after all. Most of our neighbors decided that if they were good enough for a highly educated man like Father (the only college graduate on Syringa Street), they were good enough for them. The galvanized[33] community began to look upon things in a different light and it soon became the fashion to give the Duvitches the favorable nod.

Mother invited Mrs. Duvitch to a tea party, where her delicate manners, and the fine needlework which engaged her, won the approval of the local housewives who were present. On hot days our neighbor asked one of her big boys to carry the pineapple plant (which Mother had advertised well), into the back yard; and since botanical rarities were irresistible in that town of gardens, people were soon stopping by the fence for a look at the tropical specimen. After a while Mrs. Duvitch found courage to ask these people into her house and, if Mr. Duvitch was at home, he told the visitors stories about life in the old country. It was then that the neighborhood learned about the family's European past.

The children ceased stopping their noses when Mr. Duvitch passed them by and it wasn't long before the young Duvitches were able to enjoy outside companionship when they found time to play. They blossomed out in school and they were soon shining in school plays and festivals. Even Kasimar began to take on the ways of an American dog, daring to bark and growl on occasion.

Nathan Duvitch, who was seventeen, could throw and hit a baseball as far as anybody his age in town. When I learned this, and let it be known, he was asked to join one of the local ball clubs. David, invited to play his accordion at a country dance, turned out to be a magician with the instrument and ended up being one of the community's most popular players. Mrs. Frithjof Kinsella gave One-eyed Manny an after-

---

33 galvanized: stimulated; aroused.

school job in her store and later on told Mother he was worth three boys put together.

The community presently had reason to be grateful for Mrs. Duvitch's presence. It turned out that she had a great gift for nursing, and no fear of death, no fear of disease, contagious or otherwise. In times of severe illness Dr. Switzer often suggested that she be sent for—her own girls could take over at home. There were almost no nurses in town and the nearest hospital was over a hundred miles away. When Mrs. Duvitch quietly slipped into a sickroom, she never failed to bring along a sedative[34] influence, a kind of sanity. After an hour or two of her serene presence, the patient was calmed and comforted and the family reassured.

People began to turn to the Duvitches in all kinds of trouble. A boy who got in a bad scrape, a bitter family quarrel, a baby who had come into the world deformed—the elder Duvitches, with their old-world wisdom and gift for accepting the inevitable, could sit by the hour and argue gently and convincingly against disgrace, false pride, grief, fear.

Most surprising of all, Mr. Duvitch, in one respect, turned out to be characteristically American. One Saturday afternoon when my ball team was playing Nathan's, Father met him in the local ball park.

"Chust like de American boy," Mr. Duvitch exploded when Nathan made a timely hit that drove in two runs. Our neighbor choked with pride and went on: "Nathan's battering averich three hunnert twenty-seven!"

On a cold snowy afternoon in winter Mr. Duvitch stopped at our house and presented Father (who had enormous hands, much bigger than any of the Duvitches') with a handsome pair of leather mittens, lined with fur, which had a slightly acrid[35] ashy odor.

"No doubt one of the boys resurrected them from a heap of ashes in the dump," remarked Father, drawing on the mittens, which fitted perfectly. "Why should I value them any the less? *Who* would have dreamed that the Duvitches would have so much more to offer us than we have to offer them?"

34 **sedative:** quieting; calming.

35 **acrid:** bitter.

Understanding Literature

1. The story begins with a description of the weather. How does it reflect the way people feel? Where else in the story does the weather have a connection with what is happening in the minds of the characters?

2. How does the author introduce the two families in the story? What details does he give you of what they say and do? At the beginning of the story in what respect are the families alike? How are they different?

CHARACTERIZATION

3. Two years after the Duvitches move to Syringa Street, they still have no friends in the neighborhood. In what ways do the Duvitches limit their opportunities to make friends? How do the neighborhood children and adults treat the Duvitches? Why?
4. Point out the steps by which the author presents new evidence about what the Duvitch family is like. In your answer cite specific incidents in the story.
5. How does the author show that Tom and Andy are suffering during the fishing scene?
6. Is Tom and Andy's father justified in what he does to the boys? Explain. Why are the Duvitches so moved by the presentation of the fish?
7. What change takes place in the Duvitch family? Is the change justified by what happens in the story? Explain.
8. How is Andy different at the end of the story from the way he was at the beginning? Why is the story told from Andy's point of view?

Further Activities

1. Write a paragraph describing how you changed your mind about what someone was like. Give your first impression of the person and then show how, as you got to know the person better, you changed your mind about him or her. Make very clear what the new evidence was that changed your mind.
2. It is very important for an author to pick the right person to tell his story. In one or two paragraphs discuss how the story would be different if one of the other characters had told it. For example, how different would the story be if it were told from the point of view of Tom and Andy's father?

Focusing on Words

1. *Anti-* is a prefix which you see quite often. According to the dictionary, *anti-* is defined as *opposite, against, contrary, reverse.* This story states that "the young Duvitches, like their parents, were considered antisocial." What does *antisocial* mean? Think of other words which begin with the prefix *anti-*. Can you explain what they mean? Look in a dictionary to see whether or not you are correct.
2. Another prefix is *mal-*. Mr. Duvitch's job at the rendering plant is described as being "a rather malodorous one." What does the dictionary indicate *mal-* means? Find and define other words beginning with *mal-*.

AMBROSE FLACK

A single event can often become the basis of a story. In this very brief story, a woman named Mildred tells her friend Marge what happened at work that day.

The Pocketbook Game

Alice Childress

IMPROVING YOUR READING: One way of revealing character is through what a person says. The following story is told as a monologue (only one speaker), and we learn a good deal about the speaker. We also learn a good deal about the person she is talking about. Although the person to whom Mildred is speaking has no lines, we know what she might say or do at certain times. As you read, try to imagine the whole scene.

MARGE ... Day's work is an education! Well, I mean workin' in different homes you learn much more than if you was steady in one place ... I tell you, it really keeps your mind sharp tryin' to watch for what folks will put over on you.

What? ... No, Marge, I do not want to help shell no beans, but I'd be more than glad to stay and have supper with you, and I'll wash the dishes after. Is that all right? ...

Who put anything over on who? ... Oh yes! It's like this. . . . I been working for Mrs. E ... one day a week for several months and I notice that she has some peculiar ways. Well, there was only one thing that really bothered me and that was her pocketbook habit. . . . No, not those little novels. . . . I mean her purse—her handbag.

Marge, she's got a big old pocketbook with two long straps on it. . . . and whenever I'd go there, she'd be propped up in a chair with her handbag double wrapped tight around her wrist, and from room to room she'd roam with that purse hugged to her bosom ... yes, girl! This happens every time! No, there's nobody there but me and her. . . . Marge, I couldn't say nothin' to her! It's her purse, ain't it? She can hold onto it if she wants to!

I held my peace for months, tryin' to figure out how I'd make my point. . . . Well, bless Bess! Today was the day! . . . Please, Marge, keep shellin' the beans so we can eat! I know you're listenin', but you listen with your ears, not your hands. . . . Well, anyway, I was almost ready to go home when she steps in the room hangin' onto her bag as usual and says, "Mildred, will you ask the super[1] to come up and fix the kitchen faucet?" "Yes, Mrs. E ..." I says, "as soon as I leave." "Oh, no," she says, "he may be gone by then. Please go now." "All right," I says, and out the door I went, still wearin' my Hoover apron.

1 **super:** superintendent, of an apartment building.

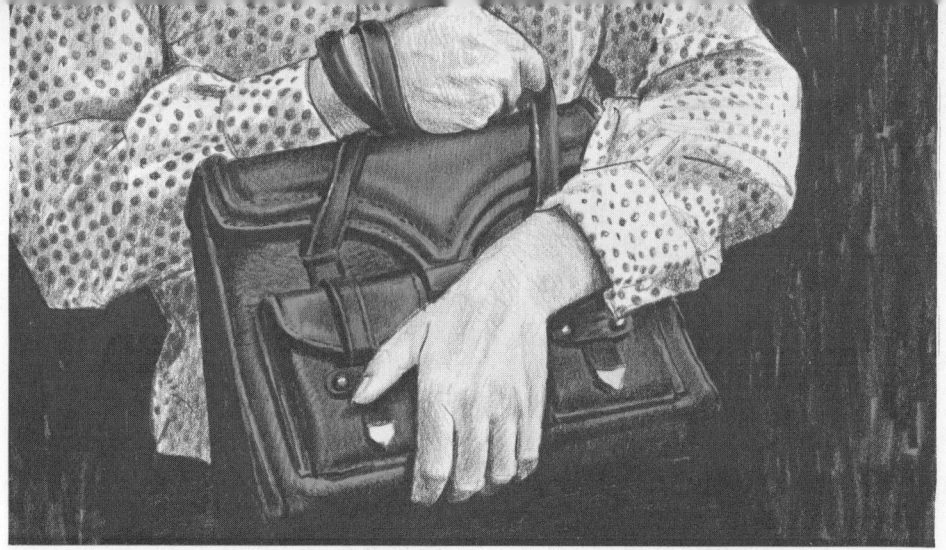

I just went down the hall and stood there a few minutes . . . and then I rushed back to the door and knocked on it as hard and frantic as I could. She flung open the door sayin', "What's the matter? Did you see the super?" . . . "No," I says, gaspin' hard for breath, "I was almost downstairs when I remembered . . . I left my pocketbook!"

With that I dashed in, grabbed my purse and then went down to get the super! Later, when I was leavin' she says real timid-like, "Mildred, I hope that you don't think I distrust you because . . ." I cut her off real quick. . . . "That's all right, Mrs. E . . ., I understand. 'Cause if I paid anybody as little as you pay me, I'd hold my pocketbook too!"

Marge, you fool . . . lookout! . . . You gonna drop the beans on the floor!

Understanding Literature

1. What kind of work does the speaker do?
2. What do you learn about the speaker?
3. What do you learn about Mrs. E?
4. Although we read none of Marge's words, can you find places where Marge probably said or did something? What did she probably say or do?
5. What do you think is the significance of the title?

Further Activity

As a whole class, rewrite this story as a dialogue (with two speakers). You will need to include what Marge was saying or doing at appropriate times. Then let two students act out the story; one student playing the part of Marge, the other playing the part of Mildred, the speaker in the story.

ALICE CHILDRESS

The Espositos are people who enjoy each other and their Sunday evenings of good music. Their favorite record is *"Celeste Aïda,"*[1] which the great singer Enrico Caruso has given to Mr. Esposito. This story is built on a problem—will the family sell the record?

The Song Caruso Sang

Patrick McCallum

IMPROVING YOUR READING: Here is another story in which you should look closely at the characterization. The father looks at life differently from the way his children do. This difference causes disagreement or a *conflict* which must be resolved. Is the resolution of the conflict real? Does it, in other words, grow out of the characters of the people? Would you expect them to act the way they do?

WELL, IT'S ALL over now and everything is okay again, although not very long ago it looked like the whole Esposito family was going to bust right up. That would have been pretty bad, because we're a big family—Mamma and Papa and six kids, counting Beppe, who is married now and last year made me an uncle.

My name is George Washington Esposito because I was born the day Papa became an American citizen. He was so proud that he named me after our first President. I sort of think he hoped some day I might be a President, too. But that was fourteen years ago, and so far there's been no sign of me heading in that direction.

What I want to tell you about is the record, and what happened to it and to the Espositos because of it. I

know it sounds crazy when I tell you all the things that a recording of *"Celeste Aïda"* by Enrico Caruso did to us, but it's the truth, all of it.

As long as I can remember anything at all, I remember the Sunday evenings in our parlor, even when I was little and we lived on the East Side of Manhattan. It's gone on the same right here in Brooklyn, too.

The whole family was always together then—Papa and Mamma, of course, and Angelina, Beppe (now with Rosa and little Peppino), Enrico, Giovanni, Mary Alice, and me, George Washington. We last two are the only Espositos who have real American names, though Mamma calls us "Maria" and "Giorgio."

Let me tell you it was a roomful, especially when the Pezzullos from next door came over. You can imagine how we squeezed together on the horsehair sofa and filled all the chairs, the straight-backed ones with

[1] *Celeste Aïda:* "Heavenly Aïda." Aïda (ä ē'dä) is the heroine in the opera of the same name by Verdi.

CHARACTERIZATION

the round knobs that pressed against our spines when we sat up straight like we ought to in them, as well as the ones from the kitchen; and still some of us had to sit on the floor. But we didn't mind. What did it matter where you sat when you were listening to beautiful music? That's something to be enjoyed anywhere.

You see, Papa had this job at Sheeler's, the big music store just off Times Square. It wasn't much of a job in those days, but even if he was only a janitor, it paid enough for him to take care of his family, and he could be near music. Before he came to America, Papa played the violincello in the string quartet at the Ristorante Ricco, one of the best places to eat in Naples in case you ever go there. But after the first big war, when times got bad, Papa wrote to Uncle Guido in America, and Uncle Guido said to come over, so he and Mamma and Beppe came to New York. That was clear back in 1920.

I was telling you about Papa's job. Like I said, he didn't mind being a janitor, because it meant he was where he could hear music all day. Mr. Sheeler took a liking to Papa and let him bring records home over the weekend, so we could all hear the wonderful music that Papa listened to every day at the store as he swept and mopped the floors.

So that's the way the Sunday evenings began. We had a phonograph, a second-hand one that Papa got at the store real cheap; not the latest model, of course, but it had a clear tone, and that's what counts. It was my job to wind it up between rec-ords, but that's as much as Papa would let any of us do; he always changed the records himself. In all the years he brought records home only one was broken and two scratched. That's pretty good, I'd say.

We all love music. From the very beginning, even back in Italy before my oldest brother, Beppe, was born, the Esposito house had music in it. And after Mamma and Papa got to America and could afford it, there was a piano, and Angelina and Beppe took lessons. Later there was a violin for Giovanni; and Mamma, who had done some singing herself before she got married, taught Enrico to sing, because he had the best voice, and maybe just a little because his name was Enrico. As for me, I'm learning to play the piccolo in the school band.

There was more than music to our Sundays in the parlor. There was the being together, and for me that was best of all. During the week we were all running in and out of the house to and from school and work; only at supper could we be together, and then only for a little while, because Angelina had her night classes at business college, and Beppe and Giovanni were turning out for basketball at the YMCA, and Enrico practiced his singing in the bedroom with the door closed, and Mary Alice and I had our homework. So it was really only Sunday in the evening that we could gather in the parlor with the lights dim and listen while Papa played the operas of Verdi and the symphonies of Beethoven.

For over an hour we would listen. Then Papa would say, "That's all tonight," and start to close down the top of the phonograph.

"But the record, Papa!" Everyone in the room chimed in. "We want to hear the record!"

Papa would look mystified, as though he didn't know what we were talking about. "The record? What record?"

"The Caruso record, Papa!" we would come back at him, everyone grinning. "You know which one we mean!"

"Ah!" He would nod as though just barely remembering. "The Caruso record." He would smile then. "Well, *bambini*, if you insist." He would shake his head. "But I do not understand why you want every time this same record."

Papa knew his part in the game. He would pick up the record, the one I mentioned before, *"Celeste Aïda,"* from the table, where he had placed it, knowing that we would demand to hear it.

To me, it is the best recording Caruso ever made of that lovely aria of Verdi's. Maybe it's because I've heard it almost every Sunday since I can remember; maybe it's because this is the only one of its kind, since no other copies were made, and it is ours.

Well, here is how it came to be: You see, long ago Papa had known Caruso in Naples, because sometimes the great tenor would come to Ricco's for a late supper when he was singing at the San Carlo. He even sang with the quartet when he felt like it —just got up in the middle of supper and sang. It was really something to hear, Papa says.

Papa had written Caruso that he and Mamma and Beppe would soon be in New York. The great man had made him promise to write if ever the Espositos came to America. He was not one to forget his old friends. If he had been, there wouldn't have been the record nor the thing that happened to us because of it.

I've heard so many times the story of Papa's meeting in New York with the man my brother Enrico was named after that now I almost feel I was there, myself, that day when Papa, following Caruso's instructions, went to the recording studio where the famous tenor was making an album of opera selections.

It was while he was singing into the big, flower-shaped horn of the recording machine that Papa entered the studio, having been permitted with the card that Caruso had sent him.

The aria was nearly over, the high, clear notes of that difficult solo going onto the soft wax disc so easily. *Ay! Mamma mia!* There was a voice straight out of heaven!

He turned away from the horn as he let go of the last note, and it was then he saw Papa through the glass and waved and smiled, crying out, *"Eh, Pasqualino, cumme stai?"*[2] and even before Papa could answer that he was fine, Caruso came rushing out of the studio and embraced him joyfully. "Come!" he said in Italian— this was before Papa knew any Eng-lish. "We shall hear the record and then have some lunch. A feast it shall be! A feast to welcome my old friend to his new home!" Then he laughed and embraced Papa again.

They sat down to listen to the record.

The last note of *"Celeste Aïda"* faded away. There was a pause, then *"Eh, Pasqualino, cumme stai?"* came out of the loud-speaker as clearly as the aria just finished.

Papa said Caruso turned speechlessly and pointed his finger at Papa and then at himself in astonishment.

The engineers in the recording room had funny looks on their faces as they hurried out. "I'm afraid you'll have to do it over, Mr. Caruso," one of them said. "It'd be pretty hard to cut out that last part without ruining the music; there isn't enough of a pause between the last note of the singing and the words you spoke afterward."

Caruso shrugged his shoulders. "Okay," he said, and grinned. "Then we do it over." He got up and started into the studio again. "I will not be long, Pasqualino," he promised. "Then we go eat."

Papa says his heart seemed to quiver and his voice would hardly come as he stopped the singer. "Enrico," he said, "what is to become of the one you just made?"

Caruso went through the motions of breaking an invisible record over his knee, grinning as he did so.

Papa nodded gravely, his voice trembling as he continued. "Enrico, may I have it?" he asked, almost in a whisper.

2 *cumme stai:* "How are you?"

The tenor did not seem to understand. "You want that record, Pasqualino?" he asked. "But why? It is no good. I can make you a better one right now."

"No, no, my friend!" Papa begged. "Please, I want only that one, the one where you speak to me and call my name."

Caruso laughed and slapped Papa on the back. "Ah, now I see!" he said. "Of course you may have it! One 'Celeste Aïda' just for you!" And he added, "With my special autograph!"

So, nearly every Sunday since, we have heard the golden voice of Enrico Caruso singing "Celeste Aïda," then felt proud and happy as we heard this greatest tenor of all time call out joyfully to our own father, "Eh, Pasqualino, cumme stai?" as if he were right in our parlor with us.

You can understand now why we all thought so much of the record. It was more than just a recording of "Celeste Aïda" by Enrico Caruso. Yet, I don't think I could tell you all the things it was to us. Like red wine on the table, the smell of garlic in the kitchen, early Mass on Sunday, and the sound of Neapolitan Italian being spoken, it was just part of our lives; we never knew any different. It isn't easy to explain things like that. . . .

Well, the years passed and we all grew older. The big boys began to shave and the girls to round out their figures. Beppe got married, and Angelina got a secretarial position, a good one with an import-export firm because she knew both English and

Italian and was a good secretary besides.

The Sunday evenings continued through all these changes in our lives. By now Papa had a better job at Sheeler's and no longer had to sweep and mop the floors; he didn't have to borrow records, either. We saved our money through the years and bought our own. One Christmas we all put together, my brothers and sisters and I, and bought Papa and Mamma a new radio-phonograph, the best there is; they were so surprised and happy that they both cried when they saw it under the tree.

Papa's record by Caruso, though, was still the prize possession of the Espositos, and it never seemed to get scratched or worn. Of course, no one touched it but Papa, and he was very careful, playing it only once a week, and always with a new needle.

It was after that first Sunday when my sister Angelina brought Dick Mantini, her boss, home to supper and our concert afterward, that things began to change. Dick's just a young guy, but he's got a swell position in this export outfit, and Angelina is his secretary. He sure got a funny look on his face when we began our act of "The record, Papa! Let us hear the record!" Then Angelina explained what it was all about, and Dick smiled politely as Papa carefully lowered the needle onto the whirling disc.

I never saw anyone spring to life as quickly as Dick when he realized that "Eh, Pasqualino, cumme stai?" was on the record.

"Hey, that's terrific!" Dick exclaimed. "There's a real collector's item, I'd say. Ought to be worth a lot of money." The parlor got real quiet when he asked Papa, "Have you ever tried to sell it?"

Papa didn't seem to understand. "Sell? What you mean, sell?"

"Why, there are people would pay you a lot of money for that record, Mr. Esposito; I couldn't say how much, but plenty, I'll bet. The singing alone, this being the only copy, would be worth a lot." He shook his head in amazement. "And with that business at the end, you could make a small fortune on it."

The room became awfully quiet, a different quiet than when we were listening to the music.

"Well," Papa sighed, "it's not for sale. It is mine, given by my friend Enrico Caruso. I will sell first my right arm."

Beppe, on the horsehair sofa with Rosa and Peppino, started to speak. "But, Papa," he began—only, when Papa looked in his direction he didn't finish what he started to say.

There was an atmosphere of uneasiness in the parlor that night and I had a feeling that Dick's idea would not just fade away by itself. . . .

The following Sunday, Beppe got up after we had heard the record and made a little speech. "Papa," he began, and everyone in the parlor knew what he was going to say.

"This week I have been thinking, and I have talked with Dick and with Enrico and Giovanni."

Papa sat up stiff but didn't say anything. Mamma looked like she'd rather be out in the kitchen making *lasagne.*

"Papa," Beppe went on, "for a long time now you've dreamed of owning a little piece of land out in Jersey, where you could have a garden and grow some grapes and fruit trees. You and Mamma have worked hard, and now it is time you took life easy. You owe it to yourselves."

Papa still did not speak. Beppe looked around him like maybe he wished Enrico or Giovanni was doing the talking.

"Well, Papa," he continued, after a pause that was nearly a sigh, "we think you ought to sell the record. Dick says he knows a man who is interested in such things and probably would give you plenty of money for it. Maybe a thousand dollars, even."

We all blinked our eyes at Beppe's words. A thousand dollars! For a record? Even if it is by Caruso? Not possible! Yet I'd never seen Beppe with a more serious expression on his face. Believe me, he wasn't kidding.

Papa spoke at last. "My record is not for sale," he said quietly but firmly. "I said before, I say again, not for a thousand or five thousand. We talk about it no more." He got up and left the parlor.

Beppe and Rosa and the baby went home, and the rest of us went to bed. I thought the talk of the record was finished and, without knowing why, I was kind of relieved. Still, letting myself dream for a minute, it would be nice to have a little farm in New Jersey. We often talked about it and dreamed of our own grapes and a few apple and cherry trees. But to sell the record? Somehow, even the little farm we wanted so much didn't seem worth that sacrifice.

It was the next day, just as I was sure the matter was closed, that Beppe came to the house all excited; while we were eating supper it was.

Beppe's eyes were bright as he told Papa about the new idea. "You wouldn't even have to sell the record, Papa!" he said breathlessly. "I talked to Dick about it again today. He says he thinks you could just sell the rights to it; you'd only have to let one of the big companies borrow the record and make a copy of it. You might get even more money than from a private collector. Think of it, Papa!" He leaned clear across the table and looked into Papa's face, waiting for him to say something.

Papa kept right on eating his supper. Then he took a sip of Chianti from the glass beside his plate, and after what seemed a long, long time, said, "I will think." But there was not even a trace of a smile on his face when he said it.

"Can I find out how to get in touch with the right party at the recording company, just in case?" Beppe asked, still leaning across the table.

Papa took another sip of wine, then nodded slowly. I could tell he wanted to forget the whole business.

Speaking of forgetting, I'd be just as glad to forget that next couple of weeks after Papa said okay to Beppe. For the first time in my memory we didn't even have the music in the parlor. You see, except for Papa and Mamma, nobody was speaking to anybody.

After Papa had agreed to Beppe's suggestion, my oldest brother contacted someone who was interested in the record and wanted to hear it. "The way they talk," Beppe explained, "I think they might give even more than a thousand for the record."

Papa finally agreed that the people from the recording company could hear the Caruso record, but they'd have to come to our house to do so; he wouldn't let the record out of the house.

It was then the unhappiness began. All my brothers and sisters, and with shame I must include myself, began thinking of the different ways we could spend the money, even before we had any idea how much it would be. Only Papa and Mamma said nothing. They were like two lost children who didn't know which way to turn; they would sit and listen to Angelina and Enrico and Giovanni and Mary Alice and me, and Beppe when he came from his house, quarreling about the money.

Giovanni wanted us to have a car, a big, new one. We'd never had a car, but he could think of all the reasons why we really needed one.

Angelina said that it would be nice to have a home out on Long Island and commute to work on the train.

Enrico thought we should all take a trip back to Italy, and he could study voice there.

Beppe and Rosa still held out for the farm in New Jersey, as it would be a good place to bring the baby on sunny weekends.

I don't think Mary Alice and I knew what we wanted, because we changed our minds every day. All of us were guilty of stretching the amount we thought we'd get for the record to cover whatever it was we wanted. . . .

The man from the recording company was coming on Sunday evening to listen to the record and decide whether or not it was what his company wanted. By that Sunday our house was not a place to be in if you were in a good mood and wanted to stay that way. Once, when I looked into Mamma's face I could tell she'd been crying, and Papa, who was always cheerful, never smiled any more.

Mamma had insisted that everybody come to dinner that Sunday, just like always, even if we were all mad at each other.

"Such faces," Papa said with a sigh as we all sat down at the table. "Only Peppino looks happy."

The little boy laughed when he heard his name. The rest of us looked down at our plates, just as we had when we were little and Papa scolded us for fighting.

"It is over two weeks now," Papa went on, "that the boss of Angelina tells us maybe we can get much money for our record. I feel this is not good, but as to give only the use of the record does not really seem bad I say nothing."

Papa sighed and shook his head sadly. "But, si, it is bad, very bad. I know this now. Ever since we think to sell I watch this family, and I see it is no more a family. Before, it is happy, and this house is filled with love and much laughing. Now there is only angry faces and fighting. Always before this time I hurry home from my work at night; now I stay away."

I could hear Mamma beginning to sniffle at the other end of the table.

"Why is this?" Papa continued. "It is because of a record, a record by my dear friend Enrico Caruso which for many years brings much joy to the Espositos." His voice sounded strange, not Papa's voice at all. "Now the thing that for many years is happiness for Pasqualino Esposito is unhappiness. I ask myself can I buy with money this happiness once again, and I find the only answer is *No.*"

You could almost hear the silence in the room. Finally Giovanni spoke. "But, Papa," he reminded, "you'd still have your record and the little farm in Jersey with the apples and grapes . . ."

"Apples and grapes I can buy at the fruit stand of Pezzullo," Papa interrupted. "A family I cannot buy in any place." He left the room.

Mamma got up, too, and looked at us as though to say something, but then she turned without saying it and followed Papa into the parlor and closed the door.

Beppe was the first to speak after they had gone. "Papa's right," he said. "It's all my fault."

"Your fault?" Giovanni asked.

Beppe nodded. "I insisted that Papa consider selling after he'd said he didn't want to. If only I'd—"

"Don't be stupid, Beppe!" Giovanni interrupted. "You were right to insist. You were just thinking of the good of the family. Once this is all over and the record is sold, Papa will see it is right. Like you said just now, he'll have his record and the money, too."

"But the family?" Beppe asked. "Didn't you hear Papa and see his face just now? And Mamma, too? That's what made me realize it. We stand a chance of losing more than we could ever gain in dollars."

They argued on, everybody pitching in, until finally Beppe banged his fist on the table and said, "We're not going to sell the record, so what's the use of arguing?"

The others stopped talking, although Giovanni did remind Beppe that in any case it was too late to call up Mr. Kamp, the man from the recording company, and tell him not to bother to come.

I found myself awfully glad about what Beppe had said. I knew now that the last thing I wanted was for us to sell the Caruso record. If it went out of our house, then something awfully important would be gone out of our family, perhaps forever. . . .

The recording-company representative, Mr. Kamp, a bald-headed little man, came on the dot of seven-thirty, just as he was supposed to. We all went into the parlor and sat down. Mr. Kamp sat alone on the horsehair sofa. The room was deadly quiet, like just before a thunderstorm.

Papa picked up the record from its place among the others on the table and put it on the turntable. It began to turn, and he lowered the needle carefully into the outside groove.

His hand was shaking noticeably.

We all looked at each other in surprise. It wasn't "Celeste Aïda" at all! In confusion, Papa had put on "Vesti la giubba," instead. Both records, the big, thick kind they used to make before I was born, looked exactly alike.

Papa asked Mr. Kamp's pardon for the mistake and took "Celeste Aïda" from the table and put it on the machine.

The little man from the recording company leaned forward and stared at the floor as he listened to the record. When it was finished he merely nodded and asked to hear it again.

Papa sat by the phonograph looking intently at each of us as Caruso sang of his love for Aïda. Following Papa's gaze, I saw Angelina and Beppe and Enrico and Giovanni and Mary Alice all with the same worried expression, one just like the next. They were not like my brothers and sisters at all, nor was this the happy time of those other Sundays.

"Best 'Celeste Aïda' ever recorded by Caruso, I'm convinced," Mr. Kamp said in a businesslike tone after hearing it the second time. He was the authority on Caruso for his company, he told us, and had heard all the great tenor's records, "but none quite like this." He was smiling for the first time. "That little personal touch at the end would make it a record seller, too," he told us, and laughed as though he thought he'd said something funny.

He got up off the sofa and, jamming his hands down into his pockets, paced across the parlor twice, his

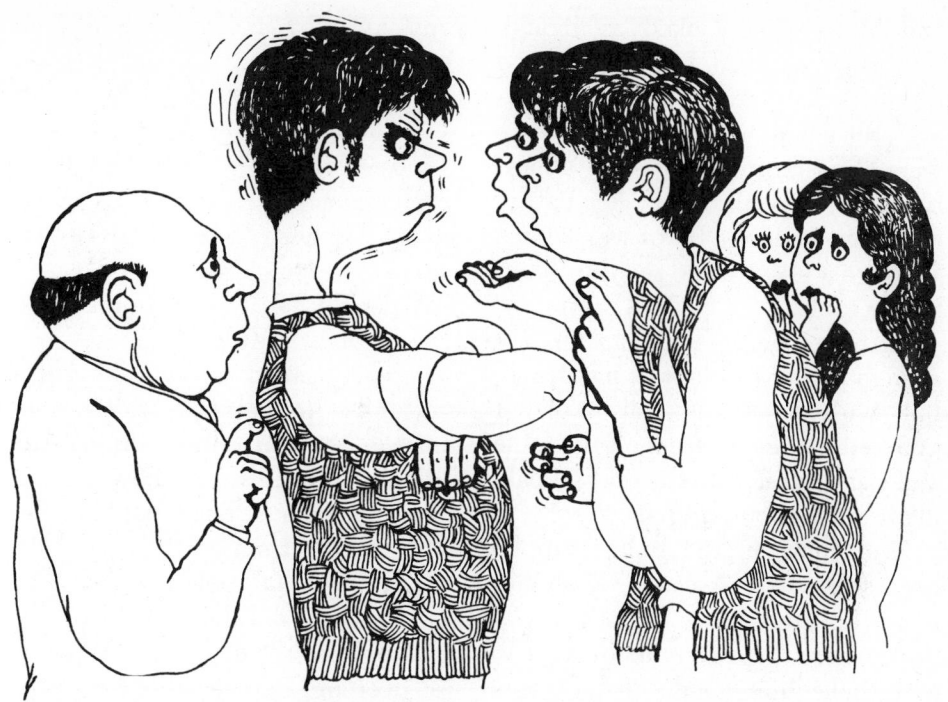

bald head almost glowing. He seemed very excited. "Mr. Esposito," he said in an even more businesslike tone than before, "my company will pay you five thousand dollars for all rights to the use of this recording if it's what we want, and I do not hesitate to assure you that it is." He began to explain the details.

There were little gasps all over the room. Five thousand dollars! We had never really dreamed of so much!

Papa nodded, but looked as though he weren't even listening to Mr. Kamp.

It was then that Beppe stood up and told Mr. Kamp the record was not for sale.

"Sorry you had to come out to Brooklyn for nothing," Beppe apologized. "We just this afternoon decided not to sell the record or the rights to it."

Both Papa and Mamma just sat looking at Beppe as though they couldn't believe what they were hearing.

Enrico and Giovanni didn't just sit there, though. They both began talking at once, each having forgotten that it would be better for the whole family, as they'd agreed, if we didn't sell our record. The offer of five thousand dollars had been too much for them. I began to tremble, and wanted to speak but couldn't.

Mr. Kamp stood up, too, as Beppe, his arms folded across his chest, stood facing Enrico and Giovanni defiantly, shaking his head. "If I might get a word in here," the record-company representative said, "I would like to tell you I have been authorized to go as high as six thousand if necessary."

"Six thousand!" Enrico and Giovanni shouted together. Angelina and Mary Alice looked as though they might weaken, but Beppe stood his ground.

I still could not speak, and there were tears in my eyes which almost blinded me. I turned my head away so no one could see that I was crying. Through a blur I could see the record on the table.

I'll never be able to explain, not even to myself, just how it happened, but, with a sob of "No! No!" I grabbed the record from off the table and slammed it onto the floor, breaking it into a thousand pieces.

Everything in the room stopped dead-still where it was. Giovanni's hands hovered above Beppe's shoulders, where they were about to grab and shake him good. Papa's face had an expression of sorrow and joy and relief all at once as he took my hand. Mamma broke the silence sobbing and saying over and over in Italian, "Good son!" The others just stood staring at me in disbelief.

Mr. Kamp finally grabbed his hat and left, muttering to himself, "Crazy as loons, all of them!"

I ran into the kitchen, no longer able to control my sobs. The others followed, all except Beppe, and they were crying and hugging me and saying I had done the right thing, that it was the only way to bring them to their senses. Papa, his arm around my shoulder, assured me, "This is a family again, and nothing else matters."

Mamma began pouring wine and passing it around, stopping only to brush away a tear from time to time; she was smiling for the first time in two weeks.

We became conscious of the sound of music drifting in from the parlor. A few seconds later Beppe appeared at the kitchen door. "Listen," he said.

We could hardly believe our ears. It was *"Celeste Aïda!"*

Beppe grinned at me. "I guess we'll have to get a new *'Vesti la giubba,'*" he said. "It seems like our old one got broken somehow."

In my rush I had grabbed the wrong record from off the table!

"Celeste Aïda" never sounded so beautiful as it did then. We listened as though for the first time. When it was over and Caruso called out, *"Eh, Pasqualino, cumme stai?"* Papa answered, "Happy again, my friend, very happy." He spoke for all of us. . . .

Well, that's all there is. We're a family again and still have the record. Maybe someday we'll save enough money to move to that farm in Jersey. Right now it's just something nice to dream about.

The Sunday evenings are once again as before, except that Angelina has married Dick, and now he also is with us every Sunday. Maybe sometime you would like to come hear the record with us, too. Caruso never sang *"Celeste Aïda"* better, and we all still get a big kick out of *"Eh, Pasqualino, cumme stai?"* at the very end.

CHARACTERIZATION

Understanding Literature

1. Which character tells the story? Why did the author choose this character to tell the story?
2. What kind of job does Papa have so that he can hear music all day? How does this job benefit the Espositos in their Sunday evening music sessions?
3. Describe the scene between Papa and Enrico Caruso at the recording studio. Why is this scene necessary to the story?
4. What is the major conflict in the story?
5. You can often tell what people are like by the kinds of things they desire. What do the various members of the Esposito family want to buy with the money? What do their plans show about their characters?
6. The record has become a part of the lives of the Esposito family. George compares the record with other things which are just naturally a part of their lives. What are they?
7. Why does George break the record? Why is the discovery of the undamaged record important to the conclusion of the story? How would the conclusion be different if the broken record had been *"Celeste Aïda"*? Would that ending be more satisfying? Why?
8. What idea does the record stand for?

Further Activity

Perhaps there is a special ceremony or tradition which is important to your family. Or maybe there is a piece of jewelry, a photograph, a book, or some other item which your family is particularly proud of or fond of. In two or three carefully planned paragraphs, tell about this tradition or item. The first paragraph should describe it. The second paragraph should probably give the background of the tradition or item, and the third paragraph could show in what ways it is precious to your family. Give your paper a title that is fitting and interesting. Be sure to proofread your paper before it is handed in. Is the spelling perfect? Are you satisfied with the punctuation? Have you used the exact word you wanted for each description?

Focusing on Words

Because the Esposito children love music, they would be able to explain the meaning of these words. With the aid of the glossary for those you do not know, define: *opera, symphony, aria, tenor, quartet.*

This story is really a story within a story. It comes from the book-length story called *Seven Arrows* and is about a mouse. Why, then, does the author have his storyteller say that it is "a Story concerning men"?

The Story of Jumping Mouse

Hyemeyohsts Storm

IMPROVING YOUR READING: The actions and speeches which authors choose reflect their *attitudes* toward their characters. As you read the story about Jumping Mouse, ask yourself: Why did Hyemeyohsts Storm have the Mouse say or do that? Why do the other animals say or do what they do? How do their actions and speeches answer the "riddle" the Chief (the storyteller) mentions at the beginning of his story? And what does this answer have to do with you?

DAY WOMAN and Prairie Rose entered Flying Cloud's lodge and hugged Dancing Water. Both girls peeked at the newborn baby before sitting down next to Dancing Water. Two Sioux women were working on buckskins, their eyes so full of tears that they could hardly work. Day Women saw the tears in Dancing Water's eyes and looked down at her hands.

"You must know quickly," said Dancing Water through her tears. "Grey Owl, Painted Elk, Four Bears, and many more are all dead." Day Women was crying hard herself now, but still she could not help but see the brightly colored material that Dancing Water dried her eyes with.

Early the next morning the men returned. Day Woman was awakened by the barking of the camp dogs. She slipped on her dress and stepped from the lodge just as Lame Bear dismounted.

"Is it true?" asked Day Woman timidly, addressing the Chief. "Do they really have leaves that talk?"

The Peace Chief raised his head and stared quietly at the distant mountains. They stood out sharply above the green landscape. "Yes," he said gently, turning to Day Woman, "they do."

"Great Father," said Hawk, looking straight into the eyes of the chief, "if they have these wonderful gifts, then why do they kill?"

"That, my son, is one of the riddles of men," answered the Chief. "Would you listen to a Story concerning men?"

"A Story?" asked Day Woman excitedly, "Great Shield, please let me run for my sister, Prairie Rose, so that she too may hear it."

"Bring as many of my children who will listen as you can!" smiled the Chief as Day Woman flew to find her friend.

Soon half a dozen children were clustered around the Story-Teller. He lit his Pipe and began:

Once there was a Mouse....

He was a Busy Mouse, Searching Everywhere, Touching his Whiskers to the Grass, and Looking. He was Busy as all Mice are, Busy with Mice things. But Once in a while he would Hear an odd Sound. He would Lift his Head, Squinting hard to See, his Whiskers Wiggling in the Air, and he would Wonder. One Day he Scurried up to a fellow Mouse and asked him, "Do you Hear a Roaring in your Ears, my Brother?"

"No, no," answered the Other Mouse, not Lifting his Busy Nose from the Ground. "I Hear Nothing. I am Busy now. Talk to me Later."

He asked Another Mouse the same Question and the Mouse Looked at him Strangely. "Are you Foolish in your Head? What Sound?" he asked and Slipped into a Hole in a Fallen Cottonwood Tree.

The little Mouse shrugged his Whiskers and Busied himself again, Determined to Forget the Whole Matter. But there was that Roaring again. It was faint, very faint, but it was there! One Day, he Decided to investigate the Sound just a little. Leaving the Other Busy Mice, he Scurried a little Way away and Listened again. There It was! He was Listening hard when suddenly, Someone said Hello.

"Hello, little Brother," the Voice said, and Mouse almost Jumped right Out of his Skin. He Arched his Back and Tail and was about to Run.

"Hello," again said the Voice. "It is I, Brother Raccoon." And sure enough, It was! "What are you Doing Here all by yourself, little Brother?" asked the Raccoon. The Mouse blushed, and put his Nose almost to the Ground. "I Hear a Roaring in my Ears and I am Investigating it," he answered timidly.

"A Roaring in your Ears?" replied the Raccoon as he Sat Down with him. "What you Hear, little Brother, is the River."

"The River?" Mouse asked curiously. "What is a River?"

"Walk with me and I will Show you the River," Raccoon said.

Little Mouse was terribly Afraid, but he was Determined to Find Out Once and for All about the Roaring. "I can Return to my Work," he thought, "after this thing is Settled, and possibly this thing may Aid me in All my Busy Examining and Collecting. And my Brothers All said it was Nothing. I will Show them. I will Ask Raccoon to Return with me and I will have Proof."

"All right Raccoon, my Brother," said Mouse. "Lead on to the River. I will Walk with you."...

Little Mouse Walked with Raccoon. His little Heart was Pounding in his Breast. The Raccoon was Taking him upon Strange Paths and little Mouse Smelled the Scent of many things that had Gone by this Way. Many times he became so Frightened he almost Turned Back. Finally, they Came to the River! It was Huge and Breathtaking, Deep and Clear in Places, and Murky in Others. Little Mouse was unable to

See Across it because it was so Great. It Roared, Sang, Cried, and Thundered on its Course. Little Mouse Saw Great and Little Pieces of the World Carried Along on its Surface.

"It is Powerful!" little Mouse said, Fumbling for Words.

"It is a Great thing," answered the Raccoon, "but here, let me Introduce you to a Friend."

In a Smoother, Shallower Place was a Lily Pad, Bright and Green. Sitting upon it was a Frog, almost as Green as the Pad it sat on. The Frog's White Belly stood out Clearly.

"Hello, little Brother," said the Frog. "Welcome to the River."

"I must Leave you Now," cut in Raccoon, "but do not Fear, little Brother, for Frog will Care for you Now." And Raccoon Left, Looking along the River Bank for Food that he might Wash and Eat.

Little Mouse Approached the Water and Looked into it. He saw a Frightened Mouse Reflected there.

"Who are you?" little Mouse asked the Reflection. "Are you not Afraid being that Far out into the Great River?"

"No," answered the Frog, "I am not Afraid. I have been Given the Gift from Birth to Live both Above and Within the River. When Winter Man Comes and Freezes this Medicine, I cannot be Seen. But all the while Thunderbird Flies, I am here. To Visit me, One must Come when the World is Green. I, my Brother, am the Keeper of the Water."

"Amazing!" little Mouse said at last, again Fumbling for Words.

"Would you like to have some Medicine Power?" Frog asked.

"Medicine Power? Me?" asked little Mouse. "Yes, yes! If it is Possible."

"Then Crouch as Low as you Can, and then Jump as High as you are Able! You will have your Medicine!" Frog said.

Little Mouse did as he was Instructed. He Crouched as Low as he Could and Jumped. And when he did, his Eyes Saw the Sacred Mountains. . . .

Little Mouse could hardly Believe his Eyes. But there They were! But then he Fell back to Earth, and he Landed in the River! . . .

Little Mouse became Frightened and Scrambled back to the Bank. He was Wet and Frightened nearly to Death.

"You have Tricked me," little Mouse Screamed at the Frog.

"Wait," said the Frog. "You are not Harmed. Do not let your Fear and Anger Blind you. What did you See?"

"I," Mouse stammered, "I, I Saw the Sacred Mountains!"

"And you have a New Name!" Frog said. "It is Jumping Mouse."

"Thank you. Thank you," Jumping Mouse said, and Thanked him again. "I want to Return to my People and Tell them of this thing that has Happened to me."

"Go. Go then," Frog said. "Return to your People. It is Easy to Find them. Keep the Sound of the Medicine River to the Back of your Head. Go Opposite to the Sound and you will Find your Brother Mice."

Jumping Mouse Returned to the World of the Mice. But he Found Disappointment. No One would Listen to him. And because he was Wet, and had no Way of explaining it because there had been no Rain, many of the other Mice were Afraid of him. They believed he had been Spat from the Mouth of Another Animal that had Tried to Eat him. And they all Knew that if he had not been Food for the One who Wanted him, then he must also be Poison for them.

Jumping Mouse Lived again among his People, but he could not Forget his Vision of the Sacred Mountains. . . .

The Memory Burned in the Mind and Heart of Jumping Mouse, and One Day he Went to the Edge of the River Place . . .

Jumping Mouse went to the Edge of the Place of Mice and Looked out onto the Prairie. He Looked up for Eagles. The Sky was Full of many Spots, each One an Eagle. But he was Determined to Go to the Sacred Mountains. He Gathered All of his Courage and Ran just as Fast as he Could onto the Prairie. His little Heart Pounded with Excitement and Fear.

He Ran until he Came to a Stand of Sage. He was Resting and trying to Catch his Breath when he Saw an Old Mouse. The Patch of Sage Old Mouse Lived in was a Haven for Mice. Seeds were Plentiful and there was Nesting Material and many things to be Busy with.

"Hello," said Old Mouse. "Welcome."

Jumping Mouse was Amazed. Such a Place and such a Mouse. "You are Truly a great Mouse," Jumping Mouse said with all the Respect he could Find. "This is Truly a Wonderful Place. And the Eagles cannot See you here, either," Jumping Mouse said.

"Yes," said Old Mouse, "and One can See All the Beings of the Prairie here: the Buffalo, Antelope, Rabbit, and Coyote. One can See them All from here and Know their Names."

"That is Marvelous," Jumping Mouse said. "Can you also See the River and the Great Mountains?"

"Yes and No," Old Mouse Said with Conviction. "I Know there is the Great River. But I am Afraid that the Great Mountains are only a Myth. Forget your Passion to See Them and Stay here with me. There is Everything you Want here, and it is a Good Place to Be."

"How can he Say such a thing?" Thought Jumping Mouse. "The Medicine of the Sacred Mountains is Nothing One can Forget."

"Thank you very much for the Meal you have Shared with me, Old Mouse, and also for sharing your Great Home," Jumping Mouse said. "But I must Seek the Mountains."

"You are a Foolish Mouse to Leave here. There is Danger on the Prairie! Just Look up there!" Old Mouse said, with even more Conviction. "See all those Spots! They are Eagles, and they will Catch you!"

It was hard for Jumping Mouse to Leave, but he Gathered his Determination and Ran hard Again. The Ground was Rough. But he Arched his Tail and Ran with All his Might. He could Feel the Shadows of the Spots upon his Back as he Ran. All those Spots! Finally he Ran into a Stand of Chokecherries. Jumping Mouse could hardly Believe his Eyes. It was Cool there and very Spacious. . . . And there were a great many things to Gather.

He was Investigating his New Domain when he Heard very Heavy Breathing. He Quickly Investigated the Sound and Discovered its Source. It was a Great Mound of Hair with Black Horns. It was a Great Buffalo. Jumping Mouse could hardly Believe the Greatness of the Being he Saw Lying there before him. He was so large that Jumping Mouse could have Crawled into One of his Great Horns. "Such a Magnificent Being." Thought Jumping Mouse, and he Crept Closer.

"Hello, my Brother," said the Buffalo. "Thank you for Visiting me."

"Hello, Great Being," said Jumping Mouse. "Why are you Lying here?"

"I am Sick and I am Dying," the Buffalo said, "And my Medicine has Told me that only the Eye of a Mouse can Heal me. But little Brother, there is no such Thing as a Mouse."

Jumping Mouse was Shocked. "One of my Eyes!" he Thought, "One of my Tiny Eyes." He scurried back into the Stand of Chokecherries. But the Breathing came Harder and Slower.

"He will Die," Thought Jumping Mouse, "If I do not Give him my Eye. He is too Great a Being to Let Die."

He Went Back to where the Buffalo Lay and Spoke. "I am a Mouse," he said with a Shaky Voice. "And you, my Brother, are a Great Being, I cannot Let you Die. I have Two Eyes, so you may have One of them."

The minute he had Said it, Jumping Mouse's Eye Flew Out of his Head and the Buffalo was Made Whole. The Buffalo Jumped to his Feet, Shaking Jumping Mouse's Whole World.

"Thank you, my little Brother," said the Buffalo. "I Know of your Quest for the Sacred Mountains and of your Visit to the River. You have Given me Life so that I may Give-Away to the People. I will be your Brother Forever. Run under my Belly and I will Take you right to the Foot of the Sacred Mountains, and you need not Fear the Spots. The Eagles cannot See you while you Run under Me. All they will See will be the Back of a Buffalo. I am of the Prairie and I will Fall on you if I Try to Go up the Mountains."

Little Mouse Ran under the Buffalo, Secure and Hidden from the Spots, but with only One Eye it was Frightening. The Buffalo's Great Hooves Shook the Whole World each time he took a Step. Finally they Came to a Place and Buffalo Stopped.

"This is Where I must Leave you, little Brother," said the Buffalo.

"Thank you very much," said Jumping Mouse. "But you Know, it was very Frightening Running under you with only One Eye. I was Constantly in Fear of your Great Earth-Shaking Hooves."

"Your Fear was for Nothing," said Buffalo. "For my Way of Walking is the Sun Dance Way, and I Always Know where my Hooves will Fall. I now must Return to the Prairie, my Brother. You can Always Find me there." . . .

Jumping Mouse Immediately Began to Investigate his New Surroundings. There were even more things here than in the Other Places, Busier things, and an Abundance of Seeds and Other things Mice Like. In his Investigation of these things, Suddenly he Ran upon a Gray Wolf who was Sitting there doing absolutely Nothing.

"Hello, Brother Wolf," Jumping Mouse said.

The Wolf's Ears Came Alert and his Eyes Shone. "Wolf! Wolf! Yes, that is what I am, I am a Wolf!" But then his mind Dimmed again and it was not long before he Sat Quietly again, completely without Memory as to who he was. Each time Jumping Mouse Reminded him who he was, he became Excited with the News, but soon would Forget again.

"Such a Great Being," thought Jumping Mouse, "but he has no Memory."

Jumping Mouse Went to the Center of this New Place and was Quiet. He Listened for a very long time to the Beating of his Heart. Then Suddenly he Made up his Mind. He Scurried back to where the Wolf Sat and he Spoke.

"Brother Wolf," Jumping Mouse said. . . .

"Wolf! Wolf," said the Wolf. . . .

"Please, Brother Wolf," said Jumping Mouse, "Please Listen to me. I Know what will Heal you. It is One of my Eyes. And I Want to Give it to you. You are a Greater Being than I. I am only a Mouse. Please Take it."

When Jumping Mouse Stopped Speaking his Eye Flew out of his Head and the Wolf was made Whole.

Tears Fell down the Cheeks of Wolf, but his little Brother could not See them, for Now he was Blind.

"You are a Great Brother," said the Wolf, "for Now I have my Memory. But Now you are Blind. I am the Guide into the Sacred Mountains. I will Take you there. There is a Great Medicine Lake there. The most Beautiful Lake in the World. All the World is Reflected there. The People, the Lodges of the People, and All the Beings of the Prairies and Skies."

"Please Take me there," Jumping Mouse said.

The Wolf Guided him through the Pines to the Medicine Lake. Jumping Mouse Drank the Water from the Lake. The Wolf Described the Beauty to him.

"I must Leave you here," said Wolf, "for I must Return so that I may Guide Others, but I will Remain with you as long as you Like."

"Thank you, my Brother," said Jumping Mouse. But although I am Frightened to be Alone, I Know you must Go so that you may Show Others the Way to this Place."

Jumping Mouse Sat there Trembling in Fear. It was no use Running, for he was Blind, but he Knew an Eagle would Find him Here. He felt a Shadow on his Back and Heard the Sound that Eagles Make. He Braced himself for the Shock. And the Eagle Hit! Jumping Mouse went to Sleep.

Then he Woke Up. The surprise of being Alive was Great, but Now he could See! Everything was Blurry, but the Colors were Beautiful.

"I can See! I can See!" said Jumping Mouse over again and again.

A Blurry Shape Came toward Jumping Mouse. Jumping Mouse Squinted hard but the Shape Remained a Blur.

"Hello, Brother," a Voice said. "Do you Want some Medicine?"

"Some Medicine for me?" asked Jumping Mouse. "Yes! Yes!"

"Then Crouch down as Low as you Can," the Voice said, "and Jump as High as you Can."

Jumping Mouse did as he was Instructed. He Crouched as Low as he Could and Jumped! The Wind Caught him and Carried him Higher.

"Do not be Afraid," the Voice called to him. "Hang on to the Wind and Trust!"

Jumping Mouse did. He Closed his Eyes and Hung on to the Wind and it Carried him Higher and Higher. Jumping Mouse Opened his Eyes and they were Clear, and the Higher he Went the Clearer they Became. Jumping Mouse Saw his Old Friend upon a Lily Pad on the Beautiful Medicine Lake. It was the Frog.

"You have a New Name," Called the Frog. "You are Eagle!"

Understanding Literature

1. Reread the first six paragraphs. What seems to have caused the sorrow at the Sioux camp?
2. Instead of directly answering Hawk's question, Chief (Great Shield) tells a story. What does he say that story is about and what question do you expect the story to answer?
3. Little Mouse seems to be afraid of practically everything. Why, then, does he leave his comfortable nest?
4. The Frog offers Little Mouse "some Medicine Power." Where else does medicine or medicine power appear in the story? Who offers it and who receives it?
5. How does Little Mouse overcome what he fears? What is the significance of the name Frog gives Mouse?
6. What do we learn about Jumping Mouse when he visits Old Mouse?
7. Why does Jumping Mouse give away his eyes? What does he gain from these two sacrifices?
8. How is Jumping Mouse like each "character" he meets?
9. What advice might the Chief be giving us in this story?

In this chapter from *Dandelion Wine*, the author presents a sketch of a woman: he tells you what she did with her life and how she influenced the lives of others.

Good-by, Grandma

Ray Bradbury

IMPROVING YOUR READING: An author must make clear whose story he or she is telling. Here Ray Bradbury keeps the focus on Great-grandma. The other people are represented only by what they say; you do not see them. This story is filled with *images,* pictures of things you can sense. This is another way of characterizing a person. When you finish reading and adding up the images, you have a clear picture of Great-grandma. It is as though you were scanning the snapshots in an album. They tell you much about the person who kept them.

SHE WAS A woman with a broom or a dustpan or a washrag or a mixing spoon in her hand. You saw her cutting piecrust in the morning, humming to it, or you saw her setting out the baked pies at noon or taking them in, cool, at dusk. She rang porcelain cups like a Swiss bell ringer, to their place. She glided through the halls as steadily as a vacuum machine, seeking, finding, and setting to rights. She made mirrors of every window, to catch the sun. She strolled but twice through any garden, trowel[1] in hand, and the flowers raised their quivering fires upon the warm air in her wake. She slept quietly and turned no more than three times in a night, as relaxed as a white glove to which, at dawn, a brisk hand will return. Waking, she touched people like pictures, to set their frames straight.

But, now . . . ?

"Grandma," said everyone. "Great-grandma."

Now it was as if a huge sum in arithmetic were finally drawing to an end. She had stuffed turkeys, chickens, squabs, gentlemen, and boys. She had washed ceilings, walls, invalids, and children. She had laid linoleum, repaired bicycles, wound clocks, stoked furnaces, swabbed iodine on ten thousand grievous wounds. Her hands had flown all around about and down, gentling this, holding that, throwing baseballs, swinging bright croquet mallets, seeding black earth, or fixing covers over dumplings, ragouts, and children wildly strewn by slumber. She had pulled down shades, pinched out candles, turned switches, and—grown old. Looking back on thirty billions of things started, carried, finished and done, it all summed up, totaled out; the last decimal was placed, the final

1 trowel: a tool for digging up small plants.

zero swung slowly into line. Now, chalk in hand, she stood back from life a silent hour before reaching for the eraser.

"Let me see now," said Great-grandma. "Let me see . . ."

With no fuss or further ado, she traveled the house in an ever-circling inventory, reached the stairs at last, and, making no special announcement, she took herself up three flights to her room where, silently, she laid herself out like a fossil imprint under the snowing cool sheets of her bed and began to die.

Again the voices:

"Grandma! Great-grandma!"

The rumor of what she was doing dropped down the stair well, hit, and spread ripples through the rooms, out doors and windows and along the street of elms to the edge of the green ravine.

"Here now, here!"

The family surrounded her bed.

"Just let me lie," she whispered.

Her ailment could not be seen in any microscope; it was a mild but ever-deepening tiredness, a dim weighting of her sparrow body; sleepy, sleepier, sleepiest.

As for her children and her children's children—it seemed impossible that with such a simple act, the most leisurely act in the world, she could cause such apprehension.[2]

"Great-grandma, now listen—what you're doing is no better than breaking a lease. This house will fall down without you. You must give us at least a year's notice!"

Great-grandma opened one eye. Ninety years gazed calmly out at her physicians like a dust-ghost from a high cupola[3] window in a fast-emptying house. "Tom . . . ?"

The boy was sent, alone, to her whispering bed.

"Tom," she said, faintly, far away, "in the Southern Seas there's a day in each man's life when he knows it's time to shake hands with all his friends and say good-by and sail away, and he does, and it's natural—it's just his time. That's how it is today. I'm so like you sometimes, sitting through Saturday matinees until nine at night when we send your dad to bring you home. Tom, when the time comes that the same cowboys are shooting the same Indians on the same mountaintop, then it's best to fold back the seat and head for the door, with no regrets and no walking backward up the aisle. So, I'm leaving while I'm still happy and still entertained."

Douglas was summoned next to her side.

"Grandma, who'll shingle the roof next spring?"

Every April for as far back as there were calendars, you thought you heard woodpeckers tapping the housetop. But no, it was Great-grandma somehow transported, singing, pounding nails, replacing shingles, high in the sky!

"Douglas," she whispered, "don't ever let anyone do the shingles unless it's fun for them."

"Yes'm."

---

2 **apprehension:** fear.

3 **cupola:** small structure built on the top of a building.

CHARACTERIZATION

"Look around come April, and say, 'Who'd like to fix the roof?' And whichever face lights up is the face you want, Douglas. Because up there on that roof you can see the whole town going toward the country and the country going toward the edge of the earth and the river shining, and the morning lake, and birds on the trees down under you, and the best of the wind all around above. Any one of those should be enough to make a person climb a weather vane some spring sunrise. It's a powerful hour, if you give it half a chance. . . ."

Her voice sank to a soft flutter.

Douglas was crying.

She roused herself again. "Now, why are you doing that?"

"Because," he said, "you won't be here tomorrow."

She turned a small hand mirror from herself to the boy. He looked at her face and himself in the mirror and then at her face again as she said, "Tomorrow morning I'll get up at seven and wash behind my ears; I'll run to church with Charlie Woodman; I'll picnic at Electric Park; I'll swim, run barefoot, fall out of trees, chew spearmint gum . . . Douglas, Douglas, for shame! You cut your fingernails, don't you?"

"Yes'm."

"And you don't yell when your body makes itself over every seven years or so, old cells dead and new ones added to your fingers and your heart. You don't mind that, do you?"

"No'm."

"Well, consider then, boy. Any man saves fingernail clippings is a fool. You ever see a snake bother to keep his peeled skin? That's about all you got here today in this bed is fingernails and snake skin. One good breath would send me up in flakes. Important thing is not the me that's lying here, but the me that's sitting on the edge of the bed looking back at me, and the me that's downstairs cooking supper, or out in the garage under the car, or in the library reading. All the new parts, they count. I'm not really dying today. No person ever died that had a family. I'll be around a long time. A thousand years from now a whole township of my offspring will be biting sour apples in the gumwood shade. That's my answer to anyone asks big questions! Quick now, send in the rest!"

At last the entire family stood, like people seeing someone off at the rail station, waiting in the room.

"Well," said Great-grandma, "there I am. I'm not humble, so it's nice seeing you standing around my bed. Now next week there's late gardening and closet-cleaning and clothes-buying for the children to do. And since that part of me which is called, for convenience, Great-grandma, won't be here to step it along, those other parts of me called Uncle Bert and Leo and Tom and Douglas, and all the other names, will have to take over, each to his own."

"Yes, Grandma."

"I don't want any Halloween parties here tomorrow. Don't want anyone saying anything sweet about me; I said it all in my time and my pride. I've tasted every victual and danced every dance; now there's one last tart I haven't bit on, one tune I haven't whistled. But I'm not afraid. I'm truly curious. Death won't get a crumb by my mouth I won't keep and savor.[4] So don't you worry over me. Now, all of you go, and let me find my sleep. . . ."

Somewhere a door closed quietly.

"That's better." Alone, she snuggled luxuriously down through the warm snowbank of linen and wool, sheet and cover, and the colors of the patchwork quilt were bright as the circus banners of old time. Lying there, she felt as small and secret as on those mornings eighty-some-odd years ago when, wakening, she comforted her tender bones in bed.

A long time back, she thought, I dreamed a dream, and was enjoying it so much when someone wakened me, and that was the day when I was born. And now? Now, let me see . . . She cast her mind back. Where was I? she thought. Ninety years

4 savor: taste with pleasure.

. . . how to take up the thread and the pattern of that lost dream again? She put out a small hand. *There* . . . Yes, that was it. She smiled. Deeper in the warm snow hill she turned her head upon her pillow. That was better. Now, yes, now she saw it shaping in her mind quietly, and with a serenity like a sea moving along an endless and self-refreshing shore. Now she let the old dream touch and lift her from the snow and drift her above the scarce-remembered bed.

Downstairs, she thought, they are polishing the silver, and rummaging the cellar, and dusting in the halls. She could hear them living all through the house.

"It's all right," whispered Great-grandma, as the dream floated her. "Like everything else in this life, it's fitting."

And the sea moved her back down the shore.

Understanding Literature

1. The author tells much of the story through a series of images, quick pictures which suggest whole scenes. In how much detail can you describe Great-grandma's house?
2. What kind of person is Great-grandma? How does she spend her time? Find phrases in the story which prove your ideas.
3. The author uses many comparisons which make the images more vivid. Instead of telling you that the window is clean, he says, "She made mirrors of every window." Explain the following comparisons which appear in the first paragraph:
   (a) glided . . . as steadily as a vacuum machine.
   (b) flowers raised their quivering fires.
   (c) as relaxed as a white glove.
   (d) she touched people like pictures, to set their frames straight.

CHARACTERIZATION

Find and explain other comparisons in the story.

4. How does Great-grandma compare her "leaving" with Tom's seeing a movie?

5. Why does Great-grandma tell Douglas not to "let anyone do the shingles unless it's fun for them"?

6. What is Great-grandma's response to Douglas's statement, "you won't be here tomorrow"?

7. Great-grandma says, "I'm not really dying today. No person ever died that had a family." Explain what is meant by her statement.

8. What does Great-grandma mean when she says, "Like everything else in this life, it's fitting"?

9. Explain the comparison made in the last line of the story, "And the sea moved her back down the shore."

10. Does it seem realistic for a person to feel the way Great-grandma does about dying? Give reasons for your answer.

Further Activity

Write a paragraph describing Great-grandma's living room as you would imagine it. Select only details which would fit her character as you have seen it in this story. You would not, for example, expect Great-grandma to have expensive-looking, showy decorations in her room nor would you expect the room to be dusty and untidy. Think about Great-grandma's character and then describe a room which you think she would be comfortable in and which she would want in her own home.

In each family a person who is ill becomes special, someone to be given extra attention and love. In this chapter from her book, *A New England Girlhood,* Nancy Hale recalls an illness and unhappiness at school during a period in her girlhood.

You Never Know

Nancy Hale

IMPROVING YOUR READING: The *flashback* technique which Nancy Hale uses is one you have probably seen on television or in movies. The author begins the story in the present, "flashes back" to the past, and concludes the story in the present. This device allows you to see the character at different times in her life: as she *is* in the present, and as she *was* in the past.

As I LIE here, trying to get over this idiotic cold before the Hansons' party, my mind becomes restless and inattentive if I try to read; I set up a game of patience[1] on a tray and even then it is as though my mind's eye were focused on some other scene; until sometimes I give up altogether trying to distract myself and simply lie here, resting, and letting my thoughts wander about as they will in my childhood, in the time when I was kept out of school so much by colds. I suppose there is a connection: I haven't had a cold in years, and I suppose this one reminds me, now, of those days when I had so many.

My mother was always very particular about taking me out of school at the first hint of a cough or a sniffle. So inconsiderate to spread a cold around, she used to say; but also my

mother was a great one for prevention; she had some terrible inner picture of complications ensuing on the common cold: the house suddenly lighted up at night, temperature's gone to 104, run for the doctor, where's the croup kettle?[2] I don't think I ever, during the period of which I speak, at least, had anything but the simplest sequence of sore throat, head cold, and the usual cough afterward.

I have no doubt but what I enjoyed staying at home, reading, and eating nice things, and not having to do anything. Any child jumps at the chance not to go to school; but my relief was a little deeper than that. This was the period when Geraldine Ames was riding high as a leader in our class, and she was the president of a club against me.

A child never knows quite why it

---

1 **game of patience:** form of the card game solitaire.

2 **croup kettle:** vaporizer for easing the breathing process during colds.

CHARACTERIZATION

is singled out as the one who is all wrong. There appear to be different reasons—in my case that my parents were painters instead of my father's being a stockbroker or banker, and that my dresses, which my mother made, had their waistlines up under my arms instead of around the hips—but the child knows inside that these are not enough. The real reason is cosmic:[3] the child is *wrong*, that's all, the herd have named her so and there is nothing, there never, never will be anything, to do about it. I would come into the varnished-oak gymnasium for prayers at the beginning of school in the morning, and Geraldine, tall and pretty with long black braids, would catch the cloth of my dress as I passed her on my way to my place and give it a tweak and whisper "Crazy . . ." with that scornful and yet abysmally beautiful smile.

I remember walking down to school in the morning, that winter, and coming to the patch in the road where it crossed the County Meadows, where the wind literally whistled across the flats and through the row of willows, and where, if the weather was zero, it was the coldest of all. It must have been January; I had on my brushed-wool cap-and-mittens set which I had been given for Christmas and which I had adored then and paraded before the mirror in, admiring its orange-and-green stripes, but which I took no further pleasure in since, one noontime after school, as I was coming down the stairs from the classrooms to the cloakroom, I had found Geraldine and one of her devotees kicking my cap around. I stood rooted to the bottom stair, watching, my heart sick. "This yours?" Geraldine asked, picking it up and tossing it at me disdainfully. "Crazy kind of a cap." I wept when I got home that day, for the beauty that had gone out of my cap-and-mittens set, and for being in the wrong. When my father got home that night, my mother told him about it. "Buck up," he said to me. "You let them see that you're as good and better than they are. Stand up for good old you." But that was impossible; he did not understand. Geraldine was beautiful and in the right, and I was in the wrong.

That morning as I crossed the bitter windy County Meadows, school seemed to loom ahead of me like a heavy woe. The January gale went through my heather-mixture coat. Suddenly I felt a tickle in the roof of my mouth. I'm getting a cold, I thought. I hesitated for a moment, and then turned around to walk home again, obedient to my mother's dictum:[4] "Always tell me at the first suggestion of a cold." I walked back up the icy street, up the hill to my warm snug home and my bed and the books that stood arrayed on my white-painted bookshelves. I don't think there is any question but that I was running away.

My mother believed in light, nourishing food for colds: poached eggs, warm and consoling on a bed of soggy

---

3 **cosmic:** vast; enormous.

4 **dictum:** command.

toast; chicken broth; baked potatoes, like hot little stoves one could hold in both hands before opening them and spreading them with butter and sprinkling them with salt; milk toast —toasted white bread laid in a soup plate, salted, with hot milk poured over it; the butter from the toast rose and floated, yellow puddles, on the white surface; cream of wheat—and as I put the cream and sugar on I would remember the game my father used to play with me when I was tiny: Once upon a time there was an island; and then white rain came, and rained and rained until it covered the island almost all up; and then it snowed, and snowed and snowed. . . .

When I stopped sneezing, and my mother could persuade herself that I was not going to develop pneumonia this time, I would sometimes leave my bed, with its white-painted arms for putting books on, and go and lie on the chaise longue[5] in her room.

Her room was papered with a white paper that had a trellis; at the top was a frieze[6] of green ivy leaves. The bureau, one of the Victorian sort decorated with carved fruit, had been painted white, by my mother, and the grapes that formed the handles painted green, with brown stems; it was very beautiful. The chaise longue upon which I lay was covered in bright green satin, and had white woodwork, traced with a line of green. I had a brown comfortable,[7] brought with me from my room,

tucked around me, and wore my old brown wool dressing gown with a pattern of Indians on it: it was two Christmases old, and I had loved it once, but I doubted all my own possessions now; perhaps that was why I so particularly enjoyed lying on the green satin chaise longue in my mother's bedroom. I stared up at the ceiling, where some long cracks and a stain made a shepherdess with sheep and an old man with a long beard, like God. It was so beautifully clear and uncluttered up there on the ceiling, with no furniture; it was easy to imagine oneself walking about upside down, with free, skating motions.

Sometimes my mother would read to me. I remember Miss Edgeworth, Mrs. Ewing, and especially the historical novels of Charlotte M. Yonge. One afternoon she was reading to me from *The Chaplet of Pearls*, which was very exciting. The setting sun of midafternoon cast a red glow on the snowdrifts outside, which reflected back through the bedroom windows, pink all over the white trellised walls. That hour, of sunset in the middle of a snowy winter afternoon, always seemed majestic, frozen, almost final. . . . My mother was reading the part where Charles IX,[8] from the staircase to his apartments in the Louvre,[9] witnesses the murder of Admiral Coligny in the Massacre of St. Bartholomew. At least that is the way I remember it. It seemed

---

5 **chaise longue** (shāz'lông'): long couch with a support for the back at one end.
6 **frieze:** ornamented border.
7 **comfortable:** quilted cover.

8 **Charles IX:** King of France from 1560 to 1574.
9 **Louvre** (lo͞o'vr): palace in Paris now used for a museum of art and for public offices.

CHARACTERIZATION

terribly real to me; I could see the carnage,[10] hear the shrieking in that frightful midnight. I stood on the staircase, I was the King, I stared down at the murder and the blood-stained Guises . . . only the stair-case was the staircase at school and the murder was being committed in the cloakroom below.

After a while my mother stopped reading and I began to play with cards, on a wooden board intended for cutting out dresses; but it was not pleasant, the kings and queens looked nasty and ferretlike;[11] I thought of the jeering stoats[12] and weasels in the Wild Wood, in *The Wind in the Willows*. My mother came and laid

10 **carnage:** slaughter; bloodshed.
11 **ferretlike:** like weasels.
12 **stoats:** ermines, small furry animals.

her hand on my forehead. "You've got a temperature again," she said, and hustled me back to my own bed. I think I was feverish all that night. My father came and stood in the door to my room when he got home. "Poor old girl," he said. "Got a tem-perament." He never called it "tem-perature."

Sometimes, when I was getting well from one of those colds, I, too, used to draw pictures, only they were not very good. What seemed to turn out best was copying colored pictures out of art books of my mother's and father's; the color was what I liked to put in. I had two water-color paintboxes, one rather limited, left from my infancy, the other large and with handsome pans for mixing the colors. My father tried to encourage me to copy Ingres and Watteau[13] in red chalk. But what I liked best to do was to copy the pictures of saints out of an old art calendar.

The reason for this was that I had been given some gold paint, and I particularly enjoyed painting the haloes round the saints' heads in thick, solid gold. I would sit at the upright black desk in my room, dressed in a great many sweaters for fear I would catch more cold, and prop the calendar, which was long and narrow, up against the pigeon-holes, to copy from. First I made a drawing on my water-color pad of the saint in pencil, long and narrow and fitting into a pointed arch as in the picture I was copying; then I opened my paintboxes and began to fill in the colors, dipping my paint-brush in the jelly glass of water beside me. Most of the saints were men, with long gray or brown beards, blue or rich purple mantles, and white garments edged with the Greek key, which also gave me an opportunity to use gold paint. I always left the halo for last, and filled it in with the grainy, sparkly gold paint very carefully, so as not to smear, or run into the hair color. Sometimes, painting a halo and taking my time over it, I would wonder what haloes were, what they were supposed to be made of: whether they were hard and thin like gold plates, or just light radiating from the saint. They seemed to be a sort of label saints wore. I imagined that the label must represent the way saints were inside; they must have something inside that was round and shining and complete. One afternoon as I was painting a halo, with the electric light, which hung from the ceiling inside a Japanese lantern, turned on because it was snowing hard outside, I began to wonder how it would feel to have a halo on, round and gold and enveloping my whole head. But all I could think of was how a cold in the head felt—round, too, as a matter of fact, and enveloping; but thick and like cotton wool.

My mother came to the door of my room and said, "Bettina Nash is downstairs and wants to see you. I told her she could, I don't think you have any germs now, but be sure to sit beside the fire out of the draft—" I didn't wait to hear her finish. I was out of that room as fast as I could dash. I slowed down to enter the living room, though, of course. Bettina was dressed in thick sweaters instead of a coat; there was still snow on her shoulders and on the top of her red skating cap. "C'mon out, why don't you? It's good coasting this after," she said.

"I can't. I'm getting over a cold," I said, dismally, and she actually seemed to sympathize with me, for she said, "Gee, that's awful. Can't you get over it quick or something?" She went away, after a while, but something had changed, a chink had opened, for she was one of Geraldine's cohorts and she had come to see me. I can't remember even going back to that boring old saint, that afternoon or ever. I was never any real good at painting, anyway.

13 Ingres (ăN′gr) and Watteau (wŏ tō′): French painters of the 19th and 18th centuries.

That afternoon a tide had turned, for me, for the next thing I remember is being one of Geraldine's cohorts myself. I don't know why she decided to accept me, but I remember basking in the precious peace of her approval, which we all sought avidly by agreeing with everything she said. "Dja see that new kid in fourth class?" she would say, as we stood about under the sighing pines in the schoolyard at recess. "She's *crazy*." "Crazy-looking thing," we would chime in; crazy meant anything wrong, anything different from the norm, which was, of course, Geraldine herself: pigtailed, gingham-dressed, belted at the hipline, scornful, *right*. I would chime in as loud as any of them, for now all was well, somebody else was crazy, not me.

These scenes, like the pictures from an old-fashioned magic lantern, are what have been running incessantly through the back of my mind as I lie here, trying to get over this stupid cold in time for Louise Hanson's party. It's too absurd; I *never* have colds. I suppose you could figure out that by having the cold I'm trying to escape from going to the party, since I know Louise hates me.

I've been told the kind of malicious thing she says behind my back.

But I'm not a child any longer, to run away. My husband says, "What do you care? If she hates you, just give her the go-by." He doesn't understand. Louise Hanson gives the best parties in town, the most important parties, and I'm not going to let hurt feelings keep me from going to this one. Besides, if there's one thing all those memories prove, it's that you never can tell. For all I know now, by this time next year I may be Louise Hanson's most intimate friend—just the way I used to get asked to stay to supper at Geraldine Ames's, long, long ago.

I wish I could throw off this cold. It's boring to stay in bed, when you're grown-up; nobody brings you trays of good things to eat, not these days. I've read all the magazines, and I can't bear games of patience, really—those horrid little faces on the cards. There isn't anything to do, just lie here with my cold filling my whole head and feeling like some kind of cotton-wool halo. I suppose I could get up, cold and all; but then, it pays to be cautious. You never know what a cold may turn into.

Understanding Literature

1. Explain the connection between the first paragraph of the story and the last three paragraphs. How is the care of this illness contrasted with the care given to the author as a child? What similarities do you notice between the person as an adult and the person as a child, seen in flashback? How do these similarities aid in weaving the threads of the story together?

2. How is the girl's cold related to the problem of her lack of acceptance by her classmates?
3. Why does the girl's brushed-wool cap-and-mittens set lose its beauty for her? In what other way could she have reacted to Geraldine's insults?
4. How is the girl's behavior, after she becomes Geraldine's friend, similar to the behavior of many people in this type of situation?

Further Activities

1. In the story Geraldine is the leader in her group. This group has power to make people comfortable or uncomfortable, accepted or rejected, happy or sad. How can such a person make others feel like "outsiders"? What qualities does such a leader have to have? Are these qualities always good ones? In what way do you think an "outsider" could become accepted by the group? Is the effort always worth the reward? Prepare to discuss these ideas.
2. The passage in which the mother's room is described is an especially vivid one. Examine this passage carefully until you are able to point out the details which make this passage so sharp and clear. Examine in the same way the passage describing the food eaten by the sick child.

In this well-known Christmas story, two young people have no money to buy Christmas gifts for each other. The spirit of giving at its best is illustrated by the sacrifice each makes to bring happiness to the other.

The Gift of the Magi

O. Henry

IMPROVING YOUR READING: An author reveals the characteristics of the people in his stories by showing them in a series of episodes or under conditions of strain and stress. Observe Della's reactions to her immediate problem and Della's and Jim's reactions to their general situation at the end of the story. What do their reactions reveal about them?

ONE DOLLAR AND eighty-seven cents. That was all. And sixty cents of it was in pennies. Pennies saved one and two at a time by bulldozing[1] the grocer and the vegetable man and the butcher until one's cheeks burned with the silent imputation of parsimony[2] that such close dealing implied. Three times Della counted it. One dollar and eighty-seven cents. And the next day would be Christmas.

There was clearly nothing to do but flop down on the shabby little couch and howl. So Della did it. Which instigates the moral reflection[3] that life is made up of sobs, sniffles, and smiles, with sniffles predominating.

While the mistress of the home is gradually subsiding from the first stage to the second, take a look at the home. A furnished flat at $8 per week. It did not exactly beggar description, but it certainly had that word[4] on the lookout for the mendicancy squad.[5]

In the vestibule below was a letter box into which no letter would go, and an electric button from which no mortal finger could coax a ring. Also appertaining thereunto[6] was a card bearing the name "Mr. James Dillingham Young."

The "Dillingham" had been flung to the breeze during a former period of prosperity when its possessor was being paid $30 per week. Now, when the income was shrunk to $20, the letters of "Dillingham" looked blurred, as though they were thinking seriously of contracting to a

---

1 **bulldozing:** bullying.
2 **imputation of parsimony:** charge of stinginess.
3 **instigates the moral reflection:** prompts the careful conclusion.

4 **that word:** beggar.
5 **mendicancy squad:** group that searches for those engaged in illegal begging.
6 **appertaining thereunto:** referring to that.

modest and unassuming D. But whenever Mr. James Dillingham Young came home and reached his flat above he was called "Jim" and greatly hugged by Mrs. James Dillingham Young, already introduced to you as Della. Which is all very good.

Della finished her cry and attended to her cheeks with the powder rag. She stood by the window and looked out dully at a gray cat walking a gray fence in a gray back yard. Tomorrow would be Christmas Day, and she had only $1.87 with which to buy Jim a present. She had been saving every penny she could for months, with this result. Twenty dollars a week doesn't go far. Expenses had been greater than she had calculated. They always are. Only $1.87 to buy a present for Jim. Her Jim. Many a happy hour she had spent planning for something nice for him. Something fine and rare and sterling—something just a little bit near to being worthy of the honor of being owned by Jim.

There was a pier glass[7] between the windows of the room. Perhaps you have seen a pier glass in an $8 flat. A very thin and very agile person may, by observing his reflection in a rapid sequence of longitudinal[8] strips, obtain a fairly accurate conception of his looks. Della, being slender, had mastered the art.

Suddenly she whirled from the window and stood before the glass. Her eyes were shining brilliantly, but her face had lost its color within twenty seconds. Rapidly she pulled down her hair and let it fall to its full length.

Now, there were two possessions of the James Dillingham Youngs in which they both took a mighty pride. One was Jim's gold watch that had been his father's and his grandfather's. The other was Della's hair. Had the Queen of Sheba lived in the flat across the airshaft, Della would have let her hair hang out the window some day to dry just to depreciate[9] Her Majesty's jewels and gifts. Had King Solomon been the janitor, with all his treasures piled up in the basement, Jim would have pulled out his watch every time he passed, just to see him pluck at his beard from envy.

So now Della's beautiful hair fell about her, rippling and shining like a cascade of brown waters. It reached below her knee and made itself almost a garment for her. And then she did it up again nervously and quickly. Once she faltered for a minute and stood still while a tear or two splashed on the worn red carpet.

On went her old brown jacket; on went her old brown hat. With a whirl of skirts and with the brilliant sparkle still in her eyes, she fluttered out the door and down the stairs to the street.

Where she stopped the sign read: "Mme. Sofronie. Hair Goods of All Kinds." One flight up Della ran, and collected herself, panting. Madame,

7 **pier glass:** narrow mirror designed to fit the wall space between two windows.
8 **longitudinal:** lengthwise.

9 **depreciate** (dǐ prē′shǐ āt′): belittle; detract from.

CHARACTERIZATION

large, too white, chilly, hardly looked the "Sofronie."

"Will you buy my hair?" asked Della.

"I buy hair," said Madame. "Take yer hat off and let's have a sight at the looks of it."

Down rippled the brown cascade.

"Twenty dollars," said Madame, lifting the mass with a practiced hand.

"Give it to me quick," said Della.

Oh, and the next two hours tripped by on rosy wings. Forget the hashed metaphor. She was ransacking the stores for Jim's present.

She found it at last. It surely had been made for Jim and no one else. There was no other like it in any of the stores, and she had turned all of them inside out. It was a platinum fob chain[10] simple and chaste in design, properly proclaiming its value by substance alone and not by meretricious[11] ornamentation—as all good things should do. It was even worthy of The Watch. As soon as she saw it she knew that it must be Jim's. It was like him. Quietness and value—the description applied to both. Twenty-one dollars they took from her for it, and she hurried home with the 87 cents. With that chain on his watch Jim might be properly anxious about the time in any company. Grand as the watch was, he sometimes looked at it on the sly on account of the old leather strap that he used in place of a chain.

When Della reached home her intoxication[12] gave way a little to prudence and reason. She got out her curling irons and lighted the gas and went to work repairing the ravages[13] made by generosity added to love. Which is always a tremendous task, dear friends—a mammoth task.

Within forty minutes her head was covered with tiny, close-lying curls that made her look wonderfully like a truant schoolboy. She looked at her reflection in the mirror long, carefully, and critically.

"If Jim doesn't kill me," she said to herself, "before he takes a second look at me, he'll say I look like a Coney Island chorus girl. But what could I do—oh! what could I do with a dollar and eighty-seven cents?"

At seven o'clock the coffee was made and the frying pan was on the back of the stove hot and ready to cook the chops.

Jim was never late. Della doubled the fob chain in her hand and sat on the corner of the table near the door that he always entered. Then she heard his step on the stair away down on the first flight, and she turned white for just a moment. She had a habit of saying little silent prayers about the simplest everyday things, and now she whispered: "Please God, make him think I am still pretty."

The door opened and Jim stepped in and closed it. He looked thin and very serious. Poor fellow, he was only twenty-two—and to be burdened with a family! He needed a

---

10 **fob chain:** short chain for watches.
11 **meretricious:** gaudy; showy.

12 **intoxication:** excitement.
13 **ravages:** damages.

new overcoat and he was without gloves.

Jim stopped inside the door, as immovable as a setter at the scent of quail. His eyes were fixed upon Della, and there was an expression in them that she could not read, and it terrified her. It was not anger, nor surprise, nor disapproval, nor horror, nor any of the sentiments that she had been prepared for. He simply stared at her fixedly with that peculiar expression on his face.

Della wriggled off the table and went for him.

"Jim, darling," she cried, "don't look at me that way. I had my hair cut off and sold it because I couldn't have lived through Christmas without giving you a present. It'll grow out again—you won't mind, will you? I just had to do it. My hair grows awfully fast. Say 'Merry Christmas!' Jim, and let's be happy. You don't know what a nice—what a beautiful, nice gift I've got for you."

"You've cut off your hair?" asked Jim, laboriously, as if he had not arrived at that patent fact yet even after the hardest mental labor.

"Cut it off and sold it," said Della. "Don't you like me just as well, anyhow? I'm me without my hair, ain't I?"

Jim looked about the room curiously.

"You say your hair is gone?" he said, with an air almost of idiocy.

"You needn't look for it," said Della. "It's sold, I tell you—sold and gone, too. It's Christmas Eve, boy. Be good to me, for it went for you. Maybe the hairs of my head were

numbered," she went on with a sudden serious sweetness, "but nobody could ever count my love for you. Shall I put the chops on, Jim?"

Out of his trance Jim seemed quickly to wake. He enfolded his Della. For ten seconds let us regard with discreet scrutiny[14] some inconsequential[15] object in the other direction. Eight dollars a week or a million a year—what is the difference? A mathematician or a wit would give you the wrong answer. The magi brought valuable gifts, but that was not among them. This dark assertion[16] will be illuminated later on.

Jim drew a package from his overcoat pocket and threw it upon the table.

"Don't make any mistake, Dell," he said, "about me. I don't think there's anything in the way of a haircut or a shave or a shampoo that could make me like my girl any less. But if you'll unwrap that package you may see why you had me going a while at first."

White fingers and nimble tore at the string and paper. And then an ecstatic scream of joy; and then, alas! a quick feminine change to hysterical tears and wails, necessitating the immediate employment of all the comforting powers of the lord of the flat.

For there lay The Combs—the set of combs, side and back, that Della had worshiped for long in a Broadway window. Beautiful combs, pure

---

14 **discreet scrutiny:** tactful inspection.
15 **inconsequential:** unimportant.
16 **assertion:** declaration.

CHARACTERIZATION

tortoise shell, with jeweled rims—just the shade to wear in the beautiful vanished hair. They were expensive combs, she knew, and her heart had simply craved and yearned over them without the least hope of possession. And now, they were hers, but the tresses that should have adorned the coveted[17] adornments were gone.

But she hugged them to her bosom, and at length she was able to look up with dim eyes and a smile and say: "My hair grows so fast, Jim!"

And then Della leaped up like a little singed cat and cried, "Oh, oh!"

Jim had not yet seen his beautiful present. She held it out to him eagerly upon her open palm. The dull precious metal seemed to flash with a reflection of her bright and ardent spirit.

"Isn't it a dandy, Jim? I hunted all over town to find it. You'll have to look at the time a hundred times a day now. Give me your watch. I want to see how it looks on it."

17 coveted: desired.

Instead of obeying, Jim tumbled down on the couch and put his hands under the back of his head and smiled.

"Dell," said he, "let's put our Christmas presents away and keep 'em a while. They're too nice to use just at present. I sold the watch to get the money to buy your combs. And now suppose you put the chops on."

The magi, as you know, were wise men—wonderfully wise men—who brought gifts to the Babe in the manger. They invented the art of giving Christmas presents. Being wise, their gifts were no doubt wise ones, possibly bearing the privilege of exchange in case of duplication. And here I have lamely related to you the uneventful chronicle of two foolish children in a flat who most unwisely sacrificed for each other the greatest treasures of their house. But in a last word to the wise of these days let it be said that of all who give gifts these two were the wisest. Of all who give and receive gifts, such as they are wisest. Everywhere they are wisest. They are the magi.

Understanding Literature

1. Select conversation from the story that helps you understand Della and Jim. What actions are shown that characterize them? What actual description of these two people is given?
2. What evidence do you have that the events in this story took place a number of years ago?
3. A metaphor is an implied comparison of two different objects which are alike in at least one way. O. Henry says "the next

two hours tripped by on rosy wings" and then calls this a "hashed metaphor." What objects are being compared? Why is the metaphor "hashed"?

4. Although the story is of a serious nature, O. Henry shows a little lightness and humor in his treatment of Della. Where and how does he do this?

5. At what point do you feel you know what the outcome of the story will be? Why?

6. Reread the last three sentences of the story. Explain what these sentences mean. Why does O. Henry, in referring to Della and Jim, say, "They are the magi"?

7. When done well, a surprise ending, though unexpected, is closely related to the characters and the events in the story. It is not an ending that is attached to the story simply to startle the reader; it satisfies him. Why is the ending of this story a particularly good one?

8. What does the title mean?

In this poem the main character represents an idea. Notice the similarity between "Abou Ben Adhem" and the previous story, "The Gift of the Magi."

Abou Ben Adhem

Leigh Hunt

Abou Ben Adhem (may his tribe increase!)
Awoke one night from a deep dream of peace,
And saw, within the moonlight in his room,
Making it rich, and like a lily in bloom,
An angel writing in a book of gold:—   5
Exceeding[1] peace had made Ben Adhem bold,
And to the presence in the room he said,
"What writest thou?" —The vision raised its head,
And with a look made of all sweet accord,[2]
Answered, "The names of those who love the Lord."   10
"And is mine one?" said Abou. "Nay, not so,"
Replied the angel. Abou spoke more low,
But cheerly still; and said, "I pray thee then,
Write me as one that loves his fellow men."

The angel wrote, and vanished. The next night   15
It came again with a great wakening light,
And showed the names whom love of God had blessed,
And lo! Ben Adhem's name led all the rest.

1 **Exceeding:** unlimited.   2 **accord:** agreement; harmony.

Understanding Literature

1. Why does Ben Adhem's name appear at the head of the list "of those who love the Lord"?
2. What idea does Abou Ben Adhem represent?

Further Activity

Write a two-paragraph theme in which you compare Abou Ben Adhem with Della and Jim in "The Gift of the Magi." You might begin the first paragraph by describing the character of Abou Ben Adhem. In the rest of the paragraph explain how the characters of Della and Jim are like or unlike Abou Ben Adhem's.

In the second paragraph explain what idea Abou Ben Adhem represents and discuss whether this idea is similar or dissimilar to the idea dramatized in "The Gift of the Magi."

The Art of Storytelling

You HAVE READ so far largely about plot and characterization. Action and people are important parts of a story, but an author is also concerned with the manner in which he tells his story, with the effect his story has on the reader, and with the meaning he wishes to convey, among many other things. If he wishes to have his characters seem like real people instead of fairy-tale heroes and heroines, he must make it clear why they act as they do and must make their reasons and actions believable. If an author wishes his readers to feel a certain way about the characters or events in his story, he must describe them in a way that will be sure to arouse that feeling. Or, on the other hand, if a writer has something important to say which he feels his readers should know about and if he chooses to say it through a story, the characters, the plot, the dialogue, and many other elements will need to contribute to his purpose. Since the author is so concerned with the way in which he tells his story and with the devices he uses, the reader will make a far better audience if he is aware of and understands these devices. In each of the following selections you will find some of the most important of these techniques explained and illustrated.

Many stories take place in imaginary worlds. As you read this story, ask yourself which parts of it could really happen and which parts are simply fantasy.

The Golden Kite, the Silver Wind

Ray Bradbury

IMPROVING YOUR READING: Authors often use *symbols*—things which stand for other things. A bird, for example, might stand for freedom; an eagle might stand for superior vision or insight. In this story you will meet many symbols: a pig, an orange, a club, a bonfire, a lake, a mouth, a needle, a sword, a scabbard, lightning, an eagle, a net, and more. How do they all connect? How do a pig and an orange end up as a "Golden Kite" and "Silver Wind"?

"IN THE SHAPE of a *pig?*" cried the Mandarin.

"In the shape of a pig," said the messenger, and departed.

"Oh, what an evil day in an evil year," cried the Mandarin. "The town of Kwan-Si, beyond the hill, was very small in my childhood. Now it has grown so large that at last they are building a wall."

"But why should a wall two miles away make my good father sad and angry all within the hour?" asked his daughter quietly.

"They build their wall," said the Mandarin, "in the shape of a pig! Do you see? Our own city wall is built in the shape of an orange. That pig will devour us, greedily!"

"Ah."

They both sat thinking.

Life was full of symbols and omens. Demons lurked everywhere, Death swam in the wetness of an eye, the turn of a gull's wing meant rain, a fan held *so*, the tilt of a roof, and, yes, even a city wall was of immense importance. Travelers and tourists, caravans, musicians, artists, coming upon these two towns, equally judging the portents, would say, "The city shaped like an orange? No! I will enter the city shaped like a pig and prosper, eating all, growing fat with good luck and prosperity!"

The Mandarin wept. "All is lost! These symbols and signs terrify. Our city will come on evil days."

"Then," said the daughter, "call in your stonemasons and temple builders. I will whisper from behind the silken screen and you will know the words."

The old man clapped his hands despairingly. "Ho, stonemasons! Ho, builders of towns and palaces!"

The men who knew marble and granite and onyx and quartz came quickly. The Mandarin faced them most uneasily, himself waiting for a

THE ART OF STORYTELLING

whisper from the silken screen behind his throne. At last the whisper came.

"I have called you here," said the whisper.

"I have called you here," said the Mandarin aloud, "because our city is shaped like an orange, and the vile city of Kwan-Si has this day shaped theirs like a ravenous pig—"

Here the stonemasons groaned and wept. Death rattled his cane in the outer courtyard. Poverty made a sound like a wet cough in the shadows of the room.

"And so," said the whisper, said the Mandarin, "you raisers of walls must go bearing trowels and rocks and change the shape of *our* city!"

The architects and masons gasped. The Mandarin himself gasped at what he had said. The whisper whispered. The Mandarin went on: "And you will change our walls into a club which may beat the pig and drive it off!"

The stonemasons rose up, shouting. Even the Mandarin, delighted at the words from his mouth, applauded, stood down from his throne. "Quick!" he cried. "To work!"

When his men had gone, smiling and bustling, the Mandarin turned with great love to the silken screen. "Daughter," he whispered, "I will embrace you." There was no reply. He stepped around the screen, and she was gone.

Such modesty, he thought. She has slipped away and left me with a triumph, as if it were mine.

The news spread through the city; the Mandarin was acclaimed. Everyone carried stone to the walls. Fireworks were set off and the demons of death and poverty did not linger, as all worked together. At the end of the month the wall had been changed. It was now a mighty bludgeon with which to drive pigs, boars, even lions, far away. The Mandarin slept like a happy fox every night.

"I would like to see the Mandarin of Kwan-Si when the news is learned. Such pandemonium and hysteria; he will likely throw himself from a mountain! A little more of that wine, oh Daughter-who-thinks-like-a-son."

But the pleasure was like a winter flower; it died swiftly. That very afternoon the messenger rushed into the courtroom. "Oh, Mandarin, disease, early sorrow, avalanches, grasshopper plagues, and poisoned well water!"

The Mandarin trembled.

"The town of Kwan-Si," said the messenger, "which was built like a pig and which animal we drove away by changing our walls to a mighty stick, has now turned triumph to winter ashes. They have built their city's walls like a great bonfire to burn our stick!"

The Mandarin's heart sickened within him, like an autumn fruit upon an ancient tree. "Oh, gods! Travelers will spurn us. Tradesmen, reading the symbols, will turn from the stick, so easily destroyed, to the fire, which conquers all!"

"No," said a whisper like a snowflake from behind the silken screen.

"No," said the startled Mandarin.

"Tell my stonemasons," said the

whisper that was a falling drop of rain, "to build our walls in the shape of a shining lake."

The Mandarin said this aloud, his heart warmed.

"And with this lake of water," said the whisper and the old man, "we will quench the fire and put it out forever!"

The city turned out in joy to learn that once again they had been saved by the magnificent Emperor of ideas. They ran to the walls and built them nearer to this new vision, singing, not as loudly as before, of course, for they were tired, and not as quickly, for since it had taken a month to rebuild the wall the first time, they had had to neglect business and crops and therefore were somewhat weaker and poorer.

There then followed a succession of horrible and wonderful days, one in another like a nest of frightening boxes.

"Oh, Emperor," cried the messenger, "Kwan-Si has rebuilt their walls to resemble a mouth with which to drink all our lake!"

"Then," said the Emperor, standing very close to his silken screen, "build our walls like a needle to sew up that mouth!"

"Emperor!" screamed the messenger. "They make their walls like a sword to break your needle!"

The Emperor held, trembling, to the silken screen. "Then shift the stones to form a scabbard to sheathe that sword!"

"Mercy," wept the messenger the following morn, "they have worked all night and shaped their walls like

lightning which will explode and destroy that sheath!"

Sickness spread in the city like a pack of evil dogs. Shops closed. The population, working now steadily for endless months upon the changing of the walls, resembled Death himself, clattering his white bones like musical instruments in the wind. Funerals began to appear in the streets, though it was the middle of summer, a time when all should be tending and harvesting. The Mandarin fell so ill that he had his bed drawn up by the silken screen and there he lay, miserably giving his architectural orders. The voice behind the screen was weak now, too, and faint, like the wind in the eaves.

"Kwan-Si is an eagle. Then our walls must be a net for that eagle. They are a sun to burn our net. Then we build a moon to eclipse their sun!"

Like a rusted machine, the city ground to a halt.

At last the whisper behind the screen cried out:

"In the name of the gods, send for Kwan-Si!"

Upon the last day of summer the Mandarin Kwan-Si, very ill and withered away, was carried into our Mandarin's courtroom by four starving footmen. The two mandarins were propped up, facing each other. Their breaths fluttered like winter winds in their mouths. A voice said:

"Let us put an end to this."

The old men nodded.

"This cannot go on," said the faint voice. "Our people do nothing but rebuild our cities to a different shape every day, every hour. They have no time to hunt, to fish, to love, to be good to their ancestors and their ancestors' children."

"This I admit," said the mandarins of the towns of the Cage, the Moon, the Spear, the Fire, the Sword and this, that, and other things.

"Carry us into the sunlight," said the voice.

The old men were borne out under the sun and up a little hill. In the late summer breeze a few very thin children were flying dragon kites in all the colors of the sun, and frogs and grass, the color of the sea and the color of coins and wheat.

The first Mandarin's daughter stood by his bed.

"See," she said.

"Those are nothing but kites," said the two old men.

"But what is a kite on the ground?" she said. "It is nothing. What does it need to sustain it and make it beautiful and truly spiritual?"

"The wind, of course?" said the others.

"And what do the sky and the wind need to make *them* beautiful?"

"A kite, of course—many kites, to break the monotony, the sameness of the sky. Colored kites, flying!"

"So," said the Mandarin's daughter. "You, Kwan-Si, will make a last rebuilding of your town to resemble nothing more nor less than the wind.

And we shall build like a golden kite. The wind will beautify the kite and carry it to wondrous heights. And the kite will break the sameness of the wind's existence and give it purpose and meaning. One without the other is nothing. Together, all will be beauty and cooperation and a long and enduring life."

Whereupon the two mandarins were so overjoyed that they took their first nourishment in days, momentarily were given strength, embraced, and lavished praise upon each other, called the Mandarin's daughter a boy, a man, a stone pillar, a warrior, and a true and unforgettable son. Almost immediately they parted and hurried to their towns, calling out and singing, weakly but happily.

And so, in time, the towns became the Town of the Golden Kite and the Town of the Silver Wind. And harvestings were harvested and business tended again, and the flesh returned, and disease ran off like a frightened jackal. And on every night of the year the inhabitants in the Town of the Kite could hear the good clear wind sustaining them. And those in the Town of the Wind could hear the kite singing, whispering, rising, and beautifying them.

"So be it," said the Mandarin in front of his silken screen.

Understanding Literature

1. At the beginning of the story, why is the Mandarin so upset by the shape of the wall of Kwan-Si?
2. What is the reasoning behind each change of shape of the cities' walls?
3. What changes take place in the Mandarin and his daughter as the building race continues? How are the townspeople affected?
4. Why did the Golden Kite and the Silver Wind succeed after all the other symbols had failed?
5. How would you complete the following statement: "The two cities in the story are like ...." Can you think of more than one answer?

Further Activity

Are the situations presented in the world of "The Golden Kite, the Silver Wind" just fantasy? Could, or do, they occur in your own world? Before answering these questions, look at the front pages of several newspapers (at least one with international events). What would the Mandarin's daughter have to say about these front-page reports?

Reading can help you to understand other people; and if you understand others, you will be better prepared to live in the world around you. In this story from *The Friendly Persuasion,* Jess Birdwell misunderstands his wife's persistence. He hates geese; Eliza loves them. A conflict is bound to develop. Jess's weakness is that he does not understand people very well. Eliza is in no such predicament; she can convince anyone of anything.

The Pacing Goose°

Jessamyn West

IMPROVING YOUR READING: Watch for the many *conflicts* which develop in this story. Jess wants one thing and Eliza wants another. Enoch, the hired man, is told to do something he does not want to do. Eliza has to win her case in court. As you wonder how each conflict will come out, you have a sense of suspense. But most of all the author is concerned with *motivation,* why people act as they do. Does the author of this story make it clear why the characters act as they do? In other words, has she motivated them?

In this story Jess and Eliza Birdwell are Quakers; that is, they belong to the Society of Friends, a religious group whose members frequently use "thee" and "thy" to all men as a mark of equality. Many Friends also refuse to take oaths and, being opposed to war, refuse to bear arms. Note how these characteristics are used in the story.

JESS SAT IN the kitchen at the long table by the west window where in winter he kept his grafting tools: the thin-bladed knife, the paper sweet with the smell of beeswax and the resin, the boxes of roots and scions.[1] Jess was a nurseryman[2] and spring meant for him not only spirits flowering—but the earth's. A week more of moderating weather and he'd be out, still in gum boots, but touching an earth that had thawed, whose riches were once again fluid enough to be sucked upward, toward those burgeonings[3] which by summer would have swelled into Early Harvests, Permains and Sweet Bows.

Spring's a various season, Jess thought, no two years the same: comes in with rains, mud deep enough to swallow horse and rider; comes in cold, snow falling so fast it weaves a web; comes in with a warm wind blowing about thy ears and bringing a smell of something flower-

1 scions (sī'ənz): shoots ready for planting.
2 nurseryman: owner of a plant nursery, where plants and trees are raised for sale.

3 burgeonings: new growths.

ing, not here, but southaways, across the Ohio, maybe, in Kentucky. Nothing here now but a smell of melting snow—which is no smell at all, but a kind of prickle in the nose, like a bygone sneeze. Comes in so various, winter put by and always so welcome.

"And us each spring so much the same."

"Thee speaking to me, Jess?"

"Nothing thee'd understand, Eliza."

Spring made Jess discontented with the human race—and with women, if anything more than men. It looked as if spring put them all in the shade: the season so resourceful and they each year meeting it with nothing changed from last year; digging up roots from the same sassafras thicket, licking sulphur and molasses from the same big-bowled spoon.

Behind him the table was set for supper, plates neatly turned to cover the bone-handled knives and forks, spoon vase aglitter with steel well burnished by brick dust, dishes of jam with more light to them than the sun, which was dwindling away, peaked and overcast outside his window.

"Spring opening up," he said, "and nobody in this house so much as putting down a line of poetry."

Eliza, who was lifting dried-peach pies from a hot oven, said nothing. She set the four of them in a neat row on the edge of her kitchen cabinet to cool, and slid her pans of cornbread into the oven. Then she turned to Jess, her cheeks red with heat, and her black eyes warm with what she had to say. "Thee'd maybe relish a nice little rhyme for thy supper, Jess Birdwell."

Jess sighed, then sniffed the pies, so rich with ripe peach flavor that the kitchen smelled like a summer orchard, nothing lacking but the sound of bees. "Now, Eliza," he said, "thee knows I wouldn't have thee anyways altered. Thee . . ."

"Thee," Eliza interrupted him, "is like all men. Thee wants to have thy poetry and eat it too."

Jess wondered how what he'd felt about spring, a season with the Lord's thumbprint fresh on it, could've led to anything so unspringlike as an argument about a batch of dried-peach pies.

"Eliza," he said firmly, "I didn't mean thee. Though it's crossed my mind sometimes as strange that none of the boys have ever turned, this time of year, to rhyming."

"Josh writes poems," Eliza said.

"Thee ever read what Josh writes, Eliza?"

Eliza nodded.

Ah, well, Jess thought, no use at this date to tell her what's the difference.

Eliza looked her husband over carefully. "Jess Birdwell," she said, "thee's full of humors.[4] Thy blood needs thinning. I'll boil thee up a good cup of sassafras tea."

Jess turned away from the green and gold sunset and the patches of snow it was gilding and fairly faced the dried-peach pies and Eliza, who

4 full of humors: moody.

THE ART OF STORYTELLING

was dropping dumplings into a pot of beans.

"That's just it, Eliza," he said. "That's just the rub."

Eliza gave him no encouragement, but he went on anyway. "Earth alters, season to season, spring comes in never two times the same, only us pounding on steady as pump bolts and not freshened by so much as a grass blade."

"Jess, thee's got spring fever."

"I could reckon time and temperature, each spring, by the way thee starts honing for geese. 'Jess, don't thee think we might have a few geese?' It's a tardy spring," Jess said. "Snow still on the ground and not a word yet from thee about geese."

Eliza pulled a chair out from the table and sat. "Jess, why's thee always been so set against geese?"

"I'm not set against geese. It's geese that's set against farming. They can mow down a half acre of sprouting corn while thee's trying to head them off—and in two minutes they'll level a row of pie plant it's taken two years to get started. No, Eliza, it's the geese that's against me."

"If thee had tight fences . . ." Eliza said.

"Eliza, I got tight fences, but the goose's never been hatched that'll admit fences exist. And an old gander'd just as soon go through a fence as hiss—and if he can't find a hole or crack in a fence he'll lift the latch."

"Jess," said Eliza flatly, "thee don't like geese."

"Well," said Jess, "I wouldn't go so far's to say I didn't like them, but I will say that if there's any meaner, dirtier animal, or one that glories in it more, I don't know it. And a thing I've never been able to understand about thee, Eliza, is what thee sees in the shifty-eyed birds."

"Geese," said Eliza, with a dreaminess unusual to her, "march along so lordly like . . . they're pretty as swans floating down a branch . . . in fall they stretch out their necks and honk to geese passing overhead as if they's wild. My father never had any trouble raising geese and I've heard him say many a time that there's no better food for a brisk morning than a fried goose egg."

Jess knew, with spring his topic, he'd ought to pass over Eliza's father and his fried goose egg but he couldn't help saying, "A fried goose egg always had a kind of bloated look to me, Eliza"—but then he went on fast. "The season's shaping up," he said. "I can see thee's all primed[5] to say, 'Jess, let's get a setting of goose eggs.'"

Eliza went over to the bean kettle and began to lift out dumplings. "It's a forwarder season than thee thinks, Jess," she said. "I got a setting under a hen now."

Jess looked at his wife. He didn't know what had made him want spring's variety in a human being— nor Eliza's substituting doing for asking. And speaking of it just now, as he had, made opposition kind of ticklish.

5 primed: prepared.

"When'd thee set them?" he asked finally.

"Yesterday," said Eliza.

"Where'd thee get the eggs?"

"Overbys'," said Eliza. The Overbys were their neighbors to the south.

"Well, they got enough for a surety," Jess said, "to give a few away."

"The Overbys don't give anything away, as thee knows. I paid for them. With my own money," Eliza added.

"How many?" Jess asked.

"Eight," Eliza said.

Jess turned back to his window. The sun had set, leaving a sad green sky and desolate black and white earth. "Five acres of corn gone," he calculated.

"Thee said," Eliza reminded him, "that what thee wanted was a little variety in me. 'Steady as a pump bolt,' were thy words."

"I know I did," Jess admitted glumly. "I talk too much."

"Draw up thy chair," Eliza said placidly, not contradicting him; "here's Enoch and the boys."

Next morning after breakfast Jess and Enoch left the kitchen together. The sun was the warmest the year had yet produced and the farm roofs were steaming; south branch, swollen by melting snow, was running so full the soft lap of its eddies[6] could be heard in the barnyard; a rooster tossed his voice into the bright air, loud and clear as if aiming to be heard by every fowl in Jennings County.

"Enoch," said Jess to his hired man, "what's thy feeling about geese?"

Enoch was instantly equipped, for the most part, with feelings on every subject. Geese was a homelier topic than he'd choose himself to enlarge upon, not one that could be much embellished[7] nor one on which Mr. Emerson,[8] so far's he could recall, had ever expressed an opinion. "In the fall of the year," he said, "long about November or December, there's nothing tastier on the table than roast goose."

"Goose on the table's not what I mean," Jess said. "I was speaking of goose on the hoof. Goose nipping off a stand of corn, Enoch, goose roistering round, honking and hissing so's thee can't hear thyself think, goose eyeing thee like a snake on stilts."

Enoch gazed at his employer for a few seconds. "Mr. Birdwell," he said, "I think that if they's an ornery bird, it's a goose. Ornery and undependable."

"I'm glad we's so like minded about them," Jess said. "Otherwise, I'd not like to ask thee to do this little job." He pulled a long darning needle from beneath the lapel of his coat.

Enoch eyed it with some mistrust. "I can't say's I've ever been handy with a needle, Mr. Birdwell."

"Thee'll be handy enough for this," Jess said with hearty conviction. "To

6 **eddies:** currents of water.

7 **embellished:** made more interesting.
8 **Mr. Emerson:** Ralph Waldo Emerson, 19th-century American essayist and poet.

THE ART OF STORYTELLING

come to it, Enoch, Eliza's set eight goose eggs. Next year with any luck she'd have two dozen. And so on. More and more. Feeling the way thee does, Enoch, about geese it's no more'n fair to give thee a chance to put a stop to this before it goes too far. One little puncture in each egg with this and the goose project's nipped in the bud and Eliza none the wiser."

"I'm mighty awkward with my hands," said Enoch, "doing fine work. Ticklish job like this I might drop an egg and break it."

"Enoch," said Jess, "thee's not developing a weakness for geese, is thee?"

"It ain't the geese," said Enoch frankly, "it's your wife. She's been mighty clever[9] to me and if she's got her heart set on geese, it'd go against the grain to disappoint her. Whyn't you do it, Mr. Birdwell?"

"Same reason," said Jess, "only more of them—and if Eliza ever asks if I tampered with that setting of eggs I figure on being able to say No." Jess held the needle nearer Enoch, who looked at it but still made no motion to take it.

"Likely no need to do a thing," Enoch said. "Two to one those eggs'll never hatch anyways. Overbys' such a fox-eared tribe they more'n likely sold her bad eggs to begin with."

"Thee's knowed about this," Jess asked, "all along?"

"Yes," Enoch said.

"Here's the needle," Jess said.

"You look at this," Enoch inquired, "not so much as a favor asked as a part of the day's work with orders from you?"

"Yes," Jess said, "that's about the way I look at it."

Enoch took the needle, held it somewhat gingerly, and with the sun glinting across its length, walked slowly toward the chickenhouse.

It takes thirty days for a goose egg to hatch, and the time, with spring work to be done, went fast. The hen Eliza had picked was a good one and kept her mind strictly on her setting. Eliza kept her mind on the hen, and Jess and Enoch found their minds oftener than they liked on Eliza and her hoped-for geese.

At breakfast on the day the geese were due to break their shells Jess said, "If I's thee, Eliza, I wouldn't bank too much on them geese. I heard Enoch say a while back he wouldn't be surprised if not an egg hatched. Thought the eggs were likely no good."

Enoch was busy pouring coffee into a saucer, then busy cooling it, but Eliza waited until he was through. "Did thee say that, Enoch?"

Enoch looked at Jess. "Yes," he said, "I kind of recollect something of the sort."

"What made thee think so, Enoch?"

"Why," said Jess, for Enoch was busy with his coffee again, "it was the Overbys. Enoch's got a feeling they's kind of unreliable. Fox-eared, I think thee said, Enoch, didn't thee?"

Enoch's work took him outside al-

9 clever: good-natured.

most at once and Jess himself said, "If thee'll just give me a little packet of food, Eliza, I won't trouble thee for anything at noon. I'm going to be over'n the south forty and it'll save time coming and going."

Eliza was surprised for Jess'd usually come twice as far for a hot dinner at midday, but she made him fried ham sandwiches and put them and some cold apple-turnovers in a bag.

"It's a pity thee has to miss thy dinner," she told him, but Jess only said, "Press of work, press of work," and hurriedly departed.

Jess came home that evening through the spring twilight, somewhat late, and found a number of things to do at the barn before he went up to the house. When he entered the kitchen nothing seemed amiss—lamps ruddy, table set, stove humming, and beside the stove a small box over which Eliza was bending. Jess stopped to look—and listen; from inside the box was coming a kind of birdlike peeping, soft and not unpleasant. Reluctantly he walked to Eliza's side. There, eating minced boiled egg, and between bites lifting its beak to Eliza, it seemed, and making those chirping sounds he'd heard was a gray-gold gosling.

Eliza looked up pleasantly. "Enoch was right," she said. "The eggs were bad. Only one hatched. I plan to call it Samantha," she told Jess. "It's a name I've always been partial to."

"Samantha," said Jess without any enthusiasm whatever for either name or gosling. "How's thee know it's a she?"

"I don't," said Eliza, "but if it's a gander it's a name easily changed to Sam."

Enoch came in just then with a load of wood for the kitchen woodbox. "Enoch," asked Jess, "has thee seen Samantha—or Sam?"

Enoch mumbled but Jess understood him to say he had.

"It was my understanding, Enoch, that thy opinion was that all those eggs were bad."

"Well, Mr. Birdwell," said Enoch, "a man could make a mistake. He could count wrong."

"A man ought to be able to count to eight without going astray," Jess said.

Eliza was paying no attention to either of them; she was making little tweeting sounds herself, bending over the chirping gosling. "Does thee know," she asked Jess, "that this is the first pet I ever had in my life?"

"Thee's got Ebony," Jess said.

"I don't mean a caged pet," Eliza said, "but one to walk beside thee. I'm reconciled the others didn't hatch. With eight I'd've had to raise geese for the table. With one only I can make Samantha a pure pet."

A pure pet was what she made of her: Samantha ate what the family ate, with the exception of articles which Eliza thought might be indigestible and would risk on humans but not on her goose. Cake, pie, corn-on-the-cob, there was nothing too good for Samantha. From

THE ART OF STORYTELLING

a big-footed, gold-downed gosling she swelled, almost at once, like a slack sail which gets a sudden breeze, into a full-rounded convexity.[10]

"Emphasis on the vexity," Jess said when he thought of this. Samantha was everything he'd disliked in the general run of geese, with added traits peculiar to herself, which vexed[11] him. Because she was fed at the doorstep, she was always underfoot. No shout, however loud, would move her before she's ready to move. If she's talked to too strong she'd flail you with her wings and pinch the calf of your leg until for some days it would look to be mortifying.[12] She'd take food out of children's hands and the pansies Jess had planted in a circle at the base of the Juneberry tree she sheared so close that there was not a naked stem left to show for all his work. And when not being crossed in any way, Jess simply looking at her and meditating, trying to fathom[13] Samantha's fascination for Eliza, the goose would suddenly extend her snakelike neck, and almost touching Jess, hiss with such a hint of icy disapprobation[14] that Jess would involuntarily recoil.

But she was Eliza's pure pet, no two ways about that, and would lift her head for Eliza to scratch, and walk beside her with the lordly roll of the known elect.

"There was some goddess," Enoch remembered, "who always had a big

---

10 **convexity:** curve.
11 **vexed:** annoyed.
12 **mortifying:** affected with gangrene.

13 **fathom:** understand.
14 **disapprobation:** disapproval; dislike.

bird with her." Jess supposed Enoch was thinking of Juno and her peacock, but the reference didn't convince him that a goose was a suitable companion for any goddess—let alone Eliza, and he couldn't honestly feel much regret when one evening toward the end of November Eliza told him Samantha was missing. "She'll turn up," Jess said. "That bird's too ornery to die young."

Eliza said nothing, but next evening she proved Jess was right. "Samantha's over at Overbys'," she said.

"Well, did thee fetch her home?" Jess asked.

"No," said Eliza with righteous indignation, "they wouldn't let me. They said they had forty geese—and forty's what they got now, and they don't think Samantha's there. They provoked me so, Jess, I told them they'd sold me seven bad eggs and now they try to take the eighth away from me."

Jess felt a little abashed[15] at this, but he asked, "How can thee be so sure Samantha's there? She might've been carried off by a varmint."

Eliza was scornful. "Thee forgets I hand-raised Samantha from a gosling. I'd know her among four hundred—let alone forty."

"Whyn't thee buy her back then," Jess asked, "if that's the only way?"

"After what I said about their eggs," Eliza answered sadly, "the Overbys say they don't want any more dealings with me."

Eliza mourned so for the lost Samantha that first Enoch and then Jess went over to the Overbys' but no one there would admit the presence of a visiting goose—forty they had, and forty you could see by counting was what they had now. Short of force there didn't seem any way of getting Samantha home again.

When Eliza heard the Overbys were going to sell geese for Christmas eating she was frantic. "Jess," she said, "I just can't bear to think of Samantha, plucked naked and resting on a table waiting to be carved. She used to sing as sweet as any bird when she was little, and she'd walk by my side taking the air. She's the only goose I ever heard of," Eliza remembered mournfully, "who'd drink tea."

In Jess's opinion a goose'd eat anything at either end of the scale, but he didn't suppose this was a suitable time to mention it to Eliza. "Eliza," he said, "short of me and Enoch's going over there and using force on old man Overby—or sneaking over at night and breaking into their chicken pen, I don't know how in the world we're going to get Samantha back for thee."

"We could sue," said Eliza.

"Thee mean go to law?" Jess asked, astounded. Quakers stayed out of courts, believing in amicable[16] settlements without recourse to law.

"Yes," said Eliza. "I'd do it for Samantha. I'd think it my duty. Going to law'd be a misery for us . . . but not so lasting a misery as being roasted would be for Samantha."

Jess couldn't deny this, but he said, "I'd have to think it over. I've

---

15 abashed: embarrassed.

16 amicable (ăm′ə kə bəl): friendly; peaceable.

never been to law yet in my life and suing for a gone goose don't seem to me a very likely place to start."

Next morning Eliza served a good but silent breakfast, not sitting herself to eat with the rest of her family.

"Thee feeling dauncy,[17] Eliza?" Jess asked.

"I just can't eat," she said, "for thinking of Samantha."

Labe and Mattie had tears in their eyes. Little Jess was mournfully bellowing. Enoch looked mighty glum. Jess felt ashamed to be swallowing victuals in the midst of so much sorrow. Eliza stood at the end of the stove where the gosling's box had rested for the first few weeks of its life, looking down, as if remembering how it had sung and lifted its beak to her.

Jess couldn't stand it. "Eliza," he said, "if thee wants to go through with it I'll go to Vernon and fee a lawyer for thee. Thee'll have to go to court, be on the witness stand—and even then I misdoubt thee'll ever get thy goose back. Does thee still want me to do it?"

Eliza came to the table and stood with her hand on Jess' shoulder. "Yes, Jess," she said, "I want thee to do it."

Jess went to Vernon, fee'd a lawyer, had a restraining order put on the Overbys so they couldn't sell or kill the goose Eliza said was Samantha, and awaited with misgivings the day of the trial. It came in mid-December.

Eliza, Jess and Enoch rode to the trial through a fall of light, fresh snow. Brilliant sunlight, crisp air, glittering snow, and Rome's spirited stepping made the occasion, in spite of its purpose, seem festive. Eliza made it seem festive. Jess, who did not forget its purpose, regarded her with some wonder. He couldn't say what it was about her—dress and bonnet appeared to be simply her First Day[18] best—but she had a holiday air.

He considered it his duty to warn her. "Eliza," he said, "thee understands thee's not going to Meeting?[19] They're not going to sit silent while thee tells them how much thee loves Samantha and how she sang when young and drank tea. Old man Overby'll have his say and he's got a lawyer hired for no other purpose than to trip thee up."

Eliza was unimpressed. "What's our lawyer fee'd for, Jess?" she asked.

Jess took another tack. "Eliza," he told her, "I don't figger thee's got a chance in a thousand to get Samantha back."

"This is a court of justice, isn't it?" Eliza asked.

"Yes," Jess said.

"Then there's no need for thee to fash[20] thyself, Jess Birdwell. I'll get Samantha back."

Not getting Samantha back wasn't what fashed Jess—he reckoned he could bear up under that mighty well. What fashed him was the whole shooting match. . . . In some

17 dauncy: sickly.
18 First Day: Sunday.
19 Meeting: Quaker religious service.
20 fash: trouble.

few cases, matters of life and death, going to court might be necessary, and he could imagine such. But a suit over a goose named Samantha wasn't one of them. And poor Eliza. Law to her was all Greek and turkey tracks . . . and here she was bound for court as chipper as if she was Chief Justice Taney[21] himself. Jess sighed and shook his head. Getting shut of Samantha would be no hardship for him, but he was downcast for Eliza's sake and the way she'd have to turn homeward empty-handed.

In the courtroom hard, clear light reflected upward from the snow fell onto what Jess thought were hard faces: courthouse hangers on; farmers whose slackening work made the diversion[22] of a trial an inviting possibility; lovers of oddity who figured a tilt between a Quaker female, preacher, to boot, and an old sinner like Milt Overby over the ownership of a goose ought to produce some enlivening quirks. They stared at Eliza, exchanged salutes with Milt Overby and inspected Samantha who in her crate awaited the court's decision.

The two lawyers, Jess considered to be on a par. Nothing fancy, either one . . . old roadsters both, gone gray in service and with a knowledge of their business. The circuit judge was something else, unaccountably young, jug-eared and dressed more sprightly than a groom for his own wedding. A city whippersnapper, born and trained north of the Mississinewa, and now, in Jess's opinion, setting a squeamish foot in backwoods provinces, and irked to find himself trying so trifling a case. Didn't know a goose from a guinea hen, like as not, and would consider tossing a coin a more suitable manner of settling such a matter—just as near right in the end—and his valuable time saved.

Eliza, Jess saw, was of no such opinion. She, too, was scanning the young judge, and Jess, who knew her, saw from the look on her face that she was taken by him. A neat, thin, pious boy—far from home—he looked, no doubt to her; a young man who could do with better cooking and more regular eating.

The young man rapped the court to order. Spitting and shuffling slackened and in a high, precise voice he read, "Birdwell versus Overby. Charge, petty larceny. Appropriation and willful withholding of goose named Samantha." The name Samantha seemed to somewhat choke him, but he got it out.

"Ready for Birdwell," said Mr. Abel Samp, Eliza's lawyer.

"Ready for Overby," said the defendant's lawyer.

Eliza was the first witness on the stand. Jess sometimes forgot what a good-looking woman Eliza was, but the interest shown on lifted faces all about him refreshed his memory.

"Swear the plaintiff in," the judge said.

Eliza, in her sweet voice, spoke directly to the judge. "I don't swear," she said.

21 Chief Justice Taney: Chief Justice of U.S. Supreme Court (1836-1864).
22 diversion: pleasant change.

The judge explained that profanity was not asked for. "I understood," said Eliza, "that thee wasn't asking for profanity. No one would think that of thee. But we Quakers do not take oaths in court. We affirm."[23]

"Permit Mrs. Birdwell to affirm," said the judge. Eliza affirmed.

Mr. Samp then proceeded to question Eliza as to Samantha's birth and habits.

"Judge," Eliza began.

"Address the judge," Mr. Samp said, "as Your Honor."

"We Quakers," Eliza told the judge, gently, "do not make use of such titles. What is thy name? I think thee'll go far in our state and thy name's one I'd like to know."

The judge appeared somewhat distraught, undecided as to whether to make the tone of the court brisk and legal (if possible) or to follow Eliza's lead of urbane[24] sociability.

"Pomeroy," he said and made a slight bow in Eliza's direction.

Eliza returned the bow, deeper and with more grace. "Friend Pomeroy," she said, "it is indeed a pleasure to know thee."

Samantha's story as Eliza told it to Friend Pomeroy was surprisingly terse.[25] Affecting, and losing nothing by Eliza's telling, but to the point.

"Mrs. Birdwell," said Samp, "how long have you had an acquaintanceship with geese and their habits?"

"Since I was a child," Eliza said.

---

23 affirm: declare something to be true.

24 urbane: well-mannered; polished.
25 terse: brief; concise.

"My father was a great fancier of geese."

"And you think you could identify this goose Samantha, which you admit in looks was similar to the defendant's?"

"I could," Eliza said with much authority.

Mr. Samp, to Jess's surprise, left the matter there. "Take the witness," he said to Overby's lawyer— but the counsel for the defendant was in no hurry to cross-examine Eliza. Instead he put his client on the stand.

"Farewell, Samantha," Jess said to Enoch.

"You relieved?" Enoch asked.

"Putting Eliza first," Jess said, "as I do, no."

Milt Overby, whose natural truculence[26] was somewhat stimulated by a nip he'd had to offset snappy weather, bellowed his way through his testimony. At one juncture he set the judge aright when he asked some elementary questions concerning the habits and configurations of geese. "Where in tarnation you from?" he snorted. "What they mean sending us judges down here who don't know Toulouse from Wyandotte,[27] or goose from gander?"

The young judge used voice and gavel to quiet the guffawing which filled the courtroom and the trial proceeded. A number of witnesses for both sides were brought to the stand and while it was shown that Overbys had maybe eaten a goose or two and neglected out of pure fondness for the creatures to count them as among the departed, still nobody had been able to positively identify Samantha.

Mr. Overby's lawyer seemed somewhat loath to cross-examine Eliza, but he put her on the stand. She'd said she knew geese and her testimony had been direct and positive. "Mrs. Birdwell," he said, "how can you be so sure your goose was with my client's geese?"

Eliza's black eyes rested confidingly upon the judge. "Friend Pomeroy," she said, "I raised Samantha from a gosling."

Jess sighed. "Here it comes," he said, "how that goose could sing and drink tea."

Eliza continued, "And there's one thing about her that always set her apart from every other goose."

"Yes, Mrs. Birdwell," said Judge Pomeroy, who was inclined to forget, with Eliza on the stand, that he was in a courtroom.

"Samantha," said Eliza, with much earnestness, "from the day she was born had a gait unlike any other goose I ever saw and one that set her apart from all her Overby connections. I picked her out at once when I went over there, because of it. Thee couldn't've missed it, Friend Pomeroy."

"Yes, Mrs. Birdwell," said the judge with interest in his voice.

"Samantha," said Eliza, "was a born pacer.[28] Thee knows what a pacer is?"

---

26 **truculence:** fierceness.
27 **Toulouse . . . Wyandotte:** Toulouse is a French breed of fowl; Wyandotte, American.

28 **pacer:** that is, she moved with slow, regular steps.

THE ART OF STORYTELLING

"Certainly," said Judge Pomeroy. "A pacer," he repeated with no surprise—and with obvious pleasure that Eliza'd hit upon so clear and differentiating an aspect of her goose and one that made identification possible.

A titter was mounting through the courtroom—Judge Pomeroy lifted his head. He had no desire to be further instructed as to the history, habits and breeds of geese, and he liked to see a trial settled by some such little and too often overlooked subtlety.[29] Judge Pomeroy brought down his gavel. "The court awards decision in favor of the plaintiff.[30] Case dismissed." While the silence that followed on his words still prevailed Judge Pomeroy stepped briskly and with obvious pleasure out through the rear door.

Jess was also brisk about departure. No use lingering until friend Pomeroy had been more thoroughly informed as to gaits in general and geese in particular. Mid-afternoon's a quiet time in any season. In winter with snow on the ground, no leaves to rustle and bare limbs rigid as rock against a cloudless sky, the hush is deepest of all. Nothing broke that hush in the surrey, except the squeak of leather and snow, the muffled footfalls of Rome Beauty. Jess and Eliza, on the front seat, rode without speaking. Enoch, in the back, seemed to meditate. Even Samantha in her crate at Enoch's feet was silent.

29 **subtlety:** delicate distinction.
30 **plaintiff:** one who made the complaint in the lawsuit.

Maple Grove Nursery was in sight before Jess spoke. "Eliza," he said, "would thee mind telling me—did thee ever see a trotting goose?"

Enoch ceased to meditate and listened. He had been wondering about this himself.

"Certainly not," said Eliza. "Thee knows as well as I, Jess Birdwell, an animal can't trot without hind feet and forefeet."

"So far, Eliza," Jess said, "we see eye to eye. Now maybe thee'd tell me—did thee ever see a goose that didn't pace?"

Eliza was truly amazed, it seemed. "Why, Jess," she said, "an ordinary goose just walks—but Samantha paces."

Jess was silent for a spell. "What'd thee say the difference is?"

"It's the swing, Jess Birdwell," said Eliza, "same as in a horse that nature's formed for a pacer . . . it's the natural bent, the way the spirit leads the beast to set his feet down. Samantha's a natural pacer."

That seemed as far as they'd likely get on the subject and Jess joined Enoch in meditation. In the barnyard, before she went up to the house, Eliza said, like an old hand at the business, "Attending court whettens the appetite. It's a little early but I thought if thee'd relish it"—and she looked at Jess and Enoch, never sparing a glance for Samantha, as if her menfolk's welfare was her sole concern—"I'd stir us up a bite to eat. Hot tea and fresh sweetcakes, say. Might fry a little sausage and open some cherry preserves. If thee'd relish it," she repeated.

Jess wasn't taken in, but he'd relish it, and so would Enoch, and they both said so. They hustled with the unhitching so they could uncrate Samantha and note her progress with eyes newly instructed as to what made a pacer. Jess dumped her in the snow, and Enoch tapped her with his hat: Samantha made for the back door.

"By sugar," said Jess, "Eliza's right. She paces." Samantha had the smooth roll of a racker[31]—there were no two ways about it. At heart she was a pacer, and what two legs could do in that line, Samantha accomplished.

"With four legs," Enoch said, "you could enter her in any county fair—

rack[32] on," he cried with enthusiasm. As they followed Samantha to the house, Enoch, for whom any event existed chiefly in its after aspects as a cud for rumination, asked, "How you feel in respect of court trials, now, Mr. Birdwell?"

"I'm still against them," Jess said, "though they's three things this trial's taught me I might never otherwise have learned. Two's about women."

Enoch revered[33] all knowledge and he had a notion that information on this subject might have a more than transcendental[34] value. "What's the two things you learned about women, Mr. Birdwell?"

"Well, Enoch, I learned first, dependability's woman's greatest vir-

---

32 rack: a framework to which animals are fastened for feeding.
33 revered: respected.
34 transcendental: abstract; remote; isolated.

31 racker: that is, she moved with the regular gait of a horse.

THE ART OF STORYTELLING

tue. Steady as a pump bolt, day in, day out. When thee finds a woman like that, Enoch, don't try to change her. Not even in spring."

"No, sir," said Enoch, "I won't."

"Second, when it's a case of woman and the law—thee don't need to waste any worry on the woman."

"No, sir," said Enoch again.

When they reached the back steps, Enoch asked, "I understood you to say you'd learned three things, Mr. Birdwell. What's the third about?"

"Hired men," said Jess.

Enoch was taken aback, but he'd asked for it. "Yes, Mr. Birdwell," he said.

"Never hire one," Jess told him, "till thee finds out first if he can count to eight. Save thyself a lot of trouble that way, Enoch."

"How's I to know the eighth'd turn out to be Samantha?" Enoch asked.

Samantha herself, who was waiting at the doorstep for an expected tidbit, reached out and unhampered by either boots or work pants nipped Enoch firmly through his thin Sunday best.

"Thee say something, Enoch?" Jess asked.

Enoch had but he didn't repeat it. Instead he said, "Pacer or no pacer, that's Samantha," and the two of them stepped out of the snow into the warm kitchen, scented with baking sweetcakes and frying sausage.

Understanding Literature

1. Why does spring make Jess "discontented with the human race," and with women in particular? What change takes place in his life? Who is for that change? Who is against it?

2. Where and why does Jess introduce geese into the conversation? What is Jess's attitude toward geese? What does Eliza mean by "I got a setting under a hen now"?

3. The second scene is between Jess and Enoch. Jess asks, "Enoch, what's thy feeling toward geese?" What is the purpose of the question? What is Enoch's real feeling as it is developed in this scene?

4. Why does the author skip thirty days before the beginning of the third scene? Why does the author have Jess go off for the day?

5. When Jess comes home that evening (fourth scene), what does he find? Why does he say, "A man ought to be able to count to eight without going astray"?

6. The fifth scene ends with Jess's agreeing to hire a lawyer to get Samantha back. How has the author made this act believable? In other words, how has she motivated it?

JESSAMYN WEST

7. In the trial scene how is the judge described? How does Jess describe him? How does Eliza describe him?
8. How does Eliza treat the judge? How does Overby treat him? What is the judge's attitude toward Eliza? Point out in the text lines which prove your answers to these questions.
9. Why does the judge award the goose to Eliza?
10. What are the three things which Jess learns from the trial? What is the purpose of his comment to Enoch, "Never hire one [a man] till thee finds out first if he can count to eight"? What is the meaning of Enoch's response to this comment?
11. Do the characters in the story seem well motivated; that is, does the author make it clear why the characters act as they do? Explain.
12. One phrase which is repeated in the story is "steady as a pump bolt." What does Jess mean by the phrase when he uses it in the first scene? What does he mean when he uses it in the last scene?

Further Activity

Choose *one* of the following topic sentences for a paragraph. Copy it onto your paper; then develop this topic sentence into a paragraph by citing evidence in the story to prove the truth of the statement.
1. Jess does not understand Eliza.
2. Eliza understands how to deal with the judge.

Even if you have never studied a musical instrument, you will understand the humor—and suffering—involved when Clarence Day's father attempted to make his son a violinist. This selection is from *Life with Father and Mother*, a well-known American story which describes family life in New York City in the late 19th century.

The Noblest Instrument

Clarence Day

IMPROVING YOUR READING: In this selection the author describes a particular group of events that played an important part in his childhood. Much of what probably happened would not interest the reader. One of the main problems for Clarence Day, therefore, as it is for any author, was *selection of detail*, for it is as important to leave things out, in this or any type of writing, as it is to put things in. Note that the author here does not give a detailed description of each day's practice, but describes only those aspects of his bout with the violin which contribute to the final impression he wants to create.

FATHER HAD BEEN away, reorganizing some old upstate railroad. He returned in an executive mood and proceeded to shake up our home. In spite of my failure as a singer, he was still bound to have us taught music. We boys were summoned before him and informed that we must at once learn to play on something. We might not appreciate it now, he said, but we should later on. "You, Clarence, will learn the violin. George, you the piano. Julian—well, Julian is too young yet. But you older boys must have lessons."

I was appalled[1] at this order. At the age of ten it seemed a disaster to lose any more of my freedom. The days were already too short for our games after school; and now here was a chunk to come out of playtime three days every week. A chunk every day, we found afterward, because we had to practice.

George sat at the piano in the parlor, and faithfully learned to pound out his exercises. He had all the luck. He was not an inspired player, but at least he had some ear for music. He also had the advantage of playing on a good robust[2] instrument, which he didn't have to be careful not to drop, and was in no danger of breaking. Furthermore, he did not have to tune it. A piano had some good points.

But I had to go through a blacker and more gruesome experience. It was bad enough to have to come in from the street and the sunlight and

1 **appalled:** shocked.　　　　2 **robust:** strong.

go down into our dark little basement where I took my lessons. But that was only the opening chill of the struggle that followed.

The whole thing was uncanny. The violin itself was a queer, fragile, cigar-boxy thing, that had to be handled most gingerly. Nothing sturdy about it. Why, a fellow was liable to crack it putting it into its case. And then my teacher, he was queer too. He had a queer pickled smell.

I dare say he wasn't queer at all really, but he seemed so to me, because he was different from the people I generally met. He was probably worth a dozen of some of them, but I didn't know it. He was one of the violins in the Philharmonic, and an excellent player; a grave, middle-aged little man—who was obliged to give lessons.

He wore a black, wrinkled frock coat, and a discolored gold watch chain. He had small, black-rimmed glasses; not tortoise shell, but thin rims of metal. His violin was dark, rich, and polished, and would do anything for him.

Mine was balky and awkward, brand-new, and of a light, common color.

The violin is intended for persons with a passion for music. I wasn't that kind of person. I liked to hear a band play a tune that we could march up and down to, but try as I would, I could seldom whistle such a tune afterward. My teacher didn't know this. He greeted me as a possible genius.

He taught me how to hold the contraption, tucked under my chin.

I learned how to move my fingers here and there on its handle or stem. I learned how to draw the bow across the strings, and thus produce sounds. . . .

Does a mother recall the first cry of her baby, I wonder? I still remember the strange cry at birth of that new violin.

My teacher, Herr M., looked as though he had suddenly taken a large glass of vinegar. He sucked in his breath. His lips were drawn back from his teeth, and his eyes tightly shut. Of course, he hadn't expected my notes to be sweet at the start; but still, there was something unearthly about that first cry. He snatched the violin from me, examined it, readjusted its pegs, and comforted it gently, by drawing his own bow across it. It was only a new and not especially fine violin, but the sounds it made for him were more natural— they were classifiable sounds. They were not richly musical, but at least they had been heard before on this earth.

He handed the instrument back to me with careful directions. I tucked it up under my chin again and grasped the end tight. I held my bow exactly as ordered. I looked up at him, waiting.

"Now," he said, nervously.

I slowly raised the bow, drew it downward. . . .

This time there were *two* dreadful cries in our little front basement. One came from my new violin and one from the heart of Herr M.

Herr M. presently came to, and smiled bravely at me, and said if I

wanted to rest a moment he would permit it. He seemed to think I might wish to lie down awhile and recover. I didn't feel any need of lying down. All I wanted was to get through the lesson. But Herr M. was shaken. He was by no means ready to let me proceed. He looked around desperately, saw the music book, and said he would now show me that. We sat down side by side on the window seat, with the book in his lap, while he pointed out the notes to me with his finger, and told me their names.

After a bit, when he felt better, he took up his own violin, and instructed me to watch him and note how he handled the strings. And then at last, he nerved himself to let me take my violin up again. "Softly, my child, softly," he begged me, and stood facing the wall. . . .

We got through the afternoon somehow, but it was a ghastly experience. Part of the time he was maddened by the mistakes I kept making, and part of the time he was plain wretched. He covered his eyes. He seemed ill. He looked often at his watch, even shook it as though it had stopped; but he stayed the full hour.

That was Wednesday. What struggles he had with himself before Friday, when my second lesson was due, I can only dimly imagine, and of course I never even gave them a thought at the time. He came back to recommence teaching me, but he had changed—he had hardened. Instead of being cross, he was stern; and instead of sad, bitter. He wasn't unkind to me, but we were no longer companions. He talked to himself, under his breath; and sometimes he took bits of paper, and did little sums on them, gloomily, and then tore them up.

During my third lesson I saw the tears come to his eyes. He went up to Father and said he was sorry but he honestly felt sure I'd never be able to play.

Father didn't like this at all. He said he felt sure I would. He dismissed Herr M. briefly—the poor man came stumbling back down in two minutes. In that short space of time he had gallantly gone upstairs in a glow, resolved upon sacrificing his earnings for the sake of telling the truth. He returned with his earnings still running, but with the look of a lost soul about him, as though he felt that his nerves and his sanity were doomed to destruction. He was low in his mind, and he talked to himself more than ever. Sometimes he spoke harshly of America, sometimes of fate.

But he no longer struggled. He accepted this thing as his destiny. He regarded me as an unfortunate something, outside the human species, whom he must simply try to labor with as well as he could. It was a grotesque experience, but he felt he must bear it.

He wasn't the only one—he was at least not alone in his sufferings. Mother, though expecting the worst, had tried to be hopeful about it, but at the end of a week or two I heard her and Margaret talking it over. I was slaughtering a scale in the front basement, when Mother came down and stood outside the door in the kitchen hall

and whispered, "Oh, Margaret!"

I watched them. Margaret was baking a cake. She screwed up her face, raised her arms, and brought them down with hands clenched.

"I don't know what we shall do, Margaret."

"The poor little feller," Margaret whispered. "He can't make the thing go."

This made me indignant. They were making me look like a lubber.[3] I wished to feel always that I could make anything go. . . .

I now began to feel a determination to master this thing. History shows us many examples of the misplaced determinations of men—they are one of the darkest aspects of human life, they spread so much needless pain: but I knew little history. And I viewed what little I did know romantically—I should have seen in such episodes their heroism, not their futility.[4] Any role that seemed heroic attracted me, no matter how senseless.

Not that I saw any chance for heroism in our front basement, of course. You had to have a battlefield or something. I saw only that I was appearing ridiculous. But that stung my pride. I hadn't wanted to learn anything whatever about fiddles or music, but since I was in for it, I'd do it, and show them I could. A boy will often put in enormous amounts of his time trying to prove he isn't as ridiculous as he thinks people think him.

Meanwhile Herr M. and I had dis-

3 **lubber:** big, clumsy person; fool.
4 **futility:** uselessness.

THE ART OF STORYTELLING

covered that I was nearsighted. On account of the violin's being an instrument that sticks out in front of one, I couldn't stand close enough to the music book to see the notes clearly. He didn't at first realize that I often made mistakes from that cause. When he and I finally comprehended that I had this defect, he had a sudden new hope that this might have been the whole trouble, and that when it was corrected I might play like a human being at last.

Neither of us ventured to take up this matter with Father. We knew that it would have been hard to convince him that my eyes were not perfect, I being a son of his and presumably made in his image; and we knew that he immediately would have felt we were trying to make

trouble for him, and would have shown an amount of resentment which it was best to avoid. So Herr M. instead lent me his glasses. These did fairly well. They turned the dim grayness of the notes into a queer bright distortion, but the main thing was they did make them brighter, so that I now saw more of them. How well I remember those little glasses. Poor, dingy old things. Herr M. was nervous about lending them to me; he feared that I'd drop them. It would have been safer if they had been spectacles: but no, they were pince-nez;[5] and I had to learn to balance them across my nose as well as I could. I couldn't wear them up near my eyes because my nose was

5 **pince-nez** (păns′nā′): eyeglasses which are clipped onto the nose.

too thin there; I had to put them about half-way down where there was enough flesh to hold them. I also had to tilt my head back, for the music stand was a little too tall for me. Herr M. sometimes mounted me on a stool, warning me not to step off. Then when I was all set, and when he without his glasses was blind, I would smash my way into the scales again.

All during the long winter months I worked away at this job. I gave no thought, of course, to the family. But they did to me. Our house was heated by a furnace, which had big warm air pipes; these ran up through the walls with wide outlets into each room, and sound traveled easily and ringingly through their roomy, tin passages. My violin could be heard in every part of the house. No one could settle down to anything while I was practicing. If visitors came they soon left. Mother couldn't even sing to the baby. She would wait, watching the clock, until my long hour of scalework was over, and then come downstairs and shriek at me that my time was up. She would find me sawing away with my forehead wet, and my hair wet and stringy, and even my clothes slowly getting damp from my exertions. She would feel my collar, which was done for, and say I must change it. "Oh, Mother! Please!"—for I was in a hurry now to run out and play. But she wasn't being fussy about my collar, I can see, looking back; she was using it merely as a barometer or gauge of my pores. She thought I had better dry my-

self before going out in the snow.

It was a hard winter for Mother. I believe she also had fears for the baby. She sometimes pleaded with Father; but no one could ever tell Father anything. He continued to stand like a rock against stopping my lessons.

Schopenhauer,[6] in his rules for debating, shows how to win a weak case by insidiously[7] transferring an argument from its right field, and discussing it instead from some irrelevant but impregnable[8] angle. Father knew nothing of Schopenhauer, and was never insidious, but, nevertheless, he had certain natural gifts for debate. In the first place his voice was powerful and stormy, and he let it out at full strength, and kept on letting it out with a vigor that stunned his opponents. As a second gift, he was convinced at all times that his opponents were wrong. Hence, even if they did win a point or two, it did them no good, for he dragged the issue to some other ground then, where he and Truth could prevail. When Mother said it surely was plain enough that I had no ear, what was his reply? Why, he said that the violin was the noblest instrument invented by man. Having silenced her with this solid premise he declared that it followed that any boy was lucky to be given the privilege of learning to play it. No boy should expect to learn it immediately. It

6 **Schopenhauer:** a 19th-century German philosopher.
7 **insidiously:** slyly; shrewdly.
8 **irrelevant but impregnable:** remote but able to resist attack.

THE ART OF STORYTELLING

required persistence. Everything, he had found, required persistence. The motto was, Never give up.

All his life, he declared, he had persevered[9] in spite of discouragement, and he meant to keep on persevering, and he meant me to, too. He said that none of us realized what he had had to go through. If he had been the kind that gave up at the very first obstacle, where would he have been now—where would any of the family have been? The answer was, apparently, that we'd either have been in a very bad way, poking round for crusts in the gutter, or else nonexistent. We might have never even been born if Father had not persevered.

Placed beside this record of Father's vast trials overcome, the little difficulty of my learning to play the violin seemed a trifle. I faithfully spurred myself on again, to work at the puzzle. Even my teacher seemed impressed with these views on persistence. Though older than Father, he had certainly not made as much money, and he bowed to the experience of a practical man who was a success. If he, Herr M., had been a success he would not have had to teach boys; and sitting in this black pit in which his need of money had placed him, he saw more than ever that he must learn the ways of this world. He listened with all his heart, as to a god, when Father shook his forefinger, and told him how to climb to the heights where financial rewards were achieved. The idea he got was

that perseverance was sure to lead to great wealth.

Consequently our front basement continued to be the home of lost causes.

Of course, I kept begging Herr M. to let me learn just one tune. Even though I seldom could whistle them, still I liked tunes; and I knew that, in my hours of practicing, a tune would be a comfort. That is, for myself. Here again I never gave a thought to the effect upon others.

Herr M., after many misgivings, to which I respectfully listened—though they were not spoken to me, they were muttered to himself, pessimistically[10]—hunted through a worn old book of selections, and after much doubtful fumbling chose as simple a thing as he could find for me—for me and the neighbors.

It was spring now, and windows were open. That tune became famous.

What would the musician who had tenderly composed this air, years before, have felt if he had foreseen what an end it would have, on Madison Avenue; and how, before death, it would be execrated[11] by that once peaceful neighborhood. I engraved it on their hearts; not in its true form but in my own eerie versions. It was the only tune I knew. Consequently I played and replayed it.

Even horrors when repeated grow old and lose part of their sting. But those I produced were, unluckily, never the same. To be sure, this tune kept its general structure the

9 **persevered:** persisted; carried on.

10 **pessimistically:** hopelessly.
11 **execrated:** detested; cursed.

same, even in my sweating hands. There was always the place where I climbed unsteadily up to its peak, and that difficult spot where it wavered, or staggered, and stuck; and then a sudden jerk of resumption[12]— I came out strong on that. Every afternoon when I got to that difficult spot, the neighbors dropped whatever they were doing to wait for that jerk, shrinking from the moment, and yet feverishly impatient for it to come.

But what made the tune and their anguish so different each day? I'll explain. The strings of a violin are wound at the end around pegs, and each peg must be screwed in and tightened till the string sounds just right. Herr M. left my violin properly tuned when he went. But suppose a string broke, or that somehow I jarred a peg loose. Its string then became slack and soundless. I had to retighten it. Not having an ear, I was highly uncertain about this.

Our neighbors never knew at what degree of tautness[13] I'd put such a string. I didn't myself. I just screwed her up tight enough to make a strong reliable sound. Neither they nor I could tell which string would thus appear in a new role each day, nor foresee the profound transformations this would produce in that tune.

All that spring this unhappy and ill-destined melody floated out through my window, and writhed in the air for one hour daily, in sunshine or storm. All that spring our neighbors and I daily toiled to its peak, and staggered over its hump, so to speak, and fell wailing through space.

12 resumption: beginning again.
13 tautness: tightness.

Things now began to be said to Mother which drove her to act. She explained to Father that the end had come at last. Absolutely. "This awful nightmare cannot go on," she said.

Father pooh-poohed her.

She cried. She told him what it was doing to her. He said that she was excited, and that her descriptions of the sounds I made were exaggerated and hysterical—must be. She was always too vehement, he shouted. She must learn to be calm. "But you're downtown, *you* don't have to hear it!"

Father remained wholly skeptical.

She endeavored to shame him. She told him what awful things the neighbors were saying about him, because of the noise I was making, for which he was responsible.

He couldn't be made to look at it that way. If there really were any unpleasantness then I was responsible. He had provided me with a good teacher and a good violin—so he reasoned. In short, he had done his best, and no father could have done more. If I made hideous sounds after all that, the fault must be mine. He said that Mother should be stricter with me, if necessary, and make me try harder.

This was the last straw. I couldn't try harder. When Mother told me his verdict I said nothing, but my body rebelled. Self-discipline had its limits—and I wanted to be out: it was spring. I skimped my hours of practice when I heard the fellows playing outside. I came home late for lessons—even forgot them. Little by little they stopped.

Father was outraged. His final argument, I remember, was that my violin had cost twenty-five dollars; if I didn't learn it the money would be wasted, and he couldn't afford it. But it was put to him that my younger brother, Julian, could learn it instead, later on. Then summer came, anyhow, and we went for three months to the seashore; and in the confusion of this Father was defeated and I was set free.

In the autumn little Julian was led away one afternoon, and imprisoned in the front basement in my place. I don't remember how long they kept him down there, but it was several years. He had an ear, however, and I believe he learned to play fairly well. This would have made a happy ending for Herr M. after all; but it was some other teacher, a younger man, who was engaged to teach Julian. Father said Herr M. was a failure.

Understanding Literature

1. In this selection Clarence Day's father is characterized in particular detail. What were some of his father's characteristics? In what way was the author similar to his father?
2. In what respects was the violin teacher, Herr M., very different from the author's father?
3. Why did the author feel, at one point, that he had to master the violin? What finally made him give up?
4. Although the violin lessons lasted for several months, Day includes only a few main incidents during this time. Why does he include these particular events?

Further Activity

Write a short essay in which you describe an incident that you think will interest a reader. You might choose your early experiences with an instrument, as Clarence Day did, a trip which you took with an older person, or an event which to you seems typical of your family. After you plan your essay, look back at the way Day wrote about his experience. He did not describe everything that happened; he chose only those details that he thought would be most interesting. Try to achieve the same goal in your essay.

Have you ever found yourself wondering about where your ancestors came from, what they were like, and why they left their native land? A family story, its most "prideful treasure," started Alex Haley wondering and traveling, traveling right into the biggest story of his life.

My Furthest-Back Person — "The African"

Alex Haley

IMPROVING YOUR READING: In "The Noblest Instrument," you noted how important it is for an author to select details carefully. Alex Haley selects key details about his "furthest-back person," repeating them as his story grows. As you read Haley's story, how does this *repetition of detail* affect you? Why are the repeated details so important?

MY GRANDMA Cynthia Murray Palmer lived in Henning, Tennessee (pop. 500), about 50 miles north of Memphis. Each summer as I grew up there, we would be visited by several women relatives who were mostly around Grandma's age, such as my Great Aunt Liz Murray who taught in Oklahoma, and Great Aunt Till Merriweather from Jackson, Tennessee, or their considerably younger niece, Cousin Georgia Anderson from Kansas City, Kansas, and some others. Always after the supper dishes had been washed, they would go out to take seats and talk in the rocking chairs on the front porch, and I would scrunch down, listening, behind Grandma's squeaky chair, with the dusk deepening into night and the lightning bugs flicking on and off above the now shadowy honeysuckles. Most often they talked about our family

—the story had been passed down for generations—until the whistling blur of lights of the southbound Panama Limited train *whooshing* through Henning at 9:05 P.M. signaled our bedtime.

So much of their talking of people, places and events I didn't understand: For instance, what was an "Ol' Massa," an "Ol' Missus" or a "plantation"? But early I gathered that white folks had done lots of bad things to our folks, though I couldn't figure out why. I guessed that all that they talked about had happened a long time ago, as now or then Grandma or another, speaking of someone in the past, would excitedly thrust a finger toward me, exclaiming, "Wasn't big as *this* 'un!" And it would astound me that anyone as old and grey-haired as they could relate to my age. But in time my head began both a recording and picturing of the more graphic scenes they would describe, just as I also visualized David killing Goliath with his slingshot, Old Pharaoh's army drowning, Noah and his ark, Jesus feeding that big multitude with nothing but five loaves and two fishes, and other wonders that I heard in my Sunday school lessons at our New Hope Methodist Church.

The furthest-back person Grandma and the others talked of—always in tones of awe, I noticed—they would call "The African." They said that some ship brought him to a place that they pronounced " 'Naplis." They said that then some "Mas' John Waller" bought him for his plantation in "Spotsylvania County, Virginia." This African kept on escaping, the fourth time trying to kill the "hateful po' cracker" slave-catcher, who gave him a choice of punishment. This African took a foot being chopped off with an ax against a tree stump, they said, and he was about to die. But his life was saved by "Mas' John's" brother —"Mas' William Waller," a doctor who was so furious about what had happened that he bought the African for himself and gave him the name "Toby."

Crippling about, working in "Mas' William's" house and yard, the African in time met "the big house cook named Bell," and there was born a girl named Kizzy. As she grew up her African daddy often showed her different kinds of things, telling her what they were in his native tongue. Pointing at a banjo, for example, the African uttered, "ko"; or pointing at

a river near the plantation, he would say "Kamby Bolong." Many of his strange words started with a "k" sound, and the little, growing Kizzy learned gradually that they identified different things.

When addressed by other slaves as "Toby," the master's name for him, the African said angrily that his name was "Kin-tay." And as he gradually learned English, he told young Kizzy some things about himself— for instance, that he was not far from his village, chopping wood to make himself a drum, when four men had surprised, overwhelmed, and kidnapped him.

So Kizzy's head held much about her African daddy when at age 16 she was sold away onto a much smaller plantation in North Carolina. Her first child, a boy, she named George. And Kizzy told her boy all about his African grandfather. George grew up to be such a game-cock fighter that he was called "Chicken George," and people would come from all over and "bet big money" on his cockfights. He and Matilda, another of Lea's slaves, had seven children, and he told them the stories and strange sounds of their African great-grandfather. And one of those children, Tom, became a blacksmith who was bought away by a "Mas' Murray" for his tobacco plantation in Alamance County, North Carolina.

There Tom met Irene, a weaver on the plantation. She also bore seven children, and Tom now told them all about their African great-great-grandfather, the faithfully passed-down knowledge of his sounds and stories having become by now the family's prideful treasure.

The youngest of that second set of seven children was a girl, Cynthia, who became my maternal Grandma (which today I can only see as fated). Anyway, all of this is how I was growing up in Henning at Grandma's, listening from behind her rocking chair as she and the other visiting old women talked of that African (never then comprehended as *my* great-great-great-great-grandfather) who said his name was *"Kin-tay,"* and said *"ko"* for banjo, *"Kamby Bolong"* for river, and a jumble of other *"k"*-beginning sounds that Grandma privately muttered, most often while making beds or cooking, and who also said that near his village he was kidnapped while chopping wood to make himself a drum.

The story had become nearly as fixed in my head as in Grandma's by the time Dad and Mama moved me and my two younger brothers, George and Julius, away from Henning to be with them at the small black agricultural and mechanical college in Normal, Alabama, where Dad taught.

To compress my next 25 years: When I was 17 Dad let me enlist as a mess boy in the U.S. Coast Guard. I became a ship's cook out in the South Pacific during World War II, and at night down by my bunk I began trying to write sea adventure stories, mailing them off to magazines and collecting rejection slips for eight years before some editors began purchasing and publishing oc-

casional stories. By 1949 the Coast Guard had made me its first "journalist"; finally with 20 years' service, I retired at the age of 37, determined to make a full time career of writing. . . .

Then one Saturday in 1965 I happened to be walking past the National Archives building in Washington. Across the interim years I had thought of Grandma's old stories —otherwise I can't think what diverted me up the Archives' steps. And when a main reading room desk attendant asked if he could help me, I wouldn't have dreamed of admitting to him some curiosity hanging on from boyhood about my slave forbears. I kind of bumbled that I was interested in census records of Alamance County, North Carolina, just after the Civil War.

The microfilm rolls were delivered, and I turned them through the machine with a building sense of intrigue, viewing in different census takers' penmanship an endless parade of names. After about a dozen microfilmed rolls, I was beginning to tire, when in utter astonishment I looked upon the names of Grandma's parents: Tom Murray, Irene Murray . . . older sisters of Grandma's as well—every one of them a name that I'd heard countless times on her front porch.

It wasn't that I hadn't believed Grandma. You just *didn't* not believe my Grandma. It was simply so uncanny actually seeing those names in print and in official U.S. Government records.

During the next several months I

THE ART OF STORYTELLING

was back in Washington whenever possible, in the Archives, the Library of Congress, the Daughters of the American Revolution Library. (Whenever black attendants understood the idea of my search, documents I requested reached me with miraculous speed.) In one source or another during 1966 I was able to document at least the highlights of the cherished family story. I would have given anything to have told Grandma, but, sadly, in 1949 she had gone. So I went and told the only survivor of those Henning front-porch storytellers: Cousin Georgia Anderson, now in her 80's in Kansas City, Kansas. Wrinkled, bent, not well herself, she was so overjoyed, repeating to me the old stories and sounds; they were like Henning echoes: "Yeah, boy, that African say his name was 'Kin-tay'; he say the banjo was 'ko,' an' the river 'Kamby-Bolong,' an he was off choppin' some wood to make his drum when they grabbed 'im!" Cousin Georgia grew so excited we had to stop her, calm her down, "You go 'head, boy! Your grandma an' all of 'em—they up there watching what you do!"

That week I flew to London on a magazine assignment. Since by now I was steeped in the old, in the past, scarcely a tour guide missed me—I was awed at so many historical places and treasures I'd heard of and read of. I came upon the Rosetta stone in the British Museum, marveling anew at how Jean Champollion, the French archaeologist, had miraculously deciphered its ancient demotic and hieroglyphic texts. . . .

The thrill of that just kept hanging around in my head. I was on a jet returning to New York when a thought hit me. Those strange, unknown-tongue sounds, always part of our family's old story . . . they were obviously bits of our original African "Kin-tay's" native tongue. What specific tongue? Could I somehow find out?

Back in New York, I began making visits to the United Nations Headquarters lobby; it wasn't hard to spot Africans. I'd stop any I could, asking if my bits of phonetic sounds held any meaning for them. A couple of dozen Africans quickly looked at me, listened, and took off—understandably dubious about some Tennesseean's accent alleging "African" sounds.

My research assistant, George Sims (we grew up together in Henning), brought me some names of ranking scholars of African linguistics. One was particularly intriguing: a Belgian- and English-educated Dr. Jan Vansina; he had spent his early career living in West African villages, studying and tape-recording countless oral histories that were narrated by certain very old African men; he had written a standard textbook, *The Oral Tradition.*

So I flew to the University of Wisconsin to see Dr. Vansina. In his living room I told him every bit of the family story in the fullest detail that I could remember it. Then, intensely, he queried me about the story's relay across the generations, about the gibberish of "*k*" sounds Grandma had fiercely muttered to herself while doing her housework, with my brothers and me giggling beyond her hearing at what we had dubbed "Grandma's noises."

Dr. Vansina, his manner very serious, finally said, "These sounds your family has kept sound very probably of the tongue called 'Mandinka.' "

I'd never head of any "Mandinka." Grandma just told of the African saying "ko" for banjo, or "Kamby Bolong" for a Virginia river.

Among Mandinka stringed instruments, Dr. Vansina said, one of the oldest was the "kora."

"Bolong," he said, was clearly Mandinka for "river." Preceded by "Kamby," it very likely meant "Gambia River."

Dr. Vansina telephoned an eminent Africanist colleague, Dr. Philip Curtin. He said that the phonetic "Kin-tay" was correctly spelled "Kinte," a very old clan that had originated in Old Mali. The Kinte men traditionally were blacksmiths, and the women were potters and weavers.

I knew I must get to the Gambia River.

The first native Gambian I could locate in the U.S. was named Ebou Manga, then a junior attending Hamilton College in upstate Clinton, New York. He and I flew to Dakar, Senegal, then took a smaller plane to Yundum Airport, and rode in a van to Gambia's capital, Bathurst. Ebou and his father assembled eight Gambia government officials. I told them Grandma's stories, every detail I could remember, as they listened intently, then reacted. "Kamby Bo-

long' of course is Gambia River!" I heard. "But more clue is your forefather's saying his name was 'Kinte.' " Then they told me something I would never even have fantasized— that in places in the back country lived very old men, commonly called griots, who could tell centuries of the histories of certain very old family clans. As for Kintes, they pointed out to me on a map some family villages, Kinte-Kundah, and Kinte-Kundah Janneh-Ya, for instance.

The Gambian officials said they would try to help me. I returned to New York dazed. It is embarrassing to me now, but despite Grandma's stories, I'd never been concerned much with Africa, and I had the routine images of African people living mostly in exotic jungles. But a compulsion now laid hold of me to learn all I could, and I began devouring books about Africa, especially about the slave trade. Then one Thursday's mail contained a letter from one of the Gambian officials, inviting me to return there.

Monday I was back in Bathurst. It galvanized me when the officials said that a griot had been located who told the Kinte clan history—his name was Kebba Kanga Fofana. To reach him, I discovered, required a modified safari: renting a launch to get upriver, two land vehicles to carry supplies by a roundabout land route, and employing finally 14 people, including three interpreters and four musicians, since a griot would not speak the revered clan histories without background music.

THE ART OF STORY TELLING

The boat *Baddibu* vibrated upriver, with me acutely tense: Were these Africans maybe viewing me as but another of the pith-helmets? After about two hours, we put in at James Island, for me to see the ruins of the once British-operated James Fort. Here two centuries of slave ships had loaded thousands of cargoes of Gambian tribespeople. The crumbling stones, the deeply oxidized swivel cannon, even some remnant links of chain seemed all but impossible to believe. Then we continued upriver to the left-bank village of Albreda, and there put ashore to continue on foot to Juffure, village of the *griot*. Once more we stopped, for me to see *toubob kolong*, "the white man's well," now almost filled in, in a swampy area with abundant, tall, saw-toothed grass. It was dug two centuries ago to "17 men's height deep" to insure survival drinking water for long-driven, famishing coffles of slaves.

Walking on, I kept wishing that Grandma could hear how her stories had led me to the *"Kamby Bolong."* (Our surviving storyteller Cousin Georgia died in a Kansas City hospital during this same morning, I would learn later.) Finally, Juffure village's playing children, sighting us, flashed an alert. The 70-odd people came rushing from their circular, thatch-roofed, mud-walled huts, with goats bounding up and about, and parrots squawking from up in the palms. I sensed him in advance somehow, the small man amid them, wearing a pillbox cap and an off-white robe—the *griot*. Then the interpreters went to him, as the villagers thronged around me.

And it hit me like a gale wind: every one of them, the whole crowd, was *jet black*. An enormous sense of guilt swept me—a sense of being some kind of hybrid . . . a sense of being impure among the pure. It was an awful sensation.

The old *griot* stepped away from my interpreters and the crowd quickly swarmed around him—all of them buzzing. An interpreter named A. B. C. Salla came to me; he whispered: "Why they stare at you so, they have never seen here a black American." And that hit me: I was symbolizing for them twenty-five millions of us they had never seen. What did they think of me—of us?

Then abruptly the old *griot* was briskly walking toward me. His eyes boring into mine, he spoke in Mandinka, as if instinctively I should understand—and A. B. C. Salla translated:

"Yes . . . we have been told by the forefathers . . . that many of us from this place are in exile . . . in that placed called America . . . and in other places."

I suppose I physically wavered, and they thought it was the heat; rustling whispers went through the crowd, and a man brought me a low stool. Now the whispering hushed —the musicians had softly begun playing *kora* and *balafon*, and a canvas sling lawn seat was taken by the *griot*, Kebba Kanga Fofana, aged 73 "rains" (one rainy season each year). He seemed to gather himself into a physical rigidity, and he began speaking the *Kinte* clan's ancestral oral history; it came rolling from his mouth across the next hours . . . 17th- and 18th-century *Kinte* lineage details, predominantly what men took wives; the children they "begot," in the order of their births; those children's mates and children.

Events frequently were dated by some proximate singular physical occurrence. It was as if some ancient scroll were printed indelibly within the *griot's* brain. Each few sentences or so, he would pause for an interpreter's translation to me. I distill here the essence:

The *Kinte* clan began in Old Mali, the men generally blacksmiths ". . . who conquered fire," and the women potters and weavers. One large branch of the clan moved to Mauretania from where one son of the clan, Kairaba Kunta Kinte, a Moslem Marabout holy man, entered Gambia. He lived first in the village of Pakali N'Ding; he moved next to Jiffarong village; ". . . and then he came here, into our own village of Juffure."

In Juffure, Kairaba Kunta Kinte took his first wife, ". . . a Mandinka maiden, whose name was Sireng. By her, he begot two sons, whose names were Janneh and Saloum. Then he got a second wife, Yaisa. By her, he begot a son, Omoro."

The three sons became men in Juffure. Janneh and Saloum went off and found a new village, Kinte-Kundah Janneh-Ya. "And then Omoro, the youngest son, when he had 30 rains, took as a wife a maiden, Binta Kebba.

"And by her, he begot four sons —Kunta, Lamin, Suwadu, and Madi. . . ."

Sometimes, a "begotten," after his naming, would be accompanied by some later-occurring detail, perhaps as ". . . in time of big water (flood), he slew a water buffalo." Having named those four sons, now the *griot* stated such a detail.

"About the time the king's soldiers came, the eldest of these four sons, Kunta, when he had about 16 rains, went away from this village, to chop wood to make a drum . . . and he was never seen again. . . ."

Goose-pimples the size of lemons seemed to pop all over me. In my knapsack were my cumulative notebooks, the first of them including how in my boyhood, my Grandma, Cousin Georgia and the others told of the African "*Kin-tay*" who always said he was kidnapped near his village—while chopping wood to make a drum. . . .

I showed the interpreter, he showed and told the *griot*, who excitedly told the people; they grew very agitated. Abruptly then they formed a human ring, encircling me, dancing and chanting. Perhaps a dozen of the women carrying their infant babies rushed in toward me, thrusting the infants into my arms —conveying, I would later learn, "the laying on of hands . . . through this flesh which is us, we are you, and you are us." The men hurried me into their mosque, their Arabic praying later being translated outside: "Thanks be to Allah for returning the long lost from among us."

THE ART OF STORYTELLING

Direct descendants of Kunta Kinte's blood brothers were hastened, some of them from nearby villages, for a family portrait to be taken with me, surrounded by actual ancestral sixth cousins. More symbolic acts filled the remaining day.

When they would let me leave, for some reason I wanted to go away over the African land. Dazed, silent in the bumping Land Rover, I heard the cutting staccato of talking drums. Then when we sighted the next village, its people came thronging to meet us. They were all—little naked ones to wizened elders—waving, beaming, amid a cacophony of crying out; and then my ears identified their words: *"Meester Kinte! Meester Kinte!"*

Let me tell you something: I am a man. But I remember the sob surging up from my feet, flinging up my hands before my face and bawling as I had not done since I was a baby . . . the jet-black Africans were jostling, staring . . . I didn't care, with the feelings surging. If you really knew the odyssey of us millions of black Americans, if you really knew how we came in the seeds of our forefathers, captured, driven, beaten, inspected, bought, branded, chained in foul ships, if you really knew, you needed weeping. . . .

Back home, I knew that what I must write, really, was our black saga, where any individual's past is the essence of the millions'. Now flat broke, I went to some editors I knew, describing the Gambian miracle, and my desire to pursue the research; Doubleday contracted to publish, and Reader's Digest to condense the projected book; then I had advances to travel further.

Annapolis, *Sept. 29, 1767.*
JUST IMPORTED,
In the Ship LORD LIGONIER, *Capt.* DAVIES, *from the River* GAMBIA, *in* AFRICA, *and to be sold by the Subscribers, in* ANNAPOLIS, *for Cash, or good Bills of Exchange, on Wednesday the 7th of October next,*

A CARGO OF CHOICE HEALTHY SLAVES. The said Ship will take TOBACCO to LONDON, on Liberty, at 6 *l.* Sterling per Ton.

/ X JOHN RIDOUT,
  DANIEL OF ST. THO'. JENIFER.

N. B. Any Person that will contract for a Quantity of Lumber, may meet with Encouragement, by applying to D. T. JENIFER.

What ship brought Kinte to Grandma's " 'Naplis" (Annapolis, Maryland, obviously)? The old *griot's* time reference to "king's soldiers" sent me flying to London. Feverish searching at last identified, in British Parliament records, "Colonel O'Hare's Forces," dispatched in mid-1767 to protect the then British-held James Fort whose ruins I'd visited. So Kunta Kinte was down in some ship probably sailing later that summer from the Gambia River to Annapolis.

Now I feel it was fated that I had taught myself to write in the U.S. Coast Guard. For the sea dramas I had concentrated on had given me years of experience searching among yellowing old U.S. maritime records. So now in English 18th Century marine records I finally tracked ships reporting themselves in and out to the Commandant of the Gambia River's James Fort. And then early one afternoon I found that a *Lord Ligonier* under a Captain Thomas

Davies had sailed on the Sabbath of July 5, 1767. Her cargo: 3,265 elephants' teeth, 3,700 pounds of beeswax, 800 pounds of cotton, 32 ounces of Gambian gold, and 140 slaves; her destination: "Annapolis."

That night I recrossed the Atlantic. In the Library of Congress the *Lord Ligonier's* arrival was one brief line in "Shipping In the Port Of Annapolis—1748-1775." I located the author, Vaughan W. Brown, in his Baltimore brokerage office. He drove to Historic Annapolis, the city's historical society, and found me further documentation of her arrival on Sept. 29, 1767. (Exactly two centuries later, Sept. 29, 1967, standing, staring seaward from an Annapolis pier, again I knew tears). More help came in the Maryland Hall of Records. Archivist Phebe Jacobsen found the *Lord Ligonier's* arriving customs declaration listing, "98 Negroes"—so in her 86-day crossing, 42 Gambians had died, one among the survivors being 16-year-old Kunta Kinte. Then the microfilmed Oct. 1, 1767, *Maryland Gazette* contained, on page two, an announcement to prospective buyers from the ship's agents, Daniel of St. Thos. Jenifer and John Ridout (the Governor's secretary): "from the River GAMBIA, in AFRICA . . . a cargo of choice, healthy SLAVES. . ."

Understanding Literature

1. Describe the evening ritual at Grandma Palmer's when relatives came to Henning. What was Alex's role at these gatherings? Did he understand every detail in the family's story? What made an impression on him?

2. Haley says that the African became very angry when other slaves addressed him as "Toby." Why do you think his real name was so important to him?

3. Which of the African's "unknown-tongue sounds" turned out to be the single most important clue to discovering his ancestral village? Why?

4. Why did the women of Juffure thrust their babies into Haley's arms? What is the significance of this gesture?

5. Haley describes being overcome with powerful emotions at several points in his travels and research. Why, at one point, does he experience "an enormous sense of guilt" and, at two other points, does he weep?

6. How did Haley's service in the Coast Guard contribute to his career as a writer?

7. Basing your opinion on "My Furthest-Back Person—'The African,'" how dependable would you say the "oral tradition" is? Under what types of circumstances do you think it might be most dependable? least dependable?

THE ART OF STORYTELLING

Gerald M. Durrell, a zoologist and a writer, combines his professions in this zany true account, in which the main character is a baboon named Georgina.

A Zoo in Suburbia

Gerald M. Durrell

IMPROVING YOUR READING: In reading "My Journey Is Still Long," you learned that an autobiography may have all of the elements of a short story. In this true account, you will see that a story's leading character may be an animal and that even in true stories things may not turn out as expected.

MOST PEOPLE who lived on our suburban road in Bournemouth could look out on their back gardens with pride, for each one resembled its neighbor's. There were minor differences, of course—some favored pansies to sweet peas, or hyacinths to lupins—but basically they were all the same. Anyone looking out at my sister's back garden, however, would have been forced to admit that it was, to say the least, unconventional. In one corner was a huge marquee, from the interior of which came a curious chorus of squeaks, whistles, grunts, and growls. Alongside it stretched a line of Dexion cages from which glowered eagles, vultures, owls, and hawks. Next to them was a large cage containing Minnie, the chimp. On the remains of what had once been a lawn, fourteen monkeys rolled and played on long leashes, while in the garage frogs croaked, touracos called throatily, and squirrels gnawed loudly on hazelnut shells. At all hours of the day the fascinated,

horrified neighbors stood trembling behind their lace curtains and watched as my sister, my mother, Sophie, Jacquie, and I trotted to and fro through the shambles of the garden, carrying little pots of bread and milk, plates of chopped fruit, or, what was worse, great hunks of gory meat or dead rats. We had, the neighbors felt, taken unfair advantage of them. If it had been a matter of a crowing cockerel, or a barking dog, or our cat having kittens in one of their best flowerbeds, they would have been able to cope with the situation. But the action of suddenly planting what amounted to a sizable zoo in their midst was so unprecedented and unnerving that it took their breath away, and so it was some time before they managed to rally their forces and start to complain.

In the meantime I had started on my search for a zoo in which to put my animals. The simplest thing to do, it occurred to me, was to go to the local council and inform them that I had the contents of a fine little zoo, and that all I wanted them to do was let me rent or purchase a suitable site on which to have it. Since I already had the animals, it seemed to me in my innocence, they would be delighted to help. It would cost them nothing, and they would be getting what was, after all, another amenity for the town. But the Powers That Be had other ideas. Bournemouth is nothing if not conservative. There had never been a zoo in the town ever since it had become a town, and so they did not see why there should be one now. This is what is known among local councils as progress. First they said that the animals would be dangerous; then they said they would smell; and then, searching their minds wildly for ideas, they said they did not have any land anyway. . . .

Then Jacquie had a brilliant idea. "Why not let's offer them to one of the big stores in town as a Christmas show?"

So I phoned up every big store in town. They were charming but unhelpful; they simply had not the space for such a show, however desirable. Then I phoned up the last on my list, the huge emporium owned by J. J. Allen. They, to my delight, evinced great interest and asked me to go and discuss it with them. And so "Durrell's Menagerie" came into being.

A large section of one of their basements was set aside, roomy cages were built with tastefully painted murals on the walls depicting a riot of tropical foliage, and the animals were moved in out of the cold and damp which had already started, into the luxury of brilliant electric light and a constant temperature. The charge for admission just covered the food bills, so the animals were warm, comfortable, and well fed without being a drain on my resources. With this worry off my mind I could turn my attention once more to the problem of getting my zoo.

It would be wearisome to go into all the details of the frustration of this period, or to make a catalogue of the number of mayors, town councillors, park superintendents, and sanitary officers I met and argued with. Suffice it to say that I felt my brain creaking at times with the effort of trying to persuade supposedly intelligent people that a zoo in any town should be considered an attraction rather than anything else. The way everyone went on, one would have thought that I wanted to set off an atomic bomb on one of the piers.

In the meantime the animals, unaware that their fate hung in the balance, did their best to make life exciting for us. There was, for example, the day that Georgina the baboon decided that she wanted to see a little more of Bournemouth than the inside of J. J. Allen's basement. Fortunately it was a Sunday morning, so there was no one in the store; I dread to think what would have happened if there had been.

I was sipping a cup of tea, preparatory to going down to the store and cleaning and feeding the animals, when the telephone rang. Without a care in the world I answered it.

"Is that Mr. Durrell?" inquired a deep, lugubrious voice.

"Yes, speaking."

"This is the police 'ere, sir. One of them monkeys of yours 'as got out, and I thought I'd better let you know."

"Good grief, which one is it?" I asked.

"I don't know sir, really. It's a big brown one. Only it looks rather fierce, sir, so I thought I'd let you know."

"Yes, thanks very much. Where is it?"

"Well, it's in one of the windows at the moment. But I don't see as 'ow it'll stay there very long. Is it liable to bite, sir?"

"Well, it may do. Don't go near it. I'll be right down," I said, slamming down the receiver.

The last thing I wanted was to get down there and find a blood-stained constable. I grabbed a taxi and we roared down to the center of the town, ignoring all speed limits. After all, I reflected, we were on police business of a sort.

As I paid off the taxi fare, the first thing that greeted my eyes was the chaos in one of the big display windows of Allen's. The window had been carefully set out to show some articles of bedroom furniture. There was a large bed, made up, a tall bed-side light, and several eiderdowns tastefully spread over the floor. At least, that was how it had looked

when the window dresser had finished it. Now it looked as if a bomb had hit it. The light had been overturned and had burned a large hole in one of the eiderdowns; the bedclothes had been stripped off the bed, and the pillow and sheets were covered with a tasteful pattern of paw marks. On the bed itself sat Georgina, bouncing up and down happily, and making ferocious faces at a crowd of scandalized church-goers who had gathered on the pavement outside the window. I went into the store and found two enormous contables lying in ambush behind a barricade of turkish toweling.

"Ah," said one with relief, "there you are, sir. We didn't like to try and catch it, see, because it didn't know us, and we thought it might make it worse, like."

"I don't think anything could make that animal worse," I said bitterly. "Actually she's harmless, but she makes ... a row and looks fierce. It's all bluff, really."

"Really?" said one of the constables, polite but unconvinced.

"I'll try and get her in the window there if I can, but if she breaks away, I want you two to 'head her off. Don't, for the love of Allah, let her get into the china department."

"She came through the china department already," said one of the constables with gloomy satisfaction.

"Did she break anything?" I asked faintly.

"No, sir, luckily. She just galloped straight through. Me and Bill was chasing 'er of course, so she didn't stop."

"Well, don't let's let her get back in there. We may not be so lucky next time."

By this time Jacquie and my sister Margo had arrived in another taxi, so our ranks had now swelled to five. We should, I thought, be able to cope with Georgina between us.

I stationed the two constables, my sister, and my wife at suitable points guarding the entrance to the china department, and then went round and entered the window in which Georgina was still bouncing up and down on the ruined bed, making obscene faces at the crowd.

"Georgina," I said in a quiet but soothing voice, "come along then, come to 'Dad."

Georgina glanced over her shoulder in surprise. She studied my face as I moved towards her, and decided that my expression belied my honeyed accents. She gathered herself and leaped through the air, over the still smoldering eiderdown, and grabbed at the top of the great rampart of turkish toweling that formed the background of the window display. This, not having been constructed to take the weight of a large baboon hurtling through the air, immediately collapsed, and Georgina fell to the ground under a cascade of many-hued toweling. She struggled madly to free herself, and succeeded in doing so just as I flung myself forward to catch her. She gave a hysterical squawk and fled out of the window into the interior of the shop. I unraveled myself from the toweling and followed.

A piercing shriek from my sister told me of Georgina's whereabouts; my sister always tends to go off like a locomotive in moments of crisis. Georgina had slipped past my sister and was now perched on a counter, surveying us with glittering eyes, thoroughly enjoying the game. We approached her in a grim-faced body. At the end of the counter, suspended from the ceiling, hung a Christmas decoration made out of holly, tinsel, and cardboard stars. It was shaped somewhat like a chandelier, and seemed, as far as Georgina was concerned, the ideal thing to swing on. She poised herself on the end of the counter and as we ran forward she leaped up and grabbed at the decoration in a manner vaguely reminiscent of the elder Fairbanks. The decoration, not having been designed for this sort of treatment, promptly gave way, and Georgina fell to the ground, leaped to her feet, and galloped off, wearing a piece of tinsel over one ear.

For the next half hour we thundered through the deserted store, always with Georgina one jump ahead of us, as it were. She knocked down a huge pile of account books in the stationery department, paused to see if a pile of lace doilies was edible, and did a large and decorative puddle at the foot of the main staircase. Then, just as the constables were beginning to breath rather stertorously,[1] and I was beginning to despair of ever catching the wretched animal, Georgina made a miscalculation. Loping easily

1 **stertorously:** in a heavy, rasping manner.

THE ART OF STORYTELLING

ahead of us, she came upon what looked like the perfect hiding place made out of rolls of linoleum arranged on end. She fled between the rolls and was lost, for the rolls had been arranged in the form of a hollow square, a three-sided trap from which there was no escape. Quickly we closed in and blocked the entrance to the linoleum trap. I advanced towards her, grim-faced, and she sat there and screamed wildly, begging for mercy. As I made a lunge to grab her she ducked under my hand, and as I swung round to prevent her escape I bumped into one of the massive rolls of linoleum. Before I could stop it, this toppled forward like a gigantic truncheon and hit one of the constables accurately on the top of his helmet. As the poor man staggered backwards, Georgina took one look at my face and decided that she was in need of police protection. She rushed to the still swaying constable and wrapped her arms tightly round his legs, looking over her shoulder at me and screaming. I jumped forward and grabbed her by her hairy legs and the scruff of her neck, and dragged her away from the constable's legs, still screaming piercingly.

"Cor!"[2] said the constable, in a voice of deep emotion, "I thought I'd 'ad me chips that time."

"Oh, she wouldn't have bitten you," I explained, raising my voice above Georgina's harsh screams. "She wanted you to protect her from me."

"Cor!" he said again. "Well, I'm glad *that's* over."

We put Georgina back in her cage, thanked the constables, cleared up the mess, cleaned and fed the animals, and then went home. But for the rest of that day, every time the phone rang I nearly jumped out of my skin.

2 **Cor:** an exclamation something like "My Lord!"

Understanding Literature

1. Author Durrell states that "Bournemouth is nothing if not conservative." Judging from the way the town reacted to the Durrells' "fine little zoo," what does "conservative" mean?
2. What was Jacquie's idea for gaining the town's goodwill?
3. Although a baboon, Georgina is still a central character in Durrell's account. Describe her.
4. How would you have reacted to the Durrells' plan if you had owned the department store?

Further Activity

Suppose that Georgina the baboon could talk and write. Write a report of the department store incident as Georgina might have reported it.

GERALD M. DURRELL

Colette, a 20th-century French writer, here presents an essay on her childhood—as she remembers it.

Where Are the Children?

Colette

IMPROVING YOUR READING: The author's *selection of detail*, the images and scenes which she chooses to recall, should give you a sense of how she feels about the memories of her house.

THE HOUSE WAS large, topped by a lofty garret. The steep gradient[1] of the street compelled the coach houses, stables, and poultry house, the laundry and the dairy, to huddle on a lower level all round a closed courtyard.

By leaning over the garden wall, I could scratch with my finger the poultry-house roof. The Upper Garden overlooked the Lower Garden—a warm, confined enclosure reserved for the cultivation of aubergines[2] and pimentos—where the smell of tomato leaves mingled in July with that of the apricots ripening on the walls. In the Upper Garden were two twin firs, a walnut tree whose intolerant shade killed any flowers beneath it, some rosebushes, a neglected lawn and a dilapidated arbor. At the bottom, along the Rue des Vignes, a boundary wall reinforced with a strong iron railing ought to have ensured the privacy of the two gardens, but I never knew those railings other

than twisted and torn from their cement foundations, and grappling in mid-air with the invincible[3] arms of a hundred-year-old wistaria.[4]

In the Rue de l'Hospice, a two-way flight of steps led up to the front door in the gloomy façade[5] with its large bare windows. It was the typical burgher's house in an old village, but its dignity was upset a little by the steep gradient of the street, the stone steps being lopsided, ten on one side and six on the other.

A large solemn house, rather forbidding, with its shrill bell and its carriage entrance with a huge bolt like an ancient dungeon, a house that smiled only on its garden side. The back, invisible to passers-by, was a sun-trap, swathed[6] in a mantle of wistaria and bignonia too heavy for the trellis of worn ironwork, which sagged in the middle like a hammock and provided shade for the

1 **gradient:** slope.
2 **aubergines** (ō'bĕr zhēnz): eggplants.
3 **invincible:** unconquerable.
4 **wistaria:** flowered vine.
5 **facade** (fə säd'): front or face of a building.
6 **swathed:** wrapped; enveloped.

THE ART OF STORYTELLING

little flagged terrace and the threshold of the sitting room.

Is it worth while, I wonder, seeking for adequate words to describe the rest? I shall never be able to conjure up[7] the splendor that adorns, in my memory, the ruddy festoons[8] of an autumn vine borne down by its own weight and clinging despairingly to some branch of the fir trees. And the massive lilacs, whose compact flowers—blue in the shade and purple in the sunshine—withered so soon, stifled by their own exuberance.[9] The lilacs long since dead will not be revived at my bidding, any more than the terrifying moonlight—silver, quicksilver, leaden-gray, with facets[10] of dazzling amethyst or scintillating[11] points of sapphire—all depending on a certain pane in the blue glass window of the summer house at the bottom of the garden.

Both house and garden are living still, I know; but what of that, if the magic has deserted them? If the secret is lost that opened to me a whole world—light, scents, birds and trees in perfect harmony, the murmur of human voices now silent forever—a world of which I have ceased to be worthy?

It would happen sometimes long ago, when this house and garden harbored a family, that a book lying open on the flagstones of the terrace or on the grass, a skipping rope twisted like a snake across the path,

or perhaps a miniature garden, pebble-edged and planted with decapitated flowers, revealed both the presence of children and their varying ages. But such evidence was hardly ever accompanied by childish shouts or laughter, and my home, though warm and full, bore an odd resemblance to those houses which, once the holidays have come to an end, are suddenly emptied of joy. The silence, the muted[12] breeze of the enclosed garden, the pages of the book stirred only by invisible fingers, all seemed to be asking, "Where are the children?"

It was then, from beneath the ancient iron trellis sagging to the left under the wistaria, that my mother would make her appearance, small and plump in those days when age had not yet wasted her. She would scan the thick green clumps and, raising her head, fling her call into the air: "Children! Where are the children?"

Where indeed? Nowhere. My mother's cry would ring through the garden, striking the great wall of the barn and returning to her as a faint exhausted echo. "Where . . . ? Children . . . ?"

Nowhere. My mother would throw back her head and gaze heavenwards, as though waiting for a flock of winged children to alight from the skies. After a moment she would repeat her call; then, grown tired of questioning the heavens, she would crack a dry poppyhead with her fingernail, rub the greenfly from

7 **conjure up:** that is, make it clear to the reader.
8 **festoons:** wreaths; garlands.
9 **exuberance:** great abundance.
10 **facets:** surfaces.
11 **scintillating:** sparkling.

12 **muted:** faint; gentle.

a rose shoot, fill her pockets with unripe walnuts, and return to the house shaking her head over the vanished children.

And all the while, from among the leaves of the walnut tree above her, gleamed the pale, pointed face of a child who lay stretched like a tomcat along a big branch, and never uttered a word. A less shortsighted mother might well have suspected that the spasmodic salutations[13] exchanged by the twin tops of the two firs were due to some influence other than that of the sudden October squalls! And in the square dormer, above the pulley for hauling up fodder, would she not have perceived, if she had screwed up her eyes, two pale patches among the hay—the face of a young boy and the pages of his book?

But she had given up looking for us, had despaired of trying to reach us. Our uncanny turbulence[14] was never accompanied by any sound. I do not believe there can ever have been children so active and so mute. Looking back at what we were, I am amazed. No one had imposed upon us either our cheerful silence or our limited sociability. My nineteen-year-old brother, engrossed in constructing some hydrotherapeutic apparatus[15] out of linen bladders, strands of wire and glass tubes, never prevented the younger, aged fourteen, from disemboweling[16] a watch

or from transposing on the piano, with never a false note, a melody or an air from a symphony heard at a concert in the county town. He did not even interfere with his junior's incomprehensible[17] passion for decorating the garden with little tombstones cut out of cardboard, and each inscribed, beneath the sign of the cross, with the names, epitaph, and genealogy[18] of the imaginary person deceased.

My sister with the too long hair might read forever with never a pause; the two boys would brush past her as though they did not see the young girl sitting abstracted[19] and entranced, and never bother her. When I was small, I was at liberty to keep up as best I could with my long-legged brothers as they ranged the woods in pursuit of swallowtails, White Admirals, Purple Emperors, or hunted for grass snakes, or gathered armfuls of the tall July foxgloves which grew in the clearings already aglow with patches of purple heather. But I followed them in silence, picking blackberries, bird cherries, a chance wild flower, or roving the hedgerows and waterlogged meadows like an independent dog out hunting on its own.

"Where are the children?" She would suddenly appear like an oversolicitous[20] mother-dog breathlessly pursuing her constant quest, head lifted and scenting the breeze. Sometimes her white linen sleeves bore

13 **spasmodic salutations:** irregular gestures of greeting.
14 **uncanny turbulence:** mysterious unrest.
15 **hydrotherapeutic apparatus:** system for treating diseases by means of baths.
16 **disemboweling:** taking apart.

17 **incomprehensible:** impossible to understand.
18 **genealogy:** line of ancestors; bloodline.
19 **abstracted:** lost in thought.
20 **oversolicitous:** too-fearful.

THE ART OF STORYTELLING

witness that she had come from kneading dough for cakes or making the pudding that had a velvety hot sauce of rum and jam. If she had been washing the Havanese dog, she would be enveloped in a long blue apron, and sometimes she would be waving a banner of rustling yellow paper, the paper used round the butcher's meat, which meant that she hoped to reassemble, at the same time as her elusive[21] children, her carnivorous[22] family of vagabond cats.

To her traditional cry she would add, in the same anxious and appealing key, a reminder of the time of day. "Four o'clock, and they haven't come in to tea! Where are the children? . . ." "Half-past six! Will they come home to dinner? Where are the children? . . ." That lovely voice; how I should weep for joy if I could hear it now! Our only sin, our single misdeed, was silence, and a kind of miraculous vanishing. For perfectly innocent reasons, for the sake of a liberty that no one denied us, we clambered over the railing, leaving behind our shoes, and returned by way of an unnecessary ladder or a neighbor's low wall.

Our anxious mother's keen sense of smell would discover on us traces of wild garlic from a distant ravine or of marsh mint from a treacherous bog. The dripping pocket of one of the boys would disgorge the bathing slip worn in malarial ponds, and the "little one," cut about the knees and skinned at the elbows, would be bleeding complacently[23] under plasters of cobweb and wild pepper bound on with rushes.

"Tomorrow I shall keep you locked up! All of you, do you hear, every single one of you!"

Tomorrow! Next day the eldest, slipping on the slated roof where he was fitting a tank, broke his collarbone and remained at the foot of the wall waiting, politely silent and half unconscious, until someone came to pick him up. Next day an eighteen-rung ladder crashed plumb on the forehead of the younger son, who never uttered a cry, but brought home with becoming modesty a lump like a purple egg between his eyes.

"Where are the children?"

Two are at rest. The others grow older day by day. If there be a place of waiting after this life, then surely she who so often waited for us has not ceased to tremble for those two who are yet alive.

For the eldest of us all, at any rate, she has done with looking at the dark windowpane every evening and saying, "I feel that child is not happy. I feel she is suffering." And for the elder of the boys she no longer listens, breathlessly, to the wheels of a doctor's trap[24] coming over the snow at night, or to the hoofbeats of the gray mare.

But I know that for the two who remain she seeks and wanders still, invisible, tormented by her inability to watch over them enough.

"Where, oh where are the children? . . ."

---

21 **elusive:** runaway; fugitive.
22 **carnivorous:** meat-eating.

23 **complacently:** in a satisfied way; contentedly.
24 **trap:** one-horse carriage.

Understanding Literature

1. Describe in your own words Colette's house and its grounds.
2. Colette shortens her descriptions by using comparisons. What do you see in your imagination when you read the following phrases?

    (a) ". . . a house that smiled only on its garden side."

    (b) ". . . a mantle of wistaria and bignonia too heavy for the trellis of worn ironwork, which sagged in the middle like a hammock. . . ."

    (c) ". . . the ruddy festoons of an autumn vine borne down by its own weight and clinging despairingly to some branch of the fir trees."

    (d) ". . . a miniature garden, pebble-edged and planted with decapitated flowers. . . ."

3. In the paragraph beginning "And all the while. . . ," where are the children?
4. Colette is offering to her readers a series of pictures, as though they were paintings of scenes. Where does each scene begin and end? Can you find the words that indicate that the scenes are taken from the past?
5. Where is she not painting pictures, but, rather, commenting directly on her life as a child?
6. What is Colette's feeling about her childhood? What evidence can you find for your answer?

Further Activity

A person is in contact with the world through his senses: sight, smell, touch, taste, and hearing. The more he uses these senses the more he is aware of what is around him in the world. A good reader should be able to follow in his mind a writer's appeals to these senses. When Colette's mother cracks a dry poppyhead, the reader should hear it; when she rubs the greenfly from a rose shoot, he should see it; when she fills her pockets with unripe walnuts, he should feel them.

List the five senses on your paper, and under each put three expressions from this essay which are appeals to that particular sense experience. When you have completed your lists, you should be able to answer this question: At what points in the essay does Colette let you see, smell, touch, taste, or hear what she does?

In this story Hamlin Garland describes the difficulties of loneliness. He places a lonely woman in a town where people try to be nice; they offer chairs and apples. But finally another woman offers something of herself to this lonely woman, and a day's pleasure is begun.

A Day's Pleasure

Hamlin Garland

IMPROVING YOUR READING: Watch for the many *contrasts* developed in this story. The leading character, Delia Markham, is contrasted to other people in the story, and she is placed in several settings which contrast with the one in which you first find her.

Observe, too, the role of the *minor characters*. Although a story is usually centered on one person, the minor characters have various functions in directing the action of the story. When you meet a minor character, you should ask, Why is he here? How does he influence the action?

WHEN MARKHAM came in from shoveling his last wagonload of corn into the crib he found that his wife had put the children to bed, and was kneading a batch of dough with the dogged action of a tired and sullen woman.

He slipped his soggy boots off his feet, and having laid a piece of wood on top of the stove, put his heels on it comfortably. His chair squeaked as he leaned back on its hinder legs, but he paid no attention; he was used to it, exactly as he was used to his wife's lameness and ceaseless toil.

"That closes up my corn," he said after a silence. "I guess I'll go to town tomorrow to git my horses shod."

"I guess I'll git ready and go along," said his wife, in a sorry[1] at-

tempt to be firm and confident of tone.

"What do you want to go to town fer?" he grumbled.

"What does anybody want to go to town fer?" she burst out, facing him. "I ain't been out o' this house fer six months, while you go an' go!"

"Oh, it ain't six months. You went down that day I got the mower."

"When was that? The tenth of July, and you know it."

"Well, mebbe 'twas. I didn't think it was so long ago. I ain't no objection to your goin', only I'm goin' to take a load of wheat."

"Well, jest leave off a sack, an' that'll balance me an' the baby," she said spiritedly.

"All right," he replied good-naturedly, seeing she was roused. "Only that wheat ought to be put up tonight if you're goin'. You won't have any time to hold sacks for me

1 **sorry:** here, pitiful.

in the morning with them young ones to get off to school."

"Well, let's go do it then," she said, sullenly resolute.

"I hate to go out agin; but I s'pose we'd better."

He yawned dismally and began pulling his boots on again, stamping his swollen feet into them with grunts of pain. She put on his coat and one of the boy's caps, and they went out to the granary. The night was cold and clear.

"Don't look so much like snow as it did last night," said Sam. "It may turn warm."

Laying out the sacks in the light of the lantern, they sorted out those which were whole, and Sam climbed into the bin with a tin pail in his hand, and the work began.

He was a sturdy fellow, and he worked desperately fast; the shining tin pail dived deep into the cold wheat and dragged heavily on the woman's tired hands as it came to the mouth of the sack, and she trembled with fatigue, but held on and dragged the sacks away when filled, and brought others, till at last Sam climbed out, puffing and wheezing, to tie them up.

"I guess I'll load 'em in the morning," he said. "You needn't wait fer me. I'll tie 'em up alone."

"Oh, I don't mind," she replied, feeling a little touched by his unexpectedly easy acquiescence to[2] her request. When they went back to the house the moon had risen.

It had scarcely set when they were wakened by the crowing roosters. The man rolled stiffly out of bed and began rattling at the stove in the dark, cold kitchen.

His wife arose lamer and stiffer than usual, and began twisting her thin hair into a knot.

Sam did not stop to wash, but went out to the barn. The woman, however, hastily soused her face into the hard limestone water at the sink, and put the kettle on. Then she called the children. She knew it was early, and they would need several callings. She pushed breakfast forward, running over in her mind the things she must have: two spools of thread, six yards of cotton flannel, a can of coffee, and mittens for Kitty. These she must have—there were oceans of things she needed.

The children soon came scudding down out of the darkness of the upstairs to dress tumultuously[3] at the kitchen stove. They humped and shivered, holding up their bare feet from the cold floor, like chickens in new-fallen snow. They were irritable, and snarled and snapped and struck like cats and dogs. Mrs. Markham stood it for a while with mere commands to "hush up," but at last her patience gave out, and she charged down on the struggling mob and cuffed them right and left.

They ate their breakfast by lamplight, and when Sam went back to his work around the barnyard it was scarcely dawn. The children, left alone with their mother, began to tease her to let them go to town also.

---

2 **acquiescence to:** acceptance of.

3 **tumultuously:** frantically; riotously.

THE ART OF STORYTELLING

"No, sir—nobody goes but baby. Your father's goin' to take a load of wheat."

She was weak with the worry of it all when she had sent the older children away to school and the kitchen work was finished. She went into the cold bedroom off the little sitting room and put on her best dress. It had never been a good fit, and now she was getting so thin it hung in wrinkled folds everywhere about the shoulders and waist. She lay down on the bed a moment to ease that dull pain in her back. She had a moment's distaste for going out at all. The thought of sleep was more alluring. Then the thought of the long, long day, and the sickening sameness of her life, swept over her again, and she rose and prepared the baby for the journey.

It was but little after sunrise when Sam drove out into the road and started for Belleplain. His wife sat perched upon the wheat sacks behind him, holding the baby in her lap, a cotton quilt under her, and a cotton horse-blanket over her knees.

Sam was disposed to be very good-natured, and he talked back at her occasionally, though she could only understand him when he turned his face toward her. The baby stared out at the passing fence posts, and wiggled his hands out of his mittens at every opportunity. He was merry at least.

It grew warmer as they went on, and a strong south wind arose. The dust settled upon the woman's shawl and hat. Her hair loosened and blew unkemptly[4] about her face. The road which led across the high, level prairie was quite smooth and dry, but still it jolted her, and the pain in her back increased. She had nothing to lean against, and the weight of the child grew greater, till she was forced to place him on the sacks beside her, though she could not loose her hold for a moment.

The town drew in sight—a cluster of small frame houses and stores on the dry prairie beside a railway station. There were no trees yet which could be called shade trees. The pitilessly severe light of the sun flooded everything. A few teams were hitched about, and in the lee[5] of the stores a few men could be seen seated comfortably, their broad hat-rims flopping up and down, their faces brown as leather.

Markham put his wife out at one of the grocery stores, and drove off down toward the elevators to sell his wheat.

The grocer greeted Mrs. Markham in a perfunctorily[6] kind manner, and offered her a chair, which she took gratefully. She sat for a quarter of an hour almost without moving, leaning against the back of the high chair. At last the child began to get restless and troublesome, and she spent half an hour helping him amuse himself around the nail-kegs.

At length she rose and went out on the walk, carrying the baby. She went into the dry-goods store and took a seat on one of the little re-

---

4 **unkemptly:** carelessly.
5 **lee:** sheltered side.
6 **perfunctorily:** mechanically; routinely.

volving stools. A woman was buying some woolen goods for a dress. It was worth twenty-seven cents a yard, the clerk said, but he would knock off two cents if she took ten yards. It looked warm, and Mrs. Markham wished she could afford it for Mary.

A pretty young girl came in and laughed and chatted with the clerk, and bought a pair of gloves. She was the daughter of the grocer. Her happiness made the wife and mother sad. When Sam came back she asked him for some money.

"What you want to do with it?" he asked.

"I want to spend it," she said.

She was not to be trifled with, so he gave her a dollar.

"I need a dollar more."

"Well, I've got to go take up that note at the bank."

"Well, the children's got to have some new underclo'es," she said.

He handed her a two-dollar bill and then went out to pay his note.

She bought her cotton flannel and mittens and thread, and then sat leaning against the counter. It was noon, and she was hungry. She went out to the wagon, got the lunch she had brought, and took it into the grocery to eat it—where she could get a drink of water.

The grocer gave the baby a stick of candy and handed the mother an apple.

"It'll kind o' go down with your doughnuts," he said.

After eating her lunch she got up and went out. She felt ashamed to sit there any longer. She entered another dry-goods store, but when the clerk came toward her saying, "Anything to-day, Mrs. ——?" she

THE ART OF STORYTELLING

answered, "No, I guess not," and turned away with foolish face.

She walked up and down the street, desolately homeless. She did not know what to do with herself. She knew no one except the grocer. She grew bitter as she saw a couple of ladies pass, holding their demi-trains[7] in the latest city fashion. Another woman went by pushing a baby carriage, in which sat a child just about as big as her own. It was bouncing itself up and down on the long slender springs, and laughing and shouting. Its clean round face glowed from its pretty fringed hood. She looked down at the dusty clothes and grimy face of her own little one, and walked on savagely.

She went into the drugstore where the soda fountain was, but it made her thirsty to sit there and she went out on the street again. She heard Sam laugh, and saw him in a group of men over by the blacksmith shop. He was having a good time and had forgotten her.

Her back ached so intolerably that she concluded to go in and rest once more in the grocer's chair. The baby was growing cross and fretful. She bought five cents' worth of candy to take home to the children, and gave baby a little piece to keep him quiet. She wished Sam would come. It must be getting late. The grocer said it was not much after one. Time seemed terribly long. She felt that she ought to do something while she was in town. She ran over her purchases—yes, that was all she had

7 **demi-trains:** short pieces of ladies' dresses which ordinarily trail behind them.

planned to buy. She fell to figuring on the things she needed. It was terrible. It ran away up into twenty or thirty dollars at the least. Sam, as well as she, needed underwear for the cold winter, but they would have to wear the old ones, even if they were thin and ragged. She would not need a dress, she thought bitterly, because she never went anywhere. She rose and went out on the street once more, and wandered up and down, looking at everything in the hope of enjoying something.

A man from Boon Creek backed a load of apples up to the sidewalk, and as he stood waiting for the grocer he noticed Mrs. Markham and the baby, and gave the baby an apple. This was a pleasure. He had such a hearty way about him. He on his part saw an ordinary farmer's wife with dusty dress, unkempt hair, and tired face. He did not know exactly why she appealed to him, but he tried to cheer her up.

The grocer was familiar with these bedraggled and weary wives. He was accustomed to see them sit for hours in his big wooden chair, and nurse tired and fretful children. Their forlorn, aimless, pathetic wandering up and down the street was a daily occurrence, and had never possessed any special meaning to him.

II

In a cottage around the corner from the grocery store two men and a woman were finishing a dainty luncheon. The woman was dressed in cool, white garments, and she seemed to make the day one of perfect comfort.

The home of the Honorable Mr. Hall was by no means the costliest in town, but his wife made it the most attractive. He was one of the leading lawyers of the county, and a man of culture and progressive views. He was entertaining a friend who had lectured the night before in the Congregational church.

They were by no means in serious discussion. The talk was rather frivolous.[8] Hall had the ability to caricature[9] men with a few gestures and attitudes, and was giving to his Eastern friend some descriptions of the old-fashioned Western lawyers he had met in his practice. He was very amusing, and his guest laughed heartily for a time.

But suddenly Hall became aware that Otis was not listening. Then he perceived that he was peering out of the window at someone, and that on his face a look of bitter sadness was falling.

Hall stopped. "What do you see, Otis?"

Otis replied, "I see a forlorn, weary woman."

Mrs. Hall rose and went to the window. Mrs. Markham was walking by the house, her baby in her arms. Savage anger and weeping were in her eyes and on her lips, and there was hopeless tragedy in her shambling walk and weak back.

In the silence Otis went on: "I saw the poor, dejected creature twice this morning. I couldn't forget her."

"Who is she?" asked Mrs. Hall, very softly.

"Her name is Markham; she's Sam Markham's wife," said Hall.

The young wife led the way into the sitting room, and the men took seats and lit their cigars. Hall was meditating a diversion[10] when Otis resumed suddenly:

"That woman came to town today to get a change, to have a little play-spell, and she's wandering around like a starved and weary cat. I wonder if there is a woman in this town with sympathy enough and courage enough to go out and help that woman? The saloonkeepers, the politicians, and the grocers make it pleasant for the man—so pleasant that he forgets his wife. But the wife is left without a word."

Mrs. Hall's work dropped, and on her pretty face was a look of pain. The man's harsh words had wounded her—and wakened her. She took up her hat and hurried out on the walk. The men looked at each other, and then the husband said:

"It's going to be a little sultry[11] for the men around these diggings. Suppose we go out for a walk."

Delia felt a hand on her arm as she stood at the corner.

"You look tired, Mrs. Markham; won't you come in a little while? I'm Mrs. Hall."

Mrs. Markham turned with a scowl on her face and a biting word on her tongue, but something in the sweet, round little face of the other woman

8 **frivolous:** unimportant.
9 **caricature:** give an exaggerated imitation of.

10 **meditating a diversion:** that is, wondering how he would entertain his guest.
11 **sultry:** stuffy; stifling.

THE ART OF STORYTELLING

silenced her, and her brow smoothed out.

"Thank you kindly, but it's most time to go home. I'm looking fer Mr. Markham now."

"Oh, come in a little while; the baby is cross and tired out; please do."

Mrs. Markham yielded to the friendly voice, and together the two women reached the gate just as two men hurriedly turned the other corner.

"Let me relieve you," said Mrs. Hall.

The mother hesitated: "He's so dusty."

"Oh, that won't matter. Oh, what a big fellow he is! I haven't any of my own," said Mrs. Hall, and a look passed like an electric spark between the two women, and Delia was her willing guest from that moment.

They went into the little sitting room, so dainty and lovely to the farmer's wife, and as she sank into an easy chair she was faint and drowsy with the pleasure of it. She submitted to being brushed. She gave the baby into the hands of the Swedish girl, who washed its face and hands and sang it to sleep, while its mother sipped some tea. Through it all she lay back in her easy chair, not speaking a word, while the ache passed out of her back, and her hot, swollen head ceased to throb.

But she saw everything—the piano, the pictures, the curtains, the wallpaper, the little tea stand. They were almost as grateful to her as the food and fragrant tea. Such housekeeping as this she had never seen. Her mother had worn her kitchen floor thin as brown paper in keeping a speckless house, and she had been in houses that were larger and costlier, but something of the charm of her hostess was in the arrangement of vases, chairs, or pictures. It was tasteful.

Mrs. Hall did not ask about her affairs. She talked to her about the sturdy little baby, and about the things upon which Delia's eyes dwelt. If she seemed interested in a vase she was told what it was and where it was made. She was shown all the pictures and books. Mrs. Hall seemed to read her visitor's mind. She kept as far from the farm and her guest's affairs as possible, and at last she opened the piano and sang to her—not slow-moving hymns, but catchy love songs full of sentiment, and then played some simple melodies, knowing that Mrs. Markham's eyes were studying her hands, her rings, and the flash of her fingers on the keys—seeing more than she heard—and through it all Mrs. Hall conveyed the impression that she, too, was having a good time.

The rattle of the wagon outside roused them both. Sam was at the gate for her. Mrs. Markham rose hastily. "Oh, it's almost sundown!" she gasped in astonishment as she looked out of the window.

"Oh, that won't kill anybody," replied her hostess. "Don't hurry. Carrie, take the baby out to the wagon for Mrs. Markham while I help her with her things."

"Oh, I've had such a good time," Mrs. Markham said as they went down the little walk.

"So have I," replied Mrs. Hall. She took the baby a moment as her guest climbed in. "Oh, you big, fat fellow!" she cried as she gave him a squeeze. "You must bring your wife in oftener, Mr. Markham," she said, as she handed the baby up.

Sam was staring with amazement.

"Thank you, I will," he finally managed to say.

"Good night," said Mrs. Markham.

"Good night, dear," called Mrs. Hall, and the wagon began to rattle off.

The tenderness and sympathy in her voice brought the tears to Delia's eyes—not hot or bitter tears, but tears that cooled her eyes and cleared her mind.

The wind had gone down, and the red sunlight fell mistily over the world of corn and stubble. The crickets were still chirping and the feeding cattle were drifting toward the farmyards. The day had been made beautiful by human sympathy.

Understanding Literature

1. Judging by the beginning of the story, how do you think Markham and his wife ordinarily live? What kind of a relationship exists between them?
2. In what ways is Mrs. Markham different from other people in the town?
3. What is the function of Mr. Otis in the story?
4. Why does Mrs. Markham "turn with a scowl" when Mrs. Hall invites her inside?
5. How is the Halls' house contrasted with the Markhams'? How is the appearance of Mrs. Hall contrasted with that of Mrs. Markham?
6. By the end of this story what has Mrs. Hall learned about herself and about others? What has Mrs. Markham learned about other people?

Further Activities

1. Prepare a short talk on how either Mrs. Hall or Mrs. Markham might spend a typical day. Be sure to prove whatever you say by some hint which you get in the story.
2. In one paragraph define what Hamlin Garland means in his story by "human sympathy." Begin your paragraph with the statement: "In 'A Day's Pleasure' human sympathy means. . . ." Go on to explain what you take the phrase to mean. In the rest of the paragraph summarize the scene in the story in which human sympathy is acted out. Be sure to include specific details which are evidence of genuine human sympathy.

Focusing on Words

You will miss much of the characterization in the story unless you know the meaning of the following italicized words. Try to define each by the way it is used in the sentence. Consult the glossary about those you are unsure of.

1. "the *dogged* action of a tired and *sullen* woman" (p. 161, col. 1)
2. "she said *spiritedly*" (p. 161, col. 2)
3. "she said, sullenly *resolute*" (p. 162, col. 1)
4. "she trembled with *fatigue*" (p. 162, col. 1)
5. "the *sickening sameness* of her life" (p. 163, col. 1)

6. "She walked up and down the street, *desolately homeless.*" (p. 165, col. 1)
7. "The grocer was familiar with these *bedraggled* and weary wives." (p. 165, col. 2)
8. "Their forlorn, *aimless, pathetic* wandering" (p. 165, col. 2)
9. "I see a *forlorn,* weary woman." (p. 166, col. 1)
10. "there was hopeless tragedy in her *shambling* walk" (p. 166, col. 1)
11. "the poor, *dejected* creature" (p. 166, col. 1)

This story by Anatole France, a French novelist and satirist, is based on an old legend that has been retold many times.

Our Lady's Juggler

Anatole France

IMPROVING YOUR READING: *Theme* refers to the central idea in a piece of literature. This story illustrates a theme. As you read, observe what the author is trying to say about the relationship between people and God.

IN THE DAYS of King Louis there was a poor juggler in France, a native of Compiègne,[1] Barnaby by name, who went about from town to town performing feats of skill and strength.

On fair days he would unfold an old worn-out carpet in the public square, and when by means of a jovial address, which he had learned of a very ancient juggler, and which he never varied in the least, he had drawn together the children and loafers, he assumed extraordinary attitudes, and balanced a tin plate on the tip of his nose. At first the crowd would feign[2] indifference.

But when, supporting himself on his hands face downwards, he threw into the air six copper balls, which glittered in the sunshine, and caught them again with his feet; or when throwing himself backwards until his heels and the nape of the neck met, giving his body the form of a perfect wheel, he would juggle in this posture with a dozen knives, a murmur of admiration would escape the spectators, and pieces of money rain down upon the carpet.

Nevertheless, like the majority of those who live by their wits, Barnaby of Compiègne had a great struggle to make a living.

Earning his bread in the sweat of his brow, he bore rather more than his share of the penalties consequent upon the misdoings of our father Adam.[3]

Again, he was unable to work as constantly as he would have been willing to do. The warmth of the sun and the broad daylight were as necessary to enable him to display his brilliant parts as to the trees if flower and fruit should be expected of them. In wintertime he was nothing more than a tree stripped of its leaves, and as it were dead. The frozen ground was hard to the juggler, and, like the grasshopper of

---

1 Compiègne (kôN pyěn′y): city in northern France.
2 feign (fān): pretend.

3 consequent . . . Adam: because of Adam's sin of disobedience.

which Marie de France[4] tells us, the inclement[5] season caused him to suffer both cold and hunger. But as he was simple-natured he bore his ills patiently.

He had never meditated on the origin of wealth, nor upon the inequality of human conditions. He believed firmly that if this life should prove hard, the life to come could not fail to redress the balance,[6] and this hope upheld him. He did not resemble those thievish and miscreant Merry Andrews[7] who sell their souls to the devil. He never blasphemed God's name; he lived uprightly, and although he had no wife of his own, he did not covet[8] his neighbor's, since woman is ever the enemy of the strong man, as it appears by the history of Samson recorded in the Scriptures.

In truth, his was not a nature much disposed to carnal[9] delights, and it was a greater deprivation to him to forsake the tankard than the Hebe[10] who bore it. For whilst not wanting in[11] sobriety, he was fond of a drink when the weather waxed[12] hot. He was a worthy man who feared God, and was very devoted to the Blessed Virgin.

Never did he fail on entering a church to fall upon his knees before the image of the Mother of God, and offer up this prayer to her:

"Blessed Lady, keep watch over my life until it shall please God that I die, and when I am dead, ensure to me the possession of the joys of paradise."

II

Now on a certain evening after a dreary wet day, as Barnaby pursued his road, sad and bent, carrying under his arm his balls and knives wrapped up in his old carpet, on the watch for some barn where, though he might not sup, he might sleep, he perceived on the road, going in the same direction as himself, a monk, whom he saluted courteously. And as they walked at the same rate they fell into conversation with one another.

"Fellow traveler," said the monk, "how comes it about that you are clothed all in green? Is it perhaps in order to take the part of a jester in some mystery play?"[13]

"Not at all, good father," replied Barnaby. "Such as you see me, I am called Barnaby, and for my calling I am a juggler. There would be no pleasanter calling in the world if it would always provide one with daily bread."

"Friend Barnaby," returned the monk, "be careful what you say. There is no calling more pleasant than the monastic life. Those who lead it are occupied with the praises of God, the Blessed Virgin, and the saints; and, indeed, the religious life

4 **Marie de France:** a French poet of the 12th century who revised some English fables.
5 **inclement** (ĭn klĕm′ənt): stormy; harsh.
6 **redress the balance:** that is, could not fail to be better.
7 **thievish . . . Andrews:** here, types of clowns who were dishonest and irreligious.
8 **covet:** wish for.
9 **carnal:** unspiritual; physical.
10 **Hebe:** cupbearer of Greek mythology.
11 **not . . . in:** not without.
12 **waxed:** grew.

13 **mystery play:** a type of medieval drama based on Biblical incidents.

THE ART OF STORYTELLING

is one ceaseless hymn to the Lord."

Barnaby replied—

"Good father, I own that I spoke like an ignorant man. Your calling cannot be in any respect compared to mine, and although there may be some merit in dancing with a penny balanced on a stick on the tip of one's nose, it is not a merit which comes within hail of your own. Gladly would I, like you, good father, sing my office day by day, and especially, the office of the most Holy Virgin, to whom I have vowed a singular[14] devotion. In order to embrace the monastic life I would willingly abandon the art by which from Soissons to Beauvais I am well known in upwards of six hundred towns and villages."

The monk was touched by the juggler's simplicity, and as he was not lacking in discernment,[15] he at once recognized in Barnaby one of those men of whom it is said in the Scriptures: "Peace on earth to men of good will." And for this reason he replied—

"Friend Barnaby, come with me, and I will have you admitted into the monastery of which I am prior.[16] He who guided St. Mary of Egypt in the desert set me upon your path to lead you into the way of salvation."

It was in this manner, then, that Barnaby became a monk. In the monastery into which he was received the religious vied[17] with one another in the worship of the Blessed Virgin, and in her honor each employed all the knowledge and all the skill which God had given him.

The prior on his part wrote books dealing according to the rules of scholarship with the virtues of the Mother of God.

Brother Maurice, with a deft[18] hand copied out these treatises upon sheets of vellum.[19]

Brother Alexander adorned the leaves with delicate miniature paintings. Here were displayed the Queen of Heaven seated upon Solomon's throne, and while four lions were on guard at her feet, around the nimbus[20] which encircled her head hovered seven doves, which are the seven gifts of the Holy Spirit, the gifts, namely, of Fear, Piety, Knowledge, Strength, Counsel, Understanding, and Wisdom. For her companions she had six virgins with hair of gold, namely, Humility, Prudence, Seclusion, Submission, Virginity, and Obedience.

At her feet were two little naked figures, perfectly white, in an attitude of supplication.[21] These were souls imploring her all-powerful intercession for their soul's health, and we may be sure not imploring in vain.

Upon another page facing this, Brother Alexander represented Eve, so that the Fall and the Redemption could be perceived at one and the same time—Eve the Wife abased,[22] and Mary the Virgin exalted.

14 **singular:** exceptional; especially pious.
15 **discernment** (dĭ sûrn′mənt): insight; accurate judgment.
16 **prior:** the head of the house of a religious order.
17 **vied:** competed.

18 **deft:** skillful.
19 **vellum:** paper similar to parchment.
20 **nimbus:** halo.
21 **in . . . supplication:** praying.
22 **abased:** humbled.

Furthermore, to the marvel of the beholder, this book contained presentments[23] of the Well of Living Waters, the Fountain, the Lily, the Moon, the Sun, and the Garden enclosed of which the Song of Songs tells us, the Gate of Heaven and the City of God, and all these things were symbols of the Blessed Virgin.

Brother Marbode was likewise one of the most loving children of Mary.

He spent all his days carving images in stone, so that his beard, his eyebrows, and his hair were white with dust, and his eyes continually swollen and weeping; but his strength and cheerfulness were not diminished, although he was now well gone in years, and it was clear that the Queen of Paradise still cherished her servant in his old age. Marbode represented her seated upon a throne, her brow encircled with an orb-shaped nimbus set with pearls. And he took care that the folds of her dress should cover the feet of her, concerning whom the prophet declared: "My beloved is as a garden enclosed."

Sometimes, too, he depicted her in the semblance[24] of a child full of grace, and appearing to say, "Thou art my God, even from my mother's womb."

In the priory, moreover, were poets who composed hymns in Latin, both in prose and verse, in honor of the Blessed Virgin Mary, and amongst the company was even a brother from Picardy who sang the miracles of Our Lady in rhymed verse and in the vulgar tongue.[25]

III

Being a witness of this emulation[26] in praise and the glorious harvest of their labors, Barnaby mourned his own ignorance and simplicity.

"Alas!" he sighed, as he took his solitary walk in the little shelterless garden of the monastery, "wretched wight[27] that I am, to be unable, like my brothers, worthily to praise the Holy Mother of God, to whom I have vowed my whole heart's affection. Alas! alas! I am but a rough man and unskilled in the arts, and I can render you in service, blessed Lady, neither edifying[28] sermons, nor treatises set out in order according to rule, nor ingenious paintings, nor statues truthfully sculptured, nor verses whose march is measured to the beat of feet.[29] No gift have I, alas!"

After this fashion he groaned and gave himself up to sorrow. But one evening, when the monks were spending their hour of liberty in conversation, he heard one of them tell the tale of a religious man who could repeat nothing other than the Ave Maria. This poor man was despised for his ignorance; but after his death there issued forth from his mouth five roses in honor of the five letters of the name Mary (Marie), and thus his sanctity was made manifest.[30]

23 **presentments:** representations; suggestions.
24 **semblance:** form.

25 **vulgar tongue:** language spoken by the general public.
26 **emulation:** rivalry; competition.
27 **wight:** creature; man.
28 **edifying:** instructive; beneficial.
29 **whose . . . feet:** which have a definite rhythm.
30 **made manifest:** shown; displayed.

THE ART OF STORYTELLING

Whilst he listened to this narrative Barnaby marveled yet once again at the loving kindness of the Virgin; but the lesson of that blessed death did not avail to console him, for his heart overflowed with zeal, and he longed to advance the glory of his Lady, who is in heaven.

How to compass[31] this he sought but could find no way, and day by day he became the more cast down, when one morning he awakened filled full with joy, hastened to the chapel, and remained there alone for more than an hour. After dinner he returned to the chapel once more.

And, starting from that moment, he repaired[32] daily to the chapel at such hours as it was deserted, and spent within it a good part of the time which the other monks devoted to the liberal and mechanical arts. His sadness vanished, nor did he any longer groan.

A demeanor[33] so strange awakened the curiosity of the monks.

These began to ask one another for what purpose Brother Barnaby could be indulging so persistently in retreat.

The prior, whose duty it is to let nothing escape him in the behavior of his children in religion, resolved to keep a watch over Barnaby during his withdrawals to the chapel. One day, then, when he was shut up there after his custom, the prior, accompanied by two of the older monks, went to discover through the chinks in the door what was going on within the chapel.

They saw Barnaby before the altar of the Blessed Virgin, head downwards, with his feet in the air, and he was juggling with six balls of copper and a dozen knives. In honor of the Holy Mother of God he was performing those feats, which aforetime had won him most renown. Not recognizing that the simple fellow was thus placing at the service of the Blessed Virgin his knowledge and skill, the two old monks exclaimed against the sacrilege.[34]

The prior was aware how stainless was Barnaby's soul, but he concluded that he had been seized with madness. They were all three preparing to lead him swiftly from the chapel, when they saw the Blessed Virgin descend the steps of the altar and advance to wipe away with a fold of her azure robe the sweat which was dropping from her juggler's forehead.

Then the prior, falling upon his face upon the pavement, uttered these words—

"Blessed are the simplehearted, for they shall see God."

"Amen!" responded the old brethren, and kissed the ground.

---

31 **to compass:** to accomplish.
32 **repaired:** here, returned.
33 **demeanor:** behavior.

34 **sacrilege:** disrespect for something sacred.

Understanding Literature

1. In the first part of the story, what do you learn about Barnaby?
2. Why does the monk apply to Barnaby the phrase "Peace on earth to men of good will"?
3. How do the different monks show their devotion to the Virgin?
4. How does the story of "a religious man who could repeat nothing other than the Ave Maria" affect Barnaby?
5. What is the main idea, the theme, illustrated by this story?

Further Activities

1. Write a single sentence in which you tell what you think is Barnaby's main character trait; that is, the most distinctive feature in his character, such as evilness or silliness. Then, in a few more sentences prove what you have said by referring to incidents in the story.
2. Write a short paragraph beginning: "In some ways Barnaby is a simple man; in other ways he is not." Prove each main idea (that he is simple and that he is not) by referring to specific incidents or ideas in the story. Organize your paper by proving, in the first part of the paragraph, that he is a simple man and by proving, in the second part, that he is *not* a simple man.

Building America

You have learned about America through her history; here you will see America in literature. Through poetry, biography, essay, and story you get closer to your subject; you watch the characters act out important parts of their lives. But even more than that, the selections which follow characterize a country; they tell you much about America's traditions, beliefs, and heroes.

You will read about the courage required by Columbus to cross an unknown ocean; about some of the people who helped America win her independence; about those who explored and developed America's West; and, finally, about the major event in 19th-century American history—the Civil War. This unit is only a glimpse at the early stages of America's history, but it is a glimpse that reveals the tremendous courage and spirit that helped to make this country great.

One of the greatest acts in American history was performed by Genoa-born Christopher Columbus, discoverer of the New World. Circumstances had fortunately brought him to Portugal at a time when that country was carrying on a thriving ocean trade throughout the known world. Columbus spent his time there as a maker of maps and talking with the old seamen, and it was in Portugal that he decided that he could reach the Indies—Eastern Asia—by sailing west. Because an unknown continent lay in his way, Columbus never reached the Indies; but Americans now honor Columbus for his accidental discovery, even though he never knew the full extent of what he had done.

To understand the persistence, the knowledge, and the courage which led Columbus to make the greatest voyage of discovery ever recorded in human history, you must know something about the situation of the time. Portugal, when Columbus lived there, was a vast seafaring empire. Its ships moved out into the Atlantic to the Azores and down the coast of Africa, trading everywhere they went and returning with rich cargoes. Its people were courageous mariners and explorers as well as expert mapmakers and navigators.

The dream of many men of the time, as it was for Columbus, was to find an ocean route to the East. The lure of Eastern Asia was great. From India, China, and other countries came small caravans over land, carrying gold and precious stones, silk and cotton, spices and perfumes across Asia to Constantinople or Levantine ports, where the cargo was then loaded on ships for distribution throughout Europe. An ocean route would make many more of these rich goods available to western markets. But while the Portuguese sought to reach India by a southern route around Africa, Columbus thought he could reach the East by sailing due west of the Azores—out into the dark, turbulent North Atlantic.

Although he correctly believed that the earth was round, Columbus made several miscalculations in his planning. The Greeks had long before divided the earth's circle into 360 degrees, but how long was a degree? The answer would depend on the size of the world. Columbus calculated a degree to be far shorter than it is, and thus he greatly underestimated the size of the world. He also miscalculated how far eastward Asia stretched. He finally estimated that 2400 nautical miles would take him from the Canary Islands to Japan. Actually the distance is 10,600 miles. If America had not lain between him and his destination, he probably would never have been heard from again.

It was in April, 1492, more than ten years after he first had his idea, that Columbus persuaded Isabella, Queen of Spain, to support his voyage of discovery. He sailed in August.

This version of the voyage is by Samuel Eliot Morison, a teacher, biographer, and sailor, who in 1939-40 organized an expedition of two sailing ships to follow the route of Columbus. The selection which follows is from Mr. Morison's book *Christopher Columbus, Mariner*.

First Crossing of the Atlantic

Samuel Eliot Morison

By THE SECOND day of August, 1492, everything at last was ready. That night every man and boy of the fleet confessed his sins, received absolution and made his communion at the church of Palos, which by happy coincidence was dedicated to Saint George, patron saint of Genoa. Columbus went on board his flagship in the small hours of Friday the third and gave the signal to get under way. Before the sun rose, all three vessels had anchors aweigh, and with sails hanging limp from their yards were floating down the Rio Tinto on the morning ebb, using their long sweeps to maintain steerageway.[1] As they swung into the Saltés and passed La Rábida close aboard, they could hear the friars chanting the ancient hymn *Iam lucis orto sidere* with its haunting refrain *Et nunc et in perpetuum,* which we render "Evermore and evermore. . . ."

Columbus's plan for the voyage was simple, and its simplicity insured his success. Not for him the boisterous head winds, the monstrous seas and the dark, unbridled waters of the North Atlantic, which had already baffled so many Portuguese. He would run south before the prevailing northerlies[2] to the Canary Islands, and there make, as it were, a right-angle turn; for he had observed on his African voyages that the winter winds in the latitude of the Canaries blew from the east, and that the ocean around them, more often than not, was calm as a millpond. An even better reason to take his departure from the Canaries was their position astride latitude 28 degrees North, which, he believed, cut Japan, passing en route the mythical Isle of Antilia,[3] which would make a good break in the westward passage. Until about a hundred years ago when chronom-

2 **northerlies**: winds blowing from the north.
3 **mythical . . . Antilia**: fabled land that Europeans once believed was located in the unknown west.

1 **steerageway**: sufficient speed to steer the boat.

eters became generally available to find longitude, sailors always tried to find the latitude of their destination and then would "run their westing" (or easting) down until they hit it. That is what Columbus proposed to do with respect to Japan, which he had figured out to be only 2400 nautical miles due west of the Canaries.

The first leg of the voyage was made in less than a week. Then, within sight of the Grand Canary, the fleet ran into a calm that lasted two or three days. Columbus decided to send *Pinta* into Las Palmas for some needed repairs while *Santa María* and *Niña* went to Gomera, westernmost of the Canaries that the Spaniards had wrested from their native inhabitants. At Gomera the Captain General (as we should call Columbus on this voyage before he made Admiral) sent men ashore to fill extra water casks, buy breadstuffs and cheese, and put a supply of native beef in pickle. He then sailed to Las Palmas to superintend *Pinta's* repairs and returned with her to Gomera.

On September 2 all three ships were anchored off San Sebastián, the port of that island. Columbus then met for the first time Doña Beatriz de Bobadilla, widow of the former captain of the island. Beatriz was a beautiful lady still under thirty, and Columbus is said to have fallen in love with her; but if that is true, he did not love her warmly enough to tarry to the next full moon. Additional ship's stores were quickly hoisted on board and struck below, and on September 6, 1492, the fleet weighed anchor for the last time in the Old World. They had still another island to pass, the lofty Ferro or Hierro. Owing to calms and variables[4] Ferro and the 12,000-foot peak of Tenerife were in sight until the ninth, but by nightfall that day, every trace of land had sunk below the eastern horizon, and the three vessels were alone on an uncharted ocean. Columbus himself gave out the course: "West; nothing to the north, nothing to the south."

Before going into the details of the voyage, let us see how those vessels were navigated, and how a day was passed at sea. Celestial navigation[5] was then in its infancy, but rough estimates of latitude could be made from the height of the North Star above the horizon and its relation to the two outer stars (the "Guards") of the Little Dipper. A meridian altitude[6] of the sun, applied to available tables of the sun's declination, also gave latitude, by a simple formula. But the instruments of observation—a solid wood or brass quadrant and the seaman's astrolabe—were so crude, and the movement of a ship threw them off to such an extent, that most navigators took their latitude sights ashore. Columbus relied almost completely on "dead reckoning," which means plotting your course and position on a chart from the three elements of direction, time and distance.

The direction he had from one or more compasses which were similar to those used in small craft until recently—a circular card graduated to the 32 points (N, N by E, NNE, NE by N, NE, and so on), with a lodestone[7] under the north point, mounted on a pin and enclosed in a binnacle with gimbals[8] so it could swing freely with the motion of the ship. Columbus's standard compass was mounted on the poop deck where the officer of the watch could see it. The helmsman, who steered with a heavy tiller attached directly to the rudder head, was below decks and could see very little. He may have had another compass to steer by, but in the smaller vessels, at least, he was conned[9] by the officer of the deck and kept a steady course by the feel of the helm. On a sailing vessel you can do that; it would be impossible in any power craft.

Time on the vessels of that day was measured by a half-hour glass which hung from a beam so the sand could flow freely from the upper to the lower half. As soon as the sand was all down, a ship's boy turned the glass and the officer of the deck recorded it by making a stroke on a slate. Eight glasses made a watch; the modern ship's bells were originally a means of marking the glasses. This half-hour-glass time could be corrected daily in fair weather by noting the moment when the sun lay due south, which was local noon.

Distance was the most variable of these three elements. Columbus had no chip log or other method of measuring the speed of his vessels. He and the watch officers merely estimated it and noted it down. By carefully checking Columbus's Journal of his First Voyage, Captain J. W. McElroy ascertained[10] that he made an average 9 per cent overestimate of his distance. This did not prevent his finding the way home, because the mistake was constant, and time and course were correct. It only resulted in Columbus placing the islands of his discovery farther west than they really were.

Even after making the proper reduction for this overestimate, the speed of his vessels is surprising. Ships of that day were expected to make 3 to 5 knots[11] in a light breeze, up to 9½ in a strong, fair gale, and at times to be capable of 12 knots. In October 1492, on the outward passage, the Columbus fleet made an average of 142 miles per day for five consecutive days, and the best day's run, 182 miles, averaged 8 knots. On the homeward passage, in February 1493, *Niña* and *Pinta* covered 198 miles one day, and at times hit it up to 11 knots. Any yachtsman today would be proud to make the records that the great Admiral did on some of his transatlantic crossings in the 15th century. Improvements in sailing vessels since 1492 have been more in seaworthiness and comfort than in speed.

One reason Columbus always

---

7 **lodestone:** magnet.
8 **binnacle with gimbals:** case with a device for suspending the compass so that it will always remain level.
9 **conned:** directed.

10 **ascertained:** discovered.
11 **knots:** A knot is a measure of speed, equal to one nautical mile per hour.

wanted two or more vessels was to have someone to rescue survivors in case of sinking. But he made an unusual record for that era by never losing a ship at sea, unless we count the *Santa María,* grounded without loss of life. Comforts and conveniences were almost totally lacking. Cooking was done on deck over a bed of sand in a wooden firebox protected from the wind by a hood. The diet was a monotonous one of salt meat, hardtack and dried peas. For drink they had wine, while it lasted, and water in casks, which often went bad. Only the Captain General and the ships' captains had cabins with bunks; the others slept where they could, in their clothes. . . .

On September 9, the day he dropped the last land below the horizon, Columbus decided to keep a true reckoning of his course for his own use and a false one to give out to the people, so that they would not be frightened at sailing so far from land. But, owing to his overestimate of speed, the "false" reckoning was more nearly correct than the "true"!

During the first ten days (September 9 to 18), the easterly trade wind blew steadily, and the fleet made 1163 nautical miles westing. This was the honeymoon of the voyage. *Que era plazer grande el gusto de las mañanas* —"What a delight was the savor of the mornings!" wrote Columbus in his Journal. That entry speaks to the heart of anyone who has sailed in the trades; it recalls the beauty of the dawn, kindling clouds and sails rose color, the smell of dew drying on a wooden deck, and, something Co-

lumbus didn't have, the first cup of coffee. Since his ships were at the northern edge of the northeast trades, where the wind first strikes the water, the sea was smooth, and the air, remarked the Captain General in his Journal, was "like April in Andalusia; the only thing wanting was to hear the song of the nightingale." But there were plenty of other birds following the ships: the little Mother Carey's chickens, dabbling for plankton in the bow waves and wakes; the boatswain bird, so called (as old seamen used to say) because it carries a marlinspike in its tail; the man-of-war or frigate bird, "thou ship of the air that never furl'st thy sails," as Walt Whitman[12] wrote; and when the fleet passed beyond the range of these birds, the big Jaeger gulls gave it a call. During this period the fleet encountered its first field of sargassum or gulfweed and found that it was no hindrance to navigation. "Saw plenty weed" was an almost daily notation in the Captain General's log. The gulfweed bothered him much less than observing a westerly variation[13] of the compass, for in European waters the variation is always easterly.

On September 19, only ten days out from Ferro, the fleet temporarily ran into an area of variable winds and rain. It was near the point on Columbus's chart where the fabled island of Antilia should have been, and all hands expected to sight land.

12 **Walt Whitman:** 19th-century American poet.
13 **variation:** a reference to the compass error due to the difference between the magnetic North Pole and the true North Pole.

The Captain General even had the deep-sea lead hove,[14] and found no bottom at 200 fathoms; no wonder, since the ocean is about 2300 fathoms deep at the point he had reached. But the seamen who, on the tenth day of the northeast trades, were beginning to wonder whether they could ever beat back home were cheered by the change of wind.

During the next five days only 234 miles were made good. During this spell of moderate weather it was easy to converse from ship to ship and to talk about this or that island, St. Brendan's or Antilia, which they might pick up. In the middle of one of these colloquies,[15] a seaman of *Pinta* gave the "Land Ho!" and everyone thought he saw an island against the setting sun. Columbus fell on his knees to thank God, ordered *Gloria in excelsis Deo* to be sung by all hands, and set a course for the island. But at dawn no island was visible; there was none. It was simply a cloud bank above the western horizon resembling land, a common phenomenon at sea. Martín Alonso Pinzón apparently wished to beat about and search for this island, but Columbus refused, because, he said, "his object was to reach the Indies, and if he delayed, it would not have made sense."

The trade wind now returned, but moderately, and during the six days September 26 to October 1, the fleet made only 382 miles. Under these circumstances the people began to mutter and grumble. Three weeks was probably more than they had ever been outside sight of land before. They were all getting on each other's nerves, as happens even nowadays on a long voyage to a known destination. There was nothing for the men to do in the light wind except to follow the ship's routine, and troll for fish. Grievances, real or imaginary, were blown up; cliques[16] were formed; Spain was farther away every minute, and what lay ahead? Probably nothing, except in the eye of that cursed Genoese. Let's make him turn back, or throw him overboard!

On the first day of October the wind increased, and in five days (October 2 to 6) the fleet made 710 miles. On the sixth, when they had passed longitude 65 degrees West and actually lay directly north of Puerto Rico, Martín Alonso Pinzón shot his agile *Pinta* under the flagship's stern and shouted, "Alter course, sir, to southwest by west . . . Japan!" Columbus did not understand whether Martín Alonso meant that he thought they had missed Japan and should steer southwest by west for China, or that Japan lay in that direction; but he knew and Pinzón knew that the fleet had sailed more than 2400 miles which, according to their calculations, lay between the Canaries and Japan. Naturally Columbus was uneasy, but he held to the west course magnetic, which, owing to the variation for which he

---

14 deep-sea . . . hove: deep-sea weight thrown overboard.
15 colloquies (kŏl'ə kwĭz): conversations.

16 cliques (klēks): small exclusive groups of people.

did not allow, was about west by south, true.

On October 7, when there was another false landfall, great flocks of birds passed over the ships, flying westsouthwest; this was the autumn migration from eastern North America to the West Indies. Columbus decided that he had better follow the birds rather than his chart, and changed course accordingly that evening. That was "good joss";[17] it was his shortest course to the nearest land. Now, every night, the men were heartened by seeing against the moon (full on October 5) flocks of birds flying their way. But by the tenth, mutiny flared up again. No land for thirty-one days. Even by the phony reckoning which Columbus gave out they had sailed much farther west than anyone had expected. Enough of this nonsense, sailing west to nowhere; let the Captain General turn back or else! Columbus, says the record, "cheered them as best he could, holding out good hope of the advantages they might gain; and, he added, it was useless to complain, *since he had come to go to the Indies, and so had to continue until he found them, with Our Lord's help.*"

That was typical of Columbus's determination. Yet even he, conscious[18] of divine guidance, could not have kept on indefinitely without the support of his captains and officers. According to one account, it was Martín Alonzo Pinzón who cheered him by shouting, *Adelante! Adelante!* which

---

17 **good joss:** slang for *good luck.*

18 **conscious:** aware.

an American poet has translated, "Sail on! Sail on!" But, according to Oviedo, one of the earliest historians who talked with the participants, it was Columbus alone who persuaded the Pinzóns and La Cosa to sail on, with the promise that if land were not found within three days, he would turn back. If this version is correct, as I believe it is, the Captain General's promise to his captains was made on October 9. Next day the trade wind blew fresher, sending the fleet along at 7 knots; it so continued on the eleventh, with a heavy following sea. But signs of land, such as branches of trees with green leaves and flowers, became so frequent that the people were content with their Captain General's decision, and the mutinous mutterings died out in the keen anticipation of making a landfall in the Indies.

As the sun set under a clear horizon October 11, the northeast trade breezed up to gale force, and the three ships tore along at 9 knots. But Columbus refused to shorten sail, since his promised time was running out. He signaled everyone to keep a particularly sharp watch, and offered extra rewards for first landfall in addition to the year's pay promised by the Sovereigns. That night of destiny was clear and beautiful with a late rising moon, but the sea was the roughest of the entire passage. The men were tense and expectant, the officers testy[19] and anxious, the Captain General serene in the confidence

that presently God would reveal to him the promised Indies.

At 10 P.M., an hour before moonrise, Columbus and a seaman, almost simultaneously, thought they saw a light "like a little wax candle rising and falling." Others said they saw it too, but most did not; and after a few minutes it disappeared. Volumes have been written to explain what this light was or might have been. To a seaman it requires no explanation. It was an illusion, created by overtense watchfulness. When uncertain of your exact position, and straining to make a night landfall, you are apt to see imaginary lights and flashes and to hear nonexistent bells and breakers.

On rush the ships, pitching, rolling, throwing spray—white waves at their bows and white wakes reflecting the moon. *Pinta* is perhaps half a mile in the lead, *Santa María* on her port quarter, *Niña* on the other side. Now one, now another forges ahead, but they are all making the greatest speed of which they are capable. With the sixth glass of the night watch, the last sands are running out of an era that began with the dawn of history. A few minutes now and destiny will turn up a glass the flow of whose sands we are still watching. Not since the birth of Christ has there been a night so full of meaning for the human race.

At 2 A.M., October 12, Rodrigo de Triana, lookout on *Pinta*, sees something like a white cliff shining in the moonlight, and sings out, *Tierra! tierra!* "Land! land!" Captain Pinzón verifies the landfall, fires a gun as

19 **testy:** impatient; easily annoyed.

agreed, and shortens sail to allow the flagship to catch up. As *Santa María* approaches, the Captain General shouts across the rushing waters, "Señor Martín Alonso, you *did* find land! Five thousand maravedis for you as a bonus!"

Yes, land it was this time, a little island of the Bahamas group. The fleet was headed for the sand cliffs on its windward side and would have been wrecked had it held course. But these seamen were too expert to allow that to happen. The Captain General ordered sail to be shortened and the fleet to jog off and on until daylight, which was equivalent to a southwesterly drift clear of the island. At dawn they made full sail, passed the southern point of the island and sought an opening on the west coast, through the barrier reef.

Before noon they found it, sailed into the shallow bay now called Long or Fernandez, and anchored in the lee of the land, in five fathoms.

Here on a gleaming beach of white coral occurred the famous first landing of Columbus. The Captain General (now by general consent called Admiral) went ashore in the flagship's boat with the royal standard of Castile displayed, the two Captains Pinzón in their boats, flying the banner of the Expedition—the green crowned cross on a white field. "And, all having rendered thanks to Our Lord, kneeling on the ground, embracing it with tears of joy for the immeasurable mercy of having reached it, the Admiral rose and gave this island the name *San Salvador*"—Holy Saviour.

Understanding Literature

1. What evidence is there in this selection which shows that the author was a sailor? What specific details does Morison use to give you a sense of a real voyage?
2. What means did Columbus use to keep his ship on course?
3. How much of Columbus's success was due to knowledge, how much to courage, how much to luck?

The name Ben Franklin is one you have heard many times and in connection with many things—government, lightning rods, diplomacy, science, the Declaration of Independence, inventions. Here you will see what Ben Franklin was like as a boy.

from That Lively Man, Ben Franklin*

Jeanette Eaton

IMPROVING YOUR READING: The following selection is biographical; it is based on the facts of Franklin's life. But the author presents these facts in fictional form; that is, much of her presentation contains details that the 20th-century biographer could not possibly know. When you read any biography, you should ask: How much of it seems to be based on fact and how much of it is certainly fiction?

"Now, BEN, my boy, we'll see how well our latest *Gazette* looks in print."

Winking at the apprentice who stood ready beside the big press, the workman lifted a lever at the side. Slowly the heavy weight rose from the inked form. Snatching up the damp paper, the man gave it a glance, nodded, and handed it to the boy.

In an absent-minded way, while his quick eye roved down the page, Ben read aloud: "The *Boston Gazette*, April twenty-second, Seventeen Hundred and Nineteen."

"The print is clear enough," said the workman. "I suppose, Ben, you'll be going over the proof before your brother does, but I'll let him take a glance at it." Striding across the long room toward a desk in the corner, he called out, "Mr. Franklin, here is a first printing of the *Gazette*."

A tall young fellow in maroon coat and knickerbockers was at that moment rising from his seat to reach from its peg his three-cornered hat. He turned and said, "Give the sheet to Ben while I'm at dinner. It's two o'clock, you know."

As he crossed the room, the door opened. On the threshold stood a young man. "Mr. James Franklin," he sang out gaily, "printer for all and sundry,[1] printer of the *Boston Gazette*, 'tis time to think of broiled cod and apple cake!"

"Aye, I'm coming, my friend," replied James.

"And you, Ben Franklin!" shouted the visitor. "Are you not faring forth also?"

From his corner Ben flashed a smile full of mischief and merriment. "Nay, sir, I spread a feast right here!"

1 all and sundry: everyone.

* From THAT LIVELY MAN, BEN FRANKLIN by Jeanette Eaton, copyright 1948 by William Morrow and Company, Inc., by permission of William Morrow and Company, Inc.

JEANETTE EATON   187

James turned to say in a harsh tone, "Don't forget, young jackanapes, I'll feast on you if you make mistakes in this proof!"

As the door closed on the two men, the chief workman, slipping off his leather apron and into his jacket, stared curiously at the apprentice. Ben had seated himself at a table by the rear window. Before him was a pitcher of milk and a cup and he was unwrapping a small package.

"Ben," said the workman, "you tell me you save part of the board money your brother pays out by dining on milk and a penny bun. What I'd like to know is what you do with your savings."

With a proud grin the boy answered, "I buy books."

"Books!" exclaimed the other. "Why, hardly a day goes by but what some bookseller's apprentice loans you by stealth one of his master's new books from London. And one of your brother's customers lets you read books from his library. What more do you want?"

"I like to have books I need not give back so fast. Look at this one!" Eagerly Ben spread out on the table a big brown volume. "Here is bound together a full year of that London newspaper, the *Spectator*. And a wittier paper was never printed. I should like to set type for such pieces as those London wits wrote, instead of this dull *Boston Gazette*."

"Hmm!" said the workman, going to the door. "Your brother is lucky to get the contract to print the *Gazette*. It brings him in a pretty penny."

Left alone, Ben munched his roll and reflected. He had been apprenticed to his brother for almost two years. Already he could set type better and faster than the journeyman printer. Moreover, he was learning to read proof, although he still made mistakes for which James cuffed him soundly. Certainly he liked this trade better than any of the others his father had urged upon him. As for the time he was apprenticed in his father's soap and candle shop—ugh, how he had hated it! The smell of boiling fat in which Josiah Franklin lived all day, to earn a good living for his large family, was revolting to his youngest son. What Ben had wanted was to go to sea. His father would not consent to that, but had agreed to let the boy change his trade and learn to be a printer.

"If only it didn't take so long to become a journeyman and earn wages!" thought Ben, as he drained his last sip of milk. "Nine years in all! Not till I'm twenty-one. That's seven long years from now."

He got up, crossed the room, and stared out through the small panes of thick glass in the front window. Passers-by on the roughly paved street were bending almost double to make headway against the cold April wind from Boston Harbor. Capes and neck scarves blew out like sails. Ben's eyes widened as he caught sight of Dr. Cotton Mather, famous preacher and member of the Assembly's Council which ruled Boston and the Massachusetts Colony. Even this stern man, who held himself so high, was buffeted[2] by the disrespectful wind.

Just then a clock on the wall of the shop chimed the quarter hour. With a start Ben strode back to his table. "I mustn't be late for school!" he thought, smiling to himself.

In another moment his quill was busily scratching away. He was trying to write an article which would be as gay and witty as those he read in the *Spectator*.

The single pupil in the Benjamin Franklin school had to work hard to please his master. Although Ben had read books ever since he could remember, he had had only a few years in the free schools and but one in the Grammar School, where he had failed in arithmetic. Now he was writing, reading, and studying with might and main to make up for lost time. Often he read far into the night.

Luckily he was strong and healthy enough to stand long hours of work. Somehow he always found time for fun. With special friends he took long walks, exploring the country for miles around the small town of Boston. What he loved best was swimming.

That year in May there was a holiday. Ben spent almost the whole afternoon in the water. When he reached home, it was nearly supper-time. He found his father and his favorite sister, little Jane, in the front bedroom, which also served as a kind of parlor.

"Mercy, Ben!" cried Jane, springing up with a swirl of the long skirts which even small girls wore in those days. "I feared you might be drowned!"

"Not I!" He laughed and looked quickly for the affectionate smile his father always turned upon his favorite son.

"Father," he said eagerly, "I tried a pretty experiment today. I made the wind draw me across the pond."

Encouraged by his listeners, the boy went on to describe his game. First he flew high in the air a big kite he had made and tied to a stout stick. Then he flung himself into the water on his back, holding the stick in both hands behind his head. Slowly the kite had pulled him across the pond to the other shore. "It was very agreeable indeed!" he wound up.

Laughing, Josiah said, "It is good to try new things, my son. Keep on using your head to judge what your eyes see. That is the way to learn."

Ben's father sometimes gave him useful criticism on writing. But Josiah had no idea of the boy's other efforts at self-education. He was trying to gain self-control in every way. He gave up eating meat to prove that he was not a slave to any sort of diet. He stopped arguing with his friends, as he so loved to do, and learned to listen to their opinions in silence, whether or not he agreed with them. His most difficult tests of self-control were caused by his brother's impatience and hot temper in the printing shop.

Late in the year 1720 an exciting change took place in the Franklin

2 **buffeted:** struck.

printing business. James lost his contract to print the *Boston Gazette*. After he had raged and worried for a bit, he decided to publish a paper of his own to be called the *Courant*. Its purpose was to discuss news and local events in a lively way. Several of his friends promised to write for the paper under assumed names.

No one was more thrilled about this venture than Ben. But when he brought his father the first issue of the *Courant*, he did so with a long face. After supper Josiah spread out the paper on the kitchen table, trimmed the candles, and began to read. Jane knelt on the wooden settle to look over his shoulder.

" 'Tis a noble-looking newspaper," she exclaimed. But when she turned to her brother, she cried out, "What ails you, Ben, that you look displeased? I thought you were happy over the *Courant!*"

"I do not hold with James in attacking those brave men who try inoculation against smallpox," he explained. "Too many people are dying of it. Why cast ridicule upon[3] an experiment which may succeed?"

Josiah put down the paper and stared at him. "Why, my son, all Boston cries out against this folly! I can hardly believe that a learned man like Dr. Mather should undertake inoculation. James pokes rare fun at him in this first issue."

"And in doing so," replied Ben with heat, "James joins the ignorant folk who fear a new idea. I believe inoculation will prove to be a good defense against this dread disease."

Opinion in Boston, however, was strongly against vaccination. The *Courant* was sold from one end of the town to the other. James was triumphant. When Ben protested against his publishing another attack in the next issue, James whacked him soundly and called him a saucy fellow. The brothers hardly spoke to one another until the *Courant* dropped the subject and turned to lighter themes.

From then on Ben delighted in the newspaper. For a year he studied carefully the gay little pieces written by James and his friends. He compared them with the *Spectator* and often thought the *Courant* might improve in wit.

Alone in the shop one afternoon, Benjamin sat reading a fresh proof of the paper. He was nibbling a large red apple as he slowly went over the contributions. Every now and then he gave a sniff which meant, "I could have put this matter better myself!" Suddenly his eyes with their heavy lids opened wide. In the silence of the empty room he whispered, "Why don't I try?"

That night and the next the candle in Ben's tiny room under the roof burned late. He was scribbling, tearing up what he had written, and beginning again. A few days later the apprentice was setting copy for the next issue of the newspaper. It was nine o'clock on a March morning. Now and then the boy turned an intent glance toward the far corner of the shop.

3 cast ridicule upon: laugh at.

At the editor's desk, James and one of the men who wrote for the *Courant* were poring over a number of closely written pages. Both men were nodding and smiling. It was plain that they were pleased with what they read. At last James strode across the room and tossed the papers to the typesetter.

"Here, Ben, set up this letter. Someone thrust it under our door last night. We want to use it in the paper at once."

Benjamin nodded and bent over the type form. Not for worlds would he have shown his delight and excitement. The letter, signed by the name Silence Dogood, was the very one he had sat up two nights to compose. It was he who had dashed down the street after supper to slip his carefully copied letter under the door of the shop. All night he had tossed and turned, wondering what James would think of it. And now his brother liked it, accepted it! The boy could hardly wait to set it up. In the issue of April 2nd, 1722, Benjamin Franklin, aged sixteen, first saw his own writing in print.

According to her maker, Silence was a respectable widow with three children. She had "a natural inclination to observe and reprove the faults of others," and intended to make good use of this talent. Describing her life in detail, the widow declared that every fortnight she was going to contribute to the readers of the *Courant* a letter which she hoped would "add somewhat to their entertainment."

Since James had accepted the first letter, thought Ben, he must be willing for the writer to keep the promise to contribute regularly. His heart thumped with the wonder of it. Now he could use his study of the *Spectator* and his practice in composition. Now all the odd and funny things he had noted so often in his walks about the town could be set down in print.

In no time at all Silence Dogood became for him almost as real as himself. She was, like the grandsons and granddaughters of the Puritans in Boston, ready to judge the wrongdoer. But she also possessed Ben Franklin's mischievous humor. Since she admitted to being a great reader, Mrs. Dogood felt free to use words and expressions worthy of a scholar.

Ben enjoyed devoting one letter to the behavior of the students at Harvard College. Silence thought too many of them, after causing their parents much trouble and expense, returned home "as great blockheads as ever, only more proud and self-conceited."

Benjamin himself tried writing ballads. Now he had Mrs. Dogood write a piece making fun of New England poetry, and his remarks were quoted by all the bookish young men of Boston. In another letter he joked gently about the bold young women who walked on Boston Common late in the evening. Men who drank too much and pretended they were sober gave Ben another chance for delightful humor. With every letter his wit and his writing improved. James looked eagerly for the contributions and published every one. The Dogood letters, indeed, became the talk of the town.

One Sunday, coming out of North Church where he had heard Cotton Mather preach, Ben was caught up in a group of gentlemen and ladies who had paused to exchange greetings. He listened with amazement to their conversation.

"Do you imagine," one fashionable lady said laughingly, "that Dr. Mather read Silence Dogood's letter about the people who only pretend to be religious? That was a pretty bit of humor."

"Who might Mrs. Dogood be, think you?" asked one of the men.

"Who indeed!" sniffed another lady, in a voice matching her prim gray woolen gown. "She writes with too bold a pen for me!"

Slowly moving on his way, Ben shook with silent glee. What would those people have said had they known that Mrs. Dogood was right there in their midst, disguised as a youth in his best Sunday suit and buckled shoes?

There were plenty of blithe spirits in Boston to enjoy the fun which Ben created. But the men in power were a sober lot. Once the Colony had been governed by leaders of the Puritan Church. But under a new charter granted in 1692, voting depended not on religion but on property. The Massachusetts legislature was elected by people who owned a certain amount of money or land. The Governor was appointed by the English King and the Council was also chosen by the English Government. The Councilors were men of education and wealth. In the early part of the 18th century they still carried on the narrow tradition of the old Puritans. They scorned and feared any effort on the part of the people to question their authority.

No wonder, therefore, that the Council kept watching this upstart newspaper called the *Courant*. Had it not held up to public laughter one of the most famous Councilors, Dr. Mather? One day an officer of the law came to the printing shop and commanded James Franklin, on order of the Council, to come at once to the Town House for questioning.

Ink-stained Benjamin rushed anxiously to the door to watch them go. He heard his brother ask in a haughty tone, "What might this inquiry be about?" Some words from the constable floated back. Ben guessed that a recent article in the newspaper showed contempt for the government. Before the day was over, news came to the shop that James had been clapped into jail.

Naturally the Franklin family was horrified. But Benjamin at once began to have a glorious time. For a whole week he was in sole charge of the paper. He hardly took time to eat or sleep. Of course Silence Dogood kept him company and composed a long article for the next issue.

"Without freedom of thought," wrote Silence, "there can be no such thing as wisdom; and no such thing as public liberty without freedom of speech."

When James came out of jail, he spoke highly of the article. "Mrs.

Dogood could not have written anything that better fitted my case," said he. His friends were pleased to find the printer in such a lighthearted mood. He sat down and wrote an amusing account of his stay in jail. For once, he was even amiable[4] to his apprentice.

Then came a morning when James reached the shop half an hour earlier than usual. He found Benjamin at a table scribbling away like fury. In two strides the printer was beside his brother.

"Why aren't you setting type?" he shouted. "What are you scrivening here?" Ben's guilty look of being caught red-handed made James snatch the paper from him. For a moment James read in silence. Then his jaw dropped. He swayed back on his heels.

"No!" he cried. "It isn't possible! What? *You!* You are Silence Dogood! You are the shrewd widow with three children!"

Benjamin looked up without speaking. His brother's face wore an expression stranger than mere anger. Jealousy was written large upon it. That a seventeen-year-old could write well enough to fool him, fool the whole town, well, it was too much to bear! James glared and slapped the paper down.

"But you have always liked these letters!" shouted Ben furiously.

A bitter argument followed. Ben was called a saucy deceiver. In turn, he called his brother a stupid tyrant. The quarrel ended in the

4 **amiable:** friendly; kindhearted.

usual way. James snatched up a ruler, took the apprentice by the collar, and gave him blow after blow.

Nevertheless, only a few months passed before James desperately needed his young brother's help. Again James wrote something offensive to the Council. This time he was forbidden to print the *Courant* or any other newspaper. To get around the grim sentence, James and his supporters decided to publish the paper under the name of Benjamin Franklin.

At first, the boy was pleased. But soon he found that it was only his name that was wanted. James scolded, commanded, and boxed the ears of the so-called publisher as if he were a stupid drudge. Day by day Ben's rebellion seethed more fiercely.

One afternoon his resentment boiled over. Flinging off his apron, he faced his brother. "James, I can no longer do with your ways. You are neither amiable nor just. I'll not stay another day to be kicked and cuffed for small reason."

"What?" James sprang from his chair in furious surprise. "You dare not break your contract! You're bound to me for four more years!"

"It matters not. I'll find work as journeyman printer at some shop. I'm skilled enough. I can bear it here no longer."

Through clenched teeth James said, "The greater fool you! You will not get one day of printing work in Boston."

It was no empty threat. James told every other master printer in the town about his faithless apprentice. No one would employ a boy who had dared break his contract. Even Josiah Franklin shook his head and told his son he had made a grave mistake. Slowly it grew clear to the rebel that there really was no chance for him in any Boston printing shop.

After many anxious days and sleepless nights, Benjamin made up his mind to run away. It seemed the only thing to do. With the help of a friend he got passage on a ship bound for New York. By selling most of his precious books, bought with such difficulty, he gathered together a little money. One evening he managed to take on board the ship his chest packed with his Sunday suit, clean shirts, stockings, and underwear. Early next morning, before anyone was awake, he tiptoed down the stairs. In the big empty kitchen he silently said good-by to his home.

Two hours later he was standing on deck as the vessel edged away from Woodman's Wharf. He could see the church spires of Boston rising above the clustered houses, the green of the Common, the sober bulk of Town House and the jail. Resentfully the youth stared at the scene.

Narrow-minded Councilmen, jealous James, skimpy living, faces that frowned on dancing and other simple joys—how glad he was to escape them all! He was not afraid to make his way by himself. Hadn't he a trade? Of course, he would miss his kind and loving parents and his sister Jane. But excitement was crowding out every other feeling. He was off to see the world!

Clutching his hat as the salt breeze swept the ship, young Franklin turned his face to the sea.

Understanding Literature

1. Reread the note at the beginning of the story. What information does the author give which she could not really know about Franklin?
2. What is the conflict or problem in this selection?
3. Cite lines which help the reader to understand what kind of person Ben was. You will notice that many of the lines which tell you something of Ben's character are not purely description. What Ben said himself, what others said about him, and the way he reacted to certain problems are all sources of information about Ben's character.

Focusing on Words

Probably there are no words in the selection from *That Lively Man, Ben Franklin* which were so new to you or so difficult that they hindered your understanding of the story. The author uses several words, however, that you will want to know more about. These are also words that aid the reader in realizing the time in which the story takes place. Define the italicized words in the following sentences:

1. "A tall young fellow in maroon coat and *knickerbockers* was at that moment rising from his seat. . . ."
2. The chief workman "stared curiously at the *apprentice*."
3. "Already he could set type better and faster than the *journeyman* printer."
4. "Jane knelt on the wooden *settle* to look over his shoulder."
5. "'Why aren't you setting type?' he shouted. 'What are you *scrivening* here?'"

Further Activities

1. Using the histories, biographies, and magazine articles in your school and town libraries, prepare a written report on Franklin and his many inventions. In the first paragraph describe briefly all his different inventions. In the second and third paragraphs describe his work on one particular invention and the use now made of this invention.
2. Use the resources of your libraries to prepare a report on Franklin's important work in the formation of the United States government.

JEANETTE EATON

Like most people, you probably think of George Washington as "the Father of his Country." In this poem you will see him as a hunter and messenger on his way to deliver a message to the French.

Young Washington

The Embassy to the French Forts, 1753
Arthur Guiterman

Tie the moccasin, bind the pack,
   Sling your rifle across your back,
Up! and follow the mountain track,
   Tread the Indian Trail.
North and west is the road we fare   5
Toward the forts of the Frenchmen, where
"Peace or War!" is the word we bear,
   Life and Death in the scale.

The leaves of October are dry on the ground,
The sheaves of Virginia are gathered and bound,   10
Her fallows are glad with the cry of the hound,
   The partridges whirr in the fern;
But deep are the forests and keen are the foes
Where Monongahela in wilderness flows;
We've labors and perils and torrents and snows   15
   To conquer before we return.

Hall and council room, farm and chase,
Coat of scarlet and frill of lace
All are excellent things in place;
   Joy in these if ye can.   20
Mine be hunting shirt, knife and gun,
Camp aglow on the sheltered run,
Friend and foe in the checkered sun;
   That's the life for a man!

Understanding Literature

1. Where is Washington going? When, why, and how is he traveling?

2. What does the second stanza add to the setting? What are the possible dangers of the trip?
3. Arthur Guiterman uses comparison and contrast in the last stanza to give his readers a better understanding of the life Washington really enjoyed as a young man. What is the comparison that is made?
4. What is the main idea within each of the three stanzas?

In the period of history in which America was fighting to win her independence from England, Paul Revere was a leading citizen of Boston. Although well-known for his skill as a silversmith, he is probably remembered far more because of his exciting midnight ride described by Longfellow.

Paul Revere's Ride

Henry Wadsworth Longfellow

IMPROVING YOUR READING: "Paul Revere's Ride" is different from many other poems in that each verse does not have the same number of lines. Some of the verses are very short, and others are quite long. The rhyme scheme, too, does not follow a set pattern, although many of the lines do rhyme with each other. The rhythm, or beat, of the poem makes it very enjoyable to hear read aloud.

Listen, my children, and you shall hear
Of the midnight ride of Paul Revere,
On the eighteenth of April, in Seventy-five;
Hardly a man is now alive
Who remembers that famous day and year.   5

He said to his friend, "If the British march
By land or sea from the town tonight,
Hang a lantern aloft in the belfry arch
Of the North Church tower as a signal light—
One, if by land, and two, if by sea;   10
And I on the opposite shore will be,
Ready to ride and spread the alarm
Through every Middlesex village and farm,
For the country folk to be up and to arm."

Then he said, "Good night!" and with muffled oar   15
Silently rowed to the Charlestown shore,
Just as the moon rose over the bay,
Where swinging wide at her moorings lay
The *Somerset*, British man-of-war;
A phantom[1] ship, with each mast and spar   20
Across the moon like a prison bar,
And a huge black hulk, that was magnified
By its own reflection in the tide.

Meanwhile, his friend, through alley and street,
Wanders and watches with eager ears,   25
Till in the silence around him he hears
The muster of men at the barrack door,
The sound of arms, and the tramp of feet,
And the measured tread of the grenadiers,
Marching down to their boats on the shore.   30

Then he climbed the tower of the Old North Church,
By the wooden stairs, with stealthy tread,
To the belfry chamber overhead,
And startled the pigeons from their perch
On the somber rafters, that round him made   35
Masses and moving shapes of shade—
By the trembling ladder, steep and tall,
To the highest window in the wall,
Where he paused to listen and look down
A moment on the roofs of the town,   40
And the moonlight flowing over all.

Beneath, in the churchyard, lay the dead,
In their night encampment on the hill,
Wrapped in silence so deep and still
That he could hear, like a sentinel's tread,   45
The watchful night wind, as it went
Creeping along from tent to tent,
And seeming to whisper, "All is well!"
A moment only he feels the spell
Of the place and the hour, and the secret dread   50

1 **phantom:** ghostlike.

Of the lonely belfry and the dead;
For suddenly all his thoughts are bent
On a shadowy something far away,
Where the river widens to meet the bay—
A line of black that bends and floats   55
On the rising tide, like a bridge of boats.

Meanwhile, impatient to mount and ride,
Booted and spurred, with a heavy stride
On the opposite shore walked Paul Revere.
Now he patted his horse's side,   60
Now gazed at the landscape far and near,
Then, impetuous, stamped the earth,
And turned and tightened his saddle girth;
But mostly he watched with eager search
The belfry tower of the Old North Church,   65
As it rose above the graves on the hill,
Lonely and spectral² and somber and still.
And lo! as he looks, on the belfry's height
A glimmer, and then a gleam of light!
He springs to the saddle, the bridle he turns,   70
But lingers and gazes, till full on his sight
A second lamp in the belfry burns!

A hurry of hoofs in a village street,
A shape in the moonlight, a bulk in the dark,
And beneath, from the pebbles, in passing, a spark   75
Struck out by a steed flying fearless and fleet:
That was all!   And yet, through the gloom and the light,
The fate of a nation was riding that night;
And the spark struck out by that steed, in his flight,
Kindled the land into flame with its heat.   80
He has left the village and mounted the steep,
And beneath him, tranquil and broad and deep,
Is the Mystic, meeting the ocean tides;
And under the alders that skirt its edge,
Now soft on the sand, now loud on the ledge,   85
Is heard the tramp of his steed as he rides.

2 **spectral:** ghostly.

HENRY WADSWORTH LONGFELLOW   **199**

It was twelve by the village clock,
When he crossed the bridge into Medford town.
He heard the crowing of the cock,
And the barking of the farmer's dog,   90
And felt the damp of the river fog,
That rises after the sun goes down.

It was one by the village clock,
When he galloped into Lexington.
He saw the gilded weathercock   95
Swim in the moonlight as he passed,
And the meetinghouse windows, blank and bare,
Gaze at him with a spectral glare,
As if they already stood aghast
At the bloody work they would look upon.   100

It was two by the village clock,
When he came to the bridge in Concord town.
He heard the bleating of the flock,
And the twitter of birds among the trees,
And felt the breath of the morning breeze   105
Blowing over the meadows brown.
And one was safe and asleep in his bed
Who at the bridge would be first to fall,
Who that day would be lying dead,
Pierced by a British musket ball.   110

You know the rest. In the books you have read,
How the British Regulars fired and fled—
How the farmers gave them ball for ball,
From behind each fence and farmyard wall,
Chasing the redcoats down the lane,   115
Then crossing the fields to emerge again
Under the trees at the turn of the road,
And only pausing to fire and load.

So through the night rode Paul Revere;
And so through the night went his cry of alarm   120
To every Middlesex village and farm—
A cry of defiance and not of fear,
A voice in the darkness, a knock at the door,
And a word that shall echo forevermore!
For, borne on the nightwind of the Past,   125

Through all our history, to the last,
In the hour of darkness and peril and need,
The people will waken and listen to hear
The hurrying hoofbeats of that steed,
And the midnight message of Paul Revere.   130

Understanding Literature

1. Read the lines which give the setting (time and place) for the action of this poem.
2. What was the purpose of the signal Paul Revere was awaiting?
3. Point out the lines in the poem which tell the reader of action that was set in motion by Paul Revere's ride.
4. Observe the rhythm of the poem, especially in lines 73-80. What effect is the poet trying to create with these lines?
5. Notice the construction of this poem. What part of the poem serves as the introduction? At what point does the climax occur? How is the suspense built up? How much of the poem would you think of as the conclusion?

Others have deserted from General Washington's army at Valley Forge. Neil is cold, hungry, and weary, and his home is but two miles away from the location of his assigned mission. Christopher, Neil's companion, is afraid Neil will not be able to resist the temptation to desert.

Patrol at Valley Forge

Russell Gordon Carter

IMPROVING YOUR READING: This story has a double plot; it has two *conflicts*, or problems, to be resolved. Identify these problems as you read, and be ready to discuss how the two plots are interwoven.

SILHOUETTED AGAINST the twilight of a winter morning early in the year 1778—bleak and bitterly cold like so many other mornings at Valley Forge during that tragic period of the Revolution—the tall sergeant filled the small doorway of the log hut as he shouted, "Private Williams an' Private Fenwood, report at once for patrol duty to Corporal Purvis at the Star Redoubt!"

As the door banged shut and his footsteps squeaked in the dry snow, Christopher Williams blinked and yawned and, still clutching his tattered blanket round him, pushed himself slowly erect, teeth chattering, slim body shivering. To his surprise, Neil Fenwood, his close companion of the past month, was already on his feet and asking for shoes. "Shoes," Neil called in a disgruntled sleep-heavy voice, "I can't go on patrol 'thout shoes!"

One of the men huddled close to the nine others on the bare ground mumbled, "Ye can wear mine." And another, lifting his head, added, "An' Christ'pher can wear mine."

"Also a jacket," Neil said. "Who'll let me borry his jacket?"

"Here, take this thing o' mine," someone grunted, and Neil bent forward.

"Christ'pher's welcome to this ragged greatcoat I have on," another voice added, but Christopher said, "Nay, I'll wear my blanket." And squeezing his head through a hole near the middle, he let the folds fall about him.

As the two Continentals,[1] both Pennsylvanians under General Wayne's command, picked up their muskets and left the hut, Christopher wondered if ever a morning had been colder or more forlorn—even at Valley Forge. The stars in the graying sky were still blue-bright and glittering,

[1] Continentals: members of the Continental army during the American Revolution.

dancing beyond the wisps of wood smoke rising from the wooden chimneys of the crudely built huts that housed Washington's half-starved and depleted[2] army—one-third the number of the British under Lord Howe living in luxury at Philadelphia, a score of miles to the southeast, and supported by British ships-of-war lying in the Delaware.

While ice particles cracked and tinkled under the feet of the two soldiers, and silent sentries wrapped in old rugs and blankets, and with legs encased in straw, stared at them with tired eyes, it seemed to Christopher that never again would he feel the warmth of summer. . . . But there was something that troubled him even more than the terrific cold, and he didn't know what to do about it.

At the Star Redoubt, to the east of Fort Washington, which crowned the summit of Mount Joy, Corporal Jacob Purvis was waiting with musket hugged against his gaunt body. He was much older than the two others and had seen service at Bunker Hill and also at Saratoga where, in October of the preceding year, the British general, Burgoyne, had surrendered with his whole army in a rare American victory.

"We have a hazardous mission," Purvis explained. " 'Tis reported there's a hogshead[3] o' shoes lying somewhere off the Old Lime Road— shoes for this army, abandoned by teamsters, 'tis said, who lacked the courage to make the full trip from York State. Mebbe the report is false like so many others, but General Washington feels 'tis worth a scouting party, as ye might say. So we three are to enter enemy territory and have a look."

"Old Lime is close to the Old York Road, eh, is it not?" Neil asked quickly—a little too quickly, Christopher thought, and glancing sidewise, he was almost certain what was in his companion's mind. More than once during recent weeks, when reports of increasing desertions had reached the hut, Neil had listened with a strange look in his eyes—so strange that several of the others had remarked upon it.

"Aye," Purvis agreed, "Old Lime lies close to Old York, an' Old York leads direct to Coryell's Ferry."

Neil cleared his throat and then was silent—and again the look was in his eyes.

As the patrol set off toward Matson's Ford across the Schuylkill, which bounded the encampment on the north, through the mind of Christopher ran the thought: "Neil has at last decided to desert! It wasn't like him to respond so readily to the sergeant's call. For some time he has been thinking of deserting, of that I am certain! And now—Coryell's Ferry and Neil's home only two miles distant on the near shore! 'Twill be easy for him to slip away from us. I wonder, ought I to speak to the corporal about it? Maybe somebody could help him."

It was a hard question. Even when the three were across the Schuylkill and beyond the Ridge Road running

<hr />

2 depleted: reduced; decreased in number.
3 hogshead: large cask.

northwest from Philadelphia to Potts Grove, Christopher was not sure what he ought to do. He liked Neil, and he knew his companion liked him, but Neil was younger by a year and a half—not yet eighteen—and at Valley Forge he had evidently seen more than was good for him. Burials, for example, day after day; three of them yesterday and five the day before. Also men ill and dying of disease and malnutrition. And then, only last week, Neil's own cousin, Private Denis Jepson, going to the hospital and having a foot amputated because of frostbite. In addition, there were the daily hardships everyone suffered: the lack of warm clothing and the scarcity and monotony of the food: no vegetables and almost no. meat, but in their place "fire cake and water"—dough paste baked in the embers and water to wash it down—along with other inadequate fare. All this because of an inefficient Quartermaster Department[4] and a Congress that had listened to men jealous of the Commander-in-Chief and felt it knew better than Washington and his generals how to wage war against the British professional soldiers.

A low word of warning from Purvis broke in upon Christopher's thoughts as the patrol was emerging from a patch of woods above Wissahickon Creek. The next instant a spurt of gold leaped against the snow across the stream, and while the valley re-echoed to the crash of a musket, the corporal spun sidewise and crumpled to the ground, a hand clutching his shoulder where crimson formed a widening stain.

"A foul plague upon it!" Purvis muttered while Christopher and Neil dragged him to a sheltered spot. "I spied the lobsterback[5] e'en whilst he was aiming his piece!" And he closed his eyes and gritted his teeth.

Kneeling beside him after they had stopped the flow of blood and bound the wound, Christopher said, "You will have to go back. Think you, you can walk?"

The corporal struggled to his feet, protesting that he didn't want to go back. Again and again he called down a foul plague upon his misfortune. Then at last, with a hand clutching a sapling, he said to Christopher, "Ah, you are right, I shall have to go back!"

"One of us will go with you," Christopher said, and looked straight at Neil.

"Nay, I can walk alone!" Purvis protested. "You two must fulfill the mission. Aye, those are my orders to you: fulfill the mission! You, Christopher Williams, are in command. And now harken and I will tell you more about the spot where 'tis said the treacherous teamsters jettisoned[6] the hogshead. Just off Old Lime, somewhere not far north o' Whitemarsh, there is a ravine with twin pines marking the opening and tow-

---

4 **Quartermaster Department:** department which provides clothing, shelter, and food for troops.

5 **lobsterback:** British soldier, so-called because of his red uniform.
6 **jettisoned:** abandoned; left behind.

ering above all other trees—" And on the palm of a trembling hand he traced an imaginary map while he gave further details.

Screened by heavy low growth, the two younger scouts stood silent as the corporal, still berating[7] his ill fortune, made his way slowly westward. When at last he was out of sight, Christopher said quietly, "We shall carry out orders and return with our report, whether favorable or unfavorable. Are you ready?"

Neil lifted somber blue eyes and glanced at the low gray sky, then with a shudder stared at the dark blood splotches in the snow where the corporal had lain. That was his only answer, and again Christopher wondered what he ought to do. Supposing he were to speak bluntly; he asked himself, could he convince his companion that desertion—even though many had already deserted from Valley Forge—was an ignoble act? He was not sure, so once more he kept the words back.

Turning, he led the way northward, taking advantage of all possible cover.

Snow was falling in slow lazy flakes when they crossed the ice-bound Wissahickon and set off up the wooded eastern slope. The Old Lime Road now was only a short distance ahead, and thanks to the corporal's directions and description, Christopher was confident of finding the ravine. It was the other thing that continued to trouble him. Somehow, even though he might have to use force, he said to himself that Neil must remain loyal!

They were deep in enemy country now, but thus far they had encountered no one except the British picket who had wounded the corporal. Halting at last on the shoulder of a low hill and taking a bite from a hard mass of dough he had tied in a corner of the blanket, Christopher motioned with his musket and said: "There below us, Neil, is the Old Lime Road, albeit 'tis hidden by thick growth—and yonder to the north I see twin pines!"

Neil nodded. "Aye," he agreed in a dull voice, "and maybe there's a ravine there, and maybe there's none— and if there be a ravine, perhaps it holds a hogshead o' shoes and perhaps it holds naught. So far as it concerns me, I can say with truth it matters little!"

Christopher's fingers tightened on his musket, but when he spoke, it was in a tone that gave no hint of his deep emotion. "At any rate, we shall do our duty," he said and, with musket quartered across his chest, set off obliquely[8] down the hillside.

A high tangle of snow-bent alders and berry bushes bordered a sharp turn almost a quarter of a mile below the twin pines, and it was there that the two scouts emerged upon the road. Christopher had snarled his blanket on a bush and was in the act

---

7 **berating:** scolding.   8 **obliquely** (ə blēk′lĭ): indirectly.

RUSSELL GORDON CARTER

205

of freeing it when, to his surprise, he heard the nearby creak of wheels. As he whirled sidewise, a heavy voice boomed upon the winter air: "Stand firm, both o' ye, and drop yer pieces!"

Then with dark eyes wide and mouth open, he was looking at a startling sight. Just at the turn stood a white horse harnessed to a light carriage with two low wheels, and beneath the folding top sat two British officers, one of them holding the reins and the other, with arm extended, aiming a pistol!

"Quick, drop yer pieces an' raise yer hands!"

Neil had already dropped his musket; now Christopher let his own slide reluctantly to the snow and slowly lifted his hands.

Slipping out of the carriage, the officer with the pistol advanced and, gathering up the weapons, tossed them into the bushes. Then with a glance toward his companion, who also had climbed out and was now at the horse's head, he suddenly laughed in a way that deepened the color in his round red mottled[9] face.

"Egad, Lieutenant!" he exclaimed. "This be comic! Remember what we talked of at mess this morning? The Third Rule o' War! Aye, the Third Rule as listed amongst the six the rebel Washington has seen fit to draw up for the benefit of better soldiers than himself. Well, here now before us is a apt picture to illustrate it: two ragged wretches who will accompany us back to Philadelphia after a very pleasant afternoon ride in our calash!"[10]

While Christopher stood with teeth clenched, and Neil motionless behind him, the British officers laughed heartily, as if never had there been greater cause for merriment. Finally the one at the horse's head said to the prisoners, "Knew ye, your rebel general had drawn up six rules o' war?"

"We have heard talk of General Washington's views on warfare," Christopher replied curtly while his gaze roved this way and that, hopefully seeking a possible means of escape.

"And know ye the Third Rule?" the florid-faced officer inquired.

Christopher shook his head. "Nay," he replied and gauged the distance between himself and the man . . . a dozen feet . . . perhaps only ten. . . . Cautiously he lowered his hands a little . . .

The officer flourished his pistol and laughed again. Then he said with mock solemnity, "Give ear now and I will quote it, the Third Rule o' War: 'The first qualification of a soldier is fortitude under fatigue and privation: courage is only the second. Hardship, poverty and actual want are the soldier's best school.' There, egad! And the two of you, one in a tattered blanket and t'other in a ragged jacket, and broken shoes upon your feet—aye, the two o' ye are pupils right out of Washington's best school—Valley Forge!" And he and

---

9 mottled: spotted.

10 calash: carriage.

his companion roared with laughter, their heads thrown back, their well-nourished bodies shaking.

But this time the laughter ended with harsh abruptness as Christopher hurled himself forward. It was a desperate chance, and he knew it—but the unexpected lunge in the midst of British hilarity caught the florid-faced officer off guard, and the pistol exploded harmlessly. Then Christopher and the man went down together, grunting, gasping, fists pounding, hands seeking a firm hold upon throats . . . while the wind caught the fluffed-up snow from their struggle and sent it flying.

Other sounds of struggle, along with the creak and clatter of wheels, trembled upon the quiet air, but for Christopher they were remote and meaningless as, with head smothered beneath the broad chest of his adversary,[11] he gasped for breath and clutched desperately at the collar of the officer's greatcoat. Long weeks of living mainly on fire cake and water had taken their toll of his strength. Nevertheless, somehow he managed at last to struggle out from under and then to jolt his enemy's chin with a short upward blow of his fist.

He was about to deliver another blow when a lean hand seized the Britisher and jerked him sidewise while a familiar voice shouted, "Surrender, or you'll get a ball from your brother officer's own pistol!" And there, snow-dusted and with a splotch of blood on his face, stood Neil!

"Surrender!" he repeated, and as he thrust the cold pistol against the

11 **adversary** (ăd′vər sĕr′ĭ): enemy.

other's temple, the officer relaxed and fell backward. Then pushing himself slowly to a sitting posture, he blinked and stared at the two Americans—just as his brother officer sprawled in the snow a few paces distant was blinking and staring at them.

Christopher rose to his feet, but before he could utter a word, Neil thrust the pistol into his hand and said hoarsely, "You can manage now!" Then he turned and went running up the road.

"Neil!" Christopher shouted after him. "Neil! Neil!"

But the only response was a few unintelligible words. Then Neil was lost to sight.

For several long seconds Christopher stood with feet apart and forehead wrinkled, his thoughts whirling like the flakes of snow in the increasing northwest wind. With a sickening sense of loss and of hurt, the explanation of Neil's conduct came to him suddenly and in a way that left no room for doubt.

"He has always had a strong liking for me," Christopher said to himself, "and that is why he attacked and disarmed the other officer and then came to my rescue—because he could not see me taken prisoner. But now, having left me able to manage, he has carried out his plan to desert!" Then he noticed that the calash was gone and, addressing the officer still sprawled on the ground, demanded, "Where is the horse?"

"Whirled and bolted in fright," was the response. "And I don't wonder! Never in all my years was I at-tacked so furiously or so savagely!" And scooping up a double handful of snow, he held it first against a great discolored lump above one eye and then against the side of his jaw.

Without taking his gaze from the prisoners, Christopher strode toward the bushes and recovered the muskets. Then standing once more before the two men, he asked himself, "Now what shall I do?" And at once came the answer: "Fulfill the mission!"

To the prisoners then he said, "Get to your feet and march—aye, up the road!" And as they quietly obeyed, it seemed to him incredible that these same two officers serving a King three thousand miles across the ocean could ever have laughed so scornfully over Washington's Third Rule of War.

Round the turn they made their way while their captor, holding the pistol in one hand and the muskets in the hollow of his arm, marched alertly half a dozen paces behind them. Along a bare stretch of straight road they marched, and then toward another turn, beyond which the twin pines rose dark and snow-mottled.

As they were rounding the second turn, Christopher suddenly caught his breath—for there near the opening of a small ravine stood the horse and calash, and in the snow alongside, where it had obviously been rolled, lay—a hogshead!

While he continued to stare, wide-eyed, Neil came striding forth from the ravine. "There's six others in there!" he announced—and something in his voice and manner made him seem altogether different from the Neil Fenwood whom Christopher had known at Valley Forge. "All six of the others also hold shoes!" Neil went on eagerly. "Seven hogsheads altogether! But a pox upon it, Christopher, we can take only the one! They'll have to send a special party after the other—"

Christopher moistened his lips, speechless. It had been a day of surprising happenings, but this, the latest, was the most surprising of all. Neil had not deserted and had no intention of deserting! Instead, leaving his companion to guard the prisoners, he had raced up the road to halt and recover the runaway horse and calash—and then had explored the ravine and found, not just one hogshead, but seven! It occurred to Christopher now that if he had caught the words Neil had flung over his shoulder, they might have explained his purpose.

Bending forward, he noted the markings on the hogshead. "Shoes," he thought. "Save for food, there is naught the army needs more!" Aloud he said to the prisoners, "Lift the hogshead into the calash."

The prisoners didn't want to lift it. They were officers, they pointed out, and should not be asked to do such menial[12] labor as lifting hogsheads. "Ne'rtheless, you will lift this one!" Christopher insisted—and noting the determined look in his eyes, they decided to obey.

Then with the hogshead filling almost the whole of the vehicle, the party set forth back along the Old Lime Road and thence westward across a bare meadow—the prisoners marching ahead, Christopher following with musket held at the alert and a loaded pistol in his waistband, then Neil with shouldered musket several paces in the rear, leading the horse and calash with its strange cargo. Onward they moved across the meadow under a darkening sky and in the teeth of the increasing storm . . . thence onward along old abandoned back roads and through stretches of woodland and across the Wissahickon . . . onward, onward, halting at times to rest or to bite off a few mouthfuls of dough paste or to make sure of direction . . . onward until the day had faded . . . then onward again through the night toward the junction of Valley Creek and the Schuylkill River.

It was mid-morning and the snow was still blowing when at last the party crossed the river at Swede's Ford and presently, to the astonishment of sentries and officers on duty, entered camp. There the two scouts yielded prisoners and calash to a detachment under one of Wayne's lieutenants and, on inquiry, learned that Corporal Purvis was secure in a hut that served as a hospital. General Wayne himself came striding down the hill a few moments later and in crisp tones asked for the story behind the capture.

Almost too weary to stand erect, Christopher managed nevertheless to give a summary account.

"Seven!" Wayne exclaimed. "Seven, you said? Seven full hogs-

12 menial: low; humble.

heads! This is something for the Commander-in-Chief to hear from your own lips! Come, both of you." And he strode toward the stone house —the former home of Isaac Potts, who had operated a forge—that General Washington now used for his headquarters.

When the three entered the doorway, Washington with the young Marquis de Lafayette beside him was seated at a long table, studying a map. Others at the table whom Christopher recognized were General Knox, chief of artillery, and the elderly Baron de Kalb, who had come from France on the same ship with Lafayette. As the Commander-in-Chief glanced up, Wayne greeted him and then told of the reason for the visit.

Washington rose to his feet—tall, easy in his movements, his face grave but serene. "You are right, General," he said to Wayne, "I wish to hear the story from the lips of the patrol leader himself."

Then once again—and in full detail this time—Christopher explained what had happened, giving enthusiastic credit to Neil for the part he had played and also mentioning how the two officers had laughed and what they had said about the Third Rule of War.

When he had finished, Washington smiled after the manner of a father to a son and stretched forth a hand first to Christopher and then to Neil.

"Both of you are a credit to the army!" he said with deep feeling. "Fortitude under fatigue and priva-tion—you nobly exemplify the maxim in your persons and in your deeds! Our enemies are correct: the two of you in a sense portray the whole army at Valley Forge! But those men were wrong to laugh. That they will discover with the passage of time."

Then turning to Wayne, he added, "See to it, General, that the six other hogsheads are soon within our possession. And see to it also that these two gallant soldiers of yours are among the first to benefit from the hogshead we already possess—and also of course that they are fed and rested." Then seating himself, he bent over the map again.

As Christopher and Neil went down the hill together a few minutes later, Neil seized his companion's hand and pressed it hard. In a voice that quivered he said, "You may never know the whole of it, Christopher, but this day—nay, yesterday—I passed a milestone in my life and am the better for it—thanks to you!"

Christopher regarded him inquiringly.

"Aye, thanks to you!" Neil repeated. "When you refused to be taken prisoner and lunged to attack, you set an example that seemed suddenly to kindle a bright fire within me! Save for you, I never could have done what I did. In truth, I—I—in truth, Christopher, I had thought of—"

"Say no more!" Christopher added quickly and put an arm across his friend's shoulders. Then he smiled. "Think of it, Neil—shoes! We are to have shoes!"

"Aye, and new ones!" Neil exclaimed.

Then for the first time in weeks, and despite hunger and fatigue, the two friends found themselves laughing while they made their way through the storm toward their log hut.

Reading Skills

1. Why is the corporal unable to complete the mission?
2. Which names of people and places do you recognize as being authentic, or real, ones?
3. Why do the two British soldiers ridicule Neil and Christopher?
4. Why does Christopher attack the British officers at the precise moment he does?
5. When does Christopher discover he is right in thinking Neil planned to desert?
6. Explain what General Washington means when he says to Neil and Christopher, "Fortitude under fatigue and privation—you nobly exemplify the maxim in your persons and in your deeds!"

Understanding Literature

1. There are really two main problems to be solved in this story. What are these two conflicts? Why would the story be weaker in plot if both problems were not presented?
2. The author has the two boys tell their story to General Washington personally instead of having someone else report the find of the seven hogsheads. Why does this give the story a more satisfactory ending?
3. What problem causes the tension and suspense in the story? Which details help to increase the suspense? What would happen to the story if Christopher simply asked Neil if he planned to desert?

Thomas Jefferson was a great man of many talents. Not only was he the author of the Declaration of Independence and one of America's greatest Presidents, but he was also a musician, scientist, mathematician, and educator. He served his country in many ways for nearly forty years. Through this poem, Rosemary and Stephen Vincent Benét tell much about the character and many achievements of Thomas Jefferson.

Thomas Jefferson

1743-1826

Rosemary and Stephen Vincent Benét

Thomas Jefferson,
What do you say
Under the gravestone
Hidden away?

"I was a giver,   5
I was a molder,
I was a builder
With a strong shoulder."

Six feet and over,
Large-boned and ruddy,   10
The eyes gray-hazel
But bright with study.

The big hands clever
With pen and fiddle
And ready, ever,   15
For any riddle.

From buying empires
To planting 'taters,
From Declarations
To trick dumb-waiters.   20

"I liked the people,
The sweat and crowd of them,
Trusted them always
And spoke aloud of them.

"I liked all learning   25
And wished to share it
Abroad like pollen
For all who merit.

"I liked fine houses
With Greek pilasters,[1]   30
And built them surely,
My touch a master's.

"I liked queer gadgets
And secret shelves,
And helping nations   35
To rule themselves.

"Jealous of others?
Not always candid?
But huge of vision
And open-handed.   40

"A wild-goose chaser?
Now and again,
Build Monticello,
You little men!

"Design my plow, sirs,   45
They use it still,
Or found my college
At Charlottesville.

1 pilasters: columns.

"And still go questing
New things and thinkers,   50
And keep as busy
As twenty tinkers.

"While always guarding
The people's freedom—
You need more hands, sir?   55
I didn't need 'em.

"They call you rascal?
They called me worse.
You'd do grand things, sir,
But lack the purse?   60

"I got no riches.
I died a debtor.
I died free-hearted
And that was better.

"For life was freakish   65
But life was fervent,
And I was always
Life's willing servant.

"Life, life's too weighty?
Too long a haul, sir?   70
I lived past eighty.
I liked it all, sir."

Understanding Literature

1. Why is part of the poem enclosed in quotation marks?
2. What were some of Thomas Jefferson's many accomplishments?
3. What do the last two verses tell you about Thomas Jefferson's character?

People other than those associated with the founding of our country, with war, and with the struggle for freedom are important to the history of America. The vastness of the West, the towering mountains, and the endlessly waving prairies lured men who were looking for adventure and wealth. Among these men were the fur trappers—and the animal they were after was the beaver.

A Wild Strain

Paul Horgan

IMPROVING YOUR READING: Different materials require different methods of reading. The stories so far in this unit are ones which you could read quickly, because there was little factual material that you would need to retain. In "A Wild Strain," however, there are more descriptions and explanations. Observe how this kind of writing differs from the other pieces in the unit. This selection is from Horgan's book *Great River: The Rio Grande in North American History.*

THE MOUNTAIN SYSTEM of the northern Rio Grande was a vast, secret world. Wandering Indians there made shrines of twig and feather and bone, and went their ways. Close to the high clouds that made their rivers, the inhuman peaks doubled the roar of thunder, or hissed with sheets of rain, or abided[1] in massive silence. Below them lay every variation of park and meadow and lost lake; gashed canyon and rocky roomlike penetralia in the stupendous temples of the high wilderness. Along hidden watercourses and in little cupped lakes lived and worked the family of a small creature destined to be the first cause of great change in the human life of the river during the early 19th century. It was the beaver.

In still pool or mild current the beaver made his house of mud and twig. Its doorway was under water. The occupants dived to enter it and came up beyond into the dry shelter of their lodge that they had built of sticks and mud, where their food was stored and where they were safe from animal predators.[2] The backwater before the den had to be three feet deep, and if this did not exist naturally, the beavers built dams to collect it. They chose a tree by the edge. Sitting upright, they chewed away bark in a belt, eating of it now and then from their paws. Down to bare wood, they gnawed away until the tree was ready to fall. Often it fell into water where it would make a stout beginning for a dam. Working in concert[3] they brought from

1 abided: existed.

2 predators (prĕd′ə tərz): plunderers.
3 in concert: together.

near-by woods bundles of stick and bush and starting out from the bank began to shore up their barrier. They dived to the bottom of the water and brought up loads of mud. This was plaster. With their broad tails they troweled mud over the laid timbers, layer upon layer, always extending the reach of the dam until it touched the opposite limit of the course or cove where they worked. At times they paused to play, racing each other in the water, diving, and loudly slapping the water with their tails.

When house and dam were finished, it was time to lay up provisions within against winter when there would be no green sprouts of willow and cottonwood and fresh grass to eat in season. The beaver clan went foraging, often far inland from their water, in search of bark. The best bark was on the smaller branches high out of reach. The beavers brought down the tree, and then stripped the tender young bark off the branches laid low. They cut the bark into three-foot strips, pulled them to their water, and there floated them to the lodge. They made little signs to guide them as they went—mounds of twig and earth which they impregnated[4] with castorum, a musk secreted[5] by the animal itself, that attracted their sense of smell and reassuringly meant *beaver* and told them where the road lay. Once in the lodge and eating, they were neat and fastidious.[6] They took out through the water doorway all the refuse of a meal and threw it into the current. Drifting away, it lodged down-current out of their way—bits of gnawed stick and knotty branch and hard root.

In the spring came the young. Leaving the mother during gestation, the male went traveling, often far away to other water, where he swam and frolicked, ate tender greens at the bank, and did not return home until the offspring were born. Then he took them in charge, trained them in work, and in the late summer led them out to forage before the sharp frosts and the thickening of their fur against the cold. Everywhere in the secret lakes and along the tributaries and in the quieter passages of the main river this lively cycle was continued by beavers in incalculable thousands, and wherever mountain and water met, evidences of it were scattered and lodged undisturbed— until the last Spanish and the first Mexican years of the Rio Grande.

For by then the beaver's fur was in great demand for the making of men's hats. The hatters of London and Paris, New York, Boston and Philadelphia consumed great cargoes of beaver pelt, and the fur trade moved westward out of St. Louis over the American continent to Astoria and the northern Rockies. While Stephen Austin[7] was completing his organized arrangements with the new government of Mexico to bring new settlers from the east nearer to the lower Rio Grande, the

---

4 **impregnated:** soaked.
5 **musk secreted:** perfumed substance given out.
6 **fastidious** (făs tĭd′ĭ əs): dainty.

7 **Stephen Austin:** a 19th-century American colonizer in Texas.

river's upper reaches knew another sort of growing infiltration by men who whether they came alone, or with a few companions, or many, still came without formal approval by the Mexican government, and with no resounding program of colonial loyalty or pious hope.

They came to take beaver in the mountain waters, in spring and autumn up north, or all through the winter in New Mexico if the season was mild. Many of them were French Canadians; the rest were from anywhere in the United States, though mostly from the frontier settlements. They outfitted themselves at St. Louis, and remembering what was commonly known out of Pike's[8] reports, crossed the plains and entered the mountains by the hundreds in the 1820's. Among their number were men who made the first trails beyond the prairies, that led overland so early as 1826, to the Pacific. Jedediah Smith, Charles Beaubien, the Roubidoux brothers, Céran St. Vrain, Bill Williams, the youthful runaway Kit Carson for whose return a reward of one cent was posted by the employer to whom he was apprenticed—such men went to the mountains after beaver skins to sell for a few dollars a pound, and all unwitting showed the way across the continent.

The movement had already had its pioneer in James Pursley, the Kentuckian, who had been detained at Santa Fe in 1805 under the Spanish governor. Others entering New Mexico from the plains were arrested, to be marched down the Rio Grande to El Paso and the prisons of Chihuahua in 1812, after confiscation of their goods, and were not released until the freeing of Mexico in 1821. Another party of trappers were taken by the provincial Spanish government in 1817, jailed in irons for forty-eight days at Santa Fe, and were finally released after being stripped of thirty thousand dollars' worth of furs and supplies. Such actions by the government were meant to protect the trapping industry already worked on a small scale by the Mexicans of the valley. Regulations declared that only permanent residents might hunt beaver. They were required to buy a hunting license, their number in any party was carefully fixed and recorded, and so were the length of time to be spent in the hunt and the weapons to be used—traps, firearms, or snares. If the early American trappers could not buy official licenses, they soon found a way to get around the law. "The North Americans began to corrupt the New Mexicans," noted a Santa Fe lawyer, "by purchasing their licenses from them," and so risked arrest.

But still the trappers came, and against other hazards. The greatest of these were the roving Indians on the prairies and the eastern upsweeps of the Rocky Mountains. For an Indian hunter could read the menace[9] that came with the white hunter; and he moved with every savagery

8 Pike's: a reference to Z. M. Pike (1779-1813), American general and explorer.

9 menace: threat.

to defend his hunting grounds. The trapper retaliated.[10] He fought the Indian with Indian ways ... and pressed westward. He fought distance, hunger, and thirst, and if he was unwary enough to be bitten by a rattlesnake, he cauterized[11] the wound by burning a thick pinch of gunpowder in it. Once in the mountains he met his second greatest adversary[12] in great numbers. This was the great grizzly bear, who was curious, fearless and gifted with a massive ursine[13] intelligence. With lumbering speed the grizzlies could travel forty miles between dawn and dark through mountains. It was not unusual for trappers to kill five or six in a day, or to see fifty or sixty, and one hunter declared that one day he saw two hundred and twenty of them. The grizzly towered above a man. His forepaws were eight or nine inches wide, and his claws six inches long. He weighed from fifteen-to-eighteen hundred pounds. His embrace was certain death. So steadily did he smell and find the trappers that in a few decades by their guns his kind was made almost extinct.

The earthen village of Ranchos de Taos near the Rio Grande was the northern town nearest the beaver waters of the mountains, and there came the mountain men to organize their supplies for the trapping seasons. They found that some men of the Ranchos de Taos already, though to a limited degree, followed the trapper's life. Seeing how swarthy they were, the newcomers thought they must be of mixed Negro and Indian blood. It was astonishing how primitive were the ways of life in Taos—the farmers used only oxen in cultivating their fields, and a miserable plow made of a Y-shaped branch from a tree, with an iron head to its end that turned the earth. Hoes, axes and other tools were all old-fashioned. There were no sawmills; no mechanical ingenuities to speed up work; and—what was oddest to the squinting and raring trappers from the East—the people seemed to have no desire for such means to change their slow, simple ways.

The mountain men encountered at Taos their first experience of the Mexican government. Taos was the seat of the northernmost customs house of Mexico. As the trappers brought little to declare in goods for sale, they were evidently allowed to go about their preparations for departure into the mountains. They bought what flour and produce they could, and recruited an occasional Taoseño to join their parties, and made ready their equipment. In the far northern Rockies the trapping parties were often large, numbering from fifty to a hundred men. Most of these were camp personnel who maintained a base for the trappers and hunters who went forward into the wilderness. The "Frenchmen" from Canada sometimes kept Indian wives, and established in the moun-

---

10 **retaliated:** returned like for like.
11 **cauterized** (kô't ə rīzd'): burned as a cure.
12 **adversary:** enemy.
13 **ursine** (ûr'sīn): bearlike.

tains a semipermanent household with rude domestic amenities.[14] Other parties were smaller, and instead of working for the great fur companies as contract employees, went their ways alone, as "free" trappers. Those who descended to the Rio Grande's northern reaches were more often than not in small units of a dozen, or three or four, or even a single man, who meant to take their furs and sell them to the highest bidder at the season's end. But all the trappers shared aspects of costume, equipment and even character, many of which grew from the tradition of the forest frontiersman of the late 18th century.

The mountain man was almost Indian-colored from exposure to the weather. His hair hung upon his shoulders. He was bearded. Next to his skin he wore a red flannel loincloth. His outer clothes were of buckskin, fringed at all the seams. The jacket sometimes reached to the knee over tight, wrinkled leggings. His feet were covered by moccasins made of deer or buffalo leather. Around his waist was a leather belt into which he thrust his flintlock pistols, his knife for skinning or scalping, and his shingling hatchet. Over one shoulder hung his bullet pouch, and over the other his powder horn. To their baldrics[15] were attached his bullet mold, ball screw, wiper and an awl for working leather. When he moved he shimmered with fringe and rang and clacked with accouter-

ments[16] of metal and wood. The most important of these were his traps, of which he carried five or six, and his firearm with its slender separate crutch of hardwood. It was always a rifle—never a shotgun, which he scorned as an effete[17] fowling piece. Made in the gun works of the brothers Jacob and Samuel Hawken, of St. Louis, the rifle had two locks for which he kept about him a hundred flints, twenty-five pounds of powder and several pounds of lead. The barrel, thirty-six inches long, was made by hand of soft iron. The recoil of its blast shocked into a hardwood stock beautifully turned and slender. Peering vividly out from under his low-crowned hat of rough wool, he was an American original, as hard as the hardest thing that could happen to him.

Alone, or with a companion or a small party, he packed his supplies on two horses and, riding a third, left Taos for the mountains in the autumn. He was wary of roaming Indians, dangerous animals—and other trapper parties. For nobody could stake a claim on hunting country, and every trapper party competed against every other. He did his best to keep his movement and direction secret, to throw others off the trail, and find the wildest country where he would be most free from rivalry. Following the groins of the foothills, the mountain men came among high slopes and rocky screens. If two worked as a pair, they sought for a

---

14 amenities (ə měn′ə tĭz): agreeable features.
15 baldrics: belts.

16 accouterments: equipment.
17 effete (ĭ fēt′): worn out.

concealed place where they could make camp and tether[18] their horses, near beaver water. There they built a shelter, and if their goal was a mountain lake, or a slow passage of stream, they set to work hacking out a cottonwood canoe. In natural forest paths they looked for the little musky mounds that marked beaver trails. They searched currents for the drift of gnawed beaver sticks. Every such sign took them closer to their prey. When they were sure they had found its little world, at evening under the pure suspended light of mountain skies they silently coasted along the shores of quiet water to set their traps.

They laid each trap two or three inches underwater on the slope of the shore, and, a little removed, they fixed a pole in deep mud and chained the trap to it. They stripped a twig of its bark and dipped one end into a supply of castorum, the beaver's own secretion that would be his bait. They fastened the twig between the open jaws of the trap leaving the musky end four inches above water. The beaver in the nighttime was drawn to it by scent. He raised his muzzle to inhale, his hind quarters went lower in the water, and the trap seized him. He threw himself into deeper water; but the trap held him, and the pole held the trap, and presently he sank to drown. In the high, still daybreak, the trappers coasted by their traps again in the canoe, and took up their catch.

Working a rocky stream from the bank the trappers lodged the trap

18 **tether:** tie; fasten.

and its chained pole in the current, where the beaver found the scent. In his struggles he might drag the trap and pole to the shore, where his burden became entangled in "thickets of brook willows," and held him till found. Sometimes he struggled to deeper midstream water, where the pole floated as a marker; and then the trappers putting off their buckskins that if saturated would dry slowly and then be hard as wood, went naked and shivering into the cold mountain stream to swim for their take. And some parties rafted down the whole length of the river in New Mexico, all the way to El Paso. Their method astonished the New Mexicans, to whom it seemed suspect because it was new. Was it proper to use a new kind of trap, and float noiselessly to a beaver site taking their catch by surprise, and spend the night in midstream with the raft moored to trees on each bank to be out of the reach of wild animals? And at the end of the journey, to sell the timbers of the raft for a good price at El Paso where wood was so scarce, take up the catch and vanish overland eastward without reporting to the government? The New Mexicans frowned at such ingenuity, energy and novelty.

When in the mountains they had exhausted a beaver site the trappers moved on to another. With their traps over their shoulders they forded streams amidst floating ice; or with their traps hanging down their backs, they scaled and descended the hard ridges between watercourses where the harder the country the better

the chance that no others had come there before them. The trap weighed about five pounds, and its chain was about five feet long. A full-grown beaver weighed between thirty and forty pounds. The catch was an awkward burden to carry back to camp for skinning. Removing the pelt from the animal, the trappers stretched it on a frame of sprung willow withes to dry. The flesh they cooked by hanging it before a fire from a thong. The carcass turned by its own weight, roasting evenly. The broad, flat tail they liked best of all. They cut it off, skinned it, toasted it at the end of a stick, and ate it with relish, as a relief from the usual hunter's diet of deer, elk, antelope, bear, lynx, or buffalo meat, or buffalo marrowbones, or buffalo blood drunk spurting and warm from the throat of a newly killed specimen.

All through the winter-fast months the mountain men worked, obedient to animal laws and themselves almost animal in their isolation, freedom and harmony with the wilderness. Their peltries were cached[19] and the piles grew, in the end to be baled with rawhide thongs. A trapper took in a good season about four hundred pounds of beaver skins. Somtimes his cache was invaded and destroyed by prowling animals, or stolen by mountain Indians; and then his months of hardship went for nothing. But if he kept his pile, he was ready to come out of the boxed mountains whose cool winds brush-

19 peltries . . . cached: skins were hidden.

ing all day over high-tilted meadows carried the scent of wild flowers down the open slopes where he descended with his haul. At five dollars a pound it would bring him two thousand dollars in the market.

But once again in Taos, he might then meet trouble with the Mexican authorities. Now that he had his cargo, they showed an interest in him. If he was unlucky, they questioned him, examined his bales, and invoking[20] regulations that nobody mentioned when he started out months before, confiscated[21] his whole catch. If he resisted he was taken to Santa Fe and jailed, with official talk about the Mexican decree of 1824 that prohibited trapping by foreigners in Mexican territory. Since there were no public warehouses hunters could only store their catches in towns by making deals with local citizens for storage space on private premises. If a Mexican citizen gave protection to a foreign trapper he was in danger from his own government. At Peña Blanca on the Río Grande in 1827 one Luís María Cabeza de Vaca hid in his house the "contraband" of beaver skins left there for safe keeping by a trapper named Young. From Santa Fe a corporal and eight soldiers of the presidial company came to seize it. Cabeza de Vaca resisted them, firing upon them in protection of his home. The soldiers returned the fire and killed him. The official report of the affair stated that "the deceased died while defending a violation of the . . . rights of the Nation," and asked exoneration[22] for the corporal and his squad.

But local officials might be bribed, and a license trumped up, and the catch restored to the trapper. In any case, after his mountain months, he was ready to burst his bonds of solitude, and he did so with raw delight. All his general passion and violence that his mountain work required him to suppress while moving lithe and crafty after watchful creatures he now broke free in the clay village where he returned among men and women. He had a frosty look of filth over him. His hair was knotted and his beard was a catch-all for the refuse of months. His clothes reeked like his body. His mouth was dry with one kind of thirst. If the one tavern in the town was full, he went to a house and asked for a corner of the packed mud floor where he could throw his gear, and was granted it. The family knew what he came to seek with his comrades. The women took kettles out of doors and built fires around them to heat water. When it was hot they brought it in, and found him waiting in his crusted skin sitting in a wooden tub. The women poured the water over him. He thrashed. He was as hairy as an animal. The water hit him and he gave the recognized cry of the mountain man—"Wagh!"—a grunt, a warning, and a boast. Bathing as violently as he did all other acts, he

20 **invoking:** appealing to.
21 **confiscated:** seized.

22 **exoneration:** release from blame.

began again to know forgotten satisfactions. As he emerged with wet light running on his skin, white everywhere but on face and hands whose weather would not wash off, he was a new man. . . .

Presently he traveled to a trading post on the prairies, or to St. Louis, to sell his catch. In the frontier cities of the United States he was a prodigal[23] spender, uneasy in their relatively ordered society, loose as it was compared to life in older and more easterly places. When the season rolled around again, he was off again to his lost lakes and rivers where obscurely content he felt most like the self he imagined until it came true.

For over three decades the trapping trade flourished. At its height the annual shipment of beaver skins from Abiquiu on the Chama and Taos on the Rio Grande was worth two hundred thousand dollars. But in the 1830's the market for beaver began to break, for the China trade out of England and New England was growing, and the clipper ships were bringing silk in great quantities to the manufacturing cities of the world. Fashion changed. Silk was offered for hats instead of fur; and the change brought the decline and finally the almost virtual abolishment of the Rocky Mountain fur trade.

The trapper was cast adrift to find new work. He could abide it only in the land of his hardy prowess, and there he found it, whether he joined the overland commercial caravans as a wagon hand, or the American Army's later surveying expeditions as a guide, or amazingly settled on river land as a farmer. He knew the craft of the wilderness and he made its first trails for the westering white man. Some of the earliest venturers in the Mexico trade were trappers; and as the trade continued to grow and establish its bases ever farther west, the trappers met it with their wares; and what had been a memorized path became a visible road; and along it moved another of the unofficial invasions of the Mexican Rio Grande that could only end by changing nations. The first sustained effort toward that end was made by the individual trapper. His greatest power to achieve it lay in his individualism. Where the Mexican was hedged by governmental authority, the trapper made his own. Where the Mexican was formal, he was wild. . . . The invasion, unorganized as it was, commercial in purpose, wild and free in its individuals, seemed to express some secret personal motive beyond the material. The trappers forecast a new, a wild, strain of human society to come to the northern river.

---

23 **prodigal** (prod′ g l): wasteful.

Reading Skills

1. What kind of men, in appearance and character, were the trappers of the northern Rio Grande? Why, and from where, did they come to trap the beaver?
2. Describe some of the hardships and hazards which the trappers had to face and overcome.
3. Paul Horgan calls the trapper "an American original." What does this phrase mean?
4. Describe the method used to trap the beaver. Why were the New Mexicans astonished and somewhat upset by this method?
5. What caused beaver trapping to decline? What then became of the trappers?
6. Although the trappers were basically interested only in returning with many furs, they unknowingly did America a service. Explain.

Abraham Lincoln hardly needs an introduction. He did many great things in his lifetime: he was the sixteenth President of the United States; he led his country through the years of the Civil War; he issued the Emancipation Proclamation; and he died in the service of his country. Such a man should be able to rest in peace. Why, then, does the poet, forty-nine years after Lincoln's death, say that "Abraham Lincoln walks at midnight"?

Abraham Lincoln Walks at Midnight

(In Springfield, Illinois)

Vachel Lindsay

IMPROVING YOUR READING: The *connotation* of a word is the implication, or suggestion, a word carries with it in addition to its literal meaning. The word *friend*, for example, literally means "one who is not an enemy." But *friend* usually suggests, or *connotes*, many other things: companionship, someone to confide in, someone to depend upon, someone who likes and trusts you. The word *friend*, therefore, has pleasant connotations; *enemy*, on the other hand, has unpleasant connotations. In "Abraham Lincoln Walks at Midnight" which words suggest, or *connote*, more than they mean literally?

It is portentous,[1] and a thing of state
That here at midnight, in our little town
A mourning figure walks, and will not rest,
Near the old courthouse pacing up and down,

Or by his homestead, or in shadowed yards   5
He lingers where his children used to play,
Or through the market, on the well-worn stones
He stalks until the dawn-stars burn away.

A bronzed, lank[2] man! His suit of ancient black,
A famous high top hat and plain worn shawl   10
Make him the quaint great figure that men love,
The prairie lawyer, master of us all.

He cannot sleep upon his hillside now.
He is among us:—as in times before!

1 **portentous:** significant; a sign of something about to happen.
2 **lank:** lean; thin.

And we who toss and lie awake for long   15
Breathe deep, and start, to see him pass the door.

His head is bowed.   He thinks on men and kings.
Yea, when the sick world cries, how can he sleep?
Too many peasants fight, they know not why,
Too many homesteads in black terror weep.   20

The sins of all the war lords burn his heart.
He sees the dreadnaughts[3] scouring every main.[4]
He carries on his shawl-wrapped shoulders now
The bitterness, the folly and the pain.

He cannot rest until a spirit-dawn   25
Shall come;—the shining hope of Europe free:
The league of sober folk, the Workers' Earth,
Bringing long peace to Cornland, Alp and Sea.

It breaks his heart that kings must murder still,
That all his hours of travail[5] here for men   30
Seem yet in vain.   And who will bring white peace
That he may sleep upon his hill again?

3 **dreadnaughts:** battleships.
4 **main:** ocean.
5 **travail:** mental and physical labor.

Understanding Literature

1. Why is Abraham Lincoln especially suitable as the main character in this poem?
2. Why is Lincoln walking at midnight? What particular things keep him from sleeping? What historical event probably moved Vachel Lindsay to write this poem?
3. What is meant by "the bitterness, the folly and the pain" which Lincoln carries on his shoulders?
4. What must happen before Lincoln will be able to "sleep upon his hill again"? What does the poet mean by "a spirit-dawn" (l. 25) and by "white peace" (l. 31)?
5. Observe the words which the poet uses in describing Lincoln. What are the connotations of these words; that is, what ideas is the poet trying to suggest about Lincoln by using these particular words: *mourning, pacing, lingers, stalks, quaint, master, bowed?* First consider the literal meaning of each word; then consider all the implications, or suggestions, of the word.

Most people are aware of the great tragedies of war. The thousands of people crippled or killed and the battles won at the cost of too many lives are the things that make newspaper headlines. But the headlines rarely tell of the other tragedies: the little skirmishes in which just two or three are killed, or the relationships between people which war twists or leaves unfulfilled. Although this story takes place during the Civil War, similar events could happen during any war.

A Gray Sleeve

Stephen Crane

IMPROVING YOUR READING: As you read "A Gray Sleeve," you will find that the author makes you feel the mystery surrounding the house. He establishes a *mood* by describing the stillness of the woods, the feeling of the unknown about the house, and the way the characters in the story react in this situation. Be ready to discuss these and other details which contribute to the mood of the story.

I

"IT LOOKS AS if it might rain this afternoon," remarked the lieutenant of artillery.

"So it does," the infantry captain assented. He glanced casually at the sky. When his eyes had lowered to the green-shadowed landscape before him, he said fretfully: "I wish those fellows out yonder would quit pelting at us. They've been at it since noon."

At the edge of a grove of maples, across wide fields, there occasionally appeared little puffs of smoke of a dull hue in this gloom of sky which expressed an impending[1] rain. The long wave of blue and steel in the field moved uneasily at the eternal barking of the far-away sharpshooters, and the men, leaning upon their rifles, stared at the grove of maples. Once a private turned to borrow some tobacco from a comrade in the rear rank, but, with his hand still stretched out, he continued to twist his head and glance at the distant trees. He was afraid the enemy would shoot him at a time when he was not looking.

Suddenly the artillery officer said: "See what's coming!"

Along the rear of the brigade of infantry a column of cavalry was sweeping at a hard gallop. A lieutenant, riding some yards to the right of the column, bawled furiously at the four troopers just at the rear of the colors. They had lost distance and made a little gap, but at the shouts of the lieutenant they urged their horses forward. The bugler,

1 impending: approaching.

careering along behind the captain of the troop, fought and tugged like a wrestler to keep his frantic animal from bolting far ahead of the column.

On the springy turf the innumerable hoofs thundered in a swift storm of sound. In the brown faces of the troopers their eyes were set like bits of flashing steel.

The long line of the infantry regiments standing at ease underwent a sudden movement at the rush of the passing squadron. The foot soldiers turned their heads to gaze at the torrent of horses and men.

The yellow folds of the flag fluttered back in silken, shuddering waves, as if it were a reluctant thing. Occasionally a giant spring of a charger would rear the firm and sturdy figure of a soldier suddenly head and shoulders above his comrades. Over the noise of the scudding hoofs could be heard the creaking of leather trappings, the jingle and clank of steel, and the tense, low-toned commands or appeals of the men to their horses; and the horses were mad with the headlong sweep of this movement. Powerful underjaws bent back and straightened, so that the bits were clamped as rigidly as vices upon the teeth, and glistening necks arched in desperate resistance to the hands at the bridles. Swinging their heads in rage at the granite[2] laws of their lives, which compelled even their angers and their ardors to chosen directions and chosen faces, their flight was as a flight of harnessed demons.

The captain's bay kept its pace at the head of the squadron with the lithe[3] bounds of a thoroughbred, and this horse was proud as a chief at the roaring trample of his fellows behind him. The captain's glance was calmly upon the grove of maples whence the sharpshooters of the enemy had been picking at the blue line. He seemed to be reflecting.[4] He stolidly[5] rose and fell with the plunges of his horse in all the indifference of a deacon's figure seated plumply in church. And it occurred to many of the watching infantry to wonder why this officer could remain imperturbable and reflective when his squadron was thundering and swarming behind him like the rushing of a flood.

The column swung in a saber-curve toward a break in a fence, and dashed into a roadway. Once a little plank bridge was encountered, and the sound of the hoofs upon it was like the long roll of many drums. An old captain in the infantry turned to his first lieutenant and made a remark, which was a compound of bitter disparagement[6] of cavalry in general and soldierly admiration of this particular troop.

Suddenly the bugle sounded, and the column halted with a jolting upheaval amid sharp, brief cries. A moment later the men had tumbled from their horses, and, carbines in hand,

2 **granite:** unchangeable.

3 **lithe** (līth): limber; flexible.
4 **reflecting:** thinking.
5 **stolidly:** inattentively; mechanically.
6 **disparagement:** criticism; condemnation.

were running in a swarm toward the grove of maples. In the road one of every four of the troopers was standing with braced legs, and pulling and hauling at the bridles of four frenzied horses.

The captain was running awkwardly in his boots. He held his saber low, so that the point often threatened to catch in the turf. His yellow hair ruffled out from under his faded cap. "Go in hard now!" he roared, in a voice of hoarse fury. His face was violently red.

The troopers threw themselves upon the grove like wolves upon a great animal. Along the whole front of woods there was the dry crackling of musketry, with bitter, swift flashes and smoke that writhed like stung phantoms. The troopers yelled shrilly and spanged bullets low into the foliage.

For a moment, when near the woods, the line almost halted. The men struggled and fought for a time like swimmers encountering a powerful current. Then with a supreme effort they went on again. They dashed madly at the grove, whose foliage from the high light of the field was as inscrutable[7] as a wall.

Then suddenly each detail of the calm trees became apparent, and with a few more frantic leaps the men were in the cool gloom of the woods. There was a heavy odor as from burned paper. Wisps of gray smoke wound upward. The men halted and, grimy, perspiring, and puffing, they searched the recesses of the woods with eager, fierce glances. Figures could be seen flitting afar off. A

7 inscrutable: here, hard to pass through.

dozen carbines rattled at them in an angry volley.

During this pause the captain strode along the line, his face lit with a broad smile of contentment. "When he sends this crowd to do anything, I guess he'll find we do it pretty sharp," he said to the grinning lieutenant.

"Say, they didn't stand that rush a minute, did they?" said the subaltern.[8] Both officers were profoundly dusty in their uniforms, and their faces were soiled like those of two urchins.

Out in the grass behind them were three tumbled and silent forms.

Presently the line moved forward again. The men went from tree to tree like hunters stalking game. Some at the left of the line fired occasionally, and those at the right gazed curiously in that direction. The men still breathed heavily from their scramble across the field.

Of a sudden a trooper halted and said: "Hello! there's a house!" Everyone paused. The men turned to look at their leader.

The captain stretched his neck and swung his head from side to side. "By George, it is a house!" he said.

Through the wealth of leaves there vaguely loomed the form of a large white house. These troopers, brown-faced from many days of campaigning, each feature of them telling of their placid confidence and courage, were stopped abruptly by the appearance of this house. There was some subtle suggestion—some tale of an unknown thing—which watched them from they knew not what part of it.

A rail fence girded a wide lawn of tangled grass. Seven pines stood along a driveway which led from two distant posts of a vanished gate. The blue-clothed troopers moved forward until they stood at the fence peering over it.

The captain put one hand on the top rail and seemed to be about to climb the fence, when suddenly he hesitated, and said in a low voice: "Watson, what do you think of it?"

The lieutenant stared at the house. "Derned if I know!" he replied.

The captain pondered. It happened that the whole company had turned a gaze of profound awe and doubt upon this edifice[9] which confronted them. The men were very silent.

At last the captain swore and said: "We are certainly a pack of fools. Derned old deserted house halting a company of Union cavalry, and making us gape like babies!"

"Yes, but there's something—something——" insisted the subaltern in a half stammer.

"Well, if there's 'something—something' in there, I'll get it out," said the captain. "Send Sharpe clean around to the other side with about twelve men, so we will sure bag your 'something—something,' and I'll take a few of the boys and find out what's in the derned old thing!"

He chose the nearest eight men for his "storming party," as the lieutenant called it. After he had waited

---

8 **subaltern:** officer of lower rank than captain.   9 **edifice:** building.

some minutes for the others to get into position, he said "Come ahead" to his eight men, and climbed the fence.

The brighter light of the tangled lawn made him suddenly feel tremendously apparent, and he wondered if there could be some mystic[10] thing in the house which was regarding this approach. His men trudged silently at his back. They stared at the windows and lost themselves in deep speculations as to the probability of there being, perhaps, eyes behind the blinds—malignant[11] eyes, piercing eyes.

Suddenly a corporal in the party gave vent to a startled exclamation, and half threw his carbine into position. The captain turned quickly, and the corporal said: "I saw an arm move the blinds—an arm with a gray sleeve!"

"Don't be a fool, Jones, now," said the captain sharply.

"I swear t'——" began the corporal, but the captain silenced him.

When they arrived at the front of the house, the troopers paused, while the captain went softly up the front steps. He stood before the large front door and studied it. Some crickets chirped in the long grass, and the nearest pine could be heard in its endless sighs. One of the privates moved uneasily, and his foot crunched the gravel. Suddenly the captain swore angrily and kicked the door with a loud crash. It flew open.

II

THE BRIGHT LIGHTS of the day flashed into the old house when the captain angrily kicked open the door. He was aware of a wide hallway, carpeted with matting and extending deep into the dwelling. There was also an old walnut hat-rack and a little marble-topped table with a vase and two books upon it. Farther back was a great, venerable[12] fireplace containing dreary ashes.

But directly in front of the captain was a young girl. The flying open of the door had obviously been an utter astonishment to her, and she remained transfixed there in the middle of the floor, staring at the captain with wide eyes.

She was like a child caught at the time of a raid upon the cake. She wavered to and fro upon her feet, and held her hands behind her. There were two little points of terror in her eyes, as she gazed up at the young captain in dusty blue, with his reddish, bronze complexion, his yellow hair, his bright saber held threateningly.

These two remained motionless and silent, simply staring at each other for some moments.

The captain felt his rage fade out of him and leave his mind limp. He had been violently angry, because this house had made him feel hesitant, wary.[13] He did not like to be wary. He liked to feel confident,

---

10 **mystic:** mysterious; hidden.
11 **malignant:** evil.

12 **venerable:** old.
13 **wary:** cautious; suspicious.

sure. So he had kicked the door open, and had been prepared to march in like a soldier of wrath.

But now he began, for one thing, to wonder if his uniform was so dusty and old in appearance. Moreover, he had a feeling that his face was covered with a compound of dust, grime, and perspiration. He took a step forward and said: "I didn't mean to frighten you." But his voice was coarse from his battle-howling. It seemed to him to have hempen fibers in it.

The girl's breath came in little, quick gasps, and she looked at him as she would have looked at a serpent.

"I didn't mean to frighten you," he said again.

The girl, still with her hands behind her, began to back away.

"Is there anyone else in the house?" he went on, while slowly following her. "I don't wish to disturb you, but we had a fight with some rebel skirmishers in the woods, and I thought maybe some of them might have come in here. In fact, I was pretty sure of it. Are there any of them here?"

The girl looked at him and said, "No!" He wondered why extreme agitation[14] made the eyes of some women so limpid[15] and bright.

"Who is here besides yourself?"

By this time his pursuit had driven her to the end of the hall, and she remained there with her back to the wall and her hands still behind her.

When she answered this question, she did not look at him but down at the floor. She cleared her voice and then said: "There is no one here."

"No one?"

She lifted her eyes to him in that appeal that the human being must make even to falling trees, crashing boulders, the sea in a storm, and said, "No, no, there is no one here." He could plainly see her tremble.

Of a sudden he bethought him that she continually kept her hands behind her. As he recalled her air when first discovered, he remembered she appeared precisely as a child detected at one of the crimes of childhood. Moreover, she had always backed away from him. He thought now that she was concealing something which was an evidence of the presence of the enemy in the house.

"What are you holding behind you?" he said suddenly.

She gave a little quick moan, as if some grim hand had throttled her.

"What are you holding behind you?"

"Oh, nothing—please. I am not holding anything behind me; indeed I'm not."

"Very well. Hold your hands out in front of you, then."

"Oh, indeed, I'm not holding anything behind me. Indeed I'm not."

"Well," he began. Then he paused and remained for a moment dubious.[16] Finally, he laughed. "Well,

---

14 **agitation:** nervousness; distress.
15 **limpid:** clear.

16 **dubious:** doubtful.

I shall have my men search the house, anyhow. I'm sorry to trouble you, but I feel sure that there is someone here whom we want." He turned to the corporal, who with the other men was gaping quietly in at the door, and said: "Jones, go through the house."

As for himself, he remained planted in front of the girl, for she evidently did not dare to move and allow him to see what she held so carefully behind her back. So she was his prisoner.

The men rummaged around on the ground floor of the house. Sometimes the captain called to them, "Try that closet," "Is there any cellar?" But they found no one, and at last they went trooping toward the stairs which led to the second floor.

But at this movement on the part of the men the girl uttered a cry—a cry of such fright and appeal that the men paused. "Oh, don't go up there! Please don't go up there!—ple—ease! There is no one there! Indeed—indeed there is not! Oh, ple—ease!"

"Go on, Jones," said the captain calmly.

The obedient corporal made a preliminary step, and the girl bounded toward the stairs with another cry.

As she passed him, the captain caught sight of that which she had concealed behind her back, and which she had forgotten in this supreme moment. It was a pistol.

She ran to the first step, and standing there, faced the men, one hand extended with perpendicular palm, and the other holding the pistol at her side. "Oh, please, don't go up there! Nobody is there—indeed, there is not! P-l-e-a-s-e!" Then suddenly she sank swiftly down upon the step, and, huddling forlornly, began to weep in the agony and with the convulsive tremors[17] of an infant. The pistol fell from her fingers and rattled down to the floor.

The astonished troopers looked at their astonished captain. There was a short silence.

Finally, the captain stooped and picked up the pistol. It was a heavy weapon of the army pattern. He ascertained[18] that it was empty.

He leaned toward the shaking girl, and said gently: "Will you tell me what you were going to do with this pistol?"

He had to repeat the question a number of times, but at last a muffled voice said, "Nothing."

"Nothing!" He insisted quietly upon a further answer. At the tender tones of the captain's voice, the phlegmatic[19] corporal turned and winked gravely at the man next to him.

"Won't you tell me?"

The girl shook her head.

"Please tell me!"

The silent privates were moving their feet uneasily and wondering how long they were to wait.

The captain said: "Please, won't you tell me?"

Then this girl's voice began in stricken tones half coherent, and amid violent sobbing: "It was grandpa's. He—he—he said he was going to shoot anybody who came in here—he didn't care if there were thousands of 'em. And—and I know he would, and I was afraid they'd kill him. And so—and—so I stole away his pistol—and I was going to hide it when you—you—you kicked open the door."

The men straightened up and looked at each other. The girl began to weep again.

The captain mopped his brow. He peered down at the girl. He mopped his brow again. Suddenly he said: "Ah, don't cry like that."

He moved restlessly and looked down at his boots. He mopped his brow again.

Then he gripped the corporal by the arm and dragged him some yards back from the others. "Jones," he said, in an intensely earnest voice, "will you tell me what in the devil I am going to do?"

The corporal's countenance[20] became illuminated with satisfaction at being thus requested to advise his superior officer. He adopted an air of great thought, and finally said: "Well, of course, the feller with the gray sleeve must be upstairs, and we must get past the girl and up there somehow. Suppose I take her by the arm and lead her——"

"What!" interrupted the captain from between his clinched teeth. As he turned away from the corporal, he said fiercely over his shoulder: "You touch that girl and I'll split your skull!"

17 **tremors:** shivering; trembling.
18 **ascertained:** made certain.
19 **phlegmatic:** weary; indifferent.

20 **countenance:** face.

STEPHEN CRANE

233

III

THE CORPORAL looked after his captain with an expression of mingled amazement, grief, and philosophy. He seemed to be saying to himself that there unfortunately were times, after all, when one could not rely upon the most reliable of men. When he returned to the group he found the captain bending over the girl and saying: "Why is it that you don't want us to search upstairs?"

The girl's head was buried in her crossed arms. Locks of her hair had escaped from their fastenings, and these fell upon her shoulder.

"Won't you tell me?"

The corporal here winked again at the man next to him.

"Because," the girl moaned—"because—there isn't anybody up there."

The captain at last said timidly: "Well, I'm afraid—I'm afraid we'll have to——"

The girl sprang to her feet again, and implored him with her hands. She looked deep into his eyes with her glance, which was at this time like that of the fawn when it says to the hunter, "Have mercy upon me!"

These two stood regarding each other. The captain's foot was on the bottom step, but he seemed to be shrinking. He wore an air of being deeply wretched and ashamed. There was a silence.

Suddenly the corporal said in a quick, low tone: "Look out, captain!"

All turned their eyes swiftly toward the head of the stairs. There had appeared there a youth in a gray uniform. He stood looking coolly down at them. No word was said by the troopers. The girl gave vent to a little wail of desolation, "O Harry!"

He began slowly to descend the stairs. His right arm was in a white sling, and there were some fresh bloodstains upon the cloth. His face was rigid and deathly pale, but his eyes flashed like lights. The girl was again moaning in an utterly dreary fashion, as the youth came slowly down toward the silent men in blue.

Six steps from the bottom of the flight he halted and said: "I reckon it's me you're looking for."

The troopers had crowded forward a trifle and, posed in lithe, nervous attitudes, were watching him like cats. The captain remained unmoved. At the youth's question he merely nodded his head and said, "Yes."

The young man in gray looked down at the girl, and then, in the same even tone which now, however, seemed to vibrate with suppressed fury, he said: "And is that any reason why you should insult my sister?"

At this sentence, the girl intervened, desperately, between the young man in gray and the officer in blue. "Oh, don't, Harry, don't! He was good to me! He was good to me, Harry—indeed he was!"

The youth came on in his quiet, erect fashion, until the girl could have touched either of the men with her hand, for the captain still remained with his foot upon the first step. She continually repeated: "O Harry! O Harry!"

The youth in gray maneuvered to glare into the captain's face, first over

one shoulder of the girl and then over the other. In a voice that rang like metal, he said: "You are armed and unwounded, while I have no weapons and am wounded; but——"

The captain had stepped back and sheathed his saber. The eyes of these two men were gleaming fire, but otherwise the captain's countenance was imperturbable. He said: "You are mistaken. You have no reason to——"

"You lie!"

All save the captain and the youth in gray started in an electric movement. These two words crackled in the air like shattered glass. There was a breathless silence.

The captain cleared his throat. His look at the youth contained a quality of singular and terrible ferocity, but he said in his stolid tone: "I

don't suppose you mean what you say now."

Upon his arm he had felt the pressure of some unconscious little fingers. The girl was leaning against the wall as if she no longer knew how to keep her balance, but those fingers—he held his arm very still. She murmured: "O Harry, don't! He was good to me—indeed he was!"

The corporal had come forward until he in a measure confronted the youth in gray, for he saw those fingers upon the captain's arm, and he knew that sometimes very strong men were not able to move hand nor foot under such conditions.

The youth had suddenly seemed to become weak. He breathed heavily and clung to the rail. He was glaring at the captain, and apparently summoning all his will power to combat his weakness. The corporal addressed him with profound straightforwardness: "Don't you be a derned fool!" The youth turned toward him so fiercely that the corporal threw up a knee and an elbow like a boy who expects to be cuffed.

The girl pleaded with the captain. "You won't hurt him, will you? He don't know what he's saying. He's wounded, you know. Please don't mind him!"

"I won't touch him," said the captain, with rather extraordinary earnestness; "don't you worry about him at all. I won't touch him!"

Then he looked at her, and the girl suddenly withdrew her fingers from his arm.

The corporal contemplated the top of the stairs, and remarked without surprise: "There's another of 'em coming!"

An old man was clambering down the stairs with much speed. He waved a cane wildly. "Get out of my house, you thieves! Get out! I won't have you cross my threshold! Get out!" He mumbled and wagged his head in an old man's fury. It was plainly his intention to assault them.

And so it occurred that a young girl became engaged in protecting a stalwart captain, fully armed, and with eight grim troopers at his back, from the attack of an old man with a walking stick!

A blush passed over the temples and brow of the captain, and he looked particularly savage and weary. Despite the girl's efforts, he suddenly faced the old man.

"Look here," he said distinctly, "we came in because we had been fighting in the woods yonder, and we concluded that some of the enemy were in this house, especially when we saw a gray sleeve at the window. But this young man is wounded, and I have nothing to say to him. I will even take it for granted that there are no others like him upstairs. We will go away, leaving your old house just as we found it! And we are no more thieves and rascals than you are!"

The old man simply roared: "I haven't got a cow nor a pig nor a chicken on the place! Your soldiers have stolen everything they could carry away. They have torn down half my fences for firewood. This afternoon some of your accursed bullets even broke my window-panes!"

The girl had been faltering: "Grandpa! O grandpa!"

The captain looked at the girl. She returned his glance from the shadow of the old man's shoulder. After studying her face a moment, he said: "Well, we will go now." He strode toward the door, and his men clanked docilely[21] after him.

At this time there was the sound of harsh cries and rushing footsteps from without. The door flew open, and a whirlwind composed of blue-coated troopers came in with a swoop. It was headed by the lieutenant. "Oh, here you are!" he cried, catching his breath. "We thought ——Oh, look at the girl!"

21 **docilely** (dŏs′əl lĭ): obediently.

The captain said intensely: "Shut up, you fool!"

The men settled to a halt with a clash and a bang. There could be heard the dulled sound of many hoofs outside of the house.

"Did you order up the horses?" inquired the captain.

"Yes. We thought——"

"Well, then, let's get out of here," interrupted the captain morosely.[22]

The men began to filter out into the open air. The youth in gray had been hanging dismally to the railing of the stairway. He now was climbing slowly up to the second floor. The old man was addressing himself directly to the serene corporal.

"Not a chicken on the place!" he cried.

"Well, I didn't take your chickens, did I?"

"No, maybe you didn't, but——"

The captain crossed the hall and stood before the girl in rather a culprit's fashion. "You are not angry at me, are you?" he asked timidly.

"No," she said. She hesitated a moment, and then suddenly held out her hand. "You were good to me—and I'm—much obliged."

The captain took her hand, and then he blushed, for he found himself unable to formulate a sentence that applied in any way to the situation.

She did not seem to heed that hand for a time.

He loosened his grasp presently, for he was ashamed to hold it so long without saying anything clever. At last, with an air of charging an intrenched brigade, he contrived to say: "I would rather do anything than frighten or trouble you."

His brow was warmly perspiring. He had a sense of being hideous in his dusty uniform and with his grimy face.

She said, "Oh, I'm so glad it was you instead of somebody who might have—might have hurt brother Harry and grandpa!"

He told her, "I wouldn't have hurt 'em for anything!"

There was a little silence.

"Well, good-by!" he said at last.

"Good-by!"

He walked toward the door past the old man, who was scolding at the vanishing figure of the corporal. The captain looked back. She had remained there watching him.

At the bugle's order, the troopers standing beside their horses swung briskly into the saddle. The lieutenant said to the first sergeant:

"Williams, did they ever meet before?"

"Hanged if I know!"

"Well, say——"

The captain saw a curtain move at one of the windows. He cantered from his position at the head of the column and steered his horse between two flower beds.

"Well, good-by!"

The squadron trampled slowly past.

"Good-by!"

They shook hands.

He evidently had something enormously important to say to her, but it seems that he could not manage it.

<hr>

22 **morosely:** disagreeably; glumly.

He struggled heroically. The bay charger, with his great mystically solemn eyes, looked around the corner of his shoulder at the girl.

The captain studied a pine tree. The girl inspected the grass beneath the window. The captain said hoarsely: "I don't suppose—I don't suppose—I'll ever see you again!"

She looked at him affrightedly and shrank back from the window. He seemed to have woefully expected a reception of this kind for his question. He gave her instantly a glance of appeal.

She said: "Why, no, I don't suppose you will."

"Never?"

"Why, no, 'tain't possible. You—you are a —Yankee!"

"Oh, I know it, but——" Eventually he continued: "Well, some day, you know, when there's no more fighting, we might——" He observed that she had again withdrawn suddenly into the shadow, so he said: "Well, good-by!"

When he held her fingers she bowed her head, and he saw a pink blush steal over the curves of her cheek and neck.

"Am I never going to see you again?"

She made no reply.

"Never?" he repeated.

After a long time, he bent over to hear a faint reply: "Sometimes—when there are no troops in the neighborhood—grandpa don't mind if I—walk over as far as that old oak tree yonder—in the afternoons."

It appeared that the captain's grip was very strong, for she uttered an exclamation and looked at her fingers as if she expected to find them mere fragments. He rode away.

The bay horse leaped a flower bed. They were almost to the drive, when the girl uttered a panic-stricken cry.

The captain wheeled his horse violently, and upon his return journey went straight through a flower bed.

The girl had clasped her hands. She beseeched him wildly with her eyes. "Oh, please, don't believe it! I never walk to the old oak tree. Indeed I don't! I never—never—never walk there."

The bridle drooped on the bay charger's neck. The captain's figure seemed limp. With an expression of profound dejection and gloom he stared off at where the leaden sky met the dark green line of the woods. The long-impending rain began to fall with a mournful patter, drop and drop. There was a silence.

At last a low voice said, "Well—I might—sometimes I might—perhaps —but only once in a great while—I might walk to the old tree—in the afternoons."

Understanding Literature

1. Describe the scene as the cavalry arrives. What is the mood at the beginning of the story?
2. How do the troopers act upon noticing the house? Describe the captain's actions.
3. Why do the brother and the grandfather appear?
4. Why does the captain have as much patience with the rebel soldier as he does?
5. What contrasts are built up between the way the captain approaches the house and the way he acts inside? between the brother and the sister? between the captain and the grandfather?
6. What effect does the girl have on the captain?
7. What is the significance of her walking "to the old tree—in the afternoons"?
8. In the opening sentence the lieutenant says that it may rain. How does the rain that begins at the end of the story fit in with the mood of the story?
9. What is the story saying about the effect of war on people?

The following is a newspaper report from *The New York Times,* introducing and report-ing a speech by Dr. Martin Luther King, a minister from Atlanta, Georgia, who led the fight for civil rights. The title "I Have a Dream" has now been given to this famous talk. The occasion was a march on Washington, D.C., August 28, 1963, made by over 200,000 people. At the time our country was being torn by racial violence; and this group, standing in front of the Lincoln Memorial, was asking peaceably for racial justice. The climax of the occasion was the speech by Dr. King.

I Have A Dream…

Dr. Martin Luther King, Jr.
as reported by James Reston

WASHINGTON, Aug. 28—Abraham Lincoln, who presided in his stone temple[1] today above the children of the slaves he emancipated, may have used just the right words to sum up the general reaction to the Negro's massive march on Washington. "I think," he wrote to Gov. Andrew G. Curtin of Pennsylvania in 1861, "the necessity of being ready increases. Look to it." Washington may not have changed a vote today, but it is a little more conscious tonight of the necessity of being ready for freedom. It may not "look to it" at once, since it is looking to so many things, but, it will be a long time before it for-gets the melodious and melancholy voice of the Rev. Dr. Martin Luther King Jr. crying out his dreams to the multitude.

It was Dr. King who, near the end of the day, touched the vast audi-ence. Until then the pilgrimage was merely a great spectacle. Only those marchers from the embattled towns in the Old Confederacy had any-thing like the old crusading zeal. For many the day seemed an adventure, a long outing in the late summer sun —part liberation from home, part Sunday School picnic, part political convention, and part fish-fry.

But Dr. King brought them alive in the late afternoon with a perora-tion[2] that was an anguished echo from all the old American reformers. Roger Williams calling for religious liberty, Sam Adams calling for poli-tical liberty, old man Thoreau de-nouncing coercion,[3] William Lloyd Garrison demanding emancipation,

---

1 This reference is to the Lincoln Memorial, which contains a large statue of Lincoln sitting. He would have appeared to be looking down on the people, even presiding over the meeting.

2 **peroration:** the conclusion of a speech in which the speaker is especially earnest and forceful.
3 **coercion** (kō ûr'shən) : restraining someone by force, or forcing someone to do something.

and Eugene V. Debs crying for economic equality—Dr. King echoed them all.

"I have a dream," he cried again and again. And each time the dream was a promise out of our ancient articles of faith; phrases from the Constitution, lines from the great anthem of the nation, guarantees from the Bill of Rights, all ending with a vision that they might one day all come true.

Dr. King touched all the themes of the day, only better than anybody else. He was full of the symbolism of Lincoln and Gandhi,[4] and the cadences of the Bible. He was both militant and sad, and he sent the crowd away feeling that the long journey had been worthwhile.

This demonstration impressed political Washington because it combined a number of things no politician can ignore. It had the force of numbers. It had the melodies of both the church and the theater. And it was able to invoke the principles of the founding fathers to rebuke[5] the inequalities and hypocrisies of modern American life.

There was a paradox[6] in the day's performance. The Negro leaders demanded equality "now," while insisting that this was only the "beginning" of the struggle. Yet it was clear that the "now," which appeared on almost every placard on Constitution Avenue, was merely an opening demand, while the exhortation[7] to increase the struggle was what was really on the leaders' minds.

It is a question whether this rally raised too many hopes among the Negroes or inspired the Negroes here to work harder for equality when they got back home. Most observers here think the latter is true, even though all the talk of "Freedom NOW" and instant integration is bound to lead to some disappointment.

The meetings between the Negro leaders on the one hand and President Kennedy and the Congressional leaders on the other also went well and probably helped the Negro cause. The Negro leaders were careful not to seem to be putting improper pressure on Congress. They made no specific requests or threats, but they argued their case in small groups and kept the crowd off Capitol Hill.

Whether this will win any new votes for the civil rights and economic legislation will probably depend on the over-all effect of the day's events on the television audience.

Above all, they got over Lincoln's point that "the necessity of being ready increases." For they left no doubt that this was not the climax of their campaign for equality but merely the beginning, that they were going to stay in the streets until they could get equality in the schools, restaurants, houses and employment agencies of the nation, and

4 Gandhi: Mahatma Gandhi—a Hindu religious leader who practiced noncooperation and passive resistance to secure political and social reforms.
5 rebuke: find fault with.
6 paradox: something that seems absurd or contradictory.

7 exhortation: urging, encouraging.

that, as they demonstrated here to-day, they had found an effective way to demonstrate for changes in the laws without breaking the law them-selves.

DR. MARTIN LUTHER KING SPEAKS

Now is the time to make real the promises of democracy. Now is the time to rise from the dark and deso-late valley of segregation to the sun-lit path of racial justice. Now is the time to lift our nation from the quicksands of racial injustice to the solid rock of brotherhood. Now is the time to make justice a reality for all of God's children.

There will neither be rest nor tran-quility in America until the Negro is granted his citizenship rights. The whirlwinds of revolt will continue to shake the foundations of our na-tion until the bright day of justice emerges.

And that is something that I must say to my people who stand on the threshold which leads to the palace of justice. In the process of gaining our rightful place we must not be guilty of wrongful deeds.

Again and again, we must rise to the majestic heights of meeting phys-ical force with soul force. The mar-velous new militancy which has engulfed the Negro community must not lead us to a distrust of all white people, for many of our white broth-ers as evidenced by their presence here today have come to realize that their destiny is tied up with our des-tiny.

There are those who are asking the devotees of civil rights, "When will you be satisfied?" We can never be satisfied as long as the Negro is the victim of the unspeakable hor-rors of police brutality. We can never be satisfied as long as our bodies, heavy with the fatigue of travel, can-not gain lodging in the motels of the highways and the hotels of the cities.

We can never be satisfied as long as our children are stripped of their selfhood and robbed of their dignity by signs saying "for whites only." We cannot be satisfied as long as the Negro in Mississippi cannot vote and the Negro in New York believes he has nothing for which to vote.

No, we are not satisfied and we will not be satisfied until justice rolls down like water and righteousness like a mighty stream.

Now, I am not unmindful that some of you have come here out of great trials and tribulations. Some of you have come fresh from narrow jail cells.

Continue to work with the faith that honor in suffering is redemp-tive.[8] Go back to Mississippi, go back to Alabama, go back to South Caro-lina, go back to Georgia, go back to Louisiana, go back to the slums and ghettos of our Northern cities, know-ing that somehow this situation can and will be changed. Let us not wallow in the valley of despair.

Now, I say to you today, my friends, so even though we face the difficulties of today and tomorrow, I still have a dream. It is a dream deeply rooted in the American

8 redemptive: rewarding.

dream. I have a dream that one day this nation will rise up and live out the true meaning of its creed: "We hold these truths to be self-evident, that all men are created equal."

I have a dream that one day on the red hills of Georgia the sons of former slaves and the sons of former slaveowners will be able to sit down together at the table of brotherhood.

I have a dream that one day even the state of Mississippi, a state sweltering with the people's injustice, sweltering with the heat of oppression, will be transformed into an oasis of freedom and justice.

I have a dream that my four little children will one day live in a nation where they will not be judged by the color of their skin, but by the content of their character.

This is our hope. This is the faith that I go back to the South with—with this faith we will be able to hew out of the mountain of despair a stone of hope.

Understanding Literature

1. As Dr. King begins to talk, he speaks of the "promises of democracy." What major promise does he want?
2. In the fifth paragraph he quotes those who say, "When will you be satisfied?" What does he say keeps his people from being satisfied?
3. What, in your own words, are the parts of Dr. King's "dream"? Read aloud the last five paragraphs of his speech and listen to the rhythm.

Further Activity

Martin Luther King gets much of his effect through the selection of words and the connotation of those words. What is particularly appropriate about the following phrases:

   (a) quicksands of racial injustice,
   (b) solid rock of brotherhood,
   (c) the threshold which leads to the palace of justice,
   (d) our children are stripped of their selfhood,
   (e) justice rolls down like water,
   (f) hew out of the mountain of despair a stone of hope.

Myths, Fables, and Legends

THROUGHOUT HISTORY questions concerning life, the world, and the universe have puzzled us. What causes the seasons? What causes storms and lightning? What happens to people after they die? Why are the deserts dry and scorched? Some of our earliest and most fascinating literature comes from a period before Christ (B.C.) in which the ancient Greeks and Romans were attempting to answer questions like these in order to understand their world better. These ancient people did not believe in one God; they attempted to answer puzzling questions by inventing many gods. These gods lived in the middle of the earth, on a high mountain named Mount Olympus, which was surrounded by a gate of clouds guarded by the goddesses named the Seasons. Ruling over the gods of Olympus as well as over the people of the earth were Jupiter and his wife Juno. These gods and goddesses of the Greek people had very exciting superhuman powers, but they also had many very human weaknesses and quarreled among themselves and played tricks not only on each other but also on the people of earth.

We know about these gods and goddesses through *myths,* many of which are ancient explanations of occurrences in nature; other myths do not explain anything in nature, but they can teach us a great deal about human nature. These myths, the origins of which are unknown, have come down to us after having been told and retold by many different people until, probably after many changes, they were written down by various poets whose works are available to us. In the pages that follow, you will read about the Greek myths as well as the myths of the Scandinavian countries.

You will also read some *fables,* which, like the myths, are not true but which have a different purpose. Instead of trying to explain life and the world as the myths do, fables usually attempt to teach or enforce some useful truth or moral, and frequently, unlike the myths, contain animals which speak and act like human beings.

The selections at the end of this unit are *legends.* Legends differ from either myths or fables. Although they are also stories which have come down from the past, many people believe them to be true, even though the facts in the legends cannot be proved.

When you have finished this unit, you will be familiar with some of the literature of several different regions—Greece, ancient Rome, England, the Scandinavian countries, India, and France. You will also be able to understand the *allusions,* or references, to many mythological and legendary figures which you will meet throughout your study of literature, and you will understand the qualities which these figures represent. As you look around you, too, you will recognize many mythological and legendary references used today—such as the Venus pencil, Atlas tires, the pictures of Mercury on advertisements, the space projects with mythological names, such as Project Mercury and Project Apollo, and many more.

The versions of the myths, fables, and legends which you are about to read were written by authors well-known for their studies of mythology. Their versions of the tales are not the only ones, but they are among the best-known. When you are finished with this unit, you might be interested in reading other versions of the same stories to see how they differ.

CHART
OF
THE GREEK GODS

*The following chart is a brief summary of the major gods
and goddesses in Greek mythology. You will want to refer
back to it as you read the myths.*

THE TITANS

CRONUS (Saturn)*	Ruler of the Titans until Zeus dethroned him
OCEAN	River encircling the earth
TETHYS (tē'thĭs)	Wife of Ocean
HYPERION	Father of the sun, the moon, and the dawn
MNEMOSYNE (nē mŏs'ə nē')	Memory
THEMIS (thē'mĭs)	Justice
IAPETUS (ī ăp'ə təs)	Father of Atlas
ATLAS	Bore the world on his shoulder
PROMETHEUS (prə mē'thē əs)	Savior of mankind

THE TWELVE GREAT
OLYMPIANS

*(lived on Mount Olympus in Thessaly,
in the northeast of Greece).*

ZEUS (zōōs) (Jupiter)	King of the gods
HERA (Juno)	Queen of the gods
POSEIDON (pō sī'dən) (Neptune)	God of the sea
HADES (Pluto)	God of the underworld
HESTIA (Vesta)	Goddess of the hearth and its fire
ARES (âr'ēz) (Mars)	God of war
PALLAS ATHENE (păl'əs ə thē'nĭ) (Minerva)	Goddess of wisdom
APOLLO (Phoebus Apollo)	God of the sun
APHRODITE (ăf'rə dī'tĭ) (Venus)	Goddess of love and beauty
HERMES (hûr'mēz) (Mercury)	Messenger of the gods; presided over any event which required skill and dexterity
ARTEMIS (är'tə mĭs) (Diana)	Goddess of the moon
HEPHAESTUS (hē fĕs'təs) (Vulcan)	Artist; made weapons for the gods

*Names in parentheses are Latin names given to the gods by the Romans.

Explanations for the creation of the earth and the creation of humankind have puzzled people throughout the ages. How does the Biblical story of creation compare with the one that follows?

This selection was written by Thomas Bulfinch, an American who died in 1867. Since his use of the English language may seem a little stiff and formal to you, you will be interested in comparing his style of telling a story with the styles of the other authors in this unit.

Prometheus and Pandora

Thomas Bulfinch

THE CREATION of the world is a problem naturally fitted to excite the liveliest interest of man, its inhabitant. The ancient pagans[1] had their own way of telling the story, which is as follows:

Before earth and sea and heaven were created, all things wore one aspect, to which we give the name of Chaos—a confused and shapeless mass, nothing but dead weight, in which, however, slumbered the seeds of things. Earth, sea, and air were all mixed up together; so the earth was not solid, the sea was not fluid, and the air was not transparent. God and Nature at last interposed, and put an end to this discord, separating earth from sea, and heaven from both. The fiery part, being the lightest, sprang up, and formed the skies; the air was next in weight and place. The earth, being heavier, sank below; and the water took the lowest place, and buoyed up the earth.

Here some god—it is not known

which—gave his good offices in arranging and disposing the earth. He appointed rivers and bays their places, raised mountains, scooped out valleys, distributed woods, fountains, fertile fields, and stony plains. The air being cleared, the stars began to appear, fishes took possession of the sea, birds of the air, and four-footed beasts of the land.

But a nobler animal was wanted, and Man was made. It is not known whether the creator made him of divine materials, or whether in the earth, so lately separated from heaven, there lurked still some heavenly seeds.

Prometheus took some of this earth, and kneading it up with water, made man in the image of the gods. He gave him an upright stature, so that while all other animals turn their faces downward, and look to the earth, he raises his to heaven, and gazes on the stars.

Prometheus was one of the Titans, a gigantic race, who inhabited the earth before the creation of man. To him and his brother Epimetheus

1 **pagans:** people who are not Christians, Jews, or Mohammedans.

was committed the office of making man, and providing him and all other animals with the faculties necessary for their preservation. Epimetheus undertook to do this, and Prometheus was to overlook his work, when it was done. Epimetheus accordingly proceeded to bestow upon the different animals the various gifts of courage, strength, swiftness, sagacity;[2] wings to one, claws to another, a shelly covering to a third, etc.

But when man came to be provided for, who was to be superior to all other animals, Epimetheus had been so prodigal[3] of his resources that he had nothing left to bestow upon him. In his perplexity he resorted to his brother Prometheus, who, with the aid of Minerva, went up to heaven, and lighted his torch at the chariot of the sun, and brought down fire to man. With this gift man was more than a match for all other animals. It enabled him to make weapons wherewith to subdue them; tools with which to cultivate the earth; to warm his dwelling, so as to be comparatively independent of climate; and to introduce the arts and to coin money, the means of trade and commerce.

Woman was not yet made. The story (absurd enough!) is that Jupiter made her, and sent her to Prometheus and his brother, to punish them for their presumption[4] in stealing fire from heaven; and man, for accepting the gift. The first woman was named Pandora. She was made in heaven, every god contributing something to perfect her. Venus gave her beauty, Mercury persuasion, Apollo music, etc. Thus equipped, she was conveyed to earth, and presented to Epimetheus, who gladly accepted her, though cautioned by his brother to beware of Jupiter and his gifts. Epimetheus had in his house a jar, in which were kept certain noxious[5] articles for which, in fitting man for his new abode, he had had no occasion.

Pandora was seized with an eager curiosity to know what this jar contained; and one day she slipped off the cover and looked in. Forthwith there escaped a multitude of plagues for hapless[6] man—such as gout, rheumatism, and colic for his body, and envy, spite, and revenge for his mind—and scattered themselves far and wide. Pandora hastened to replace the lid; but, alas! the whole contents of the jar had escaped, one thing only excepted, which lay at the bottom, and that was *hope*. So we see at this day, whatever evils are abroad, hope never entirely leaves us; and while we have *that*, no amount of other ills can make us completely wretched.

Prometheus has been a favorite subject with the poets. He is represented as the friend of mankind, who taught them civilization and the arts. But as, in so doing, he transgressed[7] the will of Jupiter, he drew down on himself the anger of the ruler of gods

2 **sagacity:** wisdom.
3 **prodigal:** wasteful.
4 **presumption:** bold venture going beyond limits imposed by the gods.

5 **noxious:** harmful.
6 **hapless:** unlucky.
7 **transgressed:** violated.

and men. Jupiter had him chained to a rock on Mount Caucasus. This state of torment might have been brought to an end at any time by Prometheus, if he had been willing to submit to his oppressor; for he possessed a secret which involved the stability[8] of Jove's throne, and if he would have revealed it, he might have been at once taken into favor. But that he disdained[9] to do. He has therefore become the symbol of magnanimous[10] endurance of unmerited suffering, and strength of will resisting oppression.

"I would not quit
This bleak ravine, these unrepentant[11] pains. . . .
Pity the self-despising slaves of Jove,
Not me, within whose mind sits peace serene."

Shelley

8 **stability:** firmness.
9 **disdained:** proudly refused.

10 **magnanimous:** honorable; noble.
11 **unrepentant:** lacking in sorrow or remorse for wrongdoing.

Understanding Literature

1. A myth may be an explanation of something about nature or the universe. What does the Prometheus myth explain? In what ways is this explanation similar to that found in the Book of Genesis in the Old Testament?
2. The word *chaos* is often used to describe confusion. What does the proper noun *Chaos* represent in this myth?
3. According to this myth, in what ways do human beings differ from the other animals of the earth?
4. In what ways does Prometheus's gift of fire benefit humankind? Why might this gift have violated the will of Jupiter?
5. In Greek mythology Pandora is the first woman on earth. What characteristic does she have which proves to be disastrous? Explain. In what ways is she similar to Eve in the Old Testament?
6. Why is it significant that *hope* is the only thing left in the jar? What is another quality that might be as important to humankind?
7. The lines quoted at the end of the selection you have just read are from a long poem, *Prometheus Unbound*, by Percy Bysshe Shelley, a 19th-century English poet. Who do you think is speaking these lines? What do they mean?
8. What do you think this myth is saying about the dangers that might be faced by people who try to do more than is expected of them? Why is Prometheus considered a hero?

Did you ever wonder why some of the months of the year are cold and bleak, whereas others are warm and good for planting? While modern science gives a different answer, the following myth gives the early Greek explanation of the origin of the seasons.

Demeter (Ceres)

Edith Hamilton

DEMETER[1] HAD an only daughter, Persephone[2] (in Latin Proserpine), the maiden of the spring. She lost her and in her terrible grief she withheld her gifts from the earth, which turned into a frozen desert. The green and flowering land was icebound and lifeless because Persephone had disappeared.

The lord of the dark underworld, the king of the multitudinous[3] dead, carried her off when, enticed[4] by the wondrous bloom of the narcissus, she strayed too far from her companions. In his chariot drawn by coal-black steeds he rose up through a chasm in the earth, and grasping the maiden by the wrist set her beside him. He bore her away, weeping, down to the underworld. The high hills echoed her cry and the depths of the sea, and her mother heard it. She sped like a bird over sea and land seeking her daughter. But no one would tell her the truth, "no man nor god, nor any sure messenger from the birds." Nine days Demeter wandered, and all that time she would not taste of ambrosia or put sweet nectar to her lips. At last she came to the Sun and he told her all the story: Persephone was down in the world beneath the earth, among the shadowy dead.

Then a still greater grief entered Demeter's heart. She left Olympus; she dwelt on earth, but so disguised that none knew her, and, indeed, the gods are not easily discerned by mortal men. In her desolate[5] wanderings she came to Eleusis and sat by the wayside near a wall. She seemed an aged woman, such as in great houses care for the children or guard the storerooms. Four lovely maidens, sisters, coming to draw water from the well, saw her and asked her pityingly what she did there. She answered that she had fled from pirates who had meant to sell her as a slave, and that she knew no one in this strange land to go to for help. They told her that any house in the town would welcome her, but that they would like best to bring her to their own if she would wait there while they went to ask their mother. The goddess bent her head in assent,[6] and the girls, filling

1 **Demeter** (dĭ mē′tər).
2 **Persephone** (pər sĕf′ə nĭ).
3 **multitudinous:** great numbers.
4 **enticed:** attracted.

5 **desolate:** lonely.
6 **assent:** approval.

their shining pitchers with water, hurried home. Their mother, Metaneira, bade them return at once and invite the stranger to come, and speeding back they found the glorious goddess still sitting there, deeply veiled and covered to her slender feet by her dark robe. She followed them, and as she crossed the threshold to the hall where the mother sat holding her young son, a divine radiance filled the doorway and awe fell upon Metaneira.

She bade Demeter be seated and herself offered her honeysweet wine, but the goddess would not taste it. She asked instead for barley-water flavored with mint, the cooling draught of the reaper at harvest time and also the sacred cup given the worshipers at Eleusis. Thus refreshed she took the child and held him to her fragrant bosom and his mother's heart was glad. So Demeter nursed Demophoön,[7] the son that Metaneira had borne to wise Celeus. And the child grew like a young god, for daily Demeter anointed him with ambrosia and at night she would place him in the red heart of the fire. Her purpose was to give him immortal youth.

Something, however, made the mother uneasy, so that one night she kept watch and screamed in terror when she saw the child laid in the fire. The goddess was angered; she seized the boy and cast him on the ground. She had meant to set him free from old age and from death, but that was not to be. Still, he had lain upon her knees and slept in her arms and therefore he should have honor throughout his life.

Then she showed herself the goddess manifest.[8] Beauty breathed about her and a lovely fragrance; light shone from her so that the great house was filled with brightness. She was Demeter, she told the awestruck women. They must build her a great temple near the town and so win back the favor of her heart.

Thus she left them, and Metaneira fell speechless to the earth and all there trembled with fear. In the morning they told Celeus what had happened and he called the people together and revealed to them the command of the goddess. They worked willingly to build her a temple, and when it was finished Demeter came to it and sat there—apart from the gods in Olympus, alone, wasting away with longing for her daughter.

That year was most dreadful and cruel for mankind over all the earth. Nothing grew; no seed sprang up; in vain the oxen drew the plowshare through the furrows. It seemed the whole race of men would die of famine. At last Zeus saw that he must take the matter in hand. He sent the gods to Demeter, one after another, to try to turn her from her anger, but she listened to none of them. Never would she let the earth bear fruit until she had seen her daughter. Then Zeus realized that his brother must give way. He told Hermes to go down to the under-

---

7 **Demophoön** (dǐ mŏf'ō ŏn).

8 **manifest:** unconcealed.

MYTHS, FABLES, AND LEGENDS

Antonakos

world and to bid the lord of it let his bride go back to Demeter.

Hermes found the two sitting side by side, Persephone shrinking away, reluctant because she longed for her mother. At Hermes's words she sprang up joyfully, eager to go. Her husband knew that he must obey the word of Zeus and send her up to earth away from him, but he prayed her as she left him to have kind thoughts of him and not be so sorrowful that she was the wife of one who was great among the immortals. And he made her eat a pomegranate[9] seed, knowing in his heart that if she did so she must return to him.

He got ready his golden car and Hermes took the reins and drove the black horses straight to the temple where Demeter was. She ran out to meet her daughter as swiftly as a Maenad runs down the mountainside. Persephone sprang into her arms and was held fast there. All day they talked of what had happened to them both, and Demeter grieved when she heard of the pomegranate seed, fearing that she could not keep her daughter with her.

Then Zeus sent another messenger to her, a great personage, none other than his revered mother Rhea, the oldest of the gods. Swiftly she hastened down from the heights of Olympus to the barren, leafless earth, and standing at the door of the temple she spoke to Demeter.

Come, my daughter, for Zeus, far-seeing,
  loud-thundering, bids you.
Come once again to the halls of the gods
  where you shall have honor.

Where you will have your desire, your
  daughter, to comfort your sorrow
As each year is accomplished and bitter
  winter is ended.
For a third part only the kingdom of darkness shall hold her.
For the rest you will keep her, you and
  the happy immortals.
Peace now. Give men life which comes
  alone from your giving.

Demeter did not refuse, poor comfort though it was that she must lose Persephone for four months every year and see her young loveliness go down to the world of the dead. But she was kind; the "Good Goddess," men always called her. She was sorry for the desolation she had brought about. She made the fields once more rich with abundant fruit and the whole world bright with flowers and green leaves. Also she went to the princes of Eleusis who had built her temple and she chose one, Triptolemus, to be her ambassador to men, instructing them how to sow the corn. She taught him and Celeus and the others her sacred rites, "mysteries which no one may utter, for deep awe checks the tongue. Blessed is he who has seen them; his lot will be good in the world to come."

In the stories of both goddesses, Demeter and Persephone, the idea of sorrow was foremost. Demeter, goddess of the harvest wealth, was still more the divine sorrowing mother who saw her daughter die each year. Persephone was the radiant maiden of the spring and the summertime, whose light step upon the dry, brown hillside was enough to make it fresh

9 **pomegranate:** thick-skinned reddish fruit.

and blooming, as Sappho[10] writes,

I heard the footfall of the flower spring . . .

—Persephone's footfall. But all the while Persephone knew how brief that beauty was; fruits, flowers, leaves, all the fair growth of earth, must end with the coming of the cold and pass like herself into the power of death. After the lord of the dark world below carried her away she was never again the gay young creature who had played in the flowery meadow without a thought of care or trouble. She did indeed rise from the dead every spring, but she brought with her the memory of where she had come from; with all her bright beauty there was something strange and awesome about her. She was often said to be "the maiden whose name may not be spoken."

The Olympians were "the happy gods," "the deathless gods," far removed from suffering mortals destined to die. But in their grief and at the hour of death, men could turn for compassion to the goddess who sorrowed and the goddess who died.

10 Sappho: ancient Greek poet.

Understanding Literature

1. Summarize the story of the origin of the seasons.
2. Demeter's care of and plans for Demophoön make a story within a story. What is the probable purpose for including this secondary story? What phenomenon of nature is explained by Demeter's absence from her duties as the harvest queen?
3. Why did men call Demeter the "Good Goddess"?
4. Why are Demeter and Persephone associated with the idea of sorrow?
5. The tone of a piece of writing depends to a great extent on the author's careful selection of words. In "Demeter" a feeling of beauty, power, and royalty is associated with the gods. For example, Persephone is described as "the maiden of the spring," and Demeter is described as the "glorious goddess." What other words or phrases do you find in this myth which seem unusually descriptive?

Why are some parts of the earth dry desert land, whereas others are moist and fertile? This myth gives one answer.

Phaethon, Son of Apollo

Olivia E. Coolidge

THOUGH APOLLO always honored the memory of Daphne, she was not his only love. Another was a mortal, Clymene,[1] by whom he had a son named Phaethon.[2] Phaethon grew up with his mother, who, since she was mortal, could not dwell in the halls of Olympus or in the palace of the sun. She lived not far from the East in the land of Ethiopia, and as her son grew up, she would point to the place where Eos, goddess of the dawn, lighted up the sky and tell him that there his father dwelt. Phaethon loved to boast of his divine father as he saw the golden chariot riding high through the air. He would remind his comrades of other sons of gods and mortal women who, by virtue of their great deeds, had themselves become gods at last. He must always be first in everything, and in most things this was easy, since he was in truth stronger, swifter, and more daring than the others. Even if he were not victorious, Phaethon always claimed to be first in honor. He could never bear to be beaten, even if he must risk his life in some rash way to win.

Most of the princes of Ethiopia willingly paid Phaethon honor, since they admired him greatly for his fire and beauty. There was one boy, however, Epaphos,[3] who was rumored to be a child of Zeus himself. Since this was not certainly proved, Phaethon chose to disbelieve it and to demand from Epaphos the deference[4] that he obtained from all others. Epaphos was proud too, and one day he lost his temper with Phaethon and turned on him, saying, "You are a fool to believe all that your mother tells you. You are all swelled up with false ideas about your father."

Crimson with rage, the lad rushed home to his mother and demanded that she prove to him the truth of the story that she had often told. "Give me some proof," he implored her, "with which I can answer this insult of Epaphos. It is a matter of life and death to me, for if I cannot, I shall die of shame."

"I swear to you," replied his mother solemnly, "by the bright orb of the sun itself that you are his son. If I swear falsely, may I never look on the sun again, but die before the

1 **Clymene** (klĭm'ə nē).
2 **Phaethon** (fā'ə thən).
3 **Epaphos** (ĕp'ə fəs).
4 **deference:** respect.

MYTHS, FABLES, AND LEGENDS

next time he mounts the heavens. More than this I cannot do, but you, my child, can go to the eastern palace of Phoebus Apollo—it lies not far away—and there speak with the god himself."

The son of Clymene leaped up with joy at his mother's words. The palace of Apollo was indeed not far. It stood just below the eastern horizon, its tall pillars glistening with bronze and gold. Above these it was white with gleaming ivory, and the great doors were flashing silver, embossed with pictures of earth, sky, and sea, and the gods that dwelt therein. Up the steep hill and the bright steps climbed Phaethon, passing unafraid through the silver doors, and stood in the presence of the sun. Here at last he was forced to turn away his face, for Phoebus sat in state on his golden throne. It gleamed with emeralds and precious stones, while on the head of the god was a brilliant diamond crown upon which no eye could look undazzled.

Phaethon hid his face, but the god had recognized his son, and he spoke kindly, asking him why he had come. Then Phaethon plucked up courage and said, "I come to ask you if you are indeed my father. If you are so, I beg you to give me some proof of it so that all may recognize me as Phoebus's son."

The god smiled, being well pleased with his son's beauty and daring. He took off his crown so that Phaethon could look at him, and coming down from his throne, he put his arms around the boy, and said, "You are indeed my son and Clymene's, and worthy to be called so. Ask of me whatever thing you wish to prove your origin to men, and you shall have it."

Phaethon swayed for a moment and was dizzy with excitement at the touch of the god. His heart leaped; the blood rushed into his face. Now he felt that he was truly divine, unlike other men, and he did not wish to be counted with men any more. He looked up for a moment at his radiant father. "Let me drive the chariot of the sun across the heavens for one day," he said.

Apollo frowned and shook his head. "I cannot break my promise, but I will dissuade you if I can," he answered. "How can you drive my chariot, whose horses need a strong hand on the reins? The climb is too steep for you. The immense height will make you dizzy. The swift streams of air in the upper heaven will sweep you off your course. Even the immortal gods could not drive my chariot. How then can you? Be wise and make some other choice."

The pride of Phaethon was stubborn, for he thought the god was merely trying to frighten him. Besides, if he could guide the sun's chariot, would he not have proved his right to be divine rather than mortal? For that he would risk his life. Indeed, once he had seen Apollo's splendor, he did not wish to go back and live among men. Therefore, he insisted on his right until Apollo had to give way.

When the father saw that nothing else would satisfy the boy, he bade the Hours bring forth his chariot and yoke the horses. The chariot was of gold and had two gold-rimmed wheels with spokes of silver. In it there was room for one man to stand and hold the reins. Around the front and sides of it ran a rail, but the back was open. At the end of a long pole there were yokes for the four horses. The pole was of gold and shone with precious jewels: the golden topaz, the bright diamond, the green emerald, and the flashing ruby. While the Hours were yoking the swift, pawing horses, rosy-fingered Dawn hastened to the gates of heaven to draw them open. Meanwhile Apollo anointed his son's face with a magic ointment, that he might be able to bear the heat of the fire-breathing horses and the golden chariot. At last Phaethon mounted the chariot and grasped the reins, the barriers were let down, and the horses shot up into the air.

At first the fiery horses sped forward up the accustomed trail, but behind them the chariot was too light without the weight of the immortal god. It bounded from side to side and was dashed up and down. Phaethon was too frightened and too dizzy to pull the reins, nor would he have known anyway whether he was on the usual path. As soon as the horses felt that there was no hand controlling them, they soared up, up with fiery speed into the heavens till the earth grew pale and cold beneath them. Phaethon shut his eyes, trembling at the dizzy, precipitous[5] height. Then the horses dropped down, more swiftly than a falling

stone, flinging themselves madly from side to side in panic because they were masterless. Phaethon dropped the reins entirely and clung with all his might to the chariot rail. Meanwhile as they came near the earth, it dried up and cracked apart. Meadows were reduced to white ashes, cornfields smoked and shriveled, cities perished in flame. Far and wide on the wooded mountains the forests were ablaze, and even the snow-clad Alps were bare and dry. Rivers steamed and dried to dust. The great North African plain was scorched until it became the desert that it is today. Even the sea shrank back to pools and caves, until dried fishes were left baking upon the white-hot sands. At last the great earth mother called upon Zeus to save her from utter destruction, and Zeus hurled a mighty thunderbolt at the unhappy Phaethon, who was still crouched in the chariot, clinging desperately to the rail. The dart cast him out, and he fell flaming in a long trail through the air. The chariot broke in pieces at the mighty blow, and the maddened horses rushed snorting back to the stable of their master, Apollo.

Unhappy Clymene and her daughters wandered over the whole earth seeking the body of the boy they loved so well. When they found him, they took him and buried him. Over his grave they wept and could not be comforted. At last the gods in pity for their grief changed them into poplar trees, which weep with tears of amber in memory of Phaethon.

5 precipitous: steep.

MYTHS, FABLES, AND LEGENDS

Understanding Literature

1. Describe the scene that prompts Phaethon to ask his mother for proof that Apollo is his father.
2. Why does Phaethon insist that Apollo carry through his promise in spite of Apollo's attempt to dissuade him?
3. In what ways does the earth suffer because of Phaethon's driving the chariot?
4. What happens to Phaethon's mother, Clymene?
5. What qualities in human nature does this myth illustrate?
6. In this myth many of the words and phrases of description are particularly fitting for the sun-god. For example, the myth states that Phaethon is admired "greatly for his *fire* and *beauty*." Another time, Phaethon is described as being "crimson with rage." Find other examples of description that are particularly appropriate in a myth about the sun-god and his son.

Further Activity

Apollo is a very important god in Greek and Roman mythology, just as the sun is a very important part of our universe. The myth that you have just read is one of many which concern this powerful god. There is a myth about how Apollo's cattle are stolen by his brother Mercury. Another myth explains the reason why Apollo always wears a wreath of laurel and relates how a laurel crown becomes the prize for athletes and musicians. Still another myth about Apollo tells of Clytie's love for him and why Clytie is changed to a sunflower. Use your library facilities to prepare a report on as many myths about Apollo as you can.

People have always wanted to fly freely through the air. Today we can do so in airplanes and even rockets, but here is a story of one boy and his father who tried it another way.

Daedalus

Olivia E. Coolidge

IN THE VERY early days it was not the mainland of Greece that was the most important, but the island of Crete, which lies below the Aegean sea, south of most of the other islands. In it there are still ruins of a great palace, almost more a city than a palace, with so many rooms and passages that it must have had many people dwelling in it. These people were evidently traders and powerful on the sea. They must have been skilled shipbuilders, and from the remains we have found, we know they were also great architects, craftsmen, and artists. In later times the island sank into unimportance, and its former prominence was forgotten. Nevertheless the story of its greatness lingers on and is associated with the skills for which we know it was famous.

In legend the king of the island of Crete was called Minos. He had a great fleet and power that extended far and wide, dominating, among other places, the city of Athens. He seems to have been a fierce tyrant, for he forced the Athenians to send him a yearly tribute of seven youths and seven maidens, whom he fed to a horrible monster that he owned.

This animal was called the Minotaur and was a creature with the head of a bull and the body of a man. To keep him safe and to prevent his victims from escaping, it was necessary to build him some special dwelling. For this purpose Minos hired a famous architect whose name was Daedalus.[1]

Daedalus, the Greeks used to say, was the first great artist, craftsman, and engineer. It was he who invented many of the tools of carpentry: the saw, the gimlet, and an efficient glue. He also was the first to make statues more lifelike than a roughly carved pillar. Before this time statues had held their legs stiffly together and their arms down by their sides. Daedalus made them stepping forward and holding something in front of them. He is said to have built a great reservoir, fortified a city, and done many other engineering works. But the most famous of all the things he made was the house he built for Minos to keep the Minotaur in. This house was a labyrinth or maze, with countless winding passages, so that it was hard to find the

1 **Daedalus** (dĕd′ə ləs).

way in or out. Perhaps the idea got into the story from a vague memory of the countless confusing passages in the Cretan palace. In any case Daedalus is supposed to have built a maze for Minos, so elaborate in its windings that no man without a clue could possibly escape from it.

Minos was delighted with his labyrinth and held the architect in great honor. Unfortunately, when the wandering artist wished to take his fee and go, the King had other ideas. There were many things that could well be made for him by the greatest craftsman in the world, and he saw no reason why he should let the man build things for someone else. Being king over an island, Minos found it easy to keep Daedalus where he was. He simply forbade all ships to give the artist passage, provided him with an elaborate workshop, and suggested that he might as well settle down and be happy.

Thus Minos gained the services of Daedalus, but the great craftsman was not content. Beyond anything else he loved freedom to wander as he pleased, seeing the world and picking up new ideas. He was not the kind of man who could easily settle down. Therefore when he saw that he could not possibly get away by ship, he turned his talents to working out something else. Minos did not visit the fine workshop he had given his artist, but if he had, he would have seen a curious sight. The whole place was deep in feathers. There were feathers of all shapes and sizes, some just thrown down anyhow as they had been brought in, and some neatly sorted into heaps. A young boy, Icarus, Daedalus's only son and companion, was doing the sorting, while Daedalus himself was busy with twine, wax, and glue, fixing the feathers together in orderly rows on a wooden framework.

Daedalus was making wings. He had seen that it would be impossible to cross the sea by boat because of Minos's order, so he had determined to fly across it. After studying the wings of birds for a long time, he designed some which he thought would support a man, and now he was working on them. Icarus was terribly excited and was helping eagerly. He did not so much dislike living in Crete, but he wanted to fly as the gods do. Think of being the first man to have wings!

The wings took a long time to finish, but at last they were done, a mighty pair for Daedalus, and a smaller one for his son. The workshop being in the top of a lofty tower, Daedalus planned that they should simply launch themselves into the air from it. As they stood there, fastening the wings onto their shoulders, Daedalus gave his excited son some last instructions.

"I shall go first," he said, "to show the way. We must go straight across the sea by the shortest route, lest we become tired and drown before we can reach land. Follow me, and remember the wings on your shoulders are not natural wings, like those of Cupid. We are men and must use tools to do what the gods can do for themselves. Even with our tools we

must always fall short of them. If you fly too near the sea, the feathers will become wet and heavy, and you will drown; if you fly up into the air as the gods do, the wax will melt in the sun long before you reach Olympus. Then your wings will fall off and you will perish. Follow me as I go through the middle of the air, neither too high nor too low. So you will be safe."

He spoke and jumped, falling like a stone till the wind caught him and he steadied. Then he began to rise again as the wings beat steadily from his shoulders. He turned and beckoned Icarus to come on. Icarus jumped. The fall was terrible; so was the sudden stop as his spread wings caught the air. Still, he had the presence of mind to work his arms as he had seen his father do, and pretty soon he was sailing ahead in long swoops over the sea.

Presently the boy began to play tricks in the air. His father flew steadily on, but it would be easy, Icarus thought, to catch up with him. Father was too old to enjoy this properly. The swoops were rather sickening, but climbing was wonderful. Up, up he went, like the lark, like the eagle, like the gods. His father called something, but the wind whistled the sound away.

Icarus realized he ought to come down, but nobody had ever been up there before, except the gods. Perhaps the real difference between gods and men was that gods could fly. If he wanted to reach Olympus, he would have to take some risk.

Up, up Icarus went, soaring into the bright sun. In vain Daedalus called to him. He was only a black speck by now. At last he was coming down. He was coming very fast, much too fast. In another second Daedalus caught sight of the boy, whirling headlong. The framework was still on his shoulders, but the feathers had all fallen off, as the hot sun had melted the wax. One moment he saw him; then with a mighty splash Icarus hit the water and was gone. Daedalus circled round over the sea, not daring to go too low lest his own wings become soaked. There was no point in both being drowned. But not even a clutching hand broke surface. The white foam hung on the water for a space; then it too disappeared.

Daedalus flew on. He reached the land at last, white-faced and exhausted, but he would neither use his wings nor teach others how to make them. He had learned man's limitations. It is not right for him to soar like the gods.

Understanding Literature

1. Describe the Minotaur. How is he fed? Where is he kept?
2. Why is Daedalus considered the first great artist?
3. Describe the method Daedalus and Icarus use to escape from Crete. What is the fate of Icarus?
4. What quality in human nature does the story of Icarus illustrate?
5. At the end of this myth we learn that Daedalus would never again use his wings nor would he teach others how to make them. "He had learned man's limitations. It is not right for him to soar like the gods." What modern examples can you think of, in addition to airplane travel, which show that this idea is not generally accepted today? Do you think that Daedalus is right to any extent? Explain.

Further Activity

In the second and third paragraphs of "Daedalus" you read about the Minotaur. To find out what happens to this horrible monster—and whether anyone ever *does* find his way out of the maze—you will want to read another famous Greek myth: the story of Theseus. *Bulfinch's Mythology* and *Mythology* by Edith Hamilton are two sources which will help you prepare a report to the class.

In literature you will find frequent references to the Gorgons, of whom Medusa is the most famous. These three female monsters have huge teeth and claws, and snakes in place of hair. They turn to stone any animal or person who looks at them.

Perseus

Thomas Bulfinch

PERSEUS[1] was the son of Jupiter and Danaë. His grandfather Acrisius, alarmed by an oracle which had told him that his daughter's child would be the instrument of his death, caused the mother and child to be shut up in a chest and set adrift on the sea. The chest floated towards Seriphus, where it was found by a fisherman who conveyed the mother and infant to Polydectes, the king of the country, by whom they were treated with kindness. When Perseus was grown up Polydectes sent him to attempt the conquest of Medusa,[2] a terrible monster who had laid waste the country. She was once a beautiful maiden whose hair was her chief glory, but as she dared to vie in beauty with Minerva, the goddess deprived her of her charms and changed her beautiful ringlets into hissing serpents. She became a cruel monster of so frightful an aspect that no living thing could behold her without being turned into stone. All around the cavern where she dwelt might be seen the stony figures of men and animals which had chanced to catch a glimpse of her and had been petrified with the sight. Perseus, favored by Minerva and Mercury, the former of whom lent him her shield and the latter his winged shoes, approached Medusa while she slept and taking care not to look directly at her, but guided by her image reflected in the bright shield which he bore, he cut off her head and gave it to Minerva, who fixed it in the middle of her Aegis.[3]

[The following is a *flashback*. It takes place before Perseus gives Medusa's head to Minerva.]

After the slaughter of Medusa, Perseus, bearing with him the head of the Gorgon, flew far and wide, over land and sea. As night came on, he reached the western limit of the earth, where the sun goes down. Here he would gladly have rested till morning. It was the realm of King Atlas, whose bulk surpassed that of all other men. He was rich in flocks and herds and had no neighbor or rival to dispute his state. But his chief pride was in his gardens, whose fruit was of gold, hanging from golden branches, half hid with golden leaves. Perseus said to him, "I come as a guest. If you honor illustrious[4] descent, I claim Jupiter for my father; if mighty deeds, I

1 **Perseus** (pûr′sūs).
2 **Medusa** (mə dū′sə).

3 **Aegis** (ē′jĭs): shield.
4 **illustrious**: famous.

MYTHS, FABLES, AND LEGENDS

plead the conquest of the Gorgon. I seek rest and food." But Atlas remembered that an ancient prophecy had warned him that a son of Jove should one day rob him of his golden apples. So he answered, "Begone! or neither your false claims of glory nor parentage shall protect you;" and he attempted to thrust him out. Perseus, finding the giant too strong for him, said, "Since you value my friendship so little, deign to accept a present;" and turning his face away, he held up the Gorgon's head. Atlas, with all his bulk, was changed into stone. His beard and hair became forests, his arms and shoulders cliffs, his head a summit, and his bones rocks. Each part increased in bulk till he became a mountain, and (such was the pleasure of the gods) heaven with all its stars rests upon his shoulders.

Perseus, continuing his flight, arrived at the country of the Ethiopians, of which Cepheus[5] was king. Cassiopeia[6] his queen, proud of her beauty, had dared to compare herself to the sea-nymphs, which roused their indignation to such a degree that they sent a prodigious[7] sea-monster to ravage the coast. To appease[8] the deities, Cepheus was directed by the oracle to expose his daughter Andromeda to be devoured by the monster. As Perseus looked down from his aerial height he beheld the virgin chained to a rock, and waiting the approach of the serpent. She was so pale and motionless that if it had not been for her flowing tears and her hair that moved in the breeze, he would have taken her for a marble statue. He was so startled at the sight that he almost forgot to wave his wings. As he hovered over her he said, "O virgin, undeserving of those chains, but rather of such as bind fond lovers together, tell me, I beseech you, your name, and the name of your country, and why you are thus bound." At first she was silent from modesty, and, if she could, would have hid her face with her hands; but when he repeated his questions, for fear she might be thought guilty of some fault which she dared not tell, she disclosed her name and that of her country, and her mother's pride of beauty. Before she had done speaking, a sound was heard off upon the water, and the sea-monster appeared, with his head raised above the surface, cleaving the waves with his broad breast. The virgin shrieked, the father and mother who had now arrived at the scene, wretched both, but the mother more justly so, stood by, not able to afford protection, but only to pour forth lamentations and to embrace the victim. Then spoke Perseus: "There will be time enough for tears; this hour is all we have for rescue. My rank as the son of Jove and my renown as the slayer of the Gorgon might make me acceptable as a suitor; but I will try to win her by services rendered, if the gods will only be propitious.[9] If she be

5 **Cepheus** (sē'fūs).
6 **Cassiopeia** (kăs'ĭ ə pē'ə).
7 **prodigious** (prə dĭj'əs): marvelous; extraordinary.
8 **appease**: calm; soothe.

9 **propitious** (prə pĭsh'əs): favorably inclined.

rescued by my valor, I demand that she be my reward." The parents consent (how could they hesitate?) and promise a royal dowry with her.

And now the monster was within the range of a stone thrown by a skillful slinger, when with a sudden bound the youth soared into the air. As an eagle, when from his lofty flight he sees a serpent basking in the sun, pounces upon him and seizes him by the neck to prevent him from turning his head round and using his fangs, so the youth darted down upon the back of the monster and plunged his sword into its shoulder. Irritated by the wound, the monster raised himself into the air, then plunged into the depth; then, like a wild boar surrounded by a pack of barking dogs, turned swiftly from side to side, while the youth eluded its attacks

by means of his wings. Wherever he can find a passage for his sword between the scales he makes a wound, piercing now the side, now the flank, as it slopes towards the tail. The brute spouts from his nostrils water mixed with blood. The wings of the hero are wet with it, and he dares no longer trust to them. Alighting on a rock which rose above the waves, and holding on by a projecting fragment, as the monster floated near he gave him a death stroke. The people who had gathered on the shore shouted so that the hills re-echoed with the sound. The parents, transported with joy, embraced their future son-in-law, calling him their deliverer and the savior of their house, and the virgin, both cause and reward of the contest, descended from the rock.

The joyful parents, with Perseus and Andromeda, repaired[10] to the palace, where a banquet was spread for them, and all was joy and festivity. But suddenly a noise was heard of warlike clamor, and Phineus,[11] the betrothed of the virgin, with a party of his adherents, burst in, demanding the maiden as his own. It was in vain that Cepheus remonstrated— "You should have claimed her when she lay bound to the rock, the monster's victim. The sentence of the gods dooming her to such a fate dissolved all engagements, as death itself would have done." Phineus made no reply, but hurled his javelin at Perseus, but it missed its mark and fell harmless. Perseus would have thrown his in turn, but the cowardly assailant ran and took shelter behind the altar. But his act was a signal for an onset by his band upon the guests of Cepheus. They defended themselves and a general conflict ensued,[12] the old king retreating from the scene after fruitless expostulations, calling the gods to witness that he was guiltless of this outrage on the rights of hospitality.

Perseus and his friends maintained for some time the unequal contest; but the numbers of the assailants were too great for them, and destruction seemed inevitable, when a sudden thought struck Perseus—"I will make my enemy defend me." Then with a loud voice he exclaimed, "If I have any friend here let him turn away his eyes!" and held aloft the Gorgon's head. "Seek not to frighten us with your jugglery," said Thescelus, and raised his javelin in the act to throw, and became stone in the very attitude. Ampyx was about to plunge his sword into the body of a prostrate foe, but his arm stiffened and he could neither thrust forward nor withdraw it. Another, in the midst of a vociferous[13] challenge, stopped, his mouth open, but no sound issuing. One of Perseus's friends, Aconteus, caught sight of the Gorgon and stiffened like the rest. Astyages struck him with his sword, but instead of wounding, it recoiled with a ringing noise.

Phineus beheld this dreadful result of his unjust aggression, and felt confounded. He called aloud to his friends, but got no answer; he touched them and found them stone. Falling on his knees and stretching out his hands to Perseus, but turning his head away, he begged for mercy. "Take all," said he, "give me but my life." "Base coward," said Perseus, "thus much I will grant you; no weapon shall touch you; moreover, you shall be preserved in my house as a memorial of these events." So saying, he held the Gorgon's head to the side where Phineus was looking, and in the very form in which he knelt, with his hands outstretched and face averted, he became fixed immovably, a mass of stone!

---

10 **repaired:** here, returned.
11 **Phineus** (fĭ′nūs).
12 **ensued:** followed.

13 **vociferous** (vō sĭf′ər əs): noisy.

Understanding Literature

1. Why does Minerva change Medusa from a beautiful maiden to a hideous monster?
2. How does Perseus avoid being turned into stone?
3. In what ways does King Atlas change after looking at Medusa's head?
4. Why is Andromeda being sacrificed?
5. According to King Cepheus, why is Phineus's engagement to Andromeda no longer binding?
6. In what way does Perseus use Medusa's head in the battle between his friends and the followers of Phineus?
7. Describe what happens to Phineus in the final scene of this battle.
8. What human frailty or weakness is illustrated by the story of the sacrifice of Andromeda?
9. What is the purpose of the several secondary stories contained within the myth of Perseus?

Further Activities

1. In many ways the myth describing Perseus and his rescue of Andromeda is not too different from modern-day hero stories. Write a brief story in which a 20th-century Perseus rescues a 20th-century Andromeda. Use a modern setting and a present-day problem.
2. According to the myths, a winged horse arises from the blood which drops to the ground when Perseus cuts off Medusa's head. This horse, named Pegasus, is later captured by Bellerophon. Using your library resources, prepare a report on the myth which describes what finally happens to Pegasus and Bellerophon.

Hercules, the great hero of Greece, has to do twelve labors, often referred to in ordinary conversation as well as in literature. The following myth explains why he has to do them and what they are.

Hercules

Edith Hamilton

THE GREATEST HERO of Greece was Hercules. He was a personage of quite another order from the great hero of Athens, Theseus.[1] He was what all Greece except Athens most admired. The Athenians were different from the other Greeks and their hero therefore was different. Theseus was, of course, bravest of the brave as all heroes are, but unlike other heroes he was as compassionate[2] as he was brave and a man of great intellect as well as great bodily strength. It was natural that the Athenians should have such a hero because they valued thought and ideas as no other part of the country did. In Theseus their ideal was embodied. But Hercules embodied what the rest of Greece most valued. His qualities were those the Greeks in general honored and admired. Except for unflinching courage, they were not those that distinguished Theseus.

Hercules was the strongest man on earth and he had the supreme self-confidence magnificent physical strength gives. He considered himself on an equality with the gods— and with some reason. They needed his help to conquer the giants. In the final victory of the Olympians over the brutish sons of Earth, Hercules's arrows played an important part. He treated the gods accordingly. Once when the priestess at Delphi gave no response to the question he asked, he seized the tripod she sat on and declared that he would carry it off and have an oracle of his own. Apollo, of course, would not put up with this, but Hercules was perfectly willing to fight him and Zeus had to intervene. The quarrel was easily settled, however. Hercules was quite good-natured about it. He did not want to quarrel with Apollo, he only wanted an answer from his oracle. If Apollo would give it the matter was settled as far as he was concerned. Apollo on his side, facing this undaunted person, felt an admiration for his boldness and made his priestess deliver the response.

Throughout his life Hercules had this perfect confidence that no matter who was against him he could never be defeated, and facts bore

1 **Theseus** (thē′sōōs).
2 **compassionate:** sympathetic.

him out. Whenever he fought with anyone the issue was certain beforehand. He could be overcome only by a supernatural force. Hera used hers against him with terrible effect and in the end he was killed by magic, but nothing that lived in the air, sea, or on land ever defeated him.

Intelligence did not figure largely in anything he did and was often conspicuously absent. Once when he was too hot he pointed an arrow at the sun and threatened to shoot him. Another time when the boat he was in was tossed about by the waves he told the waters that he would punish them if they did not grow calm. His intellect was not strong. His emotions were. They were quickly aroused and apt to get out of control, as when he deserted the *Argo* and forgot all about his comrades and the Quest of the Golden Fleece in his despairing grief at losing his young armor-bearer, Hylas. This power of deep feeling in a man of his tremendous strength was oddly endearing, but it worked immense harm, too. He had sudden outbursts of furious anger which were always fatal to the often innocent objects. When the rage had passed and he had come to himself he would show a most disarming penitence[3] and agree humbly to any punishment it was proposed to inflict on him. Without his consent he could not have been punished by anyone—yet nobody ever endured so many punishments. He spent a large part of his life expiating[4] one unfortunate deed after another and never rebelling against the almost impossible demands made upon him. Sometimes he punished himself when others were inclined to exonerate[5] him.

It would have been ludicrous[6] to put him in command of a kingdom as Theseus was put; he had more than enough to do to command himself. He could never have thought out any new or great idea as the Athenian hero was held to have done. His thinking was limited to devising a way to kill a monster which was threatening to kill him. Nevertheless he had true greatness. Not because he had complete courage based upon overwhelming strength, which is merely a matter of course, but because, by his sorrow for wrongdoing and his willingness to do anything to expiate it, he showed greatness of soul. If only he had had some greatness of mind as well, at least enough to lead him along the ways of reason, he would have been the perfect hero.

He was born in Thebes and for a long time was held to be the son of Amphitryon, a distinguished general. In those earlier years he was called Alcides, or descendant of Alcaeus who was Amphitryon's father. But in reality he was the son of Zeus. His mother, Alcmena,[7] bore two children, Hercules to Zeus and Iphicles to Amphitryon. The difference in the boys' descent was clearly shown in the way each acted in face of a

3 **disarming penitence:** touching regret for his sin.
4 **expiating:** atoning for; making up for.

5 **exonerate:** pardon.
6 **ludicrous:** ridiculous.
7 **Alcmena** (ălk mē'nə).

great danger which came to them before they were a year old. Hera, as always, was furiously jealous and she determined to kill Hercules.

One evening Alcmena gave both the children their bath and their fill of milk and laid them in their crib, caressing them and saying, "Sleep, my little ones, soul of my soul. Happy be your slumber and happy your awakening." She rocked the cradle and in a moment the babies were asleep. But at darkest midnight when all was silent in the house two great snakes came crawling into the nursery. There was a light in the room and as the two reared up above the crib, with weaving heads and flickering tongues, the children woke. Iphicles screamed and tried to get out of bed, but Hercules sat up and grasped the deadly creatures by the throat. They turned and twisted and wound their coils around his body, but he held them fast. The mother heard Iphicles's screams and, calling to her husband, rushed to the nursery. There sat Hercules laughing, in each hand a long limp body. He gave them gleefully to Amphitryon. They were dead. All knew then that the child was destined to great things. Teiresias, the blind prophet of Thebes, told Alcmena: "I swear that many a Greek woman as she cards the wool at eventide shall sing of this your son and you who bore him. He shall be the hero of all mankind."

Great care was taken with his education, but teaching him what he did not wish to learn was a dangerous business. He seems not to have liked music, which was a most important part of a Greek boy's training, or else he disliked his music master. He flew into a rage with him and brained him with his lute.[8] This was the first time he dealt a fatal blow without intending it. He did not mean to kill the poor musician; he just struck out on the impulse of the moment without thinking, hardly aware of his strength. He was sorry, very sorry, but that did not keep him from doing the same thing again and again. The other subjects he was taught, fencing, wrestling and driving, he took to more kindly, and his teachers in these branches all survived. By the time he was eighteen he was full-grown and he killed, alone by himself, a great lion which lived in the woods of Cithaeron, the Thespian lion. Ever after he wore its skin as a cloak with the head forming a kind of hood over his own head.

His next exploit was to fight and conquer the Minyans, who had been exacting a burdensome tribute from the Thebans. The grateful citizens gave him as a reward the hand of the Princess Megara. He was devoted to her and to their children and yet this marriage brought upon him the greatest sorrow of his life as well as trials and dangers such as no one ever went through, before or after. When Megara had borne him three sons he went mad. Hera, who never forgot a wrong, sent the madness upon him. He killed his children and Megara, too, as she tried to protect the youngest. Then his sanity returned. He found himself in his bloodstained hall, the dead bodies of his sons and his wife beside him. He had no idea what had happened, how they had been killed. Only a moment since, as it seemed to him, they had all been talking together. As he stood there in utter bewilderment the terrified people who were watching him from a distance saw that the mad fit was over, and Amphitryon dared to approach him. There was no keeping the truth from Hercules. He had to know how this horror had come to pass and Amphitryon told him. Hercules heard him out; then he said, "And I myself am the murderer of my dearest."

"Yes," Amphitryon answered trembling. "But you were out of your mind."

Hercules paid no attention to the implied excuse.

"Shall I spare my own life then?" he said. "I will avenge upon myself these deaths."

But before he could rush out and kill himself, even as he started to do so, his desperate purpose was changed and his life was spared. This miracle—it was nothing less—of recalling Hercules, from frenzied feeling and violent action to sober reason and sorrowful acceptance, was not wrought by a god descending from the sky. It was a miracle caused by human friendship. His friend Theseus stood before him and stretched out his hands to clasp those bloodstained hands. Thus according to the common Greek idea he would himself become defiled and have a part in Hercules's guilt.

8 lute: ancient stringed instrument.

274

"Do not start back," he told Hercules. "Do not keep me from sharing all with you. Evil I share with you is not evil to me. And hear me. Men great of soul can bear the blows of heaven and not flinch."

Hercules said, "Do you know what I have done?"

"I know this," Theseus answered. "Your sorrows reach from earth to heaven."

"So I will die," said Hercules.

"No hero spoke those words," Theseus said.

"What can I do but die?" Hercules cried. "Live? A branded man, for all to say, 'Look. There is he who killed his wife and sons!' Everywhere my jailers, the sharp scorpions of the tongue!"

"Even so, suffer and be strong," Theseus answered. "You shall come to Athens with me, share my home and all things with me. And you will give to me and to the city a great return, the glory of having helped you."

A long silence followed. At last Hercules spoke, slow, heavy words. "So let it be," he said. "I will be strong and wait for death."

The two went to Athens, but Hercules did not stay there long. Theseus, the thinker, rejected the idea that a man could be guilty of murder when he had not known what he was doing and that those who helped such a one could be reckoned defiled. The Athenians agreed and welcomed the poor hero. But he himself could not understand such ideas. He could not think the thing out at all; he could only feel. He had killed his family. Therefore he was defiled and a defiler of others. He deserved that all should turn from him with loathing. At Delphi where he went to consult the oracle, the priestess looked at the matter just as he did. He needed to be purified, she told him, and only a terrible penance[9] could do that. She bade him go to his cousin Eurystheus, King of Mycenae (of Tiryns in some stories) and submit to whatever he demanded of him. He went willingly, ready to do anything that could make him clean again. It is plain from the rest of the story that the priestess knew what Eurystheus was like and that he would beyond question purge[10] Hercules thoroughly.

Eurystheus was by no means stupid, but of a very ingenious turn of mind, and when the strongest man on earth came to him humbly prepared to be his slave, he devised a series of penances which from the point of view of difficulty and danger could not have been improved upon. It must be said, however, that he was helped and urged on by Hera. To the end of Hercules's life she never forgave him for being Zeus's son. The tasks Eurystheus gave him to do are called "the Labors of Hercules." There were twelve of them and each one was all but impossible.

The first was to kill the lion of Nemea, a beast no weapons could wound. That difficulty Hercules solved by choking the life out of him. Then he heaved the huge carcass up

9 **penance:** atonement; punishment.
10 **purge:** cleanse; purify.

on his back and carried it into Mycenae. After that, Eurystheus, a cautious man, would not let him inside the city. He gave him his orders from afar.

The second labor was to go to Lerna and kill a creature with nine heads called the Hydra which lived in a swamp there. This was exceedingly hard to do, because one of the heads was immortal and the others almost as bad, inasmuch as when Hercules chopped off one, two grew up instead. However, he was helped by his nephew Iolaus who brought him a burning brand with which he seared[11] the neck as he cut each head off so that it could not sprout again. When all had been chopped off he disposed of the one that was immortal by burying it securely under a great rock.

The third labor was to bring back alive a stag with horns of gold, sacred to Artemis, which lived in the forests of Cerynitia. He could have killed it easily, but to take it alive was another matter and he hunted it a whole year before he succeeded.

The fourth labor was to capture a great boar which had its lair on Mount Erymanthus. He chased the beast from one place to another until it was exhausted; then he drove it into deep snow and trapped it.

The fifth labor was to clean the Augean stables in a single day. Augeas had thousands of cattle and their stalls had not been cleared out for years. Hercules diverted the courses of two rivers and made them flow through the stables in a great flood that washed out the filth in no time at all.

The sixth labor was to drive away the Stymphalian birds, which were a plague to the people of Stymphalus because of their enormous numbers. He was helped by Athena to drive them out of their coverts,[12] and as they flew up he shot them.

The seventh labor was to go to Crete and fetch from there the beautiful savage bull that Poseidon had given Minos. Hercules mastered him, put him in a boat and brought him to Eurystheus.

The eighth labor was to get the man-eating mares of King Diomedes of Thrace. Hercules slew Diomedes first and then drove off the mares unopposed.

The ninth labor was to bring back the girdle[13] of Hippolyta, the Queen of the Amazons. When Hercules arrived she met him kindly and told him she would give him the girdle, but Hera stirred up trouble. She made the Amazons think that Hercules was going to carry off their queen, and they charged down on his ship. Hercules, without a thought of how kind Hippolyta had been, without any thought at all, instantly killed her, taking it for granted that she was responsible for the attack. He was able to fight off the others and get away with the girdle.

The tenth labor was to bring back the cattle of Geryon, who was a monster with three bodies living on Erythia, a western island. On his way

11 **seared:** burned.

12 **coverts:** shelters.
13 **girdle:** belt; sash.

MYTHS, FABLES, AND LEGENDS

there Hercules reached the land at the end of the Mediterranean and he set up as a memorial of his journey two great rocks, called the Pillars of Hercules (now Gibraltar and Ceuta). Then he got the oxen and took them to Mycenae.

The eleventh labor was the most difficult of all so far. It was to bring back the Golden Apples of the Hesperides, and he did not know where they were to be found. Atlas, who bore the vault of heaven upon his shoulders, was the father of the Hesperides, so Hercules went to him and asked him to get the apples for him. He offered to take upon himself the burden of the sky while Atlas was away. Atlas, seeing a chance of being relieved forever from his heavy task, gladly agreed. He came back with the apples, but he did not give them to Hercules. He told Hercules he could keep on holding up the sky, for Atlas himself would take the apples to Eurystheus. On this occasion Hercules had only his wits to trust to; he had to give all his strength to supporting that mighty load. He was successful, but because of Atlas's stupidity rather than his own cleverness. He agreed to Atlas's plan, but asked him to take the sky back for just a moment so that Hercules could put a pad on his shoulders to ease the pressure. Atlas did so, and Hercules picked up the apples and went off.

The twelfth labor was the worst of all. It took him down to the lower world, and it was then that he freed Theseus from the Chair of Forgetfulness. His task was to bring Cerberus, the three-headed dog, up from Hades. Pluto gave his permission provided Hercules used no weapons to overcome him. He could use his hands only. Even so, he forced the terrible monster to submit to him. He lifted him and carried him all the way up to the earth and on to Mycenae. Eurystheus very sensibly did not want to keep him and made Hercules carry him back. This was his last labor.

Understanding Literature

1. What incident in Hercules' childhood indicates that he is destined to do great things?
2. How is Hercules saved from killing himself after he murders his wife and children?
3. Hercules is assigned the twelve labors as atonement for his sin. Describe each labor briefly.
4. The qualities of Hercules are those the Greeks generally honored and admired. What are the qualities which make him a great hero?
5. Why is he not the perfect hero? Which of his actions are due to the flaws in his character?

6. The selection you have just read is only part of the story of Hercules. Do you think that Hercules becomes a more thoughtful and better man when his labors are done, or do you think he probably commits more rash actions? Explain. To what extent do you think people learn by their mistakes and experiences?

Further Activities

1. Using the resources in your library, prepare a brief report on the "choice of Hercules," which is not described here, and on the life of Hercules after his labors. Edith Hamilton's *Mythology*, from which this selection is taken, would be one good source for part of your report.
2. The story of Hercules's great strength is similar to that of Samson in the Bible. Read about Samson in the Book of Judges, Chapters 13-16, in the Old Testament. In one or two paragraphs describe the similarities and dissimilarities in the characters and actions of Hercules and Samson.
3. When Hercules wants to kill himself, Theseus says to him, "Men great of soul can bear the blows of heaven and not flinch." In your personal experiences you have probably met or heard of someone who endured a tragic event but was not overcome by it. Write a brief theme in which you describe who this person was, what tragic experience he had, and how he did not flinch in spite of "the blows of heaven."

   If you do not know someone whose experiences you can describe, choose an historical figure or one from a story or novel you have read.

"Was this the face that launched a thousand ships?" After hearing this famous quotation, you have probably wondered which woman was so beautiful that she could have been the cause of a war. The following myth tells of the origin of the Trojan War. This war is described in a Greek epic poem by Homer, the *Iliad*, which you will read more about later in this book.

The Judgment of Paris

Edith Hamilton

THE EVIL GODDESS of Discord, Eris, was naturally not popular in Olympus, and when the gods gave a banquet they were apt to leave her out. Resenting this deeply, she determined to make trouble—and she succeeded very well indeed. At an important marriage, that of King Peleus and the sea nymph Thetis, to which she alone of all the divinities was not invited, she threw into the banqueting hall a golden apple marked *For the Fairest*. Of course all the goddesses wanted it, but in the end the choice was narrowed down to three: Aphrodite,[1] Hera, and Pallas Athena. They asked Zeus to judge between them, but very wisely he refused to have anything to do with the matter. He told them to go to Mount Ida, near Troy, where the young prince Paris, also called Alexander, was keeping his father's sheep. He was an excellent judge of beauty, Zeus told them. Paris, though a royal prince, was doing shepherd's work because his father Priam, the King of Troy, had been warned that this prince would some day be the ruin of his country, and so had sent him away. At the moment Paris was living with a lovely nymph named Oenone.[2]

His amazement can be imagined when there appeared before him the wondrous forms of the three great goddesses. He was not asked, however, to gaze at the radiant divinities and choose which of them seemed to him the fairest, but only to consider the bribes each offered and choose which seemed to him best worth taking. Nevertheless, the choice was not easy. What men care for most was set before him. Hera promised to make him Lord of Europe and Asia; Athena, that he would lead the Trojans to victory against the Greeks and lay Greece in ruins; Aphrodite, that the fairest woman in all the world should be his. Paris, a weakling and something of a coward, too, as later events showed, chose the last. He gave Aphrodite the golden apple.

That was the Judgment of Paris,

1 Aphrodite (ăf′rə dī′tĭ).

2 Oenone (ē nō′nĭ).

famed everywhere as the real reason why the Trojan War was fought.

The fairest woman in the world was Helen, the daughter of Zeus and Leda and the sister of Castor and Pollux. Such was the report of her beauty that not a young prince in Greece but wanted to marry her. When her suitors assembled in her home to make a formal proposal for her hand they were so many and from such powerful families that her father, King Tyndareus, was afraid to select one among them, fearing that the others would unite against him. He therefore exacted first a solemn oath from all that they would champion the cause of Helen's husband, whoever he might be, if any wrong was done to him through his marriage. It was, after all, to each man's advantage to take the oath, since each was hoping he would be the person chosen, so they all bound themselves to punish to the uttermost anyone who carried or tried to carry Helen away. Then Tyndareus chose Menelaus,[3] the brother of Agamemnon,[4] and made him King of Sparta as well.

So matters stood when Paris gave the golden apple to Aphrodite. The Goddess of Love and Beauty knew very well where the most beautiful woman on earth was to be found. She led the young shepherd, with never a thought of Oenone left forlorn, straight to Sparta, where Menelaus and Helen received him graciously as their guest. The ties between guest and host were strong. Each was bound to help and never harm the other. But Paris broke that sacred bond. Menelaus trusting completely to it left Paris in his home and went off to Crete. Then,

Paris who coming
Entered a friend's kind dwelling,
Shamed the hand there that gave him food,
Stealing away a woman.

Menelaus got back to find Helen gone, and he called upon all Greece to help him. The chieftains responded, as they were bound to do. They came eager for the great enterprise, to cross the sea and lay mighty Troy in ashes.

3 **Menelaus** (měn'ə lā'əs).
4 **Agamemnon** (ăg'ə měm'nŏn).

Understanding Literature

1. How does the evil goddess of Discord, Eris, take revenge on Peleus and Thetis?
2. Who are the three beautiful goddesses whom Paris has to choose among?
3. What bribe does each offer to him? Which does Paris choose? What does Paris' choice show about his character?
4. Who is the fairest woman in the world? What oath has her father made all her suitors take? To whom is she married? In what city do they live?

Focusing on Words

1. Many of the mythological characters you have been reading about have contributed their names to form various English words. The word *cereal,* for example, comes from the name of the goddess Ceres. Can you explain why?
2. Another word that comes from a character about whom you read is *Promethean,* which means "life-giving; daringly original or creative." Why does it have these meanings?
3. Each of the following sentences contains a reference to Greek mythology. Explain what each sentence means and what it refers to.

   (*a*) He was exhausted after his Herculean labors.

   (*b*) They might have caught a glimpse of a Gorgon's head, judging from their reaction to the horrible spectacle.

   (*c*) Like the course of Phaethon, his career was brilliant but wild; it ended in disaster both for himself and those it affected.

   (*d*) Whatever he said sounded as though it were delivered from the heights of Olympus.

   (*e*) In his splendid flights of fancy, he showed as little self-restraint as Icarus.

   (*f*) She had the beauty of Helen and caused almost as much trouble.

Myths of the North

According to the poets of the Norse mythology, the Norse gods were interested mainly in heroism, especially in the essential heroic qualities of courage and bravery. These rough and powerful gods and the myths which grew about them became, for the people of the frozen North, the basis of a religion; in this religion a heroic death was a triumph, even though the hero had no heaven of eternal peace and beauty to look forward to. But with the arrival of Christianity in the Scandinavian countries, this religion built around the Norse gods was soon discarded. Although it is not definitely known where Norse myths began, it is thought that they originated in Norway, Greenland, Ireland, England, or Iceland. It *is* known, however, that they were first written down in Iceland, a cold, northern land. This fact helps to explain why Giantland is a cold, misty place.

You will more fully enjoy and understand the next two selections if you study the following names:

Asgard: Home of the gods in the center of the earth.

Giants: Spirits of frost or mountains. Giantland was a cold, misty country which lay beyond the ocean that surrounded the earth.

Odin: Allfather and sky-god who could see all the world from his throne in Asgard.

Freya or Freyja: Goddess of love and beauty.

Loki: God of fire who often used trickery to get his wishes.

Now that you have read some of the Greek and Roman myths, you will be interested in comparing them with the myths of the Scandinavian countries.

The Building of the Wall

Padraic Colum

ALWAYS THERE had been war between the giants and the gods—between the giants who would have destroyed the world and the race of men, and the gods who would have protected the race of men and would have made the world more beautiful.

There are many stories to be told about the gods, but the first one that shall be told to you is the one about the building of their city.

The gods had made their way up to the top of a high mountain and there they decided to build a great city for themselves that the giants could never overthrow. The city they would call Asgard, which means "the place of the gods." They would build it on a beautiful plain that was on the top of that high mountain. And they wanted to raise round their city the highest and strongest wall that had ever been built.

Now one day when they were be-

ginning to build their halls and their palaces a strange being came to them. Odin, the father of the gods, went and spoke to him. "What dost thou want on the mountain of the gods?" he asked the Stranger.

"I know what is in the mind of the gods," the Stranger said. "They would build a city here. I cannot build palaces, but I can build great walls that can never be overthrown. Let me build the wall round your city."

"How long will it take you to build a wall that will go round our city?" said the father of the gods.

"A year, O Odin," said the Stranger.

Now Odin knew that if a great wall could be built around it the gods would not have to spend all their time defending their city, Asgard, from the giants, and he knew that if Asgard were protected, he himself could go amongst men and teach them and help them. He thought that no payment the Stranger could ask would be too much for the building of that wall.

That day the Stranger came to the council of the gods, and he swore that in a year he would have the great wall built. Then Odin made oath that the gods would give him what he asked in payment if the wall was finished to the last stone in a year from that day.

The Stranger went away and came back on the morrow. It was the first day of summer when he started work. He brought no one to help him except a great horse.

Now the gods thought that this horse would do no more than drag blocks of stone for the building of the wall. But the horse did more than this. He set the stones in their places and mortared them together. And day and night and by light and dark the horse worked, and soon a great wall was rising round the palaces that the gods themselves were building.

"What reward will the Stranger ask for the work he is doing for us?" the gods asked one another.

Odin went to the Stranger. "We marvel at the work you and your horse are doing for us," he said. "No one can doubt that the great wall of Asgard will be built up by the first day of summer. What reward do you claim? We would have it ready for you."

The Stranger turned from the work he was doing, leaving the great horse to pile up the blocks of stone. "O

father of the gods," he said, "O Odin, the reward I shall ask for my work is the Sun and the Moon, and Freya, who watches over the flowers and grasses, for my wife."

Now when Odin heard this he was terribly angered, for the price the Stranger asked for his work was beyond all prices. He went amongst the other gods who were then building their shining palaces within the great wall and he told them what reward the Stranger had asked. The gods said, "Without the Sun and the Moon the world will wither away." And the goddesses said, "Without Freya all will be gloom in Asgard."

They would have let the wall remain unbuilt rather than let the Stranger have the reward he claimed for building it. But one who was in the company of the gods spoke. He was Loki, a being who only half belonged to the gods; his father was the Wind Giant. "Let the Stranger build the wall round Asgard," Loki said, "and I will find a way to make him give up the hard bargain he has made with the gods. Go to him and tell him that the wall must be finished by the first day of summer, and that if it is not finished to the last stone on that day the price he asks will not be given to him."

The gods went to the Stranger and they told him that if the last stone was not laid on the wall on the first day of the summer not Sol or Mani, the Sun and the Moon, nor Freya would be given him. And now they knew that the Stranger was one of the giants.

The giant and his great horse piled

up the wall more quickly than before. At night, while the giant slept, the horse worked on and on, hauling up stones and laying them on the wall with his great forefeet. And day by day the wall around Asgard grew higher and higher.

But the gods had no joy in seeing that great wall rising higher and higher around their palaces. The giant and his horse would finish the work by the first day of summer, and then he would take the Sun and the Moon, Sol and Mani, and Freya away with him.

But Loki was not disturbed. He kept telling the gods that he would find a way to prevent him from finishing his work, and thus he would make the giant forfeit the terrible price he had led Odin to promise him.

It was three days to summertime. All the wall was finished except the gateway. Over the gateway a stone was still to be placed. And the giant, before he went to sleep, bade his horse haul up a great block of stone so that they might put it above the gateway in the morning, and so finish the work two full days before summer.

It happened to be a beautiful moonlit night. Svadilfare, the giant's great horse, was hauling the largest stone he ever hauled when he saw a little mare come galloping towards him. The great horse had never seen so pretty a little mare and he looked at her with surprise.

"Svadilfare, slave," said the little mare to him and went frisking past.

Svadilfare put down the stone he was hauling and called to the little mare. She came back to him. "Why do you call me 'Svadilfare, slave'?" said the great horse.

"Because you have to work night and day for your master," said the little mare. "He keeps you working, working, working, and never lets you enjoy yourself. You dare not leave that stone down and come and play with me."

"Who told you I dare not do it?" said Svadilfare.

"I know you daren't do it," said the little mare, and she kicked up her heels and ran across the moonlit meadow.

Now the truth is that Svadilfare was tired of working day and night. When he saw the little mare go galloping off he became suddenly discontented. He left the stone he was hauling on the ground. He looked round and he saw the little mare looking back at him. He galloped after her.

He did not catch up on the little mare. She went on swiftly before him. On she went over the moonlit meadow, turning and looking back now and again at the great Svadilfare, who came heavily after her. Down the mountainside the mare went, and Svadilfare, who now rejoiced in his liberty and in the freshness of the wind and in the smell of the flowers, still followed her. With the morning's light they came near a cave and the little mare went into it. They went through the cave. Then Svadilfare caught up on the little mare and the two went wandering together, the little mare telling Svad-

ilfare stories of the Dwarfs and the Elves.

They came to a grove and they stayed together in it, the little mare playing so nicely with him that the great horse forgot all about time passing. And while they were in the grove the giant was going up and down, searching for his great horse.

He had come to the wall in the morning, expecting to put the stone over the gateway and so finish his work. But the stone that was to be lifted up was not near him. He called for Svadilfare, but his great horse did not come. He went to search for him, and he searched all down the mountainside and he searched as far across the earth as the realm of the giants. But he did not find Svadilfare.

The gods saw the first day of summer come and the gateway of the wall stand unfinished. They said to each other that if it were not finished by the evening they need not give Sol and Mani to the giant, nor the maiden Freya to be his wife. The hours of the summer day went past and the giant did not raise the stone over the gateway. In the evening he came before them.

"Your work is not finished," Odin said. "You forced us to a hard bargain and now we need not keep it with you. You shall not be given Sol and Mani nor the maiden Freya."

"Only the wall I have built is so strong I would tear it down," said the giant. He tried to throw down one of the palaces, but the gods laid hands on him and thrust him outside the wall he had built. "Go, and trouble Asgard no more," Odin commanded.

Then Loki returned to Asgard. He told the gods how he had transformed himself into a little mare and had led away Svadilfare, the giant's great horse. And the gods sat in their golden palaces behind the great wall and rejoiced that their city was now secure, and that no enemy could ever enter it or overthrow it. But Odin, the father of the gods, as he sat upon his throne was sad in his heart, sad that the gods had got their wall built by a trick; that oaths had been broken, and that a blow had been struck in injustice in Asgard.

Understanding Literature

1. Why are the giants and the gods constantly fighting one another?
2. Odin, the father of the gods, wants a wall built around Asgard for what two reasons?
3. Describe the trick that Loki plays on the Stranger and Svadilfare to keep them from finishing the wall.
4. Why is Odin the only god who is unhappy about the way the Stranger has been tricked?
5. With what in Greek mythology does Asgard compare? With whom does Odin compare?
6. Which common human qualities are portrayed in this myth?

As you read, note the difference between the climate and country in which the gods live and the climate and country of the giants.

The Apples of Idun

Olivia E. Coolidge

ALLFATHER ODIN was traveling with Loki and Honer in desolate wastes where they could discover nothing to eat. "Let us go down into this valley ahead," said Loki. "The pasture looks green by the river, and we may find deer."

"I see oxen in the shade of those oaks," replied Odin. "By all means let us go down."

The gods turned their steps to the valley, but the way was long, and the midsummer sun was at its height. Bees buzzed in the heath flowers, rabbits kicked up their heels as they fled to a safer patch of grass. Skylarks overhead filled the air with loud music. "They all feed while we stay hungry," grumbled Loki. "In Asgard we live like true gods. Here I am empty and hot, and my feet are sore. What is the use of such journeys?"

Odin smiled. "We should learn to know the earth because it is ours," he replied. "Sometimes we ride the clouds or fly on wings like the birds, but often we must travel as men do, yard by yard over stone after stone. We shall always remember these hills,

their sandy soil, their sparse yellow flowers, their little dried pines, and the green valley below."

"We shall indeed," muttered Loki. "It is a memory I well could have spared."

Dusty and hot, the travelers entered the valley as the long summer evening was drawing on. They paused to drink at the river, but they did not linger, for they were faint with hunger, and the grass was now softer under their feet. Beneath three spreading oaks they killed an ox and busied themselves preparing their meal. A pile of dry branches was collected, the ox was cut up, water fetched and thrown in the pot. At last the three gods could sit down, their feet out before them, and their backs to the trunk of a tree. On the fire rested their cooking pot, its great lid already quivering as little spurts of water escaped to fall hissing into the flames. A savory smell arose.

"I can wait no longer!" exclaimed Loki. Odin smiled as he closed his keen blue eye. Loki jumped up and, running to the fire, took a look at the stew. He seized a pointed stick to lift out one of the shoulders. "Raw!" he said in disgust. "Still perfectly raw!" He banged down the lid.

Odin smiled again. Silence fell. The skylark was weary, but the melodious thrush began her evening song. The grass was golden with buttercups. A kingfisher flashed over the stream. The smell of cooking became very pleasant and caused Odin to open his eye. "You might try the stew now," he said to Loki. "I should think we had given it time."

"I do all the work," grumbled Loki, but he got up and went to the fire. "Raw!" he said again in a fury.

This time Odin was interested and sat straight up. "Surely not," he remarked.

"Look at it!" cried Loki brandishing a piece on his stick. "Still as red as it was when we put it in. It's not reasonable!"

"It is certainly strange," replied Odin. "Well, put it back and pile up the fire."

"I am faint with hunger," complained Loki, "and everything falls on me." He piled on some more wood, still grumbling, before he came back and flung himself down on the grass.

A long time passed. The sun was behind the hills by now, and Odin drew his blue cloak about him. The three gods dozed no more, but sat with their hungry eyes fixed on the iron pot. "If it is not done by now, it never will be," said Odin at last. He got up himself, but he fared no better than Loki. The meat smelled appetizing, and the water was boiling and bubbling around it. Never-

theless when Odin lifted a piece from the pot, he found it raw and cold. "There is some magic spell at work here," he declared.

"I can cook your meat," cried a hoarse voice from above them. The three gods looked up. High in the oak tree was sitting an eagle so huge that the great branch bent beneath his weight like a tiny twig. "Give me a portion of your supper," he said. "Let me take my choice before you begin, and the meal shall be done in an instant."

"Willingly," answered Odin, uncovering the pot once more.

The creature leaped into the air with a whirring of wings and came sailing down to the fire, claws and beak outstretched. Quickly he snatched up half of the ox and was back in the tree with his dripping burden before the gods could utter a sound. He laid his prey in a crotch and swooped again to seize the other half, leaving the gods nothing but water.

Loki was beside himself with passion. "You thief!" he screamed, and snatching up one of the branches he had laid by to replenish the fire, he struck at the eagle as it turned to make for the oak. The branch hit full on the bird's back and stuck there as if glued, while Loki's hands adhered to the other end. The creature gave a sharp screech of laughter and flew off, dragging Loki after him. He skimmed over the ground so that the unfortunate god was pulled over stones and through briars, yelling that his arms were being torn from their sockets.

In a second or two his shrieks were already coming faintly, and in another moment the pair were over the hills out of hearing. "Let him go," said Odin, "and we will slaughter another ox. I can do nothing for Loki, who is in the power of a giant. He is cunning enough to get free from a dozen enchantments and will certainly join us again before we come to our journey's end."

Sure enough, on the next day Loki met them. He was covered with scratches, and the knees of his leggings were in holes, but he was well enough, though sulky.

"How did you get away?" asked his companions.

"He dropped me after a while," said Loki sullenly. "I suppose he had enough of it. My arms were almost pulled off."

"It is strange that he let you go without ransom," said Odin.

"Well he did," lied Loki, "though he might have dragged me forever for all the help I got from you." He strode on ahead, looking around furiously from time to time to see that the two gods were not laughing together behind his back.

The next day Idun,[1] the youth goddess, was sitting in her attic chamber in Asgard, looking out from her window at the flowering cherry trees. It was always spring in Idun's garden, where the scent of white mayflower lay heavy on the air. A cuckoo called in the distance, and on the window ledge perched a robin close by the goddess's hand. She looked around to see Loki entering, and her

1 **Idun** (ē'doon).

MYTHS, FABLES, AND LEGENDS

fair blue eyes lighted up with a smile. Even Loki, the faithless one, was welcome to Idun, who loved and trusted all.

"You have been on a long journey, Loki," she said gaily, "and I think you have come back for an apple from me." With that she picked up a little gold casket which sat on the bench by her side. She put her hand in and took out an apple for him, all rosy and golden. From it came a savor so sweet that with a flutter of wings the birds in the orchard came flocking to her window. Blackbirds, starlings, and doves jostled one another for space on the ledges, yet dared not come in, for fair Idun raised her arm and gently barred their path.

As Loki bit into the apple, his bruises felt no longer sore. The fruits of Idun, which were the apples of youth, sent new strength through his limbs. A wild desire seized him to go out in the sunlight, to wrestle, to swim, or even to start another of these toilsome journeys which Odin loved to make through the world.

Idun turned to the casket and shut it. As she did so, there was a faint, musical sound. "You hear," she smiled. "There is already another apple within."

"Idun," said Loki earnestly, "these are wonderful fruits, but out in the forest is a tree with apples of silver and gold. Music plays through its branches, which bear blossoms sweet as the wild rose together with the marvelous fruit. You know we eat your apples daily to keep us young, but they say that one of these others

will bring immortal youth which needs no renewal."

"It is not true," cried Idun, blushing indignantly. "There are no apples better than mine."

"Come out into the woods and look, then," begged Loki. "Bring your casket with you that we may compare the fruits."

"We must go secretly," said she. "I cannot believe you, and I would not have it said that I doubted my apples at all."

Loki and Idun stole out of Asgard into the wild, dark woods. "Come this way, Idun," said Loki, smiling down at her as he put his hand on her arm.

"The sun is sinking," said Idun. "Is the tree very far away?"

"Not so far, and the moon is rising. Besides, the golden fruit will light our path." He guided her up a steep hill. "From the top where it is rocky and bare," said he, "you can look down into the next valley and see the tree gleam. From there our road will be easy." He hurried her up the slope.

The sun had quite disappeared when Idun stood on the rock gazing out over the valley, which was half hidden in the gathering dark. "Why, there is no light to be seen!" said she in a disappointed tone. Loki made no answer, but stood looking up at the faint stars.

"Thjasse! Great Thjasse!" cried he.

"Loki," said she anxiously, pulling at his arm. "Loki, there is no light in the valley, and a cloud is covering the moon!"

"Thjasse! Great Thjasse!" cried

Loki again. "Here is Idun, the ransom I promised when you released me from the stick. Take her and let me go home."

There was no cloud over the moon, only the wings of an enormous eagle. Idun could see his red eyes and the great claws outstretched. She screamed and covered her face as the monster clutched her. Loki heard cry after cry as the two vanished into the dark.

Next morning the gods who came to the garden of Idun found it deserted, but at first they were in no wise alarmed. "She is visiting Gerd or Freyja," they said to one another. "Tomorrow she will surely be here."

The next day Idun was still absent, and in seven days more she had not returned. The blossoms on her trees had turned brown, the birds were all fled, and a chill had crept into the air. Without the magic apples of youth, Odin's hair became straggling and thin. Thor's bushy beard was streaked with gray. Fair Freyja stayed within doors, or veiled her face if she needed to walk abroad.

At last the gods met in council. All denied knowledge of Idun, Loki ... g the rest. "Well, then," said ... "where did each one of you ... er last?"

... arly all the gods had seen her ... n her chamber or her garden. ... however, replied, "Idun stole ... f Asgard with Loki as though ... wished to escape unseen."

... turned on Loki. Thor clutched ... ightly by the shoulder until he ... out in pain.

"Let me go," he cried. "I will confess that I gave her to Thjasse, the giant. It was he who, disguised as an eagle, dragged me on the end of a stick. Odin left me to ransom my life as best I could, so I promised him Idun. What else could I do?"

"Let me crush him," shouted Thor.

"By no means," answered Allfather Odin. "Release him. I think he has spoken well. Loki freed himself from the giant, but the price he paid was too high. It remains for him to rescue sweet Idun or else perish at the hands of Thor."

"Freyja," cried Loki, "lend me your garment of feathers. I will fly as a falcon to Giantland and return with fair Idun or die."

Loki flew as a falcon from Asgard, soared over the hills and the valleys, and skimmed over the bottomless sea. At last the gray cliffs of Giantland towered above him, shrouded in mist. He turned and flew to his left hand, seeking some inlet, for the cliffs went up into the clouds where he had not strength to soar. At last he found a place where a great gray river tumbled into the ocean through a gap in the dripping rocks. It seemed a forbidding inlet, but it was welcome to him, for his wings were icy and numb. He entered the gorge of the river and saw where the hall of the giant, Thjasse, towered on the hillside, a fortress of ice and rock.

The little falcon flew by the base of Thjasse's wall and alighted in a small crevice at its foot where a great bird had once built a nest. He huddled deep in the straw, while the wet mist swirled outside, and the damp icicles dripped slowly from the crags. It was dry in the little hollow, so that presently he found himself rested and warm. Now for it! he thought as he crawled out of his hole, launched himself into the air, and began the steep climb towards the upper windows where he hoped to find Idun's bower.

The falcon went spiraling upwards past the sheer face of the rocky wall which towered into the sky. Long before he came to the windows, his heart was beating fast, and his wings were failing. Here, however, the stones were smooth, and he could find no perch. Therefore, though he circled ever more slowly, he had to fly on.

At last it seemed to him he could go no higher. Every time his circle brought him close to the rock, the same worn stones met his gaze. He glanced despairingly downward. Nothing was to be seen there but mist. I dare not fall, he said to himself as with a mighty effort he rose another foot or two. This time as he approached the wall, he saw a break in the rock. It was the window of Idun's chamber above the end of the giant's great hall. Hope gave him renewed strength, and with a fierce beating of wings he circled once more, reached the ledge, and dropped half dead upon it, close beside Idun's hand.

Idun was sitting huddled up in the corner of a vast chair, her feet yards from the stone floor of the chamber, looking out into the mist. Tears ran down her cheeks as she gazed out towards Asgard, thinking of the beautiful earth, of her garden, and of the gods who loved her as though she were daughter to them all. She stretched out her hands to the bird with a cry of delight, dried it softly with her robe, set it on her shoulder, and warmed it against her cheek.

"Idun," said Loki at last in gentle tones, "I will take you to Asgard. Do not be afraid to trust me, for I come at the risk of my life."

Idun started at Loki's voice, but she answered eagerly, "I will do anything you wish if you will only carry me away."

"Where is the giant?"

"Gone forth to fish. If the catch is good, he will not return till dark."

"Trust me, then," said Loki from the window ledge. He touched her with the tip of his wing, and in an instant she and her casket shrank to the size of a thumbnail. Loki laid her gently in a walnut shell, and gathering the nut in his claws, leaped into the air.

They were over the gray sea when they came out of the mist and saw the earth as a strip of green on the distant shore. Every moment the hills became clearer until soon they were over the land. Loki cast a long look behind him and saw a black speck far off on the edge of the sky. "It is the eagle!" he said to himself as he flew on like an arrow.

Over the mountains he looked back again. The bird was much nearer by now. He could see its great wings cleaving the air, and terror gave him strength to speed like the wind. When the ramparts of Asgard came into view, he did not need to look back, for he could hear

the air whistling through the wings of the eagle behind him. With the fury of despair he raced for home.

"It is Loki!" cried the gods as they crowded the ramparts. "It is Loki, and behind him the eagle."

"Set fire on the ramparts," cried Allfather Odin. "Whether Loki is slain or not, the giant shall never escape."

Swiftly the gods heaped shavings along the walls and stood by with torches. The birds were so close by now that they could see the great beak of the eagle touch the feathers on Loki's tail. Loki felt his enemy and knew at the same time that he was almost home. With a furious spurt he shot over the ramparts and tumbled like a stone in the courtyard on the other side.

Already the gods had set fire to their shavings, and flame leaped instantly up from the wall. The eagle, coming too fast to stop himself, lurched right through the fire, setting his wings ablaze. Suddenly he fell from the air and alighted in the courtyard in his own shape of a monstrous man with his garments smoking about him and his great beard singed with flame. He glared at them all, bellowing furiously, but before he could rise, Thor swung his hammer, Mjolnir, that never missed its mark.

That night the gods drank to the rescue of Idun, and the death of the giant, while Loki sat boasting among them as if the trouble had been none of his fault.

Understanding Literature

1. What reason does Odin give Loki for their traveling on the earth?
2. What problem do Loki and Odin have as they try to cook their food and how does each react to the problem?
3. How did Loki get Idun to leave the protective walls of Asgard?
4. What are the differences between the climate and country in which the gods live and the climate and country in which the giants live?

Further Activities

1. Very often the words an author chooses will be so sharp and clear that the reader will have a distinct mental picture of the scene described. In literature this is called *visual imagery*. There are also other kinds of imagery. For example, an author may handle a description so skillfully that you can almost feel heat rising from the sands of the desert. Or the description of a newly mown field may be written so accurately and sensitively that you can almost smell the fresh grass. In other words, it is often the imagery and its appeal to the senses of sight, touch, smell, sound, or taste that move you to share in the pain, sorrow, or happiness of a work of literature.

   In "The Apples of Idun" there is imagery in the section in which Loki as a falcon flies to rescue Idun. Find passages in which you can almost feel the intense cold and dampness, and where you can actually visualize the scene described, or share the sensation of height when Loki attempts to reach Idun's chamber. What words or group of words are particularly effective in making the imagery more vivid to you?

2. Myths attempt to explain things which people find difficult to understand. Using your imagination and inventing your own gods and goddesses, create an original myth to explain how humans came to have one or two of their many good qualities, such as bravery, kindness, love, or virtue.

3. You have now read about many different gods and goddesses with many different types of power. In one or two well-organized paragraphs, tell which god or goddess you would prefer to be if by magic you could become an immortal. Explain why.

THE
FABLES
OF
ÆSOP

from The Fables of Aesop

edited by **Joseph Jacobs**

As you have seen, myths are about supernatural beings and events. They deal with religious rites and beliefs, and were used, in general, to explain the mysteries of nature.

The *fable*, another type of story, usually enforces some useful truth or moral and is frequently narrated or acted by animals; thus fables are sometimes called *beast fables*. Fables are usually connected with the name of Aesop, who is supposed to have lived between 620 and 560 B.C. While some authorities believe there was no such person, others think he is a legendary figure, that is, a man who probably lived although no one can actually prove that he did.

THE MILKMAID AND HER PAIL

PATTY, THE MILKMAID, was going to market carrying her milk in a pail on her head. As she went along she began calculating what she would do with the money she would get for the milk. "I'll buy some fowls from Farmer Brown," said she, "and they will lay eggs each morning, which I will sell to the parson's wife. With the money that I get from the sale of these eggs I'll buy myself a new dimity frock and a chip hat; and when I go to market, won't all the young men come up and speak to me! Polly Shaw will be that jealous; but I don't care. I shall just look at her and toss my head like this." As she spoke, she tossed her head back, the pail fell off it and all the milk was spilt. So she had to go home and tell her mother what had occurred.

"Ah, my child," said her mother,

"Do not count your chickens before they are hatched."

THE EAGLE AND THE ARROW

AN EAGLE WAS soaring through the air when suddenly it heard the whizz of an arrow, and felt itself wounded to death. Slowly it fluttered down to the earth, with its lifeblood pouring out of it. Looking down upon the arrow with which it had been pierced, it found that the haft[1] of the arrow had been feathered with one

1 haft: handle.

of its own plumes. "Alas!" it cried, as it died,

"We often give our enemies the means for our own destruction."

THE JAY AND THE PEACOCKS

A JAY venturing into a yard where peacocks used to walk, found there a number of feathers which had fallen from the peacocks when they were molting.[2] He tied them all to his tail and strutted down toward the peacocks. When he came near them they soon discovered the cheat, and striding up to him pecked at him and plucked away his borrowed plumes. So the jay could do no better than go back to the other jays, who had watched his behavior from a distance; but they were equally annoyed with him, and told him:

"It is not only fine feathers that make fine birds."

THE HARES AND THE FROGS

THE HARES WERE so persecuted by the other beasts, they did not know where to go. As soon as they saw a single animal approach them, off they used to run. One day they saw a troop of wild horses stampeding about, and in quite a panic all the hares scuttled off to a lake hard by, determined to drown themselves rather than live in such a continual state of fear. But just as they got near the bank of the lake, a troop of frogs, frightened in their turn by the approach of the hares, scuttled off, and jumped into the water. "Truly," said one of the hares, "things are not so bad as they seem:

"There is always someone worse off than yourself."

THE LION AND THE MOUSE

ONCE WHEN A lion was asleep a little mouse began running up and down upon him; this soon wakened the lion, who placed his huge paw upon him, and opened his big jaws to swallow him. "Pardon, O King," cried the little mouse; "forgive me this time, I shall never forget it: who knows but what I may be able to do you a turn some of these days?" The lion was so tickled at the idea of the mouse being able to help him, that he lifted up his paw and let him go. Some time after the lion was caught in a trap, and the hunters, who desired to carry him alive to the king, tied him to a tree while they went in search of a wagon to carry him on. Just then the little mouse happened to pass by, and seeing the sad plight[3] in which the lion was, went up to him and soon gnawed away the ropes that bound the king of the beasts. "Was I not right?" said the little mouse.

"Little friends may prove great friends."

THE TOWN MOUSE AND THE COUNTRY MOUSE

Now YOU MUST know that a town mouse once upon a time went on a visit to his cousin in the country.

---

2 **molting:** shedding their feathers.

3 **plight:** situation; condition.

He was rough and ready, this cousin, but he loved his town friend and made him heartily welcome. Beans and bacon, cheese and bread, were all he had to offer, but he offered them freely. The town mouse rather turned up his long nose at this country fare, and said: "I cannot understand, Cousin, how you can put up with such poor food as this, but of course you cannot expect anything better in the country; come you with me and I will show you how to live. When you have been in town a week you will wonder how you could ever have stood a country life." No sooner said than done: the two mice set off for the town and arrived at the town mouse's residence late at night. "You will want some refreshment after our long journey," said the polite town mouse, and took his friend into the grand dining room. There they found the remains of a fine feast, and soon the two mice were eating up jellies and cakes and all that was nice. Suddenly they heard growling and barking. "What is that?" said the country mouse. "It is only the dogs of the house," answered the other. "Only!" said the country mouse. "I do not like that music at my dinner." Just at that moment the door flew open, in came two huge mastiffs, and the two mice had to scamper down and run off. "Good-by, Cousin," said the country mouse. "What! Going so soon?" said the other. "Yes," he replied;

"Better beans and bacon in peace than cakes and ale in fear."

THE FOX AND THE CROW

A FOX ONCE saw a crow fly off with a piece of cheese in its beak and settle on a branch of a tree. "That's for me, as I am a fox," said Master Reynard, and he walked up to the foot of the tree. "Good day, Mistress Crow," he cried. "How well you are looking today: how glossy your feathers; how bright your eye. I feel sure your voice must surpass that of other birds, just as your figure does; let me hear but one song from you that I may greet you as the queen of birds." The crow lifted up her head and began to caw her best, but the moment she opened her mouth the piece of cheese fell to the ground, only to be snapped up by Master Fox. "That will do," said he. "That was all I wanted. In exchange for your cheese I will give you a piece of advice for the future—

"Do not trust flatterers."

Understanding Literature

1. The italicized words at the end of each of these fables explain the moral or lesson being taught. Explain each moral in your own words.
2. To what extent is each of these morals a good lesson even for the present day? In what situations might these morals be applied?

3. Certain authorities think that some of the fables were written to be used for political purposes. Could any of these fables you have just read be used in some way as advice to politicians? as advice to a country about its relationship with another country?
4. What are the characteristics of the fable which make it enjoyable reading?

Further Activity

Try to write a fable, modeled on Aesop's, to illustrate one of the following sayings:

1. Self-conceit may lead to self-destruction.
2. It is easy to be brave from a safe distance.
3. Injuries may be forgiven, but not forgotten.
4. Familiarity breeds contempt.
5. It is best to prepare for the days of necessity.
6. Appearances are deceptive.
7. United we stand, divided we fall.

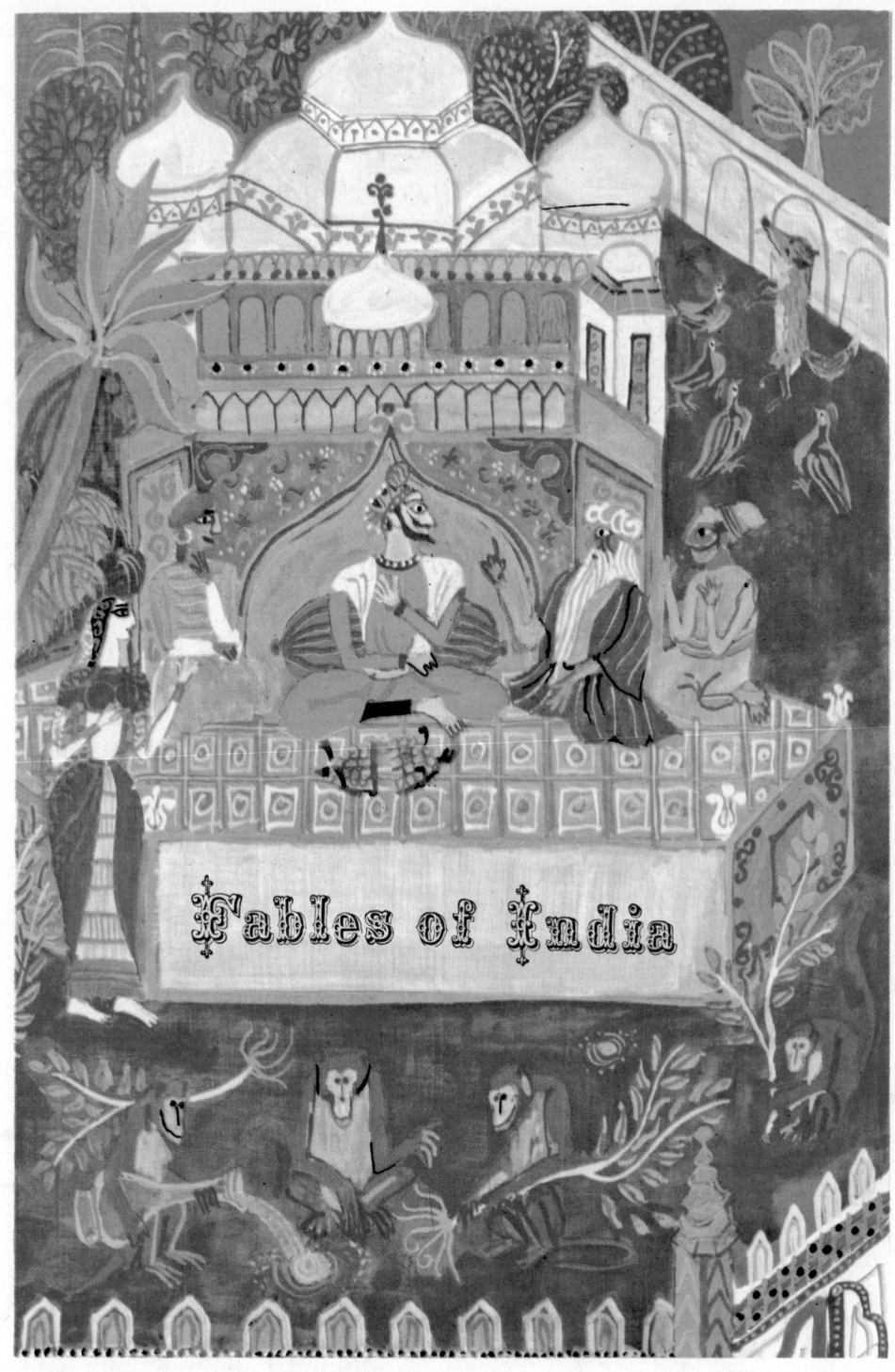

Fables of India

from The Fables of India

adapted by **Joseph Gaer**

Although Aesop is the name most of you immediately associate with fables, the Hindus of India were actually the first *fablers*. In India three main collections of fables exist. The ones which you are about to read are from *The Jataka*, a collection of stories about the many incarnations of the Buddha, the great religious teacher of India. These fables have been used to instruct the children of India.

THE MONKEY GARDENERS

IN THE ROYAL gardens of Benares,[1] a group of monkeys were allowed to roam and do as they pleased. These monkeys were great mimics. If the King came by, strolling along one of the paths, they would line up and walk behind him, just as straight and with as much dignity. If the young prince came along playing a game, they pretended they too were playing the same game. Most of all they liked to imitate the gardener. They followed him wherever he went, and whatever his task, they all imitated his motions.

A great festival was proclaimed throughout the city one day, and the gardener was eager to attend the ceremonies. But he had newly transplanted trees in the garden and did not know whom he could get to water them during the day. Then he remembered how well the monkeys imitated everything he did, and he went to their leader and said:

"His Majesty the King bestowed a great honor on you in permitting you to remain in the gardens, where you can feed on all the fruit."

"Oh, yes!" replied the monkey.

"Now there is a great festivity in the city to which I must go," the gardener went on. "To show your gratitude to His Majesty, do you think you can water the young trees while I am gone?"

"Oh, yes!" said the monkey, eagerly.

"But remember, do not waste any water," said the gardener.

"Oh, yes!" the monkey assured him.

The gardener went off to the festivities. The monkeys went happily to work and gathered together all the waterskins. They filled the containers with water and went right out to the newly planted young trees.

---

1 **Benares** (bə nä′rĭz): holy city of the Hindus in India.

"Remember," commanded the sky and opened his mouth as wide as leader, "do not waste any water!" he could.

"How shall we know how much is enough, how much is too little, and how much is too much?" asked the monkeys.

"That is very simple," said he. "First you pull up the tree and look at the size of the roots. Those with long roots need much water; those with short roots need only a little water."

"How wise you are!" said all the other monkeys.

They began industriously pulling up all the newly planted trees, and watered each according to the length of its roots, just as they had been instructed.

At this point a wise man came by and noticed what the monkeys were doing. He asked them why they pulled up the trees before they watered them.

"Because we must water them according to the length of their roots," they explained.

And the wise man (who was the Bodisat)[2] said:

"Like these monkeys turned gardeners, the ignorant and the foolish, even in their desire to do good, only succeed in doing harm."

The Fox in Saint's Clothing

ONE DAY A fox spied a flock of guinea hens and roosters. He stopped at a respectful distance, balancing himself with great skill on one foot. Then he turned his head up to the sky and opened his mouth as wide as he could.

The fowl noticed this curious pose and came closer to observe him. One cock finally asked:

"What is your name?"

"My name is Saintly," answered the fox without turning his head.

"Why do you stand on one leg?" asked a hen.

"Because my great weight would be too much for the earth to bear if I stood on it with all my four legs," answered the fox, without moving a hairsbreadth.

"Why do you keep your mouth open and swallow the wind?" asked another guinea hen.

"Because I live on air. It is my only food," the fox replied.

"Why do you keep your head turned up toward the sky?" asked a young cock.

"Because I worship the sun," answered the fox.

The guinea hens looked at the yellow skin of the scrawny fox and were convinced that he was wearing the yellow robe of a beggar monk.

"What saintliness!" they exclaimed in awe, and the entire flock paid homage[3] to him.

When they began to leave, the fox announced: "I shall be here again tomorrow to pray on this same spot, and I wish you would come and pray with me."

The next day the fox appeared in the same spot, and the flock of guinea hens came again to pay their respects and to pray with him. As they be-

2 the Bodisat: the Buddha.

3 homage (hŏm′ĭj): respect.

gan to leave, the fox watched them from the corners of his eyes. When the last of the hens was ready to follow the flock, he caught her with great dexterity,[4] quickly gobbled her up, swiftly wiped his mouth, and returned to his praying pose.

This went on for several days, until the guinea hens began to notice how their number was diminishing. One powerful cock had been suspicious of the fox from the start, and he decided to find out whether his suspicions were justified.

The next time they came to pay their respects to the pious fox, the young cock straggled behind and was the last to leave.

Whereupon the fox sprang at him. But the cock turned quickly. He flew at the fox and pecked at his eyes, crowing loud enough for all the guinea hens to hear him.

"Now we know the reason for your coming here and pretending to be a saint!"

Back trooped all the other hens and cocks and they pecked the fox to death. Then they thanked the young cock (who was the Bodisat in this form) for having saved the flock from the hypocritical[5] fox.

THE TALKATIVE TORTOISE

IN A POND in the Himalaya Mountains there once lived a handsomely marked young tortoise. He was not vicious like his cousin the snapping turtle, but he had the failing of liking to talk too much. Two wild ducks came to the pond in search of food one day, and the tortoise started to talk to them almost as soon as they alighted on the water.

Nevertheless the ducks and the tortoise became great friends, and the ducks said one day:

"We have a fine home on Mount Beautiful in the Himalayas, next to the Cave of Gold. Why don't you come and live with us, friend Tortoise?"

"How can I, a tortoise, get up to your place?"

"We thought of that," said the wild ducks. "We can take you to our home, if only you can keep from talking and not say a single word until we get there. Do you think you can do that and keep your mouth closed all that time?"

"I certainly can do that!" the tortoise assured them.

The ducks took a sturdy stick and asked the tortoise to bite hard on the center. Then they each took hold of an end of the stick with their strong bills and rose into the air, swiftly flying toward the mountains.

As they flew over the palace of the King of Benares, a number of village children saw the wild ducks in flight, carrying a tortoise on a stick.

"Look! Look! Two wild ducks are carrying a tortoise on a stick!" they shouted excitedly to their parents.

Their outcries angered the tortoise, and he wanted to shout back at them:

"If my friends want to carry me like this, what affair is that of yours, you wretches!"

But when he opened his mouth to

4 **dexterity:** quickness; skill.
5 **hypocritical:** insincere; double-dealing.

speak, he let go of the stick and fell with great force into the open courtyard of the palace; and he split in two.

The king's attendants came running up in excitement, shouting:

"A tortoise has fallen out of the sky into the courtyard!"

Everyone, including the king and his Brahman and all his courtiers, gathered around the spot where the dead tortoise lay.

The king turned and asked the Brahman: "Teacher! What made this creature fall here?"

Now, this king was very talkative and no one could ever get a word in edgewise. The Brahman gladly took this opportunity to admonish him. He answered:

"My King, his tongue killed him."

The king looked at him in amazement. And he asked: "How could his tongue bring him to his death?"

"O King, this tortoise held secure
A stick between his teeth;
But when he tried to chatter
He quickly met this fate.

Behold him, O excellent of strength,
And speak not out of season!
You see how this tortoise fell—
He talked too much and that's the reason!"

The king asked: "Are you referring to me, Teacher?"

And the teacher (who was the Bodisat born as a Brahman) replied:

"O Great King! Be it you, or be it another. Whoever talks too much sooner or later meets with disaster."

Understanding Literature

1. What are the two morals taught in "The Monkey Gardeners"?
2. What is the moral of each of the other fables?
3. In a Jataka there is always one character who is the Bodisat in disguise. What three roles does the Bodisat assume in the three fables you have just read?
4. Each of the three fables which you have just studied is compactly and concisely written. In each of them the setting and characters are made clear. What is the setting for each fable? What is the problem? Who are the main characters?
5. The Jatakas have been used to teach or instruct the children of India. Why would teaching the children through the use of fables or beast fables be more effective than issuing commands or briefly stating what is right and what is wrong?
6. In what situations would the lessons given in the three fables prove helpful?

Further Activity

In the study of literature you may often be asked to *paraphrase* a passage from a selection. To paraphrase is to restate and give the meaning of a passage in your own words. To be able to paraphrase well indicates that you understand thoroughly what you have read. Paraphrase in writing the lesson taught in each of the three Jatakas or paraphrase one complete fable. Be brief, but do not omit anything of importance.

Focusing on Words

The meaning of a word is often made partly clear by the sentence in which it occurs. Write down what you think each of the italicized words in the following sentences means; then check your answers in the glossary or a dictionary.

1. ". . . the guinea hens began to notice how their number was *diminishing*."
2. "He was not *vicious* like his cousin the snapping turtle. . . ."
3. "The Brahman gladly took this opportunity to *admonish* him."

The *Iliad* and the *Odyssey*, summarized here, are two famous epic poems believed to have been written by a Greek poet, Homer, who probably lived around 700 or 800 B.C. An *epic* is a long poem which tells a story about one hero—a human hero—and describes deeds of great or even superhuman courage. You will notice in these selections that the gods of Olympus are still powerful and influential, but the center of interest is now down on earth, on mortals.

Homer, the Great Storyteller

Eva March Tappan

A LONG, LONG time ago—perhaps three thousands years or more—there was a man named Homer. No one knows much about him; but there are legends that he was born on the island of Chios and that he was blind. He wandered about the land, homeless, but welcome wherever he chose to go, because he was a poet. He once described how a blind poet was treated at a great banquet, and probably that is the way in which people treated him. He said that when the feast was ready, a page was sent to lead in the honored guest. A silver-studded chair was brought forward for him and set against a pillar. On the pillar the page hung his harp, so near him that he could touch it if he wished. A little table was placed before him, and on it was put a tray spread with food and wine. When the feasting was at an end, he sang a glorious song of the mighty deeds of men. The Greeks liked to hear stories just as well as the people of today, and they shouted with delight. Then they all went out to the racecourse, the page leading the blind singer carefully along the way. There were races and wrestling matches and boxing and throwing of the discus. After this, the poet took his harp and stepped to the center of the circle. The young men gathered around him eagerly, and he chanted a story of Ares, the war god, and Aphrodite, goddess of beauty and love.

Homer composed two great poems. One is the *Iliad*, which takes its name from Ilium, or Troy, a town in Asia Minor. For ten long years the Greeks tried to capture Ilium. They had good reason for waging war against the Trojans, for Paris, son of the King of Troy, had stolen away the Grecian Helen, the most beautiful woman in the world. She was the wife of a Greek prince named Menelaus; and the other princes of Greece joined him in attacking Troy. They took some smaller places round about and divided the booty, as the custom was. In the tenth year of the war,

Achilles and Agamemnon, two of the greatest of the princes, quarreled about one of these divisions, and here the *Iliad* begins. Achilles was so angry that he took his followers, the Myrmidons, left the camp, and declared that he would have nothing more to do with the war, he would return to Greece.

Now the Greeks were in trouble, indeed, for Achilles was their most valiant leader, and his men were exceedingly brave soldiers. They sent his friend Patroclus to beg him to come back. Achilles would not yield, even to him; but he finally agreed to allow his followers to return and also to lend his armor and equipment to Patroclus.

When the Trojans saw the chariot and armor of Achilles, they ran for their lives, as Patroclus had expected; but at length Hector, son of King Priam, ventured to face his enemy, and Patroclus fell. Achilles was heartbroken. It was all his own fault, he declared, and he groaned so heavily that his wailing was heard in the depths of the ocean. He vowed that, come what might, he would be revenged. He went back to the camp and made up the quarrel with Agamemnon; and then he rushed forth into battle. The Trojans were so terrified that they all ran back into the city save one, Hector. But when Achilles dashed forward upon him, his heart failed, and he, too, ran for his life. Three times Achilles chased him around the walls of Troy, then thrust him through with his spear. He tied cords to the feet of his fallen enemy and dragged his body back

and forth before the eyes of the Trojans; and when the following morning had come, he dragged it twice around the tomb of Patroclus.

The Greeks believed that if a person's body had not received funeral rites, he would be condemned to wander for one hundred years on the banks of the Styx, the gloomy river of the dead; but Achilles declared in his wrath that the body of Hector should be thrown to the dogs. Then King Priam loaded into his litter rolls of handsome cloth, rich garments, and golden dishes, and made his way to the tent of the fierce warrior. "Your father is an old man like me," he pleaded. "Think of him and show pity. I have brought a wealth of ransom. Take it and give me the body of my son." The fiery Achilles yielded and even agreed to a twelve-days' truce so that the funeral might be celebrated with all due honor. The tale ends with the building of an immense pyre and the burning of the body of Hector.

Homer's second poem is the *Odyssey*. Troy finally fell into the hands of the Greeks, but Ulysses, or Odysseus,[1] one of the leaders, was unfortunate enough to be hated by Poseidon, god of the sea. His home was on the island of Ithaca; but before Poseidon would allow him to return to it, he drove the homesick wanderer back and forth over the Mediterranean Sea for ten long years and made him undergo all sorts of danger. The *Odyssey* tells the story of his wanderings and his wonderful ad-

1 **Odysseus** (ō dĭs′ūs).

MYTHS, FABLES, AND LEGENDS

ventures. First, he was driven by a storm to the land of the Lotus-eaters. Whoever ate the lotus forgot his home and friends, and cared for nothing but to stay in the lotus country and idle his life away in vain and empty dreams. Some of Odysseus's men tasted this fruit; and he had to drag them on board the ship and even tie them to the benches to keep them from staying behind.

Odysseus's second adventure was in the country of the Cyclopes,[2] monstrous giants, each having one huge eye in the middle of his forehead. One of these giants, Polyphemus,[3] found the Greeks in his cave when he drove home his sheep and goats. He devoured two of the men at once, and others on the following day. But Odysseus was planning revenge. He offered the giant a great bowl of wine, which pleased him mightily. "What is your name?" the Cyclops asked. "No man," replied Odysseus. Then Polyphemus promised him as a great favor that he should be the last of the company to be eaten. But when the giant was sleeping stupidly, Odysseus and his men took a stick of green olive wood as big as the mast of a ship, heated one end in the fire until it was a burning coal, and plunged it into the eye of Polyphemus. He roared with pain, and the other giants ran from all sides to his aid. "What is it? Who is murdering you?" they cried. "No man," howled the giant, "No man is killing me." "If it is no man," they said, "then your ill-

ness comes from Zeus, and you must bear it. We can do nothing," and they went their way.

The Greeks made their escape, but it was not long before they were in trouble again. They landed on the floating island which was the home of Aeolus, god of the winds. He was kind and friendly, and when they departed, he gave Odysseus a leathern sack tied up with a silver cord. All the stormwinds were safely shut up in this sack; but Odysseus's men supposed it was full of treasure. They were so afraid they would not get their share that while their leader slept, they tore it open. Aeolus had given them a favorable breeze, and they were so close to their own island that they could see men heaping wood on the fires, but now the stormwinds rushed out of the bag, and the vessel was driven back again over the waters.

They landed on the island of the enchantress Circe,[4] who had an unpleasant habit of changing people into the animals that they most resembled. They passed by the Sirens, beautiful, treacherous maidens who sang so sweetly from a soft green meadow near the shore that no seamen who heard them could help throwing themselves into the water to make their way nearer to the marvelous music. The wise Odysseus had himself bound to the mast and forbade his sailors to free him, whatever he might say or do. Therefore he was able to hear the magical songs in safety. Neither did he lose his

---

2 **Cyclopes** (sī′klō′ pēz).
3 **Polyphemus** (pŏl′ĭ fē′məs).

4 **Circe** (sûr′sĭ).

vessel, for he had stopped up the ears of the sailors with wax. They passed between the snaky monster Scylla and the horrible whirlpool Charybdis;[5] and after many long years of wandering and hardship Odysseus arrived on the shore of his beloved Ithaca.

Penelope, wife of Odysseus, had been tormented by a throng of suitors, who for years had been feasting upon her food and wasting her property. Her son Telemachus[6] was only a youth and not yet strong enough to drive them away. Penelope never gave up the hope that Odysseus would return, and to gain time she put the suitors off by every device in her power. When everything else had failed, she began to weave a web

in her loom, and promised that when it was done, she would choose among them. She worked at this for three years, and the suitors waited; but in the fourth year her maids found out the secret, that she was pulling out by night what she wove by day. In the very nick of time Odysseus appeared. He and Telemachus slew the wicked suitors and punished all who had been unfaithful in his absence. Then Telemachus and Penelope and the aged father of Odysseus rejoiced, for at last their lord had come to his own again.

These are bits of the stories that Homer tells in the *Iliad* and the *Odyssey;* but their greatest charm is in his manner of telling them. He seems to know just how each one of his characters feels. He understands the anger of Achilles, and he sympa-

5 **Charybdis** (kə rĭb′dĭs).
6 **Telemachus** (tə lĕm′ə kəs).

MYTHS, FABLES, AND LEGENDS

thizes with the sorrow of Hector's wife when the hero is going forth to battle. He knows how to use words so marvelously well that he can make one line sound like the tramping of horses on a plain and another like the beating of waves against the rocks. He describes every event as if he himself had seen it, and he never forgets to mention the little things which so many people pass over. Best of all, the stories are told so simply and naturally that, even after the many centuries, we can hardly help feeling that Homer is alive and is telling them directly to us.

Understanding Literature

1. Why was Homer always welcome wherever he went?
2. Summarize the cause and main events of the Trojan War as described in the *Iliad*.
3. Describe the adventures Odysseus has in traveling home after the Trojan War as related in the *Odyssey*.
4. What characteristics does Odysseus have that show the kind of man the Greeks admired and respected?
5. Tell the story of Penelope and her suitors.
6. In what ways are the gods involved in the tale?
7. Epics are often called *hero tales*. Why would the *Iliad* and the *Odyssey* be considered hero tales? How do hero tales differ from myths?
8. According to the author of this selection, why are these two great poems by Homer still enjoyed today?

Arthur may have been a real British chieftain or general who lived during the early 6th century; however, he is best known as a legendary king of Britain, famed for his virtue and valor. According to the numerous legends which grew up about him, knights rode out from his court to find adventure and to perform brave and daring deeds. In the 15th century, Sir Thomas Malory wrote a book based upon these legends about King Arthur and his court. The following selections are adapted from three of the stories in Malory's book. In these selections you will meet Arthur, Merlin the magician, the mysterious Lady of the Lake, and the treacherous Morgan le Fay.

Stories of King Arthur

Mary Macleod

THE MARVEL OF THE SWORD

WHEN UTHER PENDRAGON, King of England, died, the country for a long while stood in great danger, for every lord that was mighty gathered his forces, and many wished to be king. For King Uther's own son, Prince Arthur, who should have succeeded him, was but a child, and Merlin, the mighty magician, had hidden him away.

Now a strange thing had happened at Arthur's birth, and this was how it was.

Some time before, Merlin had done Uther a great service, on condition that the King should grant him whatever he wished for. This the King swore a solemn oath to do. Then Merlin made him promise that when his child was born it should be delivered to Merlin to bring up as he chose, for this would be to the child's own great advantage. The King had given his promise so he was obliged to agree. Then Merlin said he knew a very true and faithful man, one of

King Uther's lords, by name Sir Ector, who had large possessions in many parts of England and Wales, and that the child should be given to him to bring up.

On the night the baby was born, while it was still unchristened, King Uther commanded two knights and two ladies to take it, wrapped in a cloth of gold, and deliver it to a poor man whom they would find waiting at the postern gate of the castle. This poor man was Merlin in disguise, although they did not know it. So the child was delivered unto Merlin and he carried him to Sir Ector, and made a holy man christen him, and named him Arthur; and Sir Ector's wife cherished him as her own child.

Within two years King Uther fell sick of a great malady, and for three days and three nights he was speechless. All the barons were in much sorrow, and asked Merlin what was best to be done.

"There is no remedy," said Merlin,

"God will have His Will. But look ye all, barons, come before King Uther tomorrow, and God will make him speak."

So the next day Merlin and all the barons came before the King, and Merlin said aloud to King Uther:

"Sir, after your days shall your son Arthur be king of this realm and all that belongs to it?"

Then Uther Pendragon turned to him and said in hearing of them all:

"I give my son Arthur God's blessing and mine, and bid him pray for my soul, and righteously and honorably claim the Crown, on forfeiture of my blessing."

And with that, King Uther died.

But Arthur was still only a baby, not two years old, and Merlin knew it would be no use yet to proclaim him king. For there were many powerful nobles in England in those days, who were all trying to get the kingdom for themselves, and perhaps they would kill the little prince. So there was much strife and debate in the land for a long time.

When several years had passed, Merlin went to the Archbishop of Canterbury and counseled him to send for all the lords of the realm, and all the gentlemen of arms, that they should come to London at Christmas, and for this cause—that a miracle would show who should be rightly king of the realm. So all the lords and gentlemen made themselves ready, and came to London, and long before dawn on Christmas Day they were all gathered in the great church of Saint Paul's to pray.

When the first service was over,

there was seen in the churchyard a large stone, foursquare, like marble, and in the midst of it was like an anvil of steel, a foot high. In this was stuck by the point a beautiful sword, with naked blade, and there were letters written in gold about the sword, which said thus:

WHOSO PULLETH THIS SWORD OUT
OF THIS STONE AND ANVIL IS RIGHTLY
KING OF ALL ENGLAND.

Then the people marveled, and told it to the archbishop.

"I command," said the archbishop, "that you keep within the church, and pray unto God still; and that no man touch the sword till the service is over."

So when the prayers in church were over, all the lords went to behold the stone and the sword; and when they read the writing some of them—such as wished to be king— tried to pull the sword out of the anvil. But not one could make it stir.

"The man is not here, that shall achieve the sword," said the archbishop, "but doubt not God will make him known. But let us provide ten knights, men of good fame, to keep guard over the sword."

So it was ordained, and proclamation was made that everyone who wished might try to win the sword. And upon New Year's Day the barons arranged to have a great tournament, in which all knights who would joust or tourney might take a part. This was ordained to keep together the lords and commons, for the archbishop trusted that it would be made known who should win the sword.

How Arthur Was Crowned King

On New Year's Day, after church, the barons rode to the field, some to joust, and some to tourney, and so it happened that Sir Ector, who had large estates near London, came also to the tournament; and with him rode Sir Kay, his son, with young Arthur, his foster brother.

As they rode, Sir Kay found he had lost his sword, for he had left it at his father's lodging, so he begged young Arthur to go and fetch it for him.

"That will I, gladly," said Arthur, and he rode fast away.

But when he came to the house, he found no one at home to give him the sword, for every one had gone to see the jousting. Then Arthur was angry and said to himself:

"I will ride to the churchyard, and take the sword with me that sticketh in the stone, for my brother, Sir Kay, shall not be without a sword this day."

When he came to the churchyard he alighted, and tied his horse to the stile, and went to the tent. But he found there no knights, who should have been guarding the sword, for they were all away at the joust. Seizing the sword by the handle he lightly and fiercely pulled it out of the stone, then took his horse and rode his way, till he came to Sir Kay his brother, to whom he delivered the sword.

As soon as Sir Kay saw it, he knew well it was the sword of the Stone, so he rode to his father Sir Ector, and said:

"Sir, lo, here is the sword of the Stone, wherefore I must be king of this land."

When Sir Ector saw the sword he turned back, and came to the church, and there they all three alighted and went into the church, and he made his son swear truly how he got the sword.

"By my brother Arthur," said Sir Kay, "for he brought it to me."

"How did you get this sword?" said Sir Ector to Arthur.

And the boy told him.

"Now," said Sir Ector, "I understand you must be king of this land."

"Wherefore I?" said Arthur; "and for what cause?"

"Sir," said Ector, "because God will have it so; for never man could draw out this sword but he that shall rightly be king. Now let me see whether you can put the sword there as it was, and pull it out again."

"There is no difficulty," said Arthur, and he put it back into the stone.

Then Sir Ector tried to pull out the sword, and failed; and Sir Kay also pulled with all his might, but it would not move.

"Now you shall try," said Sir Ector to Arthur.

"I will, well," said Arthur, and pulled the sword out easily.

At this Sir Ector and Sir Kay knelt down on the ground before him.

"Alas," said Arthur, "mine own dear father and brother, why do you kneel to me?"

"Nay, nay, my lord Arthur, it is

not so; I was never your father, nor of your blood; but I know well you are of higher blood than I thought you were."

Then Sir Ector told him all, how he had taken him to bring up, and by whose command; and how he had received him from Merlin. And when he understood that Ector was not his father, Arthur was deeply grieved.

"Will you be my good, gracious lord, when you are king?" asked the knight.

"If not, I should be to blame," said Arthur, "for you are the man in the world to whom I am the most beholden, and my good lady and mother your wife, who has fostered and kept me as well as her own children. And if ever it be God's will that I be king, as you say, you shall desire of me what I shall do, and I shall not fail you; God forbid I should fail you."

"Sir," said Sir Ector, "I will ask no more of you but that you will make my son, your foster brother Sir Kay, seneschal[1] of all your lands."

"That shall be done," said Arthur, "and by my faith, never man but he shall have that office while he and I live."

Then they went to the archbishop and told him how the sword was achieved, and by whom.

On Twelfth Day all the barons came to the Stone in the churchyard, so that any who wished might try to win the sword. But not one of them all could take it out, except Arthur.

Many of them therefore were very angry, and said it was a great shame to them and to the country to be governed by a boy not of high blood, for as yet none of them knew that he was the son of King Uther Pendragon. So they agreed to delay the decision till Candlemas,[2] which is the second day of February.

But when Candlemas came, and Arthur once more was the only one who could pull out the sword, they put it off till Easter; and when Easter came, and Arthur again prevailed in presence of them all, they put it off till the Feast of Pentecost.[3]

Then by Merlin's advice the archbishop summoned some of the best knights that were to be got—such knights as in his own day King Uther Pendragon had best loved, and trusted most—and these were appointed to attend young Arthur, and never to leave him night or day till the Feast of Pentecost.

When the great day came, all manner of men once more made the attempt, and once more not one of them all could prevail but Arthur. Before all the lords and commons there assembled he pulled out the sword, whereupon all the commons cried out at once:

"We will have Arthur for our king! We will put him no more in delay, for we all see that it is God's will that he shall be our king, and he who holdeth against it, we will slay him."

And therewith they knelt down all at once, both rich and poor, and be-

---

1 **seneschal** (sĕn′ə shəl): manager of the king's estate and property.

2 **Candlemas:** religious feast day on which all candles used on church altars are blessed.

3 **Feast of Pentecost:** seventh Sunday after Easter.

MYTHS, FABLES, AND LEGENDS

sought pardon of Arthur, because they had delayed him so long.

And Arthur forgave them, and took the sword in both his hands, and offered it on the altar where the archbishop was, and so he was made knight by the best man there.

After that, he was crowned at once, and there he swore to his lords and commons to be a true king, and to govern with true justice from thenceforth all the days of his life.

The Sword Excalibur

After throwing Pellinore into an enchanted sleep, Merlin took up King Arthur, and rode forth on Pellinore's horse.

"Alas!" said Arthur, "what hast thou done, Merlin? Hast thou slain this good knight by thy crafts? There lived not so worshipful a knight as he was; I would rather than a year's income that he were alive."

"Do not be troubled," said Merlin, "for he is less hurt than you. He is only asleep, and will awake within three hours. There liveth not a greater knight than he is, and he shall hereafter do you right good service. His name is Pellinore, and he shall have two sons, that shall be passing good men—Percival of Wales, and Lamerack of Wales."

Leaving Sir Pellinore, King Arthur and Merlin went to a hermit, who was a good man, and skilled in the art of healing. He attended so carefully to the King's wounds, that in three days they were quite well, and Arthur was able to go on his way

with Merlin. Then as they rode, Arthur said, "I have no sword."

"No matter," said Merlin, "nearby is a sword that shall be yours if I can get it."

So they rode till they came to a lake, which was a fair water and broad; and in the midst of the lake, Arthur saw an arm, clothed in white samite,[1] that held in its hand a beautiful sword.

"Lo," said Merlin, "yonder is the sword I spoke of."

With that they saw a damsel rowing across the lake.

"What damsel is that?" said Arthur.

"That is the Lady of the Lake," said Merlin, "and within that lake is a rock, and therein is as fair a place as any on earth, and richly adorned. This damsel will soon come to you; then speak you fair to her, so that she will give you that sword."

Presently the damsel came to Arthur, and saluted him, and he her again.

"Damsel," said Arthur, "what sword is that which yonder the arm holdeth above the water? I would it were mine, for I have no sword."

"Sir Arthur, King," said the damsel, "that sword is mine; the name of it is Excalibur, that is as much as to say *Cut-Steel*. If you will give me a gift when I ask you, ye shall have it."

"By my faith," said Arthur, "I will give you what gift ye shall ask."

"Well," said the damsel, "go you into yonder barge, and row yourself to the sword, and take it and the

1 samite: heavy white silk fabric, interwoven with gold and silver.

scabbard[2] with you, and I will ask my gift when I see my time."

So King Arthur and Merlin alighted, and tied their horses to two trees, and went into the barge, and when they came to the sword that the hand held, Arthur lifted it by the handle, and took it with him. And the arm and hand went under the water; and so they came to the land, and rode away.

Then King Arthur looked on the sword, and liked it passing well.

"Which like you the better, the sword or the scabbard?" asked Merlin.

"I like the sword better," replied Arthur.

"You are the more unwise," said Merlin, "for the scabbard is worth ten of the sword. While you have the scabbard upon you, ye shall never lose any blood, be ye never so sorely wounded. Therefore keep well the scabbard always with you."

So they returned to Carleon, where King Arthur's knights were passing glad to see him. When they heard of his adventures they marveled that he would so jeopardy[3]

himself alone. But all men of honor said it was merry to be under such a chieftain who would put his person in adventures as other poor knights did.

Some time after this, Merlin again warned King Arthur to keep the scabbard of the sword Excalibur very securely, for as long as he had it upon him he would never lose any blood, however sorely he might be wounded. For greater safety, Arthur entrusted the sword and scabbard to his sister, Morgan le Fay. But Morgan le Fay was a false and treacherous woman. She loved another knight better than her husband King Uriens, or her brother King Arthur, and she made up a wicked plot, by which they would both be slain. Then she meant to marry this other knight, Sir Accolon, and place him on King Arthur's throne, when she herself would become queen of the whole realm. Therefore she made by enchantment another scabbard exactly like Excalibur's, which she gave to Arthur when he was going to fight; but Excalibur and its scabbard she kept for Sir Accolon.

2 **scabbard:** case for a sword.
3 **jeopardy:** endanger.

Understanding Literature: "The Marvel of the Sword" and "How Arthur Was Crowned King"

1. What is the political condition of England after Uther's death?
2. Explain the inscription on the sword. When the ambitious lords cannot stir the sword, what does the archbishop advise?
3. What incident prompts Arthur to pull the sword from the stone? How do Sir Kay and Sir Ector react to Arthur's success with the sword?

4. Why do the barons and great lords delay recognizing Arthur as king? Who finally demands that Arthur be made king?

Understanding Literature: "The Sword Excalibur"

1. What evidence of Merlin's magic powers does the reader find?
2. Merlin warns King Arthur twice about the importance of the scabbard for the sword Excalibur. What is this warning?
3. King Arthur's sister, Morgan le Fay, is described as a "false and treacherous woman." What proof of this are you given?
4. What are some of the evidences of myth or fantasy connected with the Arthurian legends that you have read?

Further Activities

1. To become a knight a person had to have a strict and rigorous education which usually began for a boy at the age of twelve. As he matured and became more skilled in certain areas, he progressed from page to squire to knight. Prepare a report on the system of knighthood with material found in your library.
2. Jousts and tournaments were military contests in which the skill and courage of the knights were tested. Prepare a report on the weapons, the armor, and the pageantry involved in these contests.
3. In much of the legendary literature of different countries you find some mystery surrounding the status and birth of the hero. What reason or reasons can you give for this?
4. The code of chivalry was the set of rules by which the knights lived. What were the chief characteristics of this code?

On the following pages are selections adapted from a famous French epic, *The Song of Roland,* set in 8th-century France. This poem, probably written during the 12th century, is set during the life of King Charlemagne,[1] an actual historical figure who lived from 742 to 814. Roland, the hero of the epic, is, however, legendary and represents a kind of ideal hero, very similar to King Arthur.

Stories of Roland

Roland Sees the King

Emeline G. Crommelin

CHARLEMAGNE, OR the Great Charles, was a powerful king of France. He had in his vast kingdom many noble knights whose brave deeds have been told again and again, ever since they were first sung by the minstrel at the famous Battle of Hastings in England, a thousand years ago.

Roland was a little beggar lad. He lived with his mother near the forest of this king's country, where he gathered the nuts for food.

"When you first see King Charlemagne," Roland's mother had often said to him, "it will be the beginning of a new life for you. You will be a beggar boy no longer."

Roland was just twelve years old when he first saw the King—and this was the way it happened: It was known that Charlemagne and his army were to be entertained at a castle in Italy. Roland, hearing this, and remembering his mother's words,

was eager to catch a glimpse of the man who was to change his life. He hastened to a hillside that overlooked the road along which the King and his men were expected to pass. Roland's only companion was Oliver, the son of the governor of the town. The two boys climbed the hillside, and there watched anxiously for the approach of their hero. Poor Roland's head and limbs were bare. His patched, scanty clothing was a strange contrast to Oliver's rich dress of a court page.

"I am sure they are coming!" shouted Roland. "I see a light among the trees. I think it must be the flashing of the sun upon their bright armor. It grows brighter and brighter as they come near."

Very soon the noise of the tramping of many feet was heard, and the rustling of dry leaves in the wood— then a cloud of dust rose above the trees. The bright shields and glittering warcoats were seen in the dis-

1 Charlemagne (shär′lə män′).

tance. The beggar boy leaned forward to see the King and his army in battle array. First came the heralds of the King, who bore the banner of France. Then followed messengers, a body of guards, and a long line of bishops and priests.

"See, Roland!" cried Oliver, "that must be the King himself." Roland knew it was King Charlemagne, for who else could bear himself so proudly and so nobly?

The two lads were so filled with admiration, they could scarcely speak. When the last gay banner had disappeared, Roland told Oliver that some day they should both be knights and ride to battle with the King. Together, by the roadside, the boys knelt, and promised to be true to each other, and to the King, as long as they should live.

As the boys rose from their knees, they sealed their promise by exchanging gifts. Oliver took from his belt a richly carved dagger, while Roland drew forth from his ragged garment a rusty old sword blade.

Thus Roland and Oliver parted at the close of that eventful day when they first saw Charlemagne, whose faithful knights they afterward became.

Roland, filled with joy, hurried to his poor dwelling, and rushing into his mother's arms, exclaimed:

"Mother, I have seen the *King!*—his knights and his peers. Would I were a knight, that I, too, might go forth to war."

Roland begged to know the secret of his life—and this is what he learned: His mother was the Princess Bertha; his father was a gallant count; and King Charlemagne, whose fame was known in all lands, was his uncle. Roland wept for joy. He bade his mother good-by, and believing that the new life had already begun, he hastened to demand his rights of the King of France.

Charlemagne and the peers of the realm were dining at the governor's castle. The courts and halls were filled with knights and squires. They talked of war, of chivalry, and of heroism. Above the voices of the feasters were heard the strains of sweet music. Suddenly, in the midst of the feast, Roland, with proud step and flashing eye, entered the banquet hall.

The King, surprised to see a half-clad boy thus interrupt the royal feast, exclaimed:

"Is not the forest a better place for you, my boy, than this castle at a royal feast?"

"The slave eats the nuts in the forest," answered Roland, proudly; "and the peasant drinks the clear water from the brook; but the best things on your table belong to my mother."

Charlemagne smiled at the boy's reply, and said:

"Your mother must be a grand lady, indeed. Has she servants? Has she a carver and a cupbearer? Has she soldiers, watchmen, and minstrels?"

"She has, indeed," the lad replied: "my two arms are her soldiers; my eyes are her watchmen; my lips are her minstrels. I should like you to see my mother, who dwells in the forest."

The King was as much puzzled as he was delighted with the child's answers. After Roland left the dining hall, Charlemagne turned to Malagis, the dwarf, and asked:

"What think you of this strange boy, who has dared interrupt our feast? Has he not a kingly bearing, in spite of his tattered garments?"

"My lord," said the dwarf, "I think the lad belongs *not* in the forest, but in the palace; for I believe that kings are his ancestors, and that royal blood flows through his veins. He will perform great deeds in the years to come. Let no harm come to him. Have him brought before you again. I see by the stars that, somehow, his life and yours are strangely mingled."

Immediately the King sent his squires to bring the boy and his mother to the castle. When they appeared before the King, he saw that Roland's mother was the Lady Bertha, his own sister, who had married against his wishes and been banished with her husband from the kingdom.

Charlemagne's joy was great. He ordered a feast to be prepared in their honor, and Roland sat at the right hand of the King. The lad was made a page in the service of a duke. His ragged clothes were exchanged for a rich gown of velvet and gold. He was no longer Roland the beggar-lad, who gathered nuts in the forest, but Roland, the nephew of the great King of France.

Roland Becomes a Knight

Emeline G. Crommelin

Some of Roland's ancestors were the noblest heroes the world had ever seen. As the dwarf in the King's court had said, surely the blood of heroes flowed in the lad's veins.

Of all the knights and warriors in Charlemagne's kingdom, Roland was the bravest and most skillful. When he reached manhood, it was right he should have suitable armor as a knight of the King. His armor was so wondrously wrought that some said it was made for him by Vulcan, the blacksmith of the Golden Age. His helmet was made of steel, inlaid with pearls, and engraved on it were strange words and battle scenes.

The metal had been taken from the earth by the dwarf-folk who lived in the North. When Roland first put on the helmet, his comrades said:

"What need has he of such wonderful armor? It would be better to give it to some one who has not a charmed life."

Roland's shield was made of steel, copper, and gold. His spurs had once belonged to King Arthur when he and his Knights of the Round Table dwelt on the earth. They were given to Roland by the fairy queen of Avalon, where King Arthur had gone to be healed of his grievous wound.

In the days when Roland lived, heroes had names for their swords. Roland called his sword Durandal, which surpassed his uncle's sword, and even the famous Excalibur, that King Arthur received from the Lady of the Lake. This sword had been carried by Hector in the battles with the Greeks. There were strange letters on one side of it, which no one but the dwarf could read:

LET HONOR BE TO HIM
WHO MOST DESERVETH IT.

On the other side of it were the words:

I AM DURANDAL, WHICH TROJAN
HECTOR WORE.

Some thought that an angel or a fairy had given the sword to Charlemagne, and told him to gird it on a young knight who had never known reproach or fear. However that may have been, Roland prized this sword beyond measure. Next to it, he cared most for his famous ivory horn, which hung from his neck by a gold chain. It was set with precious gems and inlaid with silver and gold. No one in the kingdom had ever been able to blow upon this horn. Knights had come from far and near to try; but no one had succeeded. When Roland became a knight Charlemagne was anxious to give the horn to him, and bade him try to blow a blast, saying:

"My dear nephew, you have never yet been conquered in a battle, nor have you failed in anything you have undertaken. Here is that which will test your strength. It is the horn of my grandfather. In his days, when men were stronger and seemingly more valiant than now, the most wondrous sounds were made to come forth from it. Men have grown wondrous weak of lungs—not a man in all France can blow the horn now."

When the King had finished speaking, Roland took the horn, looked at it, put it to his lips, and blew. There came forth a sound more wonderful than any one there had ever heard. It resounded through the halls of the great palace, out into the streets, over hills and mountains, and through the forest.

When the people heard it they were astonished. Some thought the end of the world had come. Others thought it was thunder filled with music.

"I give you this horn," said the King to Roland, "for you have won it fairly. No one can ever doubt your right to it. I give it to you on one condition, that you shall never blow it save in time of battle and in great distress."

When Roland had received the horn, he was fully armed as a knight for battle, with his shield and helmet, his trusty sword, and his wonderful horn.

Understanding Literature

1. Describe the ceremony Oliver and Roland perform after seeing King Charlemagne and his followers. In what ways are Oliver and Roland contrasted?
2. What does Roland's mother disclose about his relationship to King Charlemagne?
3. Describe the first meeting of Roland with King Charlemagne. What is it about this meeting which prompts Charlemagne to remark that Roland has a "kingly bearing"?
4. Which character in the story of Roland is similar to Merlin in the King Arthur stories? Explain.
5. What equipment does Roland have that corresponds with the wonderful sword Excalibur of King Arthur? What is the history of the sword of Roland?
6. Only Roland has the ability to blow the beautiful ivory horn. To what feat of King Arthur's is this similar?
7. In these selections are allusions to Vulcan and Hector, whom you read about earlier. Identify them.
8. Which parts of the story of Roland seem based on fact? Which parts are obviously fantasy? In what way does the fantasy add to the enjoyment of the story?

Further Activities

1. Prepare a report on the life and work of King Charlemagne.
2. The Battle of Hastings is mentioned in the first paragraph of "Roland Sees the King." Prepare a report on this topic, using the card catalog in your library to locate information.

A red-eyed, fearful monster demands a sacrifice of a beautiful maiden each day. As Roland journeys to Ireland at the request of King Charlemagne, he hears the story of the monster from an old Irish harper on board the ship. Roland asks the sea captain to steer straight for the Island of Ebuda, where these terrible sacrifices are taking place.

How Roland Slew a Sea Monster

James Baldwin

WHEN, AT LENGTH, the days of mourning for Duke Godfrey were passed, Ogier and the knights who were with him turned their faces southward, and rode back again to France. But Roland parted from their company, and went another way, for Charlemagne had entrusted him with a message to Oberto, the King of Ireland; and to that country he directed his course. At the nearest port on the coast a little ship awaited him; and in this he embarked, and sailed across the western sea.

For many days the vessel plowed the waters, and the sky was clear, and the wind was fair, and the voyage was a happy one. And those on board beguiled the hours with pleasant talk and with many wonderful tales of the sea. The captain was a browned and weather-beaten Norseman, who had sailed the waters for more than twoscore years, and who knew every strait and shallow and every point of land, from Gothland to the Pillars of Hercules. And he

delighted to tell of the many scenes of danger through which he had passed, and of the feats of daring which he had seen on land and sea, and of the strange beings which people the deep. One day he talked about the mermaids and the men of the sea; and he told of the great Midgard snake whom the Northmen believe to lie hidden in the deepest ocean; and he related the story of Old Aegir the Ocean King, and of his nine daughters, the white-veiled Waves. And when he had finished, Roland said that what he had told reminded him of certain stories which he had heard in the South—stories of the old pagan times, when the gods were thought to live on earth, and to take some sort of interest in the doings of men. And he spoke of Poseidon, whom the Greeks called the ruler of the sea; and of old Nereus and his fifty daughters, the silver-footed sea nymphs. And this led him to relate the beautiful fable of Andromeda, and her rescue by Perseus from the sea monster whom Poseidon had sent to devour her.

"But the gods are all dead now," said he, "and neither Aegir nor Poseidon rules the sea."

Then an old Irish harper who happened to be on shipboard spoke, and said, "Sir knight, if all reports be true, some of the sea deities still live, and are known in regions where the Christian religion has not yet been preached. Indeed, I have heard that in the Island of Ebuda, a day's sail west of Ireland, old Proteus, the servant of Poseidon, is even now imitating the deeds of his ancient master."

Then the company insisted that the harper should tell them all that he knew about this matter, and he did as they desired him.

"In the golden age," said he, "it was the task of Proteus to keep the seals and sea calves for his master Poseidon, to lead them into the pleasantest waters and to the freshest pastures, and to see that no one wilfully harmed them. When the times changed, and his old master was dethroned and no longer needed his services, he still kept on herding and caring for the seals and sea calves; for the power of habit was so strong that he could not tear himself away from his old haunts, nor change his occupation. And as he was usually very peaceable, and thought to be quite harmless, very little attention was paid to him; and he was allowed to live on, and ply his vocation, long after all the other sea deities were deposed and forgotten. One day, as he was driving about in his swan chariot, and looking after his herds, he came

to this Island of Ebuda of which I have just spoken. It chanced, that, as he drove close by the shore, the golden-haired daughter of the King of Ebuda stood on the beach. She was more passing fair than ever were the sea nymphs of old, or the mermaids, or the white-veiled daughters of Aegir. And the heart of the ancient Proteus was moved with love for the maiden, and he forthwith besought the King that he would give her to him in marriage. But the father of the maiden scorned his suit. Should he, the King of Ebuda, wed his only daughter to the last of a dying race—to the last and the least worthy of the sea-gods? Let him go back to his seals and sea calves, and never again think of making himself the peer of human beings.

"Then the love of old Proteus was changed to hate, and he vowed that he would not rest nor slumber until he had avenged the slight that had thus been put upon him. And he sent great troops of sea calves to ravage the coasts of Ebuda; and after them he caused a huge and shapeless monster, called an orc, to come, and overrun the whole island. Never was there greater distress and terror. The frightened people fled from their farms and villages, and sought safety in the walled towns; and, between famine and the ravages of the sea monsters, it seemed as if the entire nation would be destroyed. Now, it appears that there was in Ebuda some kind of an oracle, in whose decisions the people placed great trust. And the King prayed the oracle that he might know how to appease the anger of old Proteus, and turn his fearful wrath away. And the oracle answered, and said that this could be done only by offering a daily sacrifice to Proteus to be devoured by the monster orc.

" 'What shall that sacrifice be?' asked the King.

" 'The fairest maiden that can be found either in Ebuda or in the neighboring isles,' was the answer.

" 'And how long shall this fearful payment of tribute continue?' asked the King.

"And the oracle answered, 'Until a hero shall come to Ebuda's shores brave enough and strong enough to slay the orc. Then, and not till then, will Proteus withdraw the curse which he has laid upon you, and leave your people in peace.'

"And it was done as the oracle had bidden. Each day a damsel, the fairest that could be found, was offered to the orc; and the creature ceased his ravages, and allowed the people to return to their homes and farms. And each day, as a new victim was led to the horrible sacrifice, the people prayed for the coming of the hero who should save their loved ones from this dreadful doom. But he came not.

"And it is said that still in the Island of Ebuda this cruel usage is continued, and that the pagan folk who live in that land no longer look upon this sacrifice with horror and aversion, but that, grown barbarous and unfeeling, they send their ships to the neighboring coasts, and bring home scores of fair captives to be offered to the bloodthirsty orc.

Many a noble Irish maiden, I know, has been stolen from our shores, and sacrificed thus horribly by the Ebudans."

"Where sayest thou this savage Island of Ebuda lies?" asked Roland.

"In the great western ocean," answered the harper. "It lies many leagues west of green Erin."

"Turn, then, thy course, good sea captain," said Roland to the master of the ship. "Steer straight for that island kingdom. If such barbarous custom still continues there, it shall not be much longer."

But the winds, as if in league with the wrathful Proteus, hesitated to hasten the vessel on its way; and as the eagerness of the knight waxed stronger, so was the progress of the ship delayed. Sometimes the breeze died away, and there was a calm; the sails hung loose and useless upon the masts, and, had not the seamen plied their oars, the vessel would have stood still. Sometimes a west wind sprang up, and blew strong against them, and they were forced to tack about, and veer far from their intended course. And so it befell that many days passed by, ere, at length, they came in sight of the wooded shores of Ebuda, and the captain pointed out the high rock where the fair victims were daily left as food for the ravenous orc.

When they drew near the place, Roland ordered the ship's boat to be lowered; and in it he placed the largest anchor and the strongest cable that could be found. Then he sat down in the boat; and alone and unarmed, save that he carried the trusty Durandal, he rowed toward the rock. It was about the hour of sunrise—the time when the monster, they said, was wont to come for his daily meal. As the hero rowed close to the shore, he fancied that he heard faint moans, and feeble cries of distress. He looked around, and saw a maiden chained to the rock with iron links, her feet wetted by the rising tide, and her face hidden beneath the long tresses of golden hair that fell about her neck and shoulders. His heart melted with pity, and the sight nerved his arm for the strange contest which was near. He was about to speak to the maiden, when a sudden sound was heard—a roaring like that of a strong wind among the forest trees, or of the waves rolling madly into some ocean cave. He heard the loud shouts of his companions on shipboard: the breakers began to rise around his little boat. The monster was at hand, huge as a rock-built castle, dark and terrible as a thundercloud, fearless as the waves themselves.

Quickly Roland went to meet the beast; he stood up in the boat with the anchor in his hand; quietly he awaited the onset. The orc saw him, and opened his jaws to swallow both him and the boat. The red eyes of the creature glared like baleful bonfires in the morning light; his huge tail lashed the waters into a foam. It was a fearful moment, but Roland faltered not. He raised the heavy anchor still higher; and then, with the strength of a knight well trained in the use of every weapon, he

hurled it into the monster's wide-open mouth. And there it remained, propping the huge jaws apart, and so firmly fixed that the orc could by no means remove it. At nearly the same moment Roland drew his sword, the mighty Durandal; and, calling up all his strength, he struck the monster a blow which almost severed his head from his body. Then guarding the rope to which the anchor was fastened, he seized the oars, and rowed swiftly to the shore. He leaped upon the beach; and, encouraged by the shouts and cheers of his friends on board the ship, he dragged the now dead monster to the land.

And now he bethought him of the captive maiden chained to the rock, and half fallen into a swoon, scarcely knowing that she had been saved from the terrible death that had threatened her. With a single stroke of Durandal, the hero severed the iron links; and then he took her gently by the hand, and led her away from that dreadful rock, and seated her in a pleasant, sunny place high on the shore. With kind and cheerful words he sought to arouse her drooping spirits; for she seemed dazed and bewildered, as if waking from a dream, and unable for a time to remember where she was. He asked her her name, and inquired how she, so unlike the dwellers in Ebuda, had been cast on this barbarous shore and offered in sacrifice to the bloodthirsty orc. She told him that her name was Olympia, and that, in her own home beyond the seas, she was a princess, loved and

honored by hosts of subjects. And then she related, how, one day while walking alone on the seashore, she had been seized by pirates from Ebuda, and, with other fair captives, had been brought to this savage shore, and reserved as a peace offering to the monster whom the Ebudans foolishly believed to have been sent by old Proteus.

Scarcely had the princess ended her story when a new and unexpected danger threatened our hero. The folk of Ebuda had heard of the strange combat between the knight and the orc, and now in great numbers they came trooping to the shore. They stood upon the cliffs above, and along the beach, and some came down even to the water's edge, to see the dead monster and the hero who had slain him. But, although they had been freed from the terror of their lives, they were not pleased; neither felt they in the least thankful to their deliverer.

"Alas!" cried they, "this man has slain the servant of old Proteus, and now it will go hard with us who were charged with his keeping. For will not the sea-god curse us again, and send his herds of sea calves to lay waste our shores? Better it is to endure a single evil than to risk the coming of a multitude of others. The poor orc was not as bad as he might have been; and, now he is dead, there is no telling what may befall us."

"That is true," answered others; "and the only safe way for us to do is to turn away the wrath of old Proteus by punishing the man who has lifted up his sacrilegious hand against the orc. Let us pitch this busy meddler, whoever he may be, into the sea, that he may give his own account to the outraged sea-god whom we serve."

Then a great clamor and shouting arose; and those who stood highest upon the cliffs began hurling stones and darts at Roland; and those who were nearest rushed toward him with drawn swords. There is no telling what would have been the end of this affray, had not a company of armed knights rushed unexpectedly upon the scene. They were men of Ireland, who with their king, Oberto, had come with a fleet of ships to punish the savage islanders for their piracies upon the Irish shores. So great was the surprise of the Ebudans that they turned at once, and fled in wild dismay from the shore; nor did they stop in their flight until they were safely shut up within their city walls.

The meeting between Roland and King Oberto was a happy one; for they had been pages together at the court of Charlemagne, and they recognized each other as old and tried friends. And when the Irish king saw the dead orc, and heard Roland's story of the combat which had taken place, he resolved that he would return at once to his own land and leave the Ebudans in peace. And when all had gone aboard their ships again, the sails were spread, and the fleet sped gayly back toward Ireland. And Roland and the Princess Olympia were guests on board the King's own vessel. And old stories tell us that Oberto afterwards wedded Olympia, making her the Queen of Ireland; and that for many years they lived most happily together, loved and honored by all their subjects.

As for Roland, he tarried not long at the Irish court; but, having delivered the message which he bore from Charlemagne, he took ship again and hastened back to France.

Understanding Literature

1. What "fable" does Roland tell which reminds the old Irish harper of the orc and of the maidens who lived on the Island of Ebuda?
2. How does the story that the old harper tells add to the interest of Roland's actual contact with the monster and the rescue of the maiden?
3. What causes Proteus to vow revenge upon the people of Ebuda?
4. In what way does the oracle suggest that the anger of Proteus can be appeased?
5. Explain why the people of the Island of Ebuda have grown "barbarous and unfeeling" about the daily sacrifice of a maiden.
6. Describe the way in which Roland kills the fearful orc and rescues Olympia. Who is Olympia?
7. Explain why the people of Ebuda are not pleased about the death of the orc.
8. King Charlemagne is mentioned only at the very beginning of the story and at the very end. Why is it necessary to the story that he be mentioned at all?
9. What factual material may have been involved in the legend "How Roland Slew a Sea Monster"?
10. You have now read about two famous legendary heroes, King Arthur and Roland. What two great countries do they represent? In what respects are they alike and unlike? What have you learned about the people of the two periods of history represented by King Arthur and Roland?

Robin Hood, a legendary figure of 12th-century England and already well-known to you, is a different type of hero from Roland or Arthur. The tale, too, has a *mood* different from that of other legends. Filled with the roguish escapades and tricks of the gallant hero, these stories are light, humorous, and rarely serious. These selections by Howard Pyle, a noted writer and illustrator, have been retold from the old tales. Many words no longer common in modern English have been retained to add a feeling of authenticity or genuineness to the story.

Stories of Robin Hood

Robin Hood and Little John

from The Merry Adventures of Robin Hood

Howard Pyle

IN MERRY ENGLAND in the time of old, when good King Henry the Second ruled the land, there lived within the green glades of Sherwood Forest, near Nottingham Town, a famous outlaw whose name was Robin Hood. No archer ever lived that could speed a gray goose shaft with such skill and cunning as his, nor were there ever such yeomen as the sevenscore merry men that roamed with him through the greenwood shades. Right merrily they dwelt within the depths of Sherwood Forest, suffering neither care nor want, but passing the time in merry games of archery or bouts of cudgel play, living upon the King's venison, washed down with drafts of ale of October brewing.

Not only Robin himself but all the band were outlaws and dwelt apart from other men, yet they were beloved by the country people round about, for no one ever came to jolly Robin for help in time of need and went away again with an empty fist.

And now I will tell how it came about that Robin Hood fell afoul of the law.

When Robin was a youth of eighteen, stout of sinew and bold of heart, the Sheriff of Nottingham proclaimed a shooting match and offered a prize of a butt of ale to whosoever should shoot the best shaft in Nottinghamshire. "Now," quoth Robin, "will I go too, for fain would I draw a string for the bright eyes of my lass, and a butt of good October brewing." So up he got and took his good stout yew bow and a score or more of broad clothyard arrows, and started off from Locksley Town through Sherwood Forest to Nottingham.

It was at the dawn of day in the merry Maytime, when hedgerows are green and flowers bedeck the meadows; daisies pied and yellow cuckoo buds and fair primroses all along the briery hedges; when apple buds blossom and sweet birds sing, the lark at dawn of day, the throstle cock and cuckoo; when lads and lasses look upon each other with sweet thoughts; when busy housewives spread their linen to bleach upon the bright green grass. Sweet was the greenwood as he walked along its paths, and bright the green and rustling leaves, amid which the little birds sang with might and main: and blithely Robin whistled as he trudged along, thinking of Maid Marian and her bright eyes, for at such times a youth's thoughts are wont to turn pleasantly upon the lass that he loves the best.

As thus he walked along with a brisk step and a merry whistle, he came suddenly upon some foresters seated beneath a great oak tree. Fifteen there were in all, making themselves merry with feasting and drinking as they sat around a huge pasty, to which each man helped himself, thrusting his hands into the pie, and washing down that which they ate with great horns of ale which they drew all foaming from a barrel that stood nigh. Each man was clad in Lincoln green, and a fine show they made, seated upon the sward[1] beneath that fair, spreading tree. Then one of them, with his mouth full, called out to Robin, "Hulloa, where goest thou, little lad, with thy one penny bow and thy farthing shafts?"

Then Robin grew angry, for no stripling[2] likes to be taunted with his green years.

"Now," quoth he, "my bow and eke mine arrows are as good as thine; and moreover, I go to the shooting match at Nottingham Town, which same has been proclaimed by our good Sheriff of Nottinghamshire; there I will shoot with other stout yeomen, for a prize has been offered of a fine butt of ale."

Then one who held a horn of ale in his hand, said, "Ho! listen to the lad! Why, boy, thy mother's milk is yet scarce dry upon thy lips, and yet thou pratest[3] of standing up with good stout men at Nottingham butts, thou who art scarce able to draw one string of a two stone bow."

"I'll hold the best of you twenty marks," quoth bold Robin, "that I hit the clout at threescore rods,[4] by the good help of Our Lady fair."

At this all laughed aloud, and one said, "Well boasted, thou fair infant, well boasted! and well thou knowest that no target is nigh to make good thy wager."

And another cried, "He will be taking ale with his milk next."

At this Robin grew right mad. "Hark ye," said he; "yonder, at the glade's end, I see a herd of deer, even more than threescore rods distant. I'll hold you twenty marks that, by leave of Our Lady, I cause the best hart among them to die."

"Now done!" cried he who had spoken first. "And here are twenty marks. I wager that thou causest no beast to die, with or without the aid of Our Lady."

Then Robin took his good yew bow in his hand, and placing the tip

3 **pratest:** chatter.
4 **hit . . . rods:** hit the mark at 60 rods or 330 yards.

1 **sward:** grass.
2 **stripling:** young man.

at his instep, he strung it right deftly; then he nocked a broad clothyard arrow, and, raising the bow, drew the gray goose-feather to his ear; the next moment the bowstring rang and the arrow sped down the glade as a sparrowhawk skims in a northern wind. High leaped the noblest hart of all the herd, only to fall dead, reddening the green path with his heart's blood.

"Ha!" cried Robin, "how likest thou that shot, good fellow? I wot[5] the wager were mine, an it were three hundred pounds."

Then all the foresters were filled with rage, and he who had spoken the first and had lost the wager was more angry than all.

"Nay," cried he, "the wager is none of thine, and get thee gone, straightway, or, by all the saints of heaven, I'll baste thy sides until thou wilt ne'er be able to walk again."

"Knowest thou not," said another, "that thou hast killed the King's deer, and, by the laws of our gracious lord and sovereign, King Harry, thine ears should be shaven close to thy head?"

"Catch him!" cried a third.

"Nay," said a fourth, "let him e'en go because of his tender years."

Never a word said Robin Hood, but he looked at the foresters with a grim face; then, turning on his heel, strode away from them down the forest glade. But his heart was bitterly angry, for his blood was hot and youthful and prone to boil.

Now, well would it have been for him who had first spoken had he left Robin Hood alone; but his anger was hot, both because the youth had gotten the better of him and because of the deep draughts of ale that he had been quaffing. So, of a sudden, without any warning, he sprang to his feet, and seized upon his bow and fitted it to a shaft. "Ay," cried he, "and I'll hurry thee anon"; and he sent the arrow whistling after Robin.

It was well for Robin Hood that that same forester's head was spinning with ale, or else he would never have taken another step; as it was, the arrow whistled within three inches of his head. Then he turned around and quickly drew his own bow, and sent an arrow back in return.

"Ye said I was no archer," cried he aloud, "but say so now again!"

The shaft flew straight; the archer fell forward with a cry, and lay on his face upon the ground, his arrows rattling about him from out of his quiver, the gray goose shaft wet with his heart's blood. Then, before the others could gather their wits about them, Robin Hood was gone into the depths of the greenwood. Some started after him, but not with much heart, for each feared to suffer the death of his fellow; so presently they all came and lifted the dead man up and bore him away to Nottingham Town.

Meanwhile Robin Hood ran through the greenwood. Gone was all the joy and brightness from everything, for his heart was sick within him, and it was borne in upon his soul that he had slain a man.

5 **wot:** know.

"Alas!" cried he, "thou hast found me an archer that will make thy wife to wring! I would that thou hadst ne'er said one word to me, or that I had never passed thy way, or e'en that my right forefinger had been stricken off ere that this had happened! In haste I smote,[6] but grieve I sore at leisure!" And then, even in his trouble, he remembered the old saw that "What is done is done; and the egg cracked cannot be cured."

And so he came to dwell in the greenwood that was to be his home for many a year to come, never again to see the happy days with the lads and lasses of sweet Locksley Town; for he was outlawed, not only because he had killed a man, but also because he had poached upon the King's deer, and two hundred pounds were set upon his head, as a reward for whoever would bring him to the court of the King.

Now the Sheriff of Nottingham swore that he himself would bring this knave, Robin Hood, to justice, and for two reasons: first, because he wanted the two hundred pounds, and next, because the forester that Robin Hood had killed was of kin to him.

But Robin Hood lay hidden in Sherwood Forest for one year, and in that time there gathered around him many others like himself, cast out from other folk for this cause and for that. Some had shot deer in hungry wintertime, when they could get no other food, and had been seen in the act by the foresters, but had escaped, thus saving their ears; some had been turned out of their inheritance, that their farms might be added to the King's lands in Sherwood Forest; some had been despoiled by a great baron or a rich abbot or a powerful esquire—all, for one cause or another, had come to Sherwood to escape wrong and oppression.

So, in all that year, fivescore or more good stout yeomen gathered about Robin Hood, and chose him to be their leader and chief. Then they vowed that even as they themselves had been despoiled they would despoil their oppressors, whether baron, abbot, knight, or squire, and that from each they would take that which had been wrung from the poor by unjust taxes, or land rents, or in wrongful fines; but to the poor folk they would give a helping hand in need and trouble, and would return to them that which had been unjustly taken from them. Beside this, they swore never to harm a child nor to wrong a woman, be she maid, wife, or widow; so that, after a while, when the people began to find that no harm was meant to them, but that money or food came in time of want to many a poor family, they came to praise Robin and his merry men, and to tell many tales of him and of his doings in Sherwood Forest, for they felt him to be one of themselves.

Up rose Robin Hood one merry morn when all the birds were singing blithely among the leaves, and up rose all his merry men, each fellow washing his head and hands in the

6 smote: struck.

cold brown brook that leaped laughing from stone to stone. Then said Robin: "For fourteen days have we seen no sport, so now I will go abroad to seek adventures forthwith. But tarry ye, my merry men all, here in the greenwood; only see that ye mind well my call. Three blasts upon the bugle horn I will blow in my hour of need; then come quickly, for I shall want your aid."

So saying, he strode away through the leafy forest glades until he had come to the verge of Sherwood. There he wandered for a long time, through highway and byway, through dingly dell and forest skirts. Now he met a fair buxom lass in a shady lane, and each gave the other a merry word and passed their way; now he saw a fair lady upon an ambling pad,[7] to whom he doffed his cap, and who bowed sedately in return to the fair youth; now he saw a fat monk on a pannier-laden[8] ass; now a gallant knight, with spear and shield and armor that flashed brightly in the sunlight; now a page clad in crimson; and now a stout burgher from good Nottingham Town, pacing along with serious footsteps; all these sights he saw, but adventure found he none. At last he took a road by the forest skirts; a bypath that dipped toward a broad, pebbly stream spanned by a narrow bridge made of a log of wood. As he drew nigh this bridge he saw a tall stranger coming from the other side. Thereupon Robin quickened his pace, as did the stranger likewise; each thinking to cross first.

"Now stand thou back," quoth Robin, "and let the better man cross first."

"Nay," answered the stranger, "then stand back thine own self, for the better man, I wot, am I."

"That will we presently see," quoth Robin; "and meanwhile stand thou where thou art, or else, by the bright brow of Saint Aelfrida, I will show thee right good Nottingham play with a clothyard shaft betwixt thy ribs."

"Now," quoth the stranger, "I will tan thy hide till it be as many colors as a beggar's cloak, if thou darest so much as touch a string of that same bow that thou holdest in thy hands."

"Thou pratest like an ass," said Robin, "for I could send this shaft clean through thy proud heart before a curtal friar[9] could say grace over a roast goose at Michaelmastide."[10]

"And thou pratest like a coward," answered the stranger, "for thou standest there with a good yew bow to shoot at my heart, while I have nought in my hand but a plain blackthorn staff wherewith to meet thee."

"Now," quoth Robin, "by the faith of my heart, never have I had a coward's name in all my life before. I will lay by my trusty bow and eke my arrows, and if thou darest abide my coming, I will go and cut a cudgel to test thy manhood withal."

---

7 **pad:** road horse.
8 **pannier-laden:** loaded with baskets.

9 **curtal friar:** member of a religious order which dresses in short frocks.
10 **Michaelmastide:** religious feast day on September 29.

"Ay, marry,[11] that will I abide thy coming, and joyously, too," quoth the stranger; whereupon he leaned sturdily upon his staff to await Robin.

Then Robin Hood stepped quickly to the coverside and cut a good staff of ground oak, straight, without flaw, and six feet in length, and came back trimming away the tender stems from it, while the stranger waited for him, leaning upon his staff, and whistling as he gazed round about. Robin observed him furtively as he trimmed his staff, measuring him from top to toe from out the corner of his eye, and thought that he had never seen a lustier or a stouter man. Tall was Robin, but taller was the stranger by a head and a neck, for he was seven feet in height. Broad was Robin across the shoulders, but broader was the stranger by twice the breadth of a palm, while he measured at least an ell around the waist.

"Nevertheless," said Robin to himself, "I will baste thy hide right merrily, my good fellow"; then, aloud, "Lo, here is my good staff, lusty and tough. Now wait my coming, an thou darest, and meet me, an thou fearest not; then we will fight until one or the other of us tumble into the stream by dint of blows."

"Marry, that meeteth[12] my whole heart!" cried the stranger, twirling his staff above his head, betwixt his fingers and thumb, until it whistled again.

Never did the Knights of Arthur's Round Table meet in a stouter fight than did these two. In a moment Robin stepped quickly upon the bridge where the stranger stood; first he made a feint,[13] and then delivered a blow at the stranger's head that, had it met its mark, would have tumbled him speedily into the water; but the stranger turned the blow right deftly, and in return gave one as stout, which Robin also turned as the stranger had done. So they stood, each in his place, neither moving a finger's breadth back, for one good hour, and many blows were given and received by each in that time, till here and there were sore bones and bumps, yet neither thought of crying "Enough," or seemed likely to fall from off the bridge. Now and then they stopped to rest, and each thought that he never had seen in all his life before such a hand at quarterstaff. At last Robin gave the stranger a blow upon the ribs that made his jacket smoke like a damp straw thatch in the sun. So shrewd was the stroke that the stranger came within a hair's breadth of falling off the bridge; but he regained himself right quickly, and, by a dexterous blow, gave Robin a crack on the crown that caused the blood to flow. Then Robin grew mad with anger, and smote with all his might at the other; but the stranger warded the blow, and once again thwacked Robin, and this time so fairly that he fell heels over head into the water, as the queen pin falls in a game of bowls.

11 marry: indeed.
12 meeteth: suits.

13 feint: fake blow, intended to throw an opponent off balance.

MYTHS, FABLES, AND LEGENDS

"And where art thou now, my good lad?" shouted the stranger, roaring with laughter.

"Oh, in the flood and floating adown with the tide," cried Robin; nor could he forbear laughing himself at his sorry plight. Then, gaining his feet, he waded to the bank, the little fish speeding hither and thither, all frightened at his splashing.

"Give me thy hand," cried he, when he had reached the bank. "I must needs own thou art a brave and a sturdy soul, and, withal, a good stout stroke with the cudgels. By this and by that, my head hummeth like to a hive of bees on a hot June day."

Then he clapped his horn to his lips, and winded a blast that went echoing sweetly down the forest paths. "Ay, marry," quoth he again, "thou art a tall lad, and eke a brave one, for ne'er, I trow, is there a man betwixt here and Canterbury Town could do the like to me that thou hast done."

"And thou," quoth the stranger, laughing, "takest thy cudgeling like a brave heart and a stout yeoman."

But now the distant twigs and branches rustled with the coming of men, and suddenly a score or two of good stout yeomen, all clad in Lincoln green, burst from out the covert, with merry Will Stutely at their head.

"Good master," cried Will, "how is this? Truly thou art all wet from head to foot, and that to the very skin."

"Why, marry," answered jolly Robin, "yon stout fellow hath tumbled me neck and crop into the water, and hath given me a drubbing beside."

"Then shall he not go without a ducking and eke a drubbing himself!" cried Will Stutely. "Have at him, lads!"

Then Will and a score of yeomen leaped upon the stranger, but though they sprang quickly they found him ready and felt him strike right and left with his stout staff, so that, though he went down with press of numbers, some of them rubbed cracked crowns before he was overcome.

"Nay, forbear!" cried Robin, laughing until his sore sides ached again; "he is a right good man and true, and no harm shall befall him. Now hark ye, good youth, wilt thou stay with me and be one of my band? Three suits of Lincoln green shalt thou have each year, beside forty marks in fee, and share with us whatsoever good shall befall us. Thou shalt eat sweet venison and quaff the stoutest ale, and mine own good right-hand man shalt thou be, for never did I see such a cudgel player in all my life before. Speak! wilt thou be one of my good merry men?"

"That know I not," quoth the stranger, surlily, for he was angry at being so tumbled about. "If ye handle yew bow and apple shaft no better than ye do oaken cudgel, I wot ye are not fit to be called yeomen in my country; but if there be any man here that can shoot a better shaft than I, then will I bethink me of joining with you."

"Now by my faith," said Robin, "thou art a right saucy varlet, sirrah; yet I will stoop to thee as I never stooped to man before. Good Stutely, cut thou a fair white piece of bark four fingers in breadth, and set it fourscore yards distant on yonder oak. Now, stranger, hit that fairly with a gray goose shaft and call thyself an archer."

"Ay, marry, that will I," answered he. "Give me a good stout bow and a fair broad arrow, and if I hit it not strip me and beat me blue with bowstrings."

Then he chose the stoutest bow amongst them all, next to Robin's own, and a straight gray goose shaft, well-feathered and smooth, and stepping to the mark—while all the band, sitting or lying upon the greensward, watched to see him shoot—he drew the arrow to his cheek and loosed the shaft right deftly, sending it so straight down the path that it clove the mark in the very center. "Aha!" cried he, "mend thou that if thou canst"; while even the yeomen clapped their hands at so fair a shot.

"That is a keen shot, indeed," quoth Robin, "mend it I cannot, but mar it I may, perhaps."

Then taking up his own good stout bow and nocking an arrow with care he shot with his very greatest skill. Straight flew the arrow, and so true that it lit fairly upon the stranger's shaft and split it into splinters. Then all the yeomen leaped to their feet and shouted for joy that their master had shot so well.

"Now by the lusty yew bow of good Saint Withold," cried the stranger, "that is a shot indeed, and never saw I the like in all my life before! Now truly will I be thy man henceforth and for aye. Good Adam Bell[14] was a fair shot, but never shot he so!"

"Then have I gained a right good man this day," quoth jolly Robin. "What name goest thou by, good fellow?"

"Men call me John Little whence I came," answered the stranger.

Then Will Stutely, who loved a good jest, spoke up. "Nay, fair little stranger," said he, "I like not thy name and fain would I have it otherwise. Little art thou indeed, and small of bone and sinew, therefore shalt thou be christened Little John, and I will be thy godfather."

Then Robin Hood and all his band laughed aloud until the stranger began to grow angry.

"An thou make a jest of me," quoth he to Will Stutely, "thou wilt have sore bones and little pay, and that in short season."

"Nay, good friend," said Robin Hood, "bottle thine anger, for the name fitteth thee well. Little John shall thou be called henceforth, and Little John shall it be. So come, my merry men, and we will go and prepare a christening feast for this fair infant."

So turning their backs upon the stream, they plunged into the forest once more, through which they traced their steps till they reached the spot where they dwelt in the depths of the woodland. There had they built huts of bark and branches of trees, and made couches of sweet rushes spread over with skins of fallow deer. Here stood a great oak tree with branches spreading broadly around, beneath which was a seat of green moss where Robin Hood was wont to sit at feast and at merrymaking with his stout men about him. Here they found the rest of the band, some of whom had come in with a brace of fat does. Then they all built great fires and after a time roasted the does and broached a barrel of humming ale. Then when the feast was ready they all sat down, but Robin placed Little John at his right hand, for he was henceforth to be the second in the band.

Then when the feast was done Will Stutely spoke up. "It is now time, I ween, to christen our bonny babe, is it not so, merry boys?" And "Aye! Aye!" cried all, laughing till the woods echoed with their mirth.

"Then seven sponsors shall we have," quoth Will Stutely; and hunting among all the band he chose the seven stoutest men of them all.

"Now by Saint Dunstan," cried Little John, springing to his feet, "more than one of you shall rue it an you lay finger upon me."

But without a word they all ran upon him at once, seizing him by his legs and arms and holding him tightly in spite of his struggles, and they bore him forth while all stood around to see the sport. Then one came forward who had been chosen to play the priest because he had a bald crown, and in his hands he carried a brimming pot of ale. "Now who bringeth this babe?" asked he right soberly.

14 Adam Bell: famous bowman in many ballads.

"That do I," answered Will Stutely. "And what name callest thou him?"

"Little John call I him."

"Now Little John," quoth the mock priest, "thou hast not lived heretofore, but only got thee along through the world, but henceforth thou wilt live indeed. When thou livedst not thou wast called John Little, but now that thou dost live indeed, Little John shalt thou be called, so christen I thee." And at these last words he emptied the pot of ale upon Little John's head.

Then all shouted with laughter as they saw the good brown ale stream over Little John's beard and trickle from his nose and chin, while his eyes blinked with the smart of it. At first he was of a mind to be angry, but found he could not because the others were so merry; so he, too, laughed with the rest. Then Robin took this sweet, pretty babe, clothed him all anew from top to toe in Lincoln green, and give him a good stout bow, and so made him a member of the merry band.

And thus it was that Robin Hood became outlawed; thus a band of merry companions gathered about him, and thus he gained his right-hand man, Little John.

Understanding Literature

1. Describe the incident which forces Robin Hood to become an outlaw.
2. What kinds of men does Robin Hood gather into his band?
3. Describe Robin Hood's adventure with Little John.
4. From his general treatment of Little John, what can we learn about Robin Hood's character?
5. Why do the common people so readily accept Robin Hood as their hero?
6. Explain how the situations, the setting, and the vocabulary create a light, gay mood for the story of Robin Hood.
7. What is the setting of the Robin Hood stories? What paragraph is most descriptive about the setting? Which groups of words are particularly clear in forming a picture (or an image)?

In this story Robin Hood, who so enjoys playing tricks himself, is tricked by another person, King Richard the Lion-Hearted, around whom many legends have grown. At the conclusion of this story, the problems of the outlawed Robin Hood and his outlaw band seemed to be solved for the moment.

King Richard Cometh to Sherwood Forest

from The Merry Adventures of Robin Hood

Howard Pyle

NOT MORE THAN two months had passed and gone since these stirring adventures that have just been told of befell Robin Hood and Little John, when all Nottinghamshire was in a mighty stir and tumult, for King Richard of the Lion's Heart was making a royal progress through merry England, and everyone expected him to come to Nottingham Town in his journeying. Messengers went riding back and forth between the Sheriff and the King, until at last the time was fixed upon when his majesty was to stop in Nottingham, as the guest of his worship.

And now came more bustle than ever; a great running hither and thither, a rapping of hammers and a babble of voices sounded everywhere through the place, for the folk were building great arches across the streets, beneath which the King was to pass, and were draping these arches with silken banners and streamers of many colors. Great hubbub was going on in the Guild Hall of the town, also, for here a grand banquet was to be given to the King and the nobles of his train, and the best master carpenters were busy building a throne where the King and the Sheriff were to sit at the head of the table, side by side.

It seemed to many of the good folk of the place as if the day that should bring the King into the town would never come; but all the same it did come in its own season, and bright shone the sun down into the stony streets, which were all alive with a restless sea of people. On either side of the way great crowds of town and country folk stood packed as close together as dried herring in a box, so that the Sheriff's men, halberds[1] in hands, could hardly press them back to leave space for the King's riding.

"Take care whom thou pushest against!" cried a great, burly friar to one of these men. "Wouldst thou dig thine elbows into me, sirrah?

1 halberds: long-handled weapons.

By'r Lady of the Fountain, an thou dost not treat me with more deference[2] I will crack thy knave's pate[3] for thee, even though thou be one of the mighty Sheriff's men."

At this a great shout of laughter arose from a number of tall yeomen in Lincoln green that were scattered through the crowd thereabouts; but one that seemed of more authority than the others nudged the holy man with his elbow. "Peace, Tuck," said he, "didst thou not promise me, ere thou camest here, that thou wouldst put a check upon thy tongue?"

"Ay, marry," grumbled the other, "but 'a did not think to have a hard-footed knave trample all over my poor toes as though they were no more than so many acorns in the forest."

But of a sudden all this bickering ceased, for a clear sound of many bugle horns came winding down the street. Then all the people craned their necks and gazed in the direction whence the sound came, and the crowding and the pushing and the swaying grew greater than ever. And now a gallant array of men came gleaming into sight, and the cheering of the people ran down the crowd as the fire runs in dry grass.

Eight and twenty heralds in velvet and cloth of gold came riding forwards. Over their heads fluttered a cloud of snow-white feathers, and each herald bore in his hand a long silver trumpet, which he blew musically. From each trumpet hung a heavy banner of velvet and cloth of gold, with the royal arms of England emblazoned thereon. After these came riding fivescore noble knights, two by two, all fully armed, saving that their heads were uncovered. In their hands they bore tall lances, from the tops of which fluttered pennons of many colors and devices. By the side of each knight walked a page clad in rich clothes of silk and velvet, and each page bore in his hands his master's helmet, from which waved long, floating plumes of feathers. Never had Nottingham seen a fairer sight than those fivescore noble knights, from whose armor the sun blazed in dazzling light as they came riding on their great war horses, with clashing of arms and jingling of chains. Behind the knights came the barons and the nobles of the mid-country, in robes of silk and cloth of gold, with golden chains about their necks and jewels at their girdles. Behind these again came a great array of men-at-arms, with spears and halberds in their hands, and, in the midst of these, two riders side by side. One of the horsemen was the Sheriff of Nottingham in his robes of office. The other, who was a head taller than the Sheriff, was clad in a rich but simple garb, with a broad, heavy chain about his neck. His hair and beard were like threads of gold, and his eyes were as blue as the summer sky. As he rode along he bowed to the right hand and the left, and a mighty roar of voices followed him as he passed; for this was King Richard.

Then, above all the tumult and the shouting a great voice was heard

2 **deference:** respect.
3 **pate:** head.

roaring, "Heaven, its saints bless thee, our gracious King Richard! and likewise Our Lady of the Fountain, bless thee!" Then King Richard, looking toward the spot whence the sound came, saw a tall, burly, strapping priest standing in front of all the crowd with his legs wide apart as he backed against those behind.

"By my soul, Sheriff," said the King, laughing, "ye have the tallest priests in Nottinghamshire that e'er I saw in all my life. If Heaven never answered prayers because of deafness, methinks I would nevertheless have blessings bestowed upon me, for that man yonder would make the great stone image of Saint Peter rub its ears and hearken unto him. I would that I had an army of such as he."

To this the Sheriff answered never a word, but all the blood left his cheeks, and he caught at the pommel of his saddle to keep himself from falling; for he also saw the fellow that so shouted, and knew him to be Friar Tuck; and, moreover, behind Friar Tuck he saw the faces of Robin Hood and Little John and Will Scarlet and Will Stutely and Allan a Dale and others of the band.

"How now," said the King hastily, "art thou ill, Sheriff, that thou growest so white?"

"Nay, your majesty," said the Sheriff, "it was nought but a sudden pain that will soon pass by." Thus he spake, for he was ashamed that the King should know that Robin Hood feared him so little that he thus dared to come within the very gates of Nottingham Town.

Thus rode the King into Nottingham Town on that bright afternoon in the early fall season; and none rejoiced more than Robin Hood and his merry men to see him come so royally unto his own.

Eventide[4] had come; the great feast in the Guild Hall at Nottingham Town was done, and the wine passed freely. A thousand waxen lights gleamed along the board, at which sat lord and noble and knight and squire in goodly array. At the head of the table, upon a throne all hung with cloth of gold, sat King Richard with the Sheriff of Nottingham beside him.

Quoth the King to the Sheriff, laughing as he spoke, "I have heard much spoken concerning the doings of certain fellows hereabouts, one Robin Hood and his band, who are outlaws and abide in Sherwood Forest. Canst thou not tell me somewhat of them, Sir Sheriff? for I hear that thou hast had dealings with them more than once."

At these words the Sheriff of Nottingham looked down gloomily, and the Bishop of Hereford, who was present, gnawed his nether[5] lip. Quoth the Sheriff, "I can tell your majesty but little concerning the doings of those naughty fellows, saving that they are the boldest lawbreakers in all the land."

Then up spake young Sir Henry of the Lea, a great favorite with the King, under whom he had fought in Palestine. "May it please your maj-

4 **Eventide:** evening.
5 **nether:** lower.

esty," said he, "when I was away in Palestine I heard ofttimes from my father, and in most cases I heard of this very fellow, Robin Hood. If your majesty would like I will tell you a certain adventure of this outlaw."

Then the King laughingly bade him tell his tale, whereupon he told how Robin Hood had aided Sir Richard of the Lea with money that he had borrowed from the Bishop of Hereford. Again and again the King and those present roared with laughter, whilst the poor Bishop waxed cherry red in the face with vexation, for the matter was a sore thing with him. When Sir Henry of the Lea was done, others of those present, seeing how the King enjoyed this merry tale, told other tales concerning Robin and his merry men.

"By the hilt of my sword," said stout King Richard, "this is as bold and merry a knave as ever I heard tell of. Marry, I must take this matter in hand and do what thou couldst not do, Sheriff, to wit, clear the forest of him and his band."

That night the King sat in the place that was set apart for his lodging whilst in Nottingham Town. With him were young Sir Henry of the Lea and two other knights and three barons of Nottinghamshire; but the King's mind still dwelt upon Robin Hood. "Now," quoth he, "I would freely give a hundred pounds to meet this roguish fellow, Robin Hood, and to see somewhat of his doings in Sherwood Forest."

Then up spake Sir Hubert of Bingham, laughing: "If your majesty hath such a desire upon you it is not so hard to satisfy. If your majesty is willing to lose one hundred pounds, I will engage to cause you not only to meet this fellow, but to feast with him in Sherwood."

"Marry, Sir Hubert," quoth the King, "this pleaseth me well. But how wilt thou cause me to meet Robin Hood?"

"Why, thus," said Sir Hubert, "let your majesty and us here present put on the robes of seven of the Order of Black Friars, and let your majesty hang a purse of one hundred pounds beneath your gown; then let us undertake to ride from here to Mansfield Town tomorrow, and, without I am much mistaken, we will both meet with Robin Hood and dine with him before the day be passed."

"I like thy plan, Sir Hubert," quoth the King merrily, "and tomorrow we will try it and see whether there be virtue in it."

So it happened that when early the next morning the Sheriff came to where his liege lord was abiding, to pay his duty to him, the King told him what they had talked of the night before, and what merry adventure they were set upon undertaking that morning. But when the Sheriff heard this he smote his forehead with his fist. "Alas!" said he, "what evil counsel is this that hath been given thee! O my gracious lord and king, you know not what you do! This villain that you thus go to seek hath no reverence either for king or king's laws."

"But did I not hear aright when I was told that this Robin Hood hath shed no blood since he was outlawed, saving only that of that vile Guy of Gisbourne, for whose death all honest men should thank him?"

"Yea, your majesty," said the Sheriff, "you have heard aright. Nevertheless"—

"Then," quoth the King, breaking in on the Sheriff's speech, "what have I to fear in meeting him, having done him no harm? Truly, there is no danger in this. But mayhap thou wilt go with us, Sir Sheriff."

"Nay," quoth the Sheriff hastily, "Heaven forbid!"

But now seven habits such as black friars wear were brought, and the King and those about him having clad themselves therein, and his majesty having hung a purse with a hundred golden pounds in it beneath his robes, they all went forth and mounted the mules that had been brought to the door for them. Then the King bade the Sheriff be silent as to their doings, and so they set forth upon their way. Onward they traveled, laughing and jesting, until they passed through the open country; between bare harvest fields whence the harvest had been gathered home; through scattered glades that began to thicken as they went farther along, till they came within the heavy shade of the forest itself. They traveled in the forest for several miles without meeting any one such as they sought, until they had come to that part of the road that lay nearest to Newstead Abbey.

"By the holy Saint Martin," quoth the King, "I would that I had a better head for remembering things of great need. Here have we come away and brought never so much as a drop of anything to drink with us. Now I would give half a hundred pounds for somewhat to quench my thirst withal."

No sooner had the King so spoken, than out from the covert[6] at the roadside stepped a tall fellow with yellow beard and hair and a pair of merry blue eyes. "Truly, holy brother," said he, laying his hand upon the King's bridle rein, "it were an unchristian thing to not give fitting answer to so fair a bargain. We keep an inn hereabouts, and for fifty pounds we will not only give thee a good draught of wine, but will give thee as noble a feast as ever thou didst tickle thy gullet withal." So saying he put his fingers to his lips and blew a shrill whistle. Then straightway the bushes and branches on either side of the road swayed and crackled, and threescore broad-shouldered yeomen in Lincoln green burst out of the covert.

"How now, fellow," quoth the King, "who art thou, thou naughty rogue? Hast thou no regard for such holy men as we are?"

"Not a whit," quoth merry Robin Hood, for the fellow was he, "for in sooth all the holiness belonging to rich friars, such as ye are, one could drop into a thimble and the good wife would never feel it with the tip of her finger. As for my name, it is Robin Hood, and thou mayst have heard it before."

6 covert: secret place.

"Now out upon thee!" quoth King Richard. "Thou art a bold and naughty fellow and a lawless one withal, as I have often heard tell. Now, prythee, let me, and these brethren of mine, travel forward in peace and quietness."

"It may not be," said Robin, "for it would look but ill of us to let such holy men travel onward with empty stomachs. But I doubt not that thou hast a fat purse to pay thy score at our inn since thou offerest freely so much for a poor draught of wine. Show me thy purse, reverend brother, or I may perchance have to strip thy robes from thee to search for it myself."

"Nay, use no force," said the King sternly. "Here is my purse, but lay not thy lawless hands upon our person."

"Hut, tut," quoth merry Robin, "what proud words are these? Art thou the King of England, to talk so to me? Here, Will, take this purse and see what there is within."

Will Scarlet took the purse and counted out the money. Then Robin bade him keep fifty pounds for themselves, and put fifty back into the purse. This he handed to the King. "Here, brother," quoth he, "take this half of thy money, and thank Saint Martin, on whom thou didst call before, that thou hast fallen into the hands of such gentle rogues that they will not strip thee bare, as they might do. But wilt thou not put back thy cowl?[7] for I would fain see thy face."

"Nay," said the King, drawing back, "I may not put back my cowl, for we seven have vowed that we will not show our faces for four and twenty hours."

"Then keep them covered in peace," said Robin, "and far be it from me to make you break your vows."

So he called seven of his yeomen and bade them each one take a mule by the bridle; then, turning their faces toward the depths of the woodlands, they journeyed onward until they came to the open glade and the greenwood tree.

Little John, with threescore yeomen at his heels, had also gone forth that morning to wait along the roads and bring a rich guest to Sherwood glade, if such might be his luck, for many with fat purses must travel the roads at this time, when such great doings were going on in Nottinghamshire; but though Little John and so many others were gone, Friar Tuck and twoscore or more stout yeomen were seated or lying around beneath the great tree, and when Robin and the others came they leaped to their feet to meet him.

"By my soul," quoth merry King Richard, when he had gotten down from his mule and stood looking about him, "thou hast in very truth a fine lot of young men about thee, Robin. Methinks King Richard himself would be glad of such a bodyguard."

"These are not all of my fellows," said Robin, proudly, "for threescore more of them are away on business with my good right-hand man, Little

---

7 cowl: monk's hood.

MYTHS, FABLES, AND LEGENDS

John. But, as for King Richard, I tell thee, brother, there is not a man of us all but would pour out our blood like water for him. Ye churchmen cannot rightly understand our King; but we yeomen love him right loyally for the sake of his brave doings which are so like our own."

But now Friar Tuck came bustling up. "Gi' ye good den, brothers," said he. "I am right glad to welcome some of my cloth in this naughty place. Truly, methinks these rogues of outlaws would stand but an ill chance were it not for the prayers of Holy Tuck, who laboreth so hard for their well-being." Here he winked one eye slyly and stuck his tongue into his cheek.

"Who art thou, mad priest?" said the King in a serious voice, albeit he smiled beneath his cowl.

At this Friar Tuck looked all around with a slow gaze. "Look you now," quoth he, "never let me hear you say again that I am no patient man. Here is a knave of a friar calleth me a mad priest, and yet I smite him not. My name is Friar Tuck, fellow—the holy Friar Tuck."

"There, Tuck," said Robin, "thou hast said enow. Prythee, cease thy talk and bring some wine. These reverend men are athirst, and sin' they have paid so richly for their score they must e'en have the best."

Friar Tuck bridled[8] at being so checked in his speech, nevertheless he went straightway to do Robin's bidding; so presently a great crock

was brought, and wine was poured out for all the guests and for Robin Hood. Then Robin held his cup aloft. "Stay!" cried he. "Tarry in your drinking till I give you a pledge. Here is to good King Richard of great renown, and may all enemies to him be confounded."

Then all drank the King's health, even the King himself. "Methinks, good fellow," said he, "thou hast drunk to thine own confusion."

"Never a whit," quoth merry Robin, "for I tell thee that we of Sherwood are more loyal to our lord the King than those of thine order. We would give up our lives for his benefiting, whilst ye are content to lie snug in your abbeys and priories let reign who will."

At this the King laughed. Quoth he, "Perhaps King Richard's welfare is more to me than thou wottest of, fellow. But enough of that matter. We have paid well for our fare, so canst thou not show us some merry entertainment? I have oft heard that ye are wondrous archers; wilt thou not show us somewhat of your skill?"

"With all my heart," said Robin, "we are always pleased to show our guests all the sport that is to be seen. As Gaffer Swanthold sayeth, ' 'Tis a hard heart that will not give a caged starling of the best'; and caged starlings ye are with us. Ho, lads! set up a garland at the end of the glade."

Then, as the yeomen ran to do their master's bidding, Tuck turned to one of the mock friars. "Hearest thou our master?" quoth he, with a sly wink. "Whenever he cometh

8 **bridled:** was annoyed.

across some poor piece of wit he straightway layeth it on the shoulders of this Gaffer Swanthold—whoever he may be—so that the poor goodman goeth traveling about with all the odds and ends and tags and rags of our master's brain packed on his back." Thus spake Friar Tuck, but in a low voice so that Robin could not hear him, for he felt somewhat nettled at Robin's cutting his talk so short.

In the meantime the mark at which they were to shoot was set up at sixscore paces distance. It was a garland of leaves and flowers two spans in width, which same was hung upon a stake in front of a broad tree trunk. "There," quoth Robin, "yon is a fair mark, lads. Each of you shoot three arrows thereat; and if any fellow misseth by so much as one arrow, he shall have a buffet of Will Scarlet's fist."

"Hearken to him!" quoth Friar Tuck. "Why, master, thou dost bestow buffets from thy strapping nephew as though they were lovetaps from some bouncing lass. I warrant thou art safe to hit the garland thyself, or thou wouldst not be so free of his cuffing."

First David of Doncaster shot, and lodged all three of his arrows within the garland. "Well done, David!" cried Robin, "thou hast saved thine ears from a warming this day." Next Midge, the Miller, shot, and he, also, lodged his arrows in the garland. Then followed Wat, the Tinker, but alas for him! for one of his shafts missed the mark by the breadth of two fingers.

"Come hither, fellow," said Will Scarlet, in his soft, gentle voice, "I owe thee somewhat that I would pay forthwith." Then Wat, the Tinker, came forward and stood in front of Will Scarlet, screwing up his face and shutting his eyes tightly, as though he already felt his ears ringing with the buffet. Will Scarlet rolled up his sleeve, and, standing on tiptoe to give the greater swing to his arm, he struck with might and main. *"Whoof!"* came his palm against the Tinker's head, and down went stout Wat to the grass, heels over head, as the wooden image at the fair goes down when the skillful player throws a cudgel at it. Then, as the Tinker sat up upon the grass, rubbing his ear and winking and blinking at the bright stars that danced before his eyes, the yeomen roared with mirth till the forest rang. As for King Richard, he laughed till the tears ran down his cheeks. Thus the band shot, each in turn, some getting off scot free, and some winning a buffet that always sent them to the grass. And now, last of all, Robin took his place, and all was hushed as he shot. The first shaft he shot split a piece from the stake on which the garland was hung; the second lodged within an inch of the other. "By my halidom,"[9] said King Richard to himself, "I would give a thousand pounds for this fellow to be one of my guard!" And now, for the third time Robin shot; but, alas for him! the arrow was ill-feathered,

9 **By my halidom:** a mild oath.

MYTHS, FABLES, AND LEGENDS

and, wavering to one side, it smote an inch outside the garland.

At this a great roar went up, those of the yeomen who sat upon the grass rolling over and over and shouting with laughter, for never before had they seen their master so miss his mark; but Robin flung his bow upon the ground with vexation. "Now, out upon it!" cried he. "That shaft had an ill feather to it, for I felt it as it left my fingers. Give me a clean arrow, and I will engage to split the wand with it."

At these words the yeomen laughed louder than ever. "Nay, good uncle," said Will Scarlet, in his soft, sweet voice, "thou hast had thy fair chance and hast missed thine aim out and out. I swear the arrow was as good as any that hath been loosed this day. Come hither; I owe thee somewhat, and would fain pay it."

"Go, good master," roared Friar Tuck, "and may my blessing go with thee. Thou hast bestowed these love-taps of Will Scarlet's with great freedom. It were pity an thou gottest not thine own share."

"It may not be," said merry Robin. "I am King here, and no subject may raise hand against the King. But even our great King Richard may yield to the holy Pope without shame, and even take a tap from him by way of penance; therefore I will yield myself to this holy friar, who seemeth to be one in authority, and will take my punishment from him." Thus saying, he turned to the King, "I prythee, brother, wilt thou take my punishing into thy holy hands?"

"With all my heart," quoth merry King Richard, rising from where he was sitting. "I owe thee somewhat for having lifted a heavy weight of fifty pounds from my purse. So make room for him on the green, lads."

"An thou makest me tumble," quoth Robin, "I will freely give thee back thy fifty pounds; but I tell thee, brother, if thou makest me not feel grass all along my back, I will take every farthing thou hast for thy boastful speech."

"So be it," said the King, "I am willing to venture it." Thereupon he rolled up his sleeve and showed an arm that made the yeomen stare. But Robin, with his feet wide apart, stood firmly planted, waiting the other, smiling. Then the King swung back his arm, and balancing himself a moment, he delivered a buffet at Robin that fell like a thunderbolt. Down went Robin headlong upon the grass, for the stroke would have felled a stone wall. Then how the yeomen shouted with laughter till their sides ached, for never had they seen such a buffet given in all their lives. As for Robin, he presently sat up and looked all around him, as though he had dropped from a cloud and had lit in a place he had never seen before. After a while, still gazing about him at his laughing yeomen, he put his finger tips softly to his ear and felt all around it tenderly. "Will Scarlet," said he, "count this fellow out his fifty pounds; I want nothing more either of his money or of him. A murrain[10] seize him and his buffeting! I would that I had taken my dues from thee, for I verily believe he hath

deafened mine ear from ever hearing again."

Then, while gusts of laughter still broke from the band, Will Scarlet counted out the fifty pounds, and the King dropped it back into his purse again. "I give thee thanks, fellow," said he, "and if ever thou shouldst wish for another box of the ear to match the one thou hast, come to me and I will fit thee with it for nought."

So spake the merry King; but, even as he ended, there came suddenly the sound of many voices, and out from the covert burst Little John and threescore men, with Sir Richard of the Lea in the midst. Across the glade they came running, and, as they came, Sir Richard shouted to Robin: "Make haste, dear friend, gather thy band together and come with me! King Richard left Nottingham Town this very morning, and cometh to seek thee in the woodlands. I know not how he cometh, for it was but a rumor of this that reached me; nevertheless, I know that it is the truth. Therefore hasten with all thy men, and come to Castle Lea, for there thou mayst lie hidden till thy present danger passeth. Who are these strangers that thou hast with thee?"

"Why," quoth merry Robin, rising from the grass, "these are certain gentle guests that came with us from the highroad over by Newstead Abbey. I know not their names, but I have become right well acquaint with this lusty rogue's palm this morning. Marry, the pleasure of this acquaintance hath cost me a deaf ear and fifty pounds to boot!"

10 murrain: plague.

352

Sir Richard looked keenly at the tall friar, who, drawing himself up to his full height, looked fixedly back at the knight. Then of a sudden Sir Richard's cheeks grew pale, for he knew who it was that he looked upon. Quickly he leaped from off his horse's back and flung himself upon his knees before the other. At this, the King, seeing that Sir Richard knew him, threw back his cowl, and all the yeomen saw his face and knew him also, for there was not one of them but had been in the crowd in the good town of Nottingham, and had seen him riding side by side with the Sheriff. Down they fell upon their knees, nor could they say a word. Then the King looked all around right grimly, and, last of all, his glance came back and rested again upon Sir Richard of the Lea.

"How is this, Sir Richard?" said he, sternly. "How darest thou step between me and these fellows? and how darest thou offer thy knightly Castle of the Lea for a refuge to them? Wilt thou make it a hiding place for the most renowned outlaws in England?"

Then Sir Richard of the Lea raised his eyes to the King's face. "Far be it from me," said he, "to do aught that could bring your majesty's anger upon me. Yet, sooner would I face your majesty's wrath than suffer aught of harm that I could stay to fall upon Robin Hood and his band; for to them I owe life, honor, everything. Should I, then, desert him in his hour of need?"

Ere the Knight had done speaking, one of the mock friars that stood near the King came forward and knelt beside Sir Richard, and throwing back his cowl showed the face of young Sir Henry of the Lea. Then Sir Henry grasped his father's hand and said, "Here kneels one who hath served thee well, King Richard, and, as thou knowest, hath stepped between thee and death in Palestine; yet do I abide by my dear father, and here I say also, that I would freely give shelter to this noble outlaw, Robin Hood, even though it brought thy wrath upon me, for my father's honor and my father's welfare are as dear to me as mine own."

King Richard looked from one to the other of the kneeling knights, and at last the frown faded from his brow and a smile twitched at the corners of his lips. "Marry, Sir Richard," quoth the King, "thou art a bold-spoken knight, and thy freedom of speech weigheth not heavily against thee with me. This young son of thine taketh after his sire both in boldness of speech and of deed, for, as he sayeth, he stepped one time betwixt me and death; wherefore I would pardon thee for his sake even if thou hadst done more than thou hast. Rise all of you, for ye shall suffer no harm through me this day, for it were pity that a merry time should end in such a manner as to mar its joyousness."

Then all arose and the King beckoned Robin Hood to come to him. "How now," quoth he, "is thine ear still too deaf to hear me speak?"

"Mine ears would be deafened in death ere they would cease to hear your majesty's voice," said Robin.

"As for the blow that your majesty struck me, I would say that though my sins are haply many, methinks they have been paid up in full thereby."

"Thinkest thou so?" said the King with somewhat of sternness in his voice. "Now I tell thee that but for three things, to wit, my mercifulness, my love for a stout woodsman, and the loyalty thou hast avowed for me, thine ears, mayhap, might have been more tightly closed than ever a buffet from me could have shut them. Talk not lightly of thy sins, good Robin. But come, look up. Thy danger is past, for hereby I give thee and all thy band free pardon. But, in sooth, I cannot let you roam the forest as ye have done in the past; therefore I will take thee at thy word, when thou didst say thou wouldst give thy service to me, and thou shalt go back to London with me. We will take that bold knave Little John also, and likewise thy cousin, Will Scarlet, and thy minstrel, Allan a Dale. As for the rest of thy band, we will take their names and have them duly recorded as royal rangers; for methinks it were wiser to have them changed to law-abiding caretakers of our deer in Sherwood than to leave them to run at large as outlawed slayers thereof. But now get a feast ready; I would fain see how ye live in the leafy woodlands."

So Robin bade his men make ready a grand feast. Straightway great fires were kindled and burned brightly, at which savory things roasted sweetly. While this was go-ing forward, the King bade Robin call Allan a Dale for he would hear him sing. So word was passed for Allan, and presently he came, bringing his harp.

"Marry," said King Richard, "if thy singing match thy looks it is fair enough. Prythee, strike up a ditty and let us have a taste of thy skill."

Then Allan touched his harp lightly, and all words were hushed while he sang thus:

" 'Oh where hast thou been, my daughter?
  Oh where hast thou been this day,
    Daughter, my daughter?'
'Oh, I have been to the river's side,
Where the waters lie all gray and wide,
And the gray sky broods o'er the leaden
    tide,
  And the shrill wind sighs a straining.'

" 'What sawest thou there, my daughter?
  What sawest thou there this day,
    Daughter, my daughter?'
'Oh, I saw a boat come drifting nigh,
Where the quivering rushes hiss and sigh,
And the water soughs as it gurgles by,
  And the shrill wind sighs a straining.'

" 'What sailed in the boat, my daughter?
  What sailed in the boat this day,
    Daughter, my daughter?'
'Oh, there was one all clad in white,
And about his face hung a pallid light,
And his eyes gleamed sharp like the
    stars at night
  And the shrill wind sighed a straining.'

" 'And what said he, my daughter?
  What said he to thee this day,
    Daughter, my daughter?'
'Oh, said he nought, but did he this:
Thrice on my lips did he press a kiss,
And my heartstrings shrunk with an
    awful bliss,
  And the shrill wind sighed a straining.'

"'Why growest thou so cold, my daughter?
  Why growest thou so cold and white,
    Daughter, my daughter?'
Oh never a word the daughter said,
But she sat all straight with a drooping
    head,
For her heart was stilled and her face
    was dead:
  And the shrill wind sighed a straining."

All listened in silence; and when Allan a Dale had done King Richard heaved a sigh. "By the breath of my body, Allan," quoth he, "thou hast such a wondrous sweet voice that it strangely moves my heart. But what doleful ditty is this for the lips of a stout yeoman? I would rather hear thee sing a song of love and battle than a sad thing like that. Moreover, I understand it not; what meanest thou by the words?"

"I know not, your majesty," said Allan, shaking his head, "for ofttimes I sing that which I do not clearly understand mine own self."

"Well, well," quoth the King, "let it pass; only I tell thee this, Allan, thou shouldst turn thy songs to such matters as I spoke of, to wit, love or war; for in sooth thou hast a sweeter voice than Blondell, and methought he was the best minstrel that ever I heard."

But now one came forward and said that the feast was ready; so Robin Hood brought King Richard and those with him to where it lay all spread out on fair white linen cloths which lay upon the soft green grass. Then King Richard sat him down and feasted and drank, and when he was done he swore roundly that he had never sat at such a lusty repast in all his life before.

That night he lay in Sherwood Forest upon a bed of sweet green leaves, and early the next morning he set forth from the woodlands for Nottingham Town, Robin Hood and all of his band going with him. You may guess what a stir there was in the good town when all these famous outlaws came marching into the streets. As for the Sheriff, he knew not what to say nor where to look when he saw Robin Hood in such high favor with the King, whilst all his heart was filled with gall because of the vexation[11] that lay upon him.

The next day the King took leave of Nottingham Town; so Robin Hood and Little John and Will Scarlet and Allan a Dale shook hands with all the rest of the band, kissing the cheeks of each man, and swearing that they would often come to Sherwood and see them. Then each mounted his horse and rode away in the train of the King.

11 **vexation:** irritation.

Understanding Literature

1. When Robin Hood proposes a toast to King Richard, the King replies, "Methinks, good fellow, . . . thou hast drunk to thine own confusion." What does the King mean by this?
2. In all legends the hero must be skillful and adept with weapons. Robin Hood is particularly skillful with what weapon? Give proof of his skill.
3. What do you know about Will Scarlet, Allan a Dale, and Friar Tuck from their appearances in this story?
4. What is King Richard's solution to the problem of Robin Hood's escapades? What does this solution show about King Richard's character?
5. King Richard says that he does not understand Allan a Dale's song. What do you think the song is about?
6. Very often the reader will know something or be told something that the characters within a story know nothing about. This technique, used in several places in "King Richard Cometh to Sherwood Forest," makes the reader feel more involved in the story. In which situations in this selection is the reader taken into the author's confidence whereas an actual character in the story is left in ignorance?
7. Compare Robin Hood as a hero to the other legendary heroes you have read about in this unit. In what ways are they similar? In what ways are they dissimilar?

The One-Act Play

THE ONE-ACT PLAY is another way of telling a story. It differs from the short story mainly in that the play is intended to be acted out on the stage; the author is therefore limited to writing what his characters say and do. The author cannot break in to tell you what he wants you to know; he must have his characters dramatize the information, act it out. Because a play is intended to be performed on a stage, when you are reading a play you have to imagine what the actors are doing and how they would say their lines. Otherwise you are like a person who reads notes of music, but does not create any sounds or "hear" them in his imagination.

Now, what is a one-act play? First, it is a play that is brief and to the point. It takes place at one time, in one setting, and deals with one crucial situation. It supplies only enough other detail so that you understand the crucial situation. It tries to produce one impression, such as horror or humor.

The play must begin quickly. The first three or four speeches form the introduction or *exposition:* You learn when and where the action is taking place, who the characters are and how they are related to one another, and what has taken place before the curtain went up.

After the exposition is developed, the play usually moves into the complication, or *conflict*, which must be resolved in the play. The need for a solution creates the *suspense*. The action then proceeds to the *climax*, the point of greatest emotional impact. This is followed by the *resolution*, in which the problem of the play is solved and the outcome of the situation is made clear.

As the play begins, the characters talk and reveal the situation. But they are also acting in a particular *setting*, usually described by the author in italics at the beginning of the written version of the play. The setting may be a friendly country inn or a lonely one far from other people; it may be an extravagantly furnished room or a poor shack. Whatever the scene, it may tell you something about the people. It may create a happy or a mysterious atmosphere for the play. It will suggest the time of day and probably the season of the year, and these facts may have some bearing on the meaning of the play. And the setting may help to advance the plot; perhaps the story could not have happened in another setting.

In addition to a description of the setting, the author generally includes *stage directions*, the directions to the reader or actor. Do not skip over them. Sometimes the author extends these comments to tell you something about what the characters look like. He may use further stage directions at key points in the play to explain how the characters should say certain lines, or how they should react to certain situations.

As the play proceeds, the *dialogue*, the conversation of the characters, can explain things to the audience even though the characters speak only to each other. They may say something which moves the plot along; they may express ideas which the author wants to convey; and, what is most important, the characters can and often will reveal the kind of people they are by what they say.

The major element of the play is the *characterization*, the author's revelation of what his characters are like. There are several methods the playwright can use to present or characterize the people in his drama: through what they say, through what they do, and through what others say about them. Sometimes you will even find the author making direct comments about the characters in the stage directions.

Since dramas are intended to be acted for an audience, perhaps you will be able to perform or read a part in one of the plays that follows. Do not try it without rehearsing. No play is so simple that you can get up and read it adequately without asking yourself: What kind of person am I portraying? How would he say this line? What key words would he emphasize? At what point in the play would he speak happily, angrily, sadly, quickly, slowly? Study your part first and then act it. Only by thinking and practice can you become another person, and the chance to become another person, even for a short while, is one of the great attractions of the world of the theater.

After stealing a large ruby in India, the characters in this play are being pursued by three Indian priests. The thieves have settled down temporarily and safely, so they think, in a remote inn. Can they get away with the robbery?

A Night at an Inn[*]

Lord Dunsany

IMPROVING YOUR READING: This play is a *melodrama*. Its plot is romantic; it does not deal with everyday occurrences. In this type of play you are more concerned with the plot, what happens, than with the motivation of the characters, why something happens. The people are merely types; their good acts are rewarded and their bad acts are punished. In any melodrama the playwright attempts to awaken feelings of sympathy, horror, or joy. The appeal of this play is that it makes you feel a sense of horror.

CHARACTERS

A. E. SCOTT-FORTESCUE (THE TOFF),
  a dilapidated gentleman
WILLIAM JONES (BILL)
ALBERT THOMAS   } *merchant*
JACOB SMITH (SNIGGERS)   *sailors*

FIRST PRIEST OF KLESH
SECOND PRIEST OF KLESH
THIRD PRIEST OF KLESH
KLESH

(*The curtain rises on a room in an inn.* SNIGGERS *and* BILL *are talking,* THE TOFF[1] *is reading a paper.* ALBERT *sits a little apart.*)

SNIGGERS. What's his idea, I wonder?

BILL. I don't know.

SNIGGERS. And how much longer will he keep us here?

BILL. We've been here three days.

SNIGGERS. And 'aven't seen a soul.

BILL. And a pretty penny it cost us when he rented the pub.

SNIGGERS. 'Ow long did 'e rent the pub for?

BILL. You never know with him.

SNIGGERS. It's lonely enough.

BILL. 'Ow long did you rent the pub for, Toffy?

(THE TOFF *continues to read a sporting paper; he takes no notice of what is said.*)

SNIGGERS. 'E's *such* a toff.

BILL. Yet 'e's clever, no mistake.

SNIGGERS. Those clever ones are the beggars to make a muddle. Their plans are clever enough, but they don't work, and then they make a mess of things much worse than you or me.

BILL. Ah!

SNIGGERS. I don't like this place.

BILL. Why not?

SNIGGERS. I don't like the looks of it.

BILL. He's keeping us here because here those men can't find us. The three heathen priests what was looking for us so. But we want to go, and sell our ruby soon.

ALBERT. There's no sense in it.

BILL. Why not, Albert?

ALBERT. Because I gave those devils the slip in Hull.

BILL. You give 'em the slip, Albert?

ALBERT. The slip, all three of them. The fellows with the gold spots on their foreheads. I had the ruby then and I give them the slip in Hull.

BILL. How did you do it, Albert?

ALBERT. I had the ruby and they were following me. . . .

BILL. Who told them you had the ruby? You didn't show it.

ALBERT. No. . . . But they kind of know.

SNIGGERS. They kind of know, Albert?

ALBERT. Yes, they know if you've got it. Well, they sort of mouched[2] after me, and I tells a policeman and he says, Oh, they were only three poor heathens and they wouldn't hurt me. Ugh! When I thought of what they did in Malta to poor old Jim.

BILL. Yes, and to George in Bombay before we started.

SNIGGERS. Ugh!

BILL. Why didn't you give 'em in charge?

ALBERT. What about the ruby, Bill?

BILL. Ah!

ALBERT. Well, I did better than that. I walks up and down through Hull. I walks slow enough. And then I turns a corner and I runs. I never sees a corner but I turns it. But sometimes I let a corner pass just to fool them. I twists about like a hare. Then I sits down and waits. No priests.

SNIGGERS. What?

BILL. Well done, Albert!

SNIGGERS (*after a sigh of content*). Why didn't you tell us?

ALBERT. 'Cause 'e won't let you speak. 'E's got 'is plans and 'e thinks we're silly folk. Things must be done 'is way. And all the time I've give 'em the slip. Might 'ave 'ad one o' them crooked knives in him before now but for me who give 'em the slip in Hull.

BILL. Well done, Albert! Do you hear that, Toffy? Albert has give 'em the slip.

THE TOFF. Yes, I hear.

SNIGGERS. Well, what do you say to that?

2 **mouched:** sneaked; crept.

THE TOFF. O . . . Well done, Albert!

ALBERT. And what a' you going to do?

THE TOFF. Going to wait.

ALBERT. Don't seem to know what 'e's waiting for.

SNIGGERS. It's a nasty place.

ALBERT. It's getting silly, Bill. Our money's gone and we want to sell the ruby. Let's get on to a town.

BILL. But 'e won't come.

ALBERT. Then we'll leave him.

SNIGGERS. We'll be all right if we keep away from Hull.

ALBERT. We'll go to London.

BILL. But 'e must 'ave 'is share.

SNIGGERS. All right. Only let's go. (*to* THE TOFF.) We're going, do you hear? Give us the ruby.

THE TOFF. Certainly.

> (*He gives them a ruby from his waistcoat pocket; it is the size of a small hen's egg. He goes on reading his paper.*)

ALBERT. Come on, Sniggers.

> (*Exeunt* ALBERT *and* SNIGGERS.)

BILL. Good-by, old man. We'll give you your fair share, but there's nothing to do here—no girls, no halls, and we must sell the ruby.

THE TOFF. I'm not a fool, Bill.

BILL. No, no, of course not. Of course you ain't, and you've helped us a lot. Good-by. You'll say good-by?

THE TOFF. Oh, yes, good-by.

> (*Still reads his paper. Exit* BILL. THE TOFF *puts his revolver on the table beside him and goes on with his papers. After a moment the three men come rushing in again, frightened.*)

SNIGGERS (*out of breath*). We've come back, Toffy.

THE TOFF. So you have.

ALBERT. Toffy. . . . How did they get here?

THE TOFF. They walked, of course.

ALBERT. But it's eighty miles.

SNIGGERS. Did you know they were here, Toffy?

THE TOFF. Expected them about now.

ALBERT. Eighty miles!

BILL. Toffy, old man . . . what are we to do?

THE TOFF. Ask Albert.

BILL. If they can do things like this, there's no one can save us but you, Toffy. . . . I always knew you were a clever one. We won't be fools any more. We'll obey you, Toffy.

THE TOFF. You're brave enough and strong enough. There isn't many that would steal a ruby eye out of an idol's head, and such an idol as that was to look at, and on such a night. You're brave enough, Bill. But you're all three of you fools. Jim would have none of my plans, and where's Jim? And George. What did they do to him?

SNIGGERS. Don't, Toffy!

THE TOFF. Well, then, your strength is no use to you. You want cleverness; or they'll have you the way they had George and Jim.

ALL. Ugh!

THE TOFF. Those priests would follow you round the world in circles. Year after year, till they got the idol's eye. And if we died with it, they'd follow our grandchildren. That fool thinks he can escape from men like that by running round three streets in the town of Hull.

ALBERT. God's truth, *you* 'aven't escaped them, because they're *'ere*.

THE TOFF. So I supposed.

ALBERT. You *supposed*.

THE TOFF. Yes, I believe there's no announcement in the Society papers. But I took this country seat especially to receive them. There's plenty of room if you dig, it is pleasantly situated, and, what is more important, it is in a very quiet neighborhood. So I am at home to them this afternoon.

BILL. Well, *you're* a deep one.

THE TOFF. And remember, you've only my wits between you and death, and don't put your futile[3] plans against those of an educated gentleman.

ALBERT. If you're a gentleman, why don't you go about among gentlemen instead of the likes of us?

THE TOFF. Because I was too clever for them as I am too clever for you.

ALBERT. Too clever for them?

THE TOFF. I never lost a game of cards in my life.

BILL. You never lost a game?

THE TOFF. Not when there was money in it.

BILL. Well, well!

THE TOFF. Have a game of poker?

ALL. No, thanks.

THE TOFF. Then do as you're told.

BILL. All right, Toffy.

SNIGGERS. I saw something just then. Hadn't we better draw the curtains?

3 futile: useless.

THE TOFF. No.

SNIGGERS. What?

THE TOFF. Don't draw the curtains.

SNIGGERS. Oh, all right.

BILL. But, Toffy, they can see us. One doesn't let the enemy do that. I don't see why. . . .

THE TOFF. No, of course you don't.

BILL. Oh, all right, Toffy.

(*All begin to pull out revolvers.*)

THE TOFF (*putting his own away*). No revolvers, please.

ALBERT. Why not?

THE TOFF. Because I don't want any noise at my party. We might get guests that hadn't been invited. *Knives* are a different matter.

> (*All draw knives. THE TOFF signs to them not to draw them yet. TOFFY has already taken back his ruby.*)

BILL. I think they're coming, Toffy.

THE TOFF. Not yet.

ALBERT. When will they come?

THE TOFF. When I am quite ready to receive them. Not before.

SNIGGERS. I should like to get this over.

THE TOFF. Should you? Then we'll have them now.

SNIGGERS. Now?

THE TOFF. Yes. Listen to me. You shall do as you see me do. You will all pretend to go out. I'll show you how. I've got the ruby. When they see me alone they will come for their idol's eye.

BILL. How can they tell like this which of us has it?

THE TOFF. I confess I don't know, but they seem to.

Sniggers. What will you do when they come in?

The Toff. I shall do nothing.

Sniggers. What?

The Toff. They will creep up behind me. Then, my friends, Sniggers and Bill and Albert, who gave them the slip, will do what they can.

Bill. All right, Toffy. Trust us.

The Toff. If you're a little slow, you will see enacted the cheerful spectacle that accompanied the demise[4] of Jim.

Sniggers. Don't, Toffy. We'll be there, all right.

The Toff. Very well. Now watch me.

(*He goes past the windows to the inner door R. He opens it inwards, then under cover of the open door, he slips down on his knee and closes it, remaining on the inside, appearing to have gone out. He signs to the others, who understand. Then he appears to re-enter in the same manner.*)

The Toff. Now, I shall sit with my back to the door. You go out one by one, so far as our friends can make out. Crouch very low to be on the safe side. They mustn't see you through the window.

(**Bill** *makes his sham[5] exit.*)

The Toff. Remember, no revolvers. The police are, I believe, proverbially inquisitive.[6]

(*The other two follow* **Bill.** *All three are now crouching inside the door R.* **The Toff**

---

4 **demise** (dĭ mīz′): death.

5 **sham:** false.
6 **proverbially inquisitive:** commonly spoken of as curious.

puts the ruby beside him on the table. He lights a cigarette. The door at the back opens so slowly that you can hardly say at what moment it began. THE TOFF picks up his paper. A native of India wriggles along the floor ever so slowly, seeking cover from chairs. He moves L. where THE TOFF is. The three sailors are R. SNIGGERS and ALBERT lean forward. BILL's arm keeps them back. An armchair had better conceal them from the Indian. The PRIEST nears THE TOFF. BILL watches to see if any more are coming. Then he leaps forward—he has taken his boots off—and knifes the PRIEST. The PRIEST tries to shout but BILL's left hand is over his mouth. THE TOFF continues to read his sporting paper. He never looks around.)

BILL (sotto voce).[7] There's only one, Toffy. What shall we do?

THE TOFF (without turning his head). Only one?

BILL. Yes.

THE TOFF. Wait a moment. Let me think. (Still apparently absorbed in his paper.) Ah, yes. You go back, Bill. We must attract another guest. . . . Now, are you ready?

BILL. Yes.

THE TOFF. All right. You shall now see my demise at my Yorkshire residence. You must receive guests for me. (He leaps up in full view of

7 sotto voce (sŏt'ō vō'chǐ): in a whisper.

the window, flings up both arms and falls to the floor near the dead PRIEST.) Now, be ready.

(His eyes close. There is a long pause. Again the door opens, very, very slowly. Another PRIEST creeps in. He has three golden spots upon his forehead. He looks round, then he creeps up to his companion and turns him over and looks inside of his clenched hands. Then he looks at the recumbent[8] TOFF. Then he creeps toward him. BILL slips after him and knifes him like the other with his left hand over his mouth.)

BILL (sotto voce). We've only got two, Toffy.

THE TOFF. Still another.

BILL. What'll we do?

THE TOFF (sitting up). Hum.

BILL. This is the best way, much.

THE TOFF. Out of the question. Never play the same game twice.

BILL. Why not, Toffy?

THE TOFF. Doesn't work if you do.

BILL. Well?

THE TOFF. I have it, Albert. You will now walk into the room. I showed you how to do it.

ALBERT. Yes.

THE TOFF. Just run over here and have a fight at this window with these two men.

ALBERT. But they're. . . .

THE TOFF. Yes, they're dead, my perspicuous[9] Albert. But Bill and I

8 recumbent: inactive; lying down.
9 perspicuous: probably confused with perspicacious: shrewd; quick-witted.

are going to resuscitate[10] them. . . .
Come on.

> (BILL *picks up a body under the arms.*)

THE TOFF. That's right, Bill. (*Does the same.*) Come and help us, Sniggers. (SNIGGERS *comes.*) Keep low, keep low. Wave their arms about, Sniggers. Don't show yourself. Now, Albert, over you go. Our Albert is slain. Back you get, Bill. Back, Sniggers. Still, Albert. Mustn't move when he comes. Not a muscle.

> (*A face appears at the window and stays for some time. Then the door opens and, looking craftily round, the third* PRIEST *enters. He looks at his companions' bodies and turns round. He suspects something. He takes up one of the knives and with a knife in each hand he puts his back to the wall. He looks to the left and right.*)

THE TOFF. Come on, Bill.

> (*The* PRIEST *rushes to the door.* THE TOFF *knifes the last* PRIEST *from behind.*)

BILL. Well done, Toffy. Oh, you are a deep one!

ALBERT. A deep one if ever there was one.

SNIGGERS. There ain't any more, Bill, are there?

THE TOFF. No more in the world, my friend.

BILL. Aye, that's all there are. There were only three in the temple.

Three priests and their beastly idol.

ALBERT. What is it worth, Toffy? Is it worth a thousand pounds?

THE TOFF. It's worth all they've got in the shop. Worth just whatever we like to ask for it.

ALBERT. Then we're millionaires now.

THE TOFF. Yes, and, what is more important, we no longer have any heirs.

BILL. We'll have to sell it now.

ALBERT. That won't be easy. It's a pity it isn't small and we had half a dozen. Hadn't the idol any other on him?

BILL. No, he was green jade all over and only had this one eye. He had it in the middle of his forehead and was a long sight uglier than anything else in the world.

SNIGGERS. I'm sure we ought all to be very grateful to Toffy.

BILL. And, indeed, we ought.

ALBERT. If it hadn't been for him.

BILL. Yes, if it hadn't been for old Toffy. . . .

SNIGGERS. He's a deep one.

THE TOFF. Well, you see I just have a knack of foreseeing things.

SNIGGERS. I should think you did.

BILL. Why, I don't suppose anything happens that our Toff doesn't foresee. Does it, Toffy?

THE TOFF. Well, I don't think it does, Bill. I don't think it often does.

BILL. Life is no more than just a game of cards to our old Toff.

THE TOFF. Well, we've taken these fellows' trick.

SNIGGERS (*going to window*). It wouldn't do for anyone to see them.

THE TOFF. Oh, nobody will come

---

10 resuscitate: revive; recall to life.

this way. We're all alone on a moor.

BILL. Where will we put them?

THE TOFF. Bury them in the cellar, but there's no hurry.

BILL. And what then, Toffy?

THE TOFF. Why, then we'll go to London and upset the ruby business. We have really come through this job very nicely.

BILL. I think the first thing that we ought to do is to give a little supper to old Toffy. We'll bury these fellows tonight.

ALBERT. Yes, let's.

SNIGGERS. The very thing!

BILL. And we'll all drink his health.

ALBERT. Good old Toffy!

SNIGGERS. He ought to have been a general or a premier.

(*They get bottles from cupboard, etc.*)

THE TOFF. Well, we've earned our bit of a supper. (*They sit down.*)

BILL (*glass in hand*). Here's to old Toffy, who guessed everything!

ALBERT AND SNIGGERS. Good old Toffy!

BILL. Toffy, who saved our lives and made our fortunes.

ALBERT AND SNIGGERS. Hear! Hear!

THE TOFF. And here's to Bill, who saved me twice tonight.

SNIGGERS. Hear, hear! Hear! Hear!

ALBERT. He foresees everything.

BILL. A speech, Toffy. A speech from our general.

ALL. Yes, a speech.

SNIGGERS. A speech.

THE TOFF. Well, get me some water. This whisky's too much for my head, and I must keep it clear till our friends are safe in the cellar.

BILL. Water? Yes, of course. Get him some water, Sniggers.

SNIGGERS. We don't use water here. Where shall I get it?

BILL. Outside in the garden.

(*Exit* SNIGGERS.)

ALBERT. Here's to the future!

BILL. Here's to Albert Thomas, Esquire.

ALBERT. And William Jones, Esquire.

(*Re-enter* SNIGGERS, *terrified*.)

THE TOFF. Hullo, here's Jacob Smith, Esquire, J. P., alias Sniggers, back again.

SNIGGERS. Toffy, I've been thinking about my share in that ruby. I don't want it, Toffy; I don't want it.

THE TOFF. Nonsense, Sniggers. Nonsense.

SNIGGERS. You shall have it, Toffy, you shall have it yourself, only say Sniggers has no share in this 'ere ruby. Say it, Toffy, say it!

BILL. Want to turn informer, Sniggers?

SNIGGERS. No, no. Only I don't want the ruby, Toffy. . . .

THE TOFF. No more nonsense, Sniggers. We're all in together in this. If one hangs, we all hang; but they won't outwit me. Besides, it's not a hanging affair, they had their knives.

SNIGGERS. Toffy, Toffy, I always treated you fair, Toffy. I was always one to say, "Give Toffy a chance." Take back my share, Toffy.

THE TOFF. What's the matter? What are you driving at?

SNIGGERS. Take it back, Toffy.

THE TOFF. Answer me, what are you up to?

SNIGGERS. I don't want my share any more.

BILL. Have you seen the police?

(ALBERT *pulls out his knife.*)

SNIGGERS. There's no police.

THE TOFF. Well, then, what's the matter?

BILL. Out with it.

SNIGGERS. I swear to God. . . .

ALBERT. Well?

THE TOFF. Don't interrupt.

SNIGGERS. I swear I saw something *what I didn't like.*

THE TOFF. What you didn't like?

SNIGGERS (*in tears*). O Toffy, Toffy, take it back. Take my share. Say you take it.

THE TOFF. What has he seen?

(*Dead silence, only broken by* SNIGGERS' *sobs. Then steps are heard. Enter a hideous idol. It is blind and gropes its way to the ruby and picks it up and screws it into a socket in the forehead.* SNIGGERS *still weeps softly; the rest stare in horror. The idol steps out, not groping. Its steps move off, then stop.*)

THE TOFF. O great heavens!

ALBERT (*in a childish, plaintive*[11] *voice*). What is it, Toffy?

BILL. Albert, it is that obscene idol (*in a whisper*) come from India.

ALBERT. It is gone.

BILL. It has taken its eye.

SNIGGERS. We are saved.

A VOICE OFF (*with outlandish ac-* cent). Meestaire William Jones, Able Seaman.

(THE TOFF *has never spoken, never moved. He only gazes stupidly in horror.*)

BILL. Albert, Albert, what is this?

(*He rises and walks out. One moan is heard.* SNIGGERS *goes to the window. He falls back sickly.*)

ALBERT (*in a whisper*). What has happened?

SNIGGERS. I have seen it. I have seen it. Oh, I have seen it!

(*He returns to table.*)

THE TOFF (*laying his hand very gently on* SNIGGERS' *arm, speaking softly and winningly*). What was it, Sniggers?

SNIGGERS. I have seen it.

ALBERT. What?

SNIGGERS. Oh!

VOICE. Meestaire Albert Thomas, Able Seaman.

ALBERT. Must I go, Toffy, Toffy, must I go?

SNIGGERS (*clutching him*). Don't move.

ALBERT (*going*). Toffy, Toffy.

(*Exit.*)

VOICE. Meestaire Jacob Smith, Able Seaman.

SNIGGERS. I can't go, Toffy. I can't go. I can't do it. (*He goes.*)

VOICE. Meestaire Arnold Everett Scott-Fortescue, late Esquire, Able Seaman.

THE TOFF. I did not foresee it.

(*Exit.*)

CURTAIN

11 plaintive: sorrowful.

Understanding Literature

1. The play opens with a conversation between Sniggers, Bill, and Albert. Up to the time that The Toff gives them the ruby, what do you learn about the situation? Who are these people? What problem causes the suspense?

2. After The Toff gives up the ruby, why do the men come back so frightened? Why do they decide to obey The Toff? How is he different from the other three? What is his plan? How does he lure the first priest into the Inn? What are the priests after?

3. How does The Toff lure the next two priests? What happens as each enters?

4. After the priests have been done away with and all seems well, Bill says, "Why, I don't suppose anything happens that our Toff doesn't foresee." This speech becomes ironic as the action that actually occurs is the opposite of what they expected to happen. Explain the irony in terms of what they expect and what they get.

5. Why does the author have Sniggers go outside for water? How does this action affect the play?

6. How would the last scene (after Sniggers's return from outside) be acted? Why is it more effective to keep the Voice off stage? How is the last line ironic?

7. At the point when the thieves seem safe, they compare their actions to a game of cards. How is the action of the play like a game of cards?

8. Point out the qualities of this play which are characteristic of a melodrama.

This is a play about a ghost and a practical joke. The problem can be expressed in a question: Will the ghost of Jerry Bundler appear on this lonely winter night?

The Ghost of Jerry Bundler *

W. W. Jacobs and Charles Rock

IMPROVING YOUR READING: The presentation of a play, whether by amateurs or by professional actors, involves a great deal of planning and work. In addition to learning their lines and "becoming" the characters in the play, the actors must, under the guidance of a director, learn their positions on the stage. The director *blocks* the action; that is, he tells the actors where to stand or sit and when to move from one part of the stage to another. Unless these details are carefully planned, the staging of a play is awkward and confusing.

The version of "The Ghost of Jerry Bundler" printed here is an *acting edition;* it contains much more detail concerning the scene and the properties than does a reading edition, which is the version in which the other plays in this unit are printed. As you read the play you will notice stage directions such as up *C, RC,* and *L.* These are abbreviations for upstage center, right center, and left, which are divisions of the stage. This simplified diagram should make these stage positions clear.

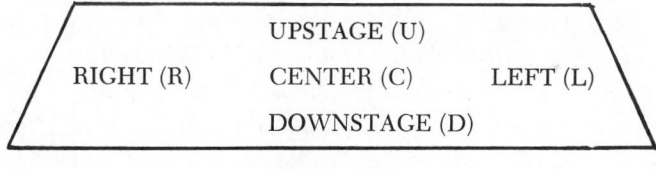

AUDIENCE

As you read this play, try to visualize in your mind where each character is. You should also keep track of the entrances and exits of the actors. The skillful playwright makes the entrances and exits believable; if a man enters or leaves the stage, he must have a reason. Watch the skill with which Jacobs and Rock move their characters around. They want some characters to know certain things, yet they must keep the information from others. Then, too, the audience must know the whole story.

CHARACTERS

HIRST	SOMERS
PENFOLD	BELDON
MALCOLM	DR. LEEK

GEORGE (a waiter)

SCENE: *The Commercial Room in an old-fashioned hotel in a small country town. An air of old-fashioned comfort is in evidence everywhere. Old sporting prints on the walls.*

On the table up c[1] *are half a dozen candlesticks, old-fashioned shape with snuffer attached. Two pairs of carpet slippers are set up within fender.[2] Red curtains to window recess. Shutters or blinds to windows. Armchair and about six other chairs in the room. One old-fashioned settle.[3] One small table. Clock. Decanter of water, half a dozen toddy tumblers. Matches, etc. The only light is a ruddy glow from the fire. Kettle on hob.[4] Moonlight from* R *of window when shutter is opened. Practical chandelier from ceiling or lights at side of mantelpiece.* DOCTOR'S *coat and muffler on chair up* L,[5] *his cap on mantelpiece.*

All lights out, dark stage. Opening music. Curtain rise—ticking of clock heard. Wind, then church clock chimes, the Lights come very slowly up, when the red glow is seen in the fireplace the low murmurs of the characters heard, and gradually get louder as lights come up to when SOMERS'S *voice tops all.*

(*The stage occupied by all characters except* GEORGE *the waiter. Discovered,* PENFOLD, *sitting in armchair* L *of fire, above it.* DOCTOR LEEK *standing above fire and leaning on mantelshelf.* HIRST *sitting on settle below fire and nearest to audience.* SOMERS *seated on settle with him but above him.* MALCOLM *and* BELDON *on chairs* RC, *facing fire.* ALL *are smoking, and drink from their respective glasses from time to time.* SOMERS *has just finished a story as Curtain rises.*)

OMNES.[6] Oh, I say, that sounds impossible, etc.

SOMERS. Haunted or not haunted, the fact remains that no one stays in the house long. It's been let to several tenants since the time of the murder, but they never completed their tenancy. The last tenant held out for a month, but at last he gave up like the rest, and cleared out, although he had done the place up thoroughly, and must have been

---

1 up C: upstage, or at the rear of the stage, in the center.
2 fender: fireplace screen.
3 settle: long wooden bench with arms, a high solid back, and a compartment below it frequently used as a chest.
4 hob: shelf at the back or side of a fireplace where things may be kept warm.
5 up L: upstage left.

6 Omnes: all; all characters speaking together.

THE ONE-ACT PLAY

pounds out of pocket[7] by the transaction.

MALCOLM. Well, it's a capital ghost story, I admit, that is, as a story, but I for one can't swallow it.

HIRST. I don't know, it is not nearly so improbable as some I have heard. Of course it's an old idea that spirits like to get into the company of human beings. A man told me once, that he traveled down by the Great Western, with a ghost as fellow passenger, and hadn't the slightest suspicion of it, until the inspector came for tickets. My friend said, the way that ghost tried to keep up appearances, by feeling in all its pockets, and even looking on the floor for its ticket, was quite touching. Ultimately it gave it up, and with a loud groan vanished through the ventilator.

(SOMERS, MALCOLM *and* LEEK *laugh heartily.*)

BELDON. Oh, I say come now, that'll do.

PENFOLD (*seriously*). Personally I don't think it's a subject for jesting. I have never seen an apparition myself, but I have known people who have, and I consider that they form a very interesting link between us and the afterlife. There's a ghost story connected with this house, you know.

OMNES. Eh! Oh? Really!

MALCOLM (*rising and going to mantelpiece, takes up his glass of toddy*). Well, I have used this house for some years now. I travel for Blennet and Burgess—wool—and

come here regularly three times a year, and I've never heard of it. (*Sits down again on his chair, holding glass in his hand.*)

LEEK. And I've been here pretty often too, though I have only been in practice here for a couple of years, and I have never heard it mentioned, and I must say I don't believe in anything of the sort. In my opinion ghosts are the invention of weak-minded idiots.

PENFOLD. Weak-minded idiots or not, there is a ghost story connected with this house, but it dates a long time back. (GEORGE, *the waiter, enters* DL, *with tray and serviette.*[8]) Oh, here's George, he'll bear me out. You've heard of Jerry Bundler, George?

GEORGE (c). Well, I've just 'eard odds and ends, sir, but I never put much count to 'em. There was one chap 'ere, who was under me when fust I come, he said he seed it, and the Guv'nor sacked him there and then. (*Goes to table by window, puts tray down, takes up glass and wipes it slowly.*)

(MEN *laugh.*)

PENFOLD. Well, my father was a native of this town, and he knew the story well. He was a truthful man and a steady churchgoer. But I have heard him declare that once in his life he saw the ghost of Jerry Bundler in this house; let me see, George, you don't remember my old dad, do you?

(GEORGE *puts down glasses over table.*)

---

7 **pounds out of pocket:** minus a considerable amount of money.

8 **serviette:** table napkin.

GEORGE. No, sir. I come here forty years ago next Easter, but I fancy he was before my time.

PENFOLD. Yes, though not by long. He died when I was twenty, and I shall be sixty-two next month, but that's neither here nor there.

(GEORGE *goes up to table* C *tidying up and listening.*)

LEEK. Who was this Jerry Bundler?

PENFOLD. A London thief, pickpocket, highwayman—anything he could turn his dishonest hand to, and he was run to earth in this house some eighty years ago. (GEORGE *puts glass down and stands listening.*) He took his last supper in this room. (PENFOLD *leans forward.* BELDON *looks round to* L *nervously.*) That night soon after he had gone to bed, a couple of Bow Street runners, the

predecessors of our present detective force, turned up here. They had followed him from London, but had lost scent a bit, so didn't arrive till late. A word to the landlord, whose description of the stranger who had retired to rest, pointed to the fact that he was the man they were after, of course enlisted his aid and that of the male servants and stable hands. The officers crept quietly up to Jerry's bedroom and tried the door, it wouldn't budge. It was of heavy oak and bolted from within. (OMNES *lean forward, showing interest.*) Leaving his comrade and a couple of grooms to guard the bedroom door, the other officer went into the yard, and, procuring a short ladder, by this means reached the window of the room in which Jerry was sleeping. The Inn servants and stable hands saw him get on to the sill and try to open the window. Suddenly there was a crash of glass, and with a cry, he fell in a heap on to the stones at their feet. Then in the moonlight, they saw the face of the highwayman peering over the sill. (OMNES *move uneasily.*) They sent for the blacksmith, and with his sledge-hammer he battered in the strong oak panels, and the first thing that met their eyes was the body of Jerry Bundler dangling from the top of the four-post bed by his own handkerchief.

> (OMNES *sit back, draw their breath, and are generally uneasy. Slight pause.*)

SOMERS. I say, which bedroom was it? (*Earnestly*).

PENFOLD. That I can't tell you, but the story goes that Jerry still haunts this house, and my father used to declare positively that the last time he slept here, the ghost of Jerry Bundler lowered itself from the top of his four-post bed and tried to strangle him.

BELDON (*jumps up, gets behind his chair, twists chair round; nervously*). O, I say, that'll do. I wish you'd thought to ask your father which bedroom it was.

PENFOLD. What for?

BELDON. Well, I should take jolly good care not to sleep in it, that's all. (*Goes to back.*)

> (PENFOLD *rising, goes to fire, and knocks out his pipe;* LEEK *gets by armchair.*)

PENFOLD. There's nothing to fear. I don't believe for a moment that ghosts could really hurt one.

(GEORGE *lights candle at table.*) In fact, my father used to say that it was only the unpleasantness of the thing that upset him, and that, for all practical purposes, Jerry's fingers might have been made of cotton wool for all the harm they could do.

> (GEORGE *hands candle, gets to door and holds it open.*)

BELDON. That's all very fine, a ghost story is a ghost story, but when a gentleman tells a tale of a ghost that haunts the house in which one is going to sleep, I call it most ungentlemanly.

> (BELDON *places his chair to* L *of table* R. PENFOLD *goes up to* C. LEEK *sits in armchair.* BELDON *goes to fireplace.*)

PENFOLD. Pooh! Nonsense. (*At table up* C.) (*During his speech* GEORGE *lights one of the candles.*) Ghosts can't hurt you. For my own part, I should rather like to see one.

OMNES. Oh, come now——(*etc.*)

PENFOLD. Well, I'll bid you good night, gentlemen.

> (*He goes toward door* L. GEORGE *opens it for him; he passes out as they all say:*)

OMNES. Good night.

> (HIRST *rises, crosses to* LC.)

BELDON (*up* R, *calling after him*). And I hope Jerry'll pay you a visit.

MALCOLM (*rises, goes to fire*). Well, I'm going to have another drink if you gentlemen will join me. I think it'll do us all good after that tale. George, take the orders.

> (GEORGE *comes down with sal-*

ver[9] *to table* R, *gathers up glasses.*)

SOMERS. Not quite so much hot water in mine.

MALCOLM. I'll have the same again, George.

BELDON. A leetle bit of lemon in mine, George.

LEEK. Soda for me, please.

HIRST. Same.

(GEORGE *goes to table* R, *collects glasses, crosses to door* L, *speaks:*)

GEORGE (*to* MALCOLM). Shall I light the gas, Mr. Malcolm? (*At door.*)

MALCOLM. No, the fire's very comfortable, unless any of you gentlemen prefer the gas.

OMNES. No, not at all—(*etc.*)

MALCOLM. Never mind, George. (*This to* GEORGE *as no one wants the gas.*) The firelight is pleasanter.

(*Exit* GEORGE *for orders* L.)

(BELDON *gets* C.)

MALCOLM (*at fire*). Does any gentleman know another——?

SOMERS (*seated* R). Well, I remember hearing——

BELDON (*up* C). Oh, I say—that'll do. (OMNES *laugh.*)

LEEK. Yes, I think you all look as if you'd heard enough ghost stories to do you the rest of your lives. And you're not all as anxious to see the real article as the old gentleman who's just gone.

HIRST (*looking to* L). Old humbug! I should like to put him to the test.

(C) (*Bus.*)[10] I say, suppose I dress up as Jerry Bundler and go and give him a chance of displaying his courage? I bet I'd make the old party sit up.

MALCOLM. Capital!

BELDON. A good idea.

LEEK. I shouldn't, if I were you.

HIRST. Just for the joke, gentlemen (C).

SOMERS. No, no—drop it, Hirst.

HIRST. Only for the joke. Look here, I've got some things that'll do very well. We're going to have some amateur theatricals at my house. We're doing a couple of scenes from THE RIVALS,[11] Somers (*pointing to* SOMERS), and I have been up to town to get the costumes, wigs, etc., today. I've got them upstairs—knee breeches, stockings, buckled shoes, and all that sort of thing. It's a rare chance. If you wait a bit, I'll give you a full dress rehearsal, entitled "Jerry Bundler, or the Nocturnal Stranger." (*At door* L.)

LEEK (*sneeringly*). You won't frighten us, will you?

HIRST. I don't know so much about that—it's a question of acting, that's all.

MALCOLM. I'll bet you a level sov,[12] you don't frighten me.

HIRST (*quietly*). A level sov. (*Pauses.*) Done. I'll take the bet to frighten you first, and the old boy afterwards. These gentlemen shall be the judges. (*Points to* LEEK *and* BELDON.)

10 BUS.: an abbreviation for *business*, a stage direction which indicates that the actor should engage in some sort of action; in this case the action is not specified. The term is sometimes written as *biz.*

11 *The Rivals*: a play by Richard Sheridan (1751-1816), an Irish dramatist.

12 SOV: sovereign, a gold coin of Great Britain.

9 salver: a tray.

THE ONE-ACT PLAY

BELDON (*up* C). You won't frighten us because we're prepared for you, but you'd better leave the old man alone. It's dangerous play. (*Appeals to* **LEEK**.)

HIRST. Well, I'll try you first. (*Moves to door and pauses.*) No gas, mind.

OMNES. No! no!

HIRST (*laughs*). I'll give you a run for your money.

(**GEORGE** *enters, holds door open.*)

(*Exit* **HIRST**.)

(**GEORGE** *passes drinks round. Five drinks.* **SOMERS** *takes the one ordered for* **HIRST** *and puts it on the table* R. **BELDON** *sits* RC. **GEORGE** *crosses to table, puts two drinks down, goes to fire and gives drinks, then up to table, puts tray down, takes up glass and begins to wipe it, gets down* L *for lines.*)

LEEK (*to* **MALCOLM**). I think you'll win your bet, sir, but I vote we give him a chance. Suppose we have cigars round, and if he's not back by the time we've finished them I must be off, as I have a quarter of an hour's walk before me. (*Looks at watch.*) He's a friend of yours, isn't he?

SOMERS. Yes, I have known him a good many years now, and I must say he's a rum chap;[13] just crazy about acting and practical joking, though I've often told him he carries the latter too far at times. In this case it doesn't matter, but I won't let him try it on the *old gentleman*. You see we know what he's going to do, and are prepared, but he doesn't, and it might lead to illness or worse; the old chap's sixty-two and such a shock might have serious consequences. But Hirst won't mind giving up that part of it, so long as he gets an opportunity of acting to us.

LEEK (*knocks pipe on grate*). Well, I hope he'll hurry up. It's getting pretty late. (*To* **SOMERS**.)

MALCOLM. Well, gentlemen, your health!

SOMERS. Good luck.

LEEK. Hurrah!

BELDON. Chin-chin!

LEEK. By the way, how is it you happen to be here tonight?

SOMERS. Oh, we missed the connection at Tolleston Junction and as the accommodation at the Railway Arms there was rather meager, the Station Master advised us to drive on here, put up for the night, and catch the Great Northern express from Exton in the morning. (*Rises, crosses to* L.) Oh, George, that reminds me —you might see that "Boots" calls us at seven sharp.

(**BELDON** *rises, goes up to them to fire.*)

GEORGE. Certainly, sir. What are your numbers?

SOMERS. 13 and 14.

GEORGE. I'll put it on the slate, special, sir. (*Goes to door* L.)

LEEK. I beg pardon, gentlemen, I forgot the cigars; George, bring some cigars back with you.

BELDON. A very mild one for me.

GEORGE. Very well, sir. (*Takes up tray from sideboard.*) (*Exit* L.)

---

13 **a rum chap:** an odd fellow.

(SOMERS *sits* RC.)

MALCOLM. I think you were very wise coming on here. (*Sits on settle* R.) I stayed at the Railway Arms, Tolleston, once—never again though. Is your friend clever at acting?

SOMERS. I don't think he's clever enough to frighten you. I'm to spend Christmas at his place, and he's asked me to assist at the theatricals he spoke of. Nothing would satisfy him till I consented, and I must honestly say I am very sorry I ever did, for I expect I shall be pretty bad. I know I have scarcely slept a wink these last few nights, trying to get the words into my head.

(GEORGE *enters backwards, pale and trembling.*)

MALCOLM. Why! Look—what the devil's the matter with George? (*Crosses to* GEORGE.)

GEORGE. I've seen it, gentlemen. (*Downstage* LC.)

OMNES. Seen who?

(BELDON *down* R *edge of table* R. LEEK *up* RC. SOMERS *up* R.)

GEORGE. The ghost. Jer—Bun—

MALCOLM. Why, you're frightened, George.

GEORGE. Yes, sir. It was the suddenness of it, and besides I didn't look for seeing it in the bar. There was only a glimmer of light there, and it was sitting on the floor. I nearly touched it.

MALCOLM (*goes to door, looks off, then returns—to others*). It must be Hirst up to his tricks. George was out of the room when he suggested it. (*To* GEORGE.) Pull yourself together, man.

GEORGE. Yes, sir—but it took me unawares. I'd never have gone to the bar myself if I'd known it was there, and I don't believe you would, either, sir.

MALCOLM. Nonsense, I'll go and fetch him in. (*Crosses to* L.)

GEORGE (*clutching him by the sleeve*). You don't know what it's like, sir. It ain't fit to look at by yourself, it ain't indeed. It's got the awfullest deathlike face, and short cropped red hair—it's—(*Smothered cry is heard.*) What's that? (*Backs to* C *and leans on chair.*)

(ALL *start, and a quick pattering of footsteps is heard rapidly approaching the room. The door flies open and* HIRST *flings himself gasping and shivering into* MALCOLM'S *arms. The door remains open. He has only his trousers and shirt on, his face very white with fear and his own hair all standing on end.* LEEK *lights the gas, then goes to* R *of* HIRST.)

OMNES. What's the matter?

MALCOLM. Why, it's Hirst. (*Shakes him roughly by the shoulder.*) What's up?

HIRST. I've seen—oh! I'll never play the fool again. (*Goes* C.)

OTHERS. Seen what?

HIRST. Him—it—the ghost—anything.

MALCOLM (*uneasily*). Rot!

HIRST. I was coming down the stairs to get something I'd forgotten, when I felt a tap—(*He breaks off suddenly gazing through open door.*) I thought I saw it again—Look—at the

foot of the stairs, can't you see anything? (*Shaking* LEEK.)

LEEK (*crosses to door peering down passage*). No, there's nothing there. (*Stays up* L.)

(HIRST *gives a sigh of relief.*)

MALCOLM (LC). Go on—you felt a tap——

HIRST (C). I turned and saw it—a little wicked head with short red hair —and a white dead face—horrible.

(*Clock chimes three-quarters.*)

(*They assist him into chair* L *of table* R.)

GEORGE (*up* C). That's what I saw in the bar—'orrid—it was devilish. (*Coming* C.)

(MALCOLM *crosses to* L. HIRST *shudders.*)

MALCOLM. Well, it's a most unaccountable thing. It's the last time I come to this house. (*Goes to* R *of* LEEK.)

GEORGE. I leave tomorrow. I wouldn't go down to that bar alone— no, not for fifty pounds. (*Goes up* R *to armchair.*)

SOMERS (*crosses to door* R *then returns to* RC). It's talking about the thing that's caused it, I expect. We've had it in our minds, and we've been practically forming a spiritualistic circle without knowing it. (*Goes to back of table* R.)

BELDON (*crosses to* RC). Hang the old gentleman. Upon my soul I'm half afraid to go to bed.

MALCOLM. Doctor, it's odd they should both think they saw something.

(*They both drop down* LC.)

GEORGE (*up* C). I saw it as plainly

as I see you, sir. P'raps if you keep your eyes turned up the passage you'll see it for yourself. (*Points.*)

(*They all look.* BELDON *goes to* SOMERS.)

BELDON. There—what was that?

MALCOLM. Who'll go with me to the bar?

LEEK. I will. (*Goes to door.*)

BELDON (*gulps*). So—will I. (*Crosses to door* L. *They go to the door. To* MALCOLM.) After you.

(*They slowly pass into the passage.* GEORGE *watching them. All exit except* HIRST *and* SOMERS.)

SOMERS. How do you feel now, old man?

HIRST (*changing his frightened manner to one of assurance*). Splendid!

SOMERS. But—(*a step back*).

HIRST. I tell you I feel splendid.

SOMERS. But the ghost—(*Steps back to* C.)

HIRST. Well, upon my word, Somers—you're not as sharp as I thought you.

SOMERS. What do you mean?

HIRST. Why, that I was the ghost George saw. (*Crosses to* LC.) By Jove, he *was* in a funk![14] I followed him to the door and overheard his description of what he'd seen, then I burst in myself and pretended I'd seen it too. I'm going to win that, bet—(VOICES *heard. Crosses to* R.) Look out, they're coming back. (*Sits.*)

SOMERS. Yes, but——

HIRST. Don't give me away—hush!

14 in a funk: frightened.

(*Re-enter* MALCOLM, LEEK, BELDON *and* GEORGE L.)

(BELDON *and* GEORGE *go up to back* C.)

HIRST. Did you see it? (*In his frightened manner.*)

MALCOLM (C). I don't know—I thought I saw something, but it might have been fancy. I'm in the mood to see anything just now. (*To* HIRST.) How are you feeling now, sir?

HIRST. Oh, I feel a bit better now. I daresay you think I'm easily scared —but you didn't see it.

MALCOLM. Well, I'm not quite sure. (*Goes to fire.*)

LEEK. You've had a bit of a shock. Best thing you can do is to go to bed.

HIRST (*finishing his drink*). Very well. Will you (*rises*) share my room with me, Somers?

(GEORGE *lights two candles.*)

SOMERS (*crosses to* LC). I will with pleasure. (*Gets up to table* C *and gets a candle.*) Provided you don't mind sleeping with the gas full on all night. (*Goes to door* L.)

LEEK (*to* HIRST). You'll be all right in the morning.

HIRST. Good night, all. (*As he crosses to door.*)

OMNES. Good night.

(ALL *talking at fire, not looking to* L *as* HIRST *and* SOMERS *exeunt;* HIRST *chuckles and gives* SOMERS *a sly dig.*)

SOMERS. Good night.

MALCOLM (*at fireplace*). Well, I suppose the bet's off, though as far as I can see I won it. I never saw a man so scared in all my life. Sort of poetic justice about it. (LEEK *with revolver in his hand, is just putting it into his pocket. Seeing him.*) Why, what's that you've got there?

LEEK. A revolver. (*At fire.*) You see I do a lot of night driving, visiting patients in outlying districts—they're a tough lot round here, and one never knows what might happen, so I have been accustomed to carry it. I just pulled it out so as to have it handy. I meant to have a pot at that ghost if I had seen him. There's no law against it, is there? I never heard of a close time for ghosts.

BELDON.—Oh, I say, never mind ghosts. Will *you* share my room? (*To* MALCOLM.)

> (GEORGE *comes down a little, holding candle.*)

MALCOLM. With pleasure. I'm not exactly frightened, but I'd sooner have company, and I daresay George here would be glad to be allowed to make up a bed on the floor.

BELDON. Certainly.

MALCOLM. Well, that's settled. A majority of three to one ought to stop any ghost. Will that arrangement suit you, George?

GEORGE. Thank you, sir. And if you gentlemen would kindly come down to the bar with me while I put out the gas, I could never be sufficiently grateful, and when (*at door*) we come back we can let the Doctor out at the front door. Will that do, sir?

LEEK. All right; I'll be getting my coat on (GEORGE *gets to door. They exit at door* L. LEEK *picks up his coat off chair up* L, *puts it on and then turns up trousers. Footsteps heard in flies,*[15] *then goes to the window* R, *pulls curtain aside and opens the shutters of the window nearest the fire. A flood of moonlight streams in from* R. *Clock strikes twelve.*) By Jove, what a lovely night. That poor devil did get a fright and no mistake. (*Crossing down to fireplace for his cap which is on the mantelpiece.* MALCOLM, BELDON *and* GEORGE *return—the door closes after them.*) Well, no sign of it, eh?

MALCOLM. No, we've seen nothing this time. Here, give me the candle, George, while you turn out the gas.

LEEK. All right, George, I'll put this one out. (*Turns out gas below fire.*)

> (MALCOLM *and* BELDON *are up at sideboard;* GEORGE, *having put the other gas out, goes up to them and is just lighting the candles for them. The* DOCTOR *is filling his pipe at mantelshelf, and stooping to get a light with a paper spill.*[16] LEEK *whistles and lights spill. The handle of the door is heard moving.* OMNES *stand motionless—* MALCOLM *and* BELDON *very frightened. They all watch. The room is lit only by the firelight which is very much fainter than it was at the beginning of the play, by the candle which* GEORGE *holds, and by the flood of moonlight from the window.*)

15 **flies:** space over the stage.
16 **spill:** a roll of paper used to light lamps or pipes.

(*The door slowly opens, a hand is seen, then a figure appears in dark breeches, white stockings, buckled shoes, white shirt, very neat in every detail with a long white or spotted handkerchief tied round the neck, the long end hanging down in front. The face cadaverous,*[17] *with sunken eyes and a leering smile, and close cropped red hair. The figure blinks at the candle, then slowly raises its hands and unties the handkerchief, its head falls on to one shoulder, it holds handkerchief out at arm's length and advances toward* MALCOLM.)
(*Just as the figure reaches the place where the moonbeams touch the floor,* LEEK *fires—he has very quietly and unobtru-sively drawn his revolver.* GEORGE *drops the candle and the figure, writhing, drops to the floor. It coughs once a choking cough.* MALCOLM *goes slowly forward, touches it with his foot, and kneels by figure, lifts figure up, gazes at it, and pulls the red wig off, discovering* HIRST. MALCOLM *gasps out* "DOCTOR." LEEK *places the revolver on chair, kneels behind* HIRST. MAL-COLM *is* LC, *kneeling. At this moment* SOMERS *enters very brightly with lighted candle*).

SOMERS. Well, did Hirst win his bet? (*Seeing* HIRST *on floor, he realizes the matter.*) You didn't—I told him not to! I told him not to! I told him—(*falls fainting into arms of* GEORGE).

17 **cadaverous** (kə dăv′ər əs): like that of a corpse; ghastly.

CURTAIN.

Understanding Literature

1. As the play opens, what attitudes are the characters taking toward ghost stories? How does Penfold's story of Jerry Bundler affect Beldon?
2. After Penfold leaves, Hirst decides to test Penfold's courage. What is his plan?
3. What bet is made between Malcolm and Hirst? Notice which people know about Hirst's plan.
4. After Hirst leaves, what do you learn about him from the talk of the others?
5. George re-enters; then Hirst. What information do they bring? How does their information affect each of the other characters?
6. While Hirst and Somers are alone, what information are you given? How would the play be different in its effect on the

audience if you did not get this information? Even when you know about the ghost, why is there still suspense in the play?

7. After Hirst and Somers leave, how does the author make it believable that Leek should be carrying a gun?

8. One version of this play has a very different ending. After Somers re-enters the room and asks if Hirst has won his bet, there is a slight pause. Then Hirst suddenly sits up and says that the doctor is a very poor shot; furthermore, Hirst wants to be paid for winning the bet. Which do you think is the better ending? Why?

In this play two average people who think that nothing exciting will ever happen to them get involved in some extraordinary events.

The Man in the Bowler Hat*

A. A. Milne

IMPROVING YOUR READING: This play makes fun of a melodramatic play. It is a *farce*, a type of comedy that contains improbable characters in improbable situations. You will see that many details quite common in melodrama are greatly exaggerated for the sake of increasing the humorous effect.

The scene is MARY's *sitting room. It is the most ordinary sitting room in the world.* JOHN *and* MARY, *two of the most ordinary people, he in the early forties, she in the late thirties, are sitting in front of the fire after dinner. He, as usual, is reading the paper; she, as usual, is knitting. They talk in a desultory[1] way.*

MARY. Did I tell you that Mrs. Patchett had just had another baby?

JOHN (*not looking up from his paper*). Yes, dear, you told me.

MARY. Did I? Are you sure?

JOHN. Last week.

1 **desultory** (dĕs′əl tôr′ĭ): aimless.

MARY. But she only had it yesterday. Mr. Patchett told me this morning when I was ordering the cauliflower.

JOHN. Ah! Then perhaps you told me she was going to have one.

MARY. Yes, I think that must have been it.

JOHN. This is the one that she was going to have?

MARY. It weighed seven pounds exactly.

JOHN. Of course, being a grocer he would have the scales ready. Boy or girl?

MARY. Boy.

JOHN. The first boy, isn't it?

MARY. The second.

JOHN. The first one that weighed seven pounds—exactly.

(*They are silent again, he reading, she knitting.*)

MARY. Anything in the paper tonight?

JOHN. A threatened strike of boiler makers.

MARY. Does that matter very much?

JOHN. It says here that the situation is extremely serious.

MARY. Tell me about it.

JOHN (*not very good at it*). Well, the—er—boiler makers are threatening to strike. (*Weightily.*) They are threatening not to make any more—er—boilers.

MARY. Kitchen boilers?

JOHN (*with an explanatory gesture*). Boilers. They are threatening not to make any more of them. And —well—that's how it is. (*Returning to his paper.*) The situation is extremely serious. Exciting scenes have been witnessed.

MARY. What sort of scenes?

JOHN. Well, naturally, when you have a lot of men threatening not to make any more boilers—and er—a lot of other men threatening that if they *don't* make any—well, exciting scenes are witnessed. *Have* been witnessed by this man, this special correspondent.

MARY (*after a pause*). It's a funny thing that nothing exciting ever happens to *us*.

JOHN. It depends what you mean by exciting. I went round in ninety-five[2] last Saturday, as I think I told you.

MARY. But I mean something really thrilling—and dangerous. Like in a novel or on a stage.

JOHN. My dear Mary, nothing like that ever happens in real life. I mean, it wouldn't happen to *us*.

MARY. Would you like it if it did?

(*He says nothing for a moment. Then he puts down his paper and sits there thinking. At last he turns to her.*)

JOHN (*almost shyly*). I used to imagine things like that happening. Years ago. Rescuing a beautiful maiden, and—and all that sort of thing. And being wrecked on a desert island with her . . . (*He turns away from her, staring into his dreams.*) Or pushing open a little green door in a long high wall and finding myself in a wonderful garden under the bluest of blue skies, and waiting, waiting—for something.

MARY. I used to imagine things too. People fighting duels because of me. Silly, isn't it? Nothing ever really happens like that.

JOHN (*still with his thoughts*). No.

(*At this moment a* STRANGE MAN *comes in. Contrary to all etiquette, he is wearing a bowler hat[3] and an overcoat, and has a half-smoked cigar in his mouth. He walks quickly across the room and sits down in a chair, with his back to the audience.* JOHN *and* MARY, *deep in their thoughts, do not notice him.*)

MARY (*looking into the fire*). I suppose we're too old for it now.

---

2 **went round in ninety-five:** golf score.

3 **bowler hat:** stiff felt hat rounded at the top.

JOHN. I suppose so.

MARY. If it had only happened once—just for the memories.

JOHN. So that we could say to each other—— Good heavens, what's that?

(*It was the crack of a revolver. No mistaking it, even by* JOHN, *who has never been much of a hand with revolvers.*)

MARY (*frightened*). John!

(*There is a scuffling noise outside the door. They look eagerly toward it. Then suddenly there is dead silence. The* MAN IN THE BOWLER HAT *flicks some of his cigar ash onto the carpet—Mary's carpet.*)

JOHN. Look!

(*Very slowly the door begins to open. Through the crack comes a long, sinuous[4] hand. The door opens farther, and the hand is followed by a long, sinuous body. Still the* Man in the Bowler Hat *says nothing. Then the door is closed, and leaning up against it, breathing rather quickly, is the* HERO, *in his hand a revolver.* JOHN *and* MARY *look at each other wonderingly.*)

JOHN (*with a preliminary cough*). I—I beg your pardon.

HERO (*turning quickly, finger to his lips*). H'sh!

JOHN (*apologetically*). I beg your pardon!

(*The* HERO *listens anxiously at the door. Then, evidently reassured for the moment, he comes toward them.*)

HERO (*to* JOHN). Quick, take this! (*He presses his revolver into* JOHN's *hand.*)

JOHN. I—er—what do I——

HERO (*to* MARY). And you! This! (*He takes another revolver from his hip pocket and presses it into* MARY's *hand.*)

MARY. Thank you. Do we——

HERO (*sternly*). H'sh!

MARY. Oh, I beg your pardon.

HERO. Listen!

(*They all listen.* JOHN *and* MARY *have never listened so intently before, but to no purpose. They hear nothing.*)

JOHN (*in a whisper*). What is it?

HERO. Nothing.

JOHN. Yes, that's what *I* heard.

HERO. Have you got a—— (*He breaks off and broods.[5]*)

MARY. A what?

HERO (*shaking his head*). No, it's too late now.

JOHN (*to* MARY). Haven't we got one?

HERO. You wait here; that will be best. I shall be back in a moment.

JOHN. What do we do?

HERO. Listen; that's all. Listen.

JOHN (*eagerly*). Yes, yes.

HERO. I shall be back directly.

(*Just as he is making for the window the door opens and the* HEROINE—*obviously—comes in. For a moment they stand gazing at each other.*)

HEROINE. Oh! (*but with a world of expression in it*).

---

4 **sinuous** (sĭn′yo͝o əs): winding; like a serpent.

5 **broods:** thinks seriously.

THE ONE-ACT PLAY

HERO. Oh! (*with even more expression*).

HEROINE. My love!

HERO. My beautiful!

(*They meet and are locked in an embrace.*)

JOHN (*to* MARY). I suppose they're engaged to be married.

MARY. Oh, I think they must be.

JOHN. They've evidently met before.

HERO (*lifting his head for a moment*). My Dolores!

JOHN (*to* MARY). I think this must be both "How do you do?" and "Good-by."

MARY (*wistfully*).[6] He is very good-looking.

JOHN (*casually*). Oh, do you think so? Now *she* is pretty, if you like.

MARY (*doubtfully*). Ye-es. Very bad style, of course.

JOHN (*indignantly*). My dear Mary——

HEROINE (*to* HERO). Quick, quick, you must go!

HERO. Never—now that I have found you again.

HEROINE. Yes, yes! My father is hot upon your tracks. He will be here at any moment in his two-seater.

HERO (*turning pale*). Your father!

HEROINE. I walked on ahead to warn you. He has come for—*It!*

JOHN (*to* MARY). What on earth's *It?*

HERO (*sinking back into a chair*). *It!*

HEROINE. Yes.

JOHN (*behind his hand to* MARY).

Income-tax collector.

HERO. The Rajah's ruby!

MARY. Oh, how exciting!

HEROINE. Yes; he knows you have it. He is determined to wrest[7] it from you.

HERO. Never!

JOHN. Well done!

HEROINE. There is no mischief he might not do if once it were in his possession. Three prominent members of society would be ruined, there would be another war in Mexico, and the exchange value of the ruble[8] would be seriously impaired.[9] Promise me you will never give it up.

HERO. I promise.

HEROINE. I must go. I am betraying my father by coming here; but I love you.

JOHN (*to* MARY). She does love him. I thought she did.

MARY. How could she help it?

HERO. I adore you!

JOHN. You see, he adores her too. It certainly looked like it.

MARY. I still don't think she's very good style.

HEROINE. Then—good-by!

(*They embrace again.*)

JOHN (*after a decent interval*). Excuse me, sir, but if you have a train to catch—I mean if your future father-in-law's two-seater is any good at all, oughtn't you to be—er——

HERO (*releasing* HEROINE). Good-by!

(*He conducts her to the door, gives her a last long, lingering look, and lets her go.*)

---

6 **wistfully:** desirously; yearningly.

7 **wrest:** snatch.
8 **ruble:** Soviet coin.
9 **impaired:** decreased.

MARY (*to herself*). Pretty, of course, in a kind of way, but I must say I don't *like* that style.

(*The* HERO *comes out of his reverie[10] and proceeds to business.*)

HERO (*briskly, to* JOHN). You have those revolvers?

JOHN. Yes.

HERO. Then wait here and listen. More than one life depends upon it.

JOHN. How many more?

HERO. If you hear the slightest noise——

JOHN (*eagerly*). Yes?

HERO. H'sh!

(*He goes to the window, waits there listening for a moment, and then slips out.* JOHN *and* MARY *remain, their ears turned attentively.*)

JOHN (*with a start*). H'sh! What's that?

MARY. What was it, dear?

JOHN. I don't know.

MARY. It's so awkward when you don't quite know what you're listening *for.*

JOHN. H'sh! We were told to listen, and we must listen. More than one life depends on it.

MARY. All right, dear.

(*They continue to listen. A little weary of it,* MARY *looks down the barrel of the revolver to see if she can see anything interesting.*)

JOHN (*observing her*). Don't do that! It's very dangerous to point a loaded revolver at yourself. If anything happened it would be too late to say afterwards that you didn't mean it.

MARY. Very well, John. Oh, look!

(*Again the door opens quickly, and a sinister gentleman in a mask inserts himself into the room. We recognize him at once as the* CHIEF VILLAIN. *Very noiselessly, his back to* JOHN *and* MARY, *he creeps along the wall toward the window.*)

JOHN (*in a whisper*). Father-in-law.

MARY. Do we—— (*indicates the revolver*).

JOHN (*doubtfully*). I—I suppose—— (*He raises his gun hesitatingly.*)

MARY. Oughtn't you say something first?

JOHN. Yes—er—— (*He clears his throat warningly.*) Ahem! (*The* CHIEF VILLAIN *continues to creep toward the window.*) You, sir!

MARY (*politely*). Do you want anything, or—or anything?

(*The* CHIEF VILLAIN *is now at the window.*)

JOHN. Just a moment, sir.

(*The* CHIEF VILLAIN *opens the window and steps out between the curtains.*)

MARY. Oh, he's gone!

JOHN. I call that very bad manners.

MARY. Do you think he'll—he'll come back?

JOHN (*with determination*). I shall shoot him like a dog if he does (*waving aside all protests*).

MARY. Yes, dear, perhaps that *would* be best.

JOHN. Look out! He's coming back.

10 reverie: daydream.

THE ONE-ACT PLAY

(He raises his revolver as the door opens. Again the CHIEF VILLAIN enters cautiously and creeps toward the window.)

MARY *(in a whisper)*. Shoot!

JOHN *(awkwardly)*. Er—I suppose it *is* the same man?

MARY. Yes, yes!

JOHN. I mean—it wouldn't be quite fair if—— *(He coughs warningly.)* Excuse me, sir!

MARY. Quick, before he goes!

JOHN *(raising his revolver nervously)*. I ought to tell you, sir—— *(To MARY.)* You know, I still think this is a different one.

(The CHIEF VILLAIN again disappears through the window.)

MARY *(in great disappointment)*. Oh, he's gone!

JOHN *(firmly)*. It was a different one. The other one hadn't got a mustache.

MARY. He had, John. It was the same man; of course it was.

JOHN. Oh! Well, if I had known that—if I had only been certain of it, I should have shot him like a dog.

A VOICE *(which sounds like the HERO's)*. Help, help!

MARY. John, listen!

JOHN. I *am* listening.

A VOICE. He-e-elp!

MARY. Oughtn't we to do something?

JOHN. We *are* doing something. We're listening. That's what he told us to do.

A VOICE. Help!

JOHN *(listening)*. That's the other man; the one who came in first.

MARY. The nice-looking one. Oh, John, we *must* do something.

JOHN. If he calls out again I shall—I shall—do something. I shall take steps. I may even have to shoot somebody. But I will *not* have——

A VOICE. Quick, quick!

MARY. There!

JOHN. Er—was that the same voice?

MARY *(moving to the door)*. Yes, of course it was. It sounded as if it were in the hall. Come along.

JOHN. Wait a moment. *(She turns round.)* We must keep cool, Mary. We mustn't be impetuous.[11] Just hold this a moment. *(He hands her his revolver.)*

MARY *(surprised)*. Why, what——

JOHN. I shall take my coat off. *(He takes off his coat very slowly.)* I'm going through with this. I'm not easily roused, but when once——

A VOICE. Help! Quick!

JOHN *(reassuringly)*. All right, my man, all right. *(Very leisurely he rolls up his sleeves.)* I'm not going to have this sort of thing going on in *my* house. I'm not going to have it. *(Doubtfully.)* I don't think I need take my waistcoat off too. What do *you* think, Mary?

MARY *(impatiently)*. No, dear, of course not; you look very nice.

JOHN *(very determined)*. Now, then, let's have that revolver. *(She gives it to him.)* I shall say, "Hands up!"—very sharply, like that—"*Hands up!*"—and then if he doesn't put his hands up I shall—I shall say, "Hands up!" again. That will show him that I'm not to be trifled with.[12] Now, then, dear, are you ready?

MARY *(eagerly)*. Yes!

11 impetuous: hasty; reckless.
12 trifled with: made light of.

JOHN. Then——

    (*But at that moment the lights go out.*)

MARY. Oh!

JOHN (*annoyed*). Now, why did you do that, Mary?

MARY. I didn't do it, dear.

JOHN. Then who did?

MARY. I don't know. They just went out.

JOHN. Then I shall write to the company tomorrow and complain. I shall complain to the company about the lights, and I shall complain to the landlord about the way people go in and out of this house, and shriek and——

MARY (*in alarm*). Oh!

JOHN. *Don't* do that! What is it?

MARY. I can feel somebody quite close to me.

JOHN. Well, that's me.

MARY. Not you, somebody else. Oh! He touched me! John!

JOHN (*addressing the darkness*). Really, sir, I must ask you not to——

MARY. Listen! I can hear breathings all round me!

JOHN. Excuse me, sir, but do you mind *not* breathing all round my wife?

MARY. There! Now I can't hear anything.

JOHN (*complacently*).[13] There you are, my dear. You see what firmness does. I wasn't going to have *that* sort of thing going on in my house.

    (*The lights go up and reveal the* **HERO** *gagged so that only his eyes are visible, and bound to a chair.*)

---

13 complacently: contentedly; with satisfaction.

THE ONE-ACT PLAY

MARY (*clinging to her husband*). Oh, John!

JOHN (*with sudden desperate bravery*). Hands up! (*He levels his revolver.*)

MARY. Don't be silly; how can he?

JOHN. All right, dear, I was only practicing. (*He blows a speck of dust off his revolver and holds it up to the light again.*) Yes; it's quite a handy little fellow. I think I shall be able to do some business with this all right.

MARY. Poor fellow! I wonder who it is.

(*The HERO tries to speak with his eyes and movements of the head.*)

JOHN. He wants something. Perhaps it's the evening paper. (*He makes a movement toward it.*)

MARY. Listen!

(*The HERO begins to tap with his feet.*)

JOHN. He's signaling something.

MARY. Dots and dashes!

JOHN. That's the Morse code; that's what that is. Where's my dictionary? (*He fetches it hastily and begins to turn over the pages.*)

MARY. Quick, dear!

JOHN (*reading*). Here we are. "1. Morse—The walrus." (*Looking at the HERO:*) No, that must be wrong. Ah, this is better! "2. Morse code signaling of telegraph operators—as 'He sends a good Morse.'"

MARY. Well? What does it say?

JOHN. Nothing. That's all. Then we come to "*Morsel*—a small piece of food, a mouthful, a bite. Also a small meal."

MARY (*brilliantly*). A mouthful!

That's what he meant. He wants the gag taken out of his mouth. (*She goes to him.*)

JOHN. That's very clever of you, Mary. I should never have thought of that.

MARY (*untying the gag*). Then! . . . Why, it's the man who came in first, the nice-looking one!

JOHN. Yes, he said he was coming back.

(*Before the HERO can express his thanks—if that is what he wants to express—the CHIEF VILLAIN, accompanied by a BAD MAN, comes in. JOHN and MARY instinctively retreat.*)

CHIEF VILLAIN (*sardonically*).[14] Ha!

JOHN (*politely*). Ha to you, sir.

(*The CHIEF VILLAIN fixes JOHN with a terrible eye.*)

JOHN (*nervously to MARY*). Say "Ha!" to the gentleman, dear.

MARY (*faintly*). Ha!

CHIEF VILLAIN. And what the Mephistopheles[15] are *you* doing here?

JOHN (*to MARY*). What are we doing here?

MARY (*bravely*). This is our house.

JOHN. Yes, this is our house.

CHIEF VILLAIN. Then siddown! (JOHN *sits down meekly.*) Is this your wife?

JOHN. Yes. (*Introducing them.*) Er—my wife—er—Mr. Er——

CHIEF VILLAIN. Then tell her to siddown too.

JOHN (*to MARY*). He wants you to siddown.   (*She does so.*)

---

14 **sardonically:** scornfully; mockingly.
15 **Mephistopheles** (mĕf'ə stŏf'ə lēz'): another name for the Devil.

CHIEF VILLAIN. That's better. (*To* BAD MAN.) Just take their guns off 'em.

BAD MAN (*taking the guns*). Do you want them tied up or gagged or anything?

CHIEF VILLAIN. No; they're not worth it.

JOHN (*humbly*). Thank you.

CHIEF VILLAIN. Now, then, to business. (*To* HERO.) Where's the Rajah's ruby?

HERO (*firmly*). I shan't tell you.

CHIEF VILLAIN. You won't?

HERO. I won't.

CHIEF VILLAIN. That's awkward. (*After much thought.*) You absolutely refuse to?

HERO. I absolutely refuse to.

CHIEF VILLAIN. Ha! (*To* BAD MAN.) Torture the prisoner.

BAD MAN (*cheerfully*). Right you are, governor. (*He feels on the lapel of his coat and then says to* MARY.) Could you oblige me with the loan of a pin, mum?

MARY. I don't think—— (*Finding one.*) Here you are.

BAD MAN. Thanks. (*He advances threateningly upon the prisoner.*)

CHIEF VILLAIN. Wait! (*To* HERO.) Before proceeding to extremities I will give you one more chance. Where is the Rajah's Raby?

BAD MAN. You mean the Rabah's Rujy, don't you, governor?

CHIEF VILLAIN. That's what I said.

JOHN (*wishing to help*). You *said* the Rubah's Rajy, but I think you meant the Rujy's——

CHIEF VILLAIN. Silence! (*To* HERO.) I ask you again—where is the Ruj—I mean where is the Rab—well, anyhow, where *is* it?

HERO. I won't tell you.

CHIEF VILLAIN. Proceed, Mr. Smithers.

BAD MAN. Well, you've asked for it, mate. (*He pushes the pin gently into the* HERO's *arm.*)

HERO. Ow!

MARY. Oh, poor fellow!

CHIEF VILLAIN. Silence! Where is—— (*The* HERO *shakes his head.*) Torture him again, Mr. Smithers.

HERO. No, no! Mercy! I'll tell you.

JOHN (*indignantly*). Oh, I say!

BAD MAN. Shall I just give him another one for luck, governor?

HERO. Certainly not!

JOHN (*to* MARY). Personally, I think he should have held out much longer.

CHIEF VILLAIN. Very well, then. Where is the Rajah's Ruby?

HERO. In the cloakroom of Waterloo Station—in a hatbox.

CHIEF VILLAIN (*doubtfully*). In the cloakroom at Waterloo Station, you say?

HERO. Yes. In a hatbox. Now release me.

CHIEF VILLAIN. How do I know it's there?

HERO. Well, how do *I* know?

CHIEF VILLAIN. True. (*Holding out his hand.*) Well, give me the ticket for it.

HERO. I haven't got it.

BAD MAN. Now, then, none of that.

HERO. I haven't, really.

JOHN. I don't think he'd say he hadn't got it if he had got it. Do you, Mary?

MARY. Oh, I'm sure he wouldn't.

Chief Villain. Silence! (*To* **Hero.**) Where is the ticket?

Hero. In the cloakroom of Paddington Station. In a hatbox.

Chief Villain. The same hatbox?

Hero. Of course not. The other one was at Waterloo Station.

Chief Villain. Well, then, where's the ticket for the hatbox in the Paddington cloakroom?

Hero. In the cloakroom at Charing Cross. In a hatbox.

Chief Villain (*annoyed*). Look here, how many hatboxes have you got?

Hero. Lots.

Chief Villain. Oh! Now let's get this straight. You say that the Rajah's Ruby is in a hatbox in the cloakroom at Paddington——

Hero. Waterloo.

Chief Villain. Waterloo; and that the ticket for that hatbox is in a hatbox in the cloakroom at Euston——

Hero. Paddington.

Chief Villain. Paddington; and that the ticket for the ticket, which is in a hatbox at Paddington, for the Ruby which is in a hatbox at King's Cross——

Bad Man. Euston.

John. St. Pancras.

Chief Villain (*angrily*). Oh, shut up! The ticket for the ticket, which is in a hatbox at Paddington, for the Ruby which is in a hatbox at—at——

John. St. Panc——

Hero. Waterloo.

Chief Villain. Waterloo, thank you. This ticket is in a hatbox at—er——

John. St. Pancras.

Chief Villain. Shut up! In a hatbox at——

Hero. Charing Cross.

Chief Villain. Exactly. (*Triumphantly.*) Then give me the ticket.

Hero. Which one?

Chief Villain (*uneasily*). The one we're talking about.

John (*helpfully*). The St. Pancras one.

Chief Villain (*in a fury*). Will you shut up? (*To* **Hero.**) Now listen. (*Very slowly and with an enormous effort of concentration:*) I want the ticket for the hatbox at Charing Cross, which contains the ticket for the hatbox at (**John's** *lips, which are forming the words "St. Pancras," are hastily smothered by the* **Bad Man's** *hand.*)—at Paddington, which contains the ticket for the hatbox at Waterloo, which contains the Rajah's Ruby. (*Proudly.*) There!

Hero. I beg your pardon?

Chief Villain (*violently*). I will *not* say it again! Give me the ticket.

Hero (*sadly*). I haven't got it.

Chief Villain (*in an awestruck whisper*). You haven't got it?

Hero. No.

Chief Villain (*after several vain attempts to speak*). Where is it?

Hero. In the cloakroom at Victoria Station.

Chief Villain (*moistening his lips and speaking very faintly*). Not—not in a hatbox?

Hero. Yes.

Chief Villain (*without much hope*). And the ticket for that?

Hero. In the cloakroom at Euston.

Chief Villain (*quite broken up*). Also in a hatbox?

HERO. Yes.

CHIEF VILLAIN. How much longer do we go on?

HERO (*cheerfully*). Oh, a long time yet.

CHIEF VILLAIN (*to* **BAD MAN**). How many London stations are there?

JOHN. Well, there's St. Pancras, and——

MARY. Liverpool Street.

BAD MAN. About twenty big ones, governor.

CHIEF VILLAIN. Twenty! And do we go round them all?

HERO. Yes.

CHIEF VILLAIN. And what do we do when we've worked through the lot?

HERO. Then we go all round them again.

CHIEF VILLAIN (*anxiously*). And— and so on?

HERO. And so on.

CHIEF VILLAIN (*his hand to his head*). This is terrible. I must think. (*To* **BAD MAN.**) Just torture him again while I think.

BAD MAN (*cheerily*). Right you are, governor. (*He approaches his victim.*)

HERO (*uneasily*). I say, look here——

JOHN. I don't think it's quite fair, you know——

MARY (*suddenly*). Give me back my pin!

BAD MAN. Must obey orders, gentlemen. (*Coaxingly to* **HERO.**) Just a little way in (*indicating with his finger*)—that much.

JOHN (*to* **MARY**). I think perhaps "that much" wouldn't matter. What do——

CHIEF VILLAIN (*triumphantly*). I've

got it! (*He rises with an air, the problem solved. They all look at him.*)

JOHN. What?

CHIEF VILLAIN (*impressively to* HERO). There is somewhere—logically, there must be somewhere—a final, an ultimate hatbox!

JOHN. By Jove! That's true!

HERO. Yes.

CHIEF VILLAIN. Where *is* that hatbox?

JOHN. St. Pancras.

CHIEF VILLAIN. Shut up! (*To* HERO.) Where is that hatbox?

HERO. In the cloakroom at Charing Cross.

CHIEF VILLAIN. Ah! (*He holds out his hand.*) Then give me the ticket for it.

BAD MAN (*threateningly*). Come on, now! The ticket!

HERO (*shaking his head sadly*). I can't.

CHIEF VILLAIN (*almost inarticulate with emotion*). You don't mean to say as you've—lost—it?

HERO (*in a whisper, with bowed head*). I've lost it.

(*With a terrible shriek the* CHIEF VILLAIN *falls back fainting into the arms of the* BAD MAN. *Instinctively* JOHN *and* MARY *embrace, sobbing to each other, "He's lost it!" And at that moment the* HEROINE *rushes in, crying, "My love, you've lost it!" and puts her arms around the* HERO. *Only the* MAN IN THE BOWLER HAT *remains unmoved. Slowly he removes the cigar from his mouth and speaks.*)

BOWLER HAT. Yes. . . . That's all right. Just a bit ragged still. . . . We'll take it again at eleven tomorrow. Second Act, please.

(*And so the rehearsal goes on.*)

CURTAIN

Understanding Literature

1. What does the conversation between John and Mary in the early part of the play (up to the entrance of the Hero) tell you about them?

2. In the section of the play dealing with the rehearsal, you see John and Mary in what they think is the real world and the actors in a stage world. What contrasts do you see in the behavior of the two groups? How does Mary react to the excitement? How does John react?

3. Much of the humor of the play arises because John keeps saying things that are the opposite of what you would expect him to say. Where do you find instances of this? Read his lines and then suggest the lines that you might have expected him to say.

A. A. MILNE

4. How would the play be different if the Man in the Bowler Hat were left out? Why is the play named after him?
5. Which characteristics of the melodrama does this play exaggerate? In what ways are the situation and the characters improbable?
6. What similarities do you see between this play and "A Night at an Inn"? What differences?

Observing Caution Notices in the Performance of Plays

As you started reading each of the previous three plays, you probably noticed a caution notice printed at the bottom of the title page. Should your class or your school decide to perform one of these plays for a school assembly program, or, in fact, for any audience, it is necessary for you to obtain permission to do so. All of these plays have been copyrighted. The caution notice is printed for the protection of the author, who deserves to receive compensation for performances of his play.

Read the following caution notice carefully. This play, unlike the others in the unit, is out of copyright in the United States. However, it is still fully protected under copyright laws in Canada, and this protection covers many types of performances.

One of the greatest of all one-act plays, "Spreading the News" was first produced in Ireland in 1904. If you read it carefully and see the mad mixture of fact and opinion, you will enjoy the spreading rumor.

Spreading the News

Lady Gregory

IMPROVING YOUR READING: This play illustrates a major characteristic of a good *plot*, that every speech or action is related to another speech or action. Each word or deed here leads to the next. The result of the tight plot construction is a fantastic piling up of comical misunderstandings.

CHARACTERS

BARTLEY FALLON	JAMES RYAN
MRS. FALLON	MRS. TARPEY
JACK SMITH	MRS. TULLY
SHAWN EARLY	A POLICEMAN (*Jo Muldoon*)
TIM CASEY	A REMOVABLE MAGISTRATE

(SCENE: *The outskirts of a Fair. An Apple Stall.* MRS. TARPEY *sitting at it.* MAGISTRATE *and* POLICEMAN *enter.*)

MAGISTRATE.[1] So that is the Fair Green. Cattle and sheep and mud. No system. What a repulsive sight!

POLICEMAN. That is so, indeed.

MAGISTRATE. I suppose there is a good deal of disorder in this place?

POLICEMAN. There is.

MAGISTRATE. Common assault?

POLICEMAN. It's common enough.

MAGISTRATE. Agrarian[2] crime, no doubt?

POLICEMAN. That is so.

MAGISTRATE. Boycotting?[3] Maiming of cattle? Firing into houses?

POLICEMAN. There was one time, and there might be again.

MAGISTRATE. That is bad. Does it go any farther than that?

POLICEMAN. Far enough, indeed.

MAGISTRATE. Homicide, then! This district has been shamefully neglected! I will change all that. When I was in the Andaman Islands,[4] my system never failed. Yes, yes, I will change all that. What has that woman on her stall?

POLICEMAN. Apples mostly—— and sweets.

MAGISTRATE. Just see if there are

1 **Magistrate:** chief government officer.
2 **Agrarian:** agricultural.

3 **Boycotting:** refusing to do business with a company.
4 **Andaman Islands:** islands in that part of the Indian Ocean called the Bay of Bengal.

any unlicensed goods underneath ——spirits or the like. We had evasions of the salt tax in the Andaman Islands.

POLICEMAN (*sniffing cautiously and upsetting a heap of apples*). I see no spirits here——or salt.

MAGISTRATE (*to* MRS. TARPEY). Do you know this town well, my good woman?

MRS. TARPEY (*holding out some apples*). A penny the half-dozen, your honor?

POLICEMAN (*shouting*). The gentleman is asking do you know the town! He's the new magistrate!

MRS. TARPEY (*rising and ducking*).[5] Do I know the town? I do, to be sure.

MAGISTRATE (*shouting*). What is its chief business?

MRS. TARPEY. Business, is it? What business would the people here have but to be minding one another's business?

MAGISTRATE. I mean what trade have they?

MRS. TARPEY. Not a trade. No trade at all but to be talking.

MAGISTRATE. I shall learn nothing here.

(JAMES RYAN *comes in, pipe in mouth. Seeing* MAGISTRATE *he retreats quickly, taking pipe from mouth.*)

MAGISTRATE. The smoke from that man's pipe had a greenish look; he may be growing unlicensed tobacco at home. I wish I had brought my telescope to this district. Come to the post office, I will telegraph for it.

5 ducking: bowing.

I found it very useful in the Andaman Islands.

(MAGISTRATE *and* POLICEMAN *go out left.*)

MRS. TARPEY. Bad luck to Jo Muldoon, knocking my apples this way and that way. (*Begins arranging them.*) Showing off he was to the new magistrate.

(*Enter* BARTLEY FALLON *and* MRS. FALLON.)

BARTLEY. Indeed it's a poor country and a scarce country to be living in. But I'm thinking if I went to America it's long ago the day I'd be dead!

MRS. FALLON. So you might, indeed.

(*She puts her basket on a barrel and begins putting parcels in it, taking them from under her cloak.*)

BARTLEY. And it's a great expense for a poor man to be buried in America.

MRS. FALLON. Never fear, Bartley Fallon, but I'll give you a good burying the day you'll die.

BARTLEY. Maybe it's yourself will be buried in the graveyard of Cloonmara before me, Mary Fallon, and I myself that will be dying unbeknownst some night, and no one anear me. And the cat itself may be gone straying through the country, and the mice squealing over the quilt.

MRS. FALLON. Leave off talking of dying. It might be twenty years you'll be living yet.

BARTLEY (*with a deep sigh*). I'm thinking if I'll be living at the end of twenty years, it's a very old man I'll be then!

THE ONE-ACT PLAY

MRS. TARPEY (*turns and sees them*). Good morrow, Bartley Fallon; good morrow, Mrs. Fallon. Well, Bartley, you'll find no cause for complaining today; they are all saying it was a good fair.

BARTLEY (*raising his voice*). It was not a good fair, Mrs. Tarpey. It was a scattered sort of a fair. If we didn't expect more, we got less. That's the way with me always; whatever I have to sell goes down and whatever I have to buy goes up. If there's ever any misfortune coming to this world, it's on myself it pitches, like a flock of crows on seed potatoes.

MRS. FALLON. Leave off talking of misfortunes and listen to Jack Smith that is coming the way, and he singing.

(*Voice of* JACK SMITH *heard singing:*)

I thought, my first love,
  There'd be but one house between you and me,
And I thought I would find
  Yourself coaxing my child on your knee.
Over the tide
  I would leap with the leap of a swan,
Till I came to the side
  Of the wife of the Red-haired man!

(JACK SMITH *comes in; he is a red-haired man, and is carrying a hayfork.*)

MRS. TARPEY. That should be a good song if I had my hearing.

MRS. FALLON (*shouting*). It's "The Red-haired Man's Wife."

MRS. TARPEY. I know it well. That's the song that has a skin on it!
(*She turns her back to them and goes on arranging her apples.*)

MRS. FALLON. Where's herself, Jack Smith?

JACK SMITH. She was delayed with her washing; bleaching the clothes on the hedge she is, and she daren't leave them, with all the tinkers that do be passing to the fair. It isn't to the fair I came myself, but up to the Five Acre Meadow I'm going, where I have a contract for the hay. We'll get a share of it into tramps[6] today. (*He lays down hayfork and lights his pipe.*)

BARTLEY. You will not get it into tramps today. The rain will be down on it by evening, and on myself too. It's seldom I ever started on a journey but the rain would come down on me before I'd find any place of shelter.

JACK SMITH. If it didn't itself, Bartley, it is my belief you would carry a leaky pail on your head in place of a hat, the way you'd not be without some cause of complaining.
(*A voice heard "Go on, now, go on out o' that. Go on I say."*)

JACK SMITH. Look at that young mare of Pat Ryan's that is backing into Shaughnessy's bullocks with the dint of the crowd! Don't be daunted, Pat, I'll give you a hand with her.
(*He goes out, leaving his hayfork.*)

MRS. FALLON. It's time for ourselves to be going home. I have all I bought put in the basket. Look at there, Jack Smith's hayfork he left after him! He'll be wanting it. (*Calls.*) Jack Smith! Jack Smith! ——He's gone through the crowd

6 tramps: stacks.

——hurry after him, Bartley, he'll be wanting it.

BARTLEY. I'll do that. This is no safe place to be leaving it. (*He takes up fork awkwardly and upsets the basket.*) Look at that now! If there is any basket in the fair upset, it must be our own basket!

(*He goes out to right.*)

MRS. FALLON. Get out of that! It is your own fault, it is. Talk of misfortunes and misfortunes will come. Glory be! Look at my new eggcups rolling in every part—— and my two pound of sugar with the paper broke——

MRS. TARPEY (*turning from stall*). God help us, Mrs. Fallon, what happened your basket?

MRS. FALLON. It's himself that knocked it down, bad manners to him. (*Putting things up.*) My grand sugar that's destroyed, and he'll not drink his tea without it. I had best go back to the shop for more, much good may it do him!

(*Enter* **TIM CASEY.**)

TIM CASEY. Where is Bartley Fallon, Mrs. Fallon? I want a word with him before he'll leave the fair. I was afraid he might have gone home by this, for he's a temperate[7] man.

MRS. FALLON. I wish he did go home! It'd be best for me if he went home straight from the fair green, or if he never came with me at all! Where is he, is it? He's gone up the road (*jerks elbow*) following Jack Smith with a hayfork.

(*She goes out to left.*)

TIM CASEY. Following Jack Smith

7 **temperate:** moderate; self-controlled.

THE ONE-ACT PLAY

with a hayfork! Did ever any one hear the like of that. (*Shouts.*) Did you hear that news, Mrs. Tarpey?

MRS. TARPEY. I heard no news at all.

TIM CASEY. Some dispute I suppose it was that rose between Jack Smith and Bartley Fallon, and it seems Jack made off, and Bartley is following him with a hayfork!

MRS. TARPEY. Is he now? Well, that was quick work! It's not ten minutes since the two of them were here, Bartley going home and Jack going to the Five Acre Meadow; and I had my apples to settle up, that Jo Muldoon of the police had scattered, and when I looked round again Jack Smith was gone, and Bartley Fallon was gone, and Mrs. Fallon's basket upset, and all in it strewed upon the ground——the tea here——the two pound of sugar there——the eggcups there——Look, now, what a great hardship the deafness puts upon me, that I didn't hear the commincement of the fight! Wait till I tell James Ryan that I see below, he is a neighbor of Bartley's, it would be a pity if he wouldn't hear the news!

(*She goes out. Enter* SHAWN EARLY *and* MRS. TULLY.)

TIM CASEY. Listen, Shawn Early! Listen, Mrs. Tully, to the news! Jack Smith and Bartley Fallon had a falling out, and Jack knocked Mrs. Fallon's basket into the road, and Bartley made an attack on him with a hayfork, and away with Jack, and Bartley after him. Look at the sugar here yet on the road!

SHAWN EARLY. Do you tell me so?

Well, that's a queer thing, and Bartley Fallon so quiet a man!

MRS. TULLY. I wouldn't wonder at all. I would never think well of a man that would have that sort of a moldering[8] look. It's likely he has overtaken Jack by this.

(*Enter* JAMES RYAN *and* MRS. TARPEY.)

JAMES RYAN. That is great news Mrs. Tarpey was telling me! I suppose that's what brought the police and the magistrate up this way. I was wondering to see them in it a while ago.

SHAWN EARLY. The police after them? Bartley Fallon must have injured Jack so. They wouldn't meddle in a fight that was only for show!

MRS. TULLY. Why wouldn't he injure him? There was many a man killed with no more of a weapon than a hayfork.

JAMES RYAN. Wait till I run north as far as Kelly's bar to spread the news!   (*He goes out.*)

TIM CASEY. I'll go tell Jack Smith's first cousin that is standing there south of the church after selling his lambs.   (*Goes out.*)

MRS. TULLY. I'll go telling a few of the neighbors I see beyond to the west.   (*Goes out.*)

SHAWN EARLY. I'll give word of it beyond at the east of the green.

(*Is going out when* MRS. TARPEY *seizes hold of him.*)

MRS. TARPEY. Stop a minute, Shawn Early, and tell me did you see red Jack Smith's wife, Kitty Keary, in any place?

8 **moldering:** crumbling; decaying.

Shawn Early. I did. At her own house she was, drying clothes on the hedge as I passed.

Mrs. Tarpey. What did you say she was doing?

Shawn Early (*breaking away*). Laying out a sheet on the hedge.

(*He goes.*)

Mrs. Tarpey. Laying out a sheet for the dead! The Lord have mercy on us! Jack Smith dead, and his wife laying out a sheet for his burying! (*Calls out.*) Why didn't you tell me that before, Shawn Early? Isn't the deafness the great hardship? Half the world might be dead without me knowing of it or getting word of it at all! (*She sits down and rocks herself.*) O my poor Jack Smith! To be going to his work so nice and so hearty, and to be left stretched on the ground in the full light of the day!

(*Enter* **Tim Casey.**)

Tim Casey. What is it, Mrs. Tarpey? What happened since?

Mrs. Tarpey. O my poor Jack Smith!

Tim Casey. Did Bartley overtake him?

Mrs. Tarpey. O the poor man!

Tim Casey. Is it killed he is?

Mrs. Tarpey. Stretched in the Five Acre Meadow!

Tim Casey. The Lord have mercy on us! Is that a fact?

Mrs. Tarpey. Without the rites of the Church or a ha' porth!

Tim Casey. Who was telling you?

Mrs. Tarpey. And the wife laying out a sheet for his corpse. (*Sits up and wipes her eyes.*) I suppose they'll wake him[9] the same as another?

(*Enter* **Mrs. Tully, Shawn Early,** *and* **James Ryan.**)

Mrs. Tully. There is great talk about this work in every quarter of the fair.

Mrs. Tarpey. Ochone![10] cold and dead. And myself maybe the last he was speaking to!

James Ryan. The Lord save us! Is it dead he is?

Tim Casey. Dead surely, and the wife getting provision for the wake.

Shawn Early. Well, now, hadn't Bartley Fallon great venom in him?

Mrs. Tully. You may be sure he had some cause. Why would he have made an end of him if he had not? (*To* **Mrs. Tarpey,** *raising her voice.*) What was it rose the dispute at all, Mrs. Tarpey?

Mrs. Tarpey. Not a one of me knows. The last I saw of them, Jack Smith was standing there, and Bartley Fallon was standing there, quiet and easy, and he listening to "The Red-haired Man's Wife."

Mrs. Tully. Do you hear that, Tim Casey? Do you hear that, Shawn Early and James Ryan? Bartley Fallon was here this morning listening to red Jack Smith's wife, Kitty Keary that was! Listening to her and whispering with her! It was she started the fight so!

Shawn Early. She must have followed him from her own house. It is likely some person roused him.

Tim Casey. I never knew, before,

---

9 **wake him:** watch over his body at night.
10 **Ochone** (əKH ōn′): Alas.

Bartley Fallon was great with Jack Smith's wife.

MRS. TULLY. How would you know it? Sure it's not in the streets they would be calling it. If Mrs. Fallon didn't know of it, and if I that have the next house to them didn't know of it, and if Jack Smith himself didn't know of it, it is not likely you would know of it, Tim Casey.

SHAWN EARLY. Let Bartley Fallon take charge of her from this out so, and let him provide for her. It is little pity she will get from any person in this parish.

TIM CASEY. How can he take charge of her? Sure he has a wife of his own. Sure you don't think he'd turn souper and marry her?

JAMES RYAN. It would be easy for him to marry her if he brought her to America.

SHAWN EARLY. With or without Kitty Keary, believe me it is for America he's making at this minute. I saw the new magistrate and Jo Muldoon of the police going to the post office as I came up—there was hurry on them—you may be sure it was to telegraph they went, the way he'll be stopped in the docks at Queenstown!

MRS. TULLY. It's likely Kitty Keary is gone with him, and not minding a sheet or a wake at all. The poor man, to be deserted by his own wife, and the breath hardly gone out yet from his body that is lying bloody in the field!

(*Enter* **MRS. FALLON.**)

MRS. FALLON. What is it the whole of the town is talking about? And what is it you yourselves are talking about? Is it about my man Bartley Fallon you are talking? Is it lies about him you are telling, saying that he went killing Jack Smith? My grief that ever he came into this place at all!

JAMES RYAN. Be easy now, Mrs. Fallon. Sure there is no one at all in the whole fair but is sorry for you!

MRS. FALLON. Sorry for me, is it? Why would anyone be sorry for me? Let you be sorry for yourselves, and that there may be shame on you forever and at the day of judgment, for the words you are saying and the lies you are telling to take away the character of my poor man, and to take the good name off of him, and to drive him to destruction! That is what you are doing!

SHAWN EARLY. Take comfort now, Mrs. Fallon. The police are not so smart as they think. Sure he might give them the slip yet, the same as Lynchehaun.

MRS. TULLY. If they do get him, and if they do put a rope around his neck, there is no one can say he does not deserve it!

MRS. FALLON. Is that what you are saying, Bridget Tully, and is that what you think? I tell you it's too much talk you have, making yourself out to be such a great one, and to be running down every respectable person! A rope, is it? It isn't much of a rope was needed to tie up your own furniture the day you came into Martin Tully's house, and you never bringing as much as a blanket, or a penny, or a suit of clothes with you, and I myself bringing seventy pounds

and two feather beds. And now you are stiffer than a woman would have a hundred pounds! It is too much talk the whole of you have. A rope, is it? I tell you the whole of this town is full of liars and schemers that would hang you up for half a glass of whiskey. (*Turning to go.*) People they are you wouldn't believe as much as daylight from without you'd get up to have a look at it yourself. Killing Jack Smith indeed! Where are you at all, Bartley, till I bring you out of this? My nice, quiet little man! My decent comrade! He that is as kind and as harmless as an innocent beast of the field! He'll be doing no harm at all if he'll shed the blood of some of you after this day's work! That much would be no harm at all. (*Calls out.*) Bartley! Bartley Fallon! Where are you? (*Going out.*) Did anyone see Bartley Fallon?

(*All turn to look after her.*)

JAMES RYAN. It is hard for her to believe any such a thing, God help her!

(*Enter* **BARTLEY FALLON** *from right, carrying hayfork.*)

BARTLEY. It is what I often said to myself, if there is ever any misfortune coming to this world, it is on myself it is sure to come!

(*All turn round and face him.*)

BARTLEY. To be going about with this fork, and to find no one to take it, and no place to leave it down, and I wanting to be gone out of this. ——Is that you, Shawn Early? (*Holds out fork.*) It's well I met you. You have no call to be leaving the fair for a while the way I have, and how can I go till I'm rid of this fork?

Will you take it and keep it until such time as Jack Smith——

SHAWN EARLY (*backing*). I will not take it, Bartley Fallon, I'm very thankful to you!

BARTLEY (*turning to apple stall*). Look at it now, Mrs. Tarpey, it was here I got it; let me thrust it in under the stall. It will lie there safe enough, and no one will take notice of it until such time as Jack Smith——

MRS. TARPEY. Take your fork out of that! Is it to put trouble on me and to destroy me you want? putting it there for the police to be rooting it out maybe.

(*Thrusts him back.*)

BARTLEY. That is a very unneighborly thing for you to do, Mrs. Tarpey. Hadn't I enough care on me with that fork before this, running up and down with it like the swinging of a clock, and afeard to lay it down in any place. I wish I never touched it or meddled with it at all!

JAMES RYAN. It is a pity, indeed, you ever did.

BARTLEY. Will you yourself take it, James Ryan? You were always a neighborly man.

JAMES RYAN (*backing*). There is many a thing I would do for you, Bartley Fallon, but I won't do that!

SHAWN EARLY. I tell you there is no man will give you any help or any encouragement for this day's work. If it was something agrarian now——

BARTLEY. If no one at all will take it, maybe it's best to give it up to the police.

TIM CASEY. There'd be a welcome for it with them, surely! (*Laughter.*)

MRS. TULLY. And it is to the police Kitty Keary herself will be brought.

MRS. TARPEY (*rocking to and fro*). I wonder now who will take the expense of the wake for poor Jack Smith?

BARTLEY. The wake for Jack Smith!

TIM CASEY. Why wouldn't he get a wake as well as another? Would you begrudge him that much?

BARTLEY. Red Jack Smith dead! Who was telling you?

SHAWN EARLY. The whole town knows of it by this.

BARTLEY. Do they say what way did he die?

JAMES RYAN. You don't know that yourself, I suppose, Bartley Fallon? You don't know he was followed and that he was laid dead with the stab of a hayfork?

BARTLEY. The stab of a hayfork!

SHAWN EARLY. You don't know, I suppose, that the body was found in the Five Acre Meadow?

BARTLEY. The Five Acre Meadow!

TIM CASEY. It is likely you don't know that the police are after the man that did it?

BARTLEY. The man that did it!

MRS. TULLY. You don't know, maybe, that he was made away with for the sake of Kitty Keary, his wife?

BARTLEY. Kitty Keary, his wife!

(*Sits down bewildered.*)

MRS. TULLY. And what have you to say now, Bartley Fallon?

BARTLEY (*crossing himself*). I to bring that fork here, and to find that news before me! It is much if I can ever stir from this place at all, or reach as far as the road!

TIM CASEY. Look, boys, at the new magistrate, and Jo Muldoon along with him! It's best for us to quit this.

SHAWN EARLY. That is so. It is best not to be mixed in this business at all.

JAMES RYAN. Bad as he is, I wouldn't like to be an informer against any man.

(*All hurry away except* MRS. TARPEY, *who remains behind her stall. Enter magistrate and policeman.*)

MAGISTRATE. I knew the district was in a bad state, but I did not expect to be confronted with a murder at the first fair I came to.

POLICEMAN. I am sure you did not, indeed.

MAGISTRATE. It was well I had not gone home. I caught a few words here and there that roused my suspicions.

POLICEMAN. So they would, too.

MAGISTRATE. You heard the same story from everyone you asked?

POLICEMAN. The same story—or if it was not altogether the same, anyway it was no less than the first story.

MAGISTRATE. What is that man doing? He is sitting alone with a hayfork. He has a guilty look. The murder was done with a hayfork!

POLICEMAN (*in a whisper*). That's the very man they say did the act; Bartley Fallon himself!

MAGISTRATE. He must have found escape difficult——he is trying to brazen it out.[11] A convict in the Andaman Islands tried the same game, but he could not escape my system! Stand aside—— Don't go far——have the handcuffs ready. (*He walks up to* BARTLEY, *folds his arms, and stands before him.*) Here, my man, do you know anything of John Smith?

BARTLEY. Of John Smith! Who is he, now?

POLICEMAN. Jack Smith, sir—— Red Jack Smith!

MAGISTRATE (*coming a step nearer and tapping him on the shoulder*). Where is Jack Smith?

BARTLEY (*with a deep sigh, and shaking his head slowly*). Where is he, indeed?

MAGISTRATE. What have you to tell?

BARTLEY. It is where he was this morning, standing in this spot, singing his share of songs—no, but lighting his pipe—scraping a match on the sole of his shoe——

MAGISTRATE. I ask you, for the third time, where is he?

BARTLEY. I wouldn't like to say that. It is a great mystery, and it is hard to say of any man, did he earn hatred or love.

MAGISTRATE. Tell me all you know.

BARTLEY. All that I know—— Well, there are the three estates; there is Limbo,[12] and there is Purgatory,[13] and there is——

MAGISTRATE. Nonsense! This is trifling! Get to the point.

11 brazen it out: face it shamelessly.
12 Limbo: according to some Christian teachings, the dwelling place of those souls unable to enter Heaven.
13 Purgatory: in some Christian teachings, the place of temporary punishment after death.

THE ONE-ACT PLAY

BARTLEY. Maybe you don't hold with the clergy so? That is the teaching of the clergy. Maybe you hold with the old people. It is what they do be saying, that the shadow goes wandering, and the soul is tired, and the body is taking a rest —— The shadow! (*Starts up.*) I was nearly sure I saw Jack Smith not ten minutes ago at the corner of the forge, and I lost him again—— Was it his ghost I saw, do you think?

MAGISTRATE (*to* POLICEMAN). Conscience-struck! He will confess all now!

BARTLEY. His ghost to come before me! It is likely it was on account of that fork! I to have it and he to have no way to defend himself the time he met with his death!

MAGISTRATE (*to* POLICEMAN). I must note down his words. (*Takes out notebook.*) (*To* BARTLEY.) I warn you that your words are being noted.

BARTLEY. If I had ha' run faster in the beginning, this terror would not be on me at the latter end! Maybe he will cast it up against me at the day of judgment—— I wouldn't wonder at all at that.

MAGISTRATE (*writing*). At the day of judgment——

BARTLEY. It was soon for his ghost to appear to me——is it coming after me always by day it will be, and stripping the clothes off in the night-time?—— I wouldn't wonder at all at that, being as I am an unfortunate man!

MAGISTRATE (*sternly*). Tell me this truly. What was the motive of this crime?

BARTLEY. The motive, is it?

MAGISTRATE. Yes; the motive; the cause.

BARTLEY. I'd sooner not say that.

MAGISTRATE. You had better tell me truly. Was it money?

BARTLEY. Not at all! What did poor Jack Smith ever have in his pockets unless it might be his hands that would be in them?

MAGISTRATE. Any dispute about land?

BARTLEY (*indignantly*). Not at all! He never was a grabber or grabbed from anyone!

MAGISTRATE. You will find it better for you if you tell me at once.

BARTLEY. I tell you I wouldn't for the whole world wish to say what it was——it is a thing I would not like to be talking about.

MAGISTRATE. There is no use in hiding it. It will be discovered in the end.

BARTLEY. Well, I suppose it will, seeing that mostly everybody knows it before. Whisper here now. I will tell no lie; where would be the use? (*Puts his hand to his mouth, and* MAGISTRATE *stoops.*) Don't be putting the blame on the parish, for such a thing was never done in the parish before——it was done for the sake of Kitty Keary, Jack Smith's wife.

MAGISTRATE (*to* POLICEMAN). Put on the handcuffs. We have been saved some trouble. I knew he would confess if taken in the right way.

(POLICEMAN *puts on handcuffs.*)

BARTLEY. Handcuffs now! Glory be! I always said, if there was ever

any misfortune coming to this place it was on myself it would fall. I to be in handcuffs! There's no wonder at all in that.

(*Enter* MRS. FALLON, *followed by the rest. She is looking back at them as she speaks.*)

MRS. FALLON. Telling lies the whole of the people of this town are; telling lies, telling lies as fast as a dog will trot! Speaking against my poor respectable man! Saying he made an end of Jack Smith! My decent comrade! There is no better man and no kinder man in the whole of the five parishes! It's little annoyance he ever gave to anyone! (*Turns and sees him.*) What in the earthly world do I see before me? Bartley Fallon in charge of the police! Handcuffs on him! O Bartley, what did you do at all at all?

BARTLEY. O Mary, there has a great misfortune come upon me! It is what I always said, that if there is ever any misfortune——

MRS. FALLON. What did he do at all, or is it bewitched I am?

MAGISTRATE. This man has been arrested on a charge of murder.

MRS. FALLON. Whose charge is that? Don't believe them! They are all liars in this place! Give me back my man!

MAGISTRATE. It is natural you should take his part, but you have no cause of complaint against your neighbors. He has been arrested for the murder of John Smith, on his own confession.

MRS. FALLON. The saints of heaven protect us! And what did he want killing Jack Smith?

MAGISTRATE. It is best you should

THE ONE-ACT PLAY

know all. He did it on account of a love affair with the murdered man's wife.

MRS. FALLON. With Jack Smith's wife! With Kitty Keary!——Ochone, the traitor!

THE CROWD. A great shame, indeed. He is a traitor, indeed.

MRS. TULLY. To America he was bringing her, Mrs. Fallon.

BARTLEY. What are you saying, Mary? I tell you——

MRS. FALLON. Don't say a word! I won't listen to any word you'll say! (*Stops her ears.*) O, isn't he the treacherous villain? Ohone go deo!

BARTLEY. Be quiet till I speak! Listen to what I say!

MRS. FALLON. Sitting beside me on the ass car coming to the town, so quiet and so respectable, and treachery like that in his heart!

BARTLEY. Is it your wits you have lost or is it I myself that have lost my wits?

MRS. FALLON. And it's hard I earned you, slaving, slaving——and you grumbling, and sighing, and coughing, and discontented, and the priest wore out anointing you, with all the times you threatened to die!

BARTLEY. Let you be quiet till I tell you!

MRS. FALLON. You to bring such a disgrace into the parish! A thing that was never heard of before!

BARTLEY. Will you shut your mouth and hear me speaking?

MRS. FALLON. And if it was for any sort of a fine handsome woman, but for a little fistful of a woman like Kitty Keary, that's not four feet high hardly, and not three teeth in her head unless she got new ones! May God reward you, Bartley Fallon, for the black treachery in your heart and the wickedness in your mind, and the red blood of poor Jack Smith that is wet upon your hand!

(*Voice of* JACK SMITH *heard singing.*)

The sea shall be dry,
  The earth under mourning and ban!
Then loud shall he cry
  For the wife of the red-haired man!

BARTLEY. It's Jack Smith's voice ——I never knew a ghost to sing before——. It is after myself and the fork he is coming! (*Goes back. Enter* JACK SMITH.) Let one of you give him the fork and I will be clear of him now and for eternity!

MRS. TARPEY. The Lord have mercy on us! Red Jack Smith! The man that was going to be waked!

JAMES RYAN. Is it back from the grave you are come?

SHAWN EARLY. Is it alive you are, or is it dead you are?

TIM CASEY. Is it yourself at all that's in it?

MRS. TULLY. Is it letting on you were to be dead?

MRS. FALLON. Dead or alive, let you stop Kitty Keary, your wife, from bringing my man away with her to America!

JACK SMITH. It is what I think, the wits are gone astray on the whole of you. What would my wife want bringing Bartley Fallon to America?

MRS. FALLON. To leave yourself, and to get quit of you she wants, Jack Smith, and to bring him away from myself. That's what the two of them had settled together.

JACK SMITH. I'll break the head of any man that says that! Who is it says it? (*To* **TIM CASEY.**) Was it you said it? (*To* **SHAWN EARLY.**) Was it you?

ALL TOGETHER (*backing and shaking their heads*). It wasn't I said it!

JACK SMITH. Tell me the name of any man that said it!

ALL TOGETHER (*pointing to* **BARTLEY**). It was *him* that said it!

JACK SMITH. Let me at him till I break his head!

    (**BARTLEY** *backs in terror. Neighbors hold* **JACK SMITH** *back.*)

JACK SMITH (*trying to free himself*). Let me at him! Isn't he the pleasant sort of a scarecrow for any woman to be crossing the ocean with! It's back from the docks of New York he'd be turned (*trying to rush at him again*), with a lie in his mouth and treachery in his heart, and another man's wife by his side, and he passing her off as his own! Let me at him, can't you.

(*Makes another rush, but is held back.*)

MAGISTRATE (*pointing to* **JACK SMITH**). Policeman, put the handcuffs on this man. I see it all now. A case of false impersonation, a conspiracy to defeat the ends of justice. There was a case in the Andaman Islands, a murderer of the Mopsa tribe, a religious enthusiast——

POLICEMAN. So he might be, too.

MAGISTRATE. We must take both these men to the scene of the murder. We must confront them with the body of the real Jack Smith.

JACK SMITH. I'll break the head of any man that will find my dead body!

MAGISTRATE. I'll call more help from the barracks. (*Blows* **POLICEMAN'S** *whistle.*)

BARTLEY. It is what I am thinking, if myself and Jack Smith are put together in the one cell for the night, the handcuffs will be taken off him, and his hands will be free, and murder will be done that time surely!

MAGISTRATE. Come on! (*They turn to the right.*)

CURTAIN

Understanding Literature

1. How does the magistrate behave as he talks with the policeman in the beginning of the play?
2. What information does partially deaf Mrs. Tarpey give them about the town? In the light of the whole play, how are her answers ironic?
3. What are Bartley and Mrs. Fallon talking about as they come on the stage?

4. As Jack Smith comes on, what is he singing about? Why does the author have him leave his hayfork behind? How does it help to tie the play together?
5. When does the play change from real action into false interpretations of the action? How do the rumors spread?
6. What does each character add to the spreading of the news? What real evidence is each character using? What false judgments does each make about the facts?
7. What does Mrs. Tarpey's partial deafness add to the play?
8. Summarize what "news" is spread. How much is fact? How much is opinion?
9. What is the situation as Bartley Fallon returns with the hayfork? How is he treated? As Bartley talks, how does the author make it seem to Bartley's listeners that he is the murderer?
10. By what steps do you arrive at the true situation?
11. How does the magistrate behave at the end of the play?

Poetry

This unit contains many different types of poems which, in turn, are concerned with many different subjects. After reading the following essay, you will know what one poet thinks poetry is all about. After reading the poems which follow it, you will be able to form your own ideas about what a poem is and what makes a good one.

Short Talk on Poetry*

*with different kinds of explanations for young people
as to how little anybody knows about poetry, how it is made,
what it is made of, how long people have been making it,
where it came from, when it began, who started it and why,
and who knows all about it.*

Carl Sandburg

WHAT IS POETRY? Is the answer hidden somewhere? Is it one of those answers locked in a box and nobody has the key? There are such questions and answers.

Once a man reading a newspaper clipped a poem written by a small boy in a school in New York City. The lines read:

There stands the elephant.
Bold and strong—
There he stands chewing his food.
We are strengthless against his strength.

And the man has kept this poem for many years. He has a feeling the boy did a good, honest piece of writing. The boy stood wondering and thinking before the biggest four-legged animal on earth today. And the boy put his wonder and thought, his personal human secret, a touch of

man's fear in the wilderness, into the nineteen words of the poem. He asked, "What does the elephant do to me when I look at him? What is my impression of the elephant?" Then he answered his own questions.

Once there was a boy went to school and learned that any two-legged animal is a biped. And he said, "Here I've been a biped all the time and I didn't know it." So there are people sometimes who talk poetry without writing it but they don't know they are talking poetry. And every child, every boy and girl, sometimes has poetry in his head and heart—even though it doesn't get written.

Once there was a wee, curly-headed boy tugged at a cornstalk, tugged till he pulled the cornstalk up all by himself and told about it to his father, who said, "I guess you're getting to be a pretty strong boy now." The little one answered, "I guess I am. The whole earth had a hold of the other end of the cornstalk and was pulling against me." Should we say this boy had imagination and what he told his father was so keen and alive it could be called poetry? Perhaps he was a poet without knowing it just like the boy who was a biped without knowing it.

Poetry is old, ancient, goes far back. It is among the oldest of human things. So old is it that no man knows how and why the first poems came.

When it shall happen sometime that men gather their gifts and go to work and write a history of language, then it may be that we shall have at the same time a history of poetry. For the first poems of man probably came about the same time the first men, women and children spoke the first human words on the earth.

Is any one surprised to hear that we do not have a history of poetry? Shall we believe that the learned men have written histories of all the important things of mankind? Surely there are many big histories yet to be written on big subjects. We do not have, for instance, a history of Money that goes back to when money first began, telling how and why. We do not have a history of Language which goes far back, telling how and why men first began to talk.

Yes, poetry is old. The first men that walked the earth, before men had learned to write, must have talked poetry to each other sometimes. Among the oldest things we have today which tell us about the Indians, the Chinese, the Egyptians,

how they lived and talked, thousands of years ago, are writings we know to be poetry. These writings have words that go along with time beats, with rhythm, one-two, one-two, or one-two-three-four, one-two-three-four. They had drums among the Indians, the Chinese, the Egyptians, thousands of years ago. And the words of their poetry move along like drumbeats, keeping time, now fast, now slow, drumming easy and slow at the opening of a war dance, drumming faster and faster, wild and furious, till it is so swift only the best-trained warriors can stand the speed of the dance that is drummed.

We have old poems, some so old no man knows how far they go back in time. One beautiful ancient English poem has no author, whose name we know. Where it came from no history books tell us. It goes like this—

On a misty moisty morning, when
    cloudy was the weather,
I chanced to meet an old man all
    clothed in leather.
He began to compliment and I began
    to grin,
"How do you do? and how do you
    do? and how do you do again?"

This is only one of many fine and strange poems we have out of the long ago. Nobody knows who wrote them or whether they were first spoken centuries before they were written down to meet our eyes in books.

What is poetry? This question no man has ever answered in such a way that all men have said, "Yes, now we know what poetry is." Many men have tried to explain what poetry is. Some men have written thick books so the question might be settled and made clear for all time. But they have all failed. Several fine poets have written essays and papers on what they believe poetry to be. Yet these poets did not do what they started out to do. They meant to explain in prose what poetry is and they ended up with writing poetry to explain poetry. This is like a man inside of a strange house trying to tell people outside who have never been in the house exactly how it feels to be in that house, which is not scientific nor exact and which is like saying, "The way to write poems is to write poems." It is only clear and understandable to those who already understand and therefore need no explanations.

When Walt Whitman[1] says, "The poet is the answerer," we are interested. If we could know just what he means by "the answerer" we would know what he means by "the poet." One poet says poetry must be "cold, lonely and distant," not knowing that some readers of poetry are glad to have books which are warm, friendly and so near that they almost breathe with life. Another poet has said poetry is "emotion remembered in tranquillity." What does that mean? It is anybody's guess what that means. To know exactly what it means we would have to know exactly what is emotion, what is tranquillity, and what we do when we remember. Otherwise it is an escape

from words into words, "passing the buck," or winding like a weasel through language that ends about where it begins. "He came out of the same hole he went in at."

There is a science called esthetics. It is the science which tries to find the laws of beauty. If as a science it ever became perfect then the books dealing with that science would become very important. Then when a builder finished a house and wished to know whether it was a beautiful house he would only have to open the books on esthetics and the books would tell him.

What is beauty? And when shall we call a thing beautiful? These, too, are questions no man has ever answered in such a way that all men have said, "Yes, now we know what beauty is and now we know how to tell the beautiful when we find it." The nearest that men have come to answering the question, "What is the beautiful?" has been in their saying the beautiful is *the appropriate*, that which serves. No hat is a beautiful hat which does not fit you and which the wind can easily blow off your head. A five-gallon hat on a cowboy riding a horse on an Arizona ranch is beautiful—but the same hat on a crowded city streetcar would be out of place, inappropriate. No song is beautiful in a room where persons desire complete quiet. No polite behavior has beauty unless it has thought and consideration for others. The most beautiful room is the one which best serves those who live in it.

The most beautiful skyscrapers are those without extras stuck on after

1 Walt Whitman: 19th-century American poet.

the real structure is finished. Why should a good, honest skyscraper have a dome or a mosque or a cement wedding cake plastered on top of it? Nearly always, what serves, what is appropriate to human use, is beautiful enough—without extras. A farm silo, a concrete grain elevator, a steel barge hauling iron ore on the Great Lakes, or a series of tall coal chutes rising as silhouettes on a moonlight night, may any one of them have as complete a beauty as the Greek Parthenon or a Gothic cathedral. Steichen, the photographer, declares he occasionally meets newspaper photographs which in design and as works of art are superior to many of the proclaimed masterpieces of painting and etching.

Now, poetry is supposed to be the esthetic art which gathers the beautiful into words. The first stuff for making poetry is words. No poems, strictly speaking, have ever been made without words. To make poems without words would be like a painter painting without paint or a bricklayer bricklaying without bricks. Of course, a feeling or a thought, or both must come to a poet before he begins using the words that make a poem. But the right words, the special and particular words for the purpose in view, these must come. For out of them the poem is made.

The words for a poem sometimes come swiftly and easily so that at last when the poem is put down on paper, the writer of them says, "I do not know how these words came. What is here was not my own abso-

lute doing any more than a dream that should come to me in a night of sleep." Yet again the words may come slowly, out of years of toil and sometimes anguish of changing phrases and arrangements.

While we do not know very much in an absolute way about the questions, "What is poetry? How is a poem made?" we do know the one little fact that poems are made of words and without words there can be no poetry. Beyond this we do not know much. However, there is one other little scientific fact we know about poetry. That is, what is poetry for any given individual depends on the individual and what his personality requires as poetry. This links up with one of the few accepted propositions of the science of esthetics: Beauty depends on personal taste. What is beauty for one person is not for another. What is poetry for one person may be balderdash or hogwash for another.

Each of us has a personality different from all others. It has even been said that as no two leaves in a forest are the same no two human characters are precisely alike. This personality that each of us has is strangely woven of millions of little facts, events, impressions out of the past and present. Your personality and mine go back to many mysterious human connections before we were born—and since. And what any one of us loves today with depth of passion, and what each of us tries to shape his life by, goes back to strange things in personality, things so darkly mixed and baffling that it is not easy for any of us at a given time to answer the question, "Why do you love this and not that? Why do you want those and not them?" The old song with its line, "I want what I want when I want it," is not entirely comic in its backgrounds.

We do not know the start of the old folk saying, "Everyone to his taste as the old woman said when she kissed the cow." We are sure a blunt Indiana philosopher knew his ground well when he wrote, "What is one man's lettuce is another man's poison ivy." These are humorous comments on the deeply serious and involved reality known as human personality. They connect directly with the fact that what is poetry for some is not poetry for others. They indicate that sometimes we cannot help it that we do not merely *dislike* some poetry; we go farther and *hate* it. And why we should hate any particular poem, thing or person is no more clear than why we love others, for hate is usually expensive in many ways and is a waste of time that belongs elsewhere. Charles Lamb[2] said he believed an old story he had heard about two men, who had never before seen each other, meeting one day in a street in London—and the moment they saw each other's faces they leaped and began fighting.

Lamb said those two men who began hitting at each other's faces the moment they saw those faces, had "imperfect sympathies." Something clicked in each one saying, "Hit him! Kill him!" They couldn't help it.

2 Charles Lamb: English essayist (1775-1834).

Though they met in a crowded street of a great city, and there was no war on, they attacked each other like two soldiers with bayonets in front-line trenches.

And exactly like those two men meeting in a London street, some of us register instantly—though not so violently—to faces we meet, buildings, colors, neckties, gowns, designs, pictures, books, plays—and poems. Something clicks in us and we know like a flash whether we like this or that new thing we meet for the first time.

And then may happen afterward a slow change of our viewpoint. What we saw nothing in to begin with takes on a glint or two we had not noticed at first; then as time passes, we gather values, intentions, gleams, that interest us and lead us on till we know we were ignorant, possessed of "imperfect sympathies," in our first impression of hate or dislike. This change of viewpoint from dislike to interest, from indifference to enthusiasm, often has happened with the finest of men and women in respect to great masterpieces of literature. Sometimes we do not know what a writer is talking about in his books because in life we have not met the people, facts, impressions which he is trying to deliver his mind and heart about in his book. Said a great modern artist, "Going along a railroad one day I see a thing I have seen many times. But this day I suddenly *see*. 'Tisn't that you *see* new, but things have prepared you for *a new vision*."

As the years pass by and experience writes out new records in our mind life, we go back to some works of art that we rejected in the early days and find values we missed. Work, love, laughter, pain, death, put impressions on us as time passes, and as we brood over what has happened.

Out of songs and scars and the mystery of personal development, we get eyes that pick out intentions we had not seen before in people, in works of art, in books and poetry.

Naturally, too, the reverse happens. What we register to at one period of life, what we find gay and full of fine nourishment at one time, we find later has lost interest for us. A few masterpieces may last across the years but we usually discard some. A few masterpieces are enough. Why this is so we do not know. For each individual his new acquisitions and old discards are different.

The books and poems at hand ready for each of us are so many and so different that we use and throw away, acquire and discard, according to personal taste, and often merely guided by whim like the man in the song, "I want what I want when I want it." Too often both among young people and grownups, there is a careless drifting and they take the easiest way in books and poetry. Millions read without asking themselves why they read and whether in all their reading they have learned anything worth the spending of their time.

It was not for nothing Thoreau[3] said an old newspaper would do for him just as well as a new one. Each of us can sit alone with our conscience for a while on the proposition of Robert Louis Stevenson that the intelligent man can find an Iliad[4] of the human race in a newspaper. And any kindly philosopher could write a thick book on why the shrewd, tolerant reader enjoys even a stupid, vain, hypocritical[5] book because the writer of the book is etching his own portrait on every page, stepping forth and talking off lines like one of the fools, clowns or pretenders in a Russian play. Healthy questions for each of us: "Why do I read books? What do books do to me? Can I improve my form as a reader? What does poetry do to me? Why do I need this or that poetry?"

We have heard much in our time about free verse being modern, as though it is a new-found style for men to use in speaking and writing, rising out of the machine age, skyscrapers, high speed and jazz. Now, if free verse is a form of writing poetry without rime, without regular meters, without established and formal rules governing it, we can easily go back to the earliest styles of poetry known to the human family— and the style is strictly free verse. Before men invented the alphabet, so that poems could be put down in writing, they spoke their poems. When one man spoke to another in

3 **Thoreau:** Henry David Thoreau, 19th-century American writer.

4 **Iliad:** a reference to the Greek epic poem by Homer. Here it means a long account of woes and disasters.

5 **hypocritical:** one that pretends to be better than it is.

a certain time beat and rhythm, if it happened that his words conveyed certain impressions and moods to his listeners, he was delivering poetry to them, whether he knew it or they knew it, and whether he or they had a name for an art which the poet was practicing on himself and them.

We may go through thousands of pages of the reports of songs, poems, and spoken dreams of American Indians as recorded in the volumes of the Bureau of Ethnology[6] of the Smithsonian Institution at Washington, and we find it all to be in the free verse style. The poems of the ancient Chinese writers Li Po, Tu Fu and others, as read in translations, and as notated by the translators, show how strange and marvelous moments of life can be captured and compressed in the manner called free verse. The Bible is one of the sublime sources of free verse. The orations of Moses, the Book of Proverbs, Ecclesiastes, the Sermon on the Mount, the "love chapter" of the Apostle Paul, these are in the free verse style of writing poetry.

If those who write in the free verse style fail at getting onto paper any lines worth reading twice, they are in the same class with those who in regular, ordered, formal verse fail to get onto paper lines worth reading twice. The crimes of free verse have been many. The same goes for sonnets, ballads, ballades, triolets, rondeaus, villanelles,[7] and the forms of verse which are governed by hexameters, pentameters, iambics,[8] strophes, and by laws which dictate how many syllables shall be permitted to perch on each line of the poem.

Perhaps no wrong is done and no temple of human justice violated in pointing out here that each authentic poet makes a style of his own. Sometimes this style is so clearly the poet's own that when he is imitated it is known who is imitated. Shakespeare, Villon,[9] Li Po, Whitman—each sent forth his language and impress of thought and feeling from a different style of gargoyle spout. In the spacious highways of great books each poet is allowed the stride that will get him where he wants to go.

Should children write poetry? Yes, whenever they feel like it. If nothing else happens they will find it a training for writing and speaking in other fields of human work and play. No novelist has been a worse writer for having practiced at poetry. Many a playwright, historian, essayist, editorial writer, could have improved his form by experimenting with poetry.

At what age should a child begin writing poetry? Any age. Poems are made of words and when a child is learning to talk, to shape words on its tongue, is a proper time for it to speak poetry—if it can.

Does it help a child poet to have praise for his poems? The child

---

6 **Ethnology:** science which studies the races of mankind.
7 **sonnets . . . villanelles:** different forms of poetry.

8 **hexameters . . . iambics:** rhythmic divisions of poetry.
9 **Villon:** Francois Villon, 15th-century French poet.

should be told that poetry is first of all for the poet, that great poets usually die saying their best work is not written. Perhaps it is wise for every child to be told that it is a mistake for either a child or a grown-up accomplished artist to be satisfied with any past performance.

The foremost American woman poet, Emily Dickinson, had scarcely any of her poetry published in her lifetime. What she wrote had to be. And it is doubtful if her poems would have had the same complete glory they have if she had been taken up and praised. On the other hand there have been poets saved to live and write beautiful pages because they found friends, an audience, and enough money to keep the wolf from sniffing round their little doorways.

The father of a great Irish poet once remarked, "What can be explained is not poetry." There are people who want a book of verse to be like the arithmetic—you turn to the back of the book and find the answers. Ken Nakazawa notes, "The poems that are obvious are like the puzzles that are already solved. They deny us the joy of seeking and creating."

Once a little girl showed to a friend a poem she had written. "Why didn't you make it longer?" asked the friend. "I could have," she answered, "but then it wouldn't have been a poem." She meant she left something in the air for the reader of the poem to linger over, as any of us do over a rose or a sunset or a face. Roses, sunsets, faces, have mystery. If we could explain them, then after having delivered our explanations we could say, "Take it from me, that's all there is to it, and there's no use your going any further for I've told you all there is and there isn't any more."

If poems could be explained, then poets would have to leave out roses, sunsets, faces, from their poems. Yet it seems that for thousands of years poets have been writing about roses, sunsets, faces, because they have mystery, significance, and a heavy or a light beauty, an appeal, a lesson and a symbolism that stays with us long as we live. It was something like this in the heart of the philosopher who declared, "What can be explained is not poetry."

Understanding Literature

1. Why, in Sandburg's opinion, are definitions of poetry unsatisfactory?
2. What is the science of esthetics?
3. What is the best definition of *the beautiful*, according to Sandburg? What are some examples of beauty that fit this definition? What is your opinion of this definition of *the beautiful*?
4. What are the only things about poetry that are really known?
5. What does Charles Lamb mean by "imperfect sympathies"? What causes a change in our sympathies?

6. What is free verse? What are some examples that Sandburg uses to prove that free verse is not a modern invention?

7. What does the statement that "what can be explained is not poetry" mean? Do you agree with this statement? Why or why not?

The Ballad

ONE OF THE OLDEST forms of poetry is the ballad, a narrative poem intended for singing or reciting and written in short stanzas. The ballad is usually about an exciting episode told in dramatic form: you see and hear the incident. These songs were made up by anonymous, or unknown, poets who traveled from town to town singing for the entertainment of groups, who were invited to join in on the refrain (repeated lines); in some instances the groups danced to the music of the ballad.

The major characteristics of ballads are that they are often about common people (though sometimes about the nobles too), that physical courage or love are frequent subjects, that they contain little characterization or description, and that action is told through dialogue (people speaking). Much of the story is left out, and you have to fill it in from what is implied, or suggested.

The ballad stanza, another main characteristic, is four lines long. The fourth line usually rhymes with the second. The rhythm is most frequently based on an unaccented sound followed by an accented one, that is, on a sound that receives no emphasis followed by one that is very much emphasized. This pattern of sound is known as iambic meter and indicated as ⌣ ′. These lines from "Robin Hood and Alan a Dale" are examples of iambic meter: "Ăs Róbĭn Hoód nĕxt mórnĭng stoód,/ Ămóngst thĕ leáves sŏ gáy." As in this example, the first and third lines of a ballad stanza usually have four accented syllables, and the second and fourth lines have three each. To read the rhythm correctly you must sometimes slur over sounds and run syllables together to make two syllables sound as one. These are general characteristics for ballads, although you will find exceptions.

Because early ballads were passed on orally from one person to another, many variations of a single ballad can be found. The names used may differ, and some of the details may vary, but the general idea of the story usually stays the same.

CARL SANDBURG

This ballad tells a story which is still being used as a plot for adventure stories. In the first line the mother (the "she" of line 1) rouses her husband (Lord Douglas) to say that their eldest daughter has gone off with her lover (Lord William). Douglas and his sons must follow and bring her back. They fight with Lord William with tragic results.

IMPROVING YOUR READING. Differences in the spelling of some words can be troublesome in reading ballads; but if you read aloud, you can understand most of the words by their sounds.

To get rhythm into his lines, a poet sometimes changes the normal order of words. For example, ". . . she saw . . . her father hard fighting, who loved her so dear" would read "her father who loved her so dear was fighting hard"; and "But a father I can never get mair" would read "But I can never get another father." If you have trouble understanding some lines, try to put the words into a more usual order.

The Douglas Tragedy

"Rise up, rise up, now, Lord Douglas," she says,
    "And put on your armor so bright;
Let it never be said that a daughter of thine
    Was married to a lord under night.

"Rise up, rise up, my seven bold sons,   5
    And put on your armor so bright,
And take better care of your youngest sister,
    For your eldest's awa' the last night."—

He's mounted her on a milk-white steed,
    And himself on a dapple gray,   10
With a bugelet horn hung down by his side,
    And lightly they rode away.

Lord William lookit o'er his left shoulder,
    To see what he could see,
And there he spy'd her seven brethren bold,   15
    Come riding o'er the lee.

"Light down,[1] light down, Lady Marg'ret," he said,
    "And hold my steed in your hand,
Until that against your seven brethren bold,
    And your father, I make a stand."—   20

She held his steed in her milk-white hand,
    And never shed one tear,
Until that she saw her seven brethren fa',[2]
    And her father hard fighting, who loved her so dear.

"O hold your hand, Lord William!" she said,   25
    "For your strokes they are wondrous sair;[3]
True lovers I can get many a ane,[4]
    But a father I can never get mair."—[5]

O, she's ta'en out her hankerchief,
    It was o' the holland sae fine,   30
And aye she dighted[6] her father's bloody wounds,
    That were redder than the wine.

"O chuse, O chuse, Lady Marg'ret," he said,
    "O whether will ye gang or bide?"—[7]
"I'll gang, I'll gang, Lord William," she said,   35
    "For you have left me no other guide."—

He's lifted her on a milk-white steed,
    And himself on a dapple gray,
With a bugelet horn hung down by his side,
    And slowly they baith[8] rade away.   40

O they rade on, and on they rade,
    And a' by the light of the moon,
Until they came to yon wan water,
    And there they lighted down.

---

1 **light down:** get down.
2 **fa':** fall.
3 **sair:** sure.
4 **ane:** another.

5 **mair:** any more.
6 **dighted:** wiped.
7 **gang or bide:** go or stay.
8 **baith:** both.

They lighted down to tak a drink 45
    Of the spring that ran sae clear;
And down the stream ran his gude heart's blood,
    And sair she 'gan to fear.

"Hold up, hold up, Lord William," she says,
    "For I fear that you are slain!"— 50
" 'Tis naething but the shadow of my scarlet cloak
    That shines in the water sae plain."—

O they rade on, and on they rade,
    And a' by the light of the moon,
Until they cam to his mother's ha'⁹ door, 55
    And there they lighted down.

"Get up, get up, lady mother," he says,
    "Get up, and let me in!—
Get up, get up, lady mother," he says,
    "For this night my fair lady I've win. 60

"O mak my bed, lady mother," he says,
    "O mak it braid¹⁰ and deep!
And lay Lady Marg'ret close at my back,
    And the sounder I will sleep."—

Lord William was dead lang ere midnight, 65
    Lady Marg'ret lang ere day—¹¹
And all true lovers that go thegither,
    May they have mair luck than they!

Lord William was buried in St Marie's kirk,¹²
    Lady Marg'ret in Marie's quire; 70
Out o' the lady's grave grew a bonny red rose,
    And out o' the knight's a brier.

And they twa met, and they twa plat,¹³
    And fain they wad be near;
And a' the warld might ken¹⁴ right weel, 75
    They were twa lovers dear.

---

9 ha': hall.
10 braid: broad.
11 lang ere day: long before daybreak.

12 kirk: church.
13 plat: intertwined.
14 ken: know.

But bye and rade the Black Douglas,[15]
    And wow but he was rough!
For he pull'd up the bonny brier,
    And flang'd in St. Mary's Loch.[16]   80

15 **Black Douglas:** Either Lady Margaret's father has recovered, or this is one of his descendents.
16 **Loch:** a deep bay.

Understanding Literature

1. What reason does the mother give for sending her husband and sons after Lord William?
2. Describe the battle. How does it end? Why does Lady Margaret choose to go on with Lord William?
3. Why does Margaret "'gan to fear"?
4. What information does Lord William give to his mother?
5. Why, would you guess, does Lady Margaret die?
6. How do the rose and brier stand for their love? In the last stanza what attitude does Douglas take toward their love?

Another ballad on love, this one characterizes cruel Barbara Allan. Can you explain her action toward the young man?

Bonny Barbara Allan

It was in and about the Martinmas[1] time,
   When the green leaves were a falling,
That Sir John Graeme, in the West Country,
   Fell in love with Barbara Allan.

He sent his men down through the town,   5
   To the place where she was dwelling:
"O haste and come to my master dear,
   Gin[2] ye be Barbara Allan."

O hooly, hooly[3] rose she up,
   To the place where he was lying,   10
And when she drew the curtain by,[4]
   "Young man, I think you're dying."

"O it's I'm sick, and very, very sick,
   And 't is a' for Barbara Allan."
"O the better for me ye's never be,   15
   Tho your heart's blood were a spilling.

"O dinna ye mind, young man," said she,
   "When ye was in the tavern a drinking,
That ye made the healths[5] gae[6] round and round,
   And slighted Barbara Allan?"   20

1 **Martinmas:** November 11, feast of Saint Martin.
2 **Gin:** if.
3 **hooly:** slowly; softly.
4 **by:** aside.
5 **healths:** drink to one's health.
6 **gae:** go.

He turned his face unto the wall,
  And death was with him dealing:
"Adieu, adieu, my dear friends all,
  And be kind to Barbara Allan."

And slowly, slowly raise she up,   25
  And slowly, slowly left him,
And sighing said, she could not stay,
  Since death of life had reft[7] him.

She had not gane a mile but twa,
  When she heard the dead-bell ringing,   30
And every jow[8] that the dead-bell geid,[9]
  It cry'd, Woe to Barbara Allan!

"O mother, mother, make my bed.
  O make it saft and narrow.
Since my love died for me today,   35
  I'll die for him tomorrow."

7 reft: robbed.   8 jow: stroke.   9 geid: gave.

Understanding Literature

1. What relation does the time of the year in which the ballad is set have to its meaning?
2. Who are the speakers in the poem? Read the complete statements made by each.
3. Why does Sir John Graeme send for Barbara Allan? Why does he die? Why does she say that she will die?
4. Why does Barbara not admit her love for Sir John?

Highwaymen were the subjects of many stories and poems written in England in days of long ago. The humorous ballad "The Crafty Farmer" tells how one highwayman was outwitted.

IMPROVING YOUR READING. Notice how much of the story here is told through *dialogue*, the speeches of the characters. The dialogue helps to advance the action of the story and to give the effect of naturalness, as if this were a report of an actual conversation.

The Crafty Farmer

The song that I'm going to sing,
   I hope it will give you content,
Concerning a silly[1] old man,
   That was going to pay his rent.

As he was riding along,   5
   Along all on the highway,
A gentleman-thief overtook him,
   And thus to him did say.

"Well overtaken!" said the thief,
   "Well overtaken!" said he;   10
And "Well overtaken!" said the old man,
   "If thou be good company."

"How far are you going this way?"
   Which made the old man for to smile;
"By my faith," said the old man,   15
   "I'm just going two mile.

1 **silly:** plain; humble.

"I'm a poor farmer," he said,
    "And I farm a piece of ground,
And my half-year's rent, kind sir,
    Just comes to forty pound.   20

"And my landlord has not been at home,
    I've not seen him this twelvemonth or more,
Which makes my rent be large;
    I've to pay him just fourscore."

"Thou shouldst not have told any body,   25
    For thieves there's ganging many;
If any should light on thee,
    They'll rob thee of thy money."

"O never mind," said the old man,
    "Thieves I fear on no side,   30
For the money is safe in my bags,
    On the saddle on which I ride."

As they were riding along,
    The old man was thinking no ill,
The thief he pulled out a pistol   35
    And bid the old man stand still.

But the old man proved crafty,
    As in the world there are many;
He threw his saddle o'er the hedge,
    Saying, "Fetch it, if thou'lt have any."   40

The thief got off his horse,
    With courage stout and bold,
To search for the old man's bag,
    And gave him horse to hold.

The old man put 's foot i' the stirrup   45
    And he got on astride;
To its side he clapt his spur up,
    You need not bid the old man ride.

"O stay!" said the thief, "O stay!
    And half the share thou shalt have." 50
"Nay, by my faith," said the old man,
    "For once I have bitten a knave."

The thief he was not content,
    But he thought there must be bags;
He out with his rusty old sword 55
    And chopt the old saddle in rags.

When he came to the landlord's house,
    This old man he was almost spent;[2]
Saying, "Come, show me a private room
    And I'll pay you a whole year's rent. 60

"I've met a fond fool by the way,
    I swapt horses and gave him no boot;
But never mind," said the old man,
    "For I got the fond fool by the foot."

He opened this rogue's portmantle,[3] 65
    It was glorious to behold;
There were three hundred pounds in silver,
    And three hundred pounds in gold.

And as he was riding home,
    And down a narrow lane, 70
He espied his mare tied to a hedge,
    Saying, "Prithee, Tib, wilt thou gang hame?"

When he got home to his wife
    And told her what he had done,
Up she rose and put on her clothes, 75
    And about the house did run.

She sung, and she sung, and she sung,
    She sung with a merry devotion,
Saying, "If ever our daughter gets wed,
    It will help to enlarge her portion." 80

2 spent: exhausted.
3 portmantle: traveling bag originally used on horseback.

Reading Skills

1. What was the purpose of the trip the farmer was taking?
2. What warning did the thief give the old man? Why did he give such a warning?
3. The farmer proves he is "crafty" in the way he handled the thieving episode. Explain.
4. What did the old man mean when he said, "For once I have bitten a knave"?
5. Explain what the farmer's wife meant at the very end of the ballad when she gaily sang:

> "If ever our daughter gets wed,
> It will help to enlarge her portion."

Understanding Literature

1. "The Crafty Farmer" has many of the qualities which you now know to be in most ballads. List and discuss the qualities which are characteristic of the ballad.
2. This ballad is fast-moving, with no superfluous or extra words. What does each stanza add to the story?
3. What are the qualities that make this ballad humorous?

Selections in the **Myths, Fables, and Legends** unit of this book show that Robin Hood has a delightful, roguish sense of humor. And as you know, Little John is always ready for any game.

IMPROVING YOUR READING. As you read, notice how a light, enjoyable *mood* is created by the poet's choice of adjectives and use of bright colors. You should see in your mind's eye the pictures suggested by the poet.

Robin Hood and Alan a Dale

Come listen to me, you gallants so free,
    All you that love mirth for to hear,
And I will you tell of a bold outlaw,
    That lived in Nottinghamshire.

As Robin Hood in the forest stood,   5
    All under the greenwood tree,
There was he ware of a brave young man,
    As fine as fine might be.

The youngster was clothed in scarlet red,
    In scarlet fine and gay,   10
And he did frisk it over the plain,
    And chanted a roundelay.[1]

As Robin Hood next morning stood,
    Amongst the leaves so gay,
There did he espy[2] the same young man   15
    Come drooping along the way.

1 **roundelay:** a song with a refrain.
2 **espy:** caught sight of.

The scarlet he wore the day before,
    It was clean cast away;
And every step he fetch a sigh,
    "Alack and a well a day!"   20

Then steppèd forth brave Little John,
    And Much the miller's son,
Which made the young man bend his bow,
    When as he saw them come.

"Stand off, stand off!" the young man said,   25
    "What is your will with me?"—
"You must come before our master straight,
    Under yon greenwood tree."

And when he came bold Robin before,
    Robin askt him courteously,   30
"O hast thou any money to spare,
    For my merry men and me?"

"I have no money," the young man said,
    "But five shillings and a ring;
And that I have kept this seven long years,   35
    To have it at my wedding.

"Yesterday I should have married a maid,
    But she is now from me tane,[3]
And chosen to be an old knight's delight,
    Whereby my poor heart is slain."   40

"What is thy name?" then said Robin Hood,
    "Come tell me, without any fail."—
"By the faith of my body," then said the young man,
    "My name it is Alan a Dale."

"What wilt thou give me," said Robin Hood,   45
    "In ready gold or fee,
To help thee to thy true-love again,
    And deliver her unto thee?"

---

3 tane: taken.

"I have no money," then quoth the young man,
    "No ready gold nor fee,
But I will swear upon a book
    Thy true servant for to be."—   50

"But how many miles to thy true-love?
    Come tell me without any guile."—[4]
"By the faith of my body," then said the young man,   55
    "It is but five little mile."

Then Robin he hasted over the plain,
    He did neither stint nor lin,[5]
Until he came unto the church
    Where Alan should keep his wedding.   60

"What dost thou do here?" the Bishop he said,
    "I prithee now tell to me:"
"I am a bold harper," quoth Robin Hood,
    "And the best in the north countrey."

"O welcome, O welcome!" the Bishop he said,   65
    "That musick best pleaseth me."—
"You shall have no musick," quoth Robin Hood,
    "Till the bride and the bridegroom I see."

With that came in a wealthy knight,
    Which was both grave and old,   70
And after him a finikin[6] lass,
    Did shine like glistering gold.

"This is no fit match," quoth bold Robin Hood,
    "That you do seem to make here;
For since we are come unto the church,   75
    The bride she shall chuse her own dear."

Then Robin Hood put his horn to his mouth,
    And blew blasts two or three;
When four and twenty bowmen bold
    Come leaping over the lee.[7]   80

4 **guile:** deceit; falsehood.   6 **finikin:** dainty.
5 **lin:** stop.   7 **lee:** probably means "plain" here; also, a shelter.

And when they came into the churchyard,
    Marching all on a row,
The first man was Alan a Dale,
    To give bold Robin his bow.

"This is thy true-love," Robin he said,   85
    "Young Alan, as I hear say;
And you shall be married at this same time,
    Before we depart away."

"That shall not be," the Bishop he said,
    "For thy word it shall not stand;   90
They shall be three times askt[8] in the church,
    As the law is of our land."

Robin Hood pull'd off the Bishop's coat,
    And put it upon Little John;
"By the faith of my body," then Robin said,   95
    "This cloath doth make thee a man."

When Little John went into the quire,[9]
    The people began for to laugh;
He askt them seven times in the church,
    Least three should not be enough.   100

"Who gives me this maid?" then said Little John;
    Quoth Robin, "That do I!
And he that doth take her from Alan a Dale
    Full dearly he shall her buy."

And thus having ended this merry wedding,   105
    The bride lookt as fresh as a queen,
And so they return'd to the merry greenwood,
    Amongst the leaves so green.

---

8 **askt:** The marriage intentions of a couple had to be announced in the church on three separate occasions.
9 **quire:** choir, part of the church set aside for the singers.

Reading Skills

1. What is the mood of the young man in the third stanza? in the fourth and fifth stanzas? What caused the change? Paraphrase (retell in your own words) the tenth stanza.
2. What agreement is made between Alan a Dale and Robin Hood? How does Robin help Alan?
3. How does Robin overcome the Bishop's objections?

Understanding Literature

1. In several lines in this ballad you can find examples of *internal rhyme*. This is rhyme within the line. "Come listen to *me*, you gallants so *free*" and "As Robin *Hood* in the forest *stood*" are examples of internal rhyme. Find other examples.
2. The author, through his choice of sounds and words, establishes the *mood* he wants the reader to feel. The mood may be a sad one; a thoughtful, pensive one; a gay one. What is the mood of "Robin Hood and Alan a Dale"? Find words which help establish the *mood*.

"Lord Randal" is one of the most famous of all ballads and has existed in different forms in all parts of Europe at various times.

IMPROVING YOUR READING. A major characteristic of ballads is the *refrain*, a verse or phrase that is usually repeated at the end of each stanza. Note here that the wording of the refrain changes near the middle of the ballad. Can you see why?

Lord Randal

"O where ha you been, Lord Randal, my son?
And where ha you been, my handsome young man?"
"I ha been at the greenwood, mother, mak my bed soon,
For I'm wearied wi hunting and fain wad[1] lie down."

"An wha met ye there, Lord Randal, my son?   5
And wha met you there my handsome young man?"
"O I met wi my true-love, mother, mak my bed soon,
For I'm wearied wi huntin an fain wad lie down."

"And what did she give you, Lord Randal, my son?
And what did she give you, my handsome young man?"   10
"Eels fried in a pan, mother, mak my bed soon,
For I'm wearied wi huntin, and fain wad lie down."

"And wha gat your leavins, Lord Randal, my son?
And wha gat your leavins, my handsome young man?"
"My hawks and my hounds, mother, mak my bed soon,   15
For I'm wearied wi hunting and fain wad lie down."

"And what becam of them, Lord Randal, my son?
And what becam of them, my handsome young man?"
"They stretched their legs out an died, mother, mak my bed
     soon,
For I'm wearied wi huntin and fain wad lie down."   20

1 **fain wad:** would gladly.

"O I fear you are poisoned, Lord Randal, my son.
I fear you are poisoned, my handsome young man."
"O yes, I am poisoned, mother, mak my bed soon,
For I'm sick at the heart and I fain wad lie down."

"What d' ye leave to your mother, Lord Randal, my son?   25
What d' ye leave to your mother, my handsome young man?"
"Four and twenty milk kye,[2] mother, mak my bed soon,
For I'm sick at the heart and I fain wad lie down."

"What d' ye leave to your sister, Lord Randal, my son?
What d' ye leave to your sister, my handsome young man?"   30
"My gold and my silver, mother, mak my bed soon,
For I'm sick at the heart, an I fain wad lie down."

"What d' ye leave to your brother, Lord Randal, my son?
What d' ye leave to your brother, my handsome young man?"
"My houses and my lands, mother, mak my bed soon,   35
For I'm sick at the heart, and I fain wad lie down."

"What d' ye leave to your true-love, Lord Randal, my son?
What d' ye leave to your true-love, my handsome young man?"
"I leave her . . . and fire, mother, mak my bed soon,
For I'm sick at the heart and I fain wad lie down."   40

2 kye: cattle.

Understanding Literature

1. What is the situation at the opening of the poem?
2. What questions are asked by the mother? How is each answered?
3. The refrain for about half the poem is "For I'm wearied wi huntin an fain wad lie down." At what point does it shift to "For I'm sick at the heart"? Why is this shift made?
4. How much of the story is told directly by the dialogue? How much is implied, or hinted at? Tell the whole story of the ballad in your own words.

Reading "The Cowboy's Dream"

Cowboy ballads are very popular in the United States. The cowboys' role of watching over the cattle on the vast prairies was an important one—and a very lonesome one. The cattle recognized the voices of the cowboys, and often if a storm was brewing, the cowboy would sing to soothe the restless cattle—and for company.

IMPROVING YOUR READING. Poetry often concerns vast questions. Writing poetry is a sensitive, thoughtful way of probing something difficult to understand. In the ballad "The Cowboy's Dream," the unknown author considers the question of what happens after death. Observe that, like the composers of other ballads, this author seeks an answer in very familiar language— in this case, that of the cowboy. The *refrain*, in this case called the Chorus, can be repeated or sung after each stanza.

The Cowboy's Dream *

Tune: "Bring Back My Bonnie to Me"

When I think of the last great roundup
On the eve of eternity's dawn,
I think of the host of cowboys
That have been with us here and have gone.

Chorus:
    Roll on, roll on,   5
  Roll on, little dogies, roll on, roll on,
    Roll on, roll on,
  Roll on, little dogies, roll on.

I think of those big-hearted fellows,
Who'll divide with you blanket and bread,   10

* Collected, adapted & arranged by John A. & Alan Lomax. Copyright 1934 and renewed 1962. Ludlow Music, Inc., New York, N.Y. Used by permission..

With a piece of stray beef well roasted,
And charge for it never a red.[1]

I wonder if any will greet me,
On the sands of that evergreen shore,
With a hearty "God bless you, old fellow,"   15
That I've met so often before.

And I often look upward and wonder
If the green fields will seem half so fair,
If any the wrong trail have taken
And will fail to be over there.   20

The trail that leads down to perdition[2]
Is paved all the way with good deeds;
But in the great roundup of ages,
Dear boys, this won't answer your needs.

The trail to green pastures, though narrow,   25
Leads straight to the home in the sky,
To the headquarters ranch of the Father
In the land of the sweet by and by.

The Inspector will stand at the gateway,
Where the herd, one and all, must go by,   30
And the roundup by the angels in judgment
Must pass 'neath His all-searching eye.

No maverick or slick[3] will be tallied
In that great book of life in His home,
For he knows all the brands and the earmarks   35
That down through all ages have come.

But, along with the strays and the sleepers,
The tailings[4] must turn from the gate;
No road brand to give them admission.
But that awful sad cry: "Too late!"   40

1 red: red cent.
2 perdition: utter loss of the soul;
loss of final happiness.

3 maverick or slick: unbranded range animals.
4 tailings: inferior ones.

But I trust in that last great roundup
When the Rider shall cut the big herd,
That the cowboy will be represented
In the earmark and brand of the Lord.

To be shipped to that bright, mystic region,   45
Over there in green pastures to lie,
And be led by the crystal still waters
To the home in the sweet by and by.

Reading Skills

1. What is a roundup? What is meant here by "the last great roundup/On the eve of eternity's dawn"?
2. What is meant here by "that evergreen shore"? by "the wrong trail"?
3. A synonym is a word that is similar in meaning to another word. List the various synonyms for God in this poem.
4. What does the line "When the Rider shall cut the big herd" mean?
5. What other title might you give the poem that would make its meaning clear?

Understanding Literature

1. What is the feeling or mood that predominates in this poem? In what way does the mood fit the subject of the poem?
2. In what ways is "The Cowboy's Dream" like the ballads you studied earlier?
3. Find examples of thought expressed in the language of the cowboy. Restate these thoughts in your own words. In this poem why is it effective to use language that is characteristic of the cowboy?

Further Activity

There are a number of people who have made a study of the ballad and its history. John A. Lomax, Alan Lomax, Carl Sandburg, Louise Pound, and Burl Ives are but a few. Prepare a report on some of the collections by these people, including information about the ballads and about the people who have collected them.

Reading "Molly Means"

One of the constant themes of literature has dealt with stories of how people have conquered evil. Sometimes they have killed dragons or fought villains or overcome the tempting devil. This next poem deals with a witch, as do many folk tales.

IMPROVING YOUR READING. This ballad does not have the usual four-line ballad stanza. It is told mostly in iambic meter and it has a refrain. The irregular spellings in the poem come from the sounds; so if you have difficulty, say the word aloud and you will probably know what it means.

Molly Means

Margaret Walker

Old Molly Means was a hag and a witch;
Chile[1] of the devil, the dark, and sitch.[2]
Her heavy hair hung thick in ropes
And her blazing eyes was black as pitch.
Imp at three and wench at 'leben   5
She counted her husbands to the number seben.
   O Molly, Molly, Molly Means
   There goes the ghost of Molly Means.

Some say she was born with a veil on her face
So she could look through unnatchal space   10
Through the future and through the past
And charm a body or an evil place
And every man could well despise
The evil look in her coal black eyes.
   Old Molly, Molly, Molly Means   15
   Dark is the ghost of Molly Means.

And when the tale begun to spread
Of evil and of holy dread:
Her black-hand arts and her evil powers
How she cast her spells and called the dead,   20

1 **chile:** child.
2 **sitch:** such.

The younguns was afraid at night
And the farmers feared their crops would blight.
    Old Molly, Molly, Molly Means
    Cold is the ghost of Molly Means.

Then one dark day she put a spell   25
On a young gal-bride just come to dwell
In the lane just down from Molly's shack
And when her husband come riding back
His wife was barking like a dog
And on all fours like a common hog.   30
    O Molly, Molly, Molly Means
    Where is the ghost of Molly Means?

The neighbors come and they went away
And said she'd die before break of day
But her husband held her in his arms   35
And swore he'd break the wicked charms;
He'd search all up and down the land
And turn the spell on Molly's hand.
    O Molly, Molly, Molly Means
    Sharp is the ghost of Molly Means.   40

So he rode all day and he rode all night
And at the dawn he come in sight
Of a man who said he could move the spell
And cause the awful thing to dwell
On Molly Means, to bark and bleed   45
Till she died at the hands of her evil deed.
    Old Molly, Molly, Molly Means
    This is the ghost of Molly Means.

Sometimes at night through the shadowy trees
She rides along on a winter breeze.   50
You can hear her holler and whine and cry.
Her voice is thin and her moan is high,
And her cackling laugh or her barking cold
Bring terror to the young and old.
    O Molly, Molly, Molly Means   55
    Lean is the ghost of Molly Means.

Understanding Literature

1. What did Molly Means look like? What evil powers did she have?
2. Tell the story in your own words.
3. Read the ballad aloud as a choral reading. Let seven students read a stanza each. The whole class can read the refrains. Make the sound reflect the meaning. After some practice, read the whole poem.

Further Activity

There are a number of people who have made a study of the ballad and its history. John A. Lomax, Alan Lomax, Carl Sandburg, Louise Pound, and Burl Ives are but a few. Prepare a report on some of the collections by these people, including information about the ballads and about the people who have collected them.

Collect some more recent ballads and compare the form and the subject of those ballads to those you have just read.

Narrative Poems

The ballads which you just studied told a story, and so do narrative poems. Narratives differ, however, in that they do not use the ballad stanza of four lines; their stanzas are usually longer. In ballads the writer usually gives the basic facts about the action of the poem without letting the reader know how he feels about it. In narratives the writer often takes a stand of approval or disapproval of the actions in the poem.

Reading "Columbus"

This poem uses several different techniques: it tells much of its story with dialogue, its setting is suggested with very few lines, and it uses a refrain, which is common in old ballads, as well as other forms of repetition. How many forms of repetition can you find?

Columbus

Joaquin Miller

Behind him lay the gray Azores,[1]
   Behind the Gates of Hercules;[2]
Before him not the ghost of shores,
   Before him only shoreless seas.
The good mate said: "Now must we pray,   5
   For lo! the very stars are gone.
Brave Adm'r'l, speak; what shall I say?"
   "Why, say: 'Sail on! sail on! and on!'"

"My men grow mutinous day by day;
   My men grow ghastly wan and weak."   10
The stout mate thought of home; a spray
   Of salt wave washed his swarthy cheek.
"What shall I say, brave Adm'r'l, say,
   If we sight naught but seas at dawn?"
"Why, you shall say at break of day: 15
   'Sail on! sail on! sail on! and on!'"

1 **Azores:** a group of nine islands belonging to Portugal in the Atlantic Ocean.
2 **Gates of Hercules:** Also called the Pillars of Hercules, these two projecting rocks are at the eastern end of the Strait of Gibraltar, a passage which lies between Spain and Africa and connects the Mediterranean Sea and the Atlantic Ocean. The Rock of Gibraltar is the more famous of the two Pillars.

They sailed and sailed, as winds might blow,
   Until at last the blanched[3] mate said:
"Why, now not even God would know
   Should I and all my men fall dead.   20
These very winds forget their way,
   For God from these dread seas is gone.
Now speak, brave Adm'r'l; speak and say——"
   He said: "Sail on! sail on! and on!"

They sailed. They sailed. Then spake the mate: 25
   "This mad sea shows its teeth tonight.
He curls his lip, he lies in wait,
   With lifted teeth, as if to bite!
Brave Adm'r'l, say but one good word;
   What shall we do when hope is gone?"   30
The words leapt as a leaping sword:
   "Sail on! sail on! sail on! and on!"

Then, pale and worn, he kept his deck,
   And peered through darkness. Ah, that night
Of all dark nights! And then a speck—   35
   A light! A light! A light! A light!
It grew, a starlit flag unfurled!
   It grew to be Time's burst of dawn.
He gained a world; he gave that world
   Its grandest lesson: "On! sail on!"   40

3 **blanched:** whitened; paled.

Understanding Literature

1. Who are the speakers in the poem?
2. What are "shoreless seas," as the phrase is used here?
3. Why is the mate "blanched"?
4. How is the sea described? How are dark and light used in the poem?
5. Put the last four lines in your own words.
6. As in some of the old ballads, a refrain is used in "Columbus." Point out examples. What is the "grandest lesson" that part of the repetitive phrases emphasize?
7. Explain the author's use of contrast to show the perseverance and faith of Columbus.

Reading "On the Loss of the Royal George"

In August of 1782 the *Royal George,* an English man-of-war, was undergoing repairs in Portsmouth Harbor, England. Suddenly the ship leaned to one side, filled with water, and sank with everyone aboard. The *Royal George,* the main vessel of Lord Howe's fleet, was commanded by Admiral Kempenfelt, who also lost his life in this tragic event. This poem by William Cowper (kōō' pər) is a tribute to the men, the ship, and England. The carefully chosen words make one feel the tragedy of the ship's sinking.

IMPROVING YOUR READING. Observe the *comparisons* made in this poem: How can a tempest give a shock? How can England have thunder? How can a ship plow?

On the Loss of the *Royal George*

William Cowper

Toll for the brave!
   The brave that are no more!
All sunk beneath the wave,
   Fast by their native shore!

Eight hundred of the brave,   5
   Whose courage well was tried,
Had made the vessel heel,
   And laid her on her side;

A land breeze shook the shrouds,[1]
   And she was overset;   10
Down went the *Royal George,*
   With all her crew complete.

---

1 shrouds: here, ropes leading from a ship's mastheads to give support to the masts. What else does this word suggest?

Toll for the brave!
   Brave Kempenfelt is gone;
His last sea fight is fought;   15
   His work of glory done.

It was not in the battle;
   No tempest gave the shock;
She sprang no fatal leak;
   She ran upon no rock;   20

His sword was in its sheath;
   His fingers held the pen,
When Kempenfelt went down,
   With twice four hundred men.

Weigh[2] the vessel up,   25
   Once dreaded by our foes!
And mingle with our cup
   The tear that England owes.

Her timbers yet are sound,
   And she may float again   30
Full-charged with England's thunder,
   And plow the distant main.

But Kempenfelt is gone;
   His victories are o'er;
And he and his eight hundred   35
   Shall plow the wave no more.

2 **Weigh:** raise; lift.

Understanding Literature

1. Explain the first line, "Toll for the brave!"
2. What caused the *Royal George* to sink?
3. The poem tells of four ways in which the ship was *not* sunk. What are they?
4. Explain the following lines:

   (a) "No tempest gave the shock."
   (b) "And mingle with our cup
        The tear that England owes."
   (c) "Full-charged with England's thunder,
        And plow the distant main."

Reading "The Revenge"

England won her reputation as a powerful nation through her achievements at sea. The ballad which you are about to read tells the story of the English ship *Revenge* and the Spanish fleet. The incident described took place in 1591. "The Revenge, a Ballad of the Fleet" was written by Alfred, Lord Tennyson while he was poet laureate[1] of England. Although this is called a ballad, you will note that it does not use the usual four-line stanza form of the "popular ballads" that you found in the group of ballads at the beginning of this unit. Tennyson calls it a ballad, however, because he is presenting, as most ballads do, one highly dramatic episode.

IMPROVING YOUR READING. *Rhyme* is produced by the repetition of sounds. In this poem there is *end rhyme,* the rhyming of words which are at the end of the line, and there is *internal rhyme,* the rhyming of words which are within a line.

A method of comparison which poets use extensively is known as *simile* (sĭm′ ə lē′). A simile is a comparison of two different objects which are alike in at least one way. In the comparison the words *like* or *as* are used. The second line of this poem, "And a pinnace, like a fluttered bird, came flying from far away," contains a simile. A pinnace, a light sailing vessel, is compared to a bird. The two objects are alike, according to the poet, in that they both have wings which flutter in the wind. If you can see in your imagination the sails of a boat flapping rapidly as the wings of a bird do, you will have fully appreciated the simile. Look for others as you read this poem.

---

1 **poet laureate:** the royal title given to the most distinguished poet in England.

The Revenge

A BALLAD OF THE FLEET

Alfred, Lord Tennyson

At Flores in the Azores Sir Richard Grenville lay,
And a pinnace, like a fluttered bird, came flying from far away:
"Spanish ships of war at sea! we have sighted fifty-three!"
Then sware Lord Thomas Howard: "'Fore God I am no coward;
But I cannot meet them here, for my ships are out of gear,[1]   5
And the half my men are sick. I must fly, but follow quick.
We are six ships of the line; can we fight with fifty-three?"

Then spake Sir Richard Grenville: "I know you are no coward;
You fly them for a moment to fight with them again.
But I've ninety men and more that are lying sick ashore.   10
I should count myself the coward if I left them, my Lord Howard,
To these Inquisition dogs and the devildoms of Spain."

So Lord Howard passed away with five ships of war that day,
Till he melted like a cloud in the silent summer heaven;
But Sir Richard bore in hand all his sick men from the land   15
Very carefully and slow,
Men of Bideford in Devon,
And we laid them on the ballast[2] down below;
For we brought them all aboard,
And they blest him in their pain, that they were not left to Spain,   20
To the thumbscrew and the stake, for the glory of the Lord.

---

1 **out of gear:** not properly rigged.
2 **ballast:** heavy material, such as sand or gravel, used to weight a ship to improve its
steadiness.

He had only a hundred seamen to work the ship and to fight,
And he sailed away from Flores till the Spaniard came in sight,
With his huge sea-castles heaving upon the weather bow.
"Shall we fight or shall we fly?   25
Good Sir Richard, tell us now,
For to fight is but to die!
There 'll be little of us left by the time this sun be set."
And Sir Richard said again: "We be all good English men.
Let us bang these dogs of Seville, the children of the devil,   30
For I never turned my back upon Don[3] or devil yet."

Sir Richard spoke and he laughed, and we roared a hurrah, and so
The little *Revenge* ran on sheer into the heart of the foe,
With her hundred fighters on deck, and her ninety sick below;
For half of their fleet to the right and half to the left were seen,   35
And the little *Revenge* ran on thro' the long sea-lane between.

Thousands of their soldiers looked down from their decks and laughed,
Thousands of their seamen made mock at the mad little craft
Running on and on, till delayed
By their mountain-like *San Philip* that, of fifteen hundred tons,   40
And up-shadowing high above us with her yawning tiers of guns,
Took the breath from our sails, and we stayed.

And while now the great *San Philip* hung above us like a cloud
Whence the thunderbolt will fall
Long and loud,   45
Four galleons drew away
From the Spanish fleet that day,
And two upon the larboard and two upon the starboard lay,
And the battle-thunder broke from them all.

But anon the great *San Philip*, she bethought herself and went,   50
Having that within her womb that had left her ill content;
And the rest they came aboard us, and they fought us hand to hand,
For a dozen times they came with their pikes and musketeers,
And a dozen times we shook 'em off as a dog that shakes his ears
When he leaps from the water to the land.   55

And the sun went down, and the stars came out far over the summer sea,
But never a moment ceased the fight of the one and the fifty-three.
Ship after ship, the whole night long, their high-built galleons came,

3 **Don:** a Spanish gentleman.

Ship after ship, the whole night long, with her battle-thunder and flame;
Ship after ship, the whole night long, drew back with her dead and her shame.   60
For some were sunk and many were shattered, and so could fight us no more—
God of battles, was ever a battle like this in the world before?

For he said, "Fight on! fight on!"
Tho' his vessel was all but a wreck;
And it chanced that, when half of the short summer night was gone,   65
With a grisly wound to be dressed he had left the deck,
But a bullet struck him that was dressing it suddenly dead,
And himself he was wounded again in the side and the head,
And he said, "Fight on! fight on!"

And the night went down, and the sun smiled out far over the summer sea,   70
And the Spanish fleet with broken sides lay round us all in a ring;
But they dared not touch us again, for they feared that we still could sting,
So they watched what the end would be.
And we had not fought them in vain,
But in perilous plight were we,   75
Seeing forty of our poor hundred were slain,
And half of the rest of us maimed for life
In the crash of the cannonades and the desperate strife;
And the sick men down in the hold were most of them stark and cold,
And the pikes were all broken or bent, and the powder was all of it spent;   80
And the masts and the rigging were lying over the side;
But Sir Richard cried in his English pride:
"We have fought such a fight for a day and a night
As may never be fought again!
We have won great glory, my men!   85
And a day less or more
At sea or ashore,
We die—does it matter when?
Sink me the ship, Master Gunner—sink her, split her in twain!
Fall into the hands of God, not into the hands of Spain!"   90

And the gunner said, "Ay, ay," but the seamen made reply:
"We have children, we have wives,
And the Lord hath spared our lives.
We will make the Spaniard promise, if we yield, to let us go;
We shall live to fight again and to strike another blow."   95
And the lion there lay dying, and they yielded to the foe.

And the stately Spanish men to their flagship bore him then,
Where they laid him by the mast, old Sir Richard caught at last,
And they praised him to his face with their courtly foreign grace;
But he rose upon their decks, and he cried: 100
"I have fought for Queen and Faith like a valiant man and true;

I have only done my duty as a man is bound to do.
With a joyful spirit I Sir Richard Grenville die!"
And he fell upon their decks, and he died.

And they stared at the dead that had been so valiant and true,   105
And had holden the power and glory of Spain so cheap
That he dared her with one little ship and his English few;
Was he devil or man? He was devil for aught they knew,
But they sank his body with honor down into the deep,
And they manned the *Revenge* with a swarthier alien crew,   110
And away she sailed with her loss and longed for her own;
When a wind from the lands they had ruined awoke from sleep,
And the water began to heave and the weather to moan,
And or ever that evening ended a great gale blew,

And a wave like the wave that is raised by an earthquake grew,   115
Till it smote on their hulls and their sails and their masts and their flags,
And the whole sea plunged and fell on the shot-shattered navy of Spain,
And the little *Revenge* herself went down by the island crags
To be lost evermore in the main.

Reading Skills

1. For what reason did Lord Thomas Howard flee the Spanish ships? Do you agree with his decision?
2. Why did Sir Richard Grenville stay to fight?
3. What was Grenville's plan of attack? Describe the battle.
4. What was the reaction of the Spanish soldiers and sailors when they saw the small *Revenge?*
5. How did Sir Richard want to end the battle? What did happen to the *Revenge?* What happened to Sir Richard?
6. What comment is the poem making on bravery and patriotism?

Understanding Literature

1. Point out examples of *end rhyme* and *internal rhyme.*
2. What examples of simile can you find in "The Revenge"? Be sure to find examples that compare different objects and use *like* or *as* in the comparison.
3. What is the effect of the repetition used in the ninth stanza?
4. "The Revenge" is called a ballad. In what ways does it differ from the common ballad form? In what ways is it like the ballads you studied earlier?

This poem once again emphasizes the importance of the ocean to the English nation.

IMPROVING YOUR READING. One of the questions you should ask of any poem is: To whom is the poem addressed? The poet here is obviously speaking to mariners of England, but which ones?

Ye Mariners of England

Thomas Campbell

Ye Mariners of England!
That guard our native seas;
Whose flag has braved, a thousand years,
The battle and the breeze!
Your glorious standard launch again   5
To match another foe!
And sweep through the deep,
While the stormy winds do blow;
While the battle rages loud and long,
And the stormy winds do blow.   10

The spirits of your fathers
Shall start from every wave!—
For the deck it was their field of fame,
And Ocean was their grave:
Where Blake[1] and mighty Nelson[2] fell,   15
Your manly hearts shall glow,
As ye sweep through the deep,
While the stormy winds do blow;
While the battle rages loud and long,
And the stormy winds do blow.   20

Britannia[3] needs no bulwark,
No towers along the steep;

1 **Blake:** Robert Blake (1599-1657), an English admiral.
2 **Nelson:** Horatio, Viscount Nelson (1758-1805), an English admiral.
3 **Britannia:** Great Britain and the dominions.

Her march is o'er the mountain-waves,
Her home is on the deep.
With thunders from her native oak,[4]   25
She quells the floods below,—
As they roar on the shore,
When the stormy winds do blow;
When the battle rages loud and long,
And the stormy winds do blow.   30

The meteor flag of England
Shall yet terrific burn;
Till danger's troubled night depart,
And the star of peace return.
Then, then, ye ocean-warriors!   35
Our song and feast shall flow
To the fame of your name,
When the storm has ceased to blow;
When the fiery fight is heard no more,
And the storm has ceased to blow.   40

4 native oak: ships made of oak.

Understanding Literature

1. To which mariners is the poem addressed?
2. In the first stanza what is the speaker asking them to do?
3. In the second stanza what comment is made on "The spirits of your fathers"?
4. How is Britain (Britannia) described in the third stanza?
5. The refrain, the last three lines of the first three stanzas, is different from the last three lines of the last stanza. What change in the situation causes the change in the refrain?
6. The words *stormy* and *storm* are repeated in the refrain. Do they have any meaning beyond that of a literal storm?
7. Re-examine "Columbus," "On the Loss of the *Royal George*," "The Revenge," and "Ye Mariners of England." Compare them with each other in terms of: (*a*) the personal qualities of the naval leaders, (*b*) the relationships between the leaders and their crews, and (*c*) the importance of the situations to the mother country.
8. The literary devices which have been called to your attention in these four poems are personification, simile, and rhyme scheme. In rereading the four poems, what examples of these techniques do you find?

Reading "Dunkirk"

In the spring of 1940 thousands of British and French troops were trapped near Dunkirk, an important seaport on the coast of France. With the help of every type of small seacraft, an air cover by fighter planes, and the discipline of the soldiers, the British government was able to evacuate more than 330,000 men to England. This famous World War II rescue operation is celebrated in the following poem.

Dunkirk

Robert Nathan

Will came back from school that day,
And he had little to say.
But he stood a long time looking down
To where the gray-green Channel water
Slapped at the foot of the little town,   5
And to where his boat, the *Sarah P*,
Bobbed at the tide on an even keel,
With her one old sail, patched at the leech.[1]
Furled like a slattern down at heel.

He stood for a while above the beach,   10
He saw how the wind and current caught her;
He looked a long time out to sea.
There was steady wind, and the sky was pale,
And a haze in the east that looked like smoke.

Will went back to the house to dress.   15
He was halfway through, when his sister Bess
Who was near fourteen, and younger than he
By just two years, came home from play.
She asked him, "Where are you going, Will?"

---

1 leech: edge.

He said, "For a good long sail."   20
"Can I come along?"

                         "No, Bess," he spoke.
"I may be gone for a night and a day."
Bess looked at him.   She kept very still.
She had heard the news of the Flanders rout,
How the English were trapped above Dunkirk,   25
And the fleet had gone to get them out—
But everyone thought that it wouldn't work.
There was too much fear, there was too much doubt.

She looked at him, and he looked at her.
They were English children, born and bred.   30
He frowned her down, but she wouldn't stir.
She shook her proud young head.
"You'll need a crew," she said.

They raised the sail on the *Sarah P,*
Like a penoncel[2] on a young knight's lance,   35
And headed the *Sarah* out to sea,
To bring their soldiers home from France.
There was no command, there was no set plan,
But six hundred boats went out with them
On the gray-green waters, sailing fast,   40
River excursion and fisherman,
Tug and schooner and racing M,
And the little boats came following last.

From every harbor and town they went
Who had sailed their craft in the sun and rain,   45
From the South Downs, from the cliffs of Kent,
From the village street, from the country lane.
There are twenty miles of rolling sea
From coast to coast, by the seagull's flight,
But the tides were fair and the wind was free,   50
And they raised[3] Dunkirk by the fall of night.

They raised Dunkirk with its harbor torn
By the blasted stern and the sunken prow;
They had raced for fun on an English tide,

---

2 **penoncel** (pĕn′ən sĕl′): small flag; streamer.
3 **raised:** sighted.

They were English children bred and born,
And whether they lived, or whether they died,
They raced for England now.

Bess was as white as the *Sarah's* sail,
She set her teeth and smiled at Will.
He held his course for the smoky veil
Where the harbor narrowed thin and long.
The British ships were firing strong.

He took the *Sarah* into his hands,
He drove her in through fire and death
To the wet men waiting on the sands.
He got his load and he got his breath,
And she came about, and the wind fought her,

He shut his eyes and he tried to pray.
He saw his England where she lay,
The wind's green home, the sea's proud daughter,
Still in the moonlight, dreaming deep,
The English cliffs and the English loam—
He had fourteen men to get away.
And the moon was clear, and the night like day
For planes to see where the white sails creep
Over the black water.

He closed his eyes and he prayed for her,
For England's hope and for England's fate;
He prayed to the men who had made her great,
Who had built her land of forest and park,
Who had made the seas an English lake;
He prayed for a fog to bring the dark;
He prayed to get home for England's sake.
And the fog came down on the rolling sea,
And covered the ships with English mist.
And diving planes were baffled and blind.

For Nelson was there in the *Victory*,[4]
With his one good eye, and his sullen twist,
And guns were out on *The Golden Hind*,[5]

---

4 **Nelson** . . . *Victory:* an allusion to Lord Nelson and the ship which he
commanded at Trafalgar in 1805 during the Napoleonic Wars.
5 *The Golden Hind:* ship commanded by Sir Francis Drake, famous 16th-
century English navigator.

Their shot flashed over the *Sarah P,*
He could hear them cheer as he came about.

By burning wharves, by battered slips,
Galleon, frigate, and brigantine,
The old dead Captains fought their ships,
And the great dead Admirals led the line.
It was England's night, it was England's sea.

The fog rolled over the harbor key.
Bess held to the stays,[6] and conned[7] him out.

And all through the dark, while the *Sarah's* wake
Hissed behind him, and vanished in foam,
There at his side sat Francis Drake,
And held him true, and steered him home.

---

6 stays: ropes supporting the mast.   **7 conned:** directed.

Understanding Literature

1. What is the mood of the poem? Which lines help to create this mood?
2. After he picks up his passengers, what does the boy pray for? To whom does he pray?
3. Why does the poet make allusions to Lord Nelson and Sir Francis Drake?
4. Why does Robert Nathan make a sixteen-year-old boy and his sister the main characters in his poem? How are pride of country and patriotism illustrated in this poem?

Reading "How They Brought the Good News from Ghent to Aix"

There is a city in Belgium named Ghent; in Germany about one hundred miles away is a city named Aix-la-Chapelle. But the ride described in "How They Brought the Good News from Ghent to Aix" never took place. Browning wrote the poem when he was at sea and thinking of the pleasure of riding his own horse.

IMPROVING YOUR READING. A poet works on your feelings not only through imagery, but also through *sound*. This poem sounds like a galloping horse. Notice, for example, the spacing of the hard, accented *g*'s in the second line. Where do you find other examples of hard sounds spaced through the lines?

How They Brought the Good News from Ghent to Aix

Robert Browning

I sprang to the stirrup, and Joris, and he;
I galloped, Dirck galloped, we galloped all three;
"Good speed!" cried the watch, as the gate bolts undrew;
"Speed!" echoed the wall to us galloping through;
Behind shut the postern,[1] the lights sank to rest,   5
And into the midnight we galloped abreast.

Not a word to each other; we kept the great pace
Neck by neck, stride by stride, never changing our place;
I turned in my saddle and made its girths tight,
Then shortened each stirrup, and set the pique[2] right,   10
Rebuckled the cheek strap, chained slacker the bit,
Nor galloped less steadily Roland a whit.

'T was moonset at starting; but while we drew near
Lokeren, the cocks crew and twilight dawned clear·
At Boom, a great yellow star came out to see;   15

---

1 postern: gate.
2 pique (pēk): apparently something peaked on the saddle, such as the pommel.

At Düffeld, 't was morning as plain as could be;
And from Mecheln church steeple we heard the half-chime,
So Joris broke silence with, "Yet there is time!"

At Aershot, up leaped of a sudden the sun,
And against him the cattle stood black every one,   20
To stare through the mist at us galloping past,
And I saw my stout galloper Roland at last,
With resolute shoulders, each butting away
The haze, as some bluff river headland its spray:

And his low head and crest, just one sharp ear bent back   25
For my voice, and the other pricked out on his track;
And one eye's black intelligence,—ever that glance
O'er its white edge at me, his own master, askance!
And the thick heavy spume-flakes which aye and anon
His fierce lips shook upwards in galloping on.   30

By Hasselt, Dirck groaned; and cried Joris, "Stay spur!
Your Roos galloped bravely, the fault 's not in her,
We 'll remember at Aix"—for one heard the quick wheeze
Of her chest, saw the stretched neck and staggering knees,
And sunk tail, and horrible heave of the flank,   35
As down on her haunches she shuddered and sank.

So, we were left galloping, Joris and I,
Past Looz and past Tongres, no cloud in the sky;
The broad sun above laughed a pitiless laugh,
'Neath our feet broke the brittle bright stubble like chaff;[3]   40
Till over by Dalhem a dome-spire sprang white,
And "Gallop," gasped Joris, "for Aix is in sight!"

"How they'll greet us!"—and all in a moment his roan
Rolled neck and croup over, lay dead as a stone;
And there was my Roland to bear the whole weight   45
Of the news which alone could save Aix from her fate,
With his nostrils like pits full of blood to the brim,
And with circles of red for his eye-sockets' rim.

---

[3] **chaff:** husks of grains separated from seed by threshing.

Then I cast loose my buffcoat, each holster let fall,
Shook off both my jack boots, let go belt and all,   50
Stood up in the stirrup, leaned, patted his ear,
Called my Roland his pet name, my horse without peer;[4]
Clapped my hands, laughed and sang, any noise, bad or good,
Till at length into Aix Roland galloped and stood.

And all I remember is—friends flocking round   55
As I sat with his head 'twixt my knees on the ground;
And no voice but was praising this Roland of mine,
As I poured down his throat our last measure of wine,
Which (the burgesses voted by common consent)
Was no more than his due who brought good news from Ghent.   60

4 **peer:** equal.

Understanding Literature

1. How does Browning show the passing of time and the progress of the journey?
2. In what ways does the third rider help his horse, Roland, over the final part of the journey to Aix?
3. Compare the sound of the first stanza with that of the last. How does the sound fit the sense?
4. Paraphrase the following:

   (*a*) "At Aershot, up leaped of a sudden the sun,
   And against him the cattle stood black every one."

   (*b*) "And there was my Roland to bear the whole weight
   Of the news which alone could save Aix from her fate."

5. Why is it not important to your enjoyment of the poem to know what the "good news" is?

This poem is a narrative of the lives of a people. Its form is
different from the others you have read. The stanzas look like
prose paragraphs, but there are strong rhythms based on repetitions of sound patterns: "Their dirges and their ditties and their
blues and jubilees." As you read, listen for other repeating patterns.

For My People

Margaret Walker

For my people everywhere singing their slave songs repeatedly: their dirges and their ditties and their blues and
jubilees, praying their prayers nightly to an unknown
god, bending their knees humbly to an unseen power;

For my people lending their strength to the years, to the   5
gone years and the now years and the maybe years,
washing ironing cooking scrubbing sewing mending
hoeing plowing digging planting pruning patching dragging along never gaining never reaping never knowing
and never understanding;   10

For my playmates in the clay and dust and sand of Alabama backyards playing baptizing and preaching and
doctor and jail and soldier and school and mama and
cooking and playhouse and concert and store and hair
and Miss Choomby and company;   15

For the cramped bewildered years we went to school to
learn to know the reasons why and the answers to and
the people who and the places where and the days when,
in memory of the bitter hours when we discovered we
were black and poor and small and different and nobody   20
cared and nobody wondered and nobody understood;

For the boys and girls who grew in spite of these things
to be man and woman, to laugh and dance and sing and
play and drink their wine and religion and success, to
marry their playmates and bear children and then die of
consumption and anemia and lynching;

For my people thronging 47th Street in Chicago and
Lenox Avenue in New York and Rampart Street in New
Orleans, lost disinherited dispossessed and happy people
filling the cabarets and taverns and other people's pockets
needing bread and shoes and milk and land and money
and something—something all our own;

For my people walking blindly spreading joy, losing time
being lazy, sleeping when hungry, shouting when burdened, drinking when hopeless, tied and shackled and
tangled among ourselves by the unseen creatures who
tower over us omnisciently and laugh;

For my people blundering and groping and floundering in
the dark of churches and schools and clubs and societies,
associations and councils and committees and conventions,
distressed and disturbed and deceived and devoured by
money-hungry glory-craving leeches, preyed on by facile[1]
force of state and fad and novelty, by false prophet and
holy believer;

For my people standing staring trying to fashion a better
way from confusion, from hypocrisy and misunderstand-
ing, trying to fashion a world that will hold all the people,
all the faces, all the adams and eves and their countless
generations;

Let a new earth rise. Let another world be born. Let a
bloody peace be written in the sky. Let a second generation full of courage issue forth; let a people loving freedom come to growth. Let a beauty full of healing and
strength of final clenching be the pulsing in our spirits
and our blood. Let the martial songs be written, let the
dirges[2] disappear. Let a race of men now rise and take
control.

1 **facile** (fas′ l): acting with ease.
2 **dirge** (derj): funeral song.

Understanding Literature

1. Each of the stanzas is on a different topic. Give a title to each stanza that indicates what each is about. What details are included in each stanza? What is the author's purpose in selecting those details?
2. Judging by this poem, what kinds of lives have Negroes led? What attitude is the author taking toward those lives?
3. What kind of life is the poet asking for in the last stanza?

Lyric Poetry

The type of poetry most frequently used by poets is the *lyric*. The word itself comes from the same root word as *lyre*, a stringed musical instrument. Lyrics were originally a kind of song accompanied by the lyre. Today they are frequently brief, melodic poems in which the writer is expressing an emotion aroused by some scene or occasion. They are usually very personal poems about ideas which have always interested people: the beauty of nature, love and friendship, patriotism, the effects of passing time, and death. They enable the reader to look at well-known things in a new way.

Reading "Hokku Poems"

The simplest kind of lyric poem is the *Haiku* (less frequently called *Hokku,* as Richard Wright names his). The term refers to a three-line poem describing a single image. The trick in writing one is to follow the scheme of five syllables in the first line, seven in the second line, and five in the third. The image used in the Haiku may appeal to one or more of our senses: seeing, hearing, touching, tasting, or smelling.

Remember, as you read, that each three lines is a separate poem.

Hokku Poems

Richard Wright

I am nobody
A red sinking autumn sun
Took my name away

Make up your mind snail!
You are half inside your house
And halfway out!

In the falling snow
A laughing boy holds out his palms
Until they are white

Keep straight down this block
Then turn right where you will find
A peach tree blooming

With a twitching nose
A dog reads a telegram
On a wet tree trunk

The spring lingers on
In the scent of a damp log
Rotting in the sun

Whose town did you leave
O wild and drowning spring rain
And where do you go?

The crow flew so fast
That he left his lonely caw
Behind in the fields

Understanding Literature

1. Supply a suitable title for each of the poems. For example, the first might be called *Beauty*. "Took my name away" could mean something like "took my breath away."
2. Find the appeals to the senses in each of the poems.
3. Try writing a three-line poem of your own. Remember to use five, seven, then five syllables per line. If you need an idea, begin with the first line of any one of Wright's poems.

Reading "Hokku Poem"

Sometimes reading a poem is like seeing a painting.

Hokku Poem

Lewis Alexander

The wind is a comb
Fixing clouds about the moon
In a strange coiffure.*

* **coiffure:** a style of arranging hair.

Understanding Literature

1. What does the writer see?

Reading "I like to see it lap the Miles"

As you read "I like to see it lap the Miles," notice how quickly you know what "it" is even though "it" is never named.

"I like to see it lap the Miles"

Emily Dickinson

I like to see it lap the Miles—
And lick the Valleys up—
And stop to feed itself at Tanks—
And then—prodigious[1] step

Around a Pile of Mountains,   5
And, supercilious[2] peer
In Shanties—by the sides of Roads—
And then a Quarry pare

To fit its Ribs
And crawl between   10
Complaining all the while
In horrid—hooting stanza—
Then chase itself down Hill—

And neigh like Boanerges[3]
Then—punctual as a Star,   15
Stop—docile and omnipotent
At its own stable door—

---

1 **prodigious** (prə dĭj′əs): marvelous; out of the course of nature.
2 **supercilious** (soo′pər sĭl′ī əs): haughty; proud.
3 **Boanerges** (bō′ə nûr′jēz): literally, sons of thunder; here, a term used for any loud or noisy speaker or orator.

Understanding Literature

1. What is the "it" in this poem?
2. After consulting the glossary for the meanings of any words that you do not know, explain what is happening in the poem.
3. What pictures or images should you see in your imagination as you read each line of this poem?
4. In this poem does Emily Dickinson feel fondness or repulsion for her subject? How do you know?

Reading "Aunt Jane Allen"

In this poem, the speaker is describing something in a new way. As you read, notice the unusual ways he describes Aunt Jane Allen. Why does he say that she "has driven her chariot to Heaven"?

Aunt Jane Allen

Fenton Johnson

State Street is lonely today. Aunt Jane Allen has driven
    her chariot to Heaven.
I remember how she hobbled along, a little woman,
    parched of skin, brown as the leather of a satchel
    and with eyes that scanned eighty years of life.   5
Have those who bore her dust to the last resting place
    buried with her the basket of aprons she went up
    and down State Street trying to sell?
Have those who bore her dust to the last resting place
    buried with her the gentle word *Son* that she gave   10
    to each of the seed of Ethiopia?

Understanding Literature

1. In figurative language, the poet tells us what has happened to Aunt Jane Allen. What has happened to her?
2. Who are the people whom Aunt Jane Allen called *Son*?
3. The last two stanzas, lines 6–11, are in the form of questions. But what do they tell us about Aunt Jane Allen?

Reading "Elysium is as far as to"

Allusion is used extensively in all literature. An allusion is a reference to a person or place which the author assumes the reader will recognize. By alluding to this person or place, the authors enrich their writing without giving wordy explanations. If Juno were alluded to, you might recall from your study of Greek mythology that she was the queen of the gods, that she was the wife of Jupiter, and that she had a jealous nature. This knowledge would certainly enrich your reading.

In the following poem there is an allusion to Elysium which, according to Greek mythology, is the place where favored heroes are made immortal. The word now suggests a paradise. Understanding this word should make Emily Dickinson's poem much clearer to you.

"Elysium is as far as to"

Emily Dickinson

Elysium is as far as to
The very nearest Room
If in that Room a Friend await
Felicity[1] or Doom—

What fortitude the Soul contains,
That it can so endure
The accent of a coming Foot—
The opening of a Door—

1 **Felicity:** happiness.

Understanding Literature

1. Paraphrase the first stanza. Why is the "very nearest Room" Elysium, or a place of paradise? Why does Emily Dickinson use the word *Elysium* instead of the word *paradise*? What does her use of the word add to the poem?
2. Paraphrase the second stanza. What does *fortitude* mean? Why is fortitude needed to endure the "accent of a coming Foot"?
3. To whom do you think the poem is addressed? Under what circumstances might the poem have been written?

Robert Louis Stevenson is probably known to you through his books *Treasure Island* and *A Child's Garden of Verses*. "The Wind" is a short poem written in a light, easy style—but it does make one wonder and pause to think.

As noted before, a poet often uses *imagery* as a way of conveying his idea. An image is any appeal to the senses: seeing, touching, hearing, tasting, and smelling. Stevenson gives us several images in this poem which appeal to some of these senses.

The Wind

Robert Louis Stevenson

I saw you toss the kites high
And blow the birds about the sky;
And all around I heard you pass,
Like ladies' skirts across the grass—
    O wind, a-blowing all day long,   5
    O wind, that sings so loud a song!

I saw the different things you did,
But always you yourself you hid.
I felt you push, I heard you call,
I could not see yourself at all—   10
    O wind, a-blowing all day long,
    O wind, that sings so loud a song!

O you that are so strong and cold,
O blower, are you young or old?
Are you a beast of field and tree,   15
Or just a stronger child than me?
    O wind, a-blowing all day long,
    O wind, that sings so loud a song!

Understanding Literature

1. What evidence does the poet give to make the reader know that there is a wind even if it cannot be seen?
2. What questions about the wind go unanswered?
3. In what ways is wind personified in the poem?
4. To what senses do the images in this poem appeal?

The following poem is from *The Tempest*, a play by William Shakespeare. Ariel, a spirit, is describing a drowned man, but the sound of the lines is more important here than the subject.

IMPROVING YOUR READING. Other kinds of sound effects used by poets are *alliteration* and *assonance*. Alliteration is the repetition of the same sound at the beginning of several words in a line. In the first line of the following poem, "Full fathom five thy father lies," the repeated *f* sound is an example of alliteration.

In the second line of the poem, "Of his bones are coral made," the poet repeats the *o* sound. This repetition of vowel sounds is called *assonance*. The sounds are often not as exact a repetition as they would be in rhymed words, and they are repeated within a line. For example, the words *bones* and *thrones* (not in this poem) are exact repetitions of the *ones* sound—they rhyme. *Five, thy,* and *lies,* on the other hand, are connected only by the repetition of the sound of the vowel *i*—an example of assonance. Read the poem aloud and listen to the sound.

Ariel's Song

William Shakespeare

Full fathom five thy father lies;
   Of his bones are coral made;
Those are pearls that were his eyes;
   Nothing of him that doth fade
But doth suffer a sea change
Into something rich and strange.
Sea nymphs hourly ring his knell:
                   Burden.[1] Ding-dong.
Hark! now I hear them—Ding-dong bell.

---

1 **Burden:** refrain.

Most people take for granted much of the beauty of nature which is theirs to enjoy merely by recognizing it. Frequently it is the poet who brings the wonders of nature to our attention.

IMPROVING YOUR READING. Often a poem is based largely on one major image—here, a field of daffodils. How many appeals to your five senses can you find in Wordsworth's imagery?

I Wandered Lonely as a Cloud

William Wordsworth

I wandered lonely as a cloud
That floats on high o'er vales and hills,
When all at once I saw a crowd,
A host, of golden daffodils;
Beside the lake, beneath the trees,   5
Fluttering and dancing in the breeze.

Continuous as the stars that shine
And twinkle on the milky way,
They stretched in never-ending line
Along the margin of a bay;   10
Ten thousand saw I at a glance,
Tossing their heads in sprightly dance.

The waves beside them danced; but they
Outdid the sparkling waves in glee;
A poet could not but be gay,   15
In such a jocund¹company;
I gazed—and gazed—but little thought
What wealth the show to me had brought:

---

1 **jocund:** merry.

For oft, when on my couch I lie
In vacant or in pensive mood,   20
They flash upon that inward eye
Which is the bliss of solitude;
And then my heart with pleasure fills,
And dances with the daffodils.

Understanding Literature

1. What do you *see* as you read the poem? Describe the scene in your own words. Do you find appeals to other senses: touch, smell, or hearing?
2. To what things does Wordsworth compare the daffodils?
3. Which words seem to suggest how the poet feels about the scene?
4. How is the last stanza related to the first three? What is a vacant or pensive mood? What is the "inward eye"? Why is it the "bliss of solitude"?

Reading "Rural Dumpheap"

This poem also tries to bring the wonders of nature to our attention and uses imagery to do so. But the tone is very different from that of "I Wandered Lonely as a Cloud."

Rural Dumpheap*

Melville Cane

This rusty mound of cans,
This scatter of tires and pans,
This litter of mattresses and twisted springs,
This rotting refuse, these abandoned things
Malodorously[1] flung,—this impudent pile   5
That dares to choke the current, to defile
The innocent season,—all are man's.

Man's inhumanity to sod
Makes countless snowdrops mourn,
And every gentle seed that's born   10
Gives battle for a dishonored god.

Within the heap and darkly, heaves
The growing mutiny of leaves,
While down the valley bird to bird
Relays the rallying word,   15
And courage calls on every breeze
To armies of anemones,[2]
And triumph scales the parapet,[3]
A host of violet.

O man, where is thy victory?   20
Despite this blight of tins,
The fern persists and cleaves and wins,
And, gladly, spring begins.

1 **Malodorously:** causing an offensive odor.   3 **parapet:** protective wall.
2 **anemones** (ə něm′ə nēz′): types of flowers.

Understanding Literature

1. What is the setting of the first stanza? What is the "innocent season"?
2. Paraphrase the second stanza. What does "sod" mean?
3. In the third stanza how does the poet use the imagery of a battle? What is fighting what?
4. In the last stanza how does "man" lose the battle?
5. To whom is this poem addressed? Why?

* From AND PASTURES NEW, copyright, 1956, by Melville Cane. Reprinted by permission of Harcourt Brace Jovanovich, Inc.

In this poem the author suggests some images and then makes a statement on what they mean.

IMPROVING YOUR READING. Your understanding of poetry will be enlarged if you determine as soon as possible the poem's *mood*. Does the poet want you to feel sad? Is the poem written in a light, gay vein? Is the subject being ridiculed? Is the poet serious about the topic? Although the following poem may seem to you to be very elementary, you will find it interesting to compare the mood of "Little Boy Blue" with that of the very different poem which follows it.

Little Boy Blue

Eugene Field

The little toy dog is covered with dust,
  But sturdy and stanch he stands;
And the little toy soldier is red with rust,
  And the musket molds in his hands.

Time was when the little toy dog was new,   5
  And the soldier was passing fair;
And that was the time when our Little Boy Blue
  Kissed them and put them there.

"Now, don't you go till I come," he said,
  "And don't you make any noise!"   10
So, toddling off to his trundle bed,
  He dreamt of the pretty toys;
And, as he was dreaming, an angel song
  Awakened our Little Boy Blue—
Oh! the years are many, the years are long,   15
  But the little toy friends are true!

Aye, faithful to Little Boy Blue they stand,
    Each in the same old place—
Awaiting the touch of a little hand,
    The smile of a little face;   20

And they wonder, as waiting the long years through
    In the dust of that little chair,
What has become of our Little Boy Blue,
    Since he kissed them and put them there.

Understanding Literature

1. What is the setting of the poem?
2. The toys "wonder" what has happened to Little Boy Blue. Point out the lines which tell the reader the answer to this.
3. What other human qualities are the toys given?
4. Point out the lines which show that time has passed.
5. What examples of alliteration do you find?
6. What is the mood of the poem?

Reading "Song"

Death is an everyday occurrence, but it is something no one truly understands. In "Little Boy Blue" by Eugene Field, death is presented in an unusual way; it is only suggested by the toys left in the boy's room. This is a sentimental presentation and one in which the word *death* is not even mentioned. In the next poem the author presents her thoughts on death in a very different way.

IMPROVING YOUR READING. In all types of literature the reader should determine the *point of view* from which the writing is done. The material may be presented by a character in the selection itself: this is the "I," or first person point of view. Or the material may be presented from the point of view of an outsider looking on and reporting events and thoughts. The material may also be presented from the author's point of view and may indicate his or her own thoughts and feelings. When the author tells the story and is free to expose the characters' ideas and opinions, to be in several different places at once, and to comment freely on characters' actions, the result, of course, is very different from that of a story which is written from the limited point of view of one of the characters in the story. Determining the point of view, being aware of the speaker in a poem or story, will aid you in a more complete understanding of the selection.

Song

Christina Rossetti

When I am dead, my dearest,
　　Sing no sad songs for me;
Plant thou no roses at my head,
　　Nor shady cypress tree:
Be the green grass above me　　　　　　　5
　　With showers and dewdrops wet:
And if thou wilt, remember,
　　And if thou wilt, forget.

I shall not see the shadows,
　　I shall not feel the rain;　　　　　　　10
I shall not hear the nightingale
　　Sing on as if in pain:
And dreaming through the twilight
　　That doth not rise nor set,
Haply[1] I may remember,　　　　　　　15
　　And haply may forget.

1 **Haply:** by chance.

Understanding Literature

1. What is the attitude of "I" in this poem toward death? Compare this attitude with that of the writer of "Little Boy Blue."
2. Who is speaking in this poem? To whom?
3. What is the meaning of line 2?
4. In lines 7 and 8 what should the person addressed "remember" and "forget"?
5. What is meant by "twilight" in the second stanza? Why does it "not rise nor set"?
6. What is the difference in mood between the first stanza and the second? How are the images in each different?

The following poem also speaks of death, but the *mood* of the poem is very different from that of the preceding poem. Claude McKay was addressing Blacks who might be killed in racial clashes in the cities. When Winston Churchill spoke to the American Congress just before our entrance into World War II, he concluded by quoting this poem.

If We Must Die

Claude McKay

If we must die—let it not be like hogs
Hunted and penned in an inglorious spot,
While round us bark the mad and hungry dogs,
Making their mock at our accursed lot.
If we must die—oh, let us nobly die,   5
So that our precious blood may not be shed
In vain; then even the monsters we defy
Shall be constrained to honor us though dead!
Oh, Kinsmen! We must meet the common foe;
Though far outnumbered, let us show us brave,   10
And for their thousand blows deal one deathblow!
What though before us lies the open grave?
Like men we'll face the murderous, cowardly pack,
Pressed to the wall, dying, but fighting back!

Understanding Literature

1. What kind of death does Claude McKay describe?
2. What contrast is made between the first four lines and the second four lines?
3. In the third line, the poet compares the enemy to dogs. What other words in the poem remind you of dogs?
4. How does the poet describe the enemy? What does the poet ask his people to do?
5. Do you think Claude McKay and Winston Churchill felt the same way about death?

This poem uses *personification,* the poetic device of giving animals, objects, or qualities the characteristics of a human being.

City: San Francisco

Langston Hughes

In the morning the city
Spreads its wings
Making a song
In stone that sings.

In the evening the city
Goes to bed
Hanging lights
About its head.

Understanding Literature

1. In what ways is the city in the morning spreading its wings? How can a city make a song in stone?
2. What picture do you get of the city in the second stanza? What is meant here by the word "head"?
3. San Francisco is a city of many hills. Does this fact make any difference in your reading of the poem? From what point might the poet be looking at the scene, from the top or bottom of a hill?
4. Judging by his choice of words in this poem, what is the author's feeling toward the city?
5. In which of the two stanzas is there an example of personification? Why is the other stanza *not* personification?

Metaphors

THE THREE LYRICAL poems which follow do not have a common subject, but they are connected in another way. Each uses a figure of speech called a *metaphor*. You have already learned that *similes* are comparisons of unlike objects and always use the words *like* or *as*. In a simile the author states directly that one thing is like another, as "My luve is like a red, red rose." In a metaphor, however, the comparison is more subtle; it is *implied* rather than stated directly. You probably use many metaphors in your daily speech, but they are so worn with use that you hardly notice them. If you say, for example, that you are boiling with anger, you are comparing the agitation and nervousness you experience when angry to the rapid bubbling of boiling water. Or when you say that an idea dawned on you, you are implying that you were able to see and understand things more clearly in much the same way that the dawn of a new day enables you to see things clearly again.

The following lines from the play *As You Like It* by William Shakespeare contain an example of poetic metaphor. Can you see what metaphor Shakespeare has used?

> All the world's a stage,
> And all the men and women merely players.
> They have their exits and their entrances,
> And one man in his time plays many parts. . . .

Shakespeare has compared the world to a stage, and people to the actors in the play on this stage. These things are similar in that men and women come to the earth when they are born and leave it when they die—in the same way that actors enter and leave the stage when their parts begin and end. And, as an actor plays many different roles in his lifetime, so does a man play different roles in his lifetime, of infant, schoolboy, and adult. Why does the poet use a metaphor here at all? Because he wants you to look at life in a new way: as a play in which every man and woman has his special part.

As you read each of the three short poems which follow, ask yourself: How are the objects similar? What effect does the poet's comparison have on the poem?

Rain

Frank Marshall Davis

Today the rain
is an aged man
a gray old man
a curious old man
in a music store   5

Today houses
are strings of a harp
soprano harp strings
bass harp strings
in a music store   10

The ancient man
strums the harp
with thin long fingers
attentively picking
a weary jingle   15
a soft jazzy jangle
then dodders away
before the boss comes 'round. . . .

Understanding Literature

1. How is the rain like a man in a music store? How are the houses like the strings of a harp?
2. What is the mood of the poem? What words suggest the mood? What sounds are suggested in the poem?
3. When the man "dodders away," what idea is being stated about the rain?
4. What is meant by the last line?

Further Activity

Try writing a similar poem about a very heavy rain with a high wind. If you want to compare the storm to a man, what kind of man will you choose? What else could you compare the storm to? In writing keep fairly close to the same length lines and to the three stanzas.

He Wishes for the Cloths of Heaven

William Butler Yeats

Had I the heavens' embroidered cloths,
Enwrought[1] with golden and silver light,
The blue and the dim and the dark cloths
Of night and light and the half light,
I would spread the cloths under your feet:
But I, being poor, have only my dreams;
I have spread my dreams under your feet;
Tread softly because you tread on my dreams.

1 **Enwrought:** ornamented; fashioned.

Understanding Literature

1. To whom might the poem be addressed?
2. What is the speaker offering to this person?
3. A metaphor is used in the first line. What things are being compared in the phrase "the heavens' embroidered cloths"? How can they be "Enwrought with golden and silver light"?
4. The speaker's dreams are used metaphorically in the last two lines. Explain the metaphor.

The Coin

Sara Teasdale

Into my heart's treasury
I slipped a coin
That time cannot take
Nor a thief purloin,[1]—
Oh, better than the minting
Of a gold-crowned king
Is the safe-kept memory
Of a lovely thing.

1 **purloin:** steal.

Understanding Literature

1. Paraphrase, or tell in your own words, what this short poem is about.
2. There is a metaphor in the first two lines. What objects are being compared? How are these objects alike?

Reading "Leaves"

"Leaves," a more complicated poem than those you have read thus far, uses the techniques of simile and metaphor that you have seen in other poems. The metaphor in this poem, however, is an *extended metaphor*. This type of metaphor is not contained within one or two lines but extends for several lines or, as in this case, for the entire length of the poem.

Leaves

Countee Cullen

One, two, and three,
Dead leaves drift from a tree.

Yesterday they loved
Wind and rain, the brush
Of wings   5
Soft and clean, that moved
Through them beyond the crush
Of things.
Yesterday they loved.

Yesterday they sang   10
Silver symphonies,
Raised high
Holy chants that rang
Leaf-wise through their trees;
As I,   15
Yesterday they sang.

Unremembered now,
They will soon lie warm
With snow;
They could grace a bough   20
Once, and love and charm,
Although
Unremembered now.

Trees so soon forget
Little leaves they had   25
Before,
Knowing spring will let
   Them wake, vernal* clad
With more;
Trees so soon forget.   30

Man dreams that he
Is more than a leaf on a tree.
   * **vernal:** of spring, or youth.

Understanding Literature

1. What human characteristics are given to the leaves?
2. How is a human life like that of the tree? of the leaves?
3. What is the meaning, in your own words, of the last two lines?

Reading "Oh, when I was in love with you"

The next group of poems deals with love and friendship, which
are also common subjects for lyric poetry.

"Oh, when I was in love with you"

A. E. Housman

Oh, when I was in love with you,
   Then I was clean and brave,
And miles around the wonder grew
   How well did I behave.

And now the fancy passes by,
   And nothing will remain,
And miles around they'll say that I
   Am quite myself again.

Understanding Literature

1. Who is the speaker in the poem?
2. In the first stanza how does the speaker behave? Why?
3. In the second stanza how does the speaker behave? Why?

In this poem the author uses one comparison after another to express his love (luve).

A Red, Red Rose

Robert Burns

O, my luve is like a red, red rose,
    That 's newly sprung in June.
O, my luve is like the melodie,
    That 's sweetly played in tune.

As fair art thou, my bonie lass,   5
    So deep in luve am I,
And I will luve thee still, my dear,
    Till a' the seas gang dry.

Till a' the seas gang dry, my dear,
    And the rocks melt wi' the sun!   10
And I will luve thee still, my dear,
    While the sands o' life shall run.

And fare thee weel, my only luve,
    And fare thee weel a while!
And I will come again, my luve,   15
    Tho' it were ten thousand mile!

Understanding Literature

1. What comparisons does the poet make to express his love? How does he exaggerate?
2. Paraphrase the last stanza.
3. Does the expression "my luve" refer to the person with whom the speaker is in love, or does it mean his love for that person?

Love is expressed in many ways. In this poem, Harlem and the sweet brown girl are both part of the love that the poet feels.

IMPROVING YOUR READING. Many poems have a pattern or rhyme scheme. Very often the repetition of a word or phrase helps establish a pattern. In "Juke Box Love Song," notice the repetition of "Take" at the beginning of the lines. Then as you read the poem aloud, find the end words that rhyme or set a pattern. Notice particularly the *personification* of the different aspects of Harlem. The poet expresses what he feels and knows about Harlem.

Juke Box Love Song

Langston Hughes

I could take the Harlem night
and wrap around you,
Take the neon lights and make a crown,
Take the Lenox Avenue buses,
Taxis, subways,   5
And for your love song tone their rumble down.
Take Harlem's heartbeat,
Make a drumbeat,
Put it on a record, let it whirl,
And while we listen to it play,   10
Dance with you till day—
Dance with you, my sweet brown Harlem girl.

Understanding Literature

1. Discuss the pattern or rhyme scheme of the poem.
2. What examples of personification do you find in the poem?
3. Remembering that images appeal to one of the five senses, what examples of imagery do you find in the poem? What senses do they appeal to?

The next two poems describe another kind of love—love of the sea.

The Sea Gypsy

Richard Hovey

I am fevered with the sunset,
I am fretful with the bay,
For the wander-thirst is on me
And my soul is in Cathay.[1]

There 's a schooner in the offing,   5
With her topsails shot with fire,
And my heart has gone aboard her
For the Islands of Desire.

I must forth again tomorrow!
With the sunset I must be   10
Hull down on the trail of rapture
In the wonder of the sea.

1 **Cathay:** China.

Understanding Literature

1. Why is the speaker "fevered" and "fretful"?
2. Explain why the speaker's "soul is in Cathay."
3. How can the schooner's topsails be "shot with fire"?
4. What are the "Islands of Desire"?
5. How can the speaker be "Hull down on the trail of rapture"?

Another recurring theme of poetry is love of country. The two following poems express this idea.

My Native Land

Sir Walter Scott

Breathes there the man, with soul so dead,
Who never to himself hath said,
   This is my own, my native land?
Whose heart hath ne'er within him burned,
As home his footsteps he hath turned   5
   From wandering on a foreign strand?[1]
If such there breathe, go, mark him well;
For him no minstrel raptures swell;
High though his titles, proud his name,
Boundless his wealth as wish can claim,—   10
Despite those titles, power, and pelf,[2]
The wretch, concentered all in self,
Living, shall forfeit fair renown,
And, doubly dying, shall go down
To the vile dust from whence he sprung,   15
Unwept, unhonored, and unsung.

1 **strand:** shore.
2 **pelf:** riches.

Understanding Literature

1. Why would a traveler have a greater appreciation for his or her native land after being away?
2. What things cannot be a substitute for a native land?
3. What is meant by "doubly dying"?
4. Why would someone without a native land be "Unwept, unhonored, and unsung"?
5. Where in this poem do you find examples of alliteration and of inverted word order?

These lines are a short excerpt from *The Tragedy of King Richard the Second,* a play by William Shakespeare. John of Gaunt, an uncle to King Richard, shows his love of England in these words spoken shortly before his death.

IMPROVING YOUR READING. This passage consists of a series of metaphors. To what different objects is England compared?

"This royal throne of kings"

William Shakespeare

This royal throne of kings, this sceptered isle,
This earth of majesty, this seat of Mars,
This other Eden, demi-paradise,
This fortress built by Nature for herself
Against infection and the hand of war,   5
This happy breed of men, this little world,
This precious stone set in the silver sea,
Which serves it in the office of a wall,
Or as a moat defensive to a house,
Against the envy of less happier lands;   10
This blessed plot, this earth, this realm, this England. . . .

Understanding Literature

1. Explain the meaning of the phrase "this sceptered isle."
2. What is suggested in the comparison of England to an "earth of majesty"?
3. In line 2 there is an allusion to Mars. Explain the allusion. Why is England called the "seat of Mars"?
4. Explain lines 4 and 5.
5. These eleven lines convey an impression of great pride in England. Point out words which help to convey this impression.
6. The last line is an especially effective one. Why?

Our country has grown strong because of people of varied backgrounds working together. In "I, Too," the poet tells of the pride he feels and of the struggle he has faced.

I, Too

Langston Hughes

I, too, sing America.

I am the darker brother.
They send me to eat in the kitchen
When company comes,
But I laugh,   5
And eat well,
And grow strong.

Tomorrow,
I'll be at the table
When company comes.   10
Nobody'll dare
Say to me,
"Eat in the kitchen,"
Then.

Besides,   15
They'll see how beautiful I am
And be ashamed—

I, too, am America.

Understanding Literature

1. Who is the "I" of the poem?
2. Does the line "They send me to eat in the kitchen" mean more than it literally says? Explain.
3. Explain "And grow strong" in line 7.
4. Who will "be ashamed"? Why?
5. What two lines are almost identical? What effect does the repetition and position of these phrases have?

Reading "Tommy"

This poem protests the way that ordinary soldiers are treated in time of peace. The English call their regular army privates Tommy Atkins, as Americans in the two World Wars referred to theirs as doughboys and GI's. The English name was originally used as a model on forms which soldiers had to fill out.

IMPROVING YOUR READING. The basis of this poem is *irony,* the contrast between what one expects and what one gets.

Tommy

Rudyard Kipling

I went into a public-'ouse to get a pint o' beer,
The publican 'e up an' sez, "We serve no red-coats here."
The girls be'ind the bar they laughed an' giggled fit to die,
I outs into the street again an' to myself sez I:
    O it 's Tommy this, an' Tommy that, an' "Tommy, go away";   5
    But it 's "Thank you, Mister Atkins," when the band begins to play,
    The band begins to play, my boys, the band begins to play,
    O it 's "Thank you, Mister Atkins," when the band begins to play.

I went into a theater as sober as could be,
They gave a drunk civilian room, but 'ad n't none for me;   10
They sent me to the gallery or round the music-'alls,
But when it comes to fightin', Lord! they 'll shove me in the stalls!
    For it's Tommy this, an' Tommy that, an' "Tommy, wait outside";
    But it 's "Special train for Atkins" when the trooper 's on the tide,
    The troopship 's on the tide, my boys, the troopship 's on the tide,   15
    O it 's "Special train for Atkins" when the trooper 's on the tide.

Yes, makin' mock o' uniforms that guard you while you sleep
Is cheaper than them uniforms, an' they 're starvation cheap;
An' hustlin' drunken soldiers when they 're goin' large a bit
Is five times better business than paradin' in full kit.   20
    Then it 's Tommy this, an' Tommy that, an' "Tommy, 'ow 's yer soul?"
    But it 's "Thin red line of 'eroes" when the drums begin to roll,
    The drums begin to roll, my boys, the drums begin to roll,
    O it 's "Thin red line of 'eroes" when the drums begin to roll.

We are n't no thin red 'eroes, nor we are n't no blackguards too,   25
But single men in barricks, most remarkable like you;
An' if sometimes our conduck is n't all your fancy paints,
Why, single men in barricks don't grow into plaster saints;
    While it 's Tommy this, an' Tommy that, an' "Tommy, fall be'ind,"
    But it 's "Please to walk in front, sir," when there 's trouble in the wind,   30
    There's trouble in the wind, my boys, there's trouble in the wind,
    O it 's "Please to walk in front, sir," when there 's trouble in the wind.

You talk o' better food for us, an' schools, an' fires, an' all:
We 'll wait for extry rations if you treat us rational.
Don't mess about the cook-room slops, but prove it to our face   35
The Widow's Uniform¹ is not the soldier-man's disgrace.
    For it 's Tommy this, an' Tommy that, an' "Chuck him out, the brute!"
    But it 's "Saviour of 'is country" when the guns begin to shoot;
    An' it 's Tommy this, an' Tommy that, an' anything you please;
    An' Tommy ain't a bloomin' fool—you bet that Tommy sees!   40

1 **Widow's Uniform:** an allusion to Queen Victoria, who was called widow by the soldiers.

Understanding Literature

1. Who is the speaker in this poem? What is his mood? What are his specific complaints?
2. The beginning of each stanza illustrates one treatment of Tommy, and the last three lines of each stanza illustrate a different treatment. What contrasts are used to show this difference? What causes the difference? How is the contrast ironic?
3. What use is made of repetition in this poem? of alliteration?
4. How does the writer feel about Tommy?

A poet is one who makes connections. Even an ordinary street scene may arouse in him memories and longing, sadness and joy. Claude McKay was born in the West Indies, but he spent many years in New York City. The sight of the tropical fruits makes him "hungry"—not for eating, but for "the old, familiar ways."

The Tropics in New York
Claude McKay

Bananas ripe and green, and gingerroot,
    Cocoa in pods and alligator pears,
And tangerines and mangoes and grapefruit,
    Fit for the highest prize at parish fairs,

Set in the window, bringing memories   5
    Of fruit trees laden by low-singing rills,[1]
And dewy dawns, and mystical blue skies
    In benediction over nunlike hills.

My eyes grew dim, and I could no more gaze;
    A wave of longing through my body swept,   10
And, hungry for the old, familiar ways,
    I turned aside and bowed my head and wept.

[1] rills: small streams.

Understanding Literature

1. The first three lines seem merely to be listing a number of tropical plants, but what *imagery* do they suggest?
2. The title of the poem places the speaker, the "I," in New York, but nowhere in the poem is the city specifically mentioned. What is the one phrase, however, that suggests a place other than the tropics?
3. In lines 7–8 the poet uses the words "mystical," "benediction," and "nunlike." What do these three words have in common? What, then, is the picture the poet presents in the phrase "mystical blue skies/In benediction over nunlike hills"?
4. Although the poem is written in three stanzas, there are only two main parts. Where does the division occur? How do you know? What is the poet doing in each part?

Although Symons uses "I," is he speaking only for himself? Or could he be speaking for all people who have this same idea of dreams?

IMPROVING YOUR READING. This poem is based on a metaphor. Note the two activities that are compared. How are they alike?

The Loom of Dreams

Arthur Symons

I broider the world upon a loom,[1]
I broider with dreams my tapestry;
Here in a little lonely room
I am master of earth and sea,
And the planets come to me,   5

I broider my life into the frame,
I broider my love, thread upon thread;
The world goes by with its glory and shame,
Crowns are bartered and blood is shed:
I sit and broider my dreams instead.   10

And the only world is the world of my dreams,
And my weaving the only happiness;
For what is the world but what it seems?
And who knows but that God, beyond our guess,
Sits weaving worlds out of loneliness?   15

[1] **loom:** frame for weaving yarn or thread into a fabric.

Understanding Literature

1. Explain the metaphors used in "The Loom of Dreams."
2. In what way is the person who dreams "master of earth and sea"?
3. What is meant by "The world goes by with its glory and shame"?
4. What does the poet mean by saying that "the only world is the world of my dreams"?
5. The poem ends with two questions which should prompt the reader to think further. What are they? What do they indicate about the poet's state of mind?

Reading "The First Snowfall"

In this poem the speaker looks out on the snow which becomes, as the poem goes on, a *symbol* of his own suffering. The poem divides into two parts: one about the actual storm and one about what it stands for, or symbolizes.

The First Snowfall

James Russell Lowell

The snow had begun in the gloaming,
   And busily all the night
Had been heaping field and highway
   With a silence deep and white.

Every pine and fir and hemlock   5
   Wore ermine too dear for an earl,
And the poorest twig on the elm tree
   Was ridged inch deep with pearl.

From sheds new-roofed with Carrara[1]
   Came Chanticleer's[2] muffled crow,   10
The stiff rails softened to a swan's-down,
   And still fluttered down the snow.

I stood and watched by the window
   The noiseless work of the sky,
And the sudden flurries of snowbirds,   15
   Like brown leaves whirling by.

I thought of a mound in sweet Auburn[3]
   Where a little headstone stood;
How the flakes were folding it gently,
   As did robins the babes in the wood.   20

1 **Carrara:** white marble.
2 **Chanticleer's:** the rooster's.

3 **Auburn:** Mount Auburn cemetery, Cambridge, Massachusetts.

Up spoke our own little Mabel,
  Saying, "Father, who makes it snow?"
And I told of the good All-father
  Who cares for us here below.

Again I looked at the snowfall,   25
  And thought of the leaden sky
That arched o'er our first great sorrow,
  When that mound was heaped so high.

I remembered the gradual patience
  That fell from that cloud like snow,   30
Flake by flake, healing and hiding
  The scar that renewed our woe.

And again to the child I whispered,
  "The snow that husheth all,
Darling, the merciful Father   35
  Alone can make it fall!"

Then, with eyes that saw not, I kissed her,
  And she, kissing back, could not know
That *my* kiss was given to her sister,
  Folded close under deepening snow.   40

Understanding Literature

1. In the second, third, and fourth stanzas the poet uses a series of images to describe the snow. Explain these images.
2. As the poet looks, what is he thinking about?
3. In the seventh stanza what is "our first great sorrow"?
4. What is the poet saying in the last stanza?
5. How is the snowfall like his sorrow?
6. Why is the poem called "The First Snowfall"?

Reading "Curfew"

Curfew means literally "the covering of the fire." In England during the Middle Ages a bell was sounded in the evening as a signal for putting out fires. Longfellow, here, uses this idea as a *symbol* of the approaching end of life.

Curfew

Henry Wadsworth Longfellow

I

Solemnly, mournfully,
  Dealing its dole,
The Curfew Bell
  Is beginning to toll.

Cover the embers,   5
  And put out the light;
Toil comes with the morning,
  And rest with the night.

Dark grow the windows,
  And quenched is the fire;   10
Sound fades into silence—
  All footsteps retire.

No voice in the chambers,
  No sound in the hall!
Sleep and oblivion   15
  Reign over all!

II

The book is completed,
   And closed, like the day;
And the hand that has written it
   Lays it away.   20

Dim grow its fancies;
   Forgotten they lie;
Like coals in the ashes,
   They darken and die.

Song sinks into silence,   25
   The story is told,
The windows are darkened,
   The hearthstone is cold.

Darker and darker
   The black shadows fall;   30
Sleep and oblivion
   Reign over all.

Understanding Literature

1. In the first four stanzas the poet is describing the actual close of a day. What images does he use?
2. In what ways do the sounds of the words used in the first stanza reflect the sound of the bell?
3. In the second part of the poem, what is the end of life compared to? How are the two things alike?
4. What other metaphors repeat the same idea?
5. How does the last stanza differ from the fourth?

Reading Light Verse

Poets are not always utterly serious. Like most human beings, they are frequently unable to resist poking fun at or laughing at many things that they see around them, as you will see in the two poems that follow. These short poems are examples of light verse, short lyric poems which are gay, clever, and written to entertain, although they sometimes have a serious purpose too.

Death at Suppertime

Phyllis McGinley

Between the dark and the daylight,
  When the night is beginning to lower,
Comes a pause in the day's occupation,
  That is known as the Children's Hour.[1]

Then endeth the skipping and skating,
  The giggles, the tantrums, and tears,
When, the innocent voices abating,
  Alert grow the innocent ears.

The little boys leap from the stairways,   5
  Girls lay down their dolls on the dot,
For promptly at five o'er the airways
  Comes violence geared to the tot.

Comes murder, comes arson, come G-men
  Pursuing unspeakable spies;   10
Come gangsters and tough-talking he-men
  With six-shooters strapped to their thighs;

Comes the corpse in the dust, comes the dictum
  "Ya' better start singin', ya' rat!"
While the torturer leers at his victim,   15
  The killer unleashes his gat.

---

1 See the poem "The Children's Hour" by Henry Wadsworth Longfellow.

With mayhem the twilight is reeling.
  Blood spatters; the tommy guns bark.
Hands reach for the sky or the ceiling
  As the dagger strikes home in the dark.   20

And lo! with what rapturous wonder
  The little ones hark to each tale
Of gambler shot down with his plunder
  Or outlaw abducting the mail.

Between the news and the tireless   25
  Commercials, while tempers turn sour,
Comes a season of horror by wireless
  That is known as the Children's Hour.

Good Sportsmanship

Richard Armour

Good sportsmanship we hail, we sing.
It's always pleasant when you spot it.
There's only one unhappy thing:
You have to lose to prove you've got it.

The cat sits;
The bat flits—
The nit-wits!

—*Samuel Hoffenstein*

Famous Characters
in Literature

FROM THE brig *Hispaniola* to the city of London; from a Missouri town on a summer morning to New England on a winter afternoon; from a quiet seaport where cannon shots once awakened the inhabitants at midnight to the English countryside where animals live the lives of humans—you can go to all these places by reading the selections in this unit.

Even more interesting than the places you can visit are the people who inhabit them. Huck Finn in the Grangerford's parlor, wondering about life and death, and art, Robinson Crusoe building his own solitary world, and Jo March fighting her worst enemy—these are the kinds of individuals you can come to know as you read.

All these people, as well as many others you will meet in this section, are characters in famous books that one day you will want to read if you have not already done so. In these selections the characters are introduced so that you can begin to know what is in store for you in many great books.

The authors of the stories lived at different times, in different places. Most of them wrote for adults, some for young people; but all the books in which these selections appear are still enjoyed by readers of all ages. Try to understand why, as you get to know the characters the authors created.

INTRODUCTION

In *The Adventures of Huckleberry Finn*, Mark Twain writes about a complex world that he knew well, about a life of boyhood adventures and about the adult world of starched shirts, formal parlors, and ceremony. In the chapter entitled "The Grangerfords Take Me In," Huck finds himself temporarily in the fancy world of the Grangerfords' parlor and completely overwhelmed by reminders of Emmeline Grangerford.

from The Adventures of Huckleberry Finn

Mark Twain

IMPROVING YOUR READING: In this chapter from Huck Finn's adventures, Huck is *characterized* mainly through his wonderings, through his reactions to things in the Grangerford parlor. As you read this chapter, try to decide what kind of person Huck is. What impresses him? What does he think is important? What does he think of Emmeline? What comments does he make on the world of adults?

IT WAS A MIGHTY nice family and a mighty nice house, too. I hadn't seen no house out in the country before that was so nice and had so much style. It didn't have an iron latch on the front door nor a wooden one with a buckskin string, but a brass knob to turn, the same as houses in town. There warn't no bed in the parlor, nor a sign of a bed, but heaps of parlors in towns has beds in them. There was a big fireplace that was bricked on the bottom, and the bricks was kept clean and red by pouring water on them and scrubbing them with another brick: sometimes they wash them over with red waterpaint that they call Spanish-brown, same as they do in town. They had big brass dog-irons that could hold up a sawlog. There was a clock on the middle of the mantelpiece, with a picture of a town painted on the bottom half of the glass front, and a round place in the middle of it for the sun, and you could see the pendulum swinging behind it. It was beautiful to hear that clock tick, and sometimes when one of these peddlers had been along and scoured her up and got her in good shape, she would start in and strike a hundred and fifty before she got tuckered out. They wouldn't took any money for her.

Well, there was a big outlandish parrot on each side of the clock, made out of something like chalk and painted up gaudy. By one of the parrots was a cat made of crockery, and a crockery dog by the other; and when you pressed down on them they squeaked but didn't open their mouths nor look different nor interested. They squeaked through underneath. There was a couple of big wild-turkey-wing fans spread out behind those things. On the table in the middle of the room was a kind of a lovely crockery basket that had apples and oranges and peaches and grapes piled up in it, which was much redder and yellower and prettier than real ones is, but they warn't real because you could see where pieces had got chipped off and showed the white chalk, or whatever it was, underneath.

This table had a cover made out of beautiful oilcloth, with a red and blue spread-eagle painted on it and a painted border all around. It come all the way from Philadelphia, they said. There was some books too, piled up perfectly exact, on each corner of the table. One was a big family Bible full of pictures. One was *Pilgrim's Progress*, about a man that left his family, it didn't say why. I read considerable in it now and then. The statements was interesting but tough. Another was *Friendship's·Offering*, full of beautiful stuff and poetry, but I didn't read the poetry. Another was Henry Clay's *Speeches*, and another was Dr. Gunn's *Family Medicine*, which told you all about what to do if a body was sick or dead. There was a hymnbook and a lot of other books. And there was nice split-bottom chairs, and perfectly sound, too—not bagged down in the middle and busted, like an old basket.

They had pictures hung on the walls—mainly Washingtons and Lafayettes, and battles, and Highland Marys, and one called "Signing the Declaration." There was some that they called crayons, which one of the daughters which was dead made her own self when she was only fifteen years old. They was different from any pictures I ever see before—blacker, mostly, than is common. One was a woman in a slim black dress, belted small under the armpits, with bulges like a cabbage in the middle of the sleeves, and a large black scoop-shovel bonnet with a black veil, and white slim ankles crossed about with black tape and very wee black slippers, like a chisel, and she was leaning pensive on a tombstone on her right elbow under a weeping willow, and her other hand hanging down her side holding a white handkerchief and a reticule, and underneath the picture it said "Shall I Never See Thee More Alas." Another one was a young lady with her hair all combed up straight to the top of her head and knotted there in front of a comb like a chairback, and she was crying into a handkerchief and had a dead bird laying on its back in her other hand with its heels up, and underneath the picture it said "I Shall Never Hear Thy Sweet Chirrup More Alas." There was one where a young lady was at a window looking up at the moon, and tears running down her cheeks; and she had an open letter in one hand with black sealing wax showing on one edge of it, and she was mashing a locket with a chain to it against her mouth and underneath the picture it said "And Art Thou Gone Yes Thou Art Gone Alas." These was all nice pictures, I reckon, but I didn't somehow seem to take to them, because if ever I was down a little they always give me the

fantods.[1] Everybody was sorry she died, because she had laid out a lot more of these pictures to do and a body could see by what she had done what they had lost. But I reckoned that with her disposition she was having a better time in the graveyard. She was at work on what they said was her greatest picture when she took sick, and every day and every night it was her prayer to be allowed to live till she got it done, but she never got the chance. It was a picture of a young woman in a long white gown, standing on the rail of a bridge all ready to jump off, with her hair all down her back, and looking up to the moon with the tears running down her face, and she had two arms folded across her breast and two arms stretched out in front and two more reaching up towards the moon—and the idea was to see which pair would look best and then scratch out all the other arms; but, as I was saying, she died before she got her mind made up and now they kept this picture over the head of the bed in her room, and every time her birthday come they hung flowers on it. Other times it was hid with a little curtain. The young woman in the picture had a kind of a nice sweet face but there was so many arms it made her look too spidery, seemed to me.

This young girl kept a scrap-book when she was alive, and used to paste obituaries and accidents and cases of patient suffering in it out of the *Presbyterian Observer*, and write poetry after them out of her own head. It was very good poetry. This is what she wrote about a boy by the name of Stephen Dowling Bots that fell down a well and was drownded:

ODE TO STEPHEN DOWLING BOTS, DEC'D[2]

And did young Stephen sicken,
  And did young Stephen die?
And did the sad hearts thicken,
  And did the mourners cry?

No; such was not the fate of
  Young Stephen Dowling Bots;
Though sad hearts round him thickened,
  'Twas not from sickness' shots.

No whooping-cough did rack his frame,
  Nor measles drear with spots;
Not these impaired the sacred name
  Of Stephen Dowling Bots.

Despised love struck not with woe
  That head of curly knots,
Nor stomach troubles laid him low,
  Young Stephen Dowling Bots.

O no. Then list with tearful eye,
  Whilst I his fate do tell.
His soul did from this cold world fly
  By falling down a well.

They got him out and emptied him;
  Alas it was too late;
His spirit was gone for to sport aloft
  In the realms of the good and great.

If Emmeline Grangerford could make poetry like that before she was fourteen, there ain't no telling what she could 'a' done by and by. Buck said she could rattle off poetry like nothing. She didn't ever have to stop to think. He said she would slap down a line, and if she couldn't

---

1 **the fantods:** frightening thoughts, "the willies."   2 **Dec'd:** deceased, dead.

find anything to rhyme with it she would just scratch it out and slap down another one and go ahead. She warn't particular; she could write about anything you choose to give her to write about just so it was sadful. Every time a man died or a woman died or a child died, she would be on hand with her "tribute" before he was cold. She called them tributes. The neighbors said it was the doctor first, then Emmeline, then the undertaker—the undertaker never got in ahead of Emmeline but once, and then she hung fire on a rhyme for the dead person's name, which was Whistler. She warn't ever the same after that; she never complained but she kind of pined away and did not live long. Poor thing, many's the time I made myself go up to the little room that used to be hers and get out her poor old scrapbook and read in it when her pictures had been aggravating me and I had soured on her a little. I liked all that family, dead ones and all, and warn't going to let anything come between us.

Understanding Literature

1. What is Huck's first impression of the Grangerford house? What things impress him? Do they impress you?
2. Compare the books and art in the Grangerford house with those you might find in any city home today. How have times changed?
3. What seems to have been Emmeline Grangerford's main interest? Does Huck share this interest?
4. What does Huck think of Emmeline's poetry? Does Twain share Huck's opinion? Cite details to support your conclusions.

Further Activity

Write a dialogue between Huck Finn and Emmeline Grangerford on what makes good poetry. Include some ambiguous phrases which clue the reader in on your own feelings about Huck's and Emmeline's standards.

Focusing on Words

Mark Twain has Huck make some comments that could be taken more than one way. We know Huck means exactly what he says, but we suspect that Twain is talking tongue-in-cheek.

FAMOUS CHARACTERS

Reread the sections in which each of the following phrases occur, citing (a) what Huck is talking about and (b) what Twain is saying (or rather, implying) about the topic under discussion.

1. "The statements was interesting but tough."
2. "I hadn't seen no house out in the country before that was so nice and had so much style."
3. "Buck said she could rattle off poetry like nothing. She didn't even have to stop to think."
4. "I liked all that family, . . . and warn't going to let anything come between us."
5. "Everybody was sorry she had died, she had laid out a lot more of these pictures to do and a body could see by what she had done what they had lost."

Little Women is a story about the March sisters—Meg, Jo, Beth, and Amy—and their friends. The girls' mother, whom they call Marmee, is the head of the family while their father is away serving as a chaplain in the army during the Civil War. Laurie—Theodore Laurence—the boy who lives next door, is a friend of all the March girls.

from Little Women

Louisa May Alcott

IMPROVING YOUR READING: Each of the March girls has a distinct personality, and although they usually get along well together they sometimes have disagreements, or conflicts. In many short stories and plays the plot involves a *conflict*, either of people, things, or ideas. In the end of the story or play the conflict is usually *resolved*, or settled. Observe how the conflict in this selection is finally resolved.

JO MEETS APOLLYON[1]

"GIRLS, WHERE ARE you going?" asked Amy, coming into their room one Saturday afternoon, and finding them getting ready to go out, with an air of secrecy which excited her curiosity.

"Never mind; little girls shouldn't ask questions," returned Jo sharply.

Now if there *is* anything mortifying to our feelings, when we are young, it is to be told that; and to be bidden to "run away, dear," is still more trying to us. Amy bridled up at this insult, and determined to find out the secret, if she teased for an

hour. Turning to Meg, who never refused her anything very long, she said coaxingly, "Do tell me! I should think you might let me go, too; for Beth is fussing over her piano, and I haven't got anything to do, and am *so* lonely."

"I can't, dear, because you aren't invited," began Meg; but Jo broke in impatiently, "Now, Meg, be quiet, or you will spoil it all. You can't go, Amy; so don't be a baby, and whine about it."

"You are going somewhere with Laurie, I know you are; you were whispering and laughing together, on the sofa, last night, and you stopped when I came in. Aren't you going with him?"

"Yes, we are; now do be still, and stop bothering."

---

1 **Apollyon:** In the Bible (the Book of Revelations), Apollyon is the angel of the bottomless pit. His name means "The Destroyer." In *Pilgrim's Progress*, a famous 17th-century book by John Bunyan, Apollyon is a fiend armed with fiery darts. He is overcome by Christian, the hero of the book, in the Valley of Humiliation.

Amy held her tongue, but used her eyes, and saw Meg slip a fan into her pocket.

"I know! I know! you're going to the theatre to see the 'Seven Castles!'" she cried; adding resolutely, "and I *shall* go, for Mother said I might see it; and I've got my rag money, and it was mean not to tell me in time."

"Just listen to me a minute, and be a good child," said Meg soothingly. "Mother doesn't wish you to go this week, because your eyes are not well enough yet to bear the light of this fairy piece. Next week you can go with Beth and Hannah, and have a nice time."

"I don't like that half as well as going with you and Laurie. Please let me; I've been sick with this cold so long, and shut up, I'm dying for some fun. Do, Meg! I'll be ever so good," pleaded Amy, looking as pathetic as she could.

"Suppose we take her. I don't believe Mother would mind, if we bundle her up well," began Meg.

"If *she* goes I shan't; and if I don't, Laurie won't like it; and it will be very rude, after he invited only us, to go and drag in Amy. I should think she'd hate to poke herself where she isn't wanted," said Jo crossly, for she disliked the trouble of overseeing a fidgety child, when she wanted to enjoy herself.

Her tone and manner angered Amy, who began to put her boots on, saying, in her most aggravating way, "I *shall* go; Meg says I may; and if I pay for myself, Laurie hasn't anything to do with it."

"You can't sit with us, for our seats are reserved, and you mustn't sit alone; so Laurie will give you his place, and that will spoil our pleasure; or he'll get another seat for you, and that isn't proper, when you weren't asked. You shan't stir a step; so you may just stay where you are," scolded Jo, crosser than ever, having just pricked her finger in her hurry.

Sitting on the floor, with one boot on, Amy began to cry, and Meg to reason with her, when Laurie called from below, and the two girls hurried down, leaving their sister wailing; for now and then she forgot her grown-up ways, and acted like a spoiled child. Just as the party was setting out, Amy called over the banisters, in a threatening tone, "You'll be sorry for this, Jo March; see if you ain't."

"Fiddlesticks!" returned Jo, slamming the door.

They had a charming time, for "The Seven Castles of the Diamond Lake" were as brilliant and wonderful as heart could wish. But, in spite of the comical red imps, sparkling elves, and gorgeous princes and princesses, Jo's pleasure had a drop of bitterness in it; the fairy queen's yellow curls reminded her of Amy; and between the acts she amused herself with wondering what her sister would do to make her "sorry for it." She and Amy had had many lively skirmishes in the course of their lives, for both had quick tempers, and were apt to be violent when fairly roused. Amy teased Jo, and Jo irritated Amy, and semi-occasional explosions occurred, of which both were much

ashamed afterward. Although the oldest, Jo had the least self-control, and had hard times trying to curb the fiery spirit which was continually getting her into trouble; her anger never lasted long, and, having humbly confessed her fault, she sincerely repented, and tried to do better. Her sisters used to say that they rather liked to get Jo into a fury, because she was such an angel afterward. Poor Jo tried desperately to be good, but her bosom enemy was always ready to flame up and defeat her; and it took years of patient effort to subdue it.

When they got home, they found Amy reading in the parlor. She assumed an injured air as they came in; never lifted her eyes from her book, or asked a single question. Perhaps curiosity might have conquered re-

sentment, if Beth had not been there to inquire, and receive a glowing description of the play. On going up to put away her best hat, Jo's first look was toward the bureau; for, in their last quarrel, Amy had soothed her feelings by turning Jo's top drawer upside down on the floor. Everything was in its place, however; and after a hasty glance into her various closets, bags, and boxes, Jo decided that Amy had forgiven and forgotten her wrongs.

There Jo was mistaken; for next day she made a discovery which produced a tempest. Meg, Beth, and Amy were sitting together, late in the afternoon, when Jo burst into the room, looking excited, and demanding breathlessly, "Has anyone taken my book?"

Meg and Beth said "No," at once

and looked surprised; Amy poked the fire, and said nothing. Jo saw her color rise, and was down upon her in a minute.

"Amy, you've got it!"

"No, I haven't."

"You know where it is, then!"

"No, I don't."

"That's a fib!" cried Jo, taking her by the shoulders, and looking fierce enough to frighten a much braver child than Amy.

"It isn't. I haven't got it, don't know where it is now, and don't care."

"You know something about it, and you'd better tell at once, or I'll make you," and Jo gave her a slight shake.

"Scold as much as you like, you'll never see your silly old book again," cried Amy, getting excited in her turn.

"Why not?"

"I burnt it up."

"What! my little book I was so fond of, and worked over, and meant to finish before Father got home? Have you really burnt it?" said Jo, turning very pale, while her eyes kindled and her hands clutched Amy nervously.

"Yes, I did! I told you I'd make you pay for being so cross yesterday, and I have, so—"

Amy got no farther, for Jo's hot temper mastered her, and she shook Amy till her teeth chattered in her head; crying, in a passion of grief and anger,—

"You wicked, wicked girl! I never can write it again, and I'll never forgive you as long as I live."

Meg flew to rescue Amy, and Beth to pacify Jo, but Jo was quite beside herself; and, with a parting box on her sister's ear, she rushed out of the room up to the old sofa in the garret, and finished her fight alone.

The storm cleared up below, for Mrs. March came home, and, having heard the story, soon brought Amy to a sense of the wrong she had done her sister. Jo's book was the pride of her heart, and was regarded by her family as a literary sprout of great promise. It was only half a dozen little fairy tales, but Jo had worked over them patiently, putting her whole heart into her work, hoping to make something good enough to print. She had just copied them with great care, and had destroyed the old manuscript, so that Amy's bonfire had consumed the loving work of several years. It seemed a small loss to others, but to Jo it was a dreadful calamity, and she felt that it never could be made up to her. Beth mourned as for a departed kitten, and Meg refused to defend her pet; Mrs. March looked grave and grieved, and Amy felt that no one would love her till she had asked pardon for the act which she now regretted more than any of them.

When the tea bell rung, Jo appeared, looking so grim and unapproachable that it took all Amy's courage to say meekly,—

"Please forgive me, Jo; I'm very, very sorry."

"I never shall forgive you," was Jo's stern answer; and, from that moment, she ignored Amy entirely.

No one spoke of the great trouble —not even Mrs. March—for all had learned by experience that when Jo was in that mood words were wasted; and the wisest course was to wait till some little accident, or her own generous nature, softened Jo's resentment, and healed the breach. It was not a happy evening; for, though they sewed as usual, while their mother read aloud from Bremer, Scott, or Edgeworth, something was wanting, and the sweet home peace was disturbed. They felt this most when singing time came; for Beth could only play, Jo stood dumb as a stone, and Amy broke down, so Meg and Mother sung alone. But, in spite of their efforts to be as cheery as larks, the flutelike voices did not seem to chord as well as usual, and all felt out of tune.

As Jo received her good-night kiss, Mrs. March whispered gently,—

"My dear, don't let the sun go down upon your anger; forgive each other, help each other, and begin again tomorrow."

Jo wanted to lay her head down on that motherly bosom, and cry her grief and anger all away; but tears were an unmanly weakness, and she felt so deeply injured that she really *couldn't* quite forgive yet. So she winked hard, shook her head, and said, gruffly because Amy was listening,—

"It was an abominable thing, and she don't deserve to be forgiven."

With that she marched off to bed, and there was no merry or confidential gossip that night.

Amy was much offended that her overtures of peace had been repulsed, and began to wish she had not humbled herself, to feel more injured than ever, and to plume herself on her superior virtue in a way which was particularly exasperating. Jo still looked like a thundercloud, and nothing went well all day. It was bitter cold in the morning; she dropped her precious turnover in the gutter, Aunt March had an attack of fidgets, Meg was pensive, Beth *would* look grieved and wistful when she got home, and Amy kept making remarks about people who were always talking about being good, and yet wouldn't try, when other people set them a virtuous example.

"Everybody is so hateful, I'll ask Laurie to go skating. He is always kind and jolly, and will put me to rights, I know," said Jo to herself, and off she went.

Amy heard the clash of skates, and looked out with an impatient exclamation,—

"There! she promised I should go next time, for this is the last ice we shall have. But it's no use to ask such a crosspatch to take me."

"Don't say that; you *were* very naughty, and it *is* hard to forgive the loss of her precious little book; but I think she might do it now, and I guess she will, if you try her at the right minute," said Meg. "Go after them; don't say anything till Jo has got good-natured with Laurie, then take a quiet minute, and just kiss her, or do some kind thing, and I'm sure she'll be friends again, with all her heart."

"I'll try," said Amy, for the advice suited her; and, after a flurry to get ready, she ran after the friends, who were just disappearing over the hill.

It was not far to the river, but both were ready before Amy reached them. Jo saw her coming, and turned her back; Laurie did not see, for he was carefully skating along the shore, sounding the ice, for a warm spell had preceded the cold snap.

"I'll go on to the first bend, and see if it's all right, before we begin to race," Amy heard him say, as he shot away, looking like a young Russian, in his fur-trimmed coat and cap.

Jo heard Amy panting after her run, stamping her feet and blowing her fingers, as she tried to put her skates on; but Jo never turned, and went slowly zigzaging down the river, taking a bitter, unhappy sort of satisfaction in her sister's troubles. She had cherished her anger till it grew strong, and took possession of her, as evil thoughts and feelings always do, unless cast out at once. As Laurie turned the bend, he shouted back,—

"Keep near the shore; it isn't safe in the middle."

Jo heard, but Amy was just struggling to her feet, and did not catch a word. Jo glanced over her shoulder, and the little demon she was harboring said in her ear,—

"No matter whether she heard or not, let her take care of herself."

Laurie had vanished round the bend; Jo was just at the turn, and Amy, far behind, striking out toward the smoother ice in the middle of the river. For a minute Jo stood still, with a strange feeling at her heart; then she resolved to go on, but something held and turned her round, just in time to see Amy throw up her hands and go down, with the sudden crash of rotten ice, the splash of water, and a cry that made Jo's heart stand still with fear. She tried to call Laurie, but her voice was gone; she tried to rush forward, but her feet seemed to have no strength in them; and, for a second, she could only stand motionless, staring, with a terror-stricken face, at the little blue hood above the black water. Something rushed swiftly by her, and Laurie's voice cried out,—

"Bring a rail; quick, quick!"

How she did it, she never knew; but for the next few minutes she worked as if possessed, blindly obeying Laurie, who was quite self-possessed, and, lying flat, held Amy up by his arm and hockey till Jo dragged a rail from the fence, and together they got the child out, more frightened than hurt.

"Now then, we must walk her home as fast as we can; pile our things on her, while I get off these confounded skates," cried Laurie, wrapping his coat round Amy, and tugging away at the straps, which never seemed so intricate before.

Shivering, dripping, and crying, they got Amy home; and, after an exciting time of it, she fell asleep, rolled in blankets, before a hot fire. During the bustle Jo had scarcely spoken; but flown about, looking pale and wild, with her things half off, her dress torn, and her hands cut and bruised by ice and rails, and refractory[2] buckles. When Amy was com-

2 **refractory:** unmanageable.

fortably asleep, the house quiet, and Mrs. March sitting by the bed, she called Jo to her, and began to bind up the hurt hands.

"Are you sure she is safe?" whispered Jo, looking remorsefully at the golden head, which might have been swept away from her sight forever under the treacherous ice.

"Quite safe, dear; she is not hurt, and won't even take cold, I think, you were so sensible in covering and getting her home quickly," replied her mother cheerfully.

"Laurie did it all; I only let her go. Mother, if she *should* die, it would be my fault"; and Jo dropped down beside the bed, in a passion of penitent tears, telling all that had happened, bitterly condemning her hardness of heart, and sobbing out her gratitude for being spared the heavy punishment which might have come upon her.

"It's my dreadful temper! I try to cure it; I think I have, and then it breaks out worse than ever. O Mother, what shall I do? what shall I do?" cried poor Jo, in despair.

"Watch and pray, dear; never get tired of trying; and never think it is impossible to conquer your fault," said Mrs. March, drawing the blowzy head to her shoulder, and kissing the wet cheek so tenderly that Jo cried harder than ever.

"You don't know, you can't guess how bad it is! It seems as if I could do anything when I'm in a passion; I get so savage, I could hurt anyone, and enjoy it. I'm afraid I *shall* do something dreadful some day, and spoil my life, and make everybody hate me. O mother, help me, do help me!"

"I will, my child, I will. Don't cry so bitterly, but remember this day, and resolve, with all your soul, that you will never know another like it. Jo, dear, we all have our temptations, some far greater than yours, and it often takes us all our lives to conquer them. You think your temper is the worst in the world; but mine used to be just like it."

"Yours, Mother? Why, you are never angry!" and, for the moment, Jo forgot remorse in surprise.

"I've been trying to cure it for forty years, and have only succeeded in controlling it. I am angry nearly every day of my life, Jo; but I have learned not to show it; and I still hope to learn not to feel it, though it may take me another forty years to do so."

The patience and the humility of the face she loved so well was a better lesson to Jo than the wisest lecture, the sharpest reproof. She felt comforted at once by the sympathy and confidence given her; the knowledge that her mother had a fault like hers, and tried to mend it, made her own easier to bear and strengthened her resolution to cure it; though forty years seemed rather a long time to watch and pray, to a girl of fifteen.

"Mother, are you angry when you fold your lips tight together, and go out of the room sometimes, when Aunt March scolds, or people worry you?" asked Jo, feeling nearer and dearer to her mother than ever before.

"Yes, I've learned to check the

hasty words that rise to my lips; and when I feel that they mean to break out against my will, I just go away a minute, and give myself a little shake, for being so weak and wicked," answered Mrs. March, with a sigh and a smile, as she smoothed and fastened up Jo's disheveled hair.

"How did you learn to keep still? That is what troubles me—for the sharp words fly out before I know what I'm about; and the more I say the worse I get, till it's a pleasure to hurt people's feelings, and say dreadful things. Tell me how you do it, Marmee dear."

"My good mother used to help me—"

"As you do us—" interrupted Jo, with a grateful kiss.

"But I lost her when I was a little older than you are, and for years had to struggle on alone, for I was too proud to confess my weakness to any one else. I had a hard time, Jo, and shed a good many bitter tears over my failures; for, in spite of my efforts, I never seemed to get on. Then your father came, and I was so happy that I found it easy to be good. But by and by, when I had four little daughters round me, and we were poor, then the old trouble began again; for I am not patient by nature, and it tried me very much to see my children wanting anything."

"Poor Mother! what helped you then?"

"Your father, Jo. He never loses patience—never doubts or complains —but always hopes, and works and waits so cheerfully, that one is ashamed to do otherwise before him.

He helped and comforted me, and showed me that I must try to practice all the virtues I would have my little girls possess, for I was their example. It was easier to try for your sakes than for my own; a startled or surprised look from one of you, when I spoke sharply, rebuked me more than any words could have done; and the love, respect, and confidence of my children was the sweetest reward I could receive for my efforts to be the woman I would have them copy."

"O Mother, if I'm ever half as good as you, I shall be satisfied," cried Jo, much touched.

"I hope you will be a great deal better, dear; but you must keep watch over your 'bosom enemy,' as Father calls it, or it may sadden, if not spoil your life. You have had a warning; remember it, and try with heart and soul to master this quick temper, before it brings you greater sorrow and regret than you have known today."

"I will try, Mother; I truly will. But you must help me, remind me, and keep me from flying out. I used to see Father sometimes put his finger on his lips, and look at you with a very kind, but sober face, and you always folded your lips tight or went away: was he reminding you then?" asked Jo softly.

"Yes; I asked him to help me so, and he never forgot it, but saved me from many a sharp word by that little gesture and kind look."

Jo saw that her mother's eyes filled and her lips trembled, as she spoke; and, fearing that she had said too much, she whispered anxiously, "Was it wrong to watch you, and to speak of it? I didn't mean to be rude, but it's so comfortable to say all I think to you, and feel so safe and happy here."

"My Jo, you may say anything to your mother, for it is my greatest happiness and pride to feel that my girls confide in me, and know how much I love them."

"I thought I'd grieved you."

"No, dear; but speaking of Father reminded me how much I miss him, how much I owe him, and how faithfully I should watch and work to keep his little daughters safe and good for him."

"Yet you told him to go, Mother, and didn't cry when he went, and never complain now, or seem as if you needed any help," said Jo, wondering. . . .

Amy stirred, and sighed in her sleep; and, as if eager to begin at once to mend her fault, Jo looked up with an expression on her face which it had never worn before.

"I let the sun go down on my anger; I wouldn't forgive her, and today, if it hadn't been for Laurie, it might have been too late! How could I be so wicked?" said Jo, half aloud, as she leaned over her sister, softly stroking the wet hair scattered on the pillow.

As if she heard, Amy opened her eyes, and held out her arms, with a smile that went straight to Jo's heart. Neither said a word, but they hugged one another close, in spite of the blankets, and everything was forgiven and forgotten in one hearty kiss.

Understanding Literature

1. What does the title of this chapter mean? Who or what is Apollyon in the story?
2. Why do the sisters like to tease Jo?
3. In what ways are Amy and Jo alike?
4. Both Amy and Jo feel they have been wronged, one by not being allowed to go to the theater, the other by having her book destroyed. With whom are you more in sympathy? Why?
5. Between what two people does the conflict occur here? How is it resolved (settled)? How might the conflict have been prevented?
6. Which person in this selection also experiences an inner conflict? What is this inner conflict?
7. Is the inner conflict of this story resolved? Explain.
8. Are Jo's and Amy's reactions and behavior believable? Explain.
9. In describing the scene at the river the author says of Jo, "she had cherished her anger till it grew strong, and took possession of her. . . ." How is this quotation related to the theme of this chapter?

"And I was going to sea myself; to sea in a schooner, with a piping boatswain, and pig-tailed singing seamen; to sea, bound for an unknown island, and to seek for buried treasures!" So young Jim Hawkins describes to himself the voyage of the *Hispaniola* just before the ship leaves Bristol, England, and shortly before you meet him and some of the crew in this chapter from *Treasure Island*.

During a series of adventures in the early part of the book, Jim comes into possession of a treasure map while his mother and he are running the Admiral Benbow Inn. Jim's friends, Dr. Livesey and Squire Trelawney, agree to fit out a ship and sail in search of the treasure, taking Jim as cabin boy. The crew has been chosen, the supplies are aboard, and the *Hispaniola* is ready to weigh anchor as you begin to read these two chapters from the middle of this famous adventure story.

from Treasure Island

Robert Louis Stevenson

IMPROVING YOUR READING: *Treasure Island* is first and foremost a good story. Stories of the sea, pirates, and lost treasure have long fascinated people, and here these ingredients are skillfully put together by Robert Louis Stevenson. There is *suspense* in the book, that quality of holding the reader almost breathless as he waits to discover the outcome of an incident. There are clear *transitions* from one scene to the next as Jim tells the story. (A transition is a way of transferring the reader's thoughts smoothly from one subject to another and showing the relationship of these two subjects to each other.) And, what is of utmost importance to any good book, the characters seem real.

THE VOYAGE

ALL THAT NIGHT we were in a great bustle getting things stowed in their place, and boatfuls of the squire's friends, Mr. Blandly and the like, coming off to wish him a good voyage and a safe return. We never had a night at the "Admiral Benbow" when I had half the work; and I was dog-tired when, a little before dawn, the boatswain[1] sounded his pipe, and the crew began to man the capstan bars.[2] I might have been twice as weary, yet I would not have left the deck; all was so new and interesting to me—the brief commands, the shrill note of the whistle, the men bustling to their places in the glimmer of the ship's lanterns.

"Now, Barbecue, tip us a stave," cried one voice.

[1] boatswain (bō′sən): officer in charge of rigging, anchors, and cables.

[2] capstan bars: revolving drums or cylinders, used on shipboard for raising the anchor by traction upon a rope or cable passing around the drum. Sailors walked around the capstan, pushing in front of them the heavy bars by which it was turned.

"The old one," cried another.

"Ay, ay, mates," said Long John, who was standing by, with his crutch under his arm, and at once broke out in the air and words I knew so well—

Fifteen men on the dead man's chest—

And then the whole crew bore chorus:

Yo-ho-ho, and a bottle of rum!

And at the third "ho!" drove the bars before them with a will.

Even at that exciting moment it carried me back to the old "Admiral Benbow" in a second; and I seemed to hear the voice of the captain piping in the chorus. But soon the anchor was short up; soon it was hanging dripping at the bows; soon the sails began to draw, and the land and shipping to flit by on either side; and before I could lie down to snatch an hour of slumber the *Hispaniola* had begun her voyage to the Isle of Treasure.

I am not going to relate that voyage in detail. It was fairly prosperous. The ship proved to be a good ship, the crew were capable seamen and the captain thoroughly understood his business. But before we came the length of Treasure Island, two or three things had happened which require to be known.

Mr. Arrow,[3] first of all, turned out even worse than the captain had feared. He had no command among the men, and people did what they pleased with him. But that was by no means the worst of it; for after a day or two at sea he began to appear

on deck with hazy eye, red cheeks, stuttering tongue, and other marks of drunkenness. Time after time he was ordered below in disgrace. Sometimes he fell and cut himself; sometimes he lay all day long in his little bunk at one side of the companion; sometimes for a day or two he would be almost sober and attend to his work at least passably.

In the meantime, we could never make out where he got the drink. That was the ship's mystery. Watch him as we pleased, we could do nothing to solve it; and when we asked him to his face, he would only laugh, if he were drunk, and if he were sober, deny solemnly that he ever tasted anything but water.

He was not only useless as an officer, and a bad influence amongst the men, but it was plain that at this rate he must soon kill himself outright; so nobody was much surprised, nor very sorry, when one dark night, with a head sea, he disappeared entirely and was seen no more.

"Overboard!" said the captain. "Well, gentlemen, that saves the trouble of putting him in irons."

But there we were, without a mate; and it was necessary, of course, to advance one of the men. The boatswain, Job Anderson, was the likeliest man aboard, and, though he kept his old title, he served in a way as mate. Mr. Trelawney had followed the sea, and his knowledge made him very useful, for he often took a watch himself in easy weather. And the coxswain,[4] Israel Hands, was a care-

---

3 **Mr. Arrow:** first mate of the *Hispaniola.*

4 coxswain (kŏk′sən, kŏk′swān): man in charge of a ship's boat and its crew.

ful, wily, old, experienced seaman, who could be trusted at a pinch with almost anything.

He was a great confidant of Long John Silver, and so the mention of his name leads me on to speak of our ship's cook, Barbecue, as the men called him.

Aboard ship he carried his crutch by a lanyard round his neck, to have both hands as free as possible. It was something to see him wedge the foot of the crutch against a bulkhead, and, propped against it, yielding to every movement of the ship, get on with his cooking like some one safe ashore. Still more strange was it to see him in the heaviest of weather cross the deck. He had a line or two rigged up to help him across the widest spaces—Long John's earrings, they were called; and he would hand himself from one place to another, now using the crutch, now trailing it alongside by the lanyard, as quickly as another man could walk. Yet some of the men who had sailed with him before expressed their pity to see him so reduced.

"He's no common man, Barbecue," said the coxswain to me. "He had good schooling in his young days, and can speak like a book when so minded; and brave—a lion's nothing alongside of Long John! I seen him grapple four, and knock their heads together—him unarmed."

All the crew respected and even obeyed him. He had a way of talking to each, and doing everybody some particular service. To me he was unweariedly kind; and always glad to see me in the galley, which

he kept as clean as a new pin; the dishes hanging up burnished, and his parrot in a cage in one corner.

"Come away, Hawkins," he would say; "come and have a yarn with John. Nobody more welcome than yourself, my son. Sit you down and hear the news. Here's Cap'n Flint— I calls my parrot Cap'n Flint, after the famous buccaneer—here's Cap'n Flint predicting success to our v'yage. Wasn't you, cap'n?"

And the parrot would say, with great rapidity, "Pieces of eight![5] pieces of eight! pieces of eight!" till John threw his handkerchief over the cage.

"Now, that bird," he would say, "is, may be, two hundred years old, Hawkins—they lives forever mostly; and if anybody's seen more wickedness, it must be the devil himself. She's sailed with England, the great Cap'n England, the pirate. She's been at Madagascar, and at Malabar, and Surinam, and Providence, and Portobello. She was at the fishing up of the wrecked plate ships.[6] It's there she learned 'Pieces of eight,' and little wonder; three hundred and fifty thousand of 'em, Hawkins! She was at the boarding of the Viceroy of the Indies out of Goa,[7] she was; and to look at her you would think she was a babby. But you smelt powder —didn't you, cap'n?"

"Stand by to go about,"[8] the parrot

5 **Pieces of eight:** large silver coins of Spain.
6 **wrecked plate ships:** refers to the theft by pirates of a vast amount of silver from wrecked Spanish ships.
7 **boarding . . . Goa:** reference to one of Captain England's exploits, the capturing of a Portuguese ship.
8 **go about:** change direction; change tack.

would scream.

"Ah, she's a handsome craft, she is," the cook would say, and give her sugar from his pocket, and then the bird would peck at the bars and swear straight on, passing belief for wickedness. "There," John would add, "you can't touch pitch and not be mucked, lad. Here's this poor old innocent bird o' mine swearing blue fire, and none the wiser, you may lay to that. She would swear the same, in a manner of speaking, before chaplain." And John would touch his forelock with a solemn way he had, that made me think he was the best of men.

In the meantime, squire and Captain Smollett were still on pretty distant terms with one another. The squire made no bones about the matter; he despised the captain. The captain, on his part, never spoke but when he was spoken to, and then sharp and short and dry, and not a word wasted. He owned, when driven into a corner, that he seemed to have been wrong about the crew, that some of them were as brisk as he wanted to see, and all had behaved fairly well. As for the ship, he had taken a downright fancy to her. "She'll lie a point nearer the wind than a man has a right to expect of his own married wife, sir. But," he would add, "all I say is we're not home again, and I don't like the cruise."

The squire, at this, would turn away and march up and down the deck, chin in air.

"A trifle more of that man," he would say, "and I should explode."

We had some heavy weather,

which only proved the qualities of the *Hispaniola*. Every man on board seemed well content, and they must have been hard to please if they had been otherwise; for it is my belief there was never a ship's company so spoiled since Noah put to sea. Double grog[9] was going on the least excuse; there was duff[10] on odd days, as, for instance, if the squire heard it was any man's birthday; and always a barrel of apples standing broached[11] in the waist, for any one to help himself that had a fancy.

"Never knew good come of it yet," the captain said to Dr. Livesey. "Spoil foc's'le[12] hands, make devils. That's my belief."

But good did come of the apple barrel, as you shall hear; for if it had not been for that, we should have had no note of warning, and might all have perished by the hand of treachery.

This was how it came about.

We had run up the trades[13] to get the wind of the island[14] we were after—I am not allowed to be more plain—and now we were running down for it with a bright lookout day and night. It was about the last day of our outward voyage, by the largest computation; some time that night, or, at latest, before noon of the morrow, we should sight the Treasure Island. We were heading S.S.W.,

and had a steady breeze abeam and a quiet sea. The *Hispaniola* rolled steadily, dipping her bowsprit now and then with a whiff of spray. All was drawing alow and aloft; everyone was in the bravest spirits, because we were now so near an end of the first part of our adventure.

Now, just after sundown, when all my work was over, and I was on my way to my berth, it occurred to me that I should like an apple. I ran on deck. The watch was all forward looking out for the island. The man at the helm was watching the luff[15] of the sail, and whistling away gently to himself; and that was the only sound excepting the swish of the sea against the bows and around the sides of the ship.

In I got bodily into the apple barrel, and found there was scarce an apple left; but, sitting down there in the dark, what with the sound of the waters and rocking movement of the ship, I had either fallen asleep, or was on the point of doing so, when a heavy man sat down with rather a clash close by. The barrel shook as he leaned his shoulders against it, and I was just about to jump up when the man began to speak. It was Silver's voice, and, before I had heard a dozen words, I would not have shown myself for all the world, but lay there, trembling and listening, in the extreme of fear and curiosity; for from these dozen words I understood that the lives of all the honest men aboard depended upon me alone.

9 **grog:** unsweetened mixture of spirits and water.
10 **duff:** pudding.
11 **broached:** opened.
12 **foc's'le:** the forward part of the vessel where the sailors live.
13 **trades:** trade winds which, on the north side of the equator, blow continually from the northeast.
14 **to . . . island:** to get to the windward of the island.

15 **luff:** forward or weather edge of the sail which the helmsman watches to be sure the sails are full.

WHAT I HEARD IN THE APPLE BARREL

"No, NOT I," said Silver. "Flint was cap'n; I was quartermaster,[16] along of my timber leg. The same broadside I lost my leg, old Pew lost his deadlights.[17] It was a master surgeon, him that ampytated me—out of college and all—Latin by the bucket, and what not; but he was hanged like a dog, and sun-dried like the rest, at Corso Castle.[18] That was Roberts's men, that was, and comed of changing names to their ships—*Royal Fortune* and so on. Now, what a ship was christened, so let her stay, I says. So it was with the *Cassandra*, as brought us all safe home from Malabar, after England took the Viceroy of the Indies; so it was with the old *Walrus*, Flint's old ship, as I've seen a-muck with the red blood and fit to sink with gold."

"Ah!" cried another voice, that of the youngest hand on board, and evidently full of admiration, "he was the flower of the flock, was Flint!"

"Davis was a man, too, by all accounts," said Silver. "I never sailed along of him; first with England, then with Flint, that's my story; and now here on my own account, in a manner of speaking. I laid by nine hundred safe, from England, and two thousand after Flint. That ain't bad for a man before the mast—all safe in bank. 'Tain't earning now, it's saving does it, you may lay to that. Where's all England's men now? I dunno. Where's Flint's? Why, most on 'em aboard here, and glad to get the duff—been begging before that, some on 'em. Old Pew, as had lost his sight, and might have thought shame, spends twelve hundred pound in a year, like a lord in Parliament. Where is he now? Well, he's dead now and under hatches; but for two year before that, shiver my timbers! the man was starving. He begged, and he stole, and he cut throats, and starved at that, by the powers!"

"Well, it aint much use, after all," said the young seaman.

"'Tain't much use for fools, you may lay to it—that, nor nothing," cried Silver. "But now, you look here: you're young, you are, but you're as smart as paint. I see that when I set my eyes on you, and I'll talk to you like a man."

You may imagine how I felt when I heard this abominable old rogue addressing another in the very same words of flattery as he had used to myself. I think, if I had been able, that I would have killed him through the barrel. Meantime, he ran on, little supposing he was overheard.

"Here it is about gentlemen of fortune. They lives rough, and they risk swinging, but they eat and drink like fighting cocks, and when a cruise is done, why, it's hundreds of pounds instead of hundreds of farthings in their pockets. Now, the most goes for rum and a good fling, and to sea again in their shirts. But that's not the course I lay. I puts it all away,

---

16 quartermaster: an officer on a ship who attends to the helm, binnacle, signals, etc. On a pirate ship this officer had much authority over the crew.
17 deadlights: sailors' slang for *eyes.*
18 Corso Castle: a British fort on the western coast of Africa.

some here, some there, and none too much anywheres, by reason of suspicion. I'm fifty, mark you; once back from this cruise, I set up gentleman in earnest. Time enough, too, says you. Ah, but I've lived easy in the meantime; never denied myself o' nothing heart desires, and slep' soft and ate dainty all my days, but when at sea. And how did I begin? Before the mast, like you!"

"Well," said the other, "but all the other money's gone now, aint it? You daren't show face in Bristol after this."

"Why, where might you suppose it was?" asked Silver, derisively.

"At Bristol, in banks and places," answered his companion.

"It were," said the cook; "it were when we weighed anchor. But my old missis has it all by now. And the 'Spy-glass' is sold, lease and goodwill and rigging; and the old girl's off to meet me. I would tell you where, for I trust you; but it 'ud make jealousy among the mates."

"And can you trust your missis?" asked the other.

"Gentlemen of fortune," returned the cook, "usually trusts little among themselves, and right they are, you may lay to it. But I have a way with me, I have. When a mate brings a slip on his cable—one as knows me, I mean—it won't be in the same world with old John. There was some that was feared of Pew, and some that was feared of Flint; but Flint his own self was feared of me. Feared he was, and proud. They was the roughest crew afloat, was Flint's; the devil himself would have been feared to go to sea with them. Well, now, I tell you, I'm not a boasting man, and you seen yourself how easy I keep company; but when I was quartermaster, *lambs* wasn't the word for Flint's old buccaneers. Ah, you may be sure of yourself in old John's ship."

"Well, I tell you now," replied the lad, "I didn't half a quarter like the job till I had this talk with you, John; but there's my hand on it now."

"And a brave lad you were, and smart, too," answered Silver, shaking hands so heartily that all the barrel shook, "and a finer figure head for a gentleman of fortune I never clapped my eyes on."

By this time I had begun to understand the meaning of their terms. By a "gentleman of fortune" they plainly meant neither more nor less than a common pirate, and the little scene that I had overheard was the last act in the corruption of one of the honest hands—perhaps of the last one left aboard. But on this point I was soon to be relieved, for Silver giving a little whistle, a third man strolled up and sat down by the party.

"Dick's square," said Silver.

"Oh, I know'd Dick was square," returned the voice of the coxswain, Israel Hands. "He's no fool, is Dick." And he turned his quid and spat. "But, look here," he went on, "here's what I want to know, Barbecue: how long are we a-going to stand off and on like a blessed bumboat? I've had a'most enough o' Cap'n Smollett; he's hazed me long enough, by thunder! I want to go into that cabin, I do. I want their pickles and wines, and that."

"Israel," said Silver, "your head aint much account, nor ever was. But you're able to hear, I reckon; leastways, your ears is big enough. Now, here's what I say: you'll berth forward, and you'll live hard, and you'll speak soft, and you'll keep sober, till I give the word; and you may lay to that, my son."

"Well, I don't say no, do I?" growled the coxswain. "What I say is, when? That's what I say."

"When! by the powers!" cried Silver. "Well now, if you want to know, I'll tell you when. The last moment I can manage; and that's when. Here's a first-rate seaman, Cap'n Smollett, sails the blessed ship for us. Here's this squire and doctor with a map and such—I don't know where it is, do I? No more do you, says you. Well, then, I mean this squire and doctor shall find the stuff, and help us to get it aboard, by the powers. Then we'll see. If I was sure of you all, sons of double Dutchmen, I'd have Cap'n Smollett navigate us halfway back again before I struck."

"Why, we're all seamen aboard here, I should think," said the lad Dick.

"We're all foc's'le hands, you mean," snapped Silver. "We can steer a course, but who's to set one? That's what all you gentlemen split on, first and last. If I had my way, I'd have Cap'n Smollett work us back into the trades at least; then we'd have no blessed miscalculations and a spoonful of water a day. But I

know the sort you are. I'll finish with 'em at the island, as soon's the blunt's on board, and a pity it is. But you're never happy till you're drunk. Split my sides, I've a sick heart to sail with the likes of you!"

"Easy all, Long John," cried Israel. "Who's a-crossin' of you?"

"Why, how many tall ships, think ye, now, have I seen laid aboard? and how many brisk lads drying in the sun at Execution Dock?"[19] cried Silver, "and all for this same hurry and hurry and hurry. You hear me? I seen a thing or two at sea, I have. If you would on'y lay your course, and p'int to windward, you would ride in carriages, you would. But not you! I know you. You'll have your mouthful of rum tomorrow, and go hang."

"Everybody know'd you was a kind of a chapling,[20] John; but there's others as could hand and steer as well as you," said Israel. "They liked a bit o' fun, they did. They wasn't so high and dry, nohow, but took their fling, like jolly companions every one."

"So?" says Silver. "Well, and where are they now? Pew was that sort, and he died a beggarman. Flint was, and he died of rum at Savannah. Ah, they was a sweet crew, they was! on'y, where are they?"

"But," asked Dick, "when we do lay 'em athwart, what are we to do with 'em, anyhow?"

19 Execution Dock: place in London where buccaneers were hanged.
20 chapling: chaplain.

FAMOUS CHARACTERS

"There's the man for me!" cried the cook, admiringly. "That's what I call business. Well, what would you think? Put 'em ashore like maroons? That would have been England's way. Or cut 'em down like that much pork? That would have been Flint's or Billy Bones's."

"Billy was the man for that," said Israel. " 'Dead men don't bite,' says he. Well, he's dead now hisself; he knows the long and short on it now; and if ever a rough hand come to port, it was Billy."

"Right you are," said Silver, "rough and ready. But mark you here: I'm an easy man—I'm quite the gentleman, says you; but this time it's serious. Dooty is dooty, mates. I give my vote—death. When I'm in Parlyment, and riding in my coach, I don't want none of these sea-lawyers in the cabin a-coming home, unlooked for, like the devil at prayers. Wait is what I say; but when the time comes, why let her rip!"

"John," cries the coxswain, "you're a man!"

"You'll say so, Israel, when you see," said Silver. "Only one thing I claim—I claim Trelawney. I'll wring his calf's head off his body with these hands, Dick!" he added, breaking off, "you just jump up, like a sweet lad, and get me an apple, to wet my pipe like."

You may fancy the terror I was in! I should have leaped out and run for it, if I had found the strength; but my limbs and heart alike misgave me. I heard Dick begin to rise, and then some one seemingly stopped him, and the voice of Hands exclaimed:

"Oh, stow that! Don't you get sucking of that bilge, John. Let's have a go of the rum."

"Dick," said Silver, "I trust you. I've a gauge on the keg, mind. There's the key; you fill a pannikin[21] and bring it up."

Terrified as I was, I could not help thinking to myself that this must have been how Mr. Arrow got the strong waters that destroyed him.

Dick was gone but a little while, and during his absence Israel spoke straight on in the cook's ear. It was but a word or two that I could catch, and yet I gathered some important news; for, besides other scraps that tended to the same purpose, this whole clause was audible: "Not another man of them'll jine." Hence there were still faithful men on board.

When Dick returned, one after another of the trio took the pannikin and drank—one "To luck;" another with a "Here's to old Flint;" and Silver himself saying, in a kind of song, "Here's to ourselves, and hold your luff, plenty of prizes and plenty of duff."

Just then a sort of brightness fell upon me in the barrel, and, looking up, I found the moon had risen, and was silvering the mizzentop and shining white on the luff of the foresail; and almost at the same time the voice of the lookout shouted, "Land ho!"

21 pannikin: cup.

Understanding Literature

1. Find evidence in the story indicating that Jim at first thought Long John Silver to be brave, respected, kind, and charming; in general, "the best of men."
2. What words might Jim have used to describe Silver after he overheard the conversation while in the apple barrel?
3. At the beginning of the chapter called "What I Heard in the Apple Barrel" how many people are talking? Who are they? What is the purpose of Long John's talk? What is it that Jim learns in the apple barrel that makes him realize that "the lives of all the honest men aboard depended upon me alone"?
4. Silver is a pirate and a leader of those who will endanger the lives of all honest men aboard the ship. But what good qualities do you see in his character?
5. Long John Silver and Jim Hawkins are the two main characters in the book, as they are in these two chapters. But there are, of course, many other characters in the book who are interesting and who help carry the story along to its outcome. Two of these minor characters are Captain Smollett and Israel

Hands, the coxswain. (*a*) How would you characterize Captain Smollett? What in the story causes you to describe him in this way? (*b*) How would you characterize Israel Hands? Explain what in the story causes you to describe him in this way. (*c*) How do you think Captain Smollett would act if the pirate members of the crew mutinied? (*d*) What role can you imagine Israel Hands playing in such a mutiny?

6. How does Stevenson create a feeling of suspense in the apple-barrel episode?

7. How is the transition made from the discussion of the loss of the ship's mate to a description of Long John Silver? How is the transition made from the captain's statement that the foc's'le hands are being spoiled to the story of Jim's being trapped in the apple barrel?

Kenneth Grahame said that he wrote for children because they are "the only really living people." But the many readers of his masterpiece, *The Wind in the Willows,* have understood that he was writing not only for children but also for all those people who are really interested in life itself. The Rat and the Mole, living in Rat's hole by the river bank, the Toad in his magnificent Toad Hall, and the Badger, who lives in the Wild Wood nearby, are the main characters in this book. In this chapter you will see how Mr. Toad lures Rat and Mole away from their beloved river to the open road and the beginning of some of their adventures.

from The Wind in the Willows

Kenneth Grahame

IMPROVING YOUR READING: Rat, Mole, Toad, Badger, and the other animals in *The Wind in the Willows* are not only animals; they are something more. They are distinctly individual characters with many of the characteristics of the people you know. In fact, each of them seems to be much more of a real "person" than many fictional people you will meet in your reading. By this fanciful treatment of animals, giving them the traits of human beings, Kenneth Grahame has enchanted children and adults while commenting on people and the way they behave.

THE OPEN ROAD

"RATTY," SAID THE Mole suddenly, one bright summer morning, "if you please, I want to ask you a favor."

The Rat was sitting on the river bank, singing a little song. He had just composed it himself, so he was very taken up with it, and would not pay proper attention to Mole or anything else. Since early morning he had been swimming in the river in company with his friends the ducks. And when the ducks stood on their heads suddenly, as ducks will, he would dive down and tickle their necks just under where their chins would be if ducks had chins, till they were forced to come to the surface again in a hurry, spluttering and angry and shaking their feathers at him, for it is impossible to say quite *all* you feel when your head is under water. At last they implored him to go away and attend to his own affairs and leave them to mind theirs. So the Rat went away, and sat on the river bank in the sun, and made up a song about them, which he called

"DUCKS' DITTY."

All along the backwater,
Through the rushes tall,
Ducks are a-dabbling,
Up tails all!

Ducks' tails, drakes' tails,
Yellow feet a-quiver,
Yellow bills all out of sight
Busy in the river!

Slushy green undergrowth
Where the roach swim—
Here we keep our larder,
Cool and full and dim.

Everyone for what he likes!
We like to be
Heads down, tails up,
Dabbling free!

High in the blue above
Swifts whirl and call—
We are down a-dabbling
Up tails all!

"I don't know that I think so *very* much of that little song, Rat," observed the Mole cautiously. He was no poet himself and didn't care who knew it; and he had a candid nature.

"Nor don't the ducks neither," replied the Rat cheerfully. "They say, 'Why can't fellows be allowed to do what they like *when* they like and *as* they like, instead of other fellows sitting on banks and watching them all the time and making remarks and poetry and things about them? What *nonsense* it all is!' That's what the ducks say."

"So it is, so it is," said the Mole, with great heartiness.

"No, it isn't!" cried the Rat indignantly.

"Well then, it isn't, it isn't," replied the Mole soothingly. "But what I wanted to ask you was, won't you take me to call on Mr. Toad? I've heard so much about him, and I do so want to make his acquaintance."

"Why, certainly," said the good-natured Rat, jumping to his feet and dismissing poetry from his mind for the day. "Get the boat out, and we'll paddle up there at once. It's never the wrong time to call on Toad. Early or late he's always the same fellow. Always good-tempered, always glad to see you, always sorry when you go!"

"He must be a very nice animal," observed the Mole, as he got into the boat and took the sculls, while the Rat settled himself comfortably in the stern.

"He is indeed the best of animals," replied Rat. "So simple, so good-natured, and so affectionate. Perhaps he's not very clever—we can't all be geniuses; and it may be that he is both boastful and conceited. But he has got some great qualities, has Toady."

Rounding a bend in the river, they came in sight of a handsome, dignified old house of mellowed red brick, with well-kept lawns reaching down to the water's edge.

"There's Toad Hall," said the Rat; "and that creek on the left, where the notice-board says, 'Private. No landing allowed,' leads to his boathouse, where we'll leave the boat. The stables are over there to the right. That's the banqueting hall you're looking at now—very old, that is. Toad is rather rich, you know, and this is really one of the nicest houses in these parts, though we never admit as much to Toad."

They glided up the creek, and the Mole shipped his sculls as they passed into the shadow of a large boathouse. Here they saw many handsome boats, slung from the crossbeams or hauled up on a slip, but none in the water; and the place had an unused and a deserted air.

The Rat looked around him. "I understand," said he. "Boating is played out. He's tired of it, and done with it. I wonder what new fad he has taken up now? Come along and let's look him up. We shall hear all about it quite soon enough."

They disembarked, and strolled across the gay flower-decked lawns in search of Toad, whom they presently happened upon resting in a wicker garden-chair, with a preoccupied expression of face, and a large map spread out on his knees.

"Hooray!" he cried, jumping up on seeing them, "this is splendid!" He shook the paws of both of them warmly, never waiting for an introduction to the Mole. "How *kind* of you!" he went on, dancing round them. "I was just going to send a boat down the river for you, Ratty, with strict orders that you were to be fetched up here at once, whatever you were doing. I want you badly—both of you. Now what will you take? Come inside and have something! You don't know how lucky it is, your turning up just now!"

"Let's sit quiet a bit, Toady!" said the Rat, throwing himself into an easy chair, while the Mole took another by the side of him and made some civil remark about Toad's "delightful residence."

"Finest house on the whole river," cried Toad boisterously. "Or anywhere else, for that matter," he could not help adding.

Here the Rat nudged the Mole. Unfortunately the Toad saw him do it, and turned very red. There was a moment's painful silence. Then Toad burst out laughing. "All right, Ratty," he said. "It's only my way, you know. And it's not such a very bad house, is it? You know you rather like it yourself. Now, look here. Let's be sensible. You are the very animals I wanted. You've got to help me. It's most important!"

"It's about your rowing, I suppose," said the Rat, with an innocent air. "You're getting on fairly well, though you splash a good bit still. With a great deal of patience, and any quantity of coaching, you may——"

"O, pooh! boating!" interrupted the Toad, in great disgust. "Silly boyish amusement. I've given that up *long* ago. Sheer waste of time, that's what it is. It makes me downright sorry to see you fellows, who ought to know better, spending all your energies in that aimless manner. No, I've discovered the real thing, the only genuine occupation for a lifetime. I propose to devote the remainder of mine to it, and can only regret the wasted years, that lie behind me, squandered in trivialities. Come with me, dear Ratty, and your amiable friend also, if he will be so very good, just as far as the stable yard, and you shall see what you shall see!"

He led the way to the stable yard accordingly, the Rat following with a most mistrustful expression; and there, drawn out of the coach house into the open, they saw a gypsy caravan, shining with newness, painted a canary-yellow picked out with green, and red wheels.

"There you are!" cried the Toad, straddling and expanding himself. "There's real life for you, embodied in that little cart. The open road, the dusty highway, the heath, the common, the hedgerows, the rolling downs! Camps, villages, towns, cities! Here today, up and off to somewhere else tomorrow! Travel, change, interest, excitement! The whole world before you, and a horizon that's always changing! And mind, this is the very finest cart of its sort that was ever built, without any exception. Come inside and look at the arrangements. Planned 'em all myself, I did!"

The Mole was tremendously interested and excited, and followed him eagerly up the steps and into the interior of the caravan. The Rat only snorted and thrust his hands deep into his pockets, remaining where he was.

It was indeed very compact and comfortable. Little sleeping-bunks—a little table that folded up against the wall—a cooking stove, lockers, bookshelves, a bird cage with a bird in it; and pots, pans, jugs and kettles of every size and variety.

"All complete!" said the Toad triumphantly, pulling open a locker. "You see—biscuits, potted lobster, sardines—everything you can possibly want. Soda water here—baccy there —letter paper, bacon, jam, cards and dominoes—you'll find," he continued, as they descended the steps again, "you'll find that nothing whatever has been forgotten, when we make our start this afternoon."

"I beg your pardon," said the Rat slowly, as he chewed a straw, "but did I overhear you say something about 'we,' and 'start,' and 'this afternoon'?"

"Now, you dear good old Ratty," said Toad imploringly, "don't begin talking in that stiff and sniffy sort of way, because you know you've *got* to come. I can't possibly manage without you, so please consider it settled, and don't argue—it's the one thing I can't stand. You surely don't mean to stick to your dull fusty old river all your life, and just live in a hole in a bank, and *boat*? I want to show you the world! I'm going to make an *animal* of you, my boy!"

"I don't care," said the Rat doggedly. "I'm not coming, and that's flat. And I *am* going to stick to my old river, *and* live in a hole, *and* boat, as I've always done. And what's more, Mole's going to stick to me and do as I do, aren't you, Mole?"

"Of course I am," said the Mole loyally. "I'll always stick to you, Rat, and what you say is to be—has got to be. All the same, it sounds as if it might have been—well, rather fun, you know!" he added wistfully. Poor Mole! The Life Adventurous was so new a thing to him, and so thrilling; and this fresh aspect of it was so tempting; and he had fallen in love at first sight with the canary-colored cart and all its little fitments.

The Rat saw what was passing in his mind, and wavered. He hated disappointing people, and he was fond of the Mole, and would do almost anything to oblige him. Toad

was watching both of them closely.

"Come along in and have some lunch," he said diplomatically, "and we'll talk it over. We needn't decide anything in a hurry. Of course, I don't really care. I only want to give pleasure to you fellows. 'Live for others!' That's my motto in life."

During luncheon—which was excellent, of course, as everything at Toad Hall always was—the Toad simply let himself go. Disregarding the Rat, he proceeded to play upon the inexperienced Mole as on a harp. Naturally a voluble[1] animal, and always mastered by his imagination, he painted the prospects of the trip and the joys of the open life and the roadside in such glowing colors that the Mole could hardly sit in his chair for excitement. Somehow, it soon seemed taken for granted by all three of them that the trip was a settled thing; and the Rat, though still unconvinced in his mind, allowed his good nature to override his personal objections. He could not bear to disappoint his two friends, who were already deep in schemes and anticipations, planning out each day's separate occupation for several weeks ahead.

When they were quite ready, the now triumphant Toad led his companions to the paddock and set them to capture the old gray horse, who, without having been consulted, and to his own extreme annoyance, had been told off by Toad for the dustiest job in this dusty expedition. He frankly preferred the paddock, and took a deal of catching. Meantime Toad packed the lockers still tighter with necessaries, and hung nose bags, nets of onions, bundles of hay, and baskets from the bottom of the cart. At last the horse was caught and harnessed, and they set off, all talking at once, each animal either trudging by the side of the cart or sitting on the shaft, as the humor took him. It was a golden afternoon. The smell of the dust they kicked up was rich and satisfying; out of thick orchards on either side the road, birds called and whistled to them cheerily; good-natured wayfarers, passing them, gave them "Good day," or stopped to say nice things about their beautiful cart; and rabbits, sitting at their front doors in the hedgerows, held up their fore paws, and said, "O my! O my! O my!"

Late in the evening, tired and happy and miles from home, they drew up on a remote common far from habitations, turned the horse loose to graze, and ate their simple supper sitting on the grass by the side of the cart. Toad talked big about all he was going to do in the days to come, while stars grew fuller and larger all around them, and a yellow moon, appearing suddenly and silently from nowhere in particular, came to keep them company and listen to their talk. At last they turned into their little bunks in the cart; and Toad, kicking out his legs, sleepily said, "Well, good night, you fellows! This is the real life for a gentleman! Talk about your old river!"

1 voluble: talkative.

KENNETH GRAHAME   533

"I *don't* talk about my river," replied the patient Rat. "You *know* I don't, Toad. But I *think* about it," he added pathetically, in a lower tone: "I think about it—all the time!"

The Mole reached out from under his blanket, felt for the Rat's paw in the darkness, and gave it a squeeze. "I'll do whatever you like, Ratty," he whispered. "Shall we run away tomorrow morning, quite early—*very* early—and go back to our dear old hole on the river?"

"No, no, we'll see it out," whispered back the Rat. "Thanks awfully, but I ought to stick by Toad till this trip is ended. It wouldn't be safe for him to be left to himself. It won't take very long. His fads never do. Good night!"

The end was indeed nearer than even the Rat suspected.

After so much open air and excitement the Toad slept very soundly, and no amount of shaking could rouse him out of bed next morning. So the Mole and Rat turned to, quietly and manfully, and while the Rat saw to the horse, and lit a fire, and cleaned last night's cups and platters, and got things ready for breakfast, the Mole trudged off to the nearest village, a long way off, for milk and eggs and various necessaries the Toad had, of course, forgotten to provide. The hard work had all been done, and the two animals were resting, thoroughly exhausted, by the time Toad appeared on the scene, fresh and gay, remarking what a pleasant easy life it was they were all leading now, after the cares and worries and fatigues of housekeeping at home.

They had a pleasant ramble that day over grassy downs and along narrow by-lanes, and camped, as before, on a common, only this time the two guests took care that Toad should do his fair share of work. In consequence, when the time came for starting next morning, Toad was by no means so rapturous about the simplicity of the primitive life, and indeed attempted to resume his place in his bunk, whence he was hauled by force. Their way lay, as before, across country by narrow lanes, and it was not till the afternoon that they came out on the high road, their first high road; and there disaster, fleet and unforeseen, sprang out on them —disaster momentous[2] indeed to their expedition, but simply overwhelming in its effect on the aftercareer of Toad.

They were strolling along the high road easily, the Mole by the horse's head, talking to him, since the horse had complained that he was being frightfully left out of it, and nobody considered him in the least; the Toad and the Water Rat walking behind the cart talking together—at least Toad was talking, and Rat was saying at intervals, "Yes, precisely; and what did *you* say to *him?*"—and thinking all the time of something very different, when far behind them they heard a faint warning hum, like the drone of a distant bee. Glancing back, they saw a small cloud of dust, with a dark center of energy, advancing on them at incredible speed, while

2 momentous: of great importance.

from out the dust a faint "Poop-poop!" wailed like an uneasy animal in pain. Hardly regarding it, they turned to resume their conversation, when in an instant (as it seemed) the peaceful scene was changed, and with a blast of wind and a whirl of sound that made them jump for the nearest ditch, it was on them! The "poop-poop" rang with a brazen shout in their ears, they had a moment's glimpse of an interior of glittering plate glass and rich morocco, and the magnificent motor car, immense, breath-snatching, passionate, with its pilot tense and hugging his wheel, possessed all earth and air for the fraction of a second, flung an enveloping cloud of dust that blinded and enwrapped them utterly, and then dwindled to a speck in the far distance, changed back into a droning bee once more.

The old gray horse, dreaming, as he plodded along, of his quiet paddock, in a new raw situation such as this simply abandoned himself to his natural emotions. Rearing, plunging, backing steadily, in spite of all the Mole's efforts at his head, and all the Mole's lively language directed at his better feelings, he drove the cart backwards toward the deep ditch at the side of the road. It wavered an instant—then there was a heart-rending crash—and the canary-colored cart, their pride and their joy, lay on its side in the ditch, an irredeemable wreck.

The Rat danced up and down in the road, simply transported with passion. "You villains!" he shouted, shaking both fists, "You scoundrels, you highwaymen, you—you—road hogs!—I'll have the law on you! I'll report you! I'll take you through all the Courts!" His homesickness had quite slipped away from him, and for the moment he was the skipper of the canary-colored vessel driven on a shoal by the reckless jockeying of rival mariners, and he was trying to recollect all the fine and biting things he used to say to masters of steam launches when their wash, as they drove too near the bank, used to flood his parlor carpet at home.

Toad sat straight down in the middle of the dusty road, his legs stretched out before him, and stared fixedly in the direction of the disappearing motor car. He breathed short, his face wore a placid, satisfied expression, and at intervals he faintly murmured "Poop-poop!"

The Mole was busy trying to quiet the horse, which he succeeded in doing after a time. Then he went to look at the cart, on its side in the ditch. It was indeed a sorry sight. Panels and windows smashed, axles hopelessly bent, one wheel off, sardine tins scattered over the wide world, and the bird in the bird cage sobbing pitifully and calling to be let out.

The Rat came to help him, but their united efforts were not sufficient to right the cart. "Hi! Toad!" they cried. "Come and bear a hand, can't you!"

The Toad never answered a word, or budged from his seat in the road; so they went to see what was the matter with him. They found him in a sort of trance, a happy smile on his face, his eyes still fixed on the dusty wake of their destroyer. At intervals he was still heard to murmur "Poop-poop!"

The Rat shook him by the shoulder. "Are you coming to help us, Toad?" he demanded sternly.

"Glorious, stirring sight!" murmured Toad, never offering to move. "The poetry of motion! The *real* way to travel! The *only* way to travel! Here today—in next week tomorrow! Villages skipped, towns and cities jumped—always somebody else's horizon! O bliss! O poop-poop! O my! O my!"

"O *stop* being an ass, Toad!" cried the Mole despairingly.

"And to think I never *knew!*" went on the Toad in a dreamy monotone. "All those wasted years that lie behind me, I never knew, never even *dreamt!* But *now*—but now that I know, now that I fully realize! O what a flowery track lies spread before me, henceforth! What dust clouds shall spring up behind me as I speed on my reckless way! What carts I shall fling carelessly into the ditch in the wake of my magnificent onset! Horrid little carts—common carts—canary-colored carts!"

"What are we to do with him?" asked the Mole of the Water Rat.

"Nothing at all," replied the Rat firmly. "Because there is really nothing to be done. You see, I know him from old. He is now possessed. He has got a new craze, and it always takes him that way, in its first stage. He'll continue like that for days now, like an animal walking in a happy dream, quite useless for all practical purposes. Never mind him. Let's go and see what there is to be done about the cart."

A careful inspection showed them that, even if they succeeded in righting it by themselves, the cart would travel no longer. The axles were in a hopeless state, and the missing wheel was shattered into pieces.

The Rat knotted the horse's reins over his back and took him by the head, carrying the bird cage and its hysterical occupant in the other hand. "Come on!" he said grimly to the Mole. "It's five or six miles to the nearest town, and we shall just have to walk it. The sooner we make a start the better."

"But what about Toad?" asked the Mole anxiously, as they set off together. "We can't leave him here, sitting in the middle of the road by himself, in the distracted state he's in! It's not safe. Supposing another Thing were to come along?"

"O, *bother* Toad," said the Rat savagely; "I've done with him!"

They had not proceeded very far on their way, however, when there was a pattering of feet behind them, and Toad caught them up and thrust a paw inside the elbow of each of them; still breathing short and staring into vacancy.

"Now, look here, Toad!" said the Rat sharply: "as soon as we get to the town, you'll have to go straight to the police station, and see if they know anything about that motor car and who it belongs to, and lodge a complaint against it. And then you'll have to go to a blacksmith's or a wheelwright's and arrange for the

KENNETH GRAHAME

cart to be fetched and mended and put to rights. It'll take time, but it's not quite a hopeless smash. Meanwhile, the Mole and I will go to an inn and find comfortable rooms where we can stay till the cart's ready, and till your nerves have recovered their shock."

"Police-station! Complaint!" murmured Toad dreamily. "Me *complain* of that beautiful, that heavenly vision that has been vouchsafed[3] me! *Mend* the *cart!* I've done with carts forever. I never want to see the cart, or to hear of it, again. O, Ratty! You can't think how obliged I am to you for consenting to come on this trip! I wouldn't have gone without you, and then I might never have seen that—that swan, that sunbeam, that thunderbolt! I might never have heard that entrancing sound, or smelt that bewitching smell! I owe it all to you, my best of friends!"

The Rat turned from him in despair. "You see what it is?" he said to the Mole, addressing him across Toad's head: "He's quite hopeless. I give it up—when we get to the town we'll go to the railway station, and with luck we may pick up a train there that'll get us back to River Bank tonight. And if ever you catch me going a-pleasuring with this provoking animal again!"—He snorted, and during the rest of that weary trudge addressed his remarks exclusively to Mole.

On reaching the town they went straight to the station and deposited Toad in the second-class waiting room, giving a porter twopence to keep a strict eye on him. They then left the horse at an inn stable, and gave what directions they could about the cart and its contents. Eventually, a slow train having landed them at a station not very far from Toad Hall, they escorted the spellbound, sleepwalking Toad to his door, put him inside it, and instructed his housekeeper to feed him, undress him, and put him to bed. Then they got out their boat from the boathouse, sculled down the river home, and at a very late hour sat down to supper in their own cozy riverside parlor, to the Rat's great joy and contentment.

The following evening the Mole, who had risen late and taken things very easy all day, was sitting on the bank fishing, when the Rat, who had been looking up his friends and gossiping, came strolling along to find him. "Heard the news?" he said. "There's nothing else being talked about, all along the river bank. Toad went up to Town by an early train this morning. And he has ordered a large and very expensive motor car."

3 **vouchsafed:** granted; given.

Understanding Literature

1. Describe the first scene of this chapter. What do you learn about Rat and Mole from what they say? from what they do?
2. You learn a good deal about Toad before you meet him. What do you learn about him from what Rat says? What do you learn about him from the description the author gives of his house, grounds, and boathouse?
3. As soon as you meet Toad, you learn even more about him from his own words and his way of talking. What does Toad's conversation before lunch reveal about his character?
4. Toad watches Mole and Rat closely after he proposes a trip in his new gypsy cart. Why does he suggest having some lunch before anything is decided?
5. How have you been prepared earlier in the story for the shift in Toad's passion for his cart to his new craze, cars?
6. Read again the description of the motor car's approach and passing. Notice the sounds that the car makes. What does it sound like in the distance? How are the sounds of the car described as it gets closer and passes? What sound do you hear again as it goes off into the distance? Notice that the author uses the name of the thing he is describing, a motor car, only once. Why do you think he uses the word just when he does in the description?
7. Why does the author capitalize the words Rat, Mole, and Toad throughout the selection?
8. Considering a real toad's appearance, why is it appropriate that the type of person which Mr. Toad resembles should be characterized in the form of a toad?
9. Turn back to Rat's song about the ducks. What does his song say about ducks? What does it imply about "everyone"? How does this song apply to the Rat and the Toad as well as to ducks? How can it apply to people as well?

Further Activities

1. ". . . that swan, that sunbeam, that thunderbolt! I might never have heard that entrancing sound, or smelt that bewitching smell!"

   Those are the words Toad uses to describe his new interest. They do *not* represent the point of view of Rat or Mole. Have you known anyone who has taken such an exaggerated interest in a new hobby, a sport, or another activity? Write a paragraph describing this interest or hobby from the point of view of the enthusiastic person.

2. The good-natured Rat did not want to go on the trip with Toad. He knew he would rather be on, in, or near the river, but he went to please his friends. If you have ever done something or gone somewhere just to please a friend, write about it, explaining why you went and the results of your doing so.

Focusing on Words

The italicized adjectives and adverbs in the following sentences all help to characterize one of the animals or the way he says something. First try to decide what you think the italicized words mean, judging from what you know of the situation being described and the character to whom they refer. Then look up each word in the glossary or a dictionary and choose the meaning which seems best suited to the use of the word in the sentence.

Words used to characterize Mole:
1. "He was no poet himself and didn't care who knew it; and he had a *candid* nature."
2. " 'Come with me, dear Ratty, and your *amiable* friend also, if he will be so very good. . . .' "
3. " 'All the same, it sounds as if it might have been—well, rather fun, you know!' he added *wistfully*."

Words used to characterize Rat:
4. " 'I don't care,' said the Rat *doggedly*. 'I'm not coming, and that's flat.' "
5. " 'Come on!' he said *grimly* to the Mole."

Words used to characterize Toad:
6. " '. . . it may be that he is both boastful and *conceited*.' "
7. " 'Finest house on the whole river,' cried Toad *boisterously*."
8. " 'Come along in, and have some lunch,' he said *diplomatically*, 'and we'll talk it over.' "
9. "Naturally a *voluble* animal, and always mastered by his imagination, he painted the prospects of the trip and the joys of the open life and the roadside in such glowing colors that the Mole could hardly sit in his chair for excitement."

Alone on an uninhabited island after a shipwreck, Robinson Crusoe faces the problem of how to survive. The adventures of Crusoe on the island are only a part of a whole book, but the island episode is the central part of the book and the best known. *The Life and Strange Surprising Adventures of Robinson Crusoe* was first published in 1719 and very soon became popular.

In the section of the book included here you will read about the first days on the island after the shipwreck. The first night ashore Crusoe slept in a tree. You meet him on the morning of the second day as he begins to solve the problems of his situation. Consider why Robinson Crusoe's nature well equips him to solve these problems.

from Robinson Crusoe

Daniel Defoe

IMPROVING YOUR READING: Robinson Crusoe's story is *fiction;* it is Defoe's imaginative account of a man's adventures. He based some of Robinson Crusoe's experiences on those of Alexander Selkirk, a sailor who did, in fact, live on an uninhabited island from 1704 to 1709. But the way that Defoe wrote his story leads the reader to believe that Robinson Crusoe's experiences actually did happen. Decide, as you read, how Defoe makes his story believable.

WHEN I WAKED it was broad day, the weather clear, and the storm abated, so that the sea did not rage and swell as before: but that which surprised me most, was, that the ship was lifted off in the night from the sand where she lay, by the swelling of tide, and was driven up almost as far as the rock which I first mentioned, where I had been so bruised by the dashing me against it; this being within about a mile from the shore where I was, and the ship seeming to stand upright still, I wished myself on board, that, at least, I might have some necessary things for my use.

When I came down from my apartment in the tree, I looked about me again, and the first thing I found was a boat, which lay as the wind and the sea had tossed her up upon the land, about two miles on my right hand. I walked as far as I could upon the shore to have got to her, but found a neck or inlet of water between me and the boat, which was about half a mile broad, so I came back for the present, being more intent upon getting at the ship, where I hoped to find something for my present subsistence.

A little after noon I found the sea very calm, and the tide ebbed so far out, that I could come within a quarter of a mile of the ship; and here I found a fresh renewing of my grief, for I saw evidently, that if we had kept on board, we had all been safe, that is to say, we had all got safe on shore, and I had not been so miserable as to be left entirely destitute of all comfort and company, as I now was; this forced tears from my eyes again, but as there was little relief in that, I resolved, if possible, to get to the ship, so I pulled off my clothes, for the weather was hot to the extremity, and took the water; but when I came to the ship, my difficulty was still greater to know how to get on board, for as she lay aground, and high out of the water, there was nothing within my reach to lay hold of. I swam round her twice, and the second time I spied a small piece of a rope, which I wondered I did not see at first, hang down by the fore-chains so low, as that with great difficulty I got hold of it, and by the help of that rope, got up into the forecastle of the ship; here I found that the ship was bulged, and had a great deal of water in her hold, but that she lay so on the side of a bank of hard sand, or rather earth, that her stern lay lifted up upon the bank, and her head low almost to the water; by this means all her quarter was free, and all that was in that part was dry; for you may be sure my first work was to search and to see what was spoiled and what was free; and first I found that all the ship's provisions were dry and untouched by the water, and being very well disposed to eat, I went to the bread-room and filled my pockets with biscuit, and eat it as I went about other things, for I had no time to lose; I also found some rum in the great cabin, of which

I took a large dram, and which I had indeed need enough of to spirit me for what was before me. Now I wanted nothing but a boat to furnish myself with many things which I foresaw would be very necessary to me.

It was in vain to sit still and wish for what was not to be had, and this extremity[1] roused my application; we had several spare yards, and two or three large spars of wood, and a spare topmast or two in the ship. I resolved to fall to work with these, and flung as many of them overboard as I could manage for their weight, tying every one with a rope that they might not drive away; when this was done I went down the ship's side, and pulling them to me, I tied four of them fast together at both ends as well as I could, in the form of a raft, and laying two or three short pieces of plank upon them crossways, I found I could walk upon it very well, but that it was not able to bear any great weight, the pieces being too light; so I went to work, and with the carpenter's saw I cut a spare topmast into three lengths, and added them to my raft, with a great deal of labor and pains, but hope of furnishing myself with necessaries encouraged me to go beyond what I should have been able to have done upon another occasion.

My raft was now strong enough to bear any reasonable weight; my next care was what to load it with, and how to preserve what I laid upon it

1 extremity: necessity.

from the surf of the sea. But I was not long considering this: I first laid all the plank or boards upon it that I could get, and having considered well what I most wanted, I first got three of the seamen's chests, which I had broken open and emptied, and lowered them down upon my raft; the first of these I filled with provisions, viz.:[2] bread, rice, three Dutch cheeses, five pieces of dried goat's flesh, which we lived much upon, and a little remainder of European corn which had been laid by for some fowls which we brought to sea with us, but the fowls were killed; there had been some barley and wheat together, but, to my great disappointment, I found afterwards that the rats had eaten or spoiled it all; as for liquors, I found several cases of bottles belonging to our skipper, in which were some cordial waters,[3] and in all about five or six gallons of rack:[4] these I stowed by themselves, there being no need to put them into the chest, nor no room for them. While I was doing this, I found the tide began to flow, though very calm, and I had the mortification to see my coat, shirt, and waistcoat, which I had left on shore upon the sand, swim away; as for my breeches, which were only linen and open-kneed, I swam on board in them and my stockings. However, this put me upon rummaging for clothes, of which I found enough, but took no more than I wanted for present use, for I had other things which my eye was more

upon, as first tools to work with on shore, and it was after long searching that I found out the carpenter's chest, which was indeed a very useful prize to me, and much more valuable than a shiploading of gold would have been at that time. I got it down to my raft, even whole as it was, without losing time to look into it, for I knew in general what it contained.

My next care was for some ammunition, and arms: there were two very good fowling pieces[5] in the great cabin, and two pistols; these I secured first, with some powder horns, and a small bag of shot, and two old rusty swords: I knew there were three barrels of powder in the ship, but knew not where our gunner had stowed them, but with much search I found them, two of them dry and good, the third had taken water; those two I got to my raft, with the arms, and now I thought myself pretty well freighted, and began to think how I should get to shore with them, having neither sail, oar, or rudder, and the least capful of wind would have overset all my navigation.

I had three encouragements, 1. A smooth calm sea, 2. The tide rising and setting in to the shore, 3. What little wind there was blew me towards the land; and thus, having found two or three broken oars belonging to the boat, and besides the tools which were in the chest, I found two saws, an ax, and a hammer, and with this cargo I put to sea. For a mile, or thereabouts, my raft

2 viz.: *videlicet,* Latin word meaning "namely."
3 cordial waters: spiritous liquors.
4 rack: arrack, an Eastern liquor made from rum and flavored with fruits and plants.

5 fowling pieces: lightweight guns.

went very well, only that I found it drive a little distant from the place where I had landed before, by which I perceived that there was some indraft of the water, and consequently I hoped to find some creek or river there, which I might make use of as a port to get to land with my cargo.

As I imagined, so it was, there appeared before me a little opening of the land, and I found a strong current of the tide set into it, so I guided my raft as well as I could to keep in the middle of the stream: but here I had like to have suffered a second shipwreck, which, if I had, I think verily would have broke my heart, for knowing nothing of the coast, my raft run aground at one end of it upon a shoal,[6] and not being aground at the other end, it wanted but a little that all my cargo had slipped off toward that end that was afloat, and so fallen into the water. I did my utmost by setting my back against the chests, to keep them in their places, but could not thrust off the raft with all my strength, neither durst I stir from the posture I was in, but holding up the chests with all my might, stood in that manner near half an hour, in which time the rising of the water brought me a little more upon a level, and a little after, the water still rising, my raft floated again, and I thrust her off with the oar I had, into the channel, and then driving up higher, I at length found myself in the mouth of a little river, with land on both sides, and a strong current or tide running up. I looked on both sides for a proper place to get to shore, for I was not willing to be driven too high up the river, hoping in time to see some ship at sea, and therefore resolved to place myself as near the coast as I could.

At length I spied a little cove on the right shore of the creek, to which with great pain and difficulty I guided my raft, and at last got so near, as that, reaching ground with my oar, I could thrust her directly in, but here I had liked to have dipped all my cargo into the sea again; for that shore lying pretty steep, that is to say sloping, there was no place to land, but where one end of my float, if it run on shore, would lie so high, and the other sink lower as before, that it would endanger my cargo again: all that I could do was to wait till the tide was at highest, keeping the raft with my oar like an anchor to hold the side of it fast to the shore, near a flat piece of ground, which I expected the water would flow over; and so it did: as soon as I found water enough, for my raft drew about a foot of water, I thrust her on upon that flat piece of ground, and there fastened or moored her by sticking my two broken oars into the ground; one on one side near one end, and one on the other side near the other end; and thus I lay till the water ebbed away, and left my raft and all my cargo safe on shore.

My next work was to view the country, and seek a proper place for my habitation, and where to stow my goods to secure them from whatever might happen; where I was I yet

6 **shoal:** sand bank where the water is shallow.

knew not, whether on the continent or on an island, whether inhabited or not inhabited, whether in danger of wild beasts or not: there was a hill not above a mile from me, which rose up very steep and high, and which seemed to overtop some other hills which lay as in a ridge from it northward; I took out one of the fowling pieces, and one of the pistols, and an horn of powder, and thus armed I traveled for discovery up to the top of that hill, where, after I had with great labor and difficulty got to the top, I saw my fate to my great affliction, (viz.) that I was in an island environed[7] every way with the sea, no land to be seen, except some rocks which lay a great way off, and two small islands less than this, which lay about three leagues to the west.

I found also that the island I was in was barren, and, as I saw good reason to believe, uninhabited, except by wild beasts, of whom however I saw none, yet I saw abundance of fowls, but knew not their kinds, neither when I killed them could I tell what was fit for food, and what not; at my coming back, I shot at a great bird which I saw sitting upon a tree on the side of a great wood: I believe it was the first gun that had been fired there since the creation of the world; I had no sooner fired, but from all the parts of the wood there arose an innumerable number of fowls of many sorts, making a confused screaming, and crying every one according to his usual note; but not one of them of any kind that I knew: as for the creature I killed, I

7 environed: surrounded.

took it to be a kind of a hawk, its color and beak resembling it, but had no talons or claws more than common: its flesh was carrion, and fit for nothing.

Contented with this discovery, I came back to my raft, and fell to work to bring my cargo on shore, which took me up the rest of that day, and what to do with myself at night I knew not, nor indeed where to rest; for I was afraid to lie down on the ground, not knowing but some wild beast might devour me, though, as I afterwards found, there was really no need for those fears.

However, as well as I could, I barricadoed[8] myself round with the chests and boards that I had brought on shore, and made a kind of a hut for that night's lodging; as for food, I yet saw not which way to supply myself, except that I had seen two or three creatures like hares run out of the wood where I shot the fowl.

I now began to consider, that I might yet get a great many things out of the ship, which would be useful to me, and particularly some of the rigging, and sails, and such other things as might come to land, and I resolved to make another voyage on board the vessel, if possible; and as I knew that the first storm that blew must necessarily break her all in pieces, I resolved to set all other things apart, until I got everything out of the ship that I could get; then I called a council, that is to say, in my thoughts, whether I should take back the raft, but this appeared impracticable; so I resolved to go as before, when the tide was down, and I did so, only that I stripped before I went from my hut, having nothing on but a checkered shirt, and a pair of linen drawers, and a pair of pumps on my feet.

I got on board the ship, as before, and prepared a second raft, and having had experience of the first, I neither made this so unwieldy, nor loaded it so hard, but yet I brought away several things very useful to me; as first, in the carpenter's stores I found two or three bags full of nails and spikes, a great screw jack,[9] a dozen or two of hatchets, and above all, that most useful thing called a grindstone; all these I secured together, with several things belonging to the gunner, particularly two or three iron crows,[10] and two barrels of musket bullets, seven muskets, and another fowling piece, with some small quantity of powder more; a large bag full of small shot, and a great roll of sheet lead: but this last was so heavy, I could not hoist it up to get it over the ship's side.

Besides these things, I took all the men's clothes that I could find, and a spare fore-topsail, a hammock, and some bedding; and with this I loaded my second raft, and brought them all safe on shore, to my very great comfort.

I was under some apprehensions during my absence from the land, that at least my provisions might be

9 **screw jack:** hoisting machine worked with a screw.
10 **crows:** bars of iron.

8 **barricadoed:** barricaded; fortified.

devoured on shore; but when I came back, I found no sign of any visitor, only there sat a creature like a wild-cat upon one of the chests, which when I came towards it, ran away a little distance, and then stood still; she sat very composed, and unconcerned, and looked full in my face, as if she had a mind to be acquainted with me; I presented my gun at her, but as she did not understand it, she was perfectly unconcerned at it, nor did she offer to stir away; upon which I tossed her a bit of biscuit, though by the way I was not very free of it, for my store was not great: however, I spared her a bit, I say, and she went to it, smelled of it, and ate it, and looked (as pleased) for more, but I thanked her, and could spare no more; so she marched off.

Having got my second cargo on shore, though I was fain[11] to open the barrels of powder, and bring them by parcels, for they were too heavy, being large casks, I went to work to make me a little tent with the sail and some poles which I cut for that purpose, and into this tent I brought everything that I knew would spoil, either with rain or sun, and I piled all the empty chests and casks up in a circle round the tent, to fortify it from any sudden attempt, either from man or beast.

When I had done this I blocked up the door of the tent with some boards within, and an empty chest set up on end without, and spreading one of the beds upon the ground, laying my two pistols just at my head, and my gun at length by me, I went to bed for the first time, and slept very quietly all night, for I was very weary and heavy, for the night before I had slept little, and had labored very hard all day, as well as to fetch all those things from the ship, as to get them on shore.

I had the biggest magazine[12] of all kinds now that ever were laid up I believe, for one man, but I was not satisfied still; for while the ship sat upright in that posture, I thought I ought to get everything out of her that I could; so every day at low water I went on board, and brought away something or other: but particularly the third time I went, I brought away as much of the rigging as I could, as also all the small ropes and rope-twine I could get, with a piece of spare canvas, which was to mend the sails upon occasion, the barrel of wet gunpowder: in a word, I brought away all the sails first and last, only that I was fain to cut them in pieces, and bring as much at a time as I could; for they were no more useful to be sails, but as mere canvas only.

But that which comforted me more still, was, that at last of all, after I had made five or six such voyages as these, and thought I had nothing more to expect from the ship that was worth my meddling with, I say, after all this, I found a great hogshead[13] of bread, and three large runlets[14] of rum or spirits, and a box

---

11 **fain:** obliged; compelled.

12 **magazine:** stock of provisions and goods.
13 **hogshead:** large cask or barrel.
14 **runlets:** casks holding about eighteen gallons.

of sugar, and a barrel of fine flour; this was surprising to me, because I had given over expecting any more provisions, except what was spoiled by the water; I soon emptied the hogshead of that bread, and wrapped it up parcel by parcel in pieces of the sails, which I cut out; and in a word, I got all this safe on shore also.

The next day I made another voyage; and now having plundered the ship of what was portable and fit to hand out, I began with the cables; and cutting the great cable into pieces, such as I could move, I got two cables and a hawser[15] on shore, with all the ironwork I could get; and having cut down the spritsail-yard, and the mizzen-yard, and everything I could to make a large raft, I loaded it with all those heavy goods, and came away. But my good luck began now to leave me; for this raft was so unwieldy, and so overladen, that after I was entered the little cove, where I had landed the rest of my goods, not being able to guide it so handily as I did the other, it overset, and threw me and all my cargo into the water; as for myself it was no great harm, for I was near the shore; but as to my cargo, it was great part of it lost, especially the iron, which I expected would have been of great use to me: however, when the tide was out, I got most of the pieces of cables ashore, and some of the iron, though with infinite labor; for I was fain to dip for it into the water, a work which fatigued me very much.

After this I went every day on board, and brought away what I could get.

I had been now thirteen days on shore, and had been eleven times on board the ship; in which time I had brought away all that one pair of hands could well be supposed capable to bring, though I believe verily, had the calm weather held, I should have brought away the whole ship piece by piece: but preparing the twelfth time to go on board, I found the wind begin to rise; however, at low water I went on board, and though I thought I had rummaged the cabin so effectually, as that nothing more could be found, yet I discovered a locker with drawers in it, in one of which I found two or three razors, and one pair of large scissors, with some ten or a dozen of good knives and forks; in another I found about thirty-six pounds[16] of value in money, some European coin, some Brazil, some pieces of eight,[17] some gold, some silver.

I smiled to myself at the sight of this money. O Drug! said I aloud, what art thou good for? thou art not worth to me, no not the taking off of the ground: one of those knives is worth all this heap: I have no manner of use for thee, e'en remain where thou art, and go to the bottom as a creature whose life is not worth saving. However, upon second thoughts, I took it away, and wrapping all this in a piece of canvas, I began to think of making another raft, but while I was preparing this, I

---

15 **hawser:** large rope used for securing a ship.

16 **pounds:** English monetary units.
17 **pieces of eight:** large silver coins of Spain.

FAMOUS CHARACTERS

found the sky overcast, and the wind began to rise, and in a quarter of an hour it blew a fresh gale from the shore; it presently occurred to me, that it was in vain to pretend to make a raft with the wind offshore, and that it was my business to be gone before the tide of flood began, otherwise I might not be able to reach the shore at all. Accordingly I let myself down into the water, and swam across the channel, which lay between the ship and the sands, and even that with difficulty enough, partly with the weight of the things I had about me, and partly the roughness of the water, for the wind rose very hastily, and before it was quite high water, it blew a storm.

But I was gotten home to my little tent, where I lay with all my wealth about me very secure. It blew very hard all the night, and in the morning when I looked out, behold no more ship was to be seen; I was a little surprised, but recovered myself with this satisfactory reflection, viz.: that I had lost no time, nor abated no diligence[18] to get everything out of her that could be useful to me, and that indeed there was little left in her that I was able to bring away if I had had more time.

I now gave over any more thoughts of the ship, or of anything out of her, except what might drive on shore from her wreck, as indeed divers[19] pieces of her afterwards did; but those things were of small use to me.

My thoughts were now wholly em-

18 nor abated no diligence: nor lessened my efforts.
19 divers: various.

ployed about securing myself against either savages, if any should appear, or wild beasts, if any were in the island; and I had many thoughts of the method how to do this, and what kind of dwelling to make, whether I should make me a cave in the earth, or a tent upon the earth: and, in short, I resolved upon both, the manner and description of which, it may not be improper to give an account of.

I soon found the place I was in was not for my settlement, particularly because it was upon a low moorish ground near the sea, and I believed would not be wholesome, and more particularly because there was no fresh water near it, so I resolved to find a more healthy and more convenient spot of ground.

I consulted several things in my situation which I found would be proper for me. 1st, health, and fresh water I just now mentioned. 2dly, shelter from the heat of the sun. 3dly, security from ravenous creatures, whether men or beasts. 4thly, a view to the sea, that if God sent any ship in sight, I might not lose any advantage for my deliverance, of which I was not willing to banish all my expectation yet.

In search of a place proper for this, I found a little plain on the side of a rising hill, whose front toward this little plain was steep as a house-side, so that nothing could come down upon me from the top; on the side of this rock there was a hollow place worn a little way in like the entrance or door of a cave, but there was not really any cave or way into the rock at all.

On the flat of the green, just before this hollow place, I resolved to pitch my tent; this plain was not above an hundred yards broad and about twice as long, and lay like a green before my door, and at the end of it descended irregularly every way down into the low-grounds by the seaside. It was on the N.N.W. side of the hill, so that I was sheltered from the heat every day, till it came to a W. and by S. sun, or thereabouts, which in those countries is near the setting.

Before I set up my tent, I drew a half circle before the hollow place, which took in about ten yards in its semidiameter from the rock, and twenty yards in its diameter, from its beginning and ending.

In this half circle I pitched two rows of strong stakes, driving them into the ground till they stood very firm like piles, the biggest end being out of the ground about five foot and a half, and sharpened on the top: the two rows did not stand above six inches from one another.

Then I took the pieces of cable which I had cut in the ship, and I laid them in rows one upon another, within the circle, between these two rows of stakes, up to the top, placing other stakes in the inside, leaning against them, about two foot and a half high, like a spur to a post, and this fence was so strong, that neither man or beast could get into it or over it. This cost me a great deal of time and labor, especially to cut the piles in the woods, bring them to the place, and drive them into the earth.

The entrance into this place I

made to be not by a door, but by a short ladder to go over the top, which ladder, when I was in, I lifted over after me, and so I was completely fenced in, and fortified, as I thought, from all the world, and consequently slept secure in the night, which otherwise I could not have done, though as it appeared afterward, there was no need of all this caution from the enemies that I apprehended danger from.

Into this fence or fortress, with infinite labor, I carried all my riches, all my provisions, ammunition and stores, of which you have the account above, and I made me a large tent, which, to preserve me from the rains that in one part of the year are very violent there, I made double, viz., one smaller tent within, and one large tent above it, and covered the uppermost with a large tarpaulin which I had saved among the sails.

And now I lay no more for a while in the bed which I had brought on shore, but in a hammock, which was indeed a very good one, and belonged to the mate of the ship.

Into this tent I brought all my provisions, and everything that would spoil by the wet, and having thus enclosed all my goods, I made up the entrance, which till now I had left open, and so passed and repassed, as I said, by a short ladder.

When I had done this, I began to work my way into the rock, and bringing all the earth and stones that I dug down out through my tent, I laid them up within my fence in the nature of a terrace, that so it raised the ground within about a foot and a half; and thus I made me a cave just behind my tent, which served me like a cellar to my house.

It cost me much labor, and many days, before all these things were brought to perfection, and therefore I must go back to some other things which took up some of my thoughts. At the same time it happened after I had laid my scheme for the setting up my tent, and making the cave, that a storm of rain falling from a thick dark cloud, a sudden flash of lightning happened, and after that a great clap of thunder, as is naturally the effect of it; I was not so much surprised with the lightning as I was with a thought which darted into my mind as swift as the lightning itself. O my powder! My very heart sunk within me, when I thought, that at one blast all my powder might be destroyed, on which, not my defense only, but the providing me food, as I thought, entirely depended; I was nothing near so anxious about my own danger, though had the powder took fire, I had never known who had hurt me.

Such impression did this make upon me, that after the storm was over, I laid aside all my works, my building, and fortifying, and applied myself to make bags and boxes to separate the powder, and keep it a little and a little in a parcel, in hope that whatever might come, it might not all take fire at once, and to keep it so apart that it should not be possible to make one part fire another. I finished this work in about a fortnight,[20] and I think my powder,

20 **a fortnight:** two weeks.

which in all was about 240 lb. weight, was divided in not less than a hundred parcels; as to the barrel that had been wet, I did not apprehend any danger from that, so I placed it in my new cave, which in my fancy I called my kitchen, and the rest I hid up and down in holes among the rocks, so that no wet might come to it, marking very carefully where I laid it.

In the interval of time while this was doing I went out once at least every day with my gun, as well to divert myself, as to see if I could kill anything fit for food, and as near as I could to acquaint myself with what the island produced. The first time I went out I presently discovered that there were goats in the island, which was a great satisfaction to me; but then it was attended with this misfortune to me, viz.: that they were so shy, so subtile, and so swift of foot, that it was the difficultest thing in the world to come at them. But I was not discouraged at this, not doubting but I might now and then shoot one, as it soon happened, for after I had found their haunts a little, I laid wait in this manner for them: I observed if they saw me in the valleys, though they were upon the rocks, they would run away as in a terrible fright; but if they were feeding in the valleys, and I was upon the rocks, they took no notice of me, from whence I concluded, that by the position of their optics,[21] their sight was so directed downward, that they did not readily see objects that were above them; so

afterward I took this method, I always climbed the rocks first to get above them, and then had frequently a fair mark. The first shot I made among these creatures, I killed a she-goat which had a little kid by her which she gave suck to, which grieved me heartily; but when the old one fell, the kid stood stock still by her till I came and took her up: and not only so, but when I carried the old one with me upon my shoulders, the kid followed me quite to my enclosure, upon which I laid down the dam, and took the kid in my arms, and carried it over my pale,[22] in hopes to have bred it up tame; but it would not eat, so I was forced to kill it and eat it myself: these two supplied me with flesh a great while, for I eat sparingly, and saved my provisions (my bread especially) as much as possibly I could. Having now fixed my habitation, I found it absolutely necessary to provide a place to make a fire in, and fuel to burn; and what I did for that, as also how I enlarged my cave, and what conveniences I made, I shall give a full account of in its place. But I must first give some little account of myself, and of my thoughts about living, which it may well be supposed were not a few.

I had a dismal prospect of my condition, for as I was not cast away upon that island without being driven, as is said, by a violent storm quite out of the course of our intended voyage, and a great way, viz. some hundreds of leagues, out of the

21 optics: eyes.

22 pale: fence.

ordinary course of the trade of mankind, I had great reason to consider it as a determination of Heaven, that in this desolate place, and in this desolate manner, I should end my life; the tears would run plentifully down my face when I made these reflections, and sometimes I would expostulate with myself, why Providence should thus completely ruin its creatures, and render them so absolutely miserable, so without help abandoned, so entirely depressed, that it could hardly be rational to be thankful for such a life.

But something always returned swift upon me to check these thoughts, and to reprove me; and particularly one day walking with my gun in my hand by the seaside, I was very pensive upon the subject of my present condition, when reason as it were expostulated with me the other way, thus: Well, you are in a desolate condition it is true, but pray remember, where are the rest of you? Did not you come eleven of you into the boat? Where are the ten? Why were not they saved and you lost? Why were you singled out? Is it better to be here or there? and then I pointed to the sea. All evils are to be considered with the good that is in them, and with what worse attends them.

Then it occurred to me again, how well I was furnished for my subsistence, and what would have been my case if it had not happened, which was an hundred thousand to one, that the ship floated from the place where she first struck and was driven so near the shore that I had time to get all these things out of her. What would have been my case, if I had been to have lived in the condition in which I at first came on shore, without necessaries of life, or necessaries to supply and procure them? Particularly, said I aloud (though to myself), what should I have done without a gun, without ammunition, without any tools to make anything, or to work with, without clothes, bedding, a tent, or any manner of covering? and that now I had all these to a sufficient quantity, and was in a fair way to provide myself in such a manner as to live without my gun when my ammunition was spent; so that I had a tolerable view of subsisting without any want as long as I lived; for I considered from the beginning how I would provide for the accidents that might happen, and for the time that was to come, even not only after my ammunition should be spent, but even after my health or strength should decay.

I confess I had not entertained any notion of my ammunition being destroyed at one blast, I mean my powder being blown up by lightning, and this made the thoughts of it so surprising to me when it lightened and thundered, as I observed just now.

And now being to enter into a melancholy relation of a scene of silent life, such perhaps as was never heard of in the world before, I shall take it from its beginning, and continue it in its order. It was, by my account, the 30th of Sept. when, in the manner as above said, I first set foot upon this horrid island, when the sun being, to us, in its autumnal equinox,[23] was almost just over my head, for I reckoned myself, by observation, to be in the latitude of 9 degrees 22 minutes north of the line.[24]

Understanding Literature

1. Crusoe's first move is to get to the ship for supplies. What kind of things does he first load into the chests on the raft? Are these the things you would expect him to take first? Why? What does he load next? Why is it a very useful prize to him?

2. How does Robinson Crusoe manage to get his raft to shore without sail, oar, or rudder? What characteristics of the man are shown by his being able to do so?

3. What factors does Robinson Crusoe take into consideration in choosing a permanent location for his home?

4. Thinking of his companions who were lost needlessly and of his own loneliness, Robinson Crusoe says, "this forced tears from my eyes again, but as there was little relief in that, I resolved, if possible, to get to the ship. . . ." What does this reaction show about Crusoe's character?

5. Cite evidence from the selection which shows that Robinson Crusoe is (a) foresighted, (b) resourceful, (c) levelheaded. Describe some of his other character traits. What makes you believe he had these traits?

6. Why would some men, given the supplies Robinson Crusoe had, have difficulty surviving on the island?

7. What things does Robinson Crusoe have which are unnecessary to support life? Name some of the modern equipment of everyday living which most people feel they cannot do without. Are these really necessities of life?

8. Why does Defoe enumerate so many of the items that Robinson Crusoe rescues from the ship? Point out other instances of Defoe's careful attention to detail.

9. Why is it particularly appropriate that the reader should see everything through Robinson Crusoe's eyes, that is, from his point of view? How does this point of view help to make the story believable?

Further Activity

Read again Defoe's description of the construction of the raft which Robinson Crusoe used to carry his first load of supplies to shore. Then reread his description of the construction of his permanent headquarters. Notice how the author explains each step in the building process so clearly and carefully that, given Crusoe's equipment, physical strength, and manual skill, you could build such a raft or home by following the steps Defoe describes.

Write a short paragraph in which you explain the way you have made something, such as a dress, a birdhouse, a cake, or a model airplane. Be sure that the explanation of your methods is so clear that someone reading your paper would be able to make the same object.

Focusing on Words

Some groups of words are seldom used except by those whose work or hobby calls for these words. Anyone, for instance, who is familiar with sailing ships and the sea would know the following italicized words used in *Robinson Crusoe*. If a reader is to understand fully stories relating to ships and the sea, he too must know these words. Which of the following italicized words do you know? Look up the meanings of those you do not know.

Words, of course, can have entirely different meanings when used in different ways. When you look up these words in the dictionary, be sure that you choose the appropriate meaning; in this case the appropriate meaning will sometimes be preceded by the abbreviation *Naut.* What does *Naut.* mean?

1. ". . . the tide *ebbed* so far out, that I could come within a quarter of a mile of the ship."
2. "[I] got up into the *forecastle* of the ship."
3. ". . . all her *quarter* was free. . . ."
4. ". . . we had several spare *yards,* and two or three large *spars* of wood. . . ."
5. My next care was "how to preserve what I laid upon [my raft] from the *surf* of the sea."
6. "[I] began to think how I should get to shore with them, having neither sail, oar, nor *rudder.* . . ."
7. ". . . my raft run aground . . . upon a *shoal.* . . ."
8. "I now began to consider, that I might yet get a great many things out of the ship . . . particularly some of the *rigging,* and sails. . . ."
9. ". . . I took all the men's clothes that I could find, and a spare *fore-topsail,* a hammock, and some bedding. . . ."

The Bad Boy of this story lived over a hundred years ago in a small seaport in northern New England. Thomas Bailey Aldrich based the story on his own boyhood, and the "I" of the story is frequently the author himself remembering the town he calls Rivermouth, his friends of that time, and what they did. The author looks back with fondness to his 19th-century New England childhood, but whether or not it was so very different in spirit from a 20th-century childhood remains for you to decide as you read this excerpt from *The Story of a Bad Boy*.

from The Story of a Bad Boy

Thomas Bailey Aldrich

IMPROVING YOUR READING: In telling the main story of the chapter—how the boys astonished Rivermouth—the author includes a great deal of the history of the cannons. At times he even treats them as people. A writer who describes inanimate objects as if they were human beings is using *personification*. Notice how the cannons are personified in this story.

HOW WE ASTONISHED
THE RIVERMOUTHIANS

Among the few changes that have taken place in Rivermouth during the past twenty years there is one which I regret. I lament the removal of all those varnished iron cannon which used to do duty as posts at the corners of streets leading from the river. They were quaintly ornamental, each set upon end with a solid shot soldered into its mouth, and gave to that part of the town a picturesqueness very poorly atoned for by the conventional wooden stakes that have deposed them.

These guns ("old sogers" the boys called them) had their story, like everything else in Rivermouth.

When that everlasting last war—the War of 1812, I mean—came to an end, all the brigs, schooners, and barks fitted out at this port as privateers were as eager to get rid of their useless twelve-pounders and swivels as they had previously been to obtain them. Many of the pieces had cost large sums, and now they were little better than so much crude iron—not so good, in fact, for they were clumsy things to break up and melt over. The government didn't want them; private citizens didn't want them; they were a drug in the market.

But there was one man, ridiculous beyond his generation, who got it into his head that a fortune was to be made out of these same guns. To buy them all, to hold on to them until war was declared again (as he had no doubt it would be in a few months), and then sell out at fabulous prices—this was the daring idea that addled the pate of[1] Silas Trefethen, "Dealer in E. & W. I. Goods and Groceries," as the faded sign over his shop door informed the public.

Silas went shrewdly to work, buying up every old cannon he could lay hands on. His back yard was soon crowded with broken-down gun carriages,[2] and his barn with guns, like an arsenal. When Silas's purpose got wind, it was astonishing how valuable that thing became which just now was worth nothing at all.

"Ha, ha!" thought Silas; "somebody else is tryin' tu git control of the market. But I guess I've got the start of *him.*"

So he went on buying and buying, oftentimes paying double the original price of the article. People in the neighboring towns collected all the worthless ordnance[3] they could find, and sent it by the cartload to Rivermouth.

When his barn was full, Silas began piling the rubbish in his cellar, then in his parlor. He mortgaged the stock of his grocery store, mortgaged his house, his barn, his horse, and would have mortgaged himself, if anyone would have taken him as security, in order to carry on the grand speculation. He was a ruined man, and as happy as a lark.

Surely poor Silas was cracked, like the majority of his own cannon. More or less crazy he must have been always. Years before this he purchased an elegant rosewood coffin, and kept it in one of the spare rooms in his residence. He even had his name engraved on the silver-plate, leaving a blank after the word "Died."

The blank was filled up in due time, and well it was for Silas that he secured so stylish a coffin in his opulent days, for when he died his worldly wealth would not have bought him a pine box, to say nothing of rosewood. He never gave up expecting a war with Great Britain. Hopeful and radiant to the last, his dying words were, *England—war—few days—great profits!*

It was that sweet old lady, Dame Jocelyn, who told me the story of Silas Trefethen; for these things happened long before my day. Silas died in 1817.

At Trefethen's death his unique collection came under the auctioneer's hammer. Some of the larger guns were sold to the town, and planted at the corners of divers[4] streets; others went off to the iron foundry; the balance, numbering twelve, were dumped down on a deserted wharf at the foot of Anchor Lane, where, summer after summer, they rested at their ease in the grass and fungi, pelted in autumn by the rain and annually buried by the winter snow. It is with these twelve guns that our story has to deal.

---

1 **addled . . . of:** confused; unbalanced.
2 **gun carriages:** wheeled bases for guns.
3 **ordnance:** artillery.

4 **divers:** several.

The wharf where they reposed was shut off from the street by a high fence—a silent, dreamy old wharf, covered with strange weeds and mosses. On account of its seclusion and the good fishing it afforded, it was much frequented by us boys.

There we met many an afternoon to throw out our lines, or play leap-frog among the rusty cannon. They were famous fellows in our eyes. What a racket they had made in the heyday of their unchastened youth! What stories they might tell now, if their puffy metallic lips could only speak! Once they were lively talkers enough; but there the grim sea dogs lay, silent and forlorn in spite of all of their former growlings.

They always seemed to me like a lot of venerable disabled tars,[5] stretched out on a lawn in front of a hospital, gazing seaward, and mutely lamenting their lost youth.

But once more they were destined to lift up their dolorous[6] voices—once more ere they keeled over and lay speechless for all time. And this is how it befell.

Jack Harris, Charley Marden, Harry Blake, and myself were fishing off the wharf one afternoon, when a thought flashed upon me like an inspiration.

"I say, boys!" I cried, hauling in my line hand over hand, "I've got something!"

"What does it pull like, youngster?" asked Harris, looking down at the taut line and expecting to see a big perch at least.

"Oh, nothing in the fish way," I returned, laughing; "it's about the old guns."

"What about them?"

"I was thinking what jolly fun it would be to set one of the old sogers on his legs and serve him out a ration of gunpowder."

Up came the three lines in a jiffy. An enterprise better suited to the disposition of my companions could not have been proposed.

In a short time we had one of the smaller cannon over on its back and were busy scraping the green rust from the touchhole.[7] The mold had spiked the gun so effectually, that for a while we fancied we should have to give up our attempt to resuscitate the old soger.

"A long gimlet[8] would clear it out," said Charley Marden, "if we only had one."

I looked to see if Sailor Ben's flag was flying at the cabin door, for he always took in the colors when he went off fishing.

"When you want to know if the Admiral's aboard, jest cast an eye to the buntin', my hearties," says Sailor Ben.

Sometimes in a jocose mood he called himself the Admiral, and I am sure he deserved to be one. The Admiral's flag was flying, and I soon procured a gimlet from his carefully kept tool chest.

5 **tars:** sailors.
6 **dolorous:** sorrowful.

7 **touchhole:** vent in the cannon through which fire was communicated to the powder.
8 **gimlet** (gĭm′lĭt): tool for boring holes.

FAMOUS CHARACTERS

Before long we had the gun in working order. A newspaper lashed to the end of a lath[9] served as a swab to dust out the bore.[10] Jack Harris blew through the touchhole and pronounced all clear.

Seeing our task accomplished so easily, we turned our attention to the other guns, which lay in all sorts of postures in the rank grass. Borrowing a rope from Sailor Ben, we managed with immense labor to drag the heavy pieces into position and place a brick under each muzzle to give it the proper elevation. When we beheld them all in a row, like a regular battery, we simultaneously conceived an idea, the magnitude of which struck us dumb for a moment.

Our first intention was to load and fire a single gun. How feeble and insignificant was such a plan compared to that which now sent the light dancing into our eyes!

"What could we have been thinking of?" cried Jack Harris. "We'll give 'em a broadside,[11] to be sure, if we die for it!"

We turned to with a will, and before nightfall had nearly half the battery overhauled and ready for service. To keep the artillery dry we stuffed wads of loose hemp into the muzzles, and fitted wooden pegs to the touchholes.

At recess the next noon the Centipedes[12] met in a corner of the school yard to talk over the proposed lark.

9 **lath:** thin, narrow strip of wood.
10 **bore:** interior of a cannon muzzle.
11 **give . . . broadside:** fire all the guns at once.
12 **Centipedes:** the name of the boys' club. Each of the twelve members wore a cent-piece on a cord around his neck.

The original projectors, though they would have liked to keep the thing secret, were obliged to make a club matter of it, inasmuch as funds were required for ammunition. There had been no recent drain on the treasury, and the society could well afford to spend a few dollars in so notable an undertaking.

It was unanimously agreed that the plan should be carried out in the handsomest manner, and a subscription to that end was taken on the spot. Several of the Centipedes hadn't a cent, excepting the one strung around their necks; others, however, were richer. I chanced to have a dollar, and it went into the cap quicker than lightning. When the club, in view of my munificence, voted to name the guns Bailey's Battery I was prouder than I have ever been since over anything.

The money thus raised, added to that already in the treasury, amounted to nine dollars—a fortune in those days; but not more than we had use for. This sum was divided into twelve parts, for it would not do for one boy to buy all the powder, not even for us all to make our purchases at the same place. That would excite suspicion at any time, particularly at a period so remote from the Fourth of July.

There were only three stores in town licensed to sell powder; that gave each store four customers. Not to run the slightest risk of remark, one boy bought his powder on Monday, the next boy on Tuesday, and so on until the requisite quantity was in our possession. This we put into a keg and carefully hid in a dry spot on the wharf.

Our next step was to finish cleaning the guns, which occupied two afternoons, for several of the old sogers were in a very congested state indeed. Having completed the task, we came upon a difficulty. To set off the battery by daylight was out of the question; it must be done at night; it must be done with fuses, for no doubt the neighbors would turn out after the first two or three shots, and it would not pay to be caught in the vicinity.

Who knew anything about fuses? Who could arrange it so the guns would go off one after the other, with an interval of a minute or so between?

Theoretically we knew that a minute fuse lasted a minute; double the quantity, two minutes; but practically we were at a standstill. There was but one person who could help us in this extremity—Sailor Ben. To me was assigned the duty of obtaining what information I could from the ex-gunner, it being left to my discretion whether or not to entrust him with our secret.

So one evening I dropped into the cabin and artfully turned the conversation to fuses in general, and then to particular fuses, but without getting much out of the old boy, who was busy making a twine hammock. Finally, I was forced to divulge the whole plot.

The Admiral had a sailor's love for a joke, and entered at once and heartily into our scheme. He volunteered to prepare the fuses himself, and I left the labor in his hands, having bound him by several extraordinary oaths—such as "Hope-I-may-die" and "Shiver-my-timbers"—not to betray us, come what would.

This was Monday evening. On Wednesday the fuses were ready. That night we were to unmuzzle Bailey's Battery. Mr. Grimshaw saw that something was wrong somewhere, for we were restless and absent-minded in the classes, and the best of us came to grief before the morning session was over. When Mr. Grimshaw announced "Guy Fawkes"[13] as the subject for our next composition, you might have knocked down the Mystic Twelve with a feather.

The coincidence was certainly curious, but when a man has committed, or is about to commit, an offense, a hundred trifles, which would pass unnoticed at another time, seem to point at him with convicting fingers. No doubt Guy Fawkes himself received many a start after he got his wicked kegs of gunpowder neatly piled up under the House of Lords.

Wednesday, as I have mentioned, was a half holiday, and the Centipedes assembled in my barn to decide on the final arrangements. These were as simple as could be. As the fuses were connected, it needed but one person to fire the train. Hereupon arose a discussion as to who

13 Guy Fawkes: a conspirator in the Gunpowder Plot, a scheme to destroy the King, Lords, and Commons of England by blowing them up on the day of the opening of Parliament. On November 5, 1605, Fawkes was about to fire the barrels of gunpowder under the House of Lords when he was seized.

FAMOUS CHARACTERS

was the proper person. Some argued that I ought to apply the match, the battery being christened after me, and the main idea, moreover, being mine. Others advocated the claim of Phil Adams as the oldest boy. At last we drew lots for the post of honor.

Twelve slips of folded paper, upon one of which was written "Thou art the man," were placed in a quart measure, and thoroughly shaken; then each member stepped up and lifted out his destiny. At a given signal we opened our billets. "Thou art the man," said the slip of paper trembling in my fingers. The sweets and anxieties of a leader were mine the rest of the afternoon.

Directly after twilight set in Phil Adams stole down to the wharf and fixed the fuses to the guns, laying a train of powder from the principal fuse to the fence, through a chink of which I was to drop the match at midnight.

At ten o'clock Rivermouth goes to bed. At eleven o'clock Rivermouth is as quiet as a country churchyard. At twelve o'clock there is nothing left with which to compare the stillness that broods over the little seaport.

In the midst of this stillness I arose and glided out of the house like a phantom bent on an evil errand; like a phantom I flitted through the silent street, hardly drawing breath until I knelt down beside the fence at the appointed place.

Pausing a moment for my heart to stop thumping, I lighted the match and shielded it with both hands until it was well under way, and then dropped the blazing splinter on the slender thread of gunpowder.

A noiseless flash instantly followed, and all was dark again. I peeped through the crevice in the fence, and saw the main fuse spitting out sparks like a conjurer. Assured that the train had not failed, I took to my heels, fearful lest the fuse might burn more rapidly than we calculated, and cause an explosion before I could get home. This, luckily, did not happen. There's a special Providence that watches over idiots, drunken men, and boys.

I dodged the ceremony of undressing by plunging into bed, jacket, boots, and all. I am not sure I took off my cap; but I know that I had hardly pulled the coverlid over me, when "Boom!" sounded the first gun of Bailey's Battery.

I lay as still as a mouse. In less than two minutes there was another burst of thunder, and then another. The third gun was a tremendous fellow and fairly shook the house.

The town was waking up. Windows were thrown open here and there and people called to each other across the streets asking what that firing was for.

"Boom!" went gun number four.

I sprung out of bed and tore off my jacket, for I heard the Captain feeling his way along the wall to my chamber. I was half undressed by the time he found the knob of the door.

"I say, sir," I cried, "do you hear those guns?"

"Not being deaf, I do," said the Captain, a little tartly—any reflection on his hearing always nettled him; "but what on earth they are for I can't conceive. You had better get up and dress yourself."

"I'm nearly dressed, sir."

"Boom! Boom"—two of the guns had gone off together.

The door of Miss Abigail's bedroom opened hastily, and that pink[14] of maidenly propriety stepped out into the hall in her nightgown—the only indecorous thing I ever knew her to do. She held a lighted candle in her hand and looked like a very aged Lady Macbeth.[15]

"O Dan'el, this is dreadful! What do you suppose it means?"

"I really can't suppose," said the Captain, rubbing his ear; "but I guess it's over now."

"Boom!" said Bailey's Battery.

Rivermouth was wide awake now, and half the male population was in the streets, running different ways, for the firing seemed to proceed from opposite points of the town. Everybody waylaid everybody else with questions; but as no one knew what was the occasion of the tumult, people who were not usually nervous began to be oppressed by the mystery.

Some thought the town was being bombarded; some thought the world was coming to an end, as the pious and ingenious Mr. Miller had predicted it would; but those who couldn't form any theory whatever were the most perplexed.

In the meanwhile Bailey's Battery bellowed away at regular intervals. The greatest confusion reigned everywhere by this time. People with lanterns rushed hither and thither. The town-watch had turned out to a man, and marched off, in admirable order, in the wrong direction. Discovering their mistake, they retraced their steps, and got down to the wharf just as the last cannon belched forth its lightning.

A dense cloud of sulphurous smoke floated over Anchor Lane, obscuring the starlight. Two or three hundred people, in various stages of excitement, crowded about the upper end of the wharf, not liking to advance farther until they were satisfied that the explosions were over. A board was here and there blown from the fence, and through the openings thus afforded a few of the more daring spirits at length ventured to crawl.

The cause of the racket soon transpired. A suspicion that they had been sold gradually dawned on the Rivermouthians. Many were exceedingly indignant, and declared that no penalty was severe enough for those concerned in such a prank; others—and these were the very people who had been terrified nearly out of their wits—had the assurance to laugh, saying that they knew all along it was only a trick.

The town-watch boldly took possession of the ground, and the crowd began to disperse. Knots of gossips lingered here and there near the place, indulging in vain surmises[16] as

14 pink: excellent example.
15 Lady Macbeth: In a scene from Shakespeare's play *Macbeth*, Lady Macbeth sleepwalks with a lighted candle in her hand.

16 surmises: guesses.

to who the invisible gunners could be.

There was no more noise that night, but many a timid person lay awake expecting a renewal of the mysterious cannonading. The Oldest Inhabitant refused to go to bed on any terms, but persisted in sitting up in a rocking chair, with his hat and mittens on, until daybreak.

I thought I should never get to sleep. The moment I drifted off in a doze I fell to laughing and woke myself up. But toward morning slumber overtook me, and I had a series of disagreeable dreams, in one of which I was waited upon by the ghost of Silas Trefethen with an exorbitant bill for the use of his guns. In another, I was dragged before a court-martial and sentenced by Sailor Ben, in a frizzled wig and three-cornered cocked hat, to be shot to death by Bailey's Battery—a sentence which Sailor Ben was about to execute with his own hand, when I suddenly opened my eyes and found the sunshine lying pleasantly across my face. I tell you I was glad!

That unaccountable fascination which leads the guilty to hover about the spot where his crime was committed drew me down to the wharf as soon as I was dressed. Phil Adams, Jack Harris, and others of the conspirators were already there, examining with a mingled feeling of curiosity and apprehension the havoc accomplished by the battery.

The fence was badly shattered and the ground plowed up for several yards round the place where the guns formerly lay—formerly lay, for now they were scattered every which way. There was scarcely a gun that hadn't burst. Here was one ripped open from muzzle to breech, and there was another with its mouth blown into the shape of a trumpet. Three of the guns had disappeared bodily, but on looking over the edge of the wharf we saw them standing on end in the tide-mud. They had popped overboard in their excitement.

"I tell you what, fellows," whispered Phil Adams, "it is lucky we didn't try to touch 'em off with punk.[17] They'd have blown us all to flinders."[18]

The destruction of Bailey's Battery was not, unfortunately, the only catastrophe. A fragment of one of the cannon had carried away the chimney of Sailor Ben's cabin. He was very mad at first, but having prepared the fuse himself he didn't dare complain openly.

"I'd have taken a reef in the blessed stovepipe," said the Admiral, gazing ruefully at the smashed chimney, "if I had known as how the Flagship was agoin' to be under fire."

The next day he rigged out an iron funnel, which, being in sections, could be detached and taken in at a moment's notice. On the whole, I think he was resigned to the demolition of his brick chimney. The stovepipe was a great deal more shipshape.

The town was not so easily appeased.[19] The selectmen determined

17 **punk:** slow-burning material used for such purposes as lighting fireworks.
18 **flinders:** pieces.
19 **appeased:** satisfied; calmed.

to make an example of the guilty parties, and offered a reward for their arrest, holding out a promise of pardon to any one of the offenders who would furnish information against the rest. But there were no faint hearts among the Centipedes. Suspicion rested for a while on several persons—on the soldiers at the fort; on a crazy fellow, known about town as "Bottle-Nose"; and at last on Sailor Ben.

"Shiver my timbers!" cried that deeply injured individual. "Do you suppose, sir, as I have lived to sixty year, an' ain't got no more sense than to go for to blaze away at my own upper riggin'? It doesn't stand to reason."

It certainly did not seem probable that Mr. Watson would maliciously knock over his own chimney, and Lawyer Hackett, who had the case in hand, bowed himself out of the Admiral's cabin convinced that the right man had not been discovered.

People living by the sea are always more or less superstitious. Stories of specter ships and mysterious beacons, that lure vessels out of their course and wreck them on unknown reefs, were among the stock legends of Rivermouth; and not a few people in the town were ready to attribute the firing of those guns to some supernatural agency. The Oldest Inhabitant remembered that when he was a boy a dim-looking sort of schooner hove to in the offing one foggy afternoon, fired off a single gun that didn't make any report, and then crumbled to nothing, spar, mast, and hulk, like a piece of burnt paper.

The authorities, however, were of the opinion that human hands had something to do with the explosions, and they resorted to deep-laid stratagems to get hold of the said hands. One of their traps came very near catching us. They artfully caused an old brass fieldpiece to be left on a wharf near the scene of our late operations. Nothing in the world but the lack of money to buy powder saved us from falling into the clutches of the two watchmen who lay secreted for a week in a neighboring sail loft.

It was many a day before the midnight bombardment ceased to be the town talk. The trick was so audacious and on so grand a scale that nobody thought for an instant of connecting us lads with it. Suspicion at length grew weary of lighting on the wrong person, and as conjecture—like the physicians in the epitaph—was in vain, the Rivermouthians gave up the idea of finding out who had astonished them.

They never did find out, and never will, unless they read this veracious[20] history. If the selectmen are still disposed to punish the malefactors,[21] I can supply Lawyer Hackett with evidence enough to convict Pepper Whitcomb, Phil Adams, Charley Marden, and the other honorable members of the Centipede Club. But really I don't think it would pay now.

20 **veracious:** truthful.
21 **malefactors** (măl'ə făk'tərs): criminals.

Understanding Literature

1. What part does Tom Bailey, the narrator, play in the planning and execution of the cannon incident? What do you learn about his character from this role?
2. How are the boys extremely lucky in their escapade?
3. You are often able to learn something about the character of the author himself from the way he writes about others. In other words, an author sometimes reveals his personality when he is describing someone else. From his descriptions of Silas and the Oldest Inhabitant do you get the impression that Thomas Bailey Aldrich has a sense of humor? Explain your answer.
4. The boys call the cannons "old sogers." When a writer describes objects as if they were human beings or gives to objects the characteristics of human beings, he is using *personification*.

   By calling the cannons "sogers," the boys are personifying the cannons, describing them in terms of people. Why is "old sogers" an appropriate name for the cannons? List all the instances in which the author compares the cannons to people, and explain why these are good comparisons.

Further Activity

In your reading you will often find a statement or an idea you immediately agree with because you yourself have had some personal experience which has led you to the same conclusion.

Consider the following statements or themes from *The Story of a Bad Boy*. Write a paragraph or two on one of these. In your paper prove the truth of the theme or statement by describing one of your own personal experiences. On the other hand, if your own experience has proved the opposite to be true, write a paragraph or two explaining why.

1. ". . . when a man has committed, or is about to commit, an offense, a hundred trifles, which would pass unnoticed at other times, seem to point at him with convicting fingers."
2. "The sweets and anxieties of a leader. . . ." (Be sure to explain what this phrase means before you proceed to agree or disagree with it.)
3. "There's a special Providence that watches over idiots, drunken men, and boys."
4. "People living by the sea are always more or less superstitious."

Sherlock Holmes, the detective hero of this story and of many others by Sir Arthur Conan Doyle, is one of the best-known characters in English literature. His stories have been made into movies and plays, and the image of the tall, thin Mr. Holmes with his double-peaked hat and his pipe has become familiar to millions of people even if they have not read the stories themselves.

This story, "The Redheaded League," is from *The Adventures of Sherlock Holmes,* which was published in 1891. *The Adventures* is a book of stories about Sherlock Holmes, each complete in itself. Here in this story you will meet Mr. Holmes and his friend and assistant, Dr. Watson, as Holmes's keen, analytical mind cuts through the confusion surrounding the Redheaded League to stop the plans of a dangerous criminal.

The Redheaded League

Sir Arthur Conan Doyle

IMPROVING YOUR READING: Notice who tells the story, from whose *point of view* you learn what happens. Why do you think the author chose to tell the story from this point of view?

Each detail and each small event should be important to every story's outcome and to the story's total effect on the reader. It is especially important in a detective story such as this that all the details, all the events, all the conversations included are there because they do contribute to the outcome of the story. Read carefully and try to predict the outcome of the mystery; that is, try to guess from everything you learn how the story will end.

I HAD CALLED upon my friend, Mr. Sherlock Holmes, one day in the autumn of last year and found him in deep conversation with a very stout, florid-faced, elderly gentleman with fiery red hair. With an apology for my intrusion, I was about to withdraw when Holmes pulled me abruptly into the room and closed the door behind me.

"You could not possibly have come at a better time, my dear Watson," he said cordially.

"I was afraid that you were engaged."

"So I am. Very much so."

"Then I can wait in the next room."

"Not at all. This gentleman, Mr. Wilson, has been my partner and helper in many of my most successful cases, and I have no doubt that he will be of the utmost use to me in yours also."

The stout gentleman half rose from his chair and gave a bob of greeting, with a quick little questioning glance from his small, fat-encircled eyes.

"Try the settee," said Holmes, relapsing into his armchair and putting his finger tips together, as was his custom when in judicial moods. "I know, my dear Watson, that you share my love of all that is bizarre and outside the conventions and humdrum routine of everyday life. You have shown your relish for it by the enthusiasm which has prompted you to chronicle,[1] and, if you will excuse my saying so, somewhat to embellish so many of my own little adventures."

"Your cases have indeed been of the greatest interest to me," I observed.

"You will remember that I remarked the other day, just before we went into the very simple problem presented by Miss Mary Sutherland, that for strange effects and extraordinary combinations we must go to life itself, which is always far more daring than any effort of the imagination."

"A proposition which I took the liberty of doubting."

"You did, Doctor, but none the less you must come round to my view, for otherwise I shall keep on piling fact upon fact on you until your reason breaks down under them and acknowledges me to be right. Now, Mr. Jabez Wilson here has been good enough to call upon me this morning, and to begin a narrative which promises to be one of the most singular which I have listened to for some time. You have heard me remark that the strangest and most unique things are very often connected not with the larger but with the smaller crimes, and occasionally, indeed, where there is room for doubt whether any positive crime has been committed. As far as I have heard, it is impossible for me to say whether the present case is an instance of crime or not, but the course of events is certainly among the most singular that I have ever listened to. Perhaps, Mr. Wilson, you would have the great kindness to recommence your narrative. I ask you not merely because my friend Dr. Watson has not heard the opening part but also because the peculiar nature of the story makes me anxious to have every possible detail from your lips. As a rule, when I have heard some slight indication of the course of events, I am able to guide myself by the thousands of other similar cases which occur to my memory. In the present instance I am forced to admit that the facts are, to the best of my belief, unique."

The portly client puffed out his chest with an appearance of some little pride and pulled a dirty and wrinkled newspaper from the inside pocket of his great-coat. As he glanced down the advertisement column, with his head thrust forward and the paper flattened out upon his knee, I took a good look at the man and endeavored, after the fashion of my companion, to read the indications which might be presented by his dress or appearance.

I did not gain very much, however, by my inspection. Our visitor bore every mark of being an average commonplace British tradesman, obese, pompous, and slow. He wore rather baggy gray shepherd's check trousers, a not overclean black frock coat, unbuttoned in the front, and a drab

1 chronicle: record.

waistcoat with a heavy brassy Albert chain, and a square pierced bit of metal dangling down as an ornament. A frayed top hat and a faded brown overcoat with a wrinkled velvet collar lay upon a chair beside him. Altogether, look as I would, there was nothing remarkable about the man save his blazing red head, and the expression of extreme chagrin and discontent upon his features.

Sherlock Holmes's quick eye took in my occupation, and he shook his head with a smile as he noticed my questioning glances. "Beyond the obvious facts that he has at some time done manual labor, that he takes snuff, that he is a Freemason,[2] that he has been in China, and that he has done a considerable amount of writing lately, I can deduce nothing else."

Mr. Jabez Wilson started up in his chair, with his forefinger upon the paper, but his eyes upon my companion.

"How, in the name of good fortune, did you know all that, Mr. Holmes?" he asked. "How did you know, for example, that I did manual labor? It's as true as gospel, for I began as a ship's carpenter."

"Your hands, my dear sir. Your right hand is quite a size larger than your left. You have worked with it, and the muscles are more developed."

"Well, the snuff, then, and the Freemasonry?"

"I won't insult your intelligence by telling you how I read that, especially as, rather against the strict rules of

your order, you use an arc-and-compass breastpin."

"Ah, of course, I forgot that. But the writing?"

"What else can be indicated by that right cuff so very shiny for five inches, and the left one with the smooth patch near the elbow where you rest it upon the desk?"

"Well, but China?"

"The fish that you have tattooed immediately above your right wrist could only have been done in China. I have made a small study of tattoo marks and have even contributed to the literature of the subject. That trick of staining the fishes' scales of a delicate pink is quite peculiar to China. When, in addition, I see a Chinese coin hanging from your watch chain, the matter becomes even more simple."

Mr. Jabez Wilson laughed heavily. "Well, I never!" said he. "I thought at first that you had done something clever, but I see that there was nothing in it, after all."

"I begin to think, Watson," said Holmes, "that I make a mistake in explaining. 'Omne ignotum pro magnifico,'[3] you know, and my poor little reputation, such as it is, will suffer shipwreck if I am so candid. Can you not find the advertisement, Mr. Wilson?"

"Yes, I have got it now," he answered with his thick red finger planted halfway down the column. "Here it is. This is what began it all. You just read it for yourself, sir."

2 **Freemason:** member of a well-known, secret society.

3 *Omne . . . magnifico:* "Whatever is unknown is magnified."

I took the paper from him and read as follows:

To the Redheaded League:

On account of the bequest of the late Ezekiah Hopkins, of Lebanon, Pennsylvania, U.S.A., there is now another vacancy open which entitles a member of the League to a salary of £ 4 a week for purely nominal services. All redheaded men who are sound in body and mind, and above the age of twenty-one years, are eligible. Apply in person on Monday, at eleven o'clock, to Duncan Ross, at the offices of the League, 7 Pope's Court, Fleet Street.

"What on earth does this mean?" I ejaculated after I had twice read over the extraordinary announcement.

Holmes chuckled and wriggled in his chair, as was his habit when in high spirits. "It is a little off the beaten track, isn't it?" said he. "And now, Mr. Wilson, off you go at scratch and tell us all about yourself, your household, and the effect which this advertisement had upon your fortunes. You will first make a note, Doctor, of the paper and the date."

"It is *The Morning Chronicle* of April 27, 1890. Just two months ago."

"Very good. Now, Mr. Wilson?"

"Well, it is just as I have been telling you, Mr. Sherlock Holmes," said Jabez Wilson, mopping his forehead; "I have a small pawnbroker's business at Coburg Square, near the City. It's not a very large affair, and of late years it has not done more than just give me a living. I used to be able to keep two assistants, but now I only keep one; and I would have a job to pay him but that he is willing to come for half wages so as to learn the business."

"What is the name of this obliging youth?" asked Sherlock Holmes.

"His name is Vincent Spaulding, and he's not such a youth, either. It's hard to say his age. I should not wish a smarter assistant, Mr. Holmes; and I know very well that he could better himself and earn twice what I am able to give him. But, after all, if he is satisfied, why should I put ideas in his head?"

"Why, indeed? You seem most fortunate in having an employee who comes under the full market price. It is not a common experience among employers in this age. I don't know that your assistant is not as remarkable as your advertisement."

"Oh, he has his faults, too," said Mr. Wilson. "Never was such a fellow for photography. Snapping away with a camera when he ought to be improving his mind, and then diving down into the cellar like a rabbit into its hole to develop his pictures. That is his main fault, but on the whole he's a good worker. There's no vice in him."

"He is still with you, I presume?"

"Yes, sir. He and a girl of fourteen, who does a bit of simple cooking and keeps the place clean—that's all I have in the house, for I am a widower and never had any family. We live very quietly, sir, the three of us; and we keep a roof over our heads and pay our debts, if we do nothing more.

"The first thing that put us out was that advertisement. Spaulding, he came down into the office just this day eight weeks, with this very paper in his hand, and he says:

" 'I wish to the Lord, Mr. Wilson, that I was a redheaded man.'

" 'Why that?' I asks.

" 'Why,' says he, 'here's another vacancy on the League of the Redheaded Men. It's worth quite a little fortune to any man who gets it, and I understand that there are more vacancies than there are men, so that the trustees are at their wits' end what to do with the money. If my hair would only change color, here's a nice little crib all ready for me to step into.'

" 'Why, what is it, then?' I asked. You see, Mr. Holmes, I am a very stay-at-home man, and as my business came to me instead of my having to go to it, I was often weeks on end without putting my foot over the door mat. In that way I didn't know much of what was going on outside, and I was always glad of a bit of news.

" 'Have you never heard of the League of the Redheaded Men?' he asked with his eyes open.

" 'Never.'

" 'Why, I wonder at that, for you are eligible yourself for one of the vacancies.'

" 'And what are they worth?' I asked.

" 'Oh, merely a couple of hundred a year, but the work is slight, and it need not interfere very much with one's other occupations.'

"Well, you can easily think that that made me prick up my ears, for the business has not been overgood for some years, and an extra couple of hundred would have been very handy.

" 'Tell me all about it,' said I.

" 'Well,' said he, showing me the advertisement, 'you can see for yourself that the League has a vacancy, and there is the address where you should apply for particulars. As far as I can make out, the League was founded by an American millionaire, Ezekiah Hopkins, who was very peculiar in his ways. He was himself redheaded, and he had a great sympathy for all redheaded men; so when he died it was found that he had left his enormous fortune in the hands of trustees, with instructions to apply the interest to the providing of easy berths to men whose hair is of that color. From all I hear it is splendid pay and very little to do.'

" 'But,' said I, 'there would be millions of redheaded men who would apply.'

" 'Not so many as you might think,' he answered. 'You see it is really confined to Londoners, and to grown men. This American had started from London when he was young, and he wanted to do the old town a good turn. Then, again, I have heard it is no use your applying if your hair is light red, or dark red, or anything but real bright, blazing, fiery red. Now, if you cared to apply, Mr. Wilson, you would just walk in; but perhaps it would hardly be worth your while to put yourself out of the way for the sake of a few hundred pounds.'

"Now, it is a fact, gentlemen, as you may see for yourselves, that my hair is of a very full and rich tint, so that it seemed to me that if there was to be any competition in the matter I stood as good a chance as any man that I had ever met. Vincent Spaulding seemed to know so much about it that I thought he might prove useful, so I just ordered him to put up the shutters for the day and to come right away with me. He was very willing to have a holiday, so we shut the business up and started off for the address that was given us in the advertisement.

"I never hope to see such a sight as that again, Mr. Holmes. From north, south, east, and west every man who had a shade of red in his hair had tramped into the city to answer the advertisement. Fleet Street was choked with redheaded folk, and Pope's Court looked like a coster's[4] orange barrow. I should not have thought there were so many in the whole country as were brought together by that single advertisement. Every shade of color they were— straw, lemon, orange, brick, Irish-setter, liver, clay; but, as Spaulding said, there were not many who had the real vivid flame-colored tint. When I saw how many were waiting, I would have given it up in despair; but Spaulding would not hear of it. How he did it I could not imagine, but he pushed and pulled and butted until he got me through the crowd, and right up to the steps which led to the office. There was a double stream upon the stair, some going up in hope, and some coming back dejected; but we wedged in as well as we could and soon found ourselves in the office."

4 **coster:** fruit seller.

"Your experience has been a most entertaining one," remarked Holmes as his client paused and refreshed his memory with a huge pinch of snuff. "Pray continue your very interesting statement."

"There was nothing in the office but a couple of wooden chairs and a deal table, behind which sat a small man with a head that was even redder than mine. He said a few words to each candidate as he came up, and then he always managed to find some fault in them which would disqualify them. Getting a vacancy did not seem to be such a very easy matter, after all. However, when our turn came the little man was much more favorable to me than to any of the others, and he closed the door as we entered, so that he might have a private word with us.

" 'This is Mr. Jabez Wilson,' said my assistant, 'and he is willing to fill a vacancy in the League.'

" 'And he is admirably suited for it,' the other answered. 'He has every requirement. I cannot recall when I have seen anything so fine.' He took a step backward, cocked his head on one side, and gazed at my hair until I felt quite bashful. Then suddenly he plunged forward, wrung my hand, and congratulated me warmly on my success.

" 'It would be injustice to hesitate,' said he. 'You will, however, I am sure, excuse me for taking an obvious precaution.' With that he seized my hair in both his hands, and tugged until I yelled with the pain. 'There is water in your eyes,' said he as he released me. 'I perceive that all is as it should be. But we have to be careful, for we have twice been deceived by wigs and once by paint. I could tell you tales of cobbler's wax which would disgust you with human nature.' He stepped over to the window and shouted through it at the top of his voice that the vacancy was filled. A groan of disappointment came up from below, and the folk all trooped away in different directions until there was not a redhead to be seen except my own and that of the manager.

" 'My name,' said he, 'is Mr. Duncan Ross, and I am myself one of the pensioners upon the fund left by our noble benefactor. Are you a married man, Mr. Wilson? Have you a family?'

"I answered that I had not.

"His face fell immediately.

" 'Dear me!' he said gravely, 'that is very serious indeed! I am sorry to hear you say that. The fund was, of course, for the propagation and spread of the redheads as well as for their maintenance. It is exceedingly unfortunate that you should be a bachelor.'

"My face lengthened at this, Mr. Holmes, for I thought that I was not to have the vacancy after all; but after thinking it over a few minutes he said that it would be all right.

" 'In the case of another,' said he, 'the objection might be fatal, but we must stretch a point in favor of a man with such a head of hair as yours. When shall you be able to enter upon your new duties?'

" 'Well, it is a little awkward, for I have a business already,' said I.

" 'Oh, never mind about that, Mr. Wilson!' said Vincent Spaulding. 'I should be able to look after that for you.'

" 'What would be the hours?' I asked.

" 'Ten to two.'

"Now a pawnbroker's business is mostly done of an evening, Mr. Holmes, especially Thursday and Friday evening, which is just before payday; so it would suit me very well to earn a little in the mornings. Besides, I knew that my assistant was a good man, and that he would see to anything that turned up.

" 'That would suit me very well,' said I. 'And the pay?'

" 'Is £4 a week.'

" 'And the work?'

" 'Is purely nominal.'⁵

" 'What do you call purely nominal?'

" 'Well, you have to be in the office, or at least in the building, the whole time. If you leave, you forfeit your whole position forever. The will is very clear upon that point. You don't comply with the conditions if you budge from the office during that time.'

" 'It's only four hours a day, and I should not think of leaving,' said I.

" 'No excuse will avail,' said Mr. Duncan Ross; 'neither sickness nor business nor anything else. There you must stay, or you lose your billet.'⁶

" 'And the work?'

" 'Is to copy out the Encyclopedia Britannica. There is the first volume of it in that press. You must find your own ink, pens, and blotting paper, but we provide this table and chair. Will you be ready tomorrow?'

" 'Certainly,' I answered.

" 'Then, good-by, Mr. Jabez Wilson, and let me congratulate you once more on the important position which you have been fortunate enough to gain.' He bowed me out of the room, and I went home with my assistant, hardly knowing what to say or do, I was so pleased at my own good fortune.

"Well, I thought over the matter all day, and by evening I was in low spirits again; for I had quite persuaded myself that the whole affair must be some great hoax or fraud, though what its object might be I could not imagine. It seemed altogether past belief that anyone could make such a will, or that they would pay such a sum for doing anything so simple as copying out the *Encyclopaedia Britannica*. Vincent Spaulding did what he could to cheer me up, but by bedtime I had reasoned myself out of the whole thing. However, in the morning I determined to have a look at it anyhow, so I bought a penny bottle of ink, and with a quill pen, and seven sheets of foolscap paper, I started off for Pope's Court.

"Well, to my surprise and delight, everything was as right as possible. The table was set out ready for me, and Mr. Duncan Ross was there to see that I got fairly to work. He started me off upon the letter *A*, and

5 nominal: trifling.
6 billet: position.

then he left me; but he would drop in from time to time to see that all was right with me. At two o'clock he bade me good day, complimented me upon the amount that I had written, and locked the door of the office after me.

"This went on day after day, Mr. Holmes, and on Saturday the manager came in and planked down four golden sovereigns for my week's work. It was the same next week, and the same the week after. Every morning I was there at ten, and every afternoon I left at two. By degrees Mr. Duncan Ross took to coming in only once of a morning, and then, after a time, he did not come in at all. Still, of course, I never dared to leave the room for an instant, for I was not sure when he might come, and the billet was such a good one, and suited me so well, that I would not risk the loss of it.

"Eight weeks passed away like this, and I had written about Abbots and Archery and Armor and Architecture and Attics, and hoped with diligence that I might get on to the B's before very long. It cost me something in foolscap, and I had pretty nearly filled a shelf with my writings. And then suddenly the whole business came to an end."

"To an end?"

"Yes, sir. And no later than this morning. I went to my work as usual at ten o'clock, but the door was shut and locked, with a little square of cardboard hammered on to the middle of the panel with a tack. Here it is, and you can read for yourself."

He held up a piece of white cardboard about the size of a sheet of note paper. It read in this fashion:

THE REDHEADED LEAGUE
IS
DISSOLVED.
October 9, 1890.

Sherlock Holmes and I surveyed this curt announcement and the rueful face behind it, until the comical side of the affair so completely overtopped every other consideration that we both burst out into a roar of laughter.

"I cannot see that there is anything very funny," cried our client, flushing up to the roots of his flaming head. "If you can do nothing better than laugh at me, I can go elsewhere."

"No, no," cried Holmes, shoving him back into the chair from which he had half risen. "I really wouldn't miss your case for the world. It is most refreshingly unusual. But there is, if you will excuse my saying so, something just a little funny about it. Pray what steps did you take when you found the card upon the door?"

"I was staggered, sir. I did not know what to do. Then I called at the offices round, but none of them seemed to know anything about it. Finally, I went to the landlord, who is an accountant living on the ground floor, and I asked him if he could tell me what had become of the Redheaded League. He said that he had never heard of any such body. Then I asked him who Mr. Duncan Ross was. He answered that the name was new to him.

" 'Well,' said I, 'the gentleman at No. 4.'

" 'What, the redheaded man?'

" 'Yes.'

" 'Oh,' said he, 'his name was William Morris. He was a solicitor and was using my room as a temporary convenience until his new premises were ready. He moved out yesterday.'

" 'Where could I find him?'

" 'Oh, at his new office. He did tell me the address. Yes, 17 King Edward Street, near St. Paul's.'

"I started off, Mr. Holmes, but when I got to that address it was a manufactory of artificial kneecaps, and no one in it had ever heard of either Mr. William Morris or Mr. Duncan Ross."

"And what did you do then?" asked Holmes.

"I went home to Saxe-Coburg Square, and I took the advice of my assistant. But he could not help me in any way. He could only say that if I waited I should hear by post. But that was not quite good enough, Mr. Holmes. I did not wish to lose such a place without a struggle, so as I had heard that you were good enough to give advice to poor folk who were in need of it, I came right away to you."

"And you did very wisely," said Holmes. "Your case is an exceedingly remarkable one, and I shall be happy to look into it. From what you have told me I think that it is possible that graver issues hang from it than might at first sight appear."

"Grave enough!" said Mr. Jabez Wilson. "Why, I have lost four pound a week."

"As far as you are personally concerned," remarked Holmes, "I do not see that you have any grievance against this extraordinary league. On the contrary, you are, as I understand, richer by some £30, to say nothing of the minute knowledge which you have gained on every subject which comes under the letter A. You have lost nothing by them."

"No, sir. But I want to find out about them, and who they are, and what their object was in playing this prank—if it was a prank—upon me. It was a pretty expensive joke for them, for it cost them two and thirty pounds."

"We shall endeavor to clear up these points for you. And, first, one or two questions, Mr. Wilson. This assistant of yours who first called your attention to the advertisement—how long had he been with you?"

"About a month then."

"How did he come?"

"In answer to an advertisement."

"Was he the only applicant?"

"No, I had a dozen."

"Why did you pick him?"

"Because he was handy and would come cheap."

"At half wages, in fact."

"Yes."

"What is he like, this Vincent Spaulding?"

"Small, stout-built, very quick in his ways, no hair on his face, though he's not short of thirty. Has a white splash of acid upon his forehead."

Holmes sat up in his chair in considerable excitement. "I thought as much," said he. "Have you ever observed that his ears are pierced for earrings?"

"Yes, sir. He told me that a gypsy had done it for him when he was a lad."

"Hum!" said Holmes, sinking back in deep thought. "He is still with you?"

"Oh, yes, sir; I have only just left him."

"And has your business been attended to in your absence?"

"Nothing to complain of, sir. There's never very much to do of a morning."

"That will do, Mr. Wilson. I shall be happy to give you an opinion upon the subject in the course of a day or two. Today is Saturday, and I hope that by Monday we may come to a conclusion."

"Well, Watson," said Holmes when our visitor had left us, "what do you make of it all?"

"I make nothing of it," I answered frankly. "It is a most mysterious business."

"As a rule," said Holmes, "the more bizarre a thing is the less mysterious it proves to be. It is your commonplace, featureless crimes which are really puzzling, just as a commonplace face is the most difficult to identify. But I must be prompt over this matter."

"What are you going to do, then?" I asked.

"To smoke," he answered. "It is quite a three pipe problem, and I beg that you won't speak to me for fifty minutes." He curled himself up in his chair, with his thin knees drawn up to his hawklike nose, and there he sat with his eyes closed and his black clay pipe thrusting out like the bill of some strange bird. I had come to the conclusion that he had dropped asleep, and indeed was nodding myself, when he suddenly sprang out of his chair with the gesture of a man who has made up his mind and put his pipe down upon the mantelpiece.

"Sarasate[7] plays at the St. James's Hall this afternoon," he remarked. "What do you think, Watson? Could your patients spare you for a few hours?"

"I have nothing to do today. My practice is never very absorbing."

"Then put on your hat and come. I am going through the City first, and we can have some lunch on the way. I observe that there is a good deal of German music on the program, which is rather more to my taste than Italian or French. It is introspective, and I want to introspect. Come along!"

We traveled by the Underground as far as Aldersgate; and a short walk took us to Saxe-Coburg Square, the scene of the singular story which we had listened to in the morning. It was a poky, little, shabby-genteel place, where four lines of dingy two-storied brick houses looked out into a small railed-in enclosure, where a lawn of weedy grass and a few clumps of faded laurel bushes made a hard fight against a smoke-laden and uncongenial atmosphere. Three gilt balls and a brown board with

7 Sarasate: a brilliant violinist.

"Jabez Wilson" in white letters, upon a corner house, announced the place where our redheaded client carried on his business. Sherlock Holmes stopped in front of it with his head on one side and looked it all over, with his eyes shining brightly between puckered lids. Then he walked slowly up the street, and then down again to the corner, still looking keenly at the houses. Finally he returned to the pawnbroker's, and, having thumped vigorously upon the pavement with his stick two or three times, he went up to the door and knocked. It was instantly opened by a bright-looking, clean-shaven young fellow, who asked him to step in.

"Thank you," said Holmes, "I only wished to ask you how you would go from here to the Strand."

"Third right, fourth left," answered the assistant promptly, closing the door.

"Smart fellow, that," observed Holmes as we walked away. "He is, in my judgment, the fourth smartest man in London, and for daring I am not sure that he has not a claim to be third. I have known something of him before."

"Evidently," said I, "Mr. Wilson's assistant counts for a good deal in this mystery of the Redheaded League. I am sure that you inquired your way merely in order that you might see him."

"Not him."

"What then?"

"The knees of his trousers."

"And what did you see?"

"What I expected to see."

"Why did you beat the pavement?"

"My dear doctor, this is a time for observation, not for talk. We are spies in an enemy's country. We know something of Saxe-Coburg Square. Let us now explore the parts which lie behind it."

The road in which we found ourselves as we turned round the corner from the retired Saxe-Coburg Square presented as great a contrast to it as the front of a picture does to the back. It was one of the main arteries which conveyed the traffic of the City to the north and west. The roadway was blocked with the immense stream of commerce flowing in a double tide inward and outward, while the footpaths were black with the hurrying swarm of pedestrians. It was difficult to realize as we looked at the line of fine shops and stately business premises that they really abutted on the other side upon the faded and stagnant square which we had just quitted.

"Let me see," said Holmes, standing at the corner and glancing along the line, "I should like just to remember the order of the houses here. It is a hobby of mine to have an exact knowledge of London. There is Mortimer's, the tobacconist, the little newspaper shop, the Coburg branch of the City and Suburban Bank, the Vegetarian Restaurant, and McFarlane's carriage-building depot. That carries us right on to the other block. And now, Doctor, we've done our work, so it's time we had some play. A sandwich and a cup of coffee, and then off to violin-land, where all is sweetness and delicacy and harmony, and there are no redheaded clients to vex us with their conundrums."[8]

My friend was an enthusiastic musician, being himself not only a very capable performer but a composer of no ordinary merit. All the afternoon he sat in the stalls wrapped in the most perfect happiness, gently waving his long, thin fingers in time to the music, while his gently smiling face and his languid, dreamy eyes were as unlike those of Holmes, the sleuth-hound, Holmes the relentless, keen-witted, ready-handed criminal agent, as it was possible to conceive. In his singular character the dual nature alternately asserted itself, and his extreme exactness and astuteness represented, as I have often thought, the reaction against the poetic and contemplative mood which occasionally predominated in him. The swing of his nature took him from extreme languor to devouring energy; and, as I knew well, he was never so truly formidable as when, for days on end, he had been lounging in his armchair amid his improvisations and his black-letter editions. Then it was that the lust of the chase would suddenly come upon him, and that his brilliant reasoning power would rise to the level of intuition, until those who were unacquainted with his methods would look askance at him as on a man whose knowledge was not that of other mortals. When I saw him that afternoon so enwrapped in the music at St. James's Hall I felt that an evil

---

8 vex . . . conundrums: annoy us with their riddles or puzzles.

time might be coming upon those whom he had set himself to hunt down.

"You want to go home, no doubt, Doctor," he remarked as we emerged.

"Yes, it would be as well."

"And I have some business to do which will take some hours. This business at Coburg Square is serious."

"Why serious?"

"A considerable crime is in contemplation. I have every reason to believe that we shall be in time to stop it. But today being Saturday rather complicates matters. I shall want your help tonight."

"At what time?"

"Ten will be early enough."

"I shall be at Baker Street at ten."

"Very well. And, I say, Doctor, there may be some little danger, so kindly put your army revolver in your pocket." He waved his hand, turned on his heel, and disappeared in an instant among the crowd.

I trust that I am not more dense than my neighbors, but I was always oppressed with a sense of my own stupidity in my dealings with Sherlock Holmes. Here I had heard what he had heard, I had seen what he had seen, and yet from his words it was evident that he saw clearly not only what had happened but what was about to happen, while to me the whole business was still confused and grotesque. As I drove home to my house in Kensington I thought over it all, from the extraordinary story of the redheaded copier of the Encyclopedia down to the visit to Saxe-Coburg Square, and the omi-

nous words with which he had parted from me. What was this nocturnal expedition, and why should I go armed? Where were we going, and what were we to do? I had the hint from Holmes that this smooth-faced pawnbroker's assistant was a formidable man—a man who might play a deep game. I tried to puzzle it out, but gave it up in despair and set the matter aside until night should bring an explanation.

It was a quarter past nine when I started from home and made my way across the Park, and so through Oxford Street to Baker Street. Two hansoms[9] were standing at the door, and as I entered the passage I heard the sound of voices from above. On entering his room I found Holmes in animated conversation with two men, one of whom I recognized as Peter Jones, the official police agent, while the other was a long, thin, sad-faced man, with a very shiny hat and oppressively respectable frock coat.

"Ha! our party is complete," said Holmes, buttoning up his pea jacket and taking his heavy hunting crop from the rack. "Watson, I think you know Mr. Jones, of Scotland Yard? Let me introduce you to Mr. Merryweather, who is to be our companion in tonight's adventure."

"We're hunting in couples again, Doctor, you see," said Jones in his consequential way. "Our friend here is a wonderful man for starting a chase. All he wants is an old dog to help him to do the running down."

9 **hansoms:** horse-drawn two-wheeled carriages; cabs.

"I hope a wild goose may not prove to be the end of our chase," observed Mr. Merryweather gloomily.

"You may place considerable confidence in Mr. Holmes, sir," said the police agent loftily. "He has his own little methods, which are, if he won't mind my saying so, just a little too theoretical and fantastic, but he has the makings of a detective in him. It is not too much to say that once or twice, as in that business of the Sholto murder and the Agra treasure, he has been more nearly correct than the official force."

"Oh, if you say so, Mr. Jones, it is all right," said the stranger with deference. "Still, I confess that I miss my rubber.[10] It is the first Saturday night for seven-and-twenty years that I have not had my rubber."

"I think you will find," said Sherlock Holmes, "that you will play for a higher stake tonight than you have ever done yet, and that the play will be more exciting. For you, Mr. Merryweather, the stake will be some £30,000; and for you, Jones, it will be the man upon whom you wish to lay your hands."

"John Clay, the murderer, thief, smasher, and forger. He's a young man, Mr. Merryweather, but he is at the head of his profession, and I would rather have my bracelets on him than on any criminal in London. He's a remarkable man, is young John Clay. His grandfather was a royal duke, and he himself has been to Eton and Oxford. His brain is as cunning as his fingers, and though we meet signs of him at every turn, we never know where to find the man himself. He'll crack a crib in Scotland one week, and be raising money to build an orphanage in Cornwall the next. I've been on his track for years and have never set eyes on him yet."

"I hope that I may have the pleasure of introducing you tonight. I've had one or two little turns also with Mr. John Clay, and I agree with you that he is at the head of his profession. It is past ten, however, and quite time that we started. If you two will take the first hansom, Watson and I will follow in the second."

Sherlock Holmes was not very communicative during the long drive and lay back in the cab humming the tunes which he had heard in the afternoon. We rattled through an endless labyrinth of gaslit streets until we emerged into Farrington Street.

"We are close there now," my friend remarked. "This fellow Merryweather is a bank director, and personally interested in the matter. I thought it as well to have Jones with us also. He is not a bad fellow, though an absolute imbecile in his profession. He has one positive virtue. He is as brave as a bulldog and as tenacious as a lobster if he gets his claws upon anyone. Here we are, and they are waiting for us."

We had reached the same crowded thoroughfare in which we had found ourselves in the morning. Our cabs were dismissed, and, following the guidance of Mr. Merryweather, we

10 rubber: round of whist, a card game.

passed down a narrow passage and through a side door, which he opened for us. Within there was a small corridor, which ended in a very massive iron gate. This also was opened, and led down a flight of winding stone steps, which terminated at another formidable gate. Mr. Merryweather stopped to light a lantern, and then conducted us down a dark, earth-smelling passage, and so, after opening a third door, into a huge vault or cellar, which was piled all round with crates and massive boxes.

"You are not very vulnerable from above," Holmes remarked as he held up the lantern and gazed about him.

"Nor from below," said Mr. Merryweather, striking his stick upon the flags which lined the floor. "Why, dear me, it sounds quite hollow!" he remarked, looking up in surprise.

"I must really ask you to be a little more quiet!" said Holmes severely. "You have already imperiled the whole success of our expedition. Might I beg that you would have the goodness to sit down upon one of those boxes, and not to interfere?"

The solemn Mr. Merryweather perched himself upon a crate, with a very injured expression upon his face, while Holmes fell upon his knees upon the floor and, with the lantern and a magnifying lens, began to examine minutely the cracks between the stones. A few seconds sufficed to satisfy him, for he sprang to his feet again and put his glass in his pocket.

"We have at least an hour before us," he remarked, "for they can hardly take any steps until the good pawnbroker is safely in bed. Then they will not lose a minute, for the sooner they do their work the longer time they will have for their escape. We are at present, Doctor—as no doubt you have divined—in the cellar of the City branch of one of the principal London banks. Mr. Merryweather is the chairman of directors, and he will explain to you that there are reasons why the more daring criminals of London should take a considerable interest in this cellar at present."

"It is our French gold," whispered the director. "We have had several warnings that an attempt might be made upon it."

"Your French gold?"

"Yes. We had occasion some months ago to strengthen our resources and borrowed for that purpose 30,000 napoleons from the Bank of France. It has become known that we have never had occasion to unpack the money, and that it is still lying in our cellar. The crate upon which I sit contains 2,000 napoleons packed between layers of lead foil. Our reserve of bullion is much larger at present than is usually kept in a single branch office, and the directors have had misgivings upon the subject."

"Which were very well justified," observed Holmes. "And now it is time that we arranged our little plans. I expect that within an hour matters will come to a head. In the meantime, Mr. Merryweather, we must put the screen over that dark lantern."

"And sit in the dark?"

"I am afraid so. I had brought a pack of cards in my pocket, and I thought that, as we were a *partie carrée*,[11] you might have your rubber after all. But I see that the enemy's preparations have gone so far that we cannot risk the presence of a light. And, first of all, we must choose our positions. These are daring men, and though we shall take them at a disadvantage, they may do us some harm unless we are careful. I shall stand behind this crate, and do you conceal yourselves behind those. Then, when I flash a light upon them, close in swiftly. If they fire, Watson, have no compunction about shooting them down."

I placed my revolver, cocked, upon the top of the wooden case behind which I crouched. Holmes shot the slide across the front of his lantern and left us in pitch darkness—such an absolute darkness as I have never before experienced. The smell of hot metal remained to assure us that the light was still there, ready to flash out at a moment's notice. To me, with my nerves worked up to a pitch of expectancy, there was something depressing and subduing in the sudden gloom, and in the cold dank air of the vault.

"They have but one retreat," whispered Holmes. "That is back through the house into Saxe-Coburg Square. I hope that you have done what I asked you, Jones?"

"I have an inspector and two officers waiting at the front door."

11 *partie carrée*: foursome.

"Then we have stopped all the holes. And now we must be silent and wait."

What a time it seemed! From comparing notes afterwards it was but an hour and a quarter, yet it appeared to me that the night must have almost gone, and the dawn be breaking above us. My limbs were weary and stiff, for I feared to change my position; yet my nerves were worked up to the highest pitch of tension, and my hearing was so acute that I could not only hear the gentle breathing of my companions, but I could distinguish the deeper, heavier inbreath of the bulky Jones from the thin, sighing note of the bank director. From my position I could look over the case in the direction of the floor. Suddenly my eyes caught the glint of a light.

At first it was but a lurid spark upon the stone pavement. Then it lengthened out until it became a yellow line, and then, without any warning or sound, a gash seemed to open and a hand appeared; a white, almost womanly hand, which felt about in the center of the little area of light. For a minute or more the hand, with its writhing fingers, protruded out of the floor. Then it was withdrawn as suddenly as it appeared, and all was dark again save the single lurid spark which marked a chink between the stones.

Its disappearance, however, was but momentary. With a rending, tearing sound, one of the broad, white stones turned over upon its side and left a square, gaping hole, through which streamed the light of a lantern. Over the edge there peeped a clean-cut, boyish face, which looked keenly about it, and then, with a hand on either side of the aperture, drew itself shoulder-high and waist-high, until one knee rested upon the edge. In another instant he stood at the side of the hole and was hauling after him a companion, lithe and small like himself, with a pale face and a shock of very red hair.

"It's all clear," he whispered. "Have you the chisel and the bags? Great Scott! Jump, Archie, jump, and I'll swing for it!"

Sherlock Holmes had sprung out and seized the intruder by the collar. The other dived down the hole, and I heard the sound of rending cloth as Jones clutched at his skirts. The light flashed upon the barrel of a revolver, but Holmes's hunting crop came down on the man's wrist, and the pistol clinked upon the stone floor.

"It's no use, John Clay," said Holmes blandly. "You have no chance at all."

"So I see," the other answered with the utmost coolness. "I fancy that my pal is all right, though I see you have got his coattails."

"There are three men waiting for him at the door," said Holmes.

"Oh, indeed! You seem to have done the thing very completely. I must compliment you."

"And I you," Holmes answered. "Your redheaded idea was very new and effective."

"You'll see your pal again presently," said Jones. "He's quicker at climbing down holes than I am. Just hold out while I fix the derbies."[12]

"I beg that you will not touch me with your filthy hands," remarked our prisoner as the handcuffs clattered upon his wrists. "You may not be aware that I have royal blood in my veins. Have the goodness, also, when you address me always to say 'sir' and 'please.' "

"All right," said Jones with a stare and a snigger. "Well, would you please, sir, march upstairs, where we can get a cab to carry your Highness to the police station?"

"That is better," said John Clay serenely. He made a sweeping bow to the three of us and walked quietly off in the custody of the detective.

"Really, Mr. Holmes," said Mr. Merryweather as we followed them from the cellar, "I do not know how the bank can thank you or repay you. There is no doubt that you have detected and defeated in the most complete manner one of the most determined attempts at bank robbery that have ever come within my experience."

"I have had one or two little scores of my own to settle with Mr. John Clay," said Holmes. "I have been at some small expense over this matter, which I shall expect the bank to refund, but beyond that I am amply repaid by having had an experience which is in many ways unique, and by hearing the very remarkable narrative of the Redheaded League."

"You see, Watson," he explained in the early hours of the morning as we sat over a glass of whisky and soda in Baker Street, "it was perfectly obvious from the first that the only possible object of this rather fantastic business of the advertisement of the League, and the copying of the Encyclopedia, must be to get this not overbright pawnbroker out of the way for a number of hours every day. It was a curious way of managing it, but, really, it would be difficult to suggest a better. The method was no doubt suggested to Clay's ingenious mind by the color of his accomplice's hair. The £4 a week was a lure which must draw him, and what was it to them, who were playing for thousands? They put in the advertisement, one rogue has the temporary office, the other rogue incites the man to apply for it, and together they manage to secure his absence every morning in the week. From the time that I heard of the assistant having come for half wages, it was obvious to me that he had some strong motive for securing the situation."

"But how could you guess what the motive was?"

"Had there been women in the house, I should have suspected a mere vulgar intrigue. That, however, was out of the question. The man's business was a small one, and there was nothing in his house which could account for such elaborate preparations, and such an expenditure as they were at. It must, then, be something out of the house. What could it be? I thought of the

12 derbies: handcuffs.

584

assistant's fondness for photography, and his trick of vanishing into the cellar. The cellar! There was the end of this tangled clue. Then I made inquiries as to this mysterious assistant and found that I had to deal with one of the coolest and most daring criminals in London. He was doing something in the cellar—something which took many hours a day for months on end. What could it be, once more? I could think of nothing save that he was running a tunnel to some other building.

"So far I had got when we went to visit the scene of action. I surprised you by beating upon the pavement with my stick. I was ascertaining whether the cellar stretched out in front or behind. It was not in front. Then I rang the bell, and, as I hoped, the assistant answered it. We have had some skirmishes, but we had never set eyes upon each other before. I hardly looked at his face. His knees were what I wished to see. You must yourself have remarked how worn, wrinkled, and stained they were. They spoke of those hours of burrowing. The only remaining point was what they were burrowing for. I walked round the corner, saw the City and Suburban Bank abutted on our friend's premises, and felt that I had solved my problem. When you drove home after the concert I called upon Scotland Yard and upon the chairman of the bank directors, with the result that you have seen."

"And how could you tell that they would make their attempt tonight?" I asked.

"Well, when they closed their League offices that was a sign that they cared no longer about Mr. Jabez Wilson's presence—in other words, that they had completed their tunnel. But it was essential that they should use it soon, as it might be discovered, or the bullion might be removed. Saturday would suit them better than any other day, as it would give them two days for their escape. For all these reasons I expected them to come tonight."

"You reasoned it out beautifully," I exclaimed in unfeigned admiration. "It is so long a chain, and yet every link rings true."

"It saved me from ennui,"[13] he answered, yawning. "Alas! I already feel it closing in upon me. My life is spent in one long effort to escape from the commonplaces of existence. These little problems help me to do so."

"And you are a benefactor of the race," said I.

He shrugged his shoulders. "Well, perhaps, after all, it is of some little use," he remarked. " 'L'homme c'est rien—l'oeuvre c'est tout,'[14] as Gustave Flaubert wrote to George Sand."[15]

13 **ennui** (än'wē): boredom.
14 **L'homme . . . tout:** "Man is nothing; his work is everything."
15 **Gustave Flaubert . . . George Sand:** 19th-century French writers.

Understanding Literature

1. From whose *point of view* is the story told?
2. The author plunges the reader immediately into the story and gives much information very quickly. What do you learn about the three characters and what they are doing in the first six short paragraphs?
3. How does Holmes's inspection of the client, Mr. Wilson, differ from Watson's? What does this difference in the way Holmes and Watson see Wilson point out about Sherlock Holmes?
4. After Holmes and Watson hear all the facts of Wilson's story and go to the pawnbroker's shop, Watson is still confused, whereas Holmes has obviously understood the whole affair and its results. Find the passage in which Watson remarks about his failure to understand the case whereas Holmes evidently has understood it completely. Considering what Watson says about himself in this passage, why do you think his *point of view* is a good one from which to tell the story? How would the story be different if Holmes had told it?
5. After you have finished the story, you understand the significance of some remarks or details that you had not understood previously. Point out in the early part of Wilson's story about himself and his business some details that Holmes makes mental note of and which help him solve the case. How do they help him solve the problem?
6. What in Mr. Wilson's description of the advertisement for the vacancy in the Redheaded League and his acceptance into the League aroused your suspicion as you read it—or that you see now *should* have aroused your suspicion?
7. At what point in the story do you first know that Sherlock Holmes has some clue as to the meaning of Wilson's story?
8. At what point were you able to begin to predict the outcome of the story? Explain what clues led you to your solution.
9. Why does Sherlock Holmes, according to his own words, work on such cases?
10. Describe Sherlock Holmes in your own words, basing your description on what Watson says about him, on what Holmes himself says, and on the way he acts. Be sure that you are able to prove all your statements about Sherlock Holmes from evidence in the story.

Author Biographies

AESOP (about 620-560 B.C.). (Pronounced ē′səp, ē′sŏp.) Although there is no positive proof that Aesop ever existed, most Greek scholars believe that a Greek slave with that name became famous for his witty retellings of Oriental animal stories. Aesop himself probably never wrote down any of these fables, but about 320 B.C. a ruler named Demetrius of Athens assembled the first known collection of Aesop's fables.

ALCOTT, LOUISA MAY (1832-1888 Louisa May Alcott wrote her first book, *Flower Fables*, for a friend's daughter. But she first became well known as a writer with *Hospital Sketches*, which first appeared in 1863. These sketches were letters which she had written to her family when she was a nurse for six weeks in a Washington hospital during the Civil War. In *Little Women* (1868) Louisa May Alcott herself appears as Jo. *Little Men* (1871) and *Jo's Boys* (1886) followed after *Little Women* and were equally popular.

ALDRICH, THOMAS BAILEY (1836-1907). Aldrich wrote about his own boyhood in Portsmouth, New Hampshire, in *The Story of a Bad Boy*. As he tells in that book, he had intended to go to college, but because of his father's death he went into business in New York. He left business for journalism, eventually returning to New England, where he was editor of *The Atlantic Monthly*, a famous magazine.

ALEXANDER, LEWIS (1900-   ). Lewis Alexander was educated in the public schools of Washington, D.C., and at Howard University where he was a member of the Howard Players. Since 1917 he has been writing poetry and specializing in Japanese forms. He played on Broadway with the Ethiopian Art Theatre and has directed the plays of two Little Theatre groups in Washington.

ARMOUR, RICHARD W. (1906-   ). Armour has had a long and distinguished career as both a teacher and a humorist. He has taught at universities in Europe and in the United States, and serves on the board of *The Writer*. Armour's children's books include *A Dozen Dinosaurs, Odd Old Mammals*, and *On Your Marks; A Package of Punctuation*. An extensive series of adult books—all spoofs—begin *It All Started with. . . .* For tired scholars he offers American *Lit. Relit, British Lit. Relit*, and *Twisted Tales of Shakespeare*, among many.

BALDWIN, JAMES (1841-1925). As he grew up in a backwoods Quaker settlement in Indiana, Baldwin developed a great affection for books and reading. At twenty-four he became a teacher; a few years later he moved up to the superintendency of the public schools of Indiana. Later he became an editor of school texts, and in his free time he wrote about fifty books, such as *The Story of Siegfried* and *The Story of Roland*.

BENÉT, ROSEMARY CARR (1898–).
See **BENÉT, STEPHEN VINCENT.**

BENÉT, STEPHEN VINCENT (1898-1943). (Pronounced bĭ nā′.) Benét's family was quite literary: his brother, William Rose Benét, was a very successful poet and novelist, as was his sister-in-law, Elinor Wylie; his wife, Rosemary Carr Benét, was a reporter for the *Chicago Tribune* when he first met her. Benét's most famous works deal with American history: *John Brown's Body* is a narrative poem about the Civil War; "The Devil and Daniel Webster" has become a classic short story.

BRADBURY, RAY (1920-). Best known as a writer of science fiction and fantasy, Bradbury writes of subjects which have interested him most of his life. At fifteen he decided that someday he should have a story of his own in a collection of *Best American Short Stories.* After graduation from high school, Bradbury sold newspapers for three years, while he wrote daily in his free time. His first published story appeared in a magazine when he was nineteen. After a few years of writing primarily for science-fiction and detective-story magazines, his earlier dream was realized when his story "The Big Black and White Game" was included in *The Best American Short Stories of 1946.*

BROWNING, ROBERT (1812-1889). Browning grew up in a London suburb, where he was given a thorough education by his intelligent, cultured parents. His early ambition was to be a poet; by the age of twelve he had written a book of poems. In 1846 Browning married Elizabeth Barrett, also a poet. Because of her poor health and the displeasure of her strong-willed father, they lived in Italy for fifteen years, until her death. Returning to England, Browning finally gained recognition for his poetry when he published *Dramatis Personae* and *The Ring and the Book.*

BULFINCH, THOMAS (1796-1867). One of eleven children of a famous architect, Bulfinch was born in Newton, Massachusetts. After graduation from Harvard in 1814, he was a teacher for a year. In 1818 the entire family moved to Washington, D.C., because the father, Charles Bulfinch, had been appointed architect of the United States Capitol. Thomas Bulfinch tried business several times, never with much success, and finally was satisfied to be a bank clerk because the job allowed so much time for study and writing. His best-known work is *The Age of Fable*, a collection of myths.

BURNS, ROBERT (1759-1796). The child who was to become the greatest of Scottish poets was born to a poor but respectable farm family in Ayrshire. Robert Burns had only a few years of formal schooling, and by the age of thirteen he was doing a man's work on the farm. Most of his life was spent in poverty, which probably contributed to his early death. Although Burns received a minimum of education in schools, he was educated, it has been said, by the traditional ballads and folk songs of Scotland. In poems like "The Cotter's Saturday Night" and songs like "Auld Lang Syne" he captures the moods and language of the Scottish people.

CAMPBELL, THOMAS (1777-1844). Born and educated in Glasgow, Scotland, Campbell became famous when he published *The Pleasures of Hope*. His best poems, such as "Ye Mariners of England," were written while he toured Germany and witnessed several battles and battle scenes. Eventually he settled in London and spent the rest of his life in various literary activities.

CANE, MELVILLE (1879-   ). Cane received his bachelor's degree from Columbia University in 1900, and a law degree in 1903. While at Columbia he edited its literary magazine. He then engaged in law practice, specializing in copyright law. Cane's interest in writing has ranged from the light verse of his early years to more recent serious poetry, articles, and short stories.

CARTER, RUSSELL GORDON (1892-1957). Born in New Jersey, Russell Gordon Carter attended Harvard, from which he graduated in 1916. He worked on several magazines and wrote numerous books based on scouting and American history.

CHILDRESS, ALICE (1920?-   ). Born in South Carolina, Alice Chil-dress grew up in Harlem where she studied acting at the American Negro Theatre. An actress and writer, she worked at times as apprentice machinist, photo-negative retoucher, governess, saleslady, and insurance agent. She has written several plays which have appeared off-Broadway and on television, and one book of topical humor, *Like One of the Family: Conversations from a Domestic's Life*.

CLEMENS, SAMUEL LANGHORNE. *See* TWAIN, MARK.

COLETTE (1873-1954). The child who was to become one of France's greatest women writers was named Gabrielle Claudine Colette when she was born in a village in Burgundy. At the age of twenty she married a music critic and novelist who used the pen name "Willy," and together the couple wrote a highly successful series of novels. During World War I, Colette converted an estate into a hospital where she worked as a nurse. Over the years she turned out an impressive list of novels and short stories, always distinguished by her ability to describe scenes, sounds, odors, and other sensations with great clarity and realism.

COLUM, PADRAIC (1881-1972). (Pronounced pô'drik kol'em.) A native of Ireland, Padraic Colum did not migrate to the United States until he had achieved moderate success as a poet and playwright in Dublin. The vast majority of his published works appeared since he came to America in 1914. Many of Colum's stories and plays are based on Irish folk tales. In 1923 he visited Hawaii to record Polynesian folk stories.

COWPER, WILLIAM (1731-1800). (Pronounced koo'per, kou'per.) Cowper's life contained a series of unfortunate events. Six years after his birth in Hertfordshire, England, his mother died. In "Tirocinium" he describes how he was bullied by the boys in his first school. He was unhappy in his London law practice and disappointed when his uncle forbade his marriage to his cousin Theodora. Throughout the rest of his life he lived with various families and wrote poetry and hymns. He is known for a humorous ballad, "John Gilpin," and a long poem, *The Task*.

CRANE, STEPHEN (1871-1900). Born in Newark, New Jersey, Stephen Crane lived in a great variety of circumstances during his short life before he died of tuberculosis in Germany. For five years he lived in New York City, sometimes among students, sometimes in the Bowery slums. Crane's first novel, written under a pseudonym, was a realistic description of the hard life of the slums. His ability to depict the terrors of war was a feature of his famous novel, *The Red Badge of Courage*, although when he wrote it, Crane had no personal experience with war.

CULLEN, COUNTEE (1903-1946). Born Countee Porter, he was orphaned at an early age and adopted by Reverend Frederick Cullen, pastor of a church in New York City. He won poetry prizes and scholastic honors in high school and at New York University. *Color*, his first volume of poetry, won the Harmon Gold Award for literature when he was only twenty-two years old. The following year, 1926, he received a Master's degree from Harvard and became a teacher, an occupation he continued all his life. His works include one novel, an anthology of American Negro poetry, and eight books of poetry. *On These I Stand*, a volume of selected poems of Countee Cullen, was published a year after his death.

DAVIS, FRANK MARSHALL (1905-   ). Born in Kansas, Frank Marshall Davis attended school there and studied journalism at Kansas State College, where he also began writing poetry. During the summers he worked on farms and on street construction crews. Much of his adult life has been spent in newspaper work—he began one paper and was its editor—and he has lived, besides Kansas, in Georgia and Hawaii. Three volumes of his poetry are *Black Man's Verse, I Am the American Negro*, and *47th Street*. He has also been a lecturer on the history of jazz.

DAY, CLARENCE S. (1874-1935). The parents of Clarence Day, Jr., are well known, not because they were famous by their own efforts, but because they are so thoroughly described in two of their son's widely read books, *Life with Father* and *Life with Mother*. Day's father was a very successful financier in the New York Stock Exchange, and after Clarence, Jr., graduated from Yale University in 1896, he joined his father's stocks and bonds brokerage. He left to join the Navy during the Spanish-American War, during which he began to be crippled by arthritis. Although confined to bed much of the time, he continued to write essays and books.

DEFOE, DANIEL (1660-1731). During the early part of his life Defoe was a London merchant. His business success ended abruptly in 1692 when he went bankrupt. He then turned to writing pamphlets, books, and newspapers. In 1719 he published *Robinson Crusoe*, his first novel. Later he produced such other well-known books as *A Journal of the Plague Year* and *Moll Flanders*.

DICKINSON, EMILY (1830-1886). Born in Amherst, Massachusetts, Emily Dickinson was the daughter of the community's leading lawyer, Edward Dickinson. After a brief formal education and an unhappy love affair, Emily Dickinson spent most of her time at home, seeing only a limited circle of friends. Her poetry was written in secret on scraps of paper and tucked away in bureau drawers. Only three or four Dickinson poems were published during her lifetime, but a collection of her poems published several years after her death was a great success. Ever since then her poetry has been admired for its sharp wit and graceful, though often irregular, rhythm.

DOYLE, SIR ARTHUR CONAN (1859-1930). Sherlock Holmes, one of the most famous characters in English literature, might never have existed if Arthur Conan Doyle, a Scottish doctor, had not needed money to supplement a meager medical practice. Doyle created Holmes as the fictional sleuth who solved crimes scientifically by careful observation and diagnosis of situations and people. The Sherlock Holmes stories were such a success that Doyle eventually gave up the practice of medicine to devote his full time to writing. The first Holmes story was *A Study in Scarlet*, published in 1887. *The Adventures of Sherlock Holmes*, a cycle of stories each complete in itself, was published in 1891.

DUNSANY, EDWARD JOHN MORETON DRAX PLUNKETT, LORD (1878-1957). Born in London, of Irish parentage, Dunsany became the 18th Baron Dunsany. He was educated at Sandhurst, the English equivalent of West Point, and applied his military training in the Boer War and World War I. His first literary ventures were in drama, but he also wrote poetry and short stories. His works often use fantasy.

DURRELL, GERALD M. (1925-   ). A noted zoologist as well as a writer, Durrell has produced many books for juveniles and is a frequent contributor to magazines and dailies. He founded the Jersey (England) Zoo

Park in 1959 and has made several zoological expeditions to the Cameroons and British Guiana. Among his writings are *A Bevy of Beasts, Menagerie Manor, My Family and Other Animals,* and *A Zoo in My Luggage.*

EATON, JEANETTE. Born in Columbus, Ohio, Jeanette Eaton earned her master's degree from Ohio State University in that city in 1910 after receiving her first degree from Vassar College in 1908. She is known chiefly as a biographer for young readers, and her books include *Young Lafayette, Jeanne d'Arc,* and *Betsy's Napoleon.*

FIELD, EUGENE (1850-1895). Field, born in St. Louis, Missouri, was sent to Massachusetts to live with relatives after his mother died when he was six. He attended several colleges, but never received a degree. Most of his adult life was spent as a newspaper reporter and columnist in several cities of the Midwest. He is known chiefly for a few children's poems which have been very popular.

FLACK, AMBROSE (1902?-   ). Flack was raised in Syracuse, New York, where he had a chance meeting with his family's idol, Theodore Roosevelt, described in a short story called "Theodore Roosevelt and My Green-Gold Fountain Pen." Flack has always enjoyed writing about children in his magazine stories.

FRANCE, ANATOLE (1844-1924). (Pronounced a na tôl' fräNs.) The son of a Paris bookseller, Jacques Anatole François Thibault was given a thorough education in the Greek and Roman classics, although he perhaps learned even more from his father's library and the discussions of artists in the family home. Throughout his life he preferred reading to writing, and the prodding of his friends was needed to make him work steadily. France's short stories and novels, such as *The Revolt of the Angels* and *Penguin Island,* are known for their insight into human nature. His observations of the good and evil in people show a keen vision and reflect his skeptical, satiric point of view.

GALE, ZONA (1874-1938). Born in Portage, Wisconsin, Zona Gale spent most of her life in her native state and used it, along with other Midwestern states, as the setting for some of her best-known writings. She was employed by newspapers in Milwaukee and New York until 1904 when she returned to Portage, where she remained for the rest of her life. She wrote novels, short stories, and plays; and for her dramatization of *Miss Lulu Bett* in 1920 she won a Pulitzer prize.

GARLAND, HAMLIN (1860-1940). Born on a farm in Wisconsin, Hamlin Garland spent his school years in Iowa, graduating from the Cedar Valley Seminary in Osage, Iowa. He farmed a homestead in North Dakota for a year, and then sold it so that he could move to Boston to prepare for a career as a teacher of

American literature. After nine years in Boston, during which he wrote a number of short stories and his first novel, *A Spoil of Office*, he returned to Wisconsin, and later lived in Chicago, New York, and Los Angeles. He is best known for his realistic description of the frontier Midwest in *A Son of the Middle Border*. Hamlin Garland was one of the first writers to describe the American Indian with accuracy, realism, and understanding.

GRAHAME, KENNETH (1859-1932). Grahame was born in Edinburgh, Scotland, but grew up in England. He did not consider writing of first importance in his life, being more concerned with his family and his work as a banker. He wrote *The Wind in the Willows* for his one son, Alistair. Except for one book of essays and a collection of writings published after his death, Grahame wrote only three books, *The Golden Age*, *Dream Days*, and *The Wind in the Willows*.

GREGORY, ISABELLA, LADY (1852-1932). In Roxborough, County Galway, Ireland, the twelfth child of Dudley Persse was named Isabella Augusta. In 1881 she married Sir William Gregory, a member of Parliament; thereafter she was known as Lady Gregory. Through her friendship with William Butler Yeats she became involved in the Irish literary revival, and together they made a success of the famous Abbey Theatre in Dublin. She collaborated with Yeats on a few plays and wrote more than thirty plays of her own, such as *Spreading the News*, *The Workhouse Ward*, and *The Rising of the Moon*.

GUITERMAN, ARTHUR (1871-1943). (Pronounced gĭt′ ər mən.) Guiterman's family lived in New York City, and he was educated at the City College of New York. In college he was active in sports, and even when he was past sixty he engaged in mountain climbing, tennis, and skating. He began his literary career as a reporter and editor, and then became a free-lance writer of poetry. He ventured into drama briefly and wrote the story and words for an opera, *A Man Without a Country*. He is perhaps best known, however, for his humorous poems, such as those in *The Laughing Muse*.

HALE, NANCY (1908-). Born in Boston, the only child of parents who were both painters, Nancy Hale studied art for a brief period. At age eleven her first publication was a short story in *The Boston Herald*. In New York City she wrote numerous magazine articles, eventually becoming assistant editor of *Vogue* and *Vanity Fair* and the first woman reporter on *The New York Times*. Her best-known writings are her short stories, which are collected in *The Earliest Dreams* and *Between the Dark and the Daylight*.

HALEY, ALEX PALMER (1921-). Alex Haley grew up in Henning, Tennessee, the son of a college professor. Stories he heard as a child turned into his best known work to date, *Roots: The Saga of an American Family*, published in 1976 as "a birthday offering to my country" (from the dedication which prefaces the book).

A high school graduation gift of a typewriter and a long service in the Coast Guard furnished Haley with the basic tools of the writer. On board ship Haley wrote love letters for less literate shipmates. To do so, he interviewed them and kept facts on file. This experience stood him in good stead later, when he became chief interviewer for a leading mid-western magazine and, more recently, in the researching of *Roots*.

HAMILTON, EDITH (1867-1963). Although she was born in Dresden, Germany, her parents were American citizens, and Edith Hamilton grew up in Fort Wayne, Indiana. With her father's encouragement, Miss Hamilton became a recognized authority on Greek, Roman, and Hebrew culture; she graduated from Bryn Mawr College in Pennsylvania. She also studied at the Universities of Leipzig and Munich in Germany, although no woman had ever before enrolled at Munich. When she returned to America, she became headmistress of the Bryn Mawr School in Baltimore. In *The Greek Way, The Roman Way*, and a collection of the Greek myths, she combined extensive knowledge with an entertaining style of writing which has made these books extremely popular.

HENRY, O. (1862-1910). William Sydney Porter, who used the pen name O. Henry, was born in Greensboro, North Carolina. When he was fifteen, he left school to go to work in an uncle's drugstore for five years. In 1882 he went to Texas, working on a ranch for two years and then becoming a bank teller. The remaining quarter-century of his life was spent in a great variety of settings—Texas, New Orleans, Honduras, Mexico, South America, and New York City. Many of his short stories were written while he was in prison in Ohio, after being convicted of embezzling funds when he was a bank teller. O. Henry is considered a master of the short story, especially those with a surprise twist at the end. Some of his short-story collections are *The Four Million, The Voice of the City, Sixes and Sevens*, and *Waifs and Strays*.

HOFFENSTEIN, SAMUEL (1890-1947). An American poet and humorist, Hoffenstein was born in Lithuania. He was a school principal, a reporter, and a drama critic. His audience is wide, ranging from elementary school children to scholars. Main works are *Poems in Praise of Practically Nothing*, and *Year In, You're Out*.

HORGAN, PAUL (1903-   ). Horgan lived in Buffalo, New York, until the age of eleven, when his family moved to Albuquerque, New Mexico. After studying music in Rochester, New York, he returned to New Mexico to join the staff of the New Mexico Military Institute.

His most successful literary effort is a two-volume history of the Rio Grande, entitled *Great River*, which won a Pulitzer prize and the Bancroft prize for history after its publication in 1954. Horgan has also written novels and short stories.

HOUSMAN, A. E. (1859-1936). The oldest of seven children, Alfred Edward Housman grew up in Worcestershire, England. He received a good formal education, including four years at Oxford University. After a decade in the civil service he became professor of Latin, first at University College, London, and later at Trinity College, Cambridge. During his lifetime he was a respected and feared literary critic and translator, but his greatness rests on his books of poetry, especially *A Shropshire Lad*.

HOVEY, RICHARD (1864-1900). After completing Dartmouth College, Hovey studied art and theology, worked as a reporter and actor, and traveled about Europe and northeastern America. He became acquainted with the Canadian poet Bliss Carman, and together they wrote a number of poems which comprise three volumes of *Songs of Vagabondia*.

HUGHES, LANGSTON (1902-1967). Langston Hughes, born in Missouri, was the class poet at Central High School in Cleveland, Ohio; and even before he graduated from Lincoln University in 1929, he was considered to be a professional writer.

His first book of poems, *The Weary Blues*, was published in 1926, and was followed by a large number of books, including a novel, short stories, and nonfiction. His works include *Not Without Laughter* (a novel), *The Ways of White Folks* (short stories), *The Big Sea* (autobiography), and several anthologies, one of the best known of which is *The Poetry of the Negro*, edited with Arna Bontemps.

HUNT, LEIGH (1784-1859). (Pronounced lē.) Born in Middlesex, England, (James Henry) Leigh Hunt was the son of parents who were driven from the United States shortly after the Revolutionary War because of their sympathy with the English monarchy. Whereas his father had favored the English rulers, Leigh Hunt and his brother John eventually got into difficulty when they criticized the English government in their weekly *Examiner*. Throughout his life Hunt spoke out in favor of freedom of speech and belief. He edited and published a variety of papers and magazines. His great contributions to literature were his campaigns to draw attention to the excellence of the writings of Keats and Shelley.

JACOBS, WILLIAM WYMARK (1863-1943). Born in London and educated in English private schools, W. W. Jacobs was employed as a civil service clerk during his early adult years. He began writing as a hobby, but when he was thirty-six he resigned from the Civil Service to devote full time to writing. Jacob's work was chiefly of two types: gentle humor and mystery. The majority of his stories concern seamen and the tales they have to tell. His spine-chilling "The Monkey's Paw" is one of the most famous short stories in English.

JOHNSON, FENTON (1888-1958). Born in Chicago, Fenton Johnson was educated in public schools of that city and at Chicago University. In 1914 he completed his first volume of poetry, *A Little Dreaming*, followed in 1916 by *Visions of the Dusk* and *Songs of the Soil*. His prose works include *Tales of Darkest America* (1920) and a book of short stories.

KING, MARTIN LUTHER, JR. (1929-1968). Born in Atlanta, Georgia, Martin Luther King, Jr., attended Morehouse College and Crozier Theological Seminary. He received a Ph.D. in Systematic Theology from Boston University, and became pastor of a church in Montgomery, Alabama. After leading the famous 1955-56 bus boycott in Montgomery, he helped found the Southern Christian Leadership Conference, a nonviolent organization whose purpose is to improve the lives of American Negroes. Dr. King became the dominant force in the nonviolent civil rights movement, and in 1964 he received the Nobel Prize for Peace. In recognition of his contribution to society, Dr. King was awarded more than two hundred honorary degrees from colleges and universities in the United States and abroad. On April 4, 1968, in Memphis, Tennessee, he was assassinated.

KIPLING, RUDYARD (1865-1936). Kipling was born in Bombay, India, of English parentage and he was educated in England. He wrote mainly about the British soldiers, government officials, and Indian natives whom he knew from personal experience. Kipling had great faith and trust in the ideals of the British Empire, and his writing often glorifies the British soldiers or officials. After marrying an American, Kipling lived in the United States for four years, and during that period he published *Many Inventions*, the book which introduced Mowgli, the boy who is raised by jungle animals. Among his well-known books are the poems of *Barrack Room Ballads* and the lively adventure stories of *Just So Stories*, *The Jungle Books*, *Puck of Pook's Hill*, and *Captains Courageous*.

LINDSAY, VACHEL (1879-1931). (Pronounced vā'chəl lĭnd'zĭ.) Lindsay's hometown, Springfield, Illinois, gave him an interest in Abraham Lincoln, whose life was closely associated with Springfield. Lindsay originally expected to be an artist, and after three years at Hiram College, he entered the Chicago Art Institute. Because he was unable to sell any of his art work, he eventually began a wanderer's tour of the country, during which he recited his poems in exchange for meals. Through much of his life he continued to recite his dramatic poetry, even after he was receiving income from several volumes of published poetry. The strong rhythms of "The Congo" and "General William Booth Enters into Heaven" were always popular with his audiences.

LONGFELLOW, HENRY WADSWORTH (1807-1882). The son of a Maine lawyer, Longfellow was the second of eight children in a family which traced its ancestors to the Pilgrims of early America. As a boy he read much from his father's excellent library, and his first poem was published when he was only thirteen. At Bowdoin College, from which he was graduated in 1825, one of his classmates was Nathaniel Hawthorne. By the time Longfellow was twenty-two he was a professor of languages at Bowdoin and had traveled in France, Spain, Germany, and Italy. In 1836 he accepted a position at Harvard, where he remained until 1854. *The Song of Hiawatha, Evangeline*, and "Paul Revere's Ride" are among his most famous poems.

LOWELL, JAMES RUSSELL (1819-1891). Son of a distinguished family in Cambridge, Massachusetts, James Russell Lowell was born in the colonial house in which he lived most of his life. He attended Harvard College, and at Harvard Law School prepared for his law career. He achieved his first public recognition with the publication of antislavery poems and articles and the *Biglow Papers*, which contained witty polit-ical comments about the Mexican War. After journeys to Europe in 1851 and 1855, he succeeded Longfellow as professor of modern languages at Harvard. He was the first editor of *The Atlantic Monthly*, and was also appointed as United States minister to Spain and England.

McGINLEY, PHYLLIS (1905-   ). Phyllis McGinley grew up in Oregon, Colorado (on a ranch), and Utah. After graduating from the University of Utah, she began teaching in Utah and New York, writing poetry when time permitted. After four or five years she left teaching to give fuller attention to writing. In 1944 her first children's book, *The Horse Who Lived Upstairs*, was published. Phyllis McGinley's light verse for adult readers has appeared in *The New Yorker* magazine. Selections from three decades of her verse appear in *Times Three*.

McKAY, CLAUDE (1891-1948). Claude McKay, born in Jamaica, was the eleventh child of a farmer. He himself studied agriculture for a time, at Tuskegee Institute and at Kansas State University, but then became interested in a literary life and moved to New York City. He had already published in Jamaica two books of poetry in Jamaican dialect. Now he began to contribute poems to American magazines, and a collection of his poems, *Harlem Shadows*, appeared in 1922. Later he turned to short stories and novels but still wrote enough verse for another volume, *Selected Poems*, published in 1953, after his death.

MILLER, JOAQUIN (1841-1913). (Pronounced wä kēn'.) While there is some uncertainty about his birth date and his middle name, there is assurance that Cincinnatus Heine (or Hiner) Miller was born in Indiana into a Quaker schoolteacher's family. The name "Joaquin" was attached to him years later when he wrote a defense of a Mexican bandit, Joaquin Murietta. After moving to Oregon with his family, Miller ran away to the California gold mines in 1855, and for most of the remainder of his life he was a wanderer who followed a great variety of temporary interests, such as law, newspaper editing, and traveling. His poetry is known for its pictures of life on the Pacific coast and various types of American people.

MILNE, A. A. (1882-1956). Born in London, Alan Alexander Milne lived in England nearly all his life. After graduation from Cambridge University, he worked as a free-lance writer for about three years; then he became assistant editor of the British magazine called *Punch*. He kept the position with *Punch* until he entered the army during World War I. When he left the service, he decided not to return to the magazine but to devote his time to writing. A. A. Milne was known through the English-speaking world as the author of a series of children's books such as *Winnie the Pooh*, *The House at Pooh Corner*, and *When We Were Very Young*.

MORISON, SAMUEL ELIOT (1887-1976). Morison, a descendant of distinguished educators on both sides of his family, received a Ph.D. from Harvard in 1913. He taught at the University of California for one year, then returned to Harvard, where he taught American history until his retirement in 1955. Although he won several prizes for his books, including a Pulitzer prize in 1942, Morison thought of himself primarily as a historian. His specialties were nautical history and the history of early New England.

NATHAN, ROBERT (1894-   ). Born in New York City, Nathan attended a private school in Geneva, Switzerland, and then went to Phillips Exeter Academy and Harvard University. After working in advertising and teaching journalism, he became a full-time writer. In addition to his several volumes of poetry and more than two dozen novels (*Portrait of Jennie* is the best-known), he has written several plays and motion-picture dramas.

POE, EDGAR ALLAN (1809-1849). The son of traveling actors, Edgar Poe was orphaned at the age of two. He was cared for until his late teens by Mr. and Mrs. John Allan, whose name he took later for his own. Poe entered the University of Virginia in 1826, but stayed for only one term, then he went off to Boston. From that time, Edgar Allan Poe's life was a tragic one. All his romances took unhappy twists, his business and literary ventures failed. Alcoholism added to his miseries. Poe is often referred to as father of the modern detective story; among his stories are "The Gold Bug," "The Purloined Letter," and "The Murders in the Rue Morgue." He also wrote poetry and was a capable literary critic.

PORTER, WILLIAM SYDNEY. *See* **HENRY, O.**

PYLE, HOWARD (1853-1911). Although he achieved his greatest recognition as an author and illustrator of children's books, Howard Pyle was for most of his professional life chiefly an artist and art teacher. Born in Wilmington, Delaware, Pyle was guided and encouraged to an artistic career by his mother. From 1894 to 1900 he taught art at Drexel Institute in Philadelphia and then returned to Wilmington to start an art school. In both his art and writing, Pyle featured chivalric characters, adventure, and the sea.

RESTON, JAMES (1909-   ). Author and newspaperman, James Reston was born in Scotland, but his family moved to America in 1910. After he was educated in Dayton, Ohio, public schools and Illinois University, he began a journalism career working for the *Springfield* (Ohio) *Daily News*, and for Ohio State University as sports publicity director. He has worked as sports writer and London correspondent for the Associated Press and has been head of the London and Washington Bureaus of the *New York Times*. Reston has received several major journalism prizes and three honorary degrees and is now with the *New York Times*.

ROSSETTI, CHRISTINA (1830-1894). The youngest of the amazing children in the Rossetti family, Christina was born in a northern section of London, where she remained for most of her life. She was educated entirely at home by her mother. Her first book of poems was published privately by her grandfather when she was twelve, but her first real publication was carried by a magazine when she was nineteen. She remained single, largely because her suitors did not share her Anglican religious views. She withdrew from society eventually, partly because of prolonged illness.

SANDBURG, CARL (1878-1967). Born in Galesburg, Illinois, Sandburg worked at a variety of jobs before becoming known as a journalist, poet, historian, and biographer. His poetry is down-to-earth, sometimes hard-hitting in its language and sometimes very folksy. He is equally well known for his six-volume biography *Abraham Lincoln*.

SANDERS, CHARLES L. (1932-   ). Charles L. Sanders is the managing editor of *Ebony*.

SCOTT, SIR WALTER (1771-1832). As a lad in Edinburgh, Scotland, Walter Scott was often unable to participate in athletic activities because he was lame. Fortunately he enjoyed listening to and telling adventure stories, and thus he developed the background which helped him to become the favorite romantic poet and adventure novelist of his day. His most well-known novels of romantic adventure are *Ivanhoe, Rob Roy,* and *Kenilworth.*

SERVICE, ROBERT W. (1874-1958). Few authors or poets traveled as widely as Robert W. Service, who was born in England, educated formally in Scotland, trained in the difficulties of life on the Pacific coast of Canada, employed as a war correspondent and ambulance driver on the mainland of Europe in World War I, and driven from France back to Canada by the Nazis in World War II. After the war he returned to France, where he continued writing until his death. His most recited and imitated poem is "The Shooting of Dan McGrew," which in style is very much like "The Cremation of Sam McGee."

SHAKESPEARE, WILLIAM (1564-1616). Literary critics agree that the greatest playwright the world has yet produced was William Shakespeare, who was born in Stratford-on-Avon about eighty miles from London, England. The facts of his early life are not known because few records were kept in the 16th century, but it is recorded that he married Anne Hathaway in 1582 and that they had three children. No one knows how he began his career as an actor and dramatist, but by 1592 he enjoyed a reputation as an actor and playwright in London, where he was then living. Among his more famous

plays are *Hamlet, Macbeth, The Merchant of Venice, Twelfth Night,* and *Romeo and Juliet.*

STEVENSON, ROBERT LOUIS (1850-1894). Stevenson's life was a restless one. It was not until six years before he died that he found a place to settle down: he lived in Samoa in the South Sea Islands from 1888 until his death. As a young man he first planned to become an engineer, but he soon left the study of engineering for that of law. After he had finished his studies, poor health sent him on frequent journeys about the world as he searched for a suitable climate. Throughout his lifetime of traveling, he continued to write essays, novels, stories, and poems. Besides *Treasure Island,* he wrote *The Strange Case of Dr. Jekyll and Mr. Hyde, Kidnapped, The Master of Ballantrae, The Black Arrow,* and a famous book of poems, *A Child's Garden of Verses.*

STORM, HYEMEYOHSTS (1935-   ). Storm, a Cheyenne, was born on Montana's Lame Deer Agency. The title of his first book, *Seven Arrows,* refers to the "teaching arrows": wisdom inherent in each of the six directions plus the Spirit of Universal Harmony.

SYMONS, ARTHUR (1865-1945). Born in Wales and educated mainly in French and Italian private schools, Arthur Symons had command of three languages from childhood. When he was twenty-one, his first book was published, but he was already recognized as an editor and literary critic. His vast knowledge of literature was demonstrated by the range of authors he edited.

TEASDALE, SARA (1844-1933). Born in St. Louis, Sara Teasdale received her education through home tutoring, attendance at a private school, and extensive travel in Europe and the Near East. She wrote several volumes of poetry and edited two anthologies of poetry for young people, *Rainbow Gold* and *Stars Tonight*. Her own poetry is known for its delicate lyric quality and careful rhythm.

TENNYSON, ALFRED, LORD (1809-1892). The fourth of seven sons of a clergyman, Alfred Tennyson was born in Lincolnshire, England. He entered Trinity College, Cambridge, in 1827, but left without a degree in 1831 when his father died. However, he had already decided that poetry writing would be his life's work, and thus he was not interested in training for any other profession. In 1850, after the death of Wordsworth, he was appointed poet laureate. In 1884 Tennyson was given a seat in the House of Lords; hence the inclusion of "Lord" in his name. Among his many famous poems are "Ulysses," *Idylls of the King* (about King Arthur), "Break, Break, Break," and *In Memoriam*.

TWAIN, MARK (1835-1910). Samuel Langhorne Clemens grew up in the small river town of Hannibal, Missouri. He used the name Mark Twain (river-boat language for two fath-

oms of water, or safe water) when he began to write later in life. He went to school in Hannibal until he was twelve years old; then his father died and he went to work in a printing office. Twain was a river-boat pilot on the Mississippi for several years and then he followed his brother west to Nevada during the Civil War. Here Twain began his writing career on the Virginia City *Enterprise*, making the pen name Mark Twain famous for the comic anecdotes of frontier life which culminated in "The Celebrated Jumping Frog of Calaveras County." Twain's fame was further extended by the dry humor of his platform lectures about places where he had traveled. *Roughing It* is Twain's account of life in the West; other books are *Tom Sawyer, the Prince and the Pauper*, and *Huckleberry Finn*.

ULLMAN, JAMES RAMSEY (1907-   ). New York-born James Ramsey Ullman graduated from Princeton University in 1929. After a trip abroad he returned to New York and became a reporter and playwright. Then he turned his attention to a different field, writing *High Conquest*, a history of mountaineering. *The White Tower* is a novel about the attempt to conquer a mountain in the Alps. Ullman has himself done much mountaineering and thus writes from firsthand experience.

WALKER, MARGARET (1915-   ). Margaret Walker graduated from Northwestern University in 1935 and obtained a master's degree in 1940 from the State University of Iowa. Her first book of poems, *For My People*, won the Yale University Younger Poets competition and was published in 1942. She has taught English at Livingstone College in Salisbury, North Carolina, and at West Virginia State College. She presently teaches at Jackson College in Mississippi, where she lives.

WEST, JESSAMYN (1907-   ). Although she was born in Indiana, Jessamyn West has lived in California since the age of six. Her first major book, *The Friendly Persuasion*, concerned a Quaker family in Indiana during the Civil War. It was made into a very successful movie in 1956. Miss West has written her autobiography, entitled *To See the Dream*. Another novel, *Of Me and Thee*, was published in 1969.

WORDSWORTH, WILLIAM (1770-1850). Wordsworth was born into a prosperous landowning family in Cumberland, England, a beautiful region of lakes and mountains. For nine years he attended school at Hawkshead in the Esthwaite Valley, and because he was able to spend much time outdoors he developed a love of nature which became the subject of many of his poems. After graduating from Cambridge University, Wordsworth became acquainted with Samuel Taylor Coleridge, and the two poets decided to work together. In 1798 they published *Lyrical Ballads;* these poems were treated unfavorably by the critics because they were written in a new style. Wordsworth's influence later became very great when this style led the Romantic movement.

WRIGHT, RICHARD (1908-1960). Born on a plantation near Natchez, Mississippi, Richard Wright was the son of a Negro mill worker and a country school teacher. When he was five, his father deserted the family; before he was ten, his mother became totally paralyzed. He lived with one relative then another; then at the age of nineteen, he went to Chicago where he held several jobs, read avidly, and began to write. In 1938, he won a five-hundred dollar prize for a magazine story, and he published his first book of short stories. *Native Son*, the novel which made him internationally famous, was published in 1940; *Black Boy*, his autobiography, appeared in 1945.

YEATS, WILLIAM BUTLER (1865-1939). (Pronounced yāts.) The son of a renowned Irish painter, William Butler Yeats was born in Dublin and educated in that city and in London. Following the family tradition, Yeats studied art but soon realized that his creative talents were more effective with words than with paints. Besides writing poetry, he was interested in drama and Irish politics. Yeats wrote a number of excellent plays and, with Lady Gregory, organized the Irish Literary Theatre, later called the Abbey Theatre, which attracted to it many of the best writers of the 20th century.

Literary Terms

Definitions for literary terms used in this book and also for certain fairly common terms not used in the text itself are given below. Page references in parentheses indicate that a term is further discussed on the pages listed. An asterisk after a word within a definition indicates that the word is defined under its own heading.

Acting Edition: An edition of a play which gives detailed instructions about staging and properties. This edition would be used by the director and actors who were putting on a play. "The Ghost of Jerry Bundler" is presented in an acting edition. (See p. 369.)

Alliteration: *See* Sound Devices.

Allusion: A reference to a person or place which the author expects the reader to recognize. Emily Dickinson's poem "Elysium" (p. 468) is based on an allusion to a place in Greek mythology. (See pp. 246, 468.)

Anecdote: A brief narrative* of a single incident. (See pp. 26, 151.)

Assonance: *See* Sound Devices.

Autobiography: An account of a person's life written by the person himself. "My Journey Is Still Long" (p. 46) is in part autobiography because it contains sections of Charles Wayo's diary.

Ballad: A narrative poem,* often meant for singing, using very simple language. Ballads usually deal with basic subjects such as love, honor, or death. The action is brief; it is often explained in dialogue,* with very little description* and characterization.* (See pp. 419, 435, 447.)

The BALLAD STANZA usually consists of four lines, with the second and fourth lines rhyming. The rhythm of each line is usually iambic meter.* Often ballads contain a refrain,* a line that is repeated at the end of each stanza. (See p. 419.)

The POPULAR BALLAD, or FOLK BALLAD, is passed down by word of mouth for generations and has no single known author. The LITERARY BALLAD has most of the characteristics of a ballad, but it has a single known author. "Bonny Barbara Allan" (p. 424) is a popular ballad; Tennyson's "The Revenge" (p. 447) is a literary ballad.

Beast Fable: A story presenting some useful truth or moral and narrated or acted by animals. (See p. 297.)

Biography: An account of a person's life written by another person. Some biographies are nonfictional; that is, they are based only on historical facts. Others, such as "That Lively Man, Ben Franklin" (p. 187), contain some fiction; that is, the author has added imaginary events or details.

Characterization: The technique of showing what a person is like. An author characterizes a person by telling what the person says, thinks, or does; by telling what others say or think about him/her; and by providing details of dress and appearance. (See pp. 54, 70, 358, 501.)

Choice of Words: The words a writer chooses in order to create a particular mood* or feeling in the reader.

Climax: The point of greatest emotional impact in a story or drama. The climax is a turning point because it leads on to a resolution of the conflict* upon which the work is based. (See pp. 26, 357.)

Comparison: The technique of showing the likenesses between two things. In "On the Loss of the *Royal George*" (p. 445) Cowper compares a ship to a plow since a ship cuts a path into the sea in the same way a plow cuts a path into the ground. Two kinds of comparisons are the metaphor* and the simile.* (See pp. 447, 479.)

Conflict: A struggle of some kind, on which drama and fiction are based. Conflict in literature may involve a struggle of man against man or man against nature; it may also be an inner conflict, in which a character attempts to understand a situation, overcome a fear, make a decision, etc. Several conflicts may be present in one work of literature. (See pp. 46, 84, 357.)

Connotation (kŏn'ə tā'shən): The emotional associations of a word, beyond the dictionary meaning of the word. For example, in describing a pleasant shade of green we might say "moss green," but we would probably not say "algae green" even though the latter might be a true description. A good writer chooses words with connotations ap-

propriate to the subject being described. (See p. 224.)

Context: The words or passages surrounding a term or passage in speech or writing. The meanings of words or passages should always be determined in context. For example, the word *match* means something quite different in these two contexts: "He beat me in the tennis *match*" and "The wet *match* would not strike easily."

Contrast: The technique of showing the differences between two things. A work of literature is often based on a contrast between characters or settings or ideas.

Dialogue (dī'ə lôg'): Conversation between two or more characters in a story, drama, or poem. Often the story of a ballad* is told entirely through dialogue. Some writers, like Jessamyn West in "The Pacing Goose" (p. 117), are skillful in using dialogue to characterize the people in a story and to present the events of the plot.* (See p. 358.)

Downstage: The front part of a stage; the part nearest the audience. (See diagram on p. 369.)

End Rhyme: *See* Sound Devices.

Epic: A long narrative poem* which tells of the adventures and achievements of a hero important to the history of his race or nation. The *Iliad* and *Odyssey* (p. 307) are Greek epics believed to have been written by Homer; Roland is an epic hero of France (*The Song of Roland*, p. 320). Since the epic hero is the principal element of an epic, an epic may also be called a hero tale.

Episode: An incident. A plot* is made up of a series of episodes, all closely related and each leading logically from one to the next. For example, the chapter from *Robinson Crusoe* (p. 541) is one episode in a series of adventures.

Exposition: Writing which explains something. The background for the plot of a short story or drama is called the exposition. In the exposition, characters are introduced and information about their backgrounds and their present situations is given. (See p. 357.)

Extended Metaphor: A metaphor,* or implied comparison between two objects, that is continued for several lines of a poem (as in Countee Cullen's "Leaves," p. 482).

Fable: Short story which teaches some useful truth or moral. Often fables contain animals which speak and act like humans; these fables may be called beast tales.* Aesop is an important writer of fables. (See pp. 246, 297.)

Falling Action: The action following the climax* of a plot;* the outcome, or resolution, of a plot. The falling action presents the solutions to the problems raised, and it resolves the conflicts* in the story or play. (See p. 357.)

Farce: A kind of play which puts very simple types of characters into ridiculous situations in order to make the audience laugh. (See p. 382.)

Fiction: Imaginative writing, rather than factual reporting of real events. The term *fiction* usually refers to novels like *Robinson Crusoe* (p. 541) and short stories like "The Gift of the Magi" (p. 103).

First Person Point of View: *See* Point of View.

Flashback: An episode* which suddenly interrupts the action of a story by shifting the scene back to an earlier time. The flashback usually explains something necessary to understanding the characters or plot. Nancy Hale uses flashback in "You Never Know" (p. 96).

Focus: The point of interest. An author will often concentrate on one character who then becomes the focus of the narrative. Ray Bradbury focuses on one character in "Good-by, Grandma" (p. 91).

Folk Ballad: *See* Ballad.

Free Verse: Poetry which does not have a uniform pattern of rhythm.* Carl Sandburg discusses free verse in his essay "Short Talk on Poetry" (p. 411).

Hero Tales: *See* Epic.

Iambic Meter: A rhythm used in poetry. It consists of an unaccented sound followed by an accented sound. For example, the word *Elaine* has iambic meter since the sound "E" is unaccented and the sound "laine" is accented. Ballads are usually written in iambic meter. (See p. 419.)

Image: A word that appeals to one of the five senses. An image creates a picture or suggests a sensation of sound, smell, taste, or touch. For example, in "Good-by, Grandma" (p. 91) Ray Bradbury associates Grandma with many images: broom, dustpan, mixing spoon, baked pies, croquet mallets, chewing gum.

Imagery (ĭm′ij rĭ): The collection of images in a work of literature. In "The Wind" (p. 469) Stevenson makes the reader feel the effect of the wind even though no one can actually see the wind. He does this by using imagery. (See p. 295.)

Internal Rhyme: *See* Sound Devices.

Irony: A contrast between what appears to be so and what really is. Irony of statement occurs when a writer or speaker appears to be saying one thing but is really saying the opposite. Irony of situation occurs when the outcome of a situation is the opposite of what one would expect, as in "The Crafty Farmer" (p. 426), when the farmer, although robbed, gets the best of the robber.

Legend: A narrative,* sometimes based on historical people or events, handed down from the past. The stories about Robin Hood (p. 333) are called legends; King Arthur (p. 312) is a legendary hero. (See p. 246.)

Light Verse: Short, lyric poems that are written to entertain but often have a serious, instructive purpose. They often use rhyme to gain a humorous effect. (See p. 498.)

Literary Ballad: *See* Ballad.

Lyric (lĭr′ĭk): A poem with a single speaker who expresses personal thoughts or emotions about a subject. For example, in "Song" (p. 476) Christina Rossetti expresses a personal point of view about death. (See p. 462.)

Melodrama: A kind of play which generally has the following characteristics: (1) the characters are either extremely good or extremely bad; (2) the ending is happy (the villain is defeated, the hero marries the heroine, etc.); (3) the plot* depends on coincidences, or chance occurrences; (4) a strong appeal is made to the audience's emotions, although in a rather shallow way (that is, the audience is supposed to like or dislike the various characters strongly, although these characters are not very realistic). Dunsany's *A Night at an Inn* (p. 359) is a melodrama.

Metaphor (mĕt′ə fər): An implied comparison of two basically different objects that are alike in at least one way. For example, in the poem "He Wishes for the Cloths of Heaven" (p. 481) Yeats compares the heavens to embroidered cloths: the silver and gold on the cloths are like the stars and sun in the sky. Both the cloths and the sky shine. (See p. 479.)

Mood: The feeling that a work of literature produces in the reader, viewer, or hearer. In "Robin Hood and Alan a Dale" (p. 430) the mood is bright and lively; in "The Telltale Heart" (p. 33) the mood is dark and mysterious. (See p. 434.)

Moral: The lesson or truth about life that a fable draws as its conclusion. The moral of Aesop's "The Fox and the Crow" (p. 299) is "Do not trust flatterers." *See* Theme. (See pp. 246, 297.)

Motivation: The reasons for a character's behavior. If an author skillfully motivates a character, the reader will believe that the character's behavior is not only possible but also probable. (See p. 54.)

Myth: A story of gods and goddesses that often explains unusual occurrences in nature. The Greeks had myths that explain the creation of the universe and the creation of humankind. (See pp. 245-246, 282.)

Mythology: The total collection of myths told by a group of people. (See p. 246.)

Narrative: A story. A narrative may be brief (see Fable) or very long, as a novel is.

Narrative Poem: A poem which tells a story and has a plot.° The ballad is one kind of narrative poem. (See pp. 43, 442.)

Narrator (nǎ rā'tər): A person who tells a story. A young girl is the narrator of "You Never Know" (p. 96); the author is the narrator of "Bill" (p. 2.) *See* Point of View.

Nonfiction: Factual reporting of real events. *See* Fiction.

Omniscient Author's Point of View: *See* Point of View.

One-Act Play: *See* pp. 357-358.

Personification: The poetic device of giving animals, objects, or qualities the characteristics of a human being. For example, in "City: San Francisco" (p. 478) Langston Hughes describes the city as going to bed and "Hanging lights/About its head."

Play: *See* pp. 357-358.

Plot: The sequence of events in a story or play. In organizing a series of incidents into a plot, the author shows the relationship between one incident and the next. (See p. 1.)

Poetry: *See* pp. 411-418, 419, 466, 498.

Point of View: The vision through which a narrative is presented; the person through whom the reader sees the action of the story. An author may handle point of view in several ways. Among these are the following:

The OMNISCIENT ("All-knowing") AUTHOR'S POINT OF VIEW, in which the author is the narrator° and can supply any information about motivation, character, or theme; can move from one place and time in the action to another; and can reveal the thoughts of any character. Most of the stories in this book are written from the omniscient author's point of view. (See p. 476.)

The FIRST PERSON POINT OF VIEW, in which the first person, "I," is narrator. The narrator may be a character in the story (Dr. Waston in "The Redheaded League," p. 566), or the narrator may be an uninvolved observer. What the first-person narrator tells is limited to what he himself would be able to see. (See p. 476.)

Popular Ballad: *See* Ballad.

Refrain: A line that is repeated at the end of the stanzas of a ballad.° "Lord Randal" (p. 435) makes use of the refrain to show the reader what has happenned. (See p. 437.)

Resolution: *See* Falling Action.

Rhyme: *See* Sound Devices.

Rhyme Scheme: *See* Sound Devices.

Rhythm (rith'əm): The beat of prose

or poetry. *See* Iambic Meter.

Rising Action: That section of a plot in which the conflict° is developed. The rising action leads to the climax° of the story or play. (See p. 357.)

Satire (săt'ir): A technique used to ridicule or make fun of human failings (such as cruelty, greed, jealousy). "The Story of Jumping Mouse" is a broad satire on the relationship between fear and power.

Scene: An episode° in a story, or a division within an act of a play.

Selection of Detail: An author's choice of details to include in a work. Because a writer cannot possibly include every fact about his subject, he must decide which to include and which to exclude. The details he selects should help to reveal his theme.° (See pp. 133, 156.)

Setting: The time and place of the action. Setting often contributes directly to the feelings aroused in the reader or to the reader's understanding of character, as in "The Strangers That Came to Town," (p. 55). (See pp. 46, 358.)

Short Story: A brief work of fiction,° designed to produce a single effect. Short stories vary in length: a short story is longer than an anecdote° and shorter than a novel. A short story shows characters (usually only a few characters) in a setting;° it develops a conflict° and reveals a theme° through its plot.°

Simile (sĭm'ə lē): A stated comparison between two basically different objects. It uses the word *as* or *like* to make the comparison. In "Columbus" (p. 443) Miller says that "The words leapt as a leaping sword." Though words are basically different from swords, they are similar in issuing a sharp, commanding challenge. (See p. 447.)

Sound Devices: Techniques for producing a musical or pleasing effect in literature, used especially in poetry. Some of the most common sound devices are the following:

ALLITERATION: The repetition of the same beginning sound in closely linked words. For example, in "Ariel's Song" (p. 470) the line "*F*ull *f*athom *f*ive thy *f*ather lies" has alliteration in the repeated *f* sound.

ASSONANCE (ăs'ə nəns): The repetition of similar vowel sounds in words that have different consonants. For example, in "Full fathom f*i*ve th*y* father l*i*es" the *i* sound is repeated to produce assonance. (See p. 470.)

RHYME: The repetition of similar or identical sounds at the ends of two words, such as h*and* and l*and*. (See p. 447.)

INTERNAL RHYME occurs when the rhyming words are in the same line of poetry. (See p. 447.)

END RHYME occurs when the rhyming words appear at the ends of lines of poetry. (See p. 447.)

RHYME SCHEME: The repeated patterns of end rhyme in the stanzas° of a poem.

Stage Directions: Instructions in a play, telling a director or actor about the arrangement of the stage, the physical location of characters and their movements, and the manner in which the actors should deliver their speeches (as *loudly, angrily*). (See p. 358.)

Stanza: A division of a poem in which each unit is usually like the others in number of lines and rhyme scheme. The beginning of a new stanza is usually indicated by skipping a line. *See* Ballad Stanza.

Surprise Ending: An unexpected ending to a short story or play. A good surprise ending should startle the reader but also satisfy him. O. Henry's "The Gift of the Magi" (p. 103 has an effective surprise ending. (See p. 108.)

Suspense: The curiosity aroused in a reader as to what will happen next. A skillful writer will try to introduce the element of suspense early in the story or drama, so that the reader will be eager to read on. Zona Gale uses suspense skillfully in "Bill" (p. 2). (See pp. 46, 357.)

Symbol: Something which stands for, or represents, something else, as a school mascot stands for the school or as the American flag represents the United States. See "The First Snowfall" (p. 494) and "The Golden Kite, the Silver Wind" (pp. 112-116).

Theme: The central idea of a work of literature. All parts of the work (characterization, plot, setting, mood) should contribute to the theme in some way. The theme is not usually stated directly, but the reader can determine it by analyzing the various elements of the work after he has finished reading it. (See p. 171.)

A moral* is the lesson which a fable teaches to the reader and is directly stated at the end of the fable. The theme, on the other hand, does not necessarily teach a lesson and is not usually directly stated. The moral of Aesop's "The Fox and the Crow" (p. 299) is "Do not trust flatterers." The theme of Scott's "My Native Land" (p. 487) is love of country.

Tone: The expression of an author's attitude toward his/her subject. Tone is revealed partly through the selection of detail* and words chosen to express ideas. Tone in literature corresponds to the tone of voice a speaker uses: a work may have an angry tone, a humorous tone, an apologetic tone.

Topic Sentence: A sentence expressing the main idea of a paragraph. The topic sentence is often the first sentence in a paragraph.

Transition: A movement from one idea or event to another. When a writer wishes to shift from one episode* to another, he must use a transitional device to help the reader follow clearly the progress of ideas or events and see the connection between them. As Jim Hawkins narrates *Treasure Island* (p. 517), he connects the various events and descriptions with transitional devices: the sound of a song in the present may remind him of a similar scene in the past, or an object like the apple barrel may appear in two episodes and link them together.

Upstage: The rear of the stage; the part farthest from the audience. (See diagram on p. 369.)

Glossary

The glossary is provided as a convenient means for looking up unfamiliar words used in this book. It may also be used in doing the *Focusing on Words* exercises. The words are defined according to their use in the book, although additional meanings of the words are also given often. Words that are footnoted in the text have not usually been included in the glossary.

The order and kinds of information to be found in an entry are shown below. Reading this information will help in using the glossary quickly and accurately.

Information given in the entry:

1. The word to be defined, divided into syllables. Example: **chro·nom·e·ter.**
2. Pronunciation of the entry. When two pronunciations are common for a word, both are usually given. Example (ä′rĭ ə, âr′ĭ ə).
3. Part of speech and, when useful, information concerning the singular or plural form.
4. Clarifying labels. These may be usage labels (example: **scriv·en** . . . *Archaic*), geographical labels (example: **set·tle** . . . *Chiefly British*), or special subject labels (example: **yard** . . . *Nautical*).
5. Definition of the entry. Where appropriate, examples may be given (as for *chimney*) or the use of the word may be illustrated (as for *abolish*).
6. Derivative parts of speech. Other parts of speech derived from nouns, verbs, or adjectives are sometimes given. Syllable divisions and accent marks for these derivative forms are always given; phonetic pronunciations are given whenever they would not be obvious. Example: **be·seech** . . . —**be·seech′ing,** *adj.* —**be·seech′ing·ly,** *adv.*

The following abbreviations are used:

adj.	adjective	l.c.	lower case
adv.	adverb	n.	noun
cap.	capital	pl.	plural
Colloq.	colloquial	prep.	preposition
conj.	conjunction	pron.	pronoun
Fr.	French	sing.	singular
Ger.	German	v.	verb

Pronunciation Key*

ă act	ī ice	ou out	y yes
ā able	j just	p page	z zeal
â air	k kept	r read	zh vision
ä art	l low	s see	ə a in *alone*
b back	m my	sh shoe	e in *system*
ch chief	n now	t ten	i in *easily*
d do	ng sing	th thin	o in *gallop*
ĕ ebb	ŏ box	th that	u in *circus*
ē equal	ō over	ŭ up	à as in Fr. *ami*
f fit	ô order	ū use	KH as in Ger. *ach*
g give	oi oil	û urge	N as in Fr. *bon*
h hit	ŏŏ book	v voice	œ as in Ger. *schon*
ĭ if	ōō ooze	w west	Y as in Ger. *uber*

a·bate (ə bāt'), *v.* to become less in amount or force.

ab·duct (ăb dŭkt'), *v.* to take away a person illegally and by force; kidnap.

a·bol·ish (ə bŏl'ish), *v.* to get rid of completely; put an end to: as, *to abolish slavery.*

ab·sorb·ing (ăb sôr'bĭng, ăb zôr'bĭng), *adj.* very interesting; holding the attention; compelling.

ac·com·plice (ə kŏm'plĭs), *n.* someone who helps another violate the law; a partner in crime.

ad·mon·ish (ăd mŏn'ĭsh), *v.* 1. to warn or advise against. 2. to scold gently; remind a person of something he should or should not do: as, *to admonish the class to be on time.*

ag·gra·vate (ăg'rə vāt'), *v.* 1. to make worse or more severe. 2. *Colloq.* to irritate, bother, or annoy; to make impatient. —**ag'gra·vat'ing,** *adj.*

aim·less (ām'lĭs), *adj.* without purpose or direction.

al·lude (ə lōōd'), *v.* to mention in a general way; refer to, but not directly. (Followed by *to.*)

al·lur·ing (ə lōōr'ĭng), *adj.* 1. very attractive; quite appealing or tempting. 2. charming.

al·ter (ôl'tər), *v.* to change; modify; make different, at least to some extent.

a·mi·a·ble (ā'mĭ ə bəl), *adj.* having a good disposition; friendly; agreeable.

an·guish (ăng'gwĭsh), *n.* great mental or physical suffering; agony.

an·tag·o·nist (ăn tăg'ə nĭst), *n.* a person who fights or competes with another; opponent.

an·tic·i·pa·tion (ăn tĭs'ə pā'shən), *n.* 1. a looking forward to; expectation. 2. a previous notion or idea.

an·ti·so·cial (ăn'tĭ sō'shəl), *adj.* 1. wishing to avoid, or avoiding, the company of other people: as, *a hermit is antisocial.* 2. harmful to the welfare of people in general.

ap·pa·ri·tion (ăp'ə rĭsh'ən), *n.* 1. something which appears suddenly and unexpectedly. 2. a phantom; ghost. 3. any act of appearing.

ap·pre·hen·sive (ăp'rĭ hĕn'sĭv), *adj.* 1. fearful about what may happen; uneasy. 2. quick to understand; learning easily or rapidly. —**ap'pre·hen'sive·ly,** *adv.* —**ap'pre·hen'sion,** *n.*

ap·pren·tice (ə prĕn'tĭs), *n.* 1. a person who is learning a craft or trade by helping a skilled master of that craft. 2. any beginner. —*v.* 3. to appoint to a position as an apprentice.

ar·dent (är'dənt), *adj.* 1. glowing; beaming. 2. glowing with enthusiasm or eagerness.

---

*The pronunciation system of *The American College Dictionary,* © Copyright 1947, 1963, Random House, Inc., New York. Used by permission.

ar·du·ous (är′joo əs), *adj.* 1. laborious; hard to do. 2. working hard; using much energy. 3. difficult to climb; steep.

a·ri·a (ä′rĭ ə, âr′ĭ ə), *n. Music.* a melody in an opera or oratorio, sung as a solo.

a·skance (ə skăns′), *adv.* 1. with a glance to the side. 2. with suspicion, doubt, or mistrust.

as·sent (ə sĕnt′), *v.* to agree; consent. —*n.* agreement.

a·stride (ə strīd′), *adj., adv.* 1. with one leg on each side: as, *sitting astride a horse.* 2. with about half lying on each side of something; straddling.

a·tone (ə tōn′), *v.* to make up for one's mistakes or sins; pay, in money, goods, or deeds, for wrong done. —**a·tone′-ment,** *n.*

at·tain (ə tān′), *v.* 1. to achieve; reach; gain. 2. to come to; arrive at: as, *to attain the age of twenty-five.*

au·dac·i·ty (ô dăs′ə tĭ), *n.* 1. bold courage; reckless daring. 2. rude boldness; impolite forwardness. —**au·da·cious** (ô dā′shəs), *adj.*

aus·tere (ô stîr′), *adj.* 1. very strict or stern in one's view of morals or behavior. 2. severe; harsh: as, *the austere living standard of the early pioneers.* 3. plain; simple; without decoration.

av·a·lanche (ăv′ə lănch′), *n.* 1. a large mass, usually of snow, that suddenly falls down a mountainside. 2. anything like an avalanche in being sudden, swift, and inescapable.

a·ver·sion (ə vŭr′zhən, ə vûr′shən), *n.* 1. a dislike; avoidance of something or someone disliked. 2. the object which is disliked.

awe (ô), *n.* a feeling which is a mixture of fear and respect, often caused by religious inspiration or great wonders of nature: as, *the view of the Grand Canyon filled the tourists with awe.*

bale·ful (bāl′fəl), *adj.* evil; harmful.

ban·ish (băn′ĭsh), *v.* 1. to force one out of the country as a punishment. 2. to get rid of; put out of one's mind.

be·drag·gled (bĭ drăg′əld), *adj.* wet and dirty; worn and limp.

bel·fry (bĕl′frĭ), *n.* the part of a tower or steeple in which a bell is hung.

be·seech (bĭ sēch′), *v.* to ask in a pleading manner; beg; request eagerly. —**be·seech′ing,** *adj.* —**be·seech′ing·ly,** *adv.*

bick·er·ing (bĭk′ər ĭng), *n.* minor argument or quarrel.

bi·zarre (bĭ zär′), *adj.* extremely odd; queer; unusual in appearance or manner; fantastic; marked by odd contrasts.

bleak (blēk), *adj.* 1. unsheltered; barren; exposed to wind: as, *the bleak winter prairie.* 2. bitterly cold and penetrating: as, *a bleak wind.* 3. cheerless; unhappy; gloomy.

blithe (blīth, blīth), *adj.* cheerful; lighthearted; gay; carefree. —**blithe′ly,** *adv.*

bois·ter·ous (boi′stər əs), *adj.* 1. rough; violent. 2. noisy; loud and lively.

boo·ty (boo′tĭ), *n.* goods taken from an enemy or a conquered people; any goods taken by force.

bra·zen (brā′zən), *adj.* 1. like brass, as in color. 2. bold; shameless in word or act.

bul·wark (bool′wərk), *n.* 1. a wall used for defense against attack. 2. a sea wall, used to break the force of the waves. 3. any defense or protection.

buoy·ant (boi′ənt, boo′yənt), *adj.* 1. tending, or having the ability, to float. 2. able to support a floating object. 3. gay; cheerful; light-spirited.

burgh·er (bûr′gər), *n.* a citizen of a town or borough.

bur·nished (bûr′nĭsht), *adj.* polished.

can·did (kăn′dĭd), *adj.* 1. saying directly just what one feels or thinks; honest; frank. 2. not biased; fair.

cas·cade (kăs kād′), *n.* 1. a small waterfall or a series of waterfalls. 2. anything which falls or showers down, such as sparks, lace, drapery, etc. —*v.* 3. to fall like a waterfall.

ce·les·tial (sə lĕs′chəl), *adj.* 1. concerning the sky or heavens. 2. of heaven; heavenly. 3. ideal or perfect: as, *celestial happiness.*

cha·grin (shə grǐn′), *n.* a feeling of disappointed embarrassment or humiliation caused by failure or the upsetting of plans.

chas·ten (chā′sən), *v.* 1. to correct behavior by punishment: as, *we chasten an unruly child.* 2. to subdue; to control the spirited emotions of (someone).

cher·ish (chĕr′ĭsh), *v.* 1. to value highly; to hold dear. 2. to treat with great care; to deal with carefully or tenderly.

chim·ney (chǐm′nǐ), *n.* 1. a structure by which smoke is carried off. 2. anything resembling a chimney (for example, the opening of a volcano or narrow rock passage).

chiv·al·ry (shǐv′əl rǐ), *n.* 1. a band of knights or noble gentlemen. 2. knighthood of the Middle Ages. 3. the code of noble behavior required of knights, such as courage, fairness, respect for women, etc.

chron·i·cle (krŏn′ə kəl), *n.* a record of events in the order that they occurred; a history. —*v.* to keep such a history.

chro·nom·e·ter (krə nŏm′ə tər), *n.* an instrument for measuring time with great precision; a very accurate watch.

ci·vil·ian (sǐ vǐl′yən), *n.* a person who is not in the armed services.

clout (klout), *n.* 1. *Archaic.* a piece of cloth or leather used for mending. 2. an archery target; a shot that hits the target. 3. *Colloq.* a blow with the hand. —*v.* 4. *Colloq.* to strike with the hand.

com·mend (kə mĕnd′), *v.* 1. to praise; mention with approval. 2. to put into the care of someone else: as, *to commend the patient to the nurse's care.*

com·pli·ance (kəm plī′əns), *n.* 1. act of carrying out, or giving in to, a wish, request, or demand. 2. a tendency to give in easily to the wishes of others.

com·pose (kəm pōz′), *v.* 1. to assemble into a combination: as, *to compose paste from flour and water.* 2. to put

in proper order. 3. to calm or settle (oneself or one's mind). 4. to write or create.

com·pute (kəm pūt′), *v.* to determine; figure by arithmetic; calculate. —**com′·pu·ta′tion**, *n.*

con·ceit·ed (kən sē′tĭd), *adj.* vain; having too high an opinion of oneself.

con·fi·dant (kŏn′fə dănt′, kŏn′fə dănt′), *n.* a trusted friend with whom secrets are shared.

con·fis·cate (kŏn′fĭs kāt′), *v.* 1. to seize property with official authority. 2. to seize; take and keep. —**con′fis·ca′tion**, *n.*

con·found·ed (kŏn foun′dĭd, kən foun′dĭd), *adj.* 1. cursed; damned; brought to ruin. 2. confused; mixed up.

con·gest·ed (kən jĕs′tĭd), *adj.* 1. blocked; obstructed; plugged up. 2. overcrowded; overfilled.

con·se·quent (kŏn′sə kwĕnt′), *adj.* coming as an effect; resulting.

con·spir·a·cy (kən spĭr′ə sĭ), *n.* 1. a secret plot by two or more persons to do something harmful, dishonest, or illegal. 2. a working together of forces. 3. a plot or plan of a group. 4. the group making such a plan.

con·spire (kən spīr′), *v.* 1. to plan secretly as a group, especially to do something evil or illegal. 2. to work together to some purpose or effect: as, *the weather and insects may conspire to ruin our picnic.*

con·stan·cy (kŏn′stən sĭ), *n.* the quality of remaining firm, steady, and unchanging; steadiness of purpose; loyalty.

con·ster·na·tion (kŏn′stər nā′shən), *n.* paralyzing fear or astonishment; dread or amazement which makes one speechless or helpless.

con·tem·plate (kŏn′təm plāt′, kən tĕm′plāt), *v.* 1. to think about; consider seriously. 2. to look at thoughtfully; gaze: as, *to contemplate a sunset.* 3. to expect; to look forward to. —**con′tem·pla′tion**, *n.*

con·temp·tu·ous (kən tĕmp′chŏō əs), *adj.*

ăct, āble, dâre, ärt; ĕbb, ēqual; ǐf, īce; hŏt, ōver, ôrder, oil, bŏŏk, ōōze, out; ŭp, ūse, ûrge; ə = a
in *alone*; **ch**, chief; **g**, give; **j**, judge; **ng**, ring; **sh**, shoe; **th**, thin; **th**, that; **zh**, vision. See the full
key at the beginning of this glossary.

GLOSSARY   **613**

showing a lack of respect; scornful; expressing the feeling that someone or something is cheap, unworthy, or evil.

con·tort (kən tôrt'), *v.* to twist or bend out of the usual shape.

con·trive (kən trīv'), *v.* 1. to think up; plan; scheme. 2. to design or invent: as, *to contrive a three-passenger bicycle.* 3. to bring about in some way; manage to do even though difficult.

con·ven·tion (kən věn'shən), *n.* 1. a meeting of members or delegates. 2. a custom; usual way of doing something; standard usage. —**con·ven'tion·al**, *adj.*

con·vic·tion (kən vĭk'shən), *n.* 1. act or process of proving or declaring the guilt of an offender. 2. a firm belief: as, *he stuck to his conviction that the lost explorers would be found.*

cor·dial (kôr'jəl), *adj.* 1. hearty; warm. —*n.* 2. anything stimulating. 3. a strong, sweet liquor. —**cor'dial·ly**, *adv.*

coun·te·nance (koun'tə nəns), *n.* 1. the expression on the face. 2. the face. —*v.* 3. to approve; give support to.

coun·ter·act (koun'tər ăkt'), *v.* to check or neutralize by a contrary action.

cour·age (kûr'ij, kŭr'ij), *n.* the quality of spirit or mind that enables a person to meet danger, pain, etc., with firmness; fearlessness; bravery.

Cov·en·try (kŏv'ən tri, kŭv'ən trĭ), *n.* a city in England. —**send to Coventry**, refuse to associate with; ostracize. [The origin of this phrase is unknown.]

cov·et (kŭv'ĭt), *v.* to desire something very much, especially something that belongs to someone else. —**cov·et·ous** (kŭv'ə təs), *adj.*

cre·mate (krē'māt), *v.* to burn a corpse.

cre·vasse (krə văs'), *n.* a deep crack or crevice in the ice of a glacier.

cudg·el (kŭj'əl), *n.* 1. a short, thick stick; a club. 2. (*pl.*) the sport of dueling with such clubs. —*v.* 3. to hit with a club.

curt (kûrt), *adj.* short; rudely brief; too abrupt to be polite. —**curt'ly**, *adv.*

cut·wa·ter (kŭt'wô'tər, kŭt'wō'tər), *n.* the front part of the bow of a ship that cuts through the water.

dar·ing (dâr'ĭng), *n.* 1. adventurous courage; boldness. —*adj.* 2. bold; adventurous. —**dar'ing·ly**, *adv.*

daunt (dônt, dänt), *v.* to frighten or discourage.

de·cap·i·tate (dĭ kăp'ə tāt'), *v.* to behead.

de·ceive (dĭ sēv'), *v.* to delude by a false appearance or statement; beguile; mislead. —**de·ceiv'er**, *n.*

de·file (dĭ fīl'), *v.* 1. to make dirty; soil. 2. to discredit the name of.

deign (dān), *v.* 1. to consider as being beneath one's dignity; lower oneself slightly. 2. to condescend.

de·ject·ed (dĭ jĕk'tĭd), *adj.* discouraged; low in spirit; downhearted. —**de·jec'tion**, *n.*

dem·o·li·tion (dĕm'ə lĭsh'ən, dē'mə lĭsh'ən), *n.* act of destroying or tearing down; destruction.

de·pose (dĭ pōz'), *v.* to remove from office; remove from a position of power: as, *to depose the king.*

de·pressed (dĭ prĕst'), *adj.* 1. sad; gloomy; downhearted; discouraged. 2. pushed down.

dep·ri·va·tion (dĕp'rə vā'shən), *n.* 1. condition in which one no longer possesses certain things which have been taken away. 2. a loss.

de·ser·tion (dĭ zûr'shən), *n.* 1. the act of leaving one's post or duty without permission. 2. abandonment of one's military duty with no intention of returning.

des·o·late (*adj.* dĕs'ə lĭt; *v.* dĕs'ə lāt'), *adj.* 1. lonely; feeling friendless; without hope. 2. deserted; without population. 3. barren; ruined; not suitable for human residence. —*v.* 4. to lay waste; to make unfit for human habitation. —**des'o·late·ly**, *adv.*

de·spoil (dĭ spoil'), *v.* to take away from by force; rob; plunder.

des·ti·ny (dĕs'tə nĭ), *n.* 1. the series of events which is bound to occur; fate; (one's) fortune, good or bad. 2. the force which seems to make things happen.

dev·as·tate (dĕv'ə stāt), *v.* to destroy; ruin: as, *World War III might devastate the earth.*

dic·tum (dĭk'təm), *n.* a forceful statement; a saying or opinion given with authority.

di·lap·i·dat·ed (dĭ lăp'ə dā'tĭd), *adj.* **1.** broken down; falling to pieces. **2.** shabby; not having as good appearance or value as in earlier times.

di·min·ish (dĭ mĭn'ĭsh), *v.* **1.** to become smaller. **2.** to make less in number or smaller in size.

dip·lo·mat·ic (dĭp'lə măt'ĭk), *adj.* able to manage negotiations with skill; suave; tactful. —**dip'lo·mat'i·cal·ly,** *adv.*

dire (dīr), *adj.* dreadful; fearful; horrible.

dis·cre·tion (dĭs krĕsh'ən), *n.* **1.** wise caution about what is said or done. **2.** the power or freedom to make decisions and to carry them out.

dis·dain·ful (dĭs dān'fəl), *adj.* feeling or showing the attitude that something is inferior, unworthy, or unimportant; scornful; aloof.

di·shev·eled (dĭ shĕv'əld), *adj.* untidy and in disorder; mussed up; not neat.

dis·mal (dĭz'məl), *adj.* **1.** causing sadness or gloom. **2.** gloomy; cheerless. **3.** dreadful.

dis·suade (dĭ swād'), *v.* to advise against something; deter.

dis·tor·tion (dĭs tôr'shən), *n.* **1.** state of being twisted out of shape. **2.** anything twisted out of shape or appearance.

dis·tract (dĭs trăkt'), *v.* **1.** to draw thoughts away to a different subject; divert attention. **2.** to confuse; mix up mentally.

di·vin·i·ty (dĭ vĭn'ə tĭ), *n.* **1.** godlike quality. **2.** a god; divine being. **3.** the study of religion. **4.** a soft, creamy candy.

doc·ile (dŏs'əl), *adj.* **1.** easy to manage, train, or teach. **2.** easy to control or discipline; quietly obedient.

dog·ged (dôg'ĭd, dŏg'ĭd), *adj.* having the stubbornness of a dog; determined;

tenacious. —**dog'ged·ly,** *adv.*

dole (dōl), *n.* **1.** money or food given to the poor or the unemployed. **2.** anything given out in small amounts. **3.** *Archaic.* sorrow; grief.

dom·i·nate (dŏm'ə nāt'), *v.* **1.** to control or rule; exercise power over. **2.** to tower over: as, *the new skyscraper will dominate the downtown area.*

drudge (drŭj), *n.* one who does tiresome, hard, unpleasant work.

ear·mark (ĭr'märk'), *n.* **1.** a mark or brand put on an animal's ear to show who owns it. **2.** any identifying mark or sign. —*v.* **3.** to put an identifying mark on.

ebb (ĕb), *n.* the receding of the tide. —*v.* flow back; to decline; fall from a better state to a worse state; waste away.

e·la·tion (ĭ lā'shən), *n.* a feeling of joy or pride; high-spirited gladness.

el·o·quent (ĕl'ə kwənt), *adj.* **1.** forceful, arousing, graceful, or persuasive, usually in speech. **2.** expressing much feeling.

em·bark (ĕm bärk'), *v.* **1.** to board a ship; put on board a ship. **2.** to begin a journey or some other venture.

em·bel·lish (ĕm bĕl'ĭsh), *v.* **1.** to decorate; adorn; add ornaments to. **2.** to improve (a story) by adding to it, especially fictional details.

en·dure (ĕn dyo͞or', ĕn do͞or'), *v.* **1.** to last or remain firm under suffering, pain, or misfortune without yielding; tolerate. **2.** to continue to exist.

en·gross (ĕn grōs'), *v.* to occupy the entire attention of; interest keenly and completely so that other things are not noticed.

en·ter·pris·ing (ĕn'tər prī'zĭng), *adj.* venturesome; willing to try new schemes; daring to take risks; bold and active.

e·nu·mer·ate (ĭ nū'mə rāt', ĭ no͞o'mə rāt'), *v.* to list one by one, as if counting.

ep·i·logue (ĕp'ə lôg', ĕp'ə lŏg'), *n.* **1.** the final part of a story or a series of events.

ăct, āble, dâre, ärt; ĕbb, ēqual; ĭf, īce; hŏt, ōver, ôrder, oil, bo͝ok, o͞oze, out; ŭp, ūse, ûrge; ə = a in *alone*; ch, chief; g, give; j, judge; ng, ring; sh, shoe; th, thin; t͟h, that; zh, vision. See the full key at the beginning of this glossary.

GLOSSARY **615**

2. a speech, usually in verse, given by an actor after the end of a play.

es·ca·pade (ĕs′kə pād′, ĕs′kə pād′), *n.* a prank; wild adventure.

e·ter·ni·ty (ĭ tûr′nə tĭ), *n.* an endless period of time without beginning or end.

e·vac·u·a·tion (ĭ văk′yŏŏ ā′shən), *n.* **1.** an emptying; a removal of the contents. **2.** withdrawal of persons from an area.

ex·ag·ger·ate (ĭg zăj′ə rāt′), *v.* to magnify an event beyond the truth; overstate.

ex·em·pli·fy (ĭg zĕm′plə fī′), *v.* to be an example of.

ex·ile (ĕg′zīl, ĕk′sīl), *v.* to force a person to leave his home territory, often as a legal punishment. *—n.* an enforced residing away from one's community.

ex·pos·tu·late (ĭk spŏs′chə lāt′), *v.* to argue with vigor; attempt to convince; reason with a person, especially to change his actions or intentions: as, *to expostulate with the referee.* *—ex·pos′tu·la′tion, n.*

ex·qui·site (ĕks′kwĭ zĭt, ĭk skwĭz′ĭt), *adj.* **1.** very beautiful, delicate, or lovely. **2.** carefully done or painstakingly made: as, *an exquisite watch.* **3.** of highest quality.

ex·traor·di·nar·y (ĭk strôr′də nĕr′ĭ), *adj.* **1.** very unusual; remarkable. **2.** exceeding the usual; quite exceptional.

ex·trem·i·ty (ĭk strĕm′ə tĭ), *n.* **1.** the farthest part; the end. **2.** the greatest degree or extent. **3.** a condition of great need or danger. **4.** a severe course of action.

ex·ul·ta·tion (ĕg′zŭl tā′shən, ĕk′sŭl tā′shən), *n.* proud rejoicing; great joy; triumphant happiness.

fa·çade (fə säd′, fă säd′), *n.* **1.** the front of a building. **2.** the front of anything, especially a front which has been made more attractive than the less visible parts of the object.

fac·ul·ty (făk′əl tĭ), *n.* **1.** any of the natural abilities of animals: as, *the faculty of hearing.* **2.** a special skill or talent: as, *a faculty for making money.* **3.** all the members of a teaching staff or other professional group.

fal·ter (fôl′tər), *v.* **1.** to hesitate; proceed in an unsure way; give way to opposition or discouragement. **2.** to walk unsteadily; stumble. **3.** to stumble in speech; stammer.

fa·tigue (fə tēg′), *n.* tiredness caused by hard work.

fer·vent (fûr′vənt), *adj.* **1.** hot; glowing. **2.** having or showing great warmth of feeling; extremely earnest.

flor·id (flôr′ĭd, flŏr′ĭd), *adj.* **1.** rosy in color; flushed with color, as the face. **2.** much decorated; showy.

fore·bod·ing (fōr bō′dĭng), *n.* a prediction of something evil or harmful; a feeling that something bad is soon to happen.

fore·cas·tle (fōk′səl, fōr′kăs′əl), *n. Nautical.* the forward section of a ship where the seamen have their quarters.

fore·top·sail (fōr′tŏp′səl), *n. Nautical.* a sail set on a forward mast of a ship.

for·lorn (fôr lôrn′), *adj.* lost; abandoned; deserted; miserable.

for·mi·da·ble (fôr′mĭ də bəl), *adj.* **1.** to be feared or dreaded; of alarming size or power. **2.** difficult to overcome; hard to handle.

for·ti·tude (fôr′tə tūd′), *n.* courage in the face of pain or disaster; patient endurance.

fur·tive (fûr′tĭv), *adj.* **1.** done in a secret, hidden way. **2.** sly; sneaky; shifty. *—fur′tive·ly, adv.*

gait (gāt), *n.* **1.** a manner of walking or running; as, *he had a stumbling gait.* **2.** any of the specific foot movements of horses: gallop, trot, pace, etc.

gar·ret (găr′ĭt), *n.* attic; unfinished room or space just under the sloping roof of a house.

ges·ta·tion (jĕs tā′shən), *n.* the act or period of carrying the unborn young in the body.

gild (gĭld), *v.* **1.** to cover with gold or a gold color. **2.** to give a bright, shiny appearance (to something). **3.** to make (something) appear more desirable than it is.

gin·ger·ly (jĭn′jər lĭ), *adv.* carefully; cautiously; timidly.

gla·cier (glā′shər), *n.* a huge mass of ice,

usually in high mountains, formed by many years of snowfall and moving slowly.

gorge (gôrj), *n.* 1. a narrow valley between steep cliffs. 2. the throat. —*v.* 3. to stuff oneself with food; eat in a greedy way.

gra·di·ent (grā′dĭ ənt), *n.* 1. a slope or incline. 2. the degree of slanting in an incline.

graft (grăft, gräft), *v.* to set a stem or bud from one plant into a cut on another plant, where it continues to grow. —*n.* the dishonest use of a job, especially in government, to acquire money for oneself.

gren·a·dier (grĕn′ə dĭr′), *n.* 1. originally, a soldier who fought by throwing grenades. 2. a member of a special regiment in the British Army.

griev·ance (grē′vəns), *n.* 1. a cause for complaint; an actual or imagined wrong or hardship. 2. complaint; resentment.

grim (grĭm), *adj.* dreadful; stern; fierce. —**grim′ly,** *adv.*

gris·ly (grĭz′lĭ), *adj.* horrible; ghastly; gruesome.

gro·tesque (grō tĕsk′), *adj.* 1. having a wildly odd or fantastic appearance. 2. so twisted in appearance as to be funny; ridiculous. 3. combining in a confused, unnatural way, as in certain types of art.

ha·lo (hā′lō), *n.* 1. a ring of light around the moon or other body in the sky. 2. a ring of light around the head of an angel or other saintly being.

heave (hēv), *v.* 1. to hoist; raise. 2. *Nautical.* to haul, draw, or pull, as by a cable (for example, *to heave up the anchor, to heave a ship*). (Past tense **heaved** or **hove.**)

hi·lar·i·ty (hĭ lăr′ə tĭ, hī lăr′ə tĭ), *n.* noisy laughter and fun.

hol·land (hŏl′ənd), *n.* a cotton or linen cloth used for children's clothing.

hos·pi·ta·ble (hŏs′pĭ tə bəl), *adj.* 1. entertaining guests in a friendly, warm manner. 2. inclined to be friendly and generous to guests or neighbors. 3. open-minded; willing to consider new ideas.

hove, *see* **heave.**

hull (hŭl), *n.* the frame or shell of a ship.

hys·te·ri·a (hĭs tĭr′ĭ ə, hĭs tĕr′ĭ ə), *n.* 1. a state of extreme emotional excitement, often with some loss of self control. 2. uncontrolled wild laughing or crying.

im·meas·ur·a·ble (ĭ mĕzh′ər ə bəl), *adj.* too large or too much to be measured; vast; boundless.

im·per·turb·a·ble (ĭm′pər tûr′bə bəl), *adj.* unable to be disturbed or upset; not excitable; calm.

im·pet·u·ous (ĭm pĕch′ŏŏ əs), *adj.* 1. moving with a wild force; rushing: as, *the impetuous flood waters.* 2. acting quickly, without much thought; acting on impulse.

im·pro·vi·sa·tion (ĭm′prə vī zā′shən, ĭm′prŏv ə zā′shən), *n.* act of preparing, composing, or making without preparation; process of doing something on the spur of the moment with the materials or facts at hand.

im·pu·dent (ĭm′pyə dənt), *adj.* lacking respect; shameless in boldness or rudeness. —**im′pu·dence,** *n.*

im·pulse (ĭm′pŭls), *n.* a sudden urge to action: as, *to act on impulse.*

in·ar·tic·u·late (ĭn′är tĭk′yə lĭt), *adj.* 1. not (expressed) in speech that is understandable: as, *an inarticulate moan.* 2. not able to speak clearly.

in·au·di·ble (ĭn ô′də bəl), *adj.* not capable of being heard.

in·cal·cu·la·ble (ĭn kăl′kyə lə bəl), *adj.* 1. too numerous or too great to be counted or measured. 2. too uncertain to be predicted; unpredictable.

in·cred·u·lous (ĭn krĕj′ə ləs), *adj.* 1. unable or unwilling to believe; doubting.

ăct, āble, dâre, ärt; ĕbb, ēqual; ĭf, īce; hŏt, ōver, ôrder, oil, bŏŏk, ōōze, out; ŭp, ūse, ûrge; ə = a in *alone*; ch, chief; g, give; j, judge; ng, ring; sh, shoe; th, thin; ᵺ, that; zh, vision. See the full key at the beginning of this glossary.

2. showing one's doubt or disbelief.
—in·cred'u·lous·ly, *adv.*

in·dec·o·rous (in děk'ə rəs, in'dĭ kōr'əs), *adj.* not proper; lacking good taste.

in·dif·fer·ent (in dĭf'ər ənt), *adj.* 1. having no interest; not caring; unconcerned. 2. having no bias, favorite, or choice; being neutral. 3. average; neither good nor bad. 4. not very good; poor.

in·dig·nant (in dĭg'nənt), *adj.* angry or scornful because of unfair, mean, or ungrateful treatment.

in·dis·pen·sa·ble (in'dĭs pĕn'sə bəl), *adj.* absolutely necessary.

in·dom·i·ta·ble (ĭn dŏm'ə tə bəl), *adj.* not easily conquered or overcome; unyielding; not giving in to defeat or discouragement.

in·duce (in dūs', in dōōs'), *v.* 1. to lead to some action or state of mind: as, *to induce a citizen to change his vote.* 2. to cause; bring about. 3. to arrive at a conclusion based on certain facts.

in·ev·i·ta·ble (in ĕv'ə tə bəl), *adj.* bound to happen; unavoidable.

in·ex·pli·ca·ble (in ĕks'plə kə bəl), *adj.* not to be accounted for or understood; unexplainable.

in·fa·mous (in'fə məs), *adj.* 1. of bad reputation; in dishonor or disgrace. 2. causing or deserving evil reputation; shameful; wicked.

in·fil·tra·tion (in'fĭl trā'shən), *n.* the act or process of passing into or through: as, *infiltration of a secret club by outsiders.*

in·gen·ious (in jēn'yəs), *adj.* 1. clever; inventive; original; skillful at designing or contriving. 2. cleverly done; showing inventiveness.

in·ge·nu·i·ty (in'jə nū'ə tĭ, in'jə nōō'ə tĭ), *n.* 1. the quality of cleverness, inventiveness, or clever skillfulness. 2. knack for clever design or construction. 3. a cleverly made device.

in·let (in'lĕt), *n.* 1. a narrow body of water running into land; a small bay. 2. a strip of water between two islands.

in·sig·nif·i·cant (in'sĭg nĭf'ə kənt), *adj.* not important; too small or of too little value to matter.

in·so·lent (in'sə lənt), *adj.* lacking respect for customs or authorities; rude; insulting.

in·su·per·a·ble (in sōō'pər ə bəl), *adj.* unable to be overcome or passed over; unconquerable.

in·ter·ces·sion (in'tər sĕsh'ən), *n.* the process of asking, pleading, or praying for someone else.

in·ter·vene (in tər vēn'), *v.* 1. to come between. 2. to come between in order to settle or adjust.

in·tol·er·a·ble (in tŏl'ər ə bəl), *adj.* unbearable; too painful, cruel, or awful to be endured. —in·tol'er·a·bly, *adv.*

in·tol·er·ant (in tŏl'ər ənt), *adj.* 1. having no patience with beliefs or ideas different from one's own. 2. making no allowance or adjustment for the ideas or needs of others.

in·tro·spect (in'trə spĕkt'), *v.* 1. to examine one's own thoughts and feelings; to look into one's own mind. 2. to observe or analyze oneself. —in'tro·spec'tive, *adj.*

in·tru·sion (in trōō'zhən), *n.* an awkward forcing in or interruption.

in·ven·to·ry (in'vən tōr'ĭ), *n.* 1. a complete list of all the goods or properties on hand. 2. a stock of goods on hand. —*v.* 3. to compile or make a list of goods; to make note of possessions.

in·vol·un·tar·y (in vŏl'ən tĕr'ĭ), *adj.* not intentional; accidental; not done by choice. —in·vol'un·tar'i·ly, *adv.*

im·plore (im plōr'), *v.* to ask with great feeling; beg.

ir·rel·e·vant (ĭ rĕl'ə vənt), *adj.* not to the point; having nothing to do with the subject.

jour·ney·man (jûr'nĭ mən), *n.* a person who has already been an apprentice at a trade but continues to work at the trade under another person.

joust (jŭst, joust), *n.* 1. a fight with lances by two knights on horseback. 2. (*pl.*) a tournament of such fights. —*v.* 3. to take part in such a fight.

jo·vi·al (jō'vĭ əl), *adj.* playful and good-humored; cheerful and jolly.

ju·di·cial (jōō dĭsh'əl), *adj.* 1. having to

do with judges, courts, or their functions. **2.** carefully considering the facts; careful in making decisions.

knick·er·bock·ers (nĭk′ər bŏk′ərz), *n.* short trousers gathered at or just below the knee.

lab·y·rinth (lăb′ə rĭnth), *n.* a series of winding passages in which it is difficult to find one's way.

lam·en·ta·tion (lăm′ən tā′shən), *n.* an outward expression of grief or sorrow; wailing; weeping.

land·fall (lănd′fôl′), *n.* **1.** the sighting of land from a vessel at sea. **2.** a landing by plane or ship.

lan·guid (lăng′gwĭd), *adj.* **1.** lacking energy, vitality, or spirit; drooping; weak. **2.** lacking interest; indifferent.

lan·guor (lăng′gər), *n.* **1.** a lack of spirit or vigor; weakness; sluggishness. **2.** a lack of interest; dullness. **3.** a tender mood.

lee (lē), *n.* **1.** the sheltered side, which the wind does not strike. **2.** a shelter. —*adj.* **3.** of or on the side which is protected from the wind.

lithe (līth), *adj.* limber; flexible; bending easily.

lit·er·al (lĭt′ər əl), *adj.* exactly true to fact; having no exaggeration or distortion.

mag·ni·tude (măg′nə tūd′, măg′nə tōōd′), *n.* largeness; importance; extent or greatness of power.

mal-, *prefix.* bad, wrongful, evil: as, *maladjustment, malpractice, malodorous.*

ma·li·cious (mə lĭsh′əs), *adj.* **1.** wishing to harm others; evil-intentioned. **2.** deliberately harmful or mischievous. —**ma·li′cious·ly,** *adv.*

mal·o·dor·ous (măl ō′dər əs), *adj.* having a bad odor.

mar·vel (mär′vəl), *n.* an amazing or wonderful thing. —*v.* to be astonished; wonder.

mate (māt), *n. Nautical.* an officer of a merchant ship who is lower in rank than the captain.

max·im (măk′sĭm), *n.* a short statement of some general truth about life.

med·i·tate (mĕd′ə tāt′), *v.* **1.** to think deeply, quietly. **2.** to plan; consider; intend.

mel·an·chol·y (mĕl′ən kŏl′ĭ), *adj.* **1.** sad; gloomy; depressed. **2.** causing sadness or gloom: as, *a melancholy fog at night.* —*n.* **3.** a state of sadness or gloom.

mol·ten (mōl′tən), *adj.* **1.** melted by heat. **2.** made by being melted and poured in a mold.

mo·nas·tic (mə năs′tĭk), *adj.* **1.** having to do with monasteries. **2.** relating to monks or nuns.

mort·gage (môr′gĭj), *n.* **1.** a claim to property, given to the lender of money as security for payment of the loan. **2.** the legal document for such a claim to property. —*v.* **3.** to pledge property when borrowing money.

mor·ti·fy (môr′tə fī), *v.* **1.** to embarrass or make ashamed; injure the pride. **2.** to subdue the body by fasting or severe self-discipline. —**mor′ti·fy′ing,** *adj.*

mul·ti·tu·di·nous (mŭl′tə tū′də nəs), *adj.* numerous; happening, or existing, in great numbers.

mut·ed (mū′tĭd), *adj.* **1.** silent; quiet. **2.** silenced; made more quiet.

mu·ti·ny (mū′tə nĭ), *n.* a fighting or rebelling against the officers or leaders of a group; revolt of sailors or soldiers against their officers. —*v.* to take part in such a revolt. —**mu′ti·nous,** *adj.*

nar·ra·tive (năr′ə tĭv), *n.* an account or story of events.

neg·lect·ed (nĭ glĕkt′ĭd), *adj.* not cared for; disregarded.

noc·tur·nal (nŏk tûr′nəl), *adj.* **1.** concerning the night. **2.** active at night; done or occurring at night. **3.** having flowers that open only at night.

ăct, āble, dâre, ärt; ĕbb, ēqual; ĭf, īce; hŏt, ōver, ôrder, oil, bŏŏk, ōōze, out; ŭp, ūse, ûrge; ə = a in *alone*; ch, chief; g, give; j, judge; ng, ring; sh, shoe; th, thin; th, that; zh, vision. See the full key at the beginning of this glossary.

nup·tials (nŭp'shəlz), *n.* a marriage ceremony; wedding.

o·blige (ə blīj'), *v.* 1. to exert a moral or legal force (on someone) to do (or not to do) something. 2. to make (a person) feel indebted because of a favor done for him.

ob·liv·i·on (ə blĭv'ĭ ən), *n.* 1. the state of being forgotten. 2. the forgetting, or the tendency to forget, something.

ob·scene (əb sēn', ŏb sēn'), *adj.* 1. indecent; shockingly immodest. 2. filthy; disgusting.

ob·scure (əb skyŏŏr'), *v.* 1. to hide from view; conceal. 2. to overshadow; confuse: as, *a bad argument can obscure the truth.* —*adj.* 3. not easily seen; hidden. 4. not easily understood. —**ob·scure'ly,** *adv.*

ob·sti·nate (ŏb'stə nĭt), *adj.* 1. stubborn; not willing to change one's mind. 2. difficult to overcome or cure: as, *an obstinate head cold.* —**ob'sti·nate·ly,** *adv.*

ob·vi·ous (ŏb'vĭ əs), *adj.* 1. easily seen; open to view. 2. easy to understand.

off·ing (ôf'ĭng), *n.* 1. a distant position at sea, as seen from the shore. 2. a distant, but still visible, spot.

om·i·nous (ŏm'ə nəs), *adj.* threatening; suggesting approaching evil or disaster.

om·nip·o·tent (ŏm nĭp'ə tənt), *adj.* all-powerful; having all possible power or authority.

op·er·a (ŏp'ər ə, ŏp'rə), *n.* a long musical production with singers, orchestra, and scenery.

op·u·lent (ŏp'yə lənt), *adj.* 1. wealthy; rich. 2. plentiful; abundant.

or·a·cle (ôr'ə kəl), *n.* 1. a place or person from which the early Greeks and Romans learned the will of the gods. 2. a message from such a place or person. 3. a very wise person.

or·dain (ôr dān'), *v.* 1. to arrange; cause to happen; establish. 2. to appoint or order by official decree.

out·crop·ping (out'krŏp'ĭng), *n.* a protrusion above the surface, as rocks which stick up above the ground.

pad·dock (păd'ək), *n.* a small field near a stable for exercising horses.

par·a·phrase (păr'ə frāz'), *v.* to restate the meaning of a passage in one's own words or in simpler words. —*n.* the words which restate the meaning of a passage.

pare (pâr), *v.* 1. to cut off an outer layer: as, *to pare an apple.* 2. to diminish; reduce; make smaller.

pas·sion (păsh'ən), *n.* a strong emotion such as intense hate or love.

pa·thet·ic (pə thĕt'ĭk), *adj.* causing one to feel pity, sympathy, or sadness.

pawn (pôn), *n.* 1. something given as security for a debt. 2. the state of being pledged as security: as, *her jewelry was in pawn.* —*v.* 3. to deposit as security.

pen·e·tra·li·a (pĕn'ə trā'lĭ ə), *n.* 1. the most inner part, as of a temple. 2. private or secret things.

pen·i·tent (pĕn'ə tənt), *adj.* sorry for a wrong done and willing to make things right.

pen·non (pĕn'ən), *n.* 1. a long, thin flag carried on the lance of a knight. 2. any pennant or flag.

pen·sive (pĕn'sĭv), *adj.* thinking deeply, seriously, or sadly; deeply thoughtful.

per·se·cute (pûr'sə kūt'), *v.* to constantly injure or distress; treat cruelly, especially because of the victim's religion, race, or politics.

per·se·ver·ance (pûr'sə vîr'əns), *n.* persistence; quality of sticking to a task until it is completed.

per·sist (pər sĭst', pər zĭst'), *v.* 1. to continue in spite of resistance or opposition; refuse to give up. 2. to say or do repeatedly: as, *to persist in teasing a younger brother.*

per·sist·ence (pər sĭs'təns, pər zĭs'təns), *n.* 1. stubborn, unyielding continuation in a course of action or thought; steady, determined pursuit of a purpose. 2. continuous going on: as, *the persistence of a heat wave.*

phe·nom·e·non (fĭ nŏm'ə nŏn'), *n.* 1. any happening or situation that can be observed and described: as, *an earthquake is a phenomenon of nature.* 2. anything that is very remarkable or unusual; a very unusual person.

pin·nace (pĭn′ĭs), *n.* a small boat which attends a large ship.

pin·na·cle (pĭn′ə kəl), *n.* a high peak, as of a mountain.

pi·ous (pī′əs), *adj.* 1. showing religious devotion; devoted to one's religion and its procedures. 2. pretending to be religious.

plac·id (plăs′ĭd), *adj.* calm; quiet; peaceful; undisturbed. —**plac′id·ly,** *adv.*

plague (plāg, plĕg), *n.* 1. a deadly, epidemic disease. 2. anything that causes trouble or pain. —*v.* 3. to torment, trouble, annoy, irritate, or bother.

plume (plo͞om), *n.* 1. a large feather. 2. one or more feathers in an ornamental arrangement. 3. a token of honor. —*v.* 4. to decorate with feathers. 5. to smooth the feathers. 6. to feel proud; take credit.

pomp (pŏmp), *n.* 1. stately, splendid, or dignified display. 2. vain or showy display.

pon·der·ous (pŏn′dər əs), *adj.* 1. bulky and heavy. 2. unwieldy or clumsy because of large size or weight. 3. dull or tiresome. —**pon′der·ous·ly,** *adv.*

pos·sessed (pə zĕst′), *adj.* influenced or governed by an evil spirit or by an overwhelming idea or emotion; crazed; mad.

prec·i·pice (prĕs′ə pĭs), *n.* a high cliff with a steep or vertical face.

pred·e·ces·sor (prĕd′ə sĕs′ər, prĕd′ə sĕs′ər), *n.* 1. one who held a job or performed a task previous to another. 2. a forefather or ancestor.

pre·lim·i·nar·y (prĭ lĭm′ə nĕr′ĭ), *adj.* coming before or leading up to; preparatory; introductory.

pres·tige (prĕs tēzh′, prĕs′tĭj), *n.* respect, status, fame, or good reputation based on approved traits or achievements.

pri·va·teer (prī′və tĭr′), *n.* 1. a privately-owned ship which is authorized by the government to attack enemy vessels. 2.

the commander or a crew member of such a ship.

pri·va·tion (prī vā′shən), *n.* lack of usual necessities and comforts of life.

pro·claim (prō klām′), *v.* to announce publicly; make public an official act or decision. —**proc·la·ma·tion** (prŏk′lə mā′shən), *n.*

pro·found (prə found′), *adj.* 1. indicating great knowledge or deep wisdom. 2. deep; far down; much below the surface. 3. intense; deeply felt: as, *the sailors showed profound joy when rescued.*

prop·o·si·tion (prŏp′ə zĭsh′ən), *n.* an idea, plan, or explanation presented for consideration.

Prov·i·dence (prŏv′ə dəns), *n.* God; one who guides or watches over human events.

pru·dence (pro͞o′dəns), *n.* 1. wisdom in practical matters; wise concern for one's own interest. 2. sensible caution; good judgment.

pub (pŭb), *n.* *British slang.* 1. a tavern. 2. an inn or hotel. [Short for *Public House.*]

punc·tu·al (pŭngk′cho͞o əl), *adj.* on time; prompt.

quar·ry (kwôr′ĭ, kwŏr′ĭ), *n.* an open pit from which stone is taken.

quar·ter (kwôr′tər), *n.* *Nautical.* the region around the stern of a ship.

quar·tet (kwôr tĕt′), *n.* 1. a group of four persons. 2. *Music.* a musical composition for four voices or instruments.

rar·e·fy (râr′ə fĭ), *v.* to become less dense; become thinner: as, *rarefied air.*

re·cess (rĭ sĕs′, rē′sĕs), *n.* 1. a hollow or indented place in a wall or surface. 2. a hidden, withdrawn, or inner place. 3. a brief stopping of work or study. —*v.* 4. to set back. 5. to halt work or study for a short time.

re·coil (rĭ koil′), *v.* 1. to jump back or

ăct, āble, dâre, ärt; ĕbb, ēqual; ĭf, īce; hŏt, ōver, ôrder, oil, bo͝ok, o͞oze, out; ŭp, ūse, ûrge; ə = a in *alone*; **ch**, chief; **g**, give; **j**, judge; **ng**, ring; **sh**, shoe; **th**, thin; **th**, that; **zh**, vision. See the full key at the beginning of this glossary.

draw back, as in fear or surprise. **2.** to fly back when released or fired, as with a spring or a gun.

re·com·mence (rē'kə mĕns'), v. to begin again; start over.

rec·on·cile (rĕk'ən sīl'), v. **1.** to make friendly again. **2.** to make fit; to bring into harmony: as, *to reconcile two descriptions of an accident.* **3.** to become willing to put up with the situation.

re·con·nais·sance (rĭ kŏn'ə səns), n. a survey or examination of an area with some purpose in mind.

re·deem (rĭ dēm'), v. **1.** to get back or buy back. **2.** to pay off, as a debt. **3.** to set free or ransom. **4.** to save or rescue from sin. **5.** to carry out a promise. **6.** to make up for (mistakes or errors).

reek (rēk), v. to have a strong, unpleasant smell; to stink. —n. a strong, bad odor.

ref·er·ence (rĕf'ər əns), n. **1.** a statement or symbol which refers the listener or reader to something. **2.** a source, usually printed, of specialized information, such as an encyclopedia. **3.** a statement about the ability or character of a person; recommendation. **4.** the person who can provide such a statement or recommendation.

re·frain (rĭ frān'), v. to keep (oneself) from doing or saying something; hold back.

ref·uge (rĕf'ūj), n. **1.** protection from danger; shelter. **2.** person, place, or thing which provides safety, shelter, or comfort.

re·lapse (rĭ lăps'), v. to fall back.

re·lent (rĭ lĕnt'), v. to become less stern, harsh, or stubborn; become more tender or forgiving.

re·morse (rĭ môrs'), n. a deep, punishing feeling of guilt or sorrow because of a wrong one has done. —**re·morse'ful,** adj. —**re·morse'ful·ly,** adv.

re·pose (rĭ pōz'), v. **1.** to lie at rest. **2.** to lie in a grave. **3.** to lay to rest. —n. **4.** a state of rest or sleep. **5.** calmness; peace of mind.

re·prove (rĭ prōōv'), v. to criticize; find fault with; scold; rebuke.

re·pulse (rĭ pŭls'), v. **1.** to drive back: as, *to repulse enemy forces.* **2.** to turn (someone) back rudely or coldly: as, *to repulse one's former friends.*

re·pul·sion (rĭ pŭl'shən), n. feeling of distaste or dislike.

re·sign (rĭ zīn'), v. **1.** to accept what happens calmly, patiently, and without complaint. **2.** to yield; give in. —**re·signed** (rĭ zīnd'), adj. —**re·sign·ed·ly** (rĭ zī'nĭd lĭ), adv.

res·o·lute (rĕz'ə lōōt'), adj. determined; not giving in; firm in holding to a purpose.

re·solve (rĭ zŏlv'), v. **1.** to decide; make up one's mind. **2.** to decide by voting; make a formal group decision. **3.** to provide an explanation or a solution. **4.** to break up into basic parts or elements. —n. **5.** determination or definite, firm intention.

re·sus·ci·tate (rĭ sŭs'ə tāt'), v. to revive; bring back to consciousness or life.

rev·e·la·tion (rĕv'ə lā'shən), n. **1.** the act of making known or revealing (something). **2.** something made known or disclosed, especially something surprising.

re·volt·ing (rĭ vōl'tĭng), adj. **1.** rebellious; taking part in a revolt. **2.** disgusting; horribly distasteful.

rid·i·cule (rĭd'ə kūl'), v. to make fun of; force people to laugh at. —n. words which make fun of something.

rig·ging (rĭg'ĭng), n. *Nautical.* the ropes and chains which keep the masts and sails of a ship in place.

rig·or·ous (rĭg'ər əs), adj. **1.** strict; harsh; severe. **2.** extremely accurate or precise: as, *rigorous control of the experiment.*

rogue (rōg), n. **1.** a wandering beggar; tramp. **2.** a rascal; dishonest or scheming person. **3.** a playful, mischievous person. **4.** an animal that lives apart from its kind and becomes unusually savage or destructive.

ro·man·tic (rō măn'tĭk), adj. pertaining to a world of fancy and pleasant dreams, rather than the world of unpleasant reality.

rud·der (rŭd′ər), *n.* a movable device for steering a boat or ship.

ru·mi·nate (rōō′mə nāt′), *v.* 1. to chew again. 2. to chew the cud, as a cow does. 3. to turn over in the mind; think quietly; keep thinking about (something). —**ru′mi·na′tion,** *n.*

sac·ri·le·gious (săk′rə lĭj′əs, săk′rə lē′jəs), *adj.* showing disrespect for things considered sacred.

same·ness (sām′nĭs), *n.* a lack of variation; boredom; monotony.

sanc·ti·ty (săngk′tə tĭ), *n.* 1. holiness; saintliness. 2. the state of being reserved for religious purposes; sacredness.

sa·vor (sā′vər), *n.* 1. a certain taste or smell; flavor. —*v.* 2. to smell or taste with pleasure. 3. to have a particular taste, smell, or quality.

sa·vor·y (sā′və rĭ), *adj.* 1. pleasant to taste or smell. 2. morally correct; respectable.

scab·bard (skăb′ərd), *n.* the cover or sheath for the blade of a sword.

scav·en·ger (skăv′ĭn jər), *n.* 1. an animal that eats garbage or decaying matter. 2. a person who collects things that others have discarded.

scep·ter (sĕp′tər), *n.* rod or wand held by a king as a symbol of his power over his country.

scriv·en (skrĭv′ən), *v. Archaic.* to write.

scull (skŭl), *n.* an oar; one of a pair of oars for a boat. —*v.* to row a boat with oars.

seethe (sēth), *v.* 1. to boil, bubble, or foam, as a liquid. 2. to be extremely excited, disturbed, or angry.

sen·ti·men·tal (sĕn′tə mĕn′təl), *adj.* appealing to the emotions, especially in an excessive way.

set·tle (sĕt′əl), *n. Chiefly British.* a long wooden bench with a high back.

sham·ble (shăm′bəl), *v.* to walk slowly and awkwardly.

shoal (shōl), *n.* 1. a shallow area in a body of water. 2. a sand bar in a river, lake, etc.

sin·is·ter (sĭn′ĭs tər), *adj.* 1. toward the left-hand side. 2. threatening the approach of evil, disaster, etc. 3. wicked or dishonest.

smug (smŭg), *adj.* satisfied with oneself; pleased with one's own goodness, cleverness, etc.

so·lem·ni·ty (sə lĕm′nə tĭ), *n.* 1. a serious, formal, or sacred ceremony. 2. a formal, serious feeling; a grave, earnest, or sacred quality.

sol·i·tude (sŏl′ə tūd′, sŏl′ə tōōd′), *n.* the state of being alone, isolated, or lonely.

som·ber (sŏm′bər), *adj.* 1. dark; dull. 2. sad; gloomy; in low spirits.

sor·did (sôr′dĭd), *adj.* 1. dirty; disgusting; trashy. 2. selfish; greedy: as, *a sordid plan to bribe officials.*

spar (spär), *n. Nautical.* a strong pole such as would be used for the mast of a ship.

spec·u·la·tion (spĕk′yə lā′shən), *n.* 1. a thought, especially of a wondering or guessing nature. 2. the process of seeking to make money by buying and selling stocks, bonds, or other valuables.

spir·it·ed (spĭr′ĭt ĭd), *adj.* lively; energetic. —**spir′it·ed·ly,** *adv.*

squeam·ish (skwē′mĭsh), *adj.* 1. easily upset by crude words or ugly sights; too particular. 2. having a stomach that is easily upset; easily made sick.

strat·a·gem (străt′ə jəm), *n.* 1. a scheme or trick used to fool an enemy. 2. any trick or device used to deceive.

sub·sist (səb sĭst′), *v.* 1. to continue to exist. 2. to continue to live; stay alive.

sub·sis·tence (səb sĭs′təns), *n.* existence; the act or state of remaining alive.

sub·tile (sŭt′əl, sŭb′tĭl), *adj.* 1. subtle. 2. crafty; sly; cunning. 3. delicate; fine; difficult to see or understand.

ăct, āble, dâre, ärt; ĕbb, ēqual; ĭf, īce; hŏt, ōver, ôrder, oil, bŏŏk, ōōze, out; ŭp, ūse, ûrge; ə = a in *alone*; **ch,** chief; **g,** give; **j,** judge; **ng,** ring; **sh,** shoe; **th,** thin; **th,** that; **zh,** vision. See the full key at the beginning of this glossary.

suit·or (soo'tər), *n.* **1.** a man who seeks the love of a woman. **2.** a person who sues or asks for something.

sul·len (sŭl'ən), *adj.* **1.** showing anger or hurt feelings by keeping to oneself and looking gloomy. **2.** sad; gloomy. — **sul'len·ly,** *adv.*

sup·press (sə prĕs'), *v.* **1.** to force or push down; to crush. **2.** to keep back; hide: as, *to suppress a smile.* **3.** to prevent or block: as, *to suppress a news story.*

sum·mit (sŭm'ĭt), *n.* the highest point that can be reached.

su·per·fi·cial (soo'pər fĭsh'əl), *adj.* **1.** touching only the surface meaning; shallow. **2.** concerning only that which is easily seen or on the surface; lacking in thoroughness; not penetrating. **3.** apparent or seeming, but not real.

su·per·nat·u·ral (soo'pər năch'ə rəl), *adj.* outside or beyond the view or experience of ordinary men; beyond the laws of nature.

sup·ple (sŭp'əl), *adj.* **1.** limber; flexible; bending easily; not rigid. **2.** easily adjustable; adaptable to new conditions or needs: as, *a supple mind.*

surf (sûrf), *n.* the foamy waves on the surface of an ocean or lake.

sward (sword), *n.* a grassy area; the grass-covered earth.

sym·met·ri·cal (sĭ mĕt'rə kəl), *adj.* balanced in design; having a regular form or arrangement, so that opposite sides are matched.

sym·pho·ny (sĭm'fə nĭ), *n. Music.* a long musical composition written for an orchestra.

syn·o·nym (sĭn'ə nĭm), *n.* a word which has the same, or almost the same, meaning as another.

tal·ly (tăl'ĭ), *v.* **1.** to count. **2.** to record a count of. —*n.* **3.** anything used to record a count or keep a score.

te·di·ous (tē'dĭ əs, tē'jəs), *adj.* long and tiresome; boring.

tem·per·a·ment (tĕm'pər ə mənt, tĕm'prə-mənt), *n.* **1.** disposition; frame of mind; usual mood or attitude. **2.** a nature that is moody or easily upset.

ten·or (tĕn'ər), *n. Music.* a male singer who can sing a high range of notes.

tink·er (tĭngk'ər), *n.* **1.** a traveling worker who mends pots and pans. **2.** a general repairman; jack-of-all-trades. **3.** a clumsy worker. —*v.* **4.** to work as an unskilled repairman. **5.** to fuss and putter around.

tol·er·a·ble (tŏl'ər ə bəl), *adj.* **1.** bearable; able to be endured. **2.** not too bad; fairly good.

tol·er·ant (tŏl'ər ənt), *adj.* **1.** willing to let others think, say, and do what they wish, even if in conflict with one's own views. **2.** free from bias or prejudice.

tran·quil (trăng'kwĭl), *adj.* **1.** calm; steady; quiet; motionless. **2.** mentally undisturbed; peaceful. —**tran'quil·ly,** *adv.* —**tran·quil'li·ty,** *n.*

trans·fix (trăns fĭks'), *v.* **1.** to pierce through, as with something pointed. **2.** to make unable to move, as though pierced through: as, *he was transfixed with fear.*

trap·pings (trăp'ĭngz), *n. pl.* **1.** decorated covering for a horse. **2.** ornamented clothing; adornments.

trav·erse (trăv'ərs, trə vûrs'), *v.* to pass over, through, or across; cross (something). —*n.* the act of crossing over, through, or across.

trem·u·lous (trĕm'yə ləs), *adj.* **1.** shaking; quivering; trembling. **2.** timid; fearful.

trib·ute (trĭb'ūt), *n.* **1.** a payment that a nation is forced to make to a stronger, or victorious, nation. **2.** any forced payment. **3.** a gift, act, or comment offered to show thanks or respect.

triv·i·al·i·ty (trĭv'ĭ ăl'ə tĭ), *n.* **1.** an unimportant thing or idea. **2.** the quality of unimportance.

ul·ti·mate·ly (ŭl'tə mĭt lĭ), *adv.* finally; in the end.

un·as·sum·ing (ŭn'ə soo'mĭng), *adj.* not bold; not pushing oneself forward; modest.

un·bri·dled (ŭn brī'dəld), *adj.* **1.** without a bridle. **2.** not under control; ungoverned.

un·chas·tened (ŭn chā'sənd), *adj.* **1.** not

restrained; not subdued; somewhat un-disciplined. **2.** not punished or cor-rected, but allowed to do what one wishes.

un·daunt·ed (ŭn dôn′tĭd), *adj.* **1.** retaining one's courage; not afraid. **2.** not hesi-tating or retreating in the face of a threat or discouragement.

un·fath·om·a·ble (ŭn făth′əm ə bəl), *adj.* **1.** too deep to be measured. **2.** not understandable; impossible to compre-hend.

un·feigned (ŭn fānd′), *adj.* genuine or real; not made up or pretended.

un·wit·ting (ŭn wĭt′ĭng), *adj.* **1.** not knowing; unaware. **2.** not intended; not done purposely: as, *an unwitting insult.*

ur·chin (ûr′chĭn), *n.* a small boy; a mis-chievous child.

ve·he·ment (vē′ə mənt), *adj.* **1.** intense; full of strong feeling. **2.** violent; force-ful. —**ve′he·ment·ly,** *adv.*

vex (vĕks), *v.* **1.** to annoy, disturb, or irritate. **2.** to worry or torment: as, *her nagging vexes her husband.*

vex·a·tion (vĕks ā′shən), *n.* **1.** state of be-ing annoyed, irritated, or provoked, usually by a small problem. **2.** some-thing that annoys or disturbs.

vice (vīs), *n.* **1.** a bad or immoral habit: as, *gambling is his worst vice.* **2.** gen-eral evil conduct.

vi·cious (vĭsh′əs), *adj.* **1.** involved in evil. **2.** spiteful; dangerously evil.

vict·ual (vĭt′əl), *n.* **1.** *Archaic or Dialect.* food or provisions, especially for human use. **2.** *(pl.) Dialect or Colloq.* articles of prepared food.

vi·per (vī′pər), *n.* a dangerous snake.

vir·tu·al (vûr′choo əl), *adj.* being some-thing in effect or power, though not in name: as, *the prime minister is a virtual king.*

vol·u·ble (vŏl′yə bəl), *adj.* talkative; fluent.

wist·ful (wĭst′fəl), *adj.* thoughtfully sad, often because of longing for something. —**wist′·ful·ly,** *adv.*

yard (yärd), *n. Nautical.* a long, tapered piece of wood which holds the square sails of a ship crosswise to the mast.

yeo·man (yō′mən), *n.* **1.** *Archaic.* a ser-vant or helper in a noble household. **2.** *Archaic.* an assistant to an official. **3.** *Archaic.* a farmer who owns his small farm. **4.** a petty officer assigned as a clerk in the U.S. Navy.

ăct, āble, dâre, ärt; ĕbb, ēqual; ĭf, īce; hŏt, ōver, ôrder, oil, bŏŏk, ōōze, out; ŭp, ūse, ûrge; ə = a in *alone*; **ch**, chief; **g**, give; **j**, judge; **ng**, ring; **sh**, shoe; **th**, thin; **th**, that; **zh**, vision. See the full key at the beginning of this glossary.

Contents by Types

Index of Authors and Titles

The number in italics after an author's name indicates the page on which a short biographical sketch of that author appears.

DEFGH   0810
PRINTED IN THE UNITED STATES OF AMERICA

Building on the Best

MEETING TODAY'S EDUCATIONAL CHALLENGES

Introduction to the Foundations of American Education
Tenth Edition

James A. Johnson, *Northern Illinois University*
Victor L. Dupuis, *The Pennsylvania State University*
Diann Musial, *Northern Illinois University*
Gene E. Hall, *University of Northern Colorado*
Donna M. Gollnick, *NCATE/National Council for the Accreditation of Teacher Education*

The best, year after year...

Few texts are as trusted as this best selling foundations of education book. Now in its tenth edition, it continues to help develop successful teachers by providing a broad introduction to the foundations of education, based upon interesting, current, and accurate discussion of important practice and theory. As always, the text offers a comprehensive overview of the historical, legal, philosophical, and social aspects of American education.

Evolving to meet the needs of a changing society...

While retaining the best from past editions, the Tenth Edition has widened its focus, addressing more fully the challenges and controversial aspects of teaching in an increasingly complex world.

Three new sociology of education chapters, co-authored by Donna Gollnick, a respected authority on multicultural education.

Greater coverage of international issues, featuring a new *Global Perspectives* section in every chapter.

Added realism and challenge, including thought-provoking *Professional Dilemmas* features, useful *Relevant Research* features and all-new, pertinent *Case Studies*.

Stronger emphasis on career development, with new *Journal/Portfolio Development* activities for each chapter to help students in their job search and teaching practice.

Plus, updated content throughout, and an unparalleled supplement package with <u>new</u> CNN Connections videotapes, <u>new</u> color transparencies, Computer Enrichment Disks, and <u>new</u> Authentic Assessment Activities in the Test Bank.

Building on the Best

RESPONDING TO A CHANGING SOCIETY

Three new chapters spotlight the expertise of co-author Donna Gollnick in exploring issues surrounding multiculturalism, democracy and schools:

Three of the four sociology chapters have been totally revised to reflect current research and theory regarding social issues and schools, and to emphasize the growing diversity of the nation. The tenth edition integrates the topic of diversity throughout the book, using examples from a variety of groups.

Chapter 4, School and Society, helps students understand the role schools play in a democracy and the value of equality. Students consider the dilemma of how to exercise individual rights while being responsible for a broader community.

- Describes power relationships between groups and the importance of group relationships in a democratic society
- Discusses institutional discrimination, racism, sexism, and homophobia
- Examines school conflicts that arise when members of communities have different values and expectations for their schools
- Outlines alternative school choices
- Compares three educational strategies for providing equality: equal education opportunity, opportunity-to-learn standards, and equality of results
- Provides a global perspective on the importance Japanese students place on studying

Chapter 5 Multicultural Society, explores culture and its influence on our lives. Students are encouraged to look at differences, examine their own ethno-centrism and prepare for teaching students from different cultural backgrounds.

- Uses culture as the basis for describing the numerous differences between individuals and groups
- Develops difference as a desirable, positive characteristic of a multicultural society
- Presents three theories that describe culturally diverse societies: assimilation, cultural pluralism, and cultural diversity
- Contrasts educational practices that reinforce assimilation, cultural pluralism, and cultural choice

- Introduces microcultural groups and the dynamic interaction of seven cultural factors: socioeconomic status, ethnicity and race, gender, language, exceptionalities, religion, and geography
- Describes some of the inequalities across microcultural groups
- Provides a global perspective on the treatment of immigrants in selected European countries
- Stresses the importance of understanding intragroup differences in working effectively with students and families

Chapter 6, Education That Is Multicultural, develops themes of diversity, social justice, and equality in delivering education in our schools. Students are challenged to think critically about practice and become involved with school, communities, and parents.

- Provides a global perspective on the debates between multicultural and anti-racist educational strategies in the United Kingdom
- Describes the importance of understanding diverse approaches to teaching and learning
- Addresses issues of inclusion in the classroom, especially the inequities that result in ability grouping
- Introduces the concept of voices and cross-cultural communications as part of multicultural education
- Presents multicultural curriculum as including multiple perspectives and confronting controversial measures
- Discusses stereotyping in and censorship of instructional resources
- Confronts inequitable practices in educational settings, such as discrimination against students in interactions with school authorities

An increased emphasis on the importance of diversity is reflected in these three chapters and throughout the textbook.

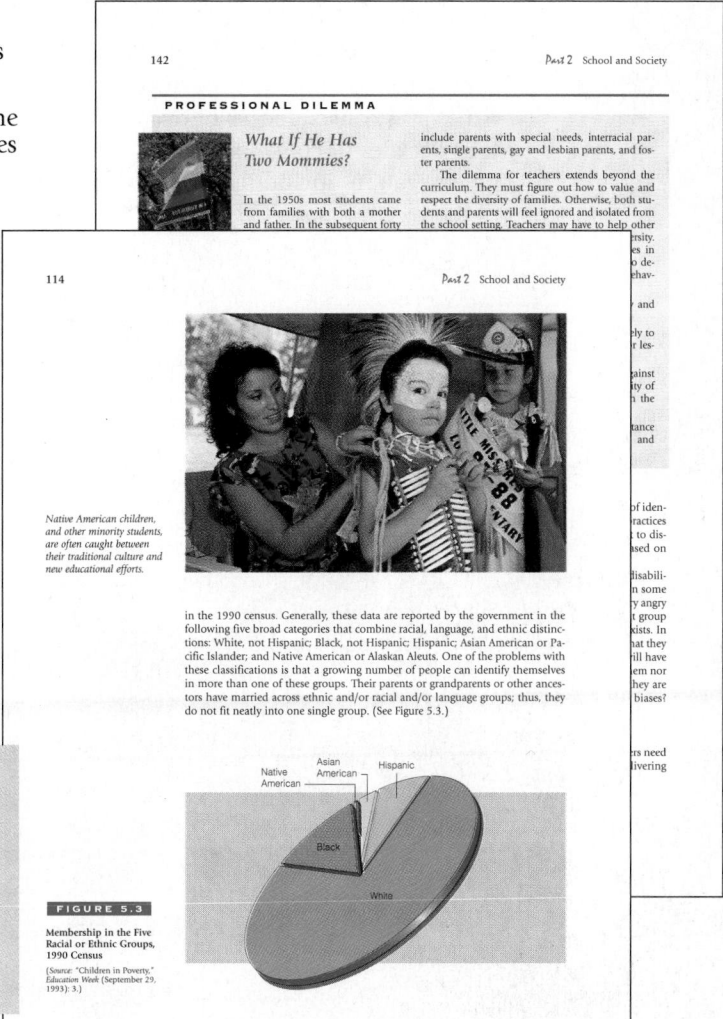

PROFESSIONAL DILEMMA

What If He Has Two Mommies?

In the 1950s most students came from families with both a mother and father. In the subsequent forty

include parents with special needs, interracial parents, single parents, gay and lesbian parents, and foster parents.

The dilemma for teachers extends beyond the curriculum. They must figure out how to value and respect the diversity of families. Otherwise, both students and parents will feel ignored and isolated from the school setting. Teachers may have to help other

Native American children, and other minority students, are often caught between their traditional culture and new educational efforts.

in the 1990 census. Generally, these data are reported by the government in the following five broad categories that combine racial, language, and ethnic distinctions: White, not Hispanic; Black, not Hispanic; Hispanic; Asian American or Pacific Islander; and Native American or Alaskan Aleuts. One of the problems with these classifications is that a growing number of people can identify themselves in more than one of these groups. Their parents or grandparents or other ancestors have married across ethnic and/or racial and/or language groups; thus, they do not fit neatly into one single group. (See Figure 5.3.)

FIGURE 5.3

Membership in the Five Racial or Ethnic Groups, 1990 Census

(*Source:* "Children in Poverty," *Education Week* (September 29, 1993): 3.)

Native American
Asian American
Hispanic
Black
White

Building on the Best

UPDATED CONTENT IN EVERY CHAPTER

New material pertaining to the teaching profession — for example, there's now a major segment on "beginning steps for developing a professional portfolio;" 1995 statistics, demographic data, and court decisions affecting education. No other text today provides as current and comprehensive discussion of the field of education as this tenth edition!

Timely coverage of issues related to the structure and finance of education — with many references to updated court decisions depicting the increased influence of the U.S. Supreme Court and the Congress in the past several years; issues of school finance at the state level; international comparisons of the public funding of schools; a new section on the four sources of law and the organization of the federal and state judicial systems; and increased emphasis on current issues and consequences of over four decades of court-ordered desegregation, including discussion of the recent Kansas City ruling. (Chs. 1,8, and 9)

Chapter 1 Teachers and Teaching as a Career

Profile of the Public School Teacher

There are 2.4 million public school teachers in the United States. Slightly over one-half of them teach at the elementary school level. Besides our large number of public school teachers, there are an additional 350,000 private school teachers and about 750,000 college and university teachers in the United States. Added to this total are over 800,000 other administrative and professional staff. It is also estimated that there are over a million education-related jobs in the United States, including such positions as education specialists in industry, instructional technologists in the military, museum educators, and training consultants in the business world.

   Altogether, we have roughly five million educators in the country, ranking education as one of the largest professions in the United States. It is estimated, however, that about 6 percent of our teachers leave the classroom each year for various reasons (retirement, resignations, poor health, etc.). So roughly 300,000 new educators are needed just to replace those leaving the profession each year.

Interest in Teaching Careers. Some experts feel that rising salaries and new respect for teachers are slowly helping to make teaching a more attractive profession. The Higher Education Research Institute at UCLA annually conducts a survey of college freshmen that, among other things, asks what career the student is planning to pursue. Figure 1.1 shows the results of this survey for the last twenty-seven years. In 1966, nearly 25 percent of freshmen were interested in becoming secondary school teachers compared to fewer than 5 percent today. Likewise, in 1966 about 9 percent of college freshmen expressed an interest in elementary teaching compared to about 5.3 percent today. Of course, this can be partly explained by the fact that our country experienced an oversupply of teachers and hence a poor job market during this period. The apparent downturn in 1993 in

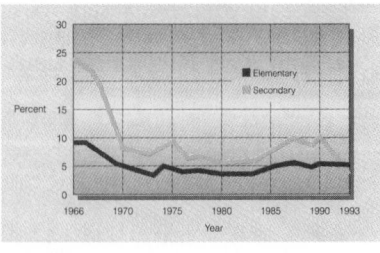

Important hot topics — including magnet schools, charter schools, year-round schools, and the use of lotteries and gaming to fund education; the rights of homeless children; student sexual harassment; AIDS and its implications for teachers and their school communities; politics in education, including the emergence of the religious right. (Chs. 8-10)

Updated philosophy chapters — including a new section on Native American philosophies, and new thinking on learner-centered educational philosophies; and discussion of the constructivist approach to education. (Chs. 14-16)

The newest innovations and changes in education — including coverage of the new national goals for education; greatly revised material on authentic assessment; new global perspective on grouping in German schools; new information on TQM, charter schools and OBE; new global segment on charter schools in England; and a new closing message to students, "Will You Be Ready?" (Chs. 17-19)

As always, this text remains a trusted preparation tool for national, state, and local teacher certification exams.

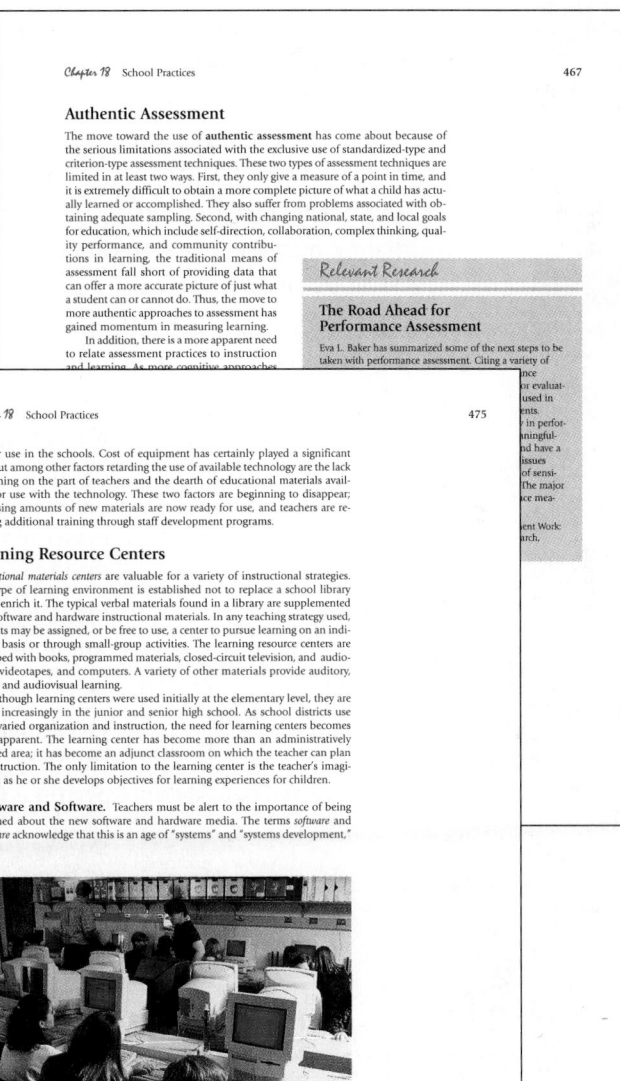

Authentic Assessment

The move toward the use of **authentic assessment** has come about because of the serious limitations associated with the exclusive use of standardized-type and criterion-type assessment techniques. These two types of assessment techniques are limited in at least two ways. First, they only give a measure of a point in time, and it is extremely difficult to obtain a more complete picture of what a child has actually learned or accomplished. They also suffer from problems associated with obtaining adequate sampling. Second, with changing national, state, and local goals for education, which include self-direction, collaboration, complex thinking, quality performance, and community contributions in learning, the traditional means of assessment fall short of providing data that can offer a more accurate picture of just what a student can or cannot do. Thus, the move to more authentic approaches to assessment has gained momentum in measuring learning.

In addition, there is a more apparent need to relate assessment practices to instruction and learning. As more cognitive approaches

Relevant Research

The Road Ahead for Performance Assessment

Eva l. Baker has summarized some of the next steps to be taken with performance assessment. Citing a variety of

regular use in the schools. Cost of equipment has certainly played a significant role, but among other factors retarding the use of available technology are the lack of training on the part of teachers and the dearth of educational materials available for use with the technology. These two factors are beginning to disappear; increasing amounts of new materials are now ready for use, and teachers are receiving additional training through staff development programs.

Learning Resource Centers

Instructional materials centers are valuable for a variety of instructional strategies. This type of learning environment is established not to replace a school library but to enrich it. The typical verbal materials found in a library are supplemented with software and hardware instructional materials. In any teaching strategy used, students may be assigned, or be free to use, a center to pursue learning on an individual basis or through small-group activities. The learning resource centers are equipped with books, programmed materials, closed-circuit television, and audio-videotapes, and computers. A variety of other materials provide auditory, and audiovisual learning.

Although learning centers were used initially at the elementary level, they are increasingly in the junior and senior high school. As school districts use varied organization and instruction, the need for learning centers becomes apparent. The learning center has become more than an administratively ed area; it has become an adjunct classroom on which the teacher can plan struction. The only limitation to the learning center is the teacher's imagination as he or she develops objectives for learning experiences for children.

Hardware and Software. Teachers must be alert to the importance of being informed about the new software and hardware media. The terms *software* and *hardware* acknowledge that this is an age of "systems" and "systems development,"

Computers in schools are becoming as basic as pencils and paper.

Building on the Best

PREPARING STUDENTS FOR TEACHING
— INNOVATIVE FEATURES SHOW THE WAY —

"Dreamcatcher" Part Openings profile master teachers from around the country who offer inspiration and advice on the teaching profession.

Every chapter includes:

Focus Questions at the beginning of each chapter help orient students to the chapter and prompt a more critical reading.

List of Key Terms at the beginning of each chapter serve as a reference for important terminology.

ALL-NEW Case Studies, based on real-world examples, set the stage for chapter material and focus attention on how chapter concepts will affect classroom practice.

NEW Professional Dilemma feature provides realistic problems students will likely face as teachers. Topics, listed on the right, are timely, controversial and intended to invite debate.

NEW! Relevant Research sections help bridge the much discussed research-practice gap. Education research related to chapter content is presented in the context of practical applications for the classroom teacher.

NEW! Global Perspectives sections help students develop a better comparative understanding of world educational practice.

Discussion Questions at the end of each chapter stimulate group discussion and encourage personal reflection.

NEW! Journal/Portfolio Development activities at the end of each chapter provide students with an opportunity to assemble their own professional portfolio for use in job interviews and teaching practice.

School–Based Experiences give students meaningful tasks that help them apply what they learn when they are in actual classroom settings.

---

instruments for use in studying learning disabilities; and statisticians devised new formulas and designs for controlling and analyzing data by using modern computers. New research tools such as regression formulas and factorial analysis yielded data that had been unobtainable earlier. On a somewhat less sophisticated level more interesting and more flexible teaching tools were developed—audiovisual devices, learning games, more beautifully illustrated books, instructional television, machines for programmed instruction, and computers. Additional personnel such as teacher aides, counselors, social workers, and school psychologists were added as well.

Relevant Research

Classroom Analysis Systems

Some of the research studies that grew out of recent educational history deal with the analysis of the teaching/learning act. Hundreds of pieces of research contributed to this research movement, including the work of Flanders* who, along with many colleagues, developed the classroom verbal interaction analysis system, which helps a teacher better understand what takes place verbally in the classroom. This system uses an observation form developed just for the purpose of recording what is taking place, moment by moment, in a classroom for a given lesson. These observations are then placed on a grid that helps a teacher better analyze and understand what took place during the lesson. Often, teachers are surprised at the results, which may be quite different from what the teacher expected. For instance, often teachers spend more time talking than they realize.

There have been many other systems developed to help teachers better understand and control what takes place in their classrooms. We encourage you to become familiar with some of these classroom observation systems and to try them in your classroom. Ask your professors and cooperating teachers in the schools where you are doing clinical work, to help you get started on this task. What classroom analysis systems have you already become familiar with? Can you locate at least six such systems? Can you experiment with the three best systems you find?

*Flanders Verbal Classroom Interaction Analysis system

Analysis of Teaching. Another emphasis found expression in the **analysis of teaching.** For half a century, researchers had been attempting to identify the characteristics and teaching styles that were most closely associated with effective instruction. Hundreds of studies had been initiated, and correlations had been done among them. During the 1950s the focus began changing from what ought to occur in teaching to what actually does occur. Flanders and other researchers developed observational scales for use in assessing verbal communications between and among teachers and students. The scales permitted observers to categorize and summarize specific actions on the part of teachers and students. These studies were followed by studies of nonverbal classroom behaviors.

Another series of investigations involving the wider range of instructional protocols was patterned after the time-motion studies used earlier for industrial processes. Dwight Allen and several other educators attempted to use some of these findings in delineating the components of effective teaching. Specific formats were used to introduce teacher candidates to the elements judged most important to good teaching. The change in focus from studies of teacher characteristics to analyses of what actually occurs in classrooms has provided us with some of our best insights into teaching and learning and given us usable instruments for further investigations of classroom behavior. We can now assess the logical, verbal, nonverbal, affective, and several attitudinal dimensions of instruction as well as the intricate aspects of cognition and concept development.

Teacher Effectiveness. Recent research has focused even more closely on the instructional patterns of effective teachers. A recent review by Powers and Beard, *Teacher Effectiveness: An Annotated Bibliography,* catalogs over three thousand

PROFESSIONAL DILEMMAS INCLUDE:

- Should There Be a National Index to Rate Schools?
- Will You Be Able to Pay Your Bills on a Teacher's Salary?
- Are Teachers Professional If They Strike?
- What If There Are Only a Few Girls in Calculus Class?
- How Much Can We Expect of Limited English Speaking Students?
- What If He Has Two Mommies?
- Can You Be a Counselor to Your Students?
- What Is the Appropriate Role for Teachers When the Politics Get Rough?
- Should Condoms Be Available to Students in Your Schools?
- What Will You Do If a Child in Your Classroom Has AIDS?
- Can You Provide Adequate Multicultural Education in Your Classroom?
- Can a Teacher Both Defend and Critique Schools?
- How Can a Teacher Better Understand the World?
- Should Ethics Be Taught in American Schools?
- Should I Use Homogeneous or Heterogeneous Ability Grouping?
- Should You Use Authentic Assessments to Grade Students?
- Can Teachers Adapt Their Classroom Philosophy to Meet the Diversity of Inclusion Students?
- Can You Prepare Authentic Assessment Tools?
- Can You Successfully Involve Parents in Their Children's Education?

PROFESSIONAL DILEMMA

Should You Use Authentic Assessments to Grade Students?

here is a growing awareness that
students should be assessed using a
that go beyond multiple-choice
ions. Teachers are being asked to
als, cooperative learning projects,
os, and other methods for assess-
an and cannot do. However, there
ing the appropriateness of using
tic ways of assessing" for grading.
nes from a Greek derivative that
oneself." When teachers grade a
only sitting beside the child, they

are also making a value judgement. Is such a value
judgement consistent with the notion of assessing
one's strengths and weaknesses?

Some educators respond positively to this question of grading authentic assessments. They believe
that society values some qualities more than others.
Hence, it is appropriate to grade a student's portfolio.
Other educators contend that such grading limits a
child's creativity; it makes the assessments less authentic because there is an implicit standard that
belongs to the teacher. Hence, teachers really are asking students to provide a certain type of portfolio; this
makes the portfolio nothing more than a large essay-
type test with portfolio entries as the correct answers.

You will need to determine your own answer to
this complex dilemma. Should you rely on authentic
assessments or merely use them as indicators of what
a child knows or can do?

CASE STUDY — PERFORMANCE-BASED SCHOOL PROGRAMS

ncreasing numbers of school districts are moving toward performance-based school
programs. These programs are the natural outgrowths of competency-based educa-
on, but are not as controversial because the local districts have greater control over
hat performance-based expectations will be. Since you, as a new teacher, have recent-
studied the pros and cons of these types of programs, you could be asked to serve
a school-district-wide committees that are contemplating these curriculum activities.
u have learned that many veteran teachers do not look favorably on these programs
because they deviate markedly from the typical school program with which these
achers have become comfortable.

As you prepare to take part in this type of school district activity, you know that
ou should do the following:

1. Talk with colleagues about their interests in individualizing instruction.
2. Prepare reading materials that discuss individualization activities with a variety of diverse learners.
3. Plan to keep communication channels open with your colleagues so they are
   informed on the status of the committee's activities.
4. Have your colleagues try and give you feedback on the sample materials that
   are investigated and developed by the committee.

Your task will not be easy because the majority of the instruction in your district
of the large group variety. Most teachers have the same set of expectations for all of

---

386   *Part 5* Philosophical Concepts, Educational Views, and Teaching Styles

free them from bondage and idolatry. Mohammed taught that Allah is a purposeful God who created things to reach certain desired goals. Those who follow
the will of Allah will be eternally rewarded in paradise, an oasis of flowing waters.
For those who do not follow the will of Allah, there is eternal suffering.

 Global Perspectives: The Fabric of Eastern Thought. As you can see,
Eastern thought is like a rich fabric of diverse ideas. It emphasizes sets of views
that are quite different from the neat categorizations of Western thought. Eastern
thought suggests that cohesive views can be achieved without the necessity of
neat, hierarchically distinct categories. Although they are quite difficult to categorize, the philosophy and thought of both the Far East and the Middle East force
us to reexamine our meanings and assumptions. As such, the study of Eastern
thought is an important part of all future educators' preparation in an increasingly multicultural society.

Native North American Thought

Just as the rich past and diverse cultures make it difficult to summarize Eastern
thought, Native North American thought is equally difficult to synthesize. **Native
North American thought** includes a varied set of beliefs, philosophical positions,
and customs that span different tribes in North America. These beliefs, positions,
and customs center on the relationship of humans to all of nature including the
earth, sun, sky, and beyond. Different tribes in different settings have developed
varied approaches to this human-to-nature relationship.

The Navajo nation is the largest United States tribe. Its early history was nomadic and its thoughts and customs are known for their unique ability to assimilate with and adapt to the thought and customs of other tribes. As with most
Native American cultures, the Navajo universe is an all-inclusive unity viewed as
an orderly system of interrelated elements. At the basis of Navajo teachings and
traditions is the value of a life lived in harmony with the natural world. Such a
view enables one to "walk in beauty." In understanding the Navajo world view,
one must note the teachings of the "inner forms" of things. These inner forms
were set in place by First Man and First Woman. The concept of "inner form" is
similar to the concept of a "spirit" or "soul" because without it, the Navajos say
the outer forms would be dead.[10]

The Native American culture of the Great Plains, of which the Lakota form
part, is based on mystical participation with the environment. Every aspect of this
ecosystem, including Earth, Sky, Night and Day, Sun and Moon, are all elements
of oneness within which life was undertaken. The Lakota celebrate the "sacred
hoop of life" and observe seven sacred rites toward the goal of ultimate communion with Wakan-Tanka, the great Spirit.[11]

The Hopi follow the path of peace, which they believe is a pure and perfect
pattern of mankind's evolutionary journey. The Road of Life of the Hopi is represented as a journey through seven universes created at the beginning. At death, the
conduct of a person in accordance with the Creator's plan determines when and
where the next step on the road will be taken. Each of the Hopi clans has a unique
role to play, and each role is an essential part of the whole. Hopis must live in
harmony with one another, with nature, and with the plan. Out of this complex
interplay, then, the plan is both created and allowed to unfold.

Chief Sequojah, author of the Cherokee alphabet

Building on the Best

ANNOTATED INSTRUCTOR'S EDITION
— YOUR PROVEN BLUEPRINT FOR A SUCCESSFUL COURSE—

New Annotated Instructor's Edition provides instructors with background information, assistance in preparation and an impressive set of resources (including updated annotations) to increase the effectiveness of their teaching. The AIE consists of two sections:

1 The Instructor's Section — a chapter-by-chapter guide

The blue-bordered Instructor's Section replaces the traditional Instructor's Manual and is conveniently bound in the instructor's text. For each chapter, the Instructor's section contains the following:

Extended Outline — all the chapter headings in one place for easy reference

Chapter Objectives — to identify primary teaching and learning goals

Strategies for Introducing Each Chapter — to spark students' initial interest in the chapter topic, including suggestions for both in-class and field activities

Chapter Overview and Analysis — a paragraph summary of the chapter's main points

Class Activities — a guide to activities including in-class activities, discussions, and projects for enhancing and applying chapter content

Transparencies — lists the appropriate items from the transparency package for the chapter

Professional Dilemma — a brief description and suggestions for using this new feature in class

Relevant Research — a brief summary and suggestions for teaching research study, highlighted in this new feature

Video Resources — descriptions and information about obtaining available videotaped material

CNN Video Guide — a summary and description of CNN Video segments for each part of the text

---

Chapter 7   Social Issues Affecting the School   IS-21

11. compare and contrast the provisions of school clinics, magnet schools, and adult literacy programs in providing for the special needs of learners.
12. examine global problems of education.

STRATEGIES FOR INTRODUCING THE CHAPTER

Identify for your class major social issues that have affected your life. Tell the class your opinions about how education has dealt with these issues. Where has education failed? This type of introduction can lead to a discussion of today's society and its impact on educational thinking. The importance of a learner's family situation should be stressed and discussed. Encourage students to share both positive and negative family experiences that have an effect on learners and learning. Use focus questions to introduce the many concepts in this chapter. Encourage students to discuss pro and con issues associated with the social issues examined in this chapter.

CHAPTER OVERVIEW AND ANALYSIS

This chapter presents the multitude of social issues that affect the school and its efforts in working with learners. The chapter provides information that identifies problems and needs, and the teacher in training should be able to grasp the magnitude of the problems that come to the doors of the school. The power and effects of the family cannot be stressed highly enough when you examine social problems of youth. Thus, the family needs to be kept utmost in mind when looking at and studying social issues. The intent of this chapter is to alert the teacher about how these problems affect the daily efforts of the teacher in the classroom.

The collage of special issues section identifies some of the more apparent issues that states and the national government have established as priorities for attention. The needs of exceptional children as protected by Public Law 94-192 and its ensuing additions and amendments should elicit teacher concerns toward all the diversity in children and not just those protected by federal law. Multicultural language issues, provisions for school clinics, magnet schools, and adult literacy programs point to the special attention being given to these issues by the American society.

CLASS ACTIVITIES

Activity 7.1: Have each student create a family profile of his or her family group. Then have the students compare their profiles with that presented by the text.
Activity 7.2: Have the students interview a teacher working in a low socioeconomic area to see what that teacher

feels is the greatest need and problem in his or her classroom.
Activity 7.3: Ask the students to investigate and discuss typical school district services that are made available to students who are involved with drugs.
Activity 7.4: Have students investigate the effectiveness of suicide prevention programs.
Activity 7.5: Have small student groups brainstorm on the topic of dropout prevention measures. Have the groups share their ideas with the whole class.
Activity 7.6: Have students debate the use of armed policemen in the schools to maintain order.
Activity 7.7: Have students in small groups prepare a statement of philosophy and guidelines for sex education in the schools. Have them share and discuss the different efforts.
Activity 7.8: Have different groups of students design programs for special needs children such as latchkey, gifted, and homeless children.
Activity 7.9: Have students (by their different certification areas) identify the kinds of learning problems bilingual children will have in the different certification areas.
Activity 7.10: Have students discuss worldwide social issues that affect global student learning in their schools.

PROFESSIONAL DILEMMA: Can You Be a Personal Counselor for Your Students?

This dilemma stretches the personal counseling activity of a regular teacher. There is little doubt that the dilemma presents a student who evidently has tremendous trust in and respect for the teacher. The instructor needs to be sure that the teacher education students are aware that they have not been trained as professional counselors. The students should meet in small groups of three to five and outline strategies for dealing with the dilemma that keep the "nontrained caveat" in mind. The strategies of the students can be shared and discussed with the whole class as to their relevance to the real world of teaching.

RELEVANT RESEARCH: How School Boards Are Responding to Violence in the Schools

This research article reports on a national survey that examined how school districts worked to prevent violence in their schools. Two significant findings emerged from this research study. First, some 82 percent of the survey respondents felt school violence was worse than it had been five years earlier. Second, there is no apparent certain method of coping with or handling violence since the survey revealed 22 different approaches were being used. The instructor can use this research article to have students debate the validity of the various reported methods being used to curb violence.

INSTRUCTOR'S SECTION

2 Fully Annotated Text Section —
with marginal annotations throughout each chapter as noted:

Focus Questions —lists the number of the Focus Question in the Instructor's Section and repeats the question for quick reference

Objectives — in the same form and content as in the Instructor's Section

Key Terms — highlights the key term that is defined in the context of the annotated paragraph and in the glossary

Transparency — corresponding title and number appear in margin, with related comments

NEW! Diversity — additional insights and information about multicultural and global issues

NEW! Journal/Portfolio Development — end-of-chapter exercises in student text are keyed to appropriate text sections

NEW! Journal Activity Masters — Journal Writing activities for students, located in the Test Bank, are described and keyed to appropriate text sections

Activity — classroom activities offer suggestions for using text in class

Videos — CNN logo in the margin indicates text material related to videotape segments

Information Note — additional background information provides instructors with options for adding depth and detail

Discussion Questions — end-of-chapter questions repeated adjacent to the related text material

Test Questions — keyed to the heading of the appropriate section by number, including NEW Authentic Assessment items

---

172

Part 2 School and Society

- Exhibition of learning problems that are foreign to expected normal behavior
- Continual early arrival at school, desire to stay late, and little desire to go home

Transparency 38:
Indicators of Child Abuse

Objective 8:
Identify child abuse practices and appropriate teacher action when child abuse is suspected.

Journal/Portfolio Development 1:
Develop a working file that contains brochure-type materials that address problems of chemical abuse, suicide, sexuality, and child abuse. Prepare a written evaluation of each of these collection topics, and assess how the brochure information can be used in your teaching.

Journal Activity Master 7.2: An In-Depth Investigation of One Key Societal Issue.
The object of this activity is to select and study one societal issue in depth and to create a program to solve the problem.

Test Questions 7.42–7.61

Focus Question 5:
Should our schools help to solve social problems? Why or why not?

Key Term:
Exceptional learners

Effects on Learning. Children who come from homes where child abuse is prevalent have extreme difficulty in the classroom. Their attention spans are seriously reduced, and they tend to look for things to do that will take them away from a task. Generally, they become very distrustful of adults, which is carried over into the classroom with the teacher. Such distrust may be manifested by extra demands on the teacher for attention, in an attempt to be sure that the teacher's learning expectations are being met, or it may be exhibited as total isolation from the teacher and the learning expectations. The child's psychological and social needs dominate his or her behavior in the classroom, and the child experiences difficulty in learning.

Teachers should not be reluctant to report these types of abnormal behaviors to the proper authorities. The national statistics on child abuse suggest that it is important for the teacher and school to become involved in suspected cases of abused children. Teachers and schools are protected from civil and criminal liability if the report of child abuse is rendered honestly from suspicion, based on behaviors listed above, and is considered valid.

A Collage of Special Issues for the School

In addition to the collage of social problems facing the teacher and the school, there is a growing list of pressing issues that the school must address as it responds to the everyday needs of its students. Although schools might not consider these issues quite as difficult to handle, they do have an effect on the learning environment. Formerly, many of these problems were not considered issues for the public schools to address because some other societal agency was responding or the issue had not yet surfaced. However, as we know more about learning and how it can be affected by physical, mental, and emotional development and the social environment, the school has had to face new, pressing issues.

Special-Needs Children

There is little doubt that the school has always encountered learners with special needs. However, schools often didn't recognize these special needs or couldn't cope with them if they were recognized. As teachers, specialists, and administrators became better trained, some of these special problems were identified. Once problems or needs could be identified, the schools could mount efforts to attend to them. It should be pointed out, however, that the degree of effort that the school employs to take care of special needs depends on the wishes of the community, state, and nation. Taking care of these needs can be controversial, and a teacher should remember that the community determines the direction of the school.

Exceptional/Handicapped Learners. With the passage in 1975 of Public Law 94-142, the special education law provided millions of **exceptional learners** with mandated public education. At the other end of the ability continuum, however, there have been only sporadic institutionalized attempts to provide special

Building on the Best

A COMPLETE LEARNING PACKAGE

Exploring Alternatives and Enrichment Simulations Software Program gives students "hands-on" experience in making professional decisions. This full-color simulations software (for Mac or IBM) allows students to analyze realistic classroom and professional situations, make decisions as "educators," and then reflect upon their actions. Every simulation includes a writing exercise that encourages student reflection and lends itself to writing assignments and class discussion.

NEW! **Enrichment Transparencies** — 100 color acetate transparencies have been created from textual material and outside sources. Each is designed to reinforce important points and visually enhance lectures.

IMPROVED! **Test Bank** — a convenient, easy-to-use testing resource of over 1000 multiple choice and true/false questions with answers, and short answer and essay questions with suggested answers — all written by the text authors. NEW to this edition of the Test Bank are **authentic assessment tools** for each chapter.

Journal Activity Masters— located in the Test Bank, allow students to practice journal writing and portfolio development.

Allyn & Bacon Computerized Testing — a computerized version of the Test Bank. Instructors can select questions that are keyed to specific chapters or sections of the test, edit and/or add questions, select by level of difficulty or question type, construct random or manual selection tests, and print up to nine versions of the same test. (for IBM and Macintosh.)

Plus... TM
NEW **CNN**
Connections Video

Add high quality video programming to your course with exclusive CNN video segments — integrated with text material!

Over 30 new videotape news clips bring to life a variety of key issues, such as cultural diversity, teacher empowerment, and legal aspects of education. Each clip is correlated directly to chapter material and available through an exclusive agreement with Cable News Network (CNN). Referenced only in the annotated instructor's edition, so instructors can decide the best way to use them, these short video segments stimulate and enliven group discussion.

Related Supplementary Texts…

An Introduction to Multicultural Education
by James A. Banks, University of Washington
Gives students a concise look at the major issues, concepts, paradigms, and teaching strategies of multicultural education.

Teacher's Problem Solving:
A Casebook of Award-Winning Teaching Cases
by James M. Cooper (editor), University of Virginia
A collection of nine award-winning cases selected for their realism, attention to cultural pluralism, style, complexity, and opportunities for using professional knowledge. They all allow for multiple courses of action.

NEW!
Modern Fiction on School Teaching: An Anthology
Edited by Jay Blanchard and Ursula Casanova, both of Arizona State University
This international anthology of fictional stories about school teaching shows just how powerful the use of fiction can be in helping students envision and evaluate what it is like to be a teacher. Stories are organized in sections that will support cross-story inquiries and discussions.

NEW EDITION!
Thoughtful Teachers, Thoughtful Schools:
Issues and Insights in Education Today,
Second Edition
by Editorial Projects in Education
This collection of up-to-date, authoritative, and high-interest articles from *Teacher Magazine* and *Education Week* covers topics such as diversity of student population and the challenges it poses, how research is changing classroom practice, the role of money, power and politics in schools today, and teacher empowerment.

ANNOTATED INSTRUCTOR'S EDITION

Introduction to the Foundations of American Education

Tenth Edition

James A. Johnson
NORTHERN ILLINOIS UNIVERSITY

Victor L. Dupuis
PENNSYLVANIA STATE UNIVERSITY

Diann Musial
NORTHERN ILLINOIS UNIVERSITY

Gene E. Hall
UNIVERSITY of NORTHERN COLORADO

Donna M. Gollnick
NATIONAL COUNCIL for ACCREDITATION of TEACHER EDUCATION

Allyn and Bacon

Boston   London   Toronto   Sydney   Tokyo   Singapore

Editor-in-Chief, Education: Nancy Forsyth
Senior Editor: Virginia Lanigan
Series Editorial Assistant: Nihad Farooq
Developmental Editor: Alicia Reilly
Marketing Manager: Kathleen Hunter
Production Administrator: Susan McIntyre
Editorial-Production Service: Kathy Smith
Composition Buyer: Linda Cox
Cover Administrator: Linda Knowles
Manufacturing Buyer: Megan Cochran

ISBN 0-205-17838-3

Printed in the United States of America
10 9 8 7 6 5 4 3 2 1   00 99 98 97 96 95

Instructor's Section Contents

Chapter 1

Teachers and Teaching as a Career

EXTENDED OUTLINE

OBJECTIVES

After reading this chapter, students will be able to:

1. articulate the importance of teachers, not only to children, but to parents and the society at large.
2. describe ways that teachers are important to children, the nation in the Information Age, and in the Global Economy.
3. discuss how teachers are viewed by students, parents, and the general public.
4. develop a general understanding of who become teachers, the conditions of teaching, and some of the important characteristics of today's teachers.
5. present a list of common reasons for becoming a teacher.

6. identify and examine key aspects of the work and career patterns of teachers.

7. understand that the profession of teaching is evolving, as is reflected in recent changes in the status, work conditions, and bases for teacher assessment.

8. provide examples of ways that the status of teaching has improved in recent years.

9. describe recent improvements in the work conditions of teachers.

10. illustrate the different strategies that teachers use to learn more about their own teaching.

11. describe the parts of a portfolio and use their own works as examples.

STRATEGIES FOR INTRODUCING THE CHAPTER

Present a short description about your own career path in the field of education. Share several personal experiences that led you to become a teacher. Ask your students about the career paths of teachers they have known. Then, invite students to share their own dreams about becoming a teacher. During the discussion, search for patterns and common themes. One theme may be that the desire to teach emerged when the students were quite young. This early career targeting may lead to a more limited perception of the world and the role of teaching in the world. If this is the case, then greater emphasis may be given to parts of this chapter that are designed to broaden perspectives on the place of teaching in society.

Divide the class into small groups and ask them to discuss the focus questions. If you want to have students begin developing group process skills, you could ask that one student be the facilitator of discussion and that another be the note taker for reporting out. When they have assembled back in a large group, have students share their discussion points and try to categorize the responses into clusters. At this point you could raise a number of questions about the work conditions of teachers. For example, "In comparison to other jobs, is teaching simple or relatively complex?" This discussion could lead into reading the Case Study: "Teaching Is Complex Work." Also, perhaps one of the CNN videos could be integrated into these discussions.

CHAPTER OVERVIEW AND ANALYSIS

This chapter introduces students to the teacher's world. Throughout the chapter an emphasis is placed on pointing out that teachers and teaching are important to a larger constituency than the children being taught. Parents, other teachers, society at large, and the nation depend on teachers doing their job well.

The chapter is designed to help future teachers begin to understand the complicated work that teachers do and to compare their interests, skills, and aspirations with those of successful educators. Although the chapter includes a number of facts and descriptions about how difficult teaching can be, the emphasis is placed on the positive aspects of teaching.

Recent changes in teaching and the status of teachers are also themes in this chapter. One important development in teaching is the increasing use of portfolios. This important tool is being used for self-reflection, as well as increasingly for evaluation and licensure. Observation and self-analytic techniques that the student can use throughout the course and their teaching career are introduced here. These techniques are linked to portfolio development so that students have the opportunity to immediately begin to use the techniques and concepts that are being introduced. The suggested activities provide additional steps that students can take to better understand and prepare for teaching in today's classrooms and schools.

CLASS ACTIVITIES

Activity 1.1: Ask students to recall one teacher from their past whom they admire. Have each student identify characteristics that made the teacher important. Then ask students to share these characteristics and compare them to those noted in the text. How do the students' reasons compare with those mentioned in the text?

Activity 1.2: Have students take on different roles in contemporary society. Assign some to be lawyers, police officers, politicians, health care workers, truck-drivers, unemployed single parents, and so on. Then ask them to identify the expectations they would have for teachers, given the role that they were assigned.

Activity 1.3: Ask students to name the top three reasons that they think drive teachers away from teaching. Then review the reasons presented in Figure 1.3. Contrast the reasons reported in the survey with those offered by your students.

Activity 1.4: Place students in small groups and ask them to make a list of the different things that teachers need to do in their job role. As they near completion, ask them to place a check by all of the items on their lists that deal directly with teaching children. Ask them to place a star by anything that pertains to events outside the classroom.

Activity 1.5: Ask students to design a slogan, such as would be used in a television ad, to enhance the stature of teachers.

Activity 1.6: Ask students to think of a time that someone "took charge" of a situation. What were the circumstances that surrounded this need to take charge? What were the characteristics of the person and the way that they took charge? Are there any implications for how teachers can take charge?

Activity 1.7: Contrast informal note taking with structured observations. Have students use both techniques during the next class.

Activity 1.8: Bring to class an example of a teacher portfolio. Use it to illustrate the way one teacher has organized a portfolio. Point out, or have students suggest, additional information that would be useful to have. Be sure to emphasize the purpose of the example portfolio. A portfolio for self-reflection will be very different from one that has been prepared to submit with an application for professional licensure.

PROFESSIONAL DILEMMA: Should There Be a National Index to Rate Schools?

We are living in a time when everything is being rated, ranked, and polled. In at least one state, Kentucky, at the end of the school year, schools that are ranked high enough are receiving a significant amount of money that they can use however they wish. The dilemma for your students is whether there should be a ranking of schools across the state and the nation. Presumably, this ranking would be published and there might be some sort of rewards as well.

RELEVANT RESEARCH: Teacher Expectations and Student Achievement

Over the last twenty-five years there has been a great deal of research and writing about "teacher expectations." One result of the earlier Rosenthal and Jacobson study and the

Rist study was increased awareness of the profound difference unconscious teacher expectations can have on student success. The new study by Goldenberg points out the importance of keeping in mind teacher behaviors. Regardless of the teacher's expectations, it is what the teacher does, and in this case did not do, that spells out the consequences for student learning.

One way to raise the importance of this issue is to ask students about their experiences of being in a class with a "teacher's pet." Have each student reflect back and visualize what it was like in that classroom for both the "pet" and the other students. Have them write down their impressions about the *expectations* that the teacher apparently held for the "pet." Ask them to describe the teacher's *behaviors* toward the "pet." Then explore the relative learning success of the "pet" versus other students in the class.

VIDEO RESOURCE

To Be a Teacher
NBC, color, 15 min.
A documentary showing the experiences of four student teachers.

TRANSPARENCIES

Transparency 1: Profile of New Teachers
Transparency 2: Reasons for Being a Teacher
Transparency 3: Essential Knowledge and Skills for Teachers
Transparency 4: Reducing the Uncertainties of Teaching
Transparency 5: What Would Have Been Most Helpful to You in Preparing to Be a Teacher?
Transparency 6: Information and Materials for a Professional Portfolio

Chapter 2

Employment Opportunities for Teachers

OBJECTIVES

After reading this chapter, students will be able to:

1. articulate pertinent information about the teacher supply picture in the United States.
2. list major factors that determine the demand for teachers in the United States.
3. analyze the fluctuating demand for teachers.
4. compare teacher salaries in typical school districts throughout the country.
5. contrast the fringe benefits, extra pay, and moonlighting options available to teachers.
6. articulate teacher certification requirements in various states.
7. internalize the variables that result in a successful job search for a typical teacher.

STRATEGIES FOR INTRODUCING THE CHAPTER

Discuss some of your personal job-searching experiences. Describe any aspect of your career that included non-teaching tasks that were related to education (i.e., writing test items for a measurement firm, presenting lectures or workshops, designing philosophy statements for school districts, writing technical manuals for computer firms, etc.). Help students see that education includes many different opportunities in addition to those directly related to the classroom.

Use the focus questions to encourage students to expand their view of education. Have the class imagine a typical week in the life of a teacher, making certain that students think about the tasks a teacher might accomplish after school hours. Then ask students to read the case study that assists them in preparing for a job interview.

CHAPTER OVERVIEW AND ANALYSIS

This second chapter is designed to help students begin to understand their eventual employment opportunities as educators. It attempts to answer two basic questions that are typically foremost in a student's mind—(1) Will I find a teaching job when I graduate?, and (2) How much money will I make as a teacher? The chapter presents in some detail the various factors that influence the teacher supply and demand picture. It points out that the demand for teachers varies greatly from time to time, subject to subject, and place to place.

Information on teacher salaries and fringe benefits is also provided in some detail. An explanation of the rather complex subject of teacher certification is presented along with suggestions for a successful job search. The basic message of the chapter is that teacher education students should learn all they can, at an early stage, about employment opportunities for teachers. The chapter offers students a wealth of information that will help them begin the arduous task of finding a teaching position.

CLASS ACTIVITIES

Activity 2.1: Use Figure 2.1 to assist students in analyzing the linear growth projection in school enrollments during the 1990 through 2000 decade. Ask students to analyze how this projected increase in student population relates to the overall decrease in the general population in the United States.

Activity 2.2: Have students develop two lists. One list should include the areas (geographical, subject, type of student) that will require fewer teaching positions. The other list should include the areas that are projected to need additional teaching positions.

Activity 2.3: Discuss the pros and cons of merit pay. Describe how it works in your own collegiate setting.

Activity 2.4: Have students identify the ways that they are most comfortable earning additional pay while teaching. Summarize the class choices in the form of a frequency chart and discuss the implications of the class profile.

Activity 2.5: Describe the specific teacher certification procedures in your state. Divide students into small groups and have them identify the strengths and weaknesses of the certification requirements. Then, ask each group to suggest one change that they believe would improve their state's certification program.

Activity 2.6: Have students prepare for a fictitious job interview. Then, interview several student volunteers and ask a panel of students to analyze the simulated interviews. At the end of the interviews ask the panel to identify the strengths of the interview candidates.

Activity 2.7: Ask students to identify an important characteristic or talent that distinguishes them. Then have them describe how this talent or characteristic would enhance their chance of getting a job.

PROFESSIONAL DILEMMA: Will You Be Able to Pay Your Bills on a Teacher's Salary?

This common professional dilemma deals with the fact that many teachers want to teach, but find they can make more money in other professions. Further complicating this dilemma is the fact that the public generally feels that teachers are already adequately paid. Also, many citizens (and school board members) feel that teachers should be paid on the basis of merit—a concept generally opposed by the education profession.

Use this professional dilemma to generate a class discussion on the topic of teacher salaries. Ask students to gather additional information about teacher salaries (perhaps in school districts where they may eventually like to teach) and share this information with the class. Also ask students to write a paper on the topic of teacher salaries, merit pay, salary schedules, etc. Finally, have students role play people taking different viewpoints regrading teacher salaries.

RELEVANT RESEARCH: Teachers Welcome Constructive Suggestions about Their Work, But Rarely Receive Them

Research has shown that teachers generally profit from specific constructive feedback on their performance; unfortunately, such feedback is typically only provided once or twice a year, and then is usually related to general performance. This Relevant Research feature provides a variety of learning opportunities about the need for educators to continually improve their performance and explore options for doing so. Ask your students to gather additional information, discuss, and/or write about related topics such as in-service teacher training, self-improvement ideas, teacher evaluation, peer evaluation, mentoring ideas, or the role of the principal (or other supervisors).

VIDEO RESOURCES

1. *Where Have All the Teachers Gone?*
   Cornell University, color, 29 min.
   Highlights the problems of American schools and the need for many excellent teachers.
2. *To Light a Fire: Great Teachers in America*
   PBS Video, color, 30 min.
   Profiles two of America's best teachers and their dynamic teaching styles.
3. *Career Builders: Education*
   Zenger Video, color, 25 min.
   Working professionals tell what it's like to teach and answer concerned questions. Guide included.

TRANSPARENCIES

Transparency 7: Projected Number of School Children to the Year 2020

Transparency 8: College Freshmen: Majors

Transparency 9: Moonlighting

Transparency 10: Relative Demand by Teaching Area

Transparency 11: Average Salary Paid Teachers

Transparency 12: Public Opinion of Teacher Salaries

Transparency 13: Characteristics Which School Systems Value

Transparency 14: Difficult Interview Questions

Chapter 3

Professional Organizations for Educators

EXTENDED OUTLINE

OBJECTIVES

After reading this chapter, students will be able to:

1. explain the role and organization of the National Education Association (NEA).
2. list the five professional initiatives of the NEA designed to improve education.
3. describe in outline form the organization of the American Federation of Teachers (AFT).
4. articulate orally and/or in writing several examples of professional activities of the AFT.
5. compare and contrast the NEA and the AFT in writing.
6. explain orally the concept of Political Action.
7. describe the purposes of existing state and local teacher organizations.
8. list specialty teacher organizations appropriate for different teacher certification areas.

STRATEGIES FOR INTRODUCING THE CHAPTER

Identify the professional organizations to which you belong, explain why they were selected, and describe the types of activities provided by the organizations. Lead a classroom discussion that helps students see that education is a profession that has many different components and services.

Use focus questions to encourage students to consider the different ways they can access organizations to assist them in their teaching career. Have the class conduct a debate that contrasts the strengths and weaknesses of teacher organizations.

CHAPTER OVERVIEW AND ANALYSIS

This chapter presents a variety of different professional organizations that teachers may join. It begins with a thoughtful description of the NEA and AFT, and outlines the organization and governance aspects of these two large teacher unions. Innovative activities of both organizations are presented as positive features. The authors stress the point that teacher unions seek to promote teacher welfare but also strive to improve the education of all students.

The chapter also discusses the state and local teacher organizations that are affiliated with the national NEA and AFT. Teacher education students are encouraged to learn all they can about these affiliated organizations and how they can be helpful to the variety of teacher certification areas.

The chapter further identifies the many specialty organizations that are available and that compete for teacher memberships. Examples are included in Appendix 3.1. Religious educational organizations are recognized in that some of the teacher education students will be teaching in nonpublic and/or religious-oriented schools. From an international perspective the chapter concludes with a discussion of the World Confederation of the Teaching Professions and the recent creation of Education International (EI).

CLASS ACTIVITIES

Activity 3.1: Have groups of students act as if they are members of the Representative Assembly of the NEA. Ask each group to develop and present one current educational policy for 2001 that is consistent with the basic purposes of the NEA.

Activity 3.2: Have several small groups of students each select one of the NEA initiatives and critique its strengths and weaknesses.

Activity 3.3: Have several small groups of students each select one of the AFT programs for professional growth and critique its strengths and weaknesses.

Activity 3.4: Have students compare the codes of ethics of the two major organizations. On the basis of this type of comparison, have students first rate their preferences for

which code they prefer and then prepare a document supporting their choices.

Activity 3.5: Split the class into two groups, one NEA and one AFT. Give each group the same school community situation: canceling extracurricular activities. Then have the groups develop an appropriate strike or sanction strategy to deal with this situation.

Activity 3.6: Select a current topic of national political debate such as charter schools. Ask the two classroom groups to research the topic and develop position statements; then compare the positions of the two groups.

Activity 3.7: Have the two groups from Activity 3.6 research this topic further in regard to two specific states and the position taken by the state governments on this topic. Then have the students discuss how they as teachers in a given state would behave if the state position on the topic were different from the position of their national organizations.

Activity 3.8: Have students discuss the international implications of EI on the NEA and AFT.

PROFESSIONAL DILEMMA: Are Teachers Professional If They Strike?

This dilemma puts the new teacher into a debatable ethical position. Should the teacher follow the dictates of his or her association or should conscience be his or her guide? The situation is almost a no-win one. The dilemma questions asked of the teacher may be used to focus on the welfare rights of the teachers or the educational rights of the students. Since both national teacher organizations speak to these issues, an organizational answer approach may be used to debate this dilemma.

RELEVANT RESEARCH: Teacher Job Satisfaction Is Important for Successful Teacher Performance

This research article focuses on the importance of having administrative support for teachers who are trying to meet the special needs of all of their students. The instructor can use this research topic to create a job satisfaction and dissatisfaction list for teachers as it relates to the expected and/or perceived supportive behaviors of the principal.

RELEVANT RESEARCH: Teachers Need to Become Active Researchers

This research article discusses how classroom teachers can become more involved in classroom research activities. It stresses the importance of teachers learning and using basic research techniques, being given administrative support for attending conferences, and being encouraged to try new research findings in the classroom. This article can be used to introduce students to the educational research literature and have them report selected research studies to the class. The studies selected can be of a general nature such as "writing across the curriculum," or they can be certification-area-specific such as "using political cartoons in teaching social studies."

VIDEO RESOURCES

1. *The Dynamics of Negotiations*
   Educational Service Bureau, color, 45 min.
   Explores the complexities of negotiations between teachers and school boards.
2. *Solving Impasses in Negotiations*
   Educational Service Bureau, color, 35 min.
   Reviews the difficult situation when negotiation impasses take place between educators and school boards.

TRANSPARENCIES

Transparency 15: NEA Structure
Transparency 16: AFT Table of Organization
Transparency 17: NEA's Nine Principles of Educational Excellence and Equity

Transparency 18: Bill of Rights for Children—NEA
Transparency 19: From Teacher Development to Student Empowerment
Transparency 20: Teacher Assessment for Preparation

COMPUTER ENRICHMENT EXPLORATION

Group Participation in Salary Negotiations. This simulation identifies the participant as a newly appointed member of a school district negotiating team. As a teacher new to the district, the teacher has certain expectations as to how this kind of effort is to be directed. The participant is initially confronted with a committee chairperson who appears to be nondemocratically directing the negotiating efforts. Confronted with this problem the participant has several options that he or she may choose to follow, and these options are branch programmed to produce different solutions to the simulation. On completion of the simulation, the participant is requested to respond on the computer as to why a certain course of action was taken and the reasons for that action. The typed computer response may be printed and handed in to the course instructor.

Chapter 4

School and Society

EXTENDED OUTLINE

OBJECTIVES

After reading this chapter, students will be able to:

1. elaborate on the contradictions inherent in democracy as practiced in the United States.
2. compare the power relationships that exist in society with those that exist in schools.
3. give examples of institutional discrimination in society and in the educational system.
4. reflect on how they are centered in discussions on racism and sexism.
5. identify different roles for the schools.
6. describe at least five purposes of schooling.
7. discuss the values that are reflected in the curriculum of schools with which they are familiar.
8. discuss the implications of meritocracy and equality on educational practices.
9. contrast equal educational opportunity, opportunity to learn standards, and equality of results efforts in education.
10. discuss the elements of the subculture of the school.
11. describe and provide examples of the informal curriculum.

STRATEGIES FOR INTRODUCING THE CHAPTER

Bring to class the newspaper from the past few days and samples of weekly news magazines like *Time* and *Newsweek*. Ask students to scan them and/or recall news reports on the radio or television over the past few days to identify the groups of people (for example, the Pope and Roman Catholics, the Black Muslims, Korean American store owners) who are being reported about in the media. Initiate a discussion about why these groups are in the news. Are there groups that are seldom mentioned? Is there a difference in the portrayal of different groups within the community?

Students should select a group with which they are not identified that has been mentioned in the news media recently. Ask them to keep a journal of the reports related to this group that they read, hear, or watch over the next week. At the end of the week, students should be able to characterize the importance and power that the group exercises in society.

CHAPTER OVERVIEW AND ANALYSIS

Democracy is the theme that integrates this chapter with an emphasis on the espoused value of equality. The dilemma between exercising our individual rights as citizens and being responsible for a broader community is explored. The overall goal is to help students both understand the role that schools play in a democracy and realize that schools themselves usually are not models of democracy.

The discussion begins with an examination of the roles of groups in society and the resulting conflict between group membership and the value of individualism that pervades much of the public rhetoric. Power and domination are critical concepts in clarifying a number of the group struggles in society. Students should begin to see where they are centered in these struggles as a result of their membership in one or more groups. In a democracy differences are valued and promoted.

The section on prejudice and discrimination further examines power by looking at the practices that have been established to help members maintain their control over many aspects of society. The idea that race makes a difference has become ingrained in the ethos of the United States over the past few centuries. Although African Americans are the primary victims of racism, others also are caught in its web. Individuals who do not look like European Americans are often treated as less important by both individuals and institutional practices. Women, gays, individuals with disabilities, limited English speakers, and others often suffer from a similar phenomenon in which they are not perceived or treated as equal to the dominant group.

The relationship between democracy and schooling is explored by reviewing the roles and purposes of schools. However, even when there is general agreement about these items, the actual implementation varies from school to school and from one region of the country to another because of the prevailing values of a community. Educators need to acknowledge that curricula, library books, extracurricular activities, and school events may be challenged by parents who believe that their values are not being reflected.

Educational implications of group membership, power, discrimination, and democracy are explored by examining ways in which differences have been treated in classroom and school settings. In some cases they are viewed as deficits to be overcome; in others, they are perceived as differences to be valued, promoted, and used to provide effective instruction. These approaches are contrasted in the presentations on equal educational opportunity, opportunity to learn standards, and equality of results.

The chapter closes by acknowledging the school culture itself as reflected in formal practices, traditions, and the informal curriculum. One aspect of schooling—studying—is presented in a view of Japanese expectations for students.

CLASS ACTIVITIES

Activity 4.1 Divide the class into small groups, and have students begin to identify the groups to which they belong that help define who they are and what their interests are. Compare commonalities and differences among class members, and identify the primary reasons for the differences. Discuss how the groups to which students belong are viewed within the social system.

Activity 4.2 Divide the class into four groups. Ask each group to develop a scenario that describes one of the following settings: (1) a school climate that is democratic; (2) a school climate that is not democratic; (3) a classroom that is democratic; and (4) a classroom that is not democratic. Compare these scenarios with the school experiences of students in the class.

Activity 4.3 Ask each student to jot down one psychological or academic need that he or she is experiencing right now. Then, have students anonymously hand in their identified needs. Place the class list in a summary chart and discuss which needs can and cannot be met in school.

Activity 4.4 Invite a school administrator to speak to the class about responding to community pressures and strategies developed to include communities in decision making about curriculum changes.

Activity 4.5 Identify a panel of students to discuss their experiences in different kinds of schools (for example, parochial, public, independent private, and alternative schools in rural, suburban, and urban areas). Class members could develop a grid to contrast the reasons for attendance at different types of schools and to compare the advantages and disadvantages of each.

Activity 4.6 Have students select a controversial issue that is receiving a great deal of coverage by the press. Have them identify any ways that schools have contributed to the controversy.

Activity 4.7 Have students prepare a debate between the value of meritocracy and equality and the way that they are reflected in schools.

Activity 4.8 Compare a community's expectations for an elementary teacher and for a secondary school teacher. Should they be different? How does the community expectation affect the professional development and commitment of the teacher?

PROFESSIONAL DILEMMA: What If There Are Only a Few Girls in the Calculus Class?

This dilemma suggests that schools play a role in perpetuating the low participation rates of girls in advanced mathematics classes. It proposes reasons that females may not be interested in the field as well as practices in schools that do not encourage females. The accompanying questions help students think about the approaches they will take in their own classrooms to equalize the involvement of females in the field of mathematics.

RELEVANT RESEARCH: Development of Racial and Gender Identity

This ethnographic study focuses on how some young people develop their racial and gender identity. The working class white males in the study constructed their own identity around their perceived relationship to others, especially females and African Americans. They believed that they had to take care of women and protect them from black men. The schooling experiences of these young men appeared not to challenge the perceptions of others as they developed their identity of themselves as white heterosexual men.

VIDEO RESOURCES

1. *Playing Fair*
   Canada Film Board (1251 Ave. of the Americas, New York, NY 10020), 15 min.
   An anti-racism series of four videotape dramas for elementary students. Central to each story is a conflict involving children from different racial and ethnic backgrounds.
2. *It's Not Easy*
   Sidewalks of New York (40 W. 27th St., New York, NY 10001), 29 min.

A powerful videotape about racism produced by teenagers currently or formerly living in homeless shelters.
3. *The Shadow of Hate*
   Teaching Tolerance (400 Washington Ave., Montgomery, AL 36104), 40 min.
   Documents episodes of intolerance toward Native Americans, European immigrants, Chinese and Japanese Americans, Latinos, African Americans, Jews, and other religious minorities.
4. *Who's Gonna Sing Our Song?*
   Video Action Fund (3034 Q Street, NW, Washington, DC 20007), 30 min.
   A documentary profiling a multimedia humanities project developed for 60 teenagers living in southeast Washington, DC.
5. *The End of Segregation: A Personal Perspective*
   Knowledge Unlimited (P. O. Box 52, Madison, WI 53701), 30 min.
   The pre-integration South of the 1940s and 50s is brought to life through a compelling interview with the critically acclaimed author of "Once Upon a Time When We Were Colored," Clifton L. Taulbert.

TRANSPARENCIES

Transparency 23: High School Completion Trends
Transparency 28: Racial Diversity of the United States
Transparency 30: Poverty and Performance

Chapter 5

<hr>

A Multicultural Society

OBJECTIVES

After reading this chapter, students will be able to:

1. define *culture* and its salient characteristics.
2. identify some of the core values of the dominant society and explain why they sometimes lead to conflicts in schools with diverse student populations.
3. identify at least seven microcultural groups in which we all participate and provide examples of how membership in one group interacts with membership in another.
4. compare assimilation, cultural pluralism, and cultural choice as descriptions of how society handles diversity.
5. describe how the ethnic diversity of the student population is changing.
6. discuss the correlation between gender and poverty and the reasons that a disproportionately large number of women are in poverty.
7. explain the need to understand the impact of religion on schools in particular regions of the country such as Utah and the Bible Belt.
8. describe why students from the same ethnic and language background may behave differently in the classroom.
9. describe how we are all multicultural.
10. explain the advantages of being able to function effectively in more than one culture.

STRATEGIES FOR INTRODUCING THE CHAPTER

Show a film or ask students to watch a documentary about a group of people in a country outside of North America. Identify the differences between this group and members of the class and categorize them by characteristics such as dress, food, interactions of adults and children, roles of men and women, religion, and values. Use these characteristics to initiate a discussion on the meaning of culture and its influence on the way we think, speak, act, and learn.

Divide students into small groups to describe characteristics of diverse groups whom they have observed or interacted with on campus or in their home communities. Focus follow-up discussion on why they were able to list the characteristics of others and whether they made value judgments about the differences based on the rightness of their own cultures.

CHAPTER OVERVIEW AND ANALYSIS

Culture and its influence on our lives provide the framework for this chapter. If teacher candidates understand the role that culture plays in even the simplest behaviors and reactions (for example, winking or frowning), they may become more accepting of differences. Otherwise, they may fall into the trap of believing that their perceptions, values, and behavior are the only *correct* way and that others' ways are inferior to their own. Unless teacher candidates can overcome their own ethnocentrism, they will have a difficult time teaching students from cultural backgrounds different than their own.

The chapter begins with an examination of culture and its characteristics. The core values of the dominant or mainstream culture guide many of the practices in schools, but may conflict with the values of other groups. The concept of microcultures is introduced to help teacher candidates understand that they and their students belong to many groups that help define who they are and their interaction with the broader society.

Three theories and ideologies of diversity in the United States are presented to provide a context for understanding school policies and practices. Although immigrant cultures have influenced the mainstream culture, assimilation requires immigrants to adopt the dominant culture. Cultural pluralism allows diverse groups to flourish separately and equally with the dominant culture. The United States is culturally diverse, but does not reflect the pure definition of culturally plural societies. The ideology of cultural choice allows individuals to move from one group to another without reprisal from the groups to which they are born or the groups with which they choose to identify.

The bulk of the chapter is devoted to discussions of the microcultural groups that have a major influence on how we see ourselves and how we are viewed by others. Differences between students in classrooms may be based on their families' socioeconomic status. Adequate resources improve their chances of being clean, well dressed, and sufficiently fed. We are all members of one or more ethnic

groups. However, our experiences in the United States have differed greatly based on our race and the way in which society responds to us, especially when we do not look like we have European roots. Although current research identifies few differences between males and females, members of the two groups are often treated differently in society and schools. Heterosexuality has been the acceptable norm of society for so long that students, teachers, and parents who are gay or lesbian often must hide their identity or face discrimination. If schools reinforce such discriminatory practices, they are not providing equal education to all students.

Language and dialectal differences contribute to the richness of a culturally diverse nation, but are often not respected in classrooms. The common goal in schools traditionally has been for all students to learn standard English and forget the second language or dialect. Growing numbers of students with disabilities are being mainstreamed into regular classrooms, but most educators have limited knowledge and skills in integrating them into the class. As a result, these students may become isolated within the classroom. For many students, religion has a great influence on their values and behavior. Teachers may find that the religious values are reflected throughout the curriculum, and will need to plan carefully to introduce multiple perspectives. Culture and schools also vary because of their location in rural, suburban, and urban areas.

In the classroom, teachers will need to monitor their reactions to students based on broad generalizations about membership in one or more of the groups mentioned above. Within every group there are intragroup differences and individuals who do not follow the norms of the group. Although we are all multicultural and have learned to function in multiple groups, most of us have not learned to function effectively in groups other than our own. Teachers who learn to be bicultural or multicultural and competent in other cultures will have an advantage in working with students from diverse backgrounds.

CLASS ACTIVITIES

Activity 5.1: Have students bring to class one representation of their culture to share with other members of the class, along with an explanation of its meaning to them or their family.

Activity 5.2: Have students develop a chart that compares the educational responses to assimilation, cultural pluralism, and cultural choice across the areas of curriculum, assessment, student-teacher interactions, and school climate.

Activity 5.3: Invite representatives from diverse student groups on campus to join a panel to discuss their experiences in schools and with teachers, highlighting good and bad experiences related to their ethnicity, gender, socio-economic status, religion, disability, and/or sexual orientation.

Activity 5.4: Ask students to participate in an ethnic event or religious service that differs from their own, record their impressions in a journal, and analyze their reactions to the experience.

Activity 5.5: Ask students to work in small groups and list on newsprint or an overhead transparency their feelings and possible reactions to entering a classroom in which the language is different than that known to members of the group. They should also indicate how they would like to be treated in a classroom in which no one else speaks their language. At the end of the exercise, reactions should be shared with the class.

Activity 5.6: Ask students to reflect on the impact of their microcultural memberships on who they are today and how they are treated by members of different groups. These reflections should be recorded as journal entries over a period of at least a month.

Activity 5.7: Have students record on a chart the advantages and disadvantages of being bicultural and bilingual. As a class or in small groups, discuss why these characteristics are often not valued in a school setting.

PROFESSIONAL DILEMMA: How Much Can We Expect of Limited English Speaking Students?

This dilemma introduces the possibility of having a number of students in the classroom whose native language is not English and presents conflicting approaches for providing educational opportunities. Teacher candidates should begin to think about how they will handle language diversity in their classrooms. This exercise might be introduced by sharing with the class statistics on the language diversity that exists in your state, region, or particular school district.

RELEVANT RESEARCH: The Interaction of Language and Culture

A North American preschool teacher wonders why she has difficulty controlling the Haitian students in her classroom while the Haitian teachers appear successful, and thus embarks on a study to improve her own teaching. She found that the language used with students differed between North American and Haitian teachers. The Haitian teachers focused on the group while North American teachers focused on the individual. The language itself was reinforced by nonverbal communications. The discussion of this study could be introduced by asking students to share examples of miscommunications between teachers and students that they have observed in their visits to schools.

VIDEO RESOURCES

1. *Painted Bride*
   City Lore (72 East First St., New York, NY 10003), 20 min.
   Immigrant women explore an extremely rich tradition in the city of New York.
2. *Black to the Promised Land*
   First Run/Icarus (153 Waverly Place, New York, NY 10014), 95 min.
   A unique documentary that challenges the myths and stereotypes fostered in both the African American and Israeli communities.
3. *Workers at the White House*
   Smithsonian Institute (Center for Folklife Programs, 955 L'Enfant Plaza, SW, Washington, DC 20560), 32 min.
   Features the occupational folklife and oral histories of a broad range of workers—butlers, maids, chefs, plumbers, and others.
4. *Cambodian Doughnut Dreams*
   First Run/Icarus (153 Waverly Place, New York, NY 10014), 27 min.
   An enlightening look at one group's pursuit of the American Dream, in the doughnut shops of Los Angeles, 10 years after Pol Pot.
5. *It Starts with a Whisper*
   Women Make Movies (462 Broadway, New York, NY 10013), 28 min.
   Touching and evocative, this film follows a young woman who has grown up on a Reserve and her decision about which path to follow in life.
6. *Living Islam*
   Ambrose Video (1290 Avenue of the Americas, New York, NY 10104), 50 min. each.
   A six-part series about Islam as a living idea and how that idea is lived. The focus is on what it means to be a Muslim in today's world.
7. *Homoteens*
   Frameline (346 Ninth St., San Francisco, CA 94103), 60 min.
   Five young gays and lesbians in New York City have produced their own vivid autobiographical portraits with the help of videomaker Joan Jubela.
8. *True Colors*
   Coronet/MTI Film & Video, color, 19 min.
   Two friends (one black, one white) take part in experiments in white, black, and mixed environments. Shows how practices maintain a second class culture in a "free" nation.

TRANSPARENCIES

Transparency 21: Ethnic Shifts in the U.S. Population
Transparency 22: Fewer Students Speak English at Home

Transparency 25: Estimated Population Growth by
    Region between 1990 and 2000
Transparency 27: Family Income and Education
Transparency 29: A Gender Wage Gap . . . Still
Transparency 31: Cultural Diversity

COMPUTER ENRICHMENT EXPLORATION

Working to Establish a Staff Development Effort Directed at Meeting the Needs of Diverse Learners. This simulation begins with the new teacher helping to plan a staff develop-

ment program in diversity for the school district. The major issue associated with this simulation is whether to take a canned program prepared by a cooperating university or to build a program based on the identified needs of the staff. Again, the participant is involved in some leadership and group conflict and must resolve that issue before moving on with the task. The simulation offers a conflict resolution task, and when the conflict is resolved to the participant's satisfaction, discussion of it can be written on the computer, printed, and handed to the course instructor.

Chapter 6

Education That Is Multicultural

OBJECTIVES

After reading this chapter, students will be able to:

1. discuss the role of diversity and equality in the education process.
2. articulate why multicultural education is for all students.
3. explain what conditions and practices exist in schools to suggest that social justice is not a principle that undergirds the educational system.
4. analyze social justice and its place in a democracy.
5. identify practices in schools that reflect social justice and those that do not reflect it.
6. identify some factors that teachers should know to help students from diverse cultural backgrounds learn the subject matter.
7. define *inclusion* as it is used in education that is multicultural.
8. describe how teachers' biases may influence their expectations for students.
9. explain why tracking of students may be an inequitable strategy.
10. provide examples of how students' voices are an integral part of education that is multicultural and democratic schools.
11. design a lesson that employs visual, perceptual characteristics rather than verbal ones.
12. reflect on the value of current student assessments and their disproportionate impact on some students.
13. create a plan for increasing knowledge about cultural diversity.

STRATEGIES FOR INTRODUCING THE CHAPTER

Ask for two male and two female volunteers to be visitors to a new culture and try to figure out differences between their culture and the new one. After the four volunteers have left the room, establish the rules for the new culture with the remainder of the class as follows:

1. Members of the culture only answer "yes" or "no" to questions from the visitors. They should not provide explanations for the answer.

2. Out of respect to males in the culture, women do not speak to males.
3. Members answer "yes" to questions if the questioner has a happy or smiling face.
4. Members answer "no" to questions if the questioner is frowning or looks very serious.
5. Male members can answer "yes" or "no" to questions from both males and females.

After members of the class understand the cultural rules and cues, invite the four volunteer visitors back into the room to interact with their classmates. Continue the interaction for fifteen to twenty minutes and ask the visitors what they learned about the culture; ask members of the host culture to describe how the visitors reacted to them. Finally, relate the experiences of both cultures to a classroom in which a student enters with a cultural background different than the teacher and most class members. How should the teacher respond to the student? How can the teacher help the student understand the dominant culture of the classroom? How can the teacher prevent the student from feeling that his or her culture is inferior to that of the other students?

CHAPTER OVERVIEW AND ANALYSIS

The importance of diversity and equality in delivering education that is multicultural in our schools is the theme of this chapter. The intent is to help teacher candidates think about these concepts as they plan lessons, interact with students, develop their repertoire of teaching strategies, assess the competence of students, and work with colleagues and parents. Future teachers need to understand that multicultural education is not a strategy for teaching students who suffer the most from discriminatory practices. It is a strategy for teaching all students more effectively by using their cultural backgrounds and prior experiences to help them learn at high levels. The values of their cultural backgrounds are reinforced by seeing themselves in instructional materials and lessons, by participating proportionately in advanced as well as special education classes, and by being treated equitably and fairly.

The early part of the chapter lays the foundation for discussion of educational strategies. Diversity is presented within the context of current public debates about multiculturalism because these are the issues that students may be struggling with as they listen to debates in the media and among students. The discussion of social justice and equality is grounded in the work of Kenneth Sirotnik on the ethics of teaching. Teacher candidates must begin to sort out the issues of diversity, social justice, and equality in order to effectively teach all students.

The major portion of the chapter focuses on the challenges faced in teaching multiculturally. Seven dimensions are presented. The first makes candidates aware of differences in the way students learn that are related to their cultural upbringing. Student learning is assisted greatly by drawing on representations of the subject matter from the background and experiences of students, rather than those of the teacher. Inclusion is addressed through discussions of the importance of high expectations and the discriminatory nature of ability grouping. The recommendation that students become more centered in the teaching process is highlighted in the discussion of respecting and encouraging diverse student voices in the dialogues of classrooms and schools. Strategies for making the curriculum reflect diversity and equality are presented. Recognizing and overcoming the biases in many instructional materials is another important component of multicultural education. At the same time, candidates should be aware that communities may not be supportive of the materials used, especially when they have not been a part of the decision-making process. The seventh dimension is the provision of equity in the instruction and assessment of students that are influenced greatly by the nature of the interactions between the teacher and students.

The chapter ends by encouraging candidates to become critical thinkers about society and educational practices. The hope is that they are able to maintain their high ideals and belief that all students can learn as they progress through their teaching career. To provide education that is multicultural will require them to continue to learn about diversity, reflect on their own practice, and adapt and change their behavior throughout their lifetime. It is a challenge that good teachers are willing to accept to ensure that their students learn.

CLASS ACTIVITIES

Activity 6.1: Have students debate the importance of social justice in society and schools.

Activity 6.2: Ask students to articulate the arguments for and against the proposition that multicultural education is divisive to the nation, and have them argue their own stand.

Activity 6.3: Invite the principal and selected teachers from a school that views itself as providing education that is multicultural to discuss the differences between their school and others and to provide recommendations to students for preparing to work in a similar setting.

Activity 6.4: Have students develop a lesson plan that incorporates the cultures of Sikh and Bosnian immigrant students. Discuss how students located information on the two cultures to help them develop the lesson plan.

Activity 6.5 Ask students to divide into one of two groups—cooperative and competitive. Have each group list a school practice that could be termed cooperative or competitive. Then have the two groups share their lists and discuss the pros and cons of each practice. Ask students if they could realistically succeed in a school that was entirely cooperative or entirely competitive.

Activity 6.6 Discuss the phrases: "For me to win, you must lose" and "For me to win, you must win." How do these phrases relate to competitive versus cooperative learning?

Activity 6.7 Ask students to design a lesson that employs visual, perceptual characteristics rather than verbal ones.

Activity 6.8 Invite teachers and/or administrators from schools that have changed their curriculum to be Afrocentric or to place Native, Latino, or Asian Americans as the center of all activities.

Activity 6.9 Have students design the major components of a rainbow curriculum. What are the criteria for including or excluding concepts or readings in the curriculum?

Activity 6.10 Why is multicultural education just as important for students who are members of the dominant group in society as for those who are members of powerless groups?

Activity 6.11 Have students role play a school board meeting in which several angry parents are concerned about the books that their children are being asked to read in their fifth and sixth grade classes. Some parents argue that the books do not reflect their values and will encourage their children to reject the family's values; other parents argue that the books introduce their children to many perspectives with which they should be aware to work effectively in a culturally diverse world. Discuss the reasons for these different perspectives and the role of schools in negotiating these differences.

Activity 6.12 Develop a list of the school practices that do not support equity, democracy, and social justice in schools. Ask students to discuss in small groups which of these they think they would be willing to confront after they begin teaching. They should discuss why they would be unwilling to confront others and the chances of these inequitable practices ever being overcome in schools.

PROFESSIONAL DILEMMA: What If He Has Two Mommies?

This dilemma begins to prepare teacher candidates for the diverse family structures from which their students will come. One of these will be a child with gay or lesbian parents. The accompanying questions raise issues that teachers may face as early as student teaching. Although some students may feel uncomfortable with such a family structure, this dilemma forces them to begin to think about how they will handle it when it does occur. The dilemma might be introduced by discussing the danger of teachers making negative judgments about students' families that may prevent the delivery of equitable education.

RELEVANT RESEARCH: The Role of Schools in Students' Construction of Ethnic Identity

This study explored students' perceptions of their ethnic identity and their interactions with students from different groups in two California schools. The students were treated differently in the two settings. One setting provided a much more equitable climate that supported diversity and had high expectations for all students. This research could be introduced by asking candidates to reflect on their own experiences or observations at some of the schools that they have visited. Can they identify school practices that either support or denigrate diversity and equality?

VIDEO RESOURCES

1. *The Spirit Travels*
   Cinema Guild (1697 Broadway, New York, NY 10019—5904), 55 min.
   A colorful, entertaining and informative look at ethnic music in America.

2. *And Then Came John*
   Scott Andrews (Industrial Center Building, Sausalito, CA 94965), 30 min.
   Challenges stereotypes about the disabled through the story of a young man with Down Syndrome who is capable of mastering everything life has to offer, including school, work, art and music.

3. *Educating Peter*
   Ambrose Video (1290 Avenue of the Americas, New York, NY 10104), 30 min.
   The story of a Down Syndrome child and his classmates testing the limits of integration (full inclusion). This film won an Oscar for best short-subject documentary.

4. *A Different Place the Intercultural Classroom*
   Intercultural Resource Corp. (78 Greylock Rd., Newtonville, MA 02160).
   A two-part video presentation and comprehensive instructional guide, which explore the intercultural classroom.

TRANSPARENCIES

Transparency 24: Approaches to Teacher Reflection
Transparency 26: SAT Scores, by Race/Ethnicity
Transparency 32: The Dimensions of Multicultural Education

Chapter 7

Social Issues Affecting the School

EXTENDED OUTLINE

OBJECTIVES

After reading this chapter, students will be able to:

1. create in writing a profile of the "family" as it currently exists in society.
2. identify the facts and issues associated with poverty.
3. identify the problems associated with chemical abuse.
4. elaborate on the issues that affect the suicide rates of young people.
5. create in writing a profile of students who are at risk to be potential dropouts.
6. identify the negative effects of crime among youth.
7. present in writing the issues associated with teenage pregnancy and AIDS.
8. identify child abuse practices and appropriate teacher action when child abuse is suspected.
9. elaborate on the needs and required practices associated with exceptional/handicapped children.
10. identify the various multicultural language programs.

11. compare and contrast the provisions of school clinics, magnet schools, and adult literacy programs in providing for the special needs of learners.
12. examine global problems of education.

STRATEGIES FOR INTRODUCING THE CHAPTER

Identify for your class major social issues that have affected your life. Tell the class your opinions about how education has dealt with these issues. Where has education failed? This type of introduction can lead to a discussion of today's society and its impact on educational thinking. The importance of a learner's family situation should be stressed and discussed. Encourage students to share both positive and negative family experiences that have an effect on learners and learning. Use focus questions to introduce the many concepts in this chapter. Encourage students to discuss pro and con issues associated with the social issues examined in this chapter.

CHAPTER OVERVIEW AND ANALYSIS

This chapter presents the multitude of social issues that affect the school and its efforts in working with learners. The chapter provides information that identifies problems and needs, and the teacher in training should be able to grasp the magnitude of the problems that come to the doors of the school. The power and effects of the family cannot be stressed highly enough when you examine social problems of youth. Thus, the family needs to be kept utmost in mind when looking at and studying social issues. The intent of this chapter is to alert the teacher about how these problems affect the daily efforts of the teacher in the classroom.

The collage of special issues section identifies some of the more apparent issues that states and the national government have established as priorities for attention. The needs of exceptional children as protected by Public Law 94-192 and its ensuing additions and amendments should elicit teacher concerns toward all the diversity in children and not just those protected by federal law. Multicultural language issues, provisions for school clinics, magnet schools, and adult literacy programs point to the special attention being given to these issues by the American society.

CLASS ACTIVITIES

Activity 7.1: Have each student create a family profile of his or her family group. Then have the students compare their profiles with that presented by the text.

Activity 7.2: Have the students interview a teacher working in a low socioeconomic area to see what that teacher feels is the greatest need and problem in his or her classroom.

Activity 7.3: Ask the students to investigate and discuss typical school district services that are made available to students who are involved with drugs.

Activity 7.4: Have students investigate the effectiveness of suicide prevention programs.

Activity 7.5: Have small student groups brainstorm on the topic of dropout prevention measures. Have the groups share their ideas with the whole class.

Activity 7.6: Have students debate the use of armed policemen in the schools to maintain order.

Activity 7.7: Have students in small groups prepare a statement of philosophy and guidelines for sex education in the schools. Have them share and discuss the different efforts.

Activity 7.8: Have different groups of students design programs for special needs children such as latchkey, gifted, and homeless children.

Activity 7.9: Have students (by their different certification areas) identify the kinds of learning problems bilingual children will have in the different certification areas.

Activity 7.10: Have students discuss worldwide social issues that affect global student learning in their schools.

PROFESSIONAL DILEMMA: Can You Be a Personal Counselor for Your Students?

This dilemma stretches the personal counseling activity of a regular teacher. There is little doubt that the dilemma presents a student who evidently has tremendous trust in and respect for the teacher. The instructor needs to be sure that the teacher education students are aware that they have not been trained as professional counselors. The students should meet in small groups of three to five and outline strategies for dealing with the dilemma that keep the "nontrained caveat" in mind. The strategies of the students can be shared and discussed with the whole class as to their relevance to the real world of teaching.

RELEVANT RESEARCH: How School Boards Are Responding to Violence in the Schools

This research article reports on a national survey that examined how school districts worked to prevent violence in their schools. Two significant findings emerged from this research study. First, some 82 percent of the survey respondents felt school violence was worse than it had been five years earlier. Second, there is no apparent certain method of coping with or handling violence since the survey revealed 22 different approaches were being used. The instructor can use this research article to have students debate the validity of the various reported methods being used to curb violence.

RELEVANT RESEARCH: Homeless Students Can Be Productive and Succeed

This research article is a case study of two homeless students who appear to have overcome the odds against them and who have successfully completed school. The instructor has two types of activities to use with the teacher education students. First, in light of the need for more classroom research (as discussed in Chapter 3), the case study type of research for classroom analyses can be discussed for its value to the teacher. Second, the instructor can work with teacher education students in developing a profile of strategies that can be employed when encountering homeless students in the regular classroom.

VIDEO RESOURCES

1. *America Hooked on Drugs*
   Coronet/MTI Film & Video, color, 20 min.
   Effects of drugs on the brain. Candid former users are interviewed. Government and community action efforts are shown.
2. *Athletes and Addiction: It's Not a Game*
   Coronet/MTI Film & Video, color, 56 min.

Winners and losers in substance abuse talk. A 29-day treatment program is revealed. Good for all, not just athletes.

TRANSPARENCIES

Transparency 33: Teenage Unemployment by Race/Ethnicity

Transparency 34: Use of Illegal Drugs Among High School Students Is Down but Drinking Remains a Problem

Transparency 35: Degrees of Delinquency

Transparency 36: Teen Sex

Transparency 37: Status of AIDS Virus and Projected Growth

Transparency 38: Indicators of Child Abuse

Transparency 39: Why Students at Risk Drop Out of School

Transparency 40: Teen Tragedy

Transparency 41: Warning Signs of Suicide and Possible Responses

Chapter 8

Structure and Finance of American Education

OBJECTIVES

After reading this chapter, students will be able to:

1. describe the overall organization of the American education system, including the relationships among local, state, and national components.
2. describe the different roles and relationships that exist in the typical school.
3. describe the major roles and relationships within public school districts.
4. describe the major roles, functions, and legal relationships of public education at the state level.
5. describe the roles, functions, and legal relationships of the federal government in education.
6. name four types of education agencies that support the purposes of schools, but that have no authority over schools.

7. name and describe at least four alternative organizational arrangements for public schools.
8. analyze contemporary issues that are related to the organization and structure of schools.
9. develop a general understanding of the current approaches and issues in the financing of public education.
10. describe the role of property taxes in the financing of public education and issues related to their use.
11. describe elements of a total system for financing public education.
12. describe at least three critical issues facing the financing of public education.

STRATEGIES FOR INTRODUCING THE CHAPTER

Take to class the gross budget figures for one or more of your nearby school districts. Outline the proportion of the school budget that is derived from state, local, and federal sources. Introduce the question of who decides how this money will be spent. What proportion will go to teacher salaries, buses, curriculum materials, and the superintendent's salary? Lead an exploratory analysis of how education is organized at the school, district, and state levels. Ask students in groups to develop a chart of their current understandings of where the money comes from, and/or where decisions are made about spending it. The purposes of this introduction are to arouse questions about and interest in learning how schools and the education system are organized, where different types of decisions are made, and where the money comes from.

This could be an important time to introduce discussion of equity. Why is it that some schools and classrooms have more resources than others? And, what could/should be done about these differences? As an assignment, students could be asked to read Jonathan Kozol's *Savage Inequalities*, or excerpts from it.

CHAPTER OVERVIEW AND ANALYSIS

Chapter 8 introduces future teachers to the organizational and financial basis of schooling in America. This chapter deals with very important concepts and principles that typically are far removed from the experiences and dominant interests of future teachers. Acknowledging the lack of "perceived relevance" does not, however, mean that the concepts and principles introduced in this chapter are not important. In fact, the concepts and principles presented in this chapter, along with the issues that are delineated, directly affect what schools are like, and what teachers can do. In an attempt to increase relevance, we have organized this chapter in an unconventional sequence!

Rather than starting from the point of view of the overarching structure of American education beginning with the U.S. Constitution and the federal government, then on down to the state level, etc., the chapter begins in the classroom of the individual school. After all, this is where education students have experience. As students, they have been in schools, and as they head toward student teaching they will think from the frame of reference of the individual classroom. Therefore, introducing students to the structure of American schools begins with the organization of classrooms and the school.

Then a nesting pattern is used, similar to a computer program, where the school is placed into the school district, the school district within the state, and the state within the federal context. One of the objectives for this chapter is to enhance the students' understanding and appreciation of the complex and intricate organizational relationships that exist between the individual school and the entire education system.

In the first half of the chapter, each of the major organizational elements of the American educational system is described. Along the way, issues and implications are referred to. This part concludes with a review of some of the more interesting and politically relevant issues. For example, politics is an increasingly important part of understanding and working in the education system. Anyone who doubts this should just review the process and outcomes of recent national elections. Special interest groups with valued agendas were clear and ever present. Many of these interest groups have agendas for the education system, whether it be from the forum of the principle of "local control," or the agenda of the religious right. Future teachers need to have an appreciation of the dynamics of the structure of the system and the politics that are internal to the system, as well as the external political pressures that can affect the directions of schooling.

The last major portion of this chapter deals with the financing of education. Students need to develop an understanding of the fiscal realities, that support for schools is dependent on the public, and that the sources of funding are a combination of local, state, and federal. Due to an array of state-by-state court actions, property taxes are increasingly becoming only one of several sources that fund schools. Issues of financing related to the increased use of state revenues and new sources of funds such as gambling are and will continue to be the focal points for intense debate.

Throughout all of the analyses and discussions of structure and financing of schools, in the last twenty to thirty years the role of the federal government has increased. Although the federal government may not be directly charged by the U.S. Constitution with financing schools, through the clever use of legislation, the federal government has played an increasing role. The movement in the early 1990s toward national standards threatened an even greater federal involvement. However, with the developing movement against "unfunded mandates" (such as asbestos abatement and aspects of special education) and other antigovernment initiatives, such as the 1995 Contract with America, there may be a gradual leveling off or even a reduction in federal involvement. However things evolve, it is very important for future teachers to be aware of the ways that the American education system is currently structured and financed. Until teachers understand the design and functioning of the system, they run the risk of being pawns rather than intelligent participants within the system.

CLASS ACTIVITIES

Activity 8.1: Ask students to draw an organization chart for the high school where they graduated. Ask some leading questions such as, Who is in charge of the school? And, where did students go for discipline problems? Once the charts are drawn, survey the class about the number of people in different roles, such as vice principals, department heads, and extracurricular roles.

Activity 8.2: If you were a principal, what duties would you like to do most of the time?

Activity 8.3: Ask students to list all the personnel roles they can think of that comprise a typical school district organizational chart. Then ask students to line up the various personnel on a hierarchical chart. What role is at the bottom?

Activity 8.4: Invite a superintendent for a question and answer session.

Activity 8.5: Find out the names of the state superintendent and state board members. Discuss their educational backgrounds. Have students discuss the pros and cons of having an elected versus an appointed state school board.

Activity 8.6: Ask students to name the Secretary of the U.S. Department of Education. Have them list the pros and cons of having education represented at the Cabinet level in the federal government. Explore the symbolic meanings of having or not having a U.S. Department of Education versus having education housed in a bureau.

Activity 8.7: Describe the activities of a regional lab, or a national research and development center in your area.

Activity 8.8: Bring to class newspaper or news magazine articles about one or more of the alternatives to public schools that is operating in your area. Describe what is happening locally with one or more of these alternatives.

Activity 8.9: Ask students to visit a private, parochial, or independent school in their area. Have them clarify how the staff is hired and the school is organized. Is the school part of a larger system?

Activity 8.10: Have students conduct a debate between local control proponents and centralization proponents.

Activity 8.11: Does a superintendent have to be politically savvy? If so, how?

Activity 8.12: Have students study, in detail, a real estate tax bill. Ask students to identify examples of regressive taxes.

Activity 8.13: Use a copy of your state's educational financial report to determine which districts are rich or poor and why. How does the property tax structure influence this picture?

Activity 8.14: Have students identify all the sources of state funding for schools: lottery money, sales and income tax, foundation programs, and so on.

Activity 8.15: Ask students to list the reasons for a taxpayer revolt.

Activity 8.16: Ask students to identify three ways that would improve accountability in the schools.

Activity 8.17: Discuss the degree to which teachers can be held accountable for student achievement.

PROFESSIONAL DILEMMA: What Is the Appropriate Role for Teachers When the Politics Get Rough?

This dilemma is based on the true story of what happened in one school district where there was an extreme shift in the educational philosophies of people elected to the school board.

The questions raised at the end of the case will stimulate discussion and thought. Most of us cannot leave our jobs, and in this case teachers cannot escape by closing their classroom doors. Thought has to be given to how to deal with this type of situation.

Lead a discussion centered around your students' reactions to this story and the questions. Ask them to seriously consider what they would do. The school board members cannot be recalled, and the next election would be in two years. The situation has to be lived with. How would they work to keep the school community alive and moving ahead? How would they use this as a learning experience? And, what would they be willing to do that is of a political nature?

One of the critical keys to handling this very difficult situation would be the leadership provided by the principal. In this case the principal was extremely skilled at masking his hurt and continuing to attempt to work not only with his school but also with the school board. He kept the best interests of his students, the school staff, and the community in mind at all times. By the way, that principal was Tim Westerberg, who is the *Dreamcatcher* discussed in the introduction to Part 3.

RELEVANT RESEARCH: State Spending Is Related to Student Achievement

Using research to respond to slogans and eighteen-second sound bites is always difficult. This problem is further compounded when dealing with taxpayer dollars. However, the study that is reported here might provide a way to respond. Wainer's study reports the states that spend more money on education have higher pupil achievement.

This is important news. Ask your students to turn this study finding into a press release. What would they be able to report about the relationship between student success and the use of taxpayer funds in their state? If their state is a high-cost-per-pupil state, the report could emphasize what the state is achieving. If it is a low-per-pupil expenditure state, the study could be used to advocate for increased spending.

It is quite likely that some of your students will not know what NAEP is. NAEP (pronounced *nape*) stands for National Assessment of Educational Progress. This is a federally financed study that takes place in every state. One strength of the study is that the items are especially constructed to test student achievement in different subjects, while the SAT has been designed to assess potential for college success. Another important advantage of the NAEP is that a representative sample of students is selected in each state, so the results are more generalizable.

VIDEO RESOURCES

1. *Learning in America: Education on Trial Part II—Are Public Schools Beyond Repair?*
   PBS Video, color, 60 min.
   Critics against educational professionals and how to determine how and who should restructure our schools.

2. *Learning in America: Education on Trial Part III—Are We Short Changing Our Schools?*
   PBS Video, color, 60 min.
   Are we throwing good money away on an unsalvageable school system?

TRANSPARENCIES

Transparency 42: The Structure of Education in the United States

Transparency 43: A School Organization Chart

Transparency 44: Sources of Revenue for School Funding

Transparency 45: Advantages and Disadvantages of Three Major Sources of Revenue for Education

Transparency 46: Public School Expenditures Per Student

Transparency 47: Government Spending for Education Worldwide

COMPUTER ENRICHMENT EXPLORATION

The School Budget and Your Classroom Supplies. This simulation exercise deals with a beginning teacher having difficulty getting what he or she feels are adequate teaching supplies and finding that the administrator is a key person in solving this issue. The participant is offered several alternatives to be taken in solving this problem and establishing a good working relationship with the principal. However this problem is solved, the participant is directed back to the text for the course and is encouraged to use text material to present a list of questions to be addressed by the principal. The questions and comments for the principal can be typed on the computer and given to the instructor in the course.

Chapter 9

Legal Aspects of Education

OBJECTIVES

After reading this chapter, students will be able to:

1. demonstrate an understanding of basic forms and structures of the American legal system.
2. describe five different sources of law.
3. describe the basic organization of the judicial system at the state and federal levels.
4. demonstrate a basic understanding of the elements and process of the legal system that impact schooling.
5. describe implications for education of three key amendments of the U.S. Constitution.
6. describe the functions of state and local government related to education.
7. describe the legal principles that allow church-based schools.
8. describe in general terms the issues and legal reasoning behind limiting religious activities in public schools.
9. describe the legal conditions that are considered in deciding whether home instruction is permissible.
10. present descriptions of a number of enduring legal issues that confront schooling.

11. trace the key court decisions that have been the basis for desegregating schools.

12. analyze the intent of contemporary judicial actions by school districts that are aimed at achieving release from desegregation court orders.

13. identify and describe features of the hiring process that could be discriminatory.

14. describe the key legislative and administrative actions aimed at providing handicapped children with an appropriate public education.

15. describe the findings and implications of key judicial actions that have defined procedures related to the education of the handicapped.

16. outline the reasoning behind the position that children with AIDS are handicapped.

17. contrast aspects of the American legal system, as it relates to schooling, with the legal aspects of schooling in other countries.

STRATEGIES FOR INTRODUCING THE CHAPTER

The legal aspects of education tend to be far removed from the minds of future teachers. Thus, in introducing this material, it is especially important to draw connections between current knowledge and past experiences of students and the myriad ways that the legal system affects the practice of teachers and schooling in America. Bring to class copies of recent articles concerning education court decisions, and the actions of Congress and state legislatures. Use the stories to illustrate the influential role of law in education. Perhaps some of the students will have had direct experience with the legal system that could be used as additional illustrations. One way to illustrate the impact of legislation on teachers (and students) would be to have them read the Case Study, which deals with their rights to photocopy copyrighted material.

As part of the introduction, point out some of the strides that have been made because of laws; then, point out some of the problems/issues that have been spawned by the growth of a litigious society. Use the focus questions to help students see how complex contemporary education is. Point out that this chapter does not deal with the *rights* of students; Chapter 10 is devoted to this topic. Conclude the chapter introduction activity by asking students to consider questions of equity in regard to handicapped children, children with AIDS, and the various forms of discrimination.

CHAPTER OVERVIEW AND ANALYSIS

Unlike many countries, legal provision for education in the United States was not directly addressed in the national constitution. Over time, the responsibility for public education has been assumed by the states. This trend has been supported through interpretation and understanding of the U.S. Constitution's First, Tenth, and Fourteenth Amendments.

The goal for this chapter is to create a beginning awareness of the legal context within which schooling exists and to introduce students to a sample of the types of schooling questions that have been and are currently being considered by legislative bodies and the courts. The chapter opens with descriptions of the various sources of law. Following this is a brief description of the federal and state judicial systems. The remainder of the chapter presents the legal basis for a number of key topics related to schooling.

One of the continuing tensions in the American legal system is the relative role and responsibility of government at the federal, state, and local levels versus the roles and responsibilities of private interests, private agencies such as parochial schools, and individual interests. Over the years the types of questions that have been asked and that the courts have clarified have increasingly narrowed the gray areas and margins among these various interests. The topics sampled in this chapter illustrate a number of these interests and related court decisions and interpretations.

Several of the court cases that have laid down guiding principles, such as the *Lemon* test and child benefit theory, are introduced. Cases related to these principles and others are introduced to help students develop an understanding and appreciation for the reasoning of the legal system. Legal precedence and linkages back to law, legislation, and constitutions are the bases for most decisions. Future teachers need to understand that this is a different form of reasoning than what is used in debates or personal arguments.

Another major emphasis in this chapter is on the relationship of public to religious interest as seen by the courts. There is a continuing set of court cases that test the limits of the public education system to include or exclude elements of religion, religious practice, and supported activities. Decisions related to release time, prayer in schools, and the opportunity for private education have been addressed in the courts. It is conceivable that while your students are studying this material, additional suits and court decisions related to these topics will take place. Also, it might be worth observing that as the appointments of justices to the court reflect particular ideological perspectives, and as the ideological perspectives of legislative bodies shift, earlier laws and court decisions may be changed or, at a minimum, be reinterpreted.

The last third of this chapter deals with a number of enduring issues and themes. During the last twenty to thirty years the courts have responded to legislative action and shifting norms and values in our society that have systematically led to the school having increasing social responsibilities in addition to the traditional educational ones. Enduring legal issues and court decisions dealing with desegregation, affirmative action, AIDS, and education of the handicapped are introduced. In this chapter future teachers are introduced to basic structures of the legal system and important education topics where the courts have played a significant role.

CLASS ACTIVITIES

Activity 9.1: Bring to class copies of newspaper articles to illustrate the legislative activity of the Congress and state branches of government. Also bring examples of executive orders and rules and regulations (including some from your state's department of education).

Activity 9.2: Bring to class copies of newspaper articles reporting on court-related activities. It is not essential that the articles deal with schooling related activity, but they should include local, state, and federal courts. Use them to illustrate the different parts of the judicial system.

Activity 9.3: Using Figure 9.1, ask students to write down one to three examples of enabling legislation that affects schools. One example should be related to the U.S. Constitution. Then ask for one to three examples of interpretive actions by local, state, or federal officials or agencies. Use these examples to make clear the sources of legal control in American education.

Activity 9.4: Provide an example of a recently passed educational law from your state. Discuss the reasons for the law's enactment, and analyze what groups and individuals fought for and against the law.

Activity 9.5: Before presenting *Everson*, ask students to write down a list of their reasons for, or against, using public tax dollars to transport students to church schools.

Activity 9.6: Have students divide into groups according to whether they are for or against "child benefit theory." Ask them to develop a list of arguments that are in support of their position that will *not be* in violation of the First Amendment.

Activity 9.7: Provide several scenarios of released-time programs, each of which has a different degree of sectarianism and a different degree of school cooperation. Have students debate the legality of each on the basis of the Illinois and New York cases.

Activity 9.8: John Holt was an advocate of home instruction because it counteracted the competitive nature of schools. Ask students to consider which aspects of public schools are competitive.

Activity 9.9: Ask students to describe their personal experiences in a school where busing was used to achieve integration. What were the benefits? What were the problems?

Activity 9.10: Ask students to list ways in which surrounding suburban districts could assist in the desegregation of large metropolitan districts. Have them design plans that they believe would be acceptable to both metropolitan and suburban school districts.

Activity 9.11: Ask students to describe examples of *de facto* discrimination that they have personally witnessed. Have the class discuss each example to determine whether there was any *de jure* segregation that could have contributed to the *de facto* example.

Activity 9.12: Bring in, or ask students to bring in, examples of announcements for teaching positions. Examine these announcements for indications of the district's efforts to employ affirmative action.

Activity 9.13: Invite a handicapped student or professor to class. Have them share their personal experiences with life in contemporary society.

Activity 9.14: Ask a regular and/or special education teacher to visit class. Have them describe the "staffing" process and the development of an IEP. Be sure to have them describe the legal parameters that frame their actions and decisions.

Activity 9.15: Have students describe any personal experiences that they may have had with AIDS. Link this discussion to the Professional Dilemma.

Activity 9.16: Ask students to share information that they may have about legal aspects of education in other countries. If possible, contrast countries where education is constituted nationally with the heavy state role in the United States.

PROFESSIONAL DILEMMA: Should Condoms Be Available to Students in Your School?

The availability of condoms in schools has been a topic of debate before. In this dilemma some recent statistics about the rates of sexual intercourse among teenagers are presented. One important statistic presented is that only half of the teenagers surveyed used condoms. These data are then juxtaposed with discussion of the threat of AIDS. The metaphor of vaccinating for polio is proposed as an alternative form of disease prevention that used to be done in schools. The presentation of the dilemma concludes with a focus on asking what the future teacher will do when his or her school has to determine an AIDS education policy and decide whether condom dispensers will be available at school.

This dilemma will, at a minimum, stimulate discussion, and more than likely will make some students uncomfortable. There also may be a lack of accurate knowledge and understanding about the risks associated with AIDS.

One way to introduce analysis of this Professional Dilemma would be to ask students to list their reasons for or against dispensing condoms at school and then, take a vote. A discussion could follow based on the students' vote. In addition to perceptions and anecdotes about personal experiences, it is quite likely that some will bring religious values and moral issues into the discussion. If the issue of AIDS does not come up, then it could be interjected at a timely moment. An important linkage should be made between the topics presented earlier in this chapter about separation of church and state. More than likely, a number of arguments will be made along religious grounds that, according to the U.S. Constitution, are not legitimate reasons for a public agency to do or not do something. Conclude the discussion by assigning the students to find out more about some aspect of the topic and come to the next class session prepared to inform the others.

RELEVANT RESEARCH: Can a Deaf Student Attending a Catholic High School Have a Government-Paid Interpreter?

This Relevant Research appears early in the chapter so that it can be used to illustrate how the legal system and process works. This case is useful for several reasons: it raises constitutional questions, it deals with parochial schools, and it is about the needs of a handicapped student. All of these elements are topics in this chapter. This case is useful also to illustrate how the reasoning in the legal system is different from our day-to-day decision making.

In this case, *Zobrest* v. *Catalina Foothills School District,* the court ruled, in a sharply divided 5–4 decision, that the Establishment Clause was not violated by the district *voluntarily* paying for a sign language interpreter for a deaf student attending a private religious school, even with the interpreter being used during prayers.

Presentation of this Relevant Research case could focus either on the different sources available and the rea-soning that is used in drawing a legal decision, or on the case specifics and whether this decision "makes sense" from a legal perspective. In terms of the sources of evidence, the case was decided on constitutional grounds, instead of the Court deciding the issue on statutory grounds of whether the IDEA requires the school district to pay for services for those students whose parents do not wish them to attend a public school. In terms of the constitutional basis, this decision would seem to suggest that the federal Establishment Clause barrier to the provision of services to private school students apparently has been removed. However, an important caution that everyone needs to keep in mind is the one-vote majority in the decision. It will be interesting to see what the Court decides in related cases.

VIDEO RESOURCE

Creation vs. Evolution: Battle in the Classroom
PBS Video, color, 58 min.
Highlights the legal debate regarding the teaching of "creation science" as opposed to evolution in our public schools.

TRANSPARENCIES

Transparency 48: Direct Aid to Nonpublic Schools—The Three-Pronged *Lemon* Test
Transparency 49: Some Categories of Disability
Transparency 50: Sources of Legal Control in American Education As They Affect the Classroom Teacher
Transparency 51: Groups with Rights and Responsibilities under the U.S. Constitution

Chapter 10

The Rights of Students and Teachers

OBJECTIVES

After reading this chapter, students will be able to:

1. demonstrate a basic understanding of the legal rights and responsibilities of school students.
2. describe the rights of school students as citizens.
3. describe the responsibilities and protections that have been established by law for school students.
4. demonstrate a basic understanding of teachers' legal rights, responsibilities, and liabilities.
5. distinguish and describe key elements of the conditions of employment including licensure, contracts, and discrimination.
6. describe the differences in rights of tenured and nontenured teachers.
7. list the essential points of academic freedom.
8. describe the meaning of liability for negligence and cite examples.
9. use the example of Taiwan to illustrate differences in the way that teachers are viewed in other countries.

STRATEGIES FOR INTRODUCING THE CHAPTER

Bring in a recent story concerning student or teacher rights. Introduce the story by raising questions about rights, responsibilities, and liabilities. Refer back to the story throughout the chapter.

    Use the focus questions to enable students to see how schools are places where the delicate balance between student and teacher rights can sometimes collide. Use the case study, which deals with censorship, as one serious example of an issue that affects both students and teachers.

CHAPTER OVERVIEW AND ANALYSIS

Chapter 9 dealt with legal issues of the school and school system. This chapter rotates the discussion to an analysis of individual student's and teacher's rights, roles, and responsibilities as defined by law. The first half of the chapter deals with the rights and responsibilities of students. The last half of the chapter addresses the rights and responsibilities of teachers, as educators and as contracted employees.

Contrary to popular opinion and the interests of some parents and teachers, students have most of the same rights as other citizens. Students cannot be thrown out of school based on an arbitrary decision of a teacher or principal; students are entitled to due process and, within limits, do have rights to free speech. At the same time, students in public schools do not have the full rights and freedoms that they have as citizens in other contexts. Schools still have authority and responsibility to see that *all* students have the opportunity to learn. Yet, as you will see in reading through the cases and topics, schools are being increasingly drawn into the larger issues of society. Topics that have been addressed in the courts in relation to students' rights and responsibilities sound familiar: sex discrimination, marriage, pregnancy, child abuse, search, and access to school records. All of these topics are reflective of issues in society at large and also represent critical points for the operation of classrooms and schools.

The second half of the chapter deals with conditions of employment of teachers and their rights and responsibilities. Teachers have a contract as a basis for employment and they are responsible for upholding their end of that contract. You should encourage teachers to read their contracts and understand what they mean, what obligations and commitments they are making when they sign. Other issues that can emerge between an employer and employee are presented in this section. The different forms of discrimination, the basis for tenure, and issues of academic freedom, collective bargaining, and the all-important area of liability and negligence are introduced. Examples are included related to each of these topics. Future teachers must become aware of the legal aspects of the role of teacher and understand the rights of students in their classrooms and schools.

CLASS ACTIVITIES

Activity 10.1: Have students divide into small groups of from five to seven. Ask some of the groups to be school boards and to write a press release informing the community of the reasons that children whose parents are illegal aliens or homeless are attending public schools. Have the other groups represent the taxpayers' group "Pay-as-you-go," with the assignment to write a press release that explains why *those* children should not be in the local public schools.

Activity 10.2: Divide the class into groups and have them develop a bill of rights for students. Then have them list the responsibilities that flow from these rights. Have each group present its bill of rights and concomitant responsibilities to the whole class.

Activity 10.3: Have students gather information concerning local statistics of child abuse and neglect cases. Ask them to prepare a chart or poster to display these data in a way that will impact a particular target audience, such as teachers, principals, or parents.

Activity 10.4: Describe the requirements for teacher certification licensure of your state. Be sure to include the steps in the process that your students need to think about now, such as background checks, fingerprinting, and the various tests.

Activity 10.5: Bring to class examples of local teaching contracts and have students examine them for components that are similar and unusual.

Activity 10.6: Using the chalk board or an overhead projector, have students list the reasons for and against teachers going on strike.

Activity 10.7: Ask a first or second-year teacher to visit class and describe the rights she or he has as an untenured teacher. Be sure to have this beginning teacher describe how she or he is being evaluated.

Activity 10.8: Have students read and review some of the books that have been the target of book banning efforts. In class, analyze the specific elements in each book that have triggered concern.

Activity 10.9: Ask students to recall personal experiences in which due care and forseeability could have been an issue for the teacher.

Activity 10.10: Divide students into groups according to their grade-level interests and ask them to brainstorm lists of situations and actions for that grade level in which a teacher could be negligent.

PROFESSIONAL DILEMMA: What Will You Do If a Child in Your Classroom Has AIDS?

This dilemma confronts the student with the likely scenario that there will be a child with AIDS in their school, and quite conceivably their classroom. Children with AIDS have the right to attend public schools; this right is guaranteed under the U.S. Constitution as well as the various statutes, rules, and regulations for the handicapped. Thus, the first part of this dilemma is thinking through how one will feel about and deal with such a child.

The second part of the dilemma focuses on the issue of teacher responsibility. The potential that another child or the teacher could become infected is real. Teachers must understand the conditions under which the virus could be transmitted and what preparations and precautions should be taken.

A critical step is to be up to date on the research about AIDS, its communicability, and the sensible things that should be done in the classroom. Teachers must continually read the latest materials, consult with physicians and other experts, and be aware of bulletins and other information made available through the Centers for Disease Control (CDC) and other health agencies. We have included in the Dilemma the 24-hour toll-free number for the CDC (800-342-2437). Also included is some of the information available at press time about what to do in the case of spilled blood. Obviously this is not the last word on the topic. The purpose of this dilemma is to heighten the students' awareness of their responsibility to learn about the potential risk, take the appropriate precautions, and at the same time keep in mind the needs of *all* students in their classrooms.

RELEVANT RESEARCH: Search of a Student's Purse

Issues related to searching students and their belongings is the focus of this Relevant Research feature. The case of *New Jersey* v. *T.L.O.* is presented in which two high school students were brought to the principal's office after they had been discovered smoking in the lavatory. In addition to finding cigarettes in one girl's purse, the vice principal found cigarette rolling papers, marijuana, and related evidence. The student and the evidence were turned over to the police. In the subsequent proceedings the student, T.L.O., contended that the search of her purse had been unlawful under the Fourteenth Amendment. The court ruling is presented in the text.

This Relevant Research feature could be introduced at the end of one class period by posing the story of the search and asking students to make notes about how they think the courts would rule. Then students could read the Relevant Research feature as an assignment in preparation for the next class. In the next class period the ruling of the Court and the reasoning could be summarized. Then pose a number of hypothetical situations where similar search problems could arise.

VIDEO RESOURCES

1. *Management of School Disruption and Violence*
   BFA and U.S. Department of Justice, color, 30 min.
   A series of four video tapes entitled (1) Management Systems for School Disruption and Violence, (2) Conflict Management, (3) Constitutional Issues, and (4) Policy/School Relations.
2. *Censorship or Selection: Choosing Books for Public Schools*
   PBS Video, color, 60 min.
   Who decides—teachers or parents—what books and what is taught? Addresses ethics in education.

TRANSPARENCIES

Transparency 52: Lawsuits Against School Districts Filed by Students

Transparency 53: Lawsuits Against School Districts Filed by Employees

Transparency 54: Risk Continua for Conducting Student Searches

Transparency 55: Teen Sexual Harrassment

Chapter 11

Antecedents of American Education

EXTENDED OUTLINE

OBJECTIVES

After reading this chapter, students will be able to:

1. describe ancient Greek education and the contributions of important Greek educational philosophers.
2. characterize the educational system found in the Roman Empire.
3. summarize the Dark Ages as they took place in the Middle Ages.
4. describe the revival of learning that occurred in Europe and the development of medieval universities.
5. articulate educational developments that transpired during the Renaissance.
6. explain the educational significance of the Protestant reformation and the contributions of Luther, Melanchthon, Ignatius of Loyola, Comenius, and Locke.
7. describe the educational events that took place during that period known as the Age of Reason.
8. list the contributions of some of the important educators who contributed to the Emergence of Common Man.

STRATEGIES FOR INTRODUCING THE CHAPTER

At the beginning of class, have students set aside all their books, notebooks, and writing implements. Have them experience the way students learned in early Greece; they had to study without the convenience of easy-to-use writing materials and without printed books. Use the Socratic dialog approach to introduce the chapters on the history of education by simply asking a series of probing questions. Use the focus questions to encourage independent thought about the history of education. Have students select a candidate for the most important educator throughout the ages. Allow them to make nominations and to explain the reasons for their nominations. Conclude the chapter introduction activity by asking students to vote for the most important educator based on the nominations. Then ask students to read the case study that presents a difficult challenge for a student teacher.

CHAPTER OVERVIEW AND ANALYSIS

This chapter briefly relates the major antecedents of American education, beginning with the early educational developments of the Eastern world, ancient Greece, and the important contributions of several famous Greek educators such as Socrates, Plato, and Aristotle. A brief look at Roman schools and the educational wisdom of Quintilian completes the first section of the chapter.

Education in the Middle Ages includes a general discussion of educational activity during that period as well as the work of Alcuin and Thomas Aquinas, both of whom made important contributions to the development of education.

Both the Renaissance and the Reformation are briefly presented as periods when great educational gains were made by many educators including Erasmus, Melanchthon, Comenius, and Locke.

The more recent antecedents of American education—those of the eighteenth and nineteenth centuries—are presented in the last section of this chapter. The writings of Voltaire and Descartes, and the educational interest of Frederick the Great during the Age of Reason are briefly discussed. The chapter concludes with a discussion of the important contributions of Rousseau, Pestalozzi, Herbart, and Froebel during the historical period known as the Emergence of Common Man. In addition to presenting a wealth of historical information, this chapter shows that many of our better education ideas were originated long ago and transported to America from other societies.

CLASS ACTIVITIES

Activity 11.1: Ask students to imagine two fictitious students who attended school in an ancient Hindu, Hebrew, Chinese, or African society. Have the students describe the two students in a short paragraph; then, discuss the various characterizations.

Activity 11.2: Use the Socratic dialog teaching approach during an entire class period. At the end of the period, have students discuss the pros and cons of the teaching method.

Activity 11.3: Ask students to design a discipline policy based on the writing of Quintilian.

Activity 11.4: Have students list the key things that they have learned in school that could be labeled "liberating." Have students share their lists of significant learning and then determine if any topics related to the trivium or quadrivium.

Activity 11.5: Ask students to identify something that they strongly believe. Then, ask them to try to develop logical arguments to convince others of their belief. Tell them that this is what Thomas Aquinas tried to do.

Activity 11.6: Ask students to select one of the educational maxims of Erasmus. Then have them modify the maxim to match their own beliefs. Collect all the revised maxims, place them on a master list, and distribute the list to the entire class.

Activity 11.7: Have students discuss Luther's argument for increased governmental support for education. What type of school funding program would Martin Luther support?

Activity 11.8: Ask students to identify one thing they would like to write on a child's *tabula rasa.*

Activity 11.9: Ask students if the three axioms of Descartes are generally believed in today's schools. Have them provide evidence for their responses.

Activity 11.10: Have students consider the teaching methods endorsed by Rousseau. Then, ask them to select one course of study that they are currently enrolled in and evaluate the teaching method in terms of Rousseau's words.

Activity 11.11: Have students design a social studies lesson according to the Herbartian teaching method.

PROFESSIONAL DILEMMA: Can You Provide an Adequate Multicultural Education in Your Classroom?

This feature deals with a common professional dilemma faced by all teachers: attempting to provide an excellent multicultural education in spite of limited background in the subject, and little time to do so. A variety of ideas are presented in this feature, and a creative instructor could use them in several different ways. You could structure a class discussion around the following questions: (1) What are the historical antecedents that have contributed to the lack of racial and ethnic understanding in our society? (2) To what degree should education programs seek to eliminate differences among individuals or to preserve and perhaps even celebrate them? (3) What can a teacher do to improve multicultural education? (4) What additional training and/or information do your students feel they need about multicultural education, and how might they obtain this information and/or training? You could also ask students to write essays on any of these important questions.

RELEVANT RESEARCH: Fewer Requirements and Lower Enrollments Are Contributing to a Decline in Students' Knowledge of the Past

Less history is being taught in our schools than in the past. This is even true in teacher education programs. Historians suggest this is an unfortunate situation, because it makes it easier for us to repeat past mistakes and more difficult for us to capitalize on past successes.

You could introduce this topic by asking students to make a list of reasons for learning history, or you could generate a discussion about the value and limitations of history. You could also ask students to select an historical topic to research, and to draw implications for education today from what they learn from their research. You could also share an example from your own professional experience where you profited from a knowledge of history.

VIDEO RESOURCES

1. *Lives in Education: The Ancient Greeks*
   Blackwell History of Education Research Collection, color, 15 min.
   Discusses the educational contributions of Sappho of Lesbos, Socrates, Plato, and Aristotle.
2. *Lives in Education: The Ancient Romans*
   Blackwell History of Education Research Collection, color, 15 min.
   Presents the educational contributions of Cicero, Quintilian, Hypatia, and Augustine.

3. *Lives in Education: The Humanists*
   Blackwell History of Education Research Collection, color, 15 min.
   Features the work of Vittorino da Feltre, Christine de Pisan, Johannes Butzback, and Erasmus.
4. *Lives in Education: The Reformers*
   Blackwell History of Education Research Collection, color, 15 min.
   Chronicles the contributions of Luther, Platter, Loyola and Comenius.

TRANSPARENCIES

Transparency 56: The Temple of Wisdom
Transparency 57: Early Christian and Medieval Education
Transparency 58: American Education Before the Civil War

COMPUTER ENRICHMENT EXPLORATION

History of Education. This exercise simulation helps teachers understand the history of education so they can capitalize on past educational successes and avoid failures. Further, it assists teachers in appreciating the important role that education has played in the historical development of our society. The historical periods studied are:
A. Antecedents of American Education
B. Colonial Education
C. Educational Development in the United States
D. Recent Educational Development

Participants in this exercise also complete a written exercise on the computer that can be given to the instructor in the course.

Chapter 12

Early American Education

EXTENDED OUTLINE

OBJECTIVES

After reading this chapter, students will be able to:

1. explain the development of schools and education in early colonial America.
2. articulate the struggle to establish universal elementary education in the United States.

3. relate the development of the Latin Grammar School, American Academy, and High School in the United States.

4. list and explain important events in the evolution of goals for our American educational system.

5. explain the reasons for the types of involvement of federal government in public education.

6. describe the historical development of programs to prepare teachers.

7. list and describe the evolution of teaching materials including the *hornbook, New England Primer, Blue-Backed Speller*, slates, and McGuffey's *Reader*.

8. describe the historical events surrounding the education of African Americans and the important pioneer work of African American educators.

9. write about the history of the education of women and the contributions of female educators.

10. describe the historical development of private education in America.

STRATEGIES FOR INTRODUCING THE CHAPTER

Obtain a copy of one of the McGuffey readers (or any other similar text from early America) and read one of the stories to the class. Have the class split up in discussion groups and identify the morals that were implied in the story. Then ask each group to discuss the list of morals and determine if they are valid for today's students.

Use the focus questions to encourage students to make connections between the issues that surrounded early American education and those that surround contemporary education. Have students select an issue that was important in early America and is still important today. Ask the class to discuss the reasons that the issue has not yet been solved. Conclude the chapter introduction activity by asking students to prepare the position paper described in the case study.

CHAPTER OVERVIEW AND ANALYSIS

Chapter 12 explains the development of education in the United States. The first section discusses colonial education including early school laws and the different types of schools that developed in the colonies, emphasizing the fact that our early educational ideas and schools were largely transplanted from Europe. The struggle to establish universal elementary education is discussed, along with the educational work of important pioneers such as Horace Mann, who came to be known as the father of common schools. The chapter also presents information on the evolution of secondary schools starting with the Latin Grammar School, the American Academy, and finally, the comprehensive High School.

The chapter then relates the evolution of the goals of our public schools, discussing the Committee of Ten, Seven Cardinal Principles, Eight Year Study, and other landmark goal statements, emphasizing that educational goals are ever-changing and often offer controversies in a democratic society. The history of federal involvement (or lack thereof) is briefly presented. Information about the U.S. Constitution, Northwest Ordinance, Morrill Land Grant, and Smith-Hughes Act as examples of the historical development of teacher education, is discussed in some detail, as is the evolution of the teaching materials that have been in the schools. Hopefully, the future teachers who read this chapter will appreciate that they are going into a profession with humble but proud traditions.

Finally, the chapter concludes with discussions on the education of special populations such as African Americans and females. The reader will quickly realize that our schools largely failed to be concerned about minority groups and females until very recently, and that prejudice, racism, and sexism are unfortunately deeply rooted in our educational history.

The last section of this chapter relates the extremely important role private schools have played, and continue to play, in our nation's development.

CLASS ACTIVITIES

Activity 12.1: Imagine being a parent of an early American family with children aged 7, 14, and 21. In which colony would you choose to settle? Discuss the reasons for your choice.

Activity 12.2: Compose a letter from parents to the school board expressing concerns about the Mennonite school teacher Christopher Dock. As a P.S. to your letter, indicate whether any of your concerns could be expressed today.

Activity 12.3: Have students describe the characteristics of the three types of secondary schools in the 1800s. Then, ask them to develop an argument supporting one of the three as a model for today's secondary schools.

Activity 12.4: Identify the many curricular areas in today's schools and relate these areas to an appropriate cardinal principle (for example, substance abuse education relates to health). Does any one principle receive more attention today?

Activity 12.5: Identify the needs of today's students; then, using this list of needs add to or subtract from the list in the Eight-Year Study.

Activity 12.6: In your opinion, how well have we followed the 1944 objectives of "Education for All American Youth"?

Activity 12.7: Prepare a position paper that argues for more or for less federal involvement in education. Conduct an in-class debate.

Activity 12.8: Prepare a resume that might be used to obtain a teaching position in the colonial school system.

Activity 12.9: Is there still a need for specialized teacher-training schools? Why or why not?

Activity 12.10: Research the hornbook. What other manipulatives were offspring of the hornbook? Are any of these offspring in use today?

Activity 12.11: Assign the class to cooperatively reproduce an early American schoolroom. List its books and materials.

Activity 12.12: How did education of African Americans by missionaries cause a conflict with the idea of slavery? Might such missionary efforts cause a conflict with today's ideas of equal educational opportunity for all?

Activity 12.13: What type of political activities would people like John Chavis, Benjamin Banneker, Frederick Douglass, Prudence Crandall, or Booker T. Washington endorse in today's society?

Activity 12.14: In what career or business would women like Mary McLeod Bethune or Emma Willard be involved today?

Activity 12.15: Research the principles of contemporary Montessori schools and compare them to the ideas of Maria Montessori.

Activity 12.16: Determine your position concerning the need for private schools. Then, examine the issue of vouchers and adopt a pro or con stance based on your position statement.

PROFESSIONAL DILEMMA: Can Teachers Both Defend and Criticize Schools?

Teachers occasionally find themselves in situations where they must defend their schools (or other teachers)—even though they may not want to. This poses an interesting professional dilemma—should the teacher always be totally honest with parents and the general public?—Or does a teacher have a professional obligation to "protect" the school and other teachers by not being overly critical? This Professional Dilemma feature explores this dilemma and asks the question—To what degree should teachers defend or criticize their school?

You could introduce this dilemma by asking students to role play teachers, parents, business people, school board members, and newspaper representatives in situations where they are discussing various school situations. Good topics might include sex education, teacher tenure, merit pay, teacher evaluation, student suspensions, or school prayer. You could also generate a class discussion about the ethics of teachers publicly criticizing their school and/or other teachers.

RELEVANT RESEARCH: Critiquing Curriculum

Much educational debate has historically revolved around the school curriculum. This Relevant Research feature describes the curriculum of the first Latin Grammar School in colonial America. This school was called the Boston Latin Grammar School, and was established in 1635. Nathanial Williams described the curriculum of this Latin Grammar School in a letter that is partially represented in this Relevant Research feature.

You could utilize this feature in several ways with your students. After reading this feature, your students could discuss, and/or write about: the apparent purposes of the colonial Latin Grammar School, differences and similarities between the Latin Grammar School and contemporary schools, the strengths and weaknesses of the Latin Grammar School curriculum, and the apparent philosophy behind the Latin Grammar School. Of course, the main purpose of this feature is to help your students better understand and appreciate the history of education.

VIDEO RESOURCES

1. *Lives in Education: The Americans*
   Blackwell History of Education Research Collection, color, 15 min.
   Presents the educational contributions of Noah Webster, Horace Mann, Henry Bernard, and Robert Owen.
2. *Lives in Education: The Outsiders*
   Blackwell History of Education Research Collection, color, 15 min.
   Discusses the important educational work of Elizabeth and Emily Blackwell, Sarah Winnemucca, Fanny Jackson Coppin, and Booker T. Washington.

TRANSPARENCIES

Transparency 59: Land Grants for Common Schools

Transparency 60: High Schools in the United States by 1860

Transparency 61: Evolution of the Essential Features of the American Public School System

Transparency 62: The Evolution of the Elementary School Curriculum and of Methods of Teaching

Chapter 13

Recent Developments in Education 1940–Present

EXTENDED OUTLINE

OBJECTIVES

After reading this chapter, students will be able to:

1. interpret the rapid growth of the educational enterprise in the United States.
2. explain the consolidation of schools, the resultant growth of school busing, expanding budgets, and curricular explosion over the past fifty years.
3. articulate the complexity of the educational enterprise in the United States.
4. list and elaborate the significant recent trends in American education.

STRATEGIES FOR INTRODUCING THE CHAPTER

Bring a copy of a complete elementary education or secondary education curriculum; one that lists the courses and all the different aspects of the academic program. Make copies for the class and have students make a list of all the types of expertise that are implied by the curriculum. For example, if students note that substance abuse is included they might identify the need for both ethical and medical expertise in order to comprehend and teach about substance abuse.

Conduct a discussion concerning the list of types of expertise identified by the class. What do students think about the expansion of curriculum and the growing list of expectations held for schools?

Use the focus questions to enable students to see how such a growing list of expectations has evolved over the past few decades. Conclude the chapter introduction activity by asking students to consider questions of equity that are implicit in the way schools are organized and in the way knowledge is presented. Once students have had an opportunity to explore how such equity questions are intertwined with school organization and curriculum, have them respond in writing to the case study.

CHAPTER OVERVIEW AND ANALYSIS

This chapter surveys important historical developments in recent history—since 1940. It begins with information about the rapid growth of the educational enterprise. Enrollment growth leads to many other types of growth—faculty, school buildings, busing, budgets, and curriculum. While schools grew in numbers, they also grew in complexity. Federal involvement in education, equal educational opportunity demands, and efforts to professionalize the educational enterprise became increasingly complex.

The chapter concludes with a discussion of recent historical trends in education. These trends include new educational emphases, analysis of the teaching and learning process, research on teacher effectiveness, increased sociological studies, and new programs for special populations. A brief look at the flood of criticism leveled at public schools over the past fifty years and litigation's increasing influence on education concludes the chapter.

Some may argue that educational events of the past few years should not be presented in the context of educational history. The authors disagree because of the extreme influence many relatively recent events have had on our schools. While we would admit that events of the last fifty years have not "stood the test of time," we believe teacher education students can learn much from these recent developments in education.

CLASS ACTIVITIES

Activity 13.1: Have students study Tables 13.1–13.4, which show tremendous growth in education. Ask them to identify the changes in school structure that occurred as a result of such growth.

Activity 13.2: Challenge students to imagine an entirely different school structure that could accommodate the massive growth of education during the past fifty-five years. Have students illustrate the structure that they propose and display the structures on the classroom walls and bulletin boards.

Activity 13.3: Have students conduct a debate on the pros and cons of school district consolidation.

Activity 13.4: Invite a special education teacher to discuss the changing roles that a special educator has had to play since 1950. Have him or her progress from specialization to least restrictive environment responsibilities to the current regular education initiative.

Activity 13.5: Invite a finance or budget professional from a school district to discuss the additional funded programs provided through federal programs. Ask the professional to discuss the pros and cons of such additional funds.

Activity 13.6: Have students develop a profile of a teacher who has specialized in a single area. Then have them develop a profile of a teacher who has a wide and varied background. Discuss the strengths and weaknesses of the two profiles.

Activity 13.7: Ask students to visit a private school in their area and comment on why they think parents might send their children there.

Activity 13.8: Describe the freedom of choice that was the foundation of A.S. Neill's educational philosophy. Compare this structure to the educational trends of today.

Activity 13.9: Ask students to list the ten top qualities that characterize an effective teacher.

Activity 13.10: After discussing the cognitive development stages cited here, have students create their own description of the learning process. Then ask them to identify which theory most closely matches theirs.

Activity 13.11: Ask students to select a leading educational critic and have them try to defend today's schools against such criticism.

PROFESSIONAL DILEMMA: How Can a Teacher Better Understand the World?

We hear much today about the need for schools to "internationalize" the curriculum; and as usual, teachers are not given much help or many resources to do so. This Professional Dilemma feature explores this challenge in a thought-provoking way.

Why not ask your students, before reading this feature, to discuss the importance of global education in our schools today? Ask them to define "international education" and to brainstorm a few ways they could include a global perspective in their future classrooms. Then, after they have read this Professional Dilemma, ask them to think about, discuss, or write about the following questions:

1. How can they, as a teacher, learn more about the world?
2. How important will global education be in their classroom?
3. How might a school help teachers infuse international education into the curriculum?

RELEVANT RESEARCH: Classroom Analysis Systems

This feature is designed to introduce the reader to at least one classroom analysis system, and to promote the idea that such systems are potentially useful as a self-improvement device for teachers. The Flanders Verbal Classroom

Interaction Analysis system is introduced as an example of a device created to help teachers better understand what happens in their classroom. Hundreds of such devices have been created by various researchers, and the reader is challenged to learn more about them because they hold the potential for helping teachers better understand and improve their professional performance.

If you have a favorite classroom analysis system, we recommend that you share it with your students at this time. Or, if teacher education students at your institution are expected to learn a certain system(s) as part of their program (even though they may do so in some other class), we suggest you review that system at this time (rather than having your students learn the Flanders system). You could also assign your students the task of learning more about several classroom analysis systems and selecting one to experiment with during an upcoming clinical experience.

VIDEO RESOURCES

1. *Lives in Education: The Critics*
   Blackwell History of Education Research Collection, color, 15 min.

Presents the lives and work of Maria Montessori, John B. Watson, Margaret Naumburg, and W. E. B. DuBois.

2. *A Day in the Life of the One Room School*
   Blackwell History of Education Research Collection, color, 15 min.
   One of a series of seven videotapes on selected topics dealing with the history of education. Other topics include hornbooks, women and teaching, Pestalozzi, religion and education, and the impact of the industrial revolution on schools.

3. *She's Nobody's Baby: A History of American Women of the 20th Century*
   Coronet/MTI Film & Video, color, 36 min.
   How women have redefined their roles and shaped the nation's history. Shows that the women's movement has been with us a long time.

TRANSPARENCIES

Transparency 63: Rates of High School Completion
Transparency 64: Stages of Cognitive Development by Jean Piaget
Transparency 65: Fundamental Ideas about Education

Chapter 14

Philosophy: The Passion to Understand

OBJECTIVES

After reading this chapter, students will be able to:

1. define philosophy and describe the methods used by philosophers.
2. identify the contributions that philosophy can make to a teacher's effectiveness.
3. list the major philosophical questions associated with the three major branches of philosophy: metaphysics, epistemology, and axiology.
4. elaborate on the major tenets of idealism, realism, pragmatism, and existentialism.
5. compare and contrast writings from philosophers who represent different schools of philosophy: Plato, Kant, and Hegel; Aristotle, Locke, and Whitehead; Peirce and Dewey; Sartre and Kierkegaard.
6. describe the characteristics of Eastern and Native North American thought.
7. elaborate on the implications for education that are associated with the different schools of philosophy.

STRATEGIES FOR INTRODUCING THE CHAPTER

Present a short scenario concerning a child who has misbehaved in school and is causing such a disruption that students are unable to concentrate. Then ask students to write down a brief statement that describes how they would respond to the situation.

Split the students into small groups and have them discuss their various responses. Then ask students to identify the underlying beliefs and values about the nature of learning in a social situation that are implied by their responses.

Have students volunteer to share some of these beliefs and values. Ask the class to try to identify which school of philosophy matches the beliefs that were shared by the volunteer students.

CHAPTER OVERVIEW AND ANALYSIS

This chapter emphasizes that philosophy is a love of wisdom. It opens with a vivid image of "passion," which is shown to be the underlying drive that gives rise to the discipline of philosophy. The chapter then clarifies that a unique set of basic questions informs the various branches of philosophy, which include metaphysics, epistemology, and axiology. Metaphysics deals with questions about the nature of reality. Epistemology deals with questions about the nature of knowing, and axiology deals with questions about values. The chapter also examines how philosophical thought is performed. This is included because students often are puzzled by the language and thought processes that philosophers use but do not clearly describe. Abstraction is shown to include a three-step linear process: (1) focusing attention on some feature within one's experience; (2) examining the precise characteristics of the feature; and (3) remembering this feature later. Imagining and generalizing are described as the altering of abstractions through the process of expanding the limits of ideas (imagination) and the simultaneous process of setting limits to these ideas (generalizing). Logic is described as a third feature of philosophical thinking and is shown to be a process of examining principles that link one argument to another.

The schools of idealism, realism, pragmatism, and existentialism comprise the next major portion of the chapter. These schools are shown to be somewhat contrived categories since no one philosopher fully represents the complete description of the school. Idealism is described as a philosophical school that holds that ideas are the only true reality. It is not that idealists reject the material world; rather, they hold that the material world is characterized by constant change and uncertainty, whereas ideas endure throughout time. Realism is shown to hold that physical entities exist in their own right. Realism's roots lie in the thinking of Aristotle.

Pragmatism is a late nineteenth-century American philosophy that affected education and social thought. It differs from most forms of idealism and realism by a belief in an open universe that is dynamic, evolving, and in a state of becoming. It is a process philosophy, which stresses becoming rather than being. For existentialists, existence (being) precedes essence (meaning). For existentialism reality is lived existence, and the final reality resides within the individual.

The chapter ends with a brief overview of Eastern and Native North American thought. No attempt is made to explore these varied and rich areas of thought in depth; rather, the chapter tries to give a "taste" for the different values and cultures that make up this complex area.

CLASS ACTIVITIES

Activity 14.1: Ask students to share their experiences from elementary school. Have them clarify how the classroom was arranged; what types of things they did during the school day; and the way discipline was handled. From the perspective of philosophy, what did these arrangements imply?

Activity 14.2: Have students identify the various ways that society views philosophy. Ask them to characterize these views by drawing a cartoon character. Have students discuss the various characters that they chose and relate them to the view that philosophy is a passion to understand. Do the cartoon characters fit or not?

Activity 14.3: Have students imagine a chair of any type. Ask them to try to write down the underlying characteristics of that chair. How do these characteristics fit other chairs? Tell them that such a process is a type of abstraction.

Activity 14.4: Ask students imagine different types of chairs. Have them try to draw a chair inside out. Now, examine the characteristics that they identified earlier and see if they still hold. This is the process of imagining and generalizing.

Activity 14.5: Compare the process of logic to that of designing a staircase. Have students clarify what statements flow from their statements about the underlying characteristics of chairs.

Activity 14.6: Share with students a statement from a school district's philosophy. Ask them to identify which schools of philosophy are represented by the statement of philosophy.

Activity 14.7: Ask students to identify the types of learning activities that would be most appropriate to the statement of philosophy discussed in Activity 14.5.

Activity 14.8: Organize students into various teams labeled realism, idealism, pragmatism, and existentialism. Present a school-related problem and have the various teams discuss a solution that is rooted in the philosophical school that they represent.

PROFESSIONAL DILEMMA: Should Ethics Be Taught in American Schools?

This professional dilemma deals with the complex question of teaching values. There is a public outcry concerning the lack of values in our contemporary society, and it would seem logical for schools to be the place to help remedy this problem. However, when asked to specify the precise values that should be taught, a dilemma occurs. Which set of values should be endorsed? How can values be specified while endorsing a multicultural society?

You can clarify this dilemma for your class by asking students to generate a personal list of values. Then have students share their lists in small discussion groups and determine similarities and differences. After this sharing, ask students to rethink their original lists and specify another list of personal values. Finally, have students consider which values on their second list they would feel comfortable teaching in their classrooms. Ask students to list them on the chalk board. Then conduct a large group discussion concerning the pros and cons for teaching these values in a contemporary classroom setting.

RELEVANT RESEARCH: The Teaching of Critical Thinking

The research surrounding critical thinking is rich with different thinking models. It is valuable for students to consider how these models compare to one another. At times, these thinking models actually conflict with one another. To help students realize the importance of examining what they mean by critical thinking, you could have them select an article about the teaching of critical thinking and summarize it. Then, have students interview one another concerning the articles they read. In pairs, have students determine the similarities and differences between the two critical thinking articles. Finally, conduct a large group discussion concerning the class findings.

VIDEO RESOURCES

1. *Lives in Education: The Ancient Greeks*
   Blackwell History of Education Research Collection, color, 15 min.
   Discusses the educational contributions of Sappho of Lesbos, Socrates, Plato, and Aristotle.
2. *Lives in Education: The Ancient Romans*
   Blackwell History of Education Research Collection, color, 15 min.
   Presents the educational contributions of Cicero, Quintilian, Hypatia, and Augustine.
3. *Lives in Education: The Humanists*
   Blackwell History of Education Research Collection, color, 15 min.
   Features the work of Vittorino da Feltre, Christine de Pisan, Johannes Butzback, and Erasmus.

TRANSPARENCIES

Transparency 66: Summary of Branches of Philosophy
Transparency 67: Thinking as a Philosopher
Transparency 68: A Socratic Dialogue
Transparency 69: Education Implications of Authoritarian Views
Transparency 71: Eastern Thought

Chapter 15

Educational Theory in American Schools: Philosophy in Action

EXTENDED OUTLINE

OBJECTIVES

After reading this chapter, students will be able to:

1. identify the major tenets of the authoritarian educational theories of perennialism, essentialism, and behaviorism.
2. identify the major tenets of the nonauthoritarian educational theories of progressivism, reconstructionism, and humanism.
3. compare and contrast authoritarian and nonauthoritarian educational theories.
4. relate educational theories to learning and curriculum development.
5. state the relationship of progressivism to democracy and society.
6. describe the major tenets of critical pedagogy and relate them to societal change.

STRATEGIES FOR INTRODUCING THE CHAPTER

Select an educational theory that you find valuable. Present the theory to the students and relate it to events in your own teaching. Explain that such theories are examples of philosophy in action. Use the focus questions to clarify how helpful theories are in the evaluation of teaching situations. Conclude the chapter introduction by asking students to reflect on the case study.

CHAPTER OVERVIEW AND ANALYSIS

This chapter discusses educational theories as examples of philosophy in action. Perennialism, essentialism, and behaviorism are shown to be authoritarian educational theories. Progressivism, reconstructionism, and humanism are shown to be nonauthoritarian educational philosophies. Educational examples of each of these theories are presented: The Great Books Program, Essential Schools, Reinforcement, Democratic Education, and Critical Pedagogy. Throughout the chapter care is exercised to display educational theory as developing and subject to change.

CLASS ACTIVITIES

Activity 15.1: Ask each student to write a list of five ideas that he or she believes are enduring. Summarize the individual lists and examine the class list. These ideas are examples of the perennialist position. How might a curriculum look if it were designed around these ideas?

Activity 15.2: Have students imagine what it means to "use your mind well." How would a curriculum look if it were designed to use one's mind well?

Activity 15.3: Bring a behavior checklist from any one of the many published observation checklists. Ask students to consider behavior as the key to understanding people. What are the strengths and weaknesses of such a position?

Activity 15.4: Jacob Getzels claimed democracy was a sacred value that people prized but failed to practice. Ask students to consider how democratic a classroom environment is. Is it a sacred or secular value?

Activity 15.5: Have students think of one societal issue that has been in the news recently. Ask them to consider how schools could make a difference with regard to the issue.

Activity 15.6: Bring to class a copy of the Carnegie Foundation on Middle School Education study about the characteristics of middle school education. The characteristics stress students working together and thinking as individuals. Ask students if this approach to learning is appropriate in high school as well. How would high schools have to be reorganized?

PROFESSIONAL DILEMMA: Should I Use Homogeneous of Heterogeneous Grouping?

This longstanding debate continues to dominate discussions about the organization of school programs. The dilemma is closely related to the problem of meeting individual needs in a group setting. It is usually easier for students to see the value of homogeneous grouping. It is important, therefore, to help future teachers understand the problems that are inherent in such grouping practices.

One way to increase students' awareness of the difficulties associated with homogeneous grouping practices is to randomly ask half of your students to wear large labels with the following terms: Slow Reader, Cannot Compute, Poor Motor Skills, Fat, and so on. Then make students with similar labels sit together. As you conduct class, give the students with the labels special attention; that is, ask them if they need assistance or review the material for them. On the following day, ask students who wore the labels to describe their feelings about wearing the labels and about the special treatment they received. Have the entire class discuss the pros and cons of such identification practices.

RELEVANT RESEARCH: The Use of Ill-Structured Problems

There is a growing body of research that indicates that the use of ill-structured problems prepares students for the problems inherent in daily life. This has major implications for teaching and learning. Generally, teachers pride themselves concerning their teaching plans. They are taught to be organized and to clearly articulate their teaching and learning objectives. Using ill-structured problems as the center of instruction requires teachers to give students more control and more responsibility for determining what the problem really means and how it will be resolved.

To help your students understand this, you could spend a class period in which you give students the task of solving an ill-structured problem. On the following day, ask students to record their feelings about the experience. Then discuss the pros and cons of the use of such problems in a contemporary classroom setting.

VIDEO RESOURCES

1. *Lives in Education: The Reformers*
   Blackwell History of Education Research Collection, color, 15 min.
   Chronicles the contributions of Luther, Platter, Loyola, and Comenius.
2. *Lives in Education: The Progressives*
   Blackwell History of Education Research Collection, color, 15 min.
   Presents the educational work of G. Stanley Hall, Francis W. Parker, John Dewey, and Ella Flagg Young.
3. *Rethinking Urban Schools: The Chicago Agenda*
   Britannica Video, color, 15 min.
   Topics include (1) rethinking urban schools, (2) building the process for learning, (3) creating an environment for learning, (4) developing the curriculum, and (5) extending the classroom.

TRANSPARENCIES

Transparency 70: Six Philosophical Orientations to Teaching

Transparency 72: Overview of Educational Thought

Transparency 73: Educational Theories: Perennialism, Essentialism, Behaviorism, Progressivism, Reconstructionism, Humanism

Transparency 74: Teachers' Thought Processes Related to Actions

Chapter 16

Building an Educational Philosophy

EXTENDED OUTLINE

OBJECTIVES

After reading the chapter, students will be able to:

1. list the characteristics of teachers as change agents.
2. provide examples of teacher leadership behaviors.
3. discuss how an educational philosophy affects classroom management and planning.
4. describe the influence of classroom practices on motivation.
5. analyze underlying differences among discipline approaches.
6. state the components of their personal philosophy of education.

STRATEGIES FOR INTRODUCING THE CHAPTER

Come to class prepared to discuss your personal philosophy of education. Discuss how you have developed it throughout the years and highlight any key experiences or theories that have altered it in a significant way. Use the focus questions to assist students in the development of their own philosophy of education.

CHAPTER OVERVIEW AND ANALYSIS

This chapter has two distinct parts; the first part analyzes the underlying meaning of being a teacher. It discusses teachers as change agents and as leaders. The second part of the chapter examines the philosophy of education as a vehicle for classroom planning and management. The intent of this chapter is to assist students in the identification of their own philosophy of education.

CLASS ACTIVITIES

Activity 16.1: Ask students to select one of the definitions of change (adaptation, rational process, reconstruction, dialectic). Using this definition, have each student design a response to the problem of illiteracy. Discuss how the responses differ.

Activity 16.2: Ask students to record their own vision for schools. Is this vision teacher-dominant or learner-supportive?

Activity 16.3: Ask students to record personal behaviors that show they model the vision for schools that they have articulated. A vision is only as effective as the way it is modeled.

Activity 16.4: Discuss the types of educational philosophy that lend themselves to each of the two teaching styles (teacher-dominant versus learner-supportive). With the class, develop a lesson plan according to each style. How do the objectives change for each style?

Activity 16.5: Split the class into three groups (interventionist, noninterventionist, and interactionist). Have each group design a discipline policy.

Activity 16.6: Have students design a teaching environment that is challenging, reinforcing, and secure. Ask them to present their designs, and have the class evaluate whether the teaching environment exhibits all three qualities.

PROFESSIONAL DILEMMA: Should You Use Authentic Assessments to Grade Students?

There is a growing awareness that students should be assessed using a variety of methods that go beyond multiple choice and essay examinations. However, there is a debate concerning the use of such assessments for grading. Actually, this dilemma relates to the larger question of assessing students with grades. Students generally understand the value of grades; they have had to deal with them throughout their many years of formal education. Therefore, it is important for students to consider what schools might be like without the use of formal grades. Ask each student to develop a method for assessment that does not use formal grades. Then have students meet in pairs to discuss their respective plans. Ask each pair to consider the pros and cons of their plans and to develop a joint plan that responds to the cons.

RELEVANT RESEARCH: Teaching Cooperation

There is a growing body of research that supports the teaching of cooperation. Business leaders consistently call on schools to develop professionals who know how to work with others. One way to help students recognize the way that such cooperation can be used in the classroom is to structure your own class activities using cooperative learning strategies. For example, you could have students prepare a group report about different educational philosophers. Have students distribute the project tasks among themselves and then deliver a group presentation. Students could indicate their specific contributions by using different color pens. You might have students study for an examination together; or you might ask students to take an examination together, with each group receiving the same score. After these experiences, ask students to discuss the pros and cons of cooperative learning.

VIDEO RESOURCES

1. *Ethics in America: Moral Education in Our Schools, The Ethics of Teaching, Censorship in a Free Society.* (series) American Humanist Association, color, 30 min. each
   A series of videotapes dealing with various philosophical questions concerning education.
2. *American Schools: Who Gives a Damn?* (2-part series) PBS Video, color, 60 min. each
   Recommended for education theory, seminars for the teaching profession, educational policy analysis and American studies.
3. *Renewing a Place Called School: A Video Series by Dr. John Goodlad—Improving Instruction.*
   Britannica Video, color, 15 min.
   Practical suggestions for starting, maintaining, and evaluating school renewal.

TRANSPARENCIES

Transparency 77: Change Is . . .
Transparency 78: Teachers as Change Agents
Transparency 79: Teachers as Leaders
Transparency 80: Developing a Philosophy of Education
Transparency 81: Educational Philosophy and Classroom Space
Transparency 75: Effective School Leadership

Chapter 17

School Programs

EXTENDED OUTLINE

OBJECTIVES

After reading this chapter, students will be able to:

1. identify the roles of education as they relate to the different types of students to be served.
2. elaborate on the tenets of the subject-centered curriculum.
3. elaborate on the tenets of the student-centered curriculum.
4. compare and contrast, using a graph matrix, the differences between the two major types of curriculum organization.
5. explain the differences and purposes of general education, exploratory education, and education for career programs of the school.
6. identify the characteristics of an effective school.
7. compare the practices of an effective school with those of the typical public school.
8. elaborate on the purposes and programs of vocational education.

9. discuss the program effects of early childhood programs on learner preparation for elementary education.
10. identify the significant need for and contributions of community education programs.

STRATEGIES FOR INTRODUCING THE CHAPTER

Relate your experiences first as a student and then as a teacher to identify the changes you have seen in education. Discuss what you perceive were the purposes of education during your student days and what they appear to be today. Have the students discuss their first twelve years of school experiences and ask them to create a list of positive and negative school feelings. Ask the students to support their feelings with specific references to school programs that they remember. Also, have them compare their earlier experiences with those of their higher education.

Using the student lists of school experience interpretations, have the students discuss and prepare a second list of what these experiences mean to them as potential teachers. Ask them to elaborate on how these experiences will lead them to different practices when they assume teaching positions.

CHAPTER OVERVIEW AND ANALYSIS

This chapter identifies some of the basic knowledge and issues that a beginning teacher needs to be concerned about during the early part of his or her career. It is not intended to be an in-depth study of the curriculum field. That type of study should come after the teacher has spent time teaching and has begun to raise professional questions about program development and procedures. Teachers will then have a need to know about and become engaged in extensive curriculum development. The information presented in this chapter will assist new teachers with their beginning preparation of teaching units and lessons for learning. It will also help them keep in mind the need to address diversity of learners as they prepare materials. As the make-up of student bodies continues to become more diverse, curriculum decisions become more significant.

Schools offer a variety of extended programs beyond the basic curriculum that most teachers employ. Therefore, beginning teachers need to know what these programs are and how they may fit into the regular program of the school. These extended programs may be impacting on regular students in contact with the beginning teacher. Additionally, some beginning teachers may want to know more about community education programs and how they can become involved in them.

CLASS ACTIVITIES

Activity 17.1: Have the students prepare a short list of purposes for a unit plan that models one of the three different roles of education (reproduction, readjustment, reconstruction).

Activity 17.2: Have students work in small teams to contact local high schools that have adopted some focus on vocational and college-bound students. Ask them to identify the differences in purpose and programs for these two groups.

Activity 17.3: Have students recall certain subjects they were taught in junior high school and how these were helpful in their education.

Activity 17.4: Have the students design a lesson in which students' interests are the basis for the lesson.

Activity 17.5: Have individual students outline a program for a specific grade level where they identify two different curriculum organizations for the same subject.

Activity 17.6: Divide the class into two groups. Have each group make a list of basic skills necessary for graduation from high school.

Activity 17.7: Have students visit a junior high school and/or middle school in the area and then identify whether they see exploratory education in practice.

Activity 17.8: Have students speculate about what they would suggest for graduation requirements if they did not have to adhere to state minimum requirements.

Activity 17.9: Have individual students select and defend what they believe the two most important elements of an effective school are.

Activity 17.10: Have students examine literature from several local vocational schools and indicate what they believe to be the critical selling points of those schools to prospective students.

Activity 17.11: Have teams of students visit a privately run preschool program and a school-operated program (if there is one), and report how they believe these schools are helping students get ready for elementary school.

Activity 17.12: Since school district community education programs have district budget support, have students debate the merits of such programs since the funds used to support community education programs could be used for basic education support.

PROFESSIONAL DILEMMA: Can Teachers Adapt Their Classroom Philosophy to Meet the Diversity of Inclusion Students?

Because of the various amendments to Public Law 94-142, the latest being the inclusion provision, this dilemma is very real for both the new teacher and the experienced teacher. The instructor should review with the students the requirements for due process and IEP creation before handling this dilemma. The special attention to this type of learner diversity has implications for the whole class. The instructor can group the students according to their different certification areas and ask them to prepare responses to the dilemma questions. Following this, the instructor can have the groups share their responses of courses of action that they would consider. The instructor can also assess the attitudes of the teacher training students toward working full time with these special students. The instructor can also have the students give a personal assessment of the additional types of teacher preparation they feel are necessary to meet these new 94-142 expectations.

RELEVANT RESEARCH: Improving Achievement of Hispanic Students

This research effort is another type of case study that a classroom teacher could conduct. It examines the growing area of inclusion of diverse students in the classroom. This shift in school enrollments will increase at an accelerated pace over the next twenty years. Again, the instructor can divide the class into certification areas and have the students address the direction of teacher effort posed by the authors of this text. The groups can then share and discuss how they would respond to the intended direction based on the findings of the study.

RELEVANT RESEARCH: Preventing Failure and Dropout Among At-Risk High School Students

This example was conducted as an action-research activity that classroom teachers could be engaged in. It points to successful findings over a seven-year period where dropout numbers were reduced significantly. The concept of a "school within a school" is not new and it exists in a variety of patterns across the country. What is different about this project is the special attention the author has given to at-risk students. The instructor can use at least two things from this study with teacher education students. First, he or she can lead a discussion on the effects of such a program on the regular students in a school. Second, he or she may have the students engage in this activity independently in small groups.

VIDEO RESOURCES

1. *Learning in America: Education on Trial* (3 part series)
   PBS Video, color, 60 min. each.
   Uses a courtroom setting to illustrate issues facing education.
2. *Renewing a Place Called School: A Video Series by Dr. John Goodlad—Enriching the Curriculum*
   PBS Video, color, 15 min.
   Practical suggestions for starting, maintaining, and evaluating school renewal.

TRANSPARENCIES

Transparency 82: Forces that Shape the Curriculum

Transparency 83: Hierarchy of Educational Aims and Objectives

Transparency 84: The Constants-Variable Program of Senior High Schools

Transparency 85: Examples of School Organization

Transparency 86: Concept Map for Effective Learning

Transparency 87: A Teacher's Instructional Repertoire

Chapter 18

School Practices

OBJECTIVES

After reading this chapter, students will be able to:

1. identify the various organizational elements of the school program.
2. elaborate on the instructional elements of the school program.
3. identify various types of learning space used in the schools.
4. discuss the different ways that teachers and related staff members can be organized for scheduling and teaching.
5. compare the issues of grouping, tracking, and classroom management associated with class size.

6. compare and contrast the different methods of learner assessment in achievement.
7. identify the taxonomies of learning and the different types of objectives for instruction.
8. compare and contrast different models of learning.
9. elaborate on the differences in using various kinds of technology to assist in teaching.
10. elaborate on how the teacher can use computers in the learning environment.

STRATEGIES FOR INTRODUCING THE CHAPTER

Using your own class syllabus, explain to the class how you will determine the overall effectiveness of your instruction and their performance. In addition, suggest ways that might enhance the effectiveness of the class, but that cannot be achieved. Solicit responses from your students about their expectations and how they can be achieved. You can also prepare a pretest that gives a readiness measure of a basic understanding of the large amount of terms and concepts associated with school practices.

CHAPTER OVERVIEW AND ANALYSIS

This chapter provides a collage of school practices that the beginning teacher can use early and throughout her or his career. Many of the practices discussed in the chapter are in use in many of the schools where beginning teachers will be employed. They will encounter some of these practices during their early field experiences and student teaching activities. Beginning teachers need to know the pros and cons of these practices so they can evaluate the intention and use of the practices in the field; this chapter helps them do that.

A major emphasis of this chapter is the importance of the growing use of technology in the classroom. The chapter identifies these technologies and discusses where and how they can be used in the learning environment. However, the chapter stresses that the most important element in any classroom is the teacher. The teacher needs to understand and appreciate that technology is an aid, but it has limitations. Teachers must learn how to direct the technology rather than have the technology direct the program and the teacher.

CLASS ACTIVITIES

Activity 18.1: Tell students that they have unlimited funds, and then ask them to draw and label their ideal classroom.

Activity 18.2: Arrange the students in random groups of three or more. Have each group be responsible for teaching one day's lesson for one grade level. Each member of each group should share the workload of the group.

Activity 18.3: Have students working in groups design a lesson for a class of five students. Then have them design the same lesson for 25 to 30 students.

Activity 18.4: Have the students compare the impact of a large class, of 100 or more students, to that of a small class of five. Have them respond to tracking, grouping, and use of materials.

Activity 18.5: Ask the students to indicate which type of grading practice they prefer. Have them use their preference with two different grade levels that are not closely related.

Activity 18.6: Ask the students to design a national grading system. They should also discuss and/or debate the purpose of these grades.

Activity 18.7: Ask students to evaluate their own style of learning. Have them list what factors are most important to their learning style.

Activity 18.8: Have groups of students choose a lesson to be taught. Then have each group suggest a way the lesson might be learned. The groups should try not to duplicate each other's method.

Activity 18.9: Have students visit a learning resource center. Ask them to identify the many different resources provided by the center and speculate how they would be beneficial to classroom learning.

Activity 18.10: Have each student give her or his own opinion on the use of computers in the classroom. Students should also formulate a list of everyday activities that can best be accomplished with computers.

PROFESSIONAL DILEMMA: Can You Prepare Authentic Assessment Tools?

Authentic assessment has become more than a popular term. As increasing numbers of states employ strategic planning requirements for schools, increased attention to outcome based learning, performance expectations, and other criterion-referenced learning expectations, the need for increased use of authentic assessment techniques has become more apparent. Couple these kinds of state expectations with a growing complex of diverse learners in the classroom and the usual types of norm-referenced assessment cease to provide meaningful information on student achievement.

The dilemma presented here accurately depicts the kinds of questions that all teachers face with diverse student bodies and state curriculum/program regulations that seek meaningful interpretations of learner performance. Additionally, this type of assessment ties directly to a teacher's objectives for learning. This dilemma will provide practice for the beginning teacher to prepare for assessment practices that go beyond the traditional testing still used in many classrooms.

RELEVANT RESEARCH: The Road Ahead for Performance Assessment

There is an increasing number of research studies looking at performance assessment and its use with learning outcomes. This particular study introduces the concept of equity in making more accurate assessments of student learning. The equity questions used in this study deal with measures that hold students' attention, the linguistic appropriateness of the measures, and the sensitivity of the measures to instruction. The instructor can have students discuss each of the three validity issues for performance assessment as they relate to some of the class activities in which students and small groups of students are working with different lessons. Also, the instructor can use this research to promote the importance of performance assessment when working with diverse groups of students.

RELEVANT RESEARCH: Videodiscs Improve Student Outcomes

This study points to the positive aspects of using technology that is tied to the intended classroom objectives and instruction. These videodiscs were developed to supplement the ongoing program rather to replace it. The instructor can use this type of research from two perspectives. First, the instructor can use the findings to discuss the "Hawthorne Effect" with innovative programs in the classroom. He or she can have the beginning teacher students discuss how long an innovative program should be in place before one can discount the Hawthorne effect. Second, the instructor might secure some samples of videodiscs for the students to examine and evaluate. If this approach is used by the instructor, then the students should be given some evaluative scheme that may be used to assess the videodiscs.

VIDEO RESOURCES

1. *Renewing a Place Called School: A Video Series by Dr. John Goodlad—The School As the Unit of Change*
   PBS Video, color, 15 min.
   Practical suggestions for starting, maintaining, and evaluating school renewal.
2. *Renewing a Place Called School: A Video Series by Dr. John Goodlad—Assessment and Long Range Planning*
   PBS video, color, 15 min.
   Practical suggestions for starting, maintaining, and evaluating school renewal.
3. *Learning in America: Education on Trial Part I—Do We Need A National Report Card?*
   PBS video, color, 60 min.
   Due to our global economy, should learning standards be national, state, or local?

TRANSPARENCIES

Transparency 88: Activity from the "Cola Can Curriculum"
Transparency 89: Two Foci of Curriculum Planning
Transparency 90: Dimensions of Classroom Life
Transparency 91: Curriculum Continuum
Transparency 92: More Computers in Schools
Transparency 93: How the Internet is Used

COMPUTER ENRICHMENT EXPLORATION

Assessing and Evaluating Students. This simulation exercise challenges the participant to choose a method for assessing student progress and evaluating that progress for reporting purposes. The participant may choose to use normative, criterion, and authentic assessment procedures or any combination of the three. The scenario presents a hypothetical class of students with baseline information and an objective for instruction. After the student makes his or her choice of assessment, he or she writes a brief paragraph on why that choice was made. Following completion of the assessment, the participant identifies and defends in writing on the computer the manner in which the assessment will be used to report to students and parents. The two written responses may be submitted to the instructor of the course.

Chapter 19

Schools for the Next Century

OBJECTIVES

After reading this chapter, students will be able to:

1. provide examples of big and little changes in today's schools.
2. develop features, along with strengths and weaknesses of restructured schools.
3. describe factors of transforming schools, including the educational rationale for each.
4. discuss the types of major changes that are occurring in more innovative high schools.
5. describe the kinds of societal conditions and reasons for the movement to establish schools as the center for delivery of coordinated services.
6. compare features of their current teacher education program with the programs espoused by the different teacher education networks.
7. describe the many ways that teachers are leaders in their schools.
8. describe and discuss the alternative career paths for teachers.
9. assess their personal readiness for entering the classroom for teaching.

STRATEGIES FOR INTRODUCING
THE CHAPTER

Share your notions of an ideal school. Suggest to your students that your expectations are realistic and that you wonder if they have any chance of coming to fruition during your students' careers. Ask them to indicate what forces may thwart the possibilities of your notions and what forces support them.

Use the focus questions to enable students to recognize how much change will be a part of their future. Have students consider and discuss their own ideas of a radically different school for learners. Conclude with the students assessing their readiness for entering the profession and providing the leadership for making the future changes they have identified.

CHAPTER OVERVIEW AND ANALYSIS

Chapter 19 has a different frame of reference than the other chapters: The emphasis is on looking forward into the future of what education and schooling can become. Teacher education students tend to be fairly conservative and traditional. They are not much unlike the professionals with whom they will work. As has been seen in this text, most schools have the same organizational arrangements and appearances as they have had for quite some time. However, there are increasing numbers of schools in the nation engaged in trying new and different types of instructional designs and practices. Our goal in this chapter is to stretch students' thinking and perspectives about the way schools could work and the future role of teachers in those schools.

The chapter opens with a discussion of the idea of change. Two key themes are developed. First, although there is a lot of talk about change, many interesting ideas are being presented, and most schools' staffs are engaged in an array of interesting activities, there is a major difference between talking about change and actually doing something about it. Second, change is a slow process and it takes several years and sometimes a generation to accomplish meaningful progress. Change comes in different sizes of innovations, and these sizes can be arrayed along a continuum from "talking" to "tinkering" to "transforming."

The remainder of the chapter introduces various transformational examples of school changes. All of these ideas and practices actually exist in one or more schools in America. These transformational activities range from schools that are engaged in implementing different roles for teachers and placing more responsibility for learning on children, to schools that are bringing together and coordinating the delivery of the various human social services. In all of these examples, educators are engaged with children, parents, and the greater community.

Finally, the chapter deals with the important concept of teacher leadership. Most teachers are not sufficiently sensitive to the major leadership responsibilities that they have beyond their classrooms. Usually, they do not think about themselves as leaders within the classroom, much less in the school or community. In fact, however, teachers should be the leaders, both within their classrooms and within the school. Their participation in community leadership sets them apart as models for their students.

CLASS ACTIVITIES

Activity 19.1: Ask students to consider their individual visions of an ideal school. Have them discuss whether their ideas are on the level of talking, tinkering, or transforming.

Activity 19.2: Bring in a local business person to discuss how he or she views business involvement in schools. Then ask students to assess whether the view presented is a tinkering or transforming idea.

Activity 19.3: Describe the work of Individually Guided Education from the 1970s and 1980s, which advocated multi-aged groupings in elementary school. Ask the students to discuss their comfort level with such ideas.

Activity 19.4: Have students redesign the Carnegie Units currently required for high school graduation. What types of learning would they require for high school students of the future?

Activity 19.5: Invite to class a staff member of a school that offers some form of coordinated school services. Have the staff member discuss the interrelationship of the various services. Does the program work smoothly?

Activity 19.6: Have students select one of the teacher education initiatives (Holmes, Renaissance), and prepare a debate about which initiative is the best.

Activity 19.7: Assign students to one of the four styles of leadership in the classroom (committee, SBDM, Consigliere, BRT), and have them consider one leadership initiative they believe could assist in transforming the student teaching experience.

Activity 19.8: Have each student chart a potential career path for his or her future. Do the paths terminate with the student still in the field of education?

Activity 19.9: Use the concluding question to the students (Will you be ready?) to have them list and analyze their own strengths and weaknesses as they prepare to begin teaching.

PROFESSIONAL DILEMMA: Can You Successfully Involve Parents in Their Childrens' Education?

This dilemma provides a real-life situation for any teacher. Getting parents to become more actively involved with their children's education is an extremely difficult task. This is particularly true of those parents who have children who are experiencing difficulty in school, whether it be social or academic. Parent involvement in their children's education tends to decrease as children move up the grade ladder. Evidence of this is seen by parental attendance at PTO meetings. As the children move into high school, fewer parents come to the school unless some serious incident has occurred and some dire consequence is being proposed. However, there is a body of school literature that suggests greater parent and/or guardian participation with the school usually leads to stronger social and intellectual development of the child.

RELEVANT RESEARCH: Moving to the Future with Our Schools

This type of futures projection description research challenges the teacher education student to look at what the school could become in the future. As such, it certainly challenges the status quo that most new teachers find when they begin their professional career. The future article suggestion that young learners be empowered in the learning environment suggests a strong emphasis on a learner-centered environment as opposed to the typical teacher-centered environment found in the overwhelming majority of schools today. If this futures assertion has any merit, there are many implications for teacher training.

RELEVANT RESEARCH: Empowering Teachers to Reform Schools

This historical research reports on an SBM approach being used in the reform of schools. There are many implications for teacher training as it relates to this type of presentation and others that are gaining popularity, at least at the talking and tinkering stages. A "bottom-up" management style is patterned after elements of the Japanese industrial management style and the hoped-for positive elements, as seen in industry, are projected to management of the schools. The teacher leadership roles in the school need to be examined as they relate to an SBM model.

VIDEO RESOURCES

1. *Parent-Teacher Communications.*
   Coronet/MTI Film and Video,color, 20 min.
   Thirteen vignettes illustrate reasonable discussions that break down when emotions are added. Gives kids' and adults' points of view.
2. *Renewing a Place Called School: A Video Series by Dr. John Goodlad—School and the Freedom to Change.*
   PBS Video, color, 15 min.
   Practical suggestions for starting, maintaining, and evaluating school renewal.

TRANSPARENCIES

Transparency 94: Parent-Child Literacy Activities
Transparency 95: Hall's Innovative Category Scale
Transparency 96: New Beginnings Services
Transparency 97: Achievement across Subjects Worldwide
Transparency 98: Deming's Fourteen Points
Transparency 99: Learning Centers
Transparency 100: Significant Forces and Trends Shaping the Future

⒞ℕℕ Videotape Guide

The CNN videotape available to users of this text contains over 30 news clips addressing important and thought-provoking issues in education. The clips are organized into six segments, corresponding to the six parts in *Introduction to the Foundations of American Education, Tenth Edition*. The clips are described individually below. You may also look in the margins of this Annotated Instructor's Edition where, for your convenience, each clip is referenced to related text content.

⒞ℕℕ *Video Summaries*

Segment I/Professional Aspects of Teaching

Teachers in this country face some of the most challenging issues in American society today: a changing population and a more complex and competitive global environment. Society asks a great deal of its teachers, but can be fickle when it comes to the specifics. How much power should teachers have? What value does society actually place on the teaching profession, and to that extent, what support are they willing to offer? The clips in Segment I visit just a few of the many issues facing educators and students today.

Clip 1/*Teach for America*

A look at recent graduates who have devoted the next two years to teaching in underprivileged schools through the intensive Teach for America program, a nonprofit, domestic educational peace corps designed to recruit, train, place, and support teachers in needy schools across the United States.

Clip 2/*Student Stress*

A comparative look at stress levels and pressure experienced by students in the United States and those in Japan and China.

Clip 3/*Kentucky Schools*

Wheeler Elementary in Louisville, Kentucky is on the cutting edge of educational reform because it gives teachers complete independence in planning their curriculum, allowing them to be extremely interactive with their students' learning process.

Clip 4/*Teacher Gap*

A teacher shortage in Los Angeles leads to an aggressive recruitment effort of "rocket scientists" and other professionals who are either out of work or seeking alternate sources of income. The results have been extremely positive, as many have made a permanent switch to the teaching profession.

Clip 5/*Kids and Learning*

The standards outlined by the Goals 2000 bill are meant to be a baseline for "what every child should know," but for failing school systems, these goals are virtually unattainable, as there is minimal money allotted for the reforms they need. Does this bill truly seek to empower schools? Or is it merely empowering the bureaucracy that governs them?

Segment II/School and Society

Among the societal issues affecting schools today, perhaps none is more significant than or as politically volatile as that of providing equal educational opportunity in a diverse society. The clips in Segment II address some ways that student diversity impacts education and life in the classroom.

Clip 6/*Sheenway School*

A small, private school in South Central Los Angeles offering personal attention and a student-centered learning environment now faces a battle for economic continuity as it becomes more difficult to "empower this community to be responsible for its children and to value education."

Clip 7/*Race and IQ*

In this controversial piece, an African American child's adoptive Caucasian mother is suing a Los Angeles school district for discrimination because the school will not allow the child to take a racially biased IQ test unless the child changes her race status from Black to White. An interesting case dealing with the responsibility of schools to provide alternative testing options for minorities.

Clip 8/*Mississippi Learning*

A look at the "Algebra Project," a privately funded math literacy program that is teaching students of the Mississippi Delta to learn math skills in their own language.

Clip 9/*Language Immersion*

Detroit's Foreign Language Immersion and Cultural Schools (FLICS) teach all subjects in only French, Spanish, and Japanese, asserting that total immersion not only promotes fluency and language acquisition, but teaches cultural appreciation to students from the very start of their educational experience.

Clip 10/*Multicultural Requirement*

In an effort to promote greater cultural understanding in schools, a group of high school seniors in Los Angeles County School District have proposed legislation requiring students to complete a multicultural semester.

Clip 11/*Immigrant Education*

A look at one of LA's "newcomer schools," which introduces immigrants to the American culture and educational system before they plunge into American public schools.

Clip 12/*Drugs in the Hood*

An uplifting report of a school drama program in Atlanta whose message is to educate students about drug abuse on their streets. Students write, produce, direct, and perform their own plays, providing solutions to problems through the arts.

Clip 13/*Dropout Prevention*

A report on community-based programs and funds in Harlem focusing on dropout prevention at an early age through encouragement and home visits by family assistants who have helped mediate the school experience.

Segment III/Governance, Organization, and Support of American Education

Teachers and students have a relationship that is both warmly intimate and coldly professional. The clips in Segment III profile situations in which the rights demanded by educators and students have tested the legal system in unique ways.

Clip 14/*Retarded Mainstreaming*

The inclusion of retarded students into public schools has become a controversial issue in New Jersey Schools as a result of a rape case involving a retarded woman; the state now faces the issue of how to protect the mentally disabled without impeding their rights to normal activities.

Clip 15/*Charter School*

A look at communities that organize and run charter schools with public funds in order to create safer learning environments for their children.

Clip 16/*Corporate Public School*

As part of a corporate experiment in education, a tuition-free private school founded and run on business principles in an impoverished Chicago district has now depleted its generous corporate funds, and is being forced to return to the Chicago public school system.

Clip 17/*Privatizing Education*

A controversial report on the political issue of privatizing education and the future of EAI (a Minnesota firm that subcontracts its services to different districts to handle the day-to-day problems of schools), which hangs in the balance of a contract with the Hartford Public School System.

Clip 18/*Desegregation Today*

Controversy over a lack of racial balance in schools has led to legal litigation followed by a massive busing program to integrate minorities into various Hartford school districts. Many question whether the funds for this program could be better spent by improving needy schools, rather than depleting their student bodies in order to integrate other schools.

Clip 19/*Kid Condom*

Condom distribution in New Haven public schools as part of a sex education program that begins at Grade 5 has communities divided; some parents applaud the program, while others feel it undermines their authority.

Clip 20/*School Book Censor*

A presentation of the censorship issue focusing on a California school district that banned literature by Alice Walker and Annie Dillard from being taught in classrooms.

Segment IV/Historical Foundations of Education

Schools can be viewed as both the agent and the product of historical trends in the United States. The clips in Segment IV look at where the American school has been, and where it might be going now.

Clip 21/*Mural of History*

A mural depicting the history of art, designed by a California artist and painted entirely by students, adorns the halls of Woodrow Wilson Middle School, and instills in students a sense of pride in their school.

Clip 22/*Ethnic Kids Books*

A look at a student who writes and illustrates children's books that represent ethnically diverse populations in order to foster and encourage crosscultural understanding.

Clip 23/*Creationism School*

A conservative school board in California wants creationism taught in social studies classrooms; this has caused a great stir in the local community.

Clip 24/*Year-Round School*

A unique Oklahoma high school that groups its diverse student body not by age but by ability, and has no summer vacation has shown surprising results—increased motivation and better student performance!

Clip 25/*Reinventing Schools*

An East Harlem school has given inner city students something to be happy about—learning. Through its unique, unstructured program, this school presents an educational philosophy that works.

Segment V/Philosophy and Education

Is there a defining philosophy in the American educational system today? How and to what extent does that philosophy and each teacher's philosophy impact life in the classroom? The clips in Segment V demonstrate how schools might reflect the values and philosophies of society at large.

Clip 26/*Quality School*

In Chicago's "Learning Center" school, the focus is on freedom. There are no bells, no principals, and no grades other than A and B in this totally student-centered environment.

Clip 27/*Pay for Profanity*

In South Central Los Angeles, one teacher has adopted a "Don't Curse" policy in her classroom, making students pay cash for each swear word they use.

Segment VI/School Programs and Practices

School programs and practices in the last few decades have undergone rapid change. The three R's are still around, but the way they are taught has certainly changed. The clips in Segment VI address some current trends in teaching and learning.

Clip 28/*Parental Grade*

In a Detroit private elementary school, parents are graded on everything from homework support to breakfast, and are asked to set goals for improvement—and their children get to sign their report cards!

Clip 29/*Parents Homework*

The technology of "mini-tel," a home monitor that links teachers, students, and parents, lets parents check their children's homework assignments, and lets students talk with their teachers and make pen pals from other schools through electronic mail.

Clip 30/*SAT Advancers*

A report on the SAT as a standard of measure that is no longer required by many colleges, despite ETS's efforts to revise the test so it is a better reflection of students' knowledge, and not just a reflection of how many prep courses they took before the actual exam day!

Clip 31/*Student Standards*

A look at "Outcomes Based Education" programs, in which students cannot advance to the next grade level until they demonstrate a set of standards measuring their ability to succeed.

Clip 32/*The Next Generation*

In Johannesburg, students of all races applaud the end of Apartheid, are hopeful about a united school of thought, and look forward to their chance to vote and make a difference in their world.

Introduction to the Foundations of American Education

Tenth Edition

James A. Johnson
NORTHERN ILLINOIS UNIVERSITY

Victor L. Dupuis
PENNSYLVANIA STATE UNIVERSITY

Diann Musial
NORTHERN ILLINOIS UNIVERSITY

Gene E. Hall
UNIVERSITY of NORTHERN COLORADO

Donna M. Gollnick
NATIONAL COUNCIL for ACCREDITATION of TEACHER EDUCATION

Introduction to the Foundations of American Education

Allyn and Bacon

BOSTON   LONDON   TORONTO   SYDNEY   TOKYO   SINGAPORE

Editor-in-Chief, Education: Nancy Forsyth
Senior Editor: Virginia Lanigan
Series Editorial Assistant: Nihad Farooq
Developmental Editor: Alicia Reilly
Marketing Manager: Kathleen Hunter
Production Administrator: Susan McIntyre
Editorial-Production Service: Kathy Smith
Text Designer: Deborah Schneck
Photo Researcher: Susan Duane
Cover Administrator: Linda Knowles
Composition Buyer: Linda Cox
Manufacturing Buyer: Megan Cochran

Library of Congress Cataloging-in-Publication Data
Introduction to the foundations of American education / James A.
   Johnson . . . [et al.]. -- 10th ed.
     p. cm.
   Includes bibliographical references and indexes.
   ISBN 0-205-16141-3
   1. Education--United States.   2. Educational sociology--United
States.   I. Johnson, James Allen.
   LB17.I59   1996
   370'.973--dc20   95-24082
                                       CIP

Printed in the United States of America
10 9 8 7 6 5 4 3 2 1   00 99 98 97 96 95

Credits continue on page 544, which should be considered an extension of the copyright page.

Contents

Chapter 2

Employment Opportunities for Teachers   29

Chapter 3 Professional Organizations for Educators   55

Part 2 **School and Society**   **76**

Chapter 4 **School and Society**   **79**

Chapter 5   # A Multicultural Society   103

Chapter 6   Education That Is Multicultural   129

Part 3 Governance and Support of American Education   182

Chapter 8 Structure and Finance of American Education   185

Chapter 9   ## Legal Aspects of Education   225

Chapter 10

The Rights of Students and Teachers   259

Chapter 12   Early American Education   313

Part 5   Philosophical Concepts, Educational Views, and Teaching Styles   366

Part 6   School Programs and Practices   428

Chapter 17   School Programs   431

Preface

Writing the tenth edition of this text has prompted us to reflect on all that has gone on in education since the first edition was published. Thirty years ago, teacher education was in a mass production mold, as teacher educators struggled to train teachers fast enough to meet the demands of a rapidly growing school population that was the result of the World War II baby boom. The student body of our schools was mainly white, middle class, and still full of the 1950s mentality of "have fun, be conventional, and prepare for the good life" during the last part of the twentieth century. Educators were largely unaware of the criticisms and pressures they would face or the changes schools would undergo during the next thirty years.

Changes included a rapid decrease in enrollment, international struggles that were to tax the very heart and soul of the United States democracy, a technological explosion that was to challenge the brightest minds associated with teaching and learning, and—most significantly—a rapidly changing demographic make-up of the United States population. The Vietnam era did away with the protective environment of the 1950s, as young people of all races in the United States took to the streets to protest war, call their educational programs into question, and ask for more meaningful school preparation for life in the twenty-first century.

Demographic changes in the United States have brought about perhaps the single most significant change to education in the last thirty years and will continue to affect education as we enter the next century. While the nonwhite school population is increasing exponentially, few teachers-in-training are part of that minority population growth. Thus, the pertinent challenge to teacher education over the next decade or so is twofold. First, how do we get more minority young people to enter the education profession? Second, how can we help nonminority teachers educate a growing minority population? The text has changed considerably over ten editions. It has remained responsive to societal changes, yet true to its mission to uphold the profession of teaching. We have also continued to recognize the importance of the learner, and the role the teacher must play in meeting the needs of students and of society.

The Contents of This Book

We have attempted to cover those areas that every teacher must know in order to be an informed, thoughtful educator: the history of education, its philosophical underpinnings; the role of education in contemporary society; the legal and financial issues that affect teachers, students, and schools; and the future of education as we look forward to the next century.

Learning Aids in This Text

We have provided several features in this text designed to enhance your understanding and provoke your interest.

The Dreamcatchers. Each major section of the text profiles master teachers from around the country who offer inspiration and advice as it relates to the dreamcatcher legend. In accordance with this Ojibwa tradition, the dreamcatcher was hung over the cradles of infants or inside the lodges of Native American people. The dreamcatcher allowed good dreams through its spiderweb-like mesh center to become part of the lives of the Ojibwa. Bad dreams were caught and perished in the web with the first light of morning.

Focus Questions. Each chapter begins with a short set of questions intended to help you find the main concepts in the chapter and orient yourself to a critical reading of the material.

Key Terms and Concepts. There is a professional language in education. At the beginning of each chapter we have identified and defined important words that will be introduced in the chapter. These terms are also boldfaced and defined in the text.

Several of our features are **new** to this edition.

Professional Dilemmas. One of the challenges of education is that there are many questions and debates for which there are no clear-cut answers. In each chapter we select one of these for your consideration. Don't expect to find the perfect answer. Instead, be prepared to understand the consequences and implications of your response to the issue, and the impact they may have on students in your classroom.

Relevant Research. Each chapter profiles an interesting example of contemporary research in education with specific relevance to chapter material.

Case Studies. Each chapter presents one or more case studies involving students and teachers in real situations, demonstrating the complexity of life within America's classrooms.

Global Perspectives. Each chapter contains one or more sections that specifically address international viewpoints related to chapter content. In addition to recognizing diversity within our own domestic borders, educators are now much more willing to look to other societies and how they approach the challenges of education.

Journal/Portfolio Development. Journals and portfolios have become valuable tools for both teachers in their own career management and for students as benchmarks of their learning accomplishments. These exercises at the end of each chapter will help you learn to use these tools to their best advantage for both yourself and your students.

School-Based Experiences. At the end of each chapter, these field activities are designed to reinforce the connection between material covered in the chapter and its classroom applications.

Sharing Ideas

We hope that as a team of authors we have been successful in pooling our ideas and presenting them to you in a useful and thought-provoking way. If you have any suggestions for us, or questions about what we have written, please send in the reader response sheet at the back of the book.

As one of the first generation of teachers for American schools in the twenty-first century, you have a special responsibility and opportunity. You and the children that you teach will be setting the direction for the future. And, as with those who have gone before you, you will be building on the work of many other educators. It is their knowledge that we pass on to you here. Best of luck in your quest to become an outstanding teacher.

Acknowledgments

We are grateful to the many people who have helped make this textbook the bestseller that it is. We thank Allyn and Bacon for supporting us as authors over the years and allowing us to deliver the message as we wished. We are also grateful to the many people who have used previous editions and who provided suggestions and materials for this edition. In particular, we are grateful to the following persons:

Morris L. Anderson, *Wayne State College*
Alan Dean, *University of Rio Grande*
Dorothy Engan-Barker, *Mankato State University*
Geneva Gay, *University of Washington*
Tyll van Geel, *University of Rochester*
John Georgeoff, *Purdue University*
Michael James, *Connecticut College*
Jane A. Newburger, *Cazenovia College*
Rosalyn Ruffner, *Kentucky Christian College*
Paul Wagner, *University of Houston—Clear Lake*
John R. Zelazek, *Central Missouri State University*

Introduction to the Foundations of American Education

Part

1

Professional Aspects of Teaching

Dreamcatcher

ANGELA is completing her student teaching and will soon graduate from her teacher education program. According to her supervisors, she has been an outstanding student teacher. And like the Native American dreamcatcher that separates good dreams from bad ones, Angela has the ability to separate good educational ideas from bad ones. We believe she has earned the title of "Dreamcatcher Student Teacher," and we have asked her to share her thoughts on student teaching with you.

When I first entered what was to become my classroom for the next five months, I saw twenty-seven eager faces staring up at me. The children were all from different backgrounds, and each one had unique ideas and goals. At that moment, dozens of questions rushed through my mind. How will I reach each child? How will I know if they understand? What will I do if a student does not comprehend? At that point, I realized my students would become my number one priority, and sleep would be my last.

As a student teacher, you are faced with three different constituents: cooperating teacher, students, and university supervisor. Engage everyone with an open mind, get involved, and be willing to try everything. Be flexible, honest, and patient, and most of all be a good listener.

Fortunately, my cooperating teacher was an experienced and knowledgeable professional with attitudes similar to mine. Both of us enjoy change and believe in doing whatever is necessary to benefit the students. She was straightforward and honest about my performance from day one.

With respect to your students, never underestimate a child's potential. Get to know each student individually. Learn how to be fair to every child. Consequences and rewards must count for everyone. If you let one child slide, all the children will think it is okay to slack off. Always acknowledge good performance, for this will help each child to succeed. Your attitude and feelings play a big part in the overall class atmosphere. Great things will happen because you believe they will happen! A positive and enthusiastic personality will go far in creating a good learning environment.

The university supervisor can be a source of encouragement and information. Keep close ties with your supervisor, and try to converse once a week about progress and problems within in the classroom.

Teaching is not a 9–3 job. You will find yourself always thinking of new ways to teach even the most basic concepts, not to mention grading papers, preparing lessons, gathering materials, and maintaining an open line of communication with parents.

Student teaching seemed overwhelming at first. There was so much to do that I often wondered how I would get it all accomplished. My advice is to stay focused, be organized, and accept the support of family and friends. A personal computer can be a big help in preparing the necessary classroom materials.

You will know you have succeeded if after five months you can honestly say you are able to accept failure. Learn from it and move on. Not every approach will succeed and not every lesson will make sense, but you will know all the time and energy has been well spent when you hear a student exclaim, "I *can* do this!"

While I will never forget Mrs. Greive and her third-grade class for giving me the opportunity to grow and learn, it was only the beginning!

Angela M. Raiff

Teachers and Teaching as a Career

Focus Questions

1. What makes teachers so important in a democratic society?
2. What are the characteristics of the best teachers you ever had?
3. Why do you want to be a teacher?
4. What can you do to effectively document what you see in schools and classrooms?
5. If you were asked to prepare a portfolio about your potential to be an outstanding teacher, what would you include?

Key Terms and Concepts

Classroom analysis systems: Clearly defined sets of procedures and written materials that can be used to analyze the interaction between teachers and students.

Educated citizenry: A goal according to which all members of our society are capable of participating intelligently in its direction and development.

Hypothesis: A proposed relationship between two or more events or qualities.

Information age: A dynamic view of society that emphasizes the problems of dealing with vast amounts of changing information.

Portfolio: A compilation for a specific purpose of the works, records, and accomplishments that a student prepares about his/her learnings, performances, and contributions.

Public confidence: The underlying trust that people have in their institutions.

Structured observations: Those judgments or impressions that are conducted according to a predetermined plan.

Teacher self-concept: How teachers view their participation in the profession of education.

Teacher stress: A condition that results from the many forces and pressures experienced through work as an educator.

Discussion Question 1:
Name three to five reasons why you want to become a teacher.

Test Questions 1.1–1.14

Objective 1:
Articulate the importance of teachers, not only to children, but to parents and the society at large.

Information Note 1.1:
There are over 2.4 million teachers in the United States. They are an important part of the work force in their community and the nation, as well as important to the children in their classrooms.

Activity 1.1:
Ask students to recall one teacher from their past whom they admire. Have each student identify characteristics that made the teacher important. Then ask students to share these characteristics and compare them to those noted in the text. How do the students' reasons compare with those mentioned in the text?

CNN Clip 1:
Teach for America

Objective 2:
Describe ways that teachers are important to children, the nation in the Information Age, and in the Global Economy.

Key Term:
Educated citizenry

Welcome to teacher education and the world of teaching. As you can see from the number of chapters and topics covered in this text, there is much to learn about becoming a teacher. In this first chapter you will begin the exploration of what you need to know to become an outstanding teacher; we will discuss the social condition of schools, list some of the positive and negative aspects of teaching, and provide a number of specific suggestions for tasks and activities that you can do to further clarify your aspirations and plans.

Teachers in America

Teachers play an extremely important role in our society. In this chapter, we will briefly explore why this is so, and we will also look at a variety of other interesting information about how the public views teachers, what teachers actually do, and how teachers view their profession.

The Importance of Teachers in Our Society

Teaching is one of the most important careers in any democratic society. In fact, a democracy is totally dependent on an **educated citizenry** that is well informed about the many political issues that must be resolved by the society. Furthermore, people in a democracy must feel that voting and participating in other ways in the democratic process are important—an attitude that must somehow be learned. Our nation looks to our teachers to provide the education essential to sustaining our democratic society.

To Our Children. It has often been said that our nation's most important natural resource is our children. Parents, legislators, and our society in general feel

Teachers play a crucial role in the lives of individuals and in the world at large.

that education is essential for our nation's children. Children must learn the basics, but they also must be cultured, nurtured, and inspired. Each child must be allowed to learn at her or his own pace, but all must be challenged—and accomplishing both tasks is extremely difficult because no two children are alike. In fact, our children—coming from multicultural backgrounds—are wonderfully diverse.

In the Information Age. Each year our society becomes more complex. In fact, we now live in what is often called an **information age**, in which knowledge has been expanded so much that managing the huge amount of available information is one of our largest problems. This rapid expansion of knowledge has required that citizens become information managers. Whom does our society expect to provide the education needed by our youth to help them function well in this capacity? If your answer is teachers, you are absolutely correct.

To Our Nation's Economy. Teachers play an extremely important role in our national economy in at least two major ways. It is well established that better educated people earn more money during their lifetimes. Teachers also contribute to the economy by providing the educated workers for our nation's businesses. Needless to say, the U.S. industrial complex simply could not function without a constant supply of workers who possess good basic skills. Interestingly, some states have recently increased their financial support of schools as catalysts for the development of high-tech industry.

In a Global Society. No longer can the role of teachers and schools be thought of only in terms of the national interest. Developing global awareness is crucial to our economic and political well-being. Teachers must understand and help their students learn about the complexities of the international system. Development of knowledge about world cultures, international events, and appreciation of the

Focus Question 1:
What makes teachers so important to a democratic society?

Key Term:
Information age

Journal Activity Master 1.1: Being a Teacher. The objective of this activity is to help the student formulate a snapshot of the teaching process through a self-reflective analysis of teaching activities.

American students today must be prepared to compete and coexist with students from all other societies in the world.

PROFESSIONAL DILEMMA

Should There Be a National Index to Rate Schools?

Should you be able to turn to your local newspaper, weekly news magazine or CNN and find a ranking of schools? We rank baseball teams and tennis players, and *U.S. News and World Report* annually offers rankings of colleges, hospitals, and mutual funds. We have the Dow Jones Index for stocks, and the odds makers in Las Vegas rank the chances of horses, football teams, and politicians being victorious. Should there also be an index for rating schools? The "Johnson-Hall" Index for schools has the high school you graduated from rated at a score of 235. The school where you will be student teaching has an index of 157.

Would having an index help you decide on the school where you want to teach? As a parent, would having an index help you choose the school where you will send your children? We don't have such a system for schools as of now, but what if we did? What kinds of factors should be built into such an index? The Dow Jones Index for the stock market is a sampling of traditional industrial stocks. There are other stock indices that look at growth stocks, computer stocks, and international markets. What would be the items you would use to construct a state or national Quality School Index?

James Gutherie[1] (1993) has proposed that a "national education index" be created. This would be a report card of how well public education is doing. Gutherie suggested the following set of composite indicators that would make up this national education index:

> *Student Performance* is the obvious place to start. The aspects chosen for inclusion in the composite indicator of student performance would require some deliberation. Would it be grades

diversities and commonalities of human values and interests are important content for the classrooms of today and essential aspects of the classrooms of the future. Developing a global perspective will mean major changes in how curriculum and courses are organized; there will be increasing emphasis on comparative and multinational perspectives, rather than on primarily American ones. The students of today will be employed in a global economy, and of necessity, they will need to have a wider knowledge base and global perspective.

Today's educators rely on the cooperation and support of parents.

How the Public Views Our Schools

Perhaps the most famous educational survey in the United States is that conducted each year by the Gallup Poll to determine the public's attitude toward our public school system. The twenty-sixth such poll has revealed a number of facts that should be of interest to people planning a teaching career.

One question that is always of interest to educators is: "Students are often given the grade A, B, C, D, and Fail to denote the quality of their work. Suppose the public schools in this community were graded in the same way? What grade would you give the public schools here—A, B, C, D, or Fail?" Table 1.1 shows the responses to this question over the past decade. The good news is that in recent years, the public has given our public schools pretty good grades. The bad news is that many Americans do not feel our public schools are doing a good job.

Another interesting question relates to what the public perceives to be the biggest problems faced by their local public schools. Table 1.2 on page 8 shows

only, or would it include a national exam? What subjects would be included? And what about using the results of individual versus group work?

Public support for education is important too. Logically, there is a link between students' doing better and the amount of community support for the schools. How would this composite indicator be measured? Would you use public opinion polls, the amount of expenditure on schools, and/or the amount of voter turnout for school board elections?

The living conditions of children are strongly related to how well they will do in school. To what extent are children seen as a resource and a critical part of the nation's long-term success? Extent of poverty, crime, family stability, attitudes, and confidence all could be included in this composite indicator.

Quality of educational service is another obvious indicator. Measurement could be made of the quality and adequacy of school buildings; the extent of professional preparation of school personnel; the kinds of science laboratories; the condition of the library; and the availability of early childhood, after-school, and extracurricular programs.

- What would be some of the advantages to having such a national index? What would be some of the disadvantages?
- What factors would you want to see included in such an index? What factors should not be included?
- Who should pay for this national index of schools? Taxpayers, the media, parents, teachers, state legislatures, or someone else?
- What difference would it make if there were a national index? More specifically, what difference would it make to you?

the responses to this question. As you can see, fighting/violence/gangs and lack of discipline are viewed as the biggest problems. These are followed by lack of proper financial support, and drug abuse and standards/quality of education. These problems are discussed in greater detail elsewhere in the book. For now, this table serves as a summary of what the public perceives to be the biggest public school problems at this time.

Objective 3:
Discuss how teachers are viewed by students, parents, and the general public.

Discussion Question 2:
What are "typical" students' impressions of teachers?

TABLE 1.1   Ratings Given the Local Public Schools

	1994	1993	1992	1991	1990	1989	1988	1987	1986	1985	1984	1983
A&B	44%	47%	40%	42%	41%	43%	40%	43%	41%	43%	42%	31%
A	9	10	9	10	8	8	9	12	11	9	10	6
B	35	37	31	32	33	35	31	31	30	34	32	25
C	30	31	33	33	34	33	34	30	28	30	35	32
D	14	11	12	10	12	11	10	9	11	10	11	13
FAIL	7	4	5	5	5	4	4	4	5	4	4	7
Don't Know	5	7	10	10	8	9	12	14	15	13	8	17

Source: Stanley M. Elan, Lowell C. Rose, and Alec M. Gallup, "The 26th Annual Gallup Poll of the Public's Attitude Toward the Public Schools." *Phi Delta Kappan,* September 1994, p. 45.

TABLE 1.2	What do you think are the biggest problems with which the public schools of this community must deal?

Problems	National Totals	No Children in School	Public School Parents	Nonpublic School Parents
Fighting/violence/gangs	18%	19%	16%	17%
Lack of discipline	18	18	17	22
Lack of proper financial support	13	12	16	9
Drug abuse	11	11	13	7
Standards/quality of education	8	8	5	11
Overcrowded schools	7	5	11	10
Lack of family structure/ problems of home life*	5	5	3	4
Crime/vandalism	4	5	4	3
Pupils' lack of interest/ truancy/poor attitudes	3	3	3	5
Parents' lack of support/ interest	3	4	2	3
Difficulty in getting good teachers	3	4	2	2
Poor curriculum/low curriculum standards	3	2	3	2
Lack of respect	3	2	3	1
Integration/segregation, racial discrimination	3	3	2	2
There are no problems	1	1	2	2
Miscellaneous**	9	9	8	13
Don't know	11	12	9	11

*New category

**A total of 33 different kinds of problems were mentioned by 2% or fewer respondents.

(Figures add to more than 100 percent because of multiple answers.)

Source: Stanley M. Elan, Lowell C. Rose, and Alec M. Gallup, "The 26th Annual Phi Delta Kappa/Gallup Poll of the Public's Attitudes Toward the Public Schools." *Phi Delta Kappan,* September 1994, p. 43.

Activity 1.2:
Have students take on different roles in contemporary society. Assign some to be lawyers, police officers, politicians, health care workers, truckdrivers, unemployed single parents, and so on. Then ask them to identify the expectations they would have for teachers, given the role that they were assigned.

Test Questions 1.15–1.35

A Look at American Teachers

Teachers are individuals and therefore differ from one another a great deal. In fact, it is very difficult to generalize about teachers in the United States. However, in an effort to help you better understand the nature of American teachers, let's look at some of their similarities and differences.

Profile of the Public School Teacher

There are 2.4 million public school teachers in the United States. Slightly over one-half of them teach at the elementary school level. Besides our large number of public school teachers, there are an additional 350,000 private school teachers and about 750,000 college and university teachers in the United States. Added to this total are over 800,000 other administrative and professional staff. It is also estimated that there are over a million education-related jobs in the United States, including such positions as education specialists in industry, instructional technologists in the military, museum educators, and training consultants in the business world.

Altogether, we have roughly five million educators in the country, ranking education as one of the largest professions in the United States. It is estimated, however, that about 6 percent of our teachers leave the classroom each year for various reasons (retirement, resignations, poor health, etc.). So roughly 300,000 new educators are needed just to replace those leaving the profession each year.

Interest in Teaching Careers. Some experts feel that rising salaries and new respect for teachers are slowly helping to make teaching a more attractive profession. The Higher Education Research Institute at UCLA annually conducts a survey of college freshmen that, among other things, asks what career the student is planning to pursue. Figure 1.1 shows the results of this survey for the last twenty-seven years. In 1966, nearly 25 percent of freshmen were interested in becoming secondary school teachers compared to fewer than 5 percent today. Likewise, in 1966 about 9 percent of college freshmen expressed an interest in elementary teaching compared to about 5.3 percent today. Of course, this can be partly explained by the fact that our country experienced an oversupply of teachers and hence a poor job market during this period. The apparent downturn in 1993 in

Objective 4:
Develop a general understanding of who become teachers, the conditions of teaching, and some of the important characteristics of today's teachers.

Information Note 1.2:
An increasing proportion of the students in teacher education are "nontraditional." In some programs they may be more than 50 percent of the students. Being over the age of twenty-five, they bring broader ranges of background experiences to teacher education and teaching.

Objective 5:
Present a list of common reasons for becoming a teacher.

Focus Question 2:
What are the characteristics of the best teachers you ever had?

Focus Question 3:
Why do you want to be a teacher?

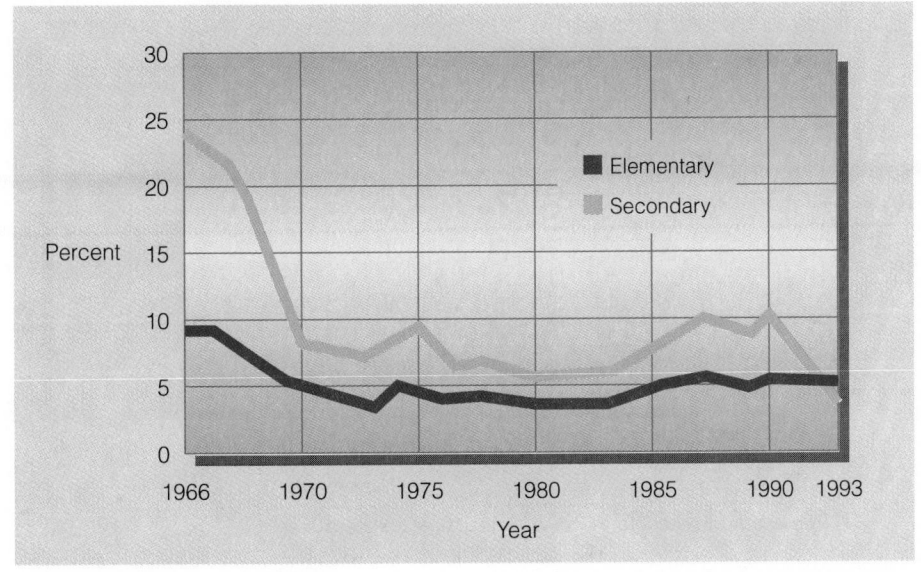

FIGURE 1.1

Freshmen Interested in Teaching Careers (percentages by level, 1966–1993)

(*Source: The American Freshman: National Norms for Fall 1993.* Higher Education Research Institute, UCLA Graduate School of Education, Los Angeles, CA 90024-1521. Reproduced with permission of the Higher Education Research Institute, Graduate School of Education, University of California, Los Angeles, CA.)

freshman interest in secondary teaching as a career could be either a short-term anomaly in the survey or an indicator that there will be fewer graduates in teacher education in the near future. If the latter is the case, then in the next several years there will once again be a shortage of teachers. Teacher demand will increase because the number of school-age children is increasing as the 1990s unfold. In fact, there are shortages already in some states and in most urban areas. This bodes well for today's teacher education students. They will likely find a strong job market, a choice of teaching positions available, and good teacher salaries upon graduation.

Transparency 2:
Reasons for Becoming a Teacher

Reasons for Becoming a Teacher. There are many reasons why people wish to become teachers. In one recent survey teachers were asked to compare their original reasons for becoming a teacher with their reasons for continuing to teach. The primary reason for deciding to teach was the desire to work with young people (70 percent), which is probably one of your reasons too. The most impressive finding from this survey is that the primary reason teachers continue to teach is the desire to work with young people (78 percent). Teaching seems to be one of the few professions where the expectations of those who wish to join are matched with what the job is really like.

Transparency 1:
Profile of New Teachers

Teacher Demographics in the United States. In the United States, public school teachers are older and more likely to have advanced degrees than are private elementary school teachers. A recent survey by the National Center for Educational Statistics points out many interesting differences between public and private school teachers in this country, some of which are shown in Figure 1.2. This report, entitled *Background Experience Characteristics of Public and Private School Teachers,* shows that private schools have fewer minority teachers than public schools.

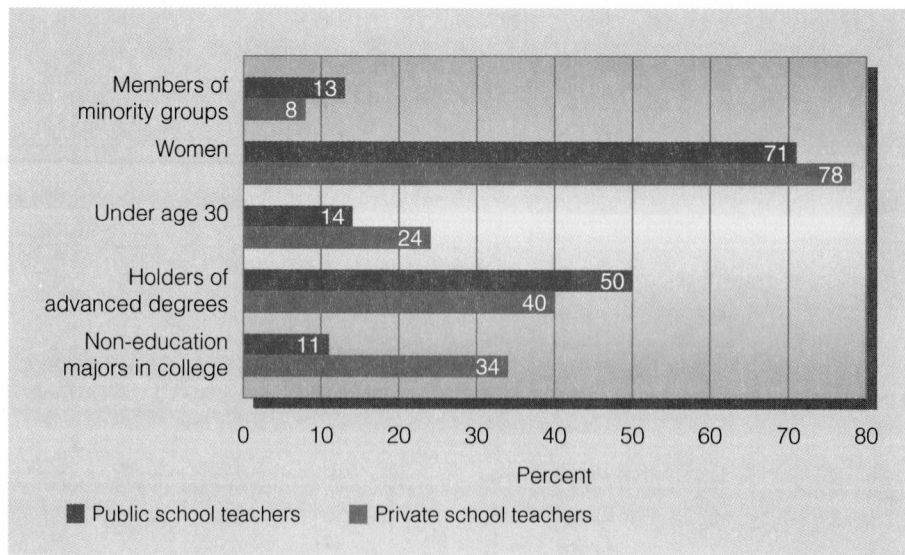

FIGURE 1.2

Differences between Public and Private School Teachers

(*Source:* The National Center for Education Statistics.)

Global Perspectives: Teaching in the United States versus in Other Countries.

American schools and student achievement are often compared with those in other countries. One recent study examined the differences in the preparation of teachers and the conditions of teaching in the United States and other economically advanced nations. Among the findings were that American teachers work longer hours and teach more classes. Elementary teachers in the United States spend more time with their students than teachers in the eighteen other countries studied. At the secondary level, teachers in the United States, Britain, and The Netherlands had the largest teaching loads—five classes, five days a week. Thus, teachers in Japan and the European nations have more time for class preparation during the school day. Interestingly, American high school teachers have less training than teachers in other countries. While U.S. high school teachers need a four-year college degree, in many European countries teachers in the upper secondary grades are required to spend five or six years in preparation at the college level. Teachers in the United States work an average of 185 days, while the international averages ranged from 190 to 195 days. However, U.S. teachers work more hours per week.[2]

CNN **Clip 2:**
Student Stress

Diversity Note 1.1:
Teaching in another country is a fantastic way to learn more about diversity.

Factors That Drive Teachers from the Classroom.

Historically, a high percentage of teachers who begin working in a classroom decide that teaching is not the profession they wish to pursue. Figure 1.3 shows that the main reasons why teachers leave the classroom are "students' social problems make teaching too difficult" and "need or want to earn more money." Other factors that contribute to teachers' leaving the classroom are "lack of administrative support" and a feeling that "teaching has become boring and less satisfying." This information reveals some of the more negative aspects of a teaching career—information you should consider seriously as you decide if you want to enter this profession.

Activity 1.3:
Ask students to name the top three reasons that they think drive teachers away from teaching. Then review the reasons presented in Figure 1.3. Contrast the reasons reported in the survey with those offered by your students.

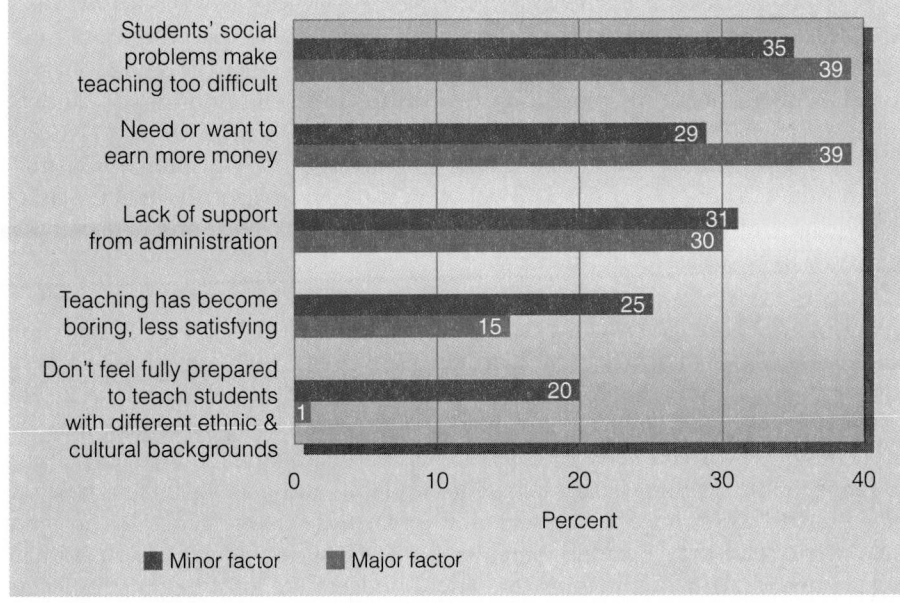

FIGURE 1.3

Factors That Drive Out Teachers

(*Source: The Metropolitan Life Survey of the American Teacher, 1991: Coming to Terms—Teachers' Views on Current Issues in Education.* New York: Louis Harris and Associates.)

Responsibilities outside the classroom such as grading papers can often be an unexpected burden for new teachers.

Objective 6:
Identify and examine key aspects of the work and career patterns of teachers.

Transparency 3:
Essential Knowledge and Skills for Teachers

More Respect for Teachers. A number of surveys have shown that teachers are respected more today than they were over the past few decades. This is probably due to the fact that teachers are better prepared and have more skills. The Carnegie Foundation recently polled 13,000 teachers to determine whether the last five years of educational reform have had any effects on the respect that teachers receive from the general public. The results of this poll indicate that, while teachers have many problems and feel a need for improvement in many aspects of their working conditions, the recent educational reform movement has brought about at least minor improvements in the working conditions of the teacher, and in the respect they command from the public.

Teachers and Teaching

It is important for you, as someone planning to be a teacher, to explore what teachers must be able to do and to find out first hand what it is like to be a beginning teacher. This information will help you decide if you have the attributes needed to be an effective teacher and what skills you will need to develop.

What a Teacher Must Be Able to Do. Whereas teaching has historically been thought of as an art, in recent years it has moved increasingly in the direction of becoming a science, thanks to the advances of research. The effective schools research, discussed further in later sections of this book, suggests that there are a number of discernible things that a teacher needs to know and be able to do to be successful. For example, the North Carolina Teacher Performance Appraisal System requires that teachers be evaluated on the following eight functions: (1) Management of instructional time, (2) Management of student behavior, (3) Instructional presentation, (4) Instructional monitoring of student performance, (5) Instructional feedback, (6) Facilitating instruction, (7) Communicating within the educational environment, and (8) Performing noninstructional duties. These categories will give you a rough idea of the major sets of knowledge and skills that you will need to learn about, practice, and perfect if you are going to be a successful teacher.

Teachers as Decision Makers. A recent study by the Carnegie Foundation for the Advancement of Teaching, based on a survey of 22,000 American teachers, helps to shed light on the type of decisions that teachers help to make in our schools. A part of this survey is shown in Table 1.3, which shows that teachers are fairly heavily involved in choosing textbooks and instructional materials, helping to shape the curriculum, setting behavior standards, and making student tracking decisions. However, this survey also shows that teachers are generally not very involved in selecting new administrators, helping to select new teachers, evaluating teacher performance, making the school budget decisions, helping to decide promotion/retention policies, or designing in-service programs. These are inter-

TABLE 1.3   Teachers and Decision Making

Activity	Involved	Not Very Involved	Most Involved	Least Involved
Choosing textbooks and instructional materials	79%	21%	93% (VT)	61% (MD)
Shaping the curriculum	63	37	85 (VT)	40 (LA)
Setting behavior standards	47	53	68 (OR)	37 (FL, NJ, RI)
Making tracking decisions	45	55	63 (MN)	36 (LA)
Designing inservice programs	43	57	82 (OK)	30 (RI)
Setting promotion/retention policies	34	66	50 (VT)	21 (FL)
Deciding school budgets	20	80	57 (HI)	8 (ND)
Evaluating teacher performance	10	90	20 (GA, UT)	6 (FL, NV, NJ, RI)
Selecting new teachers	7	93	20 (CO, NH, OR)	1 (LA)
Selecting new administrators	7	93	20 (VT)	1 (NV)

Source: The Carnegie Foundation for the Advancement of Teaching, 1987 National Survey of Public School Teachers.

esting findings, since one of the outcomes of current educational reform initiatives deals with the goal of empowering teachers in many of these areas.

Teachers as Artists.   While there are many technical skills a teacher must have, our very best teachers possess more elusive qualities that set them apart from the average educator. These qualities include a passion to help students learn, a genuine love of learning, and an overall enthusiasm for teaching that is reflected in their everyday work with students. Theorists speculate that these more ambiguous qualities of outstanding teachers cannot be taught in the same sense as technical teaching skills, but rather, are innately found in some individuals, probably partly inherited and partly gradually developed as a result of total life experiences. These qualities also give rise to the statement you have undoubtedly heard that "good teachers are born and not made." The truth is that you can learn and continue to refine technical teaching skills, as well as improve the more elusive attitudes and values that will enable you to become an outstanding educator.

Career Patterns for Educators.   People who become teachers bring a surprising variety of background experiences and interests with them to the profes-

Journal Activity Master 1.2: A Teacher Interview. This activity requires the student to interview a teacher who is in the same field as the student's major and to record and analyze the results of the interview.

Relevant Research

Teacher Expectations and Student Achievement

Researchers have studied teacher expectations for the last twenty-five years. Early studies of teacher expectations and student achievement have led educators to emphasize the importance of having high expectations for all students.

A recent study of teacher expectations by Goldenberg (1992) revealed that teacher expectations can be a mitigating factor. Goldenberg studied two first-grade Hispanic girls in the same classroom. The teacher held low expectations for one girl and high expectations for the other. Contrary to the theme of the earlier expectations studies, the student that had lower teacher expectations did well in reading achievement, while the student with high teacher expectations did not do well! Goldenberg observed the students and the teacher carefully for long periods of time and was able to explain why these unexpected findings occurred, as well as point out a very important lesson about the way more effective teachers teach.

Goldenberg observed that although the teacher held different expectations for the two students, the teacher's behaviors were not influenced in the same way. The teacher worked very hard to help the low-expectation student engage with and complete assignments. The teacher understood that this student would need extra attention. At the same time, although the high-expectation student was not completing assignments, the teacher "assumed" that she would succeed and so did not monitor and push the student. The result was that the low-expectation student succeeded and the high-expectation student did not.

Goldenberg concluded: "My principal contention is that the teacher's behavior is what matters—what a teacher expects matters less than what a teacher does" (p. 522). A teacher may rightly expect some students to do less well than others, but the teacher must make every effort to see that *all* students achieve.

Sources: R. Rosenthal and L. Jacobson. *Pygmalion in the Classroom.* New York: Holt, Rinehart & Winston, 1968.

Ray Rist, "Student Social Class and Teacher Expectations: The Self-Fulfilling Prophecy in Ghetto Education," *Harvard Educational Review 40* (1970): 411–451.

Claude Goldenberg, "The Limits of Expectations: A Case for Case Knowledge about Teacher Expectancy Effects." *American Educational Research Journal 29* (3) (1992): 517–544.

Key Term:
Teacher stress

Transparency 4:
Reducing the Uncertainties of Teaching: Four Strategies

sion. Some knew from an early age that they wanted to become teachers and concentrated on achieving that goal. Others come to teaching after having worked in business, the military, or government. Currently, a large proportion of teacher education students are *nontraditional,* that is, persons who are over the age of twenty-five. Many have had some sort of teaching-related experience before beginning their initial teacher education program. For example, many have had the opportunity to be peer tutors while in elementary or secondary school. Others have taught as a part of their work in industry, or through their church or synagogue, and some have served as classroom aides. The richer your background of teaching-related experience, the better prepared you will be to take advantage of your teacher education program.

Teacher Stress. A common condition among educators that results from the pressure-filled work they do is called **teacher stress**. Most teachers deal with large numbers of vastly different students, a shortage of time, unhappy parents, numerous colleagues, and the impossible task of teaching every student all that he or she can possibly learn regarding each subject. It is only in recent times that the education profession has come to recognize and admit that most teachers suffer from being overstressed from time to time. Most experts claim that the first step to reducing stress is to acknowledge its presence and begin to search for its source. Some larger schools are even hiring professionals to help teachers and administrators to cope with their stressful assignments. Typically, these counselors advise teachers to become more realistic about what they can accomplish. Other suggestions include the following:

- Give yourself a break. Take time off for trips to the bathroom, lunch breaks, and/or nutritious snacks. Before or after lunch, walk around the block or out to the football stadium to get some fresh air and a change of scenery.
- Prepare for discipline problems. "If you have difficult kids, work out a strategy with the guidance counselor or principal before behavior problems begin,"

Ashton urges. "That way, you'll know exactly what you're going to do ahead of time."

- Make a schedule of meetings, and then adhere to it. "Teachers have to schedule their phone calls and conferences," Ashton recommends. "They should set the meeting time, set the tone, set the agenda, and stick to it. I think that helps to diminish the sense that they're always at someone's beck and call."
- Talk to colleagues. Teachers need to find a network inside or outside of school for support and professional companionship.
- Limit the time you spend working at home. "Give yourself permission to take time off," Ashton says. Respect your limits, even if it means letting things go undone.
- Exercise. Regular exercise or activity will help release some of the tension that builds up during the day.
- Ask for help. When stress at school or home becomes overwhelming, consider talking to a professional counselor.[3]

Discussion Question 3:
What differences do you think teachers can make in your community, your state, the nation, and the world at large?

New Teacher Expectations and Ideals. Surveys of American teachers conducted by the Metropolitan Life Insurance Company indicate that teachers generally love to teach—in spite of all the problems and frustrations in our schools. In 1991 this series of teacher surveys was directed toward teachers who had just completed their first year of teaching. Since you may be in that situation in the near future, we will discuss some of the reactions new teachers had to their first year in the classroom.

This survey asked teachers who had completed their first year "what things might have been more helpful in your teacher preparation program in preparing you to be successful in the classroom?" Figure 1.4 shows the results of that question, and indicates that they could have used more help from a skilled, experienced teacher, more practical training such as a year's internship before having their own class, and better training in working with students and families from a variety of ethnic backgrounds.

Activity 1.4:
Place students in small groups and ask them to make a list of the different things that teachers need to do in their job role. As they near completion, ask them to place a check by all of the items on their lists that deal directly with teaching children. Ask them to place a star by anything that pertains to events outside the classroom.

Test Questions 1.36–1.54

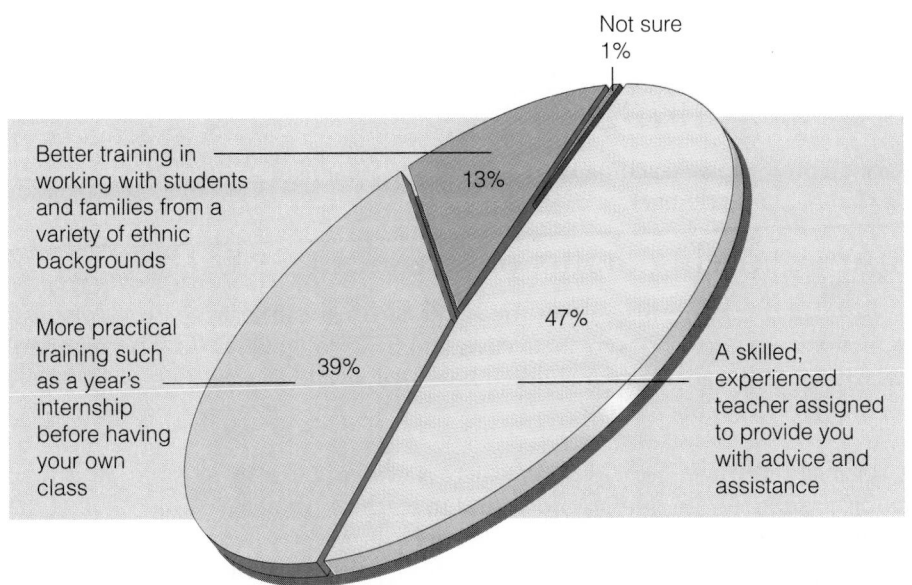

Not sure
1%

Better training in working with students and families from a variety of ethnic backgrounds

13%

More practical training such as a year's internship before having your own class

39%

47%

A skilled, experienced teacher assigned to provide you with advice and assistance

Transparency 5:
What Would Have Been Most Helpful in Preparing You to Be a Teacher?

FIGURE 1.4

What Would Have Been Most Helpful in Preparing You to Be a More Effective Teacher?

(*Source: The Metropolitan Life Survey of the American Teacher, 1991: Coming to Terms—Teachers' Views on Current Issues in Education*, p. 15.)

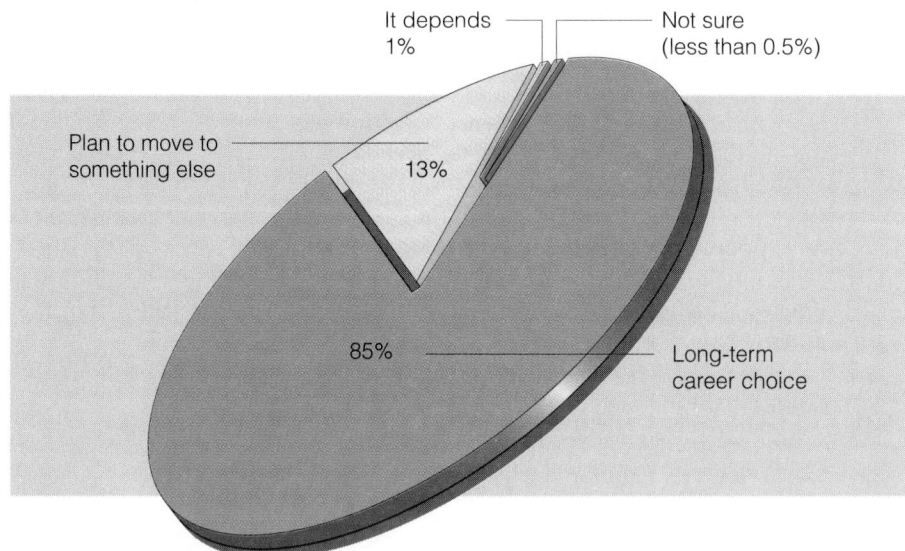

It depends
1%

Not sure
(less than 0.5%)

Plan to move to
something else

13%

85%

Long-term
career choice

FIGURE 1.5

**Career Plans of First-Year
Teachers**

(*Source: The Metropolitan Life Survey
of the American Teacher, 1991: The
First Year: New Teachers' Expectations and Ideals*, p. 19.)

Objective 7:
Understand that the profession of teaching is evolving,
as is reflected in recent
changes in the status, work
conditions, and bases for
teacher assessment.

Information Note 1.3:
Changes in the teaching profession include increased
emphasis on standards and
licensure by states. Now is
the time for future teachers to
begin compiling information
about development as a
teacher.

Diversity Note 1.2:
Population demographics are
changing too. For example,
minorities will be a majority of
Californians by the year 2000,
while Texas is projected to
turn "majority minority" before
2015.

Discussion Question 4:
What are key characteristics
of teachers you have known
that you would like to emulate? What is one thing that
you would not want to do?

This study also found out that virtually all first-year teachers believe that all children can learn, and it determined that teachers of low-income and minority students more often believe that family and other outside agencies present signif-icant barriers to student learning. Another interesting finding was that, even among the best teachers, there is a general belief that it is difficult to do an excel-lent job of teaching with more than two-thirds of the students that a typical teacher encounters.

Last, these first-year teachers were asked about their long-term plans for a teaching career. Figure 1.5 shows the response to that question and indicates that the vast majority were not discouraged by their first year in the classroom and did plan long-term careers as teachers.

Recent Changes in the Teaching Profession

Like all professions, teaching has changed considerably in recent years. Let's look at some of these changes.

The Improving Status of American Teachers

If is difficult to generalize about the status of American teachers. Everyone can remember teachers who were ineffective, and nearly all parents have been unhap-py with certain teachers their children have had. Even so, teachers have generally been respected in our society.

Increased Public Confidence. There is evidence that there is a good deal of **public confidence** in public schools and in teachers. The 1994 Gallup Poll of the Public's Attitudes toward the Public Schools shows that people generally think highly of their local schools. This information, presented in Table 1.1, also shows that people generally grade our nation's schools lower than they do their own local schools. This may be the result of a tendency of the media to dwell on the problems of schools more than the successes. It is also worth noting that the public's attitude toward our schools has been improving steadily over the past ten years. These facts should be encouraging to anyone contemplating a teaching career.

Improving Job Opportunities. An entire chapter is devoted to teacher supply and demand and salaries later in this part of the book; however, some information on these topics will be presented at this time to support a contention—that job opportunities and salaries for teachers have improved significantly in recent years. These changes have been sufficiently dramatic to improve the status of American teachers.

Objective 8:
Provide examples of ways that the status of teaching has improved in recent years.

Key Term:
Public confidence

Better Working Conditions for Teachers

The working conditions for many teachers have not always been good. Fortunately, they have improved measurably in recent years, and the following sections will show you some of the ways in which these improvements are coming about. This information represents "good news" to those who are preparing for careers in the education field.

Objective 9:
Describe recent improvements in the work conditions of teachers.

Discussion Question 5:
What can teachers do that will make a positive difference in the public's perceptions of teachers?

Better Salaries. Among the good news for new graduates of teacher education programs, teachers' salaries are improving and will likely continue to do so for some time into the future. For example, teacher salaries nationwide have risen 25 percent in recent years, according to a survey conducted by the American Federation of Teachers. Even when corrected for inflation, this figure amounts to a significant increase. We do not mean to say that teachers are currently overpaid—or for that matter, even adequately paid. Salary and its adequacy will very likely be debated as long as schools exist. The point is, however, that teachers' salaries have risen substantially. Furthermore, given the growing shortage of teachers, the laws of supply and demand will very likely continue to improve teachers' salaries for some time into the future—a phenomenon that will help to improve the status of American teachers.

Student Respect for Teachers. The extent to which students respect teachers is very difficult to determine and to generalize. Obviously, most students respect some teachers. Also, it is clear that some teachers are more respected by students than others. Likewise, the degree to which a given teacher is respected by students depends on many variables such as the given school, the nature of the students in each class, the personality and skills of the other teachers, and even the nature of the subject being taught.

A recent survey by the *Weekly Reader* of 90,000 students in grades 2 through 9 found that 55 percent of the students liked their teachers, but only 35 percent liked their school "a lot." The survey also found that younger students are generally more positive than older students.

Insight into what students like about teachers can be gleaned from a survey conducted by *Learning* magazine, which asked eighth graders in Michigan for tips for teachers. Students gave the following advice: Don't assign extra work to students who finish their work early; don't be mean; don't be overconfident; be patient; don't give up on students; let students go to the bathroom; be supportive and reassuring; have a sense of humor; don't leave the classroom; check on students while they work; correct papers with appropriate comments; be versatile; don't yell; be

TABLE 1.4   Teacher Satisfaction

Area of Satisfaction	Percent Satisfied
Contribution to society	85
Job security	84
Level of responsibility	82
Challenge	81
Appreciation by parents	68
Respect from students	67
Relaxed environment	59
Recognition from administrators	55
Prestige	38

Source: Survey of NEA K-12 Teacher Members 1985. (Washington, DC: National Education Association, p. 11.) Used by permission.

Activity 1.5:
Ask students to design a slo-gan, such as would be used in a television ad, to enhance the stature of teachers.

Key Term:
Teacher self-concept

CNN Clip 3:
Kentucky Schools

qualified in your subject area; don't be too intel-ligent; use textbooks; don't have class favorites; don't complain; dress neatly; and stay young.

In summary, there is considerable evidence to suggest that most students like and respect the majority of their teachers. This compliment should be good news to teacher education students in col-leges and universities throughout America.

Improving Teacher Self-Concept. The way teachers view their participation in their profession is commonly called **teacher self-concept.** In spite of the fact that teaching is a very demanding pro-fession, and even though educators are not paid as much as they should be, teachers generally feel good about themselves and their profession. This contention is supported by a recent study con-ducted by the National Education Association, in which teachers were asked about their level of sat-isfaction concerning a number of job variables. As Table 1.4 shows, teachers were most satisfied with their contribution to society and least satisfied with the pres-tige of their profession.

Teachers Taking Charge. A recent survey conducted by *Instructor Magazine* tallied the responses of nearly 32,000 teachers across the country regarding the degree of freedom they have as professionals.[4] One of the interesting findings of this survey concerned the freedom teachers have in selecting the instructional materials they use in the classroom. Figure 1.6 shows that 47 percent of the respondents indicated they select instructional materials in consultation with their colleagues, 41 percent indicated they have total freedom in such selection, while only 12 percent indicated they must follow a mandate when selecting instructional materials. In other words, teachers generally have considerable free-dom to select the materials that they will use in their classrooms.

Confidence, energy, and facility with a variety of teaching tools are some of the characteristics of excellent teachers.

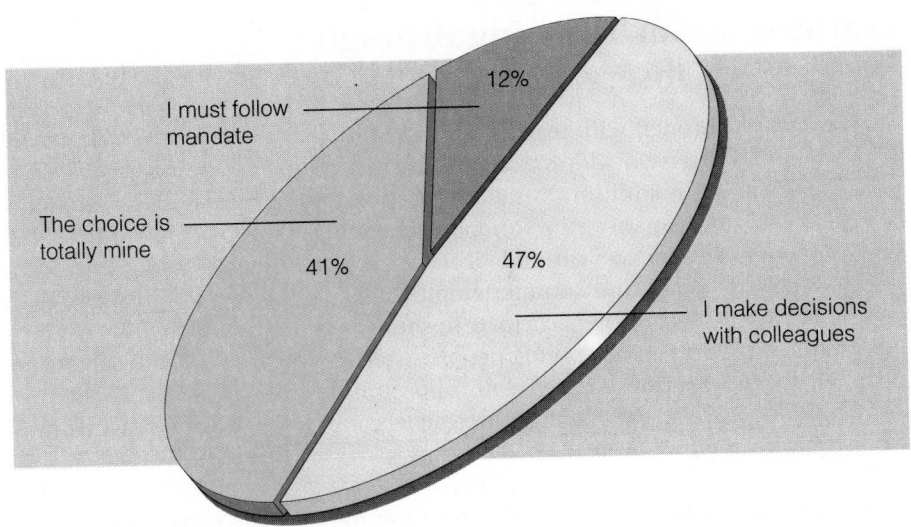

I must follow mandate

The choice is totally mine

41%

12%

47%

I make decisions with colleagues

FIGURE 1.6

How Much Freedom Do You Have in Selecting Instructional Materials?

(*Source:* Instructor Survey Results, *Instructor Magazine.* © 1990 by Scholastic Inc. Used by permission.)

Other findings from this survey include the following:

- 55 percent indicated that their schools had undergone a major shift in subject matter or instructional emphasis during the past three years.
- 73 percent indicated that the current move toward school/business partnerships is improving the educational program.
- 60 percent indicated that they did not believe that student achievement should play a role in determining the teacher's salary.
- 84 percent felt that higher teacher salaries would do more to raise the status of the teaching profession than anything else.
- 82 percent felt that the quality of teaching will improve when teachers become more involved in making curriculum decisions.

This survey, like many other typical teacher surveys, points out that teachers are slowly becoming more empowered as professional educators. This should be additional good news to college students who are preparing for careers in the teaching profession.

Activity 1.6:
Ask students to think of a time that someone "took charge" of a situation. What were the circumstances that surrounded this need to take charge? What were the characteristics of the person and the way that they took charge? Are there any implications for how teachers can take charge?

Developing Your Portfolio as You Learn about Teaching

A new educational and assessment strategy is to have students develop a **portfolio** of their accomplishments. Portfolios are compilations for a specific purpose of the works, records, and accomplishments that students prepare about what they have learned, performed, and contributed.

Portfolios are being used more frequently in teacher education too. Preservice teachers in their professional preparation programs are increasingly being asked to keep portfolios related to their development as teachers. School district employers are interested in reviewing portfolios of applicants for teaching positions, and states are requiring that teachers develop portfolios for submission when they request renewal of their teaching licenses. There are three key components to developing a professional portfolio: (1) observation and note taking, (2) reflecting on what you have done and learned, and (3) compiling the folio.

Objective 10:
Illustrate the different strategies that teachers use to learn more about their own teaching.

Key Term:
Portfolio

Learning about Teaching through Systematic Observation

Focus Question 4:
What can you do to effectively document what you see in schools and classrooms?

As you proceed through your teacher education program, you should seize every opportunity to observe a wide variety of activities related to the world of education. For instance, in addition to the observation and participation assignments that you will have as part of the formal teacher education program, you should seek out opportunities to visit and observe a wide variety of classrooms. You should also attempt to find summer employment that allows you to work with youth and/or teachers. If you participate in church or synagogue activities, perhaps you could volunteer to teach young people. We encourage you to think creatively of other ways to provide yourself with opportunities to learn more about your chosen profession by participating with teachers and by working with youth every chance you get.

Activity 1.7:
Contrast informal note taking with structured observations. Have students use both techniques during the next class.

Journal/Portfolio Development 1:
Interview a retired educator. Record and analyze his or her responses.

Informal Note Taking. One of the most common ways to collect information is by writing down your observations—in other words, taking notes. This can be done in a variety of ways. For instance, when you go into your classroom, you could start by writing a brief description of the setting, such as the physical appearance of the room, number of students, teaching devices, and so on. You can then systematically describe each of the things you observe. The more detail you can record, the more you will learn from the observations.

Create a list of questions before you begin any given observation. If you are interested in how a teacher motivates students during a particular lesson, write down the question: What techniques does the teacher use to help motivate students? You would subsequently record your observations under that question.

Observation of actual teachers in real teaching situations is a key element in good teacher training.

CASE STUDY TEACHING IS COMPLEX WORK

*C*ritics of teachers and schools often state that "anyone can teach." They point out how short the school year is, saying, "Teachers get two months of vacation." They exclaim about the short work day, "You are out of school as quick as the kids." And they harp about how simple the job of teaching is, "All you have to do is sit at a desk and tell them what you know." As much as we may wish, these simplistic stereotypes will not go away until teachers are able to explain in articulate ways what the job of teaching really entails.

A very interesting place to begin a presentation on the complexity of the work of teachers would be to look at a publication of the U.S. Department of Labor, the *Directory of Occupational Titles (DOT)*. This publication is a listing of different kinds of jobs. For each occupation, the DOT includes ratings of different aspects of the work and the needed qualifications of people who do the job. An education researcher, Brian Rowan, recently used this document to develop an analysis of how the work of teachers compared to work in other occupations.

In the DOT, three scales are used to define and analyze different occupations: (1) *worker functions*, which address the complexity of an occupation in relation to data, people, and things; (2) *general educational development*, a rating of the amount of knowledge that is required to perform the work, which includes reasoning development, mathematical development, and language development; and (3) *specific vocational preparation*, which addresses the amount of formal education and training that is required to do that occupation.

For the first Worker Functions subscale, "work with data," the highest scale options are: (0) synthesizing data, (1) coordinating, (2) compiling, (3) computing, and (4) copying. Teachers are rated a "2." On the second subscale, "work with people," the highest ranking are (0) mentoring, (1) negotiating, (2) instructing, and (3) supervising. On this subscale teachers are rated a "2." The third subscale of Worker Functions is "work with things," for which the scale rankings include (0) setting up, (2) precision working, (3) operating-controlling, (4) manipulating, (5) tending, (6) feeding-offbearing, and (7) handling. Teaching is rated a "7."

On the Knowledge and Preparation scales, again the work of teachers is seen as complex. They must be able to apply principles of logical or scientific thinking to define problems, collect data, and draw valid conclusions. Teachers must also be able to function at the highest range of skills in reading, writing, and speaking. And there is between two and four years of higher-level preparation to become a teacher.

In the concluding analysis, Rowan compared teaching with 591 occupations. When all of the occupations were rank-ordered, school teaching, both elementary and secondary, was placed just below the seventy-fifth percentile. Another way to view this analysis is that nearly 75 percent of the occupations studied were *less* complex than that of elementary and secondary school teaching.

This is a more objective analysis of how the occupation of teaching compares to many others. There are other ways that the challenges and complexities of the work of the teachers can be described and illustrated. How will you make the case when you are questioned? What aspects of teaching have you discovered already that illustrate the complexity of the work? One important dimension to consider is the number of people whose lives you will affect directly—your students and their parents. Later, these people will influence many others with what they have learned from you.

Source: Brian Rowan, "Comparing Teachers' Work with Work in Other Occupations; Notes on the Professional Status of Teaching." *Educational Researcher* 23 (6) (1994): 4–17.

Structured Observations. Observations that are conducted according to a predetermined plan are often referred to as **structured observations.** As your college or university sends you out into the schools for various laboratory experiences, you will probably be provided with guidelines that will help structure your observations. In fact, some colleges have developed written structured observations forms that will guide you when participating in clinical experiences. We recommend that you create your own structured observations forms around the questions that particularly intrigue you. In other words, if you are especially interested in classroom diversity, devise your own structured observations form that will remind you to look for details concerning that particular topic the next time you are in a classroom. In fact, it might be fun for you to create some structured observations forms that you can use with the professors in your college classes. The more aware you are of what you are looking for as you observe a classroom, the more you are likely to learn about that particular topic.

Observation Instruments. You might find it difficult to believe, but literally hundreds of structured observations instruments have been devised to help educators collect more valid data about classrooms. These observation instruments range from quite simple devices to extremely complex systems that require computers for analysis. Generally, however, they fall into two basic categories—structured interviews and classroom analysis systems.

Structured Interviews. Structured interviews consist of a series of specific questions that are asked of a respondent as well as some provision for recording the respondent's answer. You could prepare a series of important questions that you would like to ask a principal, teacher, student, parent, or anyone else connected with the educational enterprise. You must make sure that these questions are not ambiguous and that the respondent will clearly understand what you are asking. You would then seek out a number of respondents and interview them with the same structured interview technique. Obviously, the more people you surveyed through such a technique, the more representative your data would be for the population in general. If you asked only one teacher the question, "What is the single best discipline technique that you utilize in your classroom?" you would have only one idea, whereas if you asked one hundred teachers that same question, you would obtain much more representative data about effective discipline techniques used by teachers.

When doing a structured interview, you must be very careful to record your respondent's answers accurately. It is best to utilize a tape recorder, which you simply let run during your interview. In this way you obtain a complete record of the answers and can go back and listen to it many times later on. You can also write down your respondent's answers; however, unless you are adept at shorthand, it might be difficult for you to record answers accurately and completely.

Classroom Analysis Systems. Over the last fifty years, as researchers have attempted to more objectively understand what takes place in our schools, they have created many systems to study classroom activity. In general, **classroom analysis systems** come in two types: quantitative and qualitative. Quantitative systems use well-defined categories and coding procedures to count the occurrence of different teacher and student behaviors. Qualitative systems are more open ended, or descriptive.

Key Term:
Structured observation

Key Term:
Classroom analysis systems

Learning about Teaching through Observation, Analysis, and Reflection

Once you have collected observations of teaching, children, classrooms, and schools, it is very important to take time to think about what you have seen. There are several techniques for systematically analyzing your observations, but equally important is taking time to reflect on the analyses. In our rush to get everything done, we frequently fail to take time to thoughtfully examine our experiences and impressions. However, being serious about finding time to reflect is an important part of becoming an excellent teacher, and there are some processes that can be helpful.

Reflective Journals.   It is very important to keep a diary or journal in which you reflect, raise questions, and propose ideas related to your development as a teacher. You may be asked to keep a journal in some of your courses, but we encourage you to keep a professional journal regardless of course requirements. A journal is interesting to review from time to time to see how your thoughts, insights, and ideas have evolved. Do not be concerned about changes in your thoughts and opinions; the reflective journals of all outstanding teachers document a continuing evolution of questions, assumptions, and priorities.

Journal Activity Master 1.2: Interpreting Educational Data. The objective of this activity is to help the student experience (through a descriptive educational study) how first-hand data collection can challenge one's assumptions.

Summarizing Educational Information.   Regardless of the technique you use to record your educational observations, it is imperative that you take the time to study them. This is best done by rereading your recorded data many times. Once you have become thoroughly familiar with the content of your recorded data, you are ready to begin summarizing your findings. This requires an open mind. You should strive to disregard any previous prejudices you might have had on the topic. Remember that your goal is to understand objectively the accurately recorded data from your observations. It is sometimes helpful to talk with fellow students about your findings. This type of peer brainstorming will frequently allow you to see data from a slightly different and perhaps more objective viewpoint. In fact, you might want to team up with classmates who are making the same observations using the same data collection technique so that you all have the same frame of reference. The goal that you should keep in mind in summarizing your information is to draw accurate conclusions from the data you have collected.

Forming Hypotheses.   Once you have condensed and summarized your data, you are ready to draw conclusions and form **hypotheses** based on your observations. If one of your original questions was "What techniques do teachers use to motivate their students?" you would obviously develop hypotheses to answer that particular question. The hypotheses that you form at this stage in your development as an educator make worthwhile all the effort you put into observing, collecting, and analyzing data. They allow you to verify for yourself some of what you have probably been reading and hearing in your college classes. In addition, they are the basis on which you will eventually pattern your own teaching style.

Key Term:
Hypothesis

Testing Your Conclusions.   Every belief, conclusion, or hypothesis that you develop as an educator should be considered tentative. In other words, it is important to formulate such beliefs at this point in your career, but you need to keep an open mind about them and continually revalidate them. The teacher who is constantly attempting to improve is also constantly forming new or modified beliefs, hypotheses, and conclusions about teaching. That is why it is critically important for you and all educators to continually observe and analyze classroom activity so that you can constantly seek to better understand this very complex field.

Developing Folios and Portfolios

Objective 11:
Describe the parts of a portfolio and use their own works as examples.

Focus Question 5:
If you were asked to prepare a portfolio about your potential to be an outstanding teacher, what would you include?

Activity 1.8:
Bring to class an example of a teacher portfolio. Use it to illustrate the way one teacher has organized a portfolio. Point out, or have students suggest, additional information that would be useful to have. Be sure to emphasize the purpose of the example portfolio. A portfolio for self-reflection will be very different from one that has been prepared to submit with an application for professional licensure.

Transparency 6:
Information and Material for a Professional Portfolio

As you move through your teacher education program and on into your career as a teacher, you will find that you have been collecting stacks, boxes, and files of information and "stuff" related to you, your teaching, and the accomplishments of the children you have taught. If you are like most teachers you will not know for sure what to do with all of it, yet you will be reluctant to throw any of it away. Our advice is, be very careful about discarding material until you have organized a folio and anticipated the needs of various portfolios that you might have to prepare. A *folio* is the organized compilation of all the products, records, accomplishments, and testimonies of a teacher and his or her students. Imagine the folio as being a large file drawer with different compartments and file folders. Some of the material that is included is related directly to you and your background. Other items or artifacts are things that others have said about you. And some are examples of projects that your students have completed. A portfolio is assembled from the folio when there is a specific occasion or purpose, such as a job interview or application for an outstanding teacher award. The folio can be organized around three major categories of items: background and experience, attestations, and products and outcomes (see Table 1.5).

Background and Experience. There are many pieces of information about you that are factual. Demographic information, where you attended school, the states where you are licensed to teach, and the record of your work experience are examples of items that you should maintain in your folio. When organizing your folio you will identify a number of areas where you should aim to add information. Now is the time to anticipate some of the material that you might need in preparing a particular portfolio in the future. For example, when you apply for most teaching positions, a prospective employer will want to know the kinds of experiences you have had in schools and classrooms with diverse students. If you currently do not have any examples in your folio, plan to add some related experiences as your teacher education program unfolds.

Attestations. The occasions on which other people recognize your contributions and achievements are called *attestations*. Awards, letters of commendation, newspaper articles, and elected positions on committees are examples of a second category of items to keep in your folio.

Products and Outcomes. Through your efforts as a teacher, students complete assignments, produce plays, achieve on examinations, and receive awards. In this part of the folio the works and successes of those you have worked with can be compiled, along with photographs and video records of your classroom and student projects. Also include copies of committee reports, grant proposals, and other products that have resulted from your leading the efforts of other adults.

TABLE 1.5	Types of Information and Artifacts to Include in Professional Folio	
Background and Experience *(Facts)*	**Attestations** *(Recognition by others)*	**Products and Outcomes** *(Works of others based on your teaching)*
Demographics • age • birthdate • marital status Education • degrees • institutions Education Platform—philosophy Professional Credentials Work Experience Current Role and Responsibilities Multicultural Experiences Special Skills • languages • art/music Community Service • Red Cross volunteer Products • lesson plans • authored curriculum • media productions • written reflections	Awards Honorary Society Memberships Letters from • students • parents • professors • employers • colleagues Newspaper Articles about You TV Segments about You Committee Assignments Elected Offices	Examples of Student Work Photographs of Your Classroom Student Test Scores Video/audiotape of Lessons Grant Proposals Funded Student Awards Effects of Leadership • committee reports • school/class awards • curriculum developed • projects completed Subordinates Who Have Been Recognized or Promoted

Preparing a Portfolio. When the need arises to prepare a portfolio you will be delighted that you did the advance work with your folio. The time line always seems too short when a special portfolio needs to be developed. When you do the folio work along the way, you will find it relatively easy to pull specific examples and documents to fit a particular job interview, or to make final application for a teaching award. Also, when you develop the folio with the broader array of items suggested in Table 1.5, you will be able to prepare a higher quality presentation of your accomplishments.

Folio Tasks. To help you in beginning your folio we have included at the end of each chapter two "Journal/Portfolio Development" suggestions. In making the suggestions, we have anticipated some of the items that you may need to include in future portfolio presentations, and we have selected topics and tasks that are important to you at this early point in your teacher education program. In our discussions as authors we identified four components that were important to our task selections:

> *Content:* The content of the performances will be centered on the major concepts or big ideas of education.
> *Thinking:* The portfolio tasks will aim to assess a variety of thinking skills rather than focusing on just one skill within each task.

Journal/Portfolio Development 2: Your very first folio development task is to find and organize the many materials, artifacts, and records that you currently have.

Thoughtful Engaging Approaches: As much as possible, the portfolio tasks should require serious thinking and encourage more cognitive complexity.

Rich Opportunities: The performances should allow learners to solve problems in a variety of creative ways.

Summary and Implications

This chapter has briefly introduced you to the world of the teacher. We hope that it has convinced you that teaching is an extremely important profession—important to the future success of our democracy, to the happiness and welfare of our children, and to our nation's economy. It has also reminded you that teaching is one of the largest professions in America and that despite some understandable frustrations and a considerable amount of stress, teachers generally feel that their careers are fulfilling and satisfactory. Another contention of this chapter is that society, parents, and students as a rule value and respect teachers.

The last section of this chapter stressed the importance of all teachers being reflective through gathering, analyzing, and using data. We suggest that our best teachers have a natural curiosity about their work and are continually searching for better answers to the problems they face. One important recommendation is to begin developing your professional folio *now*. It is very likely that you will need to develop a portfolio before completing your teacher education program. Most certainly, you will need items from your folio as you search for your first/next teaching position.

One final implication of this chapter for those who are contemplating a career in teaching is the following: You will be entering a time-honored profession that serves an extremely important function in our society and in which most of your colleagues find fulfillment at a time when jobs are available and salaries are improving.

Discussion Questions

1. Name three to five reasons why you want to become a teacher.
2. What are "typical" students' impressions of teachers?
3. What differences do you think teachers can make in your community, your state, the nation, and the world at large?
4. What are key characteristics of teachers you have known that you would like to emulate? What is one thing that you would not want to do?
5. What can teachers do that will make a positive difference in the public's perceptions of teachers?

Journal/Portfolio Development

1. Visit with a retired teacher. Ask what school was like when he or she began teaching. What were the pay and work conditions like then? How has school and the profession of teaching changed from then to now? What kinds of changes does this teacher see for the future? After the interview, review your notes (or did you get permission and tape record?) and write a two- to three-page narrative of your thoughts, impressions, and reflections. What did you learn? What surprised you? What was new or different in the perspective of this teacher? What questions do you have now? (Don't forget to send the teacher a follow-up thank you note.)
2. Your very first folio development task is to find and organize the many materials, artifacts, and records that you currently have. If you are like most of us, the bits and pieces are stored in a number of locations. Examples of term papers, transcripts, awards, letters of recognition, and journals from trips are scattered. Take some time now to find and begin organizing these materials. Organize them by categories such as those illustrated in Table 1.5. Keep in mind the ultimate purpose for developing this folio: At various points in the future you will be drawing items out of the folio to develop a portfolio for use when you apply for a teaching position or as part of the application process to receive national certification as a master teacher.

School-Based Experiences

1. The material contained in this chapter is designed to help you decide whether you want to be a teacher. The next time you have an opportunity to be in a classroom, analyze what you observe, keeping the following three very important basic questions in mind: Do I have the talent necessary to be a good teacher? Am I willing to develop the skills I will need as a teacher? Do I really want to be teacher?

   Talk to teachers about the rewards and frustrations associated with a teaching career. Talk to students about the characteristics of their favorite teachers. Talk to parents about their educational expectations. Talk to students about their educational goals.

2. Ask ERIC. No, that is not the name of a teacher education professor. ERIC is the national database for education, which is funded through the U.S. Department of Education. ERIC consists of a number of centers and an impressive array of information retrieval systems. ERIC staff compile nearly all of the papers, research reports, and curriculum materials that are developed each year. These materials are then made available through on-line computer retrieval systems, which should be available through your college library. There are some special services for teachers in training, including two-page research synthesis publications, a 48-hour turn-around electronic question-answering service, and hundreds of lesson plans that you can access through your computer. To find out more, call 1-800-LET-ERIC. If you have an Internet ID, you can use it too. For details on locating ERIC on Internet, send an e-mail message to: askeric@ericir.syr.edu

Notes

1. James W. Gutherie, "Do America's Schools Need a 'Dow Jones Index'?" *Phi Delta Kappan 74* (7): 523–528.
2. "How U.S. Teachers Measure Up Internationally: A Comparative Study of Teacher Pay, Training, and Conditions of Service." American Federation of Teachers, Research Department, 555 New Jersey Ave. N.W., Washington, D.C. 20001.
3. D. Ladestro, "Stressed Out," *Teacher Magazine* (January 1991): 58–59.
4. "Instructor Survey Results," *Instructor Magazine* (May 1990): 23–25.

Bibliography

Clark, David L., and Astuto, Terry A. "Redirecting Reform Challenges to Popular Assumptions about Teachers and Students." *Phi Delta Kappan* (March 1994): 513–520.

Bullough, Robert V., Jr. *First-Year Teacher: A Case Study.* New York: Teachers College Press, 1989.

Edelfelt, Ray A. *Careers in Education.* Lincolnwood, IL: VGM Career Horizons, 1988.

Gutek, Gerald L. *Education and Schooling in America.* Boston: Allyn and Bacon, 1992.

Hansen, Peter. *The Joy of Stress.* New York: Andrews, McMeel and Parker, 1986.

Johansen, John; Johnson, James; and Henniger, Michael. *American Education: An Introduction to Teaching.* 7th ed. Dubuque: Wm. C. Brown, 1993.

Kaplan, Leonard, ed. *Classrooms at the Crossroads: The Washinton Post Education Companion.* Boston: Allyn and Bacon, 1993.

Kozol, Johnathan. *Savage Inequalities: Children in America's Schools.* New York: Crown Publishers, 1991.

Myers, Charles B., and Myers, Lynn K. *An Introduction to Teaching and Schools.* Fort Worth: Holt, Rinehart and Winston, 1990.

Parkey, Forrest W., and Stanford, Beverly Hardcastle. *Becoming a Teacher.* 3rd ed. Boston: Allyn and Bacon, 1995.

Posner, George J. *Field Experience: A Guide to Reflective Thinking.* New York: Longman, 1985.

Ryan, Kevin, and Cooper, James M. *Those Who Can, Teach.* 6th ed. Boston: Houghton Mifflin Co., 1992.

Smith, Tom E. C. *Introduction to Education.* 2nd ed. St. Paul: West Publishing Co., 1990.

Wragg, E. C. *An Introduction to Classroom Observation.* New York: Routledge, 1994.

Wynn, Richard, and Wynn, Joanne Lindsay. *American Education.* 9th ed. New York: Harper & Row, 1988.

Employment Opportunities for Teachers

Focus Questions

1 What factors influence the supply and demand for teachers?
2 Illustrate the ways in which lower pupil-teacher ratios would aid classroom teachers. What classes would function just as well with larger numbers of students?
3 Why are teachers reluctant to follow the general population shifts in the country? Shouldn't teachers move to areas where they are most needed?
4 How do you account for teacher shortages in some fields and oversupply in others? Why is it that the beginning salary for teachers often is lower than the salary paid the beginner in business and industry?

Key Terms and Concepts

Annual increments: Standard salary increases based on the number of years of teaching experience.

Differential pay: Extra pay or incentives (added to standard increments) awarded to teachers on the basis of merit.

Fringe benefits: Job rewards in addition to salary that may include life, professional liability, health, and dental insurance; retirement programs; and tax-free investment opportunities.

Moonlighting: Holding a second job in addition to one's primary employment; it implies working in the evening, or "under the light of the moon."

Salary schedule: Salary chart organized by teaching experience and formal education.

Teacher certification: The process whereby each state determines the requirements for obtaining a license to teach, processes applications, and issues such licenses.

Teacher supply and demand: A comparison of the projected number of school-age students with the projected number of available teachers.

*T*his chapter will explore two questions that are near and dear to the hearts of all those preparing for a teaching career: (1) Will I find a teaching job when I graduate? and (2) How much money will I make as a teacher? We will look at the factors that influence the answers to these questions and attempt to help you develop the ability to analyze the variables that will assist you in eventually finding the teaching position you want.

Factors Affecting Teacher Supply and Demand

Key Term:
Teacher supply and demand

Many factors influence **supply and demand** for teachers in the United States. Of course, these factors change from time to time as conditions in our society change. Let's briefly look at some of the main variables that determine how easy or difficult it is for teachers to find a job.

Teacher Supply

Objective 1:
Articulate pertinent information about the teacher supply picture in the United States.

The new teacher supply in a given year consists basically of two groups—new-teacher graduates and former-teacher graduates who were not employed as teachers in the previous year. New-teacher graduates have just graduated from institutions of higher education and are prepared to teach for the first time. Former-teacher graduates are prepared to teach, but do not currently hold teaching positions. Some of these former-teacher graduates taught previously; the remainder have never been employed as teachers.

Focus Question 1:
What factors influence the supply and demand for teachers?

Transparency 7:
College Freshmen: Probable Major Fields of Study

New College Graduates. American colleges and universities produced a record number of new teachers about two decades ago when they graduated over one-third of a million teachers each year. That number declined rather dramatically up until a decade ago. Over the past ten years, teacher production has modestly increased each year; now 200,000 new teachers graduate each year. Obviously, the number of newly graduated teachers is one factor in the complicated subject of teacher supply in the United States. Ironically, each year, about one-third of the new-teacher graduates do not take teaching jobs. Another third of new-teacher graduates only devote a few years to teaching before moving out of the classroom. Thus, only about one-third of all new-teacher graduates make teaching a lifetime career.

Information Note 2.1:
Fifty-five percent of the full-time working teachers have spouses who are teachers themselves.

Teachers Returning to the Classroom. Another interesting phenomenon in the question of teacher supply is that many teachers drop out of the profession for one reason or another for a period of time and then accept teaching positions later in life. An obvious example would be female teachers who begin teaching right out of college, drop out of the profession while raising young children, and return when their children become older. Many male teachers leave the teaching profession, at least temporarily, to try other occupations that typically pay larger salaries. Thus, teachers returning to the classroom also play a considerable role in the teacher supply picture in the United States. Estimates vary considerably, but it is probably a good estimate that between one-third to one-half of all newly hired teachers in each school district are experienced teachers, either returning to the classroom or moving from other school districts.

Thus, when you graduate from your teacher education program, you will be competing for teaching positions not only with other new graduates, but also with experienced teachers who are returning to the classroom or changing school districts. Teacher supply and demand is in many ways fickle, difficult to understand, and nearly impossible to predict on a long-range basis, so don't worry too much about it, because it will likely change many times during your career as an educator.

Teacher Demand

The demand for teachers in the United States varies considerably from time to time, from place to place, from subject to subject, and from grade level to grade level. Next, we will explore some of the factors that influence the demand for teachers.

Objective 2:
List major factors that determine the demand for teachers.

The School-Age Population in the United States.   One of the major factors related to the demand for teachers is the number of school-age children in the United States. This in turn is related to birth rates and school retention rates. Other factors influencing both teacher supply and demand include the amount of funds available to hire teachers, the pupil-teacher ratio, and any new programs that receive special funding. The following section will help you to better understand the variables that affect the supply and demand for teachers in the United States.

The Coming Baby Boomlet.   School enrollment is predicted to rise rather dramatically over the next decade. The U.S. Bureau of the Census prediction is

Large increases in the population of school-aged children will have far-reaching effects on the education system in general, and on teacher demand specifically.

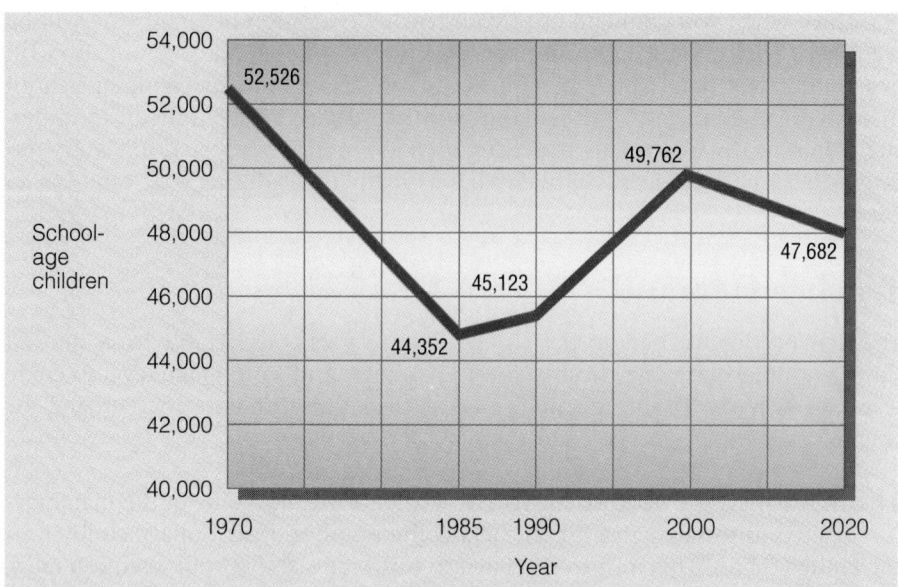

FIGURE 2.1

Number of School-Age (K-12) Children in Thousands

(*Source:* National Center for Education Statistics and U.S. Bureau of the Census.)

reflected in Figure 2.1, which shows the number of school-age children from 1970 projected into the future. As you can see, the number of school-age children in the United States bottomed out in 1985, is now at approximately 47 million plus, and is projected to reach nearly 50 million in the year 2000. This increasing number of school-age children is one of the reasons that many authorities are predicting a shortage of teachers in the United States over the next decade.

Activity 2.1:
Use Figure 2.1 to assist students in analyzing the linear growth projection in school enrollment during the decade 1990 through 2000.

Transparency 8:
Projected Number of School Children to Year 2000

U.S. Population. According to recent information presented by *Education Week,* it is projected that the population of the United States will peak at slightly over 302 million people sometime during the next fifty years. Forecasters then predict that the population will shrink to approximately 292 million people by the year 2080. The U.S. Bureau of the Census also has made the following projections for school-age populations:

For the next fifty years, the elementary school population will remain above its 1987 level of 30.8 million.

By 1995, that population (ages 5 to 13) will have grown by about 3 million, reaching 33.9 million. It will shrink again, by 2 million, between 1995 and 2005, but will not dip below the 1987 level until the year 2038. Over the subsequent four decades, it will decline to 28.3 million.

Only in the bureau's "highest" series of projections would the elementary population again reach, around the year 2010, its 1970 record level of 36.7 million. In that series, the numbers would then continue to rise, to 58.2 million in 2080.

The population of children will shrink to 16.8 million by the year 2000. It will hover between 16 and 17 million until the year 2050, and then drop slowly to 15 million by 2080, according to the mean projections.

The high school population (ages 14 to 17) declined from 14.5 million in 1987 to 13.2 million by 1990, but will rebound to the 1987 level by 1995. It will remain at or slightly above that level, according to the projections, until at least the year 2010. It will then drop slowly to 13.1 million in 2080.

The highest series projects growth in the high school population after the year 2000, up to 25.6 million in 2080; the lowest series envisions declines from the 1987 level after the year 2005—to 7.2 million in 2080.

In the Census Bureau's middle projections, the college-age population (ages 18 to 24) will never again achieve its 1987 level of 27.3 million.[1] While the overall population is on the decline, however, the population of minority children is on the increase. This demands that teachers be more sensitive to cultural differences among students and that more minority students become teachers.

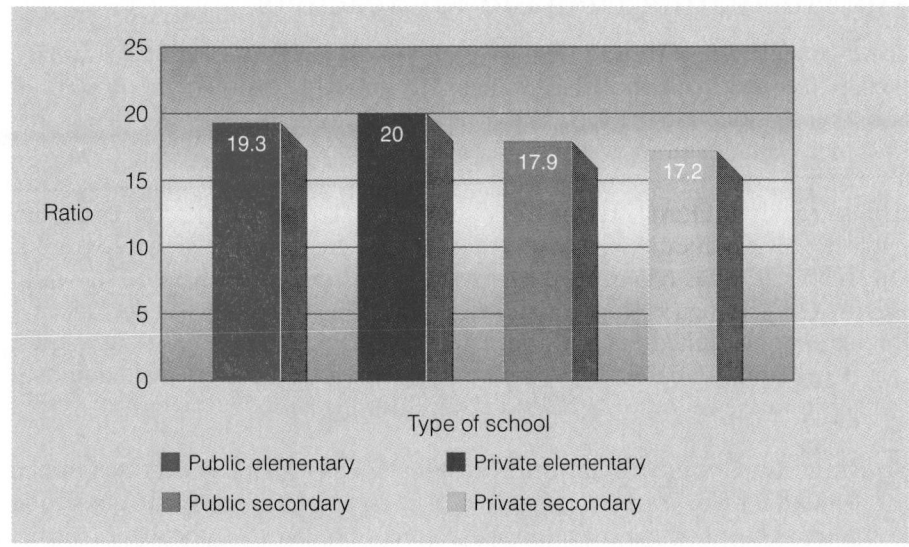

One trend in education today is the increased effort to include children with disabilities in the regular education system.

Trends in Special Education Enrollments. Our schools serve many types of handicapped students. The number of learning-disabled students has increased considerably over the last decade and now totals over four million. As a percent of the total public school enrollment, the number of special education students has risen to nearly 11 percent. This increase in the number of handicapped children served in our schools was due in large part to the Education of the Handicapped Act passed by Congress in 1975, which demands that all handicapped children be provided with a free and appropriate education.

Pupil-Teacher Ratios. The number of students taught by each teacher varies considerably from school to school and from state to state. Figure 2.2 shows pupil-teacher ratios in public and private schools for the entire United States. As

Focus Question 2:
Illustrate the ways in which lower pupil-teacher ratios would aid classroom teachers. What classes would function just as well with larger numbers of students?

FIGURE 2.2

Pupil-Teacher Ratios in Public and Private Schools

(*Source:* National Center for Education Statistics.)

Public elementary: 19.3
Private elementary: 20
Public secondary: 17.9
Private secondary: 17.2

Type of school

you can see, pupil-teacher ratios are highest in elementary schools. It is interesting to note that the pupil-teacher ratio in public schools is very similar to that in private schools and that it is somewhat lower in secondary schools than in elementary schools. Obviously, one measure of a teacher's work load is the number of students taught. Pupil-teacher ratios reflect the relationship between the number of students enrolled and the number of full-time equivalent instructional personnel available to teach them, and pupil-teacher ratios help to determine how many teachers get hired. In large school districts, lowering the pupil-teacher ratio by even one student creates a demand for many more teachers.

School Budgets. Schools never have enough money to hire all the teachers they could use. When school budgets are higher, more teachers are employed, which creates an increased demand for teachers. Unfortunately, when school budgets are limited, few teachers are hired. It has been suggested that, due to inadequate financial resources, we never have an oversupply, but rather, "underemployment" of teachers; if schools had enough money, they would hire all of the available teachers.

Global Perspectives: International Comparisons of Educational Staffing. A recent study[2] revealed interesting differences among countries regarding the amount of money devoted to hiring nonteaching school staff members. The United States hires considerably more nonteaching school staff members than any other country. In fact, more than half of the employees of U.S. schools are not teachers; they are administrators, counselors, librarians, janitors, secretaries, cooks, maintenance workers, bus drivers, and so on. This study shows that 5.6 percent of the total American labor force works in education, but teachers make up only 2.6 percent of all U.S. workers. Japan and The Netherlands have the lowest percentage of nonteaching education employees. Some of these differences can be explained by the fact that many American school children must be bused to schools, thereby requiring bus drivers and maintenance people. How else might some of these differences be explained?

The Fluctuating Demand for Teachers

Objective 3:
Analyze the fluctuating demand for teachers.

The demand for new teachers is increasing rapidly in the United States. In fact, there is a severe teacher shortage in some states, particularly in certain subjects and at certain levels and in our larger cities. Let's look more closely at the factors that influence the demand for teachers in the United States.

CNN Clip 4:
Teacher Gap

An Increasing Demand for Teachers. The U.S. Department of Education publishes many educational statistics that are of interest to professional educators. One such statistic is related to the demand for classroom teachers, as shown in Figure 2.3. This figure shows a steady increase in classroom teacher demand throughout the United States through the year 1997. These projections suggest that it will be essential for our country to recruit a large number of additional teachers into the education profession over this time period.

Shortage by Geographical and Subject Areas. As was mentioned earlier, the demand for new teachers varies from place to place, from grade to grade, and from subject to subject. Even within a given metropolitan area, one school district

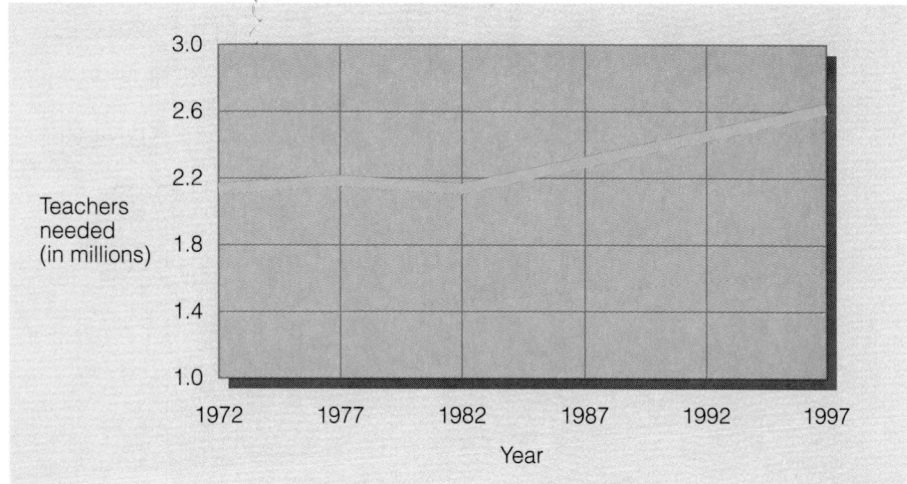

FIGURE 2.3

The Demand for Classroom Teachers Increases

(*Source:* U.S. Department of Education and National Center for Education Statistics.)

may be growing rapidly, building new schools, and hiring new teachers because of new housing developments, while the neighboring school district may be closing schools and reducing its number of teachers. Therefore, it is difficult to generalize about the nature of teacher shortages.

Generally, however, the greatest shortage of teachers exists in our larger cities—New York, Chicago, and Los Angeles, for instance—and in the southern and southwestern parts of the country.

Unfortunately, many teachers do not want to teach in large metropolitan schools, presumably because of heavy city traffic on the freeways, longer commuting time to and from work, more difficult student problems, and higher costs of living. High teacher turnover also contributes to the staffing problems of large-city schools. On the other hand, many teachers feel that teaching in a large city is challenging and fulfilling, with many advantages.

The general teacher shortage that exists in the southern and southwestern parts of the United States has come about as a result of the population shift that has occurred over the past twenty years. Many Americans have moved to the sun belt states largely because industrial development has made jobs available there. This migration has increased school enrollment, which, in turn, has created a considerable demand for teachers.

College and university placement directors suggest that students planning to become teachers should be apprised of the fact that opportunity exists in any field for the top-quality graduate. While it is true that, in times of a good supply of teachers, far more graduates are employed in elementary education, English, and social studies than in subject areas that need relatively few teachers (such as Russian language), at the same time, high-quality candidates in some teaching areas having less demand are still likely to find teaching positions, especially if they are willing to move to where vacancies exist.

Bilingual Teacher Shortage. There is a critical shortage of bilingual teachers throughout the United States. This is particularly true in our large cities and in the southern and western states where large numbers of immigrant children have no or very limited English language skills. It is estimated that 5 percent of our stu-

One of the nation's most serious teacher shortages is in bilingual education.

dents have limited English proficiency and need the services of a bilingual teacher. It is also estimated that this problem will increase in the near future.

Global Perspectives: Overseas Teaching Opportunities.   The U.S. Department of Defense operates a school system for the children of American men and women in the armed services abroad. This school system, the United States Dependents School, is one of our nation's largest school systems, enrolling about 130,000 students in over 260 schools in twenty-three countries. The approximately 7,500 teachers in this system come from every state in the union. Although not officially organized as an international education program, these U.S. Dependents Schools widen the chance for citizens of the United States and other nations to exchange cultural experiences. Opportunities for Americans to teach abroad are increasing. Demands for teachers in other nations, especially for English teachers, have heightened foreign employment. Recruiters from foreign countries have visited many college and university campuses, hoping to hire teachers from the United States.

A concise summary of opportunities for studying or teaching abroad can be found in *Educational and Cultural Exchange Opportunities,* a booklet published by the U.S. Department of State.[3]

Our Largest School Districts.   New York City has the largest school district in the United States, enrolling nearly 10,000,000 students and employing about 52,000 full-time equivalent teachers. Other extremely large school districts in the United States are Puerto Rico, Los Angeles, Chicago, Dade County in Florida, Houston, Philadelphia, and Detroit. Needless to say, these large school districts

Focus Question 3:
Why are teachers reluctant to follow the general population shifts in the country? Shouldn't teachers move to areas where they are most needed?

Focus Question 4:
How do you account for teacher shortages in some fields and oversupply in others? Why is it that the beginning salary for teachers often is lower than the salary paid to the beginner in business and industry?

Diversity Note 2.1:
There is a drastic shortage of minority teachers in the United States, at all levels.

| TABLE 2.1 | Relative Demand by Teaching Area |

Teaching Fields with Considerable Shortage (5.00–4.25)

Speech Pathology	4.48
Bilingual Education	4.45
Special Education—Multiple Handicap	4.34
Special Education—Visually Impaired	4.30
Special Educaion—Behavioral Disorders	4.28

Teaching Fields with Some Shortage (4.24–3.45)

Special Education—Hearing Impaired	4.23
Special Education—Physically Impaired	4.23
Special Education—Mentally Handicapped	4.20
Special Education—Learning Disability	4.17
Audiology	4.13
Science—Physics	3.99
Languages—Japanese	3.89
English as a Second Language	3.88
Science—Chemistry	3.82
Languages—Spanish	3.73
Psychologist (School)	3.71
Mathematics	3.62
Science—Earth/Physical	3.62
Computer Science Education	3.56
Library Science	3.50

Teaching Fields with Balanced Supply and Demand (3.44–2.65)

Science—General	3.43
Technology/Industrial Arts	3.43
Science—Biology	3.39

Social Worker (School)	3.34
Gifted/Talented Education	3.33
Counselor Education	3.23
Agriculture	3.20
Languages—French	3.15
Reading	3.15
Home Economics	3.14
Languages—German	3.12
Languages—Classics	3.05
Music—Instrumental	2.95
Music—Vocal	2.88

Teaching Fields with Some Surplus (2.64–1.85)

Journalism	2.64
Speech/Drama/Theatre	2.56
English/Language Arts	2.51
Business Education	2.49
Driver Education	2.43
Elementary—Pre-Kindergarten	2.43
Dance Education	2.38
Art/Visual	2.36
Elementary—Intermediate	2.27
Elementary—Kindergarten	2.24
Elementary–Primary	2.05
Health Education	2.02
Physical Education	1.89

Teaching Fields with Considerable Surplus (1.84–1.00)

Social Sciences/Studies	1.78

Source: The Job Search Handbook for Educators, 1995. Evanston, IL: Association for School, College and University Staffing, Inc. 1995, 11.

hire a great many new teachers each year. Furthermore, many of the best teachers' salaries are found in these school districts. Students looking forward to teaching careers should seriously consider large urban schools. Table 2.1 summarizes the current relative demand in the United States for teachers by teaching areas.

Transparency 10:
Relative Demand by Teaching Area

Teacher Salaries and Fringe Benefits

Just as many factors affect the supply of and demand for teachers, so do various factors determine educators' salary packages. Teachers' salaries, for instance, vary a great deal from one school district to another. This section discusses the variables affecting teacher salaries and fringe benefits.

Test Questions 2.25–2.41

Improving Salaries and Fringe Benefits

There is good news and bad news about salaries and fringe benefits for educators. The good news is that salaries have improved considerably in recent years and are projected to improve even more in the near future. The bad news is that teachers are still not paid as well as they should be.

Objective 4:
Compare teacher salaries in typical school districts throughout the country.

Key Term:
Salary schedule

Average Teachers' Salaries. Teachers' salaries vary considerably from state to state and from school district to school district. Table 2.2 shows the average teachers' salaries in each region of the United States.

Salary Schedules and Annual Increments. Each board of education is an agent of the state and therefore empowered to set salary levels for employees of the school district it governs. Each school system usually has a **salary schedule** that outlines the minimum and maximum salary for several levels of study

TABLE 2.2 Average Teachers' Salaries

		Elementary/Secondary		Special Education	
		Bachelors	Masters	Bachelors	Masters
Northwest	1991–1992	20,187	23,480	20,912	24,290
	1992–1993	20,196	23,266	20,048	23,671
	1993–1994	20,387	23,857	*	*
West	1991–1992	24,261	25,700	23,878	26,812
	1992–1993	24,447	26,484	24,679	27,137
	1993–1994	24,801	27,495	*	*
Rocky Mountains	1991–1992	18,528	24,087	20,017	23,775
	1992–1993	19,604	23,192	19,785	23,192
	1993–1994	20,624	22,640	*	*
Great Plains and Midwest	1991–1992	19,297	22,235	19,575	22,309
	1992–1993	20,068	23,073	20,630	23,333
	1993–1994	19,898	22,679	*	*
South Central	1991–1992	20,005	20,686	19,511	21,632
	1992–1993	20,401	21,890	20,871	22,525
	1993–1994	20,525	22,849	*	*
Southeast	1991–1992	20,083	22,361	20,483	22,785
	1992–1993	20,220	22,991	21,142	23,804
	1993–1994	21,310	24,116	*	*
Great Lakes	1991–1992	20,077	23,791	20,583	23,889
	1992–1993	21,093	24,630	21,811	25,296
	1993–1994	21,903	26,267	*	*
Middle Atlantic	1991–1992	22,235	25,426	23,228	25,972
	1992–1993	23,751	27,199	25,483	28,712
	1993–1994	24,157	27,335	*	*
Northeast	1991–1992	21,416	23,772	22,350	24,444
	1992–1993	21,022	24,718	21,067	24,632
	1993–1994	22,677	26,724	*	*
Alaska	1991–1992	30,000	34,000	30,000	34,000
	1992–1993	30,000	40,000	30,000	40,000
	1993–1994	30,540	36,486	*	*
Hawaii	1991–1992	25,100	26,990	25,100	26,990
	1992–1993	25,100	26,990	25,100	26,990
	1993–1994	25,033	27,663	*	*

*Data unavailable.

From data supplied by survey respondents. In some instances, the averages are based on limited input, and total reliability is not assured.

Source: The Job Search Handbook for Educators, 1995. Evanston, IL: Association for School, College and Univesity Staffing, Inc. 1995, 11.

beyond the bachelor's degree and for each year of teaching experience. For example, a beginning teacher with a bachelor's degree may be paid $20,000, one with a master's degree may be paid $25,000, and a beginning teacher with a master's degree and 30 additional semester hours of graduate study may be paid $30,000.

Teachers with less than a master's degree may be granted year-to-year increases for ten years; teachers with preparation beyond a master's degree may be granted **annual increments** for up to seventeen years. Therefore, teachers are rewarded both for a maximum number of years of experience and for additional education beyond the bachelor's degree. Teachers who have reached the maximum experience level for their particular education do not receive additional raises except when all the salaries listed in the salary schedule are revised upward.

Teachers' Salaries and Inflation. The overall average teacher's salary is now approximately $36,000 per year. While this figure may sound good to a beginning teacher, experienced educators feel that their purchasing power has remained relatively unchanged over the years. Figure 2.4 shows the average salary paid teachers for the past twenty years—both in current dollars and in constant (1983) dollars. As you can see, while the average teacher salary has increased from $10,000 to about $35,000, inflation has caused the constant dollar average teacher salary to remain relatively unchanged during the past twenty years. Of course, one must remember that teacher salaries vary greatly from place to place; in some school districts, teacher salaries have in fact risen considerably over the past two decades—even when corrected for inflation.

Private School Salaries. The need for private school teachers, preprimary through grade 12, will soon reach 400,000 in the United States. Thus, approximately one out of every seven teachers in the United States at the preprimary through twelfth-grade level is teaching in a private school. Many new teachers are

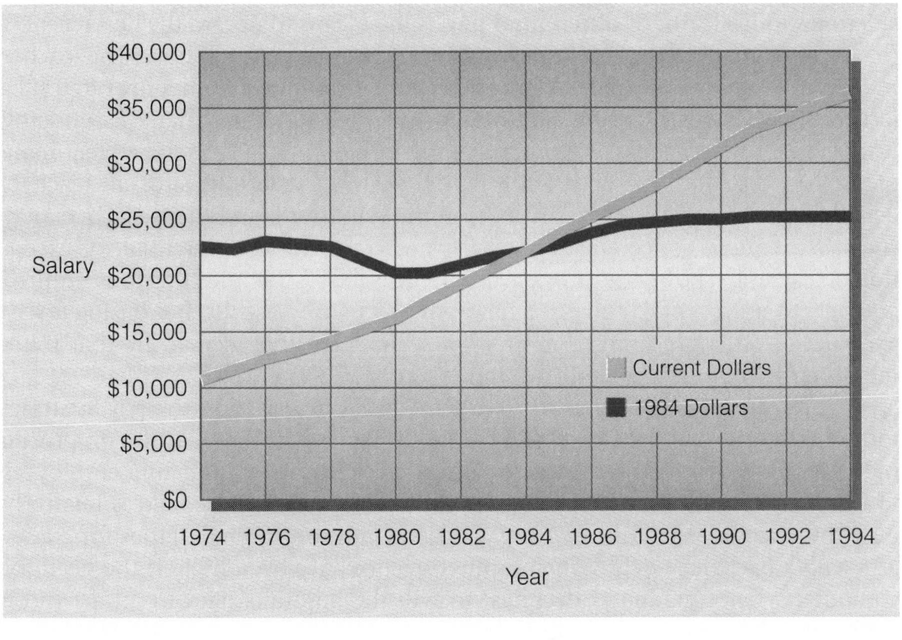

Information Note 2.3:
Just over one-half of all public school teachers lack a master's degree.

Key Term:
Annual increments

Transparency 11:
Average Salary Paid Teachers

Transparency 12:
Public Opinion of Teacher Salaries

Journal Activity Master 2.2:
A Differential Pay Schedule.
This activity requires the student to analyze a situation involving merit or differential pay.

FIGURE 2.4

Average Salary Paid Teachers

(*Source:* National Education Association, 1994. 1993–94 Estimates of School Statistics, Washington, DC: NEA. Used with permission.)

PROFESSIONAL DILEMMA

Will You Be Able to Pay Your Bills on a Teacher's Salary?

A common professional dilemma among teachers is wanting to teach, but not being able to pay the bills. The issue of whether our teachers are adequately paid is prominent in school referenda and debates over various educational bills in state legislatures throughout the nation. Obviously, people who are unemployed, or qualify for welfare programs, find it difficult to believe that teachers are underpaid. Like-wise, many retired people who are living on fixed incomes, or those who have no direct, vested interest (i.e., children), typically feel that teachers, who on the average throughout the United States make over $30,000 per year, are adequately paid. Others point out that teachers typically work only ten months a year, which makes their annual salary somewhat misleading. Add to this the feeling among many that good teachers should be better paid and poor teachers are overpaid—even though there is no conclusive evidence that better pay necessarily means better teaching.

Those who argue that teachers are not adequately paid point out that our children's and nation's future is dependent on the success of our schools. They go on to point out that you tend to "get what you pay for,"

Key Term:
Differential pay

Activity 2.3:
Discuss the pros and cons of merit pay. Describe how it works in your own collegiate setting.

hired each year to teach in private schools throughout the country. While private schools are not usually required by law to hire fully certified teachers, increasingly they are attempting to do so, and most private school teachers are fully certified.

Teachers' salaries in private schools are generally somewhat lower than those in public schools. This lower salary level is due largely to the fact that a high percentage of private schools are religious and, of course, are not tax-supported.

Students who are now enrolled in teacher education programs should keep in mind that private schools represent another career option and should become familiar with these important educational institutions.

Merit Pay–Differential Pay. School systems in a number of states are considering various forms of **differential pay** as the means to reward the best teachers for teaching excellence and to address shortages in certain disciplines. The teacher unions have historically opposed incentive plans, claiming that they are often subject to the opinions of administrators, include questionable criteria for judging teaching excellence, and cause morale problems among teachers. However, many of the best teachers realize that the typical salary schedule rewards all teachers equally regardless of their effectiveness in the classroom, and these teachers may support the merit concept as a possible way to provide a differential for exceptional teaching above the provisions of the salary schedule. Previous limited attempts to utilize merit pay plans have not proven worthwhile, but basing teachers' salaries on some form of evaluation seems plausible. It is likely that more merit plans will be developed and implemented in the future.

In any case, the need for schools to provide additional incentive pay to attract top-notch teachers to the critical shortage areas seems without question. In private industry, additional pay is always used as a mechanism for attracting employees to fill critical needs. For example, though the computer science field is relatively new, the demand is relatively strong. Consequently, beginning salaries for graduates with a bachelor's degree in computer science have been high. If the need for computer science graduates declines, so will the amounts paid to attract those employees.

and that higher teacher salaries would attract our most talented young people into the teaching profession. These proponents of higher teacher salaries believe that a typical teacher's work load is very heavy and stressful—much more so than their counterparts in most other professions—and therefore justifies a higher salary. Many feel that it is more cost-effective to spend money educating children in our schools than it is to fight crime, pay for welfare, and support correctional systems and other adult programs that purportedly result from unsuccessful or ineffectual schooling.

As you prepare for your educational career, you should think realistically about this professional dilemma. Some teachers find it difficult to remain dedicated in the face of inadequate salaries. You may face this dilemma during your career.

- Should teacher pay be based on individual ability?
- What is your image of teaching as a profession? Do you place teaching in the same professional category as medicine and law? Why or why not?
- How might teachers overcome the dilemma of inadequate pay?
- How do teachers justify working hard for low pay? Or do they?
- To what degree are you determined to teach in spite of the possibility of low or inadequate pay?

Fringe Benefits, Extra Pay, and Moonlighting

While a teacher's salary is extremely important, so are the fringe benefits and any opportunities to make additional income. This section of the book will help you better understand the more common fringe benefits, extra pay, and moonlighting opportunities available to teachers.

Objective 5:
Contrast the fringe benefits, extra pay, and moonlighting options available to teachers.

Fringe Benefits for Teachers. Almost all full-time teachers receive fringe benefits that, when added to their basic salary, constitute their total compensation package. When you pursue your first teaching position, you will want to inquire about the fringe benefits as well as the basic salary. While the salary is usually of first concern to a teacher, the fringe benefits are equally important over the long term. These **fringe benefits** vary from school to school but frequently include some type of insurance benefits—fairly complete hospitalization insurance, medical/surgical coverage, and major medical insurance. Somewhat less frequently, a teacher's medical insurance also includes dental care and prescription drugs; least frequently, it includes coverage of eyeglasses and other types of less common medical services. It is not unusual for a teacher's insurance benefits to include some type of group life insurance, although the amount can vary tremendously from school to school.

Key Term:
Fringe benefits

Information Note 2.4:
Thirty percent of teachers spend nine hours or more per month working with religious, social, civic, or professional organizations.

Many school districts also provide some type of professional liability insurance for their teachers. In fact, some states require by law that all school districts do so, presumably because parents could conceivably bring a liability lawsuit against the state, which is ultimately responsible for public education.

It is probably safe to say that all full-time public school teachers who are employed under regular continuing contracts also receive some type of retirement benefits as part of their total compensation package. As evidence of the variation in these retirement benefits, in some states, teachers receive a combination of state teacher retirement and social security retirement. In other states, a teacher's retirement may depend totally on a state program and be divorced entirely from our federal social security retirement system. It is usually possible for teachers who

Discussion Question 2:
Discuss the pros and cons of early-retirement incentive plans offered by some school districts. In your response, explain your belief about the value of young teachers and older teachers in a school.

Relevant Research

Teachers Welcome Constructive Suggestions about Their Work, But Rarely Receive Them

Research shows that when supervisors provide constructive feedback to teachers on specific skills, they help teachers become more effective and improve teacher morale. Unfortunately, a typical supervisor visit to a teacher's classroom takes place only once or twice a year and provides only general comments about the teacher's performance. This relative lack of specific supervision contributes to low morale, teacher absenteeism, and high faculty turnover. Supervision that strengthens instruction and improves teacher morale has these elements:

- agreement between supervisor and teacher on the specific skills and practices that characterize effective teaching
- frequent observation by the supervisor to see if the teacher is using these skills and practices
- a meeting between supervisor and teacher to discuss the supervisor's impressions
- agreement by the supervisor and teacher on areas for improvement
- a specific plan for improvement, jointly constructed by teacher and supervisor

We strongly encourage you to seek supervision as a beginning teacher. It will help you improve as a teacher, and may even eventually help lead to tenure and a higher salary.

Bird, T., and Little, J. S. "Instructional Leadership in Eight Secondary Schools," Final Report to the National Institute of Education. Boulder, CO: Center for Action Research, 1985, ERIC Document No. ED 263694.
Felding, G. S., and Schalock, H. S. *Promoting the Professional Development of Teachers and Administrators.* Eugene, OR: ERIC Clearinghouse on Educational Management, 1985.
Natriello, G. "Teacher's Perceptions of the Frequency of Evaluation and Assessments of Their Effort and Effectiveness," *American Educational Research Journal* 21 (3) (1984): 579–595.

Source: What Works: Research About Teaching and Learning. Washington, DC: U.S. Department of Education, 1987, 68.

Key Term:
Moonlighting

Test Questions 2.42–2.57

move from state to state to transfer their retirement benefits to the state in which they ultimately retire. In any event, a teacher's retirement program is an extremely important part of the total compensation package and needs to be well understood by everyone entering the profession.

Some schools also provide special leave provisions for their teachers, perhaps the most common being related to personal illness. Other types of leave provisions deal with family illness, emergency, and death. Another common type of leave provision deals with professional development, and, again, the conditions under which professional development leaves are granted vary considerably from school to school. Because of the high cost, relatively few public school systems allow teachers sabbatical leaves with pay in order to improve themselves professionally. This feature is much more common in colleges and universities than at the public elementary and secondary school level.

Moonlighting. A relatively large number of public school teachers **moonlight,** or hold a second job, according to a recent study by the National Center for Educational Statistics. Figure 2.5 shows some interesting data on this subject. As you can see, male teachers are more likely to moonlight than female teachers, and white, non-Hispanic teachers are more likely to moonlight than minority teachers.

Unfortunately, many moonlighting teachers indicate that they are forced to hold a second job because of relatively low salaries in the teaching profession. This is yet another factor that should be taken into account when considering a teaching career.

Getting Certified and Employed

It is never too early to start thinking about becoming certified and finding a job. There are issues about teacher certification and employment that you should know and start thinking about no matter where you are in your teacher education program. We will very briefly explore some of these topics in this section.

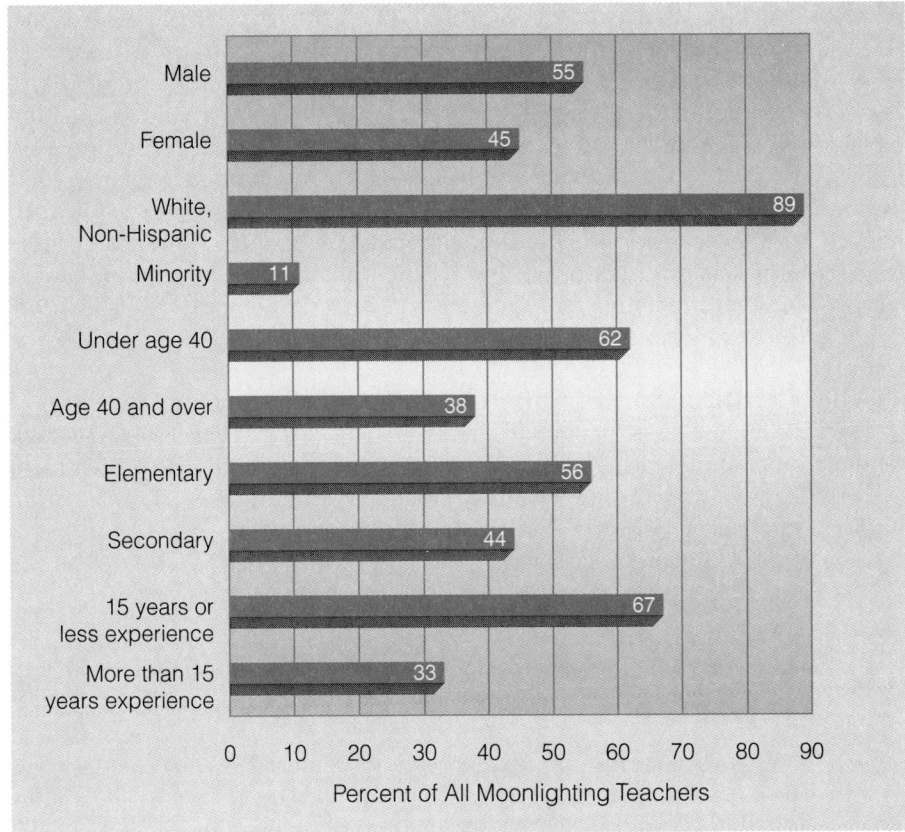

Percent of All Moonlighting Teachers

- Male — 55
- Female — 45
- White, Non-Hispanic — 89
- Minority — 11
- Under age 40 — 62
- Age 40 and over — 38
- Elementary — 56
- Secondary — 44
- 15 years or less experience — 67
- More than 15 years experience — 33

Activity 2.4:
Have students identify the ways that they are most comfortable earning additional pay while teaching. Summarize the class choices in the form of a frequency chart and discuss the implications of the class profile.

Discussion Question 3:
Many young teachers work at a second job to increase their yearly income. How do you feel about teachers holding additional jobs?

FIGURE 2.5

Moonlighting Teachers
(*Source:* Education Information Branch, Office of Educational Research and Improvement. Washington, DC: Room 300, 555 New Jersey Avenue NW, Washington, DC 20208.

Certification Requirements

All teachers must obtain an official teaching certificate before they can legally teach in our public schools. These certificates must then be periodically registered and renewed in most states.

A State Function.   Each state determines the requirements for **teacher certification** and, understandably, they vary considerably from state to state. You undoubtedly will hear a good deal about the certification requirement in the state in which you are now going to school. However, you may wish to ask more specific questions regarding the certification options available to you. You may also wish to contact the certification offices in other states in which you may be interested in working sometime in the future. Appendix 2.1 on page 49 provides the addresses and phone numbers of all the state teacher certification offices throughout the United States. You should also be aware that states change their teacher certification requirements and even create new teaching certificates from time to time. Furthermore, certification requirements are not easy to understand, since they are filled with technicalities. You should very carefully explore and understand the requirements for any certificates that you will need to teach what you want to teach, where you want to teach it.

Transparency 9:
Moonlighting

Journal/Portfolio Development 1:
Develop a portfolio (any good system for safely and neatly keeping samples of your work) and fill it with examples of your best work in all your teacher education courses. This portfolio may eventually help you get the job you want.

Objective 6:
Articulate teacher certification requirements in various states.

Key Term:
Teacher certification

Alternative Certification for School Teachers. A recent move in some states urges the development of alternative certification opportunities for people who would like to become school teachers. These alternative routes to certification have come under considerable criticism from the teacher education establishment. In some states a rather radical approach to alternative certification has been taken in which anyone with a bachelor's degree in just about any major may begin teaching with some type of provisional certificate. In other states, the alternative certification opportunity is aimed more at facilitating mid-career changes from other professions, such as business or the military, into the teaching profession. Often, such alternative certification grants career experience credits for work done in other professions.

Teacher Certification Examinations. Most states now require some type of initial examination as a part of the teacher certification process. Many states require the National Teacher Examination (NTE), which consists of a series of separate tests aimed at measuring general knowledge, communication skills, and professional knowledge. The NTE has recently undergone major revision, and now consists of the following three stages:

Stage 1: Consists of a basic skills examination designed to assess the reading, writing, and mathematical skills needed by beginning teachers. These tests will be accompanied by computer diagnostic and practice instructional modules to help prospective teachers discover and remediate any basic skills weaknesses they may have.

Stage 2: Is designed to measure professional education and subject matter knowledge. These examinations may vary somewhat from state to state to allow some flexibility. Newer testing techniques such as computer simulations and interactive video disks may be used in these examinations.

Stage 3: This stage consists of performance-based assessment devices aimed at assessing teaching skills such as planning for instruction, teaching lessons, classroom management, instructional effectiveness, and assessing student learning. These assessment sessions include observations of the teacher at work in the classroom.

National Implications. While teacher certification has historically been regulated by each state, there is increasing discussion about moving to a national teaching certificate that would presumably be recognized in all states. While a number of states now have certification reciprocity agreements whereby teachers can move without too much trouble from one state to another, a national certificate has always been appealing to teachers since it would increase their mobility. Chapter 19 will provide you with more information about some of the possible future developments concerning teacher certification.

As a future teacher, once you have determined the required certification, you should then systematically begin preparing to pass the required tests. This textbook and its ancillary materials will be helpful to you in passing any certification test that you may be required to take.

Searching for a Teaching Job

Teacher education students should start thinking about seeking employment very early in their college career. We highly recommend that if you have not already

CASE STUDY   MAXIMIZING JOB PROSPECTS

John Anderson will graduate from his teacher education program soon, and he is searching for a teaching position, preferably in a large urban school. He is a Caucasian from a small-town, middle-class family, and has heard that urban schools prefer to hire experienced minority teachers. Even so, he is determined to teach culturally diverse students in a large city school, so he is doing his best to prepare for such a position. He studied urban educational problems, and has decided he would like to accept the challenge of teaching in a large city school system, even though he did not do his student teaching in such a setting.

John read a list of ten characteristics that schools look for when hiring new teachers,* and has attempted to measure his own abilities against this list. These characteristics include:

1. The ability to make a difference in a student's life
2. A variety of life experiences
3. Classroom management experience
4. Student teaching experiences
5. Academic preparation
6. Personal appearance
7. A sense of humor
8. Adaptability
9. Maturity
10. Involvement

John honestly believes he stacks up fairly well against this list, but doesn't know how to demonstrate all his abilities to hiring officials, or what the criteria for measuring them might be. For instance, how does one demonstrate "the ability to make a difference in a student's life," or "adaptability"? He thought about editing a videotape of his best student teaching lessons, and perhaps developing a portfolio of some of his best college work for submission along with his credentials, but he isn't sure what they should contain; anyway, he has heard that many hiring officials do not take the time to really look at such material. He wishes he could think of a really good way to get the attention of the hiring officials.

1. If you were a hiring official, how would you select the best teachers?
2. Are schools justified in giving preference to minority teachers? Why or why not?
3. How and in what ways might reviewing videotapes and portfolios help hiring officials select the best teachers?
4. What advice do you have for John?
5. How might one demonstrate the ten characteristics that schools look for when hiring new teachers?
6. How will you attempt to maximize your job prospects?

*Gene Parker, "Characteristics Which School Systems Value." *1994 ASCUS Annual.* Evanston, IL: Association for School, College and University Staffing, Inc., 1994, 4.

Information Note 2.6: Many hiring officials rely mainly on the interview in selecting teachers.

Transparency 13: Characteristics That School Systems Value

Journal/Portfolio Development 2: Find a way to videotape your work in the schools. Edit these videotapes into short segments that demonstrate your skills as a teacher. Many hiring officials will be interested in seeing your tapes. Be prepared to answer questions about your performance on the videotapes.

done so, you obtain a copy of the most recent Association for School, College and University Staffing (ASCUS) annual *Job Search Handbook for Educators* from your job placement office or by writing to ASCUS, 1600 Dodge Avenue S-330, Evanston, IL 60201-3451. This handbook makes many good suggestions for college students who will eventually be seeking jobs as teachers. It points out the importance of having good grades and an excellent variety of courses that will help to make you more employable upon graduation. It also contains hints for preparing your résumé, cover letters, and letters of inquiry, and provides excellent practical suggestions for improving your interviewing techniques. This handbook also provides up-to-date information on teacher supply and demand for the various fields within the teaching profession.

Maximizing Your Job Prospects.   The most important job-hunting hint for any teacher education student is to study hard throughout college and get the best possible grades in all college classes. Also, select majors and minors that offer the most employment options. By careful planning, college students can graduate qualified to teach in a variety of fields and with more than one certificate.

All teacher education students should also seize every opportunity to gain on-the-job experience by working with children. Many volunteer programs are available in most geographical areas through schools, churches, synagogues, and various agencies that involve working with children. There are also many paid job opportunities such as summer recreation programs, youth camps, and teacher aide programs that provide opportunities to work with youths. The more experience teacher education students have in working with young people, the more they will learn about them.

The Mechanics of a Job Search.   As teacher education students approach graduation, they also need to receive job-hunting hints about developing job placement files, writing letters of application, and developing good interview techniques. Fortunately, most teacher education programs and college job placement offices automatically provide such job-hunting hints. Appendix 2.2 on page 52 provides you with a job search timetable checklist that should help you get started on your search for a teaching position.

Summary and Implications

Total school enrollment is projected to increase in the 1990s, which could result in a boom that surpasses the peak levels of the early 1970s. Consequently, a teacher shortage is a distinct possibility in the late 1990s unless more college students enroll in teacher preparation programs.

The total number of elementary and secondary teachers in the United States increased from 1970 through 1980. During this period, additional teachers were readily available, and many were hired in order to decrease the pupil-teacher ratios in previously overcrowded classrooms. Consequently, the number of elementary school teachers is now on the rise. However, the number of secondary school teachers will continue to decrease in the 1990s as previous elementary school enrollment declines affect the secondary student population. At the same time, shortages in selected discipline areas will become more pronounced in response

to the emphasis on given areas of the secondary curriculum.

Opportunities for Americans to teach abroad are increasing. The U.S. Department of Defense operates a school system for the children of American men and women in the services abroad. Teacher shortages in other nations also enhance opportunities for foreign employment.

Some school districts are attempting to devise salary incentive plans that reward the best teachers with additional merit pay. Another incentive would provide higher salaries for teachers in areas of short supply, such as special education. Although teachers' unions generally oppose such incentive plans, teachers realize that their salary schedules reward everyone equally regardless of effectiveness in the classroom. The general public and school boards tend to favor merit pay for the best teachers and extra stipends to attract well-qualified teachers in critical shortage areas. The 1990s may see more use of salary incentive plans than ever before.

More teachers will be needed in the 1990s than during the previous decade. To satisfy the clamor for improving the quality of education, these teachers will also need to be better prepared than ever before. Furthermore, teachers' salaries will be reviewed to determine ways to upgrade financial rewards for those prepared to teach in the critical shortage disciplines and for those determined to be most effective in the

classroom. Teacher organizations and teacher preparation schools are challenged to upgrade the competency levels of certified teachers now on the job and of students entering teacher preparation programs.

This chapter concluded with a number of suggestions for obtaining a teaching position, including advice on this topic from the Association for School, College and University Staffing (ASCUS), an organization that publishes an annual job-search handbook for educators.

Discussion Questions

1. Teacher shortages are reported in the areas of special education, chemistry, mathematics, and physics. Why do shortages exist in some subjects?

2. Discuss the pros and cons of the early-retirement incentive plans offered by some school districts. In your response, explain your beliefs about the value of young teachers and older teachers in a school.

3. Many young teachers work at a second job to increase their yearly income. How do you feel about teachers holding additional jobs?

4. How can colleges and departments of education better prepare beginning teachers so that their chances of employment in a tight job market will be enhanced?

5. What should be done to meet demands for teachers in areas where there are shortages?

Journal/Portfolio Development

1. Develop a portfolio (any good system for safely and neatly keeping samples of your work) and fill it with examples of your best work in all your teacher education courses. This portfolio may eventually help you get the job you want.

2. Find a way to videotape your work in the schools. Edit these videotapes into short segments that

demonstrate your skills as a teacher. Many hiring officials will be interested in seeing your tapes. Be prepared to answer questions about your performance on the videotapes.

School-Based Experiences

1. The material contained in this chapter should be very practical for you. It provides you with up-to-date information on employment opportunities available to you in the field of education when you graduate. As you have an opportunity to work in the schools, talk with the educators there about job opportunities, fringe benefits, salary schedules, merit pay, retirement benefits, and any other topics related to employment opportunities for teachers that interest you.

2. Talk to educators about moonlighting they have done in the past or are doing now. Ask why they moonlight (you may be surprised by some of the responses). Ask if their schools ever suggested that teachers should not moonlight—particularly at certain times and/or in certain jobs. Think about moonlighting you may want or have to do some day.

Notes

1. *Education Week*, 8 February 1989, 6.
2. *Education at a Glance.* Organization for Economic Cooperation and Development, 2001 L Street NW, Washington, DC 20036.

3. *Education and Cultural Exchange Opportunities.* Washington, DC: U.S. Department of State, Bureau of Cultural Affairs, 1986.

Bibliography

The American Federation of Teachers collects and distributes data on salaries and demand for educators throughout each year.

A Job Search Handbook for Educators. Published annually by the Association for School, College and University Staffing (ASCUS), 1600 Dodge Avenue S-330, Evanston, IL 60201-3451.

Gutek, Gerald L. *American Education in a Global Society.* New York: Longman, 1993.

Johansen, John J., Johnson, James A., and Henniger, Michael. *American Education: An Introduction to Teaching.* Dubuque, IA: Wm. C. Brown, 1993.

Sarason, Seymour B. *Are You Thinking of Teaching?* San Francisco: Jossey-Bass, 1993.

The National Education Association periodically publishes and reports on teacher supply, demand, and salaries.

Teacher Supply/Demand. Annual reports of the Association of School, College and University Staffing (ASCUS), 1600 Dodge Avenue S-330, Evanston, IL 60201-3451.

Appendix 2.1

U.S. Teacher Certification Offices

A teaching certificate is valid only in the state for which it is issued, and certification and testing requirements are never static. Even the very best book or chart may be out of date as soon as it is published. If you are planning to move to another state, you should contact that state's certification office, as listed below. The number code following each entry indicates the types of testing which the state required at the time of publication. . . . The key to the codes may be found at the end of the state listings.

When you write or call the state certification office, indicate the type of certificate you are receiving from your current state, which national tests you have taken, and ask for application materials and procedures for obtaining certification in the new state. Another source of information about certification requirements will be the actual districts to which you apply.

ASCUS members—career service professionals and school personnel administrators are commited to helping each other's graduates move around the country, and even around the world. For instance, each year ASCUS publishes the *National Directory of Job and Career Fairs for Educators*, listing recruiting fairs in every state. Many of these fairs are open to all interested candidates. Check your career services office for this publication. . . .

The *ASCUS Directory of Public School Systems in the United States* lists every school district in the nation by state and city. Look for it in your career planning office. . . .

Alabama
Department of Education
Division of Professional Service
5108 Gordon Persons Bldg.
50 North Ripley Street
Montgomery 36130-3901,
    205-242-9960

Alaska
Department of Education
Teacher Education and
    Certification
801 W. 10th Street, Suite 200
Juneau 99801-1894, 907-465-2031
    or 2065

Arizona (1)
Teacher Certification Unit
Department of Education
1535 W. Jefferson, Room 126
P.O. Box 85002
Phoenix 85007, 602-542-4368

Arkansas (3)
Teacher Education and Certification
Department of Education
#4 Capitol Mall, Rooms 106B/107B
Little Rock 72201, 501-682-4342

California (2)
Commission on Teacher
    Credentialing
1812 9th Street
Sacramento 94244-7000,
    916-445-7254

Colorado (1)
Teacher Education
Department of Education
201 East Colfax Ave
Denver 80203, 303-866-6628

Connecticut (2)
Bureau of Certification and
    Accreditation
State Department of Education
P.O. Box 2219
Hartford 06145, 203-566-5201

Delaware (3)
Department of Public
    Instruction
Office of Certification
Townsend Building, P.O.
    Box 1402
Dover 19903, 302-736-4686

District of Columbia (3)
Division of Teacher Services
District of Columbia Public Schools
415 12th Street, N.W., Room 1013
Washington 20004-1994,
    202-724-4250

Florida (1)
Department of Teacher Certification
325 W. Gaines Street, Room 203
Tallahassee 32399-0400, 904-488-5724

Georgia (1)
Professional Standards Commission
1452 Twin Towers East
Atlanta 30334, 404-656-2406

Hawaii (3)
State Department of Education
Office of Personnel Services
P.O. Box 2360
Honolulu 96804, 808-586-3240

Idaho (3)
State Department of Education
Teacher Education and Certification
Len B. Jordan Office Building
Boise 83720, 208-334-3475

Illinois (1)
State Teacher Certification Board
100 North First Street
Springfield 62777, 217–782–2805

Indiana (3)
Professional Standards Board
Center for Professional Development
Room 229, State House
Indianapolis 46204–2798,
   317–232–9010

Iowa
Board of Educational Examiners
Practitional Preparation and Licensure
   Bureau
Grimes State Office Building
Des Moines 50319–0416,
   515–281–3245

Kansas (3)
State Department of Education
Certification Office
120 East 10th Avenue
Topeka 66612, 913–296–2288

Kentucky (3)
State Department of Education
Division of Certification
18th Floor, Capital Plaza Tower
500 Mero Street
Frankfort 40601, 502–564–4606

Louisiana (3)
State Department of Education
Bureau of Higher Education and Teacher
   Certification
P.O Box 94064
Baton Rouge 70804–9064,
   504–342–3490

Maine (3)
Department of Education
Division of Certification and Placement
State House Station 23
Augusta 04333, 207–289–5944

Maryland (3)
State Department of Education
Division of Certification and
   Accreditation
200 West Baltimore Street, 2595
Baltimore 21201–2595, 301–333–2142

Massachusetts
State Department of Education
Division of Educational Personnel
Teacher Certification
350 Malden Street
Quincy 02168, 617–388–3300

Michigan (1)
Teacher/Administrator Preparation and
   Certification Services
Bureau of Postsecondary Education
Michigan Department of Education
P.O. Box 30008
Lansing 48909, 517–373–3310

Minnesota (3)
State Department of Education
Personnel Licensing
Capitol Square Building
550 Cedar Street
St. Paul 55101, 612–296–2046

Mississippi (3)
State Department of Education
Division of Teacher Certification
P.O. Box 771
Jackson 39205, 601–359–3483

Missouri (3)
Teacher Certification Office
Department of Elementary & Secondary
   Education
P.O. Box 480
Jefferson City 65102, 314–751–3486

Montana (3)
Office of Public Instruction
Teacher Education and Certification
Capital Building
Helena 59620, 406–444–3150

Nebraska (3)
Department of Education
Teacher Education and Certification
301 Centennial Mall South, Box 94987
Lincoln 68509, 402–471–2496

Nevada (3)
Department of Education
State Mail Room
1850 E. Sahara
Las Vegas 89158, 702–486–6455

New Hampshire
State Department of Education
Bureau of Teacher Education and
   Professional Standards
State Office Park South
101 Pleasant Street
Concord 03301–3860, 603–271–2407

New Jersey (3)
Department of Education
Division of Teacher Preparation &
   Certification
225 West State Street, CN 500
Trenton 08625–0500, 609–984–1216

New Mexico (3)
State Department of Education
Professional Licensure Unit
Education Building
Santa Fe 87501–2786, 505–827–6587

New York (1)
State Department of Education
Teacher Education and Certification
Cultural Education Center, Room 5A11
Nelson A. Rockefeller Empire State Plaza
Albany 12230, 518–474–6440

North Carolina (3)
Department of Public Instruction
Certification Section
301 N. Wilmington Street
Raleigh 27601–2825, 919–733–3077

North Dakota
Department of Public Instruction
Teacher Certification
600 East Boulevard Avenue
Bismarck 58505, 701–224–2264

Ohio (3)
Department of Education
Division of Teacher Education &
   Certification
65 S. Front Street, Room 1012
Columbus 43266–0308, 614–466–3593

Oklahoma (1)
Department of Education
Hodge Education Building
2500 North Lincoln Boulevard, Room
   211
Oklahoma City 73105–4599,
   405–521–3337

Oregon (2)
Teacher Standards and Practices
   Commission
580 State Street, Room 203
Salem 97310, 503–378–3586

Pennsylvania (3)
State Department of Education
Bureau of Teacher Preparation and
   Certification
333 Market Street, 3rd Floor
Harrisburg 17126–0333, 717–787–2967

Puerto Rico (3)
Department of Education
Certification Office
Box 759
Hato Rey 00910, 011–809–758–4949

Rhode Island (3)
Department of Education
School and Teacher Accreditation
Roger Williams Building
22 Hayes Street
Providence 02908, 401–277–2675

South Carolina (3)
State Department of Education
The Office of Education Professions
Room 1015, Rutledge Building
Columbia 29201, 803–734–8466

South Dakota
Division of Education & Cultural
    Affairs
Office of Certification
Kneip Building
700 Governor's Drive
Pierre 57501–2291, 605–773–2553

Tennessee (3)
State Department of Education
Teacher Licensing & Career Ladder
    Certification
6th Floor, North Wing
Cordell Hull Building
Nashville 37243–0377, 615–741–1644

Texas (1)
State Education Agency
Educational Personnel Records
1701 North Congress Avenue
Austin 78701–1494, 512–463–8976

Utah
State Office of Education
Certification and Personnel
    Development
250 East 500 South
Salt Lake City 84111, 801–538–7741

Vermont
State Department of Education
Educational Licensing Service
120 State Street
Montpelier 05620, 802–828–2444

Virginia (1)
Department of Education
Office of Professional Licensure
P. O. Box 6Q
Richmond 23216–2060,
    804–225–2022

Washington
Professional Education and
    Certification Office
Superintendent of Public Instruction
P. O. Box 47200
Olympia 98504–7200,
    206–753–6773

West Virginia (1)
Department of Education
Office of Professional Education
Capitol Complex, Room B-337,
    Bldg. 6
Charleston 25305, 304–558–2703

Wisconsin (3)
Department of Public Instruction
Bureau of Teacher Education, Licensing
    and Placement
Teacher Certification
125 S. Webster Street, P.O. Box 7841
Madison 53707–7841, 608–266–1879

Wyoming
State Department of Education
Certification and Licensing Unit
Hathaway Building, 2300 Capital Drive
Cheyenne 82002–0050, 307–777–6261

St. Croix District (3)
Department of Education
Educational Personnel Services
2133 Hospital Street
St. Croix, Virgin Islands 00820,
    809–773–5844

St. Thomas/St. John District (3)
Personnel Services
Department of Education
44–46 Kongens Gade
St. Thomas, Virgin Islands 00802,
    809–774–0100, ext.216

**United States Department of Defense
Overseas Dependent Section (3)**
Certification Unit
4040 N. Fairfax Drive
Arlington, Virginia 22203–1634
703–696–3081

Key to State Codes for Testing Requirements

No Code   No testing is required.
1   State requires successful completion of its own examination.
2   State requires successful completion of its own examination *plus* completion of
    one or more national tests.
3   State requires successful completion of one or more national tests. States set
    their own minimum scores.

A Note on National Testing: For many years, the Educational Testing Service (ETS) has made available two widely used national tests. The National Teacher Examinations (NTE) encompass testing in three general areas: general knowledge, communication skills and professional knowledge, as well as testing in more than 100 specific subject areas. The Pre-Professional Skills Test (PPST) is used to measure competency in reading, writing and mathematics.

Beginning in 1993, ETS began implementation of an entirely new teacher testing program: The Praxis Series: Professional Assessments for Beginning Teachers. The three parts of the Praxis Series include assessment of skills, subjects and classroom performance. Many states are currently making transitions to the Praxis Series, and we encourage all teacher candidates to contact individual state certification offices to determine exact testing requirements.

Source: The Job Search Handbook for Educators, 1995. Evanston, IL: Association for School, College and University Staffing, Inc., 1995, 32–34.

Job Search Timetable Checklist

This checklist is designed to help graduating students who are seeking teaching positions make the best use of their time as they conduct job searches. We encourage you to use this checklist in conjunction with the services and resources available from your college or university placement office.

August/September
(12 months prior to employment)

———— Attend any applicable orientations/workshops offered by your college placement office.

———— Register with your college placement office and inquire about career services.

———— Begin to define career goals by determining the types, sizes, and geographic locations of school systems in which you have an interest.

October
(11 months prior to employment)

———— Begin to identify references and ask them to prepare letters of recommendation for your credential or placement files.

———— See a counselor at your college placement office to discuss your job-search plan.

November
(10 months prior to employment)

———— Check to see that you are properly registered at your college placement office.

———— Begin developing a résumé and a basic cover letter.

———— Begin networking by contacting friends, faculty members, etc., to inform them of your career plans. If possible, give them a copy of your résumé.

December/January
(8–9 months prior to employment)

———— Finalize your résumé and make arrangements for it to be reproduced. You may want to get some tips on résumé reproduction from your college placement office.

———— Attend any career planning and placement workshops designed for education majors.

———— Use the directories available at your college placement office to develop a list of school systems in which you have an interest.

	_____ Contact school systems to request application materials.
	_____ If applying to out-of-state school systems, contact the appropriate State Departments of Education to determine testing requirements. Addresses are listed in Appendix 2.1.

February *(7 months prior to employment)*	_____ Check the status of your credential or placement file at your college placement office.
	_____ Send completed applications to school systems, with a résumé and cover letter.
	_____ Inquire about school systems which will be recruiting at your college placement office, and about the procedures for interviewing with them.

March/April *(5–6 months prior to employment)*	_____ Research school systems with which you will be interviewing.
	_____ Interview on campus and follow up with thank you letters.
	_____ Continue to follow up by phone with school systems of interest.
	_____ Begin monitoring the job vacancy listings available at your college placement office.

May/August *(1–4 months prior to employment)*	_____ Just before graduation, check to be sure you are completely registered with your college placement office, and that your credential or placement file is in good order.
	_____ Maintain communication with your network of contacts.
	_____ Subscribe to your college placement office's job vacancy bulletin.
	_____ Revise your résumé and cover letter if necessary.
	_____ Interview off campus and follow up with thank you letters.
	_____ If relocating away from campus, contact a college placement office in the area to which you are moving and inquire about available services.
	_____ Continue to monitor job vacancy listings and apply when qualified and interested.
	_____ Begin considering job offers. Ask for more time to consider offers, if necessary.
	_____ Accept the best job offer. Inform those associated with your search of your acceptance.

Adapted from material originally prepared at Miami University of Ohio.

Source: The Job Search Handbook for Educators, 1995. Evanston, IL: Association for School, College and University Staffing, Inc., 1995, 18.

3 Professional Organizations for Educators

Focus Questions

1 Do you think principals and other school workers should belong to the teachers' union? Why?
2 What do you know about labor unions? How are teacher unions similar? How are they different?
3 To what extent do you think teacher organizations should have political clout?
4 Do you know the name of the specialty studies and job-related associations that are available to teachers?
5 As an aspiring teacher, which professional associations are you joining now?

Key Terms and Concepts

American Federation of Teachers: A national teachers' organization that is primarily concerned with improving educational conditions and protecting teachers' rights.

National Education Association: The largest organization of educators; the NEA is concerned with the overall improvement of education and of the condition of educators.

Political action committees in teacher education: Various organizations that engage in political activities in support of the organizations' purposes or causes.

Professionalism and Unionism: A distinction that the NEA used in 1960 to claim that only an organization that stressed the professional aspects could represent teachers; hence a union would not be adequate, since it stressed organized labor.

Teacher power: A term that stresses organized teacher groups that lobby for improvements in education; the group embodiment of individual teacher empowerment.

World Confederation of Organizations of the Teaching Profession (WCOTP): An organization that aims to foster international understanding and goodwill, stressing peace, freedom, and respect for human dignity. Members are from approximately one hundred nations and include the AFT and the NEA.

One of the special aspects of becoming a teacher is the opportunity to join with and work along with many other well-educated and highly dedicated professionals. There are many types of professional organizations and associations that teachers can join. In most school districts, teachers are represented by their organization or union when it comes to setting the specifications for contracts and working conditions. Teachers can also join specialty associations that are dedicated to improving teaching and learning in relation to specific curricula and teaching processes. These associations include national, regional, and local-level chapters. They provide teachers with the opportunity to work with other teachers who have like concerns and interests and also enable teachers to participate in various professional leadership activities. Before the 1960s, most of these organizations and associations were small in terms of membership size and were not particularly influential. Since that time, however, organizations and associations have become major influences in terms of the development of national education policy; the determination of state policies, laws, and rules and regulations as they relate to schooling; and (at the local level) studying curriculum and negotiating labor contracts. At all of these levels, teachers are actively involved and are responsible participants as well as part of the membership that works with the resultant policy decisions and the curriculum products.

In the past thirty years, most teachers have been represented in their contract negotiations by one of the two major professional associations: the National Education Association (NEA) or the American Federation of Teachers (AFT). In either case, the typical arrangement is that the professional organization leadership works as a union and negotiates the contract and working conditions with the district. These negotiations normally take place through a dialog with the central school administration, especially the superintendent, and in the end are agreed to by the school board. Teachers usually consider the advice provided at the national level by the professional association in regard to teachers' rights, legislation favoring education, and the development of ethical codes for teacher conduct. Similarly, political involvement, promotion of education, and lobbying the legislature at the state level is normally led by the professional organizations. However, the strongest reason for an individual teacher to join a teachers' union/organization is the support for efforts at the local level. Local teachers' organizations provide representation to the school board on matters related to working conditions such as class size, salaries, and fringe benefits. Assistance to each teacher on grievance procedures and provisional legal services with due process rights gives teachers warranties against reprisals. All of these resources come with membership in the professional organization.

Teachers have plenty of opportunities to become involved in professional/specialty associations as well. These associations deal directly with design of curriculum, innovation in teaching, improving the instructional processes, and so forth. There are a number of specialty organizations that deal with targeted areas such as science teaching, mathematics teaching, English teaching, reading, middle school, and early childhood. These associations also have national, state, and local chapters. Unlike their professional organization counterparts, these associations do not deal directly with work conditions and contracts. Instead, they focus on the design of curriculum, the optimal conditions for the delivery of effective instruction, staff development and training experiences for teachers, and efforts to influence the shape of state and national policy as it relates to the particular specialty area. Interestingly, today, teacher unionism and professionalism are not mutually exclusive. As will be described later in this chapter, both of the major professional organizations, NEA and AFT, have full-time professional staffs and a number of major initiatives that are targeted toward restructuring of schools, examining alternative assessment, empowering teachers as leaders, and other commitments that do not deal with contract and work conditions per se, but instead deal with the design of the teaching and learning processes and how to create more effective teachers in the schooling context. Clearly, teachers profit from membership and participation in both professional organizations and professional/specialty associations. In this chapter, each of these types of professional organizations will be described briefly and a sampling of their activities will be presented.

Teacher Unions

In the past thirty years, teachers have joined local, regional, and national organizations as a bargaining force. In the early years of this effort, the organizations behaved very much as any other type of labor union, which caused a great deal of concern among many educators who thought of themselves as professionals. However, in order to improve the working conditions for teachers, many felt that the only recourse was to become formally organized and to engage in collective bargaining.

Like labor unions, teachers have often used collective bargaining to improve working conditions.

National Education Association (NEA)

The **National Education Association (NEA)** is by far the largest teachers' organization, with over two million members, including teachers, administrators, clerical and custodial employees, and other school personnel. The NEA has its national headquarters in Washington, DC. The basic documents for the governance of the NEA are the Constitution of the National Education Association of the United States and the Bylaws of the National Education Association of the United States.

The NEA Representative Assembly: A Legislative and Policymaking Body. The Representative Assembly is the primary legislative and policymaking body of the NEA. The executive officers are the president, vice-president, and secretary-treasurer, who are elected by the Representative Assembly and are subject to the policies established by the Representative Assembly, board of directors, and executive committee. An executive director has the primary responsibility for implementing the policies of the association and is responsible to the executive committee. Standing committees may be established and discontinued by the Representative Assembly, the board of directors, or the executive committee for the purpose of accomplishing a specific task within a limited period of time.[1]

NEA: Basic Purpose and Chronology. The basic purposes of the NEA, as stated in its charter, are to elevate the character and advance the interests of the profession of teaching and to promote education in the United States. Figure 3.1

Test Questions 3.1–3.49; 3.61

Objective 1:
Explain the role and organization of the National Education Association (NEA).

Key Term:
National Education Association

Transparency 15:
NEA Structure

Activity 3.1:
Have groups of students act as if they are members of the Representative Assembly of the NEA. Ask each group to develop and present one current educational policy for 2001 that is consistent with the basic purposes of the NEA.

Focus Question 1:
Do you think principals and other school workers should belong to the teachers' union? Why?

1857

The National Teachers' Association

Organized August 26, 1857, in Philadelphia, Pennsylvania.

Purpose   *To elevate the character and advance the interests of the profession of teaching and to promote the cause of popular education in the United States.* (The word *popular* was dropped in the 1907 Act of Incorporation.)

The name of the Association was changed at Cleveland, Ohio, on August 15, 1870, to the National Educational Association.

1870–1907

National Educational Association

Incorporated under the laws of the District of Columbia, February 24, 1886, under the name National Education Association, which was changed to National Educational Association, by certificate filed November 6, 1886.

1907–Present

National Education Association of the United States

Incorporated under a special Act of Congress, approved June 30, 1906, to succeed the National Educational Association. The Charter was accepted and Bylaws were adopted at the Fiftieth Anniversary Convention held July 10, 1907, at Los Angeles, California.

FIGURE 3.1

National Education Association 1857–Present

(*Source: NEA Handbook, 1988–89* (Washington DC: National Education Association, 1988), p. 149. Reprinted by permission.)

Information Note 3.1:
The NEA develops themes such as "NEA Mobilizes for Action" and "Advancing the Nation's Educational Agenda" in an attempt to rally people around the cause of education.

Transparency 17:
NEA's Nine Principles of Educational Excellence and Equity

Objective 2:
List the five professional initiatives of the NEA designed to improve education.

Activity 3.2:
Have several small groups of students each select one of the NEA initiatives and critique its strengths and weaknesses.

traces the organizational chronology of the NEA from its founding in 1857 as the National Teachers' Association (NTA). In 1870 the NTA united with the National Association of School Superintendents, organized in 1865, and the American Normal School Association, organized in 1858, to form the National Education Association. The organization was incorporated in 1886 in the District of Columbia as the National Education Association and was chartered in 1906 by act of Congress. The charter was officially adopted at the association's annual meeting of 1907, with the name "National Educational Association of the United States." The original statement of purpose of the NTA remains unchanged in the present NEA charter. NEA membership reached an all-time high of almost 1.9 million in 1976, stabilized at over 1.6 million in the early 1980s, and has now grown to over two million.

NEA Professional Initiatives

Given its long history of advocacy of teaching as a profession, it should not be surprising to learn that the National Education Association also has a wide portfolio of professional initiatives that are designed to introduce teachers to best practices, to facilitate teacher leadership, and to empower the restructuring of schools. The

NEA has organized a division of Educational Policy and Professional Practice, which consists of a number of areas: student assessment and accountability; professional preparation, state licensure, and certification; and governance and member activities. Each of these programs has an array of activities and initiatives to further advance teacher professionalism. In addition there is the NEA National Center for Innovation, which has a series of programs that are aimed toward the preparation of teachers and include experimental efforts in exemplary programs for schools and restructuring efforts. A sampling of the NEA professional initiatives includes the following.

Teacher TV. In a joint effort with the Learning Channel, a visionary television program is offered each Sunday for and about teachers. It is a magazine-style show that is shot on location at schools across the country and features teachers, schools, and communities that are challenging the educational status quo. Segments of the program include new education trends, teacher resources, practical tips and teaching strategies, and exploration of controversial issues.

Doubts and Certainties. *Doubts and Certainties* is a newsletter that is published bimonthly by the NEA for those who are interested in transforming schools. The newsletter continually presents descriptions of schools that engage in experimental activities. It runs feature articles that raise questions challenging conventional ways of thinking. The newsletter also includes paragraph reports from various sites around the country that are engaged in major transforming efforts. *Doubts and Certainties* also serves as a communication mechanism with the NEA School Renewal Network, which is a set of schools engaged in major experimental efforts to renew schooling.

NEA National Center for Innovation. The NEA National Center for Innovation is organized to advance the reform of public schools. It focuses on developing leadership through establishing learning communities and engaging, designing, and establishing the support of the experimental school renewal projects. The National Center includes exemplary programs in schools (Excellence in Action programs), school-based restructuring (The Mastery Learning Consortium), district-based restructuring (The Learning Laboratories Initiative), teacher preparation reform (The Teacher Education Initiative), and the use of technology and networking. There are four themes that unify all of these projects: (1) Teacher educational leaders: provisions for leadership activities; (2) National Vision: Local educational experimentation to meet national goals; (3) Restructuring: turning a fashionable idea into substantive change; and (4) Research-based risk-taking yields additional research.

Topical Publications and Reports. The NEA provides to its membership an array of reports on critical issues and topics of interest to its members. Samples of recent reports

Discussion Question 1:
Teachers' organizations defend the rights, materials, and moral interests of the teaching profession. To what extent should the organization defend a teacher's choice of reading material for classroom use? To what extent should the organization defend the rights of gay teachers?

Transparency 19:
From Teacher Development to Student Empowerment

The National Education Association is one of the major organizations overseeing and promoting the profession of teaching in the United States.

PREAMBLE

The educator, believing in the worth and dignity of each human being, recognizes the supreme importance of the pursuit of truth, devotion to excellence, and the nurture of democratic principles. Essential to these goals is the protection of freedom to learn and to teach and the guarantee of equal educational opportunity for all. The educator accepts the responsibility to adhere to the highest ethical standards.

The educator recognizes the magnitude of the responsibility inherent in the teaching process. The desire for the respect and confidence of one's colleagues, of students, of parents, and of the members of the community provides the incentive to attain and maintain the highest possible degree of ethical conduct. *The Code of Ethics of the Education Profession* indicates the aspiration of all educators and provides standards by which to judge conduct.

The remedies specified by the NEA and/or its affiliates for the violation of any provision of this Code shall be exclusive and no such provision shall be enforceable in any form other than one specifically designated by the NEA or its affiliates.

PRINCIPLE I

Commitment to the Student

The educator strives to help each student realize his or her potential as a worthy and effective member of society. The educator therefore works to stimulate the spirit of inquiry, the acquisition of knowledge and understanding, and the thoughtful formulation of worthy goals.

In fulfillment of the obligation to the student, the educator:

1. Shall not unreasonably restrain the student from independent action in the pursuit of learning.

2. Shall not unreasonably deny the student access to varying points of view.

3. Shall not deliberately suppress or distort subject matter relevant to the student's progress.

4. Shall make reasonable effort to protect the students from conditions harmful to learning or to health and safety.

5. Shall not intentionally expose the student to embarrassment or disparagement.

6. Shall not on the basis of race, color, creed, sex, national origin, marital status, political or religious beliefs, family, social or cultural background, or sexual orientation unfairly:
   a) Exclude any student from participation in any program.
   b) Deny benefits to any student.
   c) Grant any advantage to any student.

7. Shall not use professional relationships with students for private advantage.

8. Shall not disclose information about students obtained in the course of professional service, unless disclosure serves a compelling professional purpose or is required by law.

(Continued)

FIGURE 3.2

Code of Ethics of the Education Profession

(*Source:* The National Education Association, Washington, DC.)

Information Note 3.2:
Started in the fall of 1993, all high school students in Maryland were required to do 75 hours of public service. Similar experimental volunteer programs, often initiated by professional teacher groups, are springing up around the country. The current Objectives Based Education (OBE) requirements in Pennsylvania (1995) have similar student expectations.

include: Early Childhood Education in the Public Schools, Academic Tracking, and Student Testing. Each of these reports is available to members and can be of great help to school and district committees as they consider how to address current issues and concerns. Figure 3.2 presents the NEA's *Code of Ethics of the Education Profession.*

American Federation of Teachers (AFT)

The second largest teachers' union is called the **American Federation of Teachers (AFT).** The AFT, with national headquarters located in Washington, DC, is headed by a president. It was organized on April 15, 1916, and became affiliated with

PRINCIPLE II

Commitment to the Profession

The education profession is vested by the public with a trust and responsibility requiring the highest ideals of professional service.

In the belief that the quality of the services of the education profession directly influences the nation and its citizens, the educator shall exert every effort to raise professional standards, to promote a climate that encourages the exercise of professional judgment, to achieve conditions which attract persons worthy of the trust to careers in education, and to assist in preventing the practice of the profession by unqualified persons. In fulfillment of the obligation to the profession, the educator:

1. Shall not in an application for a professional position deliberately make a false statement or fail to disclose a material fact related to competency and qualifications.

2. Shall not misrepresent his/her professional qualifications.

3. Shall not assist any entry into the profession of a person known to be unqualified in respect to character, education, or other relevant attribute.

4. Shall not knowingly make a false statement concerning the qualifications of a candidate for a professional position.

5. Shall not assist a noneducator in the unauthorized practice of teaching.

6. Shall not disclose information about colleagues obtained in the course of professional service unless disclosure serves a compelling professional purpose or is required by law.

7. Shall not knowingly make false or malicious statements about a colleague.

8. Shall not accept any gratuity, gift, or favor that might impair or appear to influence professional decisions or actions.

Adopted by 1975 Representative Assembly

FIGURE 3.2 *(Continued)*

the American Federation of Labor in May 1916. John Dewey held the first membership card in the AFT. (Teachers' unions had existed earlier than 1916; for example, the Chicago Teachers' Federation was formed in 1897 and became affiliated with the American Federation of Labor in 1902.) AFT membership grew steadily from 110,522 members in 1965 to 205,323 members in 1970—almost doubling.

Membership. Membership exceeded 415,854 by 1974, reached 624,406 in May 1986, and by 1993 exceeded 806,000. The AFT has local unions in the United States, the Canal Zone, Guam, and the armed forces overseas schools for the dependents of military personnel. Besides the national federations, there are federations of teachers in most states.

Governance. The organization of the AFT includes a president, thirty-eight vice-presidents, a secretary-treasurer, an administrative staff, and eleven departments. It also includes standing committees and council committees. The Committee of Political Education (COPE) is becoming more active as the AFT participates increasingly in political discussions related to education.

Affiliation with the AFL-CIO. Since its inception the AFT has boasted of its affiliation with the AFL-CIO. The AFT has stressed that organized labor was an important force in establishing our system of free public schools and has actively supported school improvement programs at local, state, and national levels. Affiliation with organized labor gives the AFT the support of more than fifteen million members of the AFL-CIO. The support by local labor unions has often

Transparency 18: Bill of Rights for Children—NEA

Objective 3: Describe in outline form the organization of the American Federation of Teachers (AFT).

Key Term: American Federation of Teachers

Transparency 16: AFT Table of Organization

Information Note 3.3: Albert Shanker, long-time president of the AFT, continues to be a highly respected spokesperson for American education.

CODE OF ETHICS
AMERICAN FEDERATION OF TEACHERS, AFL-CIO

I. Teacher-Student Commitment

1. The Teacher works to develop each student's potential as a worthy and effective citizen.
2. The Teacher works objectively to stimulate the spirit of inquiry, the acquisition of knowledge and understanding, and the thoughtful formulation of worthy goals in each of his/her students for their advancement.
3. The Teacher works to develop and provide sound and progressively better educational opportunities for all students.

II. Teacher-Public Commitment

1. The Teacher believes that patriotism in its highest form requires dedication to the principles of our democratic heritage.
2. The Teacher shares with all other citizens the responsibility for the development of sound public policy and assumes full political and citizenship responsibilities.
3. The Teacher has the privilege and the responsibility to enhance the public image of his/her school in order to create a positive community atmosphere which will be beneficial to education.

III. Teacher-Profession Commitment

1. The Teacher believes that the quality of his/her service in the education profession directly influences the nation and its citizens.
2. The Teacher exerts every effort to raise professional standards, to improve a climate in which the exercise of professional judgment is encouraged, and to achieve conditions which attract persons worthy of the trust to careers in education.
3. The Teacher urges active participation and support in professional organizations and their programs.

IV. Teacher-District Commitment

1. The Teacher strives to do the job for which he/she was hired with honesty and to the best of his/her ability.
2. The Teacher pledges to communicate this code, along with a positive attitude toward it, to all teachers.
3. The Teacher discourages the breaching of this code and requests that all charges be presented in writing to the Union Executive Board for their deliberation and judgment.

FIGURE 3.3

Code of Ethics of the American Federation of Teachers

(*Source:* American Federation of Teachers, AFL-CIO. Used by permission.)

Discussion Question 2:
During a teachers' strike, members of a factory union from a neighboring city joined the teachers' picket line to support the teachers' demands. Do you agree or disagree with the factory union action? Explain your answer.

worked to the advantage of local AFT unions in gaining better salaries and improved fringe benefits from local boards of education. Figure 3.3 presents the AFT's code of ethics.

AFT Programs for Professional Growth

The AFT has a rich and diverse portfolio of resources available to its members. In addition to lobbying and political action activities, there are resources in the form of staff services, publications (e.g., the AFT journal, *American Educator*), and workshops related to an array of professional topics. A few of the current initiatives are described on the following page.

Education for Democracy. This project was launched at the time of the bicentennial celebration to address perceived lack of attention to the education of Americans about their democratic heritage. Since that time, Education for Democracy has taken into account the increasing diversity of our people in terms of racial, national, linguistic, and religious origins. The current thrust of the project is not only to make history relevant at the high school level, but also to emphasize history in the elementary grades. Through a series of invited papers and related materials, this project is providing teachers with information about important aspects of history that should be included in the curriculum as well as suggestions for how to make history interesting. Along the way, the theme that has developed is appreciating and understanding the importance of democracy.

Objective 4:
Articulate orally and/or in writing several examples of professional activities of the AFT.

The AFT Critical Thinking Project. This project addresses issues in the area of critical thinking. Definitions of thinking skills and dispositions are offered along with what, as research indicated, would be useful for teachers to consider. In addition, an emphasis is placed on how to develop, enhance, and assess thinking skills in children. In this program, the "turn key" model of training is used, whereby some teachers are trained at the national level and then return to the local level to train others. A thirty-five-hour program of training is available for those at the local level who wish to learn more. In one of the reports that is available out of this project, an emphasis is made on distinguishing between "knowledge" and "knowing."

It is important to stress here that in questioning the traditional reliance of the schools on a one-right-answer model of learning, the critical thinking movement is not denigrating the importance of knowledge in learning. Knowledge is essential and intrinsic to learning of all kinds. One cannot think critically without knowledge. When we think, we must always think about something. The development of critical thinking, says Cornbleth (1985), is highly knowledge dependent: We cannot think critically about the ideas we encounter unless we know something about the area in question. There is a difference, however, between memorization and understanding, as well as between "knowledge" and "knowing."

Relevant Research

Teacher Job Satisfaction Is Important for Successful Teacher Performance

A recent research project by Heller, Clay, and Perkins reported that in a national survey a majority of teachers claimed low job satisfaction.[2] Much of the dissatisfaction was associated with little academic and social support from administration, a self-perceived inability to meet student needs, and inadequate salaries. Too often, higher performance expectations and demands are not followed by supportive behaviors from administration that are geared to help teachers do a better job in meeting the needs of their diverse students. Job satisfaction is directly related to:

- the extent to which you can meet student needs,
- the degree of trust you have in your principal,
- the amount of work required of you,
- the way you interact with your students, and
- your satisfaction with your salary.

We suggest that you address these job satisfaction issues as a beginning teacher and continually during your career if you wish to be successful in meeting the needs of your students.

Source: William H. Heller; Rex J. Clay; and Cline M. Perkins, "Factors Related to Teacher Job Satisfaction and Dissatisfaction," *ERS Spectrum 10* (1) (Winter, 1992): 20–24.

Activity 3.3:
Have several small groups of students each select one of the AFT programs for professional growth and critique its strengths and weaknesses.

The AFT Educational Research and Dissemination Program. Through this program, selected findings from recent research on classroom management and effective teaching have been made available to teachers. The research findings have been tested in classrooms and found to be most useful and relevant to teachers for improving student progress. Based on the research, a set of staff development programs for teachers has been made available. The programs can be offered as a part of a statewide network, a national network, or at the local level. The program also offers various types of resources such as one-page summary sheets of exemplary programs, profiles of teachers who are making a difference through extensive use of some of the concepts, a visiting practitioner program, a glossary of expressions and terms, and a sampling of interesting information about teachers and teaching drawn from the key studies. One of the unique features of this program is the interactive and collaborative dynamic that is possible with other teachers locally, regionally, and nationally who are engaged in similar explorations and trials of the research findings.

Information Note 3.4:
Professional associations such as the AFT and NEA have become effective fund raisers for educational research and programming.

Objective 5:
Compare and contrast the NEA and AFT in writing.

Leadership for Reform Program.   The Leadership for Reform Program is designed to address the emerging plans and trends to transform schools. In this effort, participants consist of teams from the local level who respond by writing a proposal to serve as a pilot site for a special project. Out of the meetings of these teams, a set of guiding principles has been developed that addresses the range of issues that should be considered when reforming a school or a school system. This is an effort to respond to national movements such as Education 2000 and the continuing criticism of schools.

One of AFT's proposals is an answer to the emerging interest in developing a transition from the traditional preservice teacher education program on the college campus to being a full-time in-service teacher. There is an in-between phase commonly referred to as *induction*, which typically covers the first one to three years of in-service teaching experience. The AFT is proposing professional practice schools at elementary, middle, and secondary levels that are "structured, staffed, and supported to achieve three goals: student achievement, teacher induction, and supportive research directed at the continuous improvement of practice." One of the key premises in this effort is the emphasis on making student teaching more useful and relevant to the beginning teacher. The second is the continuing agenda to make teaching a self-governing profession, and the professional practice schools are seen as another lever in achieving this aspiration. The third premise of the professional practice school model is the development of more productive

The American Federation of Teachers sponsors, among other things, the continuing education of teachers.

collaborative relationships between universities and schools with the goal of establishing professional practice schools developed as a joint effort, with roles and responsibilities shared between the university and school district personnel. These professional practice schools would be like a medical teaching hospital—the teaching location for the clinical faculty and a place where university researchers could study this practice. Yet another goal for the professional practice schools is that they would demonstrate the best in teaching practice. They would provide a knowledge base to what is going on in classrooms, and there would be a heavy focus on student learning.

CASE STUDY	TEACHER ORGANIZATION SUPPORT

*T*eachers' organizations such as the AFT and NEA attempt to defend the rights, materials, and interests of educators. This aid usually comes from the local organization to which the teacher belongs, but also can be obtained from the national organization if it is necessary. A very important right that organizations protect for teachers is the "right of due process" in hiring and dismissal. If a teacher believes this right has been violated in practice with employment, he or she can begin with the local association in seeking redress.

As a new teacher in your first year of employment, you are experiencing difficulty in getting information about whether your teaching contract will be continued for the second year. You are aware that the school board has indicated to the superintendent that because of enrollment decreases and shrinking tax dollars, the district administrators are to decide which teachers will be retained for the next school year. It is now the early part of the second semester and you still have not been formally visited in your classroom by the building administrator. Since there are other new, nontenured teachers in your building, you believe that the administrator will be choosing the people she wishes to retain for the next school year.

You feel that you need to begin taking steps to protect your employment.

1. How will you approach your local association to see what help they intend to give you?
2. How do you maintain your professional relationships with your other first-year teaching colleagues, knowing that some of you may be terminated?
3. Do you have "due process" rights that need to be addressed with this issue?

Discuss a course of action that you may begin planning to satisfy your professional concerns.

NEA and AFT Compared

In the early 1960s the NEA appealed to teachers by drawing a distinction between **professionalism and unionism.** As a *professional association,* it claimed, only the NEA could truly represent teachers. A union like the AFT, on the other hand, was seen as being beneath professionalism by the NEA leadership because of its alliance with other workers within the American Federation of Labor and Congress of Industrial Organizations (AFL-CIO). The NEA has since identified itself as a union and no longer distinguishes between professionalism and unionism.

AFT: Professionalism Not Possible without Unionism. To the AFT, professionalism is not possible without unionism. A degree of self-control, the ability to help set professional standards, mastery of a specific body of knowledge, and the authority to define conditions of work are essential elements in the AFT's definition of professionalism. Since none of these can be gained without the kind of collective assertion of power that unionism makes possible, the AFT maintains that without unionism teaching can never become truly professional.

AFT Strikes, NEA Sanctions. During the 1960s the AFT was generally viewed as a collection of teachers' unions that would willingly, though illegally in most

Key Term:
Professionalism and unionism

Journal Activity Master 3.1: A Comparative Analysis of the NEA and AFT. This activity requires the student to compare the relative merits of the two largest teachers' unions.

Activity 3.4:
Have students compare the codes of ethics of the two major organizations. On the basis of this type of comparison, have students first rate their preferences for which code they prefer and then prepare a document supporting their choices.

Teachers have exercised their right to strike with mixed emotions, realizing that the resulting disruption will affect their students directly.

Focus Question 2:
What do you know about labor unions? How are teacher unions similar? How are they different?

Information Note 3.5:
Collective bargaining remains the major purpose of the NEA and the AFT. The threat of work stoppage remains one of the main tools in the collective bargaining "tool kit."

Key Term:
Teacher power

Activity 3.5:
Split the class into two groups, one NEA and one AFT. Give each group the same school community situation: canceling extracurricular activities. Then have the groups develop an appropriate strike or sanction strategy to deal with this situation.

states, close the schools by striking to gain their demands. Many educators, NEA members especially, looked on striking as a labor union technique that should not be used by "professional" teachers. At that time the NEA used a procedure termed *sanctions.* When sanctions were imposed against a school, the professional association advertised the school district as being an unacceptable place to work and discouraged association members from taking employment in the district. Teachers completed existing contractual agreements without closing the schools. Generally, several months' notice was given before sanctions were invoked, and they were applied by the NEA to local districts as well as to entire states (Oklahoma and Utah). Technically, the NEA did not have a no-strike policy at that time, but it was strongly implied. Both the AFT and NEA worked to increase **teacher power,** which stressed organizing teachers in order to enhance their ability to exert pressure for the improvement of education and teacher welfare.

Competition: AFT versus NEA. The strong competition between the AFT and NEA for memberships and bargaining rights during the late 1960s was vocally volatile and highly intense. Teacher militancy among members of both the NEA and AFT grew considerably. The strike tactic used by the AFT seemed to be more immediately effective than NEA sanctions, and as a consequence, the NEA came to embrace the strike rather than sanctions as a last resort. The NEA also came to embrace collective bargaining, which the AFT had initiated. Thus the influences of the AFT and the NEA on each other have produced a growing convergence of philosophy and purpose. Today, most teachers, administrators, and board members consider both organizations to be teachers' unions that use the tactics found most successful by the trade unions of organized labor.

However, in recent years, the NEA's emphasis on professionalism has been paralleled by the AFT's emphasis on teacher leadership. Both organizations have

PROFESSIONAL DILEMMA

Are Teachers Professional If They Strike?

Your school district association has been in negotiations with the local school board for almost one year now. Currently, you are working without a contract. It appears that the association and the board are at an impasse over salary and fringe benefits. The leader of the association has called a meeting in which she intends to discuss the potential issue of a work stoppage (strike) at the school district level. Your fall semester school term has only been in session for one and one-half months and the students are beginning to settle into a pleasant learning routine.

The community has learned of a possible strike vote and is openly against this action. Up until this time the community has always been supportive of

teacher efforts and programs. However, they do not want to see their children's educational environment being totally disrupted. Local newspaper and radio releases in support of the community are now bringing out age-old arguments supporting the notion that teachers are public servants and should not resort to work stoppages. It is apparent that the public trust between school and community is being eroded. Your association has countered that strikes, in the long run, bring about better pay for teachers, which leads to higher professional morale and greater benefits for the children.

Questions you are facing include:

- Do you think that striking is more of a legal rights or a moral rights issue?
- Is a teachers' strike any different from the strikes of other professionals such as nurses, pilots, or auto workers?
- If the association votes on a strike, how will you vote? What will you do if the strike is called?

---

increased their emphases on school improvement, the restructuring process, and the empowerment of teachers. Thus, in the 1990s both organizations maintain a balance between unionism and professionalism.

An interesting breakthrough in the competition between the AFT and the NEA occurred in California, in the fall of 1989, when the two local unions merged. The resulting organization is known as the United Educators of San Francisco, and members belong to the state and national organizations of both the AFT and the NEA. At the national level, there is open discussion about the possibility of a formal merger at some point in the future. In 1993 formal discussion of merger began between the leadership of both organizations. Such a merger would bring 3,000,000 professionals under one leadership and significantly increase their political clout on the national scene.

Political Action

An area of rapid development within teachers' organizations is that of **political action committees.** The AFT has an active Committee on Political Education (COPE). A similar NEA committee is called the Political Action Committee (NEA-PAC).

Reason for Political Action. This development was motivated by the success other unions and organizations have had through systematic political action. In the past, many organizations used moral persuasion, in which delegates

Diversity Note 3.1:
Both the AFT and NEA have consistently supported equity activities for their members. This behavior is easily seen in the governance structures of the organizations where leadership positions are held by members of both sexes, and there is racial diversity in leadership as well.

Journal Activity Master 3.2: An Analysis of Teacher Power. This activity provides students with an opportunity to analyze the various types of impact that teacher power has on society.

Objective 6:
Explain orally the concept of Political Action.

Key Term:
Political action committees in teacher education

Focus Question 3:
To what extent do you think teacher organizations should have political clout?

Discussion Question 3:
Should teacher organizations be involved in political action—for example, helping to elect political candidates who are sympathetic to their cause? Why or why not?

presented themselves to legislators or legislative committees to ask for legislation to meet organizational needs. The lessons of history show that this procedure does not work very well. Other organizations, including teachers' organizations, have found a much more effective method—helping to elect political candidates who are sympathetic to their particular needs. The political action committees monitor elected officials' voting records on education bills and analyze the platforms of new candidates. Teachers' organizations plan to support actively those candidates who will perform according to the organizations' views.

Relevant Research

Teachers Need to Become Active Researchers

There is little doubt that teachers can become competent classroom researchers. A recent study concluded that if teacher-researchers are to contribute to educational change, they need to have school and district support for accomplishing this goal. Although most teachers in the survey indicated that a researcher role for the teacher is at best a difficult task for them because of the everyday realities of their job, their attitudes toward research would change if they developed confidence and understanding of research methods. Specifically, teachers need to:

- redefine their role to include responsibilities for doing classroom research;
- be given administrative and school district support;
- be encouraged to test new research findings in their classrooms; and
- have staff development practices that include conference attendance, formal research training, and available research resources.

We encourage you, as a beginning teacher, to actively prepare yourself to do classroom reasearch. Work through your teacher association to achieve some of your goals for becoming a successful researcher.

Source: Christene K. Bennett, "Teacher-Researchers: All Dressed Up and No Place to Go?" *Educational Leadership 51* (2) (October, 1993): 69–70.

The Common Aim of National Political Committees. The state and national political action committees of the NEA and AFT have a common aim—to promote education by encouraging teachers to participate in the political life of their local, state, and national communities. These committees throughout the states are responsible for recommending political endorsements to their respective boards of directors. Interestingly, the NEA and AFT political action committees usually agree on which candidates to endorse during national elections. Both organizations have strongly endorsed Democratic party candidates, feeling that they would be more supportive of education at the national level. A significant sign of organizational professional growth, however, is the fact that national political party emphasis no longer directs COPE and PAC endorsements. Candidates of both parties are endorsed based on their support for the educational policies of both the NEA and AFT.

National teachers' union leaders continue to suggest that their political clout pays off for education. In terms of support of future political candidates, teachers' unions remain consistent in their claims that they will support

Information Note 3.6:
Many politically involved teachers serve in a variety of electioneering positions. These may include precinct committee people, county and state organization officers, and campaign workers and/or staffers for candidates.

those who seem to favor public education. Teachers' unions monitor the federal administration's actions that affect public education, and they have been vehement in their opposition to funding cuts in public education programs.

State and Local Teacher Organizations

While state and local units that are affiliated with a national organization operate under the umbrella of the parent national offices, these units are the power base of the organizations. The local association of teachers has the highest priority in the whole organization; however, the strength of any single local union lies in the solidarity in numbers, in resource personnel, and in services that the state organization provides. In the early 1960s, teachers generally became more militant regarding salary and working conditions. Classroom teachers' associations at the local level became more active in seeking assistance from state and national associations. As competition between the larger national associations grew in intensity, elections at the local level became the procedure for gaining the bargaining representation for each district. Local elections for the role of bargaining agent among competitive teacher groups remain the most important steps in the process for organizing teachers in any district, whether or not the local classroom teacher association is affiliated with a state or national organization.

Teacher Participation: Local Organization. For the most part, teachers participate directly in the affairs of local organizations. Solutions to the problems at hand are primarily the concerns of local teachers' groups. The influence of these groups would obviously be weakened without the support and resources of strong state and national parent organizations. At the same time, local organizations sometimes become indifferent about their national and state affiliation.

Local Relationships with State and National Organizations. Leadership at the national level views the problems and differences in beliefs among the local organizations as a viable part of the democratic process rather than as divisive. From the many geographic locations, grass roots views of local teacher organizations may surface through the state associations to the national level or from the local organizations directly to the national level. Decisions related to national policy are then made by majority vote with attention paid to input from all levels—local, state, and national. In some instances, local organizations have severed relations with their state and national affiliates when the members felt that their particular needs were not well met. Since the power of the state and national organizations is reduced somewhat each time a local organization withdraws state and national affiliation, state organizations especially are compelled to pay careful attention to the particular needs of local teachers' association affiliates.

Specialty Associations

There are many other associations that teachers may join, participate in, and provide leadership for that deal with their chosen profession. These specialty associations are organized around specific job assignments that teachers have (science teaching, mathematics teaching, etc.). They also relate to broad-based curriculum and school restructuring movements (effective schools, writing across the curriculum, and cooperative learning). There are a large number of these specialty associations that teachers can be a part of. An excellent listing of about 6,000 national trade associations; labor unions; professional, scientific, and technical societies; and other national organizations composed of groups united for a common purpose is given in the annual edition of *National Trade and Professional Associations of the United States* (published by Columbia Books, Inc., 1350 New York Avenue, NW, Suite 207, Washington, DC 20005). A recent edition listed 540 organizations under the "Education" heading, including those identified with specific academic disciplines, religions, and other education-related categories. Prospective teachers are encouraged to locate the most recent annual edition of this publication in their college or university library and peruse it to gain

Focus Question 4:
Do you know the name of the specialty studies and job-related associations that are available to teachers?

Journal/Portfolio Development 1:
Gather information about your state and national organizations for your teaching field (math, science, elementary). From your perspective as a new teacher, evaluate their publications, activities, and espoused agendas and how they can benefit you.

Journal/Portfolio Development 2:
Create a collection of five professional journals that will be helpful to you as a beginning teacher. Indicate how they can be useful from a content and/or instructional perspective.

Key Term:
World Confederation of Organizations of the Teaching Profession (WCOPT)

Educators United: Ready for Change

EI's First World Congress
Harare, Zimbabwe
19-23 July 1995

Global organizations such as Education International, which exists to promote the profession of teaching worldwide, indicate American educators' growing recognition of other societies.

a broader perspective of the organizations that exist to serve their individual needs and purposes.

Assignment-Related Organizations

As one would think, teacher organizations have been formed for each of the academic disciplines, as well as for each of the other curriculum areas such as vocational-technical, business, health, home economics, physical education, and driver education. We cannot attempt to list all of these organizations here. For purposes of illustration only, a few of the teaching assignment–related organizations are presented in Appendix 3.1 on page 74. These organizations typically publish professional journals, sponsor conferences, establish standards, and generally work to advance the field they represent.

Religious Education Associations

There are many religious education associations of various denominations. These national and regional religious education associations are under denominational or interdenominational control and do one or more of the following: operate sectarian schools attended by students who prefer them to public or secular private schools, supplement the public or private school program by offering educational activities for youth and adults, operate adult educational programs open to the public, and formally promote scholarships among their members. A partial listing of religious education associations is as follows:

> Association of Seventh-Day Adventists Educators
> Catholic Biblical Association of America
> Council for Jewish Education
> National Association of Episcopal Schools
> Association of Christian Schools International
> Religious Education Association

World Confederation of Organizations of the Teaching Profession

The aims of the **World Confederation of Organizations of the Teaching Profession (WCOTP)** foster a conception of education directed toward the promotion of international understanding and goodwill, with a view to safeguarding peace, freedom, and respect for human dignity. The WCOTP supports efforts to improve teaching methods, educational organizations, and the academic and professional training of teachers so as to equip them better to serve the interests of youth; to defend the rights, materials, and moral interests of the teaching profession; and to promote closer relationships among teachers in the different countries.

Member institutions of the WCOTP come from approximately a hundred nations. The NEA and AFT are members. In a study based on questionnaire data gathered by the WCOTP, many educational problems common to all nations were identified, including lack of funds, shortage of excellent teachers, the need for school buildings, and the need for compulsory and free education. The WCOTP, facing these problems with determination, holds an assembly of delegates once each year. Resolutions of the assembly have ranged widely, from intensive literary programs to free education at all levels, from increased availability and status of technical education to special and adequate provision for the educational and medical needs of the physically and mentally handicapped. The WCOTP also sponsors regional conferences. In the past these conferences have dealt with such topics as the status of the teaching profession in Niamey, Niger; teaching science in elementary schools in Asia; and the teacher's part in nation building. The WCOTP's bulletin, *Echo*, designed to promote international understanding, is published in thirteen languages. *Educational Panorama*, another WCOTP publication, is published in English, French, Spanish, Japanese, and Arabic.

Global Perspectives: Education International (EI). In January 1993, Education International (EI) officially replaced the WCOPT. EI has united more than 240 national educator unions and professional associations from around the world. This new organization brings together over 20 million elementary, secondary, and college and university staffs. In the United States, this merger brings the NEA and AFT together under a world umbrella with former NEA president Mary Hatwood Futrell as EI President and the International Federation of Free Teachers' Union (IFFTU) General Secretary, Fred Van Leeuwen, as general secretary of EI. Since the United States AFT has been an affiliate of IFFTU, this should encourage the potential merger of the NEA and AFT in the United States.

Education International's First Action Agenda. Moving now on a total global perspective, EI is focusing its efforts on:

- Improving the quality of education,
- Upgrading education employee working conditions and compensation,
- Fighting for adequate educational funding,
- Sharing curriculum,
- Safeguarding human rights,
- Fighting for gender equality, and
- Building stronger educational organizations.

Discussion Question 6:
Most public school teachers know little about religious education associations and/or the World Confederation of Organizations of the Teaching Profession. What should schools do (if anything) to provide their teachers with knowledge about these organizations? Discuss your rationale.

Activity 3.8:
Have students discuss the international implications of EI on the NEA and AFT.

Diversity Note 3.2:
Both the WCOTP and EI state that as the world gets smaller and smaller, the teaching profession must become more globally connected. As this comes to fruition, teachers of both genders and all races, colors, and creeds will interact professionally with each other.

Summary and Implications

This chapter presented the concept of teacher power as a viable force in the formulation of education-related decisions. Discussion of teacher power was followed by information about teacher organizations (local, state, and national), which are the vehicles through which teacher power is expressed. The National Education Association (NEA) with over two million members and the American Federation of Teachers (AFT) with approximately 806,000 members are the largest teacher organizations (unions). Detailed attention was given to the organizational structures of these agencies and to comparisons of the two. Perhaps the ultimate manifestation of teacher power comes from the rapidly increasing development of the respective NEA and AFT political action committees, NEA-PAC and COPE.

Attention was also given to assignment-related and specialty study, religious education, and worldwide organizations. A list of teaching assignment-related specialty study associations was presented. Similarly, several associations related to religious education were listed. Finally, a brief description of the aims and memberships of the World Confederation of Organizations of the Teaching Profession (WCOTP) was presented.

The implications are straightforward. Prospective teachers will experience concerted pressure to affiliate with the recognized teacher organizations. Each teacher must decide the advantages and disadvantages of such paid memberships. In some school districts the climate of the working environment of teachers is very similar to that of trade unions. In other districts, teachers try to keep a more scholarly, professional climate analogous to that of traditional professions like law, dentistry, and medicine. How each teacher will contribute to the organizational climate associated with a particular membership must be a personal decision.

Similarly, teachers have an opportunity as well as a professional responsibility to join one or more of the specialty study associations. Through these associations it is possible to be continually updated regarding initiatives and procedures that are being tried, as well as to develop an extended array of contacts of people within the profession who think and care about the subject as much as you do. Most of the professional associations will issue monthly or bimonthly journals or newsletters and have an annual national meeting. In addition, in most cases, there will be regional and perhaps state meetings. In all of these situations it is possible to learn more about your profession as well as to become involved as a participant, contributor, and leader.

Discussion Questions

1. Teachers' organizations defend the rights, materials, and moral interests of the teaching profession. To what extent should the organization defend a teacher's choice of reading material for classroom use? To what extent should the organization defend the rights of gay teachers?

2. During a teachers' strike, members of a factory union from a neighboring city joined the teachers' picket line to support the teachers' demands. Do you agree or disagree with the factory union action? Explain your answer.

3. Should teacher organizations be involved in political action—for example, in helping to elect political candidates who are sympathetic to their cause? Why or why not?

4. Why are the local units of teacher organizations extremely important to the national organization? Discuss.

5. A major distinction between the professional initiatives of the NEA and AFT and those of the assignment-related/specialty studies associations is their scope. NEA and AFT activities tend to focus on school-wide and district-wide initiatives while specialty studies focus on classroom and curriculum-specific topics. How do you think teachers should go about taking advantage of and integrating both of these perspectives and sets of initiatives?

6. Most public school teachers know little about religious education associations and/or the World Confederation of Organizations of the Teaching Profession. What should public schools do (if anything) to provide their teachers with knowledge about these organizations? Discuss your rationale.

Journal/Portfolio Development

1. Gather information about your state and national organizations for your teaching field (math, science, elementary). From your perspective as a new teacher, evaluate their publications, activities, and espoused agendas and how they can benefit you.

2. Create a collection of five professional journals that will be helpful to you as a beginning teacher. Indicate how they can be useful from a content and/or instructional perspective.

School-Based Experiences

This chapter provides you with information about the two major teacher organizations, the National Educational Association (NEA) and the American Federation of Teachers (AFT). When you accept a teaching position, you will most likely be asked to become a member of the NEA or the AFT. You should try to become knowledgeable about teacher organizations. When you have the opportunity to visit schools and classrooms, ask teachers and administrators their opinions about teacher organizations.

Write to a few organizations to which you might wish to belong as an educator. Ask for materials and an application form. Seriously consider joining some of these organizations as a student member (which is typically at a very reduced membership fee).

Note

1. *NEA Handbook, 1991–92.* (Washington, DC: National Education Association), 13, 159, 175.

Bibliography

American Federation of Teachers. *The AFT* v. *the NEA.* Washington, DC: American Federation of Teachers, 1989.

National Education Association. *Doubts and Certainties* 7 (4). (January/February, 1993) Washington, DC: The Association.

American Federation of Teachers. *American Teacher 77* (7). (April, 1993) Washington, DC: The Federation.

Constitution of the AFT. Washington, DC: American Federation of Teachers, AFL-CIO, 1988.

NEA Handbook, 1991–92. Washington, DC: National Education Association, 1991, 12.

American Federation of Teachers. *PSRP Reporter.* (Summer, 1993) Washington, DC: The Federation.

Nielsen, Robert M., and Polishook, Irwin H. *Academic Unions, Values and Democracy.* Pamphlet Series. Washington, DC: American Federation of Teachers, 1989.

Professional Education Associations

American Alliance for Health, Physical Education, Recreation & Dance (AALR)
1900 Association Drive
Reston, VA 22091
(703) 476–3472

American Alliance for Theatre and Education (AATE)
Theatre Arts Department
Virginia Tech.
Blacksburg, VA 24061
(703) 231–7624

American Association of Physics Teachers (AAPT)
5112 Berwyn Road
College Park, MD 20740
(301) 345–4200

American Comparative Literature Association (ACLA)
c/o Larry H. Peer, Comparative Literature Department
Brigham Young University
Provo, UT 84602
(801) 378–5529

American Council on the Teaching of Foreign Languages (ACTFL)
(Classical and Modern)
Six Executive Blvd., Upper-Level
Yonkers, NY 10701
(914) 963–8830

Association for Educational Communications and Technology (AECT)
1025 Vermont Avenue, SW, Suite 820
Washington, DC 20005
(202) 347–7834

American Federation of Teachers AFL-CIO (AFT)
555 New Jersey Avenue, NW
Washington, DC 20001
(202) 879–4400

American Home Economics Association (AHEA)
1555 King Street
Alexandria, VA 22314
(703) 655–4380 (703) 704–4600

American Speech-Language-Hearing Association (ASLHA)
10801 Rockville Place
Rockville, MD 20852
(301) 897–5700

American Vocation Association (AVA)
1410 King Street
Alexandria, VA 22314
(703) 683–3111

Association for Childhood Education International (ACEI)
11141 Georgia Avenue, Suite 200
Wheaton, MD 20902
(301) 942–2433

Association for Education in Journalism & Mass Communication (AEJMC)
1621 College Street
University of South Carolina
Columbia, SC 29208
(803) 777–2005

Association for Supervision and Curriculum Development (ASCD)
1250 N. Pitt Street
Alexandria, VA 22314
(703) 549–9110

Council for Exceptional Children (CEC)
1920 Association Drive
Reston, VA 22091
(703) 620–3660

International Reading Association (IRA)
800 Barksdale Road
P. O. Box 8139
Newark, DE 19714–8139
(302) 731–1600

International Technology Education Association (ITEA)
1914 Association Drive
Reston, VA 22091
(703) 860–2100

Modern Language Association of America (MLA)
10 Astor Place, 5th Floor
New York, NY 10003
(212) 475–9500

Music Teachers National Association (MTNA)
617 Vine Street, Suite 1432
Cincinnati, OH 45202
(513) 421–1420

National Art Education Association (NAEA)
1916 Association Drive
Reston, VA 22091
(703) 860–8000

National Association of Biology Teachers (NABT)
11250 Roger Bacon Drive, #19
Reston, VA 22090
(703) 471–1134

National Association for the Education of Young Children (NAEYC)
1834 Connecticut Avenue, NW
Washington, DC 20009
(202) 232-8777

National Association for Gifted Children (NAGC)
1155 15th Street, NW
Suite 1002
Washington, DC 20005
(202) 785-4268

National Business Education Association (NBEA)
1914 Association Drive
Reston, VA 22091
(703) 860-8300

National Council for the Social Studies (NCSS)
3501 Newark Street, NW
Washington, DC 20016
(202) 966-7840

National Council of Teachers of English (NCTE)
1111 Kenyon Road
Urbana, IL 61801
(217) 328-3870

National Council of Teachers of Mathematics (NCTM)
1906 Association Drive
Reston, VA 22091
(703) 620-9840

National Education Association (NEA)
1201 16th Street, NW
Washington, DC 20036
(202) 833-4000

National Middle Schools Association (NMSA)
4807 Evanswood Drive
Columbus, OH 43229
(614) 848-8211

National Science Teachers Association (NSTA)
1742 Connecticut Avenue
Washington, DC 20009-1171
(202) 328-5800

Dreamcatcher

JIM KUBIK has been a senior government teacher at Norfolk Senior High School in Norfolk, Nebraska since 1977. He was the 1991 Nebraska Teacher of the Year and has won numerous awards for classroom teaching. He was awarded the 1994 H. Councill Trenholm Memorial Award for Promoting Racial Understanding from the National Education Association. Kubik wrote the Nebraska Multicultural Education Act, which the Nebraska Unicameral passed in 1992; the law requires all Nebraska public schools to infuse cultural awareness into the total curriculum K-12. Several of his students helped lobby the law into reality. He took a one-year leave from teaching to work for the Nebraska Department of Education during the 1992–1993 school year to help organize the statewide implementation of the law.

When nonwhite students began appearing in my classroom as a result of a meat packing plant locating in Norfolk, I began to understand the need for more cultural awareness, not only in students, but in the whole community. I began to hear more racial jokes and stereotyping. These words were coming out of the mouths of good white students, who simply repeated what they heard at home. These students were graduating with scholarships, and yet some of them believed that all Hispanics are lazy and only blacks are on welfare. I began to wonder if we were really preparing our students for a world where they will be working with people from many different racial backgrounds. I concluded that we were not.

My nonpartisan political science club held a public forum on the issue of "Racism in Nebraska" in September of 1990. Over 1,000 people attended the forum and heard a racially diverse panel give their perspectives on race relations in Nebraska. Many of our students were so motivated by this forum that it caused them to start asking questions about multicultural education, and why they were not getting any cultural awareness education in school.

Several of these students and I approached our local school administration with the idea of infusing multicultural education into our local school district. During the next year, we tried in vain to get something started. Most of our school administrators dragged their feet and literally stalled. They felt it was just too controversial. Frustrated, my students and I approached State Senator Ernie Chambers of Omaha, the only African American state senator in the Nebraska Unicameral. We asked him to sponsor a law that would require the teaching of cultural awareness to be infused in all curriculum areas in all public schools in Nebraska. With Senator Chambers' leadership, the law passed. My students were instrumental in the lobbying efforts. This law has resulted in schools and communities thinking about the importance of cultural awareness and how it can begin to curb racial misunderstandings. Our schools will finally begin to recognize the contributions that all cultures of America have made to our great nation.

Speaking in support of multicultural education in Nebraska, at first, was not a popular thing to do, *but it was the right thing to do!* As teachers, it is our responsibility to speak out for what is right and to do what is needed to make sure *all* of our students get the best education possible.

As teachers, we have an obligation to prepare our students to appreciate the diversity that this nation has always had. This is as important as mathematics and science education.

School and Society

Focus Questions

1 What is the relationship between power and discrimination?
2 How do schools contribute to the socialization of children and youth?
3 How do schools assist in the reproduction of society?
4 Whose values are taught in schools?
5 What factors influence the subculture of a school?

Key Terms and Concepts

Discrimination: Individual or institutional practices that exclude all members of a group from certain rights, opportunities, or benefits.

Dominant group: The cultural group that has the greatest power in society; in the United States it is composed primarily of persons from a European background who are Protestant, middle class, not disabled, heterosexual, and male. This term is sometimes used synonymously with mainstream culture or group.

Equal educational opportunity: A policy to ensure that all students, regardless of their cultural background or family circumstances, are provided access to a similar education.

Equality: The state of being neither inferior nor superior.

Informal curriculum: The norms and values that define expectations for student behavior and attitudes, and that undergird the curriculum and operations of schools.

Meritocracy: A system that is based on the belief that those who achieve at the highest levels deserve the greatest rewards.

Prejudice: Preconceived negative attitudes toward the members of a group of people.

Racism: The conscious or unconscious belief that racial differences make one group superior to another, leading to discriminatory actions that limit the opportunities for members of the perceived inferior group to share in the same benefits of society.

Sexism: The conscious or unconscious belief that men are superior to women, and subsequent behavior and action that maintain the superior, powerful position of males.

Socialization: Process of learning the social norms of one's culture.

Values: Principles, standards, or qualities considered worthwhile or desirable.

**Journal/Portfolio
Development 1:**
Define democracy and write a
paper that (a) describes a
classroom that operates on
democratic principles and (b)
contrasts it with traditional
classrooms. The description
should include the set-up of
the room, the interaction
between the teacher and
students, and the interactions
of students, among other
characteristics.

Key Term:
Equality

Objective 1:
Elaborate on the contradictions inherent in democracy
as practiced in the United
States.

Information Note 4.1:
Although the number of
women in Congress has
improved greatly over the past
twenty years, only eight of the
100 members of the Senate
in the 104th Congress
(1995–1996) were women.

Test Questions 4.6–4.15

Activity 4.1:
Divide the class into small
groups and have students
begin to identify the groups to
which they belong that help
define who they are and what
their interests are. Compare
commonalities and differ-
ences among class members,
and identify the primary reasons for the differences. Discuss how the groups to which
students belong are viewed
within the social system.

Key Term:
Discrimination

The United States prides itself on being the premier model of a democratic society. Most of us would probably agree with the dictionary that defines it as "a government in which the supreme power is vested in the people and exercised by
them directly or indirectly through a system of representation usually involving
periodically held free elections."[1] The definition further describes democracy as
including the rule of the majority and practices that favor social **equality.**

Democracy has undergirded our political rhetoric for over two hundred years.
The principles of democracy teach us that we can be equal and full participants in
this democratic society. At the same time, we observe that Congress is not composed equally of men and women, nor is it representative of the ethnic, racial, religious, language, economic, or age diversity that actually exists in the nation. There
are significant differences in the education levels, types of jobs, and family incomes
across racial groups and between men and women. Children in low-income families suffer disproportionately from limited access to the best teachers, best instruction in our schools, good nutrition, safe environments, and community support
and caring.

What is the nature of groups in a democratic society? How do our interactions
with members of groups different than our own influence our ability to achieve a
democratic state supportive of egalitarian ideals? Finally, how do schools contribute to the maintenance of society and help students engage in and promote
the ideals of a democracy? We will address these issues in this chapter.

Groups in Society

A democratic society struggles with how to support individuality and yet develop
a consciousness of shared concerns and actions that promote equality. This challenge is paramount in a society like the United States that includes many groups
that impact and are impacted by political, social, and economic systems.

Some individuals are members of a group because of ascribed characteristics
at birth such as race or gender. Others belong to groups where the members share
the same national origin, native language, economic circumstances, religious affiliation, and/or residence in a specific geographic region. Of course, we each belong
to all of these groups or microcultures. At the same time, we often interact with
members of different groups in school, work, or social settings. We also may interact with others around common interests such as environmental concerns, school
funding, moving drug dealers from the block, or day care support.

Members of society view the importance of group membership differently.
Many European Americans, especially the Protestant middle class, do not identify
themselves by their racial, ethnic, gender, religious, or socioeconomic group. They
do not distinguish themselves from the larger society and often do not acknowledge the advantage that membership in these groups has provided them. On the
other hand, persons whose ancestral roots are outside of Europe, or who are recent
immigrants are more likely to identify themselves by their ethnicity, race, or religion. They or other members of their group have experienced **discrimination** in
housing, jobs, educational opportunities, or treatment by store clerks or police
officers. Their common history and experiences reinforce a group identity[2] that is
distinct from mainstream society.

Having experienced discrimination, members of excluded groups can describe
differential power relations among groups. However, members of groups who do
not normally experience discrimination have a more difficult time acknowledging

that differences in power and advantage exist. As a result, the rights of group membership versus those of individuals are debated on college campuses, in board meetings of corporations, by politicians, and in many formal and informal neighborhood meetings. These discussions focus on programs that are perceived to favor a group other than our own—affirmative action, bilingual education, and equality in funding for male and female athletes. An examination of power relationships and experiences with differences should highlight the struggles inherent in a democratic society.

Power and Domination

In 1916 John Dewey described a democratic society as one in which all of its members are able to share its benefits on equal terms.[3] Eighty years later, many persons of color, limited English speakers, women, persons with disabilities, gays and lesbians, persons with low incomes, and persons affiliated with religions other than Protestanism have still not experienced equality with members of the **dominant group.** Why have we not yet been able to achieve the egalitarian ideal that should characterize democracy? The primary factor is the inequitable power relationships that exist across groups as described by Seth Kreisberg:

> Across a broad spectrum of institutions that shape our lives, people have power over other people; that is, people have the ability to control, manipulate, and coerce other people for their own ends. These relationships of domination are not haphazardly and randomly developed. Rather, the very structures of our social institutions and the predominant norms, **values,** and beliefs of our society sanction, indeed define and reinforce, them. The ability to control and manipulate others also derives from privileged access to and control of valued resources such as education, personal wealth, housing, food, health care and weapons of war.[4]

Schools provide an example of an institution in which power relationships have been developed and maintained. Students' work and class rules are determined by teachers. Teachers are evaluated and disciplined when necessary by principals who report to a superintendent of schools. The rules and procedures for managing schools traditionally have been established by authorities who are not directly involved with the school and who may not even live in the community served by the school. Parents, especially in economically oppressed areas, often feel powerless in the education of their children.

Not only do power and domination characterize our political and economic systems, they influence relations within the family, between the sexes, among racial groups, and among members of many religious traditions. The father figure traditionally has been all powerful. Instead of there being shared relations between males and females, husbands and wives, and parents and children, one sometimes dominates the other. In these power relationships, someone or some group is viewed as inferior to another. It is no accident

CNN Clip 6:
Sheenway School

Key Term:
Dominant group

Key Term:
Values

Objective 2:
Compare the power relationships that exist in society with those that exist in schools.

The teacher-student relationship, as with many others in American society, is defined by one person having power over others

Information Note 4.2:
In an increasing number of families, men and women are sharing the job of child care, which traditionally has been the domain of the female.

Discussion Question 1:
Why is it so difficult for middle-class whites to acknowledge that their group membership historically and currently places them in a privileged position?

Discussion Question 2:
Provide examples of discriminatory practices against females, African Americans, non-native English speakers, Native Americans, the disabled, the elderly, and/or homosexuals that have become institutionalized in the educational system.

Information Note 4.3:
1990 public expenditures per student in the first through twelfth grades in the United States was $4,765, as compared to Japan's $2,624. For higher education, the United Kingdom spent $9,087 per student, as compared to $8,275 in the United States and $1,988 in Japan.

that politics, religions, and businesses have been controlled primarily by men. Until recently, they were the group more likely to be socialized to be in charge. Although this pattern is beginning to disintegrate in some families and groups, it remains so prevalent that it is often not questioned; it has been accepted as the natural way of behaving. As a result, when women are harassed, wives or children are beaten, and disproportionate numbers of African American young men are jailed, many members of the society do not react.

Many people with power in U.S. society believe that they have this status because of their individual abilities and accomplishments. They usually give no credit to their membership in the dominant group. The 1994 National Conference Survey on Inter-Group Relations[5] found that most whites do not think they have an advantage over members of other racial and ethnic groups. On the other hand, the majority of people of color in the survey characterized whites as "bigoted, bossy, and unwilling to share power."[6] There appears to be a large gap in the perceptions of power between the dominant and oppressed groups in this society.

Power not only allows domination over the powerless, it also allows access to societal benefits like good housing, tax deductions, the best schools, and social services. It is not an asset that the powerful are willing to give up or readily share with those whom they see as less deserving. A more equitable sharing of resources for schools would guarantee that all students, regardless of income or ethnic background, would have qualified teachers, sufficient books and other instructional resources, well-maintained buildings and playgrounds, and access to high-level academic knowledge. Such equality does not exist across schools that students attend today. The great disparities between schools for advantaged and underserved students have been described graphically in Jonathan Kozol's book, *Savage Inequalities: Children in America's Schools:*

> New Trier's physical setting might well make the students of Du Sable High School envious. The *Washington Post* describes a neighborhood of "circular driveways, chirping birds and white-columned homes." It is, says a student, "a maple land of beauty and civility." While Du Sable is sited on one crowded city block, New Trier students have the use of 27 acres. While Du Sable's science students have to settle for makeshift equipment, New Trier's students have superior labs and up-to-date technology. One wing of the school, a physical education center that includes three separate gyms, also contains a fencing room, a wrestling room and studios for dance instruction. In all, the school has seven gyms as well as an Olympic pool.
>
> The youngsters, according to a profile of the school in *Town and Country* magazine, "make good use of the huge, well-equipped building, which is immaculately maintained by a custodial staff of 48."
>
> It is impossible to read this without thinking of a school like Goudy, where there are no science labs, no music or art classes and no playground—and where the two bathrooms, lacking toilet paper, fill the building with their stench.[7]

Difference and Otherness

Power relationships between groups appear to influence young people's perceptions of themselves and the members of other groups. One of the struggles of youth is the construction of self, including identification and affiliation with one's gender and a racial or ethnic group. This process appears to be integrally tied to identifying "otherness," which involves assigning characteristics and behavior to members of other groups to distinguish them from oneself. The construction of others places them either in a dominating or submissive role relative to the individual. It is often dependent on stereotypes that are promoted among peers and reinforced by society.

Test Questions 4.16–4.25

Prejudice and Discrimination

Not only do our perceptions of others affect how we see ourselves in relationship to them, but they also have an influence on the treatment of members of the groups by society. **Prejudice** is a preconceived negative attitude against members of an ethnic, racial, religious, or socioeconomic group that is different from one's own. This prejudice sometimes extends to persons with disabilities or of a different sexual orientation. Such negative attitudes are based on a number of factors, including information about members of a specific group that is stereotypical and many times not true. The prejudiced individual often has had little or no direct social contact with members of the other group.

An individual's prejudice may have limited negative impact on members of the other group. However, these attitudes are passed on to children through the **socialization** process. They can be transferred into discriminatory behavior that prevents members of a group from being interviewed for a job, joining a social club, or being treated like other professionals. Prejudices are too often reinforced by schools in which a disproportionate number of students in low achieving tracks are from low-income families[8] and in special education have limited English proficiency.[9] Through this process, many students from low-income families and ethnic minority groups are prevented from gaining the skills and knowledge necessary to enter college or an apprentice trade.

> ## Relevant Research
>
> ### Development of Racial and Gender Identity
>
> The construction of identities of white males and females was the focus of a mid-1980s ethnographic study in a high school located in a city where the major factory had recently closed. The researcher collected data from students, teachers, and other school personnel in classrooms, study halls, the cafeteria, and extracurricular activities.
>
> The vast majority of the white working class males in the study believed that they would have wives and families in the future. Their descriptions of females exhibited an assumed male superiority in which females were both "other" and inferior. Their male identity was "dependent upon the construction of women as unable to take care of themselves monetarily and as having full responsibility for the day-to-day activities of children." The school appeared to offer no "sustained challenge to the vision of male dominance."
>
> The identities of these young white men not only depended on their construction of gender; they were also based on their construction of race. The goodness of white was always contrasted with the badness of black. Black men were constructed as overly sexualized individuals from whom white women must be protected. The white men in this study elaborated "their own sexuality in relation to Blacks. Black men and women [were] the foil against which they set up their own heterosexuality." On the other hand, white females did not develop their identities in relationship to blacks.
>
> *Source:* Lois Weiss, "At the Intersection of Silencing and Voice: Discursive Constructions in School," *Educational Studies 24* (1): 1–23.

Key Term:
Prejudice

Key Term:
Socialization

Institutional Discrimination

In addition to individual prejudice and discrimination, society has historically discriminated against members of powerless groups. The individuals who control and oversee our institutions are primarily members of the dominant culture. They tend to be ethnocentric in the view that their culture is superior to others, even

Objective 3:
Give examples of institutional discrimination in society and in the educational system.

Information Note 4.4:
In 1992, 97.1 percent of the superintendents of schools were white and 89.5 percent were male.

Focus Question 1:
What is the relationship between power and discrimination?

CNN Clip 7 :
Race and IQ

Key Term:
Racism

Transparency 28:
Racial Diversity of the United States.

though they have rarely experienced other cultures and have little knowledge about them. Laws and systems have been designed to promote and support the dominant culture to help maintain its superiority and the power of its members. "English only" laws that prevent official documents and communications from being printed or spoken in any language other than English is but one example of these efforts. Such practices have often become institutionalized in state and federal laws, the judicial system, schools, and other societal institutions. They have become so ingrained in the system that it is difficult to recognize them unless one is directly affected by the discriminatory policies.

Racism

Superiority is at the center of **racism,** in which members of a racial group believe that they are innately better than members of other groups. It is not a topic easily discussed in most classrooms. It is intertwined with the lived experiences of many and evokes emotions of anger, guilt, shame, and despair. Most of us learned that the United States is a just and democratic society. Therefore, it is difficult for us to confront the contradictions that support racism. Nevertheless, it is important to acknowledge the advantages or disadvantages that racism has wrought in one's life in order to overcome its negative impact on society.

Students and adults go through stages of racial identity as they address issues of discrimination and racial identification.[10] As teachers, we should be able to recognize these stages and help students in their struggle to know themselves. Cross identified five stages in black racial identity.[11] In the *preencounter stage,* an African American has assimilated into the mainstream culture, accepting many of the beliefs and values of the dominant society, including negative stereotypes about blacks. The *encounter stage* is usually entered when an individual is confronted directly by a racist act such as rejection by white peers or being the victim of racial

CASE STUDY   INTERRACIAL DATING

Revonda Bowen is president of the junior class at Randolph County High School in the small town of Wedowee, Alabama. She is also chairperson of the junior-senior prom committee and helped raise over $7,000 for the event. Revonda's mother is black and her father is white.

In February the school principal assembled the junior and senior classes and announced that he would cancel the prom if anyone came with a date of another race. Revonda asked whom she should bring since she was a mixed-race student. In front of the entire assembly, the principal told her that her parents had made a "mistake," meaning that she should not have been born. He then said that he was trying to prevent similar "mistakes" by banning interracial dates for the prom. Revonda was crushed and burst into tears.

1. What sociohistorical conditions contributed to this incident?
2. How would you have responded to interracial dating at the prom if you had been the principal?
3. As a teacher, how would you help black and white students in your class deal with this incident?

Source: Morris Dees, Memorandum from the Southern Poverty Law Center, Montgomery, AL, April 8, 1994.

slurs or attacks. In the *immersion/emersion stage,* identification as an African American becomes paramount. At first, this identification is manifested in anger against whites, but it evolves into building a knowledge base about African American history and culture. "The result of this exploration is an emerging security in a newly defined and affirmed sense of self."[12] Individuals in the fourth stage of *internalization* begin to build coalitions with members of other oppressed groups and relationships with whites who respect and acknowledge them. Those at the fifth stage of *internalization-commitment* are able to both maintain and move beyond their personal racial identity to be concerned with African Americans as a group.

The researchers who have investigated the stages of racial identity have found that it is not as linear as was described above. Individuals may move back and forth across stages as they encounter new experiences.[13] One of the first steps in this process is for us to begin to confront our own racial identity. How close are any of us to reaching an internalization stage? If we have not struggled with issues of racism, how it impacts on our lives, and how we may contribute to its perpetuation, it will be impossible for us to develop antiracist classrooms.

Sexism and Other Isms

Women, persons with disabilities, homosexuals, persons with low incomes, the elderly, and the young also suffer from discrimination and their lack of power in society. A number of individuals are members of many of these powerless groups. They may suffer double and triple indemnity as a result of racism, **sexism,** and classism. Their chances of reaching a standard of living to be comfortable in this nation are severely limited by their circumstances and group membership, as is shown in Table 4.1 on page 86.

Sexism has contributed to limited participation of young women in advanced mathematics and sciences[14]—areas that could improve their chances for attending and being successful in college. Our system, which has not viewed women's work as equal to men's work,[15] has kept women's wages lower than men's and contributed to poverty in over one-third of the households headed by women in this country.[16] Gays and lesbians continue to face legal discrimination in many areas of the nation. The young and elderly disproportionately face poverty. Policies related to child care, subsidized housing, and access to nutritious food sometimes have prevented husbands and wives of low-income families from maintaining a household together. Equality has not been achieved when great disparity in jobs, incomes, and access to quality education continues to exist among groups.

Democracy and Schooling

Children learn to function in society through a process called socialization. Parents and families are usually the primary socialization agents, especially in the early years of a child's life. Appropriate behaviors are also reinforced in religious training, the community, and even television. Upon entrance in school, whether as an infant or at age six, teachers and other school personnel take on these roles during a large portion of the student's waking hours. At this point, the family shares the teaching function with professionals in schools.

Since the beginning of the twentieth century, policies of the United States have promoted universal education for all students. Children are required to stay in school until they are sixteen years old. Approximately 87 percent of high school

Objective 4:
Reflect on how the reader is centered in discussions on racism and sexism.

Key Term:
Sexism

Information Note 4.5:
Nearly a fourth of the nation's children and 12 percent of people over sixty-five years old live below the poverty level.

Test Questions 4.26–4.45

| TABLE 4.1 | What Economists Say You Are Worth |

Age (Years)	Men			Women		
	Total	White	Nonwhite	Total	White	Nonwhite
Under 1	$ 89,645	$ 93,860	$ 57,467	$ 56,996	$ 58,065	$ 49,807
1–4	101,997	106,650	65,813	64,672	65,808	56,838
5–9	136,929	143,143	88,471	86,739	88,246	76,285
10–14	183,525	191,844	118,603	116,236	118,251	102,254
15–19	238,085	248,661	154,477	148,282	150,909	130,073
20–24	288,217	300,783	185,851	167,650	170,815	145,586
25–29	314,618	328,409	198,394	166,408	169,716	143,152
30–34	314,250	328,475	191,689	155,504	158,936	131,076
35–39	296,372	310,241	173,865	142,624	146,177	116,295
40–44	265,345	277,663	152,278	127,356	130,888	99,651
45–49	224,215	234,140	128,038	108,904	112,376	80,184
50–54	176,931	184,060	102,981	86,692	89,926	58,690
55–59	124,684	129,036	76,884	62,238	64,983	37,442
60–64	71,000	73,287	45,934	39,387	41,281	21,532
65–69	33,317	34,281	23,287	21,878	22,882	11,899
70–74	18,190	18,729	12,716	12,140	12,624	6,780
75–79	9,999	10,442	5,829	6,249	6,488	3,599
80–84	5,905	6,171	3,384	2,773	2,874	1,678
85 and over	955	999	535	357	368	236

These figures show the worth of an individual based on race and gender. They are based on a 1976 Social Security Administration paper, but have been updated to 1981.

Source: M. Sinclair, "How Does Society Put a Price Tag on Human Life?" *The Washington Post,* March 22, 1981. © 1981 *The Washington Post.* Reprinted with permission.

Activity 4.2:
Divide the class into four groups. Ask each group to develop a scenario that describes one of the following settings: (1) a school climate that is democratic; (2) a school climate that is not democratic; (3) a classroom that is democratic; and (4) a classroom that is not democratic. Compare these scenarios with the school experiences of students in the class.

Focus Question 2:
How do schools contribute to the socialization of children and youth?

Transparency 23:
High School Completion Trends.

students complete high school,[17] but we believe that even more young people should finish school. The GOALS 2000 legislation passed by Congress in 1994 calls for 90 percent of all students to graduate by the end of this century. The goal to educate nearly all of the population is an undertaking few countries attempt.

Roles of Schools

Schools serve a number of roles for society. Not only do they prepare students to be contributors to society, they also reflect good practice (universal education) and bad practice (differential achievement based on race). One's philosophical perspective determines how the roles of schools are viewed.

Reproduction. Traditionally, schools are expected to reproduce the cultural, political, social, and economic order of society. However, theorists differ in their views of how schools operate in this reproduction role. Functionalism, conflict theory, and resistance theory provide contradictory descriptions of the goals of schools as they carry out their reproductive role for society.

Functionalists view schools as important in supporting technological development, material well-being, and democracy. Since the release of the federal report *Nation at Risk* in 1983, most reports calling for the reform of schools have referred to the need for an educated workforce. A less explicit message of those reports is that schools should socialize students for their roles as workers. Schools should provide **equal educational opportunity** for all students and be a primary step for improving their social and economic status.

Conflict theorists also view schools as reproductive of society, but for purposes less noble than those granted by functionalists. Their analysis concludes that schools have been structured to maintain the power and dominance of the individuals and groups that benefit most from the current system. Rather than being benevolent institutions that provide all students an equal chance to succeed, schools legitimize existing inequities. Advantages depend greatly on ascribed characteristics. Students whose parents graduated from college are much more likely to graduate from college. Students whose parents never finished high school are themselves more likely not to finish high school. The academic tracking systems in many schools reinforce this unequal distribution. The number of middle-class students in college preparatory and advanced placement courses is disproportionately high when compared to the total school population. The number of males and students of color in special education classes is disproportionately high; students of color and those from low-income families are underrepresented in gifted and talented programs. It appears to these critics that one group is being groomed for management positions in the labor market while the second group is being prepared to labor under the direction of the first group. Thus, schools provide neither equal educational opportunity nor a chance to improve one's status to any appreciable degree (except for rare individual achievements).

Over the past decade some researchers have investigated the interactions of students and teachers as schools carry out their reproduction function. It is not an automatic process that is implemented with systematic precision. Students sometimes resist domination by school authorities. They do not readily accept their inferiority status. Kreisberg describes student resistance:

> Students resist doing homework and delay the beginning of classes. They develop intricate systems of cheating and psyching out teachers. They smoke cigarettes and marijuana in school bathrooms and sell drugs in school stairwells. They are opinionated with teachers and wear clothes that offend adults. They refuse to participate in some classes and organize to change unfair rules. (p. 17)

The resistance theory suggests much more interaction in the reproduction process than has been described in the previous two theories. It also allows for possibilities to change the system of reproduction by encouraging the development of schools that are not based on domination and submission and that actually model democracy. Students become active participants who help define and redefine schools in the process of resistance.

Reconstructionism. Some educators believe schools are able to do more than just reproduce society. They believe that schools do not need merely to reflect the inequities that prevail in the broader society; rather, schools can reconstruct or transform society. They believe that all students can learn at a high level regardless of their race, ethnicity, gender, or socioeconomic status. Education can make more of a difference in the lives of students than it currently does.

Transparency 28:
Percent of Public High School Graduates.

Information Note 4.6:
The National Center for Education Statistics reports that there is far greater variation in the mathematics, science, and literacy proficiency of students within each country than differences in averages among countries.

Objective 5:
Identify different roles for the schools.

Journal Activity Master 4.1: An Evaluation of the School as Reproducer. This activity requires students to organize a series of activities that schools exhibit into one of three roles (reproduction, adjustment, or change agent). The exercise concludes with an analytical question that helps students clarify an argument supporting one of the three roles as the predominant one schools exhibit.

Focus Question 3:
How do schools assist in the reproduction of society?

Discussion Question 3:
How do functionalists and reconstructionists expect schools to implement the purposes outlined in this chapter?

Key Term:
Equal educational opportunity

Information Note 4.7:
A number of school systems across the country are working with prominent educators to reform their schools to promote high-level learning among students. These include Ted Sizer's Coalition of Schools for Essential Learning, Alvin Pouissant's full-service schools, and Henry Levin's transformational schools.

To implement a reconstructionist approach, classrooms and schools become democratic settings in which both students and teachers are active learners and participants. Students study problems confronting society and learn the skills that allow them to attack practices that are inequitable to some students. Teachers and other school personnel actively work with the community to overcome inequities and injustices to students and their families. Social justice, human rights, human dignity, and equity are critical values that guide the work of reconstructionism. In the process the school itself should become a model of democracy that leads, rather than follows, societal practices.

Purposes of Schools

Objective 6:
Describe at least five purposes of schooling.

Activity 4.3:
Ask each student to jot down one psychological or academic need that he or she is experiencing right now. Then, have students anonymously hand in their identified needs. Place the class list in a summary chart and discuss which needs can and cannot be met in school.

Sometimes the purpose of schools reflects a perceived shortcoming in the current education system. The plethora of reports calling for the reform of education that have been written over the past two centuries have identified different purposes for schools. The five purposes described below are only a sampling of those most often mentioned by educators and the public. Most schools address each of these issues, but one may receive more prominence than others because it is a trend at a particular time.

Citizenship. Educators, parents, and policymakers agree that schools should help students become *good citizens*. There is less agreement about how schools should do this. In some schools, especially elementary schools, students receive a grade or rating on their citizenship within the classroom. Historically, students have taken a civics or government course, or they study these issues in another social studies course. The focus of citizenship education or civics and government courses is usually on the structure of the United States political system and treasured documents such as the Constitution and Bill of Rights. Patriotism and loyalty to the United States are implicit values that often undergird these courses and

Civic education usually emphasizes patriotism and national loyalty.

the hidden curriculum. A limitation of this approach is that students are seldom provided the opportunity to grapple with the problems and issues that are inherent to our democratic society. Students may learn the civic values, but never be pushed to discuss why inequities remain in society.

In a discussion of reconceptualizing civic education, Pratte[18] suggests that preparation for citizenship cannot be limited to a course. The school should promote democratic citizens who respect others; believe in human dignity; are concerned about and care for others; and fight for justice, fairness, and tolerance. Dewey also believed that good citizenship involves participating in the making of laws as well as obeying them. Through education, students should be guided to develop habits of mind that will bring about social changes without introducing disorder.[19] Students will learn through practice how to be active, involved citizens. What better place to model democratic practice and equitable participation than in our schools?

Participation in the Work Force.   One of the eight national education goals that President Clinton signed into law in 1994 stated that by the year 2000, "every American will be literate and will possess the knowledge and skills necessary to compete in a global economy." This statement parallels many of the education reform documents. A major concern expressed in these reports has been the quality of the workforce, which includes growing numbers of women and persons of color at all levels. Schools are blamed for not providing students with the skills and behaviors necessary to participate in today's economy. Some employers report that many young people do not read, write, and compute at the level needed for the jobs available. In response, these employers have sometimes established their own training to teach basic literacy.

There is a lack of agreement about the nature of these necessary skills, especially in an economy in which the greatest growth in jobs will be in the service areas, where persons of color and women have disproportionately high representation. Most high schools prepare students either to attend college or to get a job soon after graduation. Many areas of the country have vocational high schools to teach occupational skills. A number of school districts have established magnet schools with single purposes, including career preparation in the arts, health fields, computing, and service areas like foods, hotels, and tourism. A more serious dilemma is that low-income students, students of color, and females are disproportionately represented in nonacademic tracks.

Educators, policymakers, and the business community debate the "real" purpose of schools. Is the primary purpose to help students learn a trade, or learn how to learn, or learn how to take orders and follow the rules? This question is particularly important when conditions change as rapidly as they do in today's society. The vocation for which one was prepared may become obsolete. Perhaps

Information Note 4.8: The National Center for Education Statistics reported that public high school graduates in 1992 took seventeen course units in academic subjects, four in vocational subjects, and three in personal-use subjects. Males, African Americans, and Native Americans had the highest participation rates in vocational courses.

Many students begin to prepare for a job after graduation by taking vocational courses in high school or at the postsecondary level in vocational schools designed for that purpose.

John Dewey was on target in 1916 when he wrote that "a society which is mobile, which is full of channels for the distribution of changes occurring anywhere, must see to it that members are educated to personal initiative and adaptability."[20] Perhaps we should prepare students to think, adjust to change, and be active participants in their life's work.

Academic Competence. Periodically, the public becomes very concerned about the academic competence of students. This concern is reinforced by well-publicized reports of scores on achievement tests. Some school districts base their reputations on how well their students perform. Countries and their education systems are compared using performance on international tests. When the scores of U.S. students fall below those of students in other countries, policymakers become concerned. In the 1980s, concern about performance in reading, writing, and mathematics led to a back-to-basics movement in which the traditional academic subjects were emphasized. "Frills" such as the development of self-esteem, hobbies, and any other areas that took time away from academic study were condemned as a misuse of public funds. In response, a number of states and school districts increased the length of the school day so that students could have more time to learn what was expected. This emphasis reappears in two of the eight goals in GOALS 2000.

Social Development. One of the reasons that parents send their children to school is to give them the opportunity to develop interpersonal skills by interacting with other students. In this process students should learn to respect others; they also learn a set of rules for working appropriately with peers and others. Although there is usually not a course to teach skills in social development, appropriate behavior is constantly reinforced by teachers and other school personnel in the classroom and on the playground.

In our teaching we can give students opportunities to work with students from diverse cultural backgrounds and learn about those differences in the process. Interactions across groups can be encouraged through cooperative learning activities in which students from different groups are placed together. Other team projects allow us to place together students who might not seek each other out otherwise. A part of our teaching will be helping students to learn to work together positively.

Today's technology also opens many possibilities for interacting with students and adults in cultures beyond our own school boundaries. Internet and two-way video connections allow students in rural New Mexico to talk directly with students in inner city Chicago or Toyko, Japan. Many teachers have developed these linkages themselves with the assistance of other knowledgeable teachers they have met in college classes and at professional meetings. Your professor may know of easily accessible software to help you begin to make these connections across cultures.

Cultural Transmission. Schools around the world are expected to transmit the culture of their nation to young people so that they can both maintain it and pass it on to the next generation. This task often has been approached by teaching history with an emphasis on important events and heroes. As part of this process, children learn the importance of patriotism and loyalty. The formal and informal curricula have been designed to reflect and reinforce the values of the national culture.

These national values and rules are so embedded in most aspects of schooling that most participants—teachers and students alike—do not realize they exist. The only exceptions may be students who do not belong to the dominant culture or whose families have recently immigrated. In these cases, students and families quickly learn that schools do not reflect, nor do they usually support, aspects of their culture that differ from the mainstream. This dissonance between schools and families is most noticeable when students are from non-European backgrounds. Students from religious backgrounds that have not evolved from a Judeo-Christian heritage are also likely to question the culture that is being transmitted at school. The challenge for educators is to transmit the national culture while including the richness and contributions of many who do not yet see themselves as an integral part of that culture. In this way, we also begin to change and expand the national culture.

Whose Schools?

Although schools are expected to transmit the culture of the nation to the younger generation, we do not agree on *whose* culture. Is there really a national or common culture that the diverse racial, ethnic, language, and religious groups in the country accept? Dialects, behaviors, and values vary within the same cultural group as well as across groups whose members live in different regions of the country. Cultural differences are even experienced by people who move from rural areas to the city or vice versa.

How can schools begin to accommodate all of these differences? A number of conservative politicians and talk show hosts argue that schools should ignore diversity. They believe that all students should learn our common heritage and adopt the national culture as their own. In this approach, students who are not members of the dominant group are expected to leave their native language or dialect and other cultural characteristics at the doorstep of the school.

Multicultural theorists and educators argue that the diversity of students enriches the school community. They believe that cultural differences should be valued and integrated throughout the curriculum and all activities of the school. In this approach, the cultural background and experiences of students are used to teach academic and other skills at high levels.

Alternative Schools. The public schools in some districts offer options in which parents can choose the schools they deem appropriate for their children. (Similar to private schools, parents may not receive their first choice if more students have applied than there are spaces available.) In a number of large school districts, magnet schools offer specialized curriculum in the arts, languages, mathematics and science, and technical fields. Some schools have been established to place the students' ethnicity at the center of the curriculum. In an Afrocentric curriculum, for instance, African American history and experiences are the core from which the world is viewed, rather than the traditional center of Western Europe.

Some private schools were established to provide an alternative for whites who did not want their children to attend schools that were being desegregated.[21] Other private schools limit their enrollment to either males or females or to students of the same faith. The more elite boarding schools usually offer scholarships

Activity 4.4:
Invite a school administrator to speak to the class about responding to community pressures and strategies developed to include communities in decision making about curriculum changes.

Information Note 4.11:
Smaller percentages of students attend private schools as they progress from kindergarten to high school. In 1991, 60 percent of the preschoolers attended a private school as compared to 7 percent of the secondary students.

Activity 4.5:
Identify a panel of students to discuss their experiences in different kinds of schools (for example, parochial, public, independent private, and alternative schools in rural, suburban, and urban areas). Class members could develop a grid to contrast the reasons for attendance at different types of schools and to compare the advantages and disadvantages of each.

Information Note 4.12:
Racially and ethnically heterogeneous schools have the potential of improving student outcomes and intergroup relations.

Focus Question 4:
Whose values are taught in schools?

Key Term:
Informal curriculum

Journal/Portfolio Development 2:
Select a school or community in which there has been debate regarding the values to be reflected in the curriculum. (Widely publicized examples can be found in New York City, Pennsylvania, Ohio, and Kentucky). Analyze the fundamental differences between the groups in a paper, chart, or pictorial format. Identify strategies that could have prevented the conflict.

Activity 4.6:
Have students select a controversial issue that is receiving a great deal of coverage by the press. Have them identify any ways that schools have contributed to the controversy.

Discussion Question 4:
How can teachers bridge the value differences between various groups in the community? What curriculum content could spark debates in the community?

to some students who cannot afford the tuition, but are attended predominantly by children of the rich. A few public schools today have been designed for females only, with the goal of improving their academic achievement, especially in science and mathematics, and building their self-esteem. A few large cities like Detroit, Baltimore, and Minneapolis have established schools for African American and/or Native American students to provide positive gender and cultural identity models and teach skills that will empower them to overcome many of the obstacles they face. Thus, in some schools, students continue to be segregated for the purpose of avoiding integration. In other cases, the segregation has the goal of overcoming obstacles to success for members of selected powerless groups.

A growing number of parents do not enroll their children in either private or public schools. Instead, they receive permission from the state to teach their children at home. In some cases, they believe that they are more effective teachers. More often, they believe that schools teach values that they cannot support; home teaching allows them to instill the values that they think are important.

Whose Values? The selection of a private school or home schooling and support for segregated schools has been based, in part, on the values that parents believe schooling can impart. Although schools usually do not offer a course in which values are explicitly presented and discussed, values implicitly influence the formal and **informal curriculum.** They usually support the current ideological, political, and economic order of society in which individualism is much more highly regarded than the rights of the group. The Protestant work ethic is upheld in the expectation of hard work and the belief that one will be successful in life as a result. Although these may seem uncontroversial, they can be the cause of extensive debate and emotional pleas at meetings with groups of parents, school board meetings, community forums, and magazines.

Some parents are concerned that the curriculum does not reflect their religious values; often, they think that their religion is purposefully denigrated in schools. These concerns are expressed most frequently by members of some fundamentalist Christian communities, but also by Amish and Hutterite communities, and some Jewish, Muslim, and other non-Christian families and communities. On the other hand, atheists believe that religious values, especially Christian ones, pervade the school curriculum.

The emphasis on individualism and competition that is prevalent in many schools is not compatible with the cooperative patterns practiced by Native American tribes and many Latino and African American communities. These differences can lead to conflict between parents and schools and between groups within a community. The courts have often been asked to sort through these value issues since the plaintiffs believe that schools have acted inappropriately. They may also believe that either the schools do not have a democratic process in which they can be heard or the majority of the community will not support their petitions. Therefore, they turn to the justice system to help clarify the issues. School prayer, teaching creationism, banning books, sex education, and segregation are among the areas that have been tested in the courts.

Because parents and other groups in a community may vehemently disagree with the values to be reinforced in schools, we should be aware of our own values. Knowing our values as well as those of the families represented in the school should help us prepare for potential conflicts. Expectations can vary greatly from one community or school to another.

CASE STUDY | **VALUES IN EDUCATION**

*B*eginning in 1989, the Pennsylvania State Board of Education began revising its state code from Carnegie Units of coursework to student learning outcomes (sometimes called outcomes based education or OBE). Outcome #6, which was presented to the public in hearings in 1991, focused on appreciating and understanding others:

> (i) All students explore and articulate the similarities and differences among various cultures and the history and contributions of diverse cultural groups, including groups to which they belong. (ii) All students relate, in writing, speech or other media, the history and nature of prejudice to current issues facing communities, the United States, and other nations. (iii) All students develop skills of communicating, negotiating, and cooperating with others to solve interpersonal and intergroup problems and conflicts. (iv) All students work effectively with others, demonstrating respect for the dignity, worth, contributions, and equal rights of each person.

Reactions to the proposed fifty-seven core outcomes were diverse and intense. Outcome #6 was attacked by a well-organized special-interest group, Citizens for Excellence in Education. The opponents read the outcome as promoting a value system different than the student's own. "Other" was defined as alternative lifestyles, particularly homosexual. "Tolerance" was a value that they could not support.

The debate in Pennsylvania over values and OBE drew the media, and the controversy was expanded. The education reform package was defeated in January 1993. Outcome #6 and all references to attitudes and behavior were removed from the package. The revision was accepted in June 1993.

1. Why did the Citizens for Excellence in Education develop such an active interest in the Pennsylvania reform package?
2. How could a small, special-interest group take advantage of the public's lack of information on this issue?
3. How could state officials have prevented such an attack on the reform package? What impact do these debates have on local classrooms and schools?

Source: Judith McQuaide and Ann-Maureen Pliska, "The Challenge to Pennsylvania's Educational Reform," *Educational Leadership 51* (4) (December 1993/January 1994): 16–21.

Equality and Education

Test Questions 4.46–4.55

Discussion Question 5:
Contrast meritocracy and equality. What characteristics in society would be indicators that equality exists across groups in this country?

Activity 4.7:
Have students prepare a debate between the value of meritocracy and equality and the way that they are reflected in schools.

Key Term:
Meritocracy

Although equality is an espoused goal of democracy, its meaning differs based on the speaker. Many believe that each individual has an equal chance to succeed, which is measured by the dominant group in terms of wealth and accumulated material goods. This system of **meritocracy** is built on the importance of the individual. With hard work, diligence, and persistence, an individual should be able to finish school, attend college, and obtain a well-paying job. Poverty and discrimination are obstacles to be overcome by individuals.

A problem with meritocracy is that not all individuals begin the game of life from the same starting line. Whites from the middle class and above start with advantages such as the dominant culture being their own, sufficient family income to support a college education, decent housing, adequate health care, and good schools with qualified teachers. The advantages of the parents are passed on to the children, allowing them a head start in the race. In reality, the children of the

As a result of family income, some students may have a head start over others in school.

wealthy have a much greater chance of being wealthy in their adulthood than the children of low-income families. The powerful are able to ensure that their advantages are inherited by their children. Therefore, equality could only begin to be realized in this system if the children from powerless groups were provided the same or similar advantages.

Critics of the public rhetoric on equality charge that our institutions and political and economic systems are rigged to support the privileged few rather than the pluralistic majority. Both the shrinking middle class and the widening gap between wealth and poverty contribute to this critique. Nevertheless, some people still think that a more equitable society is not only desirable, but possible to achieve. Resources could begin to be more fairly distributed if all workers received a decent wage (today's minimum wage leaves families at the official poverty level). The application of civil rights laws and a drastic reduction of discriminatory practices would contribute greatly to the provision of fairness and justice in the distribution of societal benefits. In the same spirit, schools should ensure that their policies and practices are equitable. They could begin this investigation by examining whether gifted and talented programs and honors programs are accessible to students from diverse cultural groups.

If a society accepts equality as one of its primary goals, its members must be active participants in achieving the goal. One step is the refusal to accept needless human suffering and exploitation that is reflected in homelessness; inadequate minimum wage; and schools that are dangerous, unsafe, and inadequately staffed. Another step is the confrontation and elimination of racism, sexism, and other forms of discrimination.[22]

Equal Educational Opportunity

One of the policies for addressing equality in the educational system is equal educational opportunity. All students, regardless of their backgrounds, are to be provided similar opportunities to learn and benefit from schooling. The dilemma in this approach is what comprises an equal educational opportunity. On the surface, it would seem that all students should have access to quality teachers, small classes, technology, college preparatory courses, a building that supports learning, and a safe environment. In reality, most equal educational opportunity programs have struggled with overcoming educational deficiencies of underserved students by providing compensatory or remedial programs to reduce the educational gaps that have given the advantaged students a head start. The other factors that would provide equal opportunity have not been addressed by most policymakers and educators.

Even when the school has the latest technology, is clean and well-maintained, and is staffed by qualified professionals, equal opportunity is not automatically guaranteed. A number of factors need to be considered. What percentage of female and minority students are found in advanced mathematics and science classes? Who comprises the college preparatory and advanced placement classes? Who is assigned or chooses a general or vocational track? Who is referred to special education classes? Who has access to the best teachers? Who participates in which extracurricular activities? If the percentage of students from diverse groups in these classes is somewhat proportional to their representation in school, equal educational opportunity may be approaching the goal of its supporters.

Opportunity to Learn Standards

According to the *Goals 2000: Education American Act*, schools must provide all students the opportunity to learn the skills outlined in the national standards being developed for mathematics, science, English, the arts, foreign languages, history, geography, civics, and economics. The provision of remediation for the underserved is no longer the focus. The expectation is that all students can learn. Because Goals 2000 also expects U.S. students to achieve better on international tests than students in any other part of the world, we may wonder if opportunity to learn actually means the ability to perform well on some tests. More optimistically, the standards could help prevent students from being tracked into courses and programs that limit their access to higher level knowledge. They could even encourage critical thinking and viewing the world and academic subjects from multiple perspectives.

CNN Clip 5:
Kids and Learning

Equality of Results

Some theorists and educators would argue that we must not stop at just providing the opportunity to learn. This approach again places the burden on individuals in that they choose whether to take advantage of the opportunity. If the goal is to ensure an equality of results, we would be expected to develop strategies for helping all students learn at a high level. We would start our careers with the disposition or belief that all children, regardless of their group memberships and environmental circumstances, are capable of learning. Students who are not performing well academically or otherwise would become the intellectual challenges for the teacher, or even better, a team of teachers and other support personnel. The goal would become the development of strategies to ensure learning rather than simply to move students to a different class to accommodate their limitations (and limit their chances for success in school).

Information Note 4.13:
If results were equal across groups, there would not be the current gaps in SAT scores, participation in advanced mathematics and science courses, and college attendance.

PROFESSIONAL DILEMMA

What If There Are Only a Few Girls in the Calculus Class?

Many argue that the reason few females take advanced mathematics and science classes is simply that they are not interested in these fields. Few suggest that they don't participate because they are not as smart as the male students. Why are most young women not interested in these subjects?

In some cases, they may believe that there is no payoff in taking these courses, which are usually perceived to be very difficult. They may be planning to work only a short time before they marry and stay at home to raise children. Perhaps no one has encouraged them to attend college—the only reason that one would take these courses anyway. Learning the skills that will translate into a job immediately after graduation may be viewed as a more practical route to follow.

One reason that few females participate in advanced mathematics and science courses is that they do not view themselves as potential mathematicians or scientists. There are few female role models to help them develop such an identity. Teachers and other school personnel can play an important part in socializing girls to see themselves in roles other than the traditional ones of mother, wife, teacher, nurse, secre-

---

Test Questions 4.56–4.65

Objective 10:
Discuss the elements of the subculture of the school.

Journal Activity Master 4.2: An Analysis of a School's Subculture. This activity requires students to visit a school and develop a school motto, banner, or song that exhibits the school's subculture.

Focus Question 5:
What factors influence the subculture of a school?

Activity 4.8:
Compare a community's expectations for an elementary teacher and for a secondary school teacher. Should they be different? How does the community expectation affect the professional development and commitment of the teacher?

Information Note 4.14:
A number of states are in the process of developing performance-based licensure systems that will assess the teacher's actual performance in the classroom before granting a teaching license.

Culture of the School

The school itself is a cultural system that differs from the family and broader community in which we participate. Despite individual differences in ability, rate of learning, and personal interest, most students are subjected to the same type of instruction. The school's rules regulate classroom behavior as well as determine acceptable dress and speech. Common rituals are found in athletics, extracurricular clubs, graduation exercises, and school social events. The signs and emblems of the school's culture are displayed in school songs, colors, and cheers.

Formal Practices

The school operation embraces varied formal practices that are common across most schools in the nation. Students are generally assigned to grade levels on the basis of age rather than readiness, ability, or interest. Almost all children start the first grade at age six; most attend kindergarten if it is available.

The length of a high school class is relatively standard, at around 50 minutes no matter what needs to be learned and how much time it may take. The Carnegie Unit is still used to award one high school credit for 200 minutes per week for 36 weeks of class time; a student must have completed a specified number of Carnegie Units to graduate from high school. Authority is adult-centered. Students are allowed little input into the content to be taught or the way in which it is taught. Reporting of educational achievements is also formalized. Letter grades are traditionally awarded on the basis of a competitive system that compares the achievements of students.

Some schools have attempted to reduce the formal structured experiences of schools by creating learning centers, nongraded programs, and individualized learning packages based on readiness and interest. Assessments of student achievement are beginning to move beyond pencil and paper tests. Educators and test makers are designing systems that include multiple assessments that show

tary, or librarian. Too many parents, counselors, and teachers strongly encourage males to take these classes, but do not aggressively push the females to enroll in them.

Schooling contributes to this problem in other ways as well. Researchers who observe teachers' interactions with their male and female students find differences in the way teachers respond to the two groups. Teachers interacted more with males than females during lessons in mathematics. Teachers were more likely to work individually with males on classroom management, directions, and procedures. When teachers consciously changed their interactions to be more equitable, the females performed well. In fact, "the more that teachers asked high-level mathematics questions and interacted about mathematics at a high cognitive level with girls, the more girls learned about a higher cognitive level of mathematics."

■ Do you believe that males and females have different aptitudes for mathematics and science? Why?

■ How would you encourage females in your classroom to both learn and like mathematics?

■ What characteristics would you expect to find in a good, nonsexist classroom?

Source: Elizabeth Fennema and Penelope L. Peterson, "Effective Teaching for Girls and Boys: The Same or Different," in David C. Berliner and Barak V. Rosenshine, eds. *Talks to Teachers.* New York: Random House, 1987, 111–125.

much more than factual pieces of information that students can recall. They also indicate the ability to think critically and to perform effectively. They are becoming more authentic in that students are expected to perform in real life, rather than contrived, settings.

Traditions

Variations in the school culture are associated with regional influences, the social structure of a community, and location in a rural, urban, or suburban area. Some schools are influenced greatly by the religion of the children's families; others by the presence of a large military base.

Regional interests may influence the sports activities that are fueled through school spirit. In the Midwest, for example, basketball is the favored sport. In other parts of the country fierce athletic competition may be associated with football, swimming, wrestling, or gymnastics. Rural schools often emphasize Future Farmers of America clubs, agricultural programs, and 4-H clubs—activities that you are not likely to find in urban schools.

Schools with long histories have developed lasting traditions that are transferred from generation to generation. Sometimes graduates retain feelings of pride about their schools. For others, the memories are of mediocrity and of never being challenged.

Journal Activity Master 4.3: An Analysis of a Community's Impact on the School's Subculture. This activity requires students to attend an after-hours school-sponsored event. Using several structured questions, students take notes and interpret their impressions of the community's relationship to the school's subculture.

Informal Curriculum

All schools offer a formal curriculum that includes coursework in numerous academic areas. In addition, there is an informal curriculum that is seldom discussed and sometimes not acknowledged by educators. It is composed of the rules that guide the work of the school. This curriculum defines the behaviors and attitudes expected of both students and teachers, and it signifies which students are privileged by promoting their cultural values and patterns. The teacher is acknowledged

Objective 11: Describe and provide examples of the informal curriculum.

A region's special interests are often demonstrated through a school's extracurricular activities.

as the expert and is granted authority for ruling over students.[23] Critical theorists argue that these practices help maintain the status quo and current inequities in society.

For most students from the dominant culture the informal curriculum generally reinforces behaviors expected by their parents. These students fit fairly easily into the school culture. On the other hand, students from different cultural backgrounds may find school practices foreign and even contradictory to what they learn at home. The emphasis on competition between students in the classroom provides an example of one learning style being valued over another.

The informal curriculum could become more equitable and supportive of democratic principles if educators acknowledged that many school policies and practices are discriminatory because they promote and reinforce only the dominant culture. Teachers must recognize their own prejudices and discriminatory practices in teaching and management of the classroom and work to develop strategies for eliminating them.

Global Perspectives: Studying in Japan

The Japanese are among the most highly educated people in the world. All young people finish junior high school, 94 percent attend high school, and nearly a third enroll in college.[24] Students in Japan spend more time in school than U.S. students. "The school day is longer, the school week is five and a half days, and the school year is broken only by a short summer vacation of a little over a month in late July and August, a New Year's holiday, and a break before the start of the school year at the beginning of April."[25] In addition, students are assigned daily homework, beginning in the first grade, and a large percentage of them spend their summer vacation studying. Of the 600 elementary school students surveyed in Tokyo, 75 percent went to *juku* (cram school).[26] Discrepancies in the quality of education across rural, urban, and suburban schools are limited as measured by the achievements of students in higher education.

Summary and Implications

Theories of functionalism, conflict, and resistance provide different descriptions of the role of schools in reproducing culture and society. The theory of reconstructionism suggests that schools can transform society into democratic and equitable institutions. Schools serve many purposes in society. Among these purposes are the development of citizenship, preparation for work, the development of academic and social competence, and the transmission of the culture to another generation. Although most parents would agree with these purposes, they may disagree about the values that undergird the curriculum and teaching practice. It is parents' perception of the values being taught that leads to conflict in some communities.

Group membership becomes important in schooling because many students come from families and communities that do not share the culture that is reinforced in school policies, practices, and expectations. U.S. society is based primarily on the cultural traditions of western Europe. Through historical and political developments, whites have been socialized to view themselves as superior to the members of other racial groups. This power differential is also found in relations between males and females and between individuals who are relatively wealthy and those in poverty. Individual achievement is highly valued within the dominant culture. In the meritocratic system that undergirds the U.S. economic and political system, successful individuals are the ones that deserve the greatest rewards from society. Individuals who are not successful are blamed for their lack of ability or desire. Proponents of this view believe that discrimination no longer exists and they resent policies and practices that grant rights to members of a group rather than to individuals. Critics of meritocracy believe that greater equality could be achieved in society through a more equal distribution of resources, the serious application of civil rights laws, and a drastic reduction in discriminatory practices against the members of powerless groups. Educators debate the value of equal educational opportunity, opportunity to learn standards, and monitoring the equality of results in promoting greater equality in schools. As of the mid-1990s, schools are still far from providing equality for all students.

Discussion Questions

1. Why is it so difficult for middle-class whites to acknowledge that their group membership historically and currently places them in a privileged position?

2. Provide examples of discriminatory practices against females, African Americans, non-native English speakers, Native Americans, the disabled, the elderly, and/or homosexuals that have become institutionalized in the educational system.

3. How do functionalists and reconstructionists expect schools to implement the purposes outlined in this chapter?

4. How can teachers bridge the value differences between various groups in the community? What curriculum content could spark debates in the community?

5. Contrast meritocracy and equality. What characteristics in society would be indicators that equality exists across groups in this country?

Journal/Portfolio Development

1. Define democracy and write a paper that (a) describes a classroom that operates on democratic principles and (b) contrasts it with traditional classrooms. The description should include the set-up of the room, the interaction between the teacher and students, and the interactions of students, among other characteristics.

2. Select a school or community in which there has been debate regarding the values to be reflected in the curriculum. (Widely publicized examples can be found in New York City, Pennsylvania, Ohio, and Kentucky.) Analyze the fundamental differences between the groups in a paper, chart, or pictorial format. Identify strategies that could have prevented the conflict.

School-Based Experiences

1. In one of your next observations of a class in a school, identify and record the written and unwritten rules that guide the interactions of students with each other and the teacher. What values are being reinforced with these rules that make up part of the informal curriculum?

2. During one of your next visits to a school, observe how students interact with individuals from cultural backgrounds different than their own. These observations could occur in the classroom, but also in the halls, at the principal's office, and during extracurricular activities. Are students interacting

across ethnic, racial, gender, and socioeconomic groups? What is the nature of the interactions? How has the school encouraged positive, productive interactions? Students, teachers, and parents could be helpful informants in your data gathering; ask them for their perceptions.

Notes

1. *Webster's Ninth New Collegiate Dictionary.* Springfield, MA: Merriam-Webster, 1991, 338.

2. James A. Banks, *Teaching Strategies for Ethnic Studies.* 5th ed. Boston: Allyn and Bacon, 1991.

3. John Dewey, *Democracy and Education: An Introduction to the Philosophy of Education.* New York: The Free Press, 1916, 99.

4. Seth Kreisberg, *Transforming Power: Domination, Empowerment, and Education.* Albany, NY: State University of New York Press, 11.

5. The National Conference of Christians and Jews. *Taking America's Pulse: A Summary Report of the National Conference Survey on Inter-group Relations.* New York: Author, 1994.

6. Ibid, 2.

7. Jonathan Kozol, *Savage Inequalities: Children in America's Schools.* New York: Crown, 1991, 65.

8. Jennie Oakes, *Keeping Track: How Schools Structure Inequality.* New Haven, CT: Yale University Press, 1985.

9. Richard A. Figueroa and Eugene Garcia, "Issues in Testing Students from Culturally and Linguistically Diverse Backgrounds," *Multicultural Education* (Fall 1994): 10–23.

10. J. E. Helms, Ed., *Black and White Racial Identity: Theory, Research and Practice.* Westport, CT: Greenwood Press, 1990.

11. William E. Cross, Jr., *Shades of Black: Diversity in African-American Identity.* Philadelphia: Temple University Press, 1991.

12. Beverly Daniel Tatum, "Talking about Race, Learning about Racism: The Application of Racial Identity Development Theory in the Classroom," *Harvard Educational Review* 62(1) (Spring 1992): 1–24.

13. T. A. Parham, "Cycles of Psychological Negrescence," *The Counseling Psychologist* 17(2) (1989): 187–226.

14. Oakes, 1985.

15. Harriet Bradley, *Men's Work, Women's Work: A Sociological History of the Sexual Division of Labour in Employment.* Minneapolis: University of Minnesota Press, 1989.

16. United States Bureau of the Census, *Statistical Abstract of the United States: 1992.* Washington, DC: U.S. Government Printing Office, 1992.

17. Ibid.

18. Richard Pratte, *The Civic Imperative: Examining the Need for Civic Education.* New York: Teachers College Press, 1988.

19. Dewey, 1916.

20. Ibid, 88.

21. Meyer Weinberg, *A Chance to Learn: A History of Race and Education in the United States.* New York: Cambridge University Press, 1977.

22. Henry A. Giroux, "Postmodernism as Border Pedagogy: Redefining the Boundaries of Race and Ethnicity," in Henry A. Giroux, Ed., *Postmodernism, Feminism, and Cultural Politics: Redrawing Educational Boundaries.* Albany, NY: State University of New York Press, 1991, 217–256.

23. John I. Goodlad, *A Place Called School: Prospects for the Future.* New York: McGraw-Hill, 1984.

24. Edwin O. Reischauer and Marius B. Jansen, *The Japanese Today: Change and Continuing* (enlarged edition). Cambridge, MA: Harvard University Press, 1995.

25. Ibid, 190.

26. Alexander Besher, *The Pacific Rim Almanac.* New York: HarperCollins, 1991.

Bibliography

Cookson, Peter W., and Persell, Caroline Hodges. *Preparing for Power: America's Elite Boarding Schools.* New York: Basic Books, 1985.

Edelman, Marian Wright. "Winson and Dovie Hudson's Dream." *Harvard Educational Review* 63(4) (Winter 1993): 463–491.

Estrada, Kelly, and McLaren, Peter. "A Dialogue on Multiculturalism and Democratic Culture." *Educational Researcher 22*(3) (April 1993): 27–33.

Giroux, Henry A. "Postmodernism as Border Pedagogy: Redefining the Boundaries of Race and Ethnicity," in Henry A. Giroux, Ed. *Postmodernism, Feminism, and Cultural Politics: Redrawing Educational Boundaries.* Albany, NY: State University of New York Press, 1991, 217–256.

_____ *Teachers as Intellectuals: Toward a Critical Pedagogy of Learning.* Granby, MA: Bergin & Garvey, 1988.

Goodlad, John I. *A Place Called School: Prospects for the Future.* New York: McGraw-Hill, 1984.

_____ *Teachers for Our Nation's Schools.* San Francisco: Jossey-Bass, 1990.

Gutmann, Amy. *Democratic Education.* Princeton, NJ: Princeton University Press, 1987.

_____ "Democratic Education in Difficult Times." *Teachers College Record 92*(1) (Fall 1990): 7–20.

Hodge, John L. "Equality: Beyond Dualism and Oppression," in David Theo Goldberg, Ed. *Anatomy of Racism.* Minneapolis: University of Minnesota Press, 1990, 89–107.

Kozol, Jonathan. *Savage Inequalities: Children in America's Schools.* New York: Crown, 1991.

Kreisberg, Seth. *Transforming Power: Domination, Empowerment, and Education.* Albany, NY: State University of New York Press, 1992.

The National Conference of Christians and Jews. *Taking America's Pulse: A Report of the National Conference Survey on Inter-group Relations.* New York: Author, 1994.

Plank, David N., and Boyd, William Lowe. "Antipolitics, Education, and Institutional Choice: The Flight from Democracy. *American Educational Research Journal 31*(2) (Summer 1994): 263–281.

Pratte, Richard. *The Civic Imperative: Examining the Need for Civic Education.* New York: Teachers College Press, 1988.

Scheurich, James Joseph. "Toward a White Discourse on White Racism." *Educational Researcher 22*(8), (November 1993): 5–10.

Sleeter, Christine. "White Racism." *Multicultural Education* (Spring 1994): 5–8.

Weinberg, Meyer. "Diversity without Equality Equals Oppression." *Multicultural Education* (Spring 1994): 13–16.

Welch, Sharon. "An Ethic of Solidarity and Difference," in Henry A. Giroux, Ed., *Postmodernism, Feminism, and Cultural Politics: Redrawing Educational Boundaries.* Albany, NY: State University of New York Press, 1991, 83–89.

5

A Multicultural Society

Focus Questions

1   Why is culture so important in describing a group of people?
2   How do race, ethnicity, gender, and socioeconomic status interact in society to result in discrimination and inequity?
3   What impact do society and culture have on the education process?
4   What is the role of group memberships in determining one's own cultural identity?
5   What are the dangers in responding to students based only on what appears to be their ethnic group identity?

Key Terms and Concepts

Acculturation: The process of learning the cultural patterns of a second culture.

Assimilation: The process by which an immigrant group or culturally distinct group is incorporated into the dominant culture.

Cultural pluralism: A state that exists when different groups maintain their culture parallel and equal to the dominant one in a society.

Culture: The totality of socially transmitted ways of thinking, believing, feeling, and acting within a group of people that is passed from one generation to the next.

Diversity: The wide range of ways in which human groups and populations have observable and demonstrable physical and behavioral differences.[1]

Enculturation: The process of learning the characteristics of the culture of the group to which one belongs.

Ethnic group: Identification of membership in a group based on the national origin (that is, a specific country or area of the world) of one's ancestors, a shared culture, and sense of common destiny.

Ethnocentrism: The belief that members of one's group are superior to the members of other groups.

Social stratification: Levels of social class ranking based on one's income, education, occupation, wealth, and power in society.

Socioeconomic status: Criteria to describe the economic condition of individuals based on their income, occupation, and educational attainment.

Test Questions 5.1–5.3

Key Term:
Culture

Key Term:
Ethnocentrism

Discussion Question 1:
How do culture and society interact to produce inequities between diverse groups?

*O*ur actions, values, thoughts, and patterns of learning are controlled by our **culture.** Most of the time, we are not aware of the power of our cultural upbringing. This phenomenon often leads to **ethnocentrism,** in which members of a group view their culture as superior to all others. Persons from other cultural groups are perceived as odd, amusing, inferior, or immoral.[2] Ethnocentrism is sometimes promoted in emotional calls for patriotism, especially at times when a country is involved in a political conflict with another country. The other country is often denigrated by name calling based on negative stereotypes of its citizens; this occurred in the 1990 war between Iraq and the United States and its allies.

Ethnocentrism is not limited to relations with other nations; it occurs often between groups within the United States. Homosexuals are victims of abuse by radio talk show hosts and some religious groups. The religious right appears to believe that its cultural values and lifestyles are the only correct ones; alternatives are not tolerated. Historically, many members of the dominant culture have believed that their culture is superior to those with non-European roots. Ethnocentrism extends beyond individuals' views of their culture, and has led to discriminatory policies and practices that favor members of the dominant group.

One of the manifestations of ethnocentrism is the inability to accept differences among groups as natural and appropriate. Educational philosopher, Young Pai, describes this reaction to others:

> When the dominant group in a society adopts the posture that its own set of values constitutes the only idealized norm in that society, the ethnic practices or traits of minority cultures are likely to be seen as deficient patterns that must be corrected either through education or coercion. In other words, the dominant culture tends to treat the differences as *deficits.* This attitude makes it difficult for us to see that other cultures also provide effective means of dealing with the needs and problems of the respective societies.[3]

When differences are translated into a deficit model, groups that are not accepted as part of the dominant culture are expected to give up their culture in order to be accepted. Schools and other institutions marginalize members of these groups because their differences are not valued. These attitudes are translated into compensatory education for children of poverty, transitional bilingual education for students with limited English proficiency, and special education for students with disabilities.

If teachers believe that all students can learn and that teachers can ensure that learning occurs, they must confront their own ethnocentrism. Often we do not recognize that we subtly, and sometimes overtly, transmit our feelings of superiority over students and their cultural groups in our interactions in the classroom and in the curriculum content that we teach. To be effective teachers, we need to think about differences as part of our rich cultural history.

Culture and Society

Test Questions 5.4–5.10

Focus Question 1:
Why is culture so important in describing a group of people?

Society is composed of individuals and groups that share a common history, traditions, and experiences with other members of the same group. Culture provides the blueprint for how we think, feel, and behave in society. It imposes rules and order on its members by providing the patterns that help them know the meaning of their behavior. Members of the same cultural group understand the subtleties of their shared language, nonverbal communications, and ways of thinking and knowing. They often misread the cultural cues of other groups, leading to miscommunications and misunderstandings between the members of the two groups.

People around the world have the same biological and psychological needs, but the way that they meet these needs is culturally determined. The location of the group, available resources, and traditions have a great influence on the foods eaten, grooming and clothing patterns, teaching and learning styles, and interactions of men and women and parents and children. The meaning and celebration of birth, marriage, old age, and death depend on one's culture. Culture impacts on all aspects of our lives, from the simplest patterns of eating and bathing to the more complex patterns of teaching, learning, and caring for those who are less fortunate.

Characteristics of Culture

Culture is learned, shared, adapted, and dynamic. We learn our own culture through **enculturation** that parallels the socialization process. Our parents and other caretakers teach us the culture and the acceptable norms of behavior within it. We internalize our cultural patterns so well and so early that it is difficult for us to accept that there are different, but just as appropriate, ways of behaving and thinking. When we live and actively participate in a second culture, we begin to more clearly see our own unique cultural patterns. Understanding cultural differences and learning to recognize when students do not share our own cultural patterns are critical steps in the provision of an equitable learning environment. Therefore, it is important to learn much more about cultures other than our own.

Culture is not static. It is dynamic and continually adapted to serve the needs of the group. Individuals and families adapt their culture as they move from a rural to an urban area. The conditions of a geographic region may require a number of adjustments. Technological changes in the world and society can also lead to changes in our cultural patterns.

Dominant or Mainstream Culture

The dominant culture in this country is that of white, middle-class Protestants whose ancestors immigrated from western Europe. It is primarily "an urban professional and business population, college educated, and increasingly characterized in the younger age groups by double incomes."[4]

The legal system, democratic elections, and middle class values have their underpinnings in institutions and traditions of western Europe. English is a polyglot of the languages of the invaders and rulers of Great Britain throughout history. This culture has had a major impact on society's institutions because it has been the male members of the group who have dominated the political system and related government positions of authority. Historically, other cultures have not been as highly valued. Thus, through centuries of control of these systems, policies and practices have been instilled within the system to both maintain the advantages of the dominant culture and limit the influence of other cultural groups.

What are some of the characteristics of the dominant culture today? Universal education and literacy for all citizens are valued. Mass communications, which have been enhanced by the media and computer networks, influence our view of

Activity 5.1:
Have students bring to class one representation of their culture to share with other members of the class, along with an explanation of its meaning to them or their family.

Objective 1:
Define *culture* and its salient characteristics.

Key Term:
Enculturation

Discussion Question 2:
Why do we often not recognize our own cultural patterns?

Information Note 5.1:
High school students whose parents have graduated from college take more academic courses and fewer vocational courses than students whose parents completed high school only.

Objective 2:
Identify some of the core values of the dominant society and explain why they sometimes lead to conflicts in schools with diverse student populations.

ourselves and the world. A job or career must be pursued in order for a person to be recognized as successful. Fun is usually sought as a relief from work. Achievement and success are highly valued and portrayed to others by the accumulation of material goods like a house, car, boat, clothes, and vacations.

Individualism and freedom are core values that undergird the dominant culture. Members believe that individuals are totally in charge of their own destiny or success.[5] They define freedom as "being left alone by others, not having other people's values, ideas, or styles of life forced upon one, being free of arbitrary authority in work, family, and political life."[6] Members of this group rely on associations of common interest rather than strong kinship ties. They believe in absolute values of right and wrong rather than in degrees of rightness and wrongness.

Transparency 31:
Cultural Diversity

Most members of this group identify themselves as American. They do not see themselves as white, Christian, English speaking, middle class, male, or heterosexual. Many middle-class Catholics and Jews share similar values and behaviors. Although many middle-class persons of color display similar behaviors, hold the same values, and view themselves as members of this dominant group, they simultaneously maintain a strong affiliation with their own **ethnic group.** Many low-income families also hold the same values, but do not have the income to support a similar lifestyle.

Key Term:
Ethnic group

Microcultures

Objective 3:
Identify at least seven microcultural groups in which we all participate and provide examples of how membership in one group interacts with membership in another.

Our cultural identities are not determined by ethnicity and race alone. Figure 5.1 illustrates the interaction of microcultural memberships in determining our cultural identity. We are members of multiple microcultural groups, each with its own traditions and rules. We are female or male, and members of a specific socio-

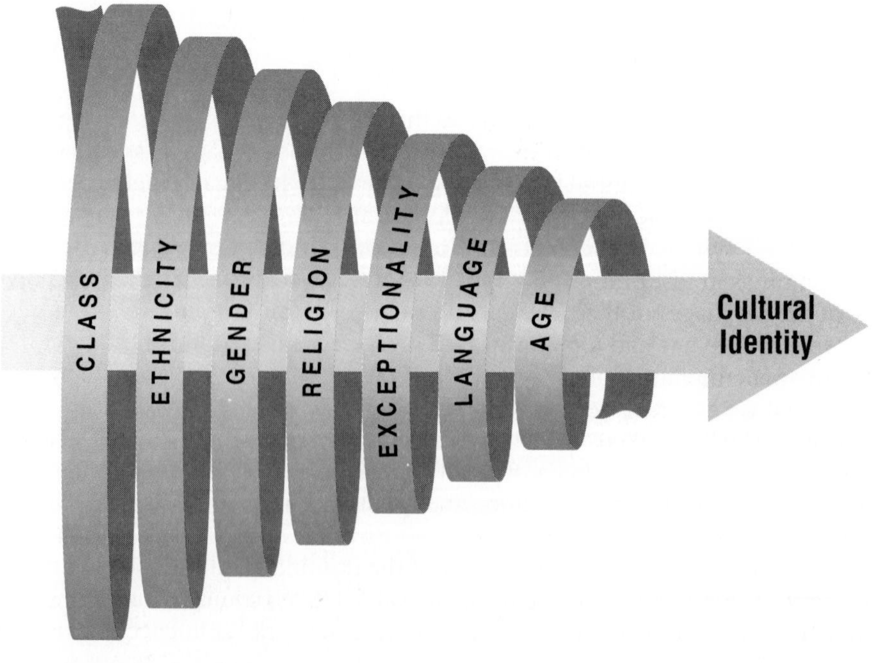

Focus Question 2:
How do race, ethnicity, gender, and socioeconomic status interact in society to result in discrimination and inequity?

FIGURE 5.1

Cultural Identity Is Based on Membership in a Number of Microcultural Groups That Interact with Each Other

(*Source:* Donna M. Gollnick and Philip C. Chinn. *Multicultural Education in a Pluralistic Society,* 4th ed. Columbus, OH: Merrill, 1994, 14. © 1994 by Merrill.)

CLASS   ETHNICITY   GENDER   RELIGION   EXCEPTIONALITY   LANGUAGE   AGE   **Cultural Identity**

economic, religious, language, geographic, and age group. In addition, we may have a disability that interacts with membership in one or more of the other microcultural groups to determine our cultural identity.

The relationship of an individual's group memberships to the dominant culture may have a great influence on how he perceives himself. Because of the importance of power relationships between groups in discussions of **diversity** and equality, educators should understand how they themselves are centered in this dialogue. Educators need to know which groups they belong to and what influence those memberships have on their own identity. A critical self-examination may be helpful in our identification of otherness and difference that pervades a culturally diverse society. This chapter is designed to explore this diversity.

Discussion Question 3:
Why might it be important to help students learn more about their own cultural background and heritage?

Key Term:
Diversity

Diversity and Education

As an educator, you are likely to encounter students from diverse ethnic, racial, religious, age, disability, and economic groups during your career. Over time, the relationship of groups to society has been described differently by sociologists, politicians, philosophers, and educators. These differing ideologies and theories have led to the development of policies and practices that range along a continuum from promotion to condemnation of group differences. **Assimilation, cultural pluralism,** and cultural choice are three of the prevalent theories and ideologies.

The translation of these theories into educational practice leads to very different strategies and outcomes. Ethnographic studies are providing valuable information about how teachers and schools interact with students in the learning process. Researchers are discovering that schools often use teaching strategies that differ from those that are effective at home, particularly as they relate to language and cognitive style.

Test Questions 5.11–5.20

Key Term:
Assimilation

Key Term:
Cultural pluralism

Activity 5.2:
Have students develop a chart that compares the educational responses to assimilation, cultural pluralism, and cultural choice across the areas of curriculum, assessment, student-teacher interactions, and school climate.

Assimilation

Assimilation is the process by which an immigrant group or culturally distinct group is incorporated into the mainstream **culture.** The group either adopts the culture of the dominant group as its own or interacts with it in a way that forges a new or different culture that is shared by both groups. Members of a group experience a number of stages in this process.

The first step involves learning the cultural patterns of the dominant group. The speed at which group members become acculturated is usually enhanced by interactions with members of this group in settings like work, school, and church. In many cases, the cultural patterns are shed—either enthusiastically or begrudgingly—and those of the dominant group are adopted. Native languages

Today's American classroom reflects the diversity present in society.

and traditions can be lost within a few generations. These steps are usually required by society for an individual to attain some modicum of financial success or achievement of the good life in the United States.

The final stage of assimilation is structural assimilation.[7] At this stage members of the immigrant or culturally distinct group interact with the mainstream group at all levels, including marriage. They no longer encounter prejudice or discrimination and share equally in the benefits of society.

At the beginning of the twentieth century, the melting pot theory emerged as a description of how immigrants contributed to the evolution of a new American culture. This theory described an egalitarian state that is central to the national rhetoric. Many immigrants believed that prejudices and inequities that they had experienced in their native countries would not exist in the United States, and that they would become valued members of the mainstream society. Although many European immigrants did melt into the mainstream, persons of color were prevented from melting—or becoming structurally assimilated—by the racist ideology that had prevented Native, African, Latino, and Asian Americans from becoming structurally assimilated for generations.

Assimilation remains the guiding principle in most schools. Immersion in the dominant culture is the **acculturation** strategy. School success depends on how well students are able to adjust to this culture. Their own cultural experiences and patterns are neither valued nor used in the teaching and learning process.

The poor academic performance of many students of color and from low-income families is sometimes explained by a cultural deficit theory in which students and their families are blamed for their failures. The problem may be that these students have not been socialized to think and act like children of the dominant culture. Proponents of this theory blame the educational deficiencies on the home environment and such factors as single parents, teenage mothers, lack of books, and poor child-rearing practices. The provision of equal educational opportunity is the policy response to this theory. Compensatory programs are offered to help the students overcome both their educational and cultural deficiencies by making them more like students from the dominant culture.

Cultural Pluralism

Cultural pluralism describes societies in which the maintenance of distinct cultural patterns, including languages, is valued and promoted. Groups may be segregated, but they have approximately equal political, economic, and educational opportunity.[8] In some cases, groups have been able to establish and maintain their own political, economic, and educational systems.

The concept of cultural pluralism does not describe the United States. Although diversity does exist, parity and equality between groups does not. Some Native American nations do have their own political and educational systems, but they do not share power and resources equally with the dominant group. Some immigrant groups choose to maintain their native culture and language. This goal is more likely to be attained if families live in communities where there is a fairly large concentration of others from a similar cultural background; Little Italy, Chinatown, Harlem, East Los Angeles, and Amish and Hutterite communities provide these settings. More often, culturally distinct groups have been forced into segregated communities because of discriminatory housing patterns.

Discussion Question 4:
How have theories describing diversity impacted on the educational process in the past decade?

Key Term:
Acculturation

Focus Question 3:
What impact do society and culture have on the education process?

Journal/Portfolio Development 1:
Contrast educational practices that have evolved to support the different theories of diversity. Develop an argument for incorporating those practices into your own teaching.

The implementation of cultural pluralism requires the recognition of the multiple cultures that comprise society. Rather than dominant culture permeating the classroom and school, the culture of the particular group or groups served by the school are the predominant focus of the curriculum. Examples include the Afrocentric and Native-centric programs that exist today in some urban areas and tribal-controlled schools. A number of ethnic and religious groups have maintained their culture and history in private schools. The Amish and Hutterites, for example, operate their own schools to limit the destruction of their cultures by the dominant group.

In this approach, a cultural difference theory is used to explain the differential achievement of students of diverse backgrounds. Disjunctures in cultural patterns between the home and school prevent academic success. Language and cognitive styles are the areas most often studied by researchers. In a review of the literature on this theory, Ana Maria Villegas found that:

> Although students and teachers in a given classroom may speak the same language, they sometimes have different ways of using it. Children whose language use at home and in their immediate community corresponds more closely to the way in which it is used in the classroom have an advantage in the learning process. For these students, prior experience transfers to the classroom and facilitates their academic performance. This seems to be the case for White, middle-class, Anglo-American students. In contrast, minority children frequently experience discontinuity in the use of language at home and in school. They are often misunderstood when applying familiar patterns of language use to classroom tasks. Of what use is prior experience to these children if their established ways of using language and making sense of the world are deemed unacceptable or prohibited in the classroom?[9]

Relevant Research

The Interaction of Language and Culture

As a North American special education teacher for preschoolers, Cynthia Ballenger began to wonder why so many Haitian students were being referred to as "wild" and having no language, especially since she found that they were responsive and intelligent. As a teacher and "fledgling" sociolinguist, she embarked on her own research as a participant-observer. She learned Creole, studied Haitian culture, and began teaching in a bilingual Haitian Creole and English preschool. She still had difficulty in controlling her class.

Ms. Ballenger learned that the Haitian teachers "emphasize[d] the group in their control talk, articulating the values and responsibilities of group membership." (p. 204) The Haitian teachers had orderly classrooms of children who, in an equally affectionate and cheerful manner, *did* follow directions and kept the confusion to a [tolerable] level (pp. 200–201).

While North American teachers differentiated between misbehaviors and connected them to their consequences (for example, "pinching hurts Ana"), Haitian teachers referred to misbehaviors as bad. The focus of North American teachers was on the individual child or family rather than on the group and what is right or wrong. With this information, the teacher-researcher began to develop different styles for handling discipline in her class. Although her style did not always match the verbal intonation and accompanying nonverbal behavior of a native Haitian, her control of the classroom improved significantly.

Source: Cynthia Ballenger, "Teaching and Practice," *Harvard Educational Review* 62(2) (Summer 1992): 199–208.

Schools in a culturally pluralistic society should be staffed by a diverse teaching force that at a minimum represents the cultures of students. Teachers from the same cultural backgrounds as students should be able to use language patterns similar to those of the students' families. Teachers from different cultural backgrounds also should be aware of multiple cultural patterns of communication and learning.

Cultural Choice

Information Note 5.2:
College enrollment in 1992 was 10 percent African American, 7 percent Latino American, 5 percent Asian American, and 1 percent Native American.

As the twentieth century draws to a close, diversity in the United States is increasing. Some immigrants plan to assimilate into the dominant culture as soon as possible. They choose to adopt the new culture and shed the old. Others do not want to shed their unique cultural identity and patterns to be successful members of society. Many learn to be bicultural and bilingual, bridging the two cultures and learning when it is appropriate to use the patterns of each. Others do not have a choice. Ideally, we could choose to assimilate, maintain our native culture, or become bi- or multicultural in our ability to function effectively in more than one cultural group. Society would support these cultural choices and not value one choice over another or discriminate based on group membership.

Unfortunately, this description does not match reality for large segments of the population. Most persons of color, such as African Americans, are acculturated, but discrimination has prevented them from becoming structurally assimilated even if they choose that route. Strong identity and affiliation with their cultural group has been necessary for solidarity purposes to fight against existing inequities and to obtain adequate housing and education. Although some members may be able to live almost solely within their distinct cultural milieu, most are forced to work within the dominant culture. Those who choose to assimilate may not be accepted by the dominant group and sometimes are rejected by the group into which they were born.

Equality across groups does not yet exist, but it continues to be a value espoused by the society. As long as discrimination against groups is tolerated by society, cultural choice will be limited primarily to male, middle-class, heterosexual whites. As the barriers to equality are reduced, there is likely to be greater individual choice and mobility across groups. "We will move toward an open society in which cultural background may influence who an individual is, but become irrelevant in public interactions, especially as the reason for institutional discrimination. In this case, cultural differences will be valued, respected, and encouraged to flourish."[10]

CNN Clip 8:
Mississippi Learning

Schools that value cultural choice promote diversity and consciously avoid the dominance of a single culture. The contributions and histories of diverse groups—particularly those represented in the school, but not limited to them—are integrated throughout the curriculum. Bilingualism and bidialectalism prevail in classrooms as well as halls. Students are the center of instruction and their cultural patterns are utilized to promote learning. Students learn to operate comfortably in both their own and other cultures, including the dominant culture. Equality is achieved as illustrated in the equal participation of all groups in courses and extracurricular activities, as well as in comparable achievement on academic assessments.

Microcultural Groups

Test Questions 5.21–5.54

Objective 4:
Compare assimilation, cultural pluralism, and cultural choice as descriptions of how society handles diversity.

Students in U.S. schools are among the most diverse in the world. By the year 2000, one-third of our students will be young people of color.[11] They are already the majority in schools in California, Texas, and the twenty-five largest cities. The native language of schools is no longer limited to English. Some school districts can identify nearly one hundred different languages that are used in the homes of their students. Religious diversity has also increased beyond the traditional Judeo-Christian heritage as immigrants from Asia, Africa, and the Middle East join our ranks. In addition, a greater number of students with disabilities are now active participants in schools and society.

Socioeconomic Status

Most people want the "good life," which allows a comfortable living. The image to many is a two-parent family who owns a home, has a stay-at-home mother and one or more children in school. In reality, only 4 percent of U.S. families fit this middle-class myth today.[12] **Socioeconomic status** is the primary determinant of the standard of living we are able to maintain. It also has a great impact on our chances of attending college and attaining a job that ensures material comfort throughout our lives.

Socioeconomic status (SES) is a criterion used by the U.S. Bureau of Census to measure the economic condition of individuals. It is determined by one's occupation, income, and educational attainment. Wealth and power are other important factors that affect the way one is able to live, but these data are difficult to measure through census data. We often can guess families' socioeconomic status if we know where they live, the type of car they drive, the schools attended by their children, and the types of vacations they take.

Social Stratification.   Most societies are characterized by **social stratification** in which individuals occupy different levels of the social structure. Wealth, income, occupation, and education help define these social positions. However, high or low rankings are not based only on the SES criteria. Race, age, gender, religion, and disability can contribute to lower rankings as well. Although members of most ethnic groups can be found at all levels of the socioeconomic status scale, those from western European backgrounds have a disproportionately high representation at the highest levels. This difference was validated in a UNESCO study that compared the standard of living in different countries. Of the nations compared, the United States ranked sixth overall. However, when the population was divided into racial groups, great differences in stratification were obvious. The living standard of U.S. whites outranked that of all other nations. On the other hand, African Americans ranked thirty-first—at the same level as an underdeveloped country.[13]

Social mobility remains one of the core values of the dominant culture. We are taught to believe "that anyone can improve social status because the social structure is open and hard work will get you there."[14] We read the Horatio Alger stories of how individuals were born in poverty, but through hard work became wealthy as a corporate president, prestigious publisher, or successful writer, athlete, or entertainer. Such dramatic upward mobility continues to occur, but the chances of moving from poverty to riches, no matter how hard one works, are rare.

Class Structure.   Traditionally, sociologists divide the population into distinct classes to study inequities in society as well as the characteristics of individuals and families at these different levels. One of the early categorization systems identified the population as lower, middle, and upper class, with finer distinctions in each of the three groups. The "underclass" is the label sometimes given to the portion of the population that lacks a stable income and is persistently poor. Indi-

Activity 5.3:
Invite representatives from diverse student groups on campus to join a panel to discuss their experiences in schools and with teachers, highlighting good and bad experiences related to their ethnicity, gender, socioeconomic status, religion, disability, and/or sexual orientation.

Key Term:
Socioeconomic status

Journal Activity Master 5.1: An Examination of Personal Social Status. In this activity, students are asked to reflect on their family background by completing a family shield. They are then given time to interpret the reasons for designing the shield the way they did.

Key Term:
Social stratification

Information Note 5.3:
There is increasing difficulty in defining what is middle class. The gap between the rich and poor is growing at the same time that the middle class is shrinking in size.

viduals who do manual work for a living are sometimes described as the "working class." When this group includes farm laborers and service workers, it represents 43 percent of the employed population.[15]

The middle class includes professionals, managers, administrators, and white-collar workers who perform nonmanual labor. Annual incomes for this class usually fall between $20,000 and $50,000 and represent about 35 percent of the individuals submitting income tax returns.[16] This level of income is often possible only because both spouses work. Families in this class live very different lifestyles at the opposite ends of the income continuum. Professionals, managers, and administrators receive the higher incomes. They are the more affluent middle class, but view their condition as universal rather than unique. They often think that most of the U.S. population shares the same affluence, advantages, and comforts.[17]

The upper class is composed of wealthy and socially prominent families. There is great disparity in the income and wealth of members of this class as compared to the others, and the gap between them is growing. For example, in 1979 corporate chief executive officers earned twenty-nine times as much as their manufacturing employees; by 1985, they earned forty times as much; and by 1988 *Business Week* reported that the multiple had grown to ninety three.[18] These great differences contribute to limited interactions with members of other classes. Children in this class rarely attend public schools, which isolates them from other social classes. Probably the greatest assimilation of lifestyles and values occurs within this class.

Discussion Question 5:
What impact does poverty have on a family's or student's cultural identity?

Poverty.   The U.S. government has established a poverty index that sets a conservative ceiling on poverty. Using this threshold, there are over 33 million persons in poverty—13.5 percent of the population. There are many myths about persons who are poor. One is that they do not work, but in reality, many work in full-time jobs that pay so poorly they cannot pull their families out of poverty. "Some two million people work year round but live in poverty and another seven million poor individuals work full time for part of the year or in part-time jobs."[19]

Children, the elderly, women, and minorities suffer disproportionately from poverty. A recent study by the United Nations found that "the percentage of children living in poverty in the United States is more than double that of other major industrialized nations . . . Other major industrialized nations have succeeded in reducing child poverty levels to below 5 percent."[20] (The comparison with other countries is shown in Figure 5.2.) This tragedy is reflected in an increase in the number of homeless families and students over the past decade. The number of homeless people is estimated at between 250,000 to three million. The estimate of the number of homeless children on any given night ranges from 68,000 to 500,000. In addition, there are nearly 14 million children living temporarily with friends or relatives.[21]

Although there are more European Americans who are below the poverty level than any other group, they represent only 11 percent of all European Americans in the country. The percentage of other racial groups in poverty is much higher. The median income of European Americans remains greater than other racial groups. African American families earn 58 percent as much as whites; Latino families earn 63 percent as much as whites.[22] The disparity in incomes between groups decreases when comparisons are made using two-income families with the same level of education, but they still are not equitable. Women also fight discriminatory practices that keep their incomes at 71 percent that of men.

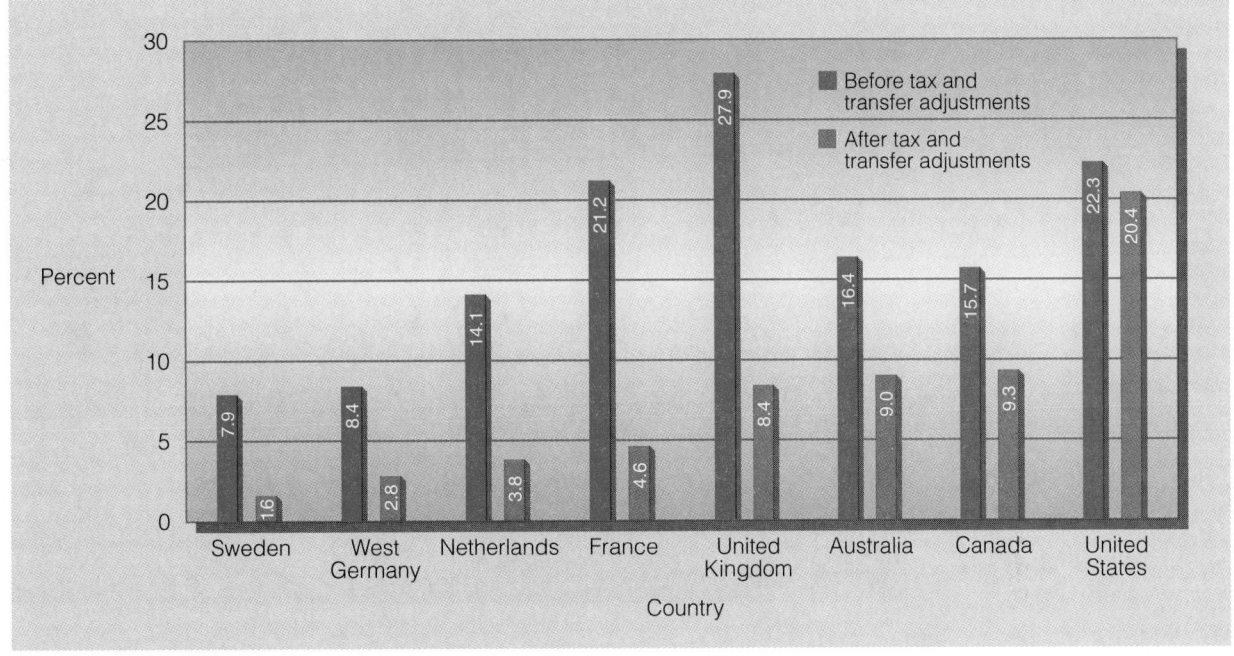

FIGURE 5.2

Percentage of Children Living in Poverty in Industrialized Nations
(*Source:* United Nations Children's Fund.)

Ethnicity and Race

National origin remains an important part of identity for many individuals. Because Native Americans are the only indigenous groups, over 99 percent of the population came from somewhere else or their ancestors did at some time during the past 500 years. Many people can identify a country of origin, although the geographical boundaries may have been moved since their ancestors immigrated. A growing number of people have mixed heritage, with ancestors from different parts of the world.

It is our national origin that determines our ethnicity. We often use continents as the broadest identification in classifications like European American, African American, South American, and Asian American. Many families can trace their heritage to specific countries (for example, Poland or Korea) and/or tribes (for example, Pueblo or Ibo). Although Latino Americans share a common language heritage of Spanish, families have come from Spain, Mexico, Central America, South America, Cuba, and Puerto Rico.

Ethnic Diversity. Within each of these broad continent classifications exist numerous ethnic groups with identities and often loyalties to a specific country. Many Americans whose ancestors immigrated either voluntarily or involuntarily identify themselves as German, Vietnamese, Hmong, Croatian, Russian, Punjabi, Argentinean, Mexican, Lebanese, or Ethiopian American. The U.S. Census Bureau asked the population to identify themselves by their ethnic origin for the first time

Objective 5:
Describe how the ethnic diversity of the student population is changing.

Native American children, and other minority students, are often caught between their traditional culture and new educational efforts.

Information Note 5.4:
Projected census data indicate that Latinos may constitute 11 percent of the population by the year 2000 and 21 percent by 2050.

Transparency 28:
Racial Diversity of the United States.

in the 1990 census. Generally, these data are reported by the government in the following five broad categories that combine racial, language, and ethnic distinctions: White, not Hispanic; Black, not Hispanic; Hispanic; Asian American or Pacific Islander; and Native American or Alaskan Aleuts. One of the problems with these classifications is that a growing number of people can identify themselves in more than one of these groups. Their parents or grandparents or other ancestors have married across ethnic and/or racial and/or language groups; thus, they do not fit neatly into one single group. (See Figure 5.3.)

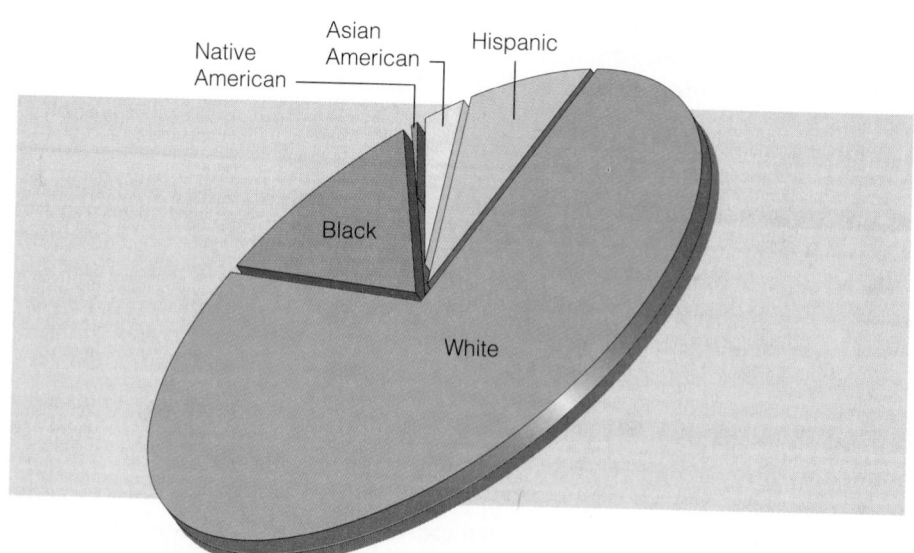

FIGURE 5.3

Membership in the Five Racial or Ethnic Groups, 1990 Census

(*Source:* "Children in Poverty," *Education Week* (September 29, 1993): 3.)

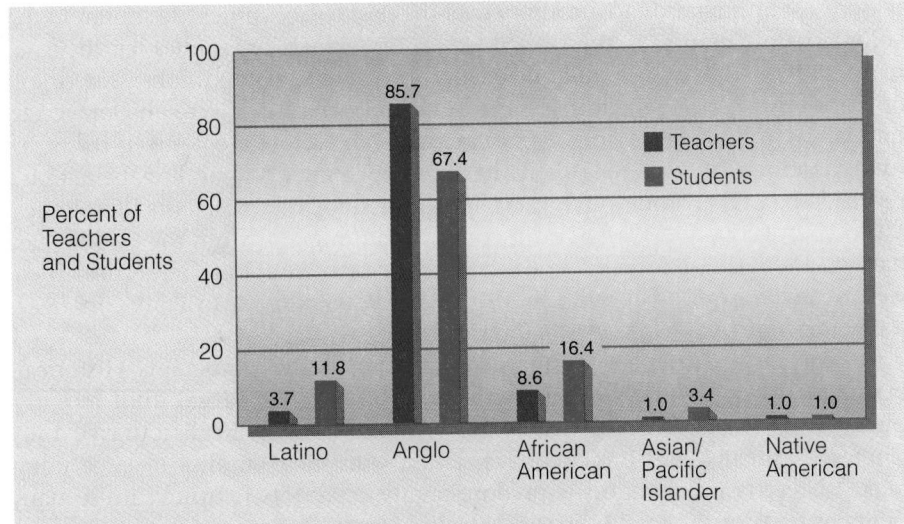

FIGURE 5.4

Distribution of Teachers and Students in U.S. K–12 Public Schools by Ethnicity, Fall 1991

(*Source:* U.S. Bureau of Labor Statistics, 1992 and U.S. Department of Education, 1993, as presented in The Tomas Rivera Center, *Resolving a Crisis in Education: Latino Teachers for Tomorrow's Classrooms.* Claremont, CA: author, 1993, 7.)

CASE STUDY   DIVERSITY IN THE TEACHING FORCE

The teaching force today is predominantly European American female, as shown in Figure 5.4. When compared with the diversity of the student population, teachers of color are currently underrepresented in teaching. These comparisons become even more disconcerting in states with large minority populations. "In California, for example, where Latinos are most heavily concentrated, Latinos comprised 33 percent of all students while Latino teachers represented only 7 percent of the state's teachers." The need for bilingual teachers in states like California, Texas, Florida, and New York is great, and shortages exist across the country.

Why is diversity in the teaching force important? Some argue that students of color would be better served by role models from their own cultural groups. Many believe that intergroup relations would be improved with the opportunities for all students to interact with teachers from both their own and other cultural groups. Even more importantly, teachers with intimate understandings of and regard for children's cultures, communities, and ways of learning and interacting appear to be more effective in helping students learn.

1. What strategies would you use to encourage more students of color to enter the teaching profession?
2. Why might it be in the best interest of the nation to attract more males and persons of color into the teaching force?
3. What should European American teachers know about cultural differences to help them be effective teachers of students of color?

Source: The Tomas Rivera Center, *Resolving a Crisis in Education: Latino Teachers for Tomorrow's Classrooms.* Claremont, CA: author, 7.

Transparency 21: Ethnic Shifts in the U.S. Population.

Information Note 5.5: Of the 22.4 million U.S. residents who identified themselves as Latino in 1990, 60 percent had roots in Mexico, 12 percent in Puerto Rico, 5 percent in Cuba, and 23 percent in other countries.

Information Note 5.6: Native American learners must learn to cope with the "Buckskin Curtain," a phrase among Natives that points out the need for the native to have one foot in the Anglo culture and one foot in the Native culture.

Global Perspectives: Diversity European Style.
The reasons for immigration and the treatment of immigrants varies around the world. As an example, let's look at the different patterns of immigration in European countries. The

reasons for immigration to a country over the past few centuries are similar to the voluntary immigration in the United States. Individuals or families left their native country because of debilitating economic or political conditions, war, or job opportunities. Often migrant workers from other countries were encouraged to immigrate to meet labor shortages. Citizens from formerly colonized countries were sometimes allowed to settle in the "mother country," expanding the nation's diversity to families from India, Pakistan, Hong Kong, Indonesia, the West Indies, Morocco, Algeria, and West African countries. Immigrants from the Middle East have greatly increased the religious diversity of many European countries. There were seven mosques in Britain in 1962 and fewer than ten in France in 1972; today there are over 600 and 1,000 respectively.[23]

European countries have responded differently to the immigrants. Historically, Italy has not encouraged immigration; in fact, it was illegal until recently. Immigration by families and reunification have been especially discouraged; only Chinese, Eritreans, and Iranians have settled with their families in large numbers.[24] Greece's immigration is predominantly expatriots returning from many different parts of the world; gypsies, Muslims from Thrace, and foreign workers also populate the country.[25] France is very diverse, but does not keep records of indigenous minorities and does not encourage the maintenance of allegiance to a second homeland.[26] Switzerland does not describe itself as an immigrant country, but over 16 percent of the population is non-Swiss from 169 countries.[27] Some eastern European countries like Croatia, Serbia, and Bosnia are undergoing a process of "ethnic cleansing," which has become an extended war, to rid their countries of persons from different ethnic or religious groups.

Although the initial intent of opening borders to guest or migrant workers was that they would eventually return to their original homeland, many subsequently settled in segregated areas, continued to use their native languages and religions, and began to raise families. Schools had to respond to students from diverse cultural backgrounds. Xenophobia and ethnocentrism abounded in policies and practices related to most of these students and their families; sometimes they face scapegoating and expulsion threats and are verbally and physically attacked.

Activity 5.4:
Ask students to participate in an ethnic event or religious service that differs from their own, record their impressions in a journal, and analyze their reactions to the experience.

Ethnic Identity.   Identification with an ethnic group helps sustain and enhance the culture of the group. Members share similar lifestyles, values, history, and common social and economic interests. There is often an identifiable dialectal and nonverbal communication system. Ethnicity is strongest when members have a high degree of interpersonal associations with other members and share common residential areas.[28]

Ethnic cohesiveness and solidarity are strengthened as members organize to fight discrimination and influence political and economic decisions that impact the group as a whole. In the 1960s these struggles with the dominant culture led to the calls for changes in institutions like schools, colleges, and government programs to support equality across ethnic groups. During this period, African, Latino, Asian, and Native Americans called for recognition of their ethnic roots in the school curriculum. By the 1970s European ethnic groups, especially those of southern and eastern origins, had also joined this movement. Ethnic studies programs were established in colleges and universities to study the history, contributions, and experiences of U.S. ethnic groups that had traditionally been excluded.

Gender

Males and females are culturally different even when they are members of the same socioeconomic, ethnic, and religious group. The ways they think and act are defined by their gender identity. The two groups are often segregated at social gatherings, located in different jobs, and expected to behave in a stereotypical fashion. "At school, at church, at work, at play, boys and girls and men and women are governed by different norms, rules of behavior and expectations; they are subject to different eligibility rules for rewards and different vulnerability to punishments."[29]

Differences between Females and Males. Learning the gender of a baby is one of the important rites of parenthood. However, the major difference between boys and girls is the way adults respond to them. There are few actual physical differences, particularly before puberty. It is the socialization process in child rearing and schools that determines gender identity and the related distinctive behaviors.

Some researchers attribute differences in mathematical, verbal, and spatial skills to different hormones that affect specific hemispheres of the brain. However, recent studies show that females and males are performing more alike, suggesting that the previously observed gender differences are not biologically determined. For example, there are no differences in quantitative abilities until the age of ten and then only slight differences that sometimes favor girls and sometimes favor boys in the middle school years. Males do perform better in high school, but the differences are declining as female students become more interested in mathematics. Gender differences in spatial abilities are declining and one's abilities in this area can be improved with training. There no longer appear to be differences in verbal abilities.[30]

By age two, children realize that they are a girl or boy; by five or six, they have learned their gender and stereotypical behavior.[31] Boys are generally socialized toward achievement and self-reliance, girls toward nurturance and responsibility. However, anthropologists have documented variations in the behaviors of males and females from culture to culture. In this country, there are differences in the expectations and behaviors of the two sexes that are rooted in their ethnicity, religion, and socioeconomic level.

A major difference between the two groups is how they are treated in society. Women tend to be equated with a natural world and men with controlling that world.[32] These power relations place men in a position of superiority, as evidenced by their disproportionate holding of the highest status and highest paying jobs. Many times this relationship extends into the home where the father and husband may both protect the family and rule over it. Sometimes this relationship leads to physical and mental abuse of women and children.

Although 90 percent of all women today will work outside the home at some time, society's view of them as inferior has contributed greatly to the current patterns of discrimination that keep many women in low prestige and low paying jobs. The jobs in which women are concentrated are those that naturally extend their role as nurturers and helpers: nursing, teaching, and secretarial work. Job and wage discrimination is a critical issue for women, especially today when a large number of families are headed by women without the advantage of a second income. These families are more likely to be in poverty than any other group; over 32 percent of the persons in these families fall below the official poverty level.[33]

Journal Activity Master 5.2: An Analysis of Gender Roles. Students are asked to examine a series of traits and determine which ones represent themselves. They are then asked to analyze these traits using a scoring system related to androgyny and to analyze the profile.

Transparency 27: Family Income and Education

Transparency 29: A Gender Wage Gap . . . Still

Objective 6: Discuss the correlation between gender and poverty and the reasons that a disproportionately large number of women are in poverty.

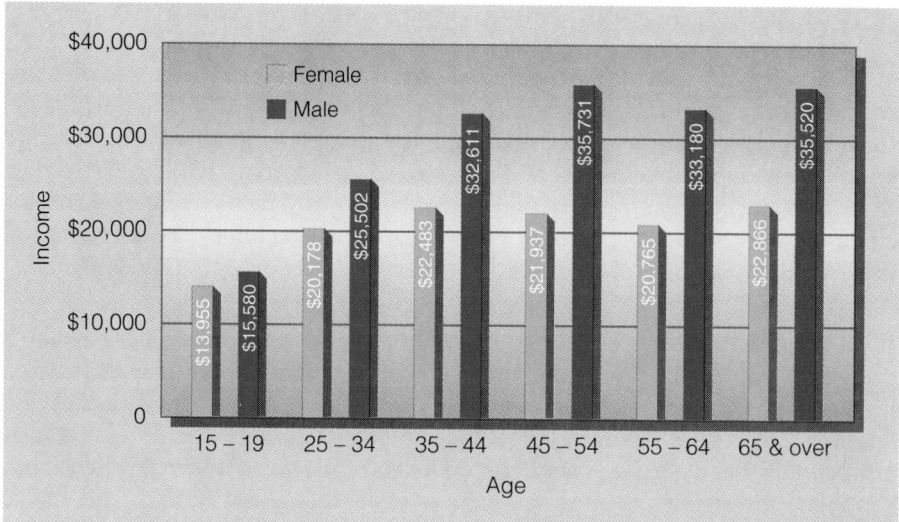

FIGURE 5.5

Differences between Male and Female Income

(*Source:* Donna M. Gollnick and Philip C. Chinn. *Multicultural Education in a Pluralistic Society,* 4th ed. Columbus, OH: Merrill, 1994, 130. © 1994 by Merrill.)

As barriers to professional education and employment are broken, the number of women in traditionally male occupations has increased. The number of female physicians increased from 6.5 percent in 1950 to 20 percent in 1991; female attorneys and judges increased from 4 to 19 percent; and female principals increased from 20 percent in 1982 to 38 percent in 1990.[34] (See Figure 5.5.)

Many males are also not well served by the current socialization patterns. Some do not fit neatly in the dominant culture's stereotypical vision of maleness. Society has not been very tolerant of deviation from the traditional masculine roles. Although much progress has been made over the past two decades, men still may be ridiculed for having "female characteristics" such as a high voice or non-aggressive behavior. Some men would feel more comfortable working as preschool teachers, nurses, or librarians—traditionally female careers—but may have learned that those jobs are inappropriate for "real men."

Young women sometimes appear ambivalent, especially as it relates to education and family relations. Some undervalue themselves and become passive and self-sacrificing. This pattern may lead them into unwanted pregnancies and unfulfilling relationships. "Young women with poor basic skills are three times more likely to become teenage parents than women with average or above-average basic skills."[35] As a result, a disproportionately large number of these women drop out of school, limiting their ability to earn a decent income. Thus, they and their children are likely to be forced into poverty at least temporarily.

Schools also reinforce behavior that is stereotypically gender specific. Female students are expected to be quiet, follow the rules, and help the teacher. Boys and young men are expected to be more rowdy and less attentive. Many working class males develop patterns of resistance to school and its authority figures because schooling is feminine and emphasizes mental rather than manual work.[36]

Sexual Orientation. Many cultural groups place high value on heterosexuality and denigrate or outlaw homosexuality. However, sexual orientation is established by age five or six;[37] it is not learned in adolescence or young adulthood, nor is it forced on others by immoral adults. It has been estimated that 5 to 10 percent of the population is homosexual.

Like other powerless groups, gays and lesbians continue to face discrimination in housing, employment, and many social institutions as evidenced when universities prohibit the establishment of gay student clubs. Some states still have laws on the books that make it illegal to engage in homosexual relations. Homophobia, as expressed in harassment and violence against gays and lesbians, is tolerated in many areas of the country. As a result of these prejudices and discriminatory practices, many gays and lesbians hide their homosexuality and have established their own social clubs, networks, and communication systems to support each other.

Isolation and loneliness are the experiences of many gay and lesbian youth. If they openly acknowledge their sexual orientation, they are likely to be harassed and face reprisals from peers and school officials. Structures within the schools do not provide homosexuals the same kind of support that is available to other students. Educators often know little about this group and have had few or no contacts with homosexuals. Students in the classroom also may be the children of gay and lesbian parents since there are 8 to 10 million children in 3 million families.[38] Without a better understanding of homosexuality, we will not be able to effectively work with gay and lesbian students or the children of homosexual parents.

Information Note 5.7:
Many gay and lesbian teachers are forced to hide their sexual orientation for fear of losing their teaching jobs.

Language

Language interacts with our ethnic and socioeconomic background to socialize us into linguistic and cultural communities. Children learn their native language by imitating adults and their peers. By age five, they have learned the syntax of language and know the meaning of thousands of words.

CNN Clip 10:
Language Immersion

When there are cultural similarities between the speaker and listener, the messages are decoded accurately. When the speaker and listener differ in ethnicity and/or class, miscommunication may occur. Even within English, a word or phrase or nonverbal gesture takes on different meanings in different cultural groups and settings. Educators need to recognize that miscommunications between them and students may be due to inaccurate decoding rather than lack of ability.

Language Differences. English is not the native language for approximately 32 million Americans.[38] Spanish, Italian, and sign language are the most common languages other than English. As immigrants assimilate into the dominant culture of the United States, the native language is often replaced with English within a few generations. The native language is more likely to be retained when schools and the community value bilingualism. As commerce and trade have become more global, professionals and administrators have realized the advantages of knowing the competitor's culture and language. They are encouraging their children to learn a second language at the same time that many of our educational policies are discouraging native speakers from using both languages. Ethnocentrism flourishes in the conservative call for "English only" usage in schools, in daily commerce, on street signs, and on official government documents. The implementation of bilingual education programs also implicitly reflects different views of the importance of a second language. Transitional bilingual programs use

Transparency 22:
Fewer Students Speak English at Home

PROFESSIONAL DILEMMA

How Much Can We Expect of Limited English Speaking Students?

The image of the United States as the land of boundless opportunity may seem a bit tarnished to many of its recession-weary citizens, but it is alive and well in many of the world's war-torn, poverty-ridden, politically oppressive countries. Indeed, immigrants from such countries are flocking to the United States in record numbers. Estimates are that some areas of the country will range from a one-third to over one-half minority, non-English-speaking population within the next few years.

A peculiar challenge arises for educators when students enter high school with little or no formal education from their native country, and with no proficiency in English. The situation may be further complicated because students come from many different countries, including Vietnam, Chile, Honduras, Ethiopia, Afghanistan, Korea, and Sierra Leone.

Immigrating late in their youth, these students are faced with a nearly impossible challenge to graduate with other students of their own age. Some educators think that the hurdle should be lowered for these students and opportunities created for them so that they may succeed and graduate with their peers. These educators see the alternative as increased frustration and dropout rates.

Others maintain that proficiency as measured by standardized tests should be retained as a requirement for all students, and that to relax these standards selectively would be patronizing and ultimately harmful to minority populations.

- How should educators' goals for limited English speakers be different than for English speakers?

- If there are several students with different native languages in your classroom, how will you ensure that they learn the concepts being taught?

- Where could you go for help in working with language diverse students?

Activity 5.5:
Ask students to work in small groups and list on newsprint or an overhead transparency their feelings and possible reactions to entering a classroom in which the language is different than that known to members of the group. They should also indicate how they would like to be treated in a classroom in which no one else speaks their language. At the end of the exercise, reactions should be shared with the class.

Information Note 5.8:
Fifty-nine percent of the students with limited English proficiency are concentrated in three states: California (33 percent), Texas (16 percent), and New York (10 percent).

the native language, especially in the early school years, to teach academic content while students concurrently learn English. As soon as possible, students move into English-only programs. There are a few schools and programs that offer bilingual maintenance programs in which English and a second language are equally valued and used for instruction.

American Sign Language (ASL) is officially recognized as a language with complex grammar and well-regulated syntax. It is the natural language developed and used for communication among deaf individuals. Like oral languages, it is learned very early by imitation of others using the language. To communicate with the hearing, many individuals who are deaf use signed English in which the oral or written word is translated into a sign. ASL is a critical factor in identification as a member of this group. The language can be more important to their cultural identity than their membership in a particular ethnic, socioeconomic, or religious group.

Dialectal Differences. Standard English is the dialect used by the majority of dominant group members for official or formal communications. However, there are numerous regional, local, ethnic, and class (or SES) dialects identifiable across this country. Each has its own set of grammatical rules that are known to its users. None is any better than another, but users of standard English are often viewed as more credible in schools and the work world. Television news anchors, reporters, and talk show hosts use standard English. Although they may be bidialectal, most teachers use standard English as the example that should be emulated by students.

Many Americans are bidialectal or multidialectal in that they use standard English at work, but use their native or local dialect at home or when they are socializing with friends. Social factors have an influence on which dialect to use in a specific situation. At one time, students were not allowed to use a dialect other than standard English in the classroom. Today, students are usually allowed to use their dialects, but are encouraged to learn standard English to provide them with an advantage in seeking employment in the dominant culture.

Exceptionalities

Twenty-five million or more Americans have been classified as having a disability or being gifted.[40] Individuals with a disability are usually identified as mentally retarded, learning disabled, speech impaired, visually impaired, hearing impaired, emotionally disturbed, behaviorally disturbed, or physically impaired. Those with physical disabilities can be readily recognized by their use of a cane, braces, wheelchair, or sign language. Some individuals are labeled very early in their school careers as mentally retarded or emotionally disturbed. Nondisabled persons often react with disdain to individuals with disabilities and view them as inferior. Critics of labeling declare the system to be demeaning and stigmatizing.

Like all other individuals, persons with disabilities want to be recognized as persons in their own right. They have the same needs for love and the same desire to be successful as the nondisabled. Instead, society has historically not accepted them as equals. Some individuals with severe disabilities are placed in institutions out of the sight of the public. Others are segregated in separate schools or classes. Too often, they are rejected and made to feel inept and limited in their abilities. Schools have contributed to this problem when they should be part of the solution.

Cultural Differences. Individuals with similar disabilities often find comfort and security with each other. Those who are hearing impaired share a language that is used by only a few of the hearing; the language provides them with a strong sense of community. In some cities like Louisville, Kentucky, many visually impaired individuals continue to live in the community near the School for the Blind where they can be close to potential work settings and provide support to each other. Individuals with mental retardation sometimes share group homes in which they can support each other and learn to be self-reliant. In these settings they establish patterns of communication and behavior that are natural to them, but may seem odd to nonmembers.

Disproportionate Placements. Some disabilities are linked to membership in one or more other microcultural groups. Individuals labeled as mentally retarded or emotionally disabled disproportionately are from low-income families. Low-income children are also overrepresented in seriously emotionally disturbed classes. Middle-class students are more likely to be classified as learning disabled. This pattern is also found in the placement of minority group members and males in special education and gifted classes. African and Native American students are overrepresented in many of the special education classes for mentally and emotionally disturbed students, as are males in general. On the other hand, Latino,

Information Note 5.9:
Males make up 64 percent of
the students in special education programs, with the largest
proportion designated as
learning disabled.

African, and Native American students are underrepresented in gifted and talented programs. Educators need to learn to monitor the reasons for their referrals of
students to be tested for placement in these classes.

Religion

Religion can have a great influence on the values and lifestyles of families and can
play an important role in the socialization of children and young people. Religious doctrines and practices often guide our beliefs about the roles of males and
females. They also provide guidance regarding birth rates, birth control, child rearing, friendships, and political attitudes.

By age five, children are able to generally identify their families' religious
affiliation. Although 90 percent of the population regards their religious beliefs
as very or fairly important,[41] less than half attend a religious service on a weekly basis. However, strong religious perspectives are reflected in the daily lives of
many families.[42]

Information Note 5.10:
Eighty-five percent of North
Americans are Christian.
However, 9 percent are not
religious, 2.5 percent are Jewish, 1.0 percent are Muslims,
0.5 percent are Hindus, and
0.2 percent are Buddhists.

Objective 7:
Explain the need to understand the impact of religion on
schools in particular regions
of the country such as Utah
and the Bible Belt.

The First Amendment.   The First Amendment of the U.S. Constitution, which
requires the separation of church and state, is a cornerstone of American democracy. When it comes to schools, there is disagreement about the meaning of the
amendment. Families appear satisfied with schools when they reflect the values
that are important in their religion. However, schools may be attacked when the
curriculum, assigned readings, holidays, and graduation exercises are perceived to
be in conflict with religious values. Many court cases over the past century have
helped sort out these issues.

Religious Pluralism.   Religious pluralism flourishes in this country. Members
of religions other than those with a Judeo-Christian heritage are increasing as
more immigrants arrive from Asia and the Middle East. Other families declare
themselves atheists or simply do not participate in an organized religion. Still
others live in cults that are established to promote and maintain a religious "calling." Some religious groups believe that their religion is the only correct and legitimate view of the world. Other groups recognize that the differences have grown
out of different historical experiences and accept the validity of diverse groups.

Although they are not as dominant as earlier in our history, Protestants are
still in the majority with 56 percent of the population. Two and one half percent
of the population are Jewish and 26 percent are Catholic. Eleven percent do not
indicate a preference. Within each of the major religious groups, there are distinct
denominations and sects that have the same general history, but can differ greatly in their beliefs and perspectives on the correct and appropriate way to live.
These western religions are compatible with the values of the dominant culture;
they usually promote patriotism and emphasize individual control of life.

With the influx of immigrants from Asia, Africa, and the Middle East over the
past few decades, religious diversity among the population has increased further
with the introduction of non-Western religions like Islam and Buddhism. The
interaction with Western religions and impact on mainstream society have yet to
be determined. In the meantime, students from diverse religious backgrounds will
appear in classrooms. Teachers will need to learn to respect these differences if
they are going to serve the students and community well.

Some religious groups, such as the Amish and Hutterites, are very closed in
that they establish their own communities and schools to help maintain the reli-

*The trend in recent years has
been to recognize and learn
more about differences, rather
than cover them up and
smooth them out.*

gion, support each other, and develop group cohesiveness. Members of some groups like Mormons promote primary relationships and interactions with other members of the same faith. Most social activities are linked to religion, and institutions have been developed to reflect and support the religious beliefs. In many rural areas the church is the center of most social and community activities. Fundamentalist churches in many urban areas expect members to spend much of their nonworking hours in church activities. For many people, religion is the essential element that determines their cultural identity.

Geography

Communities and their schools differ from one region of the country to another. We are likely to suffer culture shock in moving from one region to another. People behave differently, dress differently, and like different things even if they are from the same religious and ethnic backgrounds. An examination of differences in rural, suburban, and urban communities captures some of the cultural variation. However, differences in those communities will be found as one crosses from Northwest, Southwest, Midwest, South, and Northeast. Within these regions, an observer will find states that are culturally unique. The geography of a state like Colorado aids in the development of different cultural patterns of the population in the flat farmlands, urban centers, and mountains.

Transparency 25:
Estimated Population Growth by Region between 1990 and 2000

Rural Communities.   Rural schools are often the center of rural life. Values tend to be conservative, and the immediate rural family tends to remain a cohesive unit. The extended family, however, has begun to disappear. School children may travel long distances to school, and social interactions at school are vital. By urban and suburban standards, rural families live long distances from one another. To the rural family, however, the distances are not great, and there is a feeling of neighborliness. The social structure is less stratified than in most populous geographical areas, and everyone tends to know everyone else.

Information Note 5.11:
Recent census data suggest that the trend whereby rural areas have acquired city population may be diminishing. Mobility from the city has slowed and increased numbers of rural youth are leaving.

Although employment in these areas is scarce, increasing numbers of urban and suburban dwellers are choosing to live in the country and commute to their employment in the more populous metropolitan areas. Those who have settled in the rural areas are generally young and well educated. They are fleeing the complexities of city life to acquire self-reliance and self-confidence, to return to a physically healthier environment, or simply to be able to own an affordable home. In some instances this exodus to the country has caused problems for rural schools because the newcomers' values have clashed with those of the rural community. Family living habits and expectations for school programs differ, and some newcomers demand increased social services. In many rural communities, it takes a considerable length of time for newcomers to be accepted into the social structure.

Suburban Communities.   The suburban school is not a community school like the rural school, and recreation and social activities emanate from a variety of sources. Young people depend on the car and the telephone. Most suburban families have two cars and either an extension phone or a private phone for the children. Teenagers like to be on the move, and a car is considered a necessity.

Suburbs continue to grow in number and size, but the pattern for schooling has changed. The suburban areas close to the city are now experiencing a shift to an older population with fewer children and new middle-class minorities migrating from the cities. The schools in these areas continue to experience declining enrollments despite the baby boomlet that is affecting other schools. The boomlet is felt farther out in the newer suburbs, where property values are not as high and young parents with families can afford housing. In recent years many suburban areas have become settlement areas for southeast Asian refugee groups, who have introduced a whole new set of diversity issues for the schools to address.

Urban Communities. Urban areas provide rich cultural experiences through museums, theaters, and the arts. Although some residential areas remain segregated, many areas are ethnically and racially diverse. With the exception of segregated oppressed areas, the city provides opportunities to interact with people from diverse backgrounds in community settings and at work. Usually there are several colleges and universities in the city with libraries, lectures, sporting events, and cultural events.

Although there are many single-family homes in a city, many children live in multifamily units such as apartments or condominiums. Children who live in oppressed sections of the city are often restricted by it, having few contacts outside the area. Although affluent areas of the city may have adequate, if not beautiful, parks, libraries, and schools, some areas suffer from too few and poorly kept parks, inadequate police protection, and old, poorly maintained schools.

Cultural Identity

You, the reader, and your future students are members of at least the seven microcultures described above. The interaction of one's membership in multiple microcultures determines one's cultural identity. However, each microcultural membership is weighted differently in determining one's own cultural identity. Membership in a particular microculture can greatly influence the membership in another group. For example, some religions have strictly defined expectations for women and men that will control how they behave as adolescents, newlyweds, and a married couple. Membership in some of the microcultural groups may have little impact on how we see ourselves, while others are very important. Cultural identity is dynamic and may change over time. For example, the behavior and values of a married female with two young children may be based on her ethnic, religious, and class background. If she divorces, her identification as a woman at a different class level may become more important determinants of her own identity than they previously were.

Intragroup Differences

There are many differences within the same microcultural group. For example, all women belong to the same gender microculture, but not to the same ethnic, religious, or socioeconomic group—all of which could have a great impact on how they see themselves as females and how they are treated by society. Socioeconomic status has a great impact on how families are able to live. As a result, individuals from the same ethnic group may have very different language and behavioral patterns as well as lifestyles. Educators must be careful not to stereotype students based on a single microcultural membership.

Test Questions 5.55–5.60

Journal/Portfolio Development 2:
Prepare an autobiographical description of the importance of your membership in the microcultural groups described in this chapter to your own cultural identity. The description should indicate why membership in one or more groups is especially important in the identification of who you are.

Focus Question 4:
What is the role of group memberships in determining one's own cultural identity?

Activity 5.6:
Ask students to reflect on the impact of their microcultural memberships on who they are today and how they are treated by members of different groups. These reflections should be recorded as journal entries over a period of at least a month.

Focus Question 5:
What are the dangers in responding to students based only on what appears to be their ethnic group identity?

Objective 8:
Describe why students from the same ethnic and language background may behave differently in the classroom.

Objective 9:
Describe how we are all multicultural.

Biculturalism

Individuals who have competencies in and can operate successfully in two or more different cultures are bicultural or multicultural, and are often multilingual as well. Having proficiencies in multiple cultures does not lead to rejection of the primary cultural identification. It does allow a broad range of abilities on which one can draw as needed.

Many individuals who are not members of the dominant culture become bicultural to work or attend school and to participate effectively in their own ethnic community. Different behaviors are expected in the two settings. To be successful on the job usually requires proficiency in the ways of the dominant group. Because most schools reflect the dominant society, students are forced to adjust if they are going to be academically successful. On the other hand, many European Americans find almost total congruence between the culture of their family, schooling, and work. Most remain monocultural throughout their lives, and do not comprehend the value of becoming competent in a different culture. Thus, being multicultural and multilingual is not promoted in most communities and schools.

Information Note 5.12:
The segregation of groups in readily identifiable neighborhoods helps maintain limited interaction across groups.

Objective 10:
Explain the advantages of being able to function effectively in more than one culture.

Activity 5.7:
Have students record on a chart the advantages and disadvantages of being bicultural and bilingual. As a class or in small groups, discuss why these characteristics are often not valued in a school setting.

Summary and Implications

The way individuals behave and think is determined by their culture. Culture is so pervasive in our lives that we often are not aware that our actions and thoughts are culturally determined. Culture is learned, shared, adapted, and dynamic. Although characteristics and contributions of diverse cultural groups are reflected in society, the dominant cultural group (white, Protestant, middle-class, European Americans) has the greatest impact on societal values and behavioral expectations. Ethnocentrism takes group membership to an extreme when members believe that they are superior to members of other groups. The interaction of culture and society are critical elements in studying students, families, communities, and schools.

A number of theories have evolved to describe the nature of diversity in the United States. Assimilation has been the predominant theory during the twentieth century. To be successful in society, newcomers and other visibly distinct groups were expected to shed their cultural identities and adopt those of the dominant group. In a culturally plural society, the maintenance of distinct cultural patterns is valued, promoted, and treated as equal to the dominant culture. Cultural choice allows individuals, families, and groups to maintain their own cultures, assimilate into the dominant society, or be bicultural or multicultural. Each of these theories has been translated into educational strategies that guide a school's curriculum and the interactions of students and teachers.

Individuals belong to numerous microcultural groups, which determine their unique cultural identity. The groups that appear to be the most important in our identity are race, gender, and class or socioeconomic status. To many, religious affiliation is most critical in determining cultural patterns. One's language, disability, or sexual orientation may also be essential in the determination of cultural identity. Membership in one of these microcultural groups may be so important that it influences membership in all of the others.

Discussion Questions

1. How do culture and society interact to produce inequities between diverse groups?
2. Why do we often not recognize our own cultural patterns?
3. Why might it be important to help students learn more about their own cultural background and heritage?
4. How have theories describing diversity impacted on the educational process in the past decade?
5. What impact does poverty have on a family's or student's cultural identity?

Journal/Portfolio Development

1. Contrast educational practices that have evolved to support the different theories of diversity. Develop an argument for incorporating those practices into your own teaching.
2. Prepare an autobiographical description of the importance of your membership in the microcultural groups described in this chapter to your own cultural identity. The description should indicate why membership in one or more groups is especially important in the identification of who you are.

School-Based Experiences

1. In a school with students from diverse language backgrounds, interview a teacher about the strategies that are used to ensure that students do not fall academically behind because their native language is not English.
2. Ask a sample of students of color in a school in which they are the numerical minority how their ethnic background is reflected in the curriculum and activities of the school.

Notes

1. National Council for Accreditation of Teacher Education. NCATE *Refined Standards.* Washington, DC: Author, 1994.
2. Norman R. Yetman, *Majority and Minority: The Dynamics of Race and Ethnicity in American Life.* 4th ed. Boston: Allyn and Bacon, 1985.
3. Young Pai, *Cultural Foundation of Education.* Columbus, OH: Merrill, 1990.
4. George Spindler and Louise Spindler, *The American Cultural Dialogue and Its Transmission.* New York: Falmer Press, 1990, 38.
5. R. N. Bellah, R. Madsen, W. M. Sullivan, A. Swidler, and S. M. Tipton, *Habits of the Heart: Individualism and Commitment in American Life.* New York: Harper & Row, 1985, 23.
6. Ibid., 23.
7. Milton M. Gordon, *Assimilation in American Life: The Role of Race, Religion, and National Origins.* New York: Oxford University Press, 1964.
8. Richard Pratte, *Pluralism in Education: Conflict, Clarity, and Commitment.* Springfield, IL: Charles C. Thomas, 1979.
9. Ana Maria Villegas, *Culturally Responsive Pedagogy for the 1990s and Beyond (Trends and Issues Paper No. 6).* Washington, DC: ERIC Clearinghouse on Teacher Education, 1991.
10. Donna M. Gollnick and Philip C. Chinn, *Multicultural Education in a Pluralistic Society.* Columbus, OH: Merrill, 1994, 20.
11. American Council on Education and Education Commission of the States, *One-third of a Nation.* Washington, DC: American Council on Education, 1988.
12. Harold Hodgkinson, "The Schools We Need for the Kids We've Got" (Paper presented at the 1987 annual meeting of the American Association of Colleges for Teacher Education, February 1986).
13. R. Spencer, "U.S. Ranks 6th in Quality of Life; Japan Is 1st," *The Washington Post,* (May 18, 1993), A7.
14. Spindler and Spindler, 23.
15. Bureau of the Census, *Statistical Abstract of the United States, 1992,* 108th ed. Washington, DC: Government Printing Office, 1992.
16. Donald L. Barlett and James B. Steele, *America: What Went Wrong?* Kansas City, MO: Andrews and McMeel, 1992.
17. Stephen J. Rose, *Social Stratification in the United States: The American Profile Poster Revised and Expanded.* New York: The New Press, 1992.
18. K. P. Phillips, *The Politics of Rich and Poor.* New York: Random House, 1990 , 179–180.
19. Sar A. Levitan and Isaac Shapiro, *Working but Poor: America's Contradiction.* Baltimore, MD: The Johns Hopkins University Press, 1987, vii.
20. "Children in Poverty," *Education Week* (September 29, 1993): 3.
21. M. F. Linehan, "Children Who Are Homeless: Educational Strategies for School Personnel," *Phi Delta Kappan* 74 (1) (1992): 61–66.
22. Bureau of the Census, *Statistical Abstract of the United States, 1992.*

23. Jorgen S. Nielsen, "Muslims, Pluralism and the European Nation State," *European Journal of Intercultural Studies* 5(1) (1994): 18–22.

24. Giovanna Campani, "Intercultural Education in Italy," *European Journal of Intercultural Studies* 4(3) (1994): 44–53.

25. George Markou, "Intercultural Education in Multicultural Greece," *European Journal of Intercultural Studies* 4(3) (1994): 32–43.

26. Claude Liauza, "Interculturalism: New Lands to Discover in France," *European Journal of Intercultural Studies* 4(3) (1994): 25–31.

27. Christopher Szaday, "Schooling in Multicultural Switzerland," *European Journal of Intercultural Studies* 5(1) (1994): 38–50.

28. William L. Yancey, Eugene P. Ericksen, and Richard N. Juliani, "Emergent Ethnicity: A Review and Reformulation," in Norma R. Yetman, ed., *Majority and Minority: The Dynamics of Racial and Ethnic Relations.* Boston: Allyn and Bacon, 1985.

29. Jessie Bernard, *The Female World.* New York: Free Press, 1981, 4.

30. Myra Sadker, David Sadker, and Susan Klein, "The Issue of Gender in Elementary and Secondary Education," in Gerald Grant, ed., *Review of Research in Education,* vol. 17. Washington, DC: American Educational Research Association, 1991.

31. Bernard, 1981.

32. Pai, 1990.

33. Bureau of the Census, 1992.

34. Ibid.

35. Michelle Fine, "Sexuality, Schooling, and Adolescent Females: The Missing Discourse of Desire," *Harvard Educational Review* 58(1) (February 1988): 48.

36. P. E. Willis, *Learning to Labour: How Working Class Kids Get Working Class Jobs.* Farnborough, England: Saxon House, 1977.

37. *Joseph Acanfora* v. *Board of Education of Montgomery County, et al.* 359 F. Supp. 843 (1973); aff'd 491 F. 2nd 498 (4th Cir. 1974); cert. denied, 419 U.S. 836 (1974).

38. American Bar Association, ABA Annual Meeting Provides Forum for Family Law Experts, 13 Fam. L. Rep. (BNA), 1542, 1543, 1987. As quoted in Elaine Wickens, "Penny's Question: 'I Will Have a Child in my Class with Two Moms—What Do You Know about This?'" *Young Children* 48(3) (March 1993): 25–28.

39. Bureau of the Census, *Statistical Abstract of the United States, 1992.*

40. Gollnick and Chinn, 1994.

41. "Church Attendance Constant," *Emerging Trends* 14(3) (1992).

42. R. Bezilla, *Religion in America.* Princeton, HJ: Princeton Religion Research Center, 1993.

Bibliography

Bellah, R. N., Madsen, R., Sullivan, W. M., Swidler, A. and Tipton, S. M. *Habits of the Heart: Individualism and Commitment in American Life.* New York: Harper & Row, 1985.

Connell, R. W. "Poverty and Education." *Harvard Educational Review* 64(2) (Summer 1994): 125–149.

Corbett, Susan. "A Complicated Bias." *Young Children* 48(3) (March 1993): 29–31.

Gollnick, Donna M., and Chinn, Philip C. *Multicultural Education in a Pluralistic Society.* Columbus, OH: Merrill, 1994.

Sleeter, Christine E., ed. *Empowerment through Multicultural Education.* Albany, NY: State University of New York Press, 1991.

Spindler, George, and Spindler, Louise. *The American Cultural Dialogue and Its Transmission.* New York: Falmer Press, 1990.

Wickens, Elaine. "Penny's Question: 'I Will Have a Child in My Class with Two Moms—What Do You Know about This?'" *Young Children* 48(3) (March 1993): 25–28.

6 Education That Is Multicultural

Focus Questions

1   What philosophical beliefs support education that is multicultural?
2   What role does cultural diversity play in education that is multicultural?
3   How do teachers deliver education that is multicultural?
4   What differences could schools make in the lives of children?
5   How is education that is multicultural different from what is delivered by most good schools today?

Key Terms and Concepts

Bias: A preference or inclination that inhibits impartial judgment, leading to prejudice or discrimination.

Censorship: The condemnation of books, instructional materials, teaching content, or teaching methods because they are perceived as unsupportive of or in opposition to the values of an individual or group.

Multicultural education: An educational strategy that incorporates the teaching of exceptional and culturally diverse students, human relations, and the study of ethnic and other cultural groups in a school environment that supports diversity and equal opportunity.

Social justice: The desire for all individuals and families to share equally society's benefits.

Stereotyping: The application of common traits, characteristics, and behavior to a group of people without acknowledging individual differences within the group.

Voice: The right and opportunity to speak and be heard as an equal.

Test Questions 6.1–6.3

Objective 1:
Discuss the role of diversity
and equality in the education
process.

Diversity and equality are the perspectives through which education that is multicultural should be developed. All teaching and school activities should be designed and evaluated with these characteristics in mind. All aspects of education—including the hidden curriculum, staffing patterns, discipline, and extracurricular activities—should be viewed through these perspectives to ensure that the needs of all students are an integral part of the education process. Education must do more than reflect only dominant society; it must begin to reflect diversity and support all students. The challenge for you as an educator will be to deliver an education that is multicultural. Constant vigilance of the content and delivery of the subject matter will be required.

Key Term:
Multicultural education

Objective 2:
Articulate why multicultural
education is for all students.

Information Note 6.1:
Multicultural education is
superficial when it is limited to
tasting ethnic food and cele-
brating festivals and holidays.

Many educators have mistakenly thought that **multicultural education**[1] or education that is multicultural is only for students who are not members of the dominant group in society. Rather, it is for all students regardless of their microcultural memberships. It is as important for students and teachers of European, Protestant backgrounds as it is for those from ethnic and cultural groups that have traditionally faced discrimination in society. All content should be multicultural and presented through the viewpoints of many different groups to help students understand that there is more than one perspective on the interpretation of events and facts.

Too many educators have thought they were "doing" multicultural education simply by including information about groups other than their own in a lesson. This additive approach is evident in black history and women's history months or a highlighted section in a textbook that discusses Japanese Americans. In some schools attention to multiculturalism begins and ends with tasting ethnic foods and participating in ethnic festivals. While these activities can contribute to the development of education that is multicultural, they are side attractions and do not represent an integrated curriculum and school environment.

In education that is multicultural all teaching is multicultural and classrooms and schools are models of democracy and equity. This effort requires educators to

1. place the student at the center of the teaching and learning process;

2. promote human rights and respect for cultural differences;

3. believe that all students can learn;

4. acknowledge and build on the life histories and experiences of students' microcultural memberships;

5. critically analyze oppression and power relationships to understand racism, sexism, classism, and discrimination against the disabled, young, and aged;

6. critique society in the interest of social justice and equality; and

7. participate in collective social action to ensure a democratic society.[2]

Education that is multicultural is much more than tasting ethnic foods or participating in an ethnic festival.

Although you should begin to struggle with these issues now, the process of learning about others and reflecting on one's attitudes and actions in these areas will be a lifelong activity.

Undergirding Tenets

For centuries women, persons with low incomes, and members of oppressed ethnic and religious groups have fought for an education equal to that available to members of the dominant group. In the nineteenth century courageous educators established schools to serve some of these students, often encountering opposition from the community at the time. Nearly eighty years ago educators at the Intercultural Service Bureau in New York City were fighting for the incorporation of intercultural education into the curriculum to increase knowledge about new immigrants and to reduce the prejudice against them. In 1954 the Supreme Court declared illegal separate-but-equal education for black and white students in the *Brown* vs *Board of Education* case. The civil rights struggles in the 1960s laid the groundwork for adding content to the curriculum about African Americans, Latinos, Native Americans, and Asian Americans. Attention to equity for women, individuals with disabilities, or limited-English speakers soon followed.

These events became the foundation for education that is multicultural. A number of related beliefs about schooling and society guide the development of education that supports democracy for all. One is the belief that cultural diversity is a national strength that should be valued and promoted. Another is that **social justice** and equality remain viable goals for society and should be modeled in classrooms and schools. In this section, we will examine two of the major tenets on which multicultural education is built.

Diversity

There has been a great amount of public and academic discussion of multiculturalism in the past few years. Editorials, national news programs, radio talk shows, and debates among college students and faculty periodically focus on the importance of diversity in society and the curriculum. Simply put, the argument on one side is that the recognition and promotion of cultural and ethnic diversity will strengthen the nation. The other side argues that the promotion of diversity will divide the nation and lead to even greater conflict among groups. This second group also argues that the Western tradition is denigrated as diversity is highlighted.

The claim that multicultural education will divide the nation suggests that the nation is already united.[3] Campaigns for members of Congress, governors, and mayors in 1994 included debates about immigration, provision of services to undocumented workers and their children, the use of only English, and gay rights. Multiculturalists argue that "multicultural education is designed to help unify a deeply divided nation rather than to divide a highly cohesive one."[4] In addition, as we have the opportunity to learn more about each other and to interact on an equal basis in schools and society, members of diverse groups can maintain their ethnic and cultural diversity while developing together a common civic culture. An outgrowth of these debates has been the establishment of general education requirements in colleges and universities for ethnic, women's, and/or global studies. At least thirty-three states also expect teacher education candidates to study

Test Questions 6.3–6.18

Focus Question 1:
What philosophical beliefs support education that is multicultural?

Journal/Portfolio Development 1:
Investigate the debates related to the adoption of a multicultural curriculum in a state or local school district (New York State Department of Education's *One Nation, Many Peoples: A Declaration of Cultural Interdependence* or New York City's *Children of the Rainbow*). Prepare a paper that describes the issues involved in the debates and summarizes your recommendation for the adoption of the curriculum.

Activity 6.1:
Have students debate the importance of social justice in society and schools.

Activity 6.2:
Ask students to articulate the arguments for and against the proposition that multicultural education is divisive to the nation, and have them argue their own stand.

Information Note 6.2:
NCATE expects teacher education programs to ensure that teacher candidates can create learning experiences for students that build on their prior experiences, exceptionalities, and cultural backgrounds based on membership in ethnic, racial, gender, language, socioeconomic, community, and family groups to help all students achieve high levels of learning.

CNN Clip 10:
Multicultural Requirement

Key Term:
Social justice

Objective 3:
Explain what conditions and practices exist in schools to suggest that social justice is not a principle that undergirds the educational system.

Objective 4:
Analyze social justice and its place in a democracy.

diversity and to be able to incorporate it into their teaching.[5] The national accrediting agency for teacher education programs in colleges and universities, NCATE, has required the inclusion of multicultural content in teacher education curriculum since 1978. Most of the developing state and national standards for preschool through high school curriculum include references to diversity.

What does the public think of incorporating diversity into the curriculum of our schools? The National Conference Survey found that

> On the whole, the data suggest that cultural diversity is hardly a foreign or unfamiliar concept in contemporary American society. Asked "How important do you think it is that people from different groups learn to understand and appreciate the lifestyles, tastes, and contributions of each other's groups?" 67% of those surveyed nationwide said such understanding and appreciation is "very important," while another 25% feel it is "important." Across the board, roughly nine in ten people in all diverse groups surveyed endorse this concept, including 91% of whites.
>
> As a counterpart question, survey participants were also asked about the desirability of "teaching all students about the racial, ethnic, and cultural groups that make up America today." A substantial 57% say they find it "very desirable" and another 31% "somewhat desirable," while only 9% deem such education "undesirable," adding up to an 88% mandate from the adult public. Again, roughly 9 in 10 respondents endorse the teaching of cultural diversity in the nation's schools.
>
> These results indicate that whatever negative perceptions groups have about each other, many of the prerequisites of tolerance and inter-group cooperation are present in today's America: respect for the differences among us and a commitment to increased understanding of those differences.[6]

According to the National Conference survey, most Americans believe that diversity should be taught in schools. In another study of public perceptions of the *good society*, researchers concluded that "Pluralism does not contradict the idea of a good society, for the latter would be one that would allow a wide scope for diversity and would draw on resources from its pluralistic communities in discerning those things that are necessarily matters of the good of all."[7]

Social Justice and Equality

Peace, prosperity, freedom, and justice traditionally have defined the good society for Americans.[8] What is meant by *justice* in a society that places so much emphasis on individualism and the freedom to be left alone? Justice itself is related to fairness, moral rightness, and equity. Our judicial system is designed to guarantee legal justice for individuals and groups. **Social justice,** on the other hand, focuses on how we help others in the community who are not as advantaged as we are. In fact, most religions measure the quality of society by the justice and care given to the downtrodden—the homeless, the sick, the powerless, the uneducated.[9]

The ethic of social justice, especially as it relates to the teacher-student relationship, is essential in the profession of teaching along with moral commitments to inquiry (that is, the nurturing of thinking), knowledge, competence, and caring.[10] It requires "that schools provide equal access to and equal receipt of a quality education for *all* students. Any structures or practices that interfere with the simultaneous goals of equity and excellence, that perpetuate preexisting social and economic inequities, are subject to critique and elimination."[11] The acceptance of

Social justice is measured by the care provided to individuals in society who are not as advantaged as most.

social justice as a moral and ethical responsibility of educators and schooling is critical in the provision of education that is multicultural.

As discussed in previous chapters, schools are currently full of social injustices that need to be addressed and eliminated to provide educational equality for all students. As you reflect on the inequitable conditions in most of our schools, ask yourself the following questions:

Objective 5:
Identify practices in schools that reflect social justice and those that do not reflect it.

Discussion Question 1:
What conditions and practices exist in schools to suggest that social justice is not a principle that undergirds the educational system?

- How fair is it for some students to attend school in dilapidated, foul-smelling, crowded buildings while others attend classes in beautiful buildings with future-oriented technology and well-groomed grounds?
- How fair is it for wealthier students to have the most experienced and best qualified teachers who earn the highest salaries of all teachers?
- How fair is it that wealthier students are exposed to intellectually challenging curriculum and experiences while many low-income students do not even have an advanced placement class offered in their school?
- How fair is it that students of color, especially males, and students with disabilities or limited English proficiency are pulled out of regular classes and isolated in segregated classes during much of the school day?
- How accurate is a curriculum and pedagogy that does not reflect the rich plurality of the people, histories, experiences, and perspectives of the groups that comprise the United States and world?

These are among the numerous questions that educators should be asking themselves if they are serious about providing social justice in schools. The promise of a democratic society has been that all students have a fair chance to learn and succeed. Instead, the current system supports the same inequities that exist in society. The already advantaged student normally continues to be advantaged over students in low-income areas from the day they enter school. A theory of social justice suggests that those students with the least advantage should receive the greatest advantage in their education and schooling to begin to ensure an equal and fair playing field. The goal might be to use the best funded and successful schools as the norm for all schools, with the least advantaged receiving the greatest resources for their education.

Global Perspectives: For What Purpose? The Debate in the United Kingdom

Even the advocates for changing schools to reflect democracy and equality sometimes disagree about what to call the educational strategy. In the United Kingdom the debate between antiracists and multiculturalists began to flourish in the 1970s after the release of a number of national reports on immigrants and race relations. The differences between the two went beyond the label for what is called *multicultural education* or *education that is multicultural* in the United States. The supporters of antiracist education focused on the structure of the education system and power relationships between the dominant Anglo society and the powerless immigrant groups. The primary emphasis of the advocates for multicultural education was on the content of the curriculum. Finally, in the 1990s a synthesis of the two is evolving in which the strategy for social justice is an education that is antiracist *and* multicultural.[12]

Educational Challenges

Test Questions 6.19–6.54

Focus Question 2:
What role does cultural diversity play in education that is multicultural?

Activity 6.3:
Invite the principal and selected teachers from a school that views itself as providing education that is multicultural to discuss the differences between their school and others and to provide recommendations to students for preparing to work in a similar setting.

Focus Question 3:
How do teachers deliver education that is multicultural?

Objective 6:
Identify some factors that teachers should know to help students from diverse cultural backgrounds learn the subject matter.

The challenges for delivering education that is multicultural are many. The diversity of the student population is growing differently than in the past. By the time you start teaching, approximately one-third of the students in schools across the nation will be from ethnic groups other than European. By 2020 over 45 percent of the school-age population will be students of color.[13] Because many teacher candidates have either no or limited experience with the ethnic groups that will be in their classrooms, they will face the unknown. The tenets of diversity and social justice will require continuous learning about and with these communities to be effective teachers.

In some schools teachers may still face fairly homogeneous student populations with little exposure to diversity and the multicultural nature of the country. Even with limited ethnic diversity, most schools will have males and females from different religious and economic backgrounds. The ethic of social justice is just as important in these settings as in those with great ethnic and language diversity. To provide a well-rounded and balanced curriculum for these students, teachers will need to work harder at bringing different perspectives to presentations and discussions. Innovative strategies for providing direct exposure to diversity and issues of equality will need to be developed.

Diverse Approaches to Teaching and Learning

We all have preferred learning and teaching styles that are embedded in our cultural background and experiences. Unfortunately, most of us think that everyone else shares our learning style. Until a teacher learns to recognize these differences and develops a repertoire of different ways to teach the subject matter, some students will be deprived of appropriate assistance in the learning process.

CASE STUDY   SCIENCE SUCCESS FOR LEP STUDENTS

The city of Yakima, located in south central Washington, serves a large, rather isolated agricultural region with a culturally diverse population. One of the city's two high schools, Davis High School, enrolls Anglo (42 percent), Latino (33 percent), African American (15 percent), and Asian American (10 percent) students. Eighty-five percent of the students are eligible for free or reduced lunches.

Although the school had a fairly successful retention rate, migrant and immigrant students were not being prepared well for college, as was evidenced in their lack of success in science courses. Science faculty decided to adapt a regular chemistry course for students with limited English proficiency. The chemistry teacher participated in an intensive workshop on English as a Second Language (ESL) and then integrated ESL strategies into the curriculum. Bilingual materials were developed, and a bilingual aide was hired to work with the teacher and students. Information in class was presented visually as well as verbally, and videodiscs with English and Spanish soundtracks were used.

Students in the first class included Mexican Americans, a Peruvian, a Japanese exchange student, and an Ethiopian. They performed as well as the students in the traditional chemistry course, and some are now college students. Their self-confidence improved, as did their grades, attendance, and motivation. In addition, faculty outside the science department began to see that students with limited English proficiency could perform academically at a level equal to the other students—a fact that they had doubted in the past.

1. What components of multicultural education were integrated into the chemistry course at Davis High School?
2. What may have occurred in this course that ensured that the limited English proficient students were able to perform at a level comparable to classmates in the traditional course?
3. Why did the successful experiences of these students in science cause some teachers to rethink their expectations for them?

Source: "Davis High School: Helping Bilingual Science Students Succeed." *Rural Adult Education Forum* 5 (2) (December 1992/January 1993): 7.

Valuing Differences. Understanding the cultures of students and drawing on them to teach the subject matter is a critical component in helping students learn. Students usually can determine rather quickly whether the teacher values them and their cultures. To demonstrate a respect for the students' background and experiences, teachers should be able to help students see the relationship between the subject matter and the world in which they live. Students should be able to see themselves in the representations (that is, books, examples, word problems, and films) used by teachers. If the teaching style and representations are based totally on the culture of the teacher, it will be difficult to convince students that their cultures are also valued.

Use of students' prior knowledge and experiences with the subject matter is also critical in providing meaningful learning experiences in the classroom. Students make sense of new information in different ways. Therefore, the teacher must be able to teach the same concept by explaining it in different ways, relating it to something meaningful in the student's life and demonstrating it with multiple

Activity 6.4:
Have students develop a lesson plan that incorporates the cultures of Sikh and Bosnian immigrant students. Discuss how students located information on the two cultures to help them develop the lesson plan.

Information Note 6.3:
A key to good teaching is the thorough understanding of the subject matter. Teachers who know the subject are not dependent on a single way to teach it. If a student does not understand the concept being taught from a lecture, the teacher should be able to present an example, use an exercise, or draw an illustration to help the student learn.

CNN Clip 11:
Immigrant Education

Teachers must be able to transcend their own cultural background in the development of learning experiences that build on the cultural background of their students.

representations. For most beginning teachers, repertoires are rather limited; with experience, good teachers are able to draw on many different strategies to take advantage of a student's unique learning style and cultural patterns.

It is important to know what kind of knowledge, skills, and commitments are valued in the students' cultures. Researchers have found that some students rebel against academic study and school authority as a form of resistance against the values of dominant society and its institutions.[14] For example, some white working-class families value common sense and working with one's hands. They place less value on "book learning" than most middle-class families. Understanding these differences should help the teacher develop different strategies for presenting and discussing the subject matter.

Information Note 6.4:
Researchers at the National Center for Research on Teacher Learning warn us that we should be careful of moving from a description of behavior ("she is acting shyly") to labeling a person ("she is shy"). Are students shy or are they experiencing alienation and detachment from the activities and content of the class?

Key Term:
Stereotyping

Avoidance of Stereotyping.   After studying a program for training teachers to teach culturally different students in Los Angeles, G. Williamson McDiarmid raised a number of issues, including the fact that generalizations about culturally diverse learners are often very dangerous. Teachers need to be thoughtful about the role that culture—values, behaviors, language—may play in learning and, at the same time, avoid characterizing all students as the same because they appear to share the same ethnicity or class.[15]

At first glance, it may seem that handling diversity in a classroom would be much easier if we could just pick up a recipe book that clearly states what instruction will be effective for students from a specific group. The problem with this approach is that not only are there differences across ethnic and cultural groups, there are many differences among members within the same group. Therefore, the descriptions and recommendations of a group usually do not apply to all members of that group. The intragroup differences may be based on socioeconomic level, religion, language, and degree of assimilation. The generalizations in the recipe book would lead to **stereotyping** and prejudging students in a way that concerned McDiarmid in his Los Angeles observations.

Just like teaching itself, multicultural teaching is complex. A teacher cannot determine the learning styles, prior knowledge, or cultural experiences of students by simply knowing that they are from a specific ethnic group or socioeconomic level. The teacher will need to observe and listen to students and their parents as well as assess student performance to develop the most effective teaching strategy.

Use of Competition and Cooperation.   Traditionally classrooms have been organized with the teacher as the authority figure who lectures and controls all aspects of the learning process. In this system students compete for recognition by the teacher to answer a question and receive positive or negative reinforcement. Tests and grades are also competitive in that students compete against each other and are ranked accordingly. Competition in the classroom generally supports the learning styles of members of the dominant culture.

Cooperative learning, on the other hand, provides greater opportunities for learning by many students of color because it reflects their preferred learning style, which is group-oriented. Cooperative learning supports a more democratic climate than the traditional classroom. Students work together in small, preferably heterogeneous groups and take responsibility for themselves and other members of the group. They help each other learn and, in the process, develop skills in interpersonal relations.[16]

Inclusion in Regular Classrooms

Inclusion is a term that evolved from the work of persons with disabilities, the parents of students with disabilities, and special educators to ensure that physically and mentally challenged young people could be educated in the same classrooms as students without disabilities. In the broader society, inclusion has confronted discrimination policies and practices that have made it very difficult for some individuals to be mobile, receive a college education, and be offered jobs. As a result of the activism of these individuals, persons with disabilities have become more integrated into society. It is no longer unusual to be in meetings with professionals who are in wheelchairs or who are using sign language.

Today, inclusion is used more broadly to promote the involvement of all underrepresented groups in regular classrooms and society's institutions. In applying the ethic of social justice, one should be concerned to find white middle-class students overly represented in advanced placement classes. One should wonder why the advanced classes are intellectually stimulating and interesting while the remedial classes are usually practice oriented and dull. Why are young women and students of color underrepresented in the high-level mathematics and science courses?

Inclusion is expected in a school that provides education that is multicultural. However, it is not a common practice in many schools today. Educators have begun to accept students with mild disabilities in classrooms, but many others are transported to special schools or sent to a pull-out program within the school for much or all of the day. Although schools have been working to desegregate for forty years, the population of many urban schools is predominantly students of color while many suburban schools are predominantly white. Within desegregated schools, students are often segregated to an ever greater degree by race or language in classes. Such practices should trigger an investigation about the lack of social justice and provision of equality for all students.

High Expectations.   A key element in multicultural education is the belief that all students, regardless of their cultural backgrounds, can learn at high levels. Most persons who select teaching as their career probably want to help all students learn and believe that they can. Somewhat surprisingly, a 1994 survey of teachers in Kentucky did not support that assumption. Only about one-third of the teachers believed that all students could learn at a high level.[17]

In most cases, we also have not acknowledged our **biases** about some groups; this can have a great impact on our expectations for their ability to learn. Research on self-fulfilling prophecies has found that students perform better when the teacher has high expectations of their abilities.[18] Conversely, it is very difficult for

Activity 6.5:
Ask students to divide into one of two groups—cooperative and competitive. Have each group list a school practice that could be termed cooperative or competitive. Then have the two groups share their lists and discuss the pros and cons of each practice. Ask students if they could realistically succeed in a school that was entirely cooperative or entirely competitive.

Activity 6.6:
Discuss the phrases: "For me to win, you must lose" and "For me to win, you must win." How do these phrases relate to competitive versus cooperative learning?

Information Note 6.5:
The Individuals with Disabilities Education Act (IDEA) mandates that all children have available to them a free and appropriate education designed to meet their unique needs. This education can either be in the form of instruction in a separate classroom or mainstreaming into a regular classroom.

Objective 7:
Define *inclusion* as it is used in education that is multicultural.

Objective 8:
Describe how teachers' biases may influence their expectations for students.

Key Term:
Bias

Information Note 6.6:
The stereotype that all Asian
Americans are gifted or more
able than others does not
acknowledge that there are
intragroup differences and
that many of the recent immigrants from Asia do not have
the same background advantages as earlier immigrants.

students to overcome the teacher's low expectation. They often begin to accept that they cannot achieve, they lose interest in trying, and they take on the stereo-typical role of the nonacademic student. Thus, both teachers and students inter-act to fulfill the prophecy, even when the expectations are based on inaccurate information.

It is important that teachers develop a classroom climate that values students and makes them feel capable of academic success.[19] To be successful, this expec-tation interacts with teacher behaviors to communicate that the teacher cares about students as individuals and believes that they can learn. "The teacher ceas-es seeing his or her students as 'the other' and addresses students' psychological and social development along with their academic development."[20]

Objective 9:
Explain why tracking of stu-dents may be an inequitable strategy.

Ability Grouping. Ability grouping and tracking of students go against an ethic of social justice and equality. These practices provide the most advantaged students with the best possible school experiences while ensuring that the least advantaged students receive separate, and often ineffective, instruction. There are at least three serious repercussions of ability grouping. It "separates students along socioeconomic lines, separating rich from poor, whites from non-whites. The end result is that poor and minority children are found far more often than others in the bottom tracks. And once there, they are likely to suffer far more negative con-sequences of schooling than are their more fortunate peers."[21]

Tracking also "retard[s] the academic progress of many students—those in average and low groups. Tracking seems to foster low self-esteem among these same students and promotes school misbehavior and dropping out. Tracking also appears to lower the aspirations of students who are not in the top groups."[22] Finally, many students are placed in a track very early in their schooling—a track in which they remain throughout their school career. These unfortunate students have little opportunity to achieve academically, or even to move out of the lowest track.

Key Term:
Voice

Tracking has no place in education that is multicultural. Social justice can only exist if all students are provided equal access to educational opportunities that are high level, stimulating, and effective. Educa-tors must begin to examine why students are not learning and take on the challenge to make changes in the classroom climate and nature of instruction to promote learning by all students.

Student Voices

In a democratic classroom all participants must have a **voice**—the right and opportu-nity to speak and be heard as an equal. The dialogue cannot be dominated by teachers. They are viewed by students, especially low-income students and students of color, as rep-resenting the dominant cultural group and not being open to hearing other perspectives represented by their cultures.

Education that is multicultural encourages and validates the diverse voices of students in helping them construct their own learning.

Including student voices in the classroom dialogue is not always an easy pursuit. Students usually have limited experience in active participation in their own learning. When the classroom climate begins to include student voices, they may express anger and be confrontive; they may even test the limits of the type of language that can be used and the subjects that can be broached. Allowing student voices to be an integral part of classroom discourse often tests the patience of teachers as they and their students figure out how to listen and contribute to the learning process. At the same time, tolerance, patience with each other, and the willingness to listen will develop as student voices contribute to the exploration of the subject matter.

Discussion Question 2:
What are the potential benefits and perceived dangers of allowing student voices to be an integral part of instruction?

Affirmation of Student Voices.   Respect for differences is key in affirming student voices. For many educators it requires relinquishing the power that they have traditionally had as the voice of authority with the *right* answers. Class time can no longer be monopolized with teacher talk. The meaningful incorporation of student voices requires the development of listening skills and the validation of multiple perspectives, languages, and dialects. It should allow students to participate in the dialogue through speaking, writing, and artistic expression. It should allow them to use the modes of communicating with which they feel the most comfortable while teaching them other modes as well.

Objective 10:
Provide examples of how students' voices are an integral part of education that is multicultural and democratic schools.

Student voices are also affirmed by encouraging students to relate the subject matter to their own realities or lived experiences. Because most of us have very limited experiences in other cultures, we must expand our knowledge about them. Students can become active participants in helping others learn about their cultures and everyday experiences. Teachers can facilitate learning activities to guide students in teaching each other. If we are not able to help students see the relationship of the subject matter to their own lives, we may not be able to help them learn. Listening to them and being able to adjust our teaching strategies appropriately will help make us effective teachers.

Journal/Portfolio Development 2:
For the subject and level that you plan to teach, design a lesson that incorporates multiple voices.

The affirmation of student voices requires that educators listen to the voices of *all* students. It is particularly important to hear the voices of students of color, low-income students, girls and young women, limited English speakers, and students with disabilities. The formal and hidden curriculum has validated the voices of the dominant groups throughout their lives. One of the goals of education that is multicultural is to also validate the voices and stories of others. Teachers must ensure that these voices are not drowned out again in their classrooms. The stories or narratives of others will increase the knowledge and tolerance of differences. Many students will learn to value both their own culture and that of others. In the process we will also learn that we have much in common.[23]

Journal Activity Master 6.2: Analysis of a School Subculture. Helps student assess the multicultural flavor of a school's subculture.

Cross-Cultural Communications.   Some of the conflict in student-teacher interactions is the lack of information and understanding about cultural differences in oral and nonverbal communications. "Just as cultures differ in the structure of their language, they also differ in the structure of oral discourse. Moves made in teaching-learning discourse, who is to make them, and the sequence they should take vary from culture to culture."[24] Communicating is like other aspects of culture. We usually think that the way that we communicate with other members of the culture is "normal." We don't realize that there are many other ways to communicate that make as much sense as our own, but we have just not had the

Activity 6.7:
Ask students to design a lesson that employs visual, perceptual characteristics rather than verbal ones.

opportunity to experience them. As long as we interact only with members of the same culture, we use the same cultural cues for whose turn it is to speak, the meaning of a raised eyebrow, or the seriousness of a statement.

Often teachers do not realize that they and their students are reading the cultural cues differently. In many cases, students are punished for responding inappropriately when they may have read the teacher's intent differently based on their own cultural experiences. Recognizing that miscommunications may be based on cultural differences is the first step in improving cross-cultural communications. A next step is to be able to admit that we may be part of the problem. Next, we should be able to develop alternate means for communicating and understanding the messages from other cultures.

One approach is to systematically teach the communication patterns of the dominant culture to students who are not members of that culture. In this strategy the students' communication patterns are still valued, but they learn when it is to their advantage to use the communication patterns of the dominant group. In other words, they begin to become bicultural. However, teachers who also learn to function effectively in more than one culture will most often gain respect from students, and begin to genuinely model a multicultural pedagogy.

Multicultural Curriculum

A major dimension of education that is multicultural is the integration of diversity and equality throughout the curriculum. The curriculum for all academic areas should reflect these concepts. Adding a course on ethnic studies or women's studies to the curriculum is an easy way to introduce students to the culture, history, and experiences of others, but it is not enough. Education that is multicultural calls for the inclusion of others throughout the curriculum.

The additive approach of including a unit on one of these groups sporadically during the year suggests that they are not an integral part of society. They are somewhat interesting to study, but they are not really a part of the whole picture. As a result, the curriculum places the culture, values, history, and experiences of the dominant group at the center. The implicit message is that the dominant culture is the most important in society, and that other cultures do not count or are certainly not as important. Learning will be increased for many students if their cultures become the center of the curriculum. As they learn within their own cultural context, they see themselves and their cultures valued by the teacher and school authorities.

One-third of the students in our nation's schools do not see themselves, their families, or their communities in the curriculum. It is not only students of color who seldom find themselves at the center of the curriculum; the curriculum does not normally include information on or the stories of women, the disabled, limited English speakers, families in poverty, the elderly, or members of religions that are not Judeo-Christian. The curriculum must become more inclusive; in the process, it will begin to reflect the reality of our multicultural world rather than just the piece of it that belongs to the dominant group.

No matter how great or limited the ethnic diversity is in a school, the curriculum should be multicultural. Rural white students should have the same opportunities to view the world and subject matter from multicultural and global perspectives as students in diverse settings. Because they do not have the opportunities to interact directly with members of diverse groups, the curriculum often becomes the primary source for their exploration of diversity, social justice, and related issues.

Multiple Perspectives. The perspective of the dominant group in society has become almost universal in most textbooks, instructional materials, and teacher-student dialogue. As a result, the voice of the dominant group is centered in curriculum and instruction. Because it is the voice most prevalent, it takes on an air of superiority over all other voices and perspectives. Education that is multicultural requires an approach that validates and gives more equitable treatment to perspectives that may differ somewhat or dramatically from that of the dominant group.

The introduction and exploration of multiple perspectives are very important in the curriculum. Every historical period, as well as current events, can be viewed through the eyes of others as well as those of the dominant group. When social studies emphasizes wars, women are seldom included. Discussions of power struggles, political leaders, and business usually ignore the working class, persons of color, and women. Attention to multiple perspectives draws in the voices of the individuals and groups without power; it begins to provide them an equal voice in the interpretation of events. A study of the struggles between Native American tribes and the federal government should always include a view from the perspective of the tribes as well as the powerful influence of the government.

In the humanities multiple perspectives are available in the literature, music, and art of individuals from diverse cultural and ethnic backgrounds. The works of authors and performers can be critiqued from different perspectives as well. Reading the works of authors from diverse backgrounds, observing performances, and listening to music provides teachers and their students a more well-rounded education than possible when the voices and perspectives of those who are like them are the only ones to which they are exposed. These activities also allow students to begin to understand the experiences and feelings of others as viewed from their perspectives on the world.

Although not as readily as the social sciences and humanities, science and mathematics also lend themselves to examination from multiple experiences. For example, Native Americans' approach to science has begun to have an impact on our treatment of the earth that is very different than the industrialized Western model. As we learn to appreciate and value multiple perspectives in academic areas, we realize that there are multiple answers to many questions. As a result, our knowledge expands beyond that of the limited perspective of our family and cultural group.

Another strength of the inclusion of multiple perspectives is that it allows many voices to participate in defining a common curriculum.[25] In the process the curriculum will change from a representation predominantly of middle and upper class whites to a balanced representation of others alongside the dominant group. Diversity and equality will be valued and promoted as an inclusive curriculum and practices evolve.

Controversial Issues. Multicultural teaching helps students struggle with social problems and issues that many students face daily. Racism, sexism, classism, prejudice, and discrimination are felt differently by students of color than by members

Discussion Question 3: Why is multicultural education just as important for students who are members of the dominant group in society as for those who are members of powerless groups?

Information Note 6.8: In presenting multiple perspectives, teachers often call on the students who are members of various ethnic, socioeconomic, or religious groups to describe the perspective of the group. Although this strategy may be appropriate in some instances, it often puts students in an awkward position of speaking for a group.

Journal Activity Master 6.1: An Analysis of School Mores. In this activity students summarize the unique problems that are identified with developing a school climate that is sensitive to the needs of a multicultural population. Students are asked to design a social studies lesson in a multicultural environment.

PROFESSIONAL DILEMMA

What If He Has Two Mommies?

In the 1950s most students came from families with both a mother and father. In the subsequent forty years more and more students were being raised by single mothers, and now a growing number of single fathers. Even during this period, some students were not living with either parent, but stayed instead with relatives or in a foster home. As society becomes more tolerant of a variety of family structures and as adults become more open about their sexual orientation, teachers also will be introduced to lesbian and gay parents who may be living with a partner or separated from a partner.

The curriculum in most schools, especially at the primary and elementary levels, is often developed around the family—a nuclear family with a mother, father, and siblings. For decades now, schools have been populated with students whose families do not fit that model. The curriculum and instructional materials seldom mirror the diversity of families that may include parents with special needs, interracial parents, single parents, gay and lesbian parents, and foster parents.

The dilemma for teachers extends beyond the curriculum. They must figure out how to value and respect the diversity of families. Otherwise, both students and parents will feel ignored and isolated from the school setting. Teachers may have to help other students develop an understanding of the diversity. Sometime students respond to such differences in negative and hurtful ways. Teachers will need to develop strategies for confronting homophobic behavior from the onset.

- How could a primary teacher introduce gay and lesbian parents into a reading lesson?

- What are different ways that teachers are likely to learn that some of their students have gay or lesbian parents?

- How should a teacher with strong views against homosexual relationships approach the reality of having the children of gays and lesbians in the classroom?

- How can a school develop a climate of acceptance of all students regardless of the structure and nature of the families in which they live?

Activity 6.10:
Why is multicultural education just as important for students who are members of the dominant group in society as for those who are members of powerless groups?

of the dominant group. The ensuing anger, denial, guilt, and affirmation of identity are critical parts of learning about and struggling with the pernicious practices that permeate most of our institutions. Although it is sometimes difficult to discuss these issues in classrooms, they must be confronted in a system based on diversity and equality or changes will be impossible.

Most students of color, females, low-income students, students with disabilities, and gay students have probably already experienced discrimination in some aspect of their lives. They may have not acknowledged it or they may be very angry or frustrated by it. On the other hand, many students from the dominant group have never experienced discrimination and often do not believe that it exists. In most cases, they do not see themselves as advantaged; they do not think that they receive any more benefits from society than anyone else. These students will have a difficult time fighting social injustices if they have neither experienced them nor become aware of their existence. Are they receiving a good education if they are never exposed to the injustices that do exist or helped to confront their own biases?

Instructional Resources

Because the textbook remains a major resource in most classrooms, teachers need to know how to use it and other instructional materials effectively in delivering education that is multicultural. Almost no textbook fully integrates diversity and equality throughout the text. Therefore, the teacher often will draw on supplementary materials and discussion to provide the full, more accurate representation of an inclusive society.

As a new teacher, you may have to make a conscious effort to examine textbooks and other readings for biases, stereotyping, and the lack of coverage of diverse groups. With experience and expanding knowledge about differences, some educators quickly recognize the lack of information and intuitively counteract with appropriate adjustments to ensure a balanced exposure to multiple perspectives. It is impossible for a text or a teacher to present all perspectives on the topic or concepts presented in a lesson. However, teachers can incorporate the voices of their own students or discuss the perspectives of groups that may

Many students have faced discrimination in some aspects of their lives. They and other students should be provided an opportunity to struggle with the reality of discrimination and how to confront it in their own lives.

be in the current news. Good teachers never limit themselves and their students to the single textbook that was assigned to the course. Not only do they draw on other readings, but they often use other resources in the popular culture with which students are familiar, including movies, music, and cultural events.

Stereotyping and Unreality.   Over the past two decades, many publishers and authors have committed themselves to eliminating the **biases** and stereotypes that existed in the 1960s and before. Researchers who analyze textbooks report that there has been great improvement in many areas. Nevertheless, many instructional materials still provide superficial coverage of ethnic and cultural groups, including white ethnic groups,[26] and of issues related to diversity and equality. Real issues of poverty, AIDS, teenage pregnancy, sex education, homophobia, the great gap between the poor and the rich, homelessness, and violence against children and women are often ignored. The events of which we are most proud are highlighted, while the injustices that remain are slighted. In education that is multicultural, a balance must be provided.

When a group is stereotyped in the materials being used by students, the teacher has the responsibility for providing another representation of the group. Native Americans are most often portrayed historically.[27] The teacher should also introduce students to contemporary Native Americans who live in urban areas and on reservations, and who are scientists, lawyers, and members of Congress. Their contributions to ecology, the arts, and the dominant culture should be interwoven into the study of those topics. The intent is to present a more accurate representation of the group, to prevent one image of the group from being generalized to all members of the group, and to teach that there are many intertribal and intragroup differences. Teachers cannot undertake this task unless they first recognize that the materials are stereotyping a group.

Censorship.   Not all people believe that the curriculum and textbooks should be changed to reflect multiple perspectives of diversity. In fact, schools and teachers

Information Note 6.9: Textbooks portray social relations among groups as one of harmony and equal opportunity.

are sometimes attacked by parents and conservative groups who believe that these changes are anti-Christian and anti-American.[28] *Education Week* reported that The People for the American Way, a liberal constitutional-rights watchdog group, found **censorship** and other challenges to school materials and practices in 395 incidents in 44 states during the 1992–1993 school year. This represented the greatest number of incidents in its eleven-year history of conducting the study.[29]

Until the late 1970s, censorship attacks were usually on a specific book that the censors wanted removed from the curriculum or public and school libraries. Today the attacks have expanded to include literature series, curriculum for sex education, and programs that encourage students to take control of their own decisions related to drugs and alcohol. In addition, "many course offerings (e.g., sociology, psychology, health, and biology) as well as instruction pertaining to values clarification, self-esteem, multicultural education, evolution, AIDS education, and global education are being contested."[30] It no longer is an individual parent who is upset about the content of a book or curriculum not supporting the family's values. A number of conservative groups have undertaken well-orchestrated efforts to warn parents of the danger of certain books and teachings. To counteract the perceived denigration of their values, cases have been reviewed by the courts with limited success by the plaintiffs. The more popular approach today is to ensure that members of the group are elected to local school boards, where they can influence the adoption of curriculum.

As educators begin to implement education that is multicultural, they may face similar challenges. The most effective way of deterring such attacks is to involve parents very early in the decisions being made.[31]

Equitable Practices

Caring and fairness are two qualities that students use to describe successful teachers.[32] Students know whether teachers view them as very special or incompetent or worthless. Teacher perceptions may be based on personal characteristics of the student; sometimes, they are based on group membership. Homeless children who smell and arrive in dirty clothes may be given little chance of success. Children from one-parent homes may be pitied and their lack of academic achievement blamed on their not having two parents. Limited English speaking students are ignored until they learn English and can communicate with the teacher. Are these fair practices?

A school that provides an education that is multicultural would not tolerate such unjust practices by a teacher. Both the classroom and school would be models of democracy in which all students are treated equitably and fairly. In such a school, teachers and instructional leaders confront their own biases and develop strategies for overcoming them in their own interactions with students and colleagues. They learn to depend on each other for assistance in both developing a multicultural curriculum and ensuring that students are not subject to discrimination. In the process the classroom and school will reflect both diversity and equality. As a result, students learn to respect differences and to interact within and across ethnic and cultural groups as they struggle for social justice in the school and community.

Instruction.   Researchers have found that many teachers unknowingly discriminate between males and females and between members of their own and other ethnic groups.[33] More help is given to some students than to others. Some students are praised, while others are more likely to be corrected and disciplined. Expectations for academic success differ depending on family income or ethnic biases. However, most teachers do not deliberately set out to discriminate against certain students, especially in any harmful way. The problem is that we have been raised in a racist, sexist, and classist society in which the biases are so embedded in society that it is difficult to recognize anything other than the very overt signs. Teachers often need others to point out their discriminatory practices.

A good pattern to begin to develop even now, early in your teacher education program, is to reflect on your practice and the practice of teachers who you observe. Among the questions that might be asked are:

- Are students from different gender, economic, and ethnic groups treated differently? What are the differences?

- Are there fewer discipline and learning problems among the students who are from the same background as the teacher? What is contributing to the differences?

- Do the least advantaged students receive the most assistance from the teacher? What are the differences in instruction between the groups?

- How are the students' cultures being incorporated into the curriculum and instruction?

A key to ensuring that interactions with students are equitable is the ability to recognize one's own biases and make appropriate adjustments. Educators must be able to admit that they sometimes make mistakes. Being able to reflect on the mistakes and why they occurred should lead to the improvement of teaching.

Assessment of Students. The assessment of children begins before they are born. Physical signs of health are normally assessed while the child is in the womb; treatment is provided if necessary and available to correct serious "abnormalities" that may adversely affect the child's health for a lifetime. Even at this early stage of life, a family's income is a primary determinant of the amount and nature of assessment and care provided.

Even before many students enter a preschool or kindergarten, assessment has moved beyond monitoring the physical signs of health to also determining their

---

Relevant Research

The Role of Schools in Students' Construction of Ethnic Identity

An in-depth study of the role of ethnicity for ten students in two urban high schools included students from middle- and working-class families and represented Mexican, Vietnamese, African, Italian, and Anglo heritages.

In one school setting, most of the immigrant students reported verbal or physical assaults against them. They seldom saw students of their ethnic group in advanced classes and believed that those that were at that level had abandoned their ethnic identity. They felt ignored and discounted by most of their teachers.

None of the students in the second school had experienced abuse from Anglo students. Their ethnic peers encouraged them to both maintain their ethnic identity and be academically successful.

Ethnicity was found to be important in the students' definitions of themselves and their academic achievement, but it was dynamic, and varied with the social setting. Some students used their ethnicity as a fortress that both protected and entrapped them. Others functioned biculturally or situationally, using different patterns of interaction at home than in school. The third set of students experienced their ethnicity as a resource that helped them succeed in what they perceived to be a racist society. School practices were found to support the role of ethnicity in a student's life, encourage academic achievement for all students, and to either reduce intergroup conflict or do just the opposite.

Source: Ann Locke Dividson, Hanh Cao Yu, and Patricia Phelan, "The Ebb and Flow of Ethnicity: Constructing Identity in Varied School Settings," *Educational Foundations 7* (1) (Winter 1993): 65–87.

*Tests are as common in
schools as the textbook, but
are they used to help improve
student learning or to sort the
powerful from the powerless?*

intellectual capabilities for productivity in society. At this time some parents begin to prepare their children to attend elite universities by enrolling them in the "right" preschool, which is likely to ensure admission to the appropriate elementary school. Testing of students' potential for success in these schools begins in some settings prior to admission into a preschool or kindergarten. (The practice of testing young children for admission is not supported by the major organization of early childhood educators, the National Association for the Education of Young Children.)

Assessment in educational settings has developed into a mechanism for sorting students, rather than serving as a system to monitor progress and determine instructional strategies needed to ensure that learning occurs. Instead, assessments indicate grades, placement in special education or gifted classes, placement in college preparatory or vocational tracks, and admission into postsecondary education. Beginning as early as kindergarten, these assessments may lead to the establishment of a school life in an exciting, stimulating environment or one in dull, boring classes in which it is clear that the student is not valued.

The students who perform well on current national standardized assessments mirror the most privileged in society. For example, white middle-class male students are overrepresented in the most demanding mathematics and science courses in high schools.[34] With the exception of Asian Americans, students of color are underrepresented in the ranks of college attenders. Thus, the sorting of students appears to be based more on gender, ethnic or racial background, language, and income than on ability to perform. This conclusion is supported by research that shows that norm-referenced tests are culturally biased. The norm is the dominant society and test questions reflect the knowledge and experiences that are common to members of that group. The problem is that not all test takers, especially if they are not members of that group, have had equal or similar exposure to the content of the tests.[35]

Some political ideologues and even some researchers believe that such sorting of the population is not only appropriate, but also that it reflects the genetic differences between groups of people.[36] Others believe that current assessments only sort the privileged from other members of society. "Assessments tell people how they should value themselves and others. They open doors for some and close them for others."[37] The lower academic classes have disproportionately high representation of students of color, limited-English speakers, low-income families, and males. Is this disproportionate representation due to genetic differences, as one group suggests, or to an assessment system that is not fair to students from diverse backgrounds? If educators believe in social justice and that all students can learn regardless of their cultural backgrounds, they will develop strategies that ensure that those students who have been treated most inequitably in the system are able to compete academically with students from more privileged backgrounds. If educators believe that nonprivileged students perform poorly on tests because they are genetically inferior, the current system of sorting students will continue.

Norm-referenced, pencil-and-paper tests are rather inexpensive and easy to conduct, but they are not the only assessments available to educators. Authentic, performance-based assessments are promising. Portfolios are one example in which students and teachers compile examples of their work that can be evaluated for growth over time (see Chapter 1 for additional information). These types of assessments should encourage diversity if educators are sensitive to differences in ethnicity, language, gender, and class. "In classrooms that are taught without regard for the use of the primary language, the portfolios of limited English-speakers will provide a portrait of many futile struggles at making meaning. In classrooms that are optimal learning environments (where constructivism, biliteracy, literature, and authentic writing projects occur) the portfolio will track development and academic achievement in-context."[38]

As a teacher, you will need to decide how you will effectively use assessments in your classroom. Will you let your expectations for a student's academic success be driven by his or her performance on a national standardized test? Will you assess performance primarily to help you identify prior knowledge and experience for use in developing the most effective instructional strategies to help students learn? Will your goal be to help students learn to understand the subject matter and to think critically about it or to will it be to help them perform well on the next national test by systematically teaching the content of the test? Assessments of students and their use in the classroom provide a number of dilemmas that are influenced by a teacher's philosophical and political beliefs.

The Role of the Teacher

Education that is multicultural requires educators to be active participants in the educational process. Social justice, democracy, power, and equity become more than concepts to be discussed in class; they become guides for actions in the classroom, school, and community. Educators become advocates not only for their own empowerment, but for that of students and other powerless groups.

Thinking Critically

Educators who think critically ask questions about why inequities are occurring in their classroom and school. They wonder why girls are responding differently to the science lesson than boys. But they don't stop with wondering; they explore and try alternatives to engage the girls in the subject matter. They realize that teaching equitably does not mean teaching everyone the same way. Nor does it mean that there are thirty different lesson plans to build on the uniqueness of the learning style and cultural background of each student. It may mean that teachers help students function effectively in multiple cultural settings used by the students in the classroom. These teachers are able to draw on their vast repertoire of strategies that build on the diverse cultural backgrounds and experiences of the students, acknowledge the value of that diversity, and help them all learn.

Critical thinkers are able to challenge the philosophy and practices of the dominant society that are not supportive of equity, democracy, and social justice. They are open to alternative views, and they are not limited by the narrow parochialism that is based on absolutes and the one, right way. They question the content for accuracy and biases and value multiple perspectives. They seek explanations and attributions for the educational meanings and consequences of race, class, and gender.[39]

"When they have opportunities to raise questions about knowledge and difference, both preservice and inservice teachers report that they become increasingly committed to school and pedagogial reform, increasingly conscious of their own efficacy as individual teachers, and increasingly involved in concrete efforts to alter the educational prospects of culturally diverse populations of students."[40]

Test Questions 6.55–6.60

Transparency 24:
Approaches to Teacher Reflection

Objective 13:
Create a plan for increasing knowledge about cultural diversity.

Activity 6.12:
Develop a list of the school practices that do not support equity, democracy, and social justice in schools. Ask students to discuss in small groups which of these they think they would be willing to confront after they begin teaching. They should discuss why they would be unwilling to confront others and the chances of these inequitable practices ever being overcome in schools.

The best teachers are those who are committed to continuing to learn about their academic areas, their students, and the world. They stay current with their field and they realize when they need to seek out additional information and resources.

Involvement with Communities and Parents

Discussion Question 5: How can a teacher take advantage of the knowledge and experiences of parents to develop effective instructional strategies?

In the delivery of multicultural education, parents and the community are the essential resources on which an educator must draw to understand the cultural context in which students live. It will be impossible to develop meaningful learning experiences for students if the teacher cannot relate to the real-life experiences of students who come from different ethnic, racial, and income backgrounds than the teacher. Students usually sense very quickly when teachers view their own background as superior to that of their students.

Few beginning teachers will have had direct involvement in multiple cultural communities. Therefore, they must be open to continuing to learn about cultural differences and must depend on parents, students, and other community members to assist them. Many parents, especially those from powerless groups, are not comfortable in the school setting. Rather than waiting for them to come to a parent-teacher meeting or conference on their own, it is often necessary for the teacher to approach the parent in a nonthreatening setting. Development of a trusting relationship in which both teachers and parents work together for the benefit of the child is key in establishing positive relationships. A growing number of schools have parent advocates or liaisons who can assist the teacher in working with parents and communities. These individuals can be valuable resources in helping educators work effectively in communities with which they have little background or experience.

Learning to function effectively in several cultural communities requires participants to be comfortable with their own background. They also should understand the possible privilege they have had in society because of their race, gender, sexual orientation, or socioeconomic status. Teachers who are most successful in helping students from diverse cultural backgrounds learn are those who "struggle to confront their own histories, hear the dissonance in their own profession, and begin to construct working alliances with colleagues, parents, and communities to meet the needs of all students."[41] Teachers who provide education that is multicultural may begin to face these challenges in college, as beginning teachers, or after a number of years in the classroom.

Summary and Implications

Education that is multicultural is based on the principles of democracy and social justice to ensure that all students participate equally in the education system. It values the cultural diversity of students as reflected in their gender and ethnic, racial, language, religious, and socioeconomic backgrounds. Educators strive for the provision of educational equality in which all students are provided challenging and stimulating learning experiences. Inequalities in instruction, school environment, quality of teachers, facilities, and resources are

confronted in an effort to overcome current injustices based on privilege and power.

Educators face many challenges in delivering education that is multicultural. The teaching style of the teacher may be very effective for some students, but not for others from cultural backgrounds different from that of the teacher. To help all students learn at higher levels, the teacher must develop a wide array of strategies to build on the prior experiences and cultural backgrounds of students. The curriculum and instructional materials must continuously be critiqued and expanded to integrate diversity throughout the study of an academic area. Interactions with students must be monitored to ensure that students are not being discriminated against because of their race, gender, sexual orientation, or socioeconomic status.

The four or five years that students spend in college to prepare for teaching only begin to prepare them to work with students who are culturally diverse or to be able to deliver education that is multicultural. Beginning and experienced teachers will continue to learn about diversity and its implications for teaching and learning. Students, parents, and communities will be valuable resources in this learning process. Most educators will find it a life-long and worthwhile endeavor.

Discussion Questions

1. What conditions and practices exist in schools to suggest that social justice is not a principle that undergirds the educational system?
2. What are the potential benefits and perceived dangers of allowing student voices to be an integral part of instruction?
3. Why is multicultural education just as important for students who are members of the dominant group in society as for those who are members of powerless groups?
4. How are student assessments used by teachers and schools?
5. How can a teacher take advantage of the knowledge and experiences of parents to develop effective instructional strategies?

Journal/Portfolio Development

1. Investigate the debates related to the adoption of a multicultural curriculum in a state or local school district (New York State Department of Education's *One Nation, Many Peoples: A Declaration of Cultural Interdependence* or New York City's *Children of the Rainbow*). Prepare a paper that describes the issues involved in the debates and summarizes your recommendation for the adoption of the curriculum.
2. For the subject and level that you plan to teach, design a lesson that incorporates multiple voices.

School-Based Experiences

1. As part of an early field experience activity in your teacher education program, gather a minimum of five observational sets of data on a student of color in a classroom. In particular, look for the nature of the interaction between the student and the teacher, the communication patterns with one or two other students, the oral classroom participation patterns, and the student's engagement with the subject matter.
2. Visit an inner city school and a rural or suburban school and observe how student voices are incorporated in classes. Record the nature of the dialogue between students and teachers and among students; be able to describe the degree of equality across the voices and whether any significant patterns of differences emerged.

Notes

1. Carl A. Grant and Christine E. Sleeter, *Turning On Learning: Five Approaches for Multicultural Teaching Plans for Race, Class, Gender, and Disability.* Columbus, OH: Merrill, 1989.

2. Donna M. Gollnick and Philip C. Chinn, *Multicultural Education in a Pluralistic Society.* 4th ed. New York: Macmillan, 297.

3. James A. Banks, "Multicultural Education: Development, Dimensions, and Challenges," *Phi Delta Kappan 75* (1) (September 1993): 55–60.

4. Ibid. 23.

5. Donna M. Gollnick, "National and State Initiatives for Multicultural Education," in James A. Banks and Cherry A. McGee Banks, eds., *Handbook of Research on Multicultural Education*. New York: Macmillan, 1995, 44–64.

6. National Conference of Christians and Jews, *Taking America's Pulse: A Summary Report of the National Conference Survey on Inter-Group Relations*. New York City: Author, 1994, 9.

7. Robert N. Bellah, Richard Madsen, William M. Sullivan, Ann Swidler, and Steven M. Tipton, *The Good Society*. New York: Vintage Books, 1991.

8. Ibid.

9. Ibid.

10. Kenneth A. Sirotnik, "Society, Schooling, Teaching, and Preparing to Teach," in John I. Goodlad, Roger Soder, and Kenneth A. Sirotnik, eds., *The Moral Dimensions of Teaching*. San Francisco: Jossey-Bass, 1990, 296–327.

11. Ibid, 310.

12. Peter Figueroa, "Multicultural Education in the United Kingdom: Historical Development and Current Status," in James A. Banks and Cherry A. McGee Banks, eds., *Handbook of Research on Multicultural Education*. New York: Macmillan, 1995, 778–800.

13. Aaron M. Pallas, "The Changing Nature of the Disadvantaged Population: Current Dimensions and Future Trends," *Educational Researcher* (June/July 1989): 16–22.

14. Signithia Fordham, "Racelessness as a Factor in Black Students' School Success: Pragmatic Strategy or Pyrrhic Victory," *Harvard Educational Review* 58(1) (1988): 54–84.

15. G. Williamson McDiarmid, *What to Do About Differences? A Study of Multicultural Education for Teacher Trainees in the Los Angeles Unified School District* (Research Report 90-11). East Lansing, MI: National Center for Research on Teacher Learning, 1990.

16. Robert E. Slavin, "Cooperative Learning and Intergroup Relations," in James A. Banks and Cherry A. McGee Banks, eds., *Handbook of Research on Multicultural Education*. New York: Macmillan, 1995, 628–634.

17. "Kentuckians Show Strong Support for School Reform But Want Adjustments to Improve Program Operations." Frankfort, KY: The Kentucky Institute for Education Research, October 3, 1994.

18. Jerry E. Brophy and Thomas L. Good, *Teacher-Student Relationships: Causes and Consequences*. New York: Holt, Rinehart & Winston, 1974.

19. J. Cummins, "Empowering Minority Students: A Framework for Intervention." *Harvard Educational Review 56*: 18–36.

20. Kenneth M. Zeichner, *Educating Teachers for Cultural Diversity*. East Lansing, MI: National Center for Research on Teacher Learning, February 1993, 7.

21. Jeannie Oakes, *Keeping Track: How Schools Structure Inequality*. New Haven, CT: Yale University Press, 1985, 40.

22. Ibid.

23. Maxine Greene, "Diversity and Inclusion: Toward a Curriculum for Human Rights," *Teachers College Record 95* (2) (Winter 1993): 211–221.

24. Gollnick and Chinn, 314.

25. Michael W. Apple, "The Politics of Official Knowledge: Does a National Curriculum Make Sense?" *Teachers College Record 95* (2) (Winter 1993): 222–240.

26. Jesus Garcia, "The Changing Image of Ethnic Groups in Textbooks." *Phi Delta Kappan 75* (1) (September 1993): 29–35.

27. Christine E. Sleeter and Carl A. Grant, "Race, Class, Gender, and Disability in Current Textbooks." in Michael W. Apple, and L. K. Christian-Smith, eds., *The Politics of the Textbook*. New York: Routledge, 78–110.

28. Martha M. McCarthy, "Challenges to the Public School Curriculum: New Targets and Strategies." *Phi Delta Kappan 75* (1) (September 1993): 55–60.

29. Millicent Lawton, "Differing on Diversity." *Education Week* (December 1, 1993): 23–25.

30. McCarthy, 56.

31. Ibid.

32. Institute for Education in Transformation, *Voices from the Inside: A Report on Schooling from Inside the Classroom*. Claremont, CA: Author, 1992.

33. Myra P. Sadker and David M. Sadker, "Between Teacher and Student: Overcoming Sex Bias in Classroom Interaction," in Myra P. Sadker and David M. Sadker, eds., *Sex Equity Handbook for Schools*. New York: Longman, 1982, 96–132.

34. Oakes, 1985.

35. Richard A. Figueroa and Eugene Garcia, "Issues in Testing Students from Culturally and Linguistically Diverse Backgrounds." *Multicultural Education* (Fall 1994): 10–19.

36. Richard J. Herrnstein and Charles Murray, *The Bell Curve: Intelligence and Class Structure in American Life*. New York: Free Press, 1994.

37. Georgia Earnest Garcia and P. David Pearson, "Assessment and Diversity," *Review of Research in Education 20.* Washington, DC: American Educational Research Association, 1994, 337–391.

38. Ibid, 19.

39. Marilyn Cochran-Smith and Susan L. Lytle, "Interrogating Cultural Diversity: Inquiry and Action."

Journal of Teacher Education 43 (2) (March-April 1992): 104–115.

40. Ibid, 111.

41. Ibid, 113.

Bibliography

Apple, Michael W., and Christian-Smith, Linda K., eds. *The Politics of the Textbook.* New York: Routledge, 1991.

Garcia, Georgia Earnest, and Pearson, P. David. "Assessment and Diversity." *Review of Research in Education 20.* Washington, DC: American Educational Research Association, 1994, 337–391.

Gollnick, Donna M., and Chinn, Philip C. *Multicultural Education in a Pluralistic Society.* 4th ed. New York: Macmillan, 1994.

Goodlad, John I., Soder, Roger, and Sirotnik, Kenneth A., eds. *The Moral Dimensions of Teaching.* San Francisco: Jossey-Bass, 1990.

Grant, Carl A., and Sleeter, Christine E. *Turning on Learning: Five Approaches for Multicultural Teaching Plans for Race, Class, Gender, and Disability.* Columbus, OH: Merrill, 1989.

Lacelle-Peterson, Mark W., and Rivera, Charlene. "Is It Real for All Kids? A Framework for Equitable Assessment Policies for English Language Learners." *Harvard Educational Review 64* (1) (Spring 1994): 55–75.

Multicultural Education: The Magazine of the National Association for Multicultural Education.

"Multicultural Issues." *Phi Delta Kappan 74* (3) (November 1992): 208–227.

National Conference of Christians and Jews. *Taking America's Pulse: A Summary Report of the National Conference Survey on Inter-Group Relations.* New York City: Author, 1994.

Oakes, Jeannie. *Keeping Track: How Schools Structure Inequality.* New Haven, CT: Yale University Press, 1985.

"Race-Ethnicity-Family-Community-Student Success." *Equity and Choice* (2) (Winter 1994).

Robenstine, Clark. "The Illusion of Education Reform: The Educational System and At-Risk Students." *Educational Foundations 6* (1) (Winter 1992): 49–65.

Sobol, Thomas. "Revising the New York State Social Studies Curriculum." *Teachers College Record 95* (2) (Winter 1993): 258–272.

Chapter

7

Social Issues Affecting the School

Focus Questions

1 Why, despite increased expenditures for schools, does the dropout rate continue to be so high in the United States?
2 What is the relationship between poverty and school completion?
3 How can the school begin to combat some of the major social problems facing students?
4 What is the relationship between the social problems of youth and performance in school?
5 Should our schools help to solve social problems? Why?

Key Terms and Concepts

Chemical dependency: The habitual use, either for psychological or physical needs, of a substance such as drugs, alcohol, or tobacco.

Delinquency: A term generally ascribed to the youth culture that denotes violation of rules and regulations of the society.

Dropouts: Students who fail to complete a high school education.

Exceptional learners: A classification identification used to describe handicapped and gifted learners.

Inclusion: The federally mandated practice of placing all handicapped learners, except for profoundly handicapped, in regular classrooms where itinerant special education teachers assist the regular teacher.

Magnet schools: Specialized schools that are open to all students in a district, sometimes on a lottery basis or special needs basis.

Poverty: A relative standard of living defined by a number of complex and changing factors that may include hunger or lack of luxuries.

Poverty level: A level of family income judged by the United States Labor Department to be below the basic needs requirements of a family.

School-based clinics: Medical and advisory clinics in schools that are offered to provide personal help for students experiencing problems of sexuality.

*T*here is a considerable amount of debate over how far the schools can and should go to help solve our country's social problems. Some people believe that the schools should be concerned only with the academic development of students. Others believe that the schools are in a unique position to help solve many of the nation's pressing social problems—and should do so. While this debate continues, social problems persist and noticeably affect students and schools. In this chapter we identify a wide variety of social problems that have a direct effect on students. Note that the severity of the problem causes varying amounts of stress for learners as they move through the school program.

Problems of the Youth Culture

Young people today face numerous problems as they mature to adulthood. Changing family structures, alteration of what was once considered to be a societal set of expected values, and increased pressures to grow up quickly and be adult all have contributed to the social problems of youth. Reacting to the pressures of the time, young people have found their own ways of countering what appear to them to be circumstances with which they cannot cope. As learners in the schools, they need special attention.

Effects of the Changing Family

Objective 1:
Create in writing a profile of the "family" as it currently exists in society.

The American family has changed rather dramatically during the past four decades. The traditional description of a family with a working father, a mother at home with the children, and two or more school-age children exists for a very small part of the population. Recent reports from the U.S. Bureau of Statistics following the 1990 census suggest that about 5 percent of American families fit this description. The lifestyle of married couples with children, once the norm, is now the exception. Family descriptions are as varied as our cultural diversity. Families include a mother working with a father tending children, mothers working away from home, increasing numbers of single-parent families, increasing numbers of second marriages with unrelated children, large numbers of childless marriages (especially among the dominant white groups), unmarried couples with and without children, gay and lesbian parents, and the combinations go on. These family differences, with varying intensities of family instability, all have had their effects on the youth culture. It is little wonder that the children of these families struggle immensely in their search for their own identities and a place in life.

The latest United States census data point to the following profile for families:

- There are over 80 million households in the United States.
- Twenty-eight million married couples have no children.
- Seven out of ten women with children are in the work force.
- The divorce rate has quadrupled in the past twenty years, and the number of single-parent families is estimated at 25 percent. There are 18.2 million children being raised in single-parent families. The figure for single-parent families is estimated to grow to 30 percent by 2020.
- Sixteen percent of single-parent children have mothers under the age of 25, and 6 percent of these children have young teenage mothers.

Activity 7.1:
Have each student create a family profile of his or her family group. Then have the students compare their profiles with that presented by the text.

- Sixty-eight percent of all births to teenagers (those under age 20) occur out of wedlock.
- Sixty percent of all teenage families live in poverty as compared to 13.5 percent of the total population.
- The percentage of teenage pregnancies, with children born out of wedlock, is higher among some minority groups, but the percentage and numbers for white teenagers is increasing.
- Families without children have the highest socioeconomic status, but 50 percent of that group is 55 years and over.

Parents. In the past, parents could be described as a couple with children living in a home with room for grandparents; the couple's relationship was male-dominated, and they expected to live out their years together. There has been a rapid decline in the number of such families. As suggested in the profile above, this type of family is best described as the nuclear family. The number of nuclear families is decreasing in America.

Families are small today; average size, as projected from census reports for 1990 by the Bureau of the Census, is 3.16 members. Average household size is 2.62. However, the average figures can be deceiving because family membership size is considerably greater among the minority population. That is why the change in school population statistics for the 1990s and beyond is so significant. In 1990 *Time* magazine reported that one American in four defined himself or herself as Hispanic or nonwhite. If current birth rates continue for minority groups, the Hispanic population will increase approximately 21 percent, Asians about 22 percent, African Americans about 12 percent, Native Americans about 50 percent, and Anglo-Americans about 2 percent by the turn of the century.

Extended families are not common, except among some minority groups. The frequencies of other types of families are increasing; for example, although the divorce rate continues to escalate, four out of five divorced people remarry. The divorce rate for remarried people is higher still. There is an increase in communal living, and more single parents.

Children. All of these family changes have affected children. The family now has considerably less influence on family members' religious practices, education, and values as well as on the general socialization of the child. Although the school has assumed many of these responsibilities, other institutions also contribute to the child's socialization. These institutions include peer groups from the schools and the streets; organized groups such as scouts, 4-H, and Little League groups; and TV, radio, newspapers, and movies. The influence of the formal and informal peer groups cannot be overestimated. Because of increased female influence in the family, the family is no longer patriarchal but rather has become increasingly matriarchial and in more cases egalitarian.

The Persistence of Poverty

Poverty has existed since the human race appeared on the earth and probably will be around as long as humans are. **Poverty** in the United States is complex, and determining what factors contribute to it is difficult, if not impossible. Notions about what constitutes poverty are continually changing. One person might define poverty as physical hunger or even starvation; another might define it as a lack

Information Note 7.1:
Recent elections and national rhetoric have put considerable emphasis on the value of the family. The definition of family is broadly accepted as described in this chapter.

Focus Question 1:
Why, despite increased expenditures for schools, does the dropout rate continue to be so high in the United States?

TABLE 7.1	Percentage of Families below the Poverty Level
White	9.1%
Black	29.7
Hispanic	30.6
Native American	62.5
Total U.S.	14.7

Source: Educational Research Service, 1992.

of luxuries. In other words, poverty is relative. The poor in the United States include people who are literally starving to death as well as people who have relatively little compared to those who have very much.

Since the majority of people in the United States are not in poverty, they tend to believe that there is less poverty today than there was in the past. Not only is this not true, but in fact the number of poverty-level families is on the increase, and the increase is predominantly among minority populations. One of the difficulties in determining poverty is that its definition, based upon economic conditions, changes yearly. The government's definition of poverty is based on changing economic conditions, further adjusted by such factors as family size, sex of family head, number of children, and farm or nonfarm residence. Table 7.1 presents information about the percent of families below the poverty level in the United States. This table illustrates that the **poverty level** is greater for minority families. Table 7.2 shows the percentage of children, by race, that live in poverty.

Slightly over 14 percent of U.S. families live in poverty. African Americans suffer three times the rate of poverty of whites, and Hispanic Americans have greater than three times the poverty rate of the white population. Although there is a higher percentage of nonwhite families living in poverty, numerically there are many more impoverished white families. For instance, the per capita income of many Appalachian white families is far less than that of the rest of the country. Many Appalachian adults are unemployed, and many have very little formal schooling. The Appalachian subculture has created a way of life that keeps these mountain people impoverished. Farming and mining have traditionally furnished their livelihood; however, the mountain farms are no longer productive enough

TABLE 7.2	Percentage of Children by Race and Ethnicity That Live in Poverty		
Age	White	Black	Hispanic and Others
Total (all ages)	13.0	33.0	34.3
Under 15	17.3	46.4	40.0
15–17	14.9	44.7	35.1
18–21	15.3	40.3	30.0

Source: U.S. Bureau of the Census, 1990.

to provide a good living, and automation has largely replaced humans in the coal mines. Those who have left the mountains to go to the cities have found that their education and skills do not qualify them for desirable jobs. Many people believe that education alone cannot solve the problem. Immediate needs such as employment, housing, medical care, and legal advice must also be met. Although prompt assistance in these areas is essential to solving the problems of poverty, it cannot solve the long-range problem in the way that better education can.

Welfare.   Fortunately for people in poverty, our nation is concerned about this social dilemma. Moreover, tax money spent to eradicate poverty is a profitable investment. It costs less in the long run to help people lift themselves out of poverty than to pay the consequences of allowing them to remain impoverished. One need only check the cost of welfare programs and crime fighting to be convinced of this statement.

One of the persistent problems with the welfare programs is the lack of renewal performances in many of the families on welfare. Because of circumstances many times beyond their control, large numbers of families are second and third generation welfare families. The economic development programs associated with the many welfare programs have not been successful in providing meaningful avenues out of poverty. Thus, many young people in poverty today have known nothing but welfare during their lives and the lives of their parents. The expected development of a work ethic and the availability of jobs to promote that ethic have not taken place. The feeling of hopelessness that many young people experience today makes the job of convincing them about the importance of education very difficult.

We must realize that if we are to eradicate poverty and reduce welfare existence we must treat the disease itself, not just the symptoms. Indeed, we must try to prevent the disease in the first place, and the most effective "vaccine" at our disposal is education. It is incongruous that a nation that has amassed far more material wealth than any other in history can still contain pockets of severe poverty. Poverty prevents people from being productive citizens, from pursuing excellence, and from developing a sense of dignity. Total dependence on welfare becomes a generational "catch-all" way of life. If we are committed to the importance of democratic ideals, we must continue to work toward eliminating poverty in the United States. Fortunately, we have begun to realize the democratic, human, and economic necessity of reducing poverty, and we have initiated many immediate and long-range programs—some of which involve education—aimed at eradicating the problem.

Unemployment.   Unemployment rates in the United States are directly affected by the general economic condition of the country. However, many other factors also influence the unemployment picture. The additional women entering the labor force, the continuing high level of dropouts among minority youth, the decreasing number of young people in military service, and changing trends in college enrollments all contribute to the country's unemployment rates.

Certain groups within our society are more affected by unemployment than others. Although actual employment rates change from year to year, the relative unemployment picture for the various groups has remained essentially the same in recent history. During 1985–1989, national unemployment varied between 5 and 6 percent. Unemployment rates in late 1994 were averaging almost 6.5 percent. Generally, nonwhites and teenagers have had the highest unemployment

Transparency 33:
Teenage Unemployment by
Race/Ethnicity

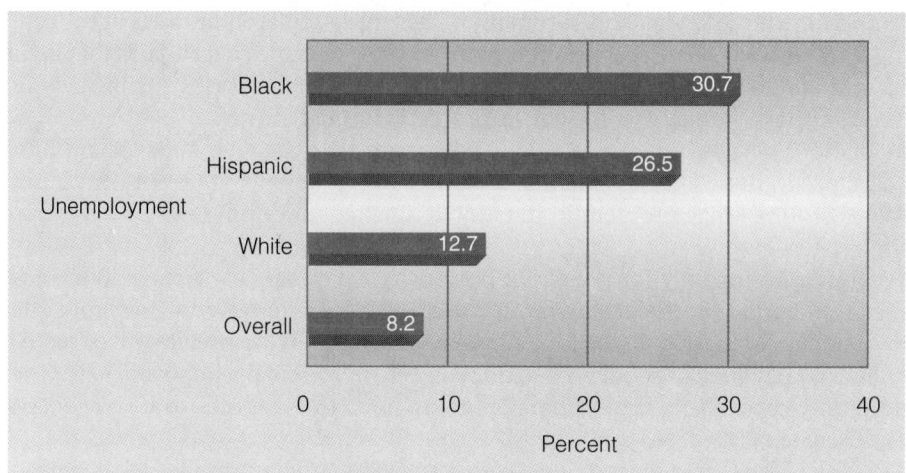

FIGURE 7.1

Teenage Unemployment by Race/Ethnicity Compared with Overall Unemployment 1994

Source: U.S. Department of Labor.

Information Note 7.3:
The Education Department of the United States Chamber of Commerce continues to report that the greater the level of education, the higher the employment rate and the higher the income.

Focus Question 3:
How can the school begin to combat some of the major social problems facing students?

Objective 3:
Identify the problems associated with chemical abuse.

Key Term:
Chemical dependency

rates. Recently, unemployment rates have increased among middle-aged workers whose industries have experienced "down-sizing" because of economic conditions. As Figure 7.1 points out, teenage unemployment rates are about three times greater than general unemployment rates. Minority teens suffer unemployment at three times the rate of white teens.

However, there is a correlation between teenage unemployment and high school completion. Inner-city teens have the highest unemployment rates, are from a variety of minority groups, and have the highest dropout rate in the nation. The job market is changing, and the changes have serious implications for the schools if poverty is to be reduced. As can be seen in Table 7.3, the majority of new jobs are in the service occupations and technology. If the schools are to contribute to the efforts to correct poverty, computer training must receive increased emphasis. As the majority population in the country becomes nonwhite, and if the school has given greater attention to meaningful job preparation, the minority unemployment figures of the 1990s should decrease significantly by the turn of the century.

Chemical Abuse

One of the most tragic social problems in America today is the misuse of drugs by young people. As reported by many recent surveys, the number one problem facing the school, in the eyes of the public, is the overuse of drugs. Alarmingly, the U.S. Public Health Service reports that about two-thirds of all high school seniors have used illicit drugs, and over 90 percent of high school seniors have used alcohol. A 1991 Gallup Poll of young people concluded that the number one problem, and the one that they were most concerned about, was the use of drugs and alcohol by themselves and the general population. It is important to note, however, that the 1993 Gallup Poll on the public attitude toward school shows that drugs in schools is no longer the number one problem. The number one problem in that poll was clearly a lack of financial support for schools. **Chemical dependency,** whether on drugs, alcohol, or tobacco, is one of the leading causes of other social and academic problems of youth. People are judged to be dependent when they find that their need for chemicals is constant and they can no longer control

TABLE 7.3	Growth of New Jobs and Occupations through 1995	
Occupations	**Number of New Jobs by 1995**	
Services	4,490,000	
Janitors		
Nurses Aides		
Sales Clerks		
Waitresses		
Clerks		
Nurses		
Secretaries		
Food Preparers		
Computer Technology	903,000	
Data Processing		
Systems Analysts		
Computer Operators		
Computer Programmers		
Software Developers		
Computer Technicians		

Source: U.S. Department of Labor.

their use. Figure 7.2 on page 160 provides information on the extent of this chemical problem in our society.

Drugs.   To counter the drug problem, schools have embarked on a variety of programs, many of which have been funded by state and federal governments and are intended to be preventive. The problem is acute and affects all age groups. In 1989 the White House launched a nationwide effort to educate the public in an attempt to curb the use of drugs. Additionally, stronger enforcement efforts were employed against the use of chemicals and their importation into the United States. Unfortunately, the rhetoric of the federal government, in the absence of adequate funding, has not put a substantial dent in the sale and use of drugs.

Many state and national programs provide students with information about drugs so that they will realize the dangers of drug abuse. The major objective of these programs is that students, as informed persons, will decide that they are better off not using illicit drugs. Generally, the most successful drug education programs are those that have been adequately funded, involve parents and students, are taught by well-trained teachers, and avoid preaching and moralizing.

Alcohol.   Student use of alcohol has risen sharply in recent years. A survey by the National Institute on Drug Abuse asked high school seniors to estimate the percentage of their friends who used various drugs and the degree of use. The survey found that alcohol was the most commonly used drug and that sizable percentages of students get drunk at least once a week. In many schools, students consume alcohol in school buildings during the day. Furthermore, medical authorities report a rapid rise in "polydrug" use—combining drugs and alcohol—

CNN Clip 12:
Drugs in the Hood

Activity 7.3:
Ask the students to investigate and discuss typical school district services that are made available to students who are involved with drugs.

Transparency 34:
Use of Illegal Drugs among High School Students Is Down But Drinking Remains a Problem.

Discussion Question 1:
How can the school help in combating the chemical problems of youth?

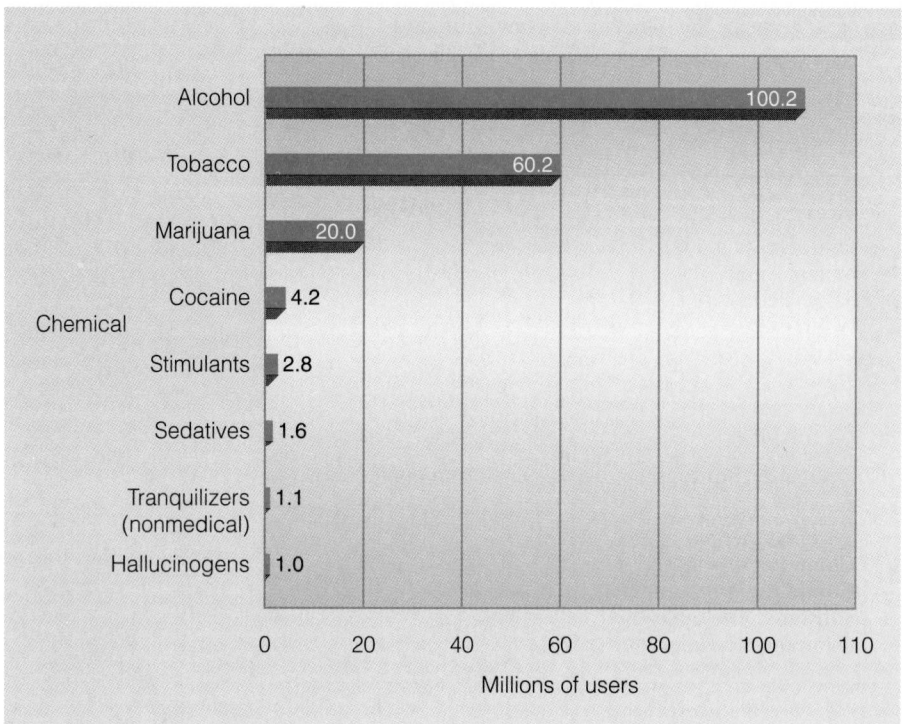

among students. Polydrug use is extremely dangerous because alcohol used with barbiturates, sedatives, or tranquilizers heightens the effect of each substance and can cause death. Clearly, alcohol and drugs have become the foremost chemical problem for young people in America.

Tobacco. Millions of American students regularly smoke cigarettes. The evidence that smoking is a serious health hazard has prompted educators to search for ways to combat this problem. National and state educational efforts directed toward the physical hazards of smoking have been successful in reducing the total number of Americans who smoke. However, young people, particularly young women, continue to smoke. This increased use of tobacco by young women has led to increased rates of female lung cancer, making the rates among the female and the male populations about equal.

Most people believe that the school is the only agency that has a chance to reduce teenage smoking significantly, and more and more schools are accepting the challenge. Some schools include a systematic study of the effects of smoking as part of their curriculum. The most promising approach to smoking education is one in which the students themselves run their own antismoking campaigns. Some schools have joined parent groups, the American Cancer Society, the American Heart Association, and the National Tuberculosis and Respiratory Diseases Association to fight teenage smoking.

Prevention. The Department of Education has created the school team approach, which was developed under the Alcohol and Drug Abuse Education

Program. Designed to help local schools prevent and reduce drug and alcohol abuse, this program has established five regional centers that provide training and technical assistance to local schools. Some other representative national efforts are being provided by the following agencies:

1. The American Council on Drug Education: This council organizes conferences and develops national media campaigns for drug education. It also provides films, books, and education kits for libraries and schools.
2. Narcotics Education, Inc.: This organization provides pamphlets, books, teaching aids, posters, audiovisual aids, and prevention magazines that can be used with preteens and teens.
3. National Federation of Parents for Drug-Free Youth: This national organization helps parent groups to get started, and provides current literature on drug legislation and resource lists for schools and libraries.
4. Target: This national federation of state high school associations, an arm of the organization of interscholastic activities associations, offers workshops, seminars, and current information on chemical abuse and prevention.
5. Toughlove: This national self-help group is for parents, children, and communities; it stresses cooperation, personal initiative, avoidance of blame, and suggested action for abusers.

These organizations and others have been assisting communities and schools in their efforts at combating the chemical problem. One such effort is Project DARE, in Los Angeles, which is operated by the school district in cooperation with the local police department. The program uses specially trained police officers to teach students how to say "no" to drugs. Other parts of the program include building self-esteem, managing stress, and developing personal skills to help resist drugs. The police work in the schools with students and also conduct parent seminars in the evening. Because of the success of this program, it has spread to other California communities and other states.

Drug and alcohol abuse awareness and prevention programs have become fairly common in schools, especially at junior and senior high school levels.

Suicide

Objective 4:
Elaborate on the issues that affect the suicide rates of young people.

Suicide rates among young people are on the rise. In fact, the rate of teen suicide has tripled during the past thirty years. By 1992, as reported by the National Institute of Mental Health, the leading cause of death for fifteen- to twenty-four-year-olds was suicide. At the same time, suicide rates for the rest of the U.S. population have remained relatively stable. Although the suicide rate is thought to be highest among lower-socioeconomic groups and many minorities, it is not. The highest-risk group for *teen suicide* is white, Protestant, and above-average in school performance. Most of these students appear to be performing normally, and many hold part-time jobs. Although many more teenage girls than teenage boys attempt suicide, the boys tend to be more successful in their attempts.

Activity 7.4:
Have students investigate the effectiveness of suicide prevention programs.

Transparency 40:
Teen Tragedy

Transparency 41:
Warning Signs of Suicide and Possible Responses

Information Note 7.4:
Since 1960 the rape rate has quadrupled, violent crime has quadrupled, teen suicide has tripled, and the delinquency rate has more than doubled. The suicide rate is highest for Native Americans.

Adolescent Perceptions. The usual cause of adolescent suicide is extreme depression. It usually appears during early adolescence, when normal physical and social development directs teenagers away from family ties. During this period, teens begin to look beyond the home for friendship and assistance in making value decisions. Chief causes that become specific contributors to attempted teen suicide are conflict with one or both parents, the breakup of boyfriend-girlfriend relationships, parental divorce, moving to a new school or area, and trouble with a teacher.

Effects of Stress. There is little doubt that young people are less able to cope with stress than older people are. Young people have not yet had enough independent life experiences to balance the stressful periods that all people endure. School relations and family relations are extremely stressful at an age when physical and psychological maturation are taking place. Effects of stress are seen in school attendance, academic performance, peer relationships, and adult encounters. Many times, students under stress seek other students who have similar types of problems, and these relationships often do not lead to good mental health. In fact, such relationships have led to a significant increase in *suicide clusters.* This type of suicide behavior is most common among teenagers. The National Institute of Mental Health has offered a list of suggestions for schools and communities to follow when there are suspicions of potential cluster suicides among young people. These are offered for study in Figure 7.3. Teachers should be especially aware of how they can be part of a preventive program against teenage suicide.

Focus Question 4:
What is the relationship between the social problems of youth and performance in school?

Warning Signs. There is a high coincidence rate between adolescent suicide and some forms of chemical dependency. Alcohol and/or drugs are used to counter depression, and when these drugs fail to deliver the desired effects, the teen is ripe for a suicide attempt. Teachers need to be especially sensitive to the early signs of depression among students. Student withdrawal behaviors, irritability, and sudden changes in work, sleep, or eating habits are all early signs of a teen going through some stage of depression and in need of professional help. The best aid that a teacher can give is to encourage the student to talk about the problem and to seek medical help. Although teen suicide is growing at an alarming rate, it can be prevented if sensitive parents and professionals seek help for an adolescent when the early signs of depression are observed.

1. Have a community plan to deal with events that could lead to cluster suicide.

2. Establish a community and school committee to coordinate the handling of suicide problems among youth.

3. Identify community people and groups who can respond quickly to problems.

4. Avoid any signs that could be interpreted as glorifying suicide, and minimize any sensationalism of any attempts.

5. Be watchful for potentially suicidal students and get them to counselors.

6. Identify elements in the environment—school, home, community—that could increase the likelihood of suicide and seek to eliminate them.

FIGURE 7.3

Suggestions for Combating Potential Cluster Suicides

(*Source:* National Institute of Mental Health.)

Dropouts: Students at Risk

Although high school and college students drop out of school for different reasons, both represent a substantial loss to our society. In most states, students must attend school until they are sixteen. They cannot drop out of school during the early years of high school. However, once they are past the compulsory attendance age, a disturbing number of them become **dropouts.** Approximately 25 percent of the eighteen-year-olds in the United States have not completed high school. This rate has not decreased in more than two decades, and it is considerably higher among minority groups. Current estimates from the Bureau of the Census data for 1990 are that 40 percent of Hispanic Americans and 25 percent of African Americans, ages eighteen to twenty-one, are dropouts. Other minority groups have even greater rates. Urban Native Americans and Puerto Ricans have dropout rates of 70–80 percent. The rate of school dropouts is particularly disturbing because most of these students cannot get jobs, many get into trouble with the law, and many do not qualify for military service. Most of them are not yet prepared to be productive citizens, and a large number are destined to become social liabilities. Figure 7.4 on page 164 shows the breakdown of various dropout groups.

Characteristics of Dropouts. Dropouts come primarily from low-income backgrounds. As Figure 7.4 shows, most come from minority groups, the exceptions being Asian Americans and Pacific Islanders. Dropouts tend to be deficient in basic reading, language arts, and mathematics skills, and often they are children of high school dropouts. Single-parent families account for a significant number of dropout students. Males tend to drop out more than females. Males often drop out to get a job, but, as was shown earlier, the highest rates of unemployment are among teenagers who have not completed high school. The major reason for females dropping out of school is early pregnancy. Most dropout students suffer

CNN **Clip 13:**
Dropout Prevention

Key Term:
Dropouts

Diversity Note 7.1:
The population growth rates of minority children are such that the (previously expected) leveling off of school enrollments over the next two decades is now projected to move upward by 35%.

Objective 5:
Create in writing a profile of students who are at risk to be potential dropouts.

Information Note 7.5:
Programs to identify potential dropouts have been successful in identification but unsuccessful in prevention.

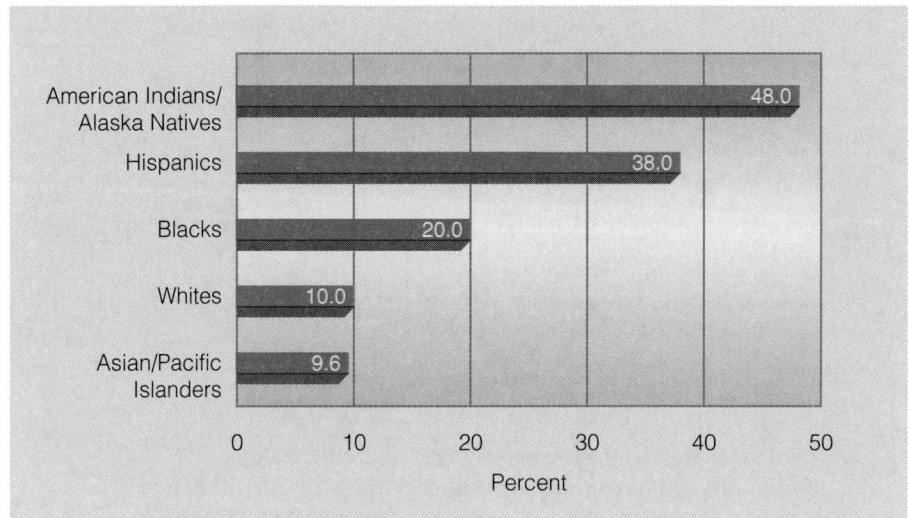

National Dropout Rates by Racial or Ethnic Group

(*Source:* National Center for Educational Statistics, 1992.)

from extremely low self-esteem and have judged themselves failures long before they drop out.

Some of the early signs of potential dropouts are seen in students who:

1. have poor school attendance,
2. lack observable interest in learning,
3. experience continuing failing grades,
4. experience continuous classroom discipline problems, and
5. have failed one or more grades in the elementary and secondary school.

Teachers need to watch for these early warning signs and seek help for a student who exhibits them before he or she becomes another dropout statistic. Schools with high dropout rates need to establish prevention programs that address the special needs of their students so that positive self-esteem and a desire to learn become part of the learner's personality.

Economic and Social Effects. The national data on dropouts point to the desperate need for the school and society to find ways to keep children in school and to teach them at least basic life skills—not only for their own good but also for the good of society. The economic cost of ignoring the problem is staggering. In 1992 the U.S. House Ways and Means Committee reported that the cost of welfare benefits and lost tax dollars is estimated to be 75 billion dollars; 60 percent of prison inmates are dropouts; and some 87 percent of pregnant teenagers are dropouts. In other words, the money spent to keep our children in school is not really an expense but an excellent long-term investment that returns handsome dividends to our society.

The gifted high school graduate who does not go to college represents still another kind of school dropout. Furthermore, half of the students who enter college never graduate. Although some of these students leave college for academic reasons, many of them have exceptional academic ability. The underdeveloped talent of these students represents a substantial loss to society. Needless to say, our society and our schools have a long way to go before they solve the school dropout problem.

Delinquency and Crime

There is a definite relationship between juvenile **delinquency** and dropping out of school. Delinquency is defined for youth as a regular behavior that violates rules and regulations of the society. Various studies of delinquency have also shown that many delinquents did failing work while in school and often were less academically able than were nondelinquents. The alarming point is that many of today's dropouts will be tomorrow's criminals, and statistics on crime in the United States are staggering. Figure 7.5 shows the dramatic increase in serious crime in recent years. To make matters worse, fewer than one in four serious crimes leads to arrest; in other words, three-fourths of the people who commit serious crimes do not get caught.

Crime Statistics. During 1985–1989, total arrests for all areas of crime were up 10 percent, according to the U.S. Government sources. Adult arrests still constituted the majority of the arrests, but those for people under the age of eighteen increased by 6 percent. Drug abuse violations grew by 14 percent during 1988–1989 alone. Five percent of all the people arrested in the United States were under the age of fifteen, 16 percent were under the age of eighteen, and 30 percent were under the age of twenty-one. As the data indicate, a significant number of young people get involved in crime. Over 80 percent of all arrests are of males. For 1988–1989, 69 percent of all arrestees were white, 30 percent were African American, and the rest were from other races. Arrest rates for children fifteen years and younger increased by 3 percent during 1988–1990. Within that increase the majority of offenses were in the areas of assault, carrying weapons, drug abuse, and vagrancy. The vast majority of these offenders were from low-socioeconomic groups and were, or were about to become, dropouts.

Cost and Effects. The President's Commission on Law Enforcement and the Administration of Justice recently reported that organized crime has become so widespread and sophisticated that it now involves narcotics, prostitution, murder, gambling, protection rackets, real estate, confidence games, politics, and the stock market. Organized crime touches every American and costs our society an

Key Term:
Delinquency

Transparency 35:
Degrees of Delinquency

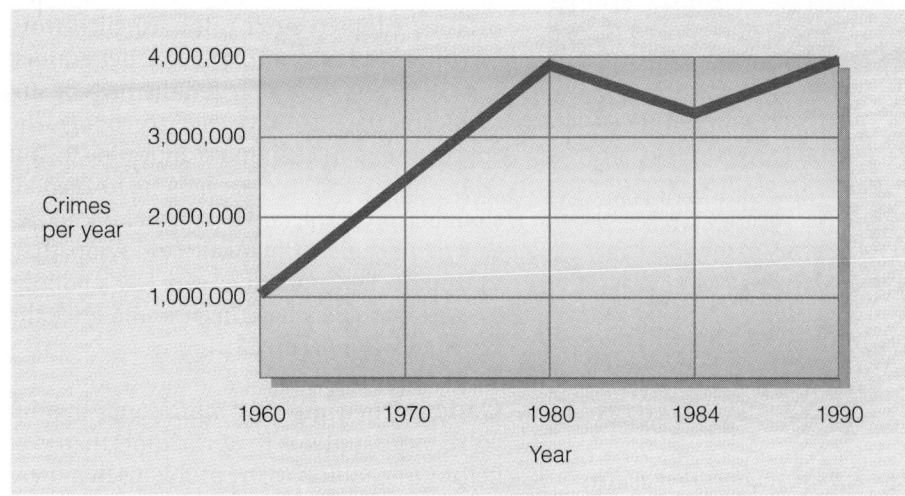

FIGURE 7.5

Growth of Serious Crime (Murder, Rape, Robbery, and Burglary) in the United States

(*Source:* U.S. Bureau of Justice Statistics.)

TABLE 7.4	Cost of Law Enforcement, 1960–1992
Year	**Cost**
1960	$3,349,000,000
1970	$8,571,000,000
1975	$17,249,000,000
1980	$27,026,000,000
1985	$32,801,000,000
1988	$38,000,000,000
1990	$40,000,000,000
1992	$43,000,000,000*

*Estimated from U.S. Bureau of Justice Statistics.

Source: U.S. Bureau of the Census, 1992.

Activity 7.6:
Have students debate the use of armed policemen in the schools to maintain order.

Discussion Question 2:
How can the school develop special programs in an attempt to curb juvenile crime?

Objective 6:
Identify the negative effects of crime among youth.

unbelievable amount of money. Table 7.4 shows the escalating cost of law enforcement. Law enforcement alone now costs every American man, woman, and child over $100 a year. Included in these figures are associated incidents of crime in the schools.

Violent Crime and Vandalism. As the world has witnessed increasing violence, so have the schools, where violence and vandalism have become very serious problems. The U.S. Senate Committee on Delinquency has estimated that school vandalism costs our nation over $600 million each year. The National Association of School Security Directors estimates that each year there are 12,000 armed robberies, 270,000 burglaries, 204,000 aggravated assaults, and 9,000 rapes in our schools. Furthermore, an estimated 70,000 serious physical assaults are made on teachers each year.

These statistics suggest the size of the problems of vandalism and violence faced by the schools. Some schools have hired police officers, adopted strict rules, expelled troublesome students, and taken a determined stance. Others have solicited the help of students and parents; have tried to change the curriculum to make it more appealing to students; have gone to great lengths to keep all students in school; and have generally adopted a democratic, humanistic, and sympathetic attitude. Unfortunately, very few solutions to these problems have been found. (See the Case Study on page 168.)

Educators have found it necessary to establish routines that address the threat of violence on school grounds.

Gangs. There are now more gangs that involve more students in our schools than ever before. In addition to the problems that these people bring to the school, they have become violent in their neighborhood communities. Gang warfare is all too common in the urban areas. It is not confined to the ghetto areas of the city but has spread to include the larger area of ethnic neighborhoods. The violence of these teen activities has led to increasing numbers of murders among the members of the gangs. The gang's quest for social control over its environment carries into the school and threatens the safety of educational staff and students who do not belong. Unfortunately, most of the gang activities are found in welfare-type areas of the community where the amenities of the culture are scarce or nonexistent and the schools are not adequately responding to the special needs of these students.

Few schools have been successful in combating violence. There are two reasons for this. First, schools lack the financial resources to make a serious, concerted attack on the problem. Second, violence has become so prevalent in American society that some social scientists believe there is simply no way to keep it out of the schools. Violence, crime, and a general disregard for the rights and welfare of others have become commonplace. The size and diversity of the violence problem can be understood only by considering a list of related problems: child abuse and neglect, spouse abuse, juvenile delinquency, television and movie violence, teen pregnancy, divorce rates, tax fraud, governmental corruption, welfare cheating, price fixing, stock manipulation, organized crime, business crime, and employee theft. Crime and violence indeed pervade both American life and the schools.

Sexuality

Sexual differences and societal expectations regarding those differences cause considerable concern for young people. The traditional roles associated with biological sexual differences no longer hold true as national norms. However, these types of cultural changes have caused difficulties for young people growing up, and these difficulties have been brought to the doors of the school. The whole issue of male and female sex roles has had a pronounced effect on self-esteem, self-concept, vocational choice, and social behavior. This has led to increased problems related to *sexuality* among young people.

Teenage Pregnancy. The youth culture of American society is experiencing a sexual revolution. *Teenage pregnancy,* venereal disease, and sex-related psychological problems are on the increase. The National Center for Health Statistics reports that teenage pregnancy is at an epidemic rate. For fifteen- to nineteen-year-olds the rate

Information Note 7.6:
The seriousness of school gang behavior is such that in some instances, a potential member of a gang can only become a member if he or she is involved in a homicide.

Relevant Research

How School Boards Are Responding to Violence in the Schools

A recent survey by the National School Boards Association examined how school districts were working to prevent violence in the schools. More than 2000 school districts responded to the survey. General findings asserted that there is an epidemic of school violence nationally and unless schools take corrective action immediately, the violent behaviors will continue to increase. A significant finding of this study was that 82 percent of the respondents indicated that violence is worse today than it was five years ago. Additional findings suggested that school efforts to curb violence did not focus on a single approach. Some twenty-two different strategies were being used by the participant schools, with the top three being suspension (78 percent), student conduct/discipline code (76 percent), and collaboration with other agencies (73 percent). Thirteen percent of the schools (near the bottom of the list) reported using volunteer parent patrols.

Reducing violence in the schools requires a team effort. Required consistency in student behavior must be enforced by the total professional staff. As a beginning teacher you need to be concerned about the safety of your workplace and involved with the school's efforts in promoting and enforcing a positive learning and working environment.

Source: National School Boards Association, "Violence in the Schools: How America's School Boards Are Safeguarding Our Children." Alexandria, VA: The Association, 1993.

Transparency 36:
Teen Sex

Activity 7.7:
Have students in small groups prepare a statement of philosophy and guidelines for sex education in the schools. Have them share and discuss the different efforts.

CASE STUDY: ACCEPTING OR NOT ACCEPTING STUDENT TRANSFERS WHO HAVE A HISTORY OF SCHOOL VIOLENCE

Schools constantly receive student transfers throughout the school year. These transfers primarily come as a result of family moves associated with job changes or social displacement. There are, however, some students who are transferred out of volatile school situations where they have been part of that volatility. It is generally thought that if the student is put into a new environment, he or she may change behavior practices and be recovered for societal inclusion. Many times, these transfers involve inner-city students being moved to suburban settings that are not experiencing problems of violence in the school.

There is little doubt that a school should accept these kinds of transfers if they are legal, but the receiving schools need to have policy in place before engaging or being forced to engage in receiving these learners. As a new teacher in a suburban school that abuts a large metropolitan area, it is highly possible that you will experience some of these types of school transfers in your classroom. You could be asked to participate in the development of a school policy to address these types of school issues. If asked to serve in this capacity, how would you respond to the following questions pertaining to such a policy?

1. What guidelines and/or rules should be established for students of this nature? Should the regular school policies (the school handbook) be the same for all students, or should there be a distinct set of policies for these students since their volatile past is a known fact?
2. What kinds of special academic and counseling help should be provided for these types of students? It is intended that these students be provided an equal opportunity to learn and achieve.
3. Should there be any special program provided for the parents and/or guardians of these students?
4. Should you as a teacher not be concerned about this type of social problem and let the school administration and school board deal with it?

You cannot run away from this problem because it will have an impact on your classroom if this type of transfer student is assigned to you. Also, you need to keep in mind the safety and benefit of the remainder of your students who will also be encountering the potential antisocial behavior of this student. What will you do?

Objective 7:
Present in writing the issues associated with teenage pregnancy and AIDS.

has risen almost 100 percent in the past fifteen years. Despite national efforts by right-to-life groups opposing abortion, teenage girls, like their older counterparts, often resort to abortion to terminate unwanted pregnancies. Although illegitimate birth rates among nonwhite teenagers are very high, white illegitimate birth rates have increased during the same period. This social phenomenon is a response to the changing sexual values of the teen culture, and it is important to note that this change in values is little different from the change in values of the general society.

Annual reports issued jointly by the American Public Health Association, the American Social Health Association, and the Venereal Disease Association continue to show increases in venereal diseases among teenagers. Gonorrhea and syphilis head the list of venereal infections. Syphilis is a medically serious venereal disease that, if left untreated, can cause serious health problems such as sterility, paralysis, blindness, heart disease, insanity, and death. Often, babies of infected mothers are born with mental and physical defects.

Motivated by the emergence of the AIDS epidemic, many schools now have programs that promote awareness about sexually transmitted diseases.

Acquired Immune Deficiency Syndrome (AIDS). Increased sexual activity among teens and adults has led to the spread of AIDS, a major, rapidly growing national health problem. At first this disease was commonly thought to be associated only with homosexuality, but the Surgeon General of the United States has reported the spread of this virus among all ages and classes of people. Figure 7.6 shows the 1979 through 1992 estimates of the expected growth of this disease. The 1993 data show these early estimates to be extremely accurate.

Transparency 37: Status of AIDS Virus and Projected Growth

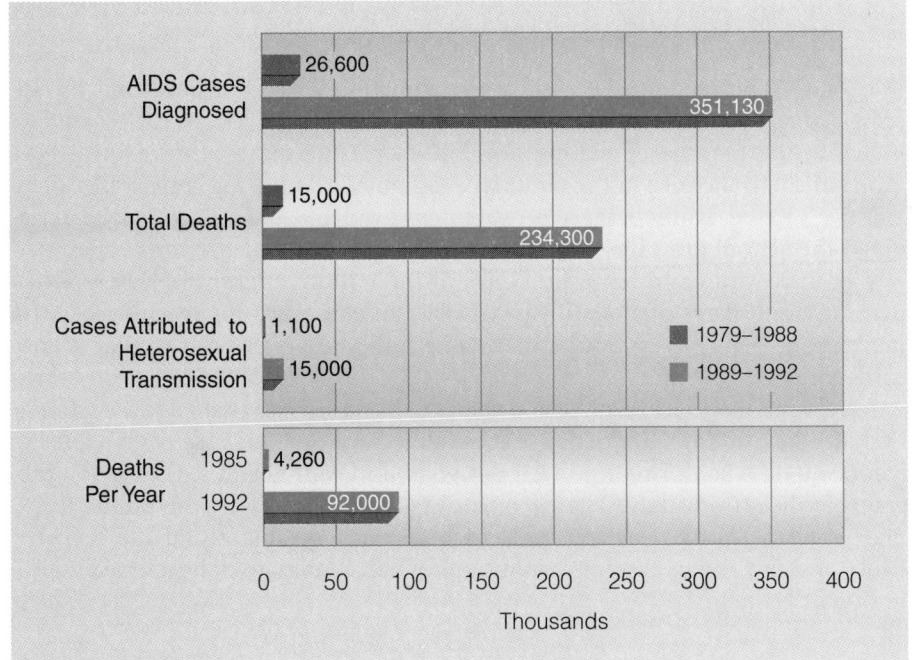

FIGURE 7.6

The Status of the AIDS Virus and Its Projected Growth

(*Source:* The Surgeon General's Report on AIDS)

PROFESSIONAL DILEMMA

Can You Be a Personal Counselor for Your Students?

In your first year of teaching you have been assigned to a middle school. All of the forewarnings of the problems and joys of working with young adolescents have proved to be accurate. As you are coming back from your lunch break one day, one of your students, a thirteen-year-old female, asks if she can have a confidential conference with you. You agree, and tell her that you will call her from class during your planning period.

You have the student called from class at the designated time, and the two of you meet in one of the guidance offices. The young girl is visibly disturbed and in tears when she comes to meet with you and it takes some time to calm her down. She is a very attractive young lady and appears to be physically and mentally more mature than other girls her age. At first, she is hesitant to say anything substantive and seems to be waiting for you to question her about her need for a private conference. With some prodding from you, she finally bursts into tears again and blurts out, "I'm pregnant and don't know what to do!"

The student tells you that her family is "highly moral" and will probably do something drastic when they find out about her problem. You move away from the family action discussion and attempt to get some additional information from her such as: How does she know she's pregnant? How far into the pregnancy does she think she is? Has she seen a doctor? Who is the male involved? She cooperates fully in telling you all you think you need to know. Thus far, you have only pursued information and served as a supportive listener.

The student, sensing your apprehension in giving advice concerning her problem, finally says, "What should I do? My life is ruined. I'll have to quit school and get a job. I'm too young to be married. I haven't told the boy and I don't know how. Should I have an abortion? Will you please help me?"

- You don't remember this type of situation being "covered" in your education courses.

- What should you do?

- What course of action should you take, and where can you turn for help in assisting this young learner?

- As a professional, what moral and ethical principles should you espouse when faced with this type of dilemma?

Discussion Question 3:
To what degree should schools be involved in AIDS education?

Some 70 percent of AIDS cases are attributed to sexual transmission—by heterosexual as well as homosexual intercourse. Some 25 percent of AIDS cases are linked to the practice of sharing needles when using drugs intravenously. The expected sharp increase in the national death rate is due to the current lack of an effective vaccine. Partly because no vaccine is available, the Surgeon General has urged the schools to offer educational programs, for which efforts are underway in most cities and school districts of the nation. *Education Week* reported that forty-one states offered at least curriculum guides for the teaching of AIDS prevention. Nine states required that this topic be part of the regular school curriculum.

Information Note 7.7:
As pessimistic as it sounds, former Surgeon General C. Everett Koop reports that he doubts that a cure will be found for AIDS.

Problems associated with sexual values will continue to challenge the schools. Even though mounting evidence suggests that these problems are often related to ignorance or misinformation, well-designed and well-taught sex education programs in the schools have not been universally supported by the public. Lacking program efforts, teachers need to be knowledgeable about the sexuality issues of youth and to recognize symptoms of behavior that can be referred to professionals for help.

Child Abuse

Largely hidden until recent years, child abuse has become a major problem for the schools. The latest national reports estimate that almost two million school-age children suffer some form of physical or mental abuse each year, including child molestation and abduction. Over one-half of the abused children are female, and the majority of abusers are parents.

Discussion Question 4:
How is learning performance affected when the learner is an abused child?

Myths and Facts. The U.S. Department of Justice reports that a child is abused every two minutes in the United States. Over 2,000 children die each year from some form of child abuse. The child abuser is most often not a dangerous stranger but a trusted friend or relative of the child. Sexual abuse is an especially insidious form of child abuse. At least one girl in four and one boy in ten will be sexually abused before they are eighteen years old, and the principal abuser will likely be a parent. Table 7.5 identifies the myths associated with sexual abuse of children. Although it is reported by the National Center of Child Abuse and Neglect that abusers are not mentally ill, the fact that they abuse children questions their mental health.

Teachers need to be watchful for possible victims of child abuse in their classrooms. The telltale signs of child abuse are the following behaviors:

- A sudden change of behavior in school learning
- No visible sign of medical attention to a child's physical or medical problems after the parents have been alerted
- Overly watchful behavior, as though the child thought something dangerous was about to happen
- Overly compliant behavior, in which the child tries to please everyone
- Behavior indicating a lack of adult supervision

Information Note 7.8:
The recent court case in Florida that awarded a child divorce from his parents because of child abuse brings up a serious issue that should be discussed.

TABLE 7.5	Myths and Facts about Sexual Abuse of Children
Myths	**Facts**
Children are sexually abused by strangers.	About 80% of children are sexually abused by family members or someone known to the child.
Sexual abuse of children is a violent act.	Only 5% of cases are acts of violence.
Persons who abuse children are mentally ill.	Not all persons who abuse children are mentally ill, but many have difficulty with appropriate child-adult relationships.
Sexual abuse of children happens only in poor families, certain ethnic groups, or uneducated families.	Child abuse takes place at all economic and educational levels of society and in all ethnic groups.
Sexual abuse does not occur in foster care.	About 25% of abuse complaints in foster care are sex-related.
Only men sexually abuse children, and the victims are always female.	Both sexes abuse children, and both male and female children are victims.

Source: The National Center of Child Abuse and Neglect.

- Exhibition of learning problems that are foreign to expected normal behavior
- Continual early arrival at school, desire to stay late, and little desire to go home

Transparency 38:
Indicators of Child Abuse

Objective 8:
Identify child abuse practices
and appropriate teacher
action when child abuse is
suspected.

**Journal/Portfolio
Development 1:**
Develop a working file that
contains brochure-type materials that address problems of
chemical abuse, suicide, sexuality, and child abuse. Prepare a written evaluation of
each of these collection topics, and assess how the
brochure information can be
used in your teaching.

**Journal Activity Master 7.2:
An In-Depth Investigation of
One Key Societal Issue.**
The object of this activity is to
select and study one societal
issue in depth and to create a
program to solve the problem.

Test Questions 7.42–7.61

Focus Question 5:
Should our schools help to
solve social problems? Why
or why not?

Effects on Learning.   Children who come from homes where child abuse is prevalent have extreme difficulty in the classroom. Their attention spans are seriously reduced, and they tend to look for things to do that will take them away from a task. Generally, they become very distrustful of adults, which is carried over into the classroom with the teacher. Such distrust may be manifested by extra demands on the teacher for attention, in an attempt to be sure that the teacher's learning expectations are being met, or it may be exhibited as total isolation from the teacher and the learning expectations. The child's psychological and social needs dominate his or her behavior in the classroom, and the child experiences difficulty in learning.

Teachers should not be reluctant to report these types of abnormal behaviors to the proper authorities. The national statistics on child abuse suggest that it is important for the teacher and school to become involved in suspected cases of abused children. Teachers and schools are protected from civil and criminal liability if the report of child abuse is rendered honestly from suspicion, based on behaviors listed above, and is considered valid.

A Collage of Special Issues for the School

In addition to the collage of social problems facing the teacher and the school, there is a growing list of pressing issues that the school must address as it responds to the everyday needs of its students. Although schools might not consider these issues quite as difficult to handle, they do have an effect on the learning environment. Formerly, many of these problems were not considered issues for the public schools to address because some other societal agency was responding or the issue had not yet surfaced. However, as we know more about learning and how it can be affected by physical, mental, and emotional development and the social environment, the school has had to face new, pressing issues.

Special-Needs Children

There is little doubt that the school has always encountered learners with special needs. However, schools often didn't recognize these special needs or couldn't cope with them if they were recognized. As teachers, specialists, and administrators became better trained, some of these special problems were identified. Once problems or needs could be identified, the schools could mount efforts to attend to them. It should be pointed out, however, that the degree of effort that the school employs to take care of special needs depends on the wishes of the community, state, and nation. Taking care of these needs can be controversial, and a teacher should remember that the community determines the direction of the school.

Key Term:
Exceptional learners

Exceptional/Handicapped Learners.   With the passage in 1975 of Public Law 94-142, the special education law provided millions of **exceptional learners** with mandated public education. At the other end of the ability continuum, however, there have been only sporadic institutionalized attempts to provide special programs for gifted and talented learners. Some states, in carrying out the federal mandates of Public Law 94-142, have included special programs for talented and gifted students. Most accelerated programs, advanced placement programs, and the like, whether they be "pull out of class" programs or enrichment programs, do little more than deliver new learning information faster and at an earlier age.

The criteria used to identify gifted and talented children are usually based on some academic norm such as I.Q. scores, achievement battery test scores, or teacher grades. The true notions of giftedness and special talents seem to get lost in the rush to provide special programs for these types of exceptional children. There is little doubt that some of the Individualized Education Program (IEP) requirements mandated for special education children by Public Law 94-142 are appropriate for gifted and talented learners, but also needed are broader criteria by which the schools identify these special learners. Exceptional learners in special education are defined as those evaluated as mentally retarded, hard of hearing, deaf, speech-impaired, visually handicapped, seriously emotionally disturbed, orthopedically impaired, other health impaired, deaf-blind, multihandicapped, or having specific learning disabilities.

Major legislation passed in recent years has given individuals with disabilities equal rights to free public education.

The main features of Public Law 94-142 are as follows:

1. All handicapped learners between the ages of three and twenty-one are to be provided with a free public education.
2. Each handicapped child is to have an Individualized Education Program (IEP), developed jointly by a school official, a teacher, the parents or guardian, and, if possible, the learner.
3. Handicapped children are not to be grouped separately unless they are severely handicapped, in which case separate facilities and programs would be deemed more appropriate. (The stress is on creation of the least restrictive environment.)
4. Tests for identification and placement are to be free of racial and cultural bias.
5. School districts are to maintain continuous efforts at identifying handicapped children.
6. School districts are to establish priorities for providing educational programs in compliance with the law.
7. Placement of the handicapped must require parental approval. Private schools are to comply with the Act.
8. Retraining or in-service training of all workers with the handicapped is required.
9. Special federal grants are available for modifying school buildings.
10. State departments of education are to be designated as the responsible state agencies for all programs for the handicapped.

Least Restrictive Environment. In addition, the law clearly explains least restrictive environment placement, Individualized Education Programs, due process protection, and teacher education. The least restrictive environment placement

Information Note 7.9:
Advocates of individualizing instruction argue for IEPs for all children. With computer technology, this is now more possible.

Journal/Portfolio Development 2:
Prepare a due-process-type IEP format that you can use in your student teaching to diagnose a regular classroom learner's needs and prescribe a learning module for him or her.

ensures that handicapped children are educated with nonhandicapped children to the maximum extent possible, and that the placement of a handicapped child outside the regular classroom occurs only when the nature or severity of the handicap is such that education in regular classes with the use of supplementary aids and services cannot be achieved satisfactorily. An Individualized Education Program must comprise written statements developed by the public agency, the child's teacher, one or both of the child's parents, and the child when appropriate. Other specialists may be involved if the parents or public agency so desires. Each written IEP must include the following:

1. The child's present level of educational performance.
2. Annual goals, including short-term instructional objectives.
3. Specific special education and related services to be provided to the child and the extent to which the child will be able to participate in regular educational programs.
4. Projected dates for initiation and anticipated duration of special services.
5. Objective criteria, evaluation procedures, and schedules for determining on at least an annual basis whether or not the short-term instructional objectives are being met.

CNN Clip 14:
Retarded Mainstreaming

Mainstreaming/Inclusion. Public Law 94-142 does not specify any requirement for mainstreaming. The law speaks strictly of the need to provide for a least restrictive environment for learning, and many times the least restrictive environment is found in the regular classroom with regular students. These classrooms, considered to be the mainstream of school learning environments, have led to the popular use of the term **mainstreaming** in placing special education students in the regular classroom for part of their instruction. Since the 1960s the Council for Exceptional Children (CEC) has directed its efforts for special education toward the provision of mainstreaming services.

Many special education services are dictated by the type of physical environment provided for the learner. Typically, regular classrooms and schools are not physically designed to accommodate many special education students. For example, few regular classrooms are built to handle the physically handicapped learner. Chalkboards are too high for learners using wheelchairs, wheelchairs don't easily fit at desks, light and sound equipment don't address special physical needs, and special ramps and elevators are often nonexistent. As new schools are built they will probably be required, as a result of Public Law 94-142, to address these kinds of physical needs in school buildings. The "new perspective," as CEC calls it, makes regular learning areas more powerful and diverse.

Objective 9:
Elaborate on the needs and required practices associated with exceptional/handicapped children.

The regular classroom environment in this plan is a model of individualized instruction for all learners. Physically, learning spaces are treated better acoustically and include amplification devices and alternative treatments of illumination. Greater use of learning centers with a multiplicity of equipment and materials is provided for special needs and preferences. Collaborative teaching is expected, in which special educators, other professionals, and aides work with regular teachers. Instruction is individualized for all learners. Special education students are moved out of the regular environment for minimal periods and only for complex individual needs.

Key Term:
Inclusion

The new stress on **inclusion** has raised serious issues for the school. Although not covered specifically by Public Law 94-142, the push nationally and statewide comes from a broader interpretation of the law. This interpretation involves putting the exceptional child in the regular classroom and bringing the special services to the classroom rather than sending the child out of the classroom for special services. This added diversity to the regular classroom has created the need for additional special education skills for the regular classroom teacher in schools moving to inclusion programs.

Homeless Students

The National Coalition for the Homeless reported in 1993 that over one million children in the United States can be classified as homeless. Like their older counterparts, the adult homeless, these young people live in shelters, abandoned buildings, welfare centers, and on the street. Half of them do not attend school regularly, and even when they do, their school performance is far from what it should be if they are to have any chance of breaking the cycle of homelessness and withstanding the social pressures on self-esteem that homeless students must surely face.

If homeless students are no longer to be the most "at-risk" students, they need to find in the school the shelter they lack at home. Unfortunately, many of these students are not allowed to attend school because they lack permanent addresses and personal records such as birth certificates and health charts and therefore cannot prove residency. The recently passed Homeless Assistance Act established a national policy, with modest funds available to the large urban areas that apply for them, that eliminates the residency requirement for homeless children and directs the schools to secure the needed documentation to get these children into the classroom.

Latchkey Children

The continuing change in family structure and living has heightened national awareness of children's problems in families in which both parents work or single-parent families in which the parent works. Almost 50 percent of working parents acknowledge that their children are home alone from after school until five-thirty in the evening (or later) when parents come home from work. Such children are referred to as latchkey (because they wear the housekey around their neck) children, and they now number six million school children, ages five to twelve. Because their parents work, latchkey children are left to care for themselves after school.

This practice has led to the development of school programs for children who have no other after-school care. The programs work with them on such issues as first aid, nutrition and health, baby-sitting, and being on their own at home. Nationally, however, the public does not seem to be willing to fund programs for

---

Relevant Research

Homeless Students Can Be Productive and Succeed

A case study report of research on the homeless points to the potential limitless strategies that can be used by the schools to accommodate homeless learners in their attempts to be successful and overcome their dire social situations. This case study reports on a young man and woman, who when given the proper chance, support, and school program were able to graduate and point their lives in a positive direction.

Living in a homeless shelter found for them by the school, the two homeless married students completed high school, including going to the prom. The school provided partial credit courses for them as they worked toward graduation. Homeless students need flexible admission criteria, course offerings, and class assignments, as well as special services and emotional support. As a professional educator you need to be flexible to accommodate all types of learners. The numbers of homeless students continue to rise, and you need to be ready to meet the needs of these special learners.

Source: Yvonne M. Vissing; Dorothy Schroepfer; and Fred Bloise, "Homeless Students, Heroic Students." *Phi Delta Kappan* 75 (7) (March, 1994): 535–539.

Activity 7.8:
Have different groups of students design programs for special needs children such as latchkey, gifted, and homeless children.

Disadvantaged and homeless students are among the large number of students at risk of not receiving the education to which they are entitled.

these children. Since the number of latchkey kids is growing, teachers must be sensitive to the fact that they may become frightened and bored and suffer from being denied normal social interaction with their peers after school.

Increasing numbers of school districts are beginning to offer after-school programs in cooperation with local churches and community groups such as the YMCA. These programs help young children to deal with such problems as how to get home from school safely, how to use the telephone and be familiar with emergency telephone numbers, what to do in case of fire, how to deal with strangers, and how to use their time wisely instead of wasting it watching soap operas and other, sometimes violent, television programs. Many latchkey children, lacking strong family influences, experience problems in school, suffer from low self-esteem, and are failing to reach their full potential. The alarming aspect of this school issue is that the nation is witnessing a growing number of such "at-risk" young learners.

Multicultural Reform

CNN Clip 10:
Multicultural Requirement

As discussed in Chapter 5, the United States is not the melting pot that we believed it was for so many decades. In fact, our differences, and multiculturalism, are growing rapidly. This change in the population makeup, which is especially pronounced among the school-age population, has created two major issues for the school and society. These are debates about, first, monolingual versus multilingual school programs and instruction and, second, English as a Second Language (ESL) for the growing numbers of non-English speakers who are gaining entrance into the United States.

Objective 10:
Identify the various multicultural language programs.

Monolingual/Bilingual. One current debate in the halls of increasing numbers of state legislatures (now estimated at over twenty-five) centers on the use of English as the national language. Passage of legislation in some states to mandate the use of English has already produced significant problems. In Florida, Spanish-speaking maintenance workers have been dismissed because they were speaking Spanish on the job, violating the English-only law in that state. (Currently, that law is being challenged in the court system.) A similar law in California whereby non-English-speaking citizens must learn the English language for everyday use if they wish to receive welfare benefits has placed considerable stress on the Los Angeles school system. The California law also mandates that the local schools must provide programs for non-English-speaking adults. This has led to a need for some 25,000 evening classes to be offered by the Los Angeles school district. Beyond the financial burden on the schools, the major problem is finding the necessary teachers to conduct these adult classes.

The U.S. English Speaking Union now seeks, at the national level, to have English declared the official language of the United States. This group wants to have bilingual ballots removed from voting and bilingual education in schools to be used only as a short-term approach to teach all citizens to use English. This move is in direct conflict with the multilingual movement supported in the schools by diverse minority and ethnic groups.

The Bilingual Education Act—Title VII of the Elementary and Secondary Education Act—was enacted into law in 1968. This Act and its various amendments were enacted to address the special needs of growing numbers of American children whose first language is not English. Originally, the Act was intended to focus on low-income learners, early childhood education, adult education, dropouts, and vocational students. Funds were also provided for preservice and in-service training of teachers for these programs.

Bilingual-bicultural education is formal instruction for learners, using their native language for learning all subjects until second-language (English) skills have been developed. This approach increases equal educational opportunities for minority children. Census reports of the 1980s indicated that the size of the non-English-language background population in the United States was 30 million people. This number is expected to increase to 39.5 million by the year 2000. People of Spanish, German, and Italian descent make up the majority of this group, the Spanish-speaking people who have migrated from Latin America and Puerto Rico comprising by far the largest portion. The Spanish-speaking portion will continue to grow. As we discussed in Chapter 5, minority populations are soon to be the majority in an increasing number of border and coastal states. The recently passed California law declaring English to be the primary language of California will face serious legal challenge as the minority numbers continue to grow there.

Bilingual programs currently in use include the following:

1. Maintenance programs are designed to teach skills needed for English that emphasize instruction in the learner's native tongue. The culture of the ethnic group receiving instruction is stressed through teaching about the group's history, literature, and art. The native language of the learner is considered an asset to society; retention of that language is a significant goal of this program.

2. Transitional programs are designed to provide intensive instruction in English, yet retain support for instruction in the native language. Learners are integrated into the regular classroom as soon as they acquire sufficient skills in English. It is critical in these programs that the learner not be disadvantaged in expected achievement areas of the curriculum.

The need for bilingual-bicultural programs will continue to grow, but how that need will be addressed by the federal and state governments in the future remains a question. As social legislation continues to suffer from financial cutbacks and the efforts to establish English as the national language are extended, attempts to provide education for non-English-speaking people may unfortunately diminish.

English as a Second Language. English As a Second Language groups have traditionally not been supported financially in their educational pursuits, as have groups advocating bilingual programs. Because rising numbers of non-English-speaking immigrants from all over the world are sending their children to Amer-

Information Note 7.10:
Currently approved curriculum regulations in Pennsylvania require students to study and master a second language before graduating from high school. This will affect the graduates of 2005.

Activity 7.9:
Have students (by their different certification areas) identify the kinds of learning problems bilingual children will have in the different certification areas.

CNN Clip 12:
Immigrant Education

ican schools, ESL programs are requiring more time during the school day if the children are to succeed in learning while using the English language.

The school finds itself in the middle of this national debate, but without clear direction from the states or national government, it cannot provide the needed leadership in program development and implementation.

School Clinics

Societal trends that have influenced the establishment of **school-based clinics** include the increasing use and misuse of illicit drugs, alcohol, and tobacco by youth; increasing suicide rates; and the sexual revolution, which has resulted in increased rates of teenage pregnancy, abortion, sexually transmitted diseases, and sex-related psychological problems. There is little doubt that these trends have had an undermining effect on the social behavior and academic success of students.

School-based clinics have emerged as a means of combating these trends. These clinics are controversial because, in addition to the regular services provided—physicals, immunizations, and first aid—they now provide birth control counseling and, in some cases, contraceptives. The clinics also provide prenatal care for pregnant teenagers and drug and alcohol abuse counseling. People who oppose these clinics do so on the basis that such services should be handled by the family, religious institutions, and community social service agencies. In fact, many people believe that because they provide birth control counseling and contraceptives, these clinics are actually promoting sexual promiscuity. Additionally, since many clinics are located in urban centers that have high proportions of low-socioeconomic students who also happen to be members of minorities, the critics argue that the clinics are using students for social engineering. Data supporting the use of such clinics in public schools suggest that, where they are in use, there are fewer teenage pregnancies and fewer instances of venereal disease. The National Academy of Science and the American Medical Association support the distribution of contraceptives to teenage youth to combat the serious problem of unwanted pregnancies. Now, with the spread of AIDS, the use of school-based clinics is even more important.

Magnet Schools

During the late 1980s, Buffalo, New York, established **magnet schools** to meet federal court requirements for desegregation that had been ordered for the city. One of the particular aims of the desegregation order in Buffalo was to provide for the growing Native American population. It had been determined that the regular school program was not providing for the special needs of Native American and African American students.

Magnet schools, as the name implies, attract particular types of students who have special educational needs. In the case of the Native American students in Buffalo, it was determined that their special needs for cultural preservation could best be handled by concentrating them in impact programs. Even though they live in concentrated neighborhoods, the regular schools do not attend to their cultural needs, because instruction is geared to the mainstream. Magnet schools attend to diversity through their programs.

Currently, there are magnet schools for African American, Native American, Greek American, and Hispanic American students in Buffalo. No one school is exclusively all Native American or all Hispanic American. The Buffalo plan calls for a maximum of 50 percent of a school's students to be members of any one minority. If the minority students do not live in the area of the designated magnet school, they are given free bus transportation. The remainder of the student body comes from the regular attendance unit of the school.

Minneapolis and St. Paul, Minnesota, have established magnet elementary schools to satisfy the special needs of the city school population. Patterned after the program for the schools in Buffalo, students are bused, in stated proportions, to the schools selected for special purposes. The magnet idea is not new. Many urban areas have had magnet-type schools at the secondary level for many years. Two such schools in New York City have been in operation for quite some time; one was highlighted in the movie *Fame.* Chicago has provided special high schools for technical, pre-engineering, and vocational training for many years. However, these schools have not been sensitive to minority differences and sometimes have become ghetto centers of education or centers of elite programs serving mostly white students. The magnet school concept, as it is currently being used, addresses social and academic needs for special programs for all kinds of students. Magnet schools are now found across the country.

Diversity Note 7.2:
Magnet schools that in addition to a large number of members of a special minority group, require other minorities and Anglos to be part of the schools, are providing excellent attention to diversity needs.

Adult Literacy

Adult education includes any course or activity taken regularly or part time by adults seventeen years of age or older. This definition is used by the federal government to identify the increasing numbers of adults taking part in programs since the early 1980s. The total number of adult participants approached thirty million in 1990. The U.S. Department of Education estimates that about 11 percent of these adult students are attempting to complete elementary requirements or high school graduation requirements. Some 17 percent are completing requirements for a vocational certificate, and the remaining adults are pursuing two-year, four-year, or postgraduate degree programs. Although these figures seem impressive, they do not fully address the literacy problems of the adult population. Eighty percent of the participants are from the white majority population and have at least a high school education. Most are already gainfully employed and have annual family incomes of $13,000 or more.

Despite what appears to be a healthy situation among adults, the Department of Education has estimated that almost 13 percent of all American adults—between eighteen million and twenty-two million people—are illiterate. Most of these people belong to minorities. These data have spurred national efforts to establish and improve adult literacy programs administered by state agencies, pub-

National efforts are aimed at improving adult literacy, which is seen as directly affecting children's literacy.

lic schools, and institutions of higher education. In addition, the national media have joined the effort to reduce adult illiteracy.

Objective 12:
Examine global problems of education.

Global Perspectives: Problems and Progress

Reporting in the *NEA Today*, UNESCO provides data on literacy gains and losses in countries around the world. While developing countries are gaining ground on literacy development, the underdeveloped countries are losing the literacy battle. Illiteracy rates are the highest in sub-saharan Africa, South Asia, and the Arab states. To a large part, this illiteracy problem is due to the fact that people spend so few years in formal education in underdeveloped countries. This lack of school time, coupled with a dire shortage of textbooks, provides about 60 to 80 days of effective schooling during the lifetime of people in the underdeveloped countries. This compares very unfavorably with sixteen years of formal education in North America.

Activity 7.10:
Have students discuss world-wide social issues that affect global student learning in their schools.

Generally, around the world, the work with illiteracy is showing positive results. The UNESCO estimates suggest that adult illiteracy in the world has fallen from 946 million in 1980 to 905 million in 1990. The forecast is that this number will fall to 869 million in the year 2000.

While the data on worldwide illiteracy are not overly positive, the overall progress in children's welfare shows considerable gains over the past ten years. Infant mortality has almost been cut in half per thousand live births, falling from 137 to 70. Life expectancy has increased during this same period from forty-six years of age to sixty-one years of age. Dropout rates in many of the developing areas (the Middle East, North Africa, East Asia/Pacific, and Central America) have improved significantly. However, the underdeveloped areas still suffer from extremely high dropout rates.

While the problems of youth in this nation appear to be insurmountable at times, this society and its educational system still provide a broader and more secure learning environment for its youth than any other country. Comparisons with other nations of the world support this assertion, despite the growing negative problems facing United States youth as they enter into and engage in their educational programs.

Summary and Implications

There are many serious social problems in the United States that have important effects on our schools. Schools cannot adequately meet the educational needs of their students without considering the society in which the young people live. Our schools and our society are so intimately related that any problem affecting one affects the other; therefore the schools alone cannot solve many of the problems confronting young people.

The implication here is clear. If we are serious about solving the problems facing young people, both society at large and our schools must work together purposefully—probably in a way not yet envisioned by planners. This effort will undoubtedly require that more money be spent on education than is currently the case. It will require that parents work much more closely with educators than they do now. And it will ask American society to make a much deeper and broader commitment to education than it has up to now.

Discussion Questions

1. How can the school help in combating the chemical problems of youth?
2. How can the school develop special programs in an attempt to curb juvenile crime?
3. To what degree should schools be involved in AIDS education?
4. How is learning performance affected when the learner is an abused child?
5. There is little doubt that the use of school-based clinics will remain controversial. What role should teachers assume in defending or not defending these clinics?

Journal/Portfolio Development

1. Develop a working file that contains brochure-type materials that address problems of chemical abuse, suicide, sexuality, and child abuse. Prepare a written evaluation of each of these collection topics, and assess how the brochure information can be used in your teaching.
2. Prepare a due-process-type IEP format that you can use in your student teaching to diagnose a regular classroom learner's needs and prescribe a learning module for him or her.

School-Based Experiences

1. When you visit a school as part of your field experience program, gather information about the numbers of children in that school who are classified as welfare children. Additionally, gather numbers on school dropouts, alcohol and drug abuse, delinquency, and child abuse. Compare your findings with national figures for these types of school problems. If your findings are lower or higher than national averages, attempt to determine what that particular school and community have or have not done to affect the statistics you have gathered. After preparing a short report on your fieldwork, share it with a teacher from the school and a few of the students. Record in writing their reactions to your findings and analyses.

2. Secure permission to examine a select set of student performance data from some school files. Examine these data in light of social activities and performances of the learners. How is school performance affected by the out-of-school activities and/or problems encountered by students?

Bibliography

Dryfoos, Joy G. *Adolescents at Risk: Prevalence and Prevention.* New York: Oxford University Press, 1990.

Gutek, Gerald L. *Education and Schooling in America.* 3rd ed. Boston: Allyn and Bacon, 1992.

Havighurst, Robert J., and Levine, Daniel U. *Society and Education.* 8th ed. Boston: Allyn and Bacon, 1992.

Hodgkinson, Harold L. *A Demographic Look At Tomorrow.* Washington, DC: Institute for Educational Leadership, 1992.

Kozol, Jonathan. *Savage Inequalities.* New York: Crown Publishers, 1991.

National Center for Educational Statistics. *Projections of Educational Statistics to 1997–99.* Washington, DC: U.S. Government Printing Office, 1991.

Rich, John Martin. *Foundations of Education: Perspectives on American Education.* New York: Macmillan Publishing Company, 1992.

Stewart, Donald. *Immigration and Education, The Crisis and Opportunities.* New York: Lexington Books, 1993.

Weatherford, James M. *Native Roots: How the Indians Enriched America.* New York: Fawcett Columbine, 1991.

Webb, L. Dean; Metha, Arlene; and Jordan, K. Forbus. *Foundations of American Education.* New York: Macmillan Publishing Company, 1991.

Dreamcatcher

*Schools are the front line of the American educational system, and one of the most important educators in each school is the principal. Therefore, our Dreamcatcher for Part 3 is a very exciting and dedicated school principal, **DR. TIM WESTERBERG**. He is principal of Littleton High School in Littleton, Colorado. Prior to becoming a principal some fifteen years earlier, he was a social studies teacher and football and track coach.*

As a principal he is a visionary leader and role model for teachers. He offers his staff ideas, a quick wit, and a participatory style of management. During the summer months he frequently works with teachers serving on teams or committees. Their frequent laughter symbolizes the collegial rather than hierarchical nature of the relationships he maintains. When a decision affecting the whole school is made, the entire staff votes. He serves on the decision-making body for the school, but does not chair it. He visits every classroom in the building on a regular basis and chats with teachers informally in their offices during planning time. He believes in a consistent, clearly articulated, and honest approach to communicating with teachers, and, as a result, they trust him.

One of Dr. Westerberg's primary values concerns his belief that students should be able to demonstrate the intellectual skills and knowledge necessary to thrive in a changing world. Consequently, he led the staff in its development of an innovative educational program where students earned graduation by demonstrating their mastery of stated school goals through such methods as exhibitions, demonstrations, and portfolios. Each student's education is an individual one based on identified personal needs, interests, and learning styles. Faculty, parents, and students work together in groups and on committees to determine through shared decision making the kinds of learning projects and activities appropriate for students in their community. Every staff person, including the principal, meets with students weekly to track their progress. To support the program, Dr. Westerberg established a school foundation that applied for and received grant monies and corporate donations that go primarily to pay teachers for their work on the project.

Dr. Westerberg believes in knowing the law fully, so that he can allow for individual differences. He feels the system should work to support people rather than people work to support systems. "Because of the guiding values in our school," Dr. Westerberg said, "I have certain expectations about how we treat people. We trust kids here, and we treat each other with trust, dignity, and respect." Instead of establishing rules, he encourages individual initiative and creativity by staff members, and he values dealing with student issues individually rather than by strict procedures. "When students leave the office, they should feel that any decision affecting them was based on their individual circumstances rather than on the school's need to comply with a predetermined set of rules." Being open to change, being a positive and enthusiastic leader for students and staff, and working to provide a climate of educational excellence characterize Dr. Westerberg's leadership at Littleton High School.

Structure and Finance of American Education

Focus Questions

1 Who is in charge of the school? How much say do teachers have?
2 What is the relationship of the school district to teachers and principals in a school?
3 What do district superintendents do? And, what is the authority relationship of the superintendent to the school board?
4 Do schools and school districts have to do what the state government says? What is the role of federal government in education?
5 How are schools paid for?
6 Property taxes have been the major source of revenue for schools. What is wrong with this?
7 In recent years there have been a large number of court cases dealing with school finance. What is the common theme in all of them?
8 How well does the spending for public schools in the United States compare with what other developed countries spend?

Key Terms and Concepts

Accountability: Holding schools responsible for what students learn.

Block grants: Federal monies that are consolidated into a broader-purpose fund from categorical funds that had more focused purposes. Block grants give more discretion to the state and local agencies that receive them.

Current expenses: Expenditures necessary for daily operation and maintenance.

Independent school: A nonpublic school that is unaffiliated with any religious institution or agency.

Intermediate unit: A level of school organization between the state and the local district; a subdivision of the elementary school including grades 4, 5 and 6.

Line: An organizational arrangement in which a subordinate is directly responsible to a supervisor.

Progressive tax: A tax scaled to the ability of the taxpayer to pay.

Property tax: A tax based on the value of property, both real estate and personal.

Regressive tax: A tax that affects low-income groups disproportionately.

Staff: An organizational arrangement in which one party is not under the direct control or authority of another.

The purpose of this chapter is to explain how the pieces making up the American education system are organized and fit together. We shall begin with the school. Our assumption is that you are familiar with schools; however, we should be able to add some important insights to your current understanding. From schools, we will move to descriptions of the structure of school districts, the organization of states, and the current role of the federal government. As you might have guessed, there are some parts of the system that don't fit nicely into this "bottom-up" story, and we will describe those parts after we have developed a picture of the whole. After the structure and organization of the American education system is presented, we will address how it is financed.

The Structure of the American Education System

Test Questions 8.1–8.33

Objective 1:
Describe the overall organization of the American education system, including the relationships among local, state, and national components.

Transparency 42:
The Structure of Education in the United States

Describing how the American education system is organized is generally done by starting at the "top" of the organization chart, with the U.S. Department of Education, moving "down" through the state structures, and ultimately arriving at the school district and school levels. This "top-down" approach reflects, in an organizational sense, that it is easier to understand the pieces when you first have a view of the whole. Also, the top-down approach indicates that there is more authority and responsibility the further up one is in the structure. In many ways this is true.

However, in education, unlike many businesses, the "bottom" is composed of professionals (teachers and principals) who know as much or more about their "business" as those who are more removed from the day-to-day life in classrooms. Thus, teachers and principals correctly advocate that they should have a great deal of say in determining what happens with their students on a day-to-day basis. Our decision to start this chapter with a description of schools, rather than at the federal level, is in some ways offering a symbolic statement that teachers can be viewed as being at the "top."

In order to avoid many of the problems implied in a vertical (top-down) picture of the American education system, a horizontal perspective, as is represented in Table 8.1, has been advocated by some theorists. One important emphasis of this horizontal Policy-to-Practice Continuum is that in order for education to

TABLE 8.1 The Policy-to-Practice Continuum in the American Education System

Federal	State	Intermediate	District	School	Classroom
President	Governor			Principal	Teacher
Congress	Legislature	Board	Superintendent	Site Council	
Secretary	Chief State School Officer	Director	Board	Teachers	Students
U.S. Department of Education	State Department of Education		District Office Staff		

improve, the agencies and people at each point along the continuum have to do their job well. A second critical feature is that all have to trust people and agencies at other points along the continuum. This means, for example, that teachers have to develop an understanding of the functions and purposes of other parts of the system. Teachers cannot stay isolated in their classrooms, unaware of the issues and expectations of the school, school district, and the state. At the other end of the continuum, it is important that policymakers learn more about the work of teachers and what goes on in schools.

Another important organizational concept to keep in mind is the difference between **line** and **staff** relationships. In any organization, some people will have the job of being supervisors, bosses, honchos, managers, or directors. Other people will "report" to these persons. The supervisor typically has the authority, at least to some degree, to direct, monitor, and evaluate the work of the subordinate. When one person has this type of authority over another there is a "line" relationship. If there is no formal organizational authority of one person over the other then they have a "staff" relationship. This distinction becomes important in education, since, in many instances, it is not clear or absolute who has the authority/responsibility to direct the work of others. For example, teachers, as professionals, legitimately can claim more independence than can employees of other organizations. But teachers are not completely free to do whatever they want. If they were, the *system* of education would break down, at least as it is experienced by students who must move through it.

Key Term:
Line

Key Term:
Staff

The Organization of Schools

The basic building block of the American education system is the school. To an amazing extent schools are organized in the same way in each state. In fact, schools are organized pretty much the same in other countries too.

Each school consists of a set of classrooms, with corridors for the movement of students, and a central office. There will be one or more large spaces for a cafeteria and gymnasium/auditorium. This building will have outside spaces for a playground, staff parking, and a driveway for dropping off and picking up students. Wherever you go you will find this basic architecture.

The design of schools is frequently criticized for being like an "egg crate." If you viewed a school building with the roof off, you would see that it resembles an egg carton from the grocery store. There are a series of cells or pockets with routes running between them. Some educational critics see this architecture as interfering with the need to introduce new educational practices. For example, the walls restrict communication between teachers and channel the flow of student traffic.

Even when a school is built with modest attempts to change the interior space, teachers and students are able to preserve the egg crate concept. For example, you may have seen an elementary school that was "open space" in design. Instead of having "self-contained" classrooms, there is an open floor plan equivalent in size to three or four classrooms. However, if you observed the arrangement of furniture, book shelves, and screens you probably noted that teachers and students had constructed zones and areas that were equivalent to having three or four self-contained classrooms.

Objective 2:
Describe the different roles and relationships that exist in the typical school.

Transparency 43:
A School Organization Chart

Focus Question 1:
Who is in charge of the
school? How much say do
teachers have?

Activity 8.1:
Ask students to draw an organization chart for the high
school where they graduated.
Ask some leading questions
such as, Who is in charge of
the school? And, where did
students go for discipline
problems? Once the charts
are drawn, survey the class
about the number of people in
different roles such as vice
principals, department heads,
and extracurricular roles.

We are not criticizing teachers for being unadaptive to new school architec-
tures; rather, we are pointing out how the organization of the space parallels the
activity of the people who use it. There are many good reasons for organizing
schools around self-contained classrooms. And in the case of open-concept space,
the noise from three or four teachers and 90 to 120 children can be so disruptive
that little learning can occur. One key to successful use of open-space plans then,
is to be sure the structure is designed in ways to control and dampen noise.

The Roles and Responsibilities of Principals.   The principal is in charge
of the school. In law the principal is the final authority at the school. The principal is typically responsible for instructional leadership, community relationships,
staff (including teachers, secretaries, and custodians), teacher selection and evaluation, pupil personnel, building and grounds, budgets, administration of personnel, provisions of contracts, administration of the attendance center office, and
business management. The principal is in a line position with the school district
superintendent. In larger school districts, the principal may have an intermediate
supervisor such as an assistant superintendent or director of elementary or secondary education.

Every year, principals are being assigned more tasks and responsibilities. For
example, there are a number of movements to increase teacher participation in the
making of school decisions. And there is a movement to increase parent and community involvement in making school decisions. Both of these movements have
led to the creation of a team or committee of teachers and parents to work with
the principal. Working with these committees places new demands on the principal's time and new expectations for the types of leadership skills a principal needs
to possess or develop.

*The principal is responsible
for the actions of all school
personnel.*

When teachers have an idea about the school, or want to try something different, it is important for them to talk with their principal. If there are department heads or team leaders, then the first discussions should be with them. In any organization, including schools, it is normal protocol to first talk with the person at the next level above. When there is a concern or problem, it is important to use the official administrative system. Contact the principal. If this method fails and there is a serious problem, then a teacher may continue up the line, by contacting the principal's supervisor—the assistant superintendent or the superintendent. If there is a serious disagreement, then a teacher may file a grievance through procedures outlined in the negotiated contract. In any instance it is wise for a beginning teacher, or one new to the system, to seek advice from experienced colleagues before taking action. In addition to knowing the system, one must know how the system works; colleagues and principals can be helpful in this regard.

Activity 8.2:
If you were a principal, what duties would you like to do most of the time?

Assistant Principals. In larger elementary schools and in most junior high schools, middle schools, and high schools, there will be one or more additional administrators. Normally they are called assistant principals, although sometimes in high schools they are titled vice principals. Large high schools will have several assistant or vice principals and some other administrators that have "director" titles, such as director of athletics and director of counseling. These administrators share in the tasks of the principal and provide additional sources of communication between teachers, students, staff, parents, community, and the district office. In elementary schools the job differentiation between the assistant principal and the principal will be less clear, and each will be a part of most operations. In the high school setting, frequently specific roles and tasks will be assigned to the different assistant principals. For example, one assistant principal will handle discipline. Another example would be the evaluation of teachers. In most districts, each teacher must be observed formally. This activity takes more time than the principal will have available, so the assistant principal(s) will observe some teachers. Normally, in the case of teacher observations, the principal will concentrate on observing the new teachers. This is especially important since the principal will be the one who makes the recommendation on rehiring beginning teachers.

Department Heads and Team Leaders. In elementary schools there will normally be another less formal level of leadership: grade level or team leaders. These persons are full-time teachers who assume a communication and coordination role for their grade level(s) or team. In junior high schools and high schools there will be department chairs. Normally the departments will be organized around the major subject areas (mathematics, science, English, and social studies), and the co-curricula (athletics and music). Teachers will be members of one of the departments, and there will be regular meetings to plan curriculum and to facilitate communication. In middle schools the leaders of the interdisciplinary teams will likely serve in the same way. In each case these department heads or team leaders will meet with the principal from time to time and meet regularly with their teachers.

Teachers. The single largest group of adults in the school are the teachers. A typical elementary school will have from fifteen to thirty-five teachers, and there will be more than one hundred in a large high school. Teachers are busy in their class-rooms working with their students, and this is where the egg crate architecture of schools can be a problem. Unless special mechanisms are used, such as team leaders or department chairs, it is very easy for individual teachers to become isolated from the school as a whole. The self-contained classroom architecture and the busy work of attending to twenty to forty students in the classroom gives each teacher little time or opportunity to communicate with other adults. As a consequence, each teacher and the principal need to work hard with the other members of the school staff to facilitate communication, and all must make an effort to work together to continually improve the school.

School Support Staff. There are personnel in a school in addition to administrators and teachers, and one of the most important of these role groups is the school secretary. Every teacher and principal will advise you to be sure to support and get along with the school secretary, who is at the nerve center of the running of the school. When a student has a problem, when a teacher needs some materials, when the principal wants a piece of information from the files, or when a student-teacher wants to know about parking a car, the first person to contact is the school secretary. Another important resource to the school are the custodians. How clean your classroom and school are will depend on the efforts of the custodians, and they also can be helpful to teachers in locating supplies and moving furniture. Keep in mind that they observe and talk with students. Frequently custodians and other support staff will know before the teachers about something that is going on. Cafeteria workers are another group of adult workers in the school who can make a positive difference in how the school feels and functions.

The School Organization Chart. All of the personnel described above are located in the school building. The principal is the single line authority for all of these adults *and* all of the students! Most experts on organizations will advocate that no more than five to seven people should be directly supervised by one administrator. Yet, in nearly all schools the principal will be responsible for a minimum of thirty adults and several hundred students. In very large schools the principal may have two hundred adults to supervise. As you can see, the simple picture of top-down direction for education breaks apart when one considers the wide array of tasks and the sheer number of people at work in each school. There have to be a number of structures for arranging the relationships between the varied role groups and facilitating coordination and communication. A typical school organization chart is presented in Figure 8.1.

Organization of the School District

Public schools in the United States are organized into school districts, which have similar purposes but widely different characteristics. Some districts provide only elementary education; others provide only high school education; still others provide both elementary and secondary education. Approximately 26 percent of the districts have fewer than 300 pupils, and their total enrollments make up about 1.3 percent of the national enrollment. Only 1.1 percent of the districts have an enrollment in excess of 25,000 students, yet these districts enroll about 28 percent of the total student population. Thousands of school districts have only one school campus; in comparison a few urban districts have as many as 500 schools.

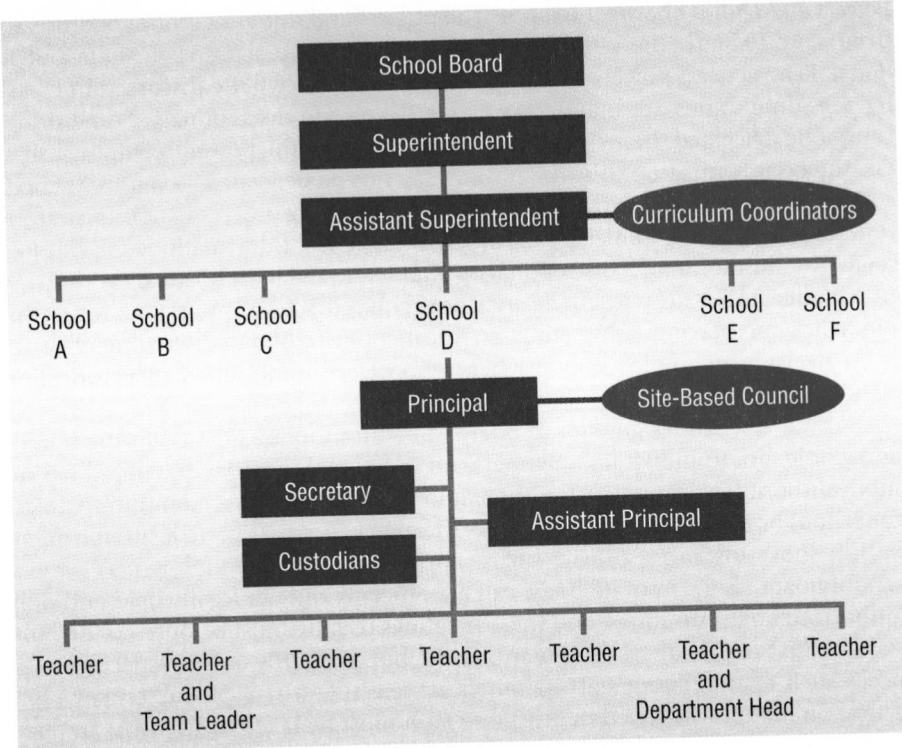

FIGURE 8.1

A School Organization Chart

The school district is governed by a school board, and its day-to-day operations are led by a superintendent. Each district will have its own district office that houses an array of administrative, instructional support, financial, and clerical support staff. As the state and federal levels of government have become active in setting educational agendas, there has been a concomitant response at the district level through an ever-increasing list of tasks that must be accomplished. These additional tasks have brought more functions and personnel to the district office.

Local Board of Education.   Legal authority for operating local school systems is given to local boards of education through state statutes. The statutes prescribe specifically how school board members are to be chosen and what duties and responsibilities they have in office. The statutes also specify the terms of board members, procedures for selecting officers of the board, duties of the officers, and procedures for filling any vacancies. Local citizens serving as school board members are official agents of the state.

About 92 percent of the school boards in the United States are elected by popular vote; most members are elected in special, nonpartisan elections. About 7 percent are appointed. The percentage of appointed school boards is higher in school districts enrolling over 25,000 pupils; yet even in three-fourths of these larger districts, the board members are elected.

Normally teachers may not be board members in the districts where they teach; however, they may be board members in districts where they live if they teach in different districts. The trend by which more teachers are becoming board members most likely results from the goal of professional associations to secure seats on school boards.

Activity 8.3:
Ask students to list all the personnel roles they can think of that comprise a typical school district organizational chart. Then ask students to line up the various personnel on a hierarchical chart. What role is at the bottom?

Information Note 8.2:
School boards are being criticized too. One proposal is to change them to "local policy boards." These new boards would establish overall direction and still hire the superintendent. But they would not be involved in curriculum development, review purchasing contracts, or be involved in staff negotiations.

Focus Question 3:
What do school district superintendents do? And, what is the authority relationship of the superintendent to the school board?

Journal Activity Master 8.1: A Summary of School Control Issues. This activity helps the student better understand the main ideas concerning school organization and control.

Activity 8.4:
Invite a superintendent for a question and answer session.

Powers and Duties of School Boards. The powers and duties of school boards vary from state to state; the school codes of the respective states spell them out in detail. (The general powers and duties of local boards will be discussed in Chapter 9.) Some duties are mandatory, while others are discretionary. Some duties cannot be delegated. If, for example, boards are given the power to employ teachers, the boards must do this; the power may not be delegated—even to a school superintendent. Boards can delegate much of the hiring process to administrators, however, and then act officially on administrative recommendations for employment. An illustration of a discretionary power left to the local board is the decision of whether or not to participate in a nonrequired school program—for example, a program of competitive athletics. Another illustration of discretionary power is the decision to employ only teachers who exceed minimum state certification standards.

Powers and duties granted to boards of education are granted to the boards as a whole, not to individual members. An individual member of a board has no more authority in school matters than any other citizen of the community unless the school board legally delegates a task through official action to a specific member; in those instances, official board approval of final actions is necessary. A school board, as a corporate body, can act officially only in legally held and duly authorized board meetings, and these meetings usually must be open to the public. Executive or private sessions may be held, but ordinarily only for specified purposes such as evaluating staff members or selecting a school site. Usually, any action on matters discussed in private session must be taken officially in an open meeting.

Superintendent of Schools.
One of the primary duties of the local board is to select its chief executive officer, the local school superintendent. There is one notable exception to the general practice of selection of the superintendent by school boards. In a few states, especially in the Southeast, school district superintendents are selected by the voters. In these situations, school superintendent selection is a political process just like that used for the election of mayors, county commissioners, some judges and others. In either case, the superintendent is responsible for the day-to-day operations of the school district, responding to school board members' interests, planning the district's budget, and setting long-term aspirations for the district. The superintendent is expected to be visible in the community and to provide overall leadership for the district.

The Importance of Leadership by the Superintendent and Board Members Cannot Be Overemphasized. The quality of the educational program of a school district is influenced strongly by the leadership that the board of education and the superintendent provide. Without the communication and support of high expectations by boards and superintendents, high-quality education is not likely to be achieved. Curriculum programs over and above state-required minimums are discretionary. For a school district to excel, the local authorities, board members, and the superintendent must convince their communities that specified school programs are needed and desirable.

The Superintendent and Central Office Staff. The superintendent of schools works with a staff to carry on the program of education. The size of the staff varies with the school district; and of course, some kind of organization is necessary. Many school systems use a line and staff organization like that shown in Figure 8.2.

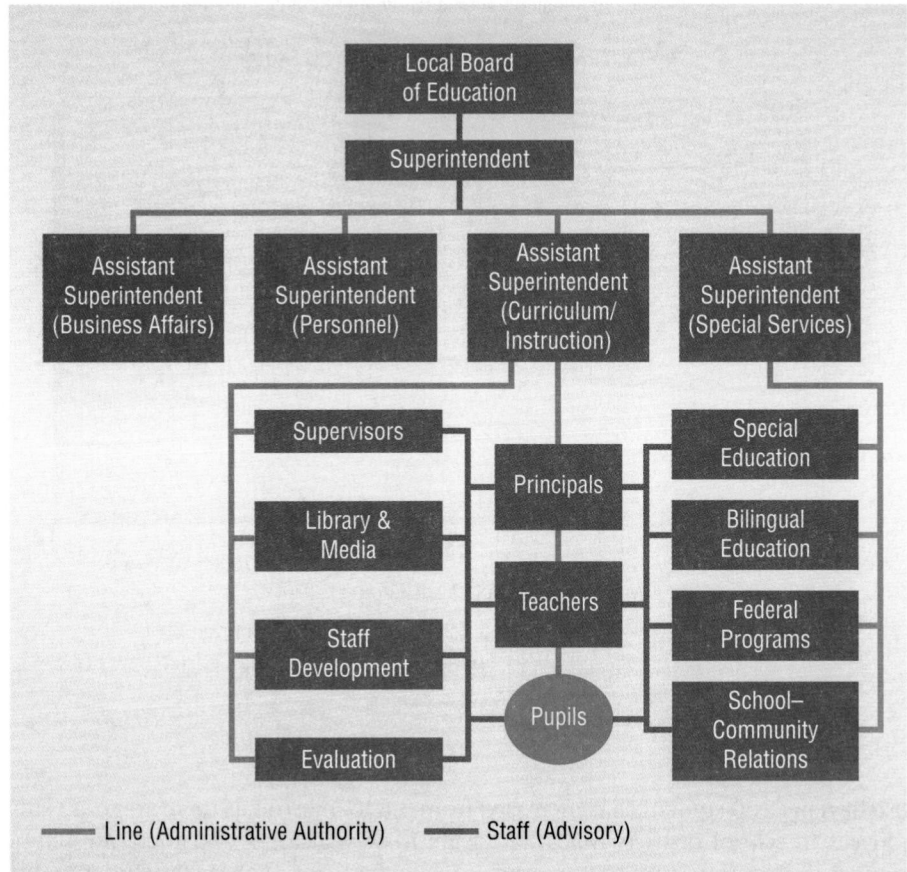

Line (Administrative Authority)   Staff (Advisory)

FIGURE 8.2

Typical School District Line
and Staff Organization

In this pattern, line officers hold the administrative power as it flows in a line from the local board of education down to the pupils. Superintendents, assistant superintendents, and principals are line officers vested with authority over the people below them on the chart. Each person is directly responsible to the official above and must work through that person in dealing with a higher official. This arrangement is frequently referred to as the "chain of command."

Administrative staff members are shown in Figure 8.2 as branching out from the direct flow of authority. Staff includes librarians, instructional supervisors, guidance officers, transportation officers, and others. They are responsible to their respective superiors, generally in an advisory relationship. Staff members usually have no authority and issue no orders. They assist and advise others from their special knowledge and abilities. Teachers are generally referred to as staff persons even though they are in the direct flow of authority. Their authority in this arrangement prevails only over pupils.

There is continuing controversy about the increasing number of people in the district office as compared to the number of teachers in schools. As can be seen in Figure 8.3 on page 194 the total number of public school staff per 100 students almost doubled between 1950 and 1981. Since then the increases have been small. During the same forty-year period the percentage of school staffs that are classroom teachers has decreased from 70 to 53 percent. However, the number of

Information Note 8.3:
The superintendency is a very vulnerable position. On average, 13 percent of the superintendencies turn over each year, and an increasing number of individuals are "exiting." They are taking other types of positions instead of seeking other superintendencies.

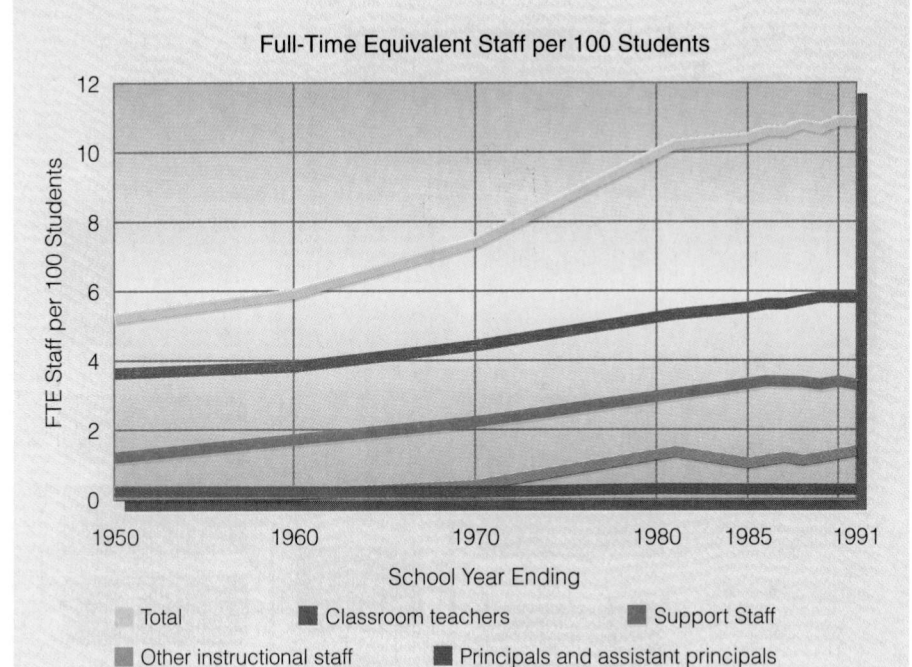

FIGURE 8.3

Full-Time Equivalent Staff per 100 Students

Note: Plotted points in each chart include school years ending: 1950, 1960, 1970, 1981, 1985–1991.

(*Source:* U.S. Department of Education, National Center for Education Statistics, *Statistics of State School Systems.* Common Core of Data, and unpublished estimates. *Digest of Educational Statistics, 1992,* tables 78 and 3.)

teachers per 100 students has increased from 3.6 to 5.8. Today, there are more employees in school districts than there were forty years ago, and there are many more staff in comparison to the number of teachers. Yet, the teacher/student ratio has changed in favor of more teachers per the number of students.

Organization of Education at the State Level

Objective 4:
Describe the major roles, functions, and legal relationships of public education at the state level.

Activity 8.5:
Find out the names of the state superintendent and state board members. Discuss their educational backgrounds. Have students discuss the pros and cons of having an elected versus an appointed state school board.

In certain countries, such as Taiwan, the national constitution specifies responsibility for education, but the U.S. Constitution does not specifically provide for public education. However, the Tenth Amendment has been interpreted as granting this power to the states. As a consequence, the states are the governmental units in the United States charged with the responsibility for education. Local school districts then receive their empowerment through state law to administer and operate the school system for the local communities. State legislatures, within the limits expressed by the federal constitution and by state constitutions, are the chief policymakers for education. State legislatures grant powers to state boards of education, state departments of education, chief state school officers, and local boards of education. These groups have only the powers granted to them by the legislature, implied powers from the specific grant of power, and the necessary powers to carry out the statutory purposes. The responsibilities and duties of intermediate units are also prescribed by the state legislatures. Figure 8.4 shows a typical state organization for education.

Stability, continuity, and leadership for education can come from the state board. However, as identified in Figure 8.4, many others are increasingly likely to

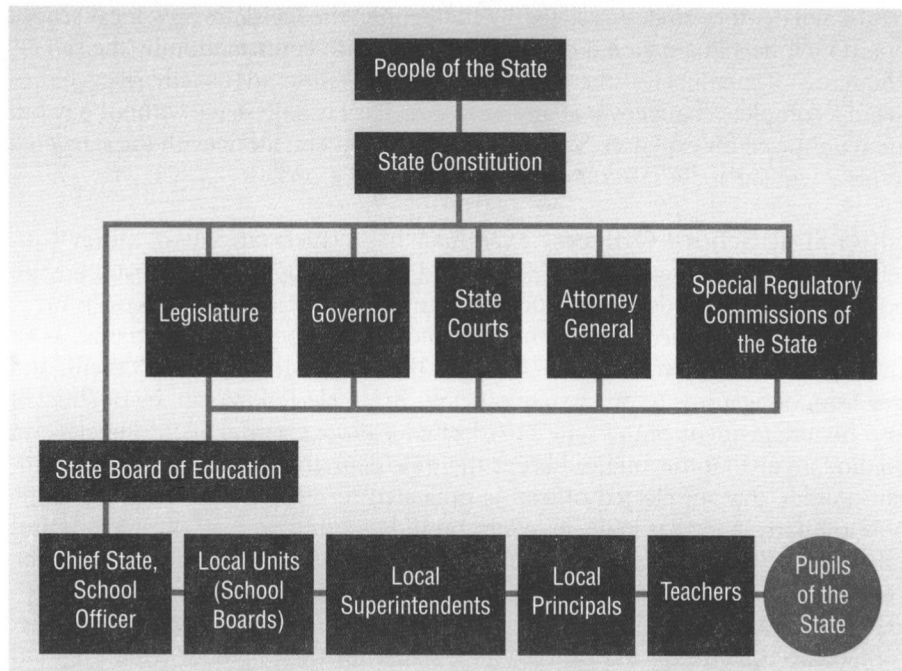

FIGURE 8.4

Typical Structure of a State School System

engage in education issues. For example, many legislators have established records of heavy influence on the direction of education. Through their initiatives new laws are established related to any and all parts of the education system. There are "education governors" as well. A number of our state leaders have been very involved in supporting and attempting to shape education in their states. Suffice it to say, there is a large number of participants, agencies, and ways to influence the shape and direction of the American education system.

State Boards of Education. State boards of education are both regulatory and advisory. Some regulatory functions are the establishment of standards for issuing and revoking teaching licenses, the establishment of standards for approving and accrediting schools, and the development and enforcement of a uniform system for gathering and reporting educational data. The advisory function includes considering the educational needs of the state, both long- and short-range, and recommending to the governor and the legislature ways of meeting these needs. State school boards, in studying school problems and in suggesting and analyzing proposals, can be invaluable to the legislature, especially since the legislature is under pressure to decide so many issues. A state board can provide a continuity in an educational program that ordinary legislative procedures don't allow for. A state board can also coordinate, supplement, and even replace study commissions appointed by a legislature for advising on educational matters. These commissions frequently include groups studying textbooks, finance, certification, school district reorganization, school building standards, and teachers' education.

State Board Membership. Members of state boards of education get their positions in various ways. Usually, they are appointed by the governor, with confirmation by the senate; they may be elected by the people, the legislature, or local school board members in a regional convention—also with confirmation by the senate. The terms of members of the state boards of education are usually staggered to avoid a complete changeover at any one time. They usually serve without pay but are reimbursed for expenses. The policy of nonpayment, along with the staggered terms, is considered a safeguard against political patronage.

Chief State School Officers. Every state has a chief state school officer. Currently, nineteen of these officers are elected by the people, twenty-seven are appointed by state boards of education, and four are appointed by the governor.

Arguments advanced for electing the chief state school officer hold that, as an elected official, the person will be close to the people, responsible to them, and free from obligations to other state officials. As an elected person, he or she will also be independent of the state board of education. Opponents of the election method argue that this method keeps the state department of education in partisan politics, that an elected official is obligated to other members of the same political party, and that many excellent candidates prefer not to engage in political contests. Those who advocate that the chief state school officer should be appointed by a state board of education claim that policymaking should be separated from policy execution, that educational leadership should not rest on the competence of one elected official, and that, with this method, recruiting and retaining qualified career workers in education would be enhanced.

Opponents of appointment by a state board of education claim mainly that the chief school officer would then not be responsible to the people. The principal objection to gubernatorial appointment is the inherent danger of the appointee's involvement in partisan politics. Another perspective on this issue is that an elected state school officer is legally an "official" of the state, whereas an officer appointed by a state board of education is generally an "employee," not a legal official.

State Departments of Education. The state government carries on its activities in education through the state department of education, which is directed by the chief state school officer. These activities have been classified in five categories: operational, regulatory, service, developmental, and public support and cooperation activities.[1] Operational activities are those in which the state department directly administers schools and services, such as schools for the blind. Regulatory activities include making sure that teacher license standards are met, that school buses are safe, and that curricular requirements are fulfilled. Service activities include advising and consulting, disseminating research, and preparing materials (on state financial aid, for example). Developmental activities are directed to improving the department itself and include planning, staffing, and research into better performance for the operational and regulatory, as well as service functions. Public support and cooperation activities involve public relations, political activities with the legislature and governor, and relations with various other governmental and nongovernmental agencies.

The Federal Government's Role in Education

Under the Tenth Amendment to the U.S. Constitution, education is a function of the states. In effect, states have the primary responsibility for education, although the schools are operated by local governmental units commonly called school districts. Although the states have the primary responsibility for education and the schools are operated at the local level, the federal government has an ever-increasing involvement in education. In the 1960s and 1970s the rationale for this interest and involvement was linked to national security and solving social problems. In the early 1990s the rationale was based on economic competitiveness. The result has been the establishment of federal agencies, programs, and laws that address various aspects of the American education system.

Leadership. The federal government has historically provided leadership in education in specific situations, usually in times of need or crises that could not be fully addressed by the leadership in states or local school districts. In the 1980s, the time was right for a more active leadership role for the federal government, such as establishing national priorities in education and raising issues such as those addressed in *A Nation at Risk*, the report prepared by the National Commission on Excellence in Education, published in 1983.

That report was not a mandate, nor was funding recommended, but it did provide recommendations to be considered by states and local school districts. The identifying of national educational issues and the encouraging of forums on these issues at the state and local levels, along with soliciting responses, are appropriate federal activities. Such activities could be made regular, rather than sporadic. Other activities include research on significant national educational issues and dissemination of exemplary practices.

The federal government also has included the Department of Education, which directly operated some education programs, funded special projects, and provided financial aid to states and local school districts.

The U.S. Department of Education. In October 1979, then President Carter signed legislation creating a cabinet-level federal agency, the Department of Education. The Department of Education took on the functions of the U.S. Office of Education, which was created in 1953 as a unit within the Department of Health, Education, and Welfare. The first-ever unit of education in the federal government, established in 1867 through the diligent efforts of Henry Barnard, was also called the Department of Education. Later, it was called the Office of Education (1869); at another time it was the Bureau of Education within the Department of the Interior. In 1939 the Office of Education became a part of the Federal Security Agency, which in 1953 became the Department of Health, Education, and Welfare, wherein the U.S. Office of Education was assigned until the new department was created in 1979.

The latest version of the Department of Education, in contrast with the first Department of Education (1867), has the potential for becoming a powerful agency. The original 1867 Department had the following stated purpose:

> To collect such statistics and facts as shall show the condition and progress of education in the several States and Territories, and to diffuse such information respecting the organization and management of schools and school systems, and methods of teaching as shall aid the people of the United States in the establishment and maintenance of efficient school systems, and otherwise promote the cause of education throughout the country.

There is no question that offering aid and awarding grants are effective ways to influence the goals of education nationally. However, there is continuing debate

Information Note 8.5:
The U.S. Department of Education is composed of a number of offices or agencies, including the Office of Educational Research and Improvement, which funds the national R&D centers, research on teaching, and a planned national education library. Special education training, research, and development is housed in the Department of Education under its own assistant secretary.

The federal government provides funding for many aspects of education, and houses organizations such as Very Special Arts, which provides programs in creative writing, and the visual and performing arts for individuals with physical and mental disabilities.

about whether the offices of the federal government should have a stronger or weaker influence on education. Some maintain that the socioeconomic forces of society are not contained within local school districts or state boundaries, and therefore direct federal intervention is needed. Others advocate dissolution of the Department.

It was within this political-educational context that the new Department of Education was created. Those who favored creating a new department felt that education was too important to be lost in the gigantic Department of Health, Education, and Welfare. Opponents took the position that a national Department of Education would result in more federal control and standardization.

In the short life of the U.S. Department of Education the influencing of education has continued to be primarily based on the use of grants and aid. However, the first several Secretaries of Education have been strong spokespersons for particular education agendas. For example, former Secretaries Bennett and Alexander were strong advocates for choice and voucher plans. The Secretaries of Education and their staffs also set funding priorities within the constraints laid down by Congress. As described next, there is a wide array of federal programs and involvement in education both within the Department of Education and within other federal agencies.

Activity 8.6:
Ask students to name the Secretary of the U.S. Department of Education. Have them list the pros and cons of having education represented at the Cabinet level in the federal government. Explore the symbolic meanings of having or not having a U.S. Department of Education versus having education housed in a bureau.

Educational Programs Operated by the Federal Government.   The federal government directly operates some school programs. For example, the public school system of the District of Columbia depends on Congress for funds. The department of the Interior has the educational responsibility for children of National Park employees, for Samoa (classified as an outlying possession), and for the trust territories of the Pacific, such as the Caroline and Marshall Islands. Many of the schools on Native American reservations are financed and managed through the Bureau of Indian Affairs of the Department of the Interior. Twenty-five of these schools have become what are called contract schools, in which the tribe determines the program and staff, but the Bureau of Indian Affairs supports the schools financially. The Department of Defense is responsible for the Military Academy at West Point, the Naval Academy at Annapolis, the Coast Guard Academy at New London, and the Air Force Academy at Colorado Springs. The Department of Defense also operates a school system for the children of the military staff wherever members are stationed. The instruction supplied in the vocational and technical training programs of the military services has made a big contribution to the education of our nation as well.

Discussion Question 1:
Some education experts are advocating a shift in thinking from "top-down" and "bottom-up" to a *horizontal* perspective. What are some possible implications of making this shift?

Categorical Aid. Another strategy for federal involvement in education is categorical financial aid. These funds are granted to be used for a specific purpose, such as compensatory education for the disadvantaged, bilingual education, education for the handicapped, and vocational education. Categorical aid is accompanied by strict rules and regulations to ensure that the aid is used for the purposes intended by Congress. The intended uses of these funds evolve from year to year as Congress and society perceive new needs.

Other Types of Education Agencies

The description of the American education system laid out so far has been in a straight line. We have described how education is organized from "bottom to top," (or is it top to bottom?). Obviously the whole system is not this simple. There are a number of related agencies and organizations that are important as well. Some of them that will play a more direct role in your work as a teacher are highlighted here.

Intermediate Units. The **intermediate unit** of school organization, which may consist of one or more counties, functions between the state department of education and the local school districts. These units have different names in different states. For example, in a number of states, such as New York and Colorado, they are called BOCES (Boards of Cooperative Educational Services); in Texas, they are called Regional Service Centers; and in California, County Education Offices.

A fundamental purpose of the intermediate unit of today is to provide two or more local districts with educational services that they cannot efficiently or economically provide individually; cooperative provisions for special education and vocational-technical education have been very successful. Other services that intermediate units can provide include audiovisual libraries, centralized purchasing, in-service training for teachers and principals, as well as other school workers, health services, instructional materials, laboratories, legal services, and special consultant services. The in-service dimension of the intermediate units has escalated in some states in the past few years, stimulated by educational reform.

Regional Educational Laboratories. The Regional Labs are a federal creation. In 1965, as part of the Elementary Secondary Education Act, authorization and funding to establish a new type of educational agency was initiated. The nation was divided into geographic regions, with each region consisting of three to seven states, and a new type of education agency was established to serve each of these regions. The purpose of these Regional Educational Laboratories is to link education personnel in schools, school districts, and state agencies with the latest findings from research and development efforts. Each lab conducts its own education research and curriculum development efforts. It also consults with educators, conducts training sessions, and organizes regional conferences. A list of the names and locations of these regional laboratories is likely available through your instructor or at your library.

National R&D Centers. Another important resource for educators has been the National Educational Research and Development (R&D) Centers. These, too, were established under President Johnson's "Great Society" program, more specifically the Elementary Secondary Education Act of 1965. For the first time in the history of the United States there was a national commitment to ongoing support for conducting research in education. To address this goal, a set of multidiscipli-

Objective 6:
Name four types of education agencies that support the purposes of schools, but that have no authority over schools.

Key Term:
Intermediate unit

Activity 8.7:
Describe the activities of a regional lab, or a national research and development center in your area.

Information Note 8.6:
Intermediate units (such as BOCES) and regional laboratories are useful sources for curriculum materials, media, education publications, and workshops for teachers and administrators.

Journal Activity Master 8.2: An Analysis of School-Based Management. An activity to analyze how decisions are impacted by school-based management techniques as well as the pros and cons of school-based management.

nary research and development centers were established. Each of these R&D centers is based at a major university and receives multi-year funding. Names and locations of the current set of national R&D centers are also likely available through your instructor or your library.

Foundations. The preceding list of agencies and involvements in education is based on public funds (tax dollars). There are also private funds that support a large number of activities in our public schools, including an impressive array of foundations. Foundations are not hamstrung by government regulations, so they are more able to support experimentation and test novel educational activities. Some are large and widely known, such as the Kellogg Foundation. Others are smaller or target their funding to particular states or particular topics. For example, the Hogg Foundation in Texas invests mainly in that state and primarily supports issues related to mental health. A new and very promising foundation in the Midwest is the Ewing Marion Kauffman Foundation in Kansas City. One of their novel projects is called Project Choice, in which eighth graders and their parents sign a contract that the student will graduate from high school on time and drug free. If the student completes the contract, the Kauffman Foundation will support the student in going to college.

Alternatives to Regular Public Schools

Currently, in many localities, parents, teachers, administrators, and children can choose from a number of alternatives to the regular school arrangement. Many of these options are being installed within public school districts, while the alternative of private schools has existed all along. Some of these options bring the opportunity for increased parent and student involvement in school decision making. All represent, in some way, a break with the traditional public school and classroom structures. The following are examples of some of the alternatives that are increasingly available.

Objective 7: Name and describe at least four alternative organizational arrangements for public schools.

Activity 8.8: Bring to class newspaper or news magazine articles about one or more of the alternatives to public schools that is operating in your area. Describe what is happening locally with one or more of these alternatives.

Information Note 8.7: One of the ironies of SBDM is that in many instances it is being mandated from the "top." For example, the state of Hawaii mandated SBDM; and in Illinois, the legislature mandated SBDM for the Chicago Public Schools. In one of the early sites, Dade County, Florida, two-thirds of the teachers in a school had to vote in favor of SBDM before the school could begin implementing it.

Site-Based Decision Making (SBDM). School-based management (SBM) or site-based decision making (SBDM) emerged in the School Restructuring movement of the 1980s. It permits individual schools within a district to be more involved in decisions related to the educational operations of that school—for example, budgeting, personnel, and curriculum. The increase in decision-making authority may be granted by the school board or the state. An example of the latter would be the Kentucky Reform Education Act, which includes a mandate for SBDM in all public schools in the state.

The concept came about in part through educational reform recommendations for greater participation of teachers in governance at the local school level. Parents' demands to have more say in the education of their children were also a factor in promoting school-based management. Two objectives of school-based management are to reduce school district regulatory control of individual schools and to empower teachers with the opportunity to participate in making decisions for their schools.

School-based management is based on two fundamental beliefs: Those who are most affected by decisions ought to play a significant role in making those decisions, and educational reform efforts will be most effective and long-lasting when carried out by people who feel a sense of ownership and responsibility

QUESTION: *Some people are concerned about the decision-making powers that reside at the federal, state, and local school boards as opposed to at the school level. In general, do you think the amount of decision-making power the local schools have is about right, too much, or too little?*

	SCHOOL LOCATION					
	Total	Inner City	Urban	Suburban	Small Town	Rural
Base	1000	123	105	258	308	205

	PERCENT					
About Right	38	30	24	39	40	45
Too Much	5	3	3	5	8	3
Too Little	57	66	71	55	52	51
Not Sure	*	*	*	*	*	*

*Less than 0.5%

FIGURE 8.5

Appropriateness of School-Based Decision-Making Authority

(*Source: The Metropolitan Life Survey of the American Teacher, 1993.* Teachers Respond to President Clinton's Education Proposals. New York: Louis Harris and Associates, Inc., 13.)

for the process. As you can see in the results of a national survey presented in Figure 8.5, these beliefs are consistent with what teachers think. More than half of all teachers surveyed and two-thirds of the inner city teachers believe that they have too little say in decision making.

What Are the Obstacles to SBDM? There are a number of obstacles in implementing school-based management. It is not a panacea for solving all of a school's or a school district's problems, and it might inspire excessively high expectations. There might be efforts by administrators and teachers to reduce administrative personnel, whereby the effectiveness of school-based management could be jeopardized. Changes in collective bargaining agreements might be necessary. Questions about educational equity might arise. Under school-based management, not all schools will have the same programs. Is that an inequity? State mandates may increase curriculum uniformity and, in so doing, stifle the educational programs developed through school-based committees. It is also possible under school-based management that teachers, principals, and other staff members might be skeptical or outright critical.[2]

Magnet Schools. Many school districts are being pressured by citizens and ordered by the courts to equalize the proportions of different racial groups in each school. One response, especially by large urban school districts such as Houston and Kansas City, has been to develop special academic programs and custom-designed facilities that will attract all students; hence, the name "magnet" schools. There are elementary, middle, and high school magnets. The program might emphasize the performing and visual arts, or math and science, or the liberal arts. Whatever the theme, the faculty, curriculum, and all students in that school are there because of their interest in the school's theme.

Discussion Question 2:
Do you think that school-based management will be effective in improving education at the elementary and secondary levels? Why or why not?

Journal/Portfolio Development 1:
Locate and interview educators involved in site-based school management.

Charter Schools. A new approach to providing communities with alternative schools that are supported by public funds is charter schools. A number of states, including California, Colorado, and Minnesota, have authorized the establishment of charter schools. The specifics are different in each state, but the basic design is that a local group of teachers (in California and Minnesota) or community members (in Colorado) develop a plan for the school that includes curriculum, staffing, and instructional expectations. This "charter" then must be accepted by the local school board and the state board of education. Charter schools function as independent public schools that students choose to attend. One of the strengths of this approach is that it is a way to be freed from many state and district regulations.

CNN Clip 24:
Year-Round School

Year-Round Schools. The normal school year of nine to ten months with the full summer off is often criticized. One concern is that students will forget too much over the summer. Critics point out that the current school year was put into place over a hundred years ago when most people lived on farms and the children were counted on to perform summer chores. One interesting solution is the year-round school. This is not an extended school year in that students attend school for more days. Rather, year-round schools spread the time in school across twelve months. One way this is done is to have multiple tracks of six to eight weeks. During any one cycle, one-fourth to one-third of the students will be on vacation and the others will be attending classes. This way, students have more frequent and shorter times away from school. An additional advantage is that the school site can handle more students on an annual basis. Year-round schools are on a steady increase. In the 1992–1993 school year, 301 public school districts in 26 states and 29 private schools had year-round programs.[3]

Activity 8.9:
Ask students to visit a private, parochial, or independent school in their area. Have them clarify how the staff is hired and the school is organized. Is the school part of a larger system?

Private, Parochial, and Independent Schools. Alternative structures of schools exist outside the public school system too. These range from elite secondary schools, mainly in the Northeast, to dynamic alternative schools for high school dropouts, to church-supported schools, to schools that are operated for profit.

Independent Schools. Private education, which preceded public education in the United States, continues to be available as an alternative to the public schools. Private schools are increasingly being referred to as independent schools. One source of information is the Council for American Private Education (CAPE), which is a coalition of fourteen private-school organizations. Another is the National Association of Independent Schools (NAIS). The following quotations, which describe independent schools and compare them to public schools, are taken from an NAIS publication.[4]

Key Term:
Independent schools

An **independent school** is a nonprofit institution governed by a board of trustees that depends almost entirely on private funds—tuition, gifts, grants—for its financial support. Most independent schools are accredited by their regional accrediting group and state departments of education. All must meet state and local health and safety standards as well as the mandatory school attendance laws. Unlike public schools, independent schools are not involved in or part of large, formal systems. They do, however, share many informal contracts among themselves and with public schools. The vast majority offer programs that prepare students for college.

Independent schools vary greatly in purpose, organization, and size, and they serve students from all racial, religious, economic, and cultural backgrounds. Some are progressive and innovative, some are conservative and traditional. They are both large and small, day and boarding, single-sex and coeducational. Independent schools have been an integral part of our nation's educational resources since colonial times.

Since each school is free to determine and practice its own philosophy of education, spirit and environment vary from school to school, even though they may display similar organizational structures and educational programs. This diversity among schools is one of their most distinctive characteristics.

Governance of Independent Schools. Each independent school is incorporated as a nonprofit, tax-exempt corporation and governed by a board of trustees that selects its own members, determines the school's philosophy, selects the chief administrative officer, and bears ultimate responsibility for the school's resources and finances. The chief administrator responsible for the day-to-day operation of the school may be called the headmaster, headmistress, president, or principal. The head's duties are comparable to those of a public school superintendent.

Issues Related to Organization and Structure

So far this description of how the American education system is organized and works has been free of discussion of issues, problems, conflicts, and ambiguities. Well, all you have to do is pick up a newspaper or watch the television news and you will be quickly confronted with one or more of the debates about what education *should* be doing or *should not* be doing. The following is a short list of topics and issues that we are grappling with in the 1990s.

Objective 8:
Analyze contemporary issues that are related to the organization and structure of schools.

Local Control. An important and unique feature of American education is local control; however, its value has been challenged recently. Some critics argue that the mobility of our population and the interdependence of social elements have undermined the traditional concept that local people should have a strong role in determining the directions of education. Some also argue that our national survival requires policies and programs laid down under centralized control by states and the federal government.

Local Control Is Challenged Each Time a Decision by a Local Board or a Local School District Is Taken to the Courts. As is discussed in Chapter 9 many court decisions dealing with the relationship between religion and the public school or with desegregation have been in response to local control. Currently, in most states, courts are ruling that local control, combined with the traditional system of financing education, has resulted in inequality of educational opportunity rather than equality.

Centralization Is the Alternative to Local Control. We have come full circle; education in large cities is already centralized, and many of these large districts are trying to solve some of their problems by decentralization. Frequently, a centralized authority does not respond well to citizens' needs and demands. Ex officio boards and councils for local community or neighborhood schools, which advise officials on large city or county boards, represent efforts to keep some form of local control in the large centralized systems.

Local school board meetings are often the main opportunity community members have to express their opinions about their children's education.

Activity 8.10:
Have students conduct a debate between local control proponents and centralization proponents.

Discussion Question 3:
How has local control of education eroded? Why has it eroded?

Activity 8.11:
Does a superintendent have to be politically savvy? If so, how?

The operational control of education today is still primarily local, carried out under the powers delegated by the states. However, federal and state involvement—both direct, through court decisions and mandates, and indirect, through federal and state aid—has been steadily increasing. How the local, state, and federal governments are related in their control is complicated and must be resolved. New and intricate relations keep forming.

Politics in Education. So far in this chapter we have provided information about the formal structures of public education at the local, state, and federal levels. Although these organizational structures illustrate the line and staff relationships, there is another set of relationships that is important to consider and understand. Each of these levels is involved in politics—the politics of education. For example, local school districts are likely to be interested in federal educational programs and grants, so they will contact members of Congress to express their opinions. The purpose is to influence their representatives' understanding of local needs and how they act on them. That is politics, partisan and nonpartisan. (Partisan politics is associated with political parties.) The same activities take place at the state level. Local school districts and professional associations follow closely what is happening in their state legislature. There is little hesitation to let members in the legislature know their opinions and urge action. It is not unusual for local school superintendents and board members to lobby their senators and representatives in person. These contacts with federal and state agencies are representative of political action. There are a number of other types of education politics that you need to be aware of as well.

Election Politics Are Becoming Increasingly Volatile. One common example of politics in elections is found in school board elections. The individuals who are on the school board can make a major difference in what you can and cannot do as a teacher. This is especially true with the concerted efforts of the Religious Right to increase their voice in school matters. They are very skilled at orchestrating campaigns to elect school board members who are favorably disposed to their interests, which include demanding curriculum changes, challenging sex education programs, pushing for prayer in the classroom, and purging reading lists in libraries. Their political strategies are good examples of what politics are about. They are well organized and use state-of-the-art combinations of fund raising, mass communication, and old-fashioned door-to-door campaigning. Since there tends not to be very much interest in school board elections, a relatively small number of people (say the membership of one or two churches) voting as a block can swing an election. The definition of what is fair in politics is not always clear. For example, the Religious Right has been criticized for running "stealth" candidates. In other words, the candidates do not

Community members may at times feel the need to air their feelings about education in a larger forum than a local school board meeting.

say explicitly what they believe and what they plan do to if elected. Still, they are using the democratic process to influence policy and practice.

Politics at the School District Level. The people who are likely to be involved in politics at the local level include board members, superintendents, and community members. Politics begins for prospective board members when they decide to run for the school board. As President John F. Kennedy said, "The first thing you need to be is elected."

A recent survey indicated that the top five motives for seeking board membership were:

- To exercise your civic duty (66 percent),
- To increase academic standards (53.4 percent),
- To improve your own child's education (40.3 percent),
- To make local schools more accountable (39.7 percent), and
- To make the schools more fiscally sound (31.7 percent).[5]

A sixth motive was to revise the curriculum. Only about 7 percent of those who sought board membership represented a special-interest group.

The motives expressed in the survey of those seeking board membership appear to be honorable. The encouragement to run for the school board by friends and neighbors, current school board members, and family members seems innocuous. In elections, however, depending on the circumstances and issues, bitterness and resentment in the school district can occur. The healing, when and if it happens, is likely to be resolved by political procedures.

School Board Politics. Board members are expected to be accountable to their public constituency. However, some board members feel that they should be accountable to the entire community, while others feel that they should be accountable only to a specific segment of the community. The two positions are not compatible and may bring about strife among board members and within the community. Political activity is the likely result.

Most school districts have at-large elections for board members. At-large elections allow the entire electorate to vote for each candidate or each board member who is running for reelection.

> When the entire electorate votes there is less chance that a minority candidate will win a seat than if voters from specific areas within the district choose their own board members. A recent survey found more minorities among appointed board members than among those who were elected.[6]

This is an issue that will continue to fester and will probably be resolved politically.

There are other political issues that board members and the public might view as more emotional and more difficult to deal with. Among them might be firing a superintendent, having a strike, closing schools, opening a school-based clinic that provides sexual advice and contraceptives to teenagers, raising taxes, reducing staff and educational opportunity, busing students, admitting a child with AIDS, desegregating schools, and having consistently losing athletic teams. Such issues are divisive and can result in political havoc until resolved.

The Superintendent and Board Politics. The superintendent is the chief executive officer of the school district. The superintendent's formal power comes from the

Information Note 8.8:
Education politics at the local level also include teacher and principal unions, the personal relationships and agenda of the leaders, and the degree of trust and respect. In some settings, there can be widespread support for experimentation and innovation. For example, in Douglas County, Colorado, the board, administration, and union agreed to support the creation and implementation of an entirely new position in each school, the Building Resource Teacher (BRT). The BRT role is a full-time position for a master teacher to provide instructional leadership and staff development within the school.

PROFESSIONAL DILEMMA

What Is the Appropriate Role for Teachers When the Politics Get Rough?

In the 1980s and 1990s teachers and school administrators have been asked to make serious efforts to change the way schools operate. In the 1980s policymakers, business leaders, and citizens at large demanded that schools "reform" and "restructure." In the late 1990s schools are engaging in "systemic reform." Yet, making major changes in the structure and operations of schools is difficult to accomplish. It is hard for teachers to give up or change what they have been doing. It takes a great deal of time to work through the process that is necessary to develop a consensus among teachers, administrators, and parents about how a

school should be restructured and what it should become. It also takes several years to work out the bugs when trying something new.

As a teacher, what would you do if, after you had spent three years in discussions and then two years in implementing a major restructuring of your school, a newly elected majority on the school board demanded that you return to the old way?

This is not a hypothetical question. After more than three years of broad-based discussions involving teachers, administrators, students, parents, and community members, the Littleton, Colorado, School Board approved alternative graduation requirements for Littleton High School. The new requirements were based on student accomplishments, instead of seat-time. Students would have to demonstrate that they had achieved the required outcomes. Littleton High School became nationally recognized for its efforts.

In November of the second year of implementation, three conservative members were elected to the

Diversity Note 8.1:
Minorities and females are severely underrepresented in school administration positions throughout the United States. Why?

board of education, but he or she also gains power through access to various sources of information. The control of information is power.

Generally, boards are considered to be policymakers, and superintendents implement the policies. Cooperative development of specific policies helps to establish the roles of both the board of education and the superintendent. However, specific education issues and others can bring about rigorous debate between the superintendent and the board and among board members. It is likely that the public will also wish to express its opinions.

The Superintendent and Staff Politics.   In addition to dealing with boards, the superintendent also works with a staff to carry on the education programs. Figure 8.1 illustrates a typical organization. The superintendent interacts directly with assistant superintendents and principals. Depending upon the school district policy, the superintendent may interact directly with the teachers' union representatives in collective bargaining. The superintendent may also be the negotiator for the school district in bargaining with the representatives of the noncertified employees, including secretaries and custodians. The more contacts the superintendent has, particularly if those contacts are controversial, the greater the potential for political activity among the staff—commonly referred to as "office politics." The staff has power in that it can also control information. The staff can initiate and spread vicious rumors, which will in time spread to the community. Enter dirty politics, full of intrigue and maneuvering. A school district involved in such political activities will suffer until the issues are resolved, which may involve dismissing personnel.

Discussion Question 4:
How can teachers affect the operations of the local school district?

The Positive Side of Politics.   Note that politics and political activities need not be negative: They can be positive and have positive results. For example, effective politicians can bring about compromises that are better solutions to issues than

five-member school board. A major theme in their election campaign was attacking the new graduation requirements, which they promised to remove. In January the new majority on the school board proceeded to implement its campaign promise. Although students from the school, parents, and school staff asked that the board not do this, or that it would at least allow the new graduation requirements to be optional, the board voted three-to-two to return to the traditional requirements. Remember that there were now students in their second year of high school who had been told that they must meet the new graduation requirements.

The school board did not stop there. In the same month, January, the superintendent, who was viewed as a very able educator and was well known and respected nationally, was terminated. By the end of the school year a number of school principals and teachers had taken positions elsewhere, and the district was running advertisements nationally for principals and teachers who held "traditional" educational values.

This may be an extreme case in some ways, but it has happened in more than one school district. And it will happen in one form or another again. If you were a teacher in Littleton High School, what would you do? Of course, it would make a difference depending on which side of the issue you were on. Either way, what would you do? Your colleagues, the school, your students, and the innovative program have been challenged. It is clear that there is the potential for casualties, including your job.

- Would you speak out, or wait for others to do so?
- What would you tell your students?
- Would you help your principal, or leave him or her on his or her own?
- How do you think you will feel the next time you are asked to invest four or five years in designing and implementing a change in your school?

any of the many singular proposals put forward. Politics are a necessary ingredient for a democracy, and a necessary ingredient for public education as well.

School-Based Management: Local Councils and Political Actions. Two issues that are likely to generate political action are the roles of the local school councils and their relationship and interaction with principals. If the members of the council are honest and sincere and, after serious debate, are willing to compromise, positive political action will have taken place. However, if some members of the council come with a special interest—such as firing the principal—political infighting is likely to happen within the council, particularly if the members are deeply entrenched and are not open to modification in their positions. Such political infighting is bound to spread into the community and thus escalate the controversy. Again, the possible solution is likely to result from political action.

The Financing of Education

A basic goal of public education in the United States is to provide an adequate education that is equally available to everyone. To achieve that goal, government must design a system of taxation that is equitable for taxpayers. The United States has not yet met the goal for public education nor achieved equitable taxation, although progress has been made.

Money to support education comes from a variety of taxes paid to local, state, and federal governments. These governments in turn distribute tax money to local school districts to operate the schools. The three principal kinds of taxes that provide revenue for schools are property taxes, sales or use taxes, and income taxes. The property tax is generally a local tax, while the sales tax generally is a state and local mix, and the income tax is collected at the state and federal levels.

Transparency 44:
Source of Revenue for School Funding

Objective 9:
Develop a general understanding of the current approaches and issues in the financing of public education.

Test Questions 8.34–8.60

Focus Question 5:
How are schools paid for?

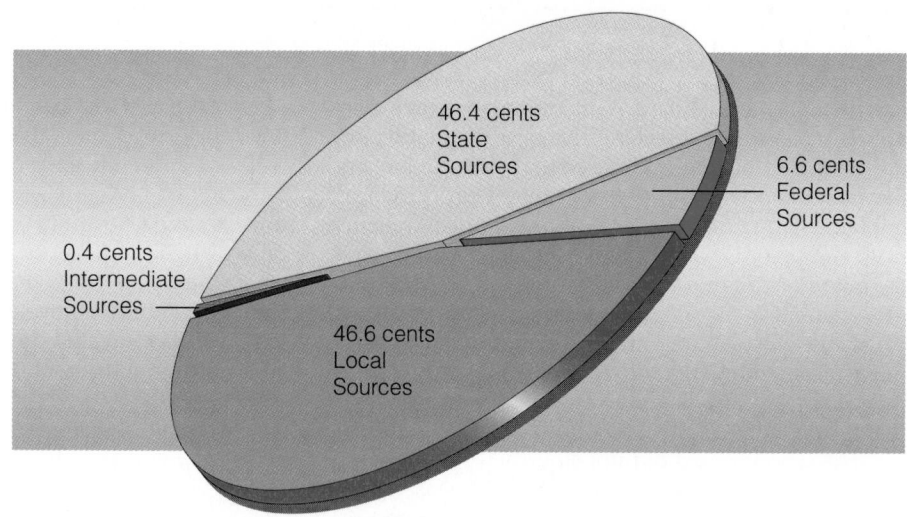

FIGURE 8.6

The Public Education Dollar: Revenues from Various Sources: School Year 1991–1992

(*Source:* National Center for Education Statistics, Common Core of Data, "National Public Education Financial Survey—Fiscal Year 1992")

Figure 8.6 portrays the percentages of education revenues received nationwide from federal, state, and local sources. As you can see, public education is primarily funded by local and state sources of revenue. Table 8.2 presents similar data for selected states. An emerging trend is indicated here: private sources of revenue. In response to budget limitations and cutbacks, schools are turning to citizens and local agencies for gifts to support special programs and services. Many school districts are establishing foundations to collect and manage these funds.

This chapter now turns to an analysis of the financing of public education through a closer look at the different sources of funding and related issues of equality of educational opportunity and taxpayer equity. It also addresses other issues related to funding for schools, including taxpayer revolts, reform in education financing, accountability, and international comparisons.

Property Taxes and Local Revenue

Objective 10:
Describe the role of property taxes in the financing of public education and issues related to their use.

Focus Question 6:
Property taxes have been the major source of revenue for schools. What is wrong with this?

Key Term:
Property tax

The **property tax** has been the primary source of local revenue for schools. It is based on the value of property, both real estate and personal. Real estate includes land holdings and buildings such as homes, commercial buildings, and factories. Personal property consists of automobiles, machinery, furniture, livestock, and intangibles, such as stocks and bonds. The property tax has both advantages and limitations.

Property Taxes: Advantages and Limitations.   The main advantage of the property tax is its stability. Although it lags behind other changes in market values, it provides a steady, regular income for the taxing agency. Also, property is fixed; that is, it is not easily moved to escape taxation, as income might be.

Limitations of Property Tax.   The property tax has numerous limitations. It bears heavily on housing: It tends to discourage rehabilitation and upkeep, since both of these would tend to raise the value of the property and therefore its taxes. It is often a deciding factor in locating a business or industry. And it is likely not to be applied equally on all properties.

TABLE 8.2   Receipts of Public Elementary and Secondary Schools by Source and by State for Selected States, Including the District of Columbia

| State | Percent of Receipts | | | |
	Local and Intermediate	State	Federal	Private
District of Columbia	91.2	—	8.6	0.3
New Hampshire	86.8	7.8	2.8	2.5
Oregon	65.6	25.4	6.1	2.9
Michigan	65.2	26.8	5.8	2.3
Nebraska	55.1	31.0	5.9	8.0
Wyoming	43.8	47.8	5.3	3.1
Illinois	59.0	31.7	6.6	2.6
U.S. Average	44.1	47.3	6.2	2.5
Florida	39.3	50.1	6.6	4.1
Minnesota	36.9	55.3	4.2	3.6
California	25.6	66.0	7.2	1.2
Mississippi	25.4	54.2	16.6	3.8
Alabama	20.6	60.1	11.1	8.2
Alaska	18.3	68.5	11.3	1.9
Washington	19.0	72.1	5.7	3.2
New Mexico	12.5	72.7	12.2	2.5
Hawaii	0.5	89.9	7.8	1.8

Source: Digest of Educational Statistics, 1993. Washington, DC: National Center for Educational Statistics, 152.

Determining the Value of Property. One difficulty with the property tax lies in determining the value of property. In some areas, assessors are local people, usually elected, with no special training in evaluating property. Their duty involves inspecting their neighbors' properties and placing values on them. In other areas, sophisticated techniques involving expertly trained personnel are used for property appraisal. In either circumstance, assessors are likely to be subject to political and informal pressures to keep values low in order to keep tax rates low.

The assessed value of property is usually only a percentage of its market value. This percentage varies from county to county and from state to state. Attempts are made within states to equalize assessments or to make certain that the same percentage of full cash value is used in assessing property throughout the state. In recent years, attempts have been made to institute full cash value for the assessed value. For the property tax to be a fair tax, equalized assessment is a necessity.

Assessed Valuations: Quality of Education. Limited tax rates for **current expenses** and limitations on indebtedness point out further the significance of assessed valuation as a factor in determining the quality of an educational program. A local school district can be making the maximum effort, taxing to the limit, and

Activity 8.12:
Have students study, in detail, a real estate tax bill. Ask students to identify examples of regressive taxes.

Key Term:
Current expenses

still not be able to offer a program comparable to what a wealthier neighboring district offers under a medium effort. The effort made by a local school district indicates the value that the citizens place on education; yet equal effort does not produce equal revenue, equal expenditures per pupil, or equal opportunity.

Expenditures per Pupil: A Wide Variance. Expenditures per pupil vary widely, partly because districts are not equally wealthy. States also differ in wealth and correspondingly in expenditures per pupil. The current average annual expenditure per pupil in the United States is $5,029. Alaska, Connecticut, New Jersey, and New York, along with the District of Columbia, all spend over $7,000 per pupil; while Alabama, Mississippi, Idaho, Tennessee, and Utah all spend less than $3,500 per pupil.[7]

Property assessment practices and formulas differ from state to state; hence, one cannot use assessed valuation per pupil as a measure in comparing the wealth of states. More accurate indices are household income and poverty rates. Eight states have household incomes greater than $35,000—Alaska, California, Connecticut, Hawaii, Maryland, Massachusetts, New Hampshire, and New Jersey. Ten states have more than 16 percent of their population below the poverty level—Alabama, Arkansas, District of Columbia, Kentucky, Louisiana, Mississippi, Montana, Oklahoma, Texas, and West Virginia.[8] In general, higher household income results in higher expenditures per pupil.

Property Tax: Proportionate and Regressive. Property tax is most generally thought of as a proportionate tax—that is, one that taxes according to ability to pay; the more wealth one has in property, the more one pays. Since assessments may be unequal and since frequently the greatest wealth is no longer related to real estate, the property tax can be regressive. **Regressive taxes,** like sales and use taxes, are those that affect low-income groups disproportionately. There is some evidence to support the contention that persons in the lowest-income groups pay a much higher proportion of their income in property taxes than persons in the highest-income groups.

Inequities of the Property Tax: What the Courts Have Said. Significant support for schools across the nation has been provided by the property tax. However, as has been described in the last several pages, because of this heavy dependence on property taxes for financing, enormous discrepancies in resources and quality have built up between schools located in rich and poor communities.

To illustrate the school finance consequences of differences in local wealth, let's look at a simple example. A school district having an assessed valuation of $30 million and a responsibility for educating 1,000 pupils would have $30,000 of assessed valuation per pupil. Since property taxes are applied to assessed valuations, a district with a high assessed valuation per pupil is in a better position to provide quality education than is one with a low assessed valuation per pupil. If school district A has an assessed valuation of $90 million and 1,000 pupils, for example, and school district B has an assessed valuation of $30 million and 1,000 pupils, a tax rate of $2 per $100 of assessed valuation would produce $1.8 million for education in district A and only $600,000 in district B. School district A could therefore spend $1,800 per pupil, compared with $600 per pupil in school district B, with the same local tax effort.

Can the Property Tax Continue to Be the Primary Base for Financing Schools (the Federal Perspective)? This question was asked of the U.S. Supreme Court in *San Antonio (Texas) Independent School District* v. *Rodriguez* (1979). Keep in mind that the U.S. Constitution does not mention education, so any litigation has to be based on indirect connections. In *Rodriguez* the challenge was initiated under the equal protection clause of the Four-teenth Amendment. This clause prohibits state action that would deny citizens equal protec-tion. The U.S. Supreme Court, in a five-to-four decision, reversed the lower court in *San Antonio Independent School District* v. *Rodriguez* and thus reaffirmed the local property tax as a basis for school financing. Justice Potter Stewart, voting with the majority, admitted that "the method of financing public schools . . . can be fairly described as chaotic and unjust." He did not, though, find it uncon-stitutional. The majority opinion, written by Justice Lewis F. Powell, Jr., stated: "We cannot say that such disparities are the product of a system that is so irrational as to be invi-diously discriminatory." The opinion also noted that the poor are not necessarily con-centrated in the poorest districts, that states must initiate fundamental reform in taxation and education, and that the extent to which quality of education varies with expenditures is inconclusive. Justice Thurgood Marshall, in the dissenting opinion, charged that the rul-ing "is a retreat from our historic commit-ment to equality of education opportunity."

Using the Property Tax to Finance Schools (the State Perspective). Equal protection challeng-es have been, or are currently being made at the state level. In some states the plaintiffs have emphasized a claim of equal protection; in others the focus has been on specific lan-guage in the education clause. In all cases the challenge is whether the state has fulfilled its constitutional obligation to provide for edu-cation. The answer by the state supreme courts in some states has been that education is not a fundamental right, and as long as there is provision for a minimally adequate education the equal protection clause is met. In *Serrano* v. *Priest* the California Supreme Court was called on to determine whether the California public school financing system, with its substantial de-pendence on local property taxes, violated the Fourteenth Amendment. In a six-to-one decision in 1971 the court held that heavy reliance on unequal local

---

Relevant Research

State Spending Is Related to Student Achievement

There is continuing discussion and debate about whether spending more money on schools results in greater out-comes with students. As with other topics, the answer one gets depends on the variables considered. The amount of money spent per student can be identified in reports from the National Center for Educational Statistics. However, does a dollar buy the same in New Jersey ($8,645 per pupil) as it does in Alabama ($3,627 per pupil)? Picking the student outcome variable is even more difficult. The measure must be standardized, the student sample must be representative, and the data must be available for all states.

One student outcome measure that has been used fre-quently is Scholastic Aptitude Test (SAT) scores. But as Wainer (1993) has pointed out, there are a number of problems in using SAT scores to compare across states. For example, the proportion of students in each state that take the SAT varies greatly. A more representative estimate of student performance would be results from the National Assessment of Educational Progress (NAEP). This measure is given to a representative sample of students in each state. When a comparison is made of the ranking of state per-pupil expenditure to student NAEP scores by state, the results indicate that increased spending is associated with higher student achievement. "We find that for every thou-sand dollars spent, a state's NAEP ranking improves by two places." (p. 24) In other words, using comparable measures, it has been shown that student achievement increases when the per-pupil expenditure increases.

Source: Howard Wainer, "Does Spending Money on Education Help? A Reaction to the Heritage Foundation and the *Wall Street Journal.*" *Educational Researcher* (December, 1993): 22–23.

property taxes "makes the quality of a child's education a function of the wealth of his parents and neighbors." Furthermore, the court declared: "Districts with small tax bases simply cannot levy taxes at a rate sufficient to produce the revenue that more affluent districts produce with a minimum effort." Officially, the California Supreme Court ruled that the system of school financing in California was unconstitutional but did not forbid the use of property taxes as long as the system of finance was neutral in the distribution of resources. Within a year of *Serrano* v. *Priest* (1971), five other courts—in Minnesota, Texas, New Jersey, Wyoming, and Arizona—ruled similarly.

Recent Challenges to School Finance within the States. The number of court cases related to school finance has increased in recent years. Some states have had new suits initiated, while others are continuing to struggle to respond to earlier court decisions and directives. In 1989 and 1990 several significant state supreme court decisions about school finance were made. In a number of states the education finance systems were knocked down by the courts, and the state legislatures were directed to remedy the wrongs.

In Montana, in *Helena Elementary School District v. State* (1989), the Montana Supreme Court ruled that the state's school finance system violated the state constitution's guarantee of equal educational opportunity. The state's constitution article mandates that the state establish an educational system that will develop the full educational potential of each person. In 1990 the court delayed the effects of its decision in order that the legislature could enact a new finance system.[9]

The Kentucky Supreme Court ruled that the entire system of school governance and finance violated the state constitution's mandate for the provision of an efficient system of common schools throughout the state (*Rose* v. *The Council for Better Education Inc.*, 1989). An excerpt from the Kentucky Supreme Court's opinion stated that "The system of common schools must be adequately funded to achieve its goals. The system of common schools must be substantially uniform throughout the state. Each child, *every child*, in this commonwealth must be provided with an equal opportunity to have an adequate education. Equality is the key word here. The children of the poor and the children of the rich, the children who live in poor districts and the children who live in the rich districts must be given the same opportunity and access to an adequate education. This obligation cannot be shifted to local counties and local school districts." The court directed the state legislature to develop a new educational system, which was adopted as the Kentucky Education Reform Act (KERA) in 1990.

It is clear that throughout the 1990s, there will continue to be suits, court actions, and legislative initiatives regarding how to best address funding inequities for public schools. Further, earlier court decisions can be revisited. For example, in a turnaround of earlier decisions, in 1994 the State Supreme Court of Arizona ruled that the state's property-tax-based school financing system was unconstitutional because it creates wide disparities between rich and poor school districts. As has been true in other states, the court is leaving it up to the legislature to rectify the problem.

Undoubtedly, changes are occurring in the state provisions for financial support for education. Equal expenditures per pupil might not, because of other factors, assure equal opportunity, but equal expenditures per pupil do, in fact, enhance the likelihood of equal opportunity.

A System of Taxation and Support for Schools

We should look at each type of tax as a part of a system. Each individual kind of tax has advantages and disadvantages, yet it is unlikely that any one of these taxes used by itself for education will be the answer. In evaluating a system of taxes, one should consider the varying ability of citizens to pay, the economic effects of the taxes on the taxpayer, the benefits that various taxpayers receive, the total yield of the tax, the economy of collection, the degree of acceptance, the convenience of paying, the problems of tax evasion, the stability of the tax, and the general adaptability of the system. It is apparent that systems of taxation are complicated; each is an intricately interdependent network.

Taxation exists to produce revenue. The allocation of revenue is complex; however, the education theme applied to allocation is equality of educational opportunity. State equalization programs were designed to accomplish this objective, and they have had limited success. Many have suggested that the logical solution to the inequities that exist in the ability of states to support education is a massive shift to federal aid.

State Sources of Revenue and Aid.   On the average in the United States, the states provide about 50 percent of the fiscal resources for local schools. This money is referred to as state aid, and within most states all of the money or a portion of this money is used to help achieve equality of opportunity.

The main sources of tax revenue for states have been classified by the Department of Commerce in four groups: sales and gross receipts, income taxes, licenses, and miscellaneous. Sales and gross receipt taxes include taxes on general sales, motor fuels, alcohol, insurance, and amusements; income taxes include both individual and corporate; licenses include those on motor vehicles, corporations, occupations, vehicle operators, hunting, and fishing. The largest miscellaneous classification includes property taxes, severance or extraction of minerals taxes, and death and gift taxes. The two largest sources of state revenues are sales and income taxes.

Sales and Income Taxes.   Sales and income taxes are lucrative sources of state revenue, and it is relatively easy to administer both. The sales tax is collected bit by bit, in a relatively painless way, by the vendor, who is responsible for keeping records. The state income tax can be withheld from wages; hence, collection is eased. Income taxes are referred to as **progressive taxes,** since they frequently are scaled to the ability of the taxpayer to pay. Sales taxes are regressive, since they affect low-income groups disproportionately. All people pay the sales tax at the same rate, so people in low-income groups pay as much tax as people in high-income groups. Part of the regression of the sales taxes and income taxes is direct and certain; they fluctuate with the economy, and they can be regulated by the legislature that must raise the money.

Gaming: A New Source of Revenue.   In 1964 New Hampshire implemented a lottery. By 1994 thirty-one states were operating lotteries. Legalized gambling in its many forms, from casinos and riverboats to horse racing, has become the newest source of state and local revenues. Gambling is an indirect source of revenue in the sense that it is not seen as a direct tax on citizens; instead, the revenues come through taxes on the games. In 1993 gamblers bet a record $394.3 billion. In

Objective 11:
Describe elements of a total system for financing public education.

Activity 8.14:
Have students identify all the sources of state funding for schools: lottery money, sales and income tax, foundation programs, and so on.

Transparency 45:
Advantages and Disadvantages of Three Major Sources of Revenue for Education

Information Note 8.10:
Gamblers bet a record $394.3 billion in 1993. 75 percent ($297.3 billion) was spent on casino table games and slot machines, 8 percent ($30.9 billion) on lotteries, and 7.4 percent ($29 billion) in Indian reservation clubs.

The link between lottery proceeds and education is not always well known to the general public.

eleven states part or all of the net proceeds from the lottery is allocated to education. In some states, such as California, the original intent was that these funds would be used for educational enhancements. However, within three years of its implementation, in a tight budget year, the California legislature had incorporated the lottery funds into the base education budget.

A recent study of the Florida lottery found the same thing. In the 1989–1990 school year the level of state funding for education decreased and approximately 56.8 percent of the lottery proceeds were used as a substitute for existing resources. The findings from the study also indicated that there was equity in the distribution of the funds. Clearly lotteries and other games represent a new source of funds.[10] It also is clear that without careful wording in the original statutes and continuous monitoring, these funds will become another revenue stream for the ongoing budget, rather than being set aside for educational enhancements.

Discussion Question 5:
What are some of the likely implications of using lotteries and limited stakes gambling to fund schools?

State Aid. State aid for education exists largely for three reasons: The state has the primary responsibility for educating its citizens, the financial ability of local school districts to support education varies widely, and personal wealth is now less related to real property than it once was. State aid can be classified as having general or categorical use. *General aid* can be used by the recipient school district as it desires; *categorical aid* is earmarked for specific purposes. Categorical aid may include, for example, money for transportation, vocational education, driver education, and programs for handicapped children. Frequently, categorical aid is given to encourage specified education programs; in some states these aid programs are referred to as incentive programs. Categorical aid funds may be granted on a matching basis; thus for each dollar of local effort, the state contributes a specified amount. Categorical aid has undoubtedly encouraged development of needed educational programs.

Diversity Note 8.2:
There is great debate over the fairness and effectiveness of aid to improve the education of minority children.

General State Aid: Equality of Opportunity. Historically, general aid was based on the idea that each child, regardless of place of residence or wealth of the local district, should be entitled to receive a basic education. General state aid was established on the principle of equality of opportunity and is usually administered through a foundation program. A *foundation program* involves determining the dollar value of the basic education opportunities desired in a state, referred to as the foundation level, and determining a minimum standard of local effort, considering local wealth. The foundation concept implies equity for taxpayers as well as equality of opportunity for students.

Foundation Programs: The Way They Work. Figure 8.7 represents graphically how a foundation program operates. The total length of each bar represents the foundation level of education required per pupil, expressed in dollars. Each school dis-

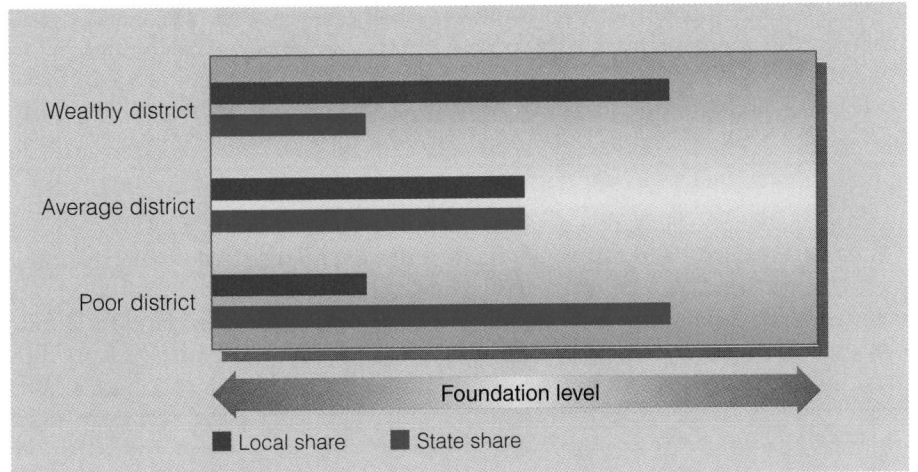

FIGURE 8.7

Equalization and the
Foundation Principle

trict must put forth the same minimum local effort to finance its schools; this effort could be a qualifying tax rate that produces the local share of the foundation level. This tax rate will produce more revenue in a wealthy district than it will in a poor district; therefore the poor district will receive more state aid than the wealthy district. Local school districts do not receive general state aid beyond that amount established as the foundation but are permitted in most instances to exceed foundation levels at their own expense.

State Foundation Programs: Limited Effectiveness. The effectiveness of the use of various state foundation programs to achieve fiscal equalization has been limited. A major limitation is that the foundation established is frequently far below the actual expenditure or far below the level needed to provide adequate educational opportunity. For example, if a state established a per-pupil foundation level of $1,500 and the average per-pupil expenditure was $3,000, equalization would not have occurred.

A second limitation is that most general state aid programs do not provide for the different expenditure levels for different pupil needs. Special education and vocational education, for example, both require more money to operate than the usual per-pupil expenditure for the typical elementary or secondary school pupil.

It is possible to replace the property tax with combinations of other sources of revenue for schools. One closely watched initiative took place in Michigan beginning in the summer of 1993 when the legislature abolished the use of property taxes as the major source of school financing without naming an alternative. Educators, the public at large, the Governor, and legislators entered into intensive discussions about the pros and cons of financing education with a new combination of taxes. In March, 1994, a statewide election was called, with one question on the ballot. Nearly 70 percent of the voters approved increasing the sales tax from 4 percent to 6 percent to finance schools. Other sources of revenue will be used as well, but the role of property taxes is greatly diminished. The new Michigan plan also includes movement toward the gradual equalizing of per-pupil expenditures, and sets a minimum $4,200 per pupil.

Discussion Question 6:
What are the advantages of using the sales and income taxes to fund elementary and secondary education instead of relying on the property tax?

Information Note 8.11:
Private fund raising groups are increasingly important to local schools as a source of funding and support for special projects. For example, the Public Education Foundation surveyed Chattanooga, Tennessee teachers about what they needed "to achieve the greatest degree of effectiveness and satisfaction." The PEF then supported teachers in developing skill training programs and in-service sessions.

In summary, the property tax is the largest local revenue source, and sales and income taxes are the largest state revenue sources. State taxes may be utilized to equalize opportunity resulting from unequal local tax bases. The need for local, state, and federal funds to support education through various kinds of taxation necessitates a tax system.

Federal Aid.   The United States has a history of federal aid to education, but it has been categorical and not general aid; it has been related to the needs of the nation at the time. Federal aid actually started before the U.S. Constitution was adopted, with the Northwest Ordinance of 1785, which provided land for public schools in "western territories." Such federal aid has continued in a steady progression to the present. Almost two hundred federal aid-to-education laws have been passed since the Northwest Ordinance. The Elementary and Secondary Education Act of 1965 has been discussed elsewhere in this book. Nevertheless, we note here one significant part of the Act: It was categorical, yet it came as close to general aid to education as federal aid ever has, and it therefore established a precedent for ways that federal aid can be used.

Educational Improvement and Consolidation Act (EICA).   Federal funding in recent years continued to be categorical until the passage of the Education Improvement and Consolidation Act (EICA) in 1981. The act consolidated twenty-eight separate federally sponsored educational programs into one **block grant.** Left out of the Act were education for the handicapped; vocational, bilingual, and adult education; impact aid; ESEA Title IV civil rights programs; and the Women's Education Equity program. ESEA Title I programs for the disadvantaged were kept as the first title of the new consolidation act, now called Chapter I. Title II of the Act consolidated the aforementioned twenty-eight programs, providing greater discretion for state and local educational agencies. The trend toward block grants is an early indication of possible transformation of the federal role in education.[11]

Federal Aid: The Controversy.   Although it is seemingly historically established, federal aid is still controversial. Advocates of federal aid point out that it is a logical answer to the need for providing equality of educational opportunity for all children regardless of wealth or residence. They point out that federal aid to education helps the national defense and general welfare, ultimately, and that these national concerns cannot be adequately pursued at the local or state level. Proponents of federal aid to education hold also that this help does not necessarily mean federal controls, citing the land grant acts and the National Defense Education Act of 1958 as federal aid that was not accompanied by control. They feel that federal aid, through the income tax, is the most equitable way of paying for public education, and for providing equal educational opportunity.

Opponents of federal aid point out that education is a state and a local function. They argue that variations in fiscal ability to pay will always exist and that the distribution of federal funds will not guarantee that whatever differences now exist will be reduced appreciably. They point out that the nation is weakened by its dependency on the federal government for funds, that categorical aid is federal control, and that states can use the income tax as effectively as the federal government.

School Finance Issues in the Late 1990s

The basic issue in school financing is not likely to be different in the late 1990s from what it has been in the past. That issue is making an adequate education equally available to everyone, along with a system of taxation designed to be equitable—that is, a system in which taxpayers are all called on to support education in proportion to their ability to pay, a progressive tax plan. Both equal opportunity and equitable taxation are difficult to achieve, as was illustrated earlier in this chapter. Some trends of the early 1990s have continued into the late 1990s. These trends include increasing enrollments, taxpayer revolt, inflation, financing educational reform, and accountability, which are likely to affect the adequacy of school funding and therefore further complicate the basic issue in school finance—providing an adequate education with equality of opportunity through an equitable system of taxation.

Objective 12:
Describe at least three critical issues facing the financing of public education.

Information Note 8.13:
54.7 percent to 63.1 percent of school budgets goes to direct services to children. Most of the remaining money is spent on functions such as building maintenance, heating, bus transportation, and administration.

Discussion Question 7:
What are three trends that could seriously affect the adequacy of school funding? Why?

Increasing Enrollments. Enrollment in elementary and secondary schools grew rapidly during the 1950s and 1960s and reached its peak in 1971. From 1971 to 1983, total enrollment decreased rapidly, reflecting the decline in the school-age population over that period. Enrollment reached a low of 39.3 million in 1984. By 2002, enrollment is projected to reach 54 million, an increase of 7 million over ten years.[12]

Increased enrollments have effects on the amount of money needed to support education adequately. While the new surge of students will be somewhat gradual, it will undoubtedly increase expenditures, and increased revenue is very likely to be needed to maintain the current level of expenditures per pupil. Furthermore, according to one educator, "the rising public school enrollments will include larger numbers and percentages of minority, limited-English-proficient, poor, and learning disabled students. All these special categories of students will require extra services to meet their needs."[13] Whether additional revenues will be available to provide educational services to the growing student population remains speculative.

Taxpayer Revolt. A most dramatic instance of taxpayer revolt occurred in California in June 1978 with the passage of Proposition 13, which limited by constitutional amendment the property tax as a source of revenue. Subsequent and similar propositions have been added in other states. The trend is toward tax limitation, which will reduce funds available for education. These efforts, along with a low success rate of local school bond referenda and the closing of school districts for periods of time because of insufficient funds to operate, indicate problems for the funding of public schools.

Activity 8.15:
Ask students to list the reasons for a taxpayer revolt.

Funding Educational Reform: Questionable. With enrollments increasing and with inflation, though modest, continuing to be a factor—along with taxpayer revolt—significant increases in funding for educational reform in the 1990s appears to be unlikely.

Accountability. Accountability in education is holding schools responsible for what students learn. This is directly related to the financing of education. Schools

Key Term:
Accountability

CASE STUDY INNOVATIVE WAYS OF FUNDING PUBLIC SCHOOLS: WHAT IS APPROPRIATE?

Colorado Springs School District 11 has approved the placement of commercial advertising on its school buses. National fast food and soft drink company logos now appear on the sides of the buses. While the district has set guidelines for the advertising it will accept, questions abound about the appropriateness of public agencies becoming involved in commercial acts. Some advocate that these are symbols that businesses are interested in education. Clearly, these activities provide the schools with monies they would not have otherwise. On the other side one can ask about the potential for a conflict of interest between the business and the needs of schools as public education entities.

More radical strategies to solve the school funding problem are being tried as well. Districts are experimenting with having certain functions "privatized," which means that instead of the work being done by school district employees, it is contracted out to a private firm. Custodial work, security provision, and bus driving are three of the services that have been privatized in a number of school districts.

In a more extreme example, the day-to-day operations of several schools and school districts have been turned over to private corporations. These for-hire corporations have contracted to run schools for a profit! For example, in 1994 a business, Education Alternatives Inc., agreed to a five-year contract to oversee the running of thirty-two public schools and the education of 25,000 students in Hartford, Connecticut. The only profit for the company will be 50 percent of any money that it saves in running the schools, which is based on the district's regular $200 million budget.

A number of issues and questions about the organization and financing of schools emerge from these many different funding experiments. For example, if the school district cannot maintain its own buildings and sustain student success, what can a for-profit corporation do that will be different? The teaching staff will be the same, the buildings will be the same, and so will the students. If there are "profits" from the use of public dollars, should they be given to a private company? Can a private corporation be held accountable in the same way that we hold public schools accountable?

1. What are your views on these issues?
2. What changes do you believe should be made in school funding?

CNN Clip 16:
Corporate Public School

CNN Clip 17:
Privatizing Education

Activity 8.16:
Ask students to identify three ways that would improve accountability in the schools.

in the 1990s will continue to be called on to be accountable. Although there are many definitions of the term *accountability*, in education it means that schools must devise a way of relating the vast expenditure made for education to the educational results. For many years the quality of education was measured by the number of dollars spent or the processes of education used. In other words, a school system that had a relatively high cost per pupil or used educational techniques judged to be effective was considered an excellent system. Seldom was the effectiveness of school systems judged by student outcomes—the educational achievements of students. Now those outcomes and a clear record of the cost of them must be accounted for.

Roots of Accountability. Accountability has its roots in two fundamental modern problems. One is the continuous escalation of educational costs, and closely related is the loss of faith in educational results. The failure of the American educational system, particularly in the cities and in some remote rural areas, has been accurately documented. The expectations of citizens for their children have not been met. Although American public schools historically have done the best job of any nation in the world in providing education for *all the children of all the people,* they still have failed for some of their constituents. Educational accountability is necessary.

When the Elementary and Secondary Education Act of 1965 went into effect, the federal government issued its first formal call for accountability; it asked to receive documented results of educational attainment.

Becoming Accountable. How can school systems become accountable? First, they must specify goals. In other words, if one goal of an elementary school is "to have pupils learn to read," then this goal must be spelled out specifically for each grade or child, whichever makes better sense, and success in meeting the goal must be measured and reported. Only in this way can results be conveyed to the public. Some states are requiring a "school report card" to be submitted to the public annually. The report cards provide information about student achievement by subject, as measured by standardized tests, along with financial and other relevant data about the school district.

Expenses and Educational Results. The second aspect of accountability, that dealing with accounting for expenses related to educational results, is easier to achieve because of modern technology. Financial accounting systems that are designed specifically to record expenditures on each educational program can effectively reveal the costs of educational results. When costs are known, one must measure them against what has been accomplished in performance. Advanced computer technology has increased the sophistication of accountability reporting systems; thus better informed educational decisions are possible, and the way is cleared for regaining the public's confidence in the educational establishment.

Teachers: Importance for Accountability. Teachers play an important role in the quest for accountability. They are the primary contact with students, and they are responsible for instruction and student achievement. Thus they are expected to do their utmost to motivate students to learn and achieve. Accountability rests on data; therefore teachers need to keep accurate records with respect to achievement, particularly if standardized tests are not utilized.

Global Perspectives: International Comparisons in Spending for Schools.

There are continuing debates about the amount of investment the United States makes in public education and how well it compares with what other countries invest. International comparisons are difficult to make. Teacher salaries are different, the way budgets and educational functions are organized is different, and measuring student success is difficult. Yet the comparisons need to be made. As can be seen in Table 8.3 on page 220 the United States is much wealthier than other countries. The number of students per teacher is higher in

Journal Activity Master 8.3: An Analysis of School Accountability. This activity provides students with an opportunity to analyze the ways schools have been held accountable.

Information Note 8.14: The demand for accountability is leading some policymakers at the state and national levels to push for state standards, national goals, and possibly national exams. Right now the National Assessment of Educational Progress (NAEP) is the only national sampling of student performance that is representative.

Activity 8.17: Discuss the degree to which teachers can be held accountable for student achievement.

Transparency 47: Government Spending for Education Worldwide

TABLE 8.3   Gross Domestic Product per Capita, Educational Expenditures, and Student-Teacher Ratios, Excluding Higher Education, 15 Industrial Countries

	Gross Domestic Product per Capita		Education Expenditures per Capita		Expenditures per Pupil		Number of Students per Teacher	
	Dollars	Rank	Dollars	Rank	Dollars	Rank	Ratio	Rank
Australia	13,523	6	646	9	2,060	15	15.7	8
Austria	11,582	15	625	11	2,972	7	9.5	2
Belgium	11,755	14	613	12	2,492	9	10.5	4
Canada	17,355	2	1,153	1	4,054	21	6.2	10
Denmark	13,218	8	969	2	3,997	3	12.2	6
France	12,791	10	723	7	2,486	10	16.9	11
Italy	12,136	13	528	15	2,320	14	11.0	5
Japan	13,137	9	635	10	2,379	13	20.0	14
Netherlands	12,196	12	723	6	2,495	8	15.5	7
Norway	16,161	3	966	3	3,636	5	8.6	1
Sweden	14,052	5	911	4	4,279	1	10.3	3
Switzerland	15,570	4	715	8	3,733	4	NA	—
United Kingdom	12,529	11	604	13	2,474	11	15.7	8
United States	18,297	1	860	5	3,398	6	18.4	13
West Germany	13,296	7	536	14	2,450	12	18.3	12
Unweighted Avg.	13,840		747		3,015		14.15	

Note: Expenditure data are for preschool through high school but exclude capital outlay and debt service. NA = not available. Original data are from OECD and UNESCO reports for 1986 and 1987. Student-teacher ratios are adjusted for part-time vocational enrollment. Various other adjustments were made to enhance comparability of the original data.

Source: Adapted from Nelson (1991), pp. 32–34, Tables 4–6 by Levine, Daniel U. "Educational Spending: International Comparisons." *Theory Into Practice 33* (2), (Spring, 1994): 126–131.

Focus Question 8:
How well does the spending for public schools in the United States compare with what other developed countries spend?

the United States than for most other developed countries. How well is the United States doing in investing in education in comparison to other countries? Clearly we are at least average, and in many ways doing well. But your answer will depend on which data you use and how you interpret them.[14]

Summary and Implications

Teaching does not take place in a classroom that is an island, disconnected from the rest of the system. All parts are intertwined. What a teacher does in his or her classroom is affected by the rest of the school, the principal, the district, the state, and the federal government. Conversely, what you do in your classroom will affect the rest of the system. Contrary to the stereotype associated with the "self-contained" classroom, American education is a highly complex system.

You need to understand how schools and school districts are organized. To be effective, you will need to know the names of the key administrators and their areas of responsibility. In time you will need to know and be able to work with these key people. Also, keep in mind that very few decisions are made in isolation from district, state, and federal rules, regulations, and policies. Most aspects of schooling have been addressed at one time or another by the various levels in the organizational charts presented in this chapter.

Another point relates to the financing of education. The brief overview of issues related to taxation, aid programs, and developing a fair and equitable system for financing education should bring you to an appreciation of the highly complex and difficult challenge we have. There are no simple solutions that will be correct. Increasing sales taxes versus tax limitations, general aid versus categorical aid, and local versus state versus federal support are basic questions.

Discussion Questions

1. Some education experts are advocating a shift in thinking from "top-down" and "bottom-up" to a *horizontal* perspective. What are some possible implications of making this shift?
2. Do you think that school-based management will be effective in improving education at the elementary and secondary levels? Why or why not?
3. How has the local control of education eroded? Why has it eroded?
4. How can teachers affect the operations of the local school district?
5. What are the advantages of using the sales and income taxes to fund elementary and secondary education instead of relying on the property tax?
6. What are some of the likely implications of using lotteries and limited stakes gambling to fund schools?
7. What are three trends that could seriously affect the adequacy of school funding? Why?

Journal/Portfolio Development

1. In order to understand more about how site-based decision making systems work, interview a council member and, if possible, observe a site-council meeting. Questions to consider include: What are the areas where the council has decision-making authority? When is it advisory? Does it have budget-making authority? What role do teachers play on the council? What do you think are the strengths and issues in having site-based councils?
2. The Republican Contract with America advocated major cuts in federal support for education programs, including free and reduced lunches and student loans. Select one of the federal education programs that you are interested in. Collect information about the program, including the amount of money budgeted by Congress and how much money the typical school/classroom/child receives. Then compile notes about the debate for and against continuation of the program and its desired level of funding. Develop a summary and conclusion of where you stand on the need for the program and the size of its budget. A useful place to gain insight into the debate can be television programs such as the Sunday morning news interview shows, CNN, MacNeil/Lehrer, and CSPAN. Insert your notes in your folio under a topic heading such as "Federal government's role in education."

School-Based Experiences

1. Visit a school and develop an organization chart for the school. Place the names of people and their roles on the chart. For one or more persons in each role group (teacher, custodian, secretary) ask

them who their supervisor is. Also, ask them if there are other persons who monitor their work. The purpose here is to determine the line and staff relationships. It is quite likely that you will find that many people have a number of relationships.

2. Seek an opportunity to study a school budget. Determine the different sources of revenue (local, state, and grants). What are the biggest line items?

Which items does the principal have authority over? Are there some monies that are discretionary for teachers? Note that in most schools, especially high schools, there will be a surprising number of activities that generate cash. Inquire about the implications of having cash on hand, and ask how these amounts are secured and what the policies are in relation to their uses.

Notes

1. Roald F. Campbell, ed; Gerald E. Stroufe; and Donald H. Layton, *Strengthening State Departments of Education.* Chicago: University of Chicago Midwest Administration, 1967, 10.

2. American Association of School Administrators and the National Associations of Elementary and Secondary School Principals, *School-Based Management: A Strategy for Better Learning.* Arlington, VA: AASA, 15–17.

3. *Directory for the National Association for Year-Round Education.* P.O. Box 711386, San Diego, CA.

4. Bobette Reed and William L. Dandridge, *Minority Leaders for Independent Schools.* Boston: National Association of Independent Schools.

5. Beatrice H. Cameron; Kenneth E. Underwood; and Jim C. Fortune, "Politics and Power: How You're Selected and Elected to Lead This Nation's Schools." *The American School Board Journal* (January 1988).

6. Cameron, Underwood, and Fortune, "It's Ten Years Later, and You've Hardly Changed at All," 20.

7. *Statistic in Brief, April, 1994.* Washington, DC: National Center for Education Statistics, 7.

8. *Digest of Educational Statistics, 1993.* Washington, DC: National Center for Education Statistics, 28.

9. *Helena Elementary School District No.1* v. *State,* 769 P.2d 684 (Mont. 1989).

10. Steven Stark; Craig R. Wood; and David S. Honeyman, "The Florida Education Lottery: Its Use as a Substitute for Existing Funds and Its Effects on the Equity of School Funding." *Journal of Education Finance* 18 (Winter, 1993): 231–242.

11. Joel S. Berke and Mary T. Moore. "A Developmental View of the Current Federal Government Role in Elementary and Secondary Education," *Phi Delta Kappan* 63 (January 1982): 337.

12. William J. Hussar, *Projections of Education Statistics to 2003.* Washington, DC: National Center for Educational Statistics, 1.

13. Allan Odden, "Sources of Funding for Education Reform." *Phi Delta Kappan* 67 (January 1986): 340.

14. Daniel U. Levine, "Educational Spending: International Comparisons." *Theory Into Practice 33* (2) (Spring, 1994): 126–131.

Bibliography

Bakalis, Michael J. "Power and Purpose in American Education." *Phi Delta Kappan* 65 (September 1983): 7–13.

Burns, Leonard T., and Howes, Jeanne. "Handing Control to Local Schools: Site-Based Management Sweeps the Country." *The School Administrator* 45 (7) (August 1988): 8–10.

Campbell, Roald F. et al. *The Organization and Control of American Schools.* 6th ed. Columbus, OH: Merrill Pub. Co. 1990.

Elmore, Richard F. and Associates. *Restructuring Schools: The Next Generation of Educational Reform.* San Francisco: Jossey-Bass. 1990.

Gordon, James, Anthony, Ward and Patricia, eds. *Who Pays for Student Diversity?: Population Change and Educational Policy.* Newbury Park, CA: Corwin Press, 1992.

Kirst, Michael. "Sustaining the Momentum of State Educational Reform: The Link Between Assessment and Financial Support." *Phi Delta Kappan 67* (January 1986): 341–345.

Odden, Allan R., ed. *Rethinking School Finance: An Agenda for the 1990's.* San Francisco: Jossey-Bass, 1992.

Slavin, Robert E. "After the Victory: Making Funding Equity Make a Difference." *Theory Into Practice 33* (2) (Spring 1994): 98–102.

Swanson, Austin D., and King, Richard A. *School Finance: Its Economics and Politics.* New York: Longman, 1991.

Legal Aspects of Education

Focus Questions

1 What are the different sources of law, and how does the judicial process work?
2 What rights are ensured under the First and Fourteenth Amendments of the U.S. Constitution?
3 Under what conditions can religious activities take place in public schools?
4 What is the difference between *de jure* and *de facto* segregation?
5 What is affirmative about Affirmative Action?
6 Does the law require that handicapped children be placed in regular classrooms?

Key Terms and Concepts

Affirmative action: A plan by which personnel policies and hiring practices do not discriminate against women and members of minority groups.

Child benefit theory: A criterion used by the U.S. Supreme Court to determine whether services provided to public and nonpublic school students benefit children and not the school or religion. If they benefit only the children, the courts have ruled that the services may be funded by public funds.

Compulsory education: School attendance that is required by law on the theory that it is for the benefit of the state or commonwealth to educate all the people.

De facto segregation: The segregation of students resulting from circumstances such as housing patterns rather than from school policy or law.

De jure segregation: The segregation of students on the basis of law, school policy, or a practice designed to accomplish such separation.

Desegregation: The process of correcting past practices of racial or any other form of illegal segregation.

Discrimination: The determination that an individual or a group of individuals has been denied constitutional rights.

Integration: The process of mixing students of different races in school to overcome segregation.

Resegregation: A situation following desegregation in which segregation returns.

Reverse discrimination: A situation in which a majority or an individual of a majority is denied certain rights because of preferential treatment provided to a minority or an individual of a minority.

*T*his chapter deals with the legal basis for and control of education at the federal, state, and local levels. Attention is directed toward the different types and sources of law, and the organization of courts and the current interpretations of the Constitution, particularly as they relate to the separation of church and state, desegregation, affirmative action, and education for the handicapped. Each of these topics includes a discussion of relevant and important rulings of the U.S. Supreme Court.

Legal Aspects of Education

There is a caution that is important for you to keep in mind while reading this chapter and whenever you are thinking about legal issues. As was pointed out in the introduction to Part 3 of this text, there are different assumptions and different rules—different frameworks—for making decisions. In this chapter, as well as the next, the framework is a legal one. Do not try simply to apply some other framework to interpret the issues that are presented here and expect to necessarily come up with the same decision. For example, a "common sense" framework, or some form of "professional judgment" framework about what is best for students will not necessarily give you the same decisions that have come from legal reasoning. The legal framework really is based in the "letter and word" of the law. When the words are questioned the courts will decide on an interpretation. And that decision will be carefully and closely linked to decisions made in past cases. Educational philosophies and everyday "logic" are not the basis for the reasoning of courts, nor are abstract definitions of what is "right." The courts' legal logic is based on precedent, as well as the rules of procedure and evidence that have been handed down from court to court and decision to decision.

Test Questions 9.1–9.10

Objective 1:
Demonstrate an understanding of basic forms and structures of the American legal system.

Focus Question 1:
What are the different sources of law, and how does the judicial process work?

Information Note 9.1:
The legal system contains a number of structures and functions in addition to those that frame schooling. For example, there are criminal and civil proceedings, which could be engaged out of apparent violations of the aspects of law that are presented here.

Objective 2:
Describe five different sources of law.

Legal Forms and Structures

There are several sources of laws at the federal and state levels, and there are several processes for addressing disputes. Some, but not all, laws are developed out of the legislative process. These are referred to as *enabling*; they provide opportunity, or make it possible for educators to do certain things. Also, laws may impose mandates or prohibitions. Once the legislation is enacted into law, if a question of interpretation is raised, then the judicial process is engaged. The judicial process can be used also when there is the appearance that a law has been violated.

To help you understand the legal aspects of education we first briefly describe the different sources of laws and the basic structure of the judicial system. Then, when you read about an interpretation of the Tenth Amendment of the U.S. Constitution, or what a state supreme court decided in a certain case, you will hopefully have a background for understanding how the whole legal system works.

Sources of Law

There are several different forms of law in the United States. Some have authority over all citizens and parts of the country, while others only apply to a specific state, type of school, or type of student and program. Some have been constructed through the democratic process of legislation and others are simply announced by designated authorities. In all cases you as an educator need to be attentive to the implication of laws for determining what you can, cannot, and should do. Five different sources of law are presented here: (1) constitution, (2) legislation, (3) case law, (4) executive order and attorney general opinion, and (5) administrative agencies.

The United States Constitution laid the groundwork for the notion of equal access to education for all.

Constitution. The U.S. Constitution and each state's constitution provide the overarching framework within which all school operational decisions are made. All policies and practices must be within the boundaries and intents of the state and U.S. constitutions. The U.S. Constitution has authority over all state constitutions in those areas that it addresses either directly or indirectly. Constitutions can be added to or changed by constructing and having amendments approved. Interestingly, there is no mention of education in the U.S. Constitution. Since nothing is said, the interpretation has been that decisions about the provision of education are primarily a state responsibility. The key question then, is What does each state's constitution say about education?

Activity 9.1:
Bring to class copies of newspaper articles to illustrate the legislative activity of the Congress and state branches of government. Also bring examples of executive orders and rules and regulations (including some from your state's department of education).

Legislation. New laws or *statutes* are constructed through the legislative process. National laws are enacted by the U.S. Congress, and each state legislature enacts laws for that state. Other levels of government, such as county and city, enact laws that apply within their jurisdiction. In general, there is a nesting of authority with the higher level of state and ultimately the federal level being able to set the laws of the land.

In the case of education, since nothing was stated, there is no constitutional authority assigned directly to the U.S. government. In order to affect education from the federal level, statutes have to be written or court cases initiated. In recent decades the federal government has increasingly involved itself in education through authoring statutes that derive authority through the offering of money or the threat of taking it away. Congress also impacts education through its authority to regulate "interstate commerce." Through this power Congress can regulate even if the entity is not receiving federal funding. Lawsuits threatened and initiated at the federal level have been on the increase as well. A clear example of federal influence in this way can be seen in the efforts to desegregate/integrate schools.

Keep in mind that the legislative process in a democratic society entails committees, public comment, draft language, and compromise, so that the final wording of a statute may not be clear or necessarily consistent. The federal government is steadily increasing its rate of producing statutes that affect education.

Case Law. Court decisions offer another source of law. When a particular question is addressed by the judicial system and a decision is made, that decision becomes a part of the record, and some cases set precedents. Subsequently when similar situations arise, there is a tendency to refer back to the earlier decision and decide the current case in the same way; thus the name *case law.* Courts rely heavily on this form of the law in making decisions. As you will read later in this chapter, in the last several decades case law at the federal level has played a major role in shaping education. Keep in mind though that for many questions different "lower" courts can make different decisions; thus there may not be one decision that applies to the entire nation until the U.S. Supreme Court renders the final decision.

Executive Orders and Attorney General Opinions.   The President of the United States and state governors can issue executive orders that apply to education. These orders can have the effect of law until such time that they are withdrawn or changed by legislative or judicial action. Often the U.S. Attorney General or a state attorney general will be asked to offer an opinion about the likely legality of a statute or educational practice. This is an advisory opinion only and may or may not be what ultimately would be decided by the judicial system. However, these opinions do save time and can help to advise and clarify points that would likely be supported in a court review.

Administrative Agencies.   Another form of law is authored by the many federal and state agencies that receive their authority through constitutional and legislative law. These administrative agencies issue guidelines, rules, and regulations, which in most cases become the details for making statutes operational. All of these "rules and regs" must be consistent with the statute on which they are based. They also add up to many pages of fine print that educators need to understand. For example, when you sign your first teaching contract, that will be a legal agreement between the employing school district/agency and you. Read it carefully. There will be reference to the law and, more than likely, there will be references to the district employee handbook, or district personnel policies. As we will explain in Chapter 10, these administrative documents are legal statements too.

Judicial Systems and Process

Objective 3:
Describe the basic organization of the judicial system at the state and federal levels.

Activity 9.2:
Bring to class copies of newspaper articles reporting on court-related activities. It is not essential that the articles deal with schooling-related activity, but they should include local, state, and federal courts. Use them to illustrate the different parts of the judicial system.

When there are disputes about whether a particular educational practice or statute is legal, the courts are asked to make a determination of the facts, review related laws, and render a decision. The first role of the judicial system is *interpretive*; the courts review relevant parts of federal and state constitutions, statutes, and case law, and draw a conclusion about what was meant and what can or cannot be done. In some cases the court will respond by writing new law.

This judicial process usually begins with a suit and trial that is heard by a *trial court,* in other words, the court of original jurisdiction. The problem, practice, or point of dispute is presented along with related facts. Relevant parts of the constitution, statutes, and case law are presented to support each side of the case. Then the court renders, usually through a jury, a decision. This decision can be appealed to a "higher court." If one of the parties is dissatisfied, the decision can be appealed to an *appellate court,* where one or more judges will review the case. If it is appealed further, ultimately the Supreme Court makes the final ruling on the legality of the point being disputed.

In the United States there are two basic judicial systems: (1) the federal court system, and (2) the state court systems. In general there are clear differences in jurisdiction. However, sometimes there are overlaps and disagreements between the two systems.

Federal Court System.   Article III, Section I of the U.S. Constitution authorizes the Supreme Court and gives authority to Congress to create other federal courts. There are federal courts with special jurisdictions such as the Tax Court, Claims Court, and the Court of International Trade. General jurisdiction is covered by three levels—district courts (which are the trial courts), circuit courts of appeal, and the Supreme Court. Each state has at least one district court, and large states such as California and New York have four district courts. Decisions at this level are usually made by one judge.

At the federal appeals level, there are twelve regional circuit courts of appeal, and one other that has national jurisdiction to handle specific claims for areas such as copyrights and international trade. These courts have from three to fifteen judges. A federal appeals court decision only applies to the state from which the appeal came; this can be a source of confusion since different appeals courts may make different decisions in regard to similar disputes.

The highest court is the U.S. Supreme Court. There is no appeal beyond this court. The Supreme Court's decisions apply across the nation and can only be changed through Congress's amending federal statutes or by subsequent decisions of the Court. One of the reasons that the U.S. Supreme Court has such an impact on education is that the Court only has jurisdiction is cases in which a state or a public official is a party to the dispute. Since education is delivered by public schools, the U.S. Constitution and the federal courts have become a vehicle for various interests to address their concerns.

State Court Systems.   In structure the state court system parallels the federal system. The provisions in each state's constitution address the structure and authority for that state's judicial system. State courts can review whatever types of controversies that state's laws allow. In most states the highest court is the supreme court, although in a few states it is called the Court of Appeals. This court normally reviews the decisions of lower courts of appeal. At the next level down are appeals courts, and at the lowest level are the trial courts, usually referred to as district courts, circuit courts, or superior courts. There can be special jurisdiction courts too, such as juvenile, probate, and small claims courts. Normally, the state judicial system only addresses issues related to that state's constitution and that state's statutes, while the federal judicial system addresses issues of federal statute and the U.S. Constitution. Thus, a key decision at the beginning of a legal challenge is whether to use federal or state laws and courts.

Legal Provisions for Education

The educational systems of the United States, both public and nonpublic, are governed by law. The U.S. Constitution is the fundamental law for the nation, and state constitutions provide the basic law for each state. A state legislature has no right to change the Constitution. When state legislatures make laws that apply to education, these laws must be in accordance with both the U.S. Constitution and the applicable state constitutions. The enabling and legislative agents of education are illustrated in the top portion of Figure 9.1 on page 230. The lower portion of Figure 9.1 shows interpretive and administrative agents. Conflicts in this system of governance are not unusual. In such instances, state and federal court systems make legal interpretations that form a body of case, or common, law.

Test Questions 9.11–9.32

Objective 4:
Demonstrate a basic understanding of the elements and process of the legal system that impact schooling.

Transparency 50:
Sources of Legal Control as They Affect the Classroom

Information Note 9.2:
Philosophy, beliefs, and changes in the times contribute to the shaping of interpretations of the law. For example, during the period of 1980–1992, the Reagan and Bush administrations appointed many conservative justices to both the U.S. Supreme Court and the federal courts. A consequence may be that some court decisions of the last twenty to thirty years will be revisited through the review of new cases. When this happens, it is possible for earlier decisions to be modified, or even reversed.

Activity 9.3:
Using Figure 9.1, ask students to write down one to three examples of enabling legislation that affects schools. One example should be related to the U.S. Constitution. Then ask for one to three examples of interpretive actions by local, state, or federal officials or agencies. Use these examples to make clear the sources of legal control in American Education.

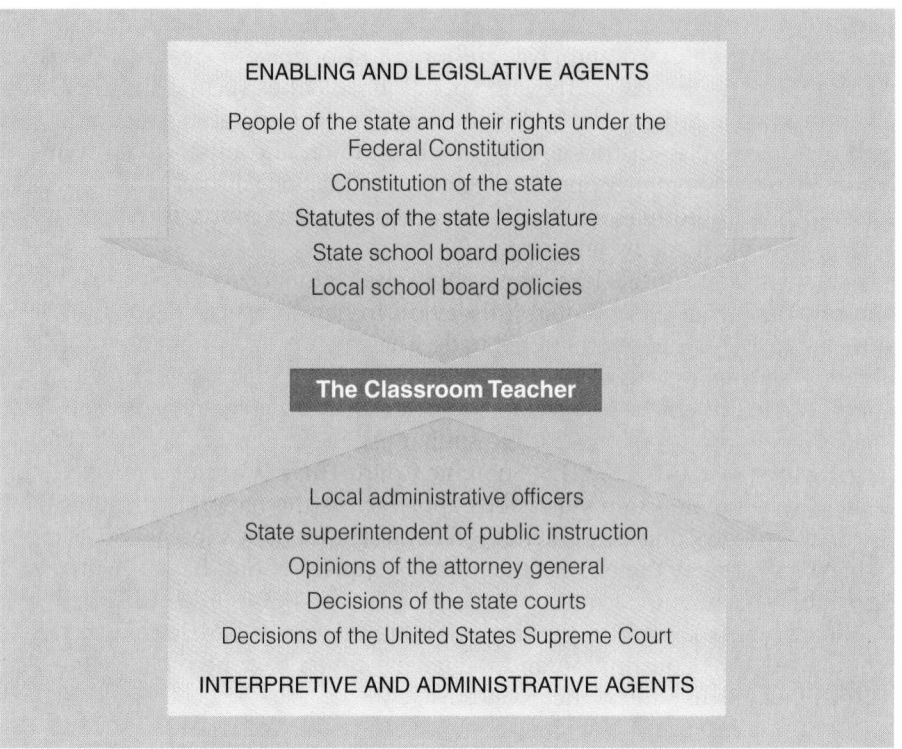

ENABLING AND LEGISLATIVE AGENTS

People of the state and their rights under the Federal Constitution

Constitution of the state

Statutes of the state legislature

State school board policies

Local school board policies

The Classroom Teacher

Local administrative officers

State superintendent of public instruction

Opinions of the attorney general

Decisions of the state courts

Decisions of the United States Supreme Court

INTERPRETIVE AND ADMINISTRATIVE AGENTS

FIGURE 9.1

Sources of Legal Control in American Education as They Affect the Classroom Teacher

U.S. Constitution

Objective 5:
Describe implications for education of three key amendments of the U.S. Constitution.

Focus Question 2:
What rights are ensured under the First and Fourteenth Amendments of the U.S. Constitution?

The rights assured to citizens of the United States by the U.S. Constitution are valid, practical, and enforceable in public schools as well. However, since much of the Bill of Rights only applies to public officials, the extent and conditions under which it applies to private schools has been a continuing source of debate and judicial interpretation. In general, when nonpublic schools accept public money, then they must abide by the requirements that accompany that acceptance. For example, they may not have discriminatory practices. However, accepting public monies does not necessarily mean that a nonpublic school has to comply with all aspects of the U.S. Constitution. The power of state government in educational matters was made quite clear by the U.S. Supreme Court as a part of its opinion in *Pierce* v. *Society of Sisters* (1925), discussed later in this chapter. The opinion stated:

Transparency 50:
Sources of Legal Control as They Affect the Classroom

> No question is raised concerning the power of the State reasonably to regulate all schools, to inspect, supervise, and examine them, their teachers, and pupils; to require that all children of proper age attend some school; that teachers shall be of good moral character and patriotic disposition; that certain studies plainly essential to good citizenship must be taught; and nothing be taught which is manifestly inimical to public welfare.

The following subsections explain how the Tenth, First, and Fourteenth Amendments of the U.S. Constitution relate to the governance of education, public and private, in the United States.

Tenth Amendment. The U.S. Constitution does not specifically provide for public education; however, the Tenth Amendment has been interpreted as granting this power to the states. The amendment specifies that "The powers not delegated to the United States by the Constitution, nor prohibited by it to the States, are reserved to the States respectively, or to the people." Therefore education is legally the responsibility and the function of each of the fifty states. Education in the United States is not nationalized as it is in many other nations of the world.

Each state, reflecting its responsibility for education in its state, has provided for education either in its constitution or its basic statutory law. For example, Section 1, Article X of the Illinois Constitution reads:

> A fundamental goal of the People of the State is the educational development of all persons to the limits of their capabilities.
>
> The State shall provide for an efficient system of high quality educational institutions and services. Education in public schools through the secondary level shall be free. There may be such other free education as the General Assembly provides by law.
>
> The State has the primary responsibility for financing the system of public education.

For example, the current Michigan Constitution states in Section 2, Article VIII:

> The Legislature shall maintain and support a system of free public elementary and secondary schools as defined by law. Each school district shall provide for the education of its pupils without discrimination as to religion, creed, race, color, or national origin.

The Utah Constitution, Section 1, Article X reads:

> The Legislature shall provide for the establishment and maintenance of a uniform system of public schools, which shall be open to all children of the State, and be free from sectarian control.

Through such statements the people of the various states commit themselves to a responsibility for education. The state legislatures are obliged to fulfill this commitment. While the interpretation of the Tenth Amendment places the responsibility for education on the states, the rights of citizens of the United States are protected by the Constitution and cannot be violated by any state.

First Amendment. The First Amendment ensures freedom of speech, of religion, and of the press, as well as the right to petition. It specifies:

> Congress shall make no law respecting an establishment of religion, or prohibiting the free exercise thereof; or abridging the freedom of speech, or of the press; or the right of the people peaceably to assemble, and to petition the Government for redress of grievances.

The application of the First Amendment to public education as considered in this chapter deals primarily with the establishment clause: "Congress shall make no law respecting an establishment of religion." In addition to ensuring other freedoms, the First Amendment ensures free practice of religion, which will be discussed in this chapter as well. The "free speech" clause of the First Amendment will be addressed more heavily in the next chapter, which focuses on teacher and student rights.

CASE STUDY   THE COPYRIGHT LAW APPLIES TO TEACHERS

*T*eachers constantly come across poems, charts, stories, photographs, and computer programs that they would like to use in their teaching. Most of the time, the material will have on it a copyright statement, or a circled ⓣ indicating that there is a registered trademark. Is it legal for a teacher to make one or more copies of this material? Legal research related to copyrights provides the answer.

Two primary sources establish the foundation quickly: The Copyright Act of 1976 and a 1991 federal court decision involving Kinko's Graphic Corporation and eight textbook publishers. The Copyright Act grants owners of copyrighted material the sole right to reproduce all or part of the work, to distribute copies, to prepare new versions based on the original work, and to perform and display the work publically. For a corporation, copyright protection lasts for seventy-five years from the date of first publication. For an individual it is the length of the author's life plus fifty years.

The court case between Kinko's and the eight textbook publishers reconfirmed the law; that is, reproduction of copyrighted materials requires that proper permissions be obtained and, if required, fees paid. The court decision also increased sensitivity to the fact that copyrights apply to multimedia, computer disks, and video and compact disk technologies.

What about a teacher who wants to make a single copy? As with many other legal questions, there are some areas where the answer is clear cut, and others where there is need for interpretation. In the Copyright Act, Congress made a provision for educators through what is called the "fair use" guideline. First of all, purchasing something that is copyrighted does not bring with it the right to make many copies. Nor does saying that it is for "educational use." However, a teacher can make a single copy of a brief part of a copyrighted work for teaching or research purposes. Multiple copies (not to exceed one per pupil) may be made for one course only if the copying meets the tests of *brevity* and *spontaneity*.

Examples of brevity would be a poem that is fewer than 250 words or an excerpt of prose that is fewer than 1,000 words or 10 percent of the work. Spontaneity means that there was inspiration and decision to use the work at a teachable moment that made it unreasonable to expect a timely reply to request for permission to copy. Another requirement in the clause is that each copy includes a notice of the copyright. Keep in mind, however, that the fair use clause is not an excuse to circumvent the Copyright Law.

Secondary sources of information about this law can be very useful to teachers. A good place to begin is with the retail copying service you use regularly. They will have guidelines for photocopying, and most stores will have standardized forms that you can use to obtain permission to make multiple copies. The larger copying services will have personnel to help you with obtaining permission, and in some cases may already have such permission on file.

In summary, the Copyright Law does apply to teachers. Teachers can make a single copy for teaching or research purposes, but in general the operating rule is, "no copying of copyrighted material without permission." The right thing to do is plan ahead and use the various services available to obtain permission. After all, one of the valued traditions in America is the creativity of its people. Their efforts should be recognized, and they are protected by law. What are your thoughts on this subject?

For information about copyrights and permissions related to textbooks contact, Association of American Publishers, Inc., 220 East 23rd St., New York, NY 10010–4685.

Fourteenth Amendment. The Fourteenth Amendment protects specified privileges of citizens. It reads in part:

> No state shall make or enforce any law which shall abridge the privileges or immunities of citizens of the United States; nor shall any State deprive any person of life, liberty, or property without due process of law; nor deny to any person within its jurisdiction the equal protection of the laws.

The application of the Fourteenth Amendment to public education as considered in this chapter deals primarily with the equal protection clause: "nor shall any State . . . deny to any person within its jurisdiction the equal protection of the laws." Equal educational opportunity is protected under the Fourteenth Amendment. In effect, the rights of citizens of the United States are ensured by the Constitution and cannot be violated by state laws or action.

State and Local Governance

State and local agencies play major roles in the governance of education. States have constitutions, with provisions for education as granted to them by the Tenth Amendment. State legislatures provide the laws that govern education within their respective states. Local school districts have boards of education whose major function is to develop policy for the local school district—policy that must be in harmony with both state and federal law.

State Legislatures. State legislatures are generally responsible for creating, operating, managing, and maintaining state school systems. The legislators are the state policymakers for education. State departments of education are created by legislatures to serve as professional advisors and to execute state policy. State legislatures, though powerful agencies, also operate under controls. The governors of many states can veto school legislation as they can other legislation; and the attorney general and the state judiciary system, when called on, will rule on the constitutionality of educational legislation.

State legislatures make decisions about how education is organized in the state; the certification standards and tenure rights of teachers; programs of study; standards of building construction for health and safety; financing of schools, including tax structure and distribution; and compulsory attendance laws.

State legislatures, in their legislative deliberations about the schools, are continually importuned by special-interest groups. These groups, realizing that the legislature is the focus of legal control of education, can exert considerable influence on individual legislators. Some of the representative influential groups are illustrated in Figure 9.2 on page 234.

It is not uncommon for over a thousand bills to be introduced each year in a state legislative session. Many of these bills originate with special-interest groups. In the past few years, state legislatures have dealt with educational bills on a wide range of topics, including: accountability, state aid, textbooks, adult basic education, length of the school year, legal holidays, lotteries, teacher and student testing, "no-pass-no-play," and school standards of various sorts.

Local Boards of Education. Local school boards are governmental units of the state, are created by the state, and are responsible to it for educating pupils

Objective 6:
Describe the functions of state and local government related to education.

Activity 9.4:
Provide an example of a recently passed educational law from your state. Discuss the reasons for the law's enactment, and analyze what groups and individuals fought for and against the law.

Information Note 9.3:
With little or no objection from educators, state legislatures continue to increase their involvement in schooling. To point out a few examples, state legislatures have set statutes about curriculum standards, no-pass-no-play rules for athletes, and licensure tests for teachers.

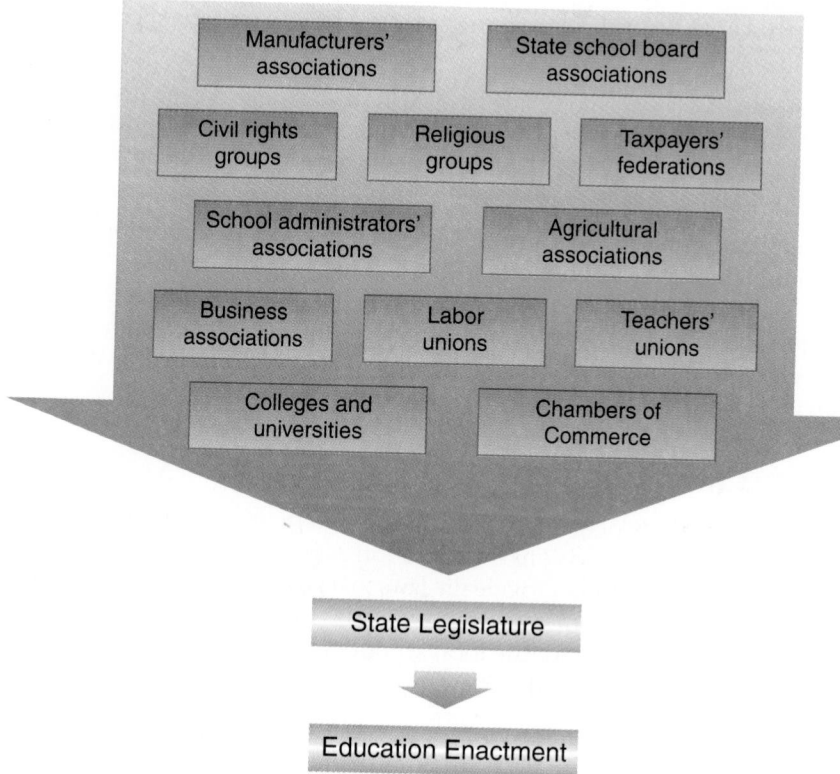

FIGURE 9.2

Influences on Legislative Decision Making

within specified local school districts. Their major function is the development of policy for the local school district—policy that must be in harmony with both federal and state law. They have only those powers granted or implied by statute that are necessary to carry out their responsibilities. Powers usually granted or implied to local school boards include the power to act as follows:

- Obtain revenue
- Maintain schools
- Purchase sites and build buildings
- Purchase materials and supplies
- Organize and provide programs of studies
- Employ necessary workers and regulate their services
- Admit and assign pupils to schools and control their conduct

Church and State

Objective 7:
Describe the legal principles that allow church-based schools.

Traditionally, the United States has strongly supported separation of church and state. Yet drawing clear lines of demarcation in terms of what can and cannot be done in schools has continued to be difficult. In part, the difficulty is due to what is and is not stated literally in the U.S. Constitution. For example, separation of church and state is not explicit in the First Amendment; instead, that is the way that Thomas Jefferson and most courts have interpreted the establishment clause. The principle was designed by our forefathers to ensure each citizen freedom to practice the religion of his or her choice. The argument then follows that education, a governmental function that is necessary if an effective democracy is to survive, must be carried on so as to preserve this basic right of religious freedom.

Our nation also has a strong religious heritage. In colonial times, education was primarily a religious matter; furthermore, much of this education was conducted in private religious schools. Many private schools today are still under religious sponsorship. Approximately 13 percent of the total school population is now enrolled in nonpublic parochial and secular schools.

Court cases concerned with separation of church and state most frequently involve both the First and Fourteenth Amendments of the U.S. Constitution. The First Amendment is interpreted as being applicable to the states by the Fourteenth Amendment. For example, a state law requiring a daily prayer to be read in classrooms throughout the state could be interpreted as "depriving persons of liberty" (see the Fourteenth Amendment due process clause) and as the state establishing a religion, or at least "prohibiting the free exercise thereof" (see the First Amendment establishment clause). States are not permitted to make laws that abridge the privileges of citizens, and the right to the free practice of religion must be insured.

Court cases related to the separation of church and state can be classified in three categories: (1) those dealing with the use of public funds to support religious education, (2) those dealing with the practice of religion in public schools, and (3) those dealing with the rights of parents to provide private education for their children. Key cases related to each of these categories are presented next.

Journal/Portfolio
Development 1:
Legal issues in our schools.

Public Funds and Parochial Education. The use of public funds to support parochial schools has been questioned on many occasions. Typically, state constitutions deny public funds to sectarian institutions or schools. However, public funds have been used to provide transportation for students to church schools and to provide textbooks for students in parochial schools. From the 1960s on, there has been renewed attention given to the use of public funds for parochial education. Other topics directly related to the use of public funds for parochial education include tuition tax credits and child benefit theory. A sampling of these cases and issues are provided here to illustrate the reasoning and to assess trends in this difficult area. The use of funds for these purposes has been challenged in many instances.

Public Funds Provide Transportation for Students of Church Schools. The landmark case on the use of public funds to provide transportation for students to church schools was *Everson* v. *Board of Education,* ruled on by the U.S. Supreme Court in 1947. The Court held that in using tax-raised funds to reimburse parents for bus fares expended to transport their children to church schools, a New Jersey school district did not violate the establishment clause of the First Amendment. The majority of the members of the Court viewed the New Jersey statute permitting free bus transportation to parochial school children as "public welfare legislation" to help get the children to and from school safely and expeditiously. Since the *Everson* decision, the highest courts in a number of states, under provisions in their own constitutions, have struck down enactments authorizing public funds to bus children attending denominational schools; others have upheld such enactments.

For example, in 1975 the U.S. Supreme Court affirmed a federal district court decision in Missouri that although a state may provide free transportation to parochial school students (*Everson* v. *Board of Education*), principles of equal protection

Activity 9.5:
Before presenting *Everson,*
ask students to write down a
list of their reasons for, or
against, using public tax dollars to transport students to
church schools.

do not require a state to do so merely because such services are provided to public school pupils. Thus a law may be in harmony with the U.S. Constitution but not with the state constitution.

Public Funds Provide Textbooks for Private Schools. A similar question exists concerning the use of public funds to provide textbooks for private schools. The landmark case originated in Louisiana, where a statute provided for textbooks to be supplied to nonpublic school children free of charge. The statute had been upheld by a state court on the theory that the children, and not the nonpublic schools, were the beneficiaries.

In *Cochran* v. *Louisiana State Board of Education* (1930) the U.S. Supreme Court held the Louisiana textbook statute valid under the Fourteenth Amendment. The Court discounted the taxpayers' contention that tax-raised funds for furnishing textbooks to private school pupils constituted a tax for a private rather than a public purpose and a deprivation of taxpayers' money without due process of law.

In a later case (*Board of Education of Central School District No. 1, Town of Greenbush v. Allen,* 1968) the Court upheld the constitutionality of a New York textbook statute. The New York law required boards of education, on individual request, to lend textbooks free to children in grades 7 through 12 in private schools if these schools complied with the state compulsory attendance law.

The Supreme Court, in its decisions in the *Everson* and *Cochran* cases, made it clear that providing transportation or textbooks per se does not violate the First Amendment.

Relevant Research

Can a Deaf Student Attending a Catholic High School Have a Government-Paid Interpreter?

Law research has a different design than other types of educational research. Instead of the researcher observing classrooms or developing and administering a student questionnaire, the legal researcher studies different sources of information related to the legal question at hand. The legal researcher works through these sources to develop an analysis of the likely legality of a particular issue.

In 1993, the question of whether it is legal to assign a government-paid interpreter to a deaf student attending a Catholic high school was tested in *Zobrest v. Catalina Foothills School District*. In a case brought by Jim Zobrest of Tucson, Arizona's Salpointe Catholic High School, the U.S. Supreme Court had to consider: (1) the Education of the Handicapped Act, a statute that requires special accommodation for the handicapped, (2) the 1971 "*Lemon* Test," which requires a court to look at a law's purpose (it should be secular), its effects on religion (it should be neutral) and whether the law results in excessive entanglement between church and state, and (3) several amendments of the U.S. Constitution (including the First and the Fourteenth). In *Zobrest* the tutor was available all day, including for religious instruction.

In a sharply divided five-to-four decision the Court has ruled that it is not unconstitutional for a public school district to send a sign language interpreter into a religious school to help a deaf student learn. This brief overview of one case illustrates the intricate array of elements that come together when you raise what seems to be a simple question about what is legal to do in your classroom.

The *Lemon* Test: Excessive Entanglement.

The *Lemon* test, emanating from *Lemon v. Kurtzman* (1971) in Pennsylvania, asks for answers to three questions: (1) Does the act have a secular purpose? (2) Does the primary effect of the act either advance or inhibit religion? (3) Does the act excessively entangle government and religion? The Court envisioned excessive entanglement between government and religion in accomplishing the necessary state supervision to ensure that the state aid would support only secular education. The Court pointed out another defect of the Pennsylvania statute—it provided for the aid to be given directly to the school. In the *Everson* case the aid was provided to the student's parents, not to the church-related school.

In 1980, by a five-to-four vote, the U.S. Supreme Court finally settled a ten-year dispute over a New York law that provided for reimbursement to private and parochial schools for record keeping and standardized testing, both required by state law. The Court envisioned no excessive entanglement and voted that testing and record keeping have neither a religious purpose nor a religious effect, nor do they violate the intent of the First Amendment.

In a 1994 case, *Board of Education of Kiryas Joel Village School District* v. *Grumet*, the U.S. Supreme Court ruled that a New York state law that created a public school to serve disabled children in a village of Hasidic Jews is a form of "religious favoritism" that violates the First Amendment. Interestingly, in this case as with some others recently, the *Lemon* case was ignored by justices in making the decision. Instead, the focus was on the legislature creating a special school and that there was no guarantee that "the next similarly situated group seeking a school district of its own will receive one." Another implication of this decision was the indication that the court would be willing to revisit *Aquilar* v. *Felton* (1985) and *Grand Rapids* v. *Ball* (1985), which invalidated sending public school teachers to private religious schools to provide supplemental instruction.

The issue of public aid to church-related schools is still in the process of being settled. Although it is clear that aid for certain secular services (such as transportation, textbooks, and—under prescribed circumstances—testing, diagnostic, therapeutic, and remedial services) can be provided, it is not yet absolutely clear what further aid will be approved. In fact, the whole body of law in this area continues to be somewhat confused and contradictory. Some state legislatures are continuing to try to find new ways to provide aid to parochial schools without violating the First Amendment. (See Table 9.1 on page 238 for a summary of U.S. Supreme Court cases in this area.)

Child Benefit Theory. The use of public funds to provide secular services has led to a concept referred to as "child benefit theory." **Child benefit theory** can be defined as providing benefits to children in parochial schools with no benefits to the schools or to a religion. More recent decisions supporting the use of public funds for transportation and textbooks for students in private schools have generally been based on the child benefit theory; this theory emerged out of commentary about the *Everson* v. *Board of Education* case. The reasoning was that transportation and books provide benefits to the children and not to the school or to a religion. Those opposed to the child benefit theory argue that aid to children receiving sectarian education instruction is effectively aiding the institution providing instruction.

The child benefit theory, as supported by the U.S. Supreme Court, has penetrated federal legislation. The Elementary and Secondary Education Act of 1965 (ESEA), for example, and its subsequent amendments provide for assistance to both public and nonpublic school children. Title I of ESEA, which dealt with assistance for the education of children from low-income families, stated that children from families attending private schools must be provided services in proportion to their numbers. As a summary, Table 9.2 on page 239 presents brief statements about the relationship of religion and public education, particularly the use of public funds for parochial education.

Another issue related to separation of church and state focuses on religious activities in public schools, which will be treated in the next section.

Information Note 9.4:
Since 1971, the *Lemon* test has provided three keys for judicial interpretations and has been regularly referred to and used as the basis for subsequent decisions. However, there is some indication in the mid- to late 1990s that this test is not being relied on as much by the courts.

Transparency 48:
Direct Aid to Nonpublic Schools—The Three-Pronged *Lemon* Test

Key Term:
Child benefit theory

Activity 9.6:
Have students divide into groups according to whether they are for or against "child benefit theory." Ask them to develop a list of arguments that are in support of their position that will *not be* in violation of the First Amendment.

TABLE 9.1	Selected U.S. Supreme Court Cases Related to the Use of Public Funds for Private Education	
Case	**Issue**	**Decision**
Everson v. *Board of Education* (1947)	Use of tax-raised funds to reimburse parents for transportation of students to church schools	Court ruled that reimbursement did not violate the First Amendment
Cochran v. *Louisiana Board of Education* (1930)	Loan of public school textbooks to children in private schools	Court ruled that state loans of secular textbooks to nonpublic school children served public purposes and did not violate the federal constitutional ban on spending public funds for private purposes
Board of Education of Central School District No. 1, Town of Greenbush v. *Allen* (1968)	Loan of public school textbooks to children in private schools	Court ruled that the loan of books did not alone demonstrate an unconstitutional degree of support for a religious institution
Lemon v. *Kurtzman* (1971)	Legislation to provide direct aid for secular services to nonpublic schools, including teacher salaries, textbooks, and instructional materials	Court ruled the legislation unconstitutional because of the excessive entanglement between government and religion
Wolman v. *Walter* (1977)	Providing nonpublic school pupils with books, standardized testing and scoring, diagnostic services, and therapeutic and remedial services	Court ruled that providing such materials and services to nonpublic school pupils was constitutional
	Provision of instructional materials and field trips to nonpublic school pupils	Court ruled that providing such materials and service to nonpublic school pupils was unconstitutional
Grand Rapids School District v. *Ball* (1985), and *Aguilar* v. *Felton* (1985)	Having public school teachers instruct nonpublic school students in supplementary education	Court ruled that the action violated the Establishment Clause in that it promoted religion
Board of Education of Kiryas Joel Village School District v. *Grumet* (1994)	New York State creating and supporting a public school district for Hasidic Jews	Court ruled it violated the Establishment Clause in that it was a form of "religious favoritism"

Religious Activities in Public Schools

Focus Question 3:
Under what conditions can religious activities take place in public schools?

Objective 8:
Describe in general terms the issues and legal reasoning behind limiting religious activities in public schools.

Four topics to be addressed with regard to religious activities in public schools are released time from regular classes for religious instruction, prayer and Bible reading in schools, the teaching of creationism or the biblical version of creation in public schools, and the use of school facilities for religious purposes.

Released Time.   Providing released time for religious instruction in public schools has been challenged and was first acted on by the U.S. Supreme Court, in 1948. The Court held that the released-time program of the Champaign, Illinois,

TABLE 9.2	Summary Statements on Church and State Related to Public Funds and Parochial Education

Laws and policies that have the effect of establishing religion in the schools will not be upheld by the courts.

Public tax funds to pay for secular textbooks for loan to students and transportation of parochial school children have been upheld by the courts.

Public tax funds to pay for salaries of teachers in parochial schools have not been upheld by the courts.

Tuition payments for parents of parochial school children have not been upheld; in Minnesota, a tax deduction has been upheld for parents of children in public *and* private schools.

Special support services such as speech and hearing teachers may be provided to parochial schools.

Parochial schools may be reimbursed for administrative costs of standardized tests, test scoring, and record keeping required by the state.

Public tax funds may not be used in support of public school teachers offering remedial or enriched instruction in parochial schools.

---

schools violated the principle of separation of church and state (*People of the State of Illinois ex rel. McCollum* v. *Board of Education of School District No. 71, Champaign, Illinois,* 1948). Four years later, the court made what initially appears to be a contradictory decision.

The Concept of Released Time Does Not Violate the First Amendment. A released-time program in New York was challenged a few years after the *McCollum* case; in *Zorach* v. *Clauson* (1952) the Supreme Court upheld a New York statute that provided for released time. The chief difference between the Champaign and New York cases is that in New York, students were released from school to go to religious centers to receive religious instruction, whereas in Champaign the instruction was given in public school classrooms. The Court indicated that the precise type of released-time program is significant; programs differ in the extent of school cooperation and in the degree of sectarianism. We can conclude that the concept of released time in and of itself does not necessarily violate the First Amendment.

Prayer and Bible Reading. The courts have rendered a number of opinions on prayer and Bible reading in the public schools. In 1962 the U.S. Supreme Court (*Engle* v. *Vitale*) held that a prayer composed by the New York State Board of Regents and used as part of the opening exercises of school violated the U.S. Constitution. The prayer read as follows: "Almighty God, we acknowledge our dependence upon Thee, and we beg Thy blessings on us, our parents, our teachers, and our country." Pupils who objected to the prayer could be excused. The Court based its decision on the establishment clause of the First Amendment: "Congress shall make no law respecting an establishment of religion, or prohibiting the free exercise thereof." Justice Hugo Black, who wrote the decision, stated:

> The constitutional prohibition against laws respecting an establishment of religion must at least mean that . . . it is no part of the business of government to impose official prayers for any group of American people to recite as a part of a religious program carried on by the government.

Discussion Question 1:
The appropriate place, if any, for prayer in public schools continues to be a source of contention. What position should public school teachers take relative to this issue? What will you say if a parent wants you to have a moment of prayer in your classroom?

Activity 9.7:
Provide several scenarios of released-time programs, each of which has a different degree of sectarianism and a different degree of school cooperation. Have students debate the legality of each on the basis of the Illinois and New York cases.

Information Note 9.5:
Political pressure continues to build for some sort of legally acceptable form of prayer in public schools. For example, a "moment of silence" is frequently discussed. With continuing pressure from the religious right, and Republican control of Congress and state legislatures, new legislative actions and court interpretations are bound to be annual events. There is not likely to be clear resolution that satisfies all interests for quite some time, if ever.

The right to pray in school, or its appropriateness in the school day routine, have been debated often in recent decades.

Other U.S. Supreme Court decisions related to Bible reading and prayer include: outlawing the reading of the Bible and reciting the Lord's Prayer as religious exercises in public schools (*Schempp* v. *School District of Abington Township,* 1963, and *Murray* v. *Curlett,* 1963); and the overturning of Alabama legislation of 1982 which authorized teachers to lead willing students in a prescribed prayer (*Wallace* v. *Jaffree,* 1985).

The constitutionality of prayer at graduation ceremonies has been considered too. In *Lee* v. *Weisman* (1992), the U.S. Supreme Court ruled, in a five-to-four decision, that it was unconstitutional to include an invocation or benediction as an official part of the program. The Court's majority reasoned that this was in violation of the establishment clause. More specifically, the effects test of *Lemon* was violated whenever government action "creates an identification of the state with a religion, or with religion in general."

Diversity Note 9.1:
Debate about whether prayer should be a part of public school is occurring in other countries as well. For example, in British schools a daily act of collective worship "of a predominantly Christian character" is mandatory. There is a "conscience clause" to let objecting parents withdraw their children. In objecting, John Habgood, Archbishop of York, observed, "It is absolutely clear that schools do not create Christians."

Lee v. *Weisman,* may settle, for the moment, the role of prayer and Bible reading as an official part of the graduation ceremony. But what about invited speakers including religious references in their remarks, or student-led prayer? A number of related cases are currently moving through lower courts. It appears that, under certain circumstances (yet to be clarified), an individual speaker may make unsolicited reference to religious views. But school officials cannot issue a vote or encourage any such action. For example, in a 1992 decision, a federal appeals court ruled on a case from Texas that graduation prayer is allowed if it is student-initiated, nonsectarian, and nonproselytizing. Since that time, legislatures in Texas, Louisiana, Mississippi, and a number of other southeastern states have passed laws with this intent. These statutes are now being challenged in the courts. Keep in mind that decisions in lower courts may well apply only in their jurisdiction; only time will tell whether any of these cases will reach the U.S. Supreme Court. There are sure to be continuing questions and court cases about the delicate balancing of the relationship between prayer and Bible reading and official school actions. For example, the current question of the legality of establishing in statutes a "moment of silence" in schools will surely be tested in the courts. For now, in these and other cases the opinions of the courts emphasize that government must remain neutral in matters of religion.

CNN Clip 23:
Creationism School

Teaching Creationism in the Public Schools. Another volatile church-state controversy pertains to teaching in public schools about the origin of humanity. The initial controversy involved the constitutionality of state prohibitions against instruction suggesting that human beings evolved through a process of natural selection from lower forms of animals. The Tennessee Supreme Court upheld such a state law in the famous 1927 Scopes "monkey trial," but the Supreme Court reached an opposite conclusion in 1968. In *Epperson* v. *Arkansas* (1968) the Court ruled that an Arkansas antievolution statute violated the First Amendment.

It declared that "the state has no legitimate interest in protecting any or all religions from views distasteful to them." It stated further that the amendment does not "permit the state to require that teaching and learning be tailor-made to the principles or prohibitions of any religious sect or dogma."

The more recent controversy has focused on the constitutionality of teaching the biblical version of creation in public schools. Creationists assert that this theory deserves equal treatment to that of the scientific theory of the evolution of life. In 1980–1981, "equal-time" provisions were introduced in the legislatures of fifteen states, with two states, (Arkansas and Louisiana) passing statutes. The intent of these initiatives was to require that each theory be given equal instructional time. The Arkansas statute was struck down by a federal district court in 1982. The judge reviewed the legislative history of the statute and concluded that it failed to satisfy the three-pronged *Lemon* test. The judge ruled that there was no evidence of secular purpose; rather it was an attempt to introduce the biblical version of creationism into the public schools. Reasoning that creation science is religious dogma, the court concluded that the only real effect of the statute was to advance religion. The court also held that the act created excessive governmental entanglement with religion because the Genesis account cannot be taught in a secular fashion.

The U.S. Supreme Court ruled in 1987 (*Edwards* v. *Aguilard*) that the Louisiana statute was in violation of the establishment clause. The act lacked a secular purpose, and it tended to show a preference for the teaching of the biblical version as opposed to the scientific version of creation. There was further evidence that the act's sponsors intended to promote religion, a violation of the *Lemon* test.

Religious Meetings in Public Schools. In 1988, President Reagan signed the Equal Process Act, which gives students—under certain, very limited circumstances—the right to hold religious meetings in public schools. This law guarantees to students the right to meet for "religious, political, philosophical, or other" discussions in any high school that allows other extracurricular activities. The U.S. Supreme Court in 1990 and again in 1993 ruled that schools must allow student Bible clubs as well as political and ideological groups to meet on campus after hours if other outside activities are held in school facilities.

Another issue related to the separation of church and state deals with the rights of parents to provide education for their children. This issue, which is discussed in the next section, is closely related to compulsory education.

Rights of Parents to Provide Private Education

The United States has a strong religious heritage. That heritage fostered the development of private religious schools and school systems dedicated to teaching religion along with secular subjects including reading, writing, and arithmetic. Some private schools are not religious-sponsored and essentially offer secular subjects. As our nation grew, sectarian private schools also grew, frequently associated with established traditional religions, such as Catholicism and Lutheranism. In recent years, many fundamentalist religious schools have been established. The fundamentalist schools have had steadily increasing enrollments. The amount of instruction of students in their homes has also escalated. The increased enrollments in fundamentalist schools and the increased amount of home instruction are attributed in part to the perceived, if not real, lack of instruction of morality in the public schools.

TABLE 9.3   Selected U.S. Supreme Court Cases Related to the Practice of Religion in Public Schools and the Right to a Private Education

Case	Issue	Decision
Creationism		
Epperson v. *State of Arkansas* (1968)	Arkansas antievolution statute	Court held that to forbid the teaching of evolution as a theory violated the First Amendment.
Edwards v. *Aguilard* (1987)	Balanced treatment of biblical and scientific creation	A state cannot require that schools teach the biblical version of creation.
Practice of Religion		
Wallace v. *Jaffree* (1985)	Legislation authorizing prayer in public schools, led by teachers; and a period of silence for meditation or voluntary prayer	Court held that state legislation authorizing a minute of silence for prayer led by teachers was unconstitutional.
Mozert v. *Hawkins County Public Schools* (1987)	Request that fundamentalist children not be exposed to basal reading series in the public schools of Tennessee	Rejected by the Sixth Circuit Court of Appeals' reasoning that the readers did not burden the students' exercise of their religious beliefs.
Board of Education of the Westside Community Schools v. *Mergens* (1990)	Holding student religious club meetings at public school	Court ruled that based on Equal Access Act (EAA) of 1984, if only one noncurriculum-related student group meets, then the school may not deny other clubs.
Lee v. *Weisman* (1992)	Conducting a religious exercise at a graduation ceremony where young graduates who object are induced to conform	Prayers as an official part of graduation exercises are unconstitutional.

Key Term:
Compulsory education

Private Education: An Alternative. The court cases having to do with the rights of parents to provide private education for their children are closely related to cases about **compulsory education.** Compulsory attendance laws generally require parents, or whoever has custody of a child between specific chronological ages, to cause the child to attend school. The constitutional objection raised regarding compulsory attendance laws is that they infringe on the individual liberty guaranteed by the Fourteenth Amendment. The constitutionality of compulsory education laws has been attacked in numerous cases, but the principle has been uniformly upheld. Courts have generally reasoned that education is so necessary to the welfare of our nation that compulsory school attendance laws are valid and desirable. Compulsory education does not mean compulsory public education, however.

Whether a state can compel children to attend a public school was settled in a case in Oregon. (See Table 9.3 for a summary of this case and other important Supreme Court cases related to the practice of religion in public schools and the right to a private education.) In 1922 the Oregon legislature passed a law requiring all children to attend public schools. The U.S. Supreme Court ruled that such a law was unconstitutional in that it infringed on the rights of parents to control the education of their children (*Pierce* v. *Society of Sisters,* 1925). This ruling established a precedent, permitting parents to have their children educated in private schools. In this same case the Court also es- tablished beyond doubt that the state may reasonably regulate all schools, public and private, and require certain subjects to be taught. It established that private schools have a right to exist, that pupils may meet the compulsory attendance laws by attending pri- vate schools, and that private schools are sub- ject to state regulation.

Parents may be granted permission to educate their children at home.

Home Instruction. The courts have also ruled that education in a child's home can meet the requirements of compulsory educa- tion. In an early case in Indiana[3] the court specified that a school is a place where edu- cation is imparted to the young; therefore a home can be a school if a qualified teacher is engaged in instruction as prescribed by the state. The state controls home instruc- tion, and the instruction generally must be equivalent to what a school provides. Home instruction must be carried out in good faith and not practiced as a sub- terfuge to avoid sending children to school.

As of 1989, every state permitted home instruction in some form, and two states, Iowa and Michigan, required that all teachers in home schools be certified. Nevertheless, there are wide differences among the states in the restrictions con- trolling home instruction and home schools. The trend is toward easing restric- tions. Various restrictions on home instruction and home schools over the years have included requiring certified teachers, following state curriculum mandates, passing the state teachers' examinations, requiring students to take annual stan- dardized achievement tests and competency tests, and setting a minimum length for the instructional day and year.

Balancing the Rights of Individuals and the Rights of the State. The interpretation of compulsory education laws indicates that a reasonable balance is sought between the rights of the individual and the rights of the state. Parents who want a religious education for their children may meet the requirement of compulsory education by enrolling their children in private or parochial schools or in approved home instruction programs. At the same time the state reserves the right to reasonably regulate private education.

Much of our discussion in this section dealt with issues associated with the separation of church and state (see Table 9.4 on page 244 for a summary) and judicial decisions made by the Supreme Court related to those issues (see Table 9.3). Frequently, the decisions made by the Court were based on the First Amend- ment. The next few pages address issues associated with segregation and desegre- gation directly related to the Fourteenth Amendment.

Enduring Legal Issues

There are a number of pressing issues where the needs of society, the laws of the land, and the role of schools intersect. These enduring issues do not have easy, sim- ple, quick, or final answers. Instead, each represents an area where difficult prob-

TABLE 9.4 Summary Statements on Church and State and the Practice of Religion in Public Schools

To teach the Bible as a religion course in the public schools is illegal, but to teach about the Bible as part of history of literature is legal.

To dismiss children from public schools for one hour once a week for religious instruction at religious centers is legal.

Reading of scripture and reciting prayers as religious exercises are in violation of the Establishment Clause.

Public schools may teach the scientific theory of evolution as a theory; a state may not require that the biblical version of evolution be taught.

Discussion Question 2:
Your state legislators offer many bills related to the operation of public schools. Are there any examples of proposed bills that you think the courts would find unconstitutional?

Objective 10:
Present descriptions of a number of enduring legal issues that confront schooling.

Information Note 9.7:
The major portion of this section addresses the phenomenon and history of desegregation court actions. The section ends with discussion of release from court orders, which many districts, including Kansas City and Denver, are striving to accomplish.

Focus Question 4:
What is the difference between *de jure* and *de facto* segregation?

CNN Clip 18:
Desegregation Today

Objective 11:
Trace the key court decisions that have been the basis for desegregating schools.

Activity 9.9:
Ask students to describe their personal experiences in a school where busing was used to achieve integration. What were the benefits? What were the problems?

Key Term:
Desegregation

Key Term:
De jure segregation

lems must be addressed through gradual development of understanding of the underlying problem(s) and experimentation with different approaches to find what will work. The pressing needs being addressed require the legal, legislative, and educational systems to work together to develop and test workable solutions. Each of these enduring issues carries with it emotion, high cost, high risk, and uncertainty as to whether the desired ends can be achieved with the legal and educational mechanisms employed. At the same time the willingness to confront these types of difficult societal problems is a strength and testimony to the confidence Americans have in their educational system. Several of these enduring issues that have been addressed through legal actions are summarized in the remainder of this chapter.

Segregation and Desegregation

Segregation in the context of this chapter refers to the separation of people by race specifically in the public schools. A major concern in the United States has been the separation of African American students from white students, resulting in segregated schools—schools that have predominantly African American students and schools that have predominantly white students. Such segregation has occurred by state law or other official action *(de jure)* and through other causes such as housing patterns *(de facto)*.

Desegregation is an effort to abolish racial segregation. For example, African American students may be transferred to predominantly white schools, and white students may be transferred to predominantly African American schools. The intent is to achieve a numerical balance of African American and white students in each school. Such a school would be referred to as an integrated school. Closely related to segregation and desegregation are the issues of busing, white flight, and resegregation, which are also discussed here.

De Jure Segregation. Before 1954, many states had laws either requiring or permitting racial segregation in public schools. Until 1954, lower courts had adhered to the doctrine of "separate but equal" as announced by the Supreme Court in 1896 (*Plessy v. Ferguson*). In *Plessy* v. *Ferguson* the Court upheld a Louisiana law that required railway companies to provide equal accommodations for the African American and white races. The Court indicated in its opinion that the Fourteenth Amendment implied political, not social, equality.

The Separate-But-Equal Doctrine Has No Place. This separate-but-equal doctrine appeared to be the rule until May 17, 1954, when the Supreme Court repudiated it in *Brown* v. *Board of Education of Topeka.* The Court said that in education the separate-but-equal doctrine has no place and that separate facilities are inherently unequal. In 1955 the Court rendered the second *Brown* v. *Board of Education of Topeka* decision, requiring that the principles of the first decision be carried out with all deliberate speed.

From 1954, the time of the *Brown* decision, to 1964, little progress was made in eliminating segregated schools. On May 25, 1964, referring to a situation in Prince Edward County, Virginia, the Supreme Court said: "There has been entirely too much deliberation and not enough speed in enforcing the constitutional rights which we held in *Brown* v. *Board of Education.* " The Civil Rights Act of 1964 added legislative power to the 1954 judicial pronouncement. The Act not only authorized the federal government to initiate court suits against school districts that were laggard in desegregating schools but also denied federal funds for programs that discriminated by race, color, or national origin.

Subsequently, many types of efforts have been made to meet the expectations of the Court decisions and legislation. The objective of these initiatives has been **integration,** that is, to achieve a representative mix of students of different races in schools. In the more than forty years since *Brown* there have been many efforts by school districts and communities, and many additional law suits.

De Facto Segregation.

De Facto **Segregation.** The U.S. Supreme Court has yet to rule on *de facto* discrimination—that is, discrimination based on causes *other than* state law or official state actions such as when the composition of neighborhood populations results in part from housing patterns.

A case heard by the U.S. Supreme Court that touched on *de facto* segregation was *Keyes* v. *School District No. 1, Denver, Colorado.* The Court, announcing its decision in 1973, sent the suit back to a district court; this court was to decide whether or not school authorities had intentionally segregated a substantial portion of the school system. If proof affirmed that the school district was operating a dual system (segregated) even though there had never been any *de jure* or legal provisions for school segregation, then the entire system would be required to desegregate. In 1974, Judge William E. Doyle of the Tenth U.S. Circuit Court of Appeals ordered integration of the city's 70,000 children. The Supreme Court, however, had not resolved the question of *de jure/de facto* segregation. In a separate opinion, Justice Powell stated: "We should abandon a distinction which long since has outlived its time, and formulate constitutional principles of national rather than merely regional applications." The Supreme Court did, however, change the concept of *de facto* segregation by turning over to federal and state trial courts the discretion to determine, as an issue of fact and not as a question of law, whether or not a local school board presides over a *de facto* or a *de jure* segregated school district. In a sense, the Supreme Court broadened the concept of *de jure* segregation.

Integration Forty Years Later.

Integration Forty Years Later. Currently, there are more than 500 formerly segregated school districts under some federal court jurisdiction. Unfortunately, while *de jure* segregation has been removed, it has been replaced in many situations with a more virulent form of segregation. The demographics and economic conditions of the country have changed in ways that have not facilitated accomplishing integration in local schools. Many strategies have been tested and there

Journal Activity Master 9.2: A Program Designed to Achieve School Integration. This activity requires students to analyze busing as a policy and to design a desegregation plan.

Key Term: Integration

Key Term: *De facto* segregation

Activity 9.10: Ask students to list ways in which surrounding suburban districts could assist in the desegregation of large metropolitan districts. Have them design plans that they believe would be acceptable to both metropolitan and suburban school districts.

Attempts to integrate students of different races by transporting them to schools outside their own neighborhoods have proven to be a difficult and emotional issue for communities.

are some indicators of success, but the goal is still a dream in many ways. One of the enduring strategies to achieve integration has been busing. Unanticipated countering points during this period include the movement of the middle class away from urban areas and the lower birth rates of whites. Also, the economic conditions and extent of racial diversity in the country have changed dramatically. These dynamic factors, along with numerous others, have not made it easy for schools and communities to achieve the desired end of desegregation.

Busing Has Been Mandated by Federal District Courts as a Means to Bring about School Desegregation. Busing has also been used voluntarily to bring about desegregation. Many school districts—including those of Boston, Seattle, Tulsa, Oklahoma City, Louisville, Austin, Dallas, Dayton, San Francisco, Los Angeles, Pontiac, and Indianapolis—have been ordered to bus school children to end segregation. But the issue remains extremely controversial.

Proponents view busing as a necessary way, and sometimes the only way, to give children of all races a chance for equality of opportunity in education. They further argue that an integrated society is essential and that if people are going to live in an integrated society, preparation must begin in school. Opponents of busing claim that it does not improve the quality of education and that it requires large expenditures that ought to go toward compensatory education.

Key Term:
Resegregation

Resegregation Generally Means a Situation in Which an Integrated School Population Becomes Almost Totally a Minority School Population. Sometimes, resegregation occurs within a school when the neighborhood from which the school's population is drawn changes from an integrated to a predominantly minority neighborhood. If the population of a city becomes predominantly minority, the schools in the city will become the same. Often the growth of the minority populations proceeds from the inner part of the city toward the outer fringe areas. Resegregation can also occur after a governmental desegregation order. In such instances, white students may withdraw or simply not reenter when the next term begins. Furthermore, white families may move to another area that is not affected by the desegregation order.

Discussion Question 3:
Segregation is illegal, yet there are many schools and school districts in which there are disproportionate numbers of minority students. What do you see as the educational implications of the continuation of these situations?

One Serious Consequence in the 1990s Is a Growing Sense of Despair in Many Minority Children. This must be understood and actively addressed by teachers such as yourself. The above description of resegregation is based on demographic and economic factors. There is another set of dynamics to resegregation that includes educational, social, and psychological factors.

Quality of education is one significant factor. As the urban areas have lost their tax base, the condition of school buildings has deteriorated. Tracking is another educational strategy that is contributing to resegregation. In some schools many minority students are scheduled out of advanced classes and clustered in more remedial classes. Minority students are experiencing less success in schools, and they have higher dropout rates as well. There also is a sense of social isolation that occurs in many schools that is defeating the goal of integration. Additionally, there is a belief among many minorities that teachers, as well as white students, do not treat them as equals. Whether or not these conditions are true, as long as students perceive that they are, the tendency to resegregate will increase.

There Is a Success Side to the Desegregation Agenda That Should Be Appreciated. For example, African Americans who graduate from integrated schools have higher incomes than those who graduate from segregated schools. They are more likely to graduate from college and to hold good jobs. And there is an increasing number of middle-class black families. Still, there is a long way to go before the dream born over forty years ago is achieved. And schools will continue to be the primary vehicle from the points of view of the courts and teachers in classrooms.

Release from Court Orders.

After forty plus years of court actions related to desegregation and school district responses, questions are now being raised about the conditions that must be in place for a school district to be released from federal court supervision. Four recent cases offer the first instances of the conditions under which the courts will back away. The *Board of Education of Oklahoma City* v. *Dowell* (1991) is important for at least three reasons. First, the U.S. Supreme Court made clear that "federal supervision of local school systems was intended as a temporary measure to remedy past discrimination." Second, the Court made clearer what was meant by unitary status: "the District Court should look not only at student assignments, but to every facet of school operations—faculty, staff, transportation, extracurricular activities and facilities." And third, for the first time, the Court ruled that a district had achieved this status:

> In the present case, a finding by the District Court that the Oklahoma City School District was being operated in compliance with the commands of the equal protection clause of the Fourteenth Amendment, and that it was unlikely that the school board would return to its former ways, would be finding that the purposes of the desegregation litigation had been fully achieved.

Two other cases add additional clarity to what the Court expects in order to release a school district from supervision. In *Freeman* v. *Pitts* (1992) the U.S. Supreme Court ruled that districts do not have to remedy racial imbalances caused by demographic changes, but the districts still have the burden of proving that their actions do not contribute to the imbalances. The third case is a return to *Brown*. The Court had ordered the 10th Circuit Court to re-examine its 1989 finding that the Topeka district remains segregated. In 1992 the Appellate Court refused to declare Topeka unitary. The court concluded that the district has done little to fulfill its duty to desegregate that was first imposed on it in 1954. The judges wrote that to expect the vestiges of segregation to "magically dissolve" with so little effort "is to expect too much."

These three cases in combination make clear that it is possible for school districts to be released from court order. The decisions also make clear that school districts have to make concerted efforts across time to address any and all remnants of *de jure* segregation. Further, it now appears that school districts are not expected to resolve those aspects of *de facto* segregation that are clearly beyond their control.

The fourth case related to achieving release from a court desegregation order has to do with the amount of effort that a school district must invest on desegre-

Activity 9.11:
Ask students to describe examples of *de facto* discrimination that they have personally witnessed. Have the class discuss each example to determine whether there was any *de jure* segregation that could have contributed to the *de facto* example.

Objective 12:
Analyze the intent of contemporary judicial actions by school districts that are aimed at achieving release from desegregation court orders.

Changing demographics in the United States have made diverse classrooms commonplace.

gation programs and the criteria for judging success. This question was addressed in an appeal by the state of Missouri in the Kansas City case. In a 1995 landmark decision, with a 5–4 vote, the Court overturned a federal judge's order that Missouri pay for two costly aspects of Kansas City's massive desegregation program. In Kansas City, the state, as well as local tax payers, has been paying for a major set of desegregation initiatives, which included construction of new school buildings with magnet programs, across-the-board teacher salary increases, and a program to help minority children reach national norms in educational achievement. This case is reputed to be the most costly in the nation, with $1.3 billion spent between 1984 and 1995.

In returning the case to federal judge Russell Clark, the Court ruled that school desegregation programs may not spend unlimited amounts of money, go on indefinitely, uniformly insist on academic achievement, or seek to lure white students from blameless suburban districts. The court's insisting on minority students achieving at national norms was seen as outside the purview of the case. Judge Rehnquist stated for the majority, "Insistence upon academic goals unrelated to the effects of (past) legal segregation unwarrantably postpones the day when the (Kansas City District) will be able to operate on its own." In reversing the lower court, Judge Rehquest criticized them for approving a desegregation goal that appeared unlimited in costs and duration.

This section has dealt with *de jure* and *de facto* segregation and with desegregation. Integration and resegregation were also discussed. (See Table 9.5 for a summary of these issues.) All of these issues have prejudice and discrimination at their core, as does the next major topic, affirmative action.

TABLE 9.5   **Summary Statements on Segregation and Desegregation**

The assignment of a child to a school on the basis of race is in violation of the equal protection clause of the Fourteenth Amendment.

Where school boards have indirectly contributed to segregated communities, the school district can be required to desegregate.

Desegregation plans that have the effect of delaying integration of the school have not been upheld by the courts.

Busing may be required for the operation of a unitary school system.

Once a school district has been fully desegregated, the school board does not need to draw up a new plan if resegregation occurs.

The merger of school districts may be required where the involved districts helped create the segregated school systems.

The neighborhood school concept is not in conflict with the equal protection clause.

Once the district has achieved unitary status, it can be released from court supervision.

Affirmative Action

Affirmative action has its basis in the protection clause of the Fourteenth Amendment, in Titles VI and VII of the Civil Rights Act of 1964, and in Title IX of the Education Amendments of 1972. Title VI of the Civil Rights Act states:

> No person in the United States shall, on the ground of race, color, or national origin, be excluded from participation in, be denied the benefits of, or be subjected to discrimination under any program or activity receiving federal financial assistance.

Title VII states:

> It shall be an unlawful employment practice for an employer (1) to fail or refuse to hire or to discharge any individual, or otherwise to discriminate against any individual with respect to his compensation, terms, conditions, or privileges of employment, because of such individual's race, color, religion, sex, or national origin; or (2) to limit, segregate, or classify his employees or applicants for employment in any way which would deprive or tend to deprive any individual of employment opportunities or otherwise adversely affect his status as an employee, because of such individual's race, color, religion, sex, or national origin.

Title IX of the Education Amendments of 1972 states:

> No person in the United States shall, on the basis of sex, be excluded from participation in, be denied the benefits of, or be subjected to discrimination under any education program or activity receiving federal financial assistance.

Discrimination and Reverse Discrimination. **Discrimination** can be defined as a determination that an individual or a group of individuals—for example, African Americans, women, or handicapped people—has been denied constitutional rights. In common usage the term applies to various minorities or individual members of a minority who lack rights typically accorded the majority. The term **reverse discrimination** implies that a majority or an individual of a majority has not been accorded certain rights because of different or preferential treatment provided to a minority or an individual of a minority.

Reverse discrimination has been cited with respect to admissions to law schools and medical schools. It has also been cited in connection with affirmative action—that is, positive efforts undertaken by society to integrate the races and to assure equal opportunities. An early test case concerned Allan Bakke, a white male, who claimed that he was discriminated against when denied admission to the University of California Medical School at Davis. In the medical school's class of one hundred students, sixteen spaces were set aside for minority applicants. The Supreme Court of California upheld Bakke's claim and ordered him admitted. Regents of the university appealed to the U.S. Supreme Court to overturn the state ruling.

In general, the arguments supporting the denial of Bakke's admission pointed out that (1) special admissions programs based on race are not quotas but goals; (2) color-sensitive admissions policies are necessary to bring minorities fully into the mainstream of American society; (3) benefits accrue to society at large from special admissions; (4) merit alone, determined by academic grades and test scores, has not been the single criterion of selection for schools; and (5) the denial did not violate the equal-protection clause of the U.S. Constitution. The arguments supporting Bakke's admission emphasized that (1) the special admissions program was a racial quota and (2) quotas are harmful to society and are unconstitutional.

Key Term:
Affirmative action

Objective 13:
Identify and describe features of the hiring process that could be discriminatory.

Activity 9.12:
Bring in, or ask students to bring in, examples of announcements for teaching positions. Examine these announcements for indications of the district's efforts to employ affirmative action.

Information Note 9.8:
The concept of "color blind" is being used increasingly to describe an ideal condition where race, gender, and ethnicity are not a regulated aspect of society. This was the original intent of the Civil Rights Act and the dream of Martin Luther King. At the same time there are serious questions about whether this is too idealistic and how color consciousness fits in.

Key Term:
Discrimination

Key Term:
Reverse discrimination

Focus Question 5:
What is affirmative about Affirmative Action?

Discussion Question 4:
What experiences have you had with Affirmative Action? What implications for teaching do you see in Affirmative Action and Equal Opportunity initiatives?

Education for the Handicapped

Discussion Question 5:
How would you define an "appropriate education" for handicapped children?

Objective 14:
Describe the key legislative and administrative actions aimed at providing handicapped children with an appropriate public education.

Transparency 49:
Some Categories of Disability

Activity 9.13:
Invite a handicapped student or professor to class. Have them share their personal experiences with life in contemporary society.

Information Note 9.9:
The implications of, and the extent and limits of the Americans with Disabilities Act are how being explored. Specifics of its meaning will be determined in time by the courts. In the interim there are implications for schools and colleges to consider. For example, ADA can be interpreted to hold that a college that places a deaf student teacher will have to provide a signing interpreter with that student teacher, and a district that employs a deaf teacher will need to provide a signing interpreter.

Another area being given extensive legal and legislative attention is the rights of the handicapped. Before the 1970s handicapped children were not necessarily entitled to a public education. The extent to which schooling was available to them was dependent on the state and community in which they resided. The amount and type of schooling available was a local government decision. Then in the early 1970s a series of court decisions and congressional acts established that handicapped children had constitutional entitlement to an "appropriate" education. Since then there have been a series of judicial decisions and legislative initiatives to define what is appropriate.

Public Law, Rules and Regulations for the Handicapped.   Three statutory initiatives serve as the cornerstones for education of the handicapped: Section 504 of the Rehabilitation Act, the Education for All Handicapped Children Act (EAHCA), also known as Public Law 94-142, and the Individuals with Disabilities Education Act (IDEA). Each of these instruments addresses student eligibilities, definition of what comprises appropriate education, and elements of due process.

Section 504 of the Rehabilitation Act.   Under this Civil Rights Act established in 1973, recipients of federal funds are prohibited from discriminating against "otherwise qualified individuals." Note that this is a federal statute and regulations, not a court decision. Three important themes addressed in Section 504 are Equal Treatment, Appropriate Education, and Handicapped Persons. Equal Treatment, as in other civil rights contexts, must be addressed. However, this does not mean the same treatment. For example, giving the same assessment procedure to handicapped and regular students may not be equal treatment. There is a "heightened standard" when making educational judgments. The measures must fit the student's circumstances, and procedural safeguards must be employed. Appropriate Education means that the school system and related parties must address indi-

As in other professions, teachers cannot be denied employment due to physical disability.

vidual needs of handicapped students as adequately as do the education approaches for regular students. In Section 504, a handicapped person is:

> Any person who (i) has a physical or mental impairment which substantial-
> ly limits one or more major life activities, (ii) has a record of such an impair-
> ment, or (iii) is regarded as having such an impairment. (34 CFR 104.3)

Public Law 94-142 (EAHCA). Passed by Congress in 1975, Public Law 94-142 has
been amended several times since. This law assures "a free appropriate public education" to all handicapped children between the ages of three and twenty-one.
Exceptional children cannot be excluded from education because of their differences. The law is very specific in describing the kind and quality of education and
in stating that each handicapped child is to have an individually planned education. (The specifics of this law are presented in Part Four of this text.) Originally,
substantial increases in funding were provided for; however, in subsequent years
the funding authorizations have been lower than the original commitment. Two
priorities for funding were identified: (1) the child who currently receives no education; and (2) the child who is not receiving all the services needed to succeed.
This direction places the emphasis on need, rather than the specific disability.

The Individuals with Disabilities Education Act (IDEA). This Act (1992) develops
tighter specifications for the delivery of education services to handicapped children. At the time, more than half of the children with disabilities were not receiving appropriate educational services. The purpose of IDEA is to make available to
all children with disabilities a free appropriate public education. IDEA establishes
at the federal level an Office of Special Education Programs headed by a Deputy
Assistant Secretary. Further, the Act makes clear that states shall not be immune
under the Eleventh Amendment of the Constitution from suit in federal court for
a violation of the Act. The Act encourages the employment of individuals with disabilities by making grants to states and local education agencies for children aged
three to five, requires the federal government to be responsive to the increasing
ethnic diversity of society and those with limited English proficiency, and funds
programs to provide education to all children with disabilities.

Handicapped Students and the Courts.
The judicial basis for the current
approaches to education of the handicapped are closely linked to the statutory
parameters of Section 504 and EAHCA, as well as the due process clause of the
Fourteenth Amendment.

Mills *v.* Board of Education *(1972).* In this case, seven children enjoined the District of Columbia Public Schools from excluding them from publicly supported
education.

> They allege that although they can profit from an education either in regular
> classrooms with supportive services or in special classes adapted to their
> needs, they have been labeled as behavioral problems, mentally retarded,
> emotionally disturbed, or hyperactive, and denied admission to the public
> schools or excluded therefrom after admission, with no provision for alter-
> native educational placement or periodical review. . . .

Up to that time the District of Columbia School District had not documented
the number of "exceptional" children that resided within the District. There were
estimates of as many as 22,000 handicapped children, with as many as 18,000 not
being provided specialized education. As typical in earlier times, the District was

Focus Question 6:
Does the law require that
handicapped children be
placed in regular classrooms?

Objective 15:
Describe the findings and
implications of key judicial
actions that have defined procedures related to the education of the handicapped.

not systematically addressing the educational needs of this student population. For example, in a 1971 report, the D.C. Public Schools estimated that 12,340 handicapped children were not going to be served in the 1971–1972 school year.

The Circuit Judge based his decision on the due process clause of the Fifteenth Amendment since this only applies to states. He concluded that the doctrine of equal educational opportunity (the education application of the equal protection clause) did apply and that due process was a binding component for the District. The Court concluded that the District was required by the Constitution, District of Columbia Code, and the District's own regulations to provide a publicly supported education for these "exceptional" children. Further, if there were not sufficient funds, then whatever funds there were must be expended equitably so that no child is entirely excluded.

> 1. That no child eligible for a publicly supported education in the District of Columbia public schools shall be excluded from a regular public school assignment by a rule, policy, or practice of the Board of Education of the District of Columbia or its agents unless such child is provided (a) adequate alternative educational services suited to the child's needs, which may include special education or tuition grants, and (b) a constitutionally adequate prior hearing and periodic review of the child's status, progress, and the adequacy of any educational alternative. . . .

> 2. The District of Columbia shall provide to each child of school age a free and suitable publicly supported education regardless of the degree of the child's mental, physical, or emotional disability or impairment. Furthermore, defendants shall not exclude any child resident in the District of Columbia from such publicly supported education on the basis of a claim of insufficient resources. . . .

Pennsylvania Association for Retarded Children (PARC) *v.* Commonwealth (1971). A consent order, issued prior to *Mills* v. *Board of Education,* required Pennsylvania to provide a free, public program of education and training appropriate to the child's capacity, within the context of a presumption that, among the alternative programs of education and training required by statute to be available, placement in a regular public school class is preferable to placement in a special public class (that is a class for "handicapped" children), and placement in a special public school class is preferable to placement in any other type of program of education and training.

Congress seems to have based much of the subsequent legislation, rules, and regulations on *Mills* and *PARC.* EAHCA and Section 504 outline procedures that must be addressed by schools, parents, and the state. For example, the most appropriate educational placement for the handicapped child must be determined using EAHCA procedures. And Section 504 is used to make judgments about whether the child is otherwise qualified to be educated in a particular setting.

The Individualized Educational Program (IEP), Which Is Mandated under EAHCA, Is the Key to Implementing Congressional Goals for Handicapped Children. Each district will have a protocol for these "staffings," during which representatives of the school district, the child's teacher, the parents or guardians, and, whenever appropriate, the disabled child meet to review the child's performance and progress. Annual goals and short-term objectives are identified and the needed instruction and services are planned. These meetings must occur at least once a year.

Activity 9.14:
Ask a regular and/or special education teacher to visit class. Have them describe the "staffing" process and the development of an IEP. Be sure to have them describe the legal parameters that frame their actions and decisions.

The intent of Congress throughout has been to build in heavy involvement of parents. There are procedural safeguards that include parents' meaningful input into all decisions affecting their child's education, the right to examine all relevant records, and prior written notice whenever a change in the child's placement is proposed, as well as a series of administrative review steps.

Throughout all of the IEP process there is a "stay put" provision, which requires that the child be continued in the current educational context. The only exception to this would be in those instances when the parent and the education agency agree that a change is desirable.

This brief summary of congressional actions and government decisions related to education of the handicapped documents the unique evolution in perspective that has occurred in the last thirty years. Education of handicapped students has moved from the option of the local district to a policy and law of the land. In an analysis of education spending the Sandia National Laboratories noted that most of the increase in educational expenditures in the last twenty years has been in special education. Altogether, these actions signify a major new commitment in American education to address individual needs.

AIDS as a Handicap. Under IDEA the courts have found that AIDS is a handicapping condition. Also, the 1990 Americans with Disabilities Act expanded the definition of "disability" in such a way as to include persons with AIDS. AIDS is an issue charged with emotion, as was desegregation. People do not always approach these difficult situations with calmness or equanimity. The courts, as well as school administrators and teachers, are constantly struggling to determine what is appropriate education for students handicapped with AIDS, and what are suitable educational environments for children with these handicaps. During this time there will be other exceptional and spiritually strong children, such as Ryan White, who challenged the educational system's capabilities. Ryan White was the Indiana adolescent with AIDS who, because of attitudes within the school, was forced to leave town. Others with handicaps will have the courage to challenge the limits of our systems. In those situations, educators, the courts, and our policymakers will be further tested but at the same time will have the opportunity to move our educational system ahead by developing creative approaches and innovative practices. Calm heads will be needed, as will wisdom from all the players in order for the education system to succeed for all its students.

The final issue in this chapter has been education for the handicapped. Prior to 1972, handicapped children received whatever level of public education was made available by their local school districts. Over the last twenty years, a series of legislative acts, rules, and regulations established that handicapped children, including those with AIDS, are entitled to an "adequate" education. The extent and meaning of "adequate" are still being worked out and will continue to be topics of discussion, contention, and legal actions in the remaining 1990s and beyond.

Global Perspectives: Legal Aspects of Education in Other Countries.

The legal aspects of school systems in other countries offer some interesting differences in comparison to the American system. For example, other democratic countries do not have the apparently never ending debates about the separation of church and state. As nearby as provinces of Canada and as far away as Belgium and The Netherlands, public dollars fund nondenominational and church-based

Objective 16:
Outline the reasoning behind the position that children with AIDS are handicapped.

Activity 9.15:
Have students describe any personal experiences that they may have had with AIDS. Link this discussion to the Professional Dilemma.

CNN Clip 19:
Kid Condom

PROFESSIONAL DILEMMA

Should Condoms Be Available to Students in Your School?

Obviously, there are moral, philosophical, religious, and ethical questions related to students having easy access to condoms. Parents would like to believe that their children are not sexually active. Most church and religious groups are opposed to premarital sex. Others are concerned that it is important to educate students about "safe sex," especially with the ever-increasing threat of AIDS.

To help you put this issue into perspective, here are some statistics: A 1991 Centers for Disease Control national survey of teenagers found that 54 percent had had sexual intercourse and that 35 percent had had two or more sexual partners. Among older teenagers, 48 percent had used condoms, while among the fifteen-year-olds, 57 percent had used condoms—which might suggest attempts at early education regarding the dangers of AIDS are having limited effect on the safe-sex practices of students.

When these questions are raised in your classroom, will you limit the discussion and the curriculum that is available to teach young people preventive health behaviors in the face of such epidemics as AIDS, or will you teach specific treatment measures for preventing communicable diseases? For comparison purposes you might be interested in knowing that there was a time when inoculations against disease, such as polio and measles, were administered at school. What about the use of condoms today?

However pressing the realities of health concerns, you and the faculty in your school will have to grapple with this critical question: "Should students have access to condoms at school?" As you might imagine, emotions will have to be placed in juxtaposition to the diverse values and beliefs of various members of the school staff and the community, as well as what the law allows.

- As a teacher, how will you respond to the request to teach about life-threatening epidemics, such as AIDS, that will stir moral controversy?

- Do you see a difference between schools administering vaccinations against disease and schools dispensing condoms to prevent disease? Explain your position.

Objective 17:
Contrast aspects of the American legal system, as it relates to schooling, with the legal aspects of schooling in other countries.

Activity 9.16:
Ask students to share information that they may have about legal aspects of education in other countries. If possible, contrast countries where education is constituted nationally with the heavy state role in the United States.

schools. In the Dutch system there are three separate school systems: public, Catholic, and Protestant. Each is supported with public funds, yet each is governed independently.

Germany incorporates instruction in religion in all schools. In fact, often there is one teacher who is hired specifically to teach religion in regularly scheduled classes. Students have to take instruction on religion, and are given a choice of Protestant or Catholic classes. In the higher grades, this instruction shifts toward more emphasis on human values.

Also in Germany there are no school boards, and there are no publicly elected state boards of education. The school system is run by government bureaucracies. The curriculum and exams are set by the state. However, parents are very actively involved in the education of their children at the school site. For example, when there is a "parent evening," *both* parents will attend. At these evenings much of the "talk" between parents will be about the homework assignments that their children have been doing. The reason is that parents are expected to help their children with homework. Yes, in Germany children have three to four hours of homework assignments *every day*. The school day ends at 1:00 P.M. Children return home and work on their homework during the afternoon.

There is a different approach to consideration of special needs children in Germany. These children either have tutors or are assigned to different schools. If a child cannot keep up with the others at a school, he or she is told "You do not belong here." The parents and the child will then either have to work harder at keeping up or move to a different school.

Another legal aspect of the education system in Germany is that teachers as government employees cannot be sued. One consequence is that teachers do not supervise children during nonteaching times. Also, as government employees, teachers are not evaluated after their first year of teaching. As this description of legal aspects of schooling in Germany illustrates, the major aspects of education and schools can be very different from country to country. Be careful to not assume that schools are the same everywhere.

Summary and Implications

The law is involved with American education, and each level of government has legal responsibilities. The U.S. Supreme Court has interpreted the Constitution in many cases related to education. Of special interest are the cases dealing with the First and Fourteenth Amendments. The First Amendment ensures freedom of speech, religion, and the press and the right to petition. Public financial support of nonpublic education and the practice of sectarian religion in public schools have persisted as issues in American education.

The Fourteenth Amendment protects specified privileges of citizens. Segregated schools existed in the United States for many years. Desegregation in the public schools began in 1954 with the U.S. Supreme court ruling on *Brown* v. *Board of Education of Topeka*. These social issues have a decided effect on how schools operate. Currently, you will observe that legal actions are increasing in attempts to be released from court desegregation orders.

The implication of court decisions based on the First and Fourteenth Amendments are many. Local boards of education must develop and adopt policies that harmonize with federal and state legislation and court decisions. The board policies guide administrators and teachers as they carry out their responsibilities. Deciding policy on sensitive subjects like religion and desegregation is often not easy. In classrooms throughout the United States, teachers will need to deal with the proper relationship between religion and public education and with the increasing diversity that is part of schools today.

As was indicated earlier in the chapter, public schools have tended to avoid some of these topics. One reason given by parents for withdrawing their children from public schools was that public schools were promulgating secular humanism and ignoring religion. Public schools cannot foster any particular religion or have religious ceremonies. They can, however, recognize the religious dimension of human existence and conduct appropriate study *about* religion. Public schools and their teachers must address rather than avoid this issue.

A third issue presented in this chapter is affirmative action. The legal basis of affirmative action is found in Titles VI and VII of the Civil Rights Act of 1964 and in Title IX of the Education Amendments of 1972. In essence, they deal with prohibiting discrimination in employment with respect to race, color, religion, sex, or national origin, particularly in educational programs or activities that receive federal financial assistance. Affirmative action also involves positive efforts to recruit and employ individuals and admit students who are underrepresented in the workplace or educational setting. Furthermore, affirmative action is involved in releasing employees. Recent court cases indicate that the courts are more lenient in issues involving hiring than in issues involving releasing employees. Members of minorities can be given preference in hiring to correct past discrimination, but they cannot be given preference over more senior employees in termination of employment.

The concluding section of this chapter described some aspects of law and schooling in Germany. In some way every country will have legal structures related to schools. You are reminded to not expect every country to view schooling, in a legal sense, in the same way.

Discussion Questions

1. The appropriate place, if any, for prayer in public schools continues to be a source of contention. What position should public school teachers take relative to this issue? What will you say if a parent wants you to have a moment of prayer in your classroom?

2. Your state legislators offer many bills related to operation of the public schools. Are there any examples of proposed bills that you think the courts would find unconstitutional?

3. Segregation is illegal, yet there are many schools and school districts in which there are disproportionate numbers of minority students. What do you see as the educational implications of the continuation of these situations?

4. What experiences have you had with Affirmative Action? What implications for teaching do you see in Affirmative Action and Equal Opportunity initiatives?

5. How would you define an "appropriate education" for handicapped children?

Journal/Portfolio Development

1. A number of enduring issues have been described in this chapter. Each has continuing legal challenges, and there is the possibility of new statutory initiatives that could have significant implications for schools. Select one of these issues that you would like to know more about and prepare an "issues brief." Search your college library for relevant material. Review related reports in news magazines and newspapers for the last two years. Develop an analysis of the issue, being sure to describe the different sides and perspectives, not just the side you prefer. In the concluding section of your brief, examine implications of different decision possibilities for you as a teacher and your classroom. Place your notes in your folio under a title such as "Legal Issues."

2. Prayer in public schools is the center for seemingly endless debates. As a teacher, you will probably be asked to offer an opinion, or asked to include a moment of silence in your classroom. Now is the time for you to prepare your position. Certainly, you have a personal position related to whether prayer should be permitted/encouraged/required in public schools. On one page make notes about the key points in your personal position. Then review the position of the courts as outlined in this chapter. Is your personal position consistent with legal precedent? Add to your page of notes where your position is supported and refuted by law. Place your notes in your folio under a title such as "Legal: Prayer in Schools."

School-Based Experiences

1. Interview a school district administrator about the effects of laws and court decisions on schools. How has the administrator had to adjust his or her workday based on the legal aspects of education? Write a report that relates what this person had to say to the legal concepts and issues that were developed in this chapter.

2. Interview a special education teacher about his or her knowledge of Section 504, PL 94–142, and

IDEA. How has the work of this teacher changed with the implementation of these laws? Is this teacher working more or less or about the same as regular classroom teachers? Write a report that contrasts what this teacher is doing with the legal expectations for providing an adequate education for the handicapped.

Notes

1. *Lemon* v. *Kurtzman* (1971).
2. *DiCenso* v. *Robinson* (1971).
3. *State* v. *Peterman* (1904).
4. *Pasadena City Board of Education* v. *Spangler* (1976).

Bibliography

Banks, James A., and Banks, Cherry A. McGree, eds. *Multicultural Education: Issues and Perspectives.* Boston: Allyn and Bacon, 1989.

Fisher, Louis; Schimmel, David; and Kelley, Cynthia. *Teacher and the Law.* New York: Longman, Inc., 1987.

LaMorte, Michael W. *School Law: Cases and Concepts.* Boston: Allyn and Bacon, 1982.

Salome, Rosemary C. *Equal Education Under Law.* New York: St. Martin's Press, 1986.

Sandia National Laboratories. "Sandia Study Helps Focus Educational Improvement Agenda." Albuquerque, NM: Sandia National Laboratories, 1991.

Zerkel, Perry. "Courtside." *Phi Delta Kappan.* (A regular feature in each issue of the *Phi Delta Kappan* providing timely and pertinent information about legal issues.)

The Rights of Students and Teachers

Focus Questions

1 Do students have the same rights as adult citizens?
2 What is the difference between procedural and substantive due process?
3 Do teachers and school administrators have to obtain a search warrant before they can search a student?
4 Is it legal for teachers to strike?
5 What is meant by the balance concept between the interest of teachers and the interest of the state?

Key Terms and Concepts

Academic freedom: The opportunity for a teacher to teach without certain coercion, censorship, or other restrictive interference.

Due process: The procedural requirements that must be followed to safeguard individuals from arbitrary, capricious, or unreasonable policies, practices, or actions.

Educational malpractice: Culpable neglect by a teacher in the performance of his or her duties as an educator.

In loco parentis: A term used to describe the implied power of schools to function in place of a parent.

Liability: The failure to use a reasonable amount of care when such conduct results in injury to another.

Teacher certification: The process whereby each state determines the requirements for obtaining a license to teach, processes applications, and issues such licenses.

Tenure: A system of school employment in which educators, after serving a probationary period, retain their positions indefinitely unless they are dismissed for legally specified reasons through clearly established procedures.

*T*eachers and students have rights and responsibilities. The U.S. Constitution again becomes the primary document and the courts the final arbiters of the extent of these rights. There are some special conditions and constraints on teachers as public employees that are narrowing in comparison to one's rights as a U.S. citizen. Students' rights are constrained due to their age and the custodial and care responsibilities that schools assume. Teachers and students still have rights, and, along with these rights responsibilities. The extent and limits of these as currently defined and adjudicated are presented in this chapter.

Students' Rights and Responsibilities

Test Questions 10.1–10.35

Objective 1:
Demonstrate a basic understanding of the legal rights and responsibilities of school students.

Focus Question 1:
Do students have the same rights as adult citizens?

Transparency 51:
Groups with Rights and Responsibilities under the U.S. Constitution and Federal Law

The rights of students have been through some dramatic shifts during the last twenty-five years. Prior to 1969, school authorities clearly had the final say as long as what they decided was seen as reasonable. A key U.S. Supreme Court decision in 1969 changed the balance by concluding that students do not "shed their constitutional rights to freedom of speech or expression at the schoolhouse gate." Going further on behalf of student rights, in 1975 the Court decided that the principle of due process applied to students. These decisions led to several successful student challenges of school policies and procedures. In the late 1980s Court decisions moved back toward increasing the authority of public school officials. Along the way student life has become more complex, not only through such threats as the increased use of drugs and the presence of weapons and gangs, but also through a diverse multicultural and shifting political context that has made it more difficult to determine what is and what is not appropriate to be able to do and say within a school environment.

To illustrate some of the issues and decisions related to student rights and responsibilities, specific court cases are presented here. Note that the cases do not necessarily constitute the last word regarding student rights, but rather are used to provide an overview of some of the issues that have been decided by our courts. Table 10.1 is a summary of key cases; however, it is not intended to provide a complete understanding of the court decisions. You should read the following narrative and pursue references provided in the Notes and Bibliography to learn more about these and other student rights issues.

Students' Rights as Citizens

Objective 2:
Describe the rights of school students as citizens.

Remember, the U.S. Constitution does not mention education. However, through a series of court decisions, all children in the United States have been granted the opportunity for a public school education. Still, as has been pointed out above, this situation is open to change, as is reflected in the 1994 California referendum vote on Proposition 187. Further, although school officials have a great deal of authority, children as students maintain many of the constitutional rights that adult citizens enjoy all the time. As obvious as each of these points may seem, each has been the subject of debate and court decision.

Students' Right to an Education. American children have a right to an education; this right is ensured in many state constitutions. It has been further defined

TABLE 10.1   Selected U.S. Supreme Court Decisions Related to Students' Rights and Responsibilities

Case	Issue	Decision
Plyler v. *Doe* (1982)	Rights to education of illegal aliens	Struck down Texas law that denied a free public education to these children.
Goss v. *Lopez* (1975)	Suspension of high school students without a hearing	Court ruled only in an emergency can a student be suspended without a hearing.
Wood v. *Strickland* (1975)	Can school board members be sued for depriving students of their constitutional rights? (suspension)?	Students can seek damages from individual school board members but not from the school district.
Tinker v. *Des Moines Independent Community School District* (1969)	Free speech rights of students to wear black armbands to protest war in Vietnam	Court ruled against school district—recognized to an extent constitutional rights of pupils.
Board of Education, Island Trees Union Free District No. 26 v. *Pico* (1982)	Challenged school board's decision to remove books from the school library	Court issued decision that, under certain circumstances, children may challenge board's decision to remove books.
Ingraham v. *Wright* (1977)	May states authorize corporal punishment without consent of the student's parent?	Yes, states may constitutionally authorize corporal punishment.
Bethel School District No. 403 v. *Fraser* (1986)	May school officials restrain student speech?	School officials may discipline a student for making lewd and indecent speech in a school assembly attended by other students.
Hazelwood School District v. *Kuhlmeier* (1988)	School district control of student expression in school newspapers, theatrical productions, and other forums	School administrators have broad authority to control student expression in the official student newspaper, which is not a public forum—considered as a part of the curriculum.
Honig v. *Doe* (1988)	Violation of the Education for All Handicapped Children Act P.L. 94–142; indefinitely suspended and attempted to expel two emotionally disturbed students	The Act authorizes officials to suspend dangerous and crippled children for a maximum of ten days. Justice Brennan said, "Congress very much meant to strip schools of unilateral authority to exclude disturbed students."
New Jersey v. *T.L.O.* (1985)	Search and seizure	School officials must have a reasonable cause when engaged in searches.

by court decisions and is now interpreted to mean that each child shall have an equal opportunity to pursue education.

The right to an education, however, is not without certain prerequisites. Citizenship alone does not guarantee a free education. Statutes that establish public school systems also generally establish how operating costs will be met. Real estate taxes are the usual source of funds, so the residence requirement is necessary for school attendance without tuition. *Residence* does not mean that the student, parent, or guardian must pay real estate taxes; it means that the student must live in the school district in which he or she wants to attend school. Residence then is a prerequisite to the right of a free public education within a specific school district.

The Children of Undocumented Illegal Aliens Have a Right to a Public Education. In *Plyler* v. *Doe* (1982) the controversial five-to-four majority decision struck down a Texas law denying a free public education to these children. The majority opinion held that the Texas law "imposes a lifetime of hardship on a discrete class of children not accountable for their disabling status and promotes the creation and perpetuation of a subclass of illiterates within our boundaries, surely adding to the problems and costs of unemployment, welfare, and crime."

As part of the continuing taxpayer revolt, the rights of children of undocumented and illegal aliens were challenged in California in the 1994 election. A citizens' referendum, Proposition 187, was approved by the voters. One aspect of this initiative directs that public services (schools) cannot be made available to children whose parents are not U.S. citizens. Although this referendum only applies to California, it is being challenged in state and federal courts and would seem to directly violate *Plyler* v. *Doe.*

Homeless Children Have the Right to Go to School.   There are over 500,000 homeless children in the United States. Since access to public school usually requires a residence address and a parent or guardian, as well as transportation, in the past homeless children were squeezed out of the system. This growing problem was addressed by Congress in 1987 with passage of the Stewart B. McKinney Homeless Assistance Act, which requires that "each State educational agency shall assure that each child of a homeless individual and each homeless youth have access to a free, appropriate public education." The law was amended in 1990 to require each school district to provide services to the homeless that are comparable to the services offered other students in the schools. These services include allowing homeless children to finish the school year in the school they were in before they lost their housing, providing transportation to school, tutoring to help catch students up, and giving the opportunity to take part in school programs offered to other children.

Students' Right to Sue.
The U.S. Supreme Court has affirmed that students may sue school board members who are guilty of intentionally depriving students of their constitutional rights. In *Wood* v. *Strickland* (1975) the Supreme Court held that school officials who discipline students unfairly cannot defend themselves against civil rights suits by claiming ignorance of pupils' basic constitutional rights. As a result of this decision, Judge Paul Williams, a federal judge in Arkansas, ordered that the students who had been suspended could seek damages from individual school board members—though not from the school district as a corporate body. The judge also ruled that the school records of the pupils must be cleared of the suspension incident. From these decisions it is apparent that the U.S. Supreme Court is taking into account the rights of students.

Rights of Students to Collect Damages.   The Supreme Court extended and clarified its ruling in *Wood* three years later when it considered the right of students to collect damages for having been suspended without a hearing.[1] The case treated two issues: under what conditions damages may be awarded to students who have been deprived of their constitutional rights and the amount of damages they can

---

Activity 10.1:
Have students divide into small groups of from five to seven. Ask some of the groups to be school boards and to write a press release informing the community of the reasons that children whose parents are illegal aliens or homeless are attending public schools. Have the other groups represent the taxpayers' group "Pay-as-you-go," with the assignment to write a press release that explains why *those* children should not be in the local public schools.

Information Note 10.1:
The McKinney Homeless Assistance Act (1990) ensures that homeless children have access to a free, appropriate public education that is the same as that provided to other children. The purpose of the law is to remove barriers—legal and practical—and to facilitate the enrollment, attendance, and success of homeless children and youth in schools.

Transparency 52:
Lawsuits Against School Districts Filed by Students

receive. The Court held that a student must first clearly establish that an injury has occurred before damages can be collected. Since that condition had not been established, the Court ruled that the students were entitled only to symbolic damages of $1.00.

Students' Right to Due Process. Much of the recent involvement of the courts with student rights has concerned due process of law for pupils. Due process is guaranteed by the Fourteenth Amendment. The protection clause states that "nor shall any State . . . deny to any person within its jurisdiction the equal protection of the laws." **Due process** of law means following those rules and principles that have been established for enforcing and protecting the rights of the accused. Due process has two connotations—procedural and substantive. *Procedural* due process has to do with whether or not the procedures used in disciplinary cases are fair; *substantive* due process is concerned with whether or not the school authorities have deprived a student of basic substantive constitutional rights such as personal liberty, property, and privacy.[2]

Focus Question 2:
What is the difference between procedural and substantive due process?

Key Term:
Due process

The application of due process to issues in schools is a recent phenomenon. Historically, schools functioned under the doctrine of ***in loco parentis*** (in place of a parent). This doctrine meant that schools could exercise almost complete control over students because they were acting as parent substitutes. Under the doctrine of *in loco parentis* the courts have usually upheld the rules and regulations of local boards of education, particularly about pupil conduct. However, the courts have not supported rules that are unconstitutionally "vague" and/or "overboard." The following cases illustrate the difficult balance between protecting students' right to due process, and at the same time allowing schools to have sufficient authority to pursue their mission.

Key Term:
In loco parentis

Procedural Due Process Is Frequently Scrutinized in Cases of Suspension and Expulsion. These cases most often result from disciplinary action taken by the school, which may or may not have violated a pupil's substantive constitutional rights. For example, in *Goss v. Lopez* (1975) the U.S. Supreme Court dealt with the suspension of high school students in Columbus, Ohio. In that case the named plaintiffs alleged that they had been suspended from public high school for up to ten days without a hearing. The action was brought up for deprivation of constitutional rights. Two students who were suspended for a semester brought suit charging that their due process rights were denied—because they were not present at the board meeting when the suspensions were handed out.

Journal Activity Master 10.1: An Analysis of Student and Teacher Rights. This activity requires the student to consider the rights of students, parents, and teachers, using gangs as a case study.

In ruling that students cannot be suspended without some kind of hearing, the Court said:

> The prospect of imposing elaborate hearing requirements in every suspension case is viewed with great concern, and many school authorities may well prefer the untrammeled power to act unilaterally, unhampered by rules about notice and hearing. But it would be a strange disciplinary system in an educational institution if no communication was sought by the disciplinarian with the student in an effort to inform him of his defalcation and to let him tell his side of the story in order to make sure than an injustice is not done. Fairness can rarely be obtained by secret, one-sided determination of the facts decisive of rights. . . . Secrecy is not congenial to truth-seeking and self-righteousness gives too slender an assurance of rightness. No better instrument has been devised for arriving at truth than to give a person in jeopardy of serious loss notice of the case against him and opportunity to meet it.

Students have frequently organized to strike for their rights.

Procedural due process cases usually involve alleged violations of the Fourteenth Amendment, which provides for the protection of specified privileges of citizens, including notice to the student, impartiality of the hearing process, and the right of representation. They may also involve alleged violations of state constitutions or statutory law that call for specific procedures. For example, many states have procedures for expulsion or suspension. Expulsion usually involves notifying parents or guardians in a specific way, perhaps by registered mail, and giving students the opportunity for a hearing before the board of education or a designated hearing officer. Suspension procedures are usually detailed as well, designating who has the authority to suspend and the length of time for suspension. Teachers and administrators should know due process regulations, including the specific regulations of the state where they are employed.

Substantive Due Process Frequently Addresses Questions of the Students' Constitutional Rights to Free Speech versus the Schools' Authority to Maintain Order in Support of Education. The *Tinker* case (*Tinker* v. *Des Moines Independent Community School District,* 1969) was significant. It involved a school board's attempt to keep students from wearing black armbands in a protest against hostilities in Vietnam. In 1969 the U.S. Supreme Court ruled against the Des Moines school board. The majority opinion of the Court was that

> the wearing of armbands in the circumstances of this case was entirely divorced from actually or potentially disruptive conduct by those participating in it. It was closely akin to "pure speech" which, we have repeatedly held, is entitled to comprehensive protection, under the First Amendment. . . .
>
> First Amendment rights, applied in the light of the special characteristics of the school environment, are available to teachers and students. It can hardly be argued that either students or teachers shed their constitutional rights to freedom at the schoolhouse gate.

In the *Tinker* opinion the Court clearly designated that the decision "does not concern aggressive, disruptive action or even group demonstrations." The decision did make it clear that whatever their age, students have constitutional rights; and the decision has had widespread effect on the operation of schools in the United States. Schools have had to pay attention to school law. Educators as well as lawyers have been guided by the principles set forth in the decision regarding the constitutional relationship between public school students and school officials.

A more recent U.S. Supreme Court decision appears to have at least narrowed the breadth of application of the *Tinker* ruling. The case involved Matthew Fraser, a high school senior in a school outside Tacoma, Washington. In the spring of 1983, Fraser was suspended from school for two days after he gave a short speech at a school assembly nominating a friend for a position in student government. School officials argued that Fraser's speech contained sexual innuendos that provoked other students to engage in disruptive behaviors unfavorable to the school setting. The U.S. District Court for the Western District of Washington held that Fraser's punishment violated his rights to free speech under the First Amendment and awarded him damages. The U.S. Court of Appeals for the Ninth Circuit affirmed the decision, holding that Fraser's speech was not disruptive under the standards of *Tinker*.[3] However, in the majority opinion in *Bethel School District No. 403* v. *Fraser* (1986), Chief Justice Warren Burger wrote: "The determination of what manner of speech in the classroom or in school assembly is inappropriate properly rests with the school board."

Attorney Thomas J. Flygare suggests that the major unanswered question appears to be whether *Fraser* will be interpreted to permit school officials to place an outright ban on political speech as "inappropriate" or whether it will be interpreted only to permit punishment for "indecent" and similar forms of speech.[4]

Efforts Have Been Made to Define Student Rights. One such effort, *A Bill of Rights for High School Students*, was developed by the American Civil Liberties Union of Maryland. It is based partly on court decisions and illustrates current thinking about student rights. It addresses, for example, freedom of expression, religion, and privacy and rights of equality of opportunity and due process. (The complete text is given in Appendix 10.1 on page 288.) Many school systems also have established their own bill of rights.

Activity 10.2:
Divide the class into groups and have them develop a bill of rights for students. Then have them list the responsibilities that flow from these rights. Have each group present its bill of rights and concomitant responsibilities to the whole class.

Discussion Question 1:
Examine "A Bill of Rights for High School Students" presented in Appendix 10.1. What are the strengths of this bill? Are there some elements of it that will be problematic for teachers?

Students' Responsibilities in School

The right, or privilege, of children to attend school also depends on their compliance with the rules and regulations of the school. To ensure the day-to-day orderly operation of schools, boards of education have the right to establish reasonable rules and regulations controlling pupils and their conduct. In a number of instances the boards' actions have been challenged. Most challenges have concerned corporal punishment, rights of married students to an education, dress codes, freedom of expression, and involvement with drugs.

Objective 3:
Describe the responsibilities and protections that have been established by law for school students.

Dress Codes and Grooming.   Lower-court cases dealing with grooming have been decided in some instances in favor of the board of education—in support of their rules and regulations—and in other instances in favor of the student. A general principle seems to be that if the dress and grooming do not incite or cause disruptive behavior or pose a health or safety problem, the court ruling is likely to support the student. Dress codes, once very much in vogue, are much less evident today. Although the U.S. Supreme Court has yet to consider a so-called long-hair case, federal courts in every circuit have issued rulings in such cases; half of them found such regulations unconstitutional, and half upheld them. In all, over a two-decade period, more than three hundred cases on this subject were decided by federal and state courts. If there is a trend, it is that students have won most of the cases that dealt with hairstyle.

The courts have usually refused to uphold dress and hair length regulations for athletic teams or extracurricular activities unless the school proves that the hair or dress interfered with a student's ability to play the sport or perform the activity.[5]

In the late 1970s and continuing through the 1980s, courts entertained fewer challenges to grooming regulations. The later decisions, however, continued to be consistent with earlier court rulings. Courts have supported school officials who attempted to regulate student appearance if the regulation could be based on disruption, health, or safety. Presumably, the controversy over the length of a student's hair or one's grooming in general is no longer critical because officials and students have a more common ground of agreement about what is acceptable. However, as the 1990s continue, new questions could be raised in relation to school efforts to control the clothing and other grooming symbols of gangs.

Journal/Portfolio Development 1: Questions about student rights.

Corporal Punishment. In 1977 the U.S. Supreme Court ruled on and finally resolved many of the issues related to corporal punishment (*Ingraham* v. *Wright*, 1977). The opinion established that states may *constitutionally* authorize corporal punishment without prior hearing or notice and without consent by the student's parents, and may as a matter of policy elect to prohibit or limit the use of corporal punishment. It also held that corporal punishment is not in violation of the Eighth Amendment.

Journal Activity Master 10.2: An Analysis of Reasonableness. This assignment requires students to evaluate the meaning of reasonableness in discipline policy.

In response to the greater sensitivity to student rights, many school districts have adopted administrative rules and regulations to restrict the occasions, nature, and manner of administering corporal punishment. In some instances, school districts specify that corporal punishment may be administered only under the direction of the principal and in the presence of another adult.

For the most part, courts have been consistent over the years in upholding school personnel in administering *reasonable* corporal punishment. Reasonableness frequently reflects local attitudes; its definition will therefore vary from region to region. In determining whether or not to administer corporal punishment, school personnel should consider these factors: age, sex, and size of pupil; size and suitability of the instrument and force employed; and the degree of the punishment in respect to the nature of the infraction. It should be noted that the lower courts across the country vary in their judgments regarding the reasonableness of corporal punishment. Teachers are cautioned to be very careful in the use of corporal punishment. Failure to exercise force with limits imposed by common law can expose a teacher to a suit for excessive use of force (battery).

Sex Discrimination. Until relatively recently, educational institutions could discriminate against females—whether they were students, staff, or faculty. In 1972 the Ninety-Second Congress enacted Title IX of the Education Amendments Act to remove sex discrimination against students and employees in federally assisted programs. The key provision in Title IX states: "No person in the United States shall, on the basis of sex, be excluded from participation in, be denied the benefits of, or be subjected to discrimination under any education program or activity receiving federal financial assistance." Title IX is enforced by the Department of Education's Office of Civil Rights. An individual or organization can allege that any policy or practice is discriminatory by writing a letter of complaint to the Secretary of Education. An administrative hearing is the next step in the process. Further steps include suing for money damages under Title IX, which the U.S. Supreme Court affirms in *Franklin* v. *Guinneth County Schools* (1992).

Marriage and Pregnancy. In the past it was not unusual for school officials to expel students who married. Some educators reasoned that marriage brought on additional responsibilities such as the establishment of a household and thus they could not perform well in school. They believed that exclusion would be a deterrent to others. Courts tended to uphold school officials in these positions. Both courts and school officials acted consistently in not rigidly enforcing compulsory attendance statutes for underage students. However, school officials today cannot prohibit a student from attending school merely because he or she is married. This position is based on the notion that every child has a right to attend school and the above-mentioned Title IX.

Public policy today encourages students to acquire as much education as they can. Not only are married students encouraged to remain in school, but they are also entitled to the same rights and privileges as unmarried students. Thus they have the right to take any course the school offers and to participate in extracurricular activities open to other students. That is, participation in extracurricular activities cannot be denied a student solely on the basis of married status. However, a student's attendance and participation rights may be removed when his or her behavior is deleterious to other students.

Today's schools also enroll more pregnant students than ever before. Title IX prohibits their exclusion from school or from participation in extracurricular activities. A number of school systems have reorganized their school programs so that courses can be offered during after-school hours or in the evenings to accommodate married and pregnant students. This arrangement makes it easier for students to work during the day and complete their education at a time convenient to them. Included in such programs are courses and topics aimed at the specific audience and a counseling program to assist students with their adjustment to marriage and family life.

Child Abuse and Neglect.

Our system of government has the right of exercising police power, which means that government is entrusted with the responsibility of looking after the health, safety, and welfare of all its citizens. In effect, a state acts as a guardian over all its people, exercising that role specifically over individuals not able to look after themselves. This guardianship extends to care for children who have been either abused or neglected by their parents. To date, all fifty states have statutes dealing with this issue. These statutes generally protect children under the age of eighteen, but the scope of protection and definitions of abuse and neglect vary considerably among the states. In 1974 Congress passed the Child Abuse Prevention and Treatment Act, which provides financial assistance to states that have developed and implemented programs for identifying, preventing, and treating instances of child abuse and neglect.

The severity of this problem has been highlighted by the requirement of mandatory reporting of suspected abuse and neglect. Formerly, this reporting was limited mainly to physicians, but today educators are also required to report instances of suspected abuse and neglect. Some teachers are reluctant to do so because they fear a breakdown in student-teacher-parent relationships and the possibility of a lawsuit based on an invasion of privacy, assault, or slander. Their fear should be diminished, however, by statutes that grant them immunity for acting in good faith.

School Records.

Before November 19, 1974, the effective date of the Buckley Amendment, the law regarding the privacy of student records was extremely unclear. Many school administrators—and most parents—do not yet realize that parents now have the right to view their children's educational records. Students over the age of eighteen also have the right to see their school records for themselves. Many teachers are not yet aware that their written comments, which they submit as part of a student's record, must be shown at a parent's request, or at a student's request if the student is eighteen or older.

Activity 10.3:
Have students gather information concerning local statistics of child abuse and neglect cases. Ask them to prepare a chart or poster to display these data in a way that will impact a particular target audience, such as teachers, principals, or parents.

Information Note 2:
The rights of children continue to increase in the eyes of the court. For example, in a 1992 child abuse case in Florida, state circuit court judge Judy Kirk ruled that an eleven-year-old boy had the right to end his relationship with his parents. This decision indicates that children have the same rights as adults to seek protection of their interests.

The new law (Public Law 93–380 as amended by Public Law 93–568) requires that schools receiving federal funds must comply with the privacy requirements or face loss of those funds. What must a school district do to comply? According to a 1976 clarification by HEW, the Buckley Amendment sets forth these main requirements that the school district must follow:

Allow all parents, even those not having custody of their children, access to each educational record that a school district keeps on their child.

Establish a district policy on how parents can go about seeing specific records.

Inform all parents what rights they have under the Amendment, how they can act on these rights according to school policy, and where they can see a copy of the policy.

Seek parental permission in writing before disclosing any personally identifiable record on a child to individuals other than professional personnel employed in the district (and others who meet certain specific requirements).[6]

Since the loss of federal funds could present serious problems to some school districts, the responsibility for procedures to meet the requirements of the Buckley Amendment is self-evident. Many school districts have carefully formulated procedures; others are striving to clarify procedures in order to prevent conflicts.

Student Publications. A significant decision relative to "underground" student newspapers was made in Illinois in 1970.[7] Students were expelled for distributing a newspaper named *Grass High*, which criticized school officials and used vulgar language. The students were expelled under an Illinois statute that empowered boards of education to expel pupils guilty of gross disobedience or misconduct. The board of education was supported by a federal court in Illinois, but on appeal the Court of Appeals for the Seventh Circuit reversed the decision. The school board was not able to validate student disruption and interference as required by *Tinker*. The plaintiffs were entitled to collect damages. An implication is the rights of students regarding newspapers they print at home are stronger.

Early in 1988, in a landmark decision (*Hazelwood School District* v. *Kuhlmeier*), the U.S. Supreme Court ruled that administrators have broad authority to control student expression in official school newspapers, theatrical productions, and other forums that are a part of the curriculum. In reaching that decision the Court determined that the *Spectrum*, the school newspaper of the Hazelwood District, was not a public forum. A school policy of the Hazelwood District required that the principal review each proposed issue of the *Spectrum*. The principal objected to two articles scheduled to appear in one issue. One of the articles was about girls at the school who had become pregnant; the other discussed the effects on students of divorce. Neither article used real names. The principal deleted two pages of the *Spectrum* rather than delete only the offending articles or require that they be modified. He stated that there was no time to make any changes in the articles and that the newspaper had to be printed immediately or not at all.

Three student journalists sued, contending that their freedom of speech had been violated. The Supreme Court upheld the principal's action. Justice Byron White decided that the *Spectrum* was not a public forum, but rather a supervised learning experience for journalism students. In effect, the censorship of a student press was upheld by the Supreme Court.

In Justice White's words,

> schools must be able to set high standards for the student speech that is disseminated under [their] auspices—standards that may be higher than those demanded by some newspaper publishers and theatrical producers in the "real" world—and may refuse to disseminate student speech that does not meet those standards.
>
> Accordingly, we hold that the standard articulated in *Tinker* for determining when a school may punish student expression need not also be the standard for determining when a school may refuse to lend its name and resources to the dissemination of student expression.

The issue of institutional control over publications has not yet been fully resolved. Student publications and their distribution have prompted school boards to write rules and regulations that will withstand judicial scrutiny. A prompt review and reasonably fast appeal procedures are vital. Students should also be advised of distribution rules and abide by them.

Focus Question 3:
Do teachers and school administrators have to obtain a search warrant before they can search a student?

Student Rights for the Handicapped.   Before the early 1970s handicapped students' access to education was left to the discretion of different levels of government. In the early 1970s court decisions established the position that handicapped students were entitled to an "appropriate" education and to procedural protections against arbitrary treatment. Congress subsequently specified a broad set of substantive and procedural rights via Section 504 of the Rehabilitation Act and the Education for All Handicapped Children Act (EAHCA). (These acts were described in Chapter 9.) Since that time there has been a continuing series of legislative and legal refinements and extensions of the intents to see that handicapped students have appropriate educational opportunities. The problem has been to define what is meant by "appropriate." This examination and clarification process continues to unfold.

CNN **Clip 14:**
Retarded Mainstreaming

The Individuals with Disabilities Education Act guarantees all students with disabilities access to an equal education.

One recent case dealing with student rights dealt with a violation of the Education for All Handicapped Children Act, PL 94-142. That law requires public school officials to keep disruptive or violent handicapped students in their current classrooms pending hearings on their behavior. In the decision made in *Honig* v. *Doe* (1988) the U.S. Supreme Court upheld lower court rulings that San Francisco school district officials violated the act in 1980 when they indefinitely suspended and then attempted to expel two emotionally disturbed students whom the officials claimed were dangerous.

The act authorizes officials to suspend dangerous handicapped children for a maximum of ten days. Longer suspensions or expulsions are permissible only if the child's parents consent to the action taken or the officials can convince a federal district judge that the child poses a danger to himself or herself or to others. The rules under which school officials must operate also are more limiting if the misbehavior is a manifestation of the student's handicap.

It is clear that Congress meant to restrain the authority that schools had traditionally used to exclude disabled students, particularly emotionally disturbed students from school. PL 94–142 did not leave school administrators powerless to deal with dangerous students.

Student and Locker Searches.   Most courts have refused to subject public school searches to the strict Fourth Amendment standards. In general, the Fourth Amendment protects individuals from search without a warrant (court order). Many lower courts have decided in favor of a more lenient interpretation of the Fourth Amendment in school searches. The rationale is that school authorities are obligated to maintain discipline and a sound educational environment and that responsibility, along with their *in loco parentis* powers, gives them the right to conduct searches and seize contraband on reasonable suspicion without a warrant. First, however, school officials may only search for evidence that a student has violated a school rule or law. Then, there must be a valid rule or law in place.

School authorities do not need a warrant to search a student's locker or a student vehicle on campus. For searches of a student's person, however, courts apply a higher standard. Where reasonable suspicion exists, a school official will likely be upheld. Reasonable suspicion exists when one has information that a student is in possession of something harmful or dangerous, or there is evidence of ille-

Relevant Research

Search of a Student's Purse

A New Jersey teacher discovered two girls smoking in a lavatory, a violation of school rules. While one of the girls admitted to smoking, the second, T.L.O. denied it. The assistant vice principal demanded to see T.L.O.'s purse., opened it, and found a pack of cigarettes. He accused her of lying and reached in to pull out the cigarette pack.

As he reached into the purse he noticed a package of cigarette rolling papers. A thorough search of the purse revealed a small amount of marijuana, a pipe, empty plastic bags, a substantial quantity of money, an index card that appeared to be a list of students who owed T.L.O. money, and two letters that implicated T.L.O. in marijuana dealing.

T.L.O. subsequently confessed to the police that she had sold marijuana at the high school, but later contended that the search of her purse had been unlawful under the Fourth Amendment.

The case was brought to the U.S. Supreme Court in *New Jersey* v. *T.L.O.* (1985). The court first held that the Fourth Amendment's prohibition of unreasonable searches and seizures does apply to public school officials. The Court then explored how to strike the balance between the student's right to privacy and the school's need to maintain a proper learning environment. The Court concluded that school officials need not obtain a warrant before searching a student and that the legality of a search should depend on the reasonableness of the search. The Court concluded that the school officials' actions were correct.

gal activities such as drug dealing (money, a list of customers, or selling papers). The second consideration is the way in which the search of a student's person is conducted. School officials are advised to have students remove contents from their clothing rather than have a teacher or administrator do it. A further caution is not to force students to remove all their clothing or undress to their underwear. To date, courts have not upheld school officials in strip searches. These cases evoke the greatest judicial sympathy toward student damages for illegal searches.[8]

The rights of students include their right to privacy. For example, should teachers be able to search a student's locker without a search warrant?

Peer Sexual Harassment Title IX prohibits sex discrimination, and this includes students harassing other students. Teasing, snapping bra straps, requesting sexual favors, making lewd comments about one's appearance or body parts, telling sexual jokes, engaging in physical abuse, and touching inappropriately are examples of sexual harassment. It is important for teachers to make it clear that sexual harassment will not be tolerated. School districts are supposed to have in place a grievance procedure for sex discrimination complaints. Students and/or their parents can file a complaint with the Office of Civil Rights also. All allegations must be investigated promptly, and immediate action must be taken in those cases where harassment behaviors have been confirmed. Keep in mind that sexual harassment is not limited to high school students; middle school and in some cases elementary school children are also sexually harassed.

Educational Malpractice. Culpable neglect by a teacher in the performance of his or her duties is called **educational malpractice.** The courts of California[9] and New York[10] dismissed suits by former students alleging indirect injury. The plaintiffs claimed that they did not achieve an adequate education and that this was the fault of the school district. In the California case the student, after graduating from high school, could barely read and write. The judge in his opinion stated:

> The science of pedagogy itself is fraught with different and conflicting theories . . . and any layman might—and commonly does—have his own emphatic viewpoints on the subject. . . . The achievement of literacy in the schools, or its failure, is influenced by a host of factors from outside the formal teaching process, and beyond the course of its ministries.

In essence, the judge stated that there is no way to assess the school's negligence. In the New York case the judge said, "The failure to learn does not bespeak a failure to teach." In the 1990s, with the push for accountability, there are likely to be more tests of the educational malpractice question.

As a summary of the discussion of this section, Table 10.2 on page 272 lists brief statements related to the rights and responsibilities of students.

Discussion Question 2:
What are your thoughts about the balancing of student rights with the need of the school officials to maintain an environment that is conducive to learning? Should school officials have more authority? Or should the students have greater freedom?

Transparency 54:
Risk Continua for Conducting Student Searches

Transparency 55:
Teen Sexual Harassment

Key Term:
Educational malpractice

| TABLE 10.2 | Summary Statements on Students' Rights and Responsibilities |

State constitutions provide that a child has the right to an education; to date, students have been unsuccessful in suing school board members on the ground that they have not learned anything.

The due process clause provides that a child is entitled to notice of charges and the opportunity for a hearing prior to being suspended from school for misbehavior.

Students enjoy freedom of speech at school unless that speech is indecent or leads to disruption; courts are in agreement that school officials can regulate the content of student newspapers. Underground newspapers are not subject to this oversight.

Students may be awarded damages from school board members for a violation of their constitutional rights if they can establish that they were injured by the deprivation and that the school official deliberately violated those rights.

The use of corporal punishment is not prohibited by the U.S. Constitution, but excessive punishment may be by the Fourteenth Amendment.

Students may be restricted in their dress when there are problems of disruption, health, or safety.

Assignments of students to activities or classes in general on the basis of sex is not consistent with Title IX. These assignments may be made in such areas as sex education classes or when sports are available for both sexes.

Restricting a student's activities on the basis of marriage or pregnancy is inconsistent with the equal protection clause and Title IX.

Teachers are required to report to proper authorities suspected instances of child abuse and neglect.

Parents have the right to examine their children's educational records; students age eighteen and older have the right to examine their records; school officials may search students, lockers, and student property without a search warrant, but they must have reasonable grounds for believing that the student is in possession of evidence of a school rule or law violation.

Teachers' Rights and Responsibilities

Test Questions 10.36–10.61

Objective 4:
Demonstrate a basic understanding of teachers' legal rights, responsibilities, and liabilities.

Teachers have the same rights as other citizens. The Fourteenth Amendment provides for substantive due process (protection against the deprivation of constitutional rights such as freedom of expression) and procedural due process (procedural protection against unjustified deprivation of substantive rights). Most court cases related to teachers evolve from either liberty or property interests. Liberty interests are created by the Constitution itself; property interests are found in some form of legal entitlement such as tenure or certification.

Teachers also have the same responsibilities as other citizens. They must abide by federal, state, and local laws and by the provisions of contracts. As professionals, they must also assume the heavy responsibility of educating young people. Specific court cases are discussed briefly to illustrate some of the issues and decisions related to aspects of teacher rights and responsibilities. Note that the cases selected do not necessarily constitute the last word regarding teacher rights but rather are used to provide an overview of some of the issues that have been decided in our courts. Table 10.3 summarizes the issues and decisions in selected cases involving teacher rights and responsibilities. This summary table is not intended to provide a complete understanding of the court decisions cited. You should read

TABLE 10.3	Selected U.S. Supreme Court Decisions Related to Teachers' Rights and Responsibilities	
Case	**Issue**	**Decision**
North Haven Board of Education v. *Bell* (1982)	Former women faculty members alleged sex discrimination	Court ruled that school employees as well as students are protected under Title IX.
Cleveland Board of Education v. *LeFleur* (1974)	Rights of pregnant teachers	Court struck down the board policy forcing all pregnant teachers to take mandatory maternity leave.
Board of Regents of State Colleges v. *Roth* (1972)	Rights of nontenured teachers	Teacher had been hired under a one-year contract. Court concluded that he did not have a property interest that would entitle him to procedural rights under the Fourteenth Amendment.
Perry v. *Sindermann* (1972)	Rights of nontenured teachers	A state employee may acquire the property interest if officially fostered customs, rules, understandings, and practices imply a contract promise to grant continuing contract status and thus establish a *de facto* tenure system.
Pickering v. *Board of Education* (1968)	Illinois teacher dismissed for criticizing a school board and superintendent in a letter published by a local newspaper	Court upheld teacher's claim that his First and Fourteenth Amendment rights were denied.
Hortonville Joint School District No. 1 v. *Hortonville Education Association* (1976)	May boards of education dismiss teachers who are striking illegally?	Court said the law gave the board power to employ and dismiss teachers as a part of the municipal labor relations balance.

the textual narrative for better comprehension. Note also that most of the court cases were decided in the 1970s and 1980s; as is illustrated in the examples, more recently new federal statutes have been the defining force.

Conditions of Employment

There are a number of conditions that must be met in order for you to be hired as a teacher. These include successfully completing a professional preparation program, being credentialed or licensed by the state, and receiving a contract from the hiring school district. In each of these instances you have rights established in law and statute, as well as responsibilities.

Teacher Certification and Licensure. The primary purpose of **teacher certification** and licensure is to make sure there are qualified and competent teachers in the public schools. All states have established requirements for teacher certification and licensure. Carrying out the policies of certification is usually a function of a state professional standards board. The board first has to make certain that

Objective 5:
Distinguish and describe key elements of the conditions of employment including licensure, contracts, and discrimination.

Focus Question 4:
Is it legal for teachers to strike?

Key Term:
Teacher certification

Transparency 53:
Lawsuits against School Districts Filed by Employees

applicants meet legal requirements; it then issues the appropriate license/certificates. Certifying agencies may not arbitrarily refuse to issue a certificate to a qualified candidate. The courts have ruled that local boards of education may prescribe additional or higher qualifications beyond the state requirements, provided that such requirements are not irrelevant, unreasonable, or arbitrary. A teaching certificate or license is a privilege granted to practice a profession—it is not a right. Teacher certification is a property interest that cannot be revoked without constitutional due process. Certification laws usually require, in addition, that the candidate show evidence of citizenship, good moral character, and good physical health. A minimum age is frequently specified.

Teacher Employment Contracts. Usually, boards of education have the statutory authority to employ teachers. This authority includes the power to enter into contracts and to fix terms of employment and compensation. In some states, only specific members of the school board may sign teacher contracts. When statutes confer the employing authority to boards of education, the authority cannot be delegated. It is usually the responsibility of the superintendent to screen and nominate candidates to the board. The board, meeting in official session, then acts officially as a group to enter into contractual agreement. Employment procedures vary from state to state, but the process is fundamentally prescribed by the legislature and must be strictly followed by local boards.

A contract usually contains the following elements: the identification of the teacher and the board of education, a statement of the legal capacity of each party to enter into contract, a definition of the assignment specified, a statement of the salary and how it is to be paid, and a provision for signature by the teacher and by the legally authorized agents of the board. In some states, contract forms are provided by state departments of education, and these forms must be used; in others, forms are optional.

A teacher may not enter into legal contract without having a valid teaching certificate issued by the state. Funds may not be legally expended under a contract with a teacher who is not legally certified. Teachers are responsible for making certain that they are legally qualified to enter into contractual agreements. Furthermore, they are responsible for carrying out the terms of the contract and abiding by them. In turn, under the contract they can legally expect proper treatment from an employer.

Discrimination. School districts are prohibited from use of discriminatory practices in the hiring, dismissal, promotion, and demotion of school personnel. In addition to court decisions, federal statutes, such as the Civil Rights Acts of 1964 and 1991, have had a defining influence on the legal basis for discrimination. For example, the 1991 law expanded protection beyond race to also include discrimination based on sex, disability, religion, and national origin. Further, employment practices must be "job-related for the position in question and consistent with business necessity." The 1991 law also places the burden on the defendant (schools) to show that a legitimate nondiscriminatory reason existed for the personnel decision.

Sex Discrimination. In *North Haven Board of Education* v. *Bell* (1982) the U.S. Supreme Court ruled that school employees as well as students are protected under Title IX. The North Haven decision involved former women faculty members who alleged sex discrimination in employment. In upholding Title IX regulations the decision not only allows the U.S. Department of Education to investigate complaints from school employees but also permits the department to cut off federal aid to institutions that discriminate.

Pay Equity. *Burkey* v. *Marshall County Board of Education* (1981) was a decision regarding pay equity. It ruled that the Marshall County school board's policy of paying the female coach of the girls' basketball team half the salary of the male coach of the boys' basketball team violated the Equal Pay Act, Title VII of the Civil Rights Act of 1964, and the Constitution. The Court also ruled that the board's policy of hiring only male teachers as coaches of boys' sports constituted illegal sex discrimination.

Racial Discrimination.   Courts will not intervene when the school board can prove that its decision not to hire or promote a minority was based on legitimate criteria, such as academic qualifications, work experience, licensing, attitude, or job performance. In Missouri, an untenured African American school teacher was laid off because of declining enrollment. When she was not recalled to fill a subsequent teaching vacancy, she sued the school board. The U.S. Court of Appeals, Eighth Circuit, denied her claim of racial discrimination, saying that the board had based its decision on the fact that she lacked permanent state licensing.[11]

Handicap Discrimination.   In another instance a legally blind librarian in Arkansas brought suit against a local school board claiming that she was unlawfully discriminated against in not being hired for a librarian position. The librarian then brought suit in a U.S. district court in Arkansas that held that although she was an "otherwise qualified handicapped individual" under Section 504 of the Rehabilitation Act, the school board had articulated genuine nondiscriminatory reasons for the failure to hire her. The court therefore concluded that the librarian was not denied employment by the school board because of her handicap and that the board had a rational basis for hiring the other applicant. Thus there was no violation of the Rehabilitation Act, and the board's decision was upheld.[12]

Teacher Pregnancy.   In *Cleveland Board of Education* v. *LaFleur* (1974), a landmark decision, the U.S. Supreme Court struck down a school board policy that forced all pregnant teachers to take mandatory maternity leave at fixed periods before and following the pregnancy term, without regard to the ability of different women to continue to work through different stages of pregnancy or recovery. School boards may reasonably regulate pregnancy situations to ensure continuity of instructional services by requiring teachers to notify the school district early in their pregnancy so that school needs may be anticipated. Board policies may not, however, establish arbitrary leave and return dates. Those decisions are best made by the teacher and her physician.

In 1979 Congress passed the Pregnancy Discrimination Act as an amendment to Title VII. The act stipulates that discrimination "because of or on the basis of pregnancy, childbirth or related medical conditions" is prohibited. Women may not be fired, denied promotions, or refused employment as a consequence of their being pregnant or having an abortion. They cannot be forced to take sick leave or exhaust their vacation time. They are entitled to the same disability or sick leave and health insurance benefits as other employees. If other employees are entitled to resume their jobs after disability leave, so too are women who have been pregnant. However, they are not guaranteed the same grade, classroom, or school.

Journal/Portfolio Development 2: Collecting and analyzing information about the rights of teachers.

Activity 10.6:
Using the chalk board or an overhead projector, have students to list the reasons for and against teachers going on strike.

Right to Bargain Collectively.

The rights of teachers to bargain collectively has been an active issue over the last three decades. In the past, teacher groups met informally with boards of education to discuss salaries and other teacher welfare provisions. Sometimes, the superintendent was even the spokesperson for such teacher groups. In recent years, formal collective procedures have evolved. These procedures have been labeled collective bargaining, professional negotiation, cooperative determination, and collective negotiation. Collective bargaining has been defined as a way of winning improved goals and not the goal itself. The right of employees to bargain collectively and the duties of the district to bargain are not constitutionally granted, but are a right typically guaranteed by statute.

A contract means that salaries, working conditions, and other matters within the scope of the collective bargaining agreement can no longer be decided unilaterally by the school administration and board of education. Instead, the contract outlines effective participation by the teachers' union and its members in formulating the school policies and programs under which they work.

The first teachers' group to bargain collectively with its local board of education was the Maywood, Illinois, Proviso Council of West Suburban Teachers, Union Local 571, in 1938. In 1957 a second local, the East St. Louis, Illinois, Federation of Teachers, was successful in negotiating a written contract. The breakthrough, however, came in December 1961, when the United Federation of Teachers, Local 2 of the American Federation of Teachers (AFT), won the right to bargain for New York City's teachers. Since then, collective bargaining agreements between boards of education and teacher groups have grown phenomenally. Both the AFT and the NEA have been active in promoting collective bargaining. Today, approximately 75 percent of the nation's teachers are covered by collective bargaining agreements.

Discussion Question 3:
Each fall there are teacher strikes somewhere in the country that delay the opening of school. Have you ever been involved in a strike? What do you think are the most critical consequences of teacher strikes? If your association leaders called for a strike, would you join the picket line or teach your classes?

Right to Strike.

Judges have generally held that public employees do not have the right to strike. For example, the Supreme Court of Connecticut,[13] and the Supreme Court of New Hampshire[14] ruled that teachers may not strike. The court opinion in Connecticut stated:

> Under our system, the government is established by and run for all of the people, not for the benefit of any person or group. The profit motive, inherent in the principle of free enterprise, is absent. It should be the aim of every employee of the government to do his or her part to make it function as efficiently and economically as possible. The drastic remedy or the organized strike to enforce the demands of unions of government employees is in direct contravention of this principle.

At least eight states—Alaska, Hawaii, Illinois, Minnesota, Ohio, Oregon, Pennsylvania, and Wisconsin—permit strikes in their collective bargaining statutes. At least twenty states have statutes that prohibit strikes. Whether or not there are specific statutes prohibiting strikes, boards of education threatened by strikes can usually get a court injunction forestalling them. Both the NEA and the AFT view the strike as a last-resort technique, although justifiable in some circumstances.

Recently, by a six-to-three vote, the U.S. Supreme Court ruled that boards of education can discharge teachers who are striking illegally. Ramifications of this decision, involving a Wisconsin public school, are potentially far-reaching. The Court viewed discharge as a policy matter rather than an issue for adjudication: "What choice among the alternative responses to the teachers' strike will best serve the interests of the school system, the interests of the parents and children who depend on the system, and the interests of the citizens whose taxes support it?"

The Court said the state law in question gave the board the power to employ and dismiss teachers as a part of the balance it had struck in municipal labor relations (*Hortonville Joint School District No. 1* v. *Hortonville Education Association*, 1976).

One can argue that strikes are unlawful when a statute is violated, that the courts in their decisions have questioned the right of public employees to strike, and that some teachers and teacher organizations consider strikes unprofessional. The question before teachers seems to be whether the strike is a justifiable and responsible means—after all other ways have been exhausted—of declaring abominable educational and working conditions and trying to remedy them.

Teacher Tenure

Teacher tenure legislation exists in most states. In many states, tenure or fair dismissal laws are mandatory and apply to all school districts without exception. In other states they do not. The various tenure laws differ not only in extent of coverage but also in provision for coverage.

Tenure laws are intended to provide security for teachers in their positions and to prevent removal of capable teachers by capricious action or political motive. Tenure statutes generally include detailed specifications necessary for attaining tenure and for dismissing teachers who have tenure. These statutes have been upheld when attacked on constitutional grounds. The courts reason that since state legislatures create school districts, they have the right to limit their power.

Objective 6:
Describe the differences in rights of tenured and non-tenured teachers.

Key Term:
Tenure

Becoming Tenured and Tenure Rights.   A teacher becomes tenured by serving satisfactorily for a stated time. This period is referred to as the probationary period and varies in length from state to state. The actual process of acquiring tenure after serving the probationary period depends on the applicable statute. In some states the process is automatic at the satisfactory completion of the probationary period; in other states, official action by the school board is necessary. Teachers may be dismissed for a number of reasons, including: "nonperformance of duty, incompetency, insubordination, conviction of crimes involving moral turpitude, failure to comply with reasonable orders, violation of contract provisions or local rules or regulations, persistent failure or refusal to maintain orderly discipline of students, and revocation of the teaching certificate."[15]

A school board in Tennessee dismissed Jane Turk from her teaching position after she was arrested for driving under the influence of alcohol (DUI).[16] Turk's appeal was upheld by the lower-court judge, since there was no evidence of an adverse effect on her capacity and fitness as a teacher. The school board appealed to the Tennessee Supreme Court, which found that the school board "acted in flagrant disregard of the statutory requirement and fundamental fairness in considering matters that should have been specifically charged in writing." Tennessee law requires that before a tenured teacher can be dismissed, "the charges shall be made in writing specifically stating the offenses which are charged." Thus teacher tenure may be affected by teacher conduct outside school as well as inside. This issue, in a sense, deals with the personal freedom of teachers; freedom to behave as other citizens do, freedom to engage in political activities, and academic freedom in the classroom.

Tenure laws are frequently attacked by those who claim that they protect incompetent teachers. There is undoubtedly some truth in the assertion, but it must be stated clearly and unequivocally that they also protect the competent and most able teachers. Teachers who accept the challenge of their profession and dare to use new methods, who inspire curiosity in their students, and who discuss controversial issues in their classrooms need protection from dismissal through political or capricious methods. Incompetent teachers, whether tenured or not, can be dismissed under the law by capable administrators and careful school boards who allow due process while evaluating teacher performance.

Rights of Nontenured Teachers.   Although due process has been applicable for years to tenured teachers, nontenured teachers do not, for the most part, enjoy the same rights. Tenured teachers enjoy two key rights—protection from dismissal except for cause as provided in state statutes and the right to prescribed procedures, also spelled out in the statutes. Nontenured teachers may also have due process rights if spelled out in state statutes, or they may be nonrenewed without any reasons being given in those states not providing for due process. If a nontenured teacher is dismissed (as distinguished from nonrenewed) before the expiration of the contract, the teacher is entitled to due process. In most states, however, provisions are only perfunctory, such as providing calendar dates for nonrenewal of contracts. Cases in Massachusetts[17] and Wisconsin[18] point to the necessity of following due process in dismissing nontenured teachers. In the Massachusetts case the court said: "The particular circumstances of a dismissal of a public school teacher provide compelling reasons for application of a doctrine of procedural due process."[19] In the Wisconsin case the court said:

> A teacher in a public elementary or secondary school is protected by the due process clause of the Fourteenth Amendment against a nonrenewal decision which is wholly without basis in fact and also against a decision which is wholly unreasoned, as well as a decision which is impermissibly based.

In 1972 the Supreme Court helped to clarify the difference in the rights of tenured and nontenured teachers. In one case (*Board of Regents* v. *Roth,* 1972) it held that nontenured teachers were assured of no rights that were not specified in state statutes. In this instance the only right that probationary teachers had was the one to be notified of nonrenewal by a specified date. In a second case the Court ruled that a nontenured teacher in the Texas system of community colleges was entitled to due process because the language of the institution's policy manual was such that an unofficial tenure system was in effect. Guidelines in the policy manual provided that a faculty member with seven years of employment in the system acquired tenure and could be dismissed only for cause (*Perry* v. *Sindermann,* 1972).

Whether a teacher is tenured or not, that person cannot be dismissed for exercise of a right guaranteed by the U.S. Constitution. A school board cannot dismiss a teacher, for example, for engaging in civil rights activities outside school, speaking on matters of public concern, belonging to a given church, or running for public office. These rights are guaranteed to all citizens, including teachers. However, if a teacher's behavior is disruptive or false, dismissal is possible without violating that teacher's right to freedom of speech.

Academic Freedom

A sensitive and vital concern to the educator is **academic freedom**—freedom to control what one will teach and to teach the truth as one discovers it, without fear of penalty. Academic freedom is thus essentially a pedagogical philosophy that has been applied to a variety of professional activities. A philosophical

Activity 10.7:
Ask a first- or second-year teacher to visit class and describe the rights she or he has as an untenured teacher. Be sure to have this beginning teacher describe how she or he is being evaluated.

Objective 7:
List the essential points of academic freedom.

Key Term:
Academic freedom

PROFESSIONAL DILEMMA

What Will You Do If a Child in Your Classroom Has AIDS?

In the fall of 1993 the national media reported two stories of children who had become infected with the AIDS virus through contact with another child who was infected. These reports once again stimulated discussion and concern among parents and students about what to do when an AIDS-infected child attends the school where they teach or that their children attend.

There are several sides to this issue. First of all, as has been pointed out in this Chapter and Chapter 9, *all* children have a legal right to attend public school (see the U.S. Constitution and your state's constitution). And the school is responsible for providing an appropriate education to all children (see PL 94–142, IDEA, and Section 504).

It is important to learn the truth about the potential for other children, and you to become infected through contact with a child who has AIDS. Becoming infected through casual contact with someone who has AIDS is impossible. To contract the AIDS virus, one must be in contact with blood or other body fluids, such as bleeding from the nose, gums, and cuts, or open sores. Transmission of AIDS through sex and the sharing of needles and razors is well documented. Even when there is contact with contaminated blood on the skin or mucus membranes in the nose or mouth, infection is rare. There are no known cases of the AIDS virus being transmitted through eating utensils or bathroom facilities. However, if an infected child is injured and starts to bleed, then preventive actions are necessary.

The Centers for Disease Control (CDC) recommends that spilled blood *always* be treated as though it contains disease. Latex gloves should be worn when wiping up blood. And, contaminated surfaces should be cleaned with a solution of 1 part bleach diluted with 10 parts water. If you want more information about AIDS, the CDC operates a 24-hour toll-free hot line seven days a week (800) 342–2437.

- What should you do to familiarize yourself with the steps and resources that your school has in place for responding to any accident that might happen?
- As a teacher, how will you respond to a child in your classroom who has been identified as HIV-positive?
- What will you do to insure that the other children in your classroom treat the infected child equitably?

---

position, however, is *not necessarily* a legal right.[20] Federal judges have generally recognized certain academic protections in the college classroom while exhibiting reluctance to recognize such rights for elementary and secondary school teachers.

The contract of a history teacher at the University of Arkansas–Little Rock was not renewed after he announced that he taught his classes from a Marxist point of view. The court ordered the teacher be reinstated in light of the university's failure to advance convincing reasons related to the academic freedom issue to warrant his nonrenewal.[21] In another case a university instructor claimed that he was denied tenure because he refused to change a student's grade. He argued that awarding a course grade was the instructor's right of academic freedom. Since the university had given several reasons for the nonrenewal of the instructor's contract, the court did not order a reinstatement.[22]

Academic Freedom for Elementary and Secondary Teachers.

Although federal courts generally have not recognized academic freedom for elementary and secondary school teachers, the most supportive ruling was made in 1980[23] in a case that involved a high school history teacher who used a simulation game to introduce her students to the characteristics of rural life during the post–Civil War

Reconstruction era. While the role playing evoked controversy in the school and community, there was no evidence that the teacher's usefulness had been impaired. Therefore the school erred in not renewing the teacher's contract, and she was ordered reinstated.

In *Pickering* v. *Board of Education* (1968) the U.S. Supreme Court dealt with academic freedom at the public school level. Pickering was a teacher in Illinois who, in a letter published by a local newspaper, criticized the school board and the superintendent for the way they had handled past proposals to raise and use new revenues for the schools. After a full hearing, the board of education terminated Pickering's employment, whereupon he brought suit under the First and Fourteenth Amendments. The Illinois courts rejected his claim. The U.S. Supreme Court, however, upheld Pickering's claim and, in its opinion, stated:

> To the extent that the Illinois Supreme Court's opinion may be read to suggest that teachers may constitutionally be compelled to relinquish the First Amendment rights they would otherwise enjoy as citizens to comment on matters of public interest in connection with the operation of the public schools in which they work, it proceeds on a premise that has been unequivocally rejected in numerous prior decisions of this Court.

In general, teachers are not free to disregard a school board's decision about which textbook to use, but they are able to participate more when it comes to their choice of supplementary methods.

Focus Question 5:

What is meant by the balance concept between the interest of teachers and the interest of the state?

Balancing the Interest of Teachers and the Interest of the State. The Court then addressed the problem of dealing with cases involving academic freedom. It held that the problem was how to arrive at a balance between the interests of the teacher, who as citizen comments on matters of public concern, and the interests of the state, which as employer promotes the efficiency of its public services through its employees. It is difficult to define precisely the limits of academic freedom. In general, the courts strongly support it yet recognize that teachers must be professionally responsible when interacting with pupils.

Generally, teachers have been supported in their rights to criticize the policies of their local school boards, wear symbols representing stated causes, participate in unpopular movements, and live unconventional lifestyles. But where the exercise of these rights can be shown to have a direct bearing on the teacher's effectiveness, respect, or discipline, these rights may have to be curtailed. For example, a teacher may have the right to wear a "punk" outfit to class, but if the wearing of the outfit leads to disruption and an inability to manage students, the teacher may be ordered to wear more traditional clothes.

Debates rage over whether books deemed objectionable can be banned from schools without interfering with the principles of free speech.

Book Banning. Ever since we have had public schools, there have been people who have taken issue with what has been taught,

CASE STUDY BOOK CENSORSHIP AND YOUR CLASSROOM

Since 1983, challenges to library books and school materials have increased by 168 percent. In the 1992–1993 school year, there were 347 attempts to censor books, plays, and other material. A number of organized groups, such as Colorado for Family Values and the Christian Action Network, are systematically targeting books and the policymaking process to have books banned that they find offensive. As a result, teachers, school boards, state boards of education, and legislatures are under intense pressure to ban various books. The established literary merit of a book makes no difference; for example, *Catcher in the Rye, Of Mice and Men, Romeo and Juliet,* and *I Know Why the Caged Bird Sings* have been challenged. Various reasons are offered as to why certain books should not be in schools, including: (1) they are frightening for children (*Scary Stories to Tell in the Dark.*); (2) they are racist (*Tom Sawyer, Little House on the Prairie,* and *Tarzan of the Apes*); and (3) they are "obscene and pornographic" (*The Bible*).

Pressure to ban and censor books comes from inside schools as well. Teachers may unwittingly withhold certain books out of fear of the possibility of controversy. In other instances, the actions of teachers are more direct. For example, teachers in Westlake Middle School in Erie, Pennsylvania (1993) used felt-tip pens to black out passages in *Gorillas in the Mist.*

Censorship and book banning is another aspect of the legal rights and responsibilities of students and teachers.

1. How will you decide if a certain book or game, such as *Where's Waldo?*, is "appropriate" for the students in your classroom?
2. What will you say when a parent pressures you to remove a book from your classroom?
3. And if fellow teachers raise questions about certain educational materials being used, how will you prepare yourself to respond?

Note: Each year a consortium of book publishers, library associations, author associations, and book seller associations publish a list of book titles that have been challenged (*Banned Books: 1994 Resource Guide*). They also make available materials for local observance of Banned Books Week in the early fall. For more association, contact the American Library Association, Office for Intellectual Freedom, 50 East Huron St., Chicago, IL 60611.

how it has been taught, and the materials used. The number of people challenging these issues and the intensity of their feeling have escalated over the past two decades. Well-organized and well-financed pressure groups have opposed the teaching of a number of topics, including political, economic, scientific, and religious theories; the teaching of values grounded in religion, morality, or ethnicity; and the portrayal of stereotypes based on gender, race, or ethnicity. Some complaints have involved differences of opinion over the central role of the school—whether it is to transmit traditional values, indoctrinate students, or teach students to do their own thinking.

A number of court cases in the last twenty years have involved the legality of removal of books from the school curriculum and school libraries. The courts have given some guidance but have not fully resolved the issue. In 1972 a court of appeals held that a book does not acquire tenure, so a school board was upheld in the removal of *Down These Mean Streets.* The seventh circuit court in 1980

CNN **Clip 20:**
School Book Censor

Activity 10.8:
Have students read and review some of the books that have been the target of book banning efforts. In class, analyze the specific elements in each book that have triggered concern.

upheld the removal of the book *Values Clarification*, ruling that local boards have considerable authority in selecting materials for schools. Removal of books on the basis of the vulgar language they contain has also been upheld.

The U.S. Supreme Court treated this issue in 1982.[24] The decision disappointed people who had hoped that the justices would issue a definitive ruling on banning of books. Instead, Justice Brennan ruled that students may sue school boards for a denial of their rights, including the right to receive information. The Court indicated that removal of a book because one disagrees with its content cannot be upheld. The net effect of this decision was that the school board decided to return the questionable books to the library.

Liability for Negligence

With about 42 million students enrolled in elementary and secondary schools, it is almost inevitable that some will be injured in educational activities. Each year, some injuries will occasion lawsuits in which plaintiffs seek damages. Such suits are often brought against both the school districts and their employees. Actions seeking monetary damages for injuries are referred to as *actions in tort*. Technically, a tort is a legal wrong—an act or the omission of an act that violates the private rights of an individual. Actions in tort are generally based on alleged negligence; the basis of tort liability or legal responsibility is negligence. Understanding the concept of negligence is essential to understanding liability.

Legally, *negligence* is the result of a failure to exercise or practice due care. It includes a factor of foreseeability of harm. Court cases on record involving negligence are numerous and varied. The negligence of teacher supervision of pupils is an important topic that includes supervision of the regular classroom, a teacher leaving a classroom, supervision of the playground, and supervision of extracurricular activities. **Liability** is the failure to use a reasonable amount of care when such conduct results in injury to another.

Negligent Chemistry Teacher. In a California high school chemistry class, pupils were injured while experimenting in the manufacture of gunpowder.[25] The teacher was in the room and had supplemented the laboratory manual instructions with his own directions. Nevertheless, an explosion occurred, allegedly caused by the failure of pupils to follow directions. A court held the teacher and the board of education liable. Negligence in this case meant the lack of supervision of laboratory work, a potentially dangerous activity requiring a high level of due care.

Field Trip Negligence. In Oregon a child was injured while on a field trip.[26] Children were playing on a large log in a relatively dry space on a beach. A large wave surged up onto the beach, dislodging the log, which began to roll. One of the children fell seaward off the log, and the receding wave pulled the log over the child, injuring him. In the subsequent court action the teacher was declared negligent for not foreseeing the possibility of such an occurrence. The court said:

> The first proposition asks this court to hold, as a matter of fact, that unusual wave action on the shore of the Pacific Ocean is a hazard so unforeseeable that there is no duty to guard against it. On the contrary, we agree with the trial judge, who observed that it is common knowledge that accidents substantially like the one that occurred in this case have occurred at beaches along the Oregon coast. Foreseeability of such harm is not so remote as to be ruled out as a matter of law.

Although negligence is a vague concept involving due care and foreseeability, it is defined more specifically each time a court decides such a case. In each instance, somewhat reflecting past decisions, courts decide what constitutes reasonable due care and adequate foresight.

Schools must deal with the issue of responsibility for student safety on field trips outside the school premises.

Governmental Immunity from Liability.

Historically, school districts have not been held liable for torts resulting from the negligence of their officers, agents, or employees while the school districts are acting in their governmental capacity. That concept was based on the doctrine that the state is sovereign and cannot be sued without consent. A school district, as an arm of state government, would therefore be immune from tort liability. Unlike school districts, employees of school districts have not been protected by the immunity school districts enjoy; teachers may be held liable for their actions. Teachers must act as reasonable and prudent people, foreseeing dangerous situations. The degree of care that is required increases with the immaturity of the pupil. Lack of supervision and foresight forms the basis of negligence charges.

There has been a trend away from governmental immunity. As of 1986, over half of the states had abrogated governmental immunity either judicially, statutorily, or through some form of legal modification. There has also been an increase in the number of lawsuits.

Liability Insurance.

Many states authorize school districts to purchase insurance to protect teachers, school districts, administrators, and school board members against suits. It is important that school districts and their employees and board members be thus protected, through either school district insurance or their own personal policies. The costs of school district liability insurance have increased so dramatically in the past few years that many school districts are contemplating the elimination of extracurricular activities. Consequently, state legislatures are being pressured to fix liability insurance rates for school districts, as well as passing laws to limit maximum liability amounts for school-related cases. For teachers, membership in the state affiliates of the NEA and membership in the AFT permit them to participate in liability insurance programs sponsored by those organizations.

As a summary of the discussion of this section, Table 10.4 on page 284 lists brief statements related to the rights and responsibilities of teachers.

Focus Question 6:
What factor must a teacher keep in mind and practice in order to reduce the possibility of being charged with negligence?

Activity 10.10:
Divide students into groups according to their grade-level interests and ask them to brainstorm lists of situations and actions for that grade level in which a teacher could be negligent.

Information Note 10.3:
Be certain to emphasize that teachers should not touch children to discipline them. Students and their parents have the right to sue for injuries both real and perceived. Also, teachers must constantly monitor their classrooms, school grounds, and all student activities to protect students from injury.

Global Perspectives: Respect for Teachers in Taiwan

In this chapter we have highlighted many of the legal rights of American teachers. You are protected by a negotiated contract, you have the right to due process as defined by the U.S. Constitution, and you have a great deal of academic freedom. In large measure what you can and cannot do as an American teacher is defined

TABLE 10.4   **Summary Statements on Teachers' Rights and Responsibilities**

Prospective teachers must fulfill the requirements of laws and policies regarding certification prior to being employed as teachers.

Boards of education have the authority to employ teachers, including the authority to enter into contracts and to fix terms of employment and compensation.

School districts are prohibited from use of discriminatory practices; discrimination in employment and salary of teachers on the basis of sex is in violation of Title IX of the Education Amendments Act.

Most states have tenure laws that provide protection for teachers against their arbitrary dismissal; rights of nontenured teachers are found in state laws.

Teachers may speak out on matters of public concern, even in criticism of their school board, as long as their speech is not disruptive or a lie.

Boards of education may remove books from library shelves under their authority to select materials for schools; however, the removal of a book merely because someone disagrees with its content was not upheld by the U.S. Supreme Court.

Many states provide for school boards and teacher unions to bargain collectively on wages, hours, and terms and conditions of employment.

Teacher strikes are unlawful when a statute is violated; in some states it is legal for teachers to strike.

Teachers are expected to exercise due care in foreseeing possible accidents and in working to prevent their occurrence; teachers may be sued for their negligence that led to pupil injury.

Teachers who administer corporal punishment must act in a way consistent with state laws, local board policies, and reasonable practices.

Objective 9:
Use the example of Taiwan to illustrate differences in the way that teachers are viewed in other countries.

Discussion Question 5:
The "Global Perspectives" section describes the respect given to teachers in Taiwan. How would you feel about having that kind of respect? Would you teach any differently? Have you had contact with teachers from other countries? If so, what have they said about the respect for teachers there?

in statute, law, and case history. What would your professional life be like if you were a teacher in another country or at another time?

Since ancient times, the Chinese have been very respectful of their teachers. You may have noticed in the movie *The Last Emperor* that only the teachers of the Emperor could ride a horse all the way into the palace. Also, the Emperor bowed to his teachers, although he did not bow to anyone else.

A country where teachers are given great respect today is Taiwan. For example, September 28, the birthday of Confucius, is a national holiday on which teachers are recognized at special ceremonies at the national, county, and local levels. At these ceremonies politicians must sit in the audience, and only teachers are allowed to sit at the head table. Another symbol of the respect for teachers in Taiwan is that teachers of the compulsory grades (K-8) do not pay any income tax! Their salaries are the same as those of high school and college teachers, but they do not have to pay income taxes.

Teachers do not have contracts in Taiwan; instead, each year the principal writes a letter of invitation to each teacher, stating the following: "On behalf of the parents I invite you to be a member of the faculty to teach their children. I hope that you will teach their children as if they were your own. . . ." How is this for showing respect for teachers and also expressing high expectations for what teachers do? Although stated differently in the United States, most parents and school administrators wish the same for teachers in this country.

Summary and Implications

Although student rights and responsibilities are being more clearly defined by court decisions, many court decisions have gone against students whose nonconformism seems to exceed a reasonable norm. American children have a right to an education but not without certain prerequisites. Boards of education have the right to establish rules and regulations provided they are reasonable, rather than arbitrary, regarding student rights. Courts are faced with determining the reasonableness of the student behavior and/or the reasonableness of board rules and regulations. Most student challenges have been related to corporal punishment, rights of married students, dress codes, and freedom of expression. Particularly in cases of suspension and expulsion, corporal punishment, dress codes, and sex discrimination, actions of school administrators and teachers may be examined regarding the due process dimensions of fairness and constitutionality. Procedures for dealing with school records, student publications, student searches, child abuse, and locker searches are being studied more thoroughly to avoid conflicts, which often end up in the courts.

Teachers have the same rights and responsibilities as other citizens. With the assistance of support organizations such as the American Civil Liberties Union (ACLU) and the teacher unions, more and more teachers are airing their grievances in court. The courts have said that a teaching certificate is a license to practice a profession and that it cannot be revoked without constitutional due process. At the same time, the courts have ruled that boards of education may prescribe requirements beyond the state requirements for certification. Teachers are responsible for making certain that they are legally certified to enter into contracts. The grounds and procedures for dismissing teachers are usually spelled out as part of the tenure statute of the respective states. Teacher dismissals by capricious

actions of boards of education are often taken to court for consideration of due process. School districts are prohibited from use of discriminatory practices in the hiring, dismissal, promotion, and demotion of school personnel. The law regarding academic freedom is unsettled, especially for elementary and secondary teachers, since federal judges have been reluctant to recognize academic freedom rights at this level. Controversy over the curriculum continues. It is expected that school boards, administrators, and teachers will continue to receive complaints about what has been taught, how it has been taught, and the materials used. The courts have clarified teachers' rights to bargain collectively and to strike (where state law permits). Court cases brought against both the school districts and their employees involving negligence are numerous and varied. Teachers should be fully aware that negligence is the result of failure to exercise or practice due care.

The implications of the actions of the courts are highly significant to the teaching profession. From the many court decisions relating to education a framework has evolved for acceptable conduct of teachers within the school setting. Today's teacher no longer can assume that personal ignorance of acceptable standards of conduct will be overlooked by the courts in adjudicating a suit brought against the teacher. (Nor should the teacher be intimidated by the courts when reasonable rules of conduct are being evolved for the practice of teaching.) Courts do not start hearings on their own efforts; school boards, school employees, or teachers must be sued before a court case can develop. However, prospective teachers need to be deliberately sensitive to the legal boundaries in teaching. Although beginning teachers need not have the knowledge and expertise of a lawyer, knowing the law well as it relates to education can contribute more than incidentally to becoming a successful teacher.

Discussion Questions

1. Examine "A Bill of Rights for High School Students" presented in Appendix 10.1. What are the strengths of this bill? Are there some elements of it that will be problematic for teachers?

2. What are your thoughts about the balancing of student rights with the need of the school officials to maintain an environment that is conducive to learning? Should school officials have more authority? Or should the students have greater freedom?

3. Each fall there are teacher strikes somewhere in the country that delay the opening of school. Have you ever been involved in a strike? What do you think are the most critical consequences of teacher strikes? If your association leaders called for a strike, would you join the picket line or teach your classes?

4. The "Global Perspectives" section describes the respect given to teachers in Taiwan. How would

you feel about having that kind of respect? Would you teach any differently? Have you had contact with teachers from other countries? If so, what have they said about the respect for teachers there?

5. What precautions should teachers take to avoid charges of negligence?

Journal/Portfolio Development

1. From time to time there will be reports in the newspapers and weekly news magazines about disagreements between students and school officials. Collect these reports, paying special attention to the legal interpretations drawn by each side, and considering the implications for you. In all instances keep in mind that both teachers and students have legal rights, as well as responsibilities. These clippings and notes might be a useful resource for you someday, when as a teacher you are confronted with a question about student and teacher rights.
2. The rights of teachers will be an ever-present theme in the background of your teaching career.

Now is the time to begin compiling notes and a file folder of clippings related to this topic. Your file could include information about teachers' rights from your state's offices of the National Education Association and the American Federation of Teachers. You also could obtain copies of teacher contracts from the school district where you went to school or where you hope to be employed. Watch the newspapers and news magazines for articles about teachers who are being sued. In reading about these cases, note the legal principles being applied as well as the specific teacher rights that are at issue.

School-Based Experiences

1. Obtain a copy of the contract agreement between the teachers' union and a school district. Develop a description and analysis of the due process rights and procedures for teachers.
2. Beginning teachers do not have the same rights as tenured teachers. Compare and contrast the rights

of beginning teachers in two school districts. Some of the items to check are: length of the probationary period, basis for tenure decision, how the tenure decision-making process works, and the rights of probationary teachers.

Notes

1. *Carey* v. *Piphus* (1978).
2. Lee O. Garber and Reynolds C. Seitz, *The Yearbook of School Law, 1971.* Danville, IL: Interstate, 1971, 253.
3. Thomas J. Flygare, "De Jure," *Phi Delta Kappan 68* (October 1986): 165–166.
4. Ibid., 165.
5. *Long* v. *Zopp* (1973).
6. Lucy Knight, "Facts about Mr. Buckley's Amendment," *American Education 13* (June 1977): 7.
7. *Scoville* v. *Board of Education* (1970).
8. William D. Valente, *Law in the Schools.* Columbus, OH: Merrill, 1980, 282.
9. *Peter W.* v. *San Francisco Unified School District* (1976).
10. *Donahue* v. *Copiague Union Free School District* (1978).
11. *1986 Deskbook Encyclopedia of American School Law.* Rosemount, MN: Data Research, 55.
12. Ibid., 61.
13. *Norwalk Teachers Association* v. *Board of Education* (1951).
14. *City of Manchester* v. *Manchester Teachers' Guild* (1957).
15. Michael La Morte, *School Law Cases and Concepts.* 4th ed. Boston: Allyn and Bacon, 1993, 190.
16. *Turk* v. *Franklin Special School District* (1982).
17. *Lucia* v. *Duggan* (1969).
18. *Gouge* v. *Joint School District No. 1* (1970).

19. Haskell C. Freedman, "The Legal Rights of Untenured Teachers," *Nolpe School Law Journal 1* (Fall 1970): 100.

20. Frank W. Kemerer, "Classroom Academic Freedom: Is It a Right?" *Kappa Delta Pi Record 19* (Summer 1983): 101.

21. *Cooper* v. *Ross* (1979).

22. *Hillis* v. *Stephen F. Austin University* (1982).

23. *Kingsville Independent School District* v. *Cooper* (1980).

24. *Board of Education, Island Trees Union Free District No. 26* v. *Pico* (1982).

25. *Mastrangelo* v. *West Side Union High School District* (1935).

26. *Morris* v. *Douglas County School District* (1966).

Bibliography

Appenzeller, Herb. *The Right to Participate.* Charlottesville, VA: Michie, 1985.

Hudgins, H. C., Jr. "The Perspective of the Courts: Their Effect on Educational Policy." *Thresholds in Education 12* (May 1986): 912.

McCarthy, Martha M., and Cambron-McCabe, Nelda H. *Public School Law: Teachers' and Students' Rights.* 3rd ed. Boston: Allyn and Bacon, 1992.

Salome, Rosemary C. *Equal Education Under Law.* New York: St. Martin's Press, 1986.

Tuthill, Doug. "Exploring the Union Contract: One Teacher's Perspective." *Phi Delta Kappan 71* (10) (June 1990): 775–780.

Zerkel, Perry. "Courtside." *Phi Delta Kappan.* (A regular feature in each issue of the *Phi Delta Kappan* providing timely and pertinent information about legal issues.)

Zerkel, Perry, and Richardson, Sharon Nalbone. *A Digest of Supreme Court Decisions Affecting Education.* 2nd ed. Bloomington, IN: Phi Delta Kappa Educational Foundation, 1988.

Appendix 10.1

A Bill of Rights for High School Students

> Neither teacher nor students shed their constitutional right to freedom of speech or expression at the schoolhouse gate. That has been the unmistakable holding of the Supreme Court for almost fifty years. (*Tinker* v. *Des Moines*, 1969)

The following statement of students' rights is intended as a guide to students, parents, teachers, and administrators who are interested in developing proper safeguards for student liberties. IT IS NOT A SUMMARY OF THE LAW, BUT SETS FORTH IN A GENERAL WAY WHAT THE ACLU THINKS *SHOULD* BE ADOPTED. . . .

Article I.   Expression
A. Students shall be free to express themselves and disseminate their views without prior restraints through speech, essays, publications, pictures, armbands, badges, and all other media of communication. Student expression may be subject to disciplinary action only in the event that such expression creates a significant physical disruption of school activities.
B. No reporter for a student publication may be required to reveal a source of information.
C. Students shall have the right to hear speakers and presentations representing a wide range of views and subjects in classes, clubs, and assemblies. Outside speakers and presentations may be limited only by considerations of time, space, and expense.
D. Students shall be free to assemble, demonstrate, and picket peacefully, to petition and to organize on school grounds or in school buildings subject only to reasonable limitations on time, place, and manner designed to avoid significant physical obstruction of traffic or significant physical disruption of school activities.
E. Students shall be free to determine their dress and grooming as they see fit, subject only to reasonable limitations designed to protect student safety or prevent significant ongoing disruption of school activities.

F. No student shall be required to participate in any way in patriotic exercises or be penalized for refusing to participate.

Article II.   Religion
A. Students shall be free to practice their own religion or no religion.
B. There shall be no school-sanctioned religious exercises or events.
C. Religious history, ideas, institutions, and literature may be studied in the same fashion as any other academic subject.

Article III.   Privacy
A. Students should be free from undercover surveillance through the use of mechanical, electronic, or other secret methods, including undercover agents, without issuance of a warrant.
B. Students should be free from warrantless searches and seizures by school officials in their personal effects, lockers, or any other facilities assigned to their personal use. General housekeeping inspections of lockers and desks shall not occur without reasonable notice.
C. Student record files
   1. A student's permanent record file shall include only information about academic competence and notification of the fact of participation in school clubs, sports, and other such school extracurricular activities. This file shall not be disclosed to any person or agency outside the school, except to the student's parents or guardian, without the student's permission.

2. Any other records (e.g., medical or psychological evaluations) shall be available only to the student, the student's parents or guardian, and the school staff. Such other records shall be governed by strict safeguards for confidentiality and shall not be available to others in or outside of the school even upon consent of the student.

3. A record shall be kept, and shall be available to the student, of any consultation of the student's files, noting the date and purpose of the consultation and the name of the person who consulted the files.

4. All records shall be open to challenge and correction by the student.

5. A student's opinions shall not be disclosed to any outside person or agency.

Article IV.   Equality

A. No organization that officially represents the school in any capacity and no curricular or extracurricular activity organized by school authorities may deny or segregate participation or award or withhold privileges on the basis of race, color, national origin, sex, religion, creed, or opinions.

Article V.   Government

A. All students may hold office and may vote in student elections. These rights shall not be denied for any reason.

B. Student government organizations and their operation, scope, and amendment procedures shall be established in a written constitution formulated with full and effective student participation.

Article VI.   Due process

A. Regulations concerning student behavior shall be formulated with full and effective student participation. Such regulations shall be published and made available to all students. Regulations shall be fully, clearly, and precisely written.

B. No student shall be held accountable by school authorities for any behavior occurring outside the organized school day or off school property (except during school-sponsored events) unless such behavior presents a clear, present, and substantial ongoing danger to persons and property in the school.

C. There shall be no cruel, unusual, demeaning, or excessive punishments. There shall be no corporal punishment.

D. No student shall be compelled by school officials to undergo psychological therapy or use medication without that student's consent. No student may be required to participate in any psychological or personality testing, research project, or experiment without that student's written, informed, and willing consent. The nature, purposes, and possible adverse consequences of the testing, project, or experiment shall be fully explained to the student.

E. A student shall have the right to due process in disciplinary and investigative proceedings. In cases that may involve serious penalties, such as suspension for more than three days, expulsion, transfer to another school, a notation on the student's record, or long-term loss of privileges:

1. A student shall be guaranteed a formal hearing before an impartial board. That student shall have the right to appeal hearing results.

2. Rules for hearings and appeals shall be written and published, and there shall be full and effective student participation in their formulation.

3. The student shall be advised in writing of any charges brought against that student.

4. The student shall have the right to present evidence and witnesses and to cross-examine adverse witnesses. The student shall have the right to have an advisor of his or her own choosing present.

5. The hearing shall be open or private as the student chooses.

6. The student shall have a reasonable time to prepare a defense.

7. A student may not be compelled to incriminate himself or herself.

8. The burden of proof, beyond a reasonable doubt, shall be upon the school.

9. A written record of all hearings and appeals shall be made available to the student, at the school's expense.

10. A student shall be free from double jeopardy.

Source: American Civil Liberties Union of Maryland, Baltimore, Md. Reprinted by permission.

Part

4

Historical Foundations of Education

Eastern Education

It is impossible to determine the date that schools first came into existence. However, the discovery of cuneiform mathematics textbooks that have been dated to 2000 B.C. suggests that some form of school probably existed in Sumeria at that time. There is also evidence to suggest that formal schools existed in China during the Hsia and Shang dynasties, perhaps as early as 2000 B.C. Let's briefly explore several examples of the origins of education.

Hindu Education. The ancient Hindu societies were deeply rooted in the caste system, in which a person's family status determined his social and vocational position in life. The Hindu religion emphasized nonearthly values, which resulted in little interest in education for anyone but boys from the highest castes. Priests were in charge of what education existed. Clues from the writing of Buddha suggest that education consisted of a heavy emphasis on morals, writing with a stick in the sand, and frequent punishments with a rod. Further education was reserved for the priestly caste, which, over the ages, gradually cultivated such disciplines as logic, rhetoric, astronomy, and mathematics. Many of our contemporary educational values, including our European languages, are partially derived from the early Hindu societies.

Hebrew Education. Perhaps no culture has valued education more than the Hebrew societies. Hebrew education was derived from their bible, which taught religious faithfulness and strict adherence to Old Testament laws. Discipline was harsh both at home and in school, justified by many Bible verses such as the proverb "He that spareth his rod, hateth his son." Early Hebrew schools taught boys to read and write, and girls to prepare food, spin, weave, sing, and dance. Teachers were greatly respected; the Talmud states "If your teacher and your father have need of your assistance, help your teacher before helping your father, for the latter has given you only the life of this world, while the former has secured for you the life of the world to come." From Hebrew society we have inherited the value we place on education.

Chinese Education. It has been said that China has been civilized longer than any other society in the world. The Chinese invented printing, gun powder, and the mariner's compass, among other things. Chinese education has always been characterized by tradition, formality, and conformity—all designed to help students to function in a regular, mechanical, and predictable routine.

In the sixth century B.C., two philosophers/reformers exerted enormous influence on Chinese thinking and education through their writings. The first of these was Lâo-tsze, who wrote:

> Certain bad rulers would have us believe that the heart and the spirit of man should be left empty, but that instead his stomach should be filled; that his bones should be strengthened rather than the power of his will; that we should always desire to have people remain in a state of ignorance, for then their demands would be few. It is difficult, they say, to govern a people that are too wise.
>
> These doctrines are directly opposed to what is due to humanity. Those in authority should come to the aid of the people by means of oral and written

Focus Question 2:
When and why do you think people first created schools?

Activity 11.1:
Ask students to imagine two fictitious students who attended school in an ancient Hindu, Hebrew, Chinese, or African society. Have the students describe the two students in a short paragraph; then, discuss the various characterizations.

Diversity Note 11.1:
Unequal educational treatment for girls existed in the ancient world.

Discussion Question 1:
What were the major factors that first caused humans to create schools, especially in the Eastern world?

instruction; so far from oppressing them and treating them as slaves, they should do them good in every possible way.

The second Chinese reformer, Hkung-tsze (551–478 B.C.), who later became known as Confucius, is the most famous Asian philosopher. Since his time, all Chinese students have been taught Confucius's five cardinal virtues (universal charity, impartial justice, conformity, rectitude of heart and mind, and pure sincerity) as well as many of his famous sayings, such as "There are three thousand crimes . . . of these no one is greater than disobedience to parents." Interestingly, early Chinese education did not include geography, history, science, language, or mathematics—all subjects so highly valued by early Western societies. Also, unlike many of their Western counterparts, early Chinese educators placed little importance on the individual. From early Chinese educational traditions we have inherited our respect for others and for authority, patience, and advances in written language.

African Education.   In Egypt, civilization and intellectual advancement occurred at a very early time. There, as in most early societies, education was provided only for the privileged males. The fact that the pyramids were built several thousand years before Christ attests to the skills of this ancient civilization. In addition, several notable Greek philosophers, including Pythagoras, Plato, Lycurgus, and Solon completed their education in Egypt.

Diversity Note 11.2:
Historians do not agree on the origin of formal education as we know it today; however, many suspect the world's educational roots lie in the Orient—probably in China.

The Egyptian society was divided into castes, with priests holding the highest position and receiving instruction in philosophy, astronomy, geometry, medicine, history, and law. The priests also provided education for others who were worthy of that privilege.

All of the great early Eastern civilizations developed educational systems long before Western civilizations did. The Eastern civilizations contributed substantially to the development of knowledge, education, and schools in the world.

The influence of ancient civilizations is felt and preserved in modern times.

Greek Education

Key Term:
Age of Pericles (455–431 B.C.)

Objective 1:
Describe ancient Greek education and the contributions of important Greek educational philosophers.

It was not until about 500 B.C. that a Western society sufficiently advanced to generate an organized concern for formal education. This happened in Greece during the **Age of Pericles.** Greece consisted of a number of city-states, one of which was Sparta—a militaristic state whose educational system was geared to support military ambitions. Infants were exposed to the elements for a stated period; if they survived the ordeal, they were judged sufficiently strong for soldiering if male or to bear healthy children if female. From the ages of eight to eighteen, boys were wards of the state. During this time they lived in barracks and received physical and moral training. Between the ages of eighteen and twenty, boys underwent rigorous war training, after which they served in the army. All men were required to marry by the age of thirty so that they might raise healthy children to serve the state. The aims of Spartan education centered on developing such ideals as courage, patriotism, obedience, cunning, and physical strength. Plutarch (A.D. 46–120), a writer of later times, said that the education of the Spartans "was calculated to make them subject to command, to endure labor, to fight, and to conquer." There was very little intellectual content in Spartan education.

In sharp contrast to Sparta was Athens, another Greek city-state, which developed an educational program that heavily stressed intellectual and aesthetic objectives. Between the ages of eight and sixteen, some Athenian boys attended a series of public schools. These schools included a grammatist school, which taught reading, writing, and counting; a gymnastics school, which taught sports and games; and a music school, which taught history, drama, poetry, speaking, and science as well as music. Because all city-states had to defend themselves against aggressors, Athenian boys received citizenship and military training between the ages of sixteen and twenty. Athenian girls were educated in the home. Athenian education stressed individual development, aesthetics, and culture.

The Western world's first great philosophers came from Athens. Of the many philosophers that Greece produced, three stand out—Socrates (470–399 B.C.), Plato (427–347 B.C.), and Aristotle (384–322 B.C.).

Relevant Research

Fewer Requirements and Lower Enrollments Are Contributing to a Decline in Students' Knowledge of the Past

Earlier generations of American students commonly learned the history of American institutions, politics, and systems of government, as well as some of the history of Greece, Rome, Europe, and the rest of the world. Today, most states require the study of only American history and other course work in social studies. Indications are that students now know and understand less about history.

In most state requirements for high school graduation, a choice is offered between history on the one hand and courses in social science and contemporary social issues on the other. Most high school students, even those in the academic track, take only one history course. Students enroll in honors courses in history at less than half the rate they enroll for honors courses in English and science. Typically, requirements have also declined for writing essays, producing research-based papers, and reading original sources. Similar declines are reported in the requirements for such reasoning skills as evaluating sources of information, drawing conclusions, and constructing logical arguments.

Sources: What Works: Research About Teaching and Learning. Washington, DC: U.S. Department of Education. 1987, 77.
Fitzgerald, F. (1979). *America Revised: History School Books in the Twentieth Century.* Boston: Atlantic Little-Brown.
Owings, J. A. (1985). "History Credits Earned by 1980 High School Sophomores Who Graduated in 1982." *High School and Beyond Tabulation.* Washington, DC: National Center for Education Statistics.
Thernstrom, S. (1985). "The Humanities and Our Cultural Challenge." In C. E. Finn, D. Ravitch, and P. Roberts (eds.). *Challenges to the Humanities.* New York: Holmes and Meier.

Of the many philosophers of ancient Greece whose teachings have lasted over time, Socrates, along with Aristotle and Plato, stands out the most.

Discussion Question 2:
What were the major differences between the Spartan and Athenian school systems? Why did these differences exist?

Key Term:
Socratic method

Activity 11.2:
Use the Socratic dialog teaching approach during an entire class period. At the end of the period, have students discuss the pros and cons of the teaching method.

Focus Question 3:
Who were some of the most important educators through the ages?

Information Note 11.1:
Early Greek philosophers are still read and respected by scholars today.

Journal Activity Master 11.1: A Socratic Lesson Plan. This activity requires students to design a lesson plan using the Socratic method.

Socrates. Socrates left no writings, but we know much about him from the writings of Xenophon and Plato. In the **Socratic method** of teaching, a teacher asks a series of questions that leads the student to a certain conclusion. This method is still commonly used by teachers today.

Socrates traveled around Athens teaching the students who gathered about him. He was dedicated to the search for truth and at times was very critical of the existing government. In fact, Socrates was eventually brought to trial for inciting the people against the government by his ceaseless questioning. He was found guilty and given a choice between ending his teaching or being put to death. Socrates chose death, thereby becoming a martyr for the cause of education. Socrates' fundamental principle, "Knowledge is virtue," has been adopted by countless educators and philosophers throughout the ages. Incidentally, some authorities speculate that Socrates may not really have existed, but rather was a mythical character created by other writers.

Plato. Plato was a student and disciple of Socrates. In his *Republic,* Plato set forth his recommendations for the ideal society. He suggested that society should contain three classes of people: artisans, to do the manual work; soldiers, to defend the society; and philosophers, to advance knowledge and to rule the society. Plato's educational aim was to discover and develop each individual's abilities. He believed that each man's abilities should be used to serve society. Plato wrote: "I call education the virtue which is shown by children when the feelings of joy or of sorrow, of love or of hate, which arise their souls, are made conformable to order." Concerning the goals of education, Plato wrote: "A good education is that which gives to the body and to the soul all the beauty and all the perfection of which they are capable."

Aristotle. Like Plato, Aristotle believed that a person's most important purpose was to serve and improve humankind. Aristotle's educational method, however, was scientific, practical, and objective, in contrast to the philosophical methods of Socrates and Plato. Aristotle believed that the quality of a society was determined by the quality of education found in that society. His writings, which include *Lyceum, Oraganon, Politics, Ethics,* and *Metaphysics,* were destined to exert greater influence on humankind throughout the Middle Ages than the writings of any other man.

Insight into some of Aristotle's views concerning education can be obtained from the following passage from *Politics:*

> There can be no doubt that children should be taught those useful things which are really necessary, but not all things; for occupations are divided into liberal and illiberal; and to young children should be imparted only such kinds of knowledge as will be useful to them without vulgarizing them. And any occupation, art, or science, which makes the body or soul or mind of the freeman less fit for the practice or exercise of virtue, is vulgar; wherefore we call those arts vulgar which tend to deform the body, and likewise all paid employments, for they absorb and degrade the mind.[1]

It was the early Greek philosophers, including Plato and Aristotle, who initiated the idea that females and slaves did not possess the intelligence to be leaders and therefore should not be educated. Unfortunately, our world's current struggle with racism and sexism is deeply rooted in Western civilization, and is traceable to the ancient world.

Roman Education

In 146 B.C. the Romans conquered Greece, and Greek teachers and their educational system were quickly absorbed into the Roman Empire. Many of the educational and philosophical advances made by the Roman Empire after that time were actually inspired by enslaved Greeks.

Objective 2:
Characterize the educational system found in the Roman Empire.

Roman Schools. Before 146 B.C., Roman children were educated primarily in the home, though some children attended schools known as *ludi,* where the rudiments of reading and writing were taught. The Greek influence on Roman education became pronounced between 50 B.C. and A.D. 200, during which time an entire system of schools developed. Some children, after learning to read and write, attended a grammaticus school to study Latin, literature, history, mathematics, music, and dialectics. These **Latin grammar schools** were somewhat like twentieth-century secondary schools in function. Students who were preparing for a career of political service received their training in schools of rhetoric, which offered courses in grammar, rhetoric, dialectics, music, arithmetic, geometry, and astronomy.

Key Term:
Latin grammar school

The Roman Empire contained numerous institutions of higher learning that were continuations of former Greek institutions. A library founded by Vespian about A.D. 70 later came to be known as the Athenaeum, and eventually offered studies in law, medicine, architecture, mathematics, and mechanics.

Information Note 11.2:
Many of the educational ideas that are popular today can be traced to the ideas of very early educators, such as Quintilian's beliefs about discipline and motivation.

Quintilian. Quintilian (A.D. 35–95) was the most influential Roman educator. In a set of twelve books, *The Institutes of Oratory,* he described current educational practices, recommended the type of educational system needed in Rome, and listed the great books in existence at that time.

Focus Question 4:
What lessons, if any, can
we learn from very early
educators?

Activity 11.3:
Ask students to design a discipline policy based on the
writing of Quintilian.

Quintilian had considerable insight into educational psychology; concerning the punishment of students, he wrote:

> I am by no means in favor of whipping boys, though I know it to be a general practice. In the first place, whipping is unseemly, and if you suppose the boys to be somewhat grown up, it is an affront to the highest degree. In the next place, if a boy's ability is so poor as to be proof against reproach he will, like a worthless slave, become insensible to blows. Lastly, if a teacher is assiduous and careful, there is no need to use force. I shall observe further that while a boy is under the rod he experiences pain and fear. The shame of this experience dejects and discourages many pupils, makes them shun being seen, and may even weary them of their lives.[2]

Regarding the motivation of students, Quintilian stated:

Discussion Question 3:
Discuss the educational
achievements of the Roman
Empire.

> Let study be made a child's diversion; let him be soothed and caressed into it, and let him sometimes test himself upon his proficiency. Sometimes enter a contest of wits with him, and let him imagine that he comes off the conqueror. Let him even be encouraged by giving him such rewards that are most appropriate to his age.[3]

These comments apply as well today as they did when Quintilian wrote them nearly two thousand years ago. Quintilian's writings were rediscovered in the 1400s and became influential in the humanistic movement in education.

The Romans had a genius for organization and for getting the job done. They made lasting contributions to architecture, and many of their roads, aqueducts, and buildings remain today. This genius for organization enabled Rome to unite much of the ancient world with a common language, a religion, and a political bond—a condition that favored the spread of education and knowledge throughout the ancient world.

Test Questions 11.18–11.31

Education in the Middle Ages (476–1300)

Information Note 11.3:
A growing number of contemporary historians believe that
the Dark Ages were, in fact,
not "dark" and that during that
time civilization and education
made a good deal of progress
that has gone unappreciated
by historians.

By A.D. 476 (the fall of the Roman Empire) the Roman Catholic Church was well on the way to becoming the greatest power in government and education. In fact, the rise of the church to a very powerful position is often cited as a main cause of the Western World's plunge into the Dark Ages. As the church stressed the importance of gaining entrance to heaven, life on earth became less important. Many people viewed earthly life as nothing more than a way to a life hereafter. We can see that a society in which this attitude prevailed would be unlikely to make intellectual advances, except perhaps in areas tangential to religion.

In this section we will briefly review the history of education in the Dark Ages and the Revival of Learning. We begin our study by examining the achievements of two educators who lived during the Dark Ages: Charlemagne and Alcuin.

The Dark Ages (400–1000)

Objective 3:
Summarize the Dark Ages as
if they took place in the Middle Ages.

As the name implies, the Dark Ages was a period when human learning and knowledge not only stood still, but actually regressed in the Western world. This was due to a variety of conditions, including political and religious oppression of the common people. However, there were some examples of human progress during this historical period.

Charlemagne. During the Dark Ages, one of the very few bright periods for education was the reign of Charlemagne (742–814). Charlemagne realized the value of education, and, as ruler of a large part of Europe, he was in a position to establish schools and encourage scholarly activity. In 768, when Charlemagne came into power, educational activity was at an extremely low ebb. The little educating that was carried on was conducted by the church, mainly to induct people into the faith and to train religious leaders. The schools in which this religious teaching took place included *catechumenal schools,* which taught church doctrine to new converts; *catechetical schools,* which at first taught the catechism but later became schools for training church leaders; and *cathedral (or monastic) schools,* which trained clergy.

Alcuin. Charlemagne sought far and wide for a talented educator who could improve education in the kingdom, finally selecting Alcuin (735–804), who had been a teacher in England. While Alcuin served as Charlemagne's chief educational advisor, he became the most famous educator of his day. His main educational writings include *On Grammar, On Orthography, On Rhetoric,* and *On Dialectics.* In addition to trying to improve education generally in the kingdom, Alcuin headed Charlemagne's Palace School in Frankland. Charlemagne himself often sat in the Palace School with the children, trying to further his own meager education.

Astronomy was one of the "seven liberal arts" taught during the time of Charlemagne and Alcuin.

Roughly during Alcuin's time, the phrase **seven liberal arts** came into common usage to describe the curriculum that was then taught in many schools. The seven liberal arts consisted of the trivium (grammar, rhetoric, and logic) and the quadrivium (arithmetic, geometry, music, and astronomy). Each of these seven subjects was defined broadly, so collectively they constituted a more comprehensive study than today's usage of the term suggests. The phrase *liberal arts* has survived time and is common now.

The Revival of Learning

Despite the efforts of men such as Charlemagne and Alcuin, very little educational progress was made during the Dark Ages. However, between 1000 and 1300—a period frequently referred to as the "Age of the Revival of Learning"—humankind slowly regained a thirst for education. This revival of interest in learning was helped by two events: first, the rediscovery of the writings of some of the ancient philosophers (mainly Aristotle) and renewed interest in them and, second, the reconciliation of religion and philosophy. Before this time the church had denounced the study of philosophy as contradictory to its teachings.

Thomas Aquinas, more than any other person, helped to change the church's views on learning. This change led to the creation of new learning institutions, such as the medieval universities.

Thomas Aquinas. The harmonization of the doctrines of the church with the doctrines of philosophy and education was rooted in the ideas of Aristotle and largely accomplished by Thomas Aquinas (1255–1274), himself a theologian. Aquinas formalized **scholasticism** (the logical and philosophical study of the beliefs of the church). His most important writing was *Summa Theologica,* which became the doctrinal authority of the Roman Catholic Church. The educational

Discussion Question 4:
What factors contributed to the decline of education during the Dark Ages?

Key Term:
Seven liberal arts

Activity 11.4:
Have students list the key things that they have learned in school that could be labeled "liberating." Have students share their lists of significant learning and then determine if any topics related to the trivium or quadrivium.

Key Term:
Scholasticism

PROFESSIONAL DILEMMA

*Can You
Provide Adequate
Multicultural
Education in
Your Classroom?*

When you become a teacher, you will be expected to provide multicultural education for your students—regardless of the age level or subjects you teach. Most teachers today face the dilemma of wanting to provide their students with a high-quality multicultural program, but being frustrated with the lack of time and support for doing so.

As indicated in chapters 11, 12, and 13, racial and ethnic prejudice and injustice have been present throughout our educational history. Unfortunately, there is still considerable racial and ethnic strife throughout the United States today, and much of this strife has filtered into the halls of education. Debates rage about how schools should meet the educational demands of a complex, multicultural society. As a teacher, you will be expected to join in this debate and help search for answers.

James Banks, a leading researcher in multicultural education at the University of Washington,

feels past efforts have been too superficial. He asserts that "additive approaches" treat multicultural material as "an appendage to the main story of the development of the nation and to the core curriculum." Instead, multicultural education should integrate multicultural perspectives throughout the curriculum, on an equal footing with white European perspectives.

Despite the lack of time and adequate school district encouragement and support, there are many things that a determined and creative teacher can do to integrate multicultural education throughout the curriculum. Teachers can also encourage the school district to develop and support comprehensive laws for multicultural education and then participate in developing these plans.

- What are the historical antecedents that have contributed to the lack of racial and ethnic understanding in our society?

- Should education programs seek to eliminate differences among individuals or to preserve and perhaps celebrate them?

- What can you do in your classroom to improve multicultural education?

- What additional information would you like about multicultural education, and where might you find such information?

Activity 11.5:
Ask students to identify something that they strongly believe in. Then, ask them to try to develop logical arguments to convince others of their belief. Tell them that this is what Thomas Aquinas tried to do.

Objective 4:
Describe the revival of learning that occurred in Europe and the development of medieval universities.

and philosophical views of Thomas Aquinas were made formal in the philosophy Thomism—a philosophy that has remained important in Roman Catholic parochial education.

Medieval Universities. The revival of learning brought about a general increase in educational activity and a growth of educational institutions, including the establishment of universities. These medieval universities, the true forerunners of our modern universities, included the University of Bologna (1158), which specialized in law; the University of Paris (1180), which specialized in theology; Oxford University (1214); and the University of Salerno (1224). By 1500, approximately eighty universities had been established in Europe.

Although the Middle Ages produced a few educational advances in the Western world, we must remember that much of the Eastern world did not experience the Dark Ages. Mohammed (569–632) led a group of Arabs through northern Africa and into southern Spain. The Eastern learning that the Arabs brought to Spain spread slowly throughout Europe over the next few centuries through the writings of such scholars as Avicenna (980–1037) and Averroes (1126–1198).

These Eastern contributions to Western knowledge included significant advances in science and mathematics, particularly the Arabic numbering system.

Education in Transition (1300–1700)

Two very important movements took place during the transition period of 1300–1700—the Renaissance and the Reformation. The Renaissance represented the protest of individuals against the dogmatic authority the church exerted over their social and intellectual life. The Renaissance started in Italy (around 1130), when humans reacquired the spirit of free inquiry that had prevailed in ancient Greece. The Renaissance slowly spread through Europe, resulting in a general revival of classical learning, called *humanism.* Erasmus (1466–1536) was one of the most famous humanist educators, and two of his books, *The Right Method of Instruction* and *The Liberal Education of Boys,* formed a humanistic theory of education.

The second movement, the Reformation, represented a reaction against certain beliefs of the Roman Catholic Church, particularly those that discouraged learning and that, in consequence, kept lay people in ignorance. We will examine both the Renaissance and the Reformation in this section.

The Renaissance

The common people were generally oppressed by wealthy landowners and royalty during the eleventh and twelfth centuries. In fact, the common people were thought to be unworthy of education and to exist primarily to serve landed gentry and royalty. The Renaissance represented a rebellion on the part of the common people against the suppression they experienced from both the church and the wealthy who controlled their lives. At that time masses of common people developed a spirit of inquiry and demanded a better life.

Vittorino da Feltre. One of the educators from the Renaissance period was a man from the eastern Alps by the name of Vittorino da Feltre (ca. 1278–1446).[4] Vittorino studied at the University of Florence, where he developed an interest in teaching. He also developed a keen interest in classical literature and, along with a number of other educators of that time, began to believe that people could be educated and also be Christians at the same time—a belief that the church generally did not share.

Vittorino established several schools, taught in a variety of others, and generally helped to advance the development of education during his lifetime. He believed that education was an important end in itself and thereby helped to rekindle an interest in the value of human knowledge during the Renaissance.

Erasmus. Erasmus has a good deal of educational insight. concerning the aims of education, he wrote:

> The duty of instructing the young includes several elements, the first and also the chief of which is that the tender mind of the child should be instructed in piety; the second, that he love and learn the liberal arts; the third, that he

Erasmus (1466–1536)

Discussion Question 5:
What were the major educational advances made during the Reformation period?

Journal/Portfolio Development 1:
Write a paper summarizing and criticizing the work and writing of one of the early educators mentioned in this chapter.

Objective 6:
Explain the educational significance of the Protestant Reformation and the contributions of Luther, Melancthon, Ignatius of Loyola, Comenius, and Locke.

Activity 11.7:
Have students discuss Luther's argument for increased governmental support for education. What type of school funding program would Martin Luther support?

be taught tact in the conduct of social life; and the fourth, that from his earliest age he accustom himself to good behavior, based on moral principles.[5]

The Reformation

It is difficult for people today to imagine the extent to which the Roman Catholic Church dominated the lives of the common people through most of what we think of as Europe during the fifteenth and sixteenth centuries. The Roman Catholic Church and the Pope had an enormous amount of influence over European royalty during this time. In fact, some historians suggest that the Pope and other officials of the Roman Catholic Church were in some ways more powerful than many individual kings and queens. After all, the Roman Catholic Church could and frequently did claim that unless members of royalty abided by its rules, they were destined to spend eternity in hell—an extremely frightening prospect for any human being. Consequently, it is understandable that the church came to be a powerful influence throughout most of Europe.

Luther and Melanchthon. The Protestant Reformation had its formal beginning in 1517, when Martin Luther (1483–1546) published his ninety-five theses, which stated his disagreement with the Roman Catholic Church. One of these disagreements held great implications for the importance of formal education. The church believed that it was not desirable for each person to read and interpret the Bible for himself or herself; rather, the church would pass on the "correct" interpretation to the laity. Luther felt not only that the church had itself misinterpreted the Bible, but also that people were intended to read and interpret the Bible for themselves. If one accepted the church's position on this matter, formal education remained unimportant. If one accepted Luther's position, however, education became necessary for all people so that they might individually read and interpret the Bible. In a sense, education became important as a way of obtaining salvation. It is understandable that Luther and his educational coworker, Melanchthon (1497–1560), soon came to stress universal elementary education. Melanchthon's most important educational writing was *Visitation Articles* (1528), in which he set forth his recommendations for schools. Luther and Melanchthon felt that education should be provided for all, regardless of class, and should be compulsory for both sexes. They also believed that it should be state-controlled, state-supported, and centered on classical languages, grammar, mathematics, science, history, music, and physical education. Luther's argument for increased governmental support for education has a familiar twentieth-century ring:

> Each city is subjected to great expense every year for the construction of roads, for fortifying its ramparts, and for buying arms and equipping soldiers. Why should it not spend an equal sum for the support of one or two schoolmasters? The prosperity of a city does not depend solely on its natural riches, on the solidity of its walls, on the elegance of its mansions, and on the abundance of arms in its arsenals; but the safety and strength of a city reside above all in a good education, which furnishes it with instructed, reasonable, honorable, and well-trained citizens.[6]

Ignatius of Loyola. To combat the Reformation movement, Ignatius of Loyola (1491–1556) organized the Society of Jesus (Jesuits) in 1540. The Jesuits worked to establish schools in which to further the cause of the Roman Catholic Church, and they tried to stem the flow of converts to the Reformation cause.

Martin Luther (1483–1546) was an early supporter of state-sponsored, state-controlled education.

Although the Jesuits' main interest was religious, they soon grew into a great teaching order and were very successful in training their own teachers. The rules by which the Jesuits conducted their schools were stated in the *Radio Studiorum;* a revised edition still guides the Jesuit schools today. The improvement of teacher training was the Jesuits' main contribution to education.

Another Catholic teaching order, the Brothers of the Christian Schools, was organized in 1684 by Jean Baptiste de la Salle (1651–1719). Unlike the Jesuits, who were primarily interested in secondary education, de la Salle and his order were interested in elementary schools and in preparing elementary school teachers. De la Salle was one of the first educators to use student teaching in the preparation of teachers.

Comenius (1592–1670)

Comenius. Among many other outstanding educators during the transition period was Johann Amos Comenius (1592–1670). Comenius is perhaps best remembered for his many textbooks, which were among the first to contain illustrations. The invention and improvement of printing during the 1400s made it possible to produce books, such as those of Comenius, more rapidly and economically—a development that was essential to the growth of education. Much of the writing of Comenius reflected the increasing interest that was then developing in science.

Locke. John Locke (1632–1704) was a very influential English educator during the late seventeenth century. He wrote many important educational works, including *Some Thoughts on Education* and *Essay Concerning Human Understanding.* He viewed a young child's mind as a blank slate (*tabula rasa*) on which an education could be imprinted. He believed that teachers needed to create a nonthreatening learning environment—a revolutionary idea at that time.

Information Note 11.6:
Ironically, Luther, like most others of his era, did not love and respect all ethnic groups equally. His writing, for instance, indicates that he was prejudiced against Jewish people because, according to the Bible, their ancient ancestors had crucified Jesus.

Activity 11.8:
Ask students to identify one thing they would write on a child's *tabula rasa.*

Modern Period (1700–Present)

As we have shown, educational progress in Europe was slow and took place in only a few places through the seventeenth century. In this section we will see why many of our current educational ideas can be traced to the early 1700s. We will look at two movements, commonly referred to as the Age of Reason and the Emergence of Common Man.

Test Questions 11.47–11.61

Objective 7:
Describe the educational events that took place during the period known as the Age of Reason.

The Age of Reason

The first movement of the early modern period that influenced education was a revolt of the intellectuals against the superstition and ignorance that dominated people's lives at the time. This movement became known as the **Age of Reason,** and Francois Marie Arouet (1745–1827), A Frenchman who wrote under the name Voltaire, was one of its leaders. Those who joined this movement became known as *rationalists* because of the faith they placed in human rational power. The implication for education in the rationalist movement is obvious: If one places greater emphasis on human ability to reason, then education takes on new importance as the way by which humans develop this power.

Key Term:
Age of Reason

Voltaire and Descartes. The work of Descartes (1596–1650) resulted in three axioms that gradually became well accepted by thinking men. These axioms were

Activity 11.9:
Ask students if the three axioms of Descartes are generally believed in today's schools. Have them provide evidence for their responses.

Information Note 11.7:
Voltaire also advocated organizing a system of public schools throughout France—an idea very advanced for that time.

(1) that reason was supreme, (2) that the laws of nature were invariable, and (3) that truth was verified by exact methods of testing. These ideas became the basis for disputing some of the traditional teaching of the church and for resisting the bonds that royalty had traditionally placed on the common people. These axioms also formed the basis of rationalism, which influenced the thinking of Voltaire. Voltaire was a very articulate writer who was also brilliant, clever, witty, and vain—qualities that helped him to become extremely influential. In fact, many authorities give him considerable credit for both the American and French Revolutions, which took place during his lifetime.

While Voltaire was not technically an educator, his writings helped to bring about a renewed interest in learning and a conviction that knowledge, and therefore schools, was extremely powerful in shaping the lives of people. His views contributed to the development of educational philosophies such as rationalism and empiricism, which helped to elevate the importance of education in the Western world.

Frederick the Great.   One of the influential leaders during the Age of Reason was Frederick the Great (1712–1786). Frederick was a friend of Voltaire and became supportive of the notion that education was of value. He was a liberal thinker for his time and was one of the few leaders who did not attempt to force the common people into a particular form of religion. Frederick also permitted an unusual amount of freedom of speech for his era and generally allowed the common people a degree of liberty that most rulers considered dangerous.

As a consequence, education was given an opportunity to develop, if not flourish, during his reign as leader of Prussia. It was during Frederick's reign that laws were passed regarding education, and teachers were required to obtain special training as well as licenses to teach.

While the progress of education during Frederick's reign was meager in comparison to what we know today, nevertheless, for his time, Frederick must be given considerable credit for contributing to the development of schools during the Age of Reason. Concerning education for all children, Frederick stated, "In the open country it is sufficient if they learn to read and write a little; if they know too much they will go to towns and become secretaries and such like." It is likewise true that Frederick did not place much value on education for young children beyond learning to read and write. It is interesting to note, however, that he was particularly interested in better training for teachers.

The Emergence of Common Man

Key Term:
Emergence of Common Man

The second movement of the early modern period that affected education was the **Emergence of Common Man.** Whereas the Age of Reason was a revolt of the learned for intellectual freedom, the Emergence of Common Man was a revolt of common people for a better life—politically, economically, socially, and educationally.

Journal/Portfolio Development 2: Make a list of historical educational ideas mentioned in this chapter that are still valid and useful for educators today.

Rousseau.   One of the leaders in this movement was Jean Jacques Rousseau (1712–1778), whose *Social Contract* (1762) became an influential book in the French Revolution. Scholars have suggested that *Social Contract* was also the basal doctrine of the American Declaration of Independence.[7] Rousseau was a philosopher, not an educator, but he wrote a good deal on the subject of education. His most important educational work was *Émile* (1762), in which he states his views concerning the ideal education for youth. Rousseau felt that the aim of education should be to return human beings to their "natural state." His view on the subject is well summed up by the opening sentence of *Émile:* "Everything is good as it comes from the hand of the author of nature: but everything degenerates in the hands of man." Rousseau's educational views came to be known as *naturalism.* Concerning the best method of teaching, Rousseau wrote:

> Do not treat the child to discourses which he cannot understand. No descriptions, no eloquence, no figures of speech. Be content to present to him appropriate objects. Let us transform our sensations into ideas. But let us not jump at once from sensible objects to intellectual objects. Let us always proceed slowly from one sensible notion to another. In general, let us never substitute the sign for the thing, except when it is impossible for us to show the thing. . . . I have no love whatever for explanations and talk. Things! Things! I shall never tire of saying that we ascribe too much importance to words. With our babbling education we make only babblers.[8]

Rousseau's most important contributions to education were his belief that it must be a natural process, not an artificial one, and his compassionate, positive view of the child. Rousseau believed that children were inherently good—a belief that was in opposition to the prevailing religiously inspired belief that children were born full of sin. The contrasting implications for teaching methods suggested by these two views are self-evident, as is the educational desirability of Rousseau's view over that which prevailed at the time. Although Rousseau never taught a day of school in his life, he likely did more to improve education through his writing than any of his contemporaries.

Pestalozzi. Johann Heinrich Pestalozzi (1746–1827) was a Swiss educator who put Rousseau's theory into practice. Pestalozzi established two schools for boys,

Jean Jacques Rousseau (1712–1778) felt that education should seek to return humans to their natural state.

Objective 8:
List the contributions of some of the important educators who contributed to the Emergence of Common Man.

Activity 11.10:
Have students consider the teaching methods endorsed by Rousseau. Then, ask them to select one course of study that they are currently enrolled in and evaluate the teaching method in terms of Rousseau.

Discussion Question 6:
What were the strengths and weaknesses of Jean Jacques Rousseau's ideas about children and education?

Johann Heinrich Pestalozzi (1746–1827)

one at Burgdorf (1800–1804) and the other at Yverdun (1805–1825). Educators came from all over the world to view Pestalozzi's schools and to study his teaching methods. Pestalozzi enumerated his educational views in a book entitled *Leonard and Gertrude*. Unlike most educators of his time, Pestalozzi believed that a teacher should treat students with love and kindness:

> I was convinced that my heart would change the condition of my children just as promptly as the sun of spring would reanimate the earth benumbed by the winter. . . . It was necessary that my children should observe, from dawn to evening, at every moment of the day, upon my brow and on my lips, that my affections were fixed on them, that their happiness was my happiness, and that their pleasures were my pleasures . . . I was everything to my children. I was alone with them from morning till night. . . . Their hands were in my hands. Their eyes were fixed on my eyes.[9]

Key concepts in the Pestalozzian method included an expression of love, understanding, and patience for children; a compassion for the poor; and the use of objects and sense perception as the basis for acquiring knowledge.

Herbart. One of the educators who studied under Pestalozzi and was influenced by him was Johann Friedrich Herbart (1776–1841). While Pestalozzi had successfully put into practice and further developed Rousseau's educational ideas, it remained for Herbart to organize these educational views into a formal psychology of education. Herbart stressed apperception (learning by association). The **Herbartian teaching method** developed into five formal steps:

1. *Preparation:* Preparing the student to receive a new idea
2. *Presentation:* Presenting the student with the new idea
3. *Association:* Assimilating the new idea with the old ideas
4. *Generalization:* The general idea deriving from the combination of the old and new ideas
5. *Application:* Applying the new knowledge

Herbart's educational ideas are contained in his *Science of Education* (1806) and *Outlines of Educational Doctrine* (1835).

Froebel. Friedrich Froebel (1782–1852) was another European educator who was influenced by Rousseau and Pestalozzi and who made a significant contribution to education. Froebel's contributions included the establishment of the first kindergarten (or *Kleinkinderbeschaftigungsanstalt*, as he called it in 1837), an emphasis on social development, a concern for the cultivation of creativity, and the concept of learning by doing. He originated the idea that women are best suited to teach young children. Froebel wrote his main educational book, *Education of Man*, in 1826.

Two developments in the late 1800s were the last important European antecedents of American education: the maturing of the scientific movement, hastened by the publication of Charles Darwin's *On the Origin of Species* (1859), and the formulation of educational psychology near the end of the century.

The student of educational history must realize that even though many educational advances have been made by 1900, the average European received a

Key Term:
Herbartian teaching method

Activity 11.11:
Have students design a social studies lesson according to the Herbartian teaching method.

Focus Question 6:
How important has education been in the history of humankind? In what ways?

Information Note 11.8:
The first kindergarten in the United States was established in Watertown, Wisconsin in 1855 by Mrs. Carl Schurg. It was conducted in German.

Journal Activity Master 11.2: Development of a Lesson Based on Froebel and Herbart. This activity requires students to redesign the Socratic lesson into one that uses the ideas of Herbart and Froebel.

pathetically small amount of formal education, even at that late date. Historically, education had been available only to the few who were fortunate enough to be born into the leisure class; the masses of people in the working class had received little or no education up to that time. What formal education the working person might have received was usually provided for religious purposes by the church.

CASE STUDY   A STUDENT TEACHER'S DILEMMA

Jean Angotti was in the middle of her student teaching assignment at the Jefferson School. As far as she knew, she was doing a good job. Both her classroom supervisor, Mrs. Serrano, and her college supervisor, Dr. Hoffman, had given her numerous compliments about her lessons, in spite of the fact that she was having some discipline problems. Mrs. Serrano had warned her at the beginning that the class was a "handful"—even for her. There were several students in the class who were difficult to motivate and, at times, disruptive.

Jean was surprised and somewhat shaken one day, when the principal, Mrs. Quanli, called her into the office to discuss a parent complaint about the lack of discipline in her classroom. This parent, who was a teacher in a nearby school district, felt that his son's learning was being inhibited by what he called "a permissive and unstructured" classroom. Mrs. Quanli told Jean that she had a policy of taking all parental complaints seriously, and of immediately sharing any parent concerns with the teachers involved. She also stated that she had visited with the classroom supervisor, Mrs. Serrano, who had told her that Jean was a very good, mature student teacher. Mrs. Serrano had recommended that Mrs. Quanli talk to Jean about the complaint before meeting with the parent again.

After visiting about the situation for a while, Mrs. Quanli asked Jean for her reaction to this parent's complaint about the lack of discipline in her classroom. Jean responded she had been impressed with the theories of Rousseau concerning children, especially his idea that children were born "good," and became "bad" only in the hands of people. This concept was revolutionary at the time and ran counter to the long-accepted religious "doctrine of original sin," which suggested that children were born "full of the devil," which sometimes had to be beaten out of them. This commonly held belief resulted in schools that were very strict, and in discipline that was very harsh. Jean felt that many of her own public school teachers had appeared to believe that students were inherently bad—as suggested by the doctrine of original sin—and therefore could not be trusted to behave or to learn on their own. In conclusion, Jean stated that she was attempting to use the Rousseauian philosophy in her student teaching—giving the students more freedom and more learning options.

1. What do you feel are Mrs. Quanli's options at this point? Of those options, which do you feel is best?
2. How do you feel about a teacher in one district complaining about a teacher in another district? In the same district?
3. How much freedom do you feel a student teacher should have to experiment with new ideas?
4. How would you feel and what would you do at this point if you were Jean's classroom supervisor, Mrs. Serrano?
5. If Jean were a close friend who asked for your advice, what suggestions would you give her? Would you recommend that Jean offer to meet with the parent?

Summary and Implications

This chapter has pointed out that many of the first educational efforts were made in China, India, and Africa, but the historical roots of our educational traditions can be traced back to Europe. People who have helped to mold Western education include Socrates, Plato, Aristotle, Qunitilian, Alcuin, Aquinas, Erasmus, Melanchthon, Rousseau, Pestalozzi, and Herbart. These and other educational pioneers labored against overwhelming odds to advance the cause of education, and many of the concepts and practices they developed are still in use today. However, perhaps their greatest contribution was in helping humankind to discover and appreciate the potential value of education. One important implication of this chapter for current ideas is that many of our contemporary educational beliefs are very old ideas. Today's teachers also have an obligation to study the history of education so that they will not repeat mistakes of the past but rather capitalize on past successes.

Discussion Questions

1. What were the major factors that first caused humans to create schools, especially in the Eastern world?
2. What were the major differences between the Spartan and Athenian school systems? Why did these differences exist?
3. Discuss the educational achievement of the Roman Empire.
4. What factors contributed to the decline of education during the Dark Ages?
5. What were the major educational advances made during the Reformation period?
6. What were the strengths and weaknesses of Jean Jacques Rousseau's ideas about children and education?

Journal/Portfolio Development

1. Write a paper summarizing and criticizing the work and writing of one of the early educators mentioned in this chapter.
2. Make a list of historical educational ideas mentioned in this chapter that are still valid and useful for educators today.

School-Based Experiences

1. Over two hundred years ago, Jean Jacques Rousseau advocated that children should be taught with love patience, understanding, and kindness. As you work in the school, experiment with this basic approach to students to see whether it is effective. You might also wish to observe experienced teachers to determine the extent to which they teach children with love, patience, understanding, and kindness. We suggest that you experiment with other ideas in this chapter as you observe and participate in the classroom.
2. As you work in schools, observe how they have changed in contrast to schools of the past. How are schools today similar to those of the past? How much and in what ways are students today similar to their historical counterparts? In what ways are they probably different?

Notes

1. Paul Monroe, *Source Book of the History of Education.* New York: Macmillan, 1901, 282.
2. Quintilian, *The Institutes of Oratory,* trans. W. Guthrie. London: Dewick and Clark, 1905, 27.
3. Ibid., 12.
4. Glenn Smith et al., *Lives in Education.* Ames, IA: Educational Studies Pres, 1984, 84–88.
5. Gabriel Compayre, *History of Pedagogy,* trans. W. H. Payne. Boston: Heath, 1888,12–13; 88–89.
6. Ibid., 115.

7. Paul Monroe, *History of Education.* New York: Macmillan, 1905, 283.

8. Gabriel Compayre, 299.

9. Ibid., 425.

Bibliography

Armytage, W. H. G. "William Byngham: A Medieval Protagonist of the Training of Teachers." *History of Education Journal 2* (1951): 107–110.

Butts, R. Freeman. *A Cultural History of Western Education.* New York: McGraw-Hill, 1955.

Chambliss, J. J., ed. *Nobility, Tragedy and Naturalism: Education in Ancient Greece.* Minneapolis: Burgess, 1971.

Cole, Luella. *A History of Education: Socrates to Montessori.* New York: Holt, Rinehart and Winston, 1950.

Compayre, Gabriel. *History of Pedagogy.* Translated by W. H. Payne. Boston: Heath, 1888.

Hamilton, E. *The Greek Way.* New York: W. W. Norton, 1930.

Keating, M. W. *Comenius.* New York: McGraw-Hill, 1931.

Lucas, Christopher J. *Our Western Educational Heritage.* New York: Macmillan, 1972.

Meyer, Adolph E. *An Educational History of the Western World.* New York: McGraw-Hill, 1965.

Painter, A. M. *A History of Education.* New York: Appleton, 1987.

12

Early American Education

Focus Questions

1 If you had been one of the early American colonists, how important would education have been to you? Why?

2 How important has our federal government been in advancing education in the United States?

3 What do you suppose life was like for the colonial school teacher?

4 What has characterized the education provided for minorities and women throughout the development of our educational history?

5 How has education improved through the history of our country?

Key Terms and Concepts

Committee of Ten: An historic NEA committee that studied secondary education in 1893.

Common elementary schools: An early attempt to provide a basic elementary education for all children.

Compulsory education: School attendance that is required by law on the theory that it is to the benefit of the state or commonwealth to educate all the people.

Dame school: A low-level primary school in the colonial and other early periods, usually conducted by an untrained woman in her own home.

Hornbook: A single printed page containing the alphabet, syllables, a prayer, and other simple words, tacked to a wooden paddle and covered with a thin transparent layer of cow's horn, used in colonial times as the beginner's first book or preprimer.

Normal school: The first American institution that was devoted exclusively to teacher training.

Old Deluder Satan Act: The first colonial educational law (1647), which required colonial towns of at least 50 households to provide education for youth.

Parochial school: An educational institution operated and controlled by a religious denomination.

Religious-affiliated school: A private school over which, in most cases, a parent church group exercises some control or to which it provides some form of subsidy.

Information Note 12.1:
The major motive of nearly all early colonial education was religious—students were taught to read so they could read the Bible and thus gain salvation.

CNN Clip 20:
Mural of History

Test Questions 12.1–12.29

Objective 1:
Explain the development of schools in early colonial America.

Focus Question 1:
If you had been one of the early American colonists, how important would education have been to you? Why?

Activity 12.1:
Imagine being a parent of an early American family with children ages 7, 14, and 21. In which colony would you choose to settle? Discuss the reason for your choice.

Discussion Question 1:
How did the development of public education differ in the northern, middle, and southern colonies?

*T*he first permanent European settlements in what is now the United States included Jamestown (1607), Plymouth (1620), Massachusetts Bay (1630), Maryland (1632), Connecticut (1635), and Providence Plantations (1636). The motives that prompted most early settlers to move to America were religious, economic, and political. Generally, these people were not dissatisfied with education in their homelands; therefore nearly all educational practices and educational materials in early colonial America were simply transplanted from the Old World.

The religious motive was very strong in colonial America, and it permeated colonial education. Colonists generally felt that a child should learn to read so that he or she could read the Bible and thus gain salvation. Beyond this desire, there was no demand for mass education. Since the clergy possessed the ability to read and write, and since the ultimate utility of education was to read the Bible, it was logical for the clergy to do much of the teaching.

Providing Education in the New World

The early settlement of the East Coast was composed of groups of colonies: the Southern Colonies, centered in Virginia; the Middle Colonies, centered in New York; and the Northern Colonies, centered in New England.

Colonial Education

The earliest settlers from Europe brought with them a sincere interest in providing at least rudimentary education for their children. Naturally, they brought their European ideas about education with them and, soon after arrival, created educational programs throughout colonial America. Let us briefly examine these early colonial school programs.

Southern Colonies. The Southern Colonies soon came to be made up of large tobacco plantations. Because of the size of the plantations, people lived far apart, and few towns were established until later in the colonial period. There was an immediate need for cheap labor to work on the plantations, and in 1619, only twelve years after Jamestown was settled, the first boatload of slaves were imported from Africa. Other sources of cheap labor for the Southern Colonies included white Europeans from a variety of backgrounds, who purchased passage to the New World by agreeing to serve a lengthy period of indentured servitude on arrival in the colonies. There soon came to be two very distinct classes of people in the South—a few wealthy landowners and a large mass of laborers, most of whom were slaves. The educational provisions that evolved from this set of conditions were precisely what one would expect. No one was interested in providing education for the slaves, with the exception of a few missionary groups, such as the English Society for the Propagation of the Gospel in Foreign Parts. Such missionary groups tried to provide some education for slaves, primarily so that they could read the Bible. The wealthy landowners usually hired tutors to teach their children at home. Distances between homes and slow transportation precluded the establishment of centralized schools. When the upper-class children grew old enough to attend college, they were usually sent to well-established schools in Europe.

Middle Colonies. The people who settled the Middle Colonies came from various national (Dutch, Swedish) and religious (Puritan, Mennonite, Catholic) backgrounds. This is why the Middle Colonies have often been called the "melting pot" of the nation. This diversity of backgrounds made it impossible for the inhabitants of the Middle Colonies to agree on a common public school system. Consequently, the respective groups established their own parochial schools. Many children received their education through an apprenticeship while learning a trade from a master already in that line of work. Some people even learned the art of teaching school through an apprenticeship.

Northern Colonies. The Northern Colonies were settled mainly by the Puritans, a religious group from Europe. In 1630, approximately one thousand Puritans settled near Boston. Unlike people in the Southern Colonies, people in New England lived close to one another. Towns sprang up and soon became centers of political and social life. Shipping ports were established, and an industrial economy developed that demanded numerous skilled and semiskilled workers—a condition that created a large middle class.

Early School Laws. These conditions of common religious views, town life, and a large middle class made it possible for the people to agree on common public schools. This agreement led to very early educational activity in the Northern Colonies. In 1642 the General Court of Massachusetts enacted a law that stated:

> This Co^t, [Court] taking into consideration the great neglect of many parents & masters in training up their children in learning . . . do hereupon order and decree, that in every towne y chosen men . . . take account from time to time of all parents and masters, and of their children, concerning their . . . ability to read & understand the principles of religion & the capitall lawes of this country. . . .

This law did nothing more than encourage citizens to look after the education of children. Five years later (1647), however, another law was enacted in Massachusetts that required towns to provide education for the youth. This law, which was often referred to as the **Old Deluder Satan Act,** because of its religious motive, stated:

Key Term:
Old Deluder Satan Act

> It being one chiefe proiect of y ould deluder, Satan, to keepe men from the knowledge of y Scriptures. . . . It is therefore orded [ordered], ye evy [every] towneship in this jurisdiction, aft y Lord hath increased y number to 50 household, shall then forthw appoint one w [with] in their towne to teach all such children as shall resort to him to write & reade . . . & it is furth ordered y where any towne shall increase to y numb [number] of 100 families or househould, they shall set up a grammar schoole, y m [aim] thereof being able to instruct youth so farr as they shall be fited for y university [Harvard]. . . .

These Massachusetts school laws of 1642 and 1647 served as models for similar laws that were soon created in other colonies.

Types of Colonial Schools. Several different kinds of elementary schools sprang up in the colonies, such as the **dame school,** which was conducted by a housewife in her home; the writing school, which taught the child to write; a variety of parochial schools; and charity, or pauper, schools taught by missionary groups.

Key Term:
Dame school

To go back a few years, in 1635 the Latin Grammar School was established in Boston—the first permanent school of this type in what is now the United States. This school was established when the people of Boston, which had been settled only five years before, voted "that our brother Philemon Pormont, shal be intreated to become scholemaster, for the teaching and nourtering of children with us." The grammar school was a secondary school, its function was college preparatory, and the idea spread quickly to other towns. Charlestown opened its first grammar school one year later, in 1636, by contracting William Witherell "to keep a school for a twelve month." Within sixteen years after the Massachusetts Bay Colony had been founded, seven or eight towns had Latin grammar schools in operation. These schools, transplanted from Europe where similar schools had existed for a long time, were traditional and designed to prepare children for college and "for the service of God, in church and commonwealth."

Harvard, the first colonial college, was established in 1636 for preparing ministers. Other early American colleges included William and Mary (1693), Yale (1701), Princeton (1746), King's College (1754), College of Philadelphia (1755), Brown (1764), Dartmouth (1769), and Queen's College (1770). The curriculum in these early colleges was traditional, with heavy emphasis on theology and the classics. An example of the extent to which the religious motive dominated colonial colleges can be found in one of the 1642 rules governing Harvard College, which stated: "Let every Student be plainly instructed, and earnestly pressed to consider well, the maine end of his life and studies is, to know God and Jesus Christ. . . ."

The Struggle for Universal Elementary Education

When the colonists arrived in this country, they simply established schools like those they had known in Europe. The objectives of colonial elementary schools were purely religious. It was commonly believed that everyone needed to be able to read the Bible to receive salvation; therefore parents were eager to have their children receive some type of reading instruction.

Christopher Dock.   A good idea of what a colonial elementary school was like, and the extent to which religion dominated its curriculum, can be gleaned from the following account of a school conducted in 1750 by Christopher Dock, a Mennonite school teacher in Pennsylvania:

> The children arrive as they do because some have a great distance to school, others a short distance, so that the children cannot assemble as punctually as they can in a city. Therefore, when a few children are present, those who can read their Testament sit together on one bench; but the boys and girls occupy separate benches. They are given a chapter which they read at sight consecutively. Meanwhile I write copies for them. Those who have read their passage of Scripture without error take their places at the table and write. Those who fail have to sit at the end of the bench, and each new arrival the same; as each one is thus released in order he takes up his slate. This process continues until they have all assembled. The last one left on the bench is a "lazy pupil."
>
> When all are together, and examined, whether they are washed and combed, they sing a psalm or morning hymn, and I sing and pray with

them. As much as they can understand of the Lord's Prayer and the Ten Commandments (according to the gift God has given them), I exhort and admonish them accordingly.[1]

Monitorial Schools.

In 1805, New York City established the first monitorial school in the United States. The monitorial school, which originated in England, represented an attempt to provide mass elementary education for large numbers of children. Typically, the teacher would teach hundreds of pupils, using the better students as helpers. By 1840, nearly all monitorial schools had been closed; the children had not learned enough to justify continuance of this type of school.

Horace Mann.

Between 1820 and 1860 an educational awakening took place in America. This movement was strongly influenced by Horace Mann (1796–1859). As secretary of the State Board of Education, Mann helped to establish **common elementary schools** in Massachusetts. These common schools were designed to provide a basic elementary education for all children. Among his many impressive educational achievements was the publication of one of the very early professional journals in this country, *The Common School Journal.* Through this journal, Mann kept educational issues before the public.

In 1852, Massachusetts passed a compulsory elementary school attendance law, the first of its kind in the country requiring all children to attend school. By 1900, thirty-two other states had passed similar **compulsory education** laws.

Global Perspectives: Educational Transplantation from Europe.

As indicated in Chapter 11, Pestalozzianism and Herbartianism considerably affected elementary education when they were introduced into the United States in the late 1800s. Pestalozzianism emphasized teaching children with love, patience, and understanding. Furthermore, children should learn from objects and firsthand experiences, not from abstractions and words. Pestalozzian concepts soon spread throughout the country. Herbartianism was imported into the United States at the Bloomington Normal School in Illinois by three students who had learned about the ideas of Herbart while studying in Germany. Herbartianism represented an attempt to make a science out of teaching. The more formal system that Herbartianism brought to the often disorganized elementary teacher was badly needed at the time. Unfortunately, Herbartianism eventually contributed to an extreme formalism and rigidity that characterized many American elementary schools in the early 1900s. One school administrator bragged that at a given moment in the school day he knew exactly what was going on in all the classrooms. One can infer from this boast that teachers often had a very strict, rigid educational program imposed on them.

If we look back at the historical development of American elementary education, we can make the following generalizations:

- Until the late 1800s the motive, curriculum, and administration of elementary education were primarily religious. The point at which elementary education began to be more secular than religious was the point at which states began to pass compulsory school attendance laws.
- Discipline has traditionally been harsh and severe in elementary schools. The classical picture of a colonial schoolmaster equipped with a frown, dunce cap, stick, whip, and a variety of abusive phrases is a more accurate picture than one

Horace Mann (1796–1859)

Information Note 12.2:
Monitorial schools were also known as Lancastrian schools, the name of an English educator who helped to create this educational mass production concept.

Key Term:
Common elementary school

Key Term:
Compulsory education

might expect. It is no wonder that children have historically viewed school as an unpleasant place. Pestalozzi had much to do with bringing about a gradual change in discipline when he advocated that love, not harsh punishment, should be used to motivate students.

- Elementary education has traditionally been formal and impersonal. The ideas of Rousseau, Pestalozzi, Herbart, and Froebel helped to change this condition gradually and make elementary education more student-centered; this was becoming apparent about 1900.
- Elementary schools have traditionally been taught by poorly prepared teachers.
- Although the aims and methodology have varied considerably from time to time, the basic content of elementary education has historically been reading, writing, and arithmetic.

The Need for Secondary Schools

Objective 3:
Relate the development of the Latin Grammar School, American Academy, and High School in the United States.

Activity 12.3:
Have students describe the characteristics of the three types of secondary schools in the 1800s. Then, ask them to develop an argument supporting one of the three as a model for today's secondary schools.

Our contemporary high schools have a long and proud tradition. They have evolved from a series of earlier forms of secondary schools that were created to serve the needs of society at various points in our history. Let us briefly review the historical need for secondary schools in the United States.

Latin Grammar School. The first form of secondary school in the colonies was the Latin grammar school mentioned previously, first established in Boston in 1635 only five years after colonists settled in the area. The Latin grammar school was concerned largely with teaching Latin and other classical subjects, such as Greek, and was strictly college preparatory.

Harvard was the only university in existence in the colonies at that time. The entrance requirements to Harvard stated:

> When any Scholar is able to understand Tully, or such like classicall Latine Author extempore, and make and speake true Latine in Verse and Prose, suo ut aiunt marte; and decline perfectly the Paradigms of Nounes and Verbes in the Greek tongue; let him then, and not before, be capable of admission into the college.

European colleges and later colonial colleges also demanded that students know Latin and Greek before they could be admitted. For instance, in the mid-eighteenth century, the requirements for admission to Yale stated:

> None may expect to be admitted into this College unless upon Examination of the President and Tutors, they shall be found able Extempore to Read, Construe, and Parce Tully, Vergil and the Greek Testament; and to write true Latin in Prose and to understand the Rules of Prosodia, and Common Arithmetic, and Shal bring Sufficient Testimony of his Blameless and inoffensive Life.

Since Latin grammar schools were designed to prepare students for college, it is little wonder that the curriculum in these schools was so classical and traditional. Needless to say, a very small percentage of children attended any Latin grammar school because very few could hope to attend college. Young women did not attend, because colleges at that time did not admit them. As late as 1785 there were only two Latin grammar schools in Boston, and the combined enrollment in these two schools was only sixty-four young men.

American Academy.   By the middle of the eighteenth century there was a need for more and better trained skilled workers. Benjamin Franklin, recognizing this need, proposed a new kind of secondary school in Pennsylvania. This proposal brought about the establishment, in Philadelphia in 1751, of the first truly American educational institution, the American Academy. Franklin established this school because he thought the existing Latin grammar schools were not providing the practical secondary education that youth needed. The philosophy, curriculum, and methodology of Franklin's academy were all geared to prepare young people for employment. Similar academies were established throughout America, and these institutions eventually replaced the Latin grammar school as the predominant secondary education institution. They were usually private schools, and many of them admitted girls as well as boys. Later on, some academies even tried to train elementary school teachers.

High School.   In 1821 an English classical school (which three years later changed its name to English High School) was opened in Boston, and another distinctively American educational institution was launched. This first high school, under the direction of George B. Emerson, consisted of a three-year course in English, mathematics, science, and history. The school later added to its curriculum the philosophy of history, chemistry, intellectual philosophy, linear drawing, logic, trigonometry, French, and the U.S. Constitution. The school enrolled about one hundred boys during its first year.

The high school was established because of a belief that the existing grammar schools were inadequate for the day and because most people could not afford to send their children to the private academies. The American high school soon replaced both the Latin grammar school and the private academy, and has been with us ever since.

About 1910 the first junior high schools were established in the United States. A survey in 1916 showed fifty-four junior high schools existing in thirty-six states. One year later a survey indicated that the number had increased to about 270. More recently, some school systems have abandoned the junior high school in favor of what is called the *middle school,* which usually consists of grades 6, 7, and 8.

Relevant Research

Critiquing Curriculum

As you prepare for your teaching career, you should have an opportunity to read and think about original historical research sources.

The following letter, written in 1712 by Nathaniel Williams, briefly describes the curriculum of the first Latin grammar school established in the colonies—the Boston Latin Grammar School, which was created in 1635, soon after the first colonists settled in that area. From "Letter from Nathaniel Williams to Nehemia Hobart," in Robert F. Seybold, *The Public Schools of Colonial Boston* (Cambridge, MA, 1935), 69–71.

Curriculum of the Boston Latin Grammar School (1712). The three first years are spent first in Learning by heart & then acc: to their capacities understanding the Accidence and Nomenclator, in construing & parsing acc: to the English rules of Syntax Sententiae Pueriles Cato & Cordcrius & Aesops Fables.

The 4th year, or sooner if their capacities allow it, they are entered upon Erasmus to which they are allou'd no English . . . & upon translating English into Latin out of m^r Garreston's Exercises.

The fifth year they are entred upon Tullies Epistles . . . the Elegancies of which are remarked and improv'd in the afternoon of the day they learn it, by translating an English which contains the phrase somthing altered, and besides recited by heart on the repetition day. . . .

The sixth year they are entred upon Tullies Offices & Luc: Flor: for the forenoon, continuing the use of Ovid's Metam: in the afternoon, & at the end of the Year they read Virgil. . . . Every week these make a Latin Epistle, the last quarter of the Year, when also they begin to learn Greek, & Rhetorick.

The seventh Year they read Tullie's Orations & Justin for the Latin & Greek Testam^t Isocrates Orat: Homer & Hesiod for the Greek in the forenoons & Virgil Horace Juyenal & Persius afternoons . . . Every fortnight they compose a theme. . . .

What was the apparent purpose of the Boston Latin Grammar School? In what ways was the curriculum similar to that in our current comprehensive high schools? In what ways was it different?

Aims of Early American Public Education

The aims of American public education have gradually changed over the years. During colonial times the overriding aim of education at all levels was to enable students to read and understand the Bible, to gain salvation, and to spread the gospel.

After independence was won from England, educational objectives—such as providing Americans with a common language, attempting to instill a sense of patriotism, developing a national feeling of unity and common purpose, and providing the technical and agricultural training our developing nation needed—became important tasks for the schools.

Committee of Ten. In 1892 a committee was established by the National Education Association to study the function of the American high school. This committee, known as the **Committee of Ten**, made an effort to set down the purposes of the high school at that time, and made the following recommendations:

- High school should consist of grades 7 through 12.
- Courses should be arranged sequentially.
- Students should be given very few electives in high school.
- One unit, called a Carnegie unit, should be awarded for each separate course that a student takes each year, provided that the course meets four or five times each week all year long.

The Committee of Ten also recommended trying to graduate high school students earlier to permit them to attend college sooner. At that time the recommendation implied that high schools had a college preparatory function. These recommendations became powerful influences in the shaping of secondary education.

Seven Cardinal Principles. Before 1900, teachers had relatively little direction in their work, since most educational goals were not precisely stated. This problem was partly overcome in 1918 when the Commission on Reorganization of Secondary Education published the report *Cardinal Principles of Secondary Education*, usually referred to as the Seven Cardinal Principles. In reality, the Seven Cardinal Principles constitute only one section of the basic principles discussed in the original text, but it is the part that has become famous. These principles stated that the student should receive an education in the following fields:

1. Health
2. Command of fundamental processes
3. Worthy home membership
4. Vocation
5. Civic education
6. Worthy use of leisure
7. Ethical character

The Eight-Year Study. The following goals of education, or "needs of youth," were listed by the Progressive Education Association in 1938 and grew out of the Eight-Year Study:

1. Physical and mental health
2. Self-assurance
3. Assurance of growth toward adult status

4. Philosophy of life
5. Wide range of personal interests
6. Esthetic appreciations
7. Intelligent self-direction
8. Progress toward maturity in social relations with age-mates and adults
9. Wise use of goods and services
10. Vocational orientation
11. Vocational competence

Activity 12.5:
Identify the needs of today's students; then, using this list, add or subtract from the Eight-Year Study.

"Purposes of Education in American Democracy."

"Purposes of Education in American Democracy." Also in 1938, the Educational Policies Commission of the National Education Association (NEA) set forth the "Purposes of Education in American Democracy." These objectives stated that students should receive an education in the four broad areas of self-realization, human relations, economic efficiency, and civic responsibility.

"Education for All American Youth."

"Education for All American Youth." In 1944 this same commission of the NEA published another statement of educational objectives, entitled "Education for All American Youth":

Activity 12.6:
In your opinion, how well have we followed the 1944 objectives of "Education for All American Youth"?

> Schools should be dedicated to the proposition that every youth in these United States—regardless of sex, economic status, geographic location, or race—should experience a broad and balanced education which will

1. equip him to enter an occupation suited to his abilities and offering reasonable opportunity for personal growth and social usefulness;
2. prepare him to assume full responsibilities of American citizenship;
3. give him a fair chance to exercise his right to the pursuit of happiness through the attainment and preservation of mental and physical health;
4. stimulate intellectual curiosity, engender satisfaction in intellectual achievement, and cultivate the ability to think rationally; and
5. help to develop an appreciation of the ethical values which should undergird all life in a democratic society.

"Imperative Needs of Youth."

"Imperative Needs of Youth." In 1952 the Educational Policies Commission made yet another statement of educational objectives, entitled the "Imperative Needs of Youth":

1. All youth need to develop salable skills and those understandings and attitudes that make the worker an intelligent productive participant in economic life. To this end most youth need supervised work experience as well as education in the skills and knowledge of their occupations.
2. All youth need to develop and maintain good health and physical fitness.
3. All youth need to understand the rights and duties of the citizen of a democratic society, and to be diligent and competent in the performance of their obligations as members of the community and citizens of the state and nation.
4. All youth need to understand the significance of the family for the individual and society and the conditions conducive to successful family life.
5. All youth need to know how to purchase and use goods and services intelligently, understanding both the values received by the consumer and the economic consequences of their acts.
6. All youth need to understand the methods of science, the influence of science on human life, and the main scientific facts concerning the nature of the world and of man.

7. All youth need opportunities to develop their capacities to appreciate beauty in literature, art, music, and nature.

8. All youth need to be able to use their leisure time well and budget it wisely, balancing activities that wield satisfactions to the individual with those that are socially useful.

9. All youth need to develop respect for other persons, to grow in their insight into ethical values and principles, and to be able to live and work cooperatively with others.

10. All youth need to grow in their ability to think rationally, to express their thoughts clearly, and to read and listen with understanding.

These various statements concerning education objectives, made over the last century, sum up fairly well the history of the aims of American public education.

History of Federal Involvement

Objective 5:
Explain the reasons for the types of involvement of federal government in education.

Activity 12.7:
Prepare a position paper that argues for more or for less federal involvement in education.

Focus Question 2:
How important has our federal government been in advancing education in the United States?

Our federal government has had a long and extensive involvement in educational affairs. In fact, it has historically supported education at all levels in a variety of ways and continues to do so today. The recent role of our federal government in educational affairs is discussed in detail elsewhere in this book. At this point we will briefly look at some of the early federal efforts to help provide education for U.S. citizens.

U.S. Constitution. The U.S. Constitution does not mention education. Therefore, by virtue of the Tenth Amendment—which states, "The powers not delegated to the United States by the Constitution, nor prohibited by it to the states, are reserved to the states respectively, or to the people"—education is a function of each state. There is some question whether the makers of the Constitution thoughtfully intended to leave education up to each state or whether they merely forgot to mention it. Some historians believe that our founding fathers wisely realized that local control of education would build a better America. Other historians believe that the framers of the Constitution were so preoccupied with what they believed were more important issues that they never thought to make national provision for education.

Information Note 12.5:
Today, many abandoned country schools can still be found standing on the sixteenth section of townships throughout rural America.

Transparency 59:
Showing Land Grants for Common Schools

Northwest Ordinance. Even though the Constitution does not refer to education, the federal government has been active in educational affairs from the very beginning. In 1785 and 1787 the Continental Congress passed the Northwest Ordinance Acts. These Acts provided for disposing of the Northwest Territory and encouraged the establishment of schools in the territory by stating: "Religion, morality and knowledge being necessary to good government and the happiness of mankind, schools and the means of education shall forever be encouraged." As the various states formed the Northwest Territory, they were required to set aside the sixteenth section of each township to be used for educational purposes.

Morrill Land Grant. In 1862, when it became apparent that existing colleges were not providing the **vocational education** needed, the federal government passed the Morrill Land Grant Act. The Hatch Act of 1887 established agricultural experimental stations across the country, and the Smith-Lever Agricultural Extension Act of 1914 carried the services of land grant colleges to the people through extension services. These early federal acts did much to improve agriculture and industry at a time when our rapidly developing nation badly needed such improvement.

Smith-Hughes Act. In 1917 the federal government passed the first act providing financial aid to public schools below the college level, the Smith-Hughes Act. This Act provided for high school vocational programs in agriculture, trades and industry, and homemaking. High schools were academically oriented then, and the Smith-Hughes Act stimulated the development of badly needed vocational programs.

The 1930s were depression days, and the government was trying to solve national economic difficulties. Legislation was enacted during these years to encourage economic development, and this legislation indirectly provided financial aid to education. Five relief agencies related to education during this time included the Civilian Conservation Corps, National Youth Administration, Federal Emergency Relief Administration, Public Works Administration, and Federal Surplus Commodities Corporation.[2]

The more recent involvements of the federal government, from 1940 to the present, are discussed in the next chapter. Appendix 13.1 on page 360 contains a chronology of the more important federal education acts.

Preparation of Teachers

Knowing that our present-day teachers have at least four—and often five to eight—years of college education, it is difficult to believe that teachers have historically had little or no training. One of the first forms of teacher training grew out of the medieval guild system, in which a young man who wished to enter a certain field of work served a lengthy period of apprenticeship with a master in the field. Some young men became teachers by serving as apprentices to master teachers, sometimes for as long as seven years.

Global Perspectives: European Beginnings of Teacher Training. The first formal teacher-training school in the Western world of which we have any record was mentioned in a request to the king of England, written by William Byngham in 1438, requesting that "he may yeve withouten fyn or fee (the) mansion ycalled Goddeshous the which he hath made and edified in your towne of Cambridge for the free herbigage of poure scolers of Gramer. . . ."[3]

Byngham was granted his request, and established Goddeshous College as a teacher-training institution on June 13, 1439. Students at this college gave demonstration lectures to fellow students to gain practice teaching. Classes were even conducted during vacations so that country schoolmasters could also attend. Byngham's college still exists today as Christ's College of Cambridge University. At that early date of 1439, Byngham made provision for two features that are still considered very important in teacher education today: scheduling classes so that teachers in service may attend and providing some kind of student teaching experience. Many present-day educators would probably be surprised to learn that these ideas are at least 550 years old.

Colonial Teachers. Elementary school teachers in colonial America were very poorly prepared; more often than not, they had received no special training at all.

Test Questions 12.30–12.48

Objective 6:
Describe the historical development of programs to prepare teachers.

Activity 12.8:
Prepare a resumé that might be used to obtain a teaching position in the colonial school system.

Focus Question 3:
What do you suppose life was like for the colonial school teacher?

Transparency 62:
The Evolution of the Elementary-School Curriculum, and Methods of Teaching

Information Note 12.6:
Some historians find it interesting and ironical that blacks from Africa and many whites from Europe were both brought to American in bondage.

The single qualification of most of them was that they themselves had been students. Most colonial college teachers, private tutors, Latin grammar school teachers, and academy teachers had received some kind of college education, usually at one of the well-established colleges or universities in Europe. A few had received their education at a colonial American college.

Teachers in the various kinds of colonial elementary schools typically had only an elementary education, but a few had attended a Latin grammar school or a private academy. It was commonly believed that to be a teacher required only that the instructor know something about the subject matter to be taught; consequently, no teacher, regardless of the level taught, received training in the methodology of teaching.

Teaching was not considered a prestigious occupation, and the pay was poor. Consequently, many school teachers viewed their jobs as only temporary. For young women who taught elementary school, the "something better" was usually marriage. Men frequently left teaching for careers in the ministry or business. Not uncommonly, career teachers in the colonies were undesirable people. Records show that many teachers lost their jobs because they paid more attention to the tavern than to the school or because of stealing, swearing, or conduct unbecoming to a person in such a position.

Since many colonial schools were conducted in connection with a church, the teacher was often considered an assistant to the minister. Besides teaching, other duties of some early colonial teachers were "to act as court messenger, to serve summonses, to conduct certain ceremonial services of the church, to lead the Sunday choir, to ring the bell for public worship, to dig the graves, and to perform other occasional duties."

Teachers as Servants. Sometimes the colonies used white indentured servants as teachers; many people who came to America bought passage by agreeing to work for some years as indentured servants. The ship's captain would then sell the indentured servant's services, more often than not by placing an ad in a newspaper. Such an ad appeared in a May 1786 edition of the *Maryland Gazette*:

Men and Women Servants

JUST ARRIVED

In the ship *Paca*, Robert Caulfield, Master, in five Weeks from Belfast and Cork, a number of healthy Men and Women SERVANTS.

Among them are several valuable tradesman, viz.

Carpenters, Shoemakers, Coopers, Blacksmiths, Staymakers, Bookbinders, Clothiers, Diers, Butchers, Schoolmasters, Millrights, and Labourers.

Their indentures are to be disposed of by the Subscribers,

Brown, and Maris
William Wilson

Teaching Apprenticeships.   Some colonial teachers learned their trade by serving as apprentices to schoolmasters. Court records reveal numerous such indentures of apprenticeship; the following was recorded in New York City in 1772:

> This Indenture witnesseth that John Campbel Son of Robert Campbel of the City of New York with the Consent of his father and mother hath put himself and by these presents doth Voluntarily put and bind himself Apprentice to George Brownell of the Same City Schoolmaster to learn the Art Trade or Mastery—for and during the term of ten years. . . . And the said George Brownell Doth hereby Covenant and Promise to teach and instruct or Cause the said Apprentice to be taught and instructed in the Art Trade or Calling of a Schoolmaster by the best way or means he or his wife may or can.

Teacher Training in Academies.   One of Benjamin Franklin's justifications for proposing an academy in Philadelphia was that some of the graduates would make good teachers. Speculating on the need for such graduates, Franklin wrote:

> A number of the poorer sort [of academy graduates] will be hereby qualified to act as Schoolmasters in the Country, to teach children Reading, Writing, Arithmetic, and the Grammar of their Mother Tongue, and being of good morals and known character, may be recommended from the Academy to Country Schools for that purpose; the Country suffering at present very much for want of good Schoolmasters, and obliged frequently to employ in their schools, vicious imported servants, or concealed Papists, who by their bad Examples and Instructions often deprave the Morals and corrupt the Principles of the children under their Care.

The fact that Franklin said some of the "poorer" graduates would make suitable teachers reflects the low regard for teachers typical of the time. The academy that Franklin proposed was established in 1751 in Philadelphia, and many graduates of academies after that time did indeed become teachers.

Normal Schools.   Many early educators recognized this country's need for better qualified teachers; however, it was not until 1823 that the first teacher-training institution was established in the United States. This private school, called a **normal school** after its European counterpart, which had existed since the late seventeenth century, was established by the Rev. Mr. Samuel Hall in Concord, Vermont. Hall's school did not produce many teachers, but it did signal the beginning of formal teacher training in the United States.

Key Term:
Normal school

The early normal school program usually consisted of a two-year course. Students typically entered the normal school right after finishing elementary school. Most normal schools did not require high school graduation for entrance until about 1900. The curriculum was much like the curriculum of the high schools of that time. Students reviewed subjects studied in elementary school, studied high school subjects, had a course in teaching (or "pedagogy" as it was then called), and did some student teaching in a model school usually operated in conjunction with the normal school. The subjects offered by a normal school in Albany, New York, in 1845 included English grammar, English composition, history, geography, reading, writing, orthography, arithmetic, algebra, geometry, trigonometry, human physiology, surveying, natural philosophy, chemistry, intellectual philosophy, moral philosophy, government, rhetoric, theory and practice of teaching, drawing, music, astronomy, and practice teaching.

Horace Mann was instrumental in establishing the first state-supported normal school, which opened in 1839 in Lexington, Massachusetts. Other public normal schools, established shortly afterwards, typically offered a two-year teacher-training program. Some of the students came directly from elementary school; others had completed secondary school. Some states did not establish state-supported normal schools until the early 1900s.

State Teachers' Colleges.   During the early part of the twentieth century, several factors caused a significant change in normal schools. For one thing, as the population of the United States increased, so did the enrollment in elementary schools, thereby creating an ever-increasing demand for elementary school teachers. Likewise, as more people attended high school, more high school teachers were needed. To meet this demand, normal schools eventually expanded their curriculum to include secondary teacher education. The establishment of high schools also created a need for teachers who were highly specialized in particular academic subjects, so normal schools established subject matter departments and developed more diversified programs. The length of the teacher education program was expanded to two, three, and finally four years, which helped to develop and diversify the normal school curriculum. The demand for teachers increased from about twenty thousand in 1900 to more than two hundred thousand in 1930.

Another factor contributed to the growth of the normal schools: The United States had advanced technologically to the point where more college-educated citizens were needed. The normal schools assumed a responsibility to help meet this need by establishing many other academic programs in addition to teacher training. As normal schools extended their programs to four years and began granting baccalaureate degrees, they also began to call themselves **state teachers' colleges.** For most institutions the change in name took place during the 1930s.

Recent Teacher Education.   Universities entered the teacher preparation business on a large scale about 1900. Before then, some graduates of universities had become high school teachers or college teachers, but not until about 1900 did universities begin to establish departments of education and add teacher education to the curriculum.

Just as the normal schools expanded in size, scope, and function to the point where they became state teachers' colleges, so did the state teachers' colleges expand to become *state colleges*. This change in name and scope took place for most institutions about 1950. The elimination of the word *teacher* really explains the story behind this transition. The new state colleges gradually expanded their programs beyond teacher education and became multipurpose institutions. One of the main reasons for this transition was that a growing number of students coming to the colleges demanded a more varied education. The state teachers' colleges developed diversified programs to try to meet their demands.

Many of these state colleges became state universities, offering doctoral degrees in a wide range of fields. Some of our largest and most highly regarded universities evolved from normal schools. Figure 12.1 pictures the evolution of American teacher preparation institutions.

Obviously, establishing the teaching profession was a long and difficult task. Preparation of teachers has greatly improved since colonial times—when anyone

Activity 12.9:
Is there still a need for specialized teacher-training schools? Why or why not?

Discussion Question 4:
How has the concept of the nature of humankind changed in the past three hundred years? What effect has this change had on teacher education?

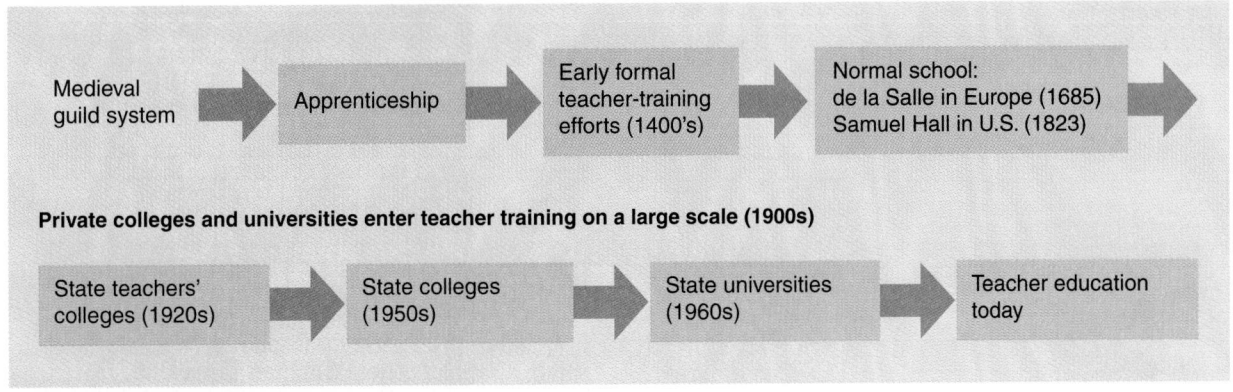

Evolution of Teacher Preparation Institutions

could be a teacher—until the present, when the rigorous requirements for permanent teacher certification cannot easily be met by everyone.

Evolution of Teaching Materials

As we have said, the first schools in colonial America were poorly equipped. In fact, the first elementary schools were usually conducted by housewives right in their homes. The only teaching materials likely to be found then were a Bible and perhaps one or two other religious books, a small amount of scarce paper, a few quill pens, and hornbooks.

The Hornbook. The **hornbook** was the most common teaching device in early colonial schools (see Figure 12.2 on page 328). Hornbooks differed widely but typically consisted of a sheet of paper, showing the alphabet, covered with a thin transparent sheet of cow's horn tacked to a paddle-shaped piece of wood. A leather cord was often looped through a hole in the paddle so that students could hang the hornbooks around their necks. Hornbooks provided students with their first reading instructions. Records indicate that hornbooks were used in Europe in the Middle Ages and were common there until the mid-1700s.

As paper became more available, the hornbook evolved into a several-page "book" called a *battledore*. The battledore, printed on heavy paper, often resembled an envelope. Like the hornbook, it typically contained the alphabet and various religious prayers and/or admonitions.

New England Primer. The first real textbook to be used in colonial elementary schools was the *New England Primer*. Records show that the first copies of this book were printed in England in the 1600s. Copies of the *New England Primer* were also printed as early as 1690 in the American colonies. The book was advertised in the *News From the Stars Almanac*, published in 1690 in Boston

Objective 7:
List and describe the evolution of teaching materials including the hornbook, *New England Primer*, slates, and McGuffey's *Reader.*

Key Term:
Hornbook

Activity 12.10:
Research the hornbook. What other manipulatives were offsprings of the hornbook? Are any of these offsprings in use today?

A Hornbook

(see Figure 12.3). The oldest extant copy of the *New England Primer* is a 1727 edition, now in the Lenox Collection of the New York Public Library.

The *New England Primer* was a small book, usually about 2 1/2 by 4 1/2 inches, with thin wooden covers covered by paper or leather. It contained 50 to 100 pages, depending on how many extra sections were added to each edition. The first pages contained the alphabet, vowels, and capital letters. Next came lists of words arranged from two to six syllables, followed by verses and tiny woodcut pictures for each letter in the alphabet. A reproduction of verses and pictures is presented in Figure 12.4. The contents of the *New England Primer* reflect the heavily religious motive in colonial education.

Advertisement (1690) for the *New England Primer*

ADVERTISEMENT.

There is now in the Prefs, and will fuddenly be extant, a Second Impreffion of *The New-England Primer enlarged*, to which is added, more *Directions for Spelling*: the *Prayer of* K. Edward the *6th.* and *Verfes made by Mr.* Rogers *the Martyr, left as a Legacy to his Children.*

Sold by *Benjamin Harris*, at the *London Coffee-House* in *Bofton*.

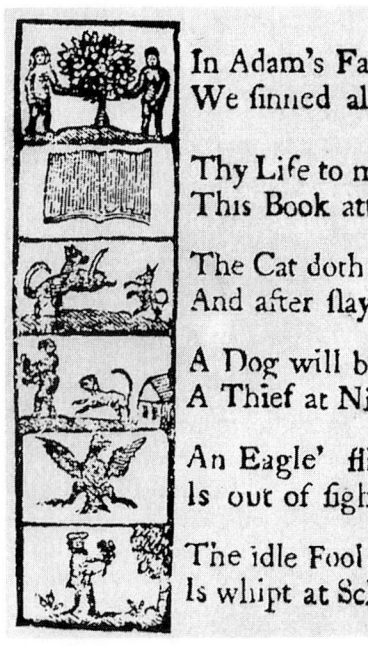

In Adam's Fall
We finned all.

Thy Life to mend,
This Book attend.

The Cat doth play,
And after flay.

A Dog will bite
A Thief at Night.

An Eagle' flight
Is out of fight.

The idle Fool
Is whipt at School

FIGURE 12.4

New England Primer

Blue-Backed Speller. The primer was virtually the only reading book used in colonial schools until about 1800, when Noah Webster published *The American Spelling Book*. This book eventually became known as the *Blue-Backed Speller* because of its blue cover. It eventually replaced the *New England Primer* as the most common elementary textbook. The speller reportedly sold over 24 million copies; its royalties supported Noah Webster and his family while he prepared his famous dictionary. The speller was approximately 4 by 6 1/2 inches; its cover was made of thin sheets of wood covered with light blue paper. The first part of the book contained rules and instructions for using the book; next came the alphabet, syllables, and consonants. The bulk of the book was taken up with lists of words arranged according to syllables and sounds. It also contained rules for reading and speaking, moral advice, and stories of various sorts. Figure 12.5 on page 330 shows a page from a *Blue-Backed Speller* printed about 1800.

Very few textbooks were available for use in colonial Latin grammar schools, academies, and colleges, though various religious books, including the Bible, were often used. A few books dealing with history, geography, arithmetic, Latin, Greek, and certain classics were available for use in colonial secondary schools and colleges during the eighteenth century. Harvard College had a large library for its day, since John Harvard, its benefactor, had bequeathed his entire library of four hundred volumes to the school.

An Early School. By 1800, nearly two hundred years after the colonies had been established, school buildings and teaching materials were still very crude and meager. You can understand something of the physical features and equipment of an 1810 New England school by reading the following description written by a teacher of that school:

Noah Webster (1758–1843)

Activity 12.11:
Assign the class to cooperatively reproduce an early American schoolroom. List its books and materials.

FIGURE 12.5

The Blue-Backed Speller

The size of the building was 22 × 20 feet. From the floor to the ceiling it was 7 feet. The chimney and entry took up about four feet at one end, leaving the schoolroom itself 18 × 20 feet. Around these sides of the room were connected desks, arranged so that when the pupils were sitting at them their faces were towards the instructor and their backs toward the wall. Attached to the sides of the desks nearest to the instructor were benches for small pupils. The instructor's desk and chair occupied the center. On this desk were stationed a rod, or ferule; sometimes both. These, with books, writings, inkstands, rules, and plummets, with a fire shovel, and a pair of tongs (often broken), were the principal furniture. . . .

The room was warmed by a large and deep fireplace. So large was it, and so efficacious in warming the room otherwise, that I have seen about one-eighth of a cord of good wood burning in it at a time. In severe weather it was estimated that the amount usually consumed was not far from a cord a week. . . .

The school was not infrequently broken up for a day or two for want of wood. The instructor or pupils were sometimes compelled to cut or saw it to prevent the closing of the school. The wood was left in the road near the house, so that it often was buried in the snow, or wet with rain. At the best, it was usually burnt green. The fires were to be kindled about half an hour before the time of beginning the school. Often, the scholar, whose lot it was, neglected to build it. In consequence of this, the house was frequently cold and uncomfortable about half of the forenoon, when, the fire being very large, the excess of heat became equally distressing. Frequently, too, we were annoyed by smoke. The greatest amount of suffering, however, arose from excessive heat, particularly at the close of the day. The pupils being in a free perspiration when they left were very liable to take cold. . . .

Instructors have usually boarded in the families of the pupils. Their compensation has varied from seven to eleven dollars a month for males; and from sixty-two and a half cents to one dollar a week for females. Within the past ten years, however, the price of instruction has rarely been less than nine dollars in the former case, and seventy-five cents in the latter. In the few instances in which instructors have furnished their own board the compensation has been about the same, it being assumed that they could work at some employment of their own enough to pay their board, especially the females.[4]

Slates.   About 1820 a new instructional device was introduced in American schools—the slate. These school slates were thin, flat pieces of slate stone framed with wood. The pencils used were also made of slate and produced a light but legible line. The wooden frames of some of the slates were covered with cloth so that noise would be minimized as students placed the slates on the desk. There were even double slates made by hinging two single slates together with cord or leather. Students wrote their assignments on the slates, just as today's students write on tablet paper. Later on, large pieces of slate made up the blackboards that were added to classrooms.

McGuffey's *Reader*.   In the same way that Noah Webster's *Blue-Backed Speller* replaced the *New England Primer,* so did the McGuffey's *Reader* eventually replace the *Blue-Backed Speller.* These readers were carefully geared to each grade and were meant to instill in children a respect for hard work, thrift, self help, and honesty. McGuffey's *Reader* dominated the elementary school book market until approximately 1900, when it was gradually replaced by newer and improved readers written by David Tower, James Fassett, William Elson, and others.

During the twentieth century, teachers have gradually adapted a variety of tools to assist them in educating American youth. This variety has come about partly through the influence of Pestalozzi, John Dewey, and others, who demonstrated that children learn best by firsthand experiences. Likewise, school buildings have become larger, more elaborate, and better designed to encourage learning. Today, many schools are equipped with an impressive array of books, laboratory equipment, movie projectors, filmstrip projectors, tape recorders, television devices, single-concept films, teaching machines, computers, programmed materials, and learning devices of all kinds. Some of the modern school buildings are not only excellent from an educational standpoint but magnificent pieces of architecture as well. One cannot help but be awed by the contrast between American education today and its humble beginning years ago.

Journal/Portfolio Development 2:
Write an essay on the importance of education in the historical development of the United States.

Information Note 12.7:
McGuffey sold millions of copies of his *Reader* and became quite wealthy.

William Holmes McGuffey (1800–1873)

CASE STUDY   LESSONS FROM THE PAST

School boards have historically been given a good deal of legal authority and responsibility for running local school districts. Most school boards are elected and therefore vary a good deal in personality and opinions about schools. Each school board eventually takes on a personality of its own. Some boards decide that their main job is to hire an excellent school superintendent, and then leave the running of the schools up to the professional education staff. In such cases, however, citizens sometimes accuse the school board of shirking their duty by simply "rubber stamping" every decision the school staff makes. Most school boards strive to set broad school policy and concentrate on the financial problems of the district. On the other hand, occasionally a school board wants to become very involved in detailed decision making and engages in activities such as interviewing all new teachers and making specific curriculum decisions.

The River View school district has the reputation of being a very conservative school district. In fact, the school board is made up mainly of rather elderly folks who are known for their conservative Christian views on life in general and on education specifically. River View is a small community of about 5,000 people, where most folks know everyone in the community and where people take a good deal of interest and pride in their schools.

Recently the school board voted to require its teachers to use the McGuffey *Eclectic Readers,* which were written in the mid-1800s, in each elementary grade. The board, which has frequently been critical of "modern" teaching methods, believes that the McGuffey *Readers* will help children learn to be more honest, patriotic, kind, punctual, and conscientious. The board has also raised questions about other curriculum questions such as creation versus evolution science, objectionable literature, and sex education.

The superintendent, Mr. Modell, in his first year in the district, has appointed a committee of teachers to study and make recommendations to the school board on these issues. As a first-year teacher in the River View School District you have been asked to serve on this committee. The Superintendent, who is chairing this committee, has asked each committee member to prepare a position paper on three basic issues [(1) the use of the McGuffey *Readers;* (2) creation versus evolution science, and (3) sex education in the schools], prior to the first meeting, which is scheduled for one week from today. What will your position paper say? Include answers to the following questions in your paper.

1. How should school curriculum be determined?
2. To what degree do you feel a school board should be involved in curriculum questions?
3. Since you are a first-year teacher without tenure, are you concerned about expressing your totally honest views on these debatable topics? Why or why not?
4. What do you think the superintendent should do in this situation?
5. What, if anything, do you feel the faculty and/or the teachers' union should do in a situation such as this?

Education for Special Populations

CNN Clip 21:
Ethnic Kids Books

Test Questions 12.49–12.61

In this section we will examine briefly the development of education of African Americans and females in the United States. We will also review the extremely important role of private education in America.

Education of African Americans

It is sad but true that, until very recently, few efforts were made in our country to provide an education for African Americans. In the following section we will briefly explore why this was the case and discuss some of the early African American educators who struggled to correct this injustice.

Slavery. In 1619, only a dozen years after Jamestown was established, the first boatload of slaves arrived in the colonies. In that year, John Rolfe wrote in his *Journal* that the captain of a Dutch ship "sold us twenty Negroes." These slaves were imported as a source of cheap labor for the new colonies.

The number of imported slaves steadily increased; between 1700 and 1750, thousands of blacks were brought to the American colonies each year. By the Revolutionary War there were approximately 700,000 blacks in the colonies; by 1860 there were about 4.5 million.

The Church's Efforts to Educate African Americans.

Probably the first organized attempts to educate the African Americans in colonial America were by French and Spanish missionaries.[5] These early missionary efforts set an example that influenced the education of both African Americans and the numerous offspring who were the result of mixed breeding. Educating slaves posed an interesting moral problem for the church. The English colonists had to find a way to overcome the idea that converting a slave to Christianity might logically lead to his or her freedom. The problem they faced was how to eliminate an unwritten law that a Christian should not be a slave. The church's governing bodies and the Bishop of London settled the matter by decreeing that conversion to Christianity did not lead to formal emancipation.

The organized church nevertheless provided the setting in which African Americans were allowed to develop skills in reading, leadership, and educating their brethren. Often African Americans and whites attended church together. Eventually, some preachers—former slaves—demonstrated exceptional skill in "spreading the gospel." The Baptists in particular, by encouraging a form of self-government, allowed African Americans to become active in the church. This move fostered the growth of African American congregations, and because of it, enslaved as well as free African Americans were given an opportunity for education and development that was not provided by many other denominations.

The efforts of the English to educate slaves were carried out largely by the Society for the Propagation of the Gospel in Foreign Parts. The Society was created by the Established Church of London in 1701. In 1705 the Reverend Samuel Thomas of Goose Creek Parish in South Carolina established a school fostered by the society, enrolling sixty African American students. Nine years later the society opened a school in New York City where two hundred African American pupils were enrolled. Despite stringent opposition from many whites, who believed that educating slaves was a "dangerous business," the society went on to establish other schools for African Americans. The degree of success of these early efforts varied greatly. Initially, many people were not generally opposed to educating African Americans; however, education seemed to make the slaves aware of their plight. In the South, much of the unrest concerning slavery was attributed to the education of slaves. Insurrections, uprisings, and threats to overseers, masters, and their

Objective 8:
Describe the historical events surrounding the education of African Americans and the important pioneer work of African American educators.

Focus Question 4:
What has characterized the education provided for minorities and women throughout the development of our educational history?

Activity 12.12:
How did education of African Americans by missionaries cause a conflict with the idea of slavery? Might such missionary efforts cause a conflict with today's idea of equal educational opportunity for all?

Information Note 12.8:
History is slowly revealing many outstanding accomplishments by early African Americans, in spite of the slavery and prejudice under which they lived.

Discussion Question 5:
What are the highlights of the history of education of African Americans?

families produced fear among the whites. Consequently, some states even passed legislation that eliminated any form of education for slaves.

John Chavis. The African Americans' individual success in acquiring education, as well as their group efforts to establish schools, was greatly enhanced by sympathetic and humanitarian white friends. John Chavis, a free man born in 1763 in Oxford, North Carolina, was an African American who was helped by whites. Chavis became a successful teacher of aristocratic whites, and his white neighbors sent him to Princeton "to see if a Negro would take a college education." His rapid advancement under Dr. Witherspoon soon indicated that the adventure was a success. He returned to Virginia and later went to North Carolina, where he preached among his own people. The success of John Chavis, even under experimental conditions, represented a small step forward in the education of African Americans.

Benjamin Banneker. Benjamin Banneker, a distinguished African American, was born in Baltimore County, Maryland, in 1731. Baltimore maintained a liberal policy toward educating African Americans, which permitted Banneker to learn to read, write, and do arithmetic at a relatively early age. He became extremely well educated. One of his accomplishments was to manufacture the first clock made in the United States in 1770. He then turned his attention specifically to astronomy. Without any instruction but with the help of books borrowed from an encouraging white inventor, Banneker soon was able to calculate eclipses of the sun and moon. His accuracy far excelled that of any other American. The outstanding works of this inventor aroused the curiosity of Thomas Jefferson, who in 1803 invited Banneker to his home, Monticello. The acknowledgment of an African American's achievement by a noted American was still another milestone in the education of the African Americans.

Frederick Douglass. Frederick Douglass, born a slave in Maryland in 1817, ran away from slavery and began talking to abolitionist groups about his experiences as a slave. He attributed his fluent speech to listening to his master talk. Douglass firmly believed that if he devoted all his efforts to improving vocational education, he could greatly improve the African Americans' plight. He thought that previous attempts by educators to combine liberal and vocational education had failed, so he emphasized vocational education solely.

One of the first northern schools established for African Americans appears to have been that of Elias Neau in New York City in 1704. Neau was an agent of the Society for the Propagation of the Gospel in Foreign Parts.

In 1807, free African Americans, including George Bell, Nicholas Franklin, and Moses Liverpool, built the first schoolhouse for African Americans in the District of Columbia. Not until 1824, however, was there an African American teacher in that district—John Adams. In 1851, Washington citizens attempted to discourage Myrtilla Miner from establishing an academy for African American girls. However, after much turmoil and harassment the white schoolmistress from New York founded her academy, and it is still functioning today.

Prudence Crandall. Prudence Crandall, a young Quaker, established an early boarding school in Canterbury, Connecticut. The trouble she ran into dramatizes some of the northern animosity to educating African Americans. Trouble arose when Sarah Harris, a "colored girl," asked to be admitted to the institution. After much deliberation, Miss Crandall finally consented, but white parents objected to

Activity 12.13:
What type of political activities would people like John Chavis, Benjamin Banneker, Frederick Douglass, Prudence Crandall, or Booker T. Washington endorse today?

Diversity Note 12.2:
There is a drastic shortage of minority teachers in the United States today.

the African American girl's attending the school and withdrew their children. To keep the school open, Miss Crandall recruited African American children. The pupils were threatened with violence, local stores would not trade with her, and the school building was vandalized. The citizens of Canterbury petitioned the state legislator to enact a law that would make it illegal to educate African Americans from out of state. Miss Crandall was jailed and tried before the state supreme court in July 1834. The court never gave a final decision because defects were found in the information prepared by the attorney for the state, and the indictment was eventually dropped. Miss Crandall continued to work for the abolition of slavery, for women's rights, and for African American education. Prudence Crandall became well known, and deserves considerable credit for the advances made by minorities and women in the United States.

Finally, Boston, the seat of northern liberalism, established a separate school for African American children in 1798. Elisha Sylvester, a white man, was in charge. The school was founded in the home of Primus Hall, a "Negro in good standing." Two years later, sixty-six free African Americans petitioned the school committee for a separate school and were refused. Undaunted, the patrons of Hall's house employed two instructors from Harvard; thirty-five years later, the school was allowed to move to a separate building. The city of Boston opened its first primary school for the education of African American children in 1820—one more milestone in the history of African American education.

African American Colleges. Unfortunately, despite these efforts, African Americans received pathetically little formal education until the Emancipation Proclamation, issued by President Abraham Lincoln on January 1, 1863. At that time the literacy rate among African Americans was estimated at 5 percent. Sunday school represented about the only opportunity most African Americans had to learn to read. In the late 1700s and early 1800s, some communities did set up separate schools for African Americans; however, only a very small percentage ever attended the schools. A few colleges such as Oberlin, Bowdoin, Franklin, Rutland, and Harvard admitted African American students; but, again, very few attended college then. There were even a few African American colleges, such as Lincoln University in Pennsylvania (1854) and Wilberforce University in Ohio (1856); however, the efforts and opportunities for the education of African Americans were pathetically few relative to the size of the African American population.

Booker T. Washington. Booker T. Washington (1856–1915) was one of the early African American educators who contributed immensely to the development of education in the United States. He realized that African American children desperately needed an education to compete in society, and he founded Tuskegee Institute in 1880. This Alabama institution provided basic and industrial education in its early years and gradually expanded to provide a wider ranging college curriculum. It stands today as a proud monument to Booker T. Washington's vision and determination concerning the education of African American youth.

Although there was no great rush to educate African Americans, the abolishment of slavery in 1865 signaled the beginning of a slow but steady effort to improve their education. By 1890, African American literacy had risen to 40 percent; by 1910 it was estimated that 70 percent of African Americans had learned to read and write. These statistics showing the rapid increase in African American literacy are impressive; however, they are compromised by a report of the U.S. Commissioner of Education showing that, by 1900, fewer than 70 of 1,000 pub-

Booker T. Washington (1856–1915)

lic high schools in the South were provided for African Americans. Ironically, while educational opportunities for African Americans were very meager, for other minority groups such as Native Americans and Hispanic Americans they were nonexistant.

The most significant developments in the education of African Americans have been in the twentieth century, and mostly since 1950. They are discussed more fully in the next chapter.

Education of Women

Objective 9:
Write about the history of the education of women and the contributions of female educators.

Historically, women have not been afforded equal educational opportunities in the United States. Furthermore, many authorities claim that our schools have traditionally been sexist institutions. Although there is much evidence to support both these assertions, it is also true that an impressive list of women have made significant contributions to our educational progress.

Colonial schools did not provide education for girls in any significant way. In some instances, girls were taught to read, but they were not admitted to Latin grammar schools, academies, or colleges. Let us look briefly at a few of the many outstanding female educators who helped to develop our country's educational system, in spite of their own limited educational opportunity.

Activity 12.14:
In what career or business would women like Mary McLeod Bethune or Emma Willard be involved today?

Information Note 12.9:
Sarah Winnemucca (1844–1891), the daughter of a Painte chief, learned English by working for an army officer. Overcoming many difficult odds, she gained an education and became an outstanding spokesperson and educational leader for Native Americans. She established her own school for Painte children and devoted her life to the cause of education.

Discussion Question 6:
What are the highlights of the history of education of women in the United States?

Emma Willard.   Emma Willard (1778–1870) was a pioneer and champion of education for females during a time when there were relatively few educational opportunities for them. While well-to-do parents hired private tutors or sent their daughters away to a girl's seminary, girls from poor families were taught only to read and write at home (provided that someone in the family had these skills). Emma Willard opened one of the first female seminaries in 1821 in Troy, New York. Her school offered an educational program equal to that of a boy's school. In a speech designed to raise funds for her school, she proposed the following benefits of seminaries for girls:

1. Females, by having their understandings cultivated, their reasoning power developed and strengthened, may be expected to act more from the dictates of reason and less from those of fashion and caprice.

2. With minds thus strengthened, they would be taught systems of morality, enforced by the sanctions of religion; and they might be expected to acquire juster and more enlarged views of their duty, and stronger and higher motives to its performance.

3. This plan of education offers all that can be done to preserve female youth from a contempt of useful labor. The pupils would become accustomed to it, in conjunction with the high objects of literature and the elegant pursuits of the fine arts; and it is to be hoped that both from habit and association they might in future life regard it as respectable.

4. The pupils might be expected to acquire a taste for moral and intellectual pleasures which would buoy them above a passion for show and parade, and which would make them seek to gratify the natural love of superiority by endeavoring to excel others in intrinsic merit rather than in the extrinsic frivolities of dress, furniture, and equipage.

5. By being enlightened in moral philosophy, and in that which teaches the operations of the mind, females would be enabled to perceive the nature and extent of that influence which they possess over their children, and the oblig-

ation which this lays them under to watch the formation of their characters with unceasing vigilance, to become their instructors, to devise plans for their improvement, to weed out the vices of their minds, and to implant and foster the virtues. And surely there is that in the maternal bosom which, when its pleadings shall be aided by education, will overcome the seductions of wealth and fashion, and will lead the mother to seek her happiness in communing with her children, and promoting their welfare. . . .[6]

Many other female institutions were established and became prominent during the mid- and late 1800s, including Mary Lyon's Mount Holyoke Female Seminary; Jane Ingersoll's Seminary in Cortland, New York; and Julia and Elias Mark's Southern Carolina Collegiate Institute at Barhamville, to name just a few. Unfortunately, not until well into the twentieth century were women generally afforded access to higher education.

Even though women eventually could attend college, they were not given equal access to all fields of study. Considerable progress has been made in recent years, but remnants of this problem still exist today.

Global Perspectives: Maria Montessori.   Maria Montessori (1870–1952), born in Italy, became first a successful physician and later a prominent educational philosopher. She developed her own theory and methods of educating young children. Her methods utilized child-size school furniture and specially designed learning materials. She emphasized independent work by children under the guidance of a trained directress. Private Montessori schools thrive in the United States today.

The fact that women have made significant contributions to our educational progress through the years has been well documented. In addition to the examples just mentioned and those discussed elsewhere in this book, we can add the following: Catherine Beecher (who founded the Hartford Female Seminary), Jane Addams (who proposed an expanded school as part of her new liberal social philosophy), Susan Anthony (who was a teacher in her early professional life), and Mrs. Carl Schurz (who founded the first kindergarten in this country).

Activity 12.15: Research the principles of contemporary Montessori schools and compare them to the ideas of Marie Montessori.

Focus Question 5: How has education improved through the history of our country?

The Nineteenth Amendment.   The first great interest in advancing the cause of females came about in the mid-1800s in the United States. At that time the women's rights convention passed twelve resolutions that attempted to spur interest in feminism and provide for females more equal participation and rights in our society. The Civil War also furthered interest in the rights of women throughout the country, very likely as a spinoff of the abolition of slavery as a basic way of improving the lives of African Americans. It is interesting to note that not all of the people who were in favor of doing away with slavery supported improved rights for women. For instance, not until 1920 was the Nineteenth Amendment passed, giving voting rights to women for the first time.

Unfortunately, the right to vote did not necessarily do much to improve the status of women, and they continued to be denied equal educational and employment opportunities for a long time. The civil rights movement after World War II served as another impetus to the women's movement and gave rise to an additional round of improvements for females in American society. Some authorities would trace the emergence of the current feminist movement to the 1960s, when a variety of activist groups coalesced to work against discrimination of all kinds in our society.

Maria Montessori (1870–1952)

PROFESSIONAL DILEMMA

Can a Teacher Both Defend and Critique Schools?

When you become a teacher, you will undoubtedly be able to find both good and bad things about your school. You will also eventually face a parent who is critical of your school and who suggests that schools used to be better in the past. You will then be faced with the common professional dilemma of having to decide to what degree you are willing to defend your classroom and/or school.

Are our schools better or worse today than they were in the "good old days"? Those who argue that schools have deteriorated often point out that the one-room school practiced many of the educational "innovations" that one reads about today. For instance, students received a considerable amount of individual attention in the small, one-room schools. Cooperative learning, which is being touted as a promising educational practice today, was commonplace, with older students helping the younger ones. Those who remember the one-room school frequently point out that values and ethics were a part of the school curriculum, and students were taught love of country, respect for law and authority, and often religious values.

On the other side of this debate, those who defend our contemporary schools point out that our society has become much more complex and that students must now receive a very different and more elaborate educational experience if they are to be successful. The small, simpler schools of the past could not possibly offer the curricular variety and experiences that are afforded students today. Defenders of contemporary schools argue that American society could not have advanced to its present state if it had been hampered by the education typically provided in the past. They point to the advancements of society as proof that public schools have provided an excellent education.

This controversy concerning whether or not our schools have improved or degenerated though history will likely continue. One of the reasons it is important for educators to understand their profession's history is to enable them to capitalize on our historical successes and to avoid our past mistakes. As a future teacher, you should consider educational history and ponder the successes and failures of our ever-evolving school system.

- Should schools return to a focus on basic skills?
- How realistic, valid, and representative are memories of the "good old days"? Is it reasonable to consider returning to an earlier state of U.S. educational history? Why or why not?
- To what degree should teachers defend or criticize their school? How and when?

Private Education in America

Private education has been extremely important in the development of America, and private schools carried on most of the education in colonial times. The first colonial colleges—Harvard, William and Mary, Yale, and Princeton—were private. Many of the other early colonial schools—which can be thought of as **religious-affiliated schools**—were operated by churches, missionary societies, and private individuals.

Key Term:
Religious-affiliated school

Objective 10:
Describe the historical development of private education in America.

CNN Clip 23:
Creationism in School

The Right of Private Schools to Exist.   In 1816 the state of New Hampshire attempted to take over Dartmouth College, which was a private institution. A lawsuit growing out of this effort ultimately resulted in the Supreme Court's first decision involving the legal rights of a private school. The Supreme Court decided that a private school's charter must be viewed as a contract and cannot be broken arbitrarily by a state. In other words, the Court decided that a private school could not be forced against its will to become a public school.

Subsequent court decisions have reconfirmed the rights of private education in a variety of ways. Generally speaking, for instance, courts have reconfirmed that private schools have a right to exist and in some cases even to share public funds as long as these funds are not used for religious purposes. Examples of such actions include the use of state funds to purchase secular textbooks and to provide transportation for students to and from private schools.

Not until after the Revolution, when there was a strong sense of nationalism, did certain educators advocate a strong public school system for the new nation. However, such recommendations were not acted on for many years.

In the meantime, some Protestant churches continued to expand their schools during the colonial period. For instance, the Congregational, Quaker, Episcopalian, Baptist, Methodist, Presbyterian, and Reform churches all, at various times and in varying degrees, established and operated schools for their youth. It was the Roman Catholics and Lutherans, however, who eventually developed elaborate parochial school systems.

Parochial Schools. As early as 1820 there were 240 Lutheran **parochial schools** in Pennsylvania. Although the number of Lutheran schools in that particular state eventually dwindled, Henry Muhlenberg and other Lutheran leaders continued to establish parochial schools until the public school system became well established. The Missouri Synod Lutheran Church has continued to maintain a well-developed parochial school system. Currently, there are approximately 1,700 Lutheran elementary and secondary schools, which enroll about 200,000 pupils, in the United States. Most of these schools are operated by the Missouri Synod Lutheran Church.

The Roman Catholic parochial school system grew rapidly after its beginnings in the 1800s. This growth continued into the twentieth century, and the Roman Catholic parochial school system in the United States is now the largest private school system in the world.

The Importance of Private Education. All of the early educational efforts undertaken in colonial America were private in nature. In fact, the concept of public education—that is, education paid for through public government—is a relatively new idea in the history of education. For many years, if parents or religious groups wanted to provide education for their children, they had to do so with their own resources. In this part of the book there have been many references to private schools and private education; at this juncture we simply wish to reiterate the tremendous importance of private education. In fact, were it not for private education as the predecessor, it is difficult to imagine that we would have evolved a public education system. Private education still plays an enormously important role at all levels of education in the United States.

It is interesting to note that in many ways the transformation from private to public education did not occur until the nineteenth century. For instance, in 1800 there was no such thing as a state system of public education anywhere in the United States—no elementary schools, secondary schools, or state colleges or universities. In fact, until the nineteenth century, all forms of education that were available were private in nature—from elementary school through graduate school. However, by the year 1900, nearly all states had developed a public system of education running from elementary school through graduate school.

Many historians suggest that the overriding motive for private education has always been religious in nature. Initially, parents wanted their children to be able

Information Note 12.10:
Private schools carried nearly the total burden of providing education in colonial America.

Discussion Question 7:
Discuss the role that private schools have played in American education.

Activity 12.16:
Determine your position concerning the need for private schools. Then, examine the issue of vouchers and adopt a pro or con stance based on your position statement.

Key Term:
Parochial schools

Journal Activity Master 12.2: An Analysis of a Contemporary School in the Light of Early American Educational Thought. This activity requires students to relate early teaching materials and educational initiatives to contemporary needs.

to read so that they could read and understand the Bible and therefore gain salvation. Even the earliest colleges were designed primarily to prepare ministers. Harvard College, for instance, was created in 1636, for the express purpose of training ministers.

Likewise, Benjamin Franklin created his unique academy as a private institution to provide technical training to young men because there was no public institution yet created to do so. It was not until 1874 that the Michigan State Supreme Court established that it was legal for school districts to tax citizens for general support of public high schools. By that time, private schools had been providing secondary education for our nation's youth for a long time.

Summary and Implications

The history of American education is filled with many messages. Some tell of successes, some of failures, others of dedicated teachers, of humble beginnings, of individuals' thirst for knowledge—even of those who have been willing to die for the truth. A chronology of these highlights of the historical development of education in the United States is presented in Appendix 13.2 on page 362.

These historical events have implications for today's educator. Teachers can learn much from our educational history if they listen carefully to these messages from the past. In particular, they will come to realize how very important education is to the preservation and progress of our society—perhaps more important than any other human endeavor.

Discussion Questions

1. How did the development of public education differ in the northern, middle, and southern colonies?
2. Discuss the evolution of elementary schools.
3. What historical conditions led to that uniquely American institution, the comprehensive high school?
4. How has the concept of the nature of humankind changed in the past three hundred years? What effect has this change had on teacher education?

5. What are the highlights of the history of education of African Americans?
6. What are the highlights of the history of education of women in the United States?
7. Discuss the roles that private schools have played in American education.

Journal/Portfolio Development

1. Summarize the evolution of the goals of public schools in Colonial America and the United States. Develop a chart that creatively portrays this evolution.

2. Write an essay on the importance of education in the historical development of the United States.

School-Based Experiences

1. George Santayana said, "Those who forget the past are doomed to repeat it." Keeping that idea in mind as you read through this chapter, try to generate a list of practical suggestions that you can use as you work in the schools. Examples might include the practical idea of Pestalozzi for working effectively with children, some of the famous historical aims

of American public education, and some of the moral wisdom espoused in early textbooks such as the *New England Primer* and McGuffey's *Reader.* During your clinical experiences in the schools, think about how applicable some of the historical ideas presented in this chapter are to today's teachers.

2. While you are in the schools, visit with older teachers and administrators to discuss the ways in which schools have changed over the years. Also ask how students have changed, how teaching methods have changed, and how parents have changed.

Notes

1. Paul Monroe, *Source Book of the History of Education.* New York: Macmillan, 1901.

2. Roe L. Johns and Edgar L. Morphet, *Financing the Public Schools.* Englewood Cliffs, NJ: Prentice-Hall, 1960, 378.

3. W. H. G. Armytage, "William Byngham: A Medieval Protagonist of the Training of Teachers," *History of Education Journal 2* (Summer 1951): 108.

4. Paul Monroe, 282.

5. Much of the material dealing with the history of African Americans up to the signing of the Emancipation Proclamation (1863) was taken from the doctoral dissertation of Samuel David, "Education, Law, and the Negro." Urbana: University of Illinois, 1970.

6. Emma Willard, "A Plan for Improving Female Education," *Women and the Higher Education.* New York: Harper & Brothers, 1893, 12–14.

Bibliography

Buetow, Harald A. *Of Singular Benefit: The Story of U.S. Catholic Education.* New York: Macmillan, 1970.

Button, H. Warren, and Provenzo, Eugene F., Jr. *History of Education and Culture in America.* 2nd ed. Englewood Cliffs, NJ: Prentice-Hall, 1989.

Butts, R. Freeman. *Public Education in the United States: From Revolution to Reform.* New York: Holt, Rinehart and Winston, 1978.

Church, Robert L., and Sedlak, Michael W. *Education in the United States: An Interpretive History.* New York: Macmillan, 1976.

Cohen, Sheldon S. *A History of Colonial Education 1607–1776.* New York: Wiley, 1974.

Cremin, Lawrence A. *American Education: The Colonial Experience 1607–1783.* New York: Harper & Row, 1970.

_____ *The Transformation of the School: Progressivism in American Education, 1876–1957.* New York: Knopf, 1961.

Cuban, L. *How Teachers Taught: Consistency and Change in American Classrooms 1890–1980.* New York: Longman, 1984.

Franklin, John Hope. *From Slavery to Freedom: A History of Negro Americans.* 4th ed. New York: Knopf, 1974.

Gartner, Lloyd P., ed. *Jewish Education in the United States: A Documentary History.* New York: Teachers College Press, 1970.

Goodsell, W. *Pioneers of Women's Education in the United States.* New York: McGraw-Hill, 1931.

Perkinson, Henry J., ed. *Two Hundred Years of American Educational Thought.* New York: David McKay, 1976.

Pulliam, John D. *History of Education in America.* Columbus, OH: Merrill, 1991.

Smith, L. Glenn. *Lives in Education: People and Ideas in the Development of Teaching.* Ames, IA: Educational Studies Press, 1993.

Szasz, Margaret Connell. *Indian Education in the American Colonies 1607–1783.* Albuquerque: U. of New Mexico Press, 1988.

Tyack, David B. *The One Best System.* Cambridge, MA: Harvard University Press, 1974.

Washington, B. T., ed. *Tuskegee and Its People: Their Ideals and Achievements.* New York: Appleton, 1905.

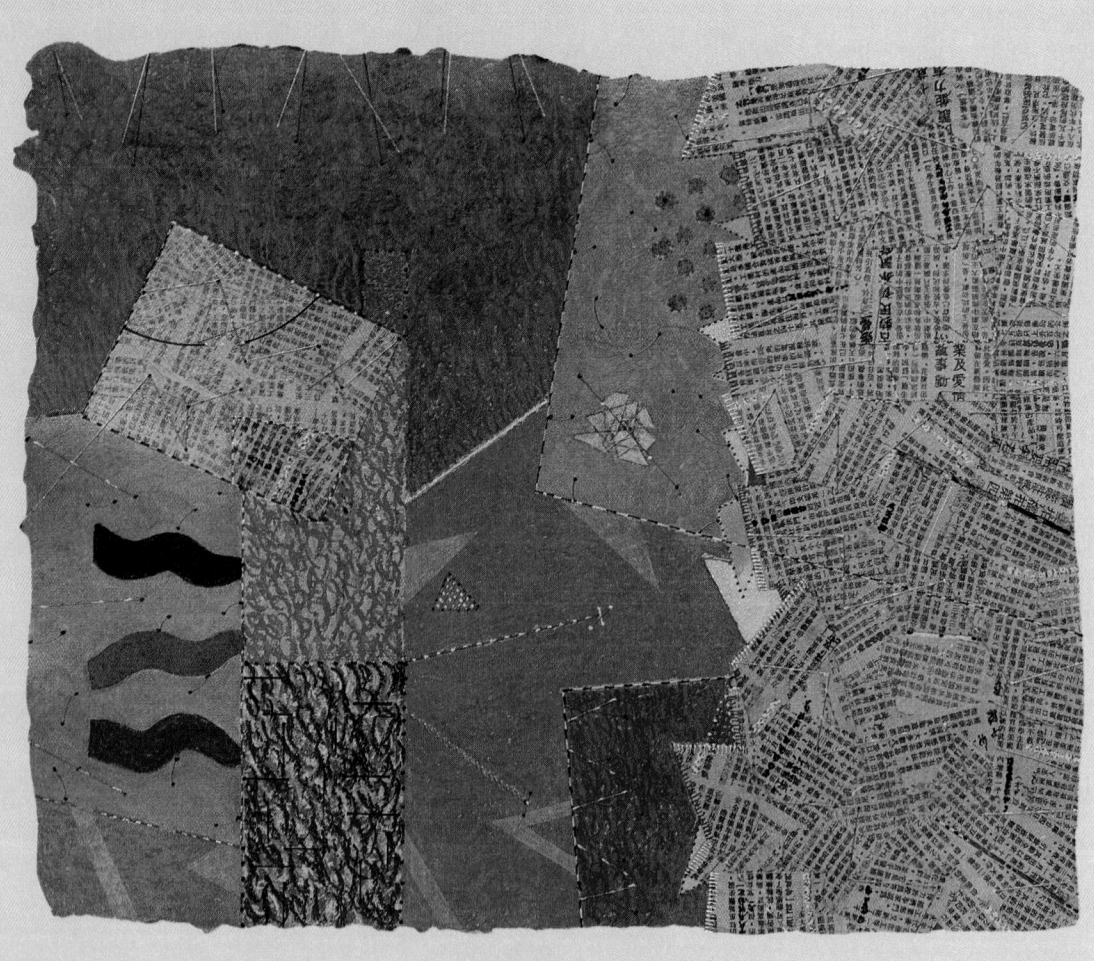

13 Recent Developments in Education 1940–Present

Focus Questions

1 What important changes have taken place in education during your lifetime?
2 How did the special education program in our schools today come into being?
3 In what ways, if any, has the federal government contributed to education in recent history?
4 What is meant by *equal educational opportunity*?
5 What role have private schools played in the United States in recent history?
6 What trends have been evident in our school system over the past fifty years?

Key Terms and Concepts

Analysis of teaching: A contemporary trend to encourage teachers to critique their own performance in the classroom.

Behavioral theory: A theory that considers the outward behavior of students to be the main target for change.

Cognitive development: A learner's acquisition of facts, concepts, and principles through intellectualization.

Effective teaching: A movement to improve teaching performance based on the outcomes of educational research.

Equal educational opportunity: Providing every student the educational opportunity to develop fully whatever talents, interests, and abilities she or he may have without regard to race, color, national origin, sex, handicap, or economic status.

One-room school: A setting in which all grade levels are taught by a single teacher in a single-room school.

More Students and Bigger Schools

There have been many changes in the American educational enterprise over the past half century. Space constraints will not allow a detailed discussion, but we will briefly examine three general topics that seem to characterize these changes since about 1940: the rapid growth of our educational system, the increasing complexity of the educational enterprise, and the recent trends in our schools.

The Rapid Growth of the Educational Enterprise

Since World War II, education has been characterized by a great deal of growth and change: growth in terms of school enrollment, educational budgets, complexity, and federal influence; change in terms of court decisions, proliferation of school laws, confusion about goals, school financial difficulties, struggle for control, and diversification of curricula. Perhaps the single most dramatic change that has occurred in education over the past half century is the growth of the educational enterprise, which took place in many ways.

Enrollment Growth. Table 13.1 shows that the total number of public school students in the United States nearly doubled from 1940 to 1990. While part of this rapid growth in school enrollment was due to overall population growth, a good part was due to the fact that greater percentages of people were going to school. Furthermore, people were staying in school much longer, as shown by the more than sixfold increased enrollment in higher education.

Need for More Teachers. Naturally, this dramatic increase in student enrollments required many additional teachers, and at times our colleges simply could not produce enough. In this situation, teacher certification requirements were lowered, sometimes to the point at which no professional education training was required at all. Over time, however, the nation seemed to meet the demand for more teachers.

As one would expect, the increased numbers of students and teachers cost a great deal more money. More schools had to be built, more buses purchased, more books and other instructional materials obtained, more school personnel hired—more of everything required to provide education was needed.

School District Consolidation

The consolidation of school districts was one development that inadvertently led to increased busing costs. Table 13.2 on page 346 shows that the number of separate school districts was reduced from 117,000 in 1940 to 16,000 in 1980. This table also shows the corresponding dramatic decline in the number of one-teacher schools over this same time period.

One-Room Schools. For many years, the **one-room school,** a single classroom taught by a single teacher and encompassing all grades, symbolized American education for millions of Americans. Although school consolidation undoubtedly

Population growth is just one of the huge differences between the schools of the twentieth century and those of early times.

Test Questions 13.1–13.21

Focus Question 1:
What important changes have taken place in education during your lifetime?

Objective 1:
Interpret the rapid growth of the educational enterprise in the United States.

Activity 13.1:
Have students study Tables 13.1–13.4, which show tremendous growth in education. Ask them to identify the changes in school structure that occurred as a result of such growth.

Activity 13.2:
Challenge students to imagine an entirely different school structure that could accommodate the massive growth of education during the past fifty years. Have students illustrate the structures that they propose and display the structures on the classroom walls and bulletin boards.

Key Term:
One-room school

TABLE 13.1   Historical Summary of Public Elementary and Secondary School Statistics: 1949–1950 to 1989–1990

Population, Pupils and Instructional Staff	1939–1940	1949–1950	1959–1960	1969–1970	1979–1980	1989–1990
Total population, in thousands	130,880	149,199	177,080	201,385	224,567	248,239
Population aged 5–17 years, in thousands	30,151	30,223	42,634	52,386	48,041	45,330
Percent of total population 5–17	23.0	20.3	24.1	26.0	21.4	18.3
Total enrollment in elementary and secondary schools, in thousands	25,434	25,111	36,087	45,550	41,651	40,543
Kindergarten and grades 1–8, in thousands	18,832	19,387	27,602	32,513	28,034	29,152
Grades 9–12 and postgraduate, in thousands	6,601	5,725	8,485	13,037	13,616	11,390
Enrollment as a percent of total population	19.4	16.8	20.4	22.6	18.5	16.3
Enrollment as a percent of 5- to 17-year-olds	84.4	83.1	84.6	87.0	86.7	89.4
Percent of total enrollment in high schools (grades 9–12 and post-graduate)	26.0	22.8	23.5	28.6	32.7	28.1
High school graduates, in thousands	1,143	1,063	1,627	2,589	2,748	2,320
Average daily attendance, in thousands	22,042	22,284	32,477	41,934	38,289	37,779
Total number of days attended by pupils enrolled, in millions	3,858	3,964	5,782	7,501	[4]6,835	—
Percent of enrolled pupils attending daily	86.7	88.7	90.0	90.4	[4]90.1	—
Average lengths of school term, in days	175.0	177.9	178.0	178.9	[4]178.5	—
Average number of days attended per pupil	151.7	157.9	160.2	161.7	[4]160.8	—

Source: 120 Years of American Education: A Statistical Portrait, U.S. Government, Office of Educational Research and Improvement. Washington, DC: U.S. Department of Education. January 1993, 34.

had many educational advantages and saved even more school dollars in some ways, it did necessitate the busing of more students over greater distances.

Dr. Mark W. DeWalt, at Susquehanna University, recently completed a study that yielded surprising results: the one-room school has made a modest comeback over the past few decades. This phenomenon is shown in Figure 13.1 on page 346, which indicates that there has been considerable growth in the number of private one-room schools since about 1970. DeWalt attributes this growth, at least in part, to the U.S. Supreme Court's decision in *Wisconsin* v. *Yoder* (1972), which upheld Amish parents' rights to educate their own children. This decision opened up the opportunity for Amish parents, as well as other parents with similar views, to establish their own private elementary schools.

Information Note 13.1:
Teacher supply and demand, as discussed more fully in chapter 2, is difficult to predict with any degree of accuracy. Candidates with excellent grades and recommendations manage to get jobs, even when there is a considerable excess of teachers.

Objective 2:
Explain the consolidation of schools, the resultant growth of school busing, expanding budgets, and curricular explosion over the past fifty years.

Journal/Portfolio Development 1:
Interview a retired teacher about the educational changes she or he has observed over the past fifty years. Ask what advice this retired educator has for beginning teachers today.

Activity 13.3:
Have students conduct a debate on the pros and cons of school district consolidation.

Information Note 13.2:
Some people believe contemporary schools would profit from emulating some of the features found in the one-room school of the past—group learning, peer teaching, independent learning, self-paced learning, and a stress on values.

Year	School Districts	One-Teacher Schools
1940	117,108	113,600
1950	83,718	59,652
1960	40,520	20,213
1970	17,995	1,815
1980	15,912	921
1990	15,358	617

TABLE 13.2 Consolidation of Public School Districts, 1940–1990

Source: 120 Years of American Education: A Statistical Portrait; U.S. Government Office of Educational Research and Improvement. Washington DC: U.S. Department of Education, January 1993, 56.

Of course, the number of one-room schools has diminished dramatically over a longer period of time. There were approximately 150,000 public one-room schools in existence in 1930, compared to just slightly over 500 today.

Growth of Busing. Both the number and percentage of students that were bused increased considerably from 1940 to 1980, as did the total cost and per-pupil cost. In addition to this general busing of students, efforts were later made to mix racial groups by busing students out of their neighborhood schools. This controversial practice is discussed elsewhere in this book.

Bigger School Budgets. The aspects of educational growth just discussed are only a few of the factors that have driven the nation's public education costs to

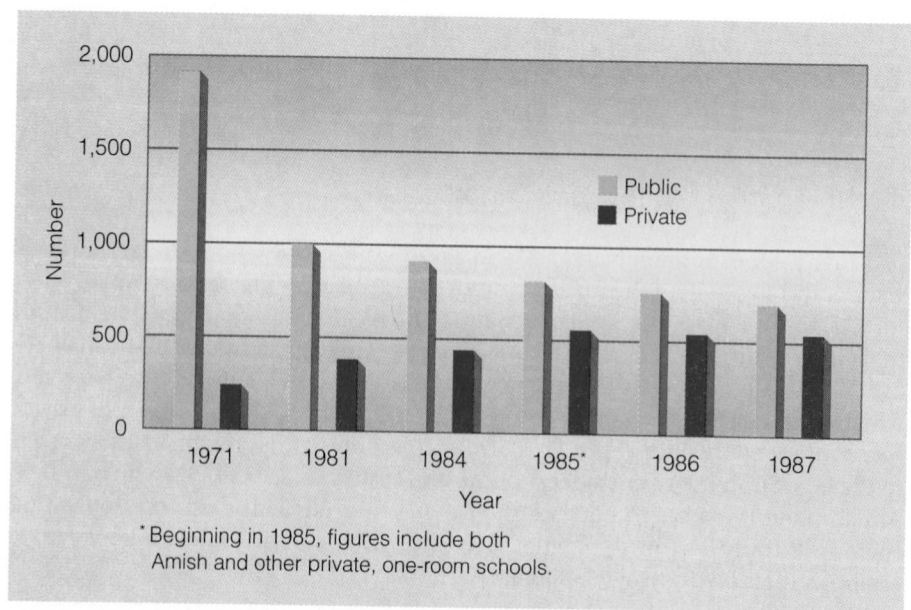

FIGURE 13.1

One-Room Schools

(*Source:* Education Week, *February 1, 1989, 3*)

* Beginning in 1985, figures include both Amish and other private, one-room schools.

record heights. This story of increasing public school budgets is vividly told by Table 13.3. Even if the figures are corrected for inflation, public education has become considerably more expensive. (The percentage of the gross national product spent on education rose from 3.5 percent in 1940 to 7 percent in 1980.[1])

Curricular Growth. The school curriculum has also experienced considerable growth during the past fifty years. This curricular growth, like most change, was the result of an accumulation of many smaller events. One such event was the publication in 1942 of the Eight-Year Study showing that students attending "progressive" schools achieved as well as students at traditional schools. This report helped to create a climate that was

Though rare, one-room school houses can still be found in contemporary education today.

more hospitable to experimentation with school curricula and teaching methodologies. The publication of a series of statements on the goals of American education (the 1938 "Purposes of Education in American Democracy," the 1944 "Education for All American Youth," and the 1952 "Imperative Needs of Youth") helped to broaden our schools' curricular offerings. (All of these goal statements were discussed more fully in the last chapter.)

Shortly after the Soviet Union launched *Sputnik*, the world's first artificial satellite, Congress passed the National Defense Education Act in 1958. This Act provided a massive infusion of federal dollars to improve our schools' science, mathematics, engineering, and foreign language programs. Eventually, innovative

CNN Clip 24:
Year Round School

Discussion Question 1:
Other than those mentioned in this chapter, what additional recent educational developments seem particularly important to you? Why are they important?

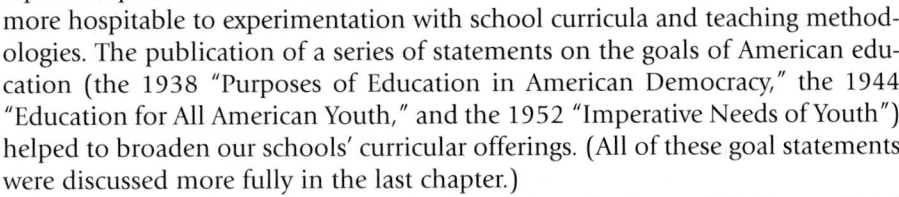

| TABLE 13.3 | **Public School Budgets, 1940–1990** | | | |

Year	Approximate Total Budget	Percentage Source		
		Federal	State	Local
1940	$2 billion	2	30	68
1950	$5 billion	3	40	57
1960	$15 billion	4	39	56
1970	$40 billion	8	40	52
1980	$97 billion	10	47	43
1990	$208 billion*	6*	47*	47*

Source: Bureau of the Census, *Digest of Educational Statistics 1982* (Washington, DC: U.S. Department of Commerce) 41.

*Estimates from: *120 Years of American Education: A Statistical Portrait,* U.S. Government Office of Educational Research and Improvement. Washington, DC: U.S. Department of Education, January 1993, 32, 34.

PROFESSIONAL DILEMMA

How Can a Teacher Better Understand the World?

Educators are admonished to "internationalize" their classrooms and their curriculum today. Most teachers really want to do so, but face the professional dilemma of developing their own understanding of the complex and richly diverse world in which we live. For one thing, while international study and travel are excellent learning opportunities for educators, it is expensive. Schools are not able to help teachers travel, and most international travel is no longer considered tax deductible by the Internal Revenue Service. Developing a better understanding of the world is difficult and expensive.

The United States played a key role in founding the United National Educational, Scientific and Cultural Organization (UNESCO) in the 1940s. Ironically, the United States withdrew its membership in UNESCO in 1983, for financial and political reasons. Teacher organizations such as the National Education Association continue to support UNESCO because of its potential to study and improve education around the globe. Understanding the world and working to improve global education is not only difficult for each teacher, but also difficult at the national level.

Still, understanding the world remains important for teachers, organizations, and nations. Accomplishing this task is a genuine professional dilemma for today's teachers. How will you cope with it? How will you internationalize your classroom and your curriculum? Will you, for instance, take international courses at a nearby college; find a way to travel outside the United States; subscribe to global publications; learn another language; take a foreign student into your home; encourage your school to offer in-service programs to help faculty better understand the world; or engage in some other activity that will help you internationalize your classroom and curriculum? We encourage you to start thinking about this professional dilemma right now—you and your future students will profit from your doing so.

Focus Question 2:
How did the special education programs we have in our schools today come into being?

Diversity Note 13.1:
"Inclusion" has become the mandate for special education students today. This requires that special students be included with all other students whenever possible.

Activity 13.4:
Invite a special education teacher to discuss the changing roles that a special educator has had to play since 1950. Have him or her progress from specialization to least restrictive environment responsibilities to the current regular education initiative.

curricula such as SMSG mathematics, BSCS biology, and PSCS physics grew out of these programs. Other school programs, such as guidance, were later funded through this Act. Note that in this case the federal government called on our schools to help solve what was perceived to be a "national defense" problem. Regardless of the motive, the NDEA represented another milestone that contributed significantly to the growth of our nation's educational enterprise.

If one were to compare today's school curriculum in nearly any subject with the curriculum in our schools fifty years ago, one would find impressive changes. The 1940 curriculum was very narrow and designed primarily for college-bound students, whereas today's curriculum is clearly broader and designed for students of all abilities. This fifty-year growth in our school curriculum has come about through the dedicated work of many people and represents one of the truly significant historical accomplishments in American education.

Growth of Special Education Programs.   Perhaps curriculum growth is best illustrated in the area of special education. The public schools historically did not provide special education programs for handicapped children; rather they simply accommodated such children as best they could, usually by placing them in regular classrooms. Teachers had little or no training to help them understand and assist the special child. In fact, relatively little was known about common handicapping conditions.

TABLE 13.4	Children Served in Special Education Programs, by Type of Disability: 1939–1940 and 1989–1990 (in thousands)					
	1939–1940	1952–1953	1962–1963	1969–1970	1979–1980	1989–1990
Percent of Public School Enrollment	1.2	1.7	3.7	5.9	9.6	11.4
Learning Disabled	1.2	1.7	3.7	5.9	9.6	11.4
Speech Impaired	—	—	—	—	1,276	2,050
Mentally Retarded	98	114	432	830	869	548
Seriously Emotionally Disturbed	10	—	80	113	329	381
Hard-of-Hearing and Deaf	13	16	46	78	80	57
Orthopedically Handicapped	[1]53	[1]29	[1]65	[1]269	80	48
Other Health Impaired	—	—	—	—	106	52
Visually Handicapped	9	9	22	24	31	22
Multihandicapped	—	—	—	—	60	86
Deaf-Blind	—	—	—	—	2	2
Preschool Handicapped	—	—	—	—	([2])	422
Other Handicapped	—	—	22	126	—	—
Total	310	475	1,469	2,677	4,005	4,641

Source: U.S. Department of Education, National Center for Educational Statistics. *Biennial Survey of Education in the United States: Digest of Educational Statistics;* Office of Special Education and Rehabilitative Services. *Annual Report to Congress on the Implementation of the Education of the Handicapped Act;* and unpublished tabulations. (This table was prepared September 1992.)

Not until the federal government passed a series of laws during the mid-twentieth century—including Public Law 94–142, Education for the Handicapped Children Act—did schools begin to develop well-designed programs for handicapped students. These new special education programs required teachers who had been trained to work with visually handicapped students, hearing-impaired students, students with behavior disorders, and so forth. States and colleges then developed a wide variety of teacher-training programs for special educators (see Table 13.4).

Special education has developed very rapidly over a relatively short period of time in our recent history. It continues to evolve rapidly today and will likely do so in the future.

Focus Question 3:
In what ways, if any, has the federal government contributed to education in recent history?

The Professionalization of Education

The field of education has taken giant strides toward becoming a profession during the past half century. In the following pages we will briefly explore the increasing complexities of our educational systems and look at some of the recent developments that have contributed to the professionalization of the field of education.

Test Questions 13.22–13.56

The Increasing Complexity of the Educational Enterprise

Our current educational system is much more complex than the school systems of the past, and this complexity is manifested in many different ways.

Objective 3:
Articulate the complexity of the educational enterprise in the United States.

Activity 13.5:
Invite a finance or budget professional from a school district to discuss the additional funded programs provided through the federal programs. Ask the professional to discuss the pros and cons of such additional funds.

Discussion Question 2:
Has the increased federal involvement in education been good or bad for our schools?

Transparency 63:
Percent of Persons 25 Years Old and Over Who Have Completed High School or College: Selected Years 1940 to 1991

Increasing Federal Involvement.   As we pointed out earlier, our federal government has played important roles in the development of national educational programs. This federal involvement in education has gradually increased over the years and it reached a crescendo during the past half century.

The 1940s saw the nation at war. The Vocational Education for National Defense Act was a crash program to prepare workers needed in industry to produce goods for national defense. The program operated through state educational agencies and trained over seven million workers. In 1941 the Lanham Act provided for building, maintaining, and operating community facilities in areas where local communities had unusual burdens because of defense and war initiatives.

GI Bill.   The GI Bill of 1944 provided for the education of veterans of World War II. Later, similar bills assisted veterans of the Korean conflict. The federal government recognized a need to help young people whose careers had been interrupted by military service. These bills afforded education to over ten million veterans at a cost of almost $20 billion. Payments were made directly to veterans and to the colleges and schools the veterans attended. In 1966, another GI Bill was passed for veterans of the war in Southeast Asia.

National Science Foundation.   The National Science Foundation, established in 1950, emphasized the need for continued support of basic scientific research. It was created to "promote the progress of science; to advance the national health, prosperity, and welfare; to secure the national defense; and for other purposes." The Cooperative Research Program of 1954 authorized the U.S. Commissioner of Education to enter into contracts with universities, colleges, and state education agencies to carry on educational research.

National Defense Education Act.   Beginning in 1957, when the first Soviet space vehicle was launched, the federal government further increased its participation in education. The National Defense Education Act of 1958, the Vocational Education Act of 1963, the Manpower Development and Training Act of 1963, the Elementary and Secondary Education Act of 1965, and the International Education Act of 1966 are examples of recently increased federal participation in educational affairs. Federally supported educational programs such as Project Head Start, National Teacher Corps, and Upward Bound are further indications of such participation.

Focus Question 4:
What is meant by *equal educational opportunity?*

Appendix 13.1 on page 360 lists some of the most important federal laws and programs that have supported education. All these Acts have involved categorical federal aid to education—that is, aid for a specific use. Some individuals believe that federal influence on education has recently been greater than either state or local influence. There can be no denying that through federal legislation, U.S. Supreme Court decisions, and federal administrative influence, the total federal effect on education is indeed great. Indications are that this effect will be even more pronounced in the future. It will remain for future historians to determine whether or not this trend in American education is a wise one.

The Struggle for Equal Educational Opportunity. The past half century has also been characterized by an increasing struggle for **equal educational opportunity** for all children, regardless of race, creed, religion, or sex. This struggle was initiated by the African American activism movement, given additional momentum by the women's rights movement, and eventually joined by many other groups such as Hispanic Americans, Native Americans, and Asian Americans. The details of this relatively recent quest for equal educational opportunity are discussed in many other parts of this book. We mention it briefly at this point simply to emphasize that the struggle for equal educational opportunity represents an important but unrealized recent historical movement in education. Today, many observers are pointing out that with the accelerated growth of minority subcultures within our nation, our economic and political survival depends to a large degree on their educational opportunities and achievements.

Key Term:
Equal educational opportunity

Discussion Question 3:
In your opinion, how much progress have we really made in providing equal educational opportunity in the United States? Defend your answer.

The Professionalization of Teaching

As we pointed out in the preceding chapter, formal teacher training is a relatively recent phenomenon. Teacher training programs were developed during the first half of this century. By the midpoint of this century, each state had established requirements for a teaching certificate. Since then, teacher training and certification have been characterized by a "refinement" or "professionalization" movement. Teacher salaries have also improved considerably over this period.

In addition to teacher education, this professionalization movement touched just about all facets of education—curriculum, teaching methodology, training of school service personnel (administrators, counselors, librarians, media and other specialists), in-service teacher training, teacher organizations, and even school building construction. To clearly understand this professionalization movement, one need only compare pictures of an old one-room country school with a modern school building, read both a 1940 and a 1994 publication of the AFT or NEA, contrast a mid-twentieth century high school curriculum with one from today, or compile a list of the teaching materials found in a 1940 school and a similar list for a typical contemporary school.

Information Note 13.3:
The current emphasis on multicultural education is being built on the same foundation on which the struggle for equal educational opportunity of the past fifty years was built.

Activity 13.6:
Have students develop a profile of a teacher who has specialized in a single area. Then have them develop a profile of a teacher who has a wide and varied background. Discuss the strengths and weaknesses of the two profiles.

Continued Importance of Private Schools

As was indicated in the preceding chapter, religion was the main purpose of education in colonial America. Children were taught to read primarily so that they could read the Bible and gain salvation. Most early colleges were established primarily to train ministers.

As the public school system developed, however, the religious nature of education gradually diminished to the point where relatively few American children attended religious schools. There have always been certain religious groups, however, that have struggled to create and maintain their own private schools so that religious instruction could permeate all areas of the curriculum. The most notable of these religious groups is the Roman Catholic Church. Over the past twenty-five

Journal Activity Master 13.1: The Development of a Personal Theory of Learning. This activity requires students to answer a series of questions so that they might clarify an underlying theory of learning. The exercise concludes with several analytical questions that clarify the historical roots that might support aspects of the theory.

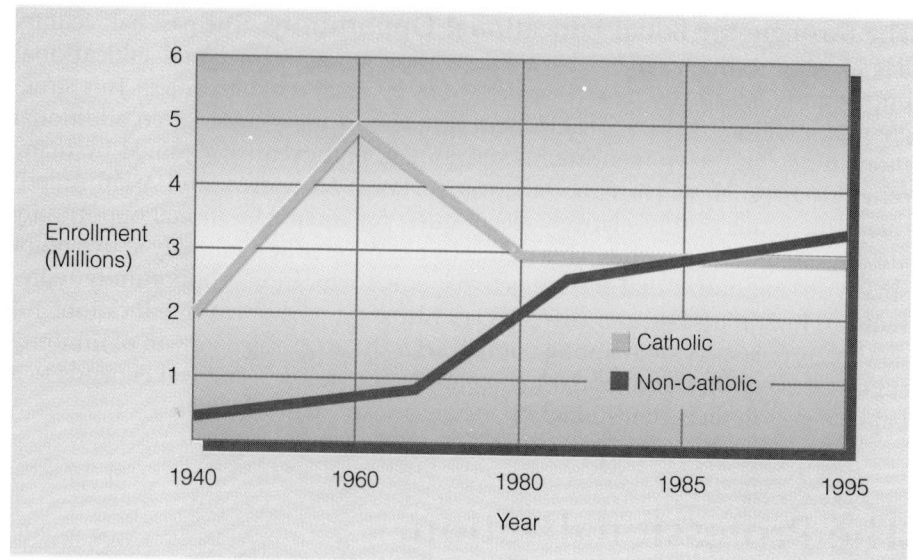

FIGURE 13.2

Estimated Private School Enrollments Since 1940

Discussion Question 4:
In what respect, if any, has education become professionalized, in your opinion?

Focus Question 5:
What role have private schools played in the United States in recent history?

Activity 13.7:
Ask students to visit a private school in their area and comment on why they think parents might send their children there.

years, though, enrollment in non-Catholic religious schools has grown dramatically while the Catholic school enrollment has declined. These changes in enrollment are reflected in Figure 13.2.

Some Roman Catholic dioceses operate extremely large school systems, sometimes larger than the public school system in the same geographical area. The Chicago Diocese operates the largest Roman Catholic school system, enrolling approximately 150,000 students.

While space does not permit a thorough discussion of contemporary private school systems, we would like to emphasize that private schools provide elementary and secondary education for a very large number of American young people.

As the public school system developed, the relative prevalance of religious education diminished.

Teacher education students should become familiar with these private school systems so that they can decide whether they might be interested in pursuing teaching positions in such schools.

Recent Trends in Education[2]

Education experienced a major change following World War II when Dewey, Counts, Bagley, Charters, Terman, and other intellectuals who held sway during the first half of the twentieth century yielded to a somewhat less philosophically oriented breed of researchers represented by Harris, Maslow, Havighurst, Bloom, Guilford, Cronbach, Bruner, McLuhan, Chomsky, and Piaget. The Progressive Education Association closed its doors, and a series of White House conferences on children, youth, and education were inaugurated in an attempt to improve education.

No school system on earth has been scrutinized, analyzed, and dissected as profoundly and as mercilessly as the American one. During the late 1940s and middle 1950s, educational institutions at all levels were not only flooded with unprecedented numbers of students but also censored and flailed unmercifully by self-ordained critics (Rickover, Bestor, Mortimer, Smith, and Flesch). In retrospect, this frantic rush to simultaneously patronize and criticize the institution seems a curious contradiction. The public schools were characterized as "Godless, soft, undisciplined, uncultured, wasteful, and disorganized." Critics who remembered the high failure rates among World War II draftees were determined to raise the levels of physical fitness and literacy; others who detected a weakening of moral and spiritual values were eager to initiate citizenship and character-education programs. The enrollments in nonpublic schools doubled, correspondence schools of all kinds sprang into existence, and the popular press carried articles and programs designed to help parents augment the basic skills within the school program. In 1955 there were an estimated 450 correspondence schools serving 700,000 students throughout the country.

New Emphases in Education.   Fortunately, though some people were highly critical of our schools, not everybody panicked. There were physical fitness programs, character-education projects, a general tightening of educational standards, and much more. Guilford, Torrence, Getzels, and others explored the boundaries of creativity; A. S. Barr and Ryans carried out exhaustive studies of teacher characteristics; and just about everybody experimented with new patterns of organization. There were primary block programs; inter-age groupings; Joplin, Stoddard, and Trump plans; core programs; and a host of other patterns or combinations of plans structured around subject areas, broad groupings of subjects, or pupil characteristics. There were programs for the gifted and the not-so-gifted, and there was a new concern for foreign language instruction as well as the functional use of English. There was also a limited resurgence of Montessori Schools and several one-of-a-kind schools such as Amidon and Summerhill. While all this was taking place within the schools, the school systems themselves were consolidating, and by 1965 there were only half as many school districts as had existed twenty years earlier.

Automation was highly regarded during the 1950s, but the tools that gave education its biggest boost were more diverse. Social psychologists provided more advanced sociometric tools that offered new insights into the functioning of groups; reading specialists and psychologists developed highly refined diagnostic

Objective 4:
List and elaborate on the significant recent trends in American education.

Journal Activity Master 13.2: An Analysis of the Historical Context Surrounding a Contemporary Trend in Education. This activity requires students to examine a series of movements and indicate those that seem to lead toward solutions and those that seem to result in more questions. Using this exercise, have students then clarify an educational trend and analyze its historical context.

Focus Question 6:
What trends have been evident in our school system over the past fifty years?

Discussion Question 5:
What is happening in education at this very moment that is likely to be written about in future books about the history of education?

Activity 13.8:
Describe the freedom of choice that was the foundation of A.S. Neill's educational philosophy. Compare this structure to the educational trends of today.

Transparency 65:
Fundamental Ideas about Education

instruments for use in studying learning disabilities; and statisticians devised new formulas and designs for controlling and analyzing data by using modern computers. New research tools such as regression formulas and factoral analysis yielded data that had been unobtainable earlier. On a somewhat less sophisticated level more interesting and more flexible teaching tools were developed—audiovisual devices, learning games, more beautifully illustrated books, instructional television, machines for programmed instruction, and computers. Additional personnel such as teacher aides, counselors, social workers, and school psychologists were added as well.

Relevant Research

Classroom Analysis Systems

Some of the research studies that grew out of recent educational history deal with the analysis of the teaching/learning act. Hundreds of pieces of research contributed to this research movement, including the work of Flanders* who, along with many colleagues, developed the classroom verbal interaction analysis system, which helps a teacher better understand what takes place verbally in the classroom. This system uses an observation form developed just for the purpose of recording what is taking place, moment by moment, in a classroom for a given lesson. These observations are then placed on a grid that helps a teacher better analyze and understand what took place during the lesson. Often, teachers are surprised at the results, which may be quite different from what the teacher expected. For instance, often teachers spend more time talking than they realize.

There have been many other systems developed to help teachers better understand and control what takes place in their classrooms. We encourage you to become familiar with some of these classroom observation systems and to try them in your classroom. Ask your professors and cooperating teachers in the schools where you are doing clinical work, to help you get started on this task. What classroom analysis systems have you already become familiar with? Can you locate at least six such systems? Can you experiment with the three best systems you find?

*Flanders Verbal Classroom Interaction Analysis system

Analysis of Teaching.   Another emphasis found expression in the **analysis of teaching.** For half a century, researchers had been attempting to identify the characteristics and teaching styles that were most closely associated with effective instruction. Hundreds of studies had been initiated, and correlations had been done among them. During the 1950s the focus began changing from what ought to occur in teaching to what actually does occur. Flanders and other researchers developed observational scales for use in assessing verbal communications between and among teachers and students. The scales permitted observers to categorize and summarize specific actions on the part of teachers and students. These studies were followed by studies of nonverbal classroom behaviors.

Another series of investigations involving the wider range of instructional protocols was patterned after the time-motion studies used earlier for industrial processes. Dwight Allen and several other educators attempted to use some of these findings in delineating the components of effective teaching. Specific formats were used to introduce teacher candidates to the elements judged most important to good teaching. The change in focus from studies of teacher characteristics to analyses of what actually occurs in classrooms has provided us with some of our best insights into teaching and learning and given us usable instruments for further investigations of classroom behavior. We can now assess the logical, verbal, nonverbal, affective, and several attitudinal dimensions of instruction as well as the intricate aspects of cognition and concept development.

Key Term:
Analysis of teaching

Teacher Effectiveness.   Recent research has focused even more closely on the instructional patterns of effective teachers. A recent review by Powers and Beard, *Teacher Effectiveness: An Annotated Bibliography*, catalogs over three thousand investigations into instructional competencies. Today's teachers, through **effective teaching,** are frequently viewed as having some important skills in common with the school teachers of sixty years ago. They are strong leaders who direct classroom activities, maximize the use of instructional time, and teach in a clear, businesslike manner.

Teachers now employ structured, carefully delineated lessons. They break larger topics into smaller, more easily grasped components, and focus on one thought, point, or direction at a time. They check prerequisite skills before introducing new skills or concepts. Step-by-step presentations are accompanied by a large number of probing questions. Teachers offer detailed explanations of difficult points, and test students on one point before moving on to the next. They provide corrective feedback where needed, and stay with the topic under study until students comprehend the major points or issues. Effective teachers use prompts and cues to assist students through the initial stages of acquisition.

This new emphasis on demonstration, prompting, and practice is a far cry from the relatively unstructured classroom activities of just ten years ago. We now emphasize carefully created learning goals and lesson sequences. It will be interesting to see whether the educational pendulum swings back to a new focus on student concerns and initiatives at some time in the future.

Sociological Studies.   A major breakthrough in education has resulted from a series of sociological studies relating to social class, social perceptions, and academic achievement. Coleman and Deutch were among the first to demonstrate that it is not the teaching equipment as much as children's social relationships that make the difference. Students' parents and peer groups at home and at school mold their perceptions and regulate their performances. These findings and those of Rosenthall and Jencks have given new direction to our efforts. Our concerns have changed, at least partially, from educational hardware to studies of pupil populations.

Study of the Learning Process.   In relatively recent years a number of leading American and European researchers have sought to analyze and describe how children learn. All of these investigators have stressed the importance of successful early learning patterns and the problems associated with serious learning deficits. They also believe that important elements within the environment may be changed or modified to promote learning.

Maria Montessori, an Italian physician, believed that children should be encouraged to teach themselves through the use of manipulative materials. She developed a wide range of educational resources, many of which could be matched or sequenced according to specific attributes (size, color, pitch, etc.). Montessori did much to promote the concept of pupil discovery and the use of tactile learning materials.

Global Perspectives: Jean Piaget.   Jean Piaget (1896–1980), a Swiss psychologist, was educated at the University of Paris. Through his work with Alfred Binet, who developed one of the first intelligence tests, Piaget became very interested in how children learn. He spent long hours observing different-aged children and eventually created a theory of mental or **cognitive development.** Piaget believed that children develop in four major stages. Up until about age two, a child is at the *sensorimotor stage* and learns mainly through the hands, mouth, and

Journal/Portfolio Development 2:
Describe and evaluate a learning experience you remember from your own elementary school days. What made it memorable, and what role did the teacher play in that learning experience?

Information Note 13.4:
Information about the teacher effectiveness movement is interwoven throughout this book. Future teachers should learn, on their own if necessary, as much as they can about this significant recent development in education.

Key Term:
Effective teaching

Activity 13.9:
Ask students to list the top ten qualities that characterize an effective teacher.

Transparency 64:
Stages of Cognitive Development by Jean Piaget

Key Term:
Cognitive development

eyes. From about two to seven years of age, a child is at the *preoperational stage* and learns primarily through language and concepts. Between the ages seven and eleven, a child's learning is characterized by *concrete operations*, which involve the use of more complex concepts such as numbers. The final learning stage identified by Piaget is called the *formal operations* phase. This stage typically begins between ages eleven and fifteen and continues throughout adulthood. During this final stage the learner employs the most sophisticated and abstract learning processes. While children do not all fit neatly into these categories, Piaget's work has contributed much to our understanding of the learning process and has helped teachers to develop more appropriate teaching strategies for students at different developmental stages.

Robert Havighurst, a University of Chicago professor, has identified specific developmental tasks that he believes children must master if they are to develop normally. He even suggests that there may be periods during which certain tasks must be mastered if they are to become an integral part of children's repertoire of responses. There may also be "teachable moments" (periods of peak efficiency for the acquisition of specific experiences) during which receptivity is particularly high. Havighurst, like Piaget, has caused us to look carefully at the motivations and needs of children.

A contemporary of Havighurst, Jerome Bruner, of Harvard, has also postulated a series of developmental steps or stages that he believes children encounter as they mature. These involve action, imagery, and symbolism. Bruner's cognitive views have stressed student inquiry and the breaking down of larger tasks into components.

Benjamin Bloom, author of Bloom's Taxonomy of Educational Objectives and Distinguished Service Professor at the University of Chicago, has attempted to identify and weigh the factors that control learning. He believes that one can predict learning outcomes by assessing three factors: (1) the cognitive entry behaviors of a student (the extent to which the pupil has mastered prerequisite skills); (2) the affective entry characteristics (the student's interest in learning the material); and (3) the quality of instruction (the degree to which the instruction offered is appropriate for the learner). We can observe Bloom's research as reflected in models of direct instruction, particularly mastery learning, in which teachers carefully explain, illustrate, and demonstrate skills and provide practice, reinforcement, corrective feedback, and remediation.

Key Term:
Behavioral theory

B. F. Skinner (1904–1990)

B. F. Skinner.   Burrhus Frederic (B. F.) Skinner (1904–1990) became one of the foremost early educational psychologists in American education. He developed a **behavioral theory** that suggested students could be successfully trained or conditioned to learn just about anything a teacher desired. This required the teacher to break down the learning into small sequential steps. Skinner even experimented with teaching machines that presented the learner with small sequential bits of information—an idea that has been revived today in computer-assisted instruction. Skinner published many works, including *The Technology of Teaching, Beyond Freedom and Dignity,* and *Walden Two.* He contributed much to our understanding of human learning and helped to advance the technology of teaching.

Educational Critics.   Another development in education was triggered by a phalanx of critics, including Edgar Friedenberg (*Coming of Age in America*), Charles Silberman (*Crisis in the Classroom*), Jonathan Kozol (*Death at an Early Age*), Ivan

CASE STUDY   THE DISCOURAGED TEACHER

Your friend, Jim, is a third-year teacher who is somewhat discouraged about the teaching profession. When he graduated from his teacher preparation program he was full of enthusiasm; in fact, he accepted a teaching position in a school with a relatively high percentage of minority students because he thought he could make a difference. However, after three years, he is disillusioned about urban schools, which he claims are making pathetically little progress toward meeting the educational needs of most urban youth. He feels that students, for the most part, are apathetic, belligerent, and unconvinced that education is worthwhile. He further states that most urban parents do not support teachers or help their children with school work. Jim is also disappointed with his school's administration, which he claims does not adequately support the teachers.

Jim believes that little, if any, progress has been made over the past fifty years to improve equal educational opportunities for minority youth. He points out that minority students drop out of school much more frequently than do nonminorities, and they have more difficulty getting into college; in addition, our schools are still sexist institutions. In fact, Jim suggests that schools have very likely made these problems worse—not better—by perpetuating a value system that does not serve minorities and females well.

Jim then asks you, as a future educator, about your opinions regarding these problems. What is your response? Include answers to the following questions in your response.

1. What lessons can we learn, if any, from history, about the education of minorities and females?
2. To what extent and in what ways do you feel Jim's perception of urban schools is correct?
3. How well do you feel our schools are serving minorities and females at this time?
4. How might schools in general better serve minorities and females in the future?
5. Should schools make special efforts and spend extra funds to improve education for special groups, or should they serve all students alike? Why or why not?
6. What are some ways that you personally might be able to improve education for minorities and female students?

Illich (*Deschooling Society*), John Holt (*How Children Fail*), and a government report, *A Nation At Risk* (1983), which focused on low educational standards. Some, like Silberman, urge us to refurbish what we already have; others, including Illich, want to abandon the schools altogether. These critics have not gone unnoticed. Friedenberg's call for alternatives to traditional education, Silberman's endorsement of open education, and Kozol's plea for equal opportunity are all reflected to some degree in innovative programs from coast to coast.

Litigation's Influence on Education. In the years since 1970 we have seen an astonishingly large segment of our school patrons and students resorting to courts of law in confrontations with school officials and teachers. Considerable space is devoted to discussing many of these law cases elsewhere in this book. Suits have been filed challenging pupil placements, grades, the failure of the school to teach properly, disciplinary actions, dress codes, and numerous other previously

CNN Clip 25:
Reinventing Schools

Journal/Portfolio Development 3:
Create a list of the most useful outcomes of American education over the past fifty years. What can you as a beginning teacher learn, if anything, from your list?

Activity 13.11:
Ask students to select a leading educational critic and have them try to defend today's education against such criticism.

Information Note 13.5:
Two chapters (9 and 10) in this book have been devoted to the important topic of the legal aspects of education. Teachers need to know a great deal about this subject—and to make sure that they have adequate professional liability insurance.

accepted educational practices. The Buckley Amendment, which gives students and their parents the right to view official school records, added immeasurably to the demands of those seeking redress of grievances. In addition, the rights of due process have been extended to include students at all levels in an effort to protect their constitutional rights. Due process requires that rules and regulations facilitate the educational goals of the school and be clearly publicized. There must also be provision for a fair hearing when regulations are violated.

It is unfortunate that legal recourse has become a major modus operandi of recent years, for legal maneuvering is generally a substitute for good faith and mutual respect. However, individual abuses have probably diminished in the wake of threatened legal sanctions.

Global Perspectives: Educators Share a World-Wide Responsibility.

These last three chapters, which have briefly reviewed the history of education, point out that many, perhaps even most, of our educational concepts and practices were first developed long ago and in various parts of the world. We contemporary teachers in the United States owe a great debt of gratitude to our historical counterparts around the globe who pioneered and developed the profession we carry on.

Diversity Note 13.2:
Many of the advances made in minority education have been initiated and/or aided by legal action.

History has shown that educators throughout the world have learned much from one another, and that education has improved and profited greatly from this sharing of educational ideas. This is even more true today than it has been in the past, and will increase as societies become ever more dependent on one another. Educators such as you will have to work even harder to share educational ideas in the future.

Summary and Implications

In this chapter we saw that the past half century has been characterized by tremendous growth, increased federal involvement, a struggle for equal educational opportunity, professionalization, litigation, and criticism. Many of the specific educational events that have taken place during this time period are listed in Appendix 13.2 on page 362.

It is difficult to draw meaningful inferences from recent events that have not yet stood the test of time. Implications of recent educational events will eventually be found in the answers to questions such as these:

- What should be the role of the federal government in education?
- How can we achieve equal educational opportunity in the United States?
- How professionalized do we want our school system to be?
- To what degree should educational policy and practice be influenced by itigation?

Discussion Questions

1. Other than those mentioned in this chapter, what additional recent educational developments seem particularly important to you? Why are they important?
2. Has the increased federal involvement in education been good or bad for our schools?
3. In your opinion, how much progress have we really made in providing equal educational opportunity in the United States? Defend your answer.

4. In what respect, if any, has education become professionalized, in your opinion?
5. What is happening in education at this very moment that is likely to be written about in future books about the history of education?

Journal/Portfolio Development

1. Interview a retired teacher about the educational changes she or he has observed over the past fifty years. Ask what advice this retired educator has for beginning teachers today.
2. Describe and evaluate a learning experience you remember from your own elementary school days.

What made it memorable, and what role did the teacher play in the learning process?
3. Create a list of the most useful outcomes of American education over the past fifty years. What can you as a beginning teacher learn, if anything, from your list?

School-Based Experiences

1. Most of the developments discussed in this chapter are so recent that they continue to influence contemporary American classrooms. As you work in the schools, look to see how our continuing struggle for equal educational opportunity is progressing. Also, analyze what you observe in order to determine the degree to which teaching has been professionalized—a movement that has gained impetus during the last fifty years. Finally, as you participate in

classrooms, look for evidence that the work of educational pioneers discussed in this chapter (such as Bloom, Montessori, Skinner, and Piaget) has made an impact in our classrooms.
2. Discuss with experienced educators the changes they have observed during their careers. Visit with older educational administrators to discuss changes they have seen in their work over the years. Ask older people about their school experiences.

Notes

1. Bureau of the Census, *Digest of Education Statistics 1982.* Washington, DC: U.S. Department of Commerce, Government Printing Office, 1982, 23.

2. We thank Dr. Donald Barnes for many of the ideas presented in this section.

Bibliography

Avrich, Paul. *The Modern School Movement: Anarchism and Education in the United States.* Princeton, NJ: Princeton University Press, 1980.
Best, John Hardin, and Sidewell, Robert T., eds. *The American Legacy of Learning: Readings in the History of Education.* Philadelphia: Lippincott, 1967.
Church, Robert L. *Education in the United States: An Interpretive History.* New York: The Free Press, 1976.
Cremin, Lawrence A. *American Education: The Metropolitan Experience 1876–1980.* New York: Harper & Row, 1988.
_____. *The Transformation of the School: Progressivism in American Education, 1876–1957.* New York: Knopf, 1961.
French, William M. *American Educational Tradition: An Interpretive History.* Boston: Heath, 1964.

Gutek, Gerald L. *Education in the United States: An Historical Perspective.* Englewood Cliffs, NJ: Prentice-Hall, 1986.
Krug, Edward. *The Shaping of the American High School.* New York: Harper & Row, 1964.
Meyer, Adolphe E. *An Educational History of the American People.* New York: McGraw-Hill, 1967.
"The Negro and American Education." *Changing Education* (a journal of the American Federation of Teachers) (Fall 1966).
Perkinson, Henry J., ed. *Two Hundred Years of American Educational Thought.* New York: David McKay, 1976.
Ravitch, Diane. *The Troubled Crusade: American Education 1945–1980.* New York: Basic Books, 1983.
Spring, Joel. *The American School 1642–1990.* White Plains, NY: Longman, 1994.

Appendix 13.1

Selected Federal Education Acts/Events

1787	Northwest Ordinance	1958	Education of Mentally Retarded Children Act
1862	First Morrill Land Grant Act		
1867	Department of Education Act	1958	Captioned Films for the Deaf Act
1887	Hatch Act	1961	Area Redevelopment Act
1890	Second Morrill Land Grant Act	1962	Manpower Development and Training Act
1911	The State Marine School Act	1962	Migration and Refugee Assistance Act
1914	Smith-Lever Agriculture Extension Act	1963	Vocational Education Act
1917	Smith-Hughes Vocational Act	1963	Higher Education Facilities Act
1918	Vocational Rehabilitation Act	1964	Civil Rights Act
1919	An act to provide for further educational facilities	1964	Economic Opportunity Act
		1965	Elementary and Secondary Education Act
1920	Smith-Bankhead Act	1965	Higher Education Act
1935	Bankhead-Jones Act	1965	Health Professions Educational Assistance Amendments
1935	Agricultural Adjustment Act		
1940	Vocational Education for National Defense Act	1965	National Foundation on the Arts and the Humanities Act
1941	Lanham Act	1965	National Technical Institute for the Deaf Act
1943	Vocational Rehabilitation Act	1965	National Vocational Student Loan Insurance Act
1944	GI Bill of Rights		
1944	Surplus Property Act	1966	International Education Act
1946	National School Lunch Act	1966	Adult Education Act
1946	George Barden Act	1966	Model Secondary School for the Deaf Act
1948	United States Information and Educational Exchange Act	1966	Elementary and Secondary Education Amendments
1949	Federal Property and Administrative Services Act	1967	Education Professions Development Act
		1968	Elementary and Secondary Education Amendments
1950	National Science Foundation		
1950	Financial assistance for local educational agencies affected by federal activities	1968	Handicapped Children's Early Education Assistance Act
		1968	Vocational Education Amendments
1950	Housing Act	1968	Higher Education Amendments
1954	Cooperative Research Act	1970	Elementary and Secondary Education Assistance Programs
1954	National Advisory Committee on Education Act		
		1970	National Commission on Libraries and Information Science Act
1954	School Milk Program Act		
1956	Library Services Act	1970	Office of Education Appropriation Act
1958	National Defense Education Act	1970	Environmental Education Act

1970   Drug Abuse Education Act
1971   Comprehensive Health Manpower Training Act
1972   Title IX Education Amendment
1972   Drug Abuse Office and Treatment Act
1972   Education Amendments
1972   Indian Education Act
1973   Older Americans Comprehensive Services Amendment
1973   Comprehensive Employment and Training Act
1974   Educational Amendments
1974   Juvenile Justice and Delinquency Prevention Act
1974   White House Conference on Library and Information Services Act
1975   Education for the Handicapped Act
1975   Indian Self-Determination and Education Assistance Act
1975   Indochina Migration and Refugee Assistance Act
1976   Education Amendments
1977   Youth Employment and Demonstration Projects Act
1978   Career Education Incentive Act

1978   Tribally Controlled Community College Assistance Act
1978   Education Amendments
1978   Middle Income Student Assistance Act
1979   Department of Education Organization Act
1980   Asbestos School Hazard Protection and Control Act
1980   Amendments to the Higher Education Act of 1965
1981   Education Consolidation and Improvement Act
1984   Education for Economic Security Act
1984   Perkins Vocational Education Act
1984   Talented Teachers Fellowship Program enacted
1986   U.S. Secretary of Education Report: *First Lessons, A Report on Elementary Education in America*
1989   Presidential Education Summit with Governors
1990   U.S. Supreme Court Decision to Allow Bible Clubs in Schools
1994   National Educational Goals: 2000 adopted by federal government

Important Dates in the History of Western Education

ca. 4000 B.C.	Written language developed
2000	First schools
1200	Trojan War
479–338	Period of Greek brilliance
469–399	Socrates
445–431	Greek Age of Pericles
427–346	Plato
404	Fall of Athens
384–322	Aristotle
336–323	Ascendancy of Alexander the Great
303	A few private Greek teachers set up schools in Rome
167	First Greek library in Rome
146	Fall of Corinth: Greece falls to Rome
A.D. 31–476	Empire of Rome
35–95	Quintilian
40–120	Plutarch
70	Destruction of Jerusalem
476	Fall of Rome in the West
734–804	Alcuin
800	Charlemagne crowned Emperor
980–1037	Avicenna
1100–1300	Crusades
1126–1198	Averroes
ca. 1150	Universities of Paris and Bologna
1209	Cambridge founded
1225–1274	St. Thomas Aquinas
1295	Voyage of Marco Polo
1384	Order of Brethren of the Common Life founded
ca. 1400	Thirty-eight universities; 108 by 1600
1423	Printing invented
1456	First book printed
1460–1536	Erasmus
1483–1546	Martin Luther
1487	Vasco de Gama discovered African route to India
1491–1556	Ignatius of Loyola
1492	Columbus lands in America
ca. 1492	Colonists begin exploiting Native Americans
ca. 1500	250 Latin grammar schools in England
1517	Luther nails theses to cathedral door; beginning of Reformation
1519–1521	Magellan first circumnavigates the globe
1534	Founding of Jesuits
1536	Sturm established his Gymnasium in Germany, the first classical secondary school
1568	Indian school established in Cuba by the Society of Jesus
1592–1600	Johann Comenius
1601	English Poor Law, established principle of tax-supported schools
1618	Holland had compulsory school law
1620	Plymouth Colony, Massachusetts, settled
1635	Boston Latin Grammar School founded
1636	Harvard founded

1642	Massachusetts law of 1642 encouraged education		1826	Froebel's *The Education of Man* published
1632–1704	John Locke		1827	Massachusetts law compelled high schools
1647	Massachusetts law of 1647 compelled establishment of schools		1837	Massachusetts had first state board, Horace Mann first secretary
1600s	Hornbooks evolved		1839	First public normal school, United States, Lexington, Massachusetts
1661	First newspaper in England		1855	First kindergarten in United States—after German model, Mrs. Schurz
1672	First teacher-training class, Father Demia, France			
1684	Brothers of the Christian Schools founded		1856–1915	Booker T. Washington
1685	First normal school, de la Salle, Rheims, France		1857–1952	John Dewey
			1861–1865	Civil War
1697	First teacher training in Germany, Francke's Seminary, Halle		1861	Oswego (New York) Normal School (Edward Sheldon)
1700–1790	Benjamin Franklin		1862	Morrill Land Grant Act: college of engineering, military science, agriculture in each state
1712–1778	Jean Rousseau			
1723	Indian student house opened by College of William and Mary		1868	Herbartian Society founded
			1870–1952	Maria Montessori
1746–1827	Johann Pestalozzi		1872	Kalamazoo Decision, made high schools legal
1751	Franklin established first academy in the United States			
			1875–1955	Mary Bethune
1758–1843	Noah Webster		1888	Teachers College, Columbia University, founded
1762	Rousseau's *Émile* published			
1775–1783	Revolution, United States		1892	Committee of Ten established
1776–1841	Johann Herbart		1896–1980	Jean Piaget
1782–1852	Friedrich Froebel		1904–1990	B. F. Skinner
1778–1870	Emma Willard		1909–1910	The first junior high schools established at Berkeley, California, and Columbus, Ohio
1789	Adoption of Constitution, United States			
1796–1859	Horace Mann		ca. 1910	The first junior colleges established at Fresno, California, and Joliet, Illinois
1798	Joseph Lancaster developed monitorial plan of education			
1799–1815	Ascendancy of Napoleon, Waterloo		1917	The Smith-Hughes Act, encouraged agriculture, industry, and home economics education in the United States
1804	Pestalozzi's Institute at Yverdon established			
1806	First Lancastrian School in New York		1932–1940	The Eight-Year Study of thirty high schools completed by the Progressive Education Association; reported favorably on the modern school
1811–1900	Henry Barnard			
1819	Dartmouth College Decision			
1821	First American high school			
1821	Troy Seminary for Women, Emma Willard, first higher education for women, United States		1941	Japanese bomb Pearl Harbor
			1941	Lanham Act
1823	First private normal school in the United States, Concord, Vermont, by Rev. Hall		1942	The Progressive Education Association published the findings of the Eight-Year Study
1825	Labor unions come on the scene			

1944–1946   Legislation by 78th U.S. Congress provided subsistence allowance, tuition fees, and supplies for the education of veterans of World War II

1945   The United National Educational, Scientific, and Cultural Organization (UNESCO) initiated efforts to improve educational standards throughout the world

1946–1947   U.S. "baby boom," eventually causing huge increase in school enrollments

1948   *McCollum v. Board of Education;* U.S. Supreme Court ruled it illegal to release children for religious classes in public school buildings

1950   The National Science Foundation founded

1952   The GI Bill's educational benefits extended to Korean War veterans

1954   U.S. Supreme Court decision required eventual racial integration of public schools

1954   Cooperative Research Program

1957   The Soviet Union launched *Sputnik*

1958   Federal Congress passed the National Defense Education Act

1959   James B. Conant wrote *The American High School Today*

1961   Federal court ruled *de facto* racial segregation illegal

1961   Peace Corps established

1961   Approximately four million college students in the United States

1962   In *Engle v. Vitale,* U.S. Supreme Court ruled compulsory prayer in public school illegal

1963   Vocational Education Act

1963   Manpower Development and Training Act

1964   The Economic Opportunity Act provided federal funds for such programs as Head Start

1964   Civil Rights Act

1965   The Elementary and Secondary Education Act allowed more federal funds for public schools

1965   Higher Education Act

1966   The GI Bill's educational benefits extended to Southeast Asia war veterans

1966   One million Americans travel abroad

1948–1966   Fulbright programs in 136 nations involving 82,500 scholars

1966   U.S. International Education Act

1966   The Coleman Report suggested that racially balanced schools did not necessarily provide a better education

1967   Education Professions Development Act

1972   Indian Education Act passed, designed to help Native Americans help themselves

1972   Title IX Education Amendment outlawing discrimination on the basis of sex

1973   In *Rodriguez* v. *San Antonio Independent School,* the U.S. Supreme Court ruled that a state's system for financing schools did not violate the Constitution although there were large disparities in per-pupil expenditure.

1975   Indochina Migration and Refugee Assistance Act (Public Law 94-23)

1975   Public Law 94-142, requiring local districts to provide education for special and handicapped children

1979   Department of Education Act

1980   The U.S. Secretary of Education became a cabinet post

1983   *High School: A Report on Secondary Education in America* by the Carnegie Foundation

1983   *A Nation at Risk: The Imperative for Educational Reform,* report by the National Commission on Excellence in Education

1983   Task Force on Education for Economic Growth, Action for Excellence, Education Commission of the States Report

1983   Task Force on Federal Elementary and Secondary Education Policy,

	Making the Grade, the Twentieth Century Fund Report	1985	NCATE Redesign Standards published
1980–1984	Fundamentalist religious movement advocating prayer in the schools and teaching of Biblical creation story	1986	Holmes Group report published
		1986	Carnegie Report of the Task Force on Teaching as a Profession
1984	Public Law 98-377 added new science and mathematics programs, magnet schools, and equal access to public schools	1989	Presidential Education Summit with Governors
		1990	U.S. Supreme Court Decision to Allow Bible Clubs in Schools
1984	Perkins Vocational Education Act to upgrade vocational programs in schools	1992	U.S. Supreme Court Decision finds officially sanctioned prayers or invocations unconstitutional
1984	Public Law 98-558 created new teacher education scholarships and continues Head Start and Follow Through programs	1994	National Educational Goals: 2000 adopted by federal government

Part 5

Philosophical Concepts, Educational Views, and Teaching Styles

Dreamcatcher

AKBAR ALI New York City Surrounded by a world of turmoil, struggle, and poverty, Akbar Ali is an educator in the fullest sense of the word. He is a musician, a language and mathematics teacher, an administrator, a counselor, and a friend to thousands of students in New York City. Throughout his twenty years of teaching, Akbar has developed a complete philosophy, one that centers on an ethical concern and compassion for all children. His approaches to learning and knowledge, to testing and grading, and to discipline and responsibility are rooted in this axiological focus on respect for the innate dignity of all persons.

I have never studied education on a formal basis, so every classroom approach has truly been an experiment of experiential learning for me and my students. During my sophomore year ar Carnegie-Mellon University, I began teaching in a high school program that was housed on campus. I was stunned by the insights about math and physics that I gained by looking through the eyes of my students. I have been teaching (and therefore learning) ever since. As a musician and composer, I was struck again by the connection between mathematical problem solving and musical problem solving in music composition and improvisation. The tensions and resolutions created through chords, rhythm, and melody reflected the same components as a logic puzzle. Connections became and remain for me a focus of understanding what learners need to experience.

Conceptually, I try to demonstrate the idea that I intend for them to grasp and then to quickly place them in a situation that will demand their use of that idea on a practical level.

I trust their ability to find their own way to the original idea and then to go beyond it. It is important to be able to recognize and support efforts of various types of intelligences and approaches. I view intelligences as mental, emotional, and physical—this is an ancient division of intelligences. I try to help students recognize which intelligence predominates in their own approach; then, after recognizing the limits of that single intelligence, I try to help them include a second intelligence. This is obviously the strength of integrated curriculum—the chance to include more than one intelligence.

I think my greatest realization about teaching is that within the content—concepts, skills, effort, and all else offered during the classroom experience—there is something else that can be transferred between teacher and student that is far more subtle and precious than skills and information. The process of sustained effort together reveals a deeper level of "education." When I can render it, my most selfless wish for what is best for them has a transforming effect on me and on my students. It is for this quality of interaction that I lovingly remember my best teachers, long after I have forgotten the literal content of their lessons. Their lessons made me a better person for living and further learning. These teachers "raised" me on many levels, like yeast in dough. It is this lesson I wish to convey within the heart of puzzles, computer programming, jazz improvisation, or any other subject that I now offer. It is to this lesson, the truest connection with my students, that I am committed.

Philosophy: The Passion to Understand

Focus Questions

1 Are you able to identify your beliefs about knowledge, human nature, and values? How might your beliefs influence your teaching?

2 Do you believe authentic learning primarily occurs in real life experiences? How would you justify your answer?

3 Do you perceive students to be innately interested in learning for its own sake? How does your response influence your teaching and learning strategies?

4 Why is it valuable for prospective teachers to study philosophy?

5 Can you identify one way that students in your classroom might tackle an issue philosophically?

Key Terms and Concepts

Abstraction: A thought process of drawing away from experience to a conceptual plane.

Axiology: An area of philosophy that deals with the nature of values. It includes questions such as "What is good?" "What is value?"

Eastern thought: A varied set of philosophies from the Far, Middle, and Near East that stress inner peace, tranquility, attitudinal development, and mysticism.

Epistemology: An area of philosophy that deals with questions about how and what we know.

Existentialism: A school of philosophy that focuses on the importance of the individual rather than external standards.

Idealism: A school of philosophy that considers ideas to be the only true reality.

Metaphysics: An area of philosophy that deals with questions about the nature of ultimate reality.

Native North American thought: A varied set of beliefs, philosophical positions, and customs that span different tribes in North America

Pragmatism: A late nineteenth-century American school of philosophy that stresses becoming rather than being.

Realism: A school of philosophy that holds that reality, knowledge, and value exist independent of the human mind. In contrast to the idealist, the realist contends that physical entities exist in their own right.

Although there are many different ways of studying philosophy, it is best thought of as a passion to understand the underlying meaning of everything. Literally derived from the Greek *philos*, which means love, and *sophos*, which means wisdom, the word *philosophy* means "love of wisdom." Early philosophers were fond of pointing out that they did not claim to be wise—they were merely lovers of wisdom. To many philosophers, conveying information is not as important as helping others in their own search for wisdom.

Searching for wisdom is closely related to the essence of multiculturalism. Philosophy demands a habit of mind that is always searching to understand and incorporate different points of view, different voices. Philosophy compels us to consider the beauty and cohesion of seemingly diverse worlds of thought and existence.

This chapter explores ideas that were generated by different thinkers. It also describes the methods that philosophers use to answer abstract and complicated questions. Finally, the chapter clarifies how philosophy is related to education and how it provides a rich resource for educators who must guide themselves and others in the pursuit of knowledge and wisdom in a complex, global society.

Structure and Methodology of Philosophy

Activity 14.1:
Ask students to share their experiences from elementary school. Have them clarify how the classroom was arranged; what types of things they did during the school day; and the way discipline was handled. From the perspective of philosophy, what did these arrangements imply?

Discussion Question 1:
How would you describe philosophy to a young child?

Education is inextricably intertwined with this passion to understand. Both philosophy and education are vitally concerned with a search for truth. By its very name education calls teachers "to lead from ignorance." Philosophy compels teachers to lead students in a direction that is meaningful and of most worth. Philosophy reminds teachers to continue the search for truth and not be satisfied with pat answers, even answers that are provided by so-called experts. To a philosopher, an expert is not one who professes truth or beauty; an expert is one who searches and questions.

Education presupposes ideas about human nature, the nature of reality, and the nature of knowledge. These questions are ultimately of a philosophical character. Teachers must constantly confront the underlying assumptions by which conduct is guided, by which value is determined, and by which the direction of all existence is influenced. Hence, the study of philosophy is at the heart of the study of education.

The Branches of Philosophy

Information Note 14.1:
The various branches of philosophy are often criticized as artificial categories. Some philosophers have called for all branches to be united under metaphysics.

Transparency 66:
Summary of the Branches of Philosophy

Philosophy is not a collection of sterile, objective facts. Rather, it can be visualized as an internal desire that drives persons to search for better answers and better understandings. At its deepest level, philosophy consists of sets of profound and basic questions that remain constant because the basic dilemmas posed by these questions are yet to be answered adequately. At this basic level, philosophy does not provide answers; rather, it offers a range of possibilities or arguments that can be examined and used to guide decisions.

Because the questions of philosophy are so important, philosophy is structured around them. Philosophy includes branches that investigate large and difficult questions—questions about reality or being, about knowledge or knowing, about goodness and beauty and living a good life. Throughout the centuries, entire branches of philosophy have evolved that specialize and center around major

Classroom organization and priorities may reflect larger educational priorities.

questions. For example, questions concerning the nature of reality or existence are examined in metaphysics; questions concerning knowledge and truth are considered in epistemology; and questions about values and goodness are central to axiology.

Metaphysics. **Metaphysics** is an area of philosophy that is concerned with questions about the nature of reality. Literally *metaphysics* means "beyond the physical." It deals with questions like: What is reality? What is existence? Is the universe rationally designed or ultimately meaningless? Metaphysics is a search for order and wholeness, applied not to particular items or experiences, but to all reality and to all existence.

In brief, metaphysics is the attempt to find coherence in the whole realm of thought and experience. Concerning the world, metaphysics includes the question of what causes events in the universe to happen, including the theories of creation and evolution. Metaphysics also involves questions concerning the nature of humans. Is human nature physical or spiritual (mind-body problem)? Does a person make free choices or do events and conditions force one into determined decisions?

The questions in metaphysics, especially those about humanity and the universe, are extremely relevant to teachers and students of education. Theories about how the universe came to be and about what causes events in the universe are crucial to interpret the physical sciences properly. George F. Kneller writes about the power of metaphysics in generating questions that lack scientific answers.[1]

Teachers often say, "If Johnnie kept his mind on his work, he would have no trouble in school." But what does the teacher mean here by "mind"? Is the

Key Term:
Metaphysics

Objective 2:
Identify the contributions that philosophy can make to a teacher's effectiveness.

Objective 3:
List the major philosophical questions associated with the three major branches of philosophy: metaphysics, epistemology, and axiology.

mind different from the body? How are the two related? Is the mind the actual source of thoughts? Perhaps what we call "mind" is not an entity at all. Physiological and psychological studies of the brain have given us factual information and cyberneticians have compared the mind (or brain) to a computer. But such comparisons are crude; they do not satisfy our concern about the ultimate nature of the mind. Here again, knowing metaphysics and being able to think metaphysically helps the teacher when considering questions of ultimate meaning.

Focus Question 1:
Are you able to identify your beliefs about knowledge, human nature, and values? How might your beliefs influence your teaching?

The answers to these questions are likely to be based on the teacher's metaphysical beliefs. If, for example, the teacher believes that very specific basic knowledge is crucial to the child's intellectual development, it is likely that this teacher will focus on the subject matter. If, on the other hand, the teacher holds that the child is more important than any specific subject matter, it is likely that this teacher will focus on the child and allow the child to provide clues as to how he or she should be instructed.

Epistemology.

Key Term:
Epistemology

Epistemology is a branch of philosophy that examines questions about how and what we know. What knowledge is true and how does knowledge take place? The epistemologist attempts to discover what is involved in the process of knowing. Is knowing a special sort of mental act; is there a difference between knowledge and belief; can we know anything beyond the objects with which our senses acquaint us? Does knowing make any difference to the object that is known?

Discussion Question 2:
In your opinion, which is the most important aspect of a given philosophy (for a teacher)—the metaphysical view, the epistemological view, or the axiological view? State the rationale for your opinion.

Because epistemological questions deal with the essence of knowledge, they are central to education. Teachers must be able to assess what is knowledge to determine if a particular piece of information should be included in the curriculum. How we know is of paramount importance to teachers because their beliefs about learning influence their classroom methods. Should teachers train students in the scientific methods, deductive reasoning, or both? Should students study logic and fallacies or follow intuition? Teachers' knowledge of how students learn influences how they will teach.

Activity 14.2:
Have students identify the various ways that society views philosophy. Ask them to characterize these views by drawing a cartoon character. Have students discuss the various characters that they chose and relate them to the view that philosophy is a passion to understand. Do the cartoon characters fit or not?

Axiology.

Axiology is an area of philosophy that deals with the nature of values. It includes questions like "What is good?" "What is value?" Questions about what should be or what values we hold are highlighted in axiology. This study of values is divided into ethics (moral values and conduct) and aesthetics (values in the realm of beauty and art). Ethics deals with such questions as "What is the good life and how ought we to behave?" Aesthetics deals with the theory of beauty and examines such questions as, "Is art imaginative and representative or is it the product of private creative imagination?"[2] Good citizenship, honesty, and correct human relations are all learned in schools. They are not always a by-product. Often, students learn ethics from *who* the teacher is as well as from *what* the teacher says. One major question to be examined is: When does the end justify any means of achieving?

Key Term:
Axiology

Journal/Portfolio Development 1:
Classroom activities that deal with what is good or bad are in the realm of axiology (values). Prepare lists of the "goods" and "evils" of the American educational system. Then pose solutions to counteract as many of the "evils" as possible.

Both ethics and aesthetics are important issues in education. Should a system of ethics be taught in the public school? If so, which system of ethics should be taught? Aesthetics questions in education involve deciding which artistic works should or should not be included in the curriculum and what kind of subject matter should be allowed or encouraged in a writing, drawing, or painting class.

Should teachers compromise their own attitudes toward a piece of artwork if their opinion differs from that of a parent or a school board?

Thinking as a Philosopher

Philosophy provides us with the tools we need to think clearly. As with any discipline, philosophy has a style of thinking as well as a set of terms and methodologies that distinguish it from other disciplines. Philosophers spend much of their energy developing symbols or terms that are both abstract (apply to many individual cases) and precise (distinguish clearly). This tension between developing ideas that embrace more and more instances (abstraction) while maintaining a clear and accurate meaning (precision) is difficult, but is at the heart of the philosopher's task. The entire process is what is meant by understanding: uncovering the underlying, the foundational, and the essential principles of reality.

In the physical sciences, experimenters try to do the same thing when they devise a theory. The major difference between the scientist who empirically examines the material world and the philosopher who examines all reality is that the physical scientist mainly targets particular events or things in the material world and then tries to explain these events by some theory. The philosopher, on the other hand, strives to clarify the underlying principles for all events, material or immaterial, that are logically related. Philosophers tend to search for concepts that are larger than what the physical scientist is researching, and they also examine not only what seems to be, but what ought to be.

Abstraction.   The notion of **abstraction** covers a multitude of meanings. The word *abstract* is derived from the Latin verb *abstrahere,* meaning to "draw away."

Transparency 67:
Thinking Philosophically

Journal Activity Master 14.1: Thinking as a Philosopher. This activity provides students with an ill-structured question. They are asked to think about the question using abstraction, imagination and generalization, and logic. Once they have recorded their thoughts using these methods, they are asked to comment on the final outcome and decide if the use of abstraction, imagination and generalization, and logic changed the way that they now think about the original question.

Key Term:
Abstraction

Contemporary philosophies of education support the notion that a classroom might just as likely be an art museum as a neat array of desks.

PROFESSIONAL DILEMMA

Should Ethics Be Taught in American Schools?

You may feel that this question demands an obvious affirmative answer. A problem arises, however, when you are asked to clarify the specific ethics that should be taught. How do you, as a teacher in a multicultural, public or private school setting, determine what values should be the focus of instruction? One school of thought, influenced largely by the work of Lawrence Kohlberg, endorses direct instruction in ethics. The educational theorists who endorse this position contend that there exists a body of professional ethics that spans all cultures. This body of ethics can be articulated at any point in time and should be taught directly to students in the public schools.

People—especially parents—may feel that children are faced with an increasingly complex and dangerous society, and that they cannot be expected simply to absorb the proper morals and values from the world around them. Because of this, the schools should step in.

Activity 14.3:
Have students imagine a chair of any type. Ask them to try to write down the underlying characteristics of that chair. How do these characteristics fit other chairs? Tell them that such a process is a type of abstraction.

Information Note 14.2:
To abstract and imagine are difficult thinking processes. Some philosophers claim that to think philosophically merely means to use logic well.

Diversity Note 14.1:
Although philosophic thinking is often connected to abstraction, cultures use and value abstract thinking differently. Some groups prefer to use symbols and metaphors rather than abstract terms.

This implies the drawing away from a concrete level of experience to a conceptual plane of principles or ideas. The process of abstraction can be thought of as a three-step process that moves thinking from singular concrete instances to more general, universal ideas. The three steps involve: (1) focusing attention on some feature within one's experience; (2) examining the precise characteristics of the feature; and (3) remembering the feature and its characteristics later so that it can be applied to other instances or combined with other ideas.

In general, philosophers distinguish between two basic types of abstraction: (1) parts, or abstractions of characteristics that could also be physically removed (features such as tabletops, legs, drawers, and the like) and (2) attributes or abstractions of characteristics that cannot be physically removed like shape, structure, or form. This second type of abstract thinking is the stuff of philosophers; they seek to understand the essential aspects of both material and immaterial things. These underlying, substantial aspects are sometimes referred to as qualities, relations, and functions.

Imagination and Generalization. According to Alexander,[3] the second step of philosophic thinking is the use of imagination. Imagination can be thought of as the altering of abstractions. In philosophy, the use of imagination assists the process of abstraction by filling in the details of an idea, selecting details, and relating ideas to one another.

Imaginative explorations occur in many different ways. Usually, they occur by first focusing on some abstraction or idea. Ideas come from making observations, reflecting about some past experience, reading, viewing a dramatic work or piece of art, or conversing with others. Once ideas are selected, imaginative explorations can be made about them. Basic assumptions about things can be examined, arguments can be justified or clarified, and ideas can be distinguished from or related to other ideas. Experiential evidence, logical consistency, and a host of other criteria can be employed. The outcome of the whole imaginative process is the development of a system of ideas that has greater clarity and more interrelationships to other ideas or sets of propositions. This last step of the imaginative exploration

In contrast to this point of view, those influenced by the educational theories proposed by Syd Simon in his text, *Values Clarification,* reject the direct instruction of ethics because democracy demands that its citizens be free to clarify their own sets of values. This philosophy calls for public schools to refrain from the direct instruction of ethics and asks teachers to help students define their own sets of individually selected values. The approach requires teachers to remain neutral in their presentations of opposing value systems. The teacher's role is simply to assist students in the clarification of the consequences of selecting any one set of ethics or values.

This difficult problem of teaching ethics is especially problematic for a democracy. Who shall select the correct set of ethics to be taught?

- If the majority is given this right, then, what becomes of the individual rights of minorities?
- Yet, is it possible to teach a value-free curriculum?
- Does the very act of instruction imply a certain value system expressed and upheld by the individual teacher? What are your responses to these questions?

process is sometimes referred to as *generalization* because it ultimately results in the development of a comprehensive set of ideas.

Generalization sets ranges and limits to the abstractions that have been altered by imagination. As one's imagination relates more and more ideas to one another, the process of generalization determines which relationships should be emphasized and de-emphasized.

As an example of the philosophical thinking process, consider a simple chair that is located in a kitchen. First, the philosopher would abstract from the chair some idea on which to focus; for instance, the idea of support. Support is an underlying substantial characteristic of all chairs. Second, the philosopher might imagine how many physical parts of a chair could be removed without destroying the chair's ability to provide support. Are four legs always necessary for support? What must be supported to be a chair? As the philosopher ponders these questions (which are spurred by the imagination), precise generalizations can be made about the basic aspects of support. New questions or hypotheses can be developed. For example, how does the support provided by chairs relate to the support that a teacher should provide to students? What does teaching support really mean? To complete this inquiry, logic is required.

Logic.   Philosophy deals with the nature of reasoning and has designated a set of principles called *logic.* Logic examines the principles that allow us to move from one argument to the next. There are many types of logic, but the two most commonly studied are deductive and inductive logic. Deduction is a type of reasoning that moves from a general statement to a specific instance. Induction is a type of reasoning that moves in the opposite direction from the particular instance to a general conclusion. Philosophy provides the tools that we need in order to think clearly. It is important for educators to have a philosophy as a means of developing their ability to think clearly about what they do on a day-to-day basis and of seeing how these things extend beyond the classroom to the whole of humanity and society. Studying philosophy enables you to recognize the underlying assumptions and principles of things so you can determine what is significant.

Focus Question 2:
Do you believe authentic learning primarily occurs in real life experiences? How would you justify your answer?

Activity 14.4:
Ask students to imagine different types of chairs. Have them try to draw a chair inside out. Now, examine the characteristics that they identified earlier and see if they still hold. This is the process of imagining and generalizing.

Activity 14.5:
Compare the process of logic to that of designing a staircase. Have students clarify what statements flow from their statements about the underlying characteristics of chairs.

Schools of Philosophy and Their Influence on Education

Test Questions 14.21–14.50

Objective 4:
Elaborate on the major tenets of idealism, realism, pragmatism, and existentialism.

Key Term:
Idealism

As philosophers attempt to answer questions, they develop answers that are clustered into different schools of thought. These schools of philosophical thought are somewhat contrived since they are merely labels developed by others who attempt to show the similarities and differences among the many answers philosophers develop. Throughout the centuries, these schools of philosophic thought have been used to explain the diversity of responses from so many thinkers. As you examine the schools of thought developed in this section, keep in mind that the philosophers who represent these schools are individual thinkers, like yourself, who do not limit their thinking to the characteristics of any one label or school of thought. Four well-known schools of thought are idealism, realism, pragmatism, and existentialism. In addition to these, Eastern thought and Native North American thought are described. Technically, these two final clusters of thought are not termed "schools" because they encompass greater diversity and often extend beyond the limits of philosophy in beliefs, customs, and group values.

Relevant Research

Teaching Critical Thinking

Teaching critical thinking is an important educational outcome; it comes as no surprise that research studies about critical thinking abound. Many schools have adopted critical thinking as a specific district outcome. There is a great deal of controversy concerning the precise meaning of critical thinking, and this confusion makes instruction difficult.

A variety of thinking models have emerged, and schools have had to carefully reflect and select which critical thinking model to adopt. This selection is not simple, for cognitive scientists are not in agreement about the proper way to conceptualize critical thinking. For many years, two researchers have investigated how schools can effectively develop students' critical thinking skills. Robert Ennis, from the University of Illinois, has concentrated his research on the proper attainment of a set of skills, whereas Richard Paul, from Sonoma State University, has focused on students' attainment of a proper set of critical thinking dispositions or attitudes. Ennis has concluded that teachers who clarify a precise set of steps in the critical thinking process can more effectively teach students to be critical thinkers. Paul has concluded that critical thinking emerges when students are encouraged and taught to think from another's perspective. He calls this the dialog, dialectic thinking process (Paul, R., 1990). As a prospective teacher, you will need to determine your own answer to the question of how critical thinking should be taught.

Sources: Robert Ennis and S. Norris. *Evaluating Critical Thinking.* Pacific Grove, California: Midwest Publications, 1989. Richard Paul. *Critical Thinking: What Every Person Needs to Survive in a Rapidly Changing World.* Rohnert Park California Center for Critical Thinking and Moral Critique, 1990.

Idealism

The roots of idealism lie in the thinking of the Greek philosopher, Plato. Generally, idealists believe that ideas are the only true reality. It is not that idealists reject the material world, but rather, they hold that the material world is characterized by constant change and uncertainty, whereas ideas endure throughout time. Hence, **idealism** is a school of philosophy that holds that ideas or concepts are the essence of all that is worth knowing. The physical world we know through our senses is only a manifestation of the spiritual world. Idealists believe in the power of reasoning and they de-emphasize the scientific method and sense perception, which they hold suspect. They search for universal or absolute truths that will remain constant throughout the centuries.

The educational philosophy of the idealist is idea-centered rather than subject-centered or child-centered because the ideal, or the idea, is the foundation of all things. Knowledge is directed toward self-consciousness and self-direction and is centered in the growth of rational processes about the big ideas. Some idealists note that the individual who is created in God's image has free will and this free will makes learning possible. The idealist believes that learning comes from within the individual rather than from without. Hence, real mental growth and spiritual growth do not occur until they are self-initiated.

Idealists' educational beliefs include an emphasis on the study of great leaders as examples for us to imitate. For idealists, the teacher is the ideal model or example for the student. Teachers pass on the cultural heritage and the unchanging content of education, such as studying the great figures of the past, the humanities, and a rigorous curriculum. Idealists emphasize the methods of lecture, discussion, and imitation, and, finally, they believe in the importance of the doctrine of ideas.

No one philosopher is an idealist. Rather, philosophers answer questions and some of their answers are similar. These similarities are what make up the different schools of philosophy. To describe adequately any one school of philosophy, such as idealism, one needs to go beyond these general characteristics and examine the subtle differences posed by individual thinkers. Plato and Socrates, Immanuel Kant, and Georg Wilhelm Frederick Hegel represent different aspects of the idealist tradition.

Plato and Socrates.   According to Plato, truth is the central reality; it is perfect, and it cannot, therefore, be found in the world of matter since the material world is both imperfect and constantly changing. Plato did not think that we create knowledge; rather, we discover it. In one of his dialogues, he conjectures that humanity once had true knowledge but lost it by being placed in a material body that distorts and corrupts that knowledge. Thus, humans have the arduous task of trying to remember what they once knew.

We only know the philosophy of Socrates through Plato, who wrote about him in a series of texts called *Dialogues*. Socrates spoke of himself as a midwife who found humans pregnant with knowledge, but knowledge that had not been born or realized. This "Doctrine of Reminiscence" speaks directly to the role of the educator. Teachers need to question students in such a way as to help them remember what they have forgotten. In the dialogue, *Meno*, Plato describes Socrates meeting a slave boy and through skillful questions leading the boy to realize that he knew the Pythagorean theorem, even though he does not know that he knows it. This emphasis on bringing forth knowledge from students through artful questioning is sometimes called the Socratic Method.

The value of Socrates' and Plato's ideas is that they have stimulated a great deal of thinking about the meaning and purpose of humankind, society, and education. Their ideas have influenced almost all philosophers who came after them whether others supported or rejected their basic ideas. Alfred North Whitehead even noted that modern philosophy is but a series of footnotes to Plato.

Writing in the *Republic*, Plato depicts his central ideas about knowledge in an allegory about human beings living in a cave. He states:

> If I am right, certain professors of education must be wrong when they say that they can put knowledge into the soul which was not there before, like sight into a blind eyes. . . .Whereas, our argument shows that the power and capacity of learning exists in the soul already; and that just as the eye was unable to turn from darkness to light without the whole body, so too the

Discussion Question 3:
Early Greek philosophers suggest that all knowledge is based on experience. Discuss the implications of this statement for teaching methodology.

Journal/Portfolio Development 2:
In idealism, character education may be enhanced through imitating exemplars—heroes in the historical record. Identify an exemplar from history and describe the way in which you could teach character through the person's example.

Information Note 14.3:
Plato also wrote a text entitled the *Republic* in which he contends that a just society requires a diversified type of school system—one that meets different types of needs.

Journal Activity Master 14.2: An Analysis of a Question from Socrates.
This activity contains a quotation from Plato, who describes Socrates in the act of questioning one of his students. Students must answer the questions posed by Socrates and reflect on the implications of their answers.

*Immanuel Kant
(1724–1804)*

*Georg Wilhelm Friedrich
Hegel (1770–1831)*

Objective 5:
Compare and contrast
writings from philosophers
who represent different
schools of philosophy:
Plato, Kant, and Hegel;
Aristotle, Locke, and Whitehead; Peirce and Dewey;
Sartre and Kierkegaard.

Key Term:
Realism

instrument of knowledge can only by the movement of the whole soul be turned from the world of becoming into that of being, and learn by degrees to endure the sight of being, and of the brightest and best of being, or in other words, of the good.[4]

Immanuel Kant. The German philosopher Immanuel Kant (1724–1804), in the *Metaphysics of Morals* and the *Critique of Practical Reason*, spelled out his idealistic philosophy. Kant believed in freedom, the immortality of the soul, and the existence of God. He wrote extensively on human reason and noted that the only way humankind can know things is through the process of reason. Hence, reality is not a thing unto itself but the interaction of reason and external sensations. Reason fits perceived objects into classes or categories according to similarities and differences. It is only through reason that we acquire knowledge of the world. Once again, it is the idea or the way that the mind works that precedes the understanding of reality.

Hegel and Marx. Georg Wilhelm Friedrich Hegel (1770–1831), another German idealist, reasoned that the ultimate reality is composed of three stages or principles—*thesis,* the Idea; *antithesis,* Nature; and *synthesis,* Mind or Spirit. The thesis and antithesis as Hegel saw them are contradictory, and the synthesis unites the positive aspects of each. Karl Marx was greatly influenced by these ideas, although he transformed the Hegelian stages or principles into a materialistic philosophical base. Marx maintained that we become alienated from our own creations, such as society and the means of production. Rather than a dialectic occurring between ideas, Marx adopted the notion of a dialectic between economic conditions and human actions, or what has been called the materialist conception of history.

Realism

Realism's roots lie in the thinking of Aristotle (384–322 B.C.). **Realism** is a school of philosophy that holds that reality, knowledge, and value exist independent of the human mind. In other words, realism rejects the idealist notion that only ideas are the ultimate reality. Refer to Figure 14.1, which illustrates the dualistic position of idealism and realism.

Realists place considerable importance on the role of the teacher in the educational process. The teacher should be a person who presents content in a systematic and organized way and should promote the idea that there are clearly defined criteria one can use in making judgments. Contemporary realists emphasize the importance of scientific research and development. Curriculum has reflected the impact of these realist thinkers through the appearance of standardized tests, serialized textbooks, and a specialized curriculum in which the disciplines are seen as separate areas of investigation.

Realists contend that the ultimate goal of education is advancement of human rationality. Schools can do this by requiring students to study organized bodies of knowledge, by teaching methods of arriving at this knowledge, and by assisting students to reason critically through observation and experimentation. Teachers must have specific knowledge about a subject so that they can order it in such a way as to teach it rationally. They must also have a broad background in order to show relationships that exist among all fields of knowledge.

IDEALISM

a. Supernatural cause as creation of universe

b. World of mental conceptions–ultimate reality in God

c. Mind

REALISM

a. Natural cause for evolution of universe

b. World of physical objects–ultimate reality in nature

c. Body

FIGURE 14.1

Dualistic Position of Idealism and Realism

The realist curriculum would be a "subject-centered" curriculum and would include natural science, social science, humanities, and instrumental subjects like logic and inductive reasoning. Realists employ experimental and observational techniques. In the school setting they would promote testing and logical, clear content. In order to understand the complexity of the realist philosophy, we must once again turn to the ideas of individual thinkers: Aristotle, Locke, and Whitehead.

Information Note 14.4:
The Committee of Ten recommended that high schools should have courses that are arranged sequentially; few electives should be available; and a Carnegie unit should be awarded for each course. Such recommendations are an example of a realistic philosophy because they tend to view learning as sequential, didactic, and orderly.

Aristotle. Aristotle (384–322 B.C.) thought that ideas (forms) are found by studying the world of matter. He believed that one could acquire knowledge of ideas or forms through an investigation of matter. He considered matter as an object of study to reach something further. In order to understand an object we must understand its absolute form, which is unchanging. To the realist, the trees of the forest exist whether or not there is a human mind to perceive them. This is an example of an independent reality. Although the ideas of a flower can exist without matter, matter cannot exist without form. Hence, each tulip shares universal properties with every other tulip and every other flower. However, the particular properties of a tulip differentiate it from all other flowers.

John Locke. John Locke (1632–1704) believed in the *tabula rasa*, blank tablet view of the mind. Locke stated that the mind of a person is blank at birth and that the person's sensory experiences make impressions on this blank tablet. John Locke distinguished between sense data and the objects they represent. The objects, or things we know, are independent of the mind or the knower insofar as thought refers to them and not merely to sense data. Ideas (round, square, tall) represent objects. Locke claimed that primary qualities (such as shapes) represent the world, while secondary qualities (such as colors) have a basis in the world but do not represent it.

The little or almost insensible, impressions on our tender infancies, have very important and lasting consequences: and there it is, as in the fountains of some rivers, where a gentle application of the hand turns the flexible waters

Aristotle (384–322 B.C.)

John Locke (1632–1704), left photo, and Alfred North Whitehead (1861–1947), right photo.

into channels, that make them at first, in the source, they received different tendencies, and arrive at last at very remote and distant places.

I imagine the minds of children as easily turned, this or that way, as water itself; and though this be the principal part and our main cure should be about the inside yet the clay cottage is not to be neglected. I shall therefore begin with the case and consider first the health of the body.[5]

Alfred North Whitehead.   Alfred North Whitehead (1861–1947), a philosopher and mathematician, attempted to reconcile some aspects of idealism and realism. He proposed "process" to be the central aspect of realism. Unlike Locke, Whitehead did not see objective reality and subjective mind as separate. He saw them as an organic unity that operates by its own principles. The universe is characterized by patterns and these patterns can be verified and analyzed through mathematics.

> Culture is activity of thought and receptiveness to beauty and humane feelings. Scraps of information have nothing to do with it. . . . In training a child to activity of thought, above all things we must beware of what I will call "inert ideas"—that is to say, ideas that are merely received into the mind without being used, or tested, or thrown into fresh combinations.
>
> In the history of education, the most striking phenomenon is the schools of learning, which at one epoch are alive with a ferment of genius, in a succeeding generation exhibit merely pedantry and routine. The reason is that they are overladen with inert ideas. Education with inert ideas is not only useless: it is, above all things, harmful—*Corruptio optimi, pessima*. Except at rare intervals of intellectual ferment, education in the past has been radically infected with inert ideas . . . Every intellectual revolution which has ever stirred humanity into greatness has been a passionate protest against inert ideas.[6]

Pragmatism

Pragmatism is a late nineteenth-century American philosophy that affected educational and social thought. It differs from most forms of idealism and realism by a belief in an open universe that is dynamic, evolving, and in a state of becoming. It is a process philosophy, which stresses becoming rather than being. Wedded as

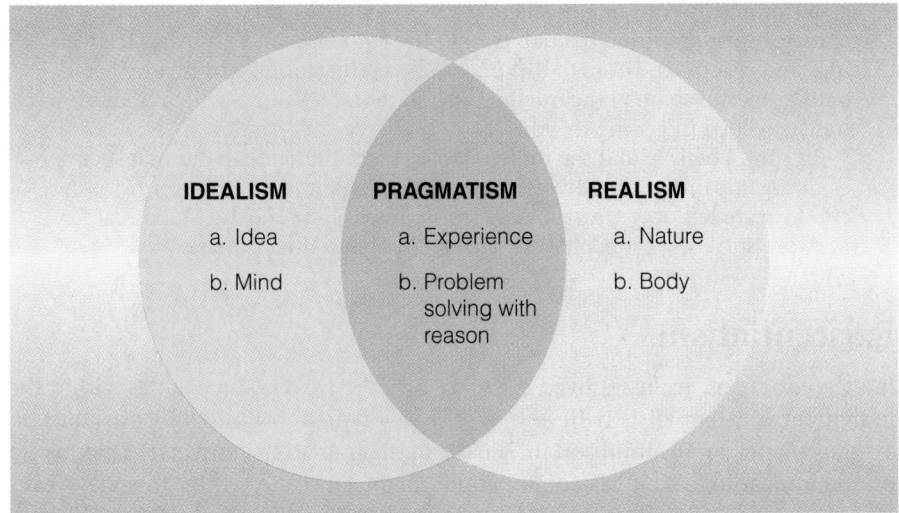

FIGURE 14.2

Relationship of Realism,
Idealism, and Pragmatism

they are to change and adaptation, pragmatists do not believe in absolute and unchanging truth. For pragmatists, truth is what works. Truth is relative because what works for one person may not for another, just as what works at one time or in one place or in one society may not work in another.

Like the realist, the pragmatist believes that we learn best through experience, but pragmatists are more willing to put that belief into practice. While realists are concerned with passing organized bodies of knowledge from one generation to the next, pragmatists stress applying knowledge—using ideas as instruments for problem solving. Realists and idealists call for a curriculum centered on academic disciplines, but pragmatists prefer a curriculum that draws the disciplines together to solve problems—an interdisciplinary approach. Refer to Figure 14.2, which illustrates the relationships among realism, idealism, and pragmatism.

Charles Sanders Peirce.   Charles Sanders Peirce (1839–1914) is considered the founder of pragmatism. He introduced the principle that belief is a habit of action undertaken to overcome indecisiveness. He believed that the purpose of thought is to produce action and that the meaning of a thought is the collection of results of actions. For example, to say that steel is "hard" is to mean that when the operation of scratch testing is performed on steel, it will not be scratched by most substances. The aim of Peirce's pragmatic method is to supply a procedure for constructing and clarifying meanings and to facilitate communication.

John Dewey.   Early in his philosophical development, John Dewey (1859–1952) related pragmatism to evolution by showing how to view ourselves as creatures who have to adapt to each other and to our environments. Dewey viewed life as a series of overlapping and interpenetrating experiences and situations, each of which has its own complete identity. The primary unit of life is the individual experience.

Dewey wrote the following selection early in his career. In it he shows his zeal for education as a social force in human affairs.

> I believe that all education proceeds by the participation of the individual in the social consciousness of the race. This process begins unconsciously almost

Transparency 69:
Educational Implications of
Authoritarian Views

Charles S. Peirce
(1839–1914)

at birth, and is continually shaping the individual's powers, saturating his consciousness, forming his habits, training his ideas, and arousing his feelings and emotions. Through this unconscious education the individual gradually comes to share in the intellectual and moral resources which humanity has succeeded in getting together. . . .

In sum, I believe that the individual is a social individual and that society is an organic union of individuals. If we eliminate the social factor from the child we are left only with an abstraction; if we eliminate the individual factor from society, we are left only with an inert and lifeless mass.[7]

Existentialism

In **existentialism,** reality is lived existence and the final reality resides within the individual. Existentialists believe that we live an alien, meaningless existence on a small planet in an unimportant galaxy in an indifferent universe. There is no ultimate meaning. Whereas some people might be paralyzed by this view, existentialists find the definition of their lives in the quest for meaning. The very meaninglessness of life compels them to instill life with meaning.

The only certainty for the existentialist is that we are free. However, this freedom is wrapped up in a search for meaning. We define ourselves, that is, we make meaning in our world, by the choices we make. In effect we are what we choose.

The existentialist believes that most schools, like other corporate symbols, deemphasize the individual and the relationship between the teacher and the student. Existentialists claim that when educators attempt to predict the behavior of students, they turn individuals into objects to be measured, quantified, and processed. Existentialists tend to feel that tracking, measurement, and standardization militate against creating opportunities for self-direction and personal choice. According to the existentialist, education is a process of developing a free, self-actualizing person centered on the feelings of the student. Therefore, education does not start with the nature of the world and with humankind, but with the human individual or self.

The existentialist educator would be a free personality engaged in projects that treat students as free personalities. The highest educational goal is to search for oneself. Teachers and students experience existential crises that involve an examination of oneself and one's life purposes. Education helps to fill in the gaps needed to fulfill those purposes; it is not a mold to which the student must be fitted. Students define themselves by their choices.

The existentialist student would have a questioning attitude and would be involved in a continuing search for self and reasons for existence. The existentialist teacher would help students become what they themselves want to become, not what outside forces such as society, other teachers, or parents want them to become.

Existentialist thinkers are as varied as the notion of individual thought and existence. There are atheistic existentialists as represented by Jean-Paul Sartre and theistic existentialists as exemplified by Sören Kierkegaard.

Jean-Paul Sartre.   Modern existentialism was born amidst the pain and disillusionment of World War II. Jean-Paul Sartre (1905–1980) broke with previous philosophers and asserted that existence (being) comes before essence (meaning).

Sartre saw no difference between being free and being human. This opens great possibilities; yet it also creates feelings of dread and nausea as one recognizes the reality of nonbeing and death as well as the great responsibilities that accompany such radical freedom to shape oneself out of one's choices. The process of answering the question "Who are we?" begins at a very crucial event in the lives of young people called the existential moment—that point somewhere toward the end of youth when we realize for the first time that we exist as an independent agent.

Sören Kierkegaard. Sören Kierkegaard (1813–1855), a Danish theologian and philosopher, criticized science, contending that its objectivity was an attempt to drive society away from the Christian faith. He described three stages to life: the aesthetic stage, in which humans live in sensuous enjoyment and emotions dominate; the ethical stage, in which humans achieve an understanding of their place and the function of life; and the religious state, for Kierkegaard the highest state, in which humans stand alone before God. It is only through faith that humans can bridge the gap between man and God. He believed that individuals must come to understand their souls, that they deny the reality of God through education. Kierkegaard maintained that individuals must accept responsibility for their choices, which they alone can make.

Eastern Thought

Most studies of Western philosophy typically begin with the Greek philosophers. Yet there is support that Platonic philosophy owed much of its development to Indian philosophy, which emphasizes the illusory quality of matter from Hinduism and Buddhism. There is much in the philosophies of the East that speaks to our concern for education. Although there are many different philosophical writings among the Far Eastern and Middle Eastern philosophers, there is one paramount idea. **Eastern thought,** unlike our Western, more empirical approach, stresses inner peace, tranquility, attitudinal development, and mysticism. Western philosophy has tended to emphasize logic and materialism while Eastern philosophy, in general, stresses the inner rather than the outer world; intuition rather than sense; and mysticism rather than scientific discoveries. This has differed from school to school, but overall Eastern thought begins with the inner world and then reaches to the outer world of phenomena.

Eastern philosophers have always concerned themselves with education, which they view as a way of achieving wisdom, maintaining the family structure, establishing the law, and providing for social and economic concerns. Instruction includes the things that one must do to achieve the good life, and education is viewed as necessary not only for this life but for achievement of the good life hereafter.

Eastern thought has not been as singular as has Western thought. One needs to study it system by system, culture by culture, and philosopher by philosopher. One good reason to study Eastern thought is that it represents a vantage point from which to examine Western thought. It encourages us to question seriously our most basic commitments to science, materialism, and nature. Eastern philosophy values order, regularity, and patience that is proportional to and in harmony with the law of nature.

Activity 14.6:
Ask students to identify the types of learning activities that would be most appropriate to the statement of philosophy discussed in Activity 14.5.

Activity 14.7:
Organize students into various teams labeled realism, idealism, pragmatism, and existentialism. Present a school-related problem and have the various teams discuss a solution that is rooted in the philosophical school that they represent.

Focus Question 4:
Why is it valuable for prospective teachers to study philosophy?

Transparency 71:
Eastern thought

Key Term:
Eastern Thought

Far Eastern Thought.   Far Eastern Indian philosophy is permeated by opposites. To the Western philosophers, these opposites need to be reconciled, but to the Eastern mind this need for consistency is unimportant. For example, great emphasis is placed on a search for wisdom, but this does not mean a rejection of worldly pleasures. Though speculation is emphasized, it has a very practical character. Far Eastern Indian philosophers insist that knowledge be used to improve both social and communal life and that people should live according to their ideals. There is a prevailing sense of universal moral justice in Far Eastern Indian philosophy by which individuals are responsible for what they are and what they become.

Hinduism, Buddhism, and Jain are three religions that provide different contexts for these philosophical principles. Hinduism does not generally encourage asceticism or a renunciation of the world, but believes that one should be able to control and regulate it. Fundamental truths include that there is an ultimate reality that is all-pervading and is the final cause of the universe. This reality is uncreated and eternal. Meditation on this ultimate reality leads to a life of virtue and righteousness. Buddhism stresses nonattachment to material things and concern for humanity; it emphasizes a sense of harmony with the universe where one is under no constraint to change forces within or without. Jain is a philosophy that rejects systems as absolutes and affirms them only as partial truths or "maybes." Jains believe that the universe has existed from all eternity, undergoing an infinite number of revolutions produced by the powers of nature. They have great respect for all life and take vows to avoid injury to any form of life.[8]

The emphasis of Far Eastern Chinese philosophy is on harmony: Correct thinking should help one achieve harmony with life. This harmony of government, business, and family should then lead toward a higher synthesis. Confucianism and Taoism provide two major contexts for Chinese thought.

Japanese thought is rooted in Shinto. This early religion of Japan encouraged nature worship. The Japanese perspective is one of acceptance and enjoyment of life and kinship with nature. Intuition is often prized over intellectualism, and there is a strong feeling for loyalty, purity, and nature. Japanese philosophy has successfully fused Confucian, Buddhist, and Taoist beliefs and practices in ways that permeate them with a distinct Japanese perspective. One example of this is the development of Zen Buddhism. Zen emphasizes a dependence on oneself rather than on an outside source for answers and wisdom; it depends more on intuition than on intellectual discovery.[9]

Middle Eastern Thought.   Many philosophies and religions (including Judaism, Christianity, and Islam) owe their origin to the Middle East. Historically, the Middle East has been a meeting ground between civilizations of the East and the West, and as such, Middle Eastern thought is more disjointed than that of the Far East. Judaism traces its origins beginning with the call of Abraham (around 1750 B.C.). Abraham believed in a God who had a special interest in humanity. Throughout the centuries Judaic thought has included a belief in one God who created the world and who cares for the world and all its creatures. In earlier conceptions of Judaism, God was viewed as possessing human qualities but later became more idealized, incorporeal. He is "I am who I am."

Christianity began as a Jewish sect, centered in Jerusalem. This sect proclaimed Jesus of Nazareth as the Messiah. The words and deeds of Jesus formed the basis of the New Testament, which was the fulfillment of Judaism. Christianity

CASE STUDY | REQUIRED STUDENT SERVICE: A FORM OF SLAVERY?

In April, 1990, Bethlehem Area School District in Eastern Pennsylvania adopted a community service graduation requirement. Under the program, every student in the district, except those in the special education program, has to perform sixty hours of community service between the start of ninth grade and the completion of twelfth grade. The school board decided to make the program mandatory based on the philosophy that education is not limited to the acquisition of knowledge. Rather, there was an underlying epistemology that knowledge included a societal component. The program was not adopted to provide benefit to the district in the form of free clerical and maintenance services. The board set the following goals for the program: (1) students will understand their responsibilities as citizens dealing with community issues, (2) they will know that their concern about people and events in the community can have positive effects, and (3) they will develop pride in assisting others.

The mandatory community service could be performed through an agency approved by the district, through an independent program selected by the district, or through an independent program selected by the student and approved by the district. Acceptable volunteer activities varied; examples included stuffing envelopes for the Lehigh Presbytery, playing with children at the Jewish Community Center, walking and grooming dogs for the Humane Society, and marching in the school band during the Halloween parade.

The parents of two Bethlehem students filed suit in federal court, claiming that the community service requirement violated their children's constitutional rights. Specifically, they alleged that the program violated the Thirteenth Amendment prohibition against involuntary servitude and the First Amendment guarantee of freedom of expression. They argued that although their children each engaged in various volunteer activities, the mandatory nature of the district's program constituted forced labor akin to slavery and compelled the students to declare, through their actions, that altruism is a desirable philosophy of life.

Although the federal lawsuit failed on the local level because the court found that the community service program was not sufficiently imbued with elements of communication to fit within the scope of constitutionally protected expression, the original parental concerns about forced labor and forced value acquisition are far from resolved. Parents who adhere to the political and religious right continue to mount challenges in various forms to the notion of mandatory community service in public schools. The original intent of the Bethlehem Area School District focused on a specific view of truth—knowledge is interconnected with society. Knowledge is not personal acquisition, but rather a shared reality.

1. Is such an epistemology legitimate in a contemporary, diverse society? Why?
2. Is knowledge value-free? Defend your answer.
3. What are the characteristics of an educated person?

---

incorporated many of the Judaic beliefs, but placed greater emphasis on the fatherhood of God and in God's concern for humanity.

Islam is the most prominent religion in the contemporary Middle East. Mohammed (A.D. 571–632) was born in Mecca. Through a revelation, Mohammed was called on to bring all people to worship Allah, the one true God. His mission was to restore to the Arabs the pure faith of their father, Abraham, and to

Objective 6:
Describe the characteristics of Eastern and Native North American thought.

Key Term:
Native North American thought

Discussion Question 4:
Describe the ways that Eastern and Native North American thought might influence what and how you teach.

Diversity Note 14.2:
Understanding the relationship among different Native American thinkers can assist teachers in valuing the underlying similarities across all cultures.

Focus Question 5:
Can you identify one way that students in your classroom might tackle an issue philosophically?

Chief Sequojah, author of the Cherokee alphabet

free them from bondage and idolatry. Mohammed taught that Allah is a purposeful God who created things to reach certain desired goals. Those who follow the will of Allah will be eternally rewarded in paradise, an oasis of flowing waters. For those who do not follow the will of Allah, there is eternal suffering.

Global Perspectives: The Fabric of Eastern Thought. As you can see, Eastern thought is like a rich fabric of diverse ideas. It emphasizes sets of views that are quite different from the neat categorizations of Western thought. Eastern thought suggests that cohesive views can be achieved without the necessity of neat, hierarchically distinct categories. Although they are quite difficult to categorize, the philosophy and thought of both the Far East and the Middle East force us to reexamine our meanings and assumptions. As such, the study of Eastern thought is an important part of all future educators' preparation in an increasingly multicultural society.

Native North American Thought

Just as the rich past and diverse cultures make it difficult to summarize Eastern thought, Native North American thought is equally difficult to synthesize. **Native North American thought** includes a varied set of beliefs, philosophical positions, and customs that span different tribes in North America. These beliefs, positions, and customs center on the relationship of humans to all of nature including the earth, sun, sky, and beyond. Different tribes in different settings have developed varied approaches to this human-to-nature relationship.

The Navajo nation is the largest United States tribe. Its early history was nomadic and its thoughts and customs are known for their unique ability to assimilate with and adapt to the thought and customs of other tribes. As with most Native American cultures, the Navajo universe is an all-inclusive unity viewed as an orderly system of interrelated elements. At the basis of Navajo teachings and traditions is the value of a life lived in harmony with the natural world. Such a view enables one to "walk in beauty." In understanding the Navajo world view, one must note the teachings of the "inner forms" of things. These inner forms were set in place by First Man and First Woman. The concept of "inner form" is similar to the concept of a "spirit" or "soul" because without it, the Navajos say the outer forms would be dead.[10]

The Native American culture of the Great Plains, of which the Lakota form part, is based on mystical participation with the environment. Every aspect of this ecosystem, including Earth, Sky, Night and Day, Sun and Moon, are all elements of oneness within which life was undertaken. The Lakota celebrate the "sacred hoop of life" and observe seven sacred rites toward the goal of ultimate communion with Wakan-Tanka, the great Spirit.[11]

The Hopi follow the path of peace, which they believe is a pure and perfect pattern of mankind's evolutionary journey. The Road of Life of the Hopi is represented as a journey through seven universes created at the beginning. At death, the conduct of a person in accordance with the Creator's plan determines when and where the next step on the road will be taken. Each of the Hopi clans has a unique role to play, and each role is an essential part of the whole. Hopis must live in harmony with one another, with nature, and with the plan. Out of this complex interplay, then, the plan is both created and allowed to unfold.

We feel that the world is good. We are grateful to be alive. We are conscious that all men are brothers. We sense that we are related to other creatures. Life is to be valued and preserved. If you see a grain of corn on the ground, pick it up and take care of it, because it has life inside. When you go out of your house in the morning and see the sun rising pause a moment to think about it. When you take water from a spring, be aware that it is a gift of nature. (Albert Yava, Big Falling Snow, Hopi)[12]

Objective 7:
Elaborate on the implications for education that are associated with the different schools of philosophy.

Summary and Implications

The study of philosophy permeates every aspect of the teacher's role and provides the underpinning for every decision. This chapter described how philosophy is related to daily teaching decisions and actions, and it clarified some of the major ideas that different philosophers have developed in their private quest for wisdom.

Philosophy was shown to revolve around three major questions: those that deal with the nature of reality (metaphysics), those that deal with knowledge and truth (epistemology), and those that deal with values (axiology). Prospective teachers are encouraged to identify the personal philosophical positions that inform their own learning and teaching. The chapter further suggests three steps that help clarify such philosophical positions: abstraction, imagination, and logic. No implied best quality is ascribed to one philosophical position over another. Rather, the most successful teachers are those who are dedicated to and thoroughly understand their preferred beliefs. Decisions about the nature of the subject matter emphasized in the curriculum are metaphysical commitments to reality—What is real? Questions related to what is true and how we know are epistemological. Classroom methods are practices that aim to assist learners in acquiring knowledge and truth in the subject area. Classroom activities

that deal with ethics (what is good or bad), beauty, and character are in the realm of axiology (values). The task of the teacher is to identify a preferred style, understand that style as thoroughly as possible, and utilize that style with a unique group of learners seeking to accomplish reasonable educational outcomes under the leadership of the teacher. The classical philosophical concepts discussed are broad categories within the vast academic realm of philosophy.

Educational inferences with regard to curricular emphasis, preferred method, character education, and developing taste for each philosophical concept may be directly drawn. The metaphysical questions about reality in philosophy serve as the basis for the curricular emphases in current educational practices. Methodology in the classroom relates to the acquisition of knowledge, which is anchored in classic epistemological considerations. Character education (morals) and developing taste (aesthetics) are value determinants extended from the axiology branches of classical philosophies. Note that the relationships presented here are drawn from many elaborate schools and systems of philosophical thought, all of which provide the foundations for the six educational theories discussed in the following chapter.

Discussion Questions

1. How would you describe philosophy to a young child?

2. In your opinion, which is the most important aspect of a given philosophy (for the teacher)—the metaphysical view, the epistemological view, or the axiological view? State the rationale for your choice.

3. Early Greek philosophers suggest that all knowledge is based on experience. Discuss the implications of this statement for teaching methodology.

4. Describe the ways that Eastern and Native North American thought might influence what and how you teach.

Journal/Portfolio Development

1. Classroom activities that deal with what is good or bad are in the realm of axiology (values). Prepare lists of the "goods" and the "evils" of the American

educational system. Then pose solutions to counteract as many of the "evils" as possible.

2. In idealism, character education may be enhanced through imitating exemplars—heroes in the historical record. Identify an exemplar educator from history and describe the way in which you could teach character through the person's example.

School-Based Experiences

1. You are about halfway through your classroom experiences. In reflecting on those experiences, you feel that you need more knowledge about philosophical concepts and views to enable you to develop your own personal educational views. Some of your colleagues have similar feelings. You may wish to encourage them to establish a study group to discuss philosophical views. The group could develop questions to ask of your supervisor. Invite the supervisor to respond to your questions in one of your study group sessions.

2. As you visit schools and classrooms, be alert for indications of philosophical concepts and different philosophical views. You might wish to talk with teachers about their personal educational views. Many schools have written statements describing their philosophy of education. You could ask a number of schools to send you a copy of their philosophy of education. When you receive them, look for similarities and differences among the philosophical statements.

Notes

1. George F. Kneller, "The Relevance of Philosophy," in *Introduction to the Philosophy of Education.* Berrien Springs, MI: Andrews University Press, 1982, 7–8.
2. Ibid., 31.
3. Herbert G. Alexander, *The Language and Logic of Philosophy.* Lanham, MD: University Press of America, 107–108.
4. Selection from Plato, *The Republic,* trans. B. Jowett. New York: Dolphin Books, 1960, 208.
5. John Locke, "Some Thoughts Concerning Education," in *The Works of John Locke* Volume X. London: Printed for W. Otridge and Son et al., 1812, 6–7.
6. Alfred North Whitehead, *The Aims of Education.* New York: The Free Press, 1929, 1957, 1–2.
7. John Dewey, "My Pedagogic Creed," *The School Journal 54* (3) (16 January 1989): 77–80. Reprinted with the permission of the Center for Dewey Studies, Southern Illinois University at Carbondale.
8. Howard A. Osman and Samuel M. Craven, *Philosophical Foundations of Education.* Columbus, OH: Merrill Publishing, 1986, 66–85.
9. Ibid.
10. Terry P. Wilson, *Navajo: Walking in Beauty.* San Franciso, CA: Chronicle Books, 1994.
11. Terry P. Wilson, *Lakota: Seeking the Great Spirit.* San Franciso, CA: Chronicle Books, 1994.
12. Terry P. Wilson, *Hopi: Following the Path of Peace.* San Franciso, CA: Chronicle Books, 1994.

Bibliography

Abel, Donald C. *Theories of Human Nature.* New York: McGraw-Hill Press, 1992.

Adler, Mortimer. "A Revolution in Education." *American Educator* 6(4) (Winter 1982): 20–24.

_____ *Ten Philosophical Mistakes: Basic Errors in Modern Thought.* New York: Macmillan Press, 1985.

Bellanca, James. *Values and the Search for Self.* Washington, DC: National Education Association, 1975.

Coleman, James S. "International Comparisons of Cognitive Achievement." *Phi Delta Kappan* (February 1985): 403–406.

Dewey, John. *Democracy and Education.* New York: Macmillan, 1916.

Ennis, Robert and Norris, S. *Evaluating Critical Thinking.* Pacific Grove, CA: Midwest Publications, 1989.

Knight, George P. *Issues and Alternatives in Educational Philosophy.* Berrien Springs, MI: Andrews University Press, 1982.

Paul, Richard. *Critical Thinking: What Every Person Needs to Survive in a Rapidly Changing World.* Rohnert Park California Center for Critical Thinking and Moral Critique, 1990.

Scheffler, Israel. *Conditions of Knowledge: An Introduction to Epistemology and Education.* Chicago: University of Chicago Press, 1978.

Soltis, Jonas F. *An Introduction to the Analysis of Educational Concepts.* 2nd rev. ed. Reading, MA: Addison-Wesley, 1978.

Taylor, A. E. *Elements of Metaphysics.* 12th ed. London: Methuen, 1946.

Whitehead, Alfred North. *The Aims of Education.* New York: The Free Press, 1929, 1957, 1–2.

Wilson, Terry P. *Navajo: Walking in Beauty.* San Franciso, CA: Chronicle Books, 1994.

Wilson, Terry P. *Lakota: Seeking the Great Spirit.* San Franciso, CA: Chronicle Books, 1994.

Wilson, Terry P. *Hopi: Following the Path of Peace.* San Franciso, CA: Chronicle Books, 1994.

Educational Theory in American Schools: Philosophy in Action

Focus Questions

1   Perennialism is an educational theory that focuses on enduring ideas and principles that transcend time. Are there universal principles that seem to be taught in many different nations? If so, identify several; if not, why?

2   How does philosophy translate into action? Provide some examples.

3   Teaching methods that are nonauthoritarian regard the learner as active and interested in learning. What are some teaching methods that foster active learning?

4   Reconstructionism calls on schools to teach students to control institutions and be organized according to democratic principles. How can schools teach people to control institutions when schools themselves are institutions?

5   Do you agree with the notion that teachers teach the way that they were taught?

Key Terms and Concepts

Behaviorism: A psychological theory that asserts that behavior represents the essence of a person; behaviorists contend that all behavior can be explained as response to stimuli.

Constructivism: An educational theory that emphasizes hands-on, activity-based teaching and learning during which students develop their own frames of thought.

Essentialism: An educational theory that holds that there is a common core of information and skills that an educated person must have; school should be organized to transmit this core of essential material.

Humanism: An educational theory that contends that humans are innately good— born free but become enslaved by institutions.

Perennialism: An educational theory that focuses on principles of knowledge that are enduring; nature, human nature, and the underlying principles of existence are considered constant, undergoing little change.

Progressivism: An educational theory that emphasizes that ideas should be tested by experimentation and that learning is rooted in answering questions developed by the learner.

Reconstructionism: An educational theory that calls on schools to teach people to control institutions and to be organized according to basic democratic ideals.

Transparency 70:
Six Philosophical Orientations
to Teaching

Transparency 72:
Overview of Educational
Thought

The philosophies presented in the previous chapter provide an overview of different ways that we can view the world: (metaphysics), knowledge (epistemology), and values (axiology). Such ideas are of little importance if they remain abstract; however, philosophic ideas are powerful forces when they are brought into action in educational theory. One can think of educational theory as the application of philosophy to the classroom. The way that curriculum is organized, the manner in which instruction is delivered, the types of school environments, and the processes of testing and grading are informed by the philosophic views held by educators, parents, and legislators. Such views vary greatly from school district to school district and from state to state. Educational theorists attempt to clarify how these different approaches to curriculum, instruction, and assessment work or do not work together. Table 15.1 describes the relationships between philosophic ideas and education.

Many teachers hold the view that the purpose of education is to train pupils' minds so that they can deal better with the intellectual concepts of life; they emphasize, in addition, the mastery of facts and information. The general notion that any child can learn any subject at any level if the subject matter is properly presented remains a strong challenge to teachers to arouse motivation for subject mastery among pupils. The concept of *mastery learning* suggests that, except for the few children who are mentally, emotionally, or physically impaired, every child can master the entire curriculum of the school when adequate time is provided. Continued attention to test scores, grade-level achievement, and other measures of subject matter competency reflect the importance that is still attached to the several views of education. School boards, parents, and the general public demand

TABLE 15.1 Educational Implications of Philosophy

Educational Aspect	Idealism	Realism	Pragmatism	Existentialism
Curricular emphasis	Subject matter of the mind: literature, intellectual history, philosophy, religion Education should be the same for everyone	Subject matter of the physical world: mathematics, science Initiative in education with the teacher	Subject matter of social experience Creation of a new social order	Subject matter of personal choice
Preferred teaching method	Teaching for the handling of ideas: lecture, discussion	Teaching for mastery of factual information and basic skills: demonstration, recitation	Problem solving: project method	Individual as entity within a social context
Character development	Imitating exemplars, heroes	Training in rules of conduct	Making group decisions in light of consequences	Individual responsibility for decisions and preferences
Art development	Studying the master-works Values of the past heritage	Studying design in nature	Participating in art projects based on cross-cultural and universal values	Personal view of the world; self-initiated activities

Source: Adapted from Van Cleve Morris and Young Pai, *Philosophy and the American School*, p. 295. Copyright © 1976 Houghton Mifflin.

more and more often that teachers provide concrete evidence that their pupils have made progress in mastering subject matter. Teachers who identify with these views are considered to be more traditional regarding teaching strategies.

In contrast, many teachers uphold John Dewey's view that the mind is not just a muscle to be developed. They accept the notion that human beings are problem solvers who profit from experience. These educators also give credence to the existential position, which emphasizes the importance of the individual and of personal awareness. Since Dewey's philosophical views have prevailed in American teachers' colleges for the past half century, it is not surprising that American schools reflect this view more than do other schools throughout the world. When teaching techniques are focused on student interactions, teachers may find that some students appear to be aimless with regard to subject matter. In such instances the teacher is challenged to arouse student interest in inquiry leading to subject content, whereas the more traditional teacher is challenged to arouse student interest in subject matter directly.

Educational theorists explain how these two different sets of teaching and learning principles differ from each other. They clarify how each set forms a cohesive whole (theory), and describe the benefits and shortcomings of adhering to either set or theory. Six educational theories considered here are perennialism, essentialism, behaviorism, progressivism, reconstructionism, and humanism. To varying degrees, each of these educational views is drawn on by classroom teachers and applied to the way teachers organize their classroom, their instruction, and their assessments. As you study these different educational theories, you will find that one or more of them clearly represents your own views. Understanding your own position in terms of known theory will be an invaluable asset as you develop your personal philosophy of education.

Test Questions 15.1–15.25

Authoritarian Educational Theories

Perennialism, essentialism, and behaviorism are different educational theories that espouse an authoritarian approach to subject matter, classroom organization, teaching methods, and assessment. Although each theory forms a distinct cohesive whole, all three are rooted in an authoritarian principle, that is, that truth and goodness are entities that are best understood by the person with expertise who is in authority. The students' role is, then, to attempt to master and follow the directions of those in power who have experience and authority.

Each theory's focus on curriculum, teaching, and learning, is presented in this chapter. In addition, representative programs are described along with an illustrative class activity.

Discussion Question 1:
What were the characteristics and behaviors of one of your favorite teachers who was authoritarian toward the students? Of a favorite teacher who was nonauthoritarian toward the students?

Perennialism

The basic educational view of **perennialism** is that the principles of knowledge are enduring. The term *perennial* may be defined as "everlasting," and the perennialist seeks everlasting truths. Although there are superficial differences from century to century, the perennialist views nature, human nature, and the underlying principles of existence as constant, undergoing little change.

Perennialists stress the importance of time-honored ideas, the great works of past and present thinkers, and the ability to reason. To know reality, perennialists

Key Term:
Perennialism

Objective 1:
Identify the major tenets of the authoritarian educational theories of perennialism, essentialism, and behaviorism.

Information Note 15.1:
The American Academy for the Advancement of Science has recently issued a report identifying the key concepts of science. They tend to be ideas that have been a topic of study for centuries.

Focus Question 1:
Perennialism is an educational theory that focuses on enduring ideas and principles that transcend time. Are there universal principles that seem to be taught in schools across many different nations? If so, identify several; if not, why?

Transparency 73:
Educational Theories

Activity 15.1:
Ask each student to write a list of five ideas that he or she believes are enduring. Summarize the individual lists and examine the class list. These ideas are examples of the perennialist position. How might a curriculum look if it were designed around these ideas?

Focus Question 2:
How does philosophy translate into action? Provide some examples.

maintain that we must examine individual things and objects around us to find their essence. To find the essence, one must discard the particulars and search for the underlying essentials. The essence of human beings lies in what they have in common—the ability to reason.

For the perennialist, the intellect does not develop merely by contact with relevant experiences. The intellect must be nourished by contact with ideas since truth ultimately resides in the nature of the things rather than in the sensory aspects of things. Perennialists contend that instead of focusing on current events or student interests, educators should teach disciplined knowledge with particular emphasis on the great ideas and works found in literature, the humanities, mathematics, science, and the arts. (See the Perennialist Class Activity box.)

Perennialist Focus of Learning. The focus of learning in perennialism lies in activities designed to discipline the mind. Subject matter of a disciplinary and spiritual nature, like mathematics, language, logic, great books, and doctrines, must be studied. The learner is assumed to be a rational and spiritual person. Difficult mental calisthenics such as reading, writing, drill, rote memory, and computations are important in training the intellect. Perennialism holds that learning to reason is also very important—an ability attained by additional mental exercises in grammar, logic, and rhetoric, as well as through use of discussion methodologies. Reasoning about human matters and about moral principles that permeate the universe is the major focus of perennialism. Such learning activities are thought to contribute to the spiritual outreaching of idealism. As the individual mind develops, the learner becomes more like a spiritual being. The learner is closer to ultimate knowledge when he or she gradually assumes the mind qualities of God. Idealism also includes some of the recent findings that stress the psychology of learning; in this realm it is believed the mind can combine pieces of learning into whole concepts that have meaning.

Perennialist Curriculum. Perennialists believe that early schooling is best directed toward preparing children for maturity, and they emphasize the three Rs in the elementary schools. In this view, perennialism and essentialism share some thoughts. Some lay and ecclesiastical perennialists consider character training, enhanced through Bible study, to be as important as the three Rs at the elementary level. A perennialist program for the secondary level is directed more toward educating the intellectually elite. Perennialism favors trade and skill training for students who are not engaged in the rigors of the general education program. Perennialists agree that the curriculum at the secondary level should provide a general educational program for the intellectually gifted and vocational training for the less gifted. However, not all perennialists agree on a curriculum design for general education.

The Great Books: A Perennialist Program. Although the Great Books program, associated with Robert M. Hutchins and Mortimer Adler, has brought much attention to perennialism, other leaders in this movement do not support the program. Proponents of the Great Books program maintain that studying the works of the leading scholars of history is the best way to a general education. Perennialists who do not agree maintain that more modern sources can be used to obtain knowledge. The ecclesiastical perennialists insist that all programs give first importance to the study of theology.

PERENNIALIST CLASS ACTIVITY

Ms. Rosemont's literature class had been studying the works of Henry David Thoreau. Today's session focused on "Reading" from *Walden*, and discussion was based on the following questions:

- Do the classics embody truth? Why or why not?
- Have all our emotions and problems been written about by great authors?
- Are none of our experiences unique? Why or why not?
- What makes a book great?
- Does popular literature ever serve a noble purpose? Why or why not?
- With whom can one talk about the best book?
- Can only great poets read the works of great poets? Why or why not?
- Does dealing with truth help us become immortal? Why or why not?
- How can we get the most benefit from our reading?

This lesson follows the Great Books procedure for questioning and could, therefore, be considered a perennialist investigation of human nature.[1]

In this perennialist class activity the nature of the learner is *active*, the nature of the subject matter is *structured*, the use of the subject matter is *cognitive*, and the behavior trend is toward *convergent thinking*.

Essentialism

Essentialism holds that there is a common core of information and skills that an educated person must have. Schools should be organized to transmit this core of essential material as effectively as possible. There are three basic principles of essentialism: a core of information, hard work and mental discipline, and teacher-centered instruction. Essentialism seeks to educate by providing training in the fundamentals, developing sound habits of mind, and learning to respect authority. The back-to-the-basics movement is a truncated form of essentialism because it focuses primarily on the three Rs and discipline.

Although essentialism shares many of the same principles as perennialism, there are several important differences. Essentialists are not so intent on transmitting underlying, basic truths; rather, they advocate the teaching of a basic core of information that will help a person live a productive life today. Hence, this core of information can and will change. This is an important difference in emphasis from the notions of everlasting truth that characterize the perennialist. In addition, essentialism stresses the disciplined development of basic skills rather than the perennialist goals of uncovering essences or underlying principles. (See the Essentialist Class Activity box on page 396.)

Essentialist Focus of Learning. Essentialism's goals are to transmit the cultural heritage and develop good citizens. It seeks to do this by emphasizing a core of fundamental knowledge and skills, developing sound habits of mental discipline, and demanding a respect for authority. Sound study habits as well as discipline are stressed in a structured learning situation. The role of the student is that of a learner. School is a place where children come to learn what they need to know, and the teacher is the person who can best instruct students in essential matters.

Key Term:
Essentialism

Focus Question 3:
Teaching methods that are nonauthoritarian regard the learner as active and interested in learning. What are some teaching methods that foster active learning?

Information Note 15.2:
The recent teaching-for-thinking movement supports the importance of teaching students to think rather than to engage in rote memorization of material presented by a teacher. This is in keeping with the educational theories of the essential schools movement.

Discussion Question 2:
When might a teacher focus on personalized situations involving such things as death or injustice to stimulate student learning? How would such a strategy relate to the back-to-basics expectations of our schools?

Activity 15.2:
Have students imagine what it means to "use your mind well." How would a curriculum look if it were designed to use one's mind well?

Journal/Portfolio Development 1:
Schools are being challenged to develop students who can achieve in a complex business world. Interview business leaders from two different companies in order to determine the importance of ethics in the operations of the businesses. Determine the extent to which the business leaders' values were influenced by teachers. List recommendations for teachers made by the business leaders. Describe a teaching approach that responds to these recommendations.

Objective 2:
Relate educational theories to learning and curriculum development.

Essentialist Curriculum.   The essentialist curriculum focuses on subject matter that includes literature, history, foreign languages, and religion. Teaching methods require formal discipline through emphasis on required reading, lectures, memorization, repetition, and examinations. Essentialists differ in their views on curriculum, but they generally agree about including subject matter of the physical world. Mathematics and the natural sciences are examples of subjects that contribute to the learners' knowledge of natural law. Activities that require mastering facts and information about the physical world are significant aspects of essentialist methodology. With truth defined as observable fact, field trips, laboratories, audiovisual materials, and nature all furnish methods of instruction. Habits of intellectual discipline are considered ends in themselves. Essentialism advocates studying the laws of nature and the accompanying universal truths of the physical world.

Essentialism envisions subject matter as the core of education. Severe criticism has been leveled at American education by those who advocate an emphasis on basic education. Essentialism assigns to the schools the task of conserving the heritage and transmitting knowledge of the physical world. In a sense the school is a curator of knowledge.

With the burgeoning of new knowledge in contemporary society, essentialism may be contributing to the slowness of educational change. In this context, essentialism is criticized as obsolete in its authoritarian tendencies. Such criticism implies that essentialism does not satisfy the twentieth-century needs of our youth. Educators within the movement deny such criticism and claim to have incorporated modern influences in the system while maintaining academic standards.

Essential Schools Movement.   The Essential Schools Movement is a contemporary school reform effort developed by Dr. Theodore Sizer. Sizer contends that there is a common core of information and skills that needs to be mastered by students, and he encourages schools to strip away the nonessentials and focus on having students "use their minds well." The Essential Schools Movement does not specify what specific content is essential. Rather, essential schools are required to analyze clearly what this core of information should be and change the curriculum to emphasize this core.

ESSENTIALIST CLASS ACTIVITY

Ms. Wright's second graders had just learned to count money. She decided to let them play several games of "musical envelopes." Although there was one envelope per student, each contained a different amount of paper "nickels," "dimes," "quarters," and "pennies." When the music stopped, students had to count the money in their envelopes. The one with the most money for each game got a special prize.[2]

In this essentialist class activity the nature of the learner is *passive,* the nature of the subject matter is *structured,* the use of the subject matter is *cognitive,* and the behavior trend is toward *convergent thinking.*

Behaviorism

B. F. Skinner, the Harvard experimental psychologist and philosopher, is the recognized leader of the movement known as **behaviorism.** Skinner verified Pavlov's stimulus-response theory with animals and, from his research, suggested that human behavior could also be explained as responses to external stimuli. (See the Behaviorist Class Activity box on page 398.) Other behaviorists' research expanded Skinner's work in illustrating the effect of the environment, particularly the interpersonal environment, in shaping individual behavior.

> Behaviorists share a common belief that a student's misbehavior can be changed and reshaped in a socially acceptable manner by directly changing the student's environment. The Behaviorist accepts the premise that students are motivated by the factor that all people will attempt to avoid experiences and stimuli that are not pleasing and will seek experiences that are pleasing and rewarding.[3]

Behaviorist Focus of Learning. Behaviorism is a psychological and educational theory that holds that one's behavior is determined by environment, not heredity. This suggests that education can contribute significantly to the shaping of the individual because the teacher can control the stimuli in a classroom and thereby influence student behavior. Behaviorists believe that the school environment must be highly organized and the curriculum based on behavioral objectives, and that knowledge is best described as behaviors that are observable. They contend that empirical evidence is essential if students are to learn and that the scientific method must be employed to arrive at knowledge. The task of education is to develop learning environments that lead to desired behaviors in students.

Reinforcement: A Behaviorist Practice. The concept of reinforcement is critical to teacher practices of behaviorism. Positive reinforcers (praise, special privileges, higher grades) are used to reward approved behavior with something desired by the student. Negative reinforcers (reprimands, extra homework, lower grades) are used to restrain behaviors that are not approved. Behaviorists generally believe that negative reinforcement is ineffective. Furthermore, they believe that learning takes place when approved behavior is observed and then positively reinforced.

When visually looking on, a teacher may provide positive reinforcement (smiling, nodding approval) or negative reinforcement (frowning, shaking the head in disapproval). Similarly, nondirective statements, questions, and directive statements may be positive or negative. Both children and adults respond to the models other people (peers, adults, heroes) represent to them by imitating the model behavior. Behaviorists contend that students tend to emulate behaviors that are rewarded.

The behaviorists have supplied a wealth of research that bears on the problems of attaining self-control, resisting temptation, and showing concern for others. Behaviorists do not attempt to learn about the causes of students' earlier problems. Rather, the teacher must ascertain what is happening in the classroom environment in order to perpetuate or extinguish the student's behavior.

CNN Clip 27:
Pay for Profanity

Journal Activity Master 15.1: An Analysis of an Educational Theory. This activity asks students to respond to a set of terms that represent a variety of educational theories. Students are asked to consider which educational theory these characteristics represent.

Information Note 15.3: Special education teachers have tended to use the ideas of behaviorism in the development of their curriculum.

Activity 15.3:
Bring a behavior checklist from any one of the many published observation checklists. Ask students to consider behavior as the key to understanding people. What are the strengths and weaknesses of such a position?

Diversity Note 15.1:
Behaviors do not imply the same meanings across cultures. Handshakes can be a welcoming gesture to some groups, while other groups consider them to be an intrusion.

Journal/Portfolio Development 2:
Describe the teaching method and classroom environment that you believe is most effective for you as a learner. Identify the educational theory or theories that would encourage the teaching method and environment that you have selected. Create a graphic that visually represents your own theory of teaching and learning.

Discussion Question 3:
The concept of reinforcement is very influential on the teacher practices of behaviorists. How would you use positive reinforcers and negative reinforcers while teaching your subject area concentration?

John Dewey (1859–1952)

BEHAVIORIST CLASS ACTIVITY

Students in Mr. Drucker's civics class were given merit tokens for coming into the room quietly, sitting at their desks, preparing notebooks and pencils for the day's lesson, and being ready to begin answering comprehension questions in their workbooks. On Fridays, students were allowed to use their tokens at an auction to buy items that Mr. Drucker knew they wanted. Sometimes, however, students had to save tokens for more than two weeks to buy what they liked best.

In this behaviorist class activity the nature of the learner is *passive,* the nature of the subject matter is *amorphous,* the use of the subject matter is *cognitive* or *affective,* and the behavior trend is toward *convergent thinking.*

Nonauthoritarian Educational Theories

Progressivism, reconstructionism, and humanism espouse a nonauthoritarian approach to subject matter, classroom organization, teaching methods, and assessment. Although each theory forms a distinct cohesive whole, all three are rooted in a nonauthoritarian principle, that is, that truth and goodness are entities that belong to all persons no matter what their station. Teachers are learners and learners are teachers, and education is the process in which individuals help one another to clarify personal meaning.

Each nonauthoritarian theory's focus or curriculum, teaching, and learning is presented in this chapter. In addition, representative programs are described along with an illustrative class activity.

Progressivism

With the rise of democracy in the late 1800s, the expansion of modern science and technology, and the need for people to be able to adjust to change, Americans had to have a new and different approach to getting knowledge to solve problems. An American philosopher, Charles S. Peirce (1839–1914), founded the philosophical system called *pragmatism.* This philosophy held that the meaning and value of ideas could be found only in their practical results. Later, William James (1842–1910) extended Peirce's theory of meaning into a theory of truth. James went further and asserted that the satisfactory working of an idea constitutes its whole truth. Pragmatism was carried much further by John Dewey (1859–1952), who was a widely known and influential philosopher and educator. Dewey insisted that ideas must always be tested by experiment. His experimental beliefs carried over into his educational philosophy, which became the basis for what was usually described as progressive education. **Progressivism** is an educational theory that emphasizes that ideas should be tested by experimentation and that learning is rooted in questions developed by the learners.[4]

Progressivism was a contemporary American educational theory. From its establishment in the mid-1920s through the mid-1950s, progressivism was the most influential educational view in America. Progressivists are basically opposed to authoritarianism and favor human experience as a basis for knowledge. Progressivism favors the scientific method of teaching and learning, allows for the beliefs of individuals, and stresses programs of student involvement that help students to learn how to think. Progressivists believe that the school should actively prepare its students for change. Progressive schools emphasize learning *how* to think rather than *what* to think. Flexibility is important in the curriculum design, and emphasis is on *experimentation,* with no single body of content stressed more than any other. Since life experience determines curriculum content, all types of content must be permitted. Certain subjects regarded as traditional are recognized as desirable for study as well. Progressivist educators would organize scientific method-oriented learning activities around the traditional subjects. Such a curriculum is called experience-centered or student-centered; the essentialism and perennialist curriculum is considered subject-centered. Experience-centered curricula stress the *process* of learning rather than the result.

Progressivism as a contemporary teaching style emphasizes the process of education in the classroom. It is more compatible with a core of problem areas across all academic disciplines than with a subject-centered approach to problem solving. It would be naive to suggest that memorization and rote practice should be ruled out. However, they are not stressed as primary learning techniques. The assertion is that interest in an intellectual activity will generate all the practice needed for learning. (See the Progressivist Class Activity box on page 400.)

Progressivism and Democracy.

Progressivism and Democracy. A tenet of progressivism is that the school, to become an important social institution, must be assigned the task of improving our way of life. To this end, experimentalism is deemed a working model of democracy. Freedom is explicit in a democracy, so it must be explicit in our schools. Certainly, freedom—rather than being a haphazard release of free will—must be organized to have meaning. Organized freedom permits each member of the school society to share in decisions, and experiences must be shared by all to ensure that the decisions are meaningful. Pupil-teacher planning is the key by which democracy in classrooms is realized and is the process that gives some freedom to students, as well as teachers, in deciding what is studied. For example, the teacher might ask students to watch a film about an issue of interest and have them list questions about the issue that were not answered by the film but that they would like to investigate. Student questions can then be analyzed by students and the teacher and refined for research. Such questions can become the basis for an inquiry and problem-solving unit of study. However, even if pupil-teacher planning is not highlighted as a specific activity, any experimentalist lesson allows students to give some of their own input in ways that influence the direction of the lesson. In that sense, progressivist lessons always involve pupil-teacher planning. For instance, asking students to make statements about life in 1908, using reprint pages from 1908 catalogues as their information source, allows students to focus on any items from the catalogues *they* choose—not items determined by the teacher.

The learner is seen as an experiencing, thinking, exploring individual. Progressivism exposes the learner to the subject matter of social experiences, social studies, projects, problems, and experiments that, when studied by the scientific method, will result in functional knowledge from all subjects. Books are regarded as tools to be used in learning rather than as sources of indisputable knowledge.

Test Questions 15.26–15.61

Objective 3:
Identify the major tenets of the nonauthoritarian educational theories of progressivism, reconstructionism, and humanism.

Key Term:
Progressivism

Objective 4:
State the relationship of progressivism to democracy and society.

Activity 15.4:
Jacob Getzels claimed democracy was a sacred value that people prized but failed to practice. Ask students to consider how democratic a classroom environment is. Is it a sacred or secular value?

PROGRESSIVIST CLASS ACTIVITY

Ms. Long's second graders read "Recipe for a Hippopotamus Sandwich" from *Where the Sidewalk Ends: Poems and Drawings of Shel Silverstein* (New York: Harper and Row, 1974). Each student was asked to draw a picture of the hippopotamus sandwich. For homework, all class members were told to read the poem to someone, show the picture, and then tell about the person's reaction on the following day.[5]

In the progressivist class activity the nature of the learner is *active,* the nature of the subject matter is *structured,* the use of the subject matter is *cognitive,* and the behavior trend is toward *divergent thinking.*

Information Note 15.4:
Jacob Getzels proposed a theory of sacred and secular values. Sacred values were those that schools teach but society does not practice. Democracy was one of these sacred values.

Progressivism and Socialization. Many people believe that the socialization aspect is the most valuable aspect of the movement. In this way, progressivism represents the leading edge of our culture and teaches us how to manage change. However, progressivism is criticized for placing so much stress on the processes of education that the ends are neglected. Its severest critics contend that it has little personal commitment to anything—producing many graduates who are uncommitted and who are content to drift through life. Progressivists counter by stating that their educational view is relatively young and therefore accepts criticism as an expected occurrence when trial-and-error methods are a part of the scientific method. The advent of progressivism as a counterview to the more traditional educational views provided exciting discussions that continue among thinkers in education.

Key Term:
Constructivism

Journal Activity Master 15.2: Philosophical Analysis of a Grading Situation.
This activity asks students to respond to a scenario involving grading and to determine how their response illustrates a certain type of educational theory.

Constructivism: A Progressivist Epistemology. **Constructivism** is an educational theory that emphasizes hands-on, activity-based teaching and learning. Recently, the American Psychological Association (APA) has encouraged teachers to reconsider the manner in which they view teaching. The APA contends that students are active learners who should be given opportunities to develop their own frames of thought. Teaching techniques should include a variety of different learning activities during which students are free to infer and discover their own answers to important questions. Teachers need to spend time designing these learning situations rather than lecturing. Learning is considered the active framing of personal meaning (by the learner) rather than framing someone else's meaning (which belongs to the teacher).

Such a view of teaching is compatible with the tenets of progressivism and has profound ramifications for the school curriculum. If students are to be encouraged to answer their own questions and develop their own thinking frame, the curriculum needs to be reconceptualized. Constructivist theorists encourage the development of critical thinking and the understanding of big ideas rather than the mastery of factual information. They contend that students who have a sound understanding of important principles that were developed through their own critical thinking will be better prepared for the complex, technological world.

CASE STUDY	AUTHENTIC SCHOOL TESTING: VALUES ON THE LOOSE

*F*or the past decade California has tried to improve its public schools by revising textbooks, recruiting quality educators, lengthening the school day, and developing alternative paths to a high school degree. Other states have been dealing with similar issues, but California stands apart because it has consistently responded to problems with more authentic, person-centered solutions. Such an orientation has enabled California educators to generate a variety of creative educational products, some of which have been adopted and implemented in other states. In a very real sense, California has become a key player in the development of student-centered educational reform.

The most recent step in the reform effort was new testing. Under the old system, elementary and high school students simply checked off answers on multiple-choice tests; these are tests of memory and fact acquisition, but hardly of coherent thought. The new assessments, called CLAS (California Learning Assessments System) are essay tests. Students are given data and a fairly long problem, and are asked questions that require independent thinking. There is often a variety of valid solutions, and students are encouraged to use personal experience to clarify their responses. The new tests are meant to assess not only how individual students are doing, but also how each school and school district is performing.

The first CLAS tests were given last year to all public school pupils in the fourth, eighth, and tenth grades. The results from approximately one million pupils showed some strength in writing, but considerable weakness in comprehension and mathematical reasoning. One would think that such tests, like other reforms, would be widely praised as an improvement over multiple choice formats. Yet, such testing reform has been highly contentious. Some parents, including the Traditional Values Coalition, objected that the reading samples in the tests might corrupt their children's moral, ethnic, or cultural views. And the essays were an unwarranted intrusion into private thought; they might reveal the values of pupils or their families, and these were none of the state's business. Parents began demanding the right to keep their children out of the tests, and some districts went to court to plead for an exemption. On June 6, 1994, a Los Angeles superior court ruled that a school could not of its own volition decide to withdraw from tests imposed by state law. The tests stay and schools must administer them. But the state has retreated on several other fronts. In the future, questions such as "How do you feel about this situation?" will not be asked. And the state has already withdrawn extracts from the writings of Alice Walker and Annie Dillard. The governor's education advisor has publicly stated that too many of the extracts reflected inner city street life.

The CLAS controversy has caused California's governor to reconsider his original $33 million infusion into the continued development of such tests. It is unclear whether such an investment is warranted, and the obvious alternatives are not attractive.

1. Should California remove those test items that seem to authentically assess complex situations? Why or why not?
2. Or should the state retreat from this type of focus (at least in its testing materials) and use test items that are more abstract, that do not require a student to build a personal answer? Why or why not?

It may be that the underlying question is not *testing* but the focus of authenticity. Testing has simply clarified the implications of such an educational focus.

Constructionist philosophies emphasize the importance of developing in students a love of learning.

Reconstructionism

Key Term:
Reconstructionism

Reconstructionism emerged in the 1930s under the leadership of George S. Counts, Harold Rugg, and Theodore Brameld. Reconstructionism recognized that progressivism had made advances beyond essentialism in teacher-pupil relations and teaching methodology. However, progressivism fixated too heavily on the needs of the child and failed to develop long-range goals for society. Spurred by the Great Depression of the 1930s, reconstructionism called for a new social order that would fulfill basic democratic ideals. Advocates believe that people should control institutions and resources and that this could happen if there were an international democracy of world government.

Objective 5:
Describe the major tenets of critical pedagogy and relate them to societal change.

Focus Question 4:
Reconstructionism calls on schools to teach students to control institutions and be organized according to democratic principles. How can schools teach people to control institutions when schools are themselves institutions?

Critical Pedagogy: A Reconstructionist Curriculum. An education for a reconstructed society would require that students be taught to critically analyze world events, explore controversial issues, and develop a vision for a new and better world. Teachers would critically examine cultural heritages, explore controversial issues, provide a vision for a new and better world, and enlist students' efforts to promote programs of cultural renewal. Although teachers would attempt to convince students of the validity of such democratic goals, they would employ democratic procedures in doing so. (See the Reconstructionist Class Activity box.)

A contemporary version of reconstructionism is rooted in the work of Henry Giroux, who views schools as vehicles for social change. He calls teachers to be transformative intellectuals and wants them to participate in creating a new society. Schools should practice **critical pedagogy,** which unites theory and practice as it provides students with the critical thinking tools to be change agents.[6]

Reconstructionism and World Reformation.
A persistent theme of reconstructionism is that public education should be the direct instrument of world reformation. As a logical extension of experimentalism, reconstructionism accepts the concept that the essence of learning is the actual experience of learning. Reconstructionism espouses a theory of social welfare that can effectively prepare learners to deal with the great crises of our time—war, inflation, rapid technological changes, depression. From the experiences of World War I, the Great Depression, and World War II, reconstructionist educators believe that the total educational effort must be seen within a social context.

As was indicated earlier, John Dewey had an immense influence on progressivism. Dewey also made major contributions to reconstructionist philosophy with his efforts to define the individual as an entity within a social context. Reconstructionists go further in stressing that individuals as entities within a social context are urged to engage in specific reform activity. Classroom teachers tend to use affective emphases and moral dilemmas in directing attention toward social reform.

Information Note 15.5:
Critical pedagogy has two major historical roots: first, from central and south America where schools are considered places of social change, and second from Germany in response to the horrors of World War II.

Activity 15.5:
Have students think of one societal issue that has been in the news recently. Ask them to consider how schools could make a difference with regard to the issue.

Diversity Note 15.2:
Some groups view the individual person as strongly connected to the larger society, while other groups consider the individual to be loosely connected to the larger society.

RECONSTRUCTIONIST CLASS ACTIVITY

Mr. Ragland asked his second graders to look at a cartoon that pictured a well-dressed man and woman in an automobile pulled by a team of two horses. The highway they were traveling along passed through rolling farmland with uncrowded meadows, trees, and clear skies in the background. He led a discussion based on the following questions:

1. What is happening in this picture?
2. Do you like what is happening in the picture? Why or why not?
3. What does it say about the way you may be living when you grow up?
4. Are you happy or unhappy about what you have described for your life as an adult?
5. How can we get people to use less gasoline now?
6. What if we could keep companies from making and selling cars that could not travel at least forty miles on one gallon of gasoline? How could we work to get a law passed to do this?[7]

In this reconstructionist class activity the nature of the learner is *active*, the nature of the subject matter is *structured*, the use of the subject matter is *affective*, and the behavior trend is toward *divergent thinking*.

Humanism

Humanism is an educational approach that is rooted in writings of Rousseau and the ideas of existentialism. Jean Jacques Rousseau (1712–1778), the father of

Key Term:
Humanism

Relevant Research

The Use of Ill-Structured Problems

For decades there has been a great deal of research surrounding the use of problems as a teaching strategy. Recently, Howard Barrows began using case studies about patients to prepare medical students for their internships. The case studies were based on the actual medical records of patients and the studies were organized around a carefully designed problem statement called an *ill-structured problem.* Ill-structured problems are questions surrounding a series of situations that have multiple solution paths. During such a problem-solving experience, medical teachers focus on the reasoning that medical students employ more than the correct diagnosis. Dr. Barrows and other medical doctors contend that it is more important to instruct medical students in critical thinking than it is to have students memorize a lot of material.

Elementary and secondary teachers have begun to use ill-structured problems. To date, the research has shown that students tend to be more motivated, more involved in learning, and more focused on the implications that learning has for society. On the other hand, data on the long-term effects on student achievement are not available. In addition, allowing students to pursue ill-structured problems can be risky. Students may develop controversial answers to some of the real problems that they encounter. Community members may find it difficult to respond to these answers; they may even disagree with the answers students employ.

If problem-based learning is going to find a place in American schools, teachers must be willing to allow students to pursue their interests, even if it means taking students beyond the confines of the curriculum. How do teachers determine when it is worthwhile to test those curricular boundaries?

Sources: H. Barrows. *How to Design a Problem-Based Learning Curriculum in the Pre-Clinical Years.* New York: Springer-Verlag, 1985.
J. O'Neil. *Rx for better thinkers: problem-based learning.* ASCD Update, Alexandria, Virginia, 1992.
W. S. Stepien, S. Gallagher, and D. Workman. "Problem-Based Learning for Traditional and Interdisciplinary Classrooms." Aurora, IL: Illinois Mathematics and Science Academy.

Romanticism, believed that the child entered the world not as a blank slate but with certain innate qualities and tendencies. In the opening sentence of *Émile,* Rousseau's famous treatise on education, he states that "God makes all things good; man meddles with them and they become evil."[8] Thus Rousseau believed in basic goodness at birth. He also believed that humans are born free but become enslaved by institutions. Humanistic education mingles some of these ideas from Rousseau with the basic ideas of existentialism.

Humanism is an educational theory that is concerned with enhancing the innate goodness of the individual. It rejects a group-oriented educational system and seeks ways to enhance the individual development of the student. Humanism adopts many of these ideas from Rousseau and mingles the ideas of existentialism to form an educational theory. (See the Humanist Class Activity box.)

Humanists believe that most schools de-emphasize the individual and the relationship between the teacher and the student. Humanists claim that as educators attempt to predict behavior of students, they turn individuals into objects to be measured. According to the humanist, education should be a process of developing a free, self-actualizing person, centered on the feelings of the student. Therefore, education does not start with great ideas, the world, or with humankind, but with the individual self.

Humanistic Curriculum. Since the goal of humanism is a completely autonomous person, education should be without coercion or prescription. Students should be active and encouraged to make their own choices. The teacher who follows humanistic theory emphasizes learning situations in which each student makes choices. Instruction and assessment are based on student interest, abilities, and needs. Students determine the rules that will govern classroom life, and they make choices about the books to read or exercises to complete.

Humanists honor divergent thinking so completely that they delay giving their own personal opinions and do not attempt to persuade students to particular points of view. Even though they emphasize the affective and thereby may make students feel a certain urgency about issues, it is always left to the individual student to decide when to take a stand, what kind of stand to take, whether a cause merits actions, and if so, what kind of action.

Humanistic School Environments. From the 1960s to the present, the influence of humanism can be identified with various creative programs and written materials. A. S. Neill proposes a "radical approach to child rearing" in his book *Summerhill.*[9] Charles E. Silberman, in his *Crisis in the Classroom,* calls for remaking American education to provide for greater consideration of the individual. Various textbooks discuss issues like the open-access curriculum, nongraded instruction, and multiage grouping, each of which attends to the uniqueness of the learner. Educators are now making various attempts in their school programs to individualize education. Block scheduling permits flexibility for students to arrange classes of their choice. Free schools, storefront schools, schools without walls, and area vocational centers provide alternatives to traditional schools. Educational programs that treat the needs of the individual are usually more costly per pupil than the traditional group-centered programs. Consequently, as taxpayer demands for accountability mount, individualized programs are often brought under unit-cost scrutiny. Nonetheless, growing numbers of educators are willing to defend increased expenditures to meet the needs of the individual learner within the instructional programs of the schools.

HUMANIST CLASS ACTIVITY

Ms. Fenway wanted her ninth graders to think about the effectiveness of television and radio advertising. She asked students to write down any five slogans or "jingles" they could remember and the products advertised. Ms. Fenway selected from their items at random and tested the class. She read each slogan, and class members had to provide answers. The test was corrected in class by the students, who were very surprised that the grading scale was reversed. Those who had all correct answers received Fs, and those who had only one correct answer received As. When asked why she had reversed the grades, Ms. Fenway responded, "Why do you think advertising is so effective?" She asked whether students resented some companies' selling tactics. Then she told students to help her make a list of questions to ask themselves in order to avoid spending money in ways they might later regret. She also asked for specific examples of spending money for items they later wished they had not bought.[10]

In this humanist class activity the nature of the learner is *active*, the nature of the subject matter is *structured*, the use of the subject matter is *affective*, and the behavior trend is toward *divergent thinking*.

Global Perspectives: Looking beyond the Boundaries. Throughout this chapter, educational theories have been represented as consistent sets of

PROFESSIONAL DILEMMA

Should I Use Homogeneous or Heterogeneous Ability Grouping?

The issue of how to group students for instruction can be very controversial. Some propose homogeneous grouping and others argue for heterogeneous grouping. Homogeneous ability grouping is a practice that seems to have merit. Permitting students who require the same level of instruction to be clustered in a single setting makes planning and resource allocation much easier. Such grouping patterns permit students to receive instruction that is tied to their specific needs since they are with others who need the same information or skill development.

Those who oppose homogeneous ability grouping contend that labeling students and placing them in similar ability groups based on their academic skill sets up structures that often inhibit future growth

and development. Both teachers and parents begin to view students according to these labels and, once tracked by ability, students seldom break out of the initial labels assigned at an early age. These individuals call for multi-ability or heterogeneous grouping. They believe that having students from a variety of backgrounds and ability levels work together is more in keeping with a democratic society. Furthermore, such multi-ability grouping permits students to more easily help one another, fostering cooperativeness and caring among those from different backgrounds. Indeed, opponents of tracking programs have pointed to the disproportionate number of minority and low-income students who seem to comprise the lower-level groups.

- List other pros and cons of homogeneous ability grouping that you can think of. List other pros and cons of heterogeneous ability grouping.

- Should one type of grouping be used in all instructional settings or circumstances, or should the types of grouping be varied according to task and context?

Objective 6:
Compare and contrast authoritarian and nonauthoritarian educational theories.

ideas linked logically together. The importance of such categorization is strongly related to the types of writings that were part and parcel of European thinkers from the eighteenth and nineteenth centuries. It is no surprise that current educational theories in the United States tend to display such clear sets of distinctions since, in large part, immigrants during these years came from Germany, Poland, Ireland, Scandinavia, England, France, Italy, and Switzerland. The last half of the twentieth century has expanded this European focus. Faster and better communication, the opening of once-closed societies, and increased interdependence has permitted differing thinking schemes to intermesh and at times conflict with one another.

Such clashes, although uncomfortable, assist in breaking or at least readjusting the limitations of categorical boundaries. The comfort of such categories can stagnate and imprison. Relying on neat sets of proven ideas provides a set of solutions. These solutions are limited by the original thinking schemes that generated them. Calling into question these categories of thought cannot be easily achieved without the infusion of other types of thinking. The influx of Asian, African, and other types of thinking are especially helpful in breaking down the rigidity of thought boundaries because many of the thinking schemes from these cultures do not require such rigid boundary sets. These flexible thinking schemes provide a different type of cohesion than that of strict logical distinctions.

Summary and Implications

This chapter provided an overview of six leading educational views utilized in part or entirely by teachers in the American schools. While one's ultimate teaching style might not be completely committed to perennialism, essentialism, behaviorism, progressivism, reconstructionism, or humanism, the basic descriptions of those views should be helpful in identifying several preferences. An individual's preferences are compatible with, if not formulated by, his or her personality. The extent to which one's teaching practices fit one's personality, and vice versa, is related to effective teaching.

Whether or not the teacher preparation program at your college or university contains formal coursework in classical or educational philosophy, we encourage you to expand your study in this area so that you may extract from the acquired knowledge meaningful beliefs to guide you in identifying preferences and methods for assisting your students.

Some classroom teachers continue to be skeptical about educational theory and proponents of theory as a basis for practice. Yet new theories about educating children continue to proliferate, while the older beliefs remain strong in today's schools. Chapter 14 presented digests of the structure and thoughts associated with selected classical philosophies. This chapter illustrated the relationship of current educational views to the classical philosophies, but described the educational views in terms of the learner, subject matter orientation, and authoritarian/nonauthoritarian tendencies. The next chapter will help you to understand how to utilize philosophy to become a better teacher.

Discussion Questions

1. What were the characteristics and behaviors of one of your favorite teachers who was authoritarian toward the students? Of a favorite teacher who was nonauthoritarian toward the students?

2. When might a teacher focus on personalized situations involving such things as death or injustice to stimulate student learning? How would such a strategy relate to the back-to-basics expectations of our schools?

3. The concept of reinforcement is very influential on the teacher practices of behaviorists. How would you use positive reinforcers and negative reinforcers while teaching your subject area concentration?

4. Experienced teachers often advise a beginning teacher: "Be firm with the students and let them know at the beginning how you intend to teach your classes." Is this advice good or bad? Discuss the pros and cons of such a procedure.

5. Humanism rules out some of the conventional notions about educating youth. Emphasis is given to the development of the individual rather than to the structure of a curriculum. What implications does humanism have for grouping students?

Journal/Portfolio Development

1. Schools are being challenged to develop students who can achieve in a complex business world. Interview business leaders from two different companies in order to determine the importance of ethics in the operations of the businesses. Determine the extent to which the business leaders' values were influenced by teachers. List recommendations for teachers made by the business leaders. Describe a teaching approach that responds to these recommendations.

2. Describe the teaching method and classroom environment that you believe is most effective for you as a learner. Identify the educational theory or theories that would encourage the teaching method and environment that you have selected. Create a graphic that visually represents your own theory of teaching and learning.

School-Based Experiences

1. This chapter contains a number of special features that give examples of classroom activities typically associated with various educational theories. As you work in the schools, take this book (or photocopies of the class activity features) with you and see whether you can determine which theory various teachers that you observe seem to be reflecting. Having done so, decide which educational theory you subscribe to and determine whether your own classroom activity is consistent with that typically associated with your personal educational philosophy.

2. Set up several interviews with teachers who organize their classrooms and teaching materials differently. Using probing questions, try to uncover the educational theory or theories that account for the differing teaching approaches.

Notes

1. Lloyd Duck, *Instructor's Manual for Teaching with Charisma.* Boston: Allyn and Bacon, 1981, Item 4, 53–54.
2. Lloyd Duck, Item A, 40.
3. Charles H. Wolfgang and Carl D. Glickman. *Solving Discipline Problems: Strategies for Classroom Teachers.* Boston: Allyn and Bacon, 1980, 121.
4. John Dewey, *Democracy and Education.* New York: Macmillan, 1916, 1–9.
5. Lloyd Duck, Item D, 41.
6. Henry A. Giroux, "Teachers as Transformative Intellectuals," *Social Education 49* (1985): 376–379.
7. Lloyd Duck, Item N, 47–48.
8. Jean Jacques Rousseau, *Émile*, trans. Alan Bloom. New York: Basic Books, 1979.
9. A. S. Neill, *Summerhill.* New York: Hart, 1960.
10. Lloyd Duck, Item C, 50–51.

Bibliography

Ackerly, Robert L. *The Reasonable Exercise of Authority.* Washington, DC: National Association of Secondary School Principals, 1969.

Bagley, William C. "An Essentialist's Platform for the Advancement of American Education." *Educational Administration and Supervision 24* (April 1938): 241–256.

Barrows, H. *How to Design a Problem-Based Learning Curriculum in the Pre-Clinical Years.* New York: Springer-Verlag, 1985.

Brameld, Theodore. *Patterns of Educational Philosophy.* New York: Holt, Rinehart and Winston, 1971.

Bricker, David C. *Classroom Life As Civic Education.* New York: Teachers College Press, 1989.

Lauderdale, William B. *Progressive Education: Lessons from Three Schools.* Phi Delta Kappa Fastback No. 166. Bloomington, IN: Phi Delta Kappa, 1981.

Morris, Van Cleve, and Pai, Young. *Philosophy and the American School.* 2nd ed. Boston: Houghton Mifflin, 1976.

O'Neil, J. *RX for Better Thinkers: Problem-Based Learning.* Alexandria, VA: ASCD Update, 1992.

Rich, John Martin. *Innovations in Education: Reformers and Their Critics.* Boston: Allyn and Bacon, 1985.

Rothman, Robert. "Standards Challenged in New Hampshire." *Education Week* (11 February 1987): 11.

Sizer, Theodore R. *Horace's Compromise: The Dilemma of the American High School.* Boston: Houghton-Mifflin, 1985.

Skinner, B. F. "Programmed Instruction Revisited." *Phi Delta Kappan* (October 1986): 103–110.

Stepien, W. S., Gallagher, S., and Workman, D. Problem-Based Learning for Traditional and Interdisciplinary Classrooms. Aurora, IL: Illinois Mathematics and Science Academy, 1992.

Strike, Kenneth A., and Soltis, Jonas F. *The Ethics of Teaching.* New York: Teachers College Press, 1985.

Wolfgang, Charles H., and Glickman, Carl D. *Solving Discipline Problems: Strategies for Classroom Teachers.* Boston: Allyn and Bacon, 1980.

16

Building an Educational Philosophy

Focus Questions

1   What does it mean to be an educational leader? In what ways could you be a leader during your first teaching assignment?

2   How do a teacher's instructional methods reflect an educational philosophy?

3   How does the organization of desks and tables in a classroom reflect an educational philosophy?

4   Why is it important for you to understand the philosophical reasoning behind your intended discipline practices?

5   During a job interview, what will you say when you are asked to state your philosophy of education?

Key Terms and Concepts

Adaptation: The promotion of a stable climate in schools so that students can attain an unbiased picture of the changes that occur in society.

Change agent: A role that emphasizes the responsibility for persons to actively participate in society.

Classroom organization: A multifaceted dimension of teaching that includes the content, method, and values that infuse the classroom environment, planning, and discipline practices.

Control theory: A theory of discipline that contends that we choose most of our behaviors to gain control of people or ourselves.

Dialectic: The conflict that occurs when opposing ideas are encountered; in change theory this conflict is the one between individual needs and societal needs.

Motivation: Internal emotion, desire, or impulse acting as an incitement to action.

Vision: A vision is a mental construction that synthesizes and clarifies what you value or consider to be of most worth.

*E*xtensive surveys of modern views of learning—as expressed in philosophy, psychology, and education journals and studies—reveal a seemingly endless and divergent range of views. Therefore, today's classroom teachers must identify their own beliefs about educating young people. Although labeling the classroom practice of any one teacher is not easy, we recommend that you, as a prospective teacher, carefully identify a personal set of operational principles with regard to classroom techniques. Whether your operational principles are drawn from the brief descriptions in this book or elsewhere, you should strive for consistent teaching behavior within the framework of sound principles—that is, behavior based on your personal philosophy of education. The previous two chapters introduced you to the philosophies from which modern educational theories have been derived. This chapter now helps you to identify your role as a teacher in society and to clarify meaningful practices for your classroom.

Educational trends, which are often identified by terms such as "the back-to-basics movement," are related to certain philosophies of education. The back-to-basics movement centers on subject matter and is clearly in the realms of essentialism and perennialism, whereas the concepts of "free schools" and "open education" are experience-based and focus on student activity as identified in progressivism and existentialism. Figure 16.1 illustrates the association of these primary educational theories with the authoritarian view, which stresses convergent thinking, and the nonauthoritarian view, which stresses divergent thinking. Note that the terms *authoritarian* and *nonauthoritarian* are meant to provide an overall view with regard to the student and subject matter and not to imply strict or permissive classroom management.

Using Philosophy to Examine Schools and Society

Transparency 77:
Change Is . . .

Objective 1:
List the characteristics of teachers as change agents.

Schools play a role within the larger society. This role is determined by a number of factors: the expectations of society's leaders, economic conditions, the ideologies of powerful lobbying groups, and the philosophies of teachers. It is especially important for educators to examine the role of the school in terms of the larger society. If such reflection does not occur, schools will merely reflect the status quo or the needs and desires of a single powerful group.

Teachers as Change Agents

An age-old question regarding the role of schools in society concerns the proper role of the school and the teacher in relation to change. Should teachers be **change agents** or should they re-emphasize eternal truths and cultural positions? This question of change versus transmission of ongoing values has been articulated in a variety or ways.

Change as Adaptation. Isaac L. Kandel (1881–1965) was a leader in the essentialist movement who advocated change as a process of **adaptation**. This approach emphasized the importance of promoting stability and adapting the

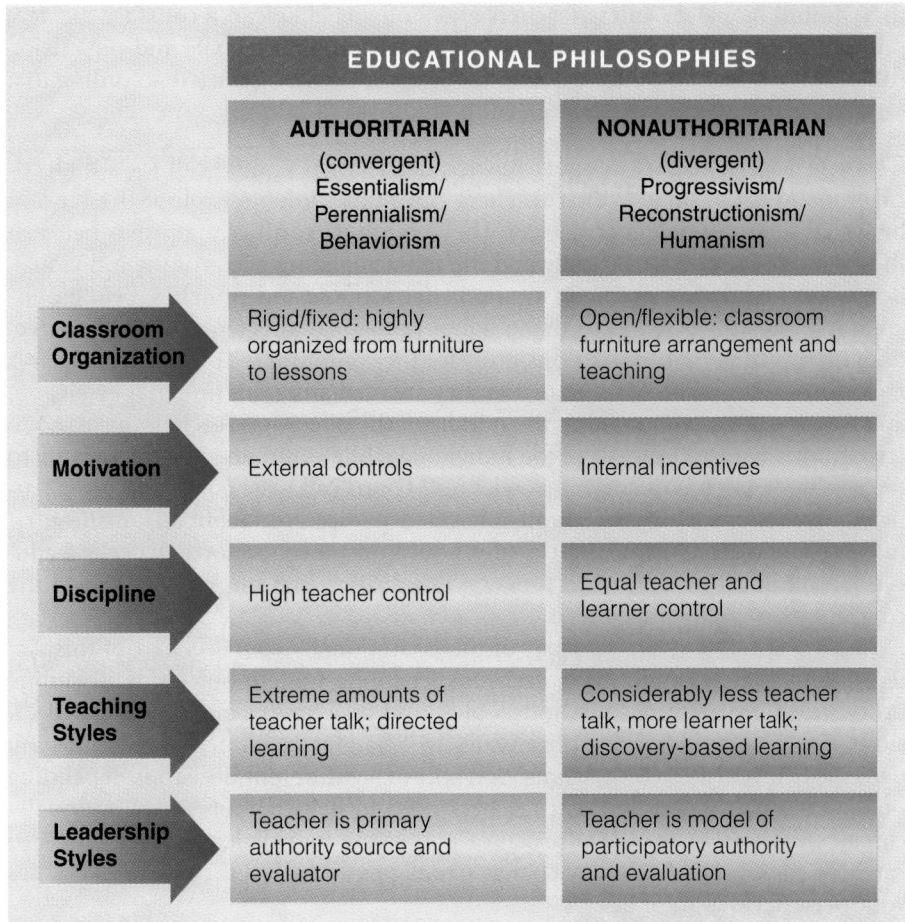

EDUCATIONAL PHILOSOPHIES

	AUTHORITARIAN (convergent) Essentialism/ Perennialism/ Behaviorism	NONAUTHORITARIAN (divergent) Progressivism/ Reconstructionism/ Humanism
Classroom Organization	Rigid/fixed: highly organized from furniture to lessons	Open/flexible: classroom furniture arrangement and teaching
Motivation	External controls	Internal incentives
Discipline	High teacher control	Equal teacher and learner control
Teaching Styles	Extreme amounts of teacher talk; directed learning	Considerably less teacher talk, more learner talk; discovery-based learning
Leadership Styles	Teacher is primary authority source and evaluator	Teacher is model of participatory authority and evaluation

FIGURE 16.1

Authoritarian versus Nonauthoritarian Views of the Classroom

individual to the environment. The school should be a place that provides students with an unbiased picture of the changes that occur in society. Hence, schools cannot educate for a new social order nor should teachers use the classroom to promote doctrine. Change occurs first in society. Schools follow the lead.[1]

Change as Rational Process. John Dewey believed school had a part in social change. He contended that change continually occurred, often without a clearly defined direction. Schools need to assume a leadership role in this change because educators have the time to study newer scientific and cultural forces, estimate the direction and outcome, and determine which changes were or were not beneficial. Schools need to provide an environment in which students can learn these analytic skills and participate in helping society determine a direction that is meaningful and of most worth.[2]

Change as Reconstruction. The reconstructionist Theodore Brameld contended that every educational system should help diagnose the causes of world problems. Schools need to do more than assess scientific and technological change;

Transparency 78:
Teachers as Change Agents

Activity 16.1:
Ask students to select one of the definitions of change (adaptation, rational process, reconstruction, dialectic). Using this definition, have each student design a response to the problem of illiteracy. Discuss how the responses differ.

Information Note 16.1:
The discussion of change as a series of different perspectives is in keeping with recent cognitive science's work on framing. These frames of thought concerning change will determine how one will act in the future.

they should be places where teachers and students alike can reconsider the very purpose of schooling and study new ways of formulating goals and organizing subject matter. Schools and society alike need to be reconstructed according to a set of human goals based on cross-cultural, universal values.[3]

Change as Dialectic.   Samuel Bowles and Herbert Gintis[4] call for a **dialectical** humanism through which teachers can help students explore the tension between the individual and society. They identify a conflict that exists between the reproductive needs of society and the self-actualizing needs of the individual. Bowles and Gintis claim that institutions like schools and churches, peer groups and town meetings are places that attempt to mediate this tension between freedom of the individual and responsibility for the community. The problem schools face is that they are often unaware that they are mediating this underlying tension, and teachers are often caught in the middle of the dilemma. Teachers are asked to respond to the unique needs of the individual while simultaneously answering to the conflicting needs of society. Bowles and Gintis call teachers to develop a participatory democracy in which all interested parties are taught to pursue their interests and resolve conflicts rationally. Educators must develop a dialectical educational philosophy that seeks a new synthesis between the individual and the community.

As a teacher, you become part of the educational system. As part of this system, you will be asked to make decisions regarding student outcomes, discipline procedures, instructional methodologies, and assessment methods. Your decisions regarding these educational issues will be greatly influenced by how you perceive teachers as change agents. You will make different decisions depending on whether you determine that teachers need to help schools adapt, rationally change the social order, reconstruct, or participate in a dialectic. Your task is to carefully consider each of these change paradigms and select the one that matches your personal system of beliefs.

Teachers may find that their own philosophies of teaching do not match those of the school where they teach.

Teachers as Leaders

Whether teachers espouse this idea or not, they serve as leaders for their students. Evidence of this can be found in the testimonials that are offered by former students when they have become adults. Most students, whether they have achieved graduate degrees or have followed vocational pursuits immediately after high school, report remembering teachers who had a personal impact on their lives. These students will usually discuss the leadership and modeling behaviors of the teachers they remember.

The idea of teachers as leaders suggests that the new teacher should be aware of the need to develop a beginning repertoire that builds strong leadership qualities to which students may look for guidance during their developmental years. These leadership qualities—and the practice of them—are highly dependent on the classroom philosophy that the new teacher puts into practice. Some beginning concepts for teacher leadership are vision, modeling behaviors, and use of power.

Vision. Classroom leadership behaviors begin with a teacher having vision and the intent to actualize that vision for the students. How a teacher actually puts that vision into practice depends wholly on the teacher's philosophical practices. A **vision** is a mental construct that synthesizes and clarifies what you value or consider to be of most worth. The clearer the vision or mental picture, the easier it is for leaders to make decisions or persuade or influence others. Formulating a vision requires reflection concerning what you believe about truth, beauty, justice, and equality. It is important to consider these issues and formulate a vision about the way schools and classrooms should be organized and implemented.

Sheive and Schoenbeit offer five steps that leaders take to put their visions into actions:[5]

1. Value your vision.
2. Be reflective and plan a course of action.
3. Articulate the vision to colleagues.
4. Develop a planning and action stage.
5. Have students become partners in the vision.

Teachers serve as leaders for their students.

Cooperative learning situations provide an alternative method for promoting student learning.

If teachers reflect on their vision, they can plan the course of action they need to use with their learners. Articulation provides teachers with an opportunity to share their vision with colleagues. In-service or staff development sessions are excellent times to articulate a classroom vision. Visions require a planning stage and an action stage if they are to become a reality. Planning and action stages should involve the students who are intended to be the receivers of this vision. For example, if a teacher wishes students to be reflective in their learning environment, then the teacher needs to help the students see that vision and become partners in the planning. The teacher may engage the students in free and open discussions of the vision and its importance to the learning environment in the classroom.

Activity 16.3:
Ask students to record personal behaviors that show that they model the vision for schools that they have articulated. A vision is only as effective as the way it is modeled.

Focus Question 1:
What does it mean to be an educational leader? In what ways could you be a leader during your first teaching assignment?

Discussion Question 2:
What characteristics or practices can you identify in a former teacher whom you would label your favorite?

Activity 16.4:
Discuss the types of educational philosophy that lend themselves to each of the two teaching styles (teacher-dominant versus learner-supportive). With the class, develop a lesson plan according to each style. How do the objectives change for each style?

Modeling. If teachers hold certain expectations of learner behaviors in the classroom, then it is imperative that they engage in modeling those behaviors with the students. If the classroom teacher is rigid and fixed in his or her classroom practices and presents an authoritarian atmosphere, then the students will probably respond in a similar fashion. On the other hand, if the teacher provides a more democratic classroom, the students will respond similarly in their classroom encounters. We would caution that a laissez-faire environment will probably produce a classroom with little or no direction on the part of the learner. Teachers should consider the modeling effect of leadership on the classroom environment and practice it on the basis of their accepted philosophy of the classroom.

Power. The concept of power in the classroom should not be considered good or bad. Power by itself has no value structure. The use of power, however, gives it a good, poor, or bad image. The nature of the teaching position entrusts a teacher with power. How a teacher uses power in the classroom or in the school building is wholly determined by the classroom philosophy the teacher wishes to project. All leaders have power that is associated with their position, but the successful leader is judicious in its use.

Teaching styles can be classified into two different uses of power: teacher dominant and learner supportive. Past and present practices in the school tend to lean heavily on the teacher-dominant style. Therefore, although many teachers in training study both categories of teaching styles, they tend to see only one major type in practice when they visit schools. We suggest that you continually study both major categories so that either can be applied as needed on the basis of classroom objectives for students and the teacher's classroom philosophy.

Teacher-dominant teaching styles are based on an authoritarian construct for the classroom. Learners are not expected to be active verbally in the learning process, but are generally expected to be receivers and practicing users of teacher-given information. Learning is very convergent. It is selected and given to the learner in the particular way in which the teacher wishes the student to acquire it.

CASE STUDY   HELPING THE FEMALES: A FORM OF SEGREGATION?

In 1994, the Illinois Mathematics and Science Academy (IMSA) completed an intensive examination of the research surrounding the success of females in higher mathematics and science. The results were astounding. Consistently, descriptive studies indicated that females dropped out or did not even attempt higher-level mathematics and science courses in high school and college. Although the research indicated that females could achieve in these courses, able female students generally refrained from the effort. The female students who did enroll in advanced science and mathematics classes tended to participate less and to drop out of these courses more often than males. Since IMSA is committed to increasing participation in science and mathematics, the faculty examined its own record. They discovered that considerably more of IMSA's female graduates majored in mathematics and science than from other high schools. This was a relief, but the faculty also discovered that while at IMSA, a significantly smaller number of females chose advanced physics electives compared to males.

Buoyed by a philosophy of equal access for all students, IMSA faculty and staff developed an exploratory research study. The physics teachers decided to conduct an all-female section of Calculus-based physics. The teachers contended that setting up such a segregated setting would assist them in clarifying what types of teaching strategies and classroom environmental characteristics were supportive of adolescent female learning. The exploratory study was designed, and twenty-one females volunteered to participate in the all-female section of Calculus-based physics for one semester.

The results of the study were generally positive. The results indicated that the all-female setting, in conjunction with a combination of hands-on teaching methods, open-ended questioning, and a cooperative learning environment, seemed to help the female students achieve and prompted them to sign up for another advanced physics course. Since the intention of this study was to implement the teaching, questioning, and environment findings in a coeducational classroom, the physics teachers used these teaching and environmental setting results in coeducational settings in subsequent semesters. However, the results have not been as powerful as they were in the coeducational setting.

Puzzled by this lack of transfer, the IMSA faculty is struggling to make sense of the entire effort. Since the original study did not completely control for a variety of factors, additional studies are being considered. It is possible, however, that these findings are only valid in an all-female setting. Such a finding is unacceptable within the context of an integrated society. Laws ban such segregation in public school settings.

1. What are the philosophical implications of this effort?
2. What is the meaning of educational equality for all?
3. How does diversity relate to equality?
4. Should one refrain from investigations that might uncover solutions that conflict with a philosophy?

Learner-supportive teaching styles view the learner as someone who is verbally active and who seeks divergence in learning. Learner-supportive teaching styles encourage the active participation of the learner in exploring learning and helping to determine the extent to which the learner will engage in alternatives. These teaching styles tend to recognize differences in learning, individual interests, and higher-order learning.

Using Philosophy in the Classroom

Test Questions 16.21–16.61

Transparency 74:
Teachers' Thought Processes
Related to Action

Transparency 76:
Influence of Teachers' Beliefs
on Teaching Behavior

Objective 3:
Discuss how an educational
philosophy affects classroom
management and planning.

Focus Question 2:
How do a teacher's instructional methods reflect an
educational philosophy?

How you manage your classroom and the content, method, and values you stress will be based on your personal view of the proper role of the teacher in society. A classroom philosophy must incorporate this larger societal view into other views that relate to student learning and behavior in the classroom. A teacher's practices in the classroom reflect his or her personal philosophy. The best goal for beginning educators is to become comfortable with a variety of classroom practices that address the needs of learners. It is not a matter of selecting one methodology over another but rather of understanding these different approaches and using them responsibly. We believe that a sound preparation for teaching addresses the need to develop a workable classroom philosophy—one that incorporates the larger role of teaching in a complex society as well as the micro role of relating to students in the classroom setting.

Classroom Organization

All teachers must be able to organize the classroom in such a way that it is conducive to teaching and learning. In fact, many school principals are quick to assert that the easiest way to predict the success of a beginning teacher is to determine his or her ability to organize the classroom. A common misconception is that good classroom organization means maintaining a controlled atmosphere and refusing to allow any behavior that even looks like it is ungoverned or unplanned. Actually **classroom organization** is a multifaced dimension of teaching that includes the content, methods, and values that infuse the classroom environment. It is a dimension of teaching that requires analysis and selection similar to that used in the identification of a preferred teaching philosophy. Figure 16.1 on page 413 shows how closely one's teaching philosophy impacts the different components of classroom organization.

Key Term:
Classroom organization

Transparency 80:
Developing a Philosophy of
Education

Information Note 16.3:
Another way of looking at
classroom organization is to
consider the *ethos*. This
Greek term encompasses the
total environment, not just the
teaching plan or approach.

**Journal/Portfolio
Development 1:**
Think about the different student seating arrangements in
various classrooms. Sketch
each seating arrangement
and describe the types of
student interaction and the
types of learning that each
seating arrangement sup-
ports. Draw a seating
arrangement that you prefer,
and describe the types of
student interaction and learning that it encourages.

Lesson Planning. Careful lesson planning is mandatory if effective teaching and learning are to follow. If the learners are considered to be passive, the lesson plan may emphasize absorbing the factual content of the subject matter. Adherents of teaching styles that consider the learners to be active participants (nonauthoritarian) would tend to emphasize processes and skills to be mastered and view the factual content of the subject matter as important but variable.

Regardless of the expectation for the learner, active or passive, the teacher needs to plan sound lessons. Every lesson should be built from a basic set of general objectives that correspond to the overall goals of the school district. This is not to suggest that every third-grade classroom in a school district should have the same daily learning objectives for the students. Daily lesson objectives can vary from classroom to classroom depending on the particular needs of the students being served. However, if those daily teaching objectives are closely related to the overall objectives of the school district, then cross-district learning will reflect the school district's overall goals.

Lessons should be tied to some form of teaching units. These units should be planned in detail to include suggestions for teaching the lessons, types of materials to be used, and specific plans for evaluation. Initially, these are all philosophic questions for the classroom teacher. How the teacher approaches these questions is very telling about his or her classroom philosophy.

The Physical Environment. The mere arrangement of classroom furniture and the use of classroom materials may be predicated on the teacher's perception of the learners as passive or active. Traditionally, the classroom has tended to be arranged in rows and columns at the elementary and secondary levels of schooling. This type of classroom arrangement has often been thought to be the best for classroom control and supervision. Often, however, the elementary teacher will rearrange the classroom into a series of small circles for special groupings in reading, mathematics, and other special subjects.

The nonauthoritarian philosophical view tends to support more open classrooms. The teacher intends learning for the students to be divergent in nature, and the student is expected to be more active in the learning process. This is not to suggest that one type of classroom arrangement is better than another or that one philosophy is superior to another, but we do suggest that the teacher in training examine classroom philosophy as it relates to the physical environment for learning.

Student Assessment. In assessing student progress and assigning grades, most teachers use a variety of techniques including examinations, term papers, project reports, group discussions, performance assessments, and various other tools. If the subject matter is treated as a bundle of information, teacher-made tests would tend to seek isolated facts and concepts as "right" answers, suggesting emphasis on convergent thinking. However, if the subject matter is treated as big ideas applicable to problem solving so as to emphasize processes and skills to arrive at several "right" answers, teacher-made tests would tend to allow for divergent thinking.

How you develop your classroom philosophy will also dictate the emphasis you place on a student's academic performance. You must decide whether a student is to be compared with his or her peers or with a set of expectations based on individual needs and differences. Generally, teachers who tend to be nonauthoritarian and look for divergence in learning will tend to place less emphasis on group norms. Teachers who favor an authoritarian role for the classroom with

Relevant Research

Teaching Cooperation

Cooperative learning is an increasingly popular approach to instruction. In cooperative learning, students work in small groups to help one another master academic material. The approach encourages teachers and students to view learning as a community process; learning is innately social and teachers as well as students depend on each other in order to create personal meaning. Studies that investigate the pros and cons of using cooperative learning techniques in the classroom have begun to emerge. Small-scale laboratory research on cooperation has a longer history than cooperative learning. This research showed that when people cooperated on different projects, they began to like one another (Slavin, 1977). Research on specific educational applications in cooperative learning began in the 1970s and is now in full swing. Studies seem to indicate that there are positive achievement and social effects if cooperative learning includes both group goals and individual accountability (Slavin, 1983, 1990). That is, groups must be working to achieve some goal or to earn rewards or recognition, and the success of the group must depend on the individual learning of every group member.

As a prospective teacher, you will need to determine how you can structure learning activities that focus on goal achievement and individual learning. One question you will need to answer is: "How does cooperative learning fit in a competitive society?"

Sources: Robert E. Slavin. "Classroom Reward Structure: An Analytical and Practical Review," *Review of Educational Research* 47: 633–650.
Robert E. Slavin. "When Does Cooperative Learning Increase Student Achievement?" *Psychological Bulletin* 94: 429–445.
Robert E. Slavin. *Cooperative Learning: Theory, Research, and Practice.* Englewood Cliffs, New Jersey: Prentice Hall, 1990.

a stress on convergence in learning will be more apt to favor student evaluation strategies based upon group norms.

Many teachers seek to inspire their students to want to learn, rather than simply to memorize information.

Objective 4:
Describe the influence of classroom practices on motivation.

Key Term:
Motivation

Discussion Question 3:
Teachers must be able to manage the classroom in such a way that the environment created is conducive to teaching and learning. How do you plan to manage your classroom to set up such an environment?

Focus Question 3:
How does the organization of desks and tables in a classroom reflect an educational philosophy?

Transparency 81:
Educational Philosophy and Classroom Space

Motivation

The meaning of **motivation** is derived from the word *motive,* which is an emotion, desire, or impulse acting as an incitement to action. This definition of motive has two parts: first it implies that motivation is internal because it relates to emotions, desires, or other internal drives and second, it implies that there is an accompanying external focus on action or behavior. Organizing a learning environment so that it relates to student needs and desires (internal) and also permits active participation in the learning process (external) is important to student motivation.

Teachers want students to be motivated to do many things: complete homework, be responsible, be life long learners, be on time, have fun, care about others, and become independent. However, it is not always clear how one sets up a classroom environment that ultimately achieves these desired outcomes. For example, if an authoritarian orientation toward teaching is employed where control is primarily in the hands of the teacher, students' motivation may suffer because they recognize that the task of teaching and the responsibility for learning is primarily the teacher's. Even if the teacher tells students that they are responsible for their own learning, students will not be internally motivated. In an authoritarian setting, motivation tends to come in the form of rules and regulations. Students are given clear directions concerning their responsibilities and they are expected to follow these directions since the teacher is in charge. For some students, this clarity of expectations and rules is comfortable. Students achieve because they must; in such a setting the second half of motivation (action) is achieved but not the first (internal desire).

In a learner-dominant setting, the responsibility for learning is primarily borne by the students. The teacher attempts to produce a climate of warmth and mutual respect. Students are encouraged to achieve specific outcomes, but ultimately, they are free to select those that most interest them. In this type of setting, the internal aspect of motivation is achieved in that students select the learning outcomes and processes that interest them; however, the second aspect of motivation (action) is not as clearly achieved in that students act according to their personal desires and these desires do not always match those of the teacher.

As a teacher you should arrange the classroom environment so that it matches your personal philosophy. Your task here is to carefully consider the "sources of power" that best reflect your philosophy of education. As many as five different power sources that relate to five different levels of motivation have been identified.[6] Power can be coercive where the motivation is "to obey." Power can take the form of rewards where the motivation is "to get." Power can be seen as legitimate where motivation takes the form of "respect." Power can be in the form of reverence where motivation is "to cooperate." Finally, power can be knowledge where the motivation is "to understand." Your philosophy of learning could include all of these sources of power. All of them may be necessary at some time or another. On the other hand, it is important to assess how you set up your classroom rules and environment and make certain that they match your personal understanding of where power should lie in the teaching and learning process.

Discipline

The attention given by the national media to disruptive behavior in the classroom has rekindled conflicting views regarding discipline. Polls of parents and teachers alike list discipline among the top issues confronting the schools. The main source of dissatisfaction for nearly two-thirds of today's teachers is the inability to manage students effectively. Teachers also are concerned about the effect disruptive behavior has on learning. The discipline dilemma—stressing more teacher control in the classroom, yet adhering to a more open philosophy that advocates less teacher control—precludes the development of a school discipline policy that would satisfy both views. Depending on the school district's expectations, the teacher may be caught between conflicting demands. Despite the personal philosophy of the teacher, he or she

Teachers may improve disipline in the classroom by involving students in management programs.

must address the wishes of the district when establishing classroom management schemes. The division of views on classroom discipline has inspired numerous books to assist teachers with discipline problems, and many special courses and workshops have been developed to deal with classroom discipline strategies. Since very few beginning teachers are given extensive exposure to discipline strategies in teacher preparation programs, the vast range of alternatives makes it difficult to decide on strategies for teachers who have yet to develop their own styles.

Glickman and Wolfgang have identified three schools of thought along a teacher-student control continuum (Figure 16.2).[7] Noninterventionists hold the view that teachers should not impose their own rules, since students are inherently capable of solving their own problems. Interactionalists suggest that students must learn that the solution to misbehavior is a reciprocal relation between student and teacher. Interventionists believe that teachers must set classroom standards for conduct and give little attention to input from the students.

Journal Activity Master 16.1: An Assessment of Classroom Environment. Via a series of probing questions, students specify and assess their own classroom environment (setting, evaluation, and discipline approach). This activity provides a grid entitled "Classroom Environment" and asks students to analyze the entire setting in terms of their philosophy of education.

Journal/Portfolio Development 2: Design a metaphor for each of the educational theories that you have studied. Then design a metaphor for your personal educational theory and clarify how it compares to the other educational theory metaphors.

Teacher Control

Student Control

Low Teacher Control	Equal Teacher Control	High Teacher Control
High Student Control	Equal Student Control	Low Student Control
Noninterventionists	Interactionists	Interventionists

FIGURE 16.2

Teacher-Student Control Continuum

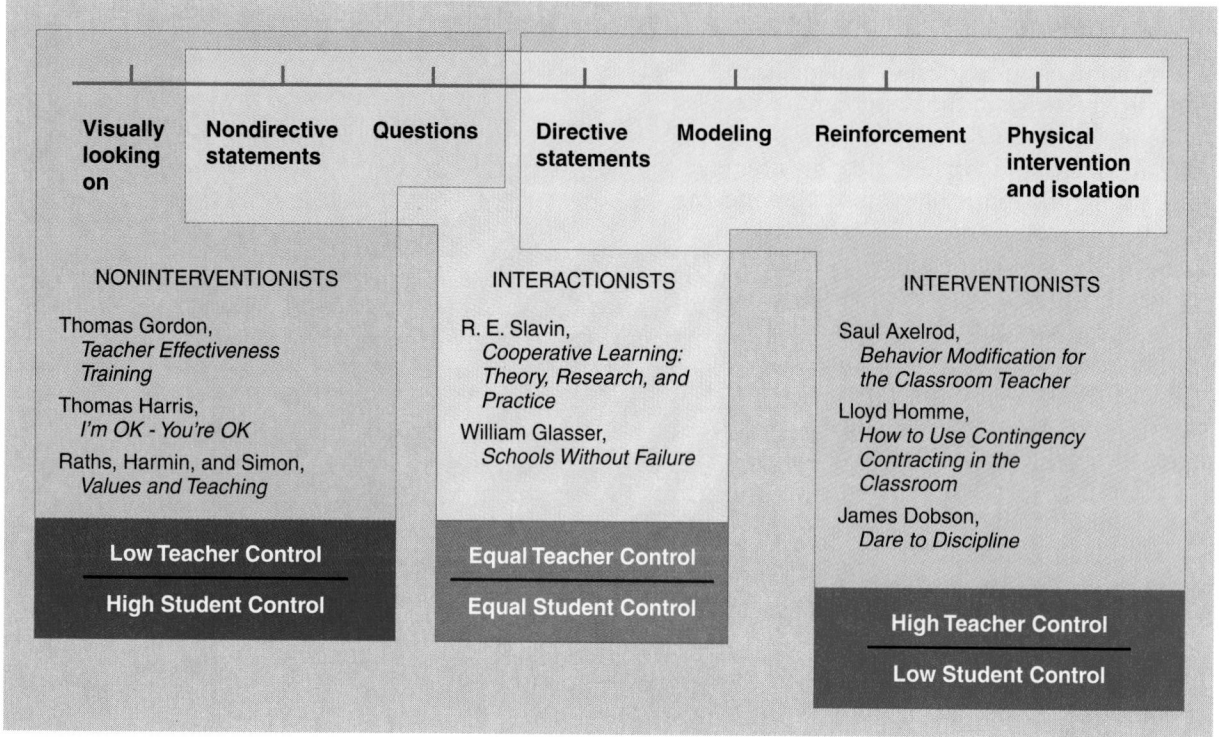

| Visually looking on | Nondirective statements | Questions | Directive statements | Modeling | Reinforcement | Physical intervention and isolation |

NONINTERVENTIONISTS	INTERACTIONISTS	INTERVENTIONISTS
Thomas Gordon, *Teacher Effectiveness Training* Thomas Harris, *I'm OK - You're OK* Raths, Harmin, and Simon, *Values and Teaching*	R. E. Slavin, *Cooperative Learning: Theory, Research, and Practice* William Glasser, *Schools Without Failure*	Saul Axelrod, *Behavior Modification for the Classroom Teacher* Lloyd Homme, *How to Use Contingency Contracting in the Classroom* James Dobson, *Dare to Discipline*
Low Teacher Control **High Student Control**	**Equal Teacher Control** **Equal Student Control**	**High Teacher Control** **Low Student Control**

FIGURE 16.3   Teacher Behavior Continuum

Focus Question 4:
Why is it important for you to understand the philosophical reasoning behind your intended discipline practices?

Objective 5:
Analyze the underlying differences among discipline approaches.

Activity 16.5:
Split the class into three groups (interventionist, noninterventionist, and interactionist). Have each group design a discipline policy.

Key Term:
Control theory

Activity 16.6:
Have students design a teaching environment that is challenging, reinforcing, and secure. Ask them to present their designs, and have the class evaluate whether the teaching environment exhibits all three qualities.

Beginning teachers are challenged to identify their own beliefs regarding discipline in the classroom in order to keep disruptive behavior at a minimum, thus enhancing the potential for learning as well as for job satisfaction. Where maintenance of discipline is the primary concern, one might choose from among the entire range of possibilities along the Wolfgang-Glickman continuum regardless of one's teaching style preference. Figure 16.3 illustrates how the major theories of classroom management relate in terms of control issues along the teacher-student control continuum. It is the professional responsibility of each classroom teacher to understand how each behavior may be used to support his or her preferred teaching philosophy. As you prepare to be a teacher, you need to examine control principles of classroom discipline.

Control Theory.   The notion of understanding **control theory** as a requisite for classroom discipline practices has been advanced by William Glasser. He suggests that a person's total behavior is composed of feelings, physiology, actions, and thoughts. How a classroom teacher controls these aspects of his or her behavior makes up an operational definition of control theory. Glasser asserts, "Control theory contends that we choose most of our total behaviors to try to gain control of people or ourselves."[8]

As a beginning teacher thinking about classroom discipline, you should recall that it is somewhat natural and human for students not to take responsibility for disrupting class or deviating from some classroom norms. As a matter of fact, teachers also find it difficult to take responsibility for some of their own behavior

PROFESSIONAL DILEMMA

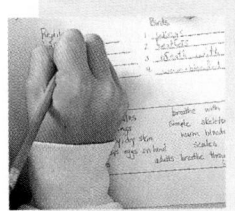

Should You Use Authentic Assessments to Grade Students?

There is a growing awareness that students should be assessed using a variety of methods that go beyond multiple-choice and essay examinations. Teachers are being asked to use students' journals, cooperative learning projects, interviews, portfolios, and other methods for assessing what a student can and cannot do. However, there is a debate concerning the appropriateness of using these more "authentic ways of assessing" for grading. The term *assess* comes from a Greek derivative that means to "sit beside oneself." When teachers grade a child, they are not only sitting beside the child, they are also making a value judgement. Is such a value judgement consistent with the notion of assessing one's strengths and weaknesses?

Some educators respond positively to this question of grading authentic assessments. They believe that society values some qualities more than others. Hence, it is appropriate to grade a student's portfolio. Other educators contend that such grading limits a child's creativity; it makes the assessments less authentic because there is an implicit standard that belongs to the teacher. Hence, teachers really are asking students to provide a certain type of portfolio; this makes the portfolio nothing more than a large essay-type test with portfolio entries as the correct answers.

You will need to determine your own answer to this complex dilemma. Should you rely on authentic assessments or merely use them as indicators of what a child knows or can do?

that deviates from the norm. It is usually being upset that causes some action and/or disruption by students and teachers. If you wish to be successful in meeting discipline challenges, you need to accept the totality of control theory. Accepting this means recognizing the elements of feelings, physiology, actions, and thoughts that make up the theory and working with students, counselors, and principals to attempt to adjust total behavior.

Discipline with Dignity.   Richard Curwin and Allen Mendler suggest that it is not enough to simply "control" students. Educators on all levels must help students learn to become decision makers and critical thinkers about their own actions. Their approach, called *Discipline with Dignity,* provides a method to teach students to take responsibility for their own behavior. The approach offers essential skills and strategies for dealing with angry, disruptive behavior while positively affecting the lives of students. The students learn to manage themselves as stress and pressures mount. The program emphasizes prevention by creating a positive classroom environment and sensitive communication. Students are viewed as partners in the process of ensuring positive, productive classroom environments.

Conflict Resolution.   Another approach to discipline, conflict resolution, focuses on the process of teaching students how to recognize problems and then productively solve them. Students are taught to be conflict managers and are trained to deal with difficulties on the playground, in the hallways, and in the classroom. They learn a specific set of skills to guide a discussion about the problem between two offenders. There are a variety of ways to train the student managers, but the underlying benefit is that the students solve their own problems with minimal assistance of adults. Advocates of conflict resolution contend that permitting students to share in the structure and even the enforcement of disci-

Diversity Note 16.2:
Home environment influences children's views about discipline. It is important to consider the community context of your school when designing discipline procedures.

Information Note 16.4:
Discipline continues to spawn a host of new approaches from assertive discipline to rational discipline. The notion of control underlies all these approaches.

Journal Activity Master 16.2: A Philosophical Analysis of a Textbook Lesson. Through a set of probing questions, students are guided through an analysis of the philosophies that underlie a textbook lesson.

Many teachers are successful with personal teaching methods.

pline policies is another way to help them learn to contribute to the school and to the society as a whole.

Discussion Question 4:
Identify some significant beginning classroom practices that a new teacher should try to develop if he or she wants to be judged a successful teacher.

Objective 6:
State the components of your personal philosophy of education.

Journal Activity Master 16.3: An Analysis of Your Own Educational Philosophy. This helps students create their own philosophy of education.

Rules for Discipline. There is no cookbook formula for establishing discipline rules and procedures for maintaining disciplined classes. There are, however, some general guidelines that will help the beginning teacher to establish some operating rules that will be accepted by students and practiced in the classroom. These guidelines are:

1. Students and teachers need to learn the importance of behavior and communication.
2. Students need to be treated with dignity. Students who are treated with dignity develop strong self-esteem.
3. Teachers need to apply critical thinking skills when creating disciplinary rules or analyzing needed disciplinary action.
4. Teachers need to examine how their actions of a social or instructional nature may have caused misbehavior.

The way the teacher introduces and uses these general principles for establishing rules for discipline will set the tone for classroom interactions, creating an environment that is conducive to learning and that minimizes classroom interruptions.

Classroom discipline strongly reflects the teacher's operating classroom philosophy. As you examine the educational philosophy that wins your interest and support, search for its applications to discipline in your classroom.

Global Perspectives: The World as Classroom. Throughout this chapter, you have been encouraged to examine your beliefs and assumptions in an effort to develop a personal philosophy of education. It is important to consider the limitations that such a philosophy can impose. For example, to what degree does your philosophy incorporate the larger world of thinkers? Does your philosophy affirm or disaffirm varied thinking schemes, varied beliefs, and varied ways of arriving at answers? Relating to our global neighbors is no longer a matter of respecting differences. If we are to truly relate and work collaboratively, our thinking schemes need to intermingle as well. Yet, a personal philosophy implies the development of a cohesive set of views about knowledge and the nature of the world. Balancing this need to intermix with the importance of clarifying an individual point of view is the challenge given us by the world classroom.

Focus Question 5:
During a job interview, what will you say when you are asked to state your philosophy of education?

Summary and Implications

While your classroom philosophy might not be completely committed to perennialism, essentialism, behaviorism, progressivism, reconstructionism, or humanism, you should be able to apply the characteristics of classroom philosophy discussed in this chapter to help you become comfortable with your own preferences for teaching. Prospective teachers, whether or not they have had educational philosophy coursework in their preparation programs, should find this practical classroom philosophy treatment a useful way to study teaching behaviors to identify trends and preferences related to a teaching style or philosophy. Perennialist, essentialist, and behaviorist teachers encourage students to view the subject matter only as experts in that field view the subject matter. Such teacher behaviors exhibit an authoritarian curriculum trend encouraging convergent thinking. Experimentalists, reconstructionists, and existentialists encourage students to use the subject matter as a means of determining more than one answer to the question at hand. This behavior can be viewed as a nonauthoritarian curriculum trend encouraging divergent thinking.

Remember that there are no perfect teaching styles or teaching methodologies. As a new teacher, you need to know how to minimize the negative effects and weaknesses associated with any particular teaching style. The styles that emphasize convergent thinking tend to reward students for giving an answer that is the exact phrase the teacher wants. Teachers using such methods must be very careful with their responses, or students will not risk participating in discussion unless they are absolutely certain that they have the exact answer. The divergent types of teaching styles may, in contrast, require students to participate in interesting activities but not make them fully aware of why they are participating or what they are learning. If students are not required to justify the generalizations they make and are not made to see that they are learning many facts and skills, they may end up feeling that all answers are so relative that problem-solving processes

are not worthwhile. Teachers who know enough about themselves and their teaching styles to show students how to succeed with both convergent thinking and divergent thinking are well on their way to reaching the ideal of being healthy eclectics.

In addition to understanding and practicing a teaching philosophy, all teachers must be prepared to integrate the several facets of classroom management in a way that is consistent with their teaching philosophy. Strategies for discipline maintenance, necessary to keep the number of problems at a minimum so that learning can occur, are very important for teaching success. Discipline is maintained when there is balancing interaction between teacher control and student participation. There are times, however, when a higher degree of teacher control is more effective.

The implications of this chapter are straightforward. Teachers who enter classrooms not understanding or knowing much about their intended teaching styles, as well as not knowing which classroom organization strategies best serve their philosophies, cannot be successful. We hope that from the material presented you will be able to begin to formulate your own classroom philosophy based on reality, knowledge, and value. Also, you should be able to envision how philosophical concepts carry over into and influence the educational views that are extant in our schools. These tasks are the theoretical, rational part of developing a personal philosophy of education.

Finally, to perceive a philosophy is one thing; to teach according to the philosophy is another. In teaching, one exhibits behavior that is compatible with a personal educational view. As long as this eclecticism serves the pedagogical purposes of the teacher and is a basis for consistent behavior by the teacher in the classroom, learning will take place. However, if eclecticism causes the teacher to change behavior frequently and with no apparent purpose, thus distracting pupils from learning, the teacher should reexamine her or his philosophy.

Discussion Questions

1. What is your vision of democracy in the classroom? To what degree should students be permitted to decide what they will study, when they will study, and how they will study? Why?
2. What characteristics or practices can you identify in a former teacher whom you would label your favorite?
3. Teachers must be able to manage the classroom in such a way that the environment created is con-

ducive to teaching and learning. How do you plan to organize your classroom to set up such an environment?

4. Identify some significant beginning classroom practices that a new teacher should try to develop if he or she wants to be judged a successful teacher.

Journal/Portfolio Development

1. Think about the different student seating arrangements in various classrooms. Sketch each seating arrangement and describe the types of student interaction and the types of learning that each seating arrangement supports. Draw a seating arrangement that you prefer, and describe the types of student interaction and learning that it encourages.

2. Design a metaphor for each of the educational theories that you have studied. Then design a metaphor for your personal educational theory and clarify how it compares to the other educational theory metaphors.

School-Based Experiences

1. While you are visiting different classrooms as part of your practicum experiences, catalog the various classroom planning and disciplinary activities that you observe. Following these observations and your recording of practices in real classrooms, classify the various styles that you have observed and identify the classroom philosophy that you feel the teacher was employing. Seek out opportunities to discuss

these findings with each of the teachers that you observe.

2. Select a teacher who has a classroom organization approach that matches your own. Set up an interview with the teacher and use probing questions to clarify the underlying reasons the teacher set up the classroom as he or she did.

Notes

1. Isaac L. Kandel, *Conflicting Theories of Education.* New York: Macmillan, 1938, 77–88.
2. John Dewey, "Education and Social Change," *The School Frontier III* (1937): 235–238.
3. Theodore Brameld, "Imperatives for a Reconstructed Philosophy of Education," *School and Society 87* (1959): 18–20.
4. Samuel Bowles and Herbert Gintis, *Schooling in Capitalistic America.* New York: Basic Books, 1975, 18–20.
5. Linda Tinelli Sheive and Marian Beauchamp Schoenbeit, "Vision and the Worklife of Educational Leaders," in *Leadership: Examining the Elusive.* Alexandria, VA: Association for Supervision and Curriculum Development, 1987, 99.
6. R. Schmuck, and P. A. Schmuck. *Group Processes in the Classroom.* William C. Brown, Dubuque, IA: 1983.
7. Carl D. Glickman and Charles H. Wolfgang, "Conflict in the Classroom: An Eclectic Model of Teacher-Child Interaction," *Elementary School Guidance and Counseling 13* (December 1978): 82–87.
8. William Glasser, *Control Theory in the Classroom.* New York: Harper and Row, 1986, 47.

Bibliography

Bloom, Benjamin. "The Search for Methods of Group Instruction," *Educational Leadership* 42 (9), (1984): 5.

Cornett, Claudia E. *What You Should Know About Teaching and Learning Styles.* Phi Delta Kappa Fastback No. 191. Bloomington, IN: Phi Delta Kappa, 1983.

Curwin, Richard L., and Mendler, Allen N. *Discipline with Dignity.* Alexandria, VA: Association for Supervision and Curriculum Development, 1988.

Glasser, William. *Control Theory in the Classroom.* New York: Harper & Row, 1986.

Howe, Kenneth R. "A Conceptual Basis for Ethics in Teacher Education." *Journal of Teacher Education* (May–June 1986): 5–11.

Kierstead, Janet, "How Teachers Manage Individual and Small Group Work in Active Classrooms," *Educational Leadership* (October 1986): 22–25.

Schmuck, R. and Schmuck, P. A. *Group Processes in the Classroom.* William C. Brown, Dubuque, IA: 1983.

Slavin, Robert E. "When Does Cooperative Learning Increase Student Achievement?" *Psychological Bulletin* 94 (1983): 429–445.

_____. *Cooperative Learning: Theory, Research and Practice.* Englewood Cliffs, NJ: Prentice Hall, 1990.

Part 6

School Programs and Practices

Dreamcatcher

SUSAN RAE BANKS is an Arapahoe Native Ameri-can from Deer Park, Washington. She received her B.A. in Special Education from Eastern Washington University and her M.Ed. from Gonzaga University. She has been a teacher in regular, special education, and integrated classroom settings working with Native American and non-Native American children. She continues her work with culturally diverse children and

their families. When she examined Section VI from the prospectus of the Dreamcatcher legend, she offered:

As an educator who has taught in a variety of settings with individuals from birth to fifty-eight years old, I have experienced the diversity among abilities and needs of students and their families. It is as this textbook tells it. One over-arching challenge that I believe new teachers must embrace with our ever-changing society and schools is to take the time to de-velop and internalize the art of flexibility. The teacher who allows for individual patterns to emerge and develop will become a stronger facil-itator of harmony and balance within the learner.

In order for the new teacher to feel confi-dent in allowing for individual patterns to develop, a knowledge base encompassing teach-ing models, strategies, and practices must be established. In addition, skills in developing and modifying curriculum to fit an individ-ual's learning path in culturally relevant ways is critical. This is especially true when one con-siders the movement of schools away from teacher-centered environments in favor of stu-dent-centered environments. This section of the text provides a solid framework from which a prospective teacher can begin to understand these practices as well as envision future educa-tional changes and challenges.

Throughout this entire text, the issue of diversity among stu-dents has been highlighted. The teacher's role is to celebrate this diversity by guiding each student through the educational web, be-ing sensitive to the potential good and bad effects of educational practices. This is as the ancients wished, with the "Dreamcatcher" that is sensitive, trapping dreams that are bad for the sleeper so only the good dreams are guided down the feather to the sleep-ing one below. Prospective teachers, follow the ways of the "Dreamcatcher" and learn the art of flexibility in gleaning the good practices for schools. In that way the learners you meet will be well served. Then, my grandmothers and their grandmothers will be happy!

School Programs

Chapter 17

Focus Questions

1 Why do beginning teachers need to be knowledgeable about issues that affect the curriculum?

2 What key questions should the teacher address before determining the type of school program needed for learners?

3 Why should teachers be able to plan school programs that address differences among learners?

4 Why should daily lesson plans and unit plans reflect the goals and aims of a school district?

5 Why should teachers continue to stress general education throughout the K-12 school program?

Key Terms and Concepts

Activity curriculum: A student-centered organizational emphasis that begins with broad topic identification for learning and weaves the related academic components into that topic.

Carnegie Unit: A measure of clock time that is used to award high school credits toward graduation.

Constants: An offering of learning experiences that make up an academic or vocational track in the secondary school.

Core curriculum: A student-centered organizational emphasis that combines broad areas of academic disciplines into manageable instructional units such as social studies and language arts for integration in learning.

Education for career: A specialty educational offering that promotes and prepares learners for postsecondary educational efforts and/or career initiation.

Exploratory education: An educational offering that is broad in scope and is used to introduce learners to a variety of learning areas that may be pursued in depth as possible career interests.

Fused curriculum: A subject-centered organizational program created with some merger of the academic disciplines such as reading, writing, and speaking into language arts as a subject for teaching.

General education: An educational offering that is common and required of all students.

Single subject curriculum: A subject-centered organizational program in which the academic disciplines are taught in isolation from each other.

Variable: An offering of elective learning experiences for secondary school students.

There is no dominant design for the specific curriculum offerings in school districts across the nation. Although the fifty state departments of education have some common elements in what they require generically for inclusion in the curriculum, considerable variance is found in specific program offerings. This variance is due to the regional differences within American society. An examination of the differences in the types of school programs is necessary for preservice teachers if they are to appreciate why these differences exist.

A key issue is how the curriculum should be organized. Teachers need to understand the differences among the broad purposes and aims of education, subject- and student-centered emphases in curriculum, and program requirements. Why and how new experiences are incorporated into school programs are vital questions for teachers if they want to create excellent learning opportunities for their students. All teachers need to grasp the intricacies of curriculum development—to know how to recognize and discard what is not useful and to adopt beneficial methods so that learners may profit.

Discussion Question 1:
Why should the general aims of education in the 1990s be different from those of the early 1900s?

Test Questions 17.1–17.15

Aims of Education and the Curriculum

The traditional purpose of education, which can be traced to the ancient liberal arts, stresses a selected set of learning skills and a vast store of selected information for students. *Traditionalists* assume that students who acquire the necessary skills and facts are "educated" and thus will behave as intelligent adults. Students are not expected or directed to use their native intelligence creatively; they are to learn passively and store knowledge for future use. Learning is the same for all: Knowledge that was relevant yesterday remains so today.

Transparency 83:
Hierarchy of Educational Aims and Objectives

CNN Clip 4:
Kids and Learning

Focus Question 1:
Why do beginning teachers need to be knowledgeable about issues that affect the curriculum?

Journal/Portfolio Development 1:
Research the National Goals for Education and assess how you can address these goals in your teaching area.

A contrasting purpose of education, stressing active student involvement in learning, evolved from the work of John Dewey and his associates after 1900. This position, referred to as *progressivism*, has not been universally accepted in practice. It is, however, still examined and studied as a school of thought; and as a theory, it has enjoyed considerable acceptance. Ideally, progressivism, expressed as learners' living and practicing in the learning environment, stresses active participation and practice during the learning period. Students are encouraged to use experience as a means to new learning. This philosophy suggests that learning is relevant; learning is life; students learn best by participating in learning.

New National Goals for education were proposed and passed in 1990, and the current Administration bases its educational recommendations and funding on these goals. The goals are as follows:

By the year 2000,

1. All children in America will start school ready to learn;
2. The high school graduation rate will increase to at least 90 percent;
3. American students will leave grades 4, 8, and 12 having gained competency in challenging subject matter;
4. American students will be first in the world in science and mathematics achievement;
5. Every adult American will be literate and possess the knowledge and skills necessary to compete in a global economy and to exercise the rights and responsibilities of citizenship;

6. Every school in America will be free of drugs and violence and will offer a disciplined environment conducive to learning.

Education for the remainder of this century has a monumental task if these goals are to be achieved.

Roles for Education

In formulating what the school has to do, curriculum planners frequently find that planning is easy but actualizing that planning is not. National, regional, and state commissions have all expressed their thoughts about what education should be. The school may see its job as reproduction, readjustment, or reconstruction—or some combination of these. These tasks are examined here as they relate to the philosophical concepts that prescribe the school and curriculum.

Information Note 17.1:
In a pluralistic society, the emphasis on one or two combinations of these roles varies by locale, state, and region.

Reproduction. If the school merely elects the role of *reproduction*, then its task is to transmit simply and unquestioningly our nation's cultural heritage to its youth. The subject matter that is selected should be what has survived through the ages. If the school is to fulfill only the reproductive function, the teacher must consider whether the subject matter has withstood the test of time and therefore should be included in the curriculum or whether irrelevant material may have survived along with the relevant. The teacher must also decide whether the relevant subject matter of yesterday is enough for today's youth. The problems associated with making this decision are increased by the vast and continually growing amount of knowledge that is available in our society. In addition to the old knowledge that must be passed on, there is new knowledge that continues to press for its rightful place in the curriculum.

Activity 17.1:
Have the students prepare a short list of purposes for a unit plan that models one of the three different roles of education (reproduction, readjustment, reconstruction).

Readjustment. Sole attention to *readjustment* calls for the school to gear its curriculum to social usefulness and efficiency. A curriculum for readjustment is concerned with preparing students for present-day adult life; it stresses civic training and social responsibility. Readjustment demands that the school retain parts of the past and also suggests that the school must do a certain amount of readjusting to meet current needs. Concentrating purely on this function may ignore some of the principles of child development and currently accepted psychology of learning. The child's need to understand and direct personal actions, the need to be able to adapt and organize in the light of prior experience, and the critical need for individual attention may be neglected when the theme of social utility is forced on the school. Readjustment, if it is the sole role of the schools, may tend to inhibit personal behavior changes that are necessary for adult life.

Reconstruction. The school that adopts the educational role of *reconstruction* establishes a curriculum that moves to the forefront of current thought and practice in society and strives to change the status quo. The school then undertakes not only to prepare young people for the future but also to prepare the future for young people. The school practicing this role is attempting to lead society; however, to date, schools in the United States have not accepted this role. In designing the curriculum the teacher must be aware of the pitfalls of this extreme approach and the hidden danger that past and current interests, traditions, and values may be sacrificed for the sake of change.

Focus Question 2:
What key questions should the teacher address before determining the type of school program needed for learners?

Objective 1:
Identify the roles of education as they relate to the different types of students to be served.

Information Note 17.2:
Remember that classification schemes often neglect overlap and intersection. They do, however, afford an opportunity for examining things systematically.

Discussion Question 2:
How should the school curriculum be altered to address problems of basic literacy and development of survival skills?

Activity 17.2:
Have students work in small teams to contact local high schools that have adopted some focus on vocational and college-bound students. Ask them to identify the differences in purpose and programs for these two groups.

Combination of Roles. Overemphasizing any one of the three roles for schooling—reproduction, readjustment, or reconstruction—would produce a top-heavy operational and philosophical concept that is inconsistent with the eclecticism needed today. These three functions must be constantly blended so that students will have the best opportunity to become self-supporting, self-respecting, and self-directing participants in American and world society.

Students to Be Served

In meeting these roles for the school, the teacher must recognize at least five broad categories of students that attend school. The number and kinds of these students will vary from school district to school district, but every school district has some mix of these types of students. Although the categories appear to be distinctly different, students may fall into one—or more than one—of them. In tending to multicultural concerns, keep in mind that these different types of students are found in all cultural groups.

Terminal Students—At Risk. These students, for various reasons, drop out along the way and have to be absorbed by society. Currently, national high-school dropout rates are between 25 and 30 percent, with minority groups having considerably higher rates. In fact, the minority dropout rate may approach 60 percent in many of the large cities of this country.

College-Bound Students. These students are preparing for higher education. Nationally, approximately 50 percent of high school graduates pursue study beyond high school. This figure is misleading, however, because it does not account for students who have dropped out before graduating from high school. The preparatory programs for the 50 percent must be varied because of the range of post–high school educational desires and opportunities. These students may

Recent trends seem to reflect a healthy job market for high-school graduates from vocational technical education programs.

attend two-year community colleges leading to terminal associate degrees or four-year institutions leading to baccalaureate degrees. The drop in higher education enrollments in the 1990s is due in part to the changes in family size during the 1970s and early 1980s. The number will probably be reduced even further because of declining secondary enrollments and young people finding an increasingly lower correlation between college education and job placement.

Focus Question 3:
Why should teachers be able to plan school programs that address differences among learners?

Vocational-Technical Students. These students are primarily preparing for jobs while in a comprehensive or vocational-technical high school. Some of these students, however, may further their education later on, formally or informally. Although the percentage of students who fall into this category varies according to the criteria used, it appears to be on the increase. Data on job placement for college-trained students suggest a job shortage, whereas data for vocational-technical students suggest a healthy job market.

Destination Unknown. These are students who have native ability but do not realize an expected level of achievement during high school. They are often referred to as "late bloomers," and it is not uncommon to find, in follow-up studies of these students, that increasing numbers of them are pursuing some form of postsecondary educational programs. Because many of these students did not focus on career goals while in high school, they often lack the prerequisite preparation for further schooling and find that they must fill in the gaps before they can go on.

Special Students. These students are identified as emotionally, mentally, or physically handicapped. Court decisions of the 1970s ordered that many special students be included as regular school students and accommodated by the regular curriculum. As was explained earlier in the discussion of Public Law 94-142, this federal law now mandates a least restrictive environment for learning for exceptional children. Many such students are now being mainstreamed and infused into the regular curriculum.

Relevant Research

Improving Achievement of Hispanic Students

Citing many of the familiar problems associated with the achievement problems of Hispanic youth, Christopher Howe's case study research reports on two exploratory studies that offered suggestions for addressing the needs of Hispanic youth and thus improving their achievement. The two studies found that:

- Successful programs placed value on the students' language and culture.
- These programs set high expectations for language-minority students.
- These programs had effective staff development efforts for the teachers.
- The programs had special counselors available.
- Minority parents were involved in the programs.
- The staff encouraged minority student empowerment.

As the Hispanic population continues to grow nationally, teachers need to improve their efforts to meet the needs of these students.

Source: Christopher K. Howe, "Improving the Achievement of Hispanic Students," *Educational Leadership* 51 (8) (May, 1994): 42–44.

Diversity Note 17.1:
As this section suggests, minority students are in all schools. The concept of "minority" encompasses more than race, culture, and language.

The best analysis of the current average school curriculum suggests that the needs of college-bound students continue to receive majority attention. If priorities were otherwise, the national dropout rate—especially for urban areas—would probably not be so alarmingly high. Some people feel the most slighted learner is the gifted child. Therefore, curriculum development should proceed from some special diagnostic attempts to identify the various kinds of students the curriculum is intended to serve.

PROFESSIONAL DILEMMA

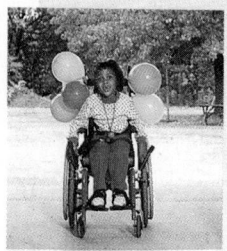

Can Teachers Adapt Their Classroom Philosophy to Meet the Diversity of Inclusion Students?

Except for the basic knowledge preparation you received about P. L. 94-142 in your teacher education program, you were probably never adequately prepared to accommodate and teach the full range of exceptional students. The school district where you have just begun your first year of teaching has moved to an inclusion program for exceptional learners. In your class are three students with exceptionalities of mildly learning disabled, emotionally disturbed, and cerebral palsy gifted. Prior to teaching you had assumed that these "special" learners would be accommodated for most of their learning in a separate

learning area designated as special education, with their own teacher, and if mainstreamed with you, it would only be for social and emotional growth purposes. Now, you have these special students for all of their learning activities; an itinerant special education teacher will come to your class as you need him or her.

Your dilemma at this point is:

- How will you redirect your classroom philosophy to handle this type of classroom diversity?
- How will you prepare a separate curriculum for these students or modify the regular one so the special students can share with the regular students?
- Where will you go for help with this problem?
- How will you work with the nondisabled students in their development of positive attitudes and behaviors toward the special learners?

Keep in mind that the best teachers value all of their students and that this attitude is visible to those they teach.

Test Questions 17.16–17.38

Transparency 89:
Two Foci of Curriculum Planning

Transparency 82:
Forces that Shape the School Curriculum

Objective 2:
Elaborate on the tenets of the subject-centered curriculum.

Information Note 17.3:
Outcomes Based Education (OBE) tends to lean heavily on subject-centered structures.

Activity 17.3:
Have students recall certain subjects they were taught in junior high school and how these were helpful in their education.

Key Term:
Single subject curriculum

Curriculum Structure

Any school system can choose its own pattern of curriculum organization. These patterns tend to range between the extremes of a *subject-centered* and a *student-centered* organization. Between the two extremes a continuum of curricular programs exists, and schools use various elements from either extreme or both. In general, curricular organization that tends to be subject-centered is content-oriented; if it uses a student-centered pattern, it is learner-oriented.

Subject-Centered Organization

By analyzing the curriculum continuum (see Figure 17.1), we can categorize patterns that offer separate courses for the various academic disciplines and those that fuse the disciplines under the broad heading "subject-centered patterns of curriculum organization." Correlated programs and activity programs are classified as student-centered organizations. You will recognize that the patterns of curricular organizations used by various schools often tend to be eclectic, borrowing from many sources. How a school district organizes its curriculum is related strongly to its philosophical position on the purposes of education.

Single Subject Curriculum. The **single subject curriculum** is the oldest and still most widely used in U.S. schools. In the modern, single subject curriculum, all the subjects for instruction are separated. In the extreme use of this approach,

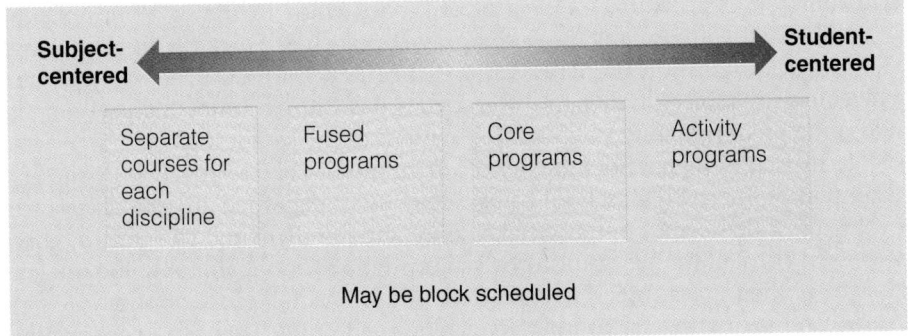

FIGURE 17.1

A Curriculum Continuum

the disciplines of knowledge are taught in isolation with no attempt at integration. The intent is to provide a discipline for students that alerts them to set classifications and to recognize arrangements of facts and ideas. An important criterion in selecting ideas for study is to choose those that have proved beneficial for solving problems of investigation in research. These facts and ideas are the ones that have lasted over time.

This curriculum calls for extensive explanation and oral discourse. The curriculum uses a formal, step-by-step study of ideas and facts; rarely are students expected or encouraged to explore or experiment on their own. The teaching methods include extensive verbal activities—lectures, discussions, questions, and answers—and written exercises such as term papers.

Supporters and defenders of the single subject curriculum argue that subjects that have withstood the test of time are the most worthy. They also contend that just because some children do not learn well in such a curriculum does not imply any inherent weakness in the curriculum organization. Supporters of this type of curriculum espouse an essentialistic philosophy of education, and advocates point out that not everything can be studied at once, nor can any study be all-inclusive. With the rapid increase in knowledge there simply has to be an ordered, segmented approach if one is to study a subject effectively. The separated subjects are a convenient way to clarify this knowledge so that it can be comprehended by students.

Fused Curriculum. The **fused curriculum** is an attempt to decrease the number of separate subjects that have gradually been brought into the single subject curriculum. In place of separate classes in reading, writing, spelling, grammar, speech, and literature, for example, the fused curriculum combines these subjects under English or language arts. The single subject curriculum remains almost intact, but students are introduced to the field as a whole rather than to bits and pieces. Subject matter goals are left whole, but the fused approach provides teachers and students more latitude within a broad subject area.

The fused curriculum has enjoyed its greatest success at the elementary level. Separate subjects, once taught for short periods during the day, are now more apt to be taught in a fused fashion over longer periods. Common fused studies in the elementary school center on language arts, social studies, general science, mathematics, art, music, and physical education and health.

In the past, junior high schools developed several variations of the fused program. Some schools combined language arts and social studies with block

Journal Activity Master 17.1: An Analysis of the Impact of Different Curriculum Organizations. Requires students to distinguish between subject-centered and student-centered lesson plans.

Activity 17.5: Have individual students outline a program for a specific grade level where they identify two different curriculum organizations for the same subject.

Key Term: Fused curriculum

Information Note 17.4: As one moves from fusion-type programs, the philosophy of what is important to be learned becomes more Gestalt-oriented.

scheduling, thus providing a longer period for teaching these two groups of subjects. Block scheduling puts two fused programs such as language arts and social studies back-to-back in the daily school schedule. However, in recent years the movement of subject matter to lower grades has caused junior high schools to adopt the predominantly single subject pattern of the senior high school.

In the senior high school the fused curriculum has had relatively little success. Examples of the few high school courses that are so patterned are general science, problems of democracy in the social studies, and family living. The greatest effect the fused curriculum has had on the senior high school is probably the integration of unified areas into single subject courses. Many high school teachers of American history now try to interlace a certain amount of geography and political science into their history courses.

Student-Centered Organization

Objective 3:
Elaborate on the tenets of the student-centered curriculum.

Focus Question 4:
Why should daily lesson plans and unit plans reflect the goals and aims of a school district?

Information Note 17.5:
The student-centered approach to curriculum offers the best chance of meeting diverse needs of learners.

Activity 17.6:
Divide the class into two groups. Have each group make a list of basic skills necessary for graduation from high school.

The concern for students' needs and interests has produced the *student-centered organization*. A student-centered organization describes either a core curriculum or an activity curriculum. In the past, and also today to some extent, these curricula have had both social and psychological interpretations. The current needs of youth are generally defined as what society expects of maturing young adults. While an extreme interpretation of the subject-centered organization stresses that learning is most effective if it is rigorous and difficult, the student-centered organization emphasizes encouraging students' interest in learning and their appreciation for it. When the interests and needs of learners are incorporated in the curriculum, motivation tends to become intrinsic rather than extrinsic. However, this description does not imply that the student-centered organization is directed by the whims of the learner; rather, it is based on the premise that learning is more successfully achieved if it is built on the interests the learner has developed before formal education begins. As you read about core and activity programs, compare and contrast the student-centered organization with the subject-centered organization.

Core Curriculum. The core curriculum grew out of a general dissatisfaction with the piecemeal learning promoted by the subject-centered organization. In trying to offer students a more enriching education, proponents of the core curriculum believe that subjects should be unified and new methods should be adopted. Since society has become increasingly fragmented, with more emphasis on science and technology, proponents of the core curriculum feel that the only logical approach to developing social values and social vision is through a core organization. The core curriculum may have different degrees of organization and may cross broader subject lines, but it places even greater stress than the fused curriculum on the need to integrate subject matter.

Key Term:
Core curriculum

The **core curriculum** emphasizes social values, and much time is given to studying the culture and its moral content. This curriculum promotes problem solving as a learning method; within this approach, facts, descriptive principles, socioeconomic conditions, and moral rules of conduct and behavior are stressed. In its purest form, the core is basically normative in its presentation; major focus is on topics such as the social needs of today.

CASE STUDY	PERFORMANCE-BASED SCHOOL PROGRAMS

*I*ncreasing numbers of school districts are moving toward performance-based school programs. These programs are the natural outgrowths of competency-based education, but are not as controversial because the local districts have greater control over what performance-based expectations will be. Since you, as a new teacher, have recently studied the pros and cons of these types of programs, you could be asked to serve on school-district-wide committees that are contemplating these curriculum activities. You have learned that many veteran teachers do not look favorably on these programs because they deviate markedly from the typical school program with which these teachers have become comfortable.

As you prepare to take part in this type of school district activity, you know that you should do the following:

1. Talk with colleagues about their interests in individualizing instruction.
2. Prepare reading materials that discuss individualization activities with a variety of diverse learners.
3. Plan to keep communication channels open with your colleagues so they are informed on the status of the committee's activities.
4. Have your colleagues try and give you feedback on the sample materials that are investigated and developed by the committee.

Your task will not be easy because the majority of the instruction in your district is of the large group variety. Most teachers have the same set of expectations for all of their students, and little differentiation is made between students with greater and lesser abilities. What are your views on these ideas?

Activity Curriculum. At the extreme right of the curriculum organization continuum is the **activity curriculum** (see Figure 17.1 on page 437). In its purest form it operates with the child as the sole center of learning. Since education, like life, is ever-changing, the activity curriculum expects to change continually. Students' needs and interests are assessed, and the curriculum is built on that assessment. The psychology of learning in this approach is based on the emotional involvement of the learner. Thus, if a child develops an interest in something and becomes emotionally involved with it, learning is enhanced.

The activity curriculum encompasses all subject matter. Completely flexible, the activity for the early learner may center on topics such as play, pets, toys, boats, letter carriers, or police officers. Emphasis is placed on observation, play, stories, and handiwork. This curriculum has several characteristics that make it distinctive. First, the interests and purposes of children determine the educational program. Second, common learning (general education) comes about as a result of individual interest. Third, this curriculum is not planned in advance, but guidelines are established to help the students choose alternatives intelligently as they progress through the program. Activities are planned cooperatively by students and teachers, and what they plan and pursue may or may not have any deliberate social direction. In the pursuit of planned goals, solving problems becomes the principal teaching method. Little or no need for extracurricular activities develops because all interests are accommodated within the regular program.

Key Term:
Activity curriculum

Activity 17.4:
Have the students design a lesson in which students' interests are the basis of the lesson.

Curriculum Contrasts

The subject-centered organization and the student-centered organization represent the two extremes of a curriculum continuum. These two organizational patterns can be contrasted in the following manner:

Objective 4:
Compare and contrast, using a graph matrix, the differences between the two major types of curriculum organization.

Journal Activity Master 17.2: An Analysis of Achievement Testing.
Helps students interpret different types of tests.

Subject-centered curriculum	*Student-centered curriculum*
Centered on subjects within the academic disciplines	Centered on learners and their diagnosed needs
Emphasis on subject matter to be learned	Emphasis on promoting all-around growth of learners
Subject matter selected and organized before it is taught	Subject matter selected and organized cooperatively by learners and teachers during the learning period
Controlled by the teacher or someone representing authority external to the learning situation	Controlled and directed cooperatively by learners (pupils, teachers, parents, supervisors, principals, and others) in the learning situation
Emphasis on facts, information, knowledge for its own sake or for possible future use; generally, lower-order learning	Emphasis on learning things to improve living and to solve day-to-day problems
Emphasis on specific habits and skills as separate aspects of learning	Emphasis on habits and skills as integral parts of larger experiences
Emphasis on improving methods of teaching specific subject matter	Emphasis on understanding and improving through the process of learning
Emphasis on uniformity of exposure to learning and uniformity of learning results	Emphasis on variability in exposure to learning and in results expected
Education conforming to set patterns	Education aiding each child to build a socially creative individuality
Education considered schooling	Education considered a continuous, intelligent process of growth

Global Perspectives: A Student-Centered Curriculum in New Zealand

Test Questions 17.39–17.54

New Zealand has the highest literacy rate in the world. The National Ministry of Education credits this achievement to the whole-language approach that is used in the schools and supported by teachers, parents, communities, teacher-training programs, and the national government. Although the system is legally controlled by the national government, there is a remarkable degree of autonomy encouraged and practiced by the local schools. In a sense, the local schools are like "charter" schools in England and those that are struggling to begin in the United States. The national government totally finances the schools, but local schools determine how the funds will be used. Nationally, the schools practice site-based management.

Children in New Zealand start school at the age of five. They come to school on their birthday, celebrate their birthday party, and move into the learning environment with the other children. The school environment includes: cooperative learning with an emphasis on small group and pair learning; multicultural immersion with special attention given to Maori, the indigenous people of New Zealand; use of journals in expression and evaluation; and total attention to readiness for learning and individual differences.

Teachers have a remarkable degree of autonomy in the schools of New Zealand. Although there is a printed national curriculum, the teachers are free to use it in any way they feel is appropriate for the special needs of their children. Teaching materials are not dictated nationally, but are developed at the local levels; however, the national government pays for the creation and support of these materials. Curriculum revision is led by the Ministry of Education, with considerable input from both professionals and the general public. Recent curriculum goal efforts for the country were begun using survey forms that were placed in and collected from McDonald's fast food chain outlets; customers responded to six questions about goals printed on the placemats. The data from this survey became the basis for further analysis and comment nationally.

Many of the current educational practices in New Zealand continue to be discussed as innovative practices in the United States. We have much to learn as we look at global efforts in education that seem to be successful at this time.

Journal/Portfolio Development 2:
Examine promising educational practices in one or two of the global nations and assess the impact of those practices on those nations' educational programs.

Program Requirements

Embedded in the operating program of the school are three broad academic components that constitute the function of the educational program: general education, exploratory education, and education for career. Their placement and emphasis depend wholly on the learner's needs as they relate to growth and development, the psychology of learning, instructional strategies, and various administrative arrangements.

General Education

General education is the broad area of the school program that is concerned primarily with developing common learning. Its central purpose is helping students to become participating citizens and well-adjusted individuals. Although general education is concentrated in the elementary school, some elements of it persist throughout the entire period of formal education. Although the other two broad areas of the school program, exploratory and personal education, include general education outcomes, they are not organized primarily for that purpose.

Basic Skills. The general education program concentrates on developing *basic skills* and introduces students to basic studies that include reading, composition, listening, speaking, and computing. Learners are expected to acquire creative and disciplined thinking skills that include different methods of inquiry and applying knowledge. General education also encompasses the humanities—an appreciation

The general education program concentrates on the basic skills of reading, composition, listening, speaking, and computing.

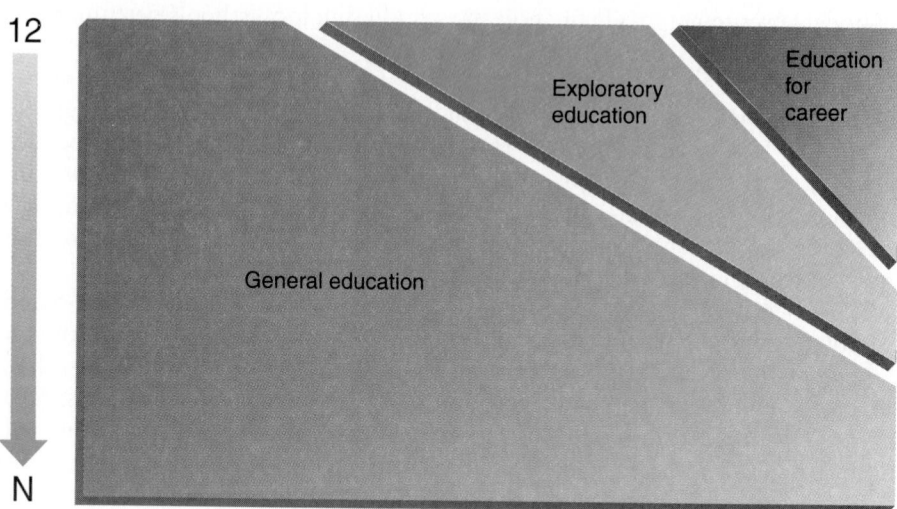

FIGURE 17.2

Educational Emphasis in the N-12 Program

Objective 5:
Explain the differences and purposes of general education, exploratory education, and education for career programs of the school.

Key Term:
General education

Focus Question 5:
Why should teachers continue to stress general education throughout the K-12 school program?

Information Note 17.6:
Attention to basic skills needs to address basic life skills also. Those skills are found in the curriculum requirements presented by Pennsylvania in its Outcomes Based Education programs.

Discussion Question 3:
Which type of curriculum, subject-centered or student-centered, do you prefer? Why?

for literature, music, and the visual arts—and the social and natural sciences. Within a general education program, learners are expected to acquire the essential, adult basic performance skills that are needed to function successfully in society. The way general education is accomplished varies among school districts. The identified components of common learning provide the core of general education in the elementary school and are improved and developed further throughout the total formal program of education. Figure 17.2 illustrates the general education emphasis for the formal N-12 structure.

One of the most perplexing problems facing general education planners is maintaining the placement sequence in the total scheme of education. As we have just seen, the number of years of schooling devoted to general education is determined by changing economic factors as well as by society's concern with efficiency and productivity. The people who demand accountability from today's schools have joined those who call for more general education. In the very recent past, the need for specialization caused a slackening of interest in general education and an increased emphasis on specialized studies and the applied fields. In contrast, the decades of the 1980s and the 1990s have shown more attention to the pressure for accountability in general education.

Career and Life Skills.   During the 1960s and 1970s, increasing public pressure caused some subjects to be presented earlier in the curriculum. Advanced skills and some special training, previously reserved for the secondary school, were introduced into the elementary school. It is now a regular practice to introduce the formal teaching of career and life skills such as foreign language, principles of economics, chemical and sex education, advanced principles of mathematics, and introductory programs for vocational career choices in elementary school. Although there are justifiable reasons for this introduction, they do not change the nature and purpose of common learning in the elementary program. Because of this expanded common learning for younger students, educators must reassess the general education program and possibly redefine the concept of common learning.

As preschool and early-childhood education receive increased philosophical and financial support, the general education program, identified as common learning for all, should probably be redistributed over a broader continuum, from nursery school through grade 12.

Exploratory Education

The **exploratory education** program is designed primarily for an educational organization unique to the United States: the junior high school. Depending on school district organization, the junior high, intermediate, or middle school continues general education and introduces students, on a limited basis, to a variety of specialized subjects. It is expected that the students will take these exploratory experiences and utilize them in making career decisions that they will pursue in senior high school and beyond.

Key Term:
Exploratory education

Junior High School. Following are five reasons for the existence of junior high school and for exploratory education programs:

1. The junior high school provides a transitional period, easing students' transfer from the elementary school to the high school. Junior high school is designed for students who are entering early adolescence, a trying period of growth and development. Since the transition period from childhood to adulthood is so critical, the junior high school is planned to accommodate the special physical, emotional, and social problems of this age group. In general, the students have come from an administrative unit that is child-centered, and they are preparing to enter one that is subject-centered. The junior high school has been planned to foster a gradual development of independence in learning and self-discipline. So that students have a "home base," block scheduling is sometimes used for the language arts-social studies program, and the teacher for this block has a better chance than others to know and help the students. Junior high school students also take several courses taught by specialists; in this way they are gradually introduced to the departmentalized, single subject senior high school.

2. The junior high school allows for the exploration of interests, aptitudes, and abilities, thus aiding the students in vocational and educational planning. The program introduces, in concentrated periods, such subjects as art, music, home economics, vocational education, and speech. The intention is that as the students progress toward senior high school, they will explore subjects in which they may specialize later. These exploratory programs may last nine weeks or one semester and are often offered on a rotating basis.

3. Junior high school students are introduced to an elaborate program of guidance and counseling that continues

The junior and senior high school programs should be designed to suit all students, regardless of their future plans for college or career.

through senior high school. This program is intended to help students plan intelligently for adult life. By using specially trained guidance personnel, the junior high school emphasizes development of wholesome attitudes for mental, emotional, and social growth among the student body.

4. Providing for variety in junior high helps to lower the school dropout rate. Variable programming considers the differing special abilities of youth, and its rationale stresses the important effects of the students' socioeconomic background on their interests, aptitudes, needs, and personality development.

5. Articulation of the total twelve-year school program may be stimulated by the junior high school. This administrative unit has the advantage of examining the elementary program and planning for articulation with the senior high school. Articulation is successful when all teachers within the school system work together to understand and appreciate the special tasks each must perform.

Like the elementary school, the junior high school has had to find ways to accommodate the continuing movement toward an earlier exposure for subjects. There is little doubt that the pressure of content requirements from the senior high school and the accompanying problems associated with Carnegie units of credits have caused the junior high school to become, as some say, "a senior high school in short pants."

The Middle School. By way of returning to the initial philosophy that guided the junior high school, many school districts have put the ninth grade back in the senior high school and created a new administrative organization of 5–8, 6–8, or 7–8, labeled the intermediate or middle school. The new *middle school* is intended to provide for the exploratory learning that the junior high school never quite achieved. Many of the early intentions of the junior high school continue for the middle school, with the exception of the ninth grade. Because of societal changes, improvements in health and nutrition, and more accelerated rates of physical and social maturation, ninth graders are much more like senior high school students today than they were when the original junior high school idea was conceived.

Middle schools are enjoying phenomenal growth during the 1990s. Since their early growth during the 1960s when 1000 such schools were reported across the nation, estimates for numbers of these schools today are over 12,000.[1] These schools emphasize problem-solving skills, reflective thinking processes, and individualized learning programs. Curriculum content is easily integrated, and the emphasis in instruction is that the teacher is a personal guide and facilitator of learning as opposed to a dispenser of knowledge. These schools stress the use of interdisciplinary teaching teams, greater attention to advisory programs, and increased exploratory exposure to unified arts programs. There is a decreased emphasis on content and competition so commonly found in the junior and senior high school.

Education for Career

The senior high school assumes the special task of uniting the foundations of general education with the introductions to exploratory education, culminating in a

Activity 17.7:
Have students visit a junior high school and/or middle school in the area and then identify whether they see exploratory education in practice.

Because of the large number of high school students who go on to college, high schools have tended to emphasize college preparatory programs.

rounded education that prepares one for an **education for career.** The senior high school will terminate formal education for many students, but it will prepare others for more advanced and specialized education in college or for special post–high school training. Because a large number of high school graduates go on to college, school systems are tempted to overemphasize the college preparatory program. However, the high school should offer programs designed to suit all students. Attention should be given to individual choice in establishing various programs. Although students can register in certain programs, they may take subjects in another curriculum. Presumably, each designation refers to special interest education.

Constants-Variable Program. The basic high school course requirements, more commonly referred to as **constants,** are required for all students; and many electives, the **variable** program offerings, become required coursework for a particular avenue of learning. Within the constants, however, additional provisions take into account the special needs, interests, and abilities of students. For example, a high school requiring three years of English may allow its students relative freedom in meeting this requirement. Other elective programs have, until recent years, provided this flexibility.

In continuing the program for general education (see Figure 17.2 on page 442), the high school has an established core of general courses required for all students. These requirements have traditionally accounted for seven to nine of the sixteen to twenty Carnegie units required for graduation. The national concern with the quality of education, as expressed in the many national commission reports, has led to an increase in the number of general education requirements for graduation. However, the requirements vary from state to state. Increasing numbers of states now require four units of English instead of three, two or three units of mathematics instead of one, and two or three units of science instead of one. The emphasis on mathematics and science is particularly heavy and comes at a time when there is a shortage of highly qualified teachers in these disciplines.

Carnegie Units. One **Carnegie unit** of credit is awarded for each class that meets for two hundred minutes of formal education a week for thirty-six weeks in the school year. The remainder of the units required for graduation are satisfied

Discussion Question 4:
How do purposes of general education and exploratory education differ?

Information Note 17.7:
Many of the tenets of the middle school are equally applicable to the junior high school.

Key Term:
Education for career

Relevant Research

Preventing Failure and Dropout among At-Risk High School Students

An action-research project was established in the Des Moines public schools to intervene against the failure and dropout rate of at-risk students in the middle and high schools. In this "school within a school" program, at-risk students were identified and assigned to smaller classes, with teachers giving greater personal attention to the students. The major goal of the program is to promote the social/emotional growth of the students. The program is also tied in to community programs and agencies for student referral activities. During the seven years that the program has been in operation, the dropout rate for the schools has decreased from 11 percent to 5 percent. Achievement and attendance rates for these students has reached the normal rate for the secondary schools.

This study suggests common-sense interventions for at-risk students. When given special services and modifications to the regular program, these students demonstrate success. It probably can be extrapolated from this study that the regular students would perform better if they also received benefits similar to those provided by this program.

Source: Randy Gordon, "The School within a School Program: Preventing Failure and Dropout among At-Risk High School Students." *ERS Spectrum* II (1) (Winter, 1993): 27–30.

Key Term:
Constants

Transparency 84:
Constants—Variable Program of the Senior High School

Key Term:
Variable

The senior high school will terminate formal education for many students, but it will prepare others for more advanced and specialized education.

by the elective programs for specialization and enrichment. The special programs vary in name, sequence, and scope, but the two most usual within the comprehensive senior high school are the tracking program and the constants-variable program. The main difficulty with the Carnegie unit system is that it does not take into account the research on student learning, which states that students do not all learn at the same rate, nor do they maintain a constant learning rate. Yet most American secondary schools continue to schedule students in established time modules that are consistent with the definition of a Carnegie unit given for time devoted to a particular experience. School systems simply do not apply sound reasoning supported by research when they conclude that all students need two hundred minutes a week of varied instruction for thirty-six weeks to accomplish one Carnegie unit successfully. If learning objectives are clearly specified, some students meet them in less time than others. The criterion for success should not be time or attendance; rather, it should be the successful attainment of the clearly specified learning objectives and minimum requirements. Many feel when students meet the objectives, they should be awarded the credit determined for the objectives.

Activity 17.8:
Have students speculate about what they would suggest for graduation requirements if they did not have to adhere to state minimum requirements.

Key Term:
Carnegie Unit

Journal Activity Master 17.2: Repeat activity for student-centered curriculum.

Information Note 17.8:
Outcomes Based Education (OBE) has begun to challenge the age-old Carnegie Unit system. States that are moving toward OBE are still mandating 180-plus-day school years, but let the expected outcomes drive the time-on-task with academic learning.

Test Questions 17.55–17.61

Objective 6:
Identify the characteristics of an effective school.

Transparency 86:
Concept Map for Effective Teaching

Extended Programs

Schools may be directly or indirectly involved in one or several programs that extend beyond the regular K-12 structure. These programs provide differing emphases in school organization and instruction, educational opportunities for very young children, job opportunity training for older adolescents and adults, and outlets for avocational interests for community members who live in the school district. The extent of these programs depends upon the wealth and desires of the community.

Effective Schools

The plethora of national school studies that have focused on the characteristics of excellence in education has spawned the *effective schools* research studies that have identified the characteristics and practices that hallmark an effective school. These studies have been gleaned from school district data that show high student achievement and are marked by certain characteristics that contribute to this achievement.

Program Characteristics.   The program characteristics of an effective school are as follows:

- The instructional program is goal oriented. Students know exactly what is expected of them as they pursue learning.

- There is constant and consistent assessment and monitoring of student progress. There is immediate feedback on student performance.
- Instruction is appropriate to the learner. Individual differences are given prime attention.
- The program gives emphasis to basic skills, including both academic and life skills.
- There is continuity of instruction across the grades. The staff works together to provide common types of learning experiences in all parts of the curriculum.
- There is effective grouping for instruction. Where grouping practices are used, they are flexible and correspond to the task at hand and the individual differences by task.
- Instructional time is organized to maximize the effectiveness of the "teachable moments." Students experience different time modules for learning.
- All lessons are adjusted to the students' needs. Teachers are concerned about the concept of "time on task" in learning.

Environment Characteristics. The environment characteristics are as follows:

- There is democratic administrative leadership. Fairness in leadership and fairness in decision making create a healthy environment that promotes sound mental health among teachers and learners.
- There is an orderly, safe environment. The social and academic environment is free from fear for safety for both learners and teachers.
- There is clear, firm, and consistent discipline. Learners know what is expected of them and practice that policy.
- There is a cooperative/family atmosphere. Students are encouraged to become part of an interactive family.
- There are few classroom interruptions. School announcements, visitors, and the like do not disturb the learning environment.
- There is parental involvement in student learning. Parents are encouraged and expected to be partners in their children's learning.
- The school exhibits positive community relations. The school invites community members to participate in the regular program and uses community resources.
- There are adequate facilities and learning materials. School district budgets provide teachers and learners with the type of materials and amount of equipment needed for each school's objectives.
- The school plant is well kept. Plant facilities are attractive and kept at a high degree of maintenance.

Expectations. School programs that encourage and enhance the professional sharing of ideas among teachers and provide inducements for those behaviors to occur become more effective for students. The "Pygmalion" effect is ever present in effective schools. When teachers hold realistic, yet high, expectations for their students, those students usually reach those expectations.

Discussion Question 5:
Why should every school be an effective school?

Information Note 17.9:
The Coalition of Essential Schools, with its philosophy of "relearning," is espoused by Ted Sizer. His coalition of schools has incorporated many of the elements of effective schools.

Vocational Education

The narrowness of the typical track program in senior high schools has undoubtedly contributed to the continuing shortage of high school graduates who are well prepared in the vocational-technical fields. All too often, students drift into the

Activity 17.9:
Have individual students select and defend what they believe the two most important elements of an effective school are.

Objective 7:
Compare the practices of an effective school with those of the typical public school.

Objective 8:
Elaborate on the purposes and programs of vocational education.

Activity 17.10:
Have students examine literature from several local vocational schools and indicate what they believe to be the critical selling points of those schools to prospective students.

vocational track because they cannot meet certain academic standards. Sometimes, educators forget that this kind of training requires students who are capable of both academic and vocational-technical work. But the constants-variable program can include training for students that has meaning for new industry and the changing economy. Too often in the past, and even today, vocational-technical training has tended to be obsolescent. However, the constants-variable program can stress work experience and on-the-job training that relate to school experience. Although general enrollments in education dropped dramatically during the 1970s and into the 1980s, shifts in enrollments to vocational education were tremendous. During this period, enrollments in career education increased by over 200 percent.

School Criteria. A well-conceived vocational-technical program meets the following twelve criteria:

1. The program is directly related to employment opportunities, as determined by school officials in cooperation with occupational experts and other competent individuals and groups.
2. The course content is confirmed or changed by periodic analysis of the occupations.
3. The courses for a specific occupation are set up and maintained with the advice and cooperation of the various occupational groups concerned.
4. The facilities and equipment used in instruction are comparable to what is found in the particular occupation.
5. The conditions for instruction duplicate, as nearly as possible, desirable conditions in the occupation itself and at the same time provide effective learning.
6. The length of teaching periods and total hours of instruction are determined by the requirements of the occupation and the needs of the students.
7. Training in a particular occupation develops marketable skills, abilities, attitudes, work habits, and appreciation to the point at which the trainee can obtain and hold a job in that occupation.
8. Day and evening classes are scheduled at hours and during seasons that are convenient to potential students.
9. Instruction is offered only to individuals who need and want it and who can profit from it occupationally.
10. The teachers are competent in the occupation and are professionally qualified for teaching.
11. Vocational guidance, including effective follow-up on all students who finish or drop out of a course, is an integral and continuing part of the program.
12. Continuous research is an integral part of the program.

Program Types. Gene Bottoms and Patricia Copa[2] list five types of general vocational programs and four types of occupationally specific programs. The general programs are as follows:

1. Consumer/homemaking, focusing on family life.
2. Prevocational as introductory or exploratory.
3. Prevocational basic skills.
4. Related instruction in occupational service, mathematics, and communication skills needed for specific jobs.

5. Employability skills for cooperative work programs.

The occupationally specific programs include the following:

1. Occupational cluster programs of comprehensive high schools. These programs provide for a broader curricular approach, such as the study of the field of electronics.

2. Occupation-specific programs for one particular occupation. An example of this type of program is computer technology.

3. Job-specific programs for an individual job within a broader cluster of occupations.

4. Employer-specific programs as needed or requested by particular employers.

The latter three specific programs are usually found in community colleges and vocational-technical schools.

This type of vocational training has brought about significant changes in the comprehensive high school. Since it is extremely difficult and costly for a local school district to provide adequate vocational training in the regular high schools, area vocational schools have been developed for students from several participating school districts. The area vocational-technical school can provide a great variety of career clusters for vocational curricula. They can also provide a far more comprehensive program than a local high school that attempts by itself to serve the needs of all its vocational students. Federal funding has assisted in this type of vocational training but not to the degree needed.

Early-Childhood Education

Numerous research studies have emphasized the benefits of early learning for preschool learners, and, as a result, early-childhood educational programs have grown in number and kind. Originally, early-childhood programs were viewed primarily as child care programs for working families; but they have now assumed, in addition to providing for that continuing need, additional tasks in the formal education of young children. Although they are found in a variety of settings from sponsored day-care programs to private self-supporting schools, their aims tend to be similar in their offerings for young children.

Objective 9:
Discuss the program effects of early childhood programs on learner preparation for elementary education.

Program Types. Current trends identify at least three types of early-childhood programs for young children. The first can be labeled traditional in nature, and it promotes a program that is not uncommon for most kindergarten programs in the United States. Depending on the age of the child, the program provides a readiness activity for the child as a preparatory stage for entering the public school structure. The philosophy of these pro-

Early childhood activities that develop children's curiosity and interest in learning contribute significantly to later success in school.

grams is similar to that practiced in the public schools and is basically essentialist.

A second type of program is associated with the behaviorist philosophy of education and, generally, is a behavior modification program. This program also provides day care for very young children and a preschool program for older early learners who are about to enter the public school system. The major difference between this program and a traditional one is its emphasis on a reward system for expected institutional performance of the learners. Reinforcement tactics predominate, and the young learner is schooled in the expected readiness competencies for the kindergarten.

The third major type of early-childhood program is referred to as the child development approach. Some of the current early-childhood theorists refer to it as a play curriculum. Its roots are embedded in the activity curriculum discussed earlier in this chapter, and it uses the play concept to help children get ready for the more formal learning atmosphere of the regular kindergarten. It, too, provides a day-care program for very young children, but it introduces more formal learning activities, via play activities, for the older preschool child.

Placement in the Curriculum. All of these programs remain outside the formal K-12 structure of the regular school, but program efforts have increasingly come to be seen as part of the educational continuum for learners. The promise of these programs is that they do promote individual growth in learners, and they undoubtedly have some important implications for the kindergarten and regular elementary program. That is, young children are entering the formal school structure with improved degrees of readiness. These individual differences among young learners are creating increasing demands on the elementary school to accommodate broader differences in readiness among learners who are beginning the kindergarten and first-grade programs.

Community Education

At the other end of the spectrum are adult learners who may or may not have completed their high school education. Increasing numbers of this group have also completed some form of post-high school education. As the U.S. population becomes older, the need for community education programs will grow. Pioneered by the Mott Foundation during the 1960s, community education programs have grown substantially since that time. Additionally, while the majority of early-education programs are not part of the regular school system's efforts, the community education programs are.

Adult Clientele. There are three types of adults whom community education programs must accommodate. The first is the returning adult student who seeks to complete his or her high school diploma. Growing numbers of these students are attending community education programs in order to increase their opportunities for worthwhile employment. The data that relate economic self-sufficiency with level of education are most compelling to individuals who have not completed a high school education. Many of these students seek the General Education Diploma (GED) offered by the community program, but some students are also returning to the regular classroom.

A second type of adult for whom community education programs attempt to provide is contemplating a career or job change. These programs may be offered in the evening at the regular high school or at a nearby vocational school or community college. The offerings may provide vocational training or a review of some of the basic skills that are needed to gain admission to some post–high school institution. The number of adult students returning to college and university campuses is on the increase, and colleges and universities are recruiting these students as the number of young applicants for admission declines.

The third type of adult to be accommodated by community education programs is seeking an avocational outlet for his or her leisure hours. As the adult population continues to increase, and as the percentage who complete high school and some form of occupational education increases, the need for community education programs that provide avocational offerings will also grow.

Future of Community Education. We see that the expression "education from birth to death" will take on new meaning as we move toward the turn of the century. Community education programs will surely be on the increase. However, the biggest deterrent to growth of these types of programs is finance. When recession periods and taxpayer unrest set in, the community education program is the first program whose viability in the school district will be challenged.

Diversity Note 17.2:
Adult students of the present and future will be heavily represented by minority parts of the population as these people attempt to fulfill education needs lost in the past. Some may even be returning to the regular high school, and teachers need to be prepared to meet the needs of this new type of clientele for the school.

Summary and Implications

Issues for the curriculum are constantly changing as society acquires new expectations. The teacher working in program development must be knowledgeable about current issues and how those issues bear on the purposes and aims of the school program. Applications of this knowledge assist the teacher in designing a curriculum with student- or subject-centered emphases. Within this structure, student needs must be addressed through general education, exploratory education, and education for careers.

The implications for program development are associated with increasing demands on the education program. Schools must still provide for the individual differences of learners. Increasing state requirements for general education place greater stress on members of the student population who have had difficulty in meeting traditional academic standards. If increased requirements lead to increased standards of academic performance for all, the school may find that it has an increase in dropout rates. How teachers meet this challenge depends wholly on how well they accept special responsibility for curriculum development. Students may be expected to participate in more courses in general education—namely, mathematics, science, and English—but the reality and applicability of these subjects to the real world of the learner will have to be addressed.

Discussion Questions

1. Why should the general aims of education in the 1990s be different from those of the early 1900s?

2. How should the school curriculum be altered to address problems of basic literacy and development of survival skills?

3. Which type of curriculum, subject-centered or student-centered, do you prefer? Why?

4. How do the purposes of general education and exploratory education differ?

5. Why should every school be an effective school?

Journal/Portfolio Development

1. Research the National Goals for Education and assess how you can address these goals in your teaching area.
2. Examine promising educational practices in one or two of the global nations and assess the impact of those practices on those nations' educational programs.

School-Based Experiences

1. When making a visit to a school for one of your practicum experiences, plan to secure a copy of the school's curriculum guide. Make an analysis of the guide to determine whether the school has implemented a subject-centered or student-centered curriculum. Then, observe several teachers in classrooms to see whether the classroom practices support your analysis of the printed curriculum. Discuss your findings with the teachers you observed and record their perceptions of the guide and their efforts to practice what the guide prescribes.

2. When visiting a school as part of your practicum experiences, secure permission to visit and observe two classroom teachers. Before visiting the classes, meet with each of the teachers and discuss their school's curriculum with them. In particular, ask them how their program provides for the general education needs of their students. Have them identify two such provisions for you. Observe their classes to see if you can identify the general education provisions that they enumerated for you.

Notes

1. Sylvester Kohut, Jr., *The Middle School: A Bridge Between Elementary and High Schools,* 2nd ed. Washington, DC: National Education Association, 1988, 7.

2. Gene Bottoms and Patricia Copa, "A Perspective on Vocational Education Today," *Phi Delta Kappan 64* (5) (January, 1983): 349–350.

Bibliography

Brewer, Jo Ann. *Introduction to Early Childhood Education*. Boston: Allyn and Bacon, 1992.

Elmore, Richard F., and Fuhrman, Susan H. *The Governance of Curriculum*. 1994 Yearbook. Alexandria, VA: Association for Supervision and Curriculum Development, 1994.

Fullan, Michael, and Stiegelbauer, Steve. *The New Meaning of Educational Change*. New York: Teachers College Press, 1991.

George, Paul S.; Stevenson, Chris; Thomason, Julia; and Bean, James. *The Middle School and Beyond*. Alexandria, VA: Association for Supervision and Curriculum Development, 1992.

Glasser, William. *The Quality School: Managing Students without Coercion*. New York: Harper & Row, 1990.

Oliva, Peter F. *Developing the Curriculum*. 3rd ed. New York: HarperCollins Publishers, 1992.

Tanner, Daniel, and Tanner, Laurel. *History of the School Curriculum*. New York: Macmillan Publishing Company, 1990.

Chapter 18

School Practices

Focus Questions

1 How do graded and nongraded schools differ?
2 How does the use of space affect the instructional program?
3 What are some of the important practices that teachers should look for when visiting schools?
4 What conclusions can be drawn about the grouping or nongrouping of students?
5 Why are testing and evaluating such difficult tasks for teachers?

Key Terms and Concepts

Articulation: The manner in which the various parts of the school program compliment each other in their relationship to a student's learning.

Authentic Assessment: An assessment of student learning that is based on real-world practice and attempts to measure learning in the same way it was acquired by the learner.

Continuity: Vertical articulation.

Graded schools: Schools that contain year-long levels such as first grade, second grade, tenth grade and the like.

Grouping: A practice whereby students are put into learning groups with others who have like abilities and interests.

Modules for learning: Time periods for learning that are in the daily schedule of the school.

Tracking: A method of placing students according to their ability levels in homogeneous classes or learning experiences where they all follow the same curriculum—that is, college preparatory or vocational.

When asked to describe an American school, one needs to create a picture that depicts the organization of space; the materials being used; the observed teacher, learner, and specialist behaviors; the grouping and learning patterns of students; the staffing arrangements of teachers; the pieces of written evidence that explain how things occur and what children learn; and so on. This brief list and many other pieces of observable, touchable, and experimental data constitute a patchwork portrait of the school. The interesting thing about this picture is that there will be as many different versions of it as there are people who are asked to describe the school. This chapter examines some of the easily identifiable school practices and discusses their impact on the teachers and learners.

Teachers and Space

The school building and the staff comprise the material and human resources of the school. How these resources are used determines the type of program that is offered to the student. It is important to remember that one of the most precious elements of the school is the professional staff. As a professional, you will want to take an active part in determining how your school organizes its staff and students for instruction and how the staff can get the maximum use of assigned space for instruction. Despite the fact that practices within an organizational structure and planned space vary from school building to school building, there are some commonalities among all American schools. We will discuss those in this section.

Organizational Arrangements

Test Questions 18.1–18.26

Objective 1:
Identify the various organizational elements of the school program.

School organizations vary from school district to school district, and various degrees of emphasis on particular practices will be found in any description of the American school. There are, however, general categories of operation that are found in all schools. What is different is how these categories are emphasized. That difference can be attributed to the diversity of practices, size and wealth of the community, geographical location, and community expectations.

Another point to consider is the school plant itself. During periods of rapid pupil population growth, school districts experienced a constant and growing building program. Various building styles addressed intended programs of the time. As enrollment growth dipped and stabilized during the late 1970s and the 1980s, school space became fixed. Currently, only districts that are experiencing growth because of the "baby boomlet" are again building new schools. Some of the urban districts are also facing the need to replace extremely old buildings that have been condemned for some time by safety experts. However, in all of these cases the economic implications for the districts dictate how creative a district may be in its organizational arrangements.

The school building and staff comprise the material and human resources that determine what kinds of programs and practices can be used with students.

Graded Schools. The **graded school** is a borrowed European concept for organizing pupils in some orderly fashion by chronological age. Historically, children in the United States have usually begun formal schooling at the age of five or six. In almost every state of the nation that practice continues today. A few states mandate the age of seven as the starting age for compulsory education, but most use the age of five or six. It became only natural that children starting their first year of formal schooling should be called "first graders." When they returned for a second year of schooling, they were called "second graders." Gradually, requirements and standards were established for each of the formal years of schooling, and the twelve-year graded school emerged. Because of the graded requirements, however, not all students spend twelve years in graded schools. Students who fail to meet some of the graded requirements along the way must repeat a grade or several grades, and they may spend more than twelve years in school if they wish to receive a secondary school diploma. The diploma, however, typically indicates the equivalent of a minimum of twelve years of successful formal education.

Most schools in the United States are graded schools. They provide organization of pupils by ages and have established standards for each grade. Some of the problems with this type of school organization are:

1. Graded schools do not account for differences in learners with regard to either academic readiness or social, mental, and physical maturity. For example, it does not necessarily follow that thirteen-year-old girls and boys, who are vastly different physically, mentally, and emotionally, should be grouped together as seventh or eighth graders in an intermediate school. Girls are typically more mature at this age than are boys, yet they are grouped with boys for learning. Nor are all five- or six-year-olds similar in maturity.

2. Graded schools do not account positively for what a child actually has learned when the school decides that grade-level requirements have not been met and the child is forced to repeat the whole grade the following year. As a result, early failure rates among young learners help to contribute to school dropout rates later in the graded school. Individual differences in learning rates and achievement are seldom attended to, and learners suffer the greatest diversity differences in these types of schools. Although many elementary schools attempt to address this problem, few secondary schools do anything about it.

3. Since most graded schools tend to use group rather than individual expectations for test performance, and since so few of the tests that are used meet accepted criteria for good test making, learners who do not meet standards for grade levels may be unfairly penalized by these tests.

Nongraded Schools. The *nongraded school,* as now defined, involves a school organization that allows each child to progress through the system at an individual rate of development. The lockstep grade-level concept, with its set curriculum for each grade, is abandoned in favor of an individual, flexible, and continuous educational program. Sometimes referred to as "continuous progress education," this plan guides students through a series of stages of development geared to readiness for learning. Students are grouped flexibly according to age, ability, maturity, achievement, and other developmental factors. Within this grouping, students are encouraged to move ahead through each subject at their own speed; their grouping varies with the progress they make.

The nongraded curriculum makes the final move toward complete dissolution of the lockstep graded system. When an elementary school becomes nongraded, the kindergarten and early grades are often simply designated as the primary school. The upper elementary school—grades 5, 6, 7, and 8—becomes a new unit

Information Note 18.1:
School programs should direct organizational arrangements rather than arrangements directing programs.

Key Term:
Graded schools

Focus Question 1:
How do graded and nongraded schools differ?

of organization labeled the intermediate or middle school, and the high school discards its strict traditional approach and graded pattern in favor of phases of learning and sequential development.

The nongraded school tries to minimize the shortcomings of the graded system, and the conventional grade designations of the typical American school are consequently discarded. With grade-level designations gone, able students can theoretically advance at a rate commensurate with ability. Whereas in the graded system it takes five years to teach the formal learning skills expected for grades K-4, children in nongraded schools might complete this learning in three, four, or five years. In addition, in the nongraded school, less able students may not have to experience psychological fear of failure or suffer the minimal learning associated with grade placement. They may take five or more years to master the necessary skills.

Most of the nongrading has appeared at the elementary level, although some high schools have attempted it. If nongrading were applied to all formal education, the curriculum could be divided into four parts: primary education, intermediate education, secondary education, and higher education. All these separate groups could be nongraded and could provide a continuous education organized around the individual progress of pupils. This type of organization more easily meets the needs of diverse students.

Instructional Organizational Elements

Teachers who are examining the operations of school organization should look for evidence of **articulation,** or interrelation, of the educational program. Too often, teachers tend to teach their own subject with little concern for what is taking place in other subjects in the same grade. Then teachers complain that there is little, if any, horizontal transfer of learning. However, a closer examination of this problem of poor articulation points to a lack of cooperative planning among teachers of the various academic disciplines. For instance, ninth-grade social studies teachers might feel little obligation to correct a student's careless English. In class the social sciences are emphasized, and teachers can easily ignore incorrect English usage.

Information Note 18.2:
A beginning form of non-grading can be made around primary units for five- to eight-year-olds; intermediate units around nine- to thirteen-year-olds; and advanced units around fourteen- to eighteen-year-olds.

Key Term:
Articulation

Objective 2:
Elaborate on the instructional elements of the school program.

Articulation Types. The same lack of horizontal articulation occurs between the mathematics teacher and the science teacher. The science teacher focuses on scientific inquiry and tends to slight mathematical exactness. Just as important as horizontal articulation among subjects is articulation within each subject. In many large schools where several teachers teach the same subject at the same level, they do not try to coordinate their presentations. Course guides and outlines, which theoretically could greatly improve the articulation within courses, do not even exist in many schools. Teachers tend to teach and emphasize what they want. With little or no supervision they go their own separate ways under the cloak of academic freedom. This lack of articulation also exists in large elementary schools among self-

Teachers can support students more effectively if they support one another.

Chronological Ages	4 - 8				8 - 12			12 - 15			15 - 18			IDENTIFIED CURRICULUM CONCEPTS
Grade Levels	K.	1	2	3	4	5	6	7	8	9	10	11	12	
	I	I	I	E	E	Re	Re	E	DS	DS	DS	DS		Concept 1
			I	I	I	I	I	E	E	E	E	Re	Re	Concept 2
														Concept 3
	I	Re	I	I	Re	I	Re	I	I	DS	DS	DS	DS	Concept 4
														Concept K

Key: I = Introduction to concept   E = Exploratory work in the concept
       Re = Reinforcement   DS = Depth study of the concept

FIGURE 18.1

Vertical Articulation in the Curriculum

contained classrooms. Rarely do elementary teachers confer with one another to correlate the educational program. Any constructive move toward horizontal articulation should probably begin within the narrower confines of the subjects themselves before addressing the interdisciplinary aspects of the problem.

Continuity.   Within the school's curriculum, **continuity** refers to vertical articulation. In addition to considering horizontal articulation, the teacher must be concerned with the interrelatedness of all grade levels of the school program and how they provide students with continuous learning. Figure 18.1 suggests one way of examining the vertical articulation of the total curriculum. It applies whether the school district uses grade levels or nongraded organization. Every discipline comprises established concepts that can be identified. Because some concepts are easier to grasp than others, some can be studied at an early stage of a learner's development, while others must be introduced at a later date. The teaching staff determines what concepts will be taught and to whom, at what stage they should be introduced, and their rate of study.

Space for Learning

Since we work on the principle of mass education, the school manages and directs large numbers of staff and students at any given time during the school year. The way space is used within the learning environment has psychological implications. Humans—teachers and pupils—are very protective of their space, and teaching and

Key Term:
Continuity

Transparency 91:
Curriculum Continuum

Information Note 18.3:
These types of articulation and balance issues are best solved by employing team approaches.

Activity 18.1:
Tell students that they have unlimited funds, and then ask them to draw and label their ideal classroom.

Objective 3:
Identify various types of learning space used in the schools.

Journal Activity Master 18.1: An Analysis of a Competitive and a Cooperative Learning Environment. Helps students clarify that teaching strategies have implicit social objectives.

Focus Question 2:
How does the use of space affect the instructional program?

learning have a better chance of being successful when space is allocated in a way that is sensitive to such personal needs. As humans, we do not like overcrowding, and we do not like to have our personal space violated. It is important to address this psychological need when we look at space and staffing for the school program.

Fixed Space. Most school buildings have been constructed along conventional lines with large corridors and self-contained classrooms on both sides of the corridors. Library, physical education, and other resource rooms are conveniently located for easy access to students. Use of *fixed space* in this way usually supports a grade-level type of school organization. Flexible space for instruction is often lacking, and there is often little or no cooperation among teachers regarding space utilization.

Open Space. Open-space facilities tend to be larger instructional areas with movable walls, flexible learning environments, and instructional organizations that are nongraded. However, this type of space does not automatically guarantee an instructional program that is developed around the philosophy of open education. It does provide the capacity for nongraded organization. Instead of having corridors faced by small classrooms, with about thirty students per room, a school plant has large instructional spaces that can be kept completely open for varieties of instruction or can be reduced to smaller areas through the use of movable walls and furniture. A school that is configured like this tends to be more conducive to diversified instructional and grouping patterns. Although its popularity has increased rapidly during the past fifteen years, the open-space facility is still found primarily at the elementary and middle school levels.

One of the biggest problems associated with the intended use of open-space facilities is the lack of adequate preparation of teachers. When school districts contemplate the use of open-space facilities, they should plan for adequate in-service staff development. If teachers learn how to be more comfortable in open space, they are more likely to use it as it was intended.

Staffing and Scheduling

School districts have complete flexibility in determining how to use their staffs. Except for the requirement that they must use appropriately certified teachers to teach the assigned offerings in the curriculum, the districts may arrange the teachers in any feasible configuration for instruction. Most schools are organized around a line and staff concept with teachers reporting to department heads or grade level chairpersons who in turn report to the administrator of the building. This has been common for schools for many years, but following are other ways to organize staff for instruction.

Objective 4:
Discuss the different ways that teachers and related staff members can be organized for scheduling and teaching.

Team Teaching. The needs of students are more apt to be met when the students are exposed to varied learning experiences. In team teaching, learning can be most successful when large-group instruction (100 to 150 students), small-group instruction (eight to ten students), and independent study are combined. A teaching team, organized by subject or by a combination of subjects, can provide these three kinds of experiences. The distribution of time among the large groups, the small groups, and the independent study will vary according to the subject studied. Advocates of team teaching have suggested that, on the average, students should spend 40 percent of their time in large-group instruction, 30 percent in small-group discussion, and 30 percent in independent study.

Team teaching in both elementary and secondary schools may take different forms; the size and composition of the team may vary; and the teams may teach one subject or may cross subject lines. Some of the specific advantages offered by team teaching include the following:

1. The specialization of teaching, whereby the particular talents of a teacher are used to the fullest,
2. The improvement of supervisory arrangements, whereby team teachers critique one another's teaching performance,
3. The use of nonprofessional aides for routine duties, and
4. The expanded and multiple uses of many of the new teaching devices that aid the teacher.

The teaching team can be organized in two general ways. The first, a formal approach, is referred to as a *hierarchical* team organization. This approach is a line-staff organization in which a leader heads a team composed of regular teachers and teachers' aides. The second type of organization is referred to as a *collegial*, or equalitarian, team. There is no formal structure to this organization; leadership is shared or exchanged voluntarily, and all teachers receive the same pay and have equal responsibility and similar duties. Team organization is binding, however, in that although teachers enjoy a more informal organization, they must work together at a common task.

Differentiated Staffing. *Differentiated* staffing has added a new dimension to the pattern for team teaching. However, it is merely a refinement of hierarchical teaching. Specifically, it establishes a career ladder that links the paraprofessional job with the superintendent's office. Different levels of instructional personnel are created, and each level requires certain kinds of training and experience. The director of curriculum and instruction becomes the school district program team leader. Each instructional and research staff assignment carries specific instructional responsibilities.

Modular and Flexible Scheduling. The organizational terms *modular* and *flexible* refer to two different concepts in scheduling and should not be considered the same thing. *Modular scheduling* has existed for some time in both elementary and secondary schools. At the elementary level it has usually been associated with thirty-minute time blocks **(modules for learning)** and at the secondary level, with forty- to sixty-minute time blocks. The secondary school time blocks are tied to the instructional time allocation of the Carnegie unit. A modular schedule is just as rigid as the six- to eight-period schedule used for so many years in the secondary schools. In contrast, *flexible scheduling* uses smaller time blocks (mods), but the schedule changes regularly during the school year as students' needs and teaching objectives are altered for particular periods and types of instruction. Combining these two organizational concepts—modular and flexible scheduling—implies that the traditional organization for instruction can be changed to meet changing needs and concepts of learning as students pass through the school.

The regime of the six- or eight-period day of the typical high school does not allow enough flexibility for the best use of teacher and student resources and abilities. Classes tend to be the same size for everything, and the concern is maintaining an average teacher load. An increasing number of educators question the wisdom of devoting the same amount of time to each subject. Some subjects can be taught best in shorter blocks of time for fewer periods a week; others can best

Activity 18.2:
Arrange the students in random groups of three or more. Have each group be responsible for teaching one day's lesson for one grade level. Each member of each group should share in the workload of the group.

Information Note 18.4:
Teaming practices afford greater opportunities to meet special needs of diverse students.

Discussion Question 1:
How do different teacher scheduling arrangements affect student learning environments?

Key Term:
Modules for learning

be taught in longer blocks. Some classes may be intentionally kept small; others may exceed the regular thirty-pupil classrooms. The size of the class is best determined by the intended objectives.

Modular and flexible schedules have unlimited possibilities regardless of how the curriculum is organized—that is, whether it is subject-centered or student-centered. However, as one introduces flexibility into the pattern for instruction, a theoretical shift begins to take place; the philosophical rationale adopted for flexibility tends to direct programs toward student-centered needs rather than subject-centered goals.

Student Placement and Evaluation

Test Questions 18.27–18.49

During the past thirty or so years a vast collection of research has accumulated that consistently suggests that children do not all learn at the same rate or in the same way. However, schools have tended to ignore that research and to group children in manageable-sized clusters of twenty-five to thirty students per teacher, without regard to learning progress. The practice is based on tradition. As a beginning teacher, you will want to address the individual differences among your students. As we discussed in Part Two of this text, the student body with which you will interact over the next thirty or so years will increase in its diversity. Your concern for that diversity will be reflected in your practices to recognize and attend to individual differences.

Class Size

Objective 5:
Compare the issues of grouping, tracking, and classroom management associated with class size.

Focus Question 3:
What are some of the important practices that teachers should look for when visiting schools?

Determining the optimal class size for elementary and secondary schools continues to be an uncertain exercise. There is little doubt that if all classes could have a one-to-one ratio with teacher and student, learning and teaching conditions would approach an ideal setting. However, there are valid arguments that can be offered for learning environments that are something other than a tutorial approach with a teacher. Significant numbers of studies on class size conducted over the past forty or so years have concluded little other than the notion that students can learn in a variety of class sizes. Valid arguments can be offered for group learning activities in which the student is expected and encouraged to interact with his or her peers. In addition, for some learning objectives the student is expected to receive significant amounts of information, and this can best be delivered in large groups. The problems associated with "inclusion" of special education learners creates a new question for classroom size research.

Information Note 18.5:
A philosophy of classroom management is crucial for placement of students.

Instructional Management. Some guidelines that educational theorists have proposed for class size tend to be related to the intended objectives of the teacher. For example, if the learning objective is to have the student be a receiver of information, then class size may be any size that is manageable according to available space or attending personnel. But if the learning objective is to have students use information with other students in discussion, then the class size should be small enough that all members can participate with equal time. Classes for this type of learning environment probably should not exceed ten or twelve students. This size not only allows each student to become an active participant but also allows the teacher to observe critically each student's degree of participation as well as assess the quality of that participation.

Students often enjoy and benefit from interaction with other students.

Grouping. The special problems of ability grouping are closely related to any examination of a school's curriculum practices. Ability **grouping** refers to the way in which student groups are created for instruction. Generally, ability grouping has been defended as a way in which the teacher can provide more adequately for individual differences. Elementary schools have tended to group pupils by subject area within the self-contained classroom, and secondary schools have tended to group students by subject, as learners develop and pursue special interests. The usual effects of grouping have caused special and separate classes to be established for the academically talented, the slow learners, and the average learners.

Philosophy of Grouping. The position that school systems take on ability grouping depends largely on their conception of the individual child and of the general purpose of education. If the philosophical position of the school is focused on a predetermined curriculum, the school is more likely to support *homogeneous* ability grouping. In homogeneous grouping, the school uses some set of criteria (such as intelligence scores or achievement tests) to group like students. If, in contrast, the school is concerned about the personal and social development of students and believes in diversity as a technique of stimulating education, it is more likely to favor *heterogeneous* grouping. In heterogeneous grouping, the school intentionally puts students with a variety of abilities and interests together.

Despite the usual defense for ability grouping—that is, provision for individual differences—school programs still tend to be group-oriented, and individual differences are not given sufficient attention. Although ability grouping has been defended as a way to help increase learners' achievement levels, this defense is only weakly substantiated by research findings. Although many studies report positive achievement results for more able students, other studies report negative findings for less able students. One rather consistent type of research finding suggests more positive affective learning in heterogeneous grouping.

Key Term:
Grouping

Discussion Question 2:
What are the pros and cons of ability grouping?

Activity 18.3:
Have students working in groups design a lesson for a class of five students. Then have them design the same lesson for 25 to 30 students.

Diversity Note 18.1:
When grouping children on the basis of ability (intelligence testing) and achievement measures, minority children suffer because of a lack of equity in the social and learning environments of their lives.

Journal/Portfolio Development 1:
Develop a personal philosophy about your concepts and preferences in grouping students. In particular, base your philosophical tenets on your beliefs about students, their learning needs, their diversity, and their intellectual differences.

One of the chief difficulties in establishing truly homogeneous groups is the imprecise measurement instruments used to establish groups. Another constraint is the lack of flexible class and teaching assignments: It is almost impossible to select a completely homogeneous class when every class must have thirty students and when scheduling conflicts and student interests cause potentially valid diagnostic-testing data to be discarded. If the student population of a school district is a sample of the total population and if that sample is a mirror of some normal curve distribution, then class sizes cannot all be the same and still be classified as homogeneous for learning purposes.

Global Perspectives: Multi-Year Grouping in German Schools. German schools have not embraced behaviorism in learning to the extent that American schools have. Like many other European school systems, German schools emphasize studying the bigger ideas and theories, as opposed to learning the facts. Many German schools place students in heterogeneous classrooms and keep them with the same teacher for three or four years. This longer working relationship is potentially beneficial to both the teacher and the learner.

Since the teachers get to know the students better, they have a greater grasp of their students' learning patterns, interests, social skills, and emotional stability. This enriched knowledge of their students helps the teacher to prepare more meaningful learning activities and provide greater attention to individual differences. The multi-year grouping helps the students also. They get to know their peers better and are able to develop in a more socially safe environment where they can learn together and critique each other. All of this leads to greater understanding patterns on the part of the German students. This type of positive learning encourages thinking, risk taking, and personal involvement in the learning environment.

We know that grouping of this type exists in some schools in the United States, but it is far from the norm. As this country seeks to develop more heuristic approaches to be used in learning, the use of different grouping patterns may be considered. If students are to become better thinkers, perhaps they need environments where they can experience these behaviors in a safe, secure manner.

Grouping Problems. The potential for problems generated by ability grouping far outweighs the scant benefits to be gained by rigid grouping. Some of the serious problems associated with rigid homogeneous grouping are the following:

1. Teachers tend to favor teaching average or above-average groups rather than groups of low ability. Low-ability groups, however, are not always filled with low-ability students. These groups also become dumping grounds for learners with discipline problems, some of whom are not of low ability.
2. Students who are given labels of low ability usually perform poorly because of the teacher's low expectation of them.
3. Problems associated with social-class and minority group differences are usually increased with ability grouping.
4. Ability grouping tends to reinforce unfavorable self-concepts among children placed in low-ability groups.
5. Negative self-concepts are more severe among minority group learners who are assigned to low-ability groups.
6. For the learners, ability grouping does not enhance the value and acceptance of differences in society.
7. Although academically talented students achieve better in high-ability groups, low-ability students tend to perform poorly in low-ability groups.

Focus Question 4:
What conclusions can be drawn about the grouping or nongrouping of students?

Diversity Note 18.2:
Grouping as we know it in the United States is not generally followed in international settings. Generally, students of differing abilities and achievements learn together, many times in cooperative settings. This approach has much to offer to minority children with differing abilities.

Despite the many negative aspects of ability grouping, the advantage of using some limited and flexible grouping pattern is that it can contribute to teaching effectiveness. There is little doubt that the task of instruction—and the general intent to provide individualized programs—is made easier if the range of abilities and interests is reduced through grouping. If grouping remains flexible and is based on abilities, needs, interests, and social practices, and if students are not locked into fixed groups, the teacher can arrange instruction to achieve a set of appropriate objectives for a particular group.

Tracking. **Tracking** provides rigid, specified programs built on a system of prerequisite courses. A student who is identified with a particular high school program (such as college prep or business) stays "on the track" to complete the program and does not benefit from the flexibility associated with a constants-variable program. Rigid grouping practices are added, and the track becomes more specific. Although tracking programs were thought to provide for individual differences, they have introduced a rigid program of constants, with little elective participation by the student. For instance, one of the common tracks, the college preparatory program, has become a rigorous intellectual curriculum designed to prepare the student for more advanced learning. In so doing, it has tended to limit the student's development in aesthetics and appreciation of art and music.

The typical college preparatory program requires the student to satisfy requirements of four units in English, three in social studies, three to four in science, three to four in mathematics, three in foreign language, and at least two in physical education and health. These requirements total eighteen to twenty Carnegie units; therefore very little time is available for courses in art, music, drama, or practical skills such as computer science or driver education. These programs provide little other than instruction in the three Rs. The broader aspects of the basic, life-coping skills, aesthetic appreciations, the understanding of others, and any sense of the necessity for economic productivity are simply ignored in these rigid tracking programs. As state and local curriculum requirements continue to reflect tighter college-type programs for all learners, the nonacademic survival and appreciation skills may be placed in serious jeopardy.

Key Term:
Tracking

Activity 18.4:
Have the students compare the impact of a large class of 100 or more students, to that of a small class of five students. Have them respond to tracking, grouping, and use of materials.

Information Note 18.6:
Tracking programs have proven to be the greatest deterrent to providing for diversity. Diverse students usually are assigned to the "low" track and fail to receive the type of programs they need to become better educated citizens.

Measurement and Evaluation

Teachers have a variety of techniques to appraise the curriculum and student achievement. Using classroom tests, they can evaluate whether or not specific objectives set forth for a certain subject have been achieved. Although test results are used primarily for teaching and for determining grades, they also aid teachers in adjusting methodology and course content. Additionally, they may be used to diagnose learners' readiness before beginning instruction. Standardized tests give the school system perspective about its relationship to the state, regional, or national picture. A few words of caution should be offered, however, about standardized tests: They should not be considered an effective method of evaluating students, and they should not be thought so important that they alone determine the curriculum. If tests were to determine the curriculum, the program would lose the depth of richness it can enjoy with a creative teacher.

The teacher can conditionally evaluate progress toward educational objectives—associated with students' social development, educational and social interest, and values—by checklists, rating scales, inventories, and questionnaires. Teachers and guidance counselors can also assess the effect of certain kinds of cur-

Objective 6:
Compare and contrast the different methods of learner assessment in achievement.

Journal Activity Master 18.2: What Does Effective Mean? This activity helps to clarify the definition of effective schools.

CNN Clip 30:
SAT Advancers

TABLE 18.1   Norm-Referenced and Criterion-Referenced Data Contrasts

Norm-Referenced Data	Criterion-Referenced Data
Are gathered from instruments established from local, state, or national norms	Gathered from instruments established from local instructional objectives
Indicate how a learner or a group of learners has performed in comparison with peers	Indicate the degree to which a learner has achieved a particular learning objective or set of objectives
Tend to be valid and reliable according to some national expectations or norms	Have a high degree of validity to a set of learner objectives; reliability of the data, by usual measurement standards, is questionable
Indicate a student's overall performance, aptitude, or attitude on some broad continuum or domain—usually used for ordering pupils	Indicate a specific level of competency or development as expected by previously stated objectives; usually used for individual diagnosis and prescription

ricular changes by observation, interview, anecdotal records, sociometrics, sociodrama, and student autobiographies. The school system can use opinion polls, interview community employers, and follow up on graduates to judge how effective the total school program is.

Normative Testing. *Norm-referenced* (or normative) *data*—that is, data that are compared to local, state, or national norms—are easily obtained when teachers use standardized tests. In addition to the precautions mentioned earlier with regard to using them, an ever-present question is how effectively these tests measure a particular school program. They should be used with some degree of caution for student placement, and unless such caution is exercised in identifying and interpreting student progress, these tests may be detrimental in evaluating the curriculum.

Criterion Testing. *Criterion-referenced* data are gathered from instruments that have been specially designed to measure expected learning changes. Whereas the learner performance in norm-referenced testing is compared to the performance of other learners, criterion-referenced testing shows performance of the student against himself or herself. Criterion-referenced measuring instruments involve stated operational learning objectives. They do not yield test scores that indicate a percentage of achievement based on some class standards or norms; they do indicate how well a particular student has met the stated learning objectives of the teacher. If these tests are planned specifically to show minimum levels of learner competence, they can be valuable to the teacher, the student, and the parents. For instance, criterion-referenced tests not only yield total scores but also indicate how well each objective was reached. If certain objectives have not been reached, the students repeat the learning activity for those objectives only and do not repeat the activities that have been completed successfully. Instead of assigning grades for achievement, the teacher assesses pupil progress on a pass/fail basis. When these measuring instruments are used along with norm-referenced instruments, the evaluation of a curriculum, especially pupil progress, becomes much more accurate. Table 18.1 shows the difference between norm-referenced and criterion-referenced data.

Authentic Assessment

The move toward the use of **authentic assessment** has come about because of the serious limitations associated with the exclusive use of standardized-type and criterion-type assessment techniques. These two types of assessment techniques are limited in at least two ways. First, they only give a measure of a point in time, and it is extremely difficult to obtain a more complete picture of what a child has actually learned or accomplished. They also suffer from problems associated with obtaining adequate sampling. Second, with changing national, state, and local goals for education, which include self-direction, collaboration, complex thinking, quality performance, and community contributions in learning, the traditional means of assessment fall short of providing data that can offer a more accurate picture of just what a student can or cannot do. Thus, the move to more authentic approaches to assessment has gained momentum in measuring learning.

In addition, there is a more apparent need to relate assessment practices to instruction and learning. As more cognitive approaches to teaching and learning replace behavioral theories, it has become more important to assess learning in a more holistic manner, rather than just gathering data on discrete bits of knowledge acquired by a learner. Conventional types of test formats (objective and subjective) serve an important purpose for some pictures of learning, but they just don't provide the whole picture.

Authentic assessment is considered authentic when it directly examines student performance on a learned task. A collection of these assessment techniques (sometimes called *performance assessment*) makes up the total authentic assessment approach. This is accomplished by using a context or situation that directly displays what the student has learned. This text has proposed (with an introduction in Chapter 1 and portfolio activities at the end of each chapter) that you engage in a beginning form of authentic assessment by developing your own professional portfolio that shows what you have learned and what kinds of performances you have exhibited. We encourage you to think about how these techniques can be used with your students when you begin teaching.

To be authentic, assessment activities must resemble actual classroom and life tasks. Characteristics of authentic assessment are:

- The assessment closely resembles the way the student will encounter the task or use the knowledge in real life.
- The teacher and the student constantly examine what has been learned, and they jointly determine the limits of that learning.
- The assessment has the learner display learning in a variety of contexts, not just one.

Focus Question 5:
Why are testing and evaluating such difficult tasks for teachers?

Key Term:
Authentic assessment

Relevant Research

The Road Ahead for Performance Assessment

Eva L. Baker has summarized some of the next steps to be taken with performance assessment. Citing a variety of studies that have been conducted with performance assessment, Baker's research lays out the issues for evaluating the forms and quality of the measures to be used in challenging the advocates of alternative assessments.

The first challenge is the promotion of equity in performance. Equity is discussed as it refers to the meaningfulness of measures that hold students' attention and have a specific purpose that makes sense. Other equity issues include linguistic appropriateness and the issue of sensitivity that the measurement has for instruction. The major concern of this research report is that performance measures be subjected to the strict tenets of validity.

Source: Eva L. Baker, "Making Performance Assessment Work: The Road Ahead," *Educational Leadership* 51 (6) (March, 1994) pp. 58–62.

Information Note 18.7:
OBE programs call for the use of this type of assessment procedures.

One significant change in contemporary school practices is the variety of methods by which students are allowed to demonstrate their learning.

■ Assessment provides for active collaborative reflection by both teacher and student.

Methods Used for Authentic Assessment.   Traditional type test data can be used to provide part of the picture for authentic assessment. However, these types of data should be strongly supported by learning journals and logs that contain written descriptions, drawings, reminders, data, charts, conclusions, inferences, generalizations, and any other collection of notes and artifacts that have been developed and gathered by the learner during the learning process. Interviews and observations conducted by other students and the teacher can be recorded for immediate and later discussions. All of these activities need to be ongoing so that when examined collectively, real changes in learning behavior can be easily seen. Finally, this holistic set of authentic data should be collected and displayed in a portfolio. Teachers working with students in this type of authentic assessment approach will need to help learners acquire the skills necessary to gather and report these types of data. When successful, this measuring technique will replace the weekly student test approach and occur continuously.

Using a Portfolio.   Portfolios act as a compilation of a student's work based on a variety of criteria. They may contain beginning and ending performances on work or only the student's best work. They are collections of student performances that can be shared with parents, teachers, other students, and even employers. (The portfolio you are keeping with this text could be shared with a hiring school district.) The Northwest Evaluation Association offers this definition of a portfolio.

> A portfolio is a purposeful collection of student work that tells the story of the student's efforts, progress, or achievement in (a) given area(s). This collection must include student participation in selection of portfolio content; the guidelines for selection; the criteria for judging merit; and evidence of student self-reflection."[1]

PROFESSIONAL DILEMMA

Can You Prepare Authentic Assessment Tools?

As you start your first year of teaching, you are confronted with a very diverse class. In particular, the class has been heterogeneously grouped, and in addition to several Hispanic students who have a poor command of English, you have two inclusion students. Your principal has informed you that the district places a heavy emphasis on authentic assessment for students.

You have some initial breathing room because the supervisor is not requiring you to provide polished authentic assessment strategies for your first unit of instruction; however, she wants you to be more fully involved with this type of assessment as you start your second unit of instruction. You have about six weeks to get ready for your next unit, and the supervisor wants to see your assessment plans before you begin that unit.

Your dilemma is multifold.

- What will your second unit be?
- How will you determine what authentic assessments to use?
- Where can you turn for help as you prepare for the second unit?

Assess some of the techniques you can use with your class, and prepare some samples for the supervisor to evaluate. In particular, address the heterogeneous makeup of your class.

Some of the problems to be aware of when using portfolios are representativeness of materials, clear criteria for assessing, authentic work and extraneous response requirements, differences in interpretations, and conclusions reached by student and teacher. Portfolios should have purpose and be linked to instruction. They should be carefully managed and have *a priori* decisions made about storage and transfer, as well as ownership and access.

Authentic assessment is an attempt to make testing, both in and out of the classroom, more precise and less restricted. Its very name implies attempting to determine what students have really learned. When you are working with diverse groups of learners, this type of assessment yields superior data on what changes in learning behavior have occurred and to what level skills have been developed.

Grading. Evaluating student learning, or *grading,* is one of the most difficult tasks that teachers face. In a very real sense the teacher is labeling the student when an evaluation takes place. One of the major difficulties of grading students involves the evidence that the teacher has gathered on the student's performance. This evidence is usually obtained from paper-and-pencil test performance or some planned program of teacher observation of student performance. Two questions with which teachers must wrestle as they prepare to evaluate their students are the following:

1. Are the measuring instruments or other means of assessment that were used to evaluate student performance valid and reliable? In other words, do the classroom tests, or other procedures of authentic assessment that are used to determine grades, accurately and consistently measure what has or has not been learned?
2. Has the teacher sampled enough of the learning behavior to determine that whatever has been observed or measured truly reflects a student's performance?

Activity 18.5:
Ask the students to indicate which type of grading practice they prefer. Have them use their preference with two different grade levels that are not closely related.

Activity 18.6:
Ask the students to design a national grading system. They should also discuss and/or debate the purpose of these grades.

Grading is not an easy task, and many experienced teachers continue to have difficulty with it. How a teacher determines the grades for his or her students tends to be wholly related to the teacher's personal philosophy. A school district may determine what constitutes an A or B or C in a course, but the teacher learns how to adjust a predetermined grading program to his or her personal philosophy. Good teachers constantly search for fair and consistent approaches to grading.

Planning for Instruction

Test Questions 18.50–18.60

The key to success for any planned curriculum is how the intended curriculum learning experiences are delivered to the learner. Instructional practices in the schools may vary considerably, depending on expectations for student performance and the teacher's repertoire of instructional skills. The expectations for student performance should be based on clusters of learning objectives by discipline, grade-level, or combinations of disciplines in a nongraded school organization. Well-planned objectives assist the teacher in planning for instruction.

Types of Learning

Objective 7:
Identify the taxonomies of learning and the different types of objectives for instruction.

The broad aims that the many national committees and commissions have developed are valuable only if they have some relation to specific learning outcomes planned for the school. Teachers who are preparing to plan the curriculum, teach the subjects, and evaluate the intended outcomes should understand how planned objectives for learning are reached. Expected types of learning change as the world adjusts to change. Planning for different types of learning is never finished. The instructional planning activity is an active process.

Activity 18.7:
Ask students to evaluate their own style of learning. Have them list what factors are most important to their learning style.

Taxonomies. There have been several attempts to clarify and develop educational objectives. One is the comprehensive approach of Bloom and others—the taxonomy of educational objectives. These educators classified the objectives in three groups, or domains, according to the kind of learning to be produced: cognitive, affective, and psychomotor.

Information Note 18.8:
In the 1920s Ralph Tyler first proposed writing objectives addressing these types of learning outcomes.

- *Cognitive* objectives are concerned with remembering, recognizing knowledge, and developing intellectual abilities and skills.
- *Affective* objectives are concerned with interests, attitudes, opinions, appreciations, values, and emotional sets.
- *Psychomotor* objectives are concerned with the development of muscular and motor skills. These three domains are presented in Appendix 18.1 on page 483.

Convergent Learning. Teachers work with learners to develop at least two types of learning practice and behavior: convergent and divergent. These behaviors are associated with the lower and higher levels of the taxonomies. The sole objective of *convergent* learning is that the learner experience the discovery and manipulation of new (for the learner) knowledge but then arrive at closure and acceptance of a single solution or generalization before moving on to new learning. This type of learning is anticipated when the teacher's intent is to work with the learner at the lower levels of the cognitive taxonomy.

Divergent Learning. *Divergent* learning encourages the learner to explore, develop hypotheses, gather information to test those hypotheses, and arrive at a defensible conclusion. The student does not have to search for the one "right" conclusion because there is not one. This type of learning practice prepares students to search for and accept answers that are different from one another. Objectives that focus on divergent learning are derived from the higher levels of the cognitive taxonomy.

Models of Learning

Students are different. They learn at different rates; they have differing abilities; some are more able and some are less able; some learn more easily through some mediums of instruction, and others learn more easily through other mediums of instruction. Teachers should consider using appropriate models of mastery learning, programmed learning, and individualized learning in order to meet the different needs of their students.

Objective 8:
Compare and contrast different models of learning.

Mastery Learning Model. The *mastery learning model* attempts to address problems of learning rate and differences in ability. Although students of differing abilities and learning rates may work with the same or similar objectives, they are all still expected to acquire mastery or satisfactory achievement of the objective. Some students may be given more time than others, and some may be provided with opportunities at different levels of mastery in order to achieve the expectations. One of the keys to the success of a mastery learning model is the teacher's diagnostic and prescriptive work. Teachers must be realistic in their expectations for learners and be reasonably confident that what they desire in learning outcomes is achievable by the students with whom they interact. If mastery learning is planned to be sequential, then the student success rate is particularly important. Students need to experience success in learning.

Mastery learning models are difficult to employ if the school curriculum is rigidly fixed by grade level and all students are expected to master certain objectives every year. They are most effective in nongraded school programs in which time (by the year) is not as crucial. These programs are more flexible, and differences in learning rates can be attended to with fewer problems. Specific objectives for learners are still used, however, and clusters of students or individual students work with those objectives.

Programmed Models. *Programmed learning* can be traced to the early work of Sidney Pressy during the 1920s. Pressy was unable to promote his ideas to any extent during the 1930s, but B. F. Skinner presented them thirty years later. Since then, programmed instruction has gained significant acceptance. Although this model can be and has been used for application learning behaviors, it is perhaps best used for developing expected knowledge and comprehension.

Two approaches to programmed instruction are important for teaching. The first, linear programming, uses constructed-response frames for which the student must supply an answer. The student may receive immediate feedback to a single response or feedback only after a planned series of responses. In the second method, branch programming, the student proceeds to additional frames for learning only after correct responses are recorded; the learner is directed along an

Teaching practices now often favor interactive and hands-on learning experiences that engage students in learning.

alternative route for remedial or reinforcement activities. This branching technique is designed to help the student correct and understand his or her errors before moving on to an advanced series of frames.

Programmed instruction is considered to have the following advantages:

1. Students are free to learn at rates commensurate with their own abilities. Programmed instruction permits individual study. Fundamental subject matter can be presented through a program, providing the teacher additional time to work with pupils on an individual basis.
2. The confirmation-correction feature of the program provides reinforcement of learning and builds student interest.
3. Programs can be designed to instruct in affective as well as cognitive areas of learning.
4. Programming helps students to understand a sequence of complex material and has the potential for doing so in less time than formal classroom instruction.

One of the primary considerations to be made in using programmed materials is the student's reading level. Since programmed learning relies on the printed word, there may be damaging effects on the poor reader. Another consideration is that although programs can be designed for learning appreciation as well as for skills, not very much has been done for learning appreciation so far.

Individualized Models. Audiotutorial and *individually prescribed instruction (IPI)* models provide for individual pacing of learning activities. Direct student-teacher contact is at a minimum except when the teacher provides remedial, developmental, or enrichment services to the learner as a result of some diagnosis. One of the chief characteristics of these strategies is test-teach-test. From predetermined instructional objectives, curricular modules for individualized instruction are developed. For each module a diagnostic test is developed to measure, before instruction starts, how well the learner can reach the module objectives. After diagnosis, the learner proceeds through the instructional package and is retested at completion. If learners reach the expected criterion for the learning package, they go ahead at their own rate. The learning packages become individual tutors for the students. The task of the teacher is to monitor learner progress through diagnostic activities and testing.

The term *audiotutorial* refers to audiotape recorders for the instructional delivery system, whereas IPI may use a whole host of instructional delivery systems ranging from paper materials to computers. Teachers using IPI generally follow these steps:

Step 1: Administer a diagnostic test for the learning module, and establish entering behavior.
Step 2: Have the learner experience the elements of the learning module indicated by an entry-level test.
Step 3: Test the learner as he or she completes the module.
Step 4: If the expected criterion for the module has been attained, move the student to the next module and pretest.

Individually guided education (IGE) was developed by the Kettering Foundation's Institute for the Development of Educational Activities (IDEA) and the Sears Roebuck Foundation. The current activities of IGE are disseminated through two major

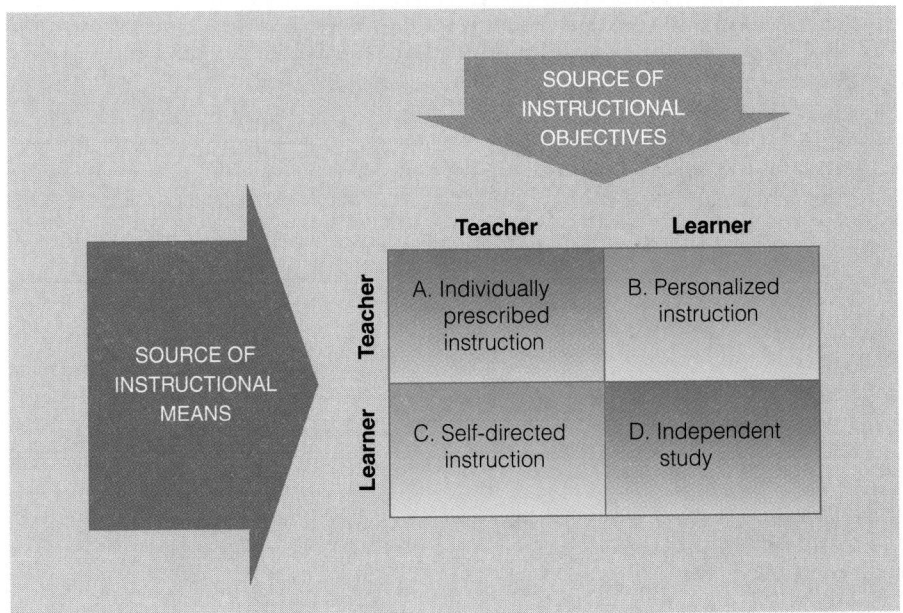

FIGURE 18.2

Individualized Learning
Matrix

national groups. One is the IGE Teacher Education Project at the University of Wisconsin, and the other is the national IGE Project operating out of IDEA in Dayton, Ohio. Whereas IPI takes all learners through the same preplanned program with identical objectives, IGE promotes different specific objectives for individual learners and is heavily process-oriented. Objectives are planned by the teacher and student. IGE strongly emphasizes both individualized and group learning.

There are many types of instructional models that offer a variety of approaches to individualized learning. Cecil Trueblood[2] developed a model for categorizing these varieties (Figure 18.2). The model illuminates the sources of objectives and the sources of means of instruction as a classification matrix for individualized learning. Programs in which the teacher determines the objectives and means of instruction are described as category A. Programs in which the learner cooperates on either objectives or the means of instruction are described as categories B and C, respectively. The most sophisticated type of individualized learning is one in which the learner determines his or her own objectives and means of instruction, category D.

Thinking Skills Model. A *thinking skills model* has at last assumed its rightful place among the learning models for instruction. Because it has been regarded for countless years to be part of the language arts program of the elementary school, little has been done formally in the classroom; it has generally been assumed that thinking skills have been taught by the teacher and acquired by the learner during the normal process of teaching and learning. Teachers now know, as a continued emphasis on learning theory enriches the teacher preparation program, that if you want learners to know and practice how to think, that process must be taught. Students must become more responsible for their own learning if learning is to continue after the student leaves the teacher.

Discussion Question 4:
How is the mastery learning model different from the thinking skills model?

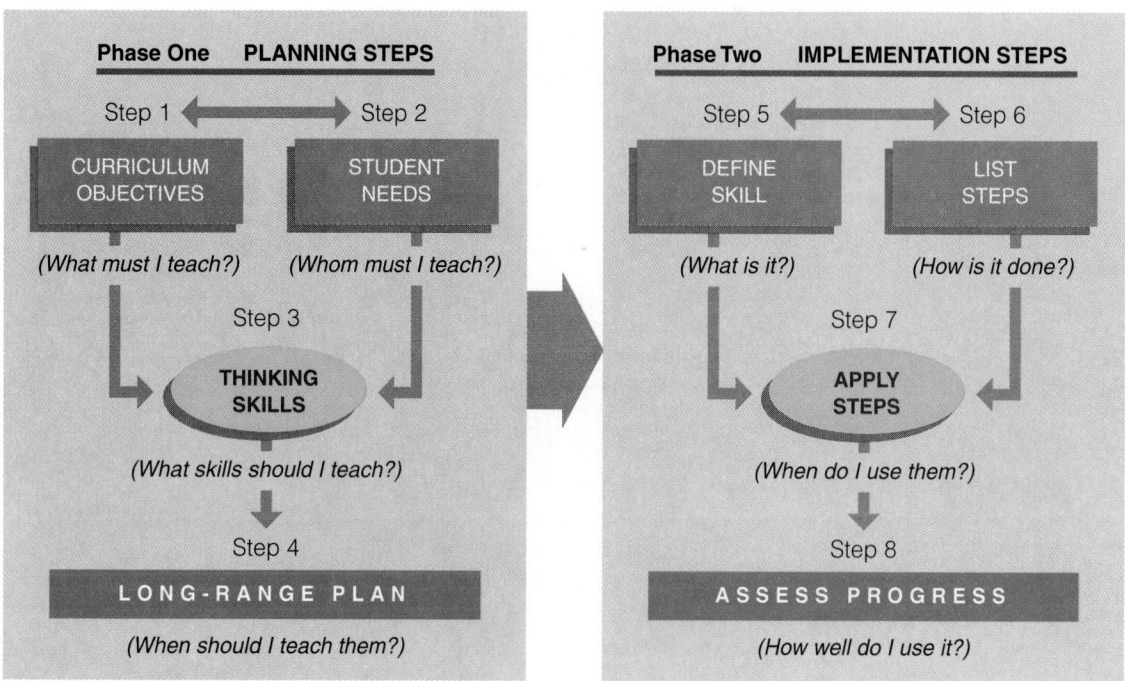

Thinking Skills Model

(Source: Antoinette Worsham, "A 'Grow As You Go' Thinking Skills Model," *Educational Leadership.* (April, 1988): 56–57.)

Activity 18.8:
Have groups of students choose a lesson to be taught. Then have each group suggest a way that the lesson might be learned. The groups should try not to duplicate each other's method.

Antoinette Worsham[3] has developed a thinking skills model, which is shown in Figure 18.3. Her model presents an eight-step approach for teachers to use if they wish to develop thinking skills while delivering their instructional program. As the figure shows, the model has two phases, a planning phase and an implementation phase. As the teacher works with the students, he or she uses an inductive process to work on skills. Students are instructed in how to ask the questions that are appropriate to skill development and content acquisition. Interestingly enough, this type of learning model holds great promise for transfer from one academic class to another. The model can be used with the cognitive domain levels to help students move from lower-level learning to higher-level learning. If the teacher has objectives for learning that can be ascribed to the hierarchy of learning, then the thinking skills model can be used to increase the achievement of those objectives. Students are encouraged to be reflective in their learning and keep logs of what they learned and how they learned it. The greatest strength of this model is that the students, if they have acquired the requisite skills, see its applicability to all of their learning encounters and the relationships in learning among the many disciplines they study.

Use of Technology

Test Questions 18.61–18.79

The past and current decades have witnessed an explosion in the creation of technological aids for teachers. This technology, however, has been slow in gaining regular use in the schools. Cost of equipment has certainly played a significant role, but among other factors retarding the use of available technology are the lack of training on the part of teachers and the dearth of educational materials available for use with the technology. These two factors are beginning to disappear; increasing amounts of new materials are now ready for use, and teachers are receiving additional training through staff development programs.

Learning Resource Centers

Instructional materials centers are valuable for a variety of instructional strategies. This type of learning environment is established not to replace a school library but to enrich it. The typical verbal materials found in a library are supplemented with software and hardware instructional materials. In any teaching strategy used, students may be assigned, or be free to use, a center to pursue learning on an individual basis or through small-group activities. The learning resource centers are equipped with books, programmed materials, closed-circuit television, and audiotapes, videotapes, and computers. A variety of other materials provide auditory, visual, and audiovisual learning.

Although learning centers were used initially at the elementary level, they are found increasingly in the junior and senior high school. As school districts use more varied organization and instruction, the need for learning centers becomes more apparent. The learning center has become more than an administratively planned area; it has become an adjunct classroom on which the teacher can plan for instruction. The only limitation to the learning center is the teacher's imagination as he or she develops objectives for learning experiences for children.

Hardware and Software. Teachers must be alert to the importance of being informed about the new software and hardware media. The terms *software* and *hardware* acknowledge that this is an age of "systems" and "systems development,"

Objective 9:
Elaborate on the differences in using various kinds of technology to assist in teaching.

Activity 18.9:
Have students visit a learning resource center. Ask them to identify the many different resources provided by the center and speculate how they would be beneficial to classroom learning.

Computers in schools are becoming as basic as pencils and paper.

but in their application in education they refer to human resources and learning materials and their uses. Examples of software are books, filmstrips, audiotapes, and transparencies. Examples of hardware are projectors, television monitors, and computers.

Such products have greater significance today for learning than ever before. With the acceleration of the amount of knowledge, and the effect of this on the curriculum, the American educational system has to keep finding ways to incorporate this new knowledge systematically into planned programs. American inventive genius and advanced technology have produced a vast number of devices, programs, organizations for instruction, and materials to help the teacher do a better job. While the lay person, the educator, and the academician have recognized and clarified the disciplines of knowledge, technological genius has produced mechanical aids ranging from very simple recording equipment to complex computers. Many of the new instructional media have become part of the vast educational team that will continue to produce more advanced hardware and software materials to improve learning.

Television.   *Instructional television* can be used as an open- or closed-circuit medium as an aid to instruction. With closed-circuit units, most often used within a school building or within a district, school districts can create their own instructional materials as local needs dictate while providing all learners with access to the best teachers in the school system. Open-circuit units usually receive television communication on a broader scale and not specific to a district. In both cases the television units use live or taped instructional packages for classroom use. The Communication Satellite System (COMSAT) has now opened new possibilities for mass education through television transmission anywhere in the United States. For formal class presentation, television has the capacity for reaching extraordinarily large groups of students. However, if instructional television is to be used successfully, it should fit into the general scheme of teaching. To allow it to become dominant in instruction is to misuse the medium, and if the misuse is allowed, the instructional value of television becomes as questionable as the single-textbook approach or overuse of the motion picture. Continuous evaluation of television instruction is all important, since as a medium of large-group instruction, its potential for misdirected learning or group indoctrination is ever present. Its primary emphasis should always be directed toward education—and not toward television for itself.

Microteaching.   Another use of television is to help teachers improve in instructional practices. Although television is not an integral part of many staff development programs, those programs whose main objective is the improvement of instruction will find the use of videotape equipment very beneficial. An increasing number of teacher-training institutions have adopted television, or *microteaching*, techniques. If the early efforts of teacher training are to be successful, school districts should provide television equipment and help for teachers who are trying to improve teaching skills. Through videotapes, teachers can watch their classroom performance and thus identify and modify or eliminate teaching weaknesses. Television is a valuable tool for the in-service training of teachers. Through videotape, many outside consultants can be brought to the school district, where in-service training is most effective.

Dial-Access Systems.   Dial-access audio and video systems provide more ways of individualizing instruction. *Dial-access systems* use a phone-type system to "dial up" preprepared learning packages that are used on an individual basis. These systems can be used either as the sole method of instruction for some parts of the curriculum or as a supplement to regular classroom instruction. Dial-access equipment was first used, on an experimental basis, in 1961 at the University of Michigan. Since then, it has been used primarily for language study. Use seems to be divided evenly between teacher-mediated instruction (instruction that is part of the teacher's planned lessons) and enrichment instruction (instruction that is provided for students who have completed all of the required work planned for all students). The dial-access carrels are conveniently placed in the school so that students can get direct help from a teacher if it is needed. The curriculum is built with instructional objectives, and students progress at individual rates based on diagnostic test batteries.

This particular use of technology creates time for small-group learning activities with teachers; students can pursue the required common learning through individualized dial-access systems. Another use of dial-access equipment is listening laboratories that accommodate small groups of students. These laboratories can utilize records or audiotapes. A more expanded use of existing language laboratories in many schools could provide similar instructional services that are being delivered by dial-access systems.

Videodiscs. *Videodiscs*, which resemble the old 78-rpm phonograph records, offer another significant advance in technology. These disks carry prerecorded video material or can be used to tape specific television programs for instructional use. Among the distinct features of this technology are the capacity for instant access to any part of a program and the high quality of still pictures.

Videodiscs, like videotapes, can be used for simulation programs and can help the teacher to move a step closer to the individualization of instruction. The combined use of these disks with microcomputers is currently being refined. The computer can be used to manage the individualizing of the instruction as the student proceeds through the videodisc frames.

Computers

Computer-assisted instruction has opened a new vista for individualized learning. When a computer is used, individual learning is limited only by what the programmer has put into the machine. The established techniques of linear and branch programming can accommodate individual or small-group learning sessions in a variety of ways. The computer now acts as a tutor in the learning environment. Through *computer-assisted instruction* a teacher can serve a large number of pupils and still have instantaneous

---

Relevant Research

Videodiscs Improve Student Outcomes

Optical Data Corporation, through its Educational Research Partnerships program, conducted a videodisc study in elementary science with their participating schools. The program is intended as a resource supplement to the regular program and features photographs, diagrams, movie clips, and animations. The videodisc program can be used for elementary, middle school, high school, and college level school programs. Optical Data provided staff development activities for the schools using the program.

Teachers using the program collected the data for Optical Data; it included both standardized type assessment and portfolio data. After one year of operation, the data indicated that students using the videodiscs had higher achievement levels than students not using the discs. Videodisc students had higher lab scores and better attitudes toward science. This study is continuing, but thus far, it suggests that students can do better in science when the regular program is augmented by videodiscs created for resource use.

Source: Heidi Marie Rock and Alysa Cummings, "Can Videodiscs Improve Student Outcomes?" *Educational Leadership 51* (7) (April, 1994): 46–50.

Objective 10:
Elaborate on how the teacher can use computers in the learning environment.

| CASE STUDY | SELECTING TECHNOLOGY |

School use of technology continues to have a significant influence on the school program. As new generations of minicomputers continue to emerge and costs come down, the use and impact of this technology presents an increasing demand on the schools. Add to this the fact that increasing percentages (estimated at 30 to 40 percent currently) of children are beginning school with a sophisticated degree of computer literacy. This is due to the increased numbers of computers in homes. There is a caveat to this growth among school learners, however. There is a growing discrepancy between the learners who come from the middle class and above, and those children who are coming from lower class poverty families. Many of the children of this latter group are also diversity children, and this has had an impact on the direction the school takes with regard to computers for learners. Despite this difference in learners, schools are continuing to increase their use of computers in the classroom.

You have been asked to serve on a school committee to evaluate and determine the technology needs for your school building. Most of the technology now in use centers around overhead projectors, film projectors and the like, and some closed-circuit television receivers. You have become a strong computer advocate since your undergraduate teacher education program. However, many of the teachers in your building have not fully accepted computers and retain some phobias about this technology. Your student body is somewhat diverse and has a significant number of students who are coming from homes without computers.

1. As a committee member, what tactics will you employ to win support of your colleagues in giving considerable emphasis toward computer technology?
2. What assumptions can you explore about the financial feasibility of technology enhancement for your school?
3. What plans should your committee address about how the school should begin to use computers with the diverse student body described above?
4. Should you try and involve the parents of children attending the school? Why?

The principal has indicated that he wants a report from the committee in time for a superintendent's meeting in the near future.

---

evaluation of pupil progress readily at hand. Thus the role of the teacher takes on new dimensions. Instead of merely dispensing knowledge, the teacher can be, with increased precision, diagnostician, prescriber of learning materials, and devotee of increased teacher-learner interaction.

Discussion Question 5:
Discuss the significance of the computer in individualizing instruction.

Simulation/Interactive Video.   Simulation programs for the classroom computer can be developed by the teacher with minimal knowledge of computer operation. *Simulations* present the learner with lifelike situations and are very successful ways to reach the higher levels of the cognitive domain of learning while having an effect on the affective domain of learning. When combined with computers for interactive video programs, simulation techniques can be made as real as life. As a teacher in preparation for a full career, you should be preparing yourself not only to be computer literate, but also to use the computer to assist in your regularly planned classroom instruction. Computers are now found in almost every school district of the nation. In fact, as reported by Quality Education Data of Denver, Colorado, twenty-one of the states plus the District of Columbia now mandate computer instruction in the schools. Some of these mandates are built around competency tests for graduating seniors, and others call for at least a mandatory offering in computer literacy.

Record-Keeping and Management. Just as the computer can deliver instruction, it can also manage the whole instructional and record-keeping program of a school district. Records of student performance and accompanying reports, use of materials, management of scheduling, and records of learners' progress are but a few of the possibilities of computer-managed instruction. The computer management system operating in the Admiral Peary Vocational-Technical School in Ebensburg, Pennsylvania, for example, monitors learning progress for the teacher. As students complete prescribed tasks, modules, and units of learning, the students' progress is recorded and stored. On completion of a specified vocational program the student is given, in addition to a regular high school transcript, a printout that shows the level of competency development for the whole program—the sort of information that is most meaningful to prospective employers. With this technology now available for use, you might think that teaching has been greatly simplified. On the contrary, teachers must now face curricular issues that were previously reserved for administrators and supervisors.

Mainframes. Many early computer applications required an expensive mainframe computer with accompanying terminals for student use. As the technology developed, schools had to keep changing models with each new generation of mainframes—a costly exercise. For a considerable period of time, computer-assisted or computer-managed instruction was therefore severely limited by cost, but the introduction of microcomputers has reduced this problem.

Microcomputers

The microcomputers that are now increasingly being used in the schools cost considerably less than the huge mainframe computers of the recent past. The popular Apples, IBMs, and the like, with their floppy and hard disks, are being utilized to answer the need for computer literacy and individualized instruction. The newer microcomputers use less sophisticated and more easily learned program languages for curriculum development. In addition, the computer industry has developed a vast storehouse of academic programs for use with computers.

Boons and Banes. There are three significant difficulties associated with the use of microcomputers for instruction. First, technology is expanding so rapidly that the market is continually being flooded with new, more sophisticated hardware. The question of which computer to buy is tied not only to the original cost but also to the life cycle of the model. For instance, in the short span of five years the Apple computer evolved through five models, each more capable than its predecessor. The PC market has seen the same type of growth.

The second problem is that software tends to be developed for use with a specific type of microcomputer and is not always compatible with other types. As newer models are introduced, there is increased compatibility of available software; but the problem still remains. Third, and perhaps most important, instructional staffs are not trained to program or use microcomputers as they were intended. Teachers cannot willy-nilly buy software and inflict it on learners. They

Activity 18.10:
Have each student give his or her own opinion on the use of computers in the classroom. Students should also formulate a list of everyday activities that can be accomplished with computers.

Transparency 92:
More Computers in Schools

Journal/Portfolio Development 2:
Select two pieces of software that can be used in your teaching field. Assess their appropriateness for a particular grade level of students, as well as their appropriateness as supplemental resource material or stand-alone instructional material.

need to be retrained to evaluate software in light of both planned objectives for the curriculum and learner models.

Microcomputers can be used in many of the same activities that initially required mainframe computers. Teachers who have become computer literate and have microcomputers available to them can now manage instruction with their computers and maintain sophisticated records on students. As teachers develop test items for the programs they teach, these items can easily be programmed into a computer for random selection when testing students. Software houses have developed voluminous amounts of computer software to be used in the classroom in all of the content areas, and teachers need to know how to evaluate software. Instructional programs and games are now available for mathematics, science, social studies, foreign languages, and the language arts.

Microcomputers have become a popular delivery system for meeting the needs of special education learners. The special education teacher can prepare the required IEP with the computer and then provide programs for the learner to use. The common expression in the microcomputer field today is "user friendly," and the stress in development is to provide simple, uncomplicated software that encourages teacher and student use.

Kyle Peck and Denise Dorricott offer ten cogent reasons for schools to increase their use of computers.[4] They believe computers provide:

1. Greater attention to students' developing and learning at different rates;
2. Assistance in students' acquiring proficiency in accessing, evaluating, and communicating information;
3. Help in improving the quality and quantity of students' thinking and writing;
4. Assistance in students' learning problem-solving skills;
5. A nurturing of students' artistic expression;
6. Help in students' developing global awareness and the ability to use resources that exist outside the school;
7. Opportunities for students' doing meaningful work;
8. Access to high-level and high-interest courses;
9. A comfortable relationship with the tools of the information age; and
10. Increased productivity and efficiency for schools.

Computer Futures. Computer literacy for the 1990s and beyond has become a new basic skill for all learners at all levels. Every daily encounter is somehow affected by computer technology. Current estimates suggest that by the year 2000, 98 percent of all households in the United States will have computers, which will be used for a wide variety of home activities. So why should you as a teacher prepare yourself to use the computer as a professional? Let us share with you at least five cogent reasons for you to become a computer user.

1. **Word processing.** As a teacher, you will constantly be producing reading materials for teaching—course outlines, handouts, tests, and so on. You will also be responsible for written student evaluations, communications with parents, and other paperwork. Word processing allows you instant creation and revision. If your written materials are kept on disk, you have the capability of easy revisions from semester to semester and year to year. As a side benefit, you will be modeling for your students a very practical use of the computer as they compose and write in the learning environment.
2. **Database information.** As a teacher, you constantly use data that you share with your students. The computer assists you in collecting and developing

databases that can be useful in your instruction in mathematics, social studies, business, language arts—with literary analyses and vocabulary building, science experiments, and many other areas. Additionally, the database information practice can be of assistance in the preparation of materials as well as determining how they were used and the outcomes of their use.

3. **Spreadsheet information.** As a teacher, you will also be a record keeper. The use of spreadsheets will free you from the traditional gradebook and help you to keep a considerably more accurate and up-to-date record of your students' performances. Routine activities at the end of a grading period, such as averaging grades, can be done automatically by pressing a few keys. Students who come and go during the year can easily be accommodated by your spreadsheet. The more literate you become in the use of the spreadsheet, the more you reduce your nonteaching load. As a professional, you want time to plan and teach, not to be a recordkeeper. Computers can help you to become a more effective professional.

4. **Use of CD-ROMS.** Many data-based programs are now available on a CD-ROM; they contain reading material, pictures, encyclopedia information, and stand-alone instructional lessons.

5. **Communication NETworks.** Through the use of Bitnet and Internet, teachers can now communicate with other teachers and programs around the country. The computer modem allows teachers to access libraries and their information storage facilities via telephone connection.

More than ever, teachers need to be computer literate. This textbook revision, for example, has been undertaken with the aid of computer technology. New word-processing programs now aid the authors in composing and editing text. Use of the typewriter has passed into oblivion. Thus the computer is more than just a tool for teachers to use in instruction. It is an instrument capable of mass communication and instantaneous decision making.

Transparency 93:
How the Internet Is Used

Summary and Implications

In examining the program of the school the teacher needs to consider several factors. Whether the school is graded or nongraded will affect the curriculum, the teacher, and the learner. Space, whether fixed or open, affects the type of operating school program. Scheduling practices affect both the teacher and the learner in the learning environment. How teachers test, the types of tests they use, and the way in which they evaluate students are all aspects of the picture of schooling. The instructional organization of the teachers' day yields further information about the operating philosophy of the school program. Technology holds the day in modern educational practice; how it is used depends on the teacher.

The implications of school practices are important for you as a beginning, and later a practicing, professional. You must have some knowledge of all of these areas in order to become an evaluator of school practices. Schools exist for learners; the learning atmosphere and the practices of the school reflect the attention given to the practice of quality learning environments. Finally, how the teacher uses technology will determine whether that technology is a sophisticated aid to the teacher or has become the teacher for the student.

Discussion Questions

1. How do different teacher scheduling arrangements affect student learning environments?

2. What are the pros and cons of ability grouping?

3. What do you think about authentic assessment practices?

4. How is the mastery learning model different from the thinking skills model?

5. Discuss the significance of the computer in individualizing instruction.

Journal/Portfolio Development

1. Develop a personal philosophy about your concepts and preferences in grouping students. In particular, base your philosophical tenets on your beliefs about students, their learning needs, their diversity, and their intellectual differences.

2. Select two pieces of software that can be used in your teaching field. Assess their appropriateness for a particular grade level of students; as well as their appropriateness as supplemental resource material or stand-alone instructional material.

School-Based Experiences

1. Visit a school and observe how teachers work differently with students as a result of homogeneous grouping. Discuss your observations with the teacher after you have had an opportunity to have the teacher explain his or her goals for different students.

2. Visit an elementary and a secondary school and observe the different uses of space. Write a paper that compares and contrasts the different uses of space in the two schools. Use organizational and instructional criteria for space as the basis for your comparisons. Verify your analysis with the administrators of the two schools.

Notes

1. Arter, Judith A., and Vicki Spandel, "Using Portfolios of Student Work in Instruction and Assessment," *Educational Measurement Issues and Practices* (Spring, 1992): 36–44.

2. Cecil R. Trueblood, "A Model for Using Diagnosis in Individualizing Mathematics Instruction in the Elementary Classroom," *The Arithmetic Teacher* (November, 1971): 507.

3. Antoinette Worsham, "A 'Grow As You Go' Thinking Skills Model," *Educational Leadership* 45 (7) (April, 1988): 56–58.

4. Peck, Kyle L., and Denise Dorricott, "Why Use Technology?" *Educational Leadership* 51 (7) (April, 1994): 11–14.

Bibliography

Educational Research Service. *Ability Grouping.* 2nd ed. Arlington, VA: Educational Research Service, 1990.

Joyce, Bruce, and Weil, Marsha, w/Showers, Beverly. *Models of Teaching.* 4th ed. Boston: Allyn and Bacon, 1992.

Marzano, Robert J., Pickering, Debra, and McTighe, Jay. *Assessing Student Outcomes.* Alexandria, VA: Association for Supervision and Curriculum Development, 1993.

Means, Barbara, and Olson, Kerry. *Technology and Education Reform: The Reality Behind the Promise.* San Francisco: Jossey-Bass, 1994.

Perleman, Lew. *School's Out: Hyper Learning, The New Technology, and The End of Education.* New York: William Morrow, 1992.

Sizer, Theodore. *Horace's School: Redesigning the American High School.* Boston: Houghton Mifflin, 1992.

U.S. Department of Education. *America 2000: An Education Strategy.* Washington, DC: U.S. Government Printing Office, 1991.

Wittrock, Merlin C, and Baker, Eva L. *Testing and Cognition.* Englewood Cliffs, NJ: Prentice Hall, 1991.

Appendix 18.1

Domains of Learning

The levels of cognitive learning are numerically ordered from the most superficial to the most advanced to establish a hierarchical arrangement for evaluating depth of learning.

Cognitive

1.00	Knowledge
1.10	Knowledge of specifics
1.20	Knowledge of ways and means of dealing with specifics
1.30	Knowledge of the universals and abstractions in a field
2.00	Comprehension
2.10	Translation
2.20	Interpolation
2.30	Extrapolation
3.00	Application
4.00	Analysis
4.10	Analysis of elements
4.20	Analysis of relationships
4.30	Analysis of organizational principles
5.00	Synthesis
5.10	Production of a unique communication
5.20	Production of a plan or proposed set of operations
5.30	Derivation of a set of abstract relations
6.00	Evaluation
6.10	Judgments in terms of internal evidence
6.20	Judgments in terms of external criteria

Source: Benjamin S. Bloom, ed., *Taxonomy of Educational Objectives* (New York: Longmans, Green, 1956), pp. 6–8.

Affective

1.00	Receiving (attending)
1.10	Awareness
1.20	Willingness to receive
1.30	Controlled or selected attention
2.00	Responding
2.10	Acquiescence in responding
2.20	Willingness to respond
2.30	Satisfaction in response
3.00	Valuing
3.10	Acceptance of a value
3.20	Preference for a value
3.30	Commitment
4.00	Organization
4.10	Conceptualization of a value
4.20	Organization of a value system
5.00	Characterization by a value or value complex
5.10	Generalized set
5.20	Characterization

Source: David R. Krathwohl, Benjamin S. Bloom, and Bertram B. Masia, *Taxonomy of Educational Objectives* (New York: McKay, 1964), pp. 176–193.

Psychomotor

1.00	Reflex movements
1.10	Segmental reflexes
1.20	Intersegmental reflexes
1.30	Suprasegmental reflexes
2.00	Basic-fundamental movements
2.10	Locomotor movements
2.20	Nonlocomotor movements
2.30	Manipulative movements
3.00	Perceptual abilities
3.10	Kinesthetic discrimination
3.20	Visual discrimination
3.30	Auditory discrimination
3.40	Tactile discrimination
3.50	Coordinated abilities
4.00	Physical abilities
4.10	Endurance
4.20	Strength
4.30	Flexibility
4.40	Agility
5.00	Skilled movements
5.10	Simple adaptive skills
5.20	Compound adaptive skills
5.30	Complex adaptive skills
6.00	Nondiscursive communication
6.10	Expressive movement
6.20	Interpretive movement

Source: Anita J. Harrow, *Taxonomy of the Psychomotor Domain* (New York: McKay, 1972), pp. 1–2.

Schools for the Next Century

Focus Questions

1 There are a few schools where major transformations are taking place. Describe the features of these schools.

2 What do you think society should do to address the social and emotional needs of children?

3 What kinds of changes in schools do you expect to see during your career as a teacher?

4 Leadership is an important part of school success. How do you think teacher leadership can make a difference?

5 In the past there were few career advancement opportunities for teachers that did not require them to leave the classroom. Do you know of career advancement possibilities today that allow you to continue being a teacher?

Key Terms and Concepts

Career ladder: A career path for teachers consisting of a number of rungs, or job roles, that carry with them increasing responsibility and performance of more complex professional tasks.

Core values: Statements of principles about teaching and learning that are fundamental to one's philosophy of schooling.

Metaphors: The use of words, images, and examples from one's experiences and background to explain and illustrate an idea.

Restructuring: An umbrella label for talking about a number of innovations and themes related to Site-Based Decision Making that are intended to improve school operations and, through these, student performance.

Second change facilitator/consigliere: A special leadership role in a school whereby a teacher offers facilitating assistance to other teachers during the unfolding of a school-based change process.

Transforming: Major restructuring, redesigning, or significantly changing the shape and function of schools.

In reading the first eighteen chapters of this book you have learned a lot about schooling. You have had the opportunity to learn about different philosophical bases and educational points of view, and you have explored the relationships between school and society. You have examined how schools are organized and governed, as well as their financial and legal structures. In the last two chapters, we have looked at contemporary school programs and practices. All of these chapters have summarized how American education has developed and evolved into the 1990s.

However, this cannot be the end of the story. In your career as a teacher, you will be participating in the continuing evolution and further development of American education. You will have the opportunity to test many exciting new approaches and technologies. In addition, as an American educator, you will have the opportunity to be creative and to employ innovative practices in your classroom. It will even be possible to share your experiences with many others across the land.

All types of exciting changes will take place for you in your career as a teacher. Changes around us are coming rapidly and have enormous impact on our lives. In the last several years we have witnessed the breakup of the Soviet Union, a number of multinational peace-keeping initiatives, the birth of a global economy, ever smaller and faster computers, new technologies for the home and the classroom, and exciting breakthroughs in medicine. This truly is a time of change and it is clear that, in your career as a teacher, you will be a key part of the dynamic and exciting world of change in education.

Change Is All around Us

Test Questions 19.1–19.17

Activity 19.1:
Ask students to consider their individual visions of an ideal school. Have them discuss whether their ideas are on the level of talking, tinkering, or transforming.

One of the challenges you will face during your career will be to accept change and nurture the many innovations that will be introduced. Further, we hope you will be creative and contribute your own novel ideas for improving schools. Therefore, in this last chapter, we will introduce you to some of the innovative practices and resources that are being created for schools as they move into the twenty-first century. Everything that is described here is already in operation somewhere in America. However, as you will realize, most of the ideas have not touched the majority of classrooms and many educators are still unaware of these interesting, novel, and promising practices. We offer them here to *stretch* your thinking about schooling, teaching, and your role as a teacher in the next century.

Big Change or Little Change?

Information Note 19.1:
A number of education policy experts are not talking about systemic reform. They believe that past reform efforts have dealt only with parts of the education system. With systemic reform, teaching, learning, and governance are to be rethought all at the same time rather than separately.

Objective 1:
Provide examples of big and little changes in today's schools.

At this point in your life, you have spent many years in schools, and chances are they were rather typical schools in terms of how they were organized and the types of curriculum and teaching processes that were used. In many ways, the typical school has retained the worst features of the historical one-room schoolhouse; there is one teacher in a classroom with four walls, a chalkboard at the front, and twenty or more children are sitting in chairs arranged in rows. However, typical schools of today have lost such promising educational features of the one-room schoolhouse as children of a wide age range in the same classroom, children teaching children, flexible schedules, community involvement in the school, and teachers as leading members of the community. These very important educational features were lost early in the twentieth century as ideas from the industrial revolution were applied to the "business of schools." For example, the fifty-minute class period and ringing bells for class change are reflections of the efficient assembly line. In this image of schooling, students are "products," teachers are the "workers," and principals are "management." As you read the remainder of this chapter, keep in mind your images of the one-room schoolhouse. In many ways, the restructuring and transforming of schools that is taking place in the 1990s is a return to some of those "lost features."

The Focus on Learning. There is enormous pressure, from the changes that are taking place in society, to have schools respond in kind. The dynamics of the world are creating increasingly international and global perspectives. There are a number of trends in terms of work, the characteristics of the family, distribution of wealth, and the diversity

One of the challenges students and teachers of the future will face is adapting to rapid changes in technology.

of our students and population. All of these features are impacting what schools will become. Whether we are reading newsmagazines, listening to industrial leaders and politicians, or watching the evening news on television, it is impossible to escape the concern about the quality of American education and the demand for change. These demands are not for small tinkerings with schools; rather, there is an expectation for large-scale redesign. The wished-for changes have to do with the approaches to teaching, the design of the curriculum, the organization of schools, how states are organized to support schooling, changes in the roles of teachers and principals, and the redesign of teacher education programs.

There is also a major shift in the **metaphors** used to address schools. Metaphors are the images, examples, and models that are used to compare schools with other parts of society. For example, the metaphor of the school as a factory is undergoing a major change. Instead of our seeing the school as an assembly line, stamping out students as products, we now see students as the "workers," teachers and principals as "managers" of the instructional environment, and the "product" as a "student learning." This perspective change represents a dramatic shift in how one thinks about the role of teachers and students. Changing how one views the work of schools leads directly to changes in the roles and responsibilities of teachers and students, as well as the way schools are organized. Schools of the future will have different structures and role relationships. Such symbols as bells ringing every forty-eight minutes will be replaced by new symbols, such as students carrying lap-top computers instead of books and papers.

A Scale for Assessing the Size of Change. Changes come in various forms and sizes. Just as in industry, change in schools can be vast and sweeping, or small and insignificant. Another aspect in considering change is that, in many instances, planned changes are not actually implemented: There is a great deal of talk, but

Transparency 87:
A Teacher's Instructional Repertoire

Key Term:
Metaphors

the change itself is never really put into practice in classrooms. In other cases, there are very small changes that do not make a major difference in what students learn. Thus, a distinction can be made between talking about change and tinkering with relatively small changes. The critics of schools, as well as many educators, are asking for **transforming** types of changes—ones that would dramatically influence the shape, structure, and operations of schools and classrooms.

One way to view the different magnitudes of change is illustrated in Figure 19.1. In some recent research and writing, Hall has proposed a scale—similar to the Richter scale for grading the size of earthquakes—for grading the size of innovations. In this case, the sizes of different changes in schools are being compared. Referred to as the HIC scale, this ten-point scale goes from "Talking" to "Tinkering" to "Transforming." At the Talking end of the scale, there are speeches, press announcements, and published commission reports, but there is little if any change in classrooms. As one moves toward the middle levels of the scale, the Tinkering section, changes take place in schools and in classrooms; however, they are of modest impact. The categories of change at the Transforming end represent major, wide-ranging restructurings, redesigns, and alternative configurations of what schools and school practices can be like.

Key Term:
Transforming

Journal Activity Master 19.1: My Dream School. Requires students to design an ideal school for the future.

Discussion Question 1: Some have referred to the coordinated services school as the "one-stop shopping school." What other metaphors describe a school of this type?

	LEVEL	NAME	EXAMPLES
Talking	0	Cruise Control	1950s Teacher in same classroom for many years
	1	Whisper	Pronouncements by officials Commission reports
	2	Tell	New rules and more regulations of old practices
	3	Yell	Prescriptive policy mandates
Tinkering	4	Shake	New texts Revised curriculum
	5	Rattle	Change principal Team teaching
	6	Roll	Change teacher's classroom Change grade configurations
	7	Redesign	Evening kindergarten Integrated curriculum
Transforming	8	Restructure	Site-based decision making Differentiated staffing
	9	Mutation	Teacher and principal belong to the same union Changing the role of school boards Coordinated services
	10	Reconstruction	Local constitutional convention Glasnost

FIGURE 19.1

Hall's Innovation Category Scale (HIC's)

(Source: G. E. Hall, "Examining the Relative Size of Innovations: A Scale and Implications." Greeley, CO: College of Education, University of Northern Colorado, 1993.)

Think about the changes in schools that you are aware of and the ones you have read about in this text. How many of the ideas for change that you know about have been put into practice? We suspect that you know of many good ideas that are not implemented in most schools. This is because change is difficult, and large-scale change is personally uncomfortable—as well as a lot of work. Also, the truly Transforming types of changes take many years to implement. Further, many of the Transforming changes tend to be seen as wild and crazy. Ideas such as placing schools in shopping centers, or having high school students teach elementary students, represent major shifts from schools as we know them. Truly Transforming ideas, such as having public schools begin with children at birth, or high school students taking two months to do an independent project away from the school, are hard to accept as "doable." Yet, an increasing number of Transforming innovations are being tried.

In the remainder of this chapter, various Transforming types of educational innovations are described. The purpose is to stretch your thinking and to increase your awareness of the vast variety of major changes that already exist in some American schools. As we move toward the twenty-first century, more of these Transforming types of innovations will be taking place, and in your career as a teacher, you will have the opportunity to participate in the implementation of many of them. At the very least, it is likely that you will experience working in a school district where one or more schools will be incorporating some of these types of practices. Perhaps, as your career unfolds, you will have the opportunity to create additional innovations in teaching, curriculum, and classroom and school operation.

Relevant Research

Moving to the Future with Our Schools

A futures researcher declares that critical mass changes are needed for the schools of the immediate future. Tying the concepts of childhood and schooling together, Dixon lays out a futures school that is learner based rather than adult based. Using examples of strong child influences on everything in their lives—influences from major industries, running households, creating and establishing social norms, and in the final analysis determining what they will or will not learn in school—he offers an empowerment to young learners in their educational development.

Some of the hallmarks of his futures school are: teachers who are leaders in defining education (rather than followers of corporate giants); students who govern in schools rather than "play" at governing; classrooms that are referred to as "living rooms"; and teachers who are human interactors, consultants, and tutors. This provides a challenge for the new teacher to explore. Are you getting ready professionally to become a practicing visionary?

Source: R. G. Des Dixon, "Future Schools and How to Get There from Here," *Phi Delta Kappan* 75 (5): 360–365.

Restructuring Schools

The current theme for bringing about major changes in schools is called **restructuring**. Restructuring is an umbrella label that encompasses a number of different innovations and themes. In the larger perspective, the restructuring movement addresses how to make schools more successful in relation to student learning. A number of the changes have been directed at student learning by introducing new tests, increasing the rigor of old tests, and using alternative assessment procedures such as portfolios. Other restructuring innovations have been directed at the design of the teaching-learning situation by changing the curriculum materials and introducing different teaching strategies, such as the 4MAT Program, TESA, and Madelyn Hunter's Essential Elements of Instruction.[1] Still other initiatives

Key Term:
Restructuring

Transparency 85:
Examples of School Organization

have been directed more toward organizational systems through emphasizing the instructional leader role of the principal and establishing interdisciplinary teacher teams. All three of these dimensions have extensive research bases to justify their use, and all have been directly associated with student success, teacher success, and schools that are more positive places for teaching and learning.

There are a number of concrete implications of the restructuring movement. One is that the role of the school principal changes dramatically. The principal can no longer be the authoritarian directive leader, but instead has to work in more collegial and collaborative ways—not only with the Site-Based Decision Making council, but also with the rest of the professionals and support staff in the building. A second implication in restructuring is related to the design of curriculum. For example, more academic courses are being required for high school graduation. Up to this time, high school students have been able to graduate with a relative minimum of courses in basic subject areas such as mathematics and science, and, in many instances, English as well. With the restructuring movement, increasing expectations for academic preparation for high school graduation are being put into place. Other innovations under the restructuring umbrella are described here.

Site-Based Decision Making (SBDM)

Parts of SBDM were covered in Chapter 8. The SBDM school council can include teachers, classified personnel, the principal, community representatives, business representatives, parents, and perhaps others. The premise is that all of the participants serving on the council will work together to make more informed decisions at the local site. A wide array of decision-making responsibilities is possible. Also, the composition of the site-based council can vary dramatically. One effort to summarize these components and variations of the innovation of Site-Based Decision Making is presented in Appendix 19.1 on page 515.

Another theme out of the restructuring movement is increased involvement of parents in schools. Through the SBDM process, parents have a more direct say in decisions affecting the school. Also, parents' increasing participation as aides in classrooms and in the development of projects and activities helps provide the school with more resources. This latter activity is becoming increasingly important with the serious cutbacks in funding that education is experiencing in the 1990s. Parent involvement in schools is happening not only in schools with children from well-to-do families. The increased concern about the failure to educate low-income and minority children has resulted in many educators, political leaders, and community groups advocating parent involvement in all schools. This trend toward a more shared responsibility between parents and schools is very promising.

Historically, there was a perceived separation by which schools dealt only with academic issues while parents and the community dealt with the social and emotional development of children. Now there is an understanding that the school, community, and the parents have to work together to address four domains: academic, social, physical, and emotional development of children. The situation has been driven by the demographics of our student population, which have been reported throughout this book. For example: 40 percent of today's school children will have lived with a single parent by the time they reach age eighteen. More than 20 percent live in poverty. Fifteen percent speak a native language other than

---

Information Note 19.2:
An increasing number of schools and school districts are being run by businesses. After all, American education has an annual budget of some $450 billion. One large business plan is the Edison Project, proposed by Christopher Whittle, who was the founder of Channel One. He plans to open more schools with a budget cost of $5,500 per student per year.

Objective 2:
Develop features, along with strengths and weaknesses, of restructured schools.

CNN Clip 28:
Parental Grade

There are a number of ways in which parents can become involved in the education of their children.

PROFESSIONAL DILEMMA

Can You Successfully Involve Parents in Their Children's Education?

Throughout your professional training you learned about the importance of having parents involved with their children's learning. This text has strongly emphasized how important that involvement is for minority and single-parent children. You will be faced with this type of diversity in your classroom wherever you begin your professional teaching career. You will also encounter increasing school district demands that you take the time to reach out to parents and have them become partners with you in meeting the educational needs of their children. Successful accomplishment of this professional expectation takes considerable planning and time.

At the end of the first month of your initial teaching year, your principal approaches you and indicates that he wants you and your colleagues to begin this reach-out behavior with the community. The group of students that you teach are representative of the total student body: You interact regularly with able and less able students, you have nonminority and minority students who come from two-parent and single-parent families, and you even have two homeless students in one of your classes. The principal asks you to prepare a parent/school involvement program for your students, and he would like to discuss some of your plans with him in one month.

Your dilemma at this point is:

- Where do you begin? The principal suggests that you identify two or three students and prepare a case study approach to this task.
- What kinds of students will you select?
- How will you make preparations for this important venture?

English, and 15 percent have physical or mental disabilities. All of these data indicate that the complexion of the school classroom has changed dramatically. As a result, how we teach has to change in equally dramatic ways.

There are a number of ways that parents can become involved in schools. An example of direct involvement is parents being able to select the school their children will attend. Another is influencing the decision making that goes on in schools by participating on SBDM councils. A third way of involving parents in schools is through *parent training programs*, in which parents can develop new skills in such areas as communication, how to work effectively with children of different ages, how to help children develop self-discipline, and achievement orientation. Parents also learn guidance techniques for helping their children develop study habits and attend to homework. Parents can also be involved in the *development of resource and support programs*. These can range from the above-mentioned developing and soliciting financial and resource supports for the school to assisting in providing services to other parents in the school community. In addition, parents can be effective in working in counseling, training, advising in regard to substance abuse, and other types of *support and discussion group activities* that relate to the larger mission of today's schools.

Business Involvement in Schools

Another increasingly important set of school partnerships are those that are developing between businesses and schools. In the past, more of a one-way perspective existed in the relationships between businesses and schools. There were various

Focus Question 1:
There are a few schools where major transformations are taking place. Describe features of these schools.

Activity 19.7:
Assign students to one of the four styles of leadership in the classroom (committee, SBDM, Consigliere, BRT), and have them consider one leadership initiative they believe could assist in transforming the student teaching experience.

Transparency 94:
Parent–Child Literacy Patterns

Discussion Question 2:
What do you think will happen to the role of the teacher in a school that is serving as the center for the delivery of coordinated services?

CNN Clip 29:
Parents' Homework

Activity 19.2:
Bring in a local business person to discuss how he or she views business involvement in school. Then ask students to assess whether the view presented is a tinkering or transforming idea.

types of "adopt-a-school" programs, where businesses would send often obsolete equipment and other types of resources to the schools. In many ways these programs treated schools as some sort of underprivileged client that businesses could assist; however, that simplistic one-way perspective has changed dramatically in the 1990s. Now there truly are reciprocal partnerships between businesses and schools. The business community is recognizing that not only do they have things to offer schools, but also schools have many types of resources to offer to the business community in return. One of the expanding steps in the ongoing dialogue between businesses and schools has been the number of chief executive officers, such as the former president of Xerox, David Kearns, former CEO of IBM John Akers, and the previous CEO of US West, Jack MacAllister, who have been advocates for schools. They have continued to express their interest in and support for schools, and they have invested in changing schools. These types of testimonies and initiatives by business leaders have kept public attention focused on the need to improve schools.

Transforming Schools

Test Questions 19.18–19.42

Discussion Question 3:
Develop answers to TQM questions: Who are the customers for teachers? What is the product of schools? What is the product of your classroom?

There are a small number of experimental efforts that are truly about transforming schools. In each instance, a local staff of teachers, principals, parents, and community representatives are struggling to implement a model of what all schools can become. Each of these schools has been through a two-to-four year process of developing images for what they want to be. In many instances they have had to confront school district and state policies that prohibit the types of transformations that they wish to implement. In response, some states are making major changes in their education policies and procedures to encourage more change. In all cases, transformed schools are being established that offer hints regarding what schools could be like for you in your career as a teacher. All of these transforming efforts have major implications for the preparation of teachers, such as yourself. It is important to note that at the same time schools are changing, there will be transforming efforts in relation to the design of teacher education programs. Further, as a teacher, you will be in a position to facilitate and lead change efforts. This section describes some current transforming activities.

Objective 3:
Describe factors of transforming schools, including the educational rationale for each.

Key Term:
Core values

Information Note 19.3:
The New American School Development Corporation has funded eleven design teams to develop "blueprints" for a new generation of American schools. Key requirements for these schools are that they meet world-class standards and that they operate fiscally on a budget comparable to that of regular schools.

In the late 1980s and early 1990s many of the efforts to transform schools were made under the label of "restructuring." As we summarized above, the so-called restructuring movement focused on a number of elements for making schools more responsive and effective, such as Site-Based Decision Making, cooperative learning, and the use of particular curriculum philosophies, such as whole language. A small number of the schools have gone far beyond those elements to entirely new school models. These transforming schools incorporate a number of different features and designs. The design of each school is based on a set of **core values** or beliefs. In each case the school has developed a statement and list of principles about teaching and learning that have guided the decision making for transforming the school. These statements include descriptions of what a particular community believes is important about children, the role of teachers, and expectations about the responsibilities of students. In nearly all instances, the key determinant for making changes has been judgments about what would most optimally affect student success. Note that success is not always determined in terms of narrow measures such as standardized achievement tests. In most of the

> ## CASE STUDY   CLASSROOM STRATEGIC PLANNING
>
> Strategic planning has become as commonplace for schools as it is for business and industry, government, and many growing church groups. In education, this can be a very strong professional growth activity or it can degenerate into a "busy-work" activity that meets some state mandate for filing a plan. However, most strategic activities are meaningful and give a school district a chance to stand back; take a fresh look at the whole school operation; and assess the needs of the students, the community, and the nation. With these types of baseline data for a school district, teachers and staff can plan for district-wide change, school building change, and classroom changes.
>
> As a new teacher, you should constantly be involved in planning your classroom program. As you have seen, student needs change, the makeup of classroom diversity changes, and knowledge and needed basic skill requirements change. This requires you to be flexible in what you propose to do with your students in their learning environment. You will find that wherever you teach, your building administrator will have continuous expectations for you to keep your professional activities current with the changing times.
>
> Prepare a plan of action to keep your classroom strategic planning up to date, using a teaching assignment perspective. Indicate how you will correlate your individual strategic planning efforts with those of your school building and the school district. How will you correlate your efforts with your classroom colleagues at a given grade level or discipline level? Where does all of this activity fit into what you believe about learning and student diversity? How will you seek evaluation of what you do, and will that evaluation alter your plans? How can you demonstrate leadership throughout this whole activity?

transforming schools, there is a broader, more robust perspective of what students need to accomplish and achieve. One example of a statement of principles is presented as Figure 19.2 on page 494. This set of principles was developed by a coalition of child advocacy groups that is collectively referred to as the National Coalition of Advocates for Students.

Education Family Style

One of the transformed schools that is implementing a wide array of features is the Laboratory School at the University of Northern Colorado. The basic theme for the restructuring of this school has been "Education Family Style." The emphasis on family is a direct reaction to the Laboratory School staff's concern that the lives of the typical student of the 1990s is filled with disruptions. In many ways, the typical school adds further disruption to the life of American students. For example, every fall students are placed with a new set of classmates and with a new teacher. From the students' point of view, instead of there being continuity from year to year, the school year begins with disruption. Then, nine months later, more disruption is introduced by breaking up the class; and the following fall the cycle begins anew.

In response to this, the staff at the UNC laboratory School has created families whereby 50–100 students of a two-to-three-year age span can stay together across a number of years. This "family" has two-to-three teachers who are also permanent across time. Thus, one source of disruption is minimized and a number

Journal/Portfolio Development 19.1: Select one of the "transformation of schools" topics and assess its potential for becoming a regular part of the school operation. Contrast it with the current school operation.

1. Children are entitled to have parents, advocates, and concerned educators included in all decisions affecting their education.

2. Children are entitled to learn in an integrated, heterogeneous setting responsive to different learning styles and abilities.

3. Children are entitled to comprehensible, culturally supportive, and developmentally appropriate curriculum and teaching strategies.

4. Children are entitled to access to a common body of knowledge and the opportunity to acquire higher-order skills.

5. Children are entitled to a broadly based assessment of their academic progress and grading structures that enhance individual strengths and potential.

6. Children are entitled to a broad range of support services that address individual needs.

7. Children are entitled to attend a school that is safe, attractive, and free from prejudice.

8. Children are entitled to attend school every day unless they pose a danger to other children or school staff.

9. Children are entitled to instruction by teachers who hold high expectations for all students and who are fully prepared to meet the challenges inherent in diverse classrooms.

10. Children are entitled to an equal education opportunity supported by provision of greater resources to schools serving low-income, minority, differently abled or immigrant students.

FIGURE 19.2

Ten Student Entitlements for Educational Success

(*Source: The National Coalition of Advocates for Students,* 1992.)

of new stabilizing elements are introduced. As you can see, the creation of families adds a number of new dimensions to the schooling context, one of the more salient factors being that children of multiple ages are together in the same class(es). Another difference is that, instead of working in isolation, teachers work together as an interdisciplinary team with their family of students. An overall picture of the design of the UNC Laboratory School is presented as Figure 19.3.

Vision 20-20. Another feature of the UNC Laboratory School is the absence of the typical grade-level structure. Instead of having kindergarten, first grade, second grade, freshman, and senior year, the Laboratory School has five levels. These levels cover the range from early childhood to young adult, conceivably from 20 days to 20 years. In other words, the staff in this school are exploring what the schooling environment can be like for children from very young ages to young adulthood; hence, the theme—Vision 20-20. In contrast to traditional grade levels, the five developmental levels reflect current research and theory about the age at which the typical transition points in learning style and perspective take place. The Lab School staff propose that a school be organized around these developmental levels, rather than the typical grade levels correlated directly with age and birth dates.

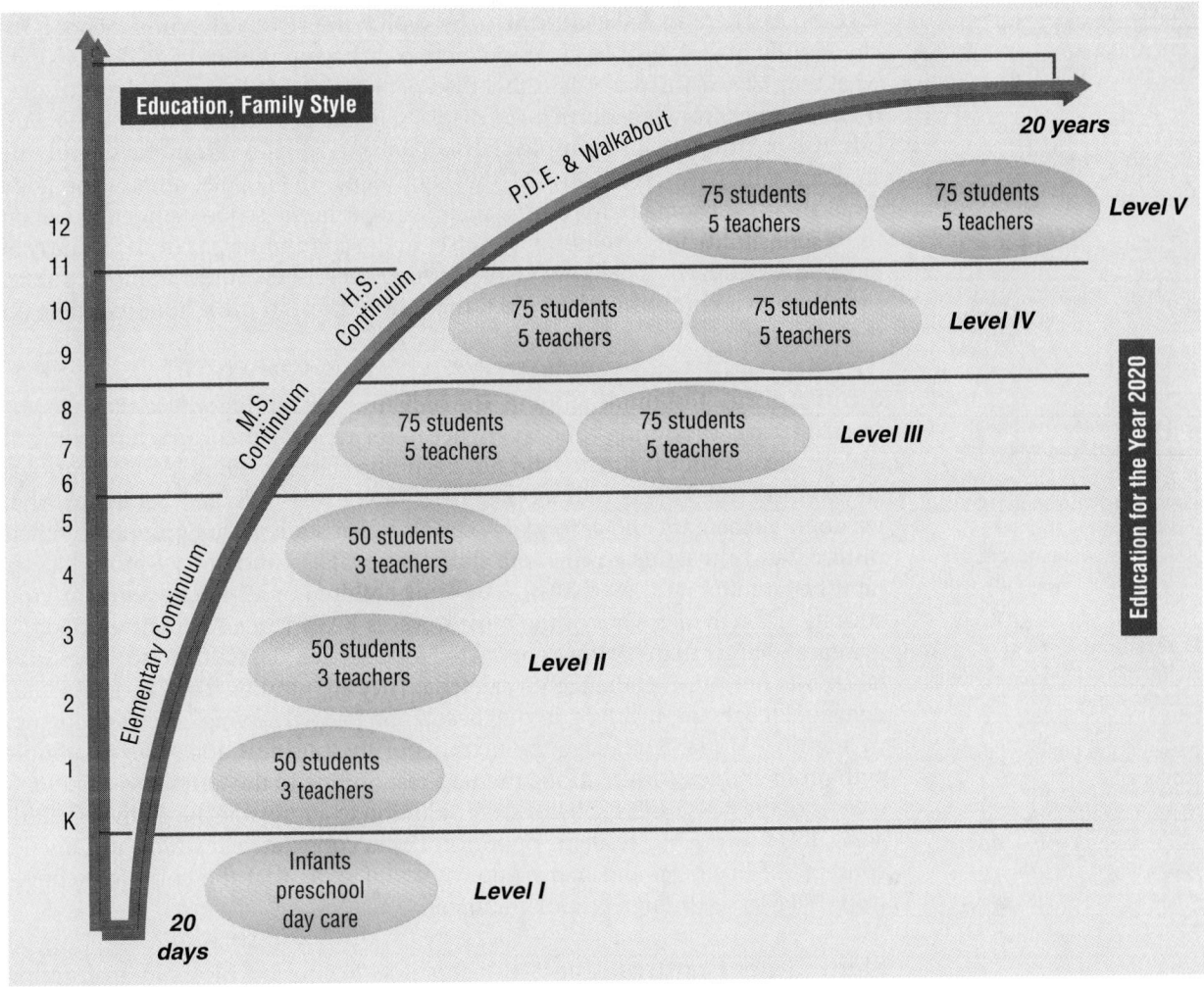

Education, Family Style

P.D.E. & Walkabout

20 years

H.S. Continuum

M.S. Continuum

Elementary Continuum

Education for the Year 2020

75 students 5 teachers	75 students 5 teachers	**Level V**
75 students 5 teachers	75 students 5 teachers	**Level IV**
75 students 5 teachers	75 students 5 teachers	**Level III**

50 students 3 teachers

50 students 3 teachers — **Level II**

50 students 3 teachers

Infants preschool day care — **Level I**

12
11
10
9
8
7
6
5
4
3
2
1
K

20 days

FIGURE 19.3

Organizing Framework for the University of Northern Colorado Laboratory School

Autonomous Learning. The UNC Laboratory School places a strong emphasis on students assuming major responsibility for their own learning. In addition, parents are directly drawn into the work of the school through the development of *Personal Learning Plans*. Each six weeks the parent and the teachers, along with the student, meet to review the student's accomplishments, to clarify objectives, and to set the list of tasks to be accomplished in the next interval. Heavy emphasis is placed on the expectation that the students will be self-directed, as well as individually guided by teachers, in their learning. Teachers have a responsibility to help students develop confidence and independence in order to become lifelong learners. At the same time, it is assumed that students will increasingly assume more responsibility and initiative in relation to what they learn and how they learn it, especially if they have more of a role in managing the process.

Focus Question 2:
What do you think society should do to address the social and emotional needs of children?

CNN Clip 31:
SAT Advancers

Use of Authentic Assessment. The staff at the UNC Laboratory School, including the high school level, are interested in having the students demonstrate what they have learned in ways other than paper and pencil tests. Students display their learning through performances, displays, media productions, and other methods. It is envisioned, for example, that as part of graduation from the school, the students will have accomplished the equivalent of the Australian aborigine's "walkabout." At some point during their last year in the school, students take on the responsibility for developing a project in the community, or in the country at large, that is directly related to their learning objectives. Students move out on their own to accomplish this project, then they return to the school to report on the outcome.

Multi-Aging. Just think about it! The only time in your life when you were segregated by age was during your experience in the typical American school. In your college classes, your instructor did not begin the class by saying "All 21-year-olds sit over here. All 37-year-olds sit over here. All 42-year-olds. . . ." Yet this is what we do in elementary and secondary schools when students are grouped by their birth dates. In reaction to this, the staff of the UNC Laboratory School has established a number of mechanisms to bring children of all ages together around educational activities. One of the most novel is KAFE (Kids Alternative Food Experience). Rather than having a contracted food service, the staff and students have taken over operation of the school cafeteria. They are running it as a business! Students of all ages are involved in purchasing, preparing, serving, and cleaning up. In addition, students manage the finances of the business and have to grapple with profit and loss, while, along the way, responding to the tastes and food preferences of their customers. Obviously, in addition to addressing the theme of multi-aging, KAFE also offers students opportunities in cooperative learning, arithmetic, concepts of business, and many other types of skills that the critics of schools would like to see in high school graduates.

Activity 19.3:
Describe the work of Individually Guided Education from the 1970s and 1980s, which advocated multi-aged groupings in elementary school. Ask the students to discuss their comfort level with such ideas.

Diversity Note 19.1:
Authentic exhibition and multi-age grouping practices provide valuable assistance in meeting the needs of diverse students.

Many Other Features. The UNC Laboratory School is typical of transforming schools in that many of the individual innovative themes that have been described in earlier chapters have been brought together into one comprehensive plan. Some of the other themes at the UNC Laboratory School include: appropriate technology (there is a difference between being "high tech" and including "appropriate uses" of technology), business and community education, developmental grouping, early-childhood education, global and community awareness, interdisciplinary education, Site-Based Decision Making, and social responsibility and service. Schools of this type truly are at the higher ends of the HIC scale. They are engaged in transforming what schooling can be about, and they are responding to the unique needs of students in the 1990s.

Transforming High Schools

Transparency 97:
Achievement across Subjects Worldwide

Objective 4:
Discuss the types of major changes that are occurring in more innovative high schools.

There is widespread agreement that it is more difficult to bring about change in high schools than in elementary or middle schools. There are a number of reasons for this, including the fact that many high schools are large, teachers tend to be more focused on their subject matter, and program offerings are more complex—because of the combination of basic disciplines, co-curricular activities, athletics, music, and drama that are offered in the comprehensive high school. Other factors that make change difficult include Carnegie units, fifty-minute time blocks, and the diversity of students and adults. However, transformations of high schools are happening too.

Essential Schools. One of the most promising efforts to bring about significant change in high schools is being lead by Ted Sizer and his colleagues in *The Coalition of Essential Schools*. This effort is based on an earlier study of high schools that was conducted by Sizer. The Coalition, which was a network of twelve high schools attempting to bring about significant change, joined with the Education Commission of the States, which is a national agency that brings together staffs of the governors' offices around major initiatives. The merged coalition is now called *Re-Learning*. In this nationwide effort, member high schools must address nine common principles, and school communities who wish to transform their high schools must agree to share in and work on achieving them. Through the Coalition it is possible for the schools to receive support from each other, learning more about the developmental work that needs to be done with the community and the staff, as well as with students, to bring about significant change. There are Re-Learning schools in most states. The leaders of this transforming effort have found that certain principles receive the most resistance and therefore have to be addressed most systematically.

Information Note 19.4: Restructuring the curriculum in high schools includes the design of integrated curriculum, the organization of curriculum around big ideas, cooperative learning, problem-based learning, and alternative assessment techniques.

Total Quality Management (TQM). The American business paradigm is being confronted with major challenges too. The challenge to the American way of doing business has many names, but in general it is referred to as Japanese management or Total Quality Management (TQM). Since World War II the Japanese have put together a very different way of thinking about doing business. TQM brings with it a different set of assumptions about business, and currently a number of educators are considering how TQM can be applied to schools. The TQM paradigm clearly confronts the current way American schools are run. To illustrate this comparison, think about the old impressions of Japanese products that were imported into the United States and contrast those with current impressions.

Early Japanese Products	*Japanese Products of Today*
Low tech	High tech
Cheap	High priced
Poor quality	High quality
Unreliable	Maintenance free

As you can see from these examples there has been a major metamorphosis in what we think of products made in Japan. The reason for this paradigm shift was the involvement of a number of American consultants in working with the Japanese to rebuild their economy following World War II. The most prominent of these consultants was W. Edwards Deming, who brought to Japan a very different set of assumptions about how to approach manufacturing. His whole thrust was to place the emphasis on building a quality product and to focus on *continuously improving* the quality of the product. Further, Dr. Deming emphasized collecting data about every aspect of the manufacturing process and using these data to make changes and to evaluate the success of efforts to improve quality.

This paradigm is very different from the way American business has been run. In American business, the assumptions, focus, and attitudes have been on producing products as cheaply as possible and in large quantities. The focus has been on making things at lower costs instead of on increasing the quality. In the American business paradigm, improvement has to do with how to make things more cheaply in order in order to increase profits. The TQM model assumes that increasing quality will result in decreased costs and therefore higher profits. Let us see what this would mean in terms of thinking about schools. Consider the following as attributes of regular schools and a paradigm TQM school:

Regular Schools	TQM Schools
Nine-month time module	Eighteen-year module (womb to graduation)
Self-contained classroom	Shopping mall school
Education only	Integrated services
Emphasis is on teaching	Emphasis is on learning
Each school year the same	Each year changes based on data about last year's teaching and learning
No systematic use of data, but students are graded	Data about students, teaching, and curriculum are constantly analyzed and used to change teaching and the curriculum
No feedback about how your students did after leaving class	Direct feedback on how your students do the next year
No feedback on student success in the next higher level of schooling	Direct feedback on how students do in subsequent schools
Teacher pay based on years of teaching	Teacher pay based on how successful your students are in subsequent years and adjusted by track record of the students once they leave school
Annual evaluation by the principal	No annual evaluation; instead, continuous feedback to individuals and staff as a whole about the effects of improvement efforts
Telling students what they need to know	Asking students, parents, and the community what future adults need to be able to do

As you can see, the emphases and assumptions of these two paradigms of schooling are quite different. They represent the kind of paradigm shift you will experience in your career. The emphasis on continuous improvement is especially important. The focus on learning, the multiyear perspective, and the idea that there needs to be cooperation among all members of the organization to improve quality are different from what goes on in the regular school paradigm. In the TQM model, three important questions that can be translated and applied to schools are:

1. Who are your customers?
2. What is your product?
3. How can the manufacturing processes be changed to improve the quality of the product?

As you explore these questions and develop your own answers, you will find that they represent a very different way of thinking. For example, who are your

Activity 19.4:
Have students redesign the Carnegie Units currently required for high school graduation. What types of learning would they require for high school students of the future?

customers? You probably are giving the quick answer that they are your students, or the parents, or the community. In some cases this is true; however, have you thought about the fact that the teacher who receives your students next year is your customer? The product you deliver to that teacher is your student. Thus, in the TQM model, among the important customers you need to be interacting with and considering as consumers are the teachers at the next grade level.

Charter Schools. In 1989, Minnesota was one of the first states to pass legislation in favor of parents choosing schools for their children. Ten years earlier, a strong national debate arose over the concept of school vouchers. During the 1990s school choice came into active existence as charter schools emerged in California, Texas, Wisconsin, and Arkansas in addition to Minnesota. The debates about this issue continue in many other states today.

Charter schools allow parents to choose what they perceive to be high quality education for their children—education they feel is not being given by the local public schools. They are different from the voucher concept in that the public school district financial vouchers are for parents to use in selecting educational experiences for their children. In Minnesota the law allows a charter school to operate with a contract with the local school board. This is an educational agreement between a charter school and the school board, with the board spelling out goals, objectives, and responsibilities of both parties, the board and the charter school.

With charter schools, there is a power shift in governance, funding, and accountability. The granting school board provides the funds for operation of the charter school, but the charter school has its own governing body (school board), teachers, and administrators. In situations in which charter schools house students from the regular school district, the local school district budget is reduced and shifted for use by the charter school. Charter schools must compete for students; thus, there is a high degree of accountability in their operation or they will not survive.

Global Perspectives: Charter Schools in England. Charter schools began in England in 1989. Since the English system of public education is a national system, the Department of Education issues direct grants for the formation of charter schools. These charter schools move through a transitional period before being granted permanent status. Once the school has moved to a corporation basis it receives yearly grants of funds from the national education ministry for school operation and school plant services.

CNN **Clip 32:**
The Next Generation

The charter schools of England are completely different from those described for Minnesota in that they, like their public school counterparts, are responsible to the state and not to the local school district where they are located. This appears to be more a function of a centralized system of schooling as opposed to the U.S. system, in which local autonomy has been granted by the state governments for operation of the schools. The charter schools of both countries, however, serve the same purpose—providing a quality educational alternative to learners.

Outcomes Based Education (OBE). The philosophy of Outcomes Based Education is usually associated with William Spady. Outcomes Based Education differs from performance-type programs in that it is intended to address meaningful culminating experiences. The demonstrations of outcomes being achieved must occur in some contest or performance setting; they must be of high quality; and they are expected to occur at culminatng periods such as at fifth, eighth, and twelfth

Focus Question 3:
What kinds of changes in schools do you expect to see during your career as a teacher?

grade levels. The demonstrations of competence need to take place in an aura of what Spady calls the "Demonstration Mountain." This "mountain" contains the *traditional zone,* which is structured task performances with discrete content skills; the *transitional zone,* which is complex unstructured task performances with higher order competencies; and the *transformational zone,* which is life-role functioning with complex role performances.

Outcomes based education students are expected to be implementors and performers, problem finders and solvers, planners and designers, creators and producers, learners and thinkers, listeners and communicators, teachers and mentors, supporters and contributors, team members and partners, and listeners and organizers. In 1991 Pennsylvania moved to OBE and mandated all school districts to prepare their district strategic planning along OBE guidelines. The big issue with a movement of this type is determining what the desired outcomes will be. In Pennsylvania, "Moral Right" organizations and groups opposed the notion of affective outcomes that addressed values and morals leading to students' accepting homosexuality as a healthy lifestyle. Temporarily shelved because of the efforts of these critics, the Pennsylvania OBE program goes on, but it is muted in the affective areas of learning.

Schools as the Center for Delivery of Coordinated Services

Transparency 99:
Learning Centers

Objective 5:
Describe the kinds of societal conditions and reasons for the movement to establish schools as the center for delivery of coordinated services.

Up to this point, we have looked at schools as if they were the single agency that deals with children. However, this is not the image of schools that will exist in the very near future. As a matter of fact, there are a number of very exciting initiatives under way at this time in which schools are serving as the center for coordination and delivery of a wide range of social, educational, and human service functions. Unlike the past, and for most of the schools in the present, schools in the future will be dramatically transformed from a single purpose to full service. Increasingly they will become the center for access to many services including emotional health, welfare, education, criminal justice, health, and dental services. Instead of attempting to address the educational needs of children in isolation of other needs and their families, some schools have already become holistic family resource centers.[2]

This is a dramatic move away from the array of individual agencies that have dealt with distinct parts of the child. Each of these agencies may have been performing well, but none dealt with the child as a whole person. In fact, it has not been uncommon to have on average five different social service agencies addressing the needs of one at-risk child. Typically, none of these agencies would communicate with the others concerning their knowledge of the child or the child's family, nor would they communicate about the interventions that were being made. In addition, the various levels of federal, state, and local human service agencies complicate the delivery of services. For example, in the California state government, there are 160 different programs and 35 state agencies that deal with services to children. The whole child is not seen by any one agency, as each is specialized in delivery of its service.

Obviously, when there are this many different agencies involved, with all of the associated professions and related policies, rules, and regulations, it is highly unlikely that any one child can be addressed as a whole, nor that all children will be receiving equal access to the available service resources. In fact, in many cases, agencies are required by law to withhold information from other agencies. There have been no means for developing linkages, communication, or coordination. Think about your own preparation to become a teacher. Has it been typical in your program for each of the human service professions to be aware of the work of the other professionals involved with other aspects of the child? For example, it is a typical pattern on college and university campuses for teacher education students to have no formal contact or training with social work, nursing, counseling, or criminal justice students. From the point of view of an at-risk student, all of these services and the related professional personnel are addressing the same child and his or her family. The need to address this compounding picture is obvious. The solution that is being tested across the country is coordinated or integrated services.

Services Problems. Many children are not receiving the needed services that are available. More and more children are at risk and so are an increasing number of families. Yet we have not made the transformation from the old way of doing business to new ways of addressing the increasingly prevalent and urgent needs. Melaville and Blank[3] have developed a report and analysis of this emerging effort to structure interagency partnerships so that children and families can receive these comprehensive services. In their report, they identify five reasons for the failures typical of our current system.

1. Most services are crisis oriented.
2. The current social welfare system divides the problems of children and families into rigid and distinct categories that fail to reflect interrelated causes and solutions.
3. The inability to adequately meet the needs of children and families reflects a lack of functional communication.
4. Specialized agencies are unable to easily craft comprehensive solutions for complex problems.
5. The existing services are insufficiently funded.

This set of indicators is obvious. The consequences of this condition are clear when one thinks about children and families and the experiences they can have in trying to seek help to resolve problems. Few if any of our systems are set up to be preventive. Instead, we focus on issues and problems once they reach crisis proportions. Also, in the past, as a problem was identified, a discrete agency or a set of professionals were trained and organized to deal with that specific problem area. Funding guidelines and accountability requirements, based upon the specific service area, would then follow. With time, each of these professions developed its own bureaucracy, vertical lines of communication, and professional standards. No mechanisms for communication *across* agencies with regard to functions and with regard to the needs and services offered to specific children and families were developed. In many ways, each of these professions is in *competition* with the others for funding, for policy support, and for coordination of interventions that its agency specializes in making. In general, there still are no mechanisms for these agencies to communicate and exchange ideas with each other. And of course, as the number of families and children in crisis has risen, funding support has not kept pace.

Given the enormity of the problem, it is clear that there needs to be a major transformation that will result in a comprehensive service delivery system. In their

Information Note 19.5: Vandell and Posner, of the Wisconsin Center for Educational Research, have found that low-income third graders who went to formal after-school programs did better at mathematics and reading and had better grade point averages than children who were cared for by parents or other adults or were left unsupervised.

Journal Activity Master 19.2: An Analysis of Change Style. Helps students better understand change in our schools.

Activity 19.5: Invite to class a staff member of a school that offers some form of coordinated school services. Have the staff member discuss the interrelationship of the various services. Does the program work smoothly?

Discussion Question 4:
What are some of the basic principles about schooling and the role of teachers and students that you would advocate as the basis for transforming a school?

analysis, Melaville and Blank[4] offered the following features that should be part of a revised system.

1. There needs to be a wide array of prevention treatment and support services.
2. Comprehensive service delivery must include techniques to ensure that children and their families actually receive the services they need.
3. There must be a focus on the whole family.
4. High-quality services must empower children and families.
5. Effectiveness and high-quality prevention support of treatment services must be measured by the impact these interventions have on the lives of children and families they serve.

Promising Examples of Coordinated Services.   The key to accomplishing the delivery of coordinated services must be partnerships and collaboration. No longer can we afford to have schools moving along with their own agenda without consultation with other social services, such as health care, mental health, social work and juvenile justice. Fortunately, there are a number of promising experimental efforts that are modeling how these new forms of interagency collaboratives can work. In most cases, the school is the central agency for the coordination and delivery of these services. The following are brief descriptions.

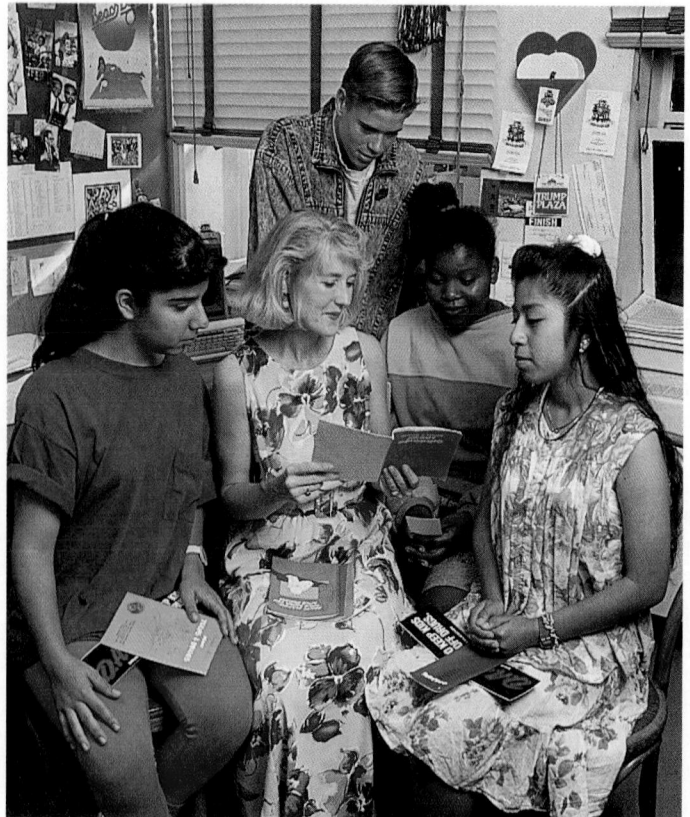

Schools attempt to help students understand how to address the challenges presented by a complex and changing society.

South Central School District #406, Tuckwila, Washington is working to coordinate services across the entire school district. In this community on the south central side of Seattle, an array of services is being centered around the school. A part of this work is built on defining what is meant by children at risk (those who experience an inability to participate successfully in the main institutions of society—family, home, school, community, and work force). In this school district, comprehensive services teachers and instructional assistants provide instruction to students both within and outside of the regular classroom. A case management system has been put into place for diagnosing student needs, designing interventions, monitoring, evaluating, and communicating about student success. Learning-support services are being funded through a combination of federal, state, and local dollars, which results in a more efficient and effective service approach. The program also includes a heavy component of involvement with hundreds of parents and other patrons who volunteer their time to be in schools and to serve on committees to assist teachers and to work one-on-one with students.

New Beginnings Integrated Services for Children and Family has been established in San

Diego. The goals of this project are to develop and test an integrated collaborative system of services for families and children. The types of services provided in the collaborative agency and the array of agencies working together to support this experimental effort is summarized in Figure 19.4 on page 504. In San Diego, Alexander Hamilton Elementary School is becoming a living model of the integration of school with social service agencies. In this one school setting, families are able to access health care, job training, welfare payments, English as a second language, adult classes, public housing referrals, and more. The ambitiousness of this experimental effort is reflected in some of the dramatic statistics about the needs of the Hamilton School community. For example, in 1987–88, about 28 percent of the children were at the school for less than 60 days. And only 40 percent were enrolled for the full year! These data clearly indicate the need for re-thinking how educational and other services are delivered and the need for communication and coordination through integrated services. In a model such as Hamilton, it is possible for at-risk students and their families to gain much needed support. The core beliefs for the New Beginnings project in San Diego are listed here and are characteristic of other integrated service initiatives:

We believe that . . .

- Children and families in our community are a valuable resource and their healthy development is essential to the social and economic future of San Diego;
- The number of children and families that live in poverty and are at risk of not developing to their potential is growing in our community;
- The family is the primary care-giver and source of social learning, and must be supported and strengthened;
- Families cannot be assisted effectively and strengthened through fragmented services provided by public agencies in isolation from each other;
- The best hope for helping families and children comes through early intervention and continuing development services;
- Each public agency in the community, including the City of San Diego, County of San Diego, San Diego Community College District, San Diego Unified School District, and the San Diego Housing Commission, has a critical role in supporting children and families;
- Only an integrated service system involving all of these agencies and a full resource of professional staff can meet the complex needs of children and families in our community; and
- Such a system must not be dependent on short-term special funding, but must represent a fundamental restructure of existing resources.[5]

Intermediate School 218, Manhattan, New York opened in 1992 to 1,100 students, mothers, fathers, and other children in the neighborhood. Among the services offered are dental treatment, drug counseling, tutoring, after-school programs, eye and physical exams, and mental health and social work counseling. The school offers workshops on such topics as pregnancy prevention, racial awareness, parenting skills, and AIDS. This school is a joint project of both public and private agencies. It was launched as a partnership between the school district and the Children's Aid Society, a nonprofit organization based in Manhattan. Cooperative efforts of this type save each agency money in operating costs and facilities, and the professionals in the different social services are able to deliver in their area of expertise. This means, for example, that teachers can focus more on teaching and

Transparency 96:
New Beginnings Services

Diversity Note 19.2:
At-risk learners are found in considerably higher proportions among minority children. When compared to the typical school, transformation programs are much more successful with these learners.

Transparency 88:
Activity from the Cola Can Curriculum

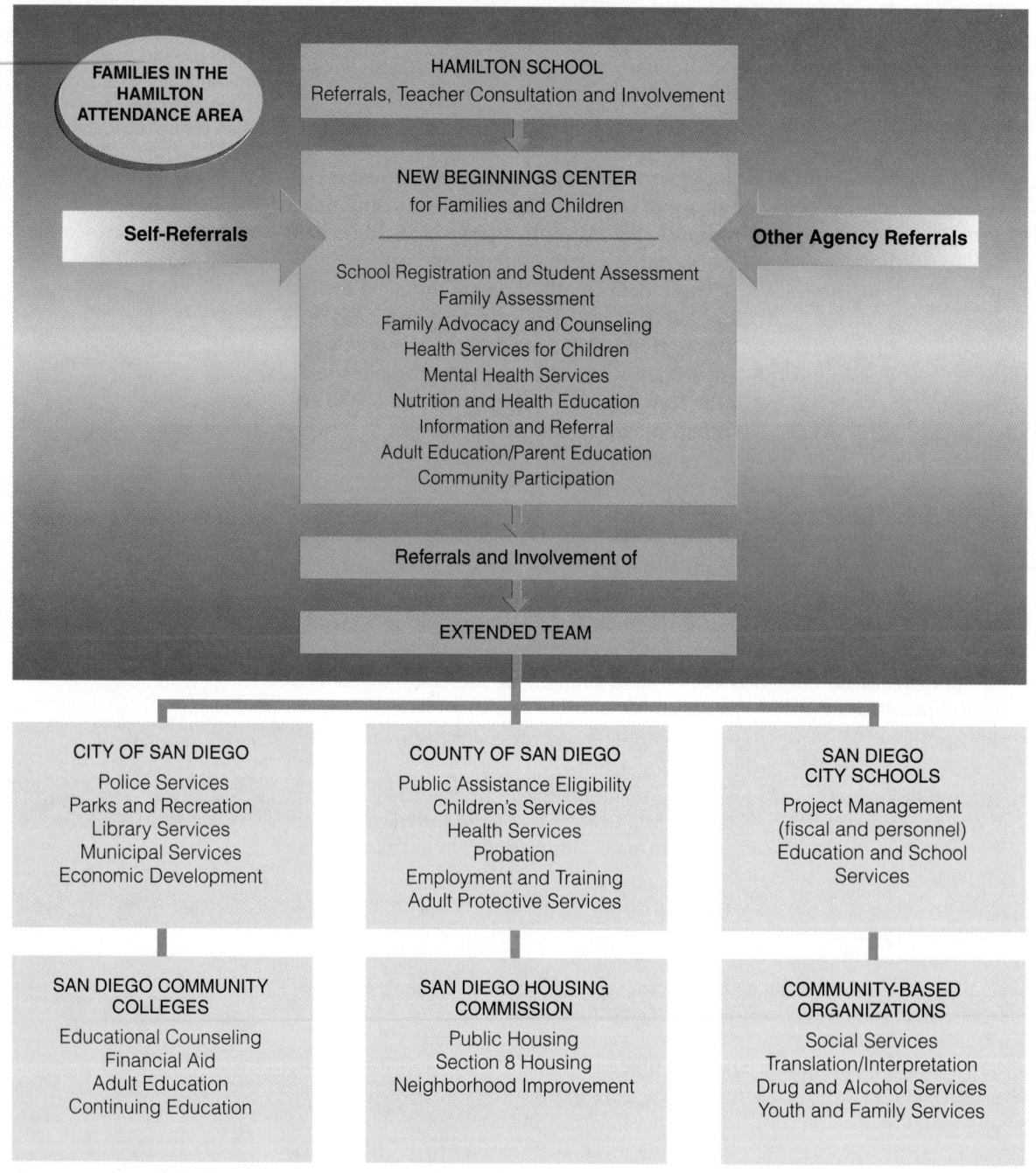

NEW BEGINNINGS SERVICES

FAMILIES IN THE HAMILTON ATTENDANCE AREA

HAMILTON SCHOOL
Referrals, Teacher Consultation and Involvement

NEW BEGINNINGS CENTER
for Families and Children

Self-Referrals   Other Agency Referrals

School Registration and Student Assessment
Family Assessment
Family Advocacy and Counseling
Health Services for Children
Mental Health Services
Nutrition and Health Education
Information and Referral
Adult Education/Parent Education
Community Participation

Referrals and Involvement of

EXTENDED TEAM

CITY OF SAN DIEGO
Police Services
Parks and Recreation
Library Services
Municipal Services
Economic Development

COUNTY OF SAN DIEGO
Public Assistance Eligibility
Children's Services
Health Services
Probation
Employment and Training
Adult Protective Services

SAN DIEGO CITY SCHOOLS
Project Management (fiscal and personnel)
Education and School Services

SAN DIEGO COMMUNITY COLLEGES
Educational Counseling
Financial Aid
Adult Education
Continuing Education

SAN DIEGO HOUSING COMMISSION
Public Housing
Section 8 Housing
Neighborhood Improvement

COMMUNITY-BASED ORGANIZATIONS
Social Services
Translation/Interpretation
Drug and Alcohol Services
Youth and Family Services

FIGURE 19.4

Organization of Collaborative Agencies to Deliver Coordinated Services to Hamilton School, San Diego, California that the children will attend school both better prepared and better supported to learn. The schedule for Intermediate School 218 is interesting as well. The school is open six days a week, 52 weeks a year, and after 3:00 P.M. the school turns into a community center that offers courses, workshops, and tutors. On average, the school is open fifteen hours a day.

Teacher Education Is Changing

Clearly, if schools are going to be different, then teachers who will be working in those schools will need to be thinking differently and performing differently. This has direct implications for the initial preparation of teachers. A number of initiatives are under way at major universities, state universities, private universities, and small liberal arts colleges to redesign teacher education programs. As has been illustrated with many of the other initiatives for changing schools in changing times, the development of collaborative efforts, coalitions, and national networks is a pattern in the restructuring of teacher education. Three of the major national initiatives to reform teacher education are the Holmes Group, the Renaissance Group and the National Network for Educational Renewal.

The Holmes Group.   The Holmes Group is a national consortium of schools of education dedicated to the reform of teacher education. This group has taken its name from Henry W. Holmes, who was Dean of Harvard University's Graduate School of Education, from 1920 to 1940. Holmes was a strong supporter of teacher education reform. The Holmes Group had its beginning in 1983, when a small number of deans of education in research-oriented institutions met to explore and debate their shared understandings and to develop a common agenda. Currently the Holmes Group consists of over ninety institutions from across the country. Membership is restricted to those institutions that place a heavy emphasis on research productivity, and the key member in the Holmes Group is the dean of each member institution. Out of their initial deliberations, the Holmes Group identified five goals for the reform of teacher education. These are:

1. To make education of teachers intellectually more solid.
2. To recognize differences in teachers' knowledge, skill, and commitment, in their education, certification, and work.
3. To create standards of entry to the profession—examinations and educational requirements—that are professionally relevant and intellectually defensible.
4. To connect our own institutions to schools.
5. To make schools better places for teachers to work, and to learn.[6]

One of the more controversial premises of the Holmes Group is that teacher education should be a post-baccalaureate program. In other words, those who wish to become teachers would first receive a bachelor's degree in a discipline, then move into a fifth year or post-baccalaureate teacher education program. The controversy is based on the fact that the expectation would add to the amount of time that it takes to become a teacher, as well as incurring the expense of another year of higher education, thus discouraging minorities and low-income students from the profession.

Objective 6:
Compare features of their current teacher education program with the programs espoused by the different teacher education networks.

Information Note 19.6:
Outcomes-based education is coming to teacher education programs. These programs will challenge teachers in training to integrate knowledge (of what they teach) and develop a commitment to a style of thinking in a discipline.

CNN Clip 31:
Student Standards

Activity 19.6:
Have students select one of the teacher education initiatives (Holmes, Renaissance), and prepare a debate about which initiative is the best.

Another focus of the Holmes Group is the creation of Professional Development Schools—local schools where innovative practices and the best quality of teaching will be occurring. It is in these schools that the clinical experiences for future teachers, such as student teaching, would take place. In the development of the teacher, the Holmes Group places strong emphasis on a liberal education, which takes place through professional core studies. They also place heavy emphasis on the importance of clinical practice, guided opportunities, and focused practice in order to work toward the goal of high entry levels.

The Renaissance Group. Another network of universities that is focusing on the reform of teacher education is the Renaissance Group. The membership of this group comes predominantly from those state universities that historically had been normal schools. As you remember, normal schools were the first formal teacher education colleges in America. In recent years, these institutions have become multipurpose universities, consisting of a number of professional schools and offering an array of master's degrees, and in many instances doctoral degrees. The primary participants in the Renaissance Group are the presidents, vice presidents for academic affairs, and the deans of schools/colleges of education; a unique difference from the Holmes Group is that presidents and vice presidents are expected to be ongoing active participants in the efforts to redesign teacher education. This triad of members is particularly important in addressing the first of the twelve principles of the Renaissance Group. Like many of the restructuring efforts in schools, the Renaissance Group has identified a set of core values or belief statements to guide the work. These principles are:

1. The education of teachers is an all-campus responsibility.
2. Programs for the preparation of teachers thrive in a university culture that values quality teaching.
3. Decisions concerning the education of teachers are the shared responsibility of the university faculty, practitioners, and other related professionals.
4. The initial preparation of teachers is integrated throughout a student's university experience and is not segmented or reserved to the student's final year.
5. The appropriate role of the state is to establish outcome expectations for teacher education graduates; the appropriate role of the university is to determine the curriculum, standards, and internal policies for teacher education programs.
6. Rigorous learning expectations and exit requirements characterize the program to educate teachers.
7. The academic preparation of teachers includes a rigorous general education program, in-depth subject matter preparation, and both general and content-specific preparation in teaching methodology.
8. Teacher education programs reflect American diversity and prepare graduates to teach in a pluralistic and multicultural society.
9. The education of teachers incorporates extensive and sequenced field and clinical experiences.
10. Quality teacher preparation programs have faculty who are active in scholarly and professional endeavors.
11. The continuing professional development of teachers and other education personnel is a shared responsibility of the university faculty and other education professionals.
12. Programs to educate teachers for the new world have sufficient support to implement these principles.[7]

One of the interesting principles of the Renaissance Group agenda for reform of teacher education is the theme that all university faculty are teacher educators— not just those in the school/college of education. An assumption of the Renaissance Group is that the faculty in the disciplines (e.g., chemistry, history, English) are models of the teaching of that discipline for future teachers. As a result, the Renaissance Group places heavy emphasis on teacher education as a campus-wide responsibility, as well as the need for all faculty to be aware of their being pedagogical as well as content models for future teachers.

National Network for Educational Renewal. The newest network of teacher education institutions has been assembled around the shared support for nineteen postulates that have been proposed by John Goodlad.[8] These postulates were based on extensive study of schools and teacher education institutions in twelve states. Institution members of this network are committed to redesigning their teacher education programs in ways that will address the nineteen postulates. Two examples of these postulates are:

Transparency 98:
Deming's Fourteen Points

> *Postulate eight.* Programs for the education of educators must provide extensive opportunities for future teachers to move beyond being students of organized knowledge to become teachers who will inquire into both knowledge and teaching.

> *Postulate nine.* Programs for the education of educators must be characterized by a socialization process through which candidates transcend their self-oriented student preoccupations to become much more other-oriented in identifying with a culture of teaching.

These and the other seventeen postulates then become the guiding assumptions for the design and organization of more relevant, effective, and rigorous teacher education programs. Again, there is a trend away from individual, isolated courses and experiences within particular institutions toward a more collaborative, interactive, and principled approach to education.

Teacher Leadership Is the Key

You are aware of the continuing concern about American schools and the education of children: The media run features about novel approaches to schooling and report the latest test results; politicians refer to themselves as the "education" president/governor/senator; leaders of business and industry continue to express concerns about the ability of American schools to produce skilled workers. You may not have thought about the reasons and assumptions underlying this persistent theme of concern and critiquing of American education. One of the key assumptions is Americans' basic faith that education and schooling can make a difference. While faith has been lost in many of our institutions, schools continue to be viewed as critical and essential to the opportunity for the individual, as well as society as a whole, to improve and advance.

The most important key to the success of the schools is teachers. The reason for the focus of so much attention on teachers is the understanding of parents, political leaders, industrialists, and the society at large that teachers do make a difference. And teachers make a difference beyond their own classrooms. How teachers work together within the school and provide leadership across the school district, the state, and the nation sets the themes and directions for schooling.

Test Questions 19.43–19.61

Focus Question 4:
Leadership is an important part of school success. How do you think teacher leadership can make a difference?

Transparency 90:
Dimensions of Classroom Life

Without well-educated and dedicated teachers who are willing to provide leadership, the faith and hope that Americans place in schooling would be unfounded.

As a teacher you will have many opportunities—and the responsibility—to provide leadership in your classroom, across your school and your district, and for the profession at large. Do not enter the profession of teaching thinking that all you have to do is close the door to your classroom and teach "your" children. The leadership role of a teacher is a critical, exciting, and challenging part of the job.

Teacher Leadership in Schools

Objective 7:
Describe the many ways that teachers are leaders in their schools.

All too frequently teachers think only about what goes on in their classrooms and do not develop perspectives about the school as a whole. This is unfortunate, since teachers are an integral part of the larger organization, and only to the extent to which they are able to work together and to assist each other can they make a major difference in the success of students. From the students' point of view, they attend the total school, and teachers need to develop this school-wide perspective too. There are many ways that teachers can be involved in leadership activities. Obviously, they must first think about what leadership means in their classroom. In addition, there are many opportunities to be involved in leadership functions across the school, ranging from participating on various committees, to chairing committees, to serving in key roles in regard to particular change processes and school improvement efforts. Some examples of the different opportunities for teachers to be involved in leadership are described here.

Discussion Question 5:
How do you feel about some of the school-transforming ideas that have been introduced in this chapter? Which of these ideas would you want to become involved with as a teacher?

Transformational Leadership. Of the many models of leadership, traditionally, the "top down" model was preferred. In this model the "boss" made the decisions and directed the "followers." More recently, the concept of "empowerment" has emerged. In professional organizations, such as schools, the principal cannot work as the "boss," and organizational norms must be developed across the school that facilitate teachers' work and allow them to learn and grow along with their students. Currently, the model of "transformational leadership" is being examined. In this perspective it is the responsibility of every member of the organization to help transform it and to see there is learning and growing. This, of course, requires that every member in the organization be a learner. Thus, teacher leadership entails not only thinking about how the students in your classroom learn and grow, but also thinking about how fellow teachers and the school as a whole are learning and growing. This growth must be in ways that empower the members of the organization to continually improve in job performance. As a teacher, you have not only the opportunity but also the responsibility to participate in leadership activities in your classroom, the school, and in larger arenas.

Advanced technologies notwithstanding, the teacher will continue to be the single most important element in the education of our children.

Leadership in the Classroom. You may not have thought about a teacher as the classroom leader; however, that is the case. Within the classroom, you have an amazing amount of leadership responsibility. You will have from twenty to thirty-five students for whom you are responsible. In high school you are responsible for groups of students for fifty minutes at a time, with well over one hundred students that you will be leading during a school day. In addition, other adults will be part of your classroom. You may have an aide, there may be student teachers, and there may be various "pull out" programs that identify selected students for special instruction. In all cases, you as the teacher will be the leader of the activities and the work of these people. How you provide direction and guidance and facilitate their work will make the difference in the success of their learning outcomes. This guidance of other people and their work is leadership. In other words, your job is not just to teach the children; it is also to be a manager of learning and a facilitator of the other managers who are there to assist in this important work.

Information Note 19.7:
A new professional association has been created for teachers who have leadership roles. It is called the Leadership Institute for the Future of Teaching (LIFT).

School Committees. In your very first meetings in your school there will be opportunities to become involved in many of the working committees. At the beginning, you will probably serve as a member of one or more of these committees. Some are charged with addressing curriculum and instruction issues. There may be a social committee. There likely will be committees that work as liaisons with the community. In many committees it will be necessary to liaison with the district office and other schools. In all cases, as a member of the committee, you will be in a leadership role, because it is not just the chair of the committee who provides leadership. All members have a responsibility to carry out their part in making the committee effective. This includes setting a good example in terms of meeting attendance, being prepared, and participating. It also means being sensitive to the ideas and interests of the other members, and striving to facilitate the development of a consensus of all committee members about the directions that should be taken.

Relevant Research

Empowering Teachers to Reform Schools

Using a historical research base, Midgley and Wood offer a Site-Based Management (SBM) approach that can be used in the reform of schools.[10] The model is built around the notion of empowering teachers. Defining SBM as a "bottom up" as opposed to a "top down" management model, they set out the research needed to create such a management model. The tenets of their model include establishing a common vision for change, altering the school culture, collaborating, defining roles of leadership teams, having a task-focused environment, and finally, empowering staff.

As increasing numbers of schools are moving into SBM, teachers need to become better versed in their roles, relationships, and expectations. Change will come either in some organized and logical fashion or haphazardly. You must decide how you will prepare for and accept this change.

Source: Carol Midgley and Stewart Wood, "Beyond Site-Based Management: Empowering Teachers to Reform Schools," *Phi Delta Kappan* 75 (3) (November, 1993): 245–252.

Site-Based Decision Making (SBDM) has been talked about at a number of points in this book. Earlier in this chapter we introduced a Configuration Component Checklist for Site-Based Decision Making (see Appendix 19.1). In this Component Checklist, note Components 1, 2, 3, 12, 13, and 16. In each of these components there is a direct expectation for teachers to provide leadership. There are other school-wide councils and committees that deal with the governance and operation of the school as well. For example, many schools and school districts have engaged in "school improvement" processes, which include a committee made up of teachers, their principal, and perhaps others. In each of these configurations of SBDM, there is the expectation of across-the-school leadership by teachers.

Second Change Facilitator/Consigliere. Another important role, which is less official but found in every school, is that of **second change facilitator,** or

Key Term:
Second change facilitator/consigliere

consigliere. In extensive research on the change process, Shirley Hord, Gene Hall,[9] and their colleagues have observed that whenever a school is engaged in a substantial change effort, a special role exists for a teacher to provide day-to-day leadership for implementation of the change. Of course, the principal is most likely to serve as the *first* change facilitator. However, in most instances, a teacher will be identified to serve as a key resource to all teachers in the school. Hord and Hall have called this person the *consigliere* or *second change facilitator.* This person is most likely to have some released time to work as a facilitator and coach for other teachers and will tend to have more expertise and interest in the area of the change. For example, the teacher who is very interested in language arts could have the assignment of serving as the second change facilitator/consigliere for the implementation of whole language or a writing process curriculum. Perhaps a particular department chair with a great deal of interest in computers and educational technology takes on the role of consigliere to assist other teachers and chairs in the implementation of interactive video technology. Here, again, a role for teacher leadership has been identified that is important to school and student success.

Teacher Career Paths

Objective 8:
Describe and discuss the alternative career paths for teachers.

Information Note 19.8:
Teachers need to think more about career opportunities in higher education. They may serve as clinical faculty or teaching education faculty. They may also serve as discipline-oriented faculty. These positions usually require the terminal academic degree, D.Ed. or Ph.D.

In the "old days" teachers had one position, teacher. They were assigned as a regular teacher from the first day they entered the classroom, they were a teacher five years later, ten years later, twenty years later. . . . Unlike any other profession, there were no different levels of role and responsibility, and there was only one pay scale. Historically, teachers at the beginning of their career would have the same level of responsibility as those who had twenty-five to thirty years of experience. This is no longer the case. Today, there are exciting career advancement possibilities for teachers. The following brief descriptions are offered to encourage you to remember that your training—and learning about your profession—are not over with the completion of your initial teacher education program. There are many exciting avenues for professional growth, increased professional status, wider ranges of responsibility, and higher levels of salary through the career paths that are available to teachers today.

Levels of Certificates/Licenses. Most states now differentiate between inexperienced and more experienced teachers by the type of license or credential that is issued. The increasingly common practice is that with the completion of your teacher education program and recommendation to the state you will receive a *provisional* certificate/license, which will allow you to begin your career as a regular teacher. States vary on the requirements for moving beyond the initial license. In most cases your provisional status will conclude following three years of successful experience as a beginning teacher and the completion of some amount of advanced training. More than likely you will be expected to do some study toward a master's degree, and perhaps even completion of a masters degree will be expected. The next level up the career path will be a *regular* certificate/ license. Typically this will be issued to teachers after the requisite three years of successful teaching experience and a recommendation from their principal or school district. Normally this license will be renewable every five years. There will be an expectation that you continue to study and to do advanced training, which can include study in higher education and/or training offered by your school district. In some states there is a third level of certificate that is referred to as a *master* teacher, mentor, or professional certificate/license. This advanced level of licensure will require more

Focus Question 5:
In the past there were few career advancement opportunities for teachers that did not require them to leave the classroom. Do you know of career possibilities that still allow you to be a teacher?

This plan would provide a "career ladder" that could lead to salaries equivalent to mid-management pay ranges for teachers. The plan has a probationary period for teachers that stresses professional development. During the initial probationary period, teachers must complete in-service requirements equivalent to a master's degree and have satisfactory on-the-job performance evaluations. Changes made in the tenure system extend the probationary period to four to six years, but provide a flexible time frame for achieving tenure status.

PROBATIONARY STATUS:

First year	All teachers are probationary
Second year	Advance to career nominee status, continue as probationary teacher, or be terminated
Third year	Advance to career candidate, advance to career nominee, remain career nominee, or be terminated
Fourth year	Advance to career candidate status, remain as career nominee, or be terminated
Fifth year	Be awarded tenure, advance to career candidate, remain a career candidate, or be terminated
Sixth year	Be awarded tenure, remain a career candidate, or be terminated
Seventh year	Become tenured or be terminated

LEVELS FOR TENURED TEACHER:

Career Level I This first step for tenured teachers would provide an extra $2,000 per year. Teachers would be reevaluated every three years. Each evaluation that is satisfactory would provide another $2,000 increment. Teachers in this level would teach, evaluate curriculum materials, and work with probationary teachers.

Career Level II After three years' experience at the first level, teachers could move to Level II. The salary level would be approximately $2,000 above the Level I teachers. In addition to classroom teaching, these teachers would help with assigned projects, possibly assist in numerous schools, conduct research, or work on in-service projects.

Career Level III These teachers would work as curriculum specialists or on in-service projects. They would still serve as classroom teachers. They should be able to carry out research projects as needed by the district. The salary would be approximately $2,000 above the Level II teacher.

FIGURE 19.5 Charlotte-Mecklenburg Schools Career Development Plan

advanced study, a series of superior evaluations, and a track record of accomplishment in professional activities.

An expanded career plan for teachers, called a **career ladder,** has been proposed in a number of states, including Texas and Tennessee. In these models there are more steps and levels of advancement for teachers. With each level comes increased salary, increased roles and responsibilities, and more complex tasks. The best articulation of the career ladder perspective is by Schlecty and Crowell[10] (see Figure 19.5). In their model of the career ladder, each level represents a broader

Key Term:
Career ladder

range of responsibilities and more complex professional tasks in relation to teaching and working with other teachers. From a professional point of view, this represents an idealized career path. Unfortunately, to date, very few school districts have experimented with implementation of this model.

There are other roles and career paths open to teachers. For example, becoming a team leader, where you work with two to six other teachers, offers an important opportunity for leadership. Teaming can be done for the purpose of exchanging lesson plans or co-teaching a discipline, and in a middle school an interdisciplinary team can be responsible for instruction in all areas for a set of students. Teachers also move to various roles in the district office. For example, in larger districts there will be positions for curriculum coordinators and specialists in gifted education, bilingual education, Chapter One, and compensatory education. In all of these examples, expert teachers have the opportunity to work with other teachers, principals, and children in different schools. In addition, all of these positions require leadership skills and place an emphasis on improving teaching and learning.

Will You Be Ready? Becoming a teacher is something special. Few people, even those in a teacher preparation program, really grasp the significance of this service profession. Despite the general public concerns about the overall quality of American education and the professional concerns about overburdened classrooms and learning environments and general financial support of education, teaching is a critical base for the maintenance of the American society. For that matter, it is a significant base for any society. A nation advances or declines on the basis of its educational development. A society's schools and teachers wield a tremendous impact on the future of the nation and the world.

The twenty-first century, close at hand, will mark over a two hundred-year history of this nation's growth from a small group of rebel people in the thirteen colonies to that of an international world leader in economic development; scientific achievement in medicine, agriculture, nutrition, knowledge creation, and cybernetics; and with one of the highest standards of living in the world. All of this can be linked to a nation committed to the importance of education for all people. In examining the foundations of American education, the authors of this text have provided you with all the boons, banes, and anodynes of American education. As we have indicated, the system has not been and is not a perfect one. However, the system has been somewhat elastic in nature and has successfully adjusted to the needs of the society it has served. The critical challenge for the third century of its history is how it will continue to adjust to the needs of a society growing closer in an interdependent world.

Our educational achievements tell us that there is little that we cannot learn or do. Teachers are better prepared than ever in our history, and our learners are more capable than ever before. Our educational history and societal development has led us to this point. We know that teachers will learn and teach differently than before, and that learners will acquire and use knowledge differently than before. The challenge to the new teachers of the twenty-first century is to move boldly into educational endeavors that we have read about and studied but never tried. That attitude, if put into practice, will stretch our efforts far beyond where we have been. The career of teaching will assume an added level of importance to the continued success and growth of this nation.

Journal/Portfolio Development 19.2:
Develop a career ladder for yourself and establish a personal management plan for achieving that goal. Indicate the importance of each step along the way.

Transparency 95:
Hall's Innovative Category Scale

Activity 19.8:
Have each student chart a potential career path for his or her future. Do the paths terminate with the student still in the field of education?

Transparency 100:
Significant Forces and Trends Facing the Future

Objective 9:
Assess their personal readiness for entering the classroom for teaching.

Activity 19.9:
Use the concluding question to the students (Will You Be Ready?) to have them list and analyze their own strengths and weaknesses as they begin to enter teaching.

Summary and Implications

We live in a time of change. In this chapter we have highlighted some of the ways of thinking about change in schools. Unfortunately, too much of the time we just talk about change, and when we attempt to change we accomplish small tinkerings. Transforming is what we have to be about. Examples of transforming in schools have been presented. Probably the most important of these, for the 1990s, is the idea of the school serving as the center for the coordinated delivery of human services: the "full-service school." There are an increasing number of models of how this can work around the nation. It is an exciting and challenging opportunity to bring together professionals from education, social work, criminal justice, dental and health care, and in some cases the performing and visual arts, to focus on the growth and development of children and their families. There is a hint of movement toward the return of a sense of community and an interest in dealing with the wholeness of family life.

Schools will not continue to be as they were when you went through them. Our societies will continue to change. You will be a participant in the change process. Teachers are leaders, and teachers are a part of the leadership team for their schools. Your role begins in your classroom but extends beyond to the school, to the community, and to your profession at large. As your career unfolds, participate, share in leadership, and contribute your energies and creativity to continually improving what occurs in your classroom, your school, and your community. In other words, "Go for it!" "Do Something!" And good luck to you.

Discussion Questions

1. Some have referred to the coordinated services school as the "one-stop shopping" school. What other metaphors might describe a school of this type?
2. What do you think will happen to the role of the teacher in a school that is serving as the center for the delivery of coordinated services?
3. Develop answers to TQM questions: Who are the customers for teachers? What is the product of schools? What is the product of your classroom?
4. What are some of the basic principles about schooling and the role of teachers and students that you would advocate as the basis for transforming a school?
5. How do you feel about some of the school-transforming ideas that have been introduced in this chapter? Which of the ideas would you want to become involved with as a teacher?

Journal/Portfolio Development

1. Select one of the "transformation of schools" topics and assess its potential for becoming a regular part of the school operation. Contrast it with the current school operation.
2. Develop a career ladder for yourself and establish a personal management plan for achieving that goal. Indicate the importance of each step along the way.

School-Based Experiences

1. Visit a school that is doing innovative things. Develop a report of what is going on and use the HIC Scale to assess how different the school is.
2. Visit a school that is using Site-Based Decision Making. Complete the Checklist in Appendix 19.1. Do a comparison of what you have read about SBDM with what you find. What are implications you see for the leadership role of the teacher?

Notes

1. Madelyn Hunter, "Knowing, Teaching and Supervising," in *Using What We Know About Schools,* ed. P. L. Hosford. Alexandria, VA: Association for Supervisor and Curriculum Development, 1984, 169–192.

2. M. W. Kirst, "Improving Children's Services, Overcoming Barriers, Creating New Opportunities," *Phi Delta Kappan* (1991).

3. A. I. Melaville and M. J. Blank, *What It Takes: Structuring Interagency Partnerships to Connect Children and Families with Comprehensive Services.* Washington, DC: Education and Human Services Consortium c/o IEL, 1991.

4. Ibid.

5. "New Beginnings Statement of Philosophy." San Diego, CA: 1990.

6. "Tomorrow's Teachers: A Report of the Holmes Group." East Lansing, MI: 1986.

7. "The Twelve Principles Guiding Renaissance Group Activities." Cedar Falls, IA: The Renaissance Group, University of Northern Iowa, 1991.

8. J. I. Goodlad, *Teachers for Our Nations Schools.* San Francisco, CA: Jossey-Bass Publishers, 1990.

9. G. E. Hall and S. M. Hord, *Change in Schools: Facilitating the Process.* Albany, NY: State University of New York Press, 1989.

10. P. Schlecty and D. Crowell, *Staff Development and School Improvement: A School District Examines Its Potential for Excellence.* National Institute of Education, U.S. Department of Education (NIE Contract 400-79-0056).

Bibliography

Bechtol, William M. and Sorenson, Juanita S. *Restructuring Schooling for Individual Students.* Boston: Allyn and Bacon, 1993.

Kirst, M. W. "Improving Children's Services, Overcoming Barriers, Creating New Opportunities." *Phi Delta Kappan,* 1991.

Kuhn, T. S. *The Structure of Scientific Revolution.* 2nd ed. Chicago: The University of Chicago Press, 1970.

Melaville, A. I. and Blank, M. J. *What It Takes: Structuring Interagency Partnerships to Connect Children and Families with Comprehensive Services.* Washington, DC: Education and Human Services Consortium c/o IEL, 1991.

Sergiovanni, T. J. *Value Added Leadership: How to Get Extraordinary Performance in Schools.* San Diego, CA: Harcourt, Brace and Jovanovich, 1990.

Tripp, Robert L. *The Game of School.* Reston, VA: Extended Vision Press, 1993.

Weber, Robert J. *Forks, Photographs, and Hot Air Balloons.* Portsmouth, NH: Heinemann, 1993.

Ysselddyke, James E. and Thurlow, Martha L. *Self-Study Guide to the Development of Educational Outcomes and Indicators.* Minneapolis: University of Minnesota National Center on Educational Outcomes, 1993.

Configuration Component Checklist for Site-Based Decision Making

---

IMPLEMENTATION REQUIREMENTS

Staff Development

____ Initial training for principal   ____ Initial training for council   ____ On-going coaching

Context Support

____ Mechanisms to release site from traditional policies and procedures
____ Active accommodation by School Board
____ District office personnel role shifts to accommodate and support SBDM
____ Installation of new parallel systems for evaluation and accountability
____ Commitment of chairman level
____ Presumption in favor of granting waivers by reviewing party

---

SBDM OPERATIONAL COMPONENTS AND VARIATIONS

COUNCIL STRUCTURES AND PROCESSES

1. *Participant Representation of School Council* (indicate number of each)

____ Teachers	____ Custodians	____ Students	____ District administrators
____ Parents	____ Principal	____ Instructional aids	____ School board member
____ Business persons			

2. *Strategies to Support Teacher Participation*

____ Team teaching	____ Part-time teachers	____ Volunteers
____ Instructional aids	____ After-school meetings	____ Early release day

3. *Decision-making Process*

    (a) Consensus   (b) Vote

4. *Participants Solicited in Decision-Making*

____ Other teachers   ____ Other parents   ____ Students
____ District office   ____ State   ____ Business persons

5. *Decision Sequence*

____ Prework by task force   ____ School decisions final
____ Council recommends to whole faculty   ____ School decisions have to be confirmed by district office
____ Council decision final   ____ School board has final say
____ Council recommends to principal,   ____ State has final say
      has final decision

6. *Council Procedures*

____ Have minutes of previous meetings   ____ Provide members complete information
      available ahead of time
____ Publish agenda in advance   ____ Procedures are followed
____ Work load is shared by all members

7. *Council Meeting Process*

____ Steer discussions toward important agenda items
____ Chair sees that all have an opportunity to speak
____ Procedures are used to keep track of ideas, issues, and recommendations

8. *Waiver Process*

(a) Board   (b) Request goes   (c) District   (d) Committee   (e) A multi-   (f) Waivers
    receives   to one admin-   committee   reviews and   component   are not
    request and   istrator then   reviews then   recommends to   proposal and   permitted
    acts on   board   recommends   superintendent,   multiple review
    quickly   to board   who takes to   process is
                                                          board   required

9. *Types of Waivers Sought*

____ Testing   ____ District policies
____ Teacher load   ____ District rules and regulations
____ Class schedules   ____ State policies
____ School calendar   ____ State rules and regulations
____ Textbooks   ____ Federal policies
____ Staff development   ____ Federal rules and regulations
____ Teacher contract variations   ____ Court rulings
____ Other contract variations

10. *Scope of Council Work*

____ Curriculum   ____ Coordination of social services
____ Staffing   ____ School improvement implementations
____ Budget   ____ Coordination of criminal justice system
____ Testing   ____ Coordination of community action
____ Teaching   ____ Legal and regulatory issues
____ School improvement planning

11. *Curriculum* (Authority: ____ Set ____ Advise ____ No Role)

    (a) Selection of   (b) Selection of materials   (c) Selection of teacher   (d) Combination of
        goals only   including texts only   Delivery approaches   _____

12. *Budget Topics* (Authority: ____ Set ____ Advise ____ No Role)

    ____ Principal salary   ____ Curriculum material purchases   ____ Teacher salaries
    ____ Lunchroom personnel   ____ Supplies   ____ Other _____

13. *Staff Evaluations* (Authority: ____ Set ____ Advise ____ No Role)

    ____ of principal   ____ of teachers   ____ of aides   ____ of others _____

14. *Teacher Assignments/Scheduling* (Authority: ___ Set ____ Advise ____ No Role)

    (a) Decide   (b) Advise   (c) No role

15. *Hirings* (Authority: ____ Set ____ Advise ____ No Role)

    (a) All school   (b) Principal   (c) Teachers   (d) Classified   (e) No say
        employees   staff

16. *Teacher Work Hours/Work Week* (Authority: ____ Set ____ Advise ____ No Role)

    (a) All   (b) Non-student contact   (c) Student contact   (d) No say

17. *Testing*

    (a) Site has full authority   (b) Site must receive   (c) Site must receive   (d) Combination
        to set testing   district approval   state approval   of (b) and (c)

Based on the earlier Innovation Configuration Component Checklist presented in:
G. E. Hall and G. R. Galluzzo, *Site-Based Decision Making: Changing Policy into Practice* (WV: Appalachia Educational Laboratory, 1991).

For more information on Innovation Configuration Component Checklists, see:
G. E. Hall and S. M. Hord, *Change in Schools, Facilitating the Process* (Albany, NY: State University of New York Press, 1987).

Glossary

Abstraction: A thought process of drawing away from experience to a conceptual plane.

Academic freedom: The opportunity for a teacher to teach without certain coercion, censorship, or other restrictive interference.

Accountability: Holding schools responsible for what students learn.

Acculturation: The process of learning the cultural patterns of a second culture.

Activity curriculum: A student-centered organizational emphasis that begins with broad topic identification for learning and weaves the related academic components into that topic.

Adaptation: The promotion of a stable climate in schools so that students can attain an unbiased picture of the changes that occur in society.

Affirmative action: A plan by which personnel policies and hiring practices do not discriminate against women and members of minority groups.

Age of Pericles (455–431 B.C.): A period of Greek history in which sufficiently great strides were made in human advancement to generate an organized concern for formal education.

Age of Reason: The beginning of the modern period of educational thought that emphasizes the importance of reason. The writings of Voltaire strongly influenced this movement and formed the basis for rationalism.

American Federation of Teachers: A national teachers' organization that is primarily concerned with improving educational conditions and protecting teachers' rights.

Analysis of teaching: A contemporary trend to encourage teachers to critique their own performance in the classroom.

Annual increments: Standard salary increases based on the number of years of teaching experience.

Articulation: The manner in which the various parts of the school program compliment each other in their relationship to a student's learning.

Assimilation: The process by which an immigrant group or culturally distinct group is incorporated into the dominant culture.

Authentic assessment: An assessment of student learning that is based on real-world practice and attempts to measure learning in the same way it was acquired by the learner.

Axiology: An area of philosophy that deals with the nature of values. It includes questions such as "What is good?" "What is value?"

Behavioral theory: A theory that considers the outward behavior of students to be the main target for change.

Behaviorism: A psychological theory that asserts that behavior represents the essence of a person; behaviorists contend that all behavior can be explained as response to stimuli.

Bias: A preference or inclination that inhibits impartial judgment, leading to prejudice or discrimination.

Block grants: Federal monies that are consolidated into a broader-purpose fund from categorical funds that had more focused purposes. Block grants give more discretion to the state and local agencies that receive them.

Career ladder: A career path for teachers consisting of a number of rungs, or job roles, that carry with them increasing responsibility and performance of more complex professional tasks.

Carnegie Unit: A measure of clock time that is used to award high school credits toward graduation.

Censorship: The condemnation of books, instructional materials, teaching content, or teaching methods because they are perceived as unsupportive of or in opposition to the values of an individual or group.

Change agent: A role that emphasizes the responsibility for persons to actively participate in society.

Chemical dependency: The habitual use, either for psychological or physical needs, of a substance such as drugs, alcohol, or tobacco.

Child benefit theory: A criterion used by the U.S. Supreme Court to determine whether services provided to public and nonpublic school students benefit children and not the school or religion. If they benefit only the children, the courts have ruled that the services may be funded by public funds.

Classroom analysis systems: Clearly defined sets of procedures and written materials that can be used to analyze the interaction between teachers and students.

Classroom organization: A multifaceted dimension of teaching that includes the content, method, and values that infuse the classroom environment, planning, and discipline practices.

Cognitive development: A learner's acquisition of facts, concepts, and principles through intellectualization.

Committee of Ten: An historic NEA committee that studied secondary education in 1893.

Common elementary schools: An early attempt to provide a basic elementary education for all children.

Compulsory education: School attendance that is required by law on the theory that it is to the benefit of the state or commonwealth to educate all the people.

Constants: An offering of learning experiences that make up an academic or vocational track in the secondary school.

Constructivism: An educational theory that emphasizes hands-on, activity-based teaching and learning during which students develop their own frames of thought.

Continuity: Vertical articulation.

Control theory: A theory of discipline that contends that we choose most of our behaviors to gain control of people or ourselves.

Core curriculum: A student-centered organizational emphasis that combines broad areas of academic disciplines into manageable instructional units such as social studies and language arts for integration in learning.

Core values: Statements of principles about teaching and learning that are fundamental to one's philosophy of schooling.

Cultural pluralism: A state that exists when different groups maintain their culture parallel and equal to the dominant one in a society.

Culture: The totality of socially transmitted ways of thinking, believing, feeling, and acting within a group of people that is passed from one generation to the next.

Current expenses: Expenditures necessary for daily operation and maintenance.

Dame school: A low-level primary school in the colonial and other early periods, usually conducted by an untrained woman in her own home.

De facto **segregation:** The segregation of students resulting from circumstances such as housing patterns rather than from school policy or law.

De jure **segregation:** The segregation of students on the basis of law, school policy, or a practice designed to accomplish such separation.

Delinquency: A term generally ascribed to the youth culture that denotes violation of rules and regulations of the society.

Desegregation: The process of correcting past practices of racial or any other form of illegal segregation.

Dialectic: The conflict that occurs when opposing ideas are encountered; in change theory this conflict is the one between individual needs and societal needs.

Differential pay: Extra pay or incentives (added to standard increments) awarded to teachers on the basis of merit.

Discrimination: Individual or institutional practices that exclude all members of a group from certain rights, opportunities, or benefits.

Diversity: The wide range of ways in which human groups and populations have observable and demonstrable physical and behavioral differences.

Dominant group: The cultural group that has the greatest power in society; in the United States it is composed primarily of persons from a European background who are Protestant, middle class, not disabled, heterosexual, and male. This term is sometimes used synonymously with mainstream culture or group.

Dropouts: Students who fail to complete a high school education.

Due process: The procedural requirements that must be followed to safeguard individuals from arbitrary, capricious, or unreasonable policies, practices, or actions.

Eastern thought: A varied set of philosophies from the Far, Middle, and Near East that stress inner peace, tranquility, attitudinal development, and mysticism.

Educated citizenry: A goal according to which all members of our society are capable of participating intelligently in its direction and development.

Education for career: A specialty educational offering that promotes and prepares learners for postsecondary educational efforts and/or career initiation.

Educational malpractice: Culpable neglect by a teacher in the performance of his or her duties as an educator.

Effective teaching: A movement to improve teaching performance based on the outcomes of educational research.

Emergence of Common Man: Coincides with the Age of Reason and emphasizes the rights of the common people for a better life, politically, economically, socially, and educationally. Rousseau was a leader in this movement.

Enculturation: The process of learning the characteristics of the culture of the group to which one belongs.

Epistemology: An area of philosophy that deals with questions about how and what we know.

Equal educational opportunity: A policy to ensure that all students, regardless of their cultural background or family circumstances, are provided access to a similar education.

Equality: The state of being neither inferior nor superior.

Essentialism: An educational theory that holds that there is a common core of information and skills that an educated person must have; school should be organized to transmit this core of essential material.

Ethnic group: Identification of membership in a group based on the national origin (that is, a specific country or area of the world) of one's ancestors, a shared culture, and sense of common destiny.

Ethnocentrism: The belief that members of one's group are superior to the members of other groups.

Exceptional learners: A classification identification used to describe handicapped and gifted learners.

Existentialism: A school of philosophy that focuses on the importance of the individual rather than external standards.

Exploratory education: An educational offering that is broad in scope and is used to introduce learners to a variety of learning areas that may be pursued in depth as possible career interests.

Fringe benefits: Job rewards in addition to salary that may include life, professional liability, health, and dental insurance; retirement programs; and tax-free investment opportunities.

Fused curriculum: A subject-centered organizational program created with some merger of the academic disciplines such as reading, writing, and speaking into language arts as a subject for teaching.

General education: An educational offering that is common and required of all students.

Graded schools: Schools that contain year-long levels such as first grade, second grade, tenth grade and the like.

Grouping: A practice whereby students are put into learning groups with others who have like abilities and interests.

Herbartian teaching method: An organized teaching method based on the principles of Pestalozzi that stresses learning by association and consists of five steps (preparation, presentation, association, generalization, and application).

Historical interpretation: Different ways to study and understand history, such as celebrationist, liberal, revisionist, and postmodernist historians would tend to do.

Hornbook: A single printed page containing the alphabet, syllables, a prayer, and other simple words, tacked to a wooden paddle and covered with a thin transparent layer of cow's horn, used in colonial times as the beginner's first book or preprimer.

Humanism: An educational theory that contends that humans are innately good—born free but become enslaved by institutions.

Hypothesis: A proposed relationship between two or more events or qualities.

Idealism: A school of philosophy that considers ideas to be the only true reality.

Inclusion: The federally mandated practice of placing all handicapped learners, except for profoundly handicapped, in regular classrooms where itinerant special education teachers assist the regular teacher.

Independent school: A nonpublic school that is unaffiliated with any religious institution or agency.

Informal curriculum: The norms and values that define expectations for student behavior and attitudes, and that undergird the curriculum and operations of schools.

Information age: A dynamic view of society that emphasizes the problems of dealing with vast amounts of changing information.

In loco parentis: A term used to describe the implied power of schools to function in place of a parent.

Integration: The process of mixing students of different races in school to overcome segregation.

Intermediate unit: A level of school organization between the state and the local district; a subdivision of the elementary school including grades 4, 5, and 6.

Latin grammar school: An early type of school that emphasized the study of Latin, literature, history, mathematics, music, and dialectics.

Liability: The failure to use a reasonable amount of care when such conduct results in injury to another.

Line: An organizational arrangement in which a subordinate is directly responsible to a supervisor.

Magnet schools: Specialized schools that are open to all students in a district, sometimes on a lottery basis or special needs basis.

Meritocracy: A system that is based on the belief that those who achieve at the highest levels deserve the greatest rewards.

Metaphors: The use of words, images, and examples from one's experiences and background to explain and illustrate an idea.

Metaphysics: An area of philosophy that deals with questions about the nature of ultimate reality.

Modules for learning: Time periods for learning that are in the daily schedule of the school.

Moonlighting: Holding a second job in addition to one's primary employment; it implies working in the evening, or "under the light of the moon."

Motivation: Internal emotion, desire, or impulse acting as an incitement to action.

Multicultural education: An educational strategy that incorporates the teaching of exceptional and culturally diverse students, human relations, and the study of ethnic and other cultural groups in a school environment that supports diversity and equal opportunity.

National Education Association: The largest organization of educators; the NEA is concerned with the overall improvement of education and of the condition of educators.

Native North American thought: A varied set of beliefs, philosophical positions, and customs that span different tribes in North America

Normal school: The first American institution that was devoted exclusively to teacher training.

Old Deluder Satan Act: The first colonial educational law (1647), which required colonial towns of at least 50 households to provide education for youth.

One-room school: A setting in which all grade levels are taught by a single teacher in a single-room school.

Parochial school: An educational institution operated and controlled by a religious denomination.

Perennialism: An educational theory that focuses on principles of knowledge that are enduring; nature, human nature, and the underlying principles of existence are considered constant, undergoing little change.

Political action committees in teacher education: Various organizations that engage in political activities in support of the organizations' purposes or causes.

Portfolio: A compilation for a specific purpose of the works, records, and accomplishments that a student prepares about his/her learnings, performances, and contributions.

Poverty: A relative standard of living defined by a number of complex and changing factors that may include hunger or lack of luxuries.

Poverty level: A level of family income judged by the United States Labor Department to be below the basic needs requirements of a family.

Pragmatism: A late nineteenth-century American school of philosophy that stresses becoming rather than being.

Prejudice: Preconceived negative attitudes toward the members of a group of people.

Professionalism and Unionism: A distinction that the NEA used in 1960 to claim that only an organization that stressed the professional aspects could represent teachers; hence a union would not be adequate, since it stressed organized labor.

Progressive tax: A tax scaled to the ability of the taxpayer to pay.

Progressivism: An educational theory that emphasizes that ideas should be tested by experimentation and that learning is rooted in answering questions developed by the learner.

Property tax: A tax based on the value of property, both real estate and personal.

Public confidence: The underlying trust that people have in their institutions.

Racism: The conscious or unconscious belief that racial differences make one group superior to another, leading to discriminatory actions that limit the opportunities for members of the perceived inferior group to share in the same benefits of society.

Realism: A school of philosophy that holds that reality, knowledge, and value exist independent of the human mind. In contrast to the idealist, the realist contends that physical entities exist in their own right.

Reconstructionism: An educational theory that calls on schools to teach people to control institutions and to be organized according to basic democratic ideals.

Regressive tax: A tax that affects low-income groups disproportionately.

Religious-affiliated school: A private school over which, in most cases, a parent church group exercises some control or to which it provides some form of subsidy.

Resegregation: A situation following desegregation in which segregation returns.

Restructuring: An umbrella label for talking about a number of innovations and themes related to Site-Based Decision Making that are intended to improve school operations and, through these, student performance.

Reverse discrimination: A situation in which a majority or an individual of a majority is denied certain rights because of preferential treatment provided to a minority or an individual of a minority.

Salary schedule: Salary chart organized by teaching experience and formal education.

Scholasticism: The logical and philosophical study of the beliefs of the church.

School-based clinics: Medical and advisory clinics in schools that are offered to provide personal help for students experiencing problems of sexuality.

Second change facilitator/consigliere: A special leadership role in a school whereby a teacher offers facilitating assistance to other teachers during the unfolding of a school-based change process.

Seven liberal arts: A curriculum that consisted of the trivium (grammar, rhetoric, logic) and the quadrivium (arithmetic, geometry, music, astronomy).

Sexism: The conscious or unconscious belief that men are superior to women, and subsequent behavior and action that maintain the superior, powerful position of males.

Single subject curriculum: A subject-centered organizational program in which the academic disciplines are taught in isolation from each other.

Socialization: Process of learning the social norms of one's culture.

Social justice: The desire for all individuals and families to share equally society's benefits.

Social stratification: Levels of social class ranking based on one's income, education, occupation, wealth, and power in society.

Socioeconomic status: Criteria to describe the economic condition of individuals based on their income, occupation, and educational attainment.

Socratic method: A way of teaching that centers on the use of questions by the teacher to lead students to certain conclusions.

Staff: An organizational arrangement in which one party is not under the direct control or authority of another.

Stereotyping: The application of common traits, characteristics, and behavior to a group of people without acknowledging individual differences within the group.

Structured observations: Those judgments or impressions that are conducted according to a predetermined plan.

Teacher certification: The process whereby each state determines the requirements for obtaining a license to teach, processes applications, and issues such licenses.

Teacher power: A term that stresses organized teacher groups that lobby for improvements in education; the group embodiment of individual teacher empowerment.

Teacher self-concept: How teachers view their participation in the profession of education.

Teacher stress: A condition that results from the many forces and pressures experienced through work as an educator.

Teacher supply and demand: A comparison of the projected number of school-age students with the projected number of available teachers.

Tenure: A system of school employment in which educators, after serving a probationary period, retain their positions indefinitely unless they are dismissed for legally specified reasons through clearly established procedures.

Tracking: A method of placing students according to their ability levels in homogeneous classes or learning experiences where they all follow the same curriculum—that is, college preparatory or vocational.

Transforming: Major restructuring, redesigning, or significantly changing the shape and function of schools.

Values: Principles, standards, or qualities considered worthwhile or desirable.

Variable: An offering of elective learning experiences for secondary school students.

Vision: A mental construction that synthesizes and clarifies what you value or consider to be of most worth.

Voice: The right and opportunity to speak and be heard as an equal.

World Confederation of Organizations of the Teaching Profession (WCOTP): Former name of the organization, now known as *Educational International,* that aims to foster international understanding and goodwill, stressing peace, freedom, and respect for human dignity. Members are from approximately one hundred nations and include the AFT and the NEA.

Name Index

Subject Index

Reader Feedback

We would sincerely appreciate your suggestions for improving *Introduction to the Foundations of American Education*, tenth edition. Please respond briefly to the following questions and return this form to Allyn & Bacon, 160 Gould St., Needham Heights, MA 02194-2310, or fax it to us care of Education Editor, 617/455–1294. Thank you.

1. What is the name of the course for which you used this book?

2. What is you general reaction to this book?

3. What were the most useful features of this book?

4. What were the least useful features?

5. Were all the chapters of the book assigned? If not, which ones were omitted?

6. Do you plan to keep this book after you finish this course? Why or why not?

7. Other comments or suggestions for improving this book.